THE ROUTLEDGE COMPANION TO NEWS AND JOURNALISM

The Routledge Companion to News and Journalism presents an authoritative, comprehensive assessment of diverse forms of news media reporting – past, present and future.

Including 60 chapters, written by an outstanding team of internationally respected authors, the *Companion* provides scholars and students with a reliable, historically informed guide to news media and journalism studies.

The new paperback edition of this *Companion* includes four new chapters, focusing on news framing, newsmagazines, digital radio news, and social media – such as Twitter – in real-time news.

The *Companion* has the following features:

- It is organised to address a series of themes pertinent to the ongoing theoretical and methodological development of news and journalism studies around the globe.
- The focus encompasses news institutions, production processes, texts and audiences.
- Individual chapters are problem-led, seeking to address 'real world' concerns that cast light on an important dimension of news and journalism – and show why it matters.
- Chapters draw on a range of academic disciplines to explore pertinent topics, particularly around the role of journalism in democracy, such as citizenship, power and public trust.
- Discussion revolves primarily around academic research conducted in the UK and the US, with further contributions from other national contexts, thereby allowing international comparisons to be made.

The Routledge Companion to News and Journalism provides an essential guide to key ideas, issues, concepts and debates, while also stressing the value of reinvigorating scholarship with a critical eye to developments in the professional realm.

Contributors: G. Stuart Adam, Stuart Allan, Chris Atton, Brian Baresch, Geoffrey Baym, W. Lance Bennett, Rodney Benson, S. Elizabeth Bird, R. Warwick Blood, Tanja Bosch, Raymond Boyle, Bonnie Brennen, Qing Cao, Cynthia Carter, Anabela Carvalho, Deborah Chambers, Lilie Chouliaraki, Lisbeth Clausen, James R. Compton, Simon Cottle, Ros Coward, Andrew Crisell, Mark Deuze, Roger Dickinson, Wolfgang Donsbach, Mats Ekström, Mohammed el-Nawawy, James S. Ettema, Natalie Fenton, Bob Franklin, Herbert J. Gans, Mark Glaser, Mark Hampton, Joseph Harker, Jackie Harrison, John Hartley, Alfred Hermida, Andrew Hoskins, Shih-Hsien Hsu,

Dale Jacquette, Bengt Johansson, Richard Kaplan, Douglas Kellner, Carolyn Kitch, Larsåke Larsson, Justin Lewis, Jake Lynch, Brian McNair, Mirca Madianou, Donald Matheson, Heidi Mau, Kaitlynn Mendes, Máire Messenger Davies, Toby Miller, Martin Montgomery, Marguerite Moritz, Henrik Örnebring, Julian Petley, Greg Philo, Shawn Powers, Stephen D. Reese, Barry Richards, David Rowe, Philip Seib, Jane B. Singer, Guy Starkey, Linda Steiner, Daya Kishan Thussu, John Tulloch, Howard Tumber, Silvio Waisbord, Gary Whannel, Andrew Williams, Barbie Zelizer

Stuart Allan is Professor of Journalism in the Media School, Bournemouth University, UK. Recent books include *News Culture* (3rd edition, 2010), *Keywords in News and Journalism Studies* (co-authored with Barbie Zelizer, 2010), *Digital War Reporting* (co-authored with Donald Matheson, 2009) and *Citizen Journalism: Global Perspectives* (co-edited with Einar Thorsen, 2009).

THE
ROUTLEDGE COMPANION
TO NEWS AND JOURNALISM

REVISED EDITION

Edited by
Stuart Allan

Routledge
Taylor & Francis Group

LONDON AND NEW YORK

First published 2010
by Routledge

First published in paperback 2012
by Routledge
2 Park Square, Milton Park, Abingdon, Oxon OX14 4RN

Simultaneously published in the USA and Canada
by Routledge
711 Third Avenue, New York, NY 10017

Routledge is an imprint of the Taylor & Francis Group, an informa business

British Library Cataloguing in Publication Data
A catalogue record for this book is available from the British Library

Library of Congress Cataloging in Publication Data
The Routledge companion to news and journalism studies / edited by Stuart Allan.
p. cm.
1. Journalism. 2. Mass media. I. Allan, Stuart, 1962-
PN4731.R68 2009
070.4071'1--dc22
2009013227

ISBN: 978-0-415-46529-8 (hbk)
ISBN: 978-0-415-66953-5 (pbk)
ISBN: 978-0-203-86946-8 (ebk)

Typeset in Goudy Old Style
by Fakenham Prepress Solutions, Fakenham, Norfolk NR21 8NN

MIX
Paper from
responsible sources
FSC
www.fsc.org   FSC® C004839

Printed and bound in Great Britain by
TJ International Ltd, Padstow, Cornwall

CONTENTS

CONTENTS

CONTENTS

LIST OF CONTRIBUTORS

G. Stuart Adam is Professor Emeritus of Journalism at Carleton University, Ottawa, Canada, and an Affiliate of the Poynter Institute, St Petersburg, Florida, USA. A former newspaper reporter, his academic appointments included being Director of Carleton's School of Journalism (1973–87). His publications include *A Sourcebook of Canadian Media Law* (with Robert Martin, 1989) and *Notes Towards a Definition of Journalism* (1993). He is also co-author and editor, with Roy Peter Clark, of *Journalism: The Democratic Craft* (2006).

Stuart Allan is Professor of Journalism in the Media School at Bournemouth University, UK. He is the author of *News Culture* (3rd edition, 2010), *Media, Risk and Science* (2002), *Online News: Journalism and the Internet* (2006), and co-author of *Nanotechnology, Risk and Communication* (2009) and *Digital War Reporting* (2009). His previous collections include *News, Gender and Power* (1998), *Environmental Risks and the Media* (2000), *Journalism After September 11* (2002), *Reporting War: Journalism in Wartime* (2004), *Journalism: Critical Issues* (2005) and *Citizen Journalism: Global Perspectives* (2009).

Chris Atton is Professor of Media and Culture in the School of Arts and Creative Industries at Edinburgh Napier University, UK. His research specialises in alternative media, and he is the author of four books, including *Alternative Media* (2002) and *Alternative Journalism* (2008), as well as over fifty articles and book chapters. He has made special studies of fanzines, the media of new social movements and popular music journalism.

Brian Baresch is a PhD candidate in the School of Journalism at the University of Texas at Austin, USA. In addition to news framing, he is researching how the people formerly known as the audience are spreading news and related information, as well as the implications the new news ecosystem has for society. He has 20 years of experience as a professional and freelance editor for various news organizations.

Geoffrey Baym is Associate Professor of Media Studies at the University of North Carolina Greensboro, USA. The author of several works examining 'real' and 'fake' forms of broadcast journalism, his interests lie with the changing styles and standards of news media and political discourse. His most recent work, *From Cronkite to Colbert: The Evolution of Broadcast News* (2009), explores the decline of high-modern journalism, the rise of postmodern infotainment, and the emergence of hybrid, 'neo-modern' forms of news and public affairs.

W. Lance Bennett is Professor of Political Science and Ruddick C. Lawrence Professor of Communication at the University of Washington, Seattle, USA, where he also serves as Director of the Center for Communication and Civic Engagement. He has been recognised with the Distinguished Scholar Award for lifetime achievement in human communication research by the (US) National Communication Association, and the American Political Science Association has given him the Ithiel de Sola Pool and Murray Edelman awards. Among numerous books and articles, he is co-author of *When the Press Fails: Political Power and the News Media from Iraq to Katrina.*

Rodney Benson is Associate Professor of Media, Culture, and Communication and Affiliated Faculty Member in Sociology at New York University, USA. He has published numerous articles on comparative media systems and the sociology of news, focusing on the US and French press, in such leading journals as *The American Sociological Review, Political Communication* and the *European Journal of Communication.* He is the co-editor, with Erik Neveu, of *Bourdieu and the Journalistic Field* (2005).

S. Elizabeth Bird is Professor, Department of Anthropology, University of South Florida, USA. Her books include *For Enquiring Minds: A Cultural Study of Supermarket Tabloids* (1992), *Dressing in Feathers: The Construction of the Indian in American Popular Culture* (1996), *The Audience in Everyday Life* (2003), and the forthcoming *Anthropology of News and Journalism: Global Perspectives.* She has also published over 50 articles and chapters in media studies, popular culture, and folklore.

R. Warwick Blood is Professor of Communication, News Research Group, University of Canberra, Australia. He researches risk theory and socio-cultural risk communication, especially news representations of health issues – including suicide and mental illness, licit and illicit drugs, overweight and obesity, and casualties of conflict. Current research includes a National Health and Medical Research Council public health grant – The Australian Health News Research Collaboration. He is writing *Images of War, Terror and Risk* with John Tulloch.

Tanja Bosch is Lecturer in the Centre for Film and Media Studies at the University of Cape Town, South Africa. She completed her MA in International Affairs while a Fulbright Scholar at Ohio University, where she also completed a PhD in Mass Communication, writing her thesis on community radio and identity. She researches and teaches radio studies, mobile media and youth.

Raymond Boyle is a Senior Lecturer in media and cultural policy at the Centre for Cultural Policy Research at the University of Glasgow, UK. He writes on media and sports issues and is author of a number of books in this area, including *Sports Journalism: Context and Issues* (2006) and, with Richard Haynes, *Power Play: Sport the Media and Popular Culture* (2nd edition, 2009) and *Football in the New Media Age* (2004).

Bonnie Brennen is the Nieman Professor of Journalism in the Diederich College of Communication at Marquette University, USA. Her research focuses on journalism history and cultural studies of the relationship between media and society. She is the author of *For the Record: An Oral History of Rochester, New York Newsworkers* (2001), and co-editor, with Hanno Hardt, of *Picturing the Past: Media, History & Photography* (1999) and *Newsworkers: Toward a History of the Rank and File* (1995).

Qing Cao is Senior Lecturer in Chinese Studies at Liverpool John Moores University, UK. Previously he taught at SOAS, University of London. His research focuses on Chinese media and politics and Western representations of China. His publications have appeared in major international journals and as book chapters by Routledge, Palgrave and University of Hong Kong Press.

Cynthia Carter is Senior Lecturer in the Cardiff School of Journalism, Media and Cultural Studies, Cardiff University, UK. Her research interests include children and news, feminist media studies, and media violence. She is co-author of *Violence and the Media* (2003) and recently co-edited *Critical Readings: Media and Gender* (2004) and *Critical Readings: Violence and the Media* (2006). She is a founding co-editor of *Feminist Media Studies* and an editorial board member of various journals.

Anabela Carvalho is Associate Professor at the University of Minho, Portugal. She has published in a number of journals and edited books and is editor of *Communicating Climate Change: Discourses, Mediations and Perceptions, As Alterações Climáticas, os Media e os Cidadãos* and of special issues of the journals *Comunicação e Sociedade* and *Environmental Communication*. She is Chair of the Science and Environment Communication Section of the European Communication Research and Education Association (ECREA).

Deborah Chambers is Professor of Media and Cultural Studies at Newcastle University, UK. Her research areas intersect sociology and media and cultural studies with a focus on social and cultural theory, gender, identities, the sociology of journalism, the family and changing intimate relationships. Her publications include *Representing the Family* (2001), *Women & Journalism* (with Linda Steiner and Carole Fleming, Routledge, 2004) and *New Social Ties: Contemporary Connections in a Fragmented Society* (2006).

Lilie Chouliaraki is Professor of Media and Communications at the Department of Media and Communications, London School of Economics and Political Science, UK. Her recent publications include *The Spectatorship of Suffering* (2006), *The Soft Power of War* (2007) and *Media, Organisations, Identity* (2009).

Lisbeth Clausen is an Associate Professor at Copenhagen Business School at the Department of Intercultural Management and Communication and the Vice-Director of the Asian Studies Program (Copenhagen Business School),

Denmark. Her research interest is newsroom studies, news flow and audience reception. She is the author of the book *Global News Production* concerning international news production in Japanese newsrooms. Her media and communication research has appeared in journals such as *Media, Culture and Society*, *Nordicom Review* and *Keio Communication Review*.

James R. Compton is Associate Professor in the Faculty of Information and Media Studies at the University of Western Ontario, Canada. He is author of *The Integrated News Spectacle: A Political Economy of Cultural Performance* (2004), and co-editor of *Converging Media, Diverging Politics: A Political Economy of News Media in the United States and Canada* (2005). He is a former reporter/editor with the Canadian Press/ Broadcast News wire service.

Simon Cottle is Professor of Media and Communications, Deputy Head of School and Director of the Mediatised Conflict Research Group in the School of Journalism, Media and Cultural Studies (JOMEC) at Cardiff University, UK. His latest book is *Global Crisis Reporting: Journalism in the Global Age* (2009). He is the series editor for Global Crises and the Media, a major new international series of books commissioned by Peter Lang Publisher, New York.

Ros Coward is Professor of Journalism at Roehampton University, UK. She is the author of several books, including *Language and Materialism* (with John Ellis, 1976), *Female Desire: How Women's Sexuality is Packaged and Consumed* (1984); *The Whole Truth: The Myth of Alternative Health* (1990), *Our Treacherous Hearts: How Women Let Men Get Their Way* (1992), *Diana: The Authorised Portrait* (2004); and co-author of *Mandela: The Authorised Portrait* (2006). As a journalist, she is best known for her columns on the 'Comment and Analysis' pages of the *Guardian*, and for her column 'Looking After Mother' about caring for a parent with dementia.

Andrew Crisell is Professor of Broadcasting Studies at Sunderland University, UK. He wrote *Understanding Radio* (1994), *An Introductory History of British Broadcasting* (2002) and *A Study of Modern Television* (2006), co-authored *Radio Journalism* (2009) with Guy Starkey, and edited *More than a Music Box: Radio Cultures and Communities in a Multi Media World* (2004). He is also a member of the editorial boards of the *Radio Journal* and the *Journal of Media Business Studies*.

Mark Deuze holds a joint appointment as Associate Professor in Telecommunications at Indiana University's Department of Telecommunications in Bloomington, USA, and as Professor of Journalism and New Media at Leiden University, The Netherlands. Publications of his work include five books, including *Media Work* (2007), as well as guest-edited special issues of journals on convergence culture (*Convergence*, 2008; *International Journal of Cultural Studies*, 2009), and articles in journals such as *The Information Society*, *New Media & Society* and *Journalism Studies*.

Roger Dickinson is Senior Lecturer in the Department of Media & Communication at the University of Leicester, UK. He is Director of the Distance Learning programme in media and communications. He is currently working on a study of journalist training.

Wolfgang Donsbach is Professor of Communication at Dresden University of Technology, Germany. He has been president of the World Association for Public Opinion Research (1995–96) and of the International Communication Association (2004–05). He was managing editor of the *International Journal of Public Opinion Research* (1999–2007) and is the general editor of the 12-volume *International Encyclopedia of Communication* (2008). His main research interests are in journalism, political communication, public opinion, and exposure to communication.

Mats Ekström is Professor of Media and Communication at Örebro University, Sweden. He has performed extensive research on journalism, media discourse and the relations between media and politics. His recent publications include the book, co-edited with Åsa Kroon and Mats Nylund, *News from the Interview Society* (2006), as well as articles in *Media, Culture and Society*, *Journalism Studies* and the *Journal of Language and Politics*, amongst others.

Mohammed el-Nawawy is the Knight-Crane endowed chair in the School of Communication at Queens University of Charlotte, USA. His research interests are focused on the new media in the Middle East, particularly satellite channels and the Internet, and their impact on the Arab public sphere. His work on Arab media in general, and Al-Jazeera in particular, has attracted the attention of the popular press inside and outside the US. He is the founding editor of the *Journal of Middle East Media* and serves on the editorial board of *Media, War and Conflict*. He is also a board member on the Arab–US Association for Communication Educators.

James S. Ettema is Professor of Communication Studies at Northwestern University, USA, where his work focuses on the social organisation and cultural impact of media. He is a past chair of Communication Studies and a co-founder of the Media, Technology and Society graduate programme. Among his books is *Custodians of Conscience: Investigative Journalism and Public Virtue*, written with Theodore L. Glasser of Stanford University, which won the Frank Luther Mott-Kappa Tau Alpha Award from the National Journalism and Mass Communication Honor Society and the Sigma Delta Chi Award for research on journalism from the Society of Professional Journalists, among other awards.

Natalie Fenton is Reader in Media and Communications in the Department of Media and Communication, Goldsmiths, University of London, UK. She is also Co-Director of the Goldsmiths Media Research Centre, Spaces, Connections, Control, funded by the Leverhulme Trust, and Co-Director of the Goldsmiths

Centre for the Study of Global Media and Democracy. She has published widely on issues relating to new media, politics and democracy. Her latest book is the edited collection *New Media, Old News: Journalism and Democracy in the Digital Age* (2009).

Bob Franklin is Professor of Journalism Studies at Cardiff University, UK. He is the Editor of *Journalism Studies* and *Journalism Practice* and co-editor of a new series *Journalism Studies: Key Texts* published by Sage. Publications include *The Future of Newspapers* (2009), *Pulling Newspapers Apart; Analysing Print Journalism* (2008), *Local Journalism and Local Media; Making the Local News* (2006), *Television Policy; The MacTaggart Lectures* (2005), *Key Concepts in Journalism Studies* (2005) and *Packaging Politics: Political Communication in Britain's Media Democracy* (2004).

Herbert J. Gans is the Robert S. Lynd Professor Emeritus of Sociology at Columbia University, USA. He is the author of 18 books and monographs, including *Deciding What's News* (1979), *Democracy and the News* (2003) and, most recently, *Imagining America in 2033* (2008). A past president of the American Sociological Association, he received the Association's Career of Distinguished Scholarship Award in 2006.

Mark Glaser, a long-time freelance journalist, is executive editor of PBS MediaShift and PBS Idea Lab websites. From 2001 to 2005, he wrote a weekly column for USC Annenberg School of Communication's *Online Journalism Review*, and he still writes the OPA Intelligence Report email newsletter for the Online Publishers Association. He has written essays for Harvard's *Nieman Reports* and the website for the Yale Center for Globalization, and written for numerous magazines and newspapers such as *Conde Nast Traveler, Entertainment Weekly* and the *New York Times*. He was the lead writer for the Industry Standard's award-winning 'Media Grok' daily email newsletter during the dot-com heyday, and a finalist for a 2004 Online Journalism Award in the Online Commentary category for his *OJR* column.

Mark Hampton is Associate Professor of History at Lingnan University in Hong Kong and a co-editor of the journal *Media History*. He is the author of *Visions of the Press in Britain, 1850–1950* (2004) and co-editor of *Anglo–American Media Interactions, 1850–2000* (2007). He is currently writing a book on Hong Kong and Britishness, 1945–97.

Joseph Harker is an editor and columnist on the *Guardian's* comment section in London, UK. He also coordinates the diversity and inclusion strategy for the paper's editorial department. He is a former managing editor of the *Guardian's* features department. In 2008, he edited its Black History Month poster series, and in 1994 edited the book *The Legacy of Apartheid*, to mark South Africa's first free elections. Before joining the *Guardian*, he was editor and publisher of the weekly newspaper *Black Briton*, and previous to that assistant editor at *The Voice*.

Jackie Harrison is Professor of Public Communication, Head of the Department of Journalism Studies and Chair of the Centre for Freedom of the Media at the University of Sheffield, UK. She is researching the architecture, culture and role of European news and the failures and abuses of news media freedom and standards it faces. She is the author of *News* (Routledge, 2006) and *European Broadcasting Law and Policy* (2007) and is editor of *Mediating Europe: Mass media in contemporary European culture* (2009).

John Hartley is the author/editor of many books and articles on popular culture, media and journalism, most recently *Television Truths* (2008), *The Uses of Digital Literacy* (2009), and *Story Circle: Digital Storytelling Around the World* (2009). He is editor of the *International Journal of Cultural Studies*. Hartley is a Federation Fellow (Australian Research Council), and Research Director of the ARC Centre of Excellence for Creative Industries & Innovation at Queensland University of Technology, Australia.

Alfred Hermida is an award-winning online news pioneer, digital media scholar and journalism educator. An Associate Professor at the Graduate School of Journalism at the University of British Columbia, Canada, his research interests include digital journalism and social media. He is a co-author of *Participatory Journalism: Guarding Open Gates at Online Newspapers* (2011). Hermida spent 16 years at BBC News and was a founding news editor of the BBC News website.

Andrew Hoskins is Associate Professor in Sociology at the University of Warwick, UK. He is founding co-editor of the journal *Media, War & Conflict*, founding editor-in-chief of the journal *Memory Studies* and Director of the Warwick Centre for Memory Studies. He is co-author of *Television and Terror: Conflicting Times and the Crisis of News Discourse* (2007) and co-editor of *Save As... Digital Memories* (2009).

Shih-Hsien Hsu is a PhD candidate in the School of Journalism at the University of Texas at Austin, USA. Hsu received her master's in journalism from National Chengchi University and her bachelor's in political science from National Taiwan University. Her research interests include the construction of media discourse and the effect of new media on the political communication process.

Dale Jacquette is Lehrstuhl ordentlicher Professur für Philosophie, Schwerpunkt theoretische Philosophie (Senior Professorial Chair in Theoretical Philosophy), at Universität Bern, Switzerland. He is the author of numerous articles on logic, metaphysics, philosophy of mind and aesthetics, and has recently published *Ontology* (2002), *David Hume's Critique of Infinity* (2001), *The Philosophy of Schopenhauer* (2005) and *Journalistic Ethics: Moral Responsibility in the Media* (2007).

Bengt Johansson is Associate Professor at University of Gothenburg, Sweden. His research focuses on different aspects of political communication, such as election news reporting, media effects, political scandals and political campaigning/ advertising. Articles published in international journals include 'Talk Scandals', *Media, Culture & Society* (with Mats Ekström, 2007), 'Electoral Cycles and the Mobilizing Effects of Elections: The Swedish Case', *Journal of Elections, Public Opinions and Parties* (with Jesper Strömbäck, 2007).

Richard Kaplan, an independent scholar, is the author of *Politics and the American Press: The Rise of Objectivity, 1865–1920* (2002) and numerous articles on media history, including 'American Journalism Goes to War, 1898–2001: A Manifesto on Media and Empire' in *Media History* (2003).

Douglas Kellner is George Kneller Chair in the Philosophy of Education at UCLA, USA. He is the author of many books, including *Camera Politica: The Politics and Ideology of Contemporary Hollywood Film* (co-authored with Michael Ryan); *Critical Theory, Marxism, and Modernity; Jean Baudrillard: From Marxism to Postmodernism and Beyond;* works in cultural studies such as *Media Culture and Media Spectacle;* a trilogy of books on postmodern theory with Steve Best; and a trilogy of books on the media and the Bush administration, encompassing *Grand Theft 2000, From 9/11 to Terror War* and *Media Spectacle and the Crisis of Democracy.* Kellner is editing the collected papers of Herbert Marcuse, four volumes of which have appeared with Routledge. His latest book is *Guys and Guns Amok: Domestic Terrorism and School Shootings from the Oklahoma City Bombings to the Virginia Tech Massacre.*

Carolyn Kitch is Professor of Journalism at Temple University in Philadelphia, USA, and the author of three books about media history and memory: *The Girl on the Magazine Cover: The Origins of Visual Stereotypes in American Mass Media* (2001); *Pages from the Past: History and Memory in American Magazines* (2005); and, with Janice Hume, *Journalism in a Culture of Grief* (2008). She is a former magazine editor and writer for *McCall's, Good Housekeeping* and *Reader's Digest.*

Larsåke Larsson is Professor of Media and Communication Studies at Örebro University, Sweden. He is researching in journalism, public relations and crisis communication. His primary research deals with the relations between journalists and politicians. His recent publications include the books *Opionionsmakarna (The Opinion Makers,* 2005) and *Kris och lärdom (Crisis and learning,* 2008) together with articles in local journalism and PR in *Journalism Studies, Journal of Communication Management* and *Nordicom.*

Justin Lewis is Professor of Communication at the Cardiff School of Journalism, Media and Cultural Studies. He has written several books about media and politics, his most recent being *Shoot First and Ask Questions Later: Media Coverage of the War* *in Iraq* (2006), *Constructing Public Opinion* (Columbia University Press, 2001) and *Citizens or Consumers* (Open University Press, 2005).

Jake Lynch is Director of the Centre for Peace and Conflict Studies at the University of Sydney, Australia. He is the author, with Annabel McGoldrick, of the landmark text, *Peace Journalism*, as well as numerous other books, book chapters and articles. He convened the inaugural peace journalism commission of the International Peace Research Association, and is an executive member of the Sydney Peace Foundation. Before taking up an academic career, he was a professional journalist, having worked as a presenter for BBC World television news, a Political Correspondent for Sky News and the Sydney correspondent for the *Independent*.

Brian McNair is Professor of Journalism and Communication at the University of Strathclyde, and the founding Director of the Strathclyde School of Journalism and Communication, UK. He is the author of many books and essays on journalism, including *News & Journalism in the UK* (Fifth edition, Routledge, 2008); *Cultural Chaos: journalism, news and power in a globalised world* (Routledge, 2006); and *The Sociology of Journalism* (1998). His work has been widely translated, and is standard reading on journalism and media studies courses all over the world. His book-length study, *Journalists in Film: Heroes and Villains*, is published in 2010.

Mirca Madianou is Lecturer in the Department of Sociology, University of Cambridge and a Fellow of Lucy Cavendish College, UK. She is the author of *Mediating the Nation* (2005) and several other articles on news audiences as well as on nationalism, transnationalism and the media. She is currently the Principal Investigator on the ESRC-funded project 'Migration, ICTs and Transnational Families'.

Donald Matheson is Senior Lecturer in Media and Communication at the University of Canterbury, New Zealand. He is author of *Media Discourses: Analysing Media Texts* (2005) and co-author of *Digital War Reporting* (2009). He co-edits the journal *Ethical Space: The International Journal of Communication Ethics* and writes on journalism's textual practices, particularly in digital media.

Heidi Mau is a PhD candidate in the Mass Media and Communication program at Temple University, Philadelphia, USA. Her research interests centre on the critical examination of mass media and memory, technology and popular culture. She has screened work as an independent media artist in the US and Europe, and has taught media production and criticism at various US universities, including the University of Oklahoma, the University of Pennsylvania and Temple University.

Kaitlynn Mendes is Lecturer in Journalism at De Montfort University, UK. Her main research interests are gender and media, and also children, news and new media technology. She is currently the 'Commentary and Criticism' Co-Editor for the journal *Feminist Media Studies* (Routledge), and is an active member of the Media,

Cultural and Communications Association (MeCCSA). She currently sits on the MeCCSA Women's Network Steering Committee, and is the immediate past chair for the Post-Graduate Network.

Máire Messenger Davies is Director of the Centre for Media Research at the University of Ulster in Northern Ireland, UK. A former journalist, she has taught in universities on both sides of the Atlantic. Her books include *'Dear BBC': Children, television-storytelling and the public sphere* (2001) and *Television is Good for your Kids* (1989, 2001). She is currently conducting research funded by the AHRC and BBC, in collaboration with Bournemouth, Cardiff and De Montfort universities into children and news.

Toby Miller is Professor of Media & Cultural Studies at the University of California, Riverside, USA. His teaching and research cover the media, sport, labour, gender, race, citizenship, politics and cultural policy. He is the author and editor of over 20 volumes, and has published essays in well over 100 journals and books. His current research covers the success of Hollywood overseas, the links between culture and citizenship, and anti-Americanism.

Martin Montgomery is Reader in English Studies at the University of Strathclyde, UK, where he teaches and researches in the School of Journalism and Communication. He is the author of many books and articles on language and communication, including *The Discourse of Broadcast News* (Routledge, 2007) and *An Introduction to Language and Society* (3rd edition, Routledge, 2008). He is currently working on a book on language and the media.

Marguerite Moritz is Professor and UNESCO Chair in International Journalism Education at the University of Colorado, Boulder, USA. Her research looks at professional codes and practices in contemporary news media, including LGBT representations. She was writer and story consultant for the documentary *Scouts Honor*, which examines the Boy Scouts of America's anti-gay policies. The film won the audience award for best documentary and the Freedom of Expression Award at the Sundance Film Festival in 2001.

Henrik Örnebring is Axess Research Fellow in Comparative European Journalism at the Reuters Institute for the Study of Journalism, UK. He is also a Research Associate at the Oxford Internet Institute. He has published several journal articles and book chapters on the topics of journalism, journalism history and television history, and recently guest edited an issue of the journal *Journalism Studies* (2009) on European journalism.

Julian Petley is Professor of Screen Media and Journalism in the School of Arts at Brunel University, UK. His most recent books are *Censoring the Moving Image* (co-written with Philip French) and *Censorship: a Beginner's Guide*. He is a member of the editorial board of the *British Journalism Review* and chair of the Campaign for Press and Broadcasting Freedom.

Greg Philo is Professor of Communications and Research Director of the Glasgow University Media Group, UK. He was co-author of the Glasgow Media Group books *Bad News* (1976), *More Bad News* (1980), *Really Bad News* (1982) and *War and Peace News* (1985). He is editor of *Message Received* (1999), *Media and Mental Distress* (1996) and *The Glasgow Media Group, Volume II* (1995), and the author of *Seeing and Believing: the Influence of Television* (1990) and *Market Killing* (with David Miller, 2001). His most recent books are *Bad News From Israel* (with Mike Berry, 2004) and *Israel and Palestine: Competing Histories* (with Mike Berry, 2006).

Shawn Powers is a PhD candidate at USC Annenberg, USA, and a Research Associate at the USC Center on Public Diplomacy, USA. His research interests focus on the use of media in times of war and conflict, and the potential roles media technologies play in resolving cross-cultural disagreements and international tensions. Previously he worked at the Center for Strategic and International Studies in Washington, DC, and has conducted field and media research in the Middle East, Eastern Europe and Southeast Asia. He is currently a visiting Assistant Professor at the USC Annenberg School of Communication program in London, UK.

Stephen D. Reese is Jesse H. Jones Professor of Journalism and Associate Dean for Academic Affairs in the College of Communication at the University of Texas at Austin, USA. His research, published in numerous articles, chapters and books, focuses on the sociology of news, the framing of political issues and the transformation of journalism under globalization. Most recently he was section editor for 'Media Production and Content' in the ICA *Encyclopedia of Communication*.

Barry Richards is Professor of Public Communication in the Media School at Bournemouth University, UK. Previously he was Professor and Head of the Department of Human Relations at the University of East London. His books include *Disciplines of Delight: The Psychoanalysis of Popular Culture* (1994), and *Emotional Governance: Politics, Media and Terror* (2007). His major interests are in the emotional dimensions of politics, particularly in relation to conflict, security and extremism.

David Rowe is Professor in the Centre for Cultural Research (CCR), University of Western Sydney, Australia, and from 2006–9 was CCR's Director. He has published on media and popular culture in many journals, including *Media, Culture & Society*, *Journalism* and *Social Semiotics*. His books include *Popular Cultures: Rock Music, Sport and the Politics of Pleasure* (1995) and *Sport, Culture and the Media: The Unruly Trinity* (2nd edition, 2004).

Philip Seib is Professor of Journalism and Public Diplomacy, and Professor of International Relations, at the University of Southern California, USA. He is author or editor of numerous books, including, most recently, *The Al Jazeera Effect: How the New Global Media Are Reshaping World Politics*. He is editor of the Palgrave Macmillan Series in International Political Communication and is co-editor of the journal *Media, War & Conflict*.

Jane B. Singer is the Johnston Press Chair in Digital Journalism at the University of Central Lancashire, UK, and Associate Professor in the University of Iowa School of Journalism and Mass Communication, USA. Her research explores digital journalism, including changing roles, perceptions and practices. Before earning her PhD in journalism from the University of Missouri, she was the first news manager of Prodigy Interactive Services. She also has worked as a newspaper reporter and editor.

Guy Starkey is a former radio practitioner with 20 years' experience in media education, management and research in the UK. He is the author of *Local Radio, Going Global* (2011), *Balance and Bias in Journalism: Representation, Regulation and Democracy* (2007) and *Radio in Context* (2004). He is co-author with Andrew Crisell of *Radio Journalism* (2009). The Chair of the Radio Research Section of the European Communication Research and Education Association (ECREA), he is also a member of the steering committee of the Radio Studies Network within the Media, Communication and Cultural Studies Association (MeCCSA).

Linda Steiner is Professor of Journalism and Director of Doctoral and Research Studies at the University of Maryland's College of Journalism, USA. Previously, she was Professor of Media Studies at Rutgers University. Her most recent books are *Key Concepts in Critical Cultural Studies* (co-edited); and *Women and Journalism* (co-authored). She has published 30 book chapters, as well as refereed articles in a variety of journalism and media studies journals. She serves on nine editorial boards.

Daya Kishan Thussu is Professor of International Communication at the University of Westminster in London, UK. He is the Founder and Managing Editor of the journal *Global Media and Communication*. Among his main publications are *Electronic Empires* (1998), *International Communication: Continuity and Change* (2nd edition, 2006), *War and the Media: Reporting Conflict 24/7* (2003), *Media on the Move: Global Flow and Contra-flow* (2007), *News as Entertainment* (2007) and *Internationalizing Media Studies* (2009).

John Tulloch has been Research Professor of Sociology and Communications, Director of the University Research Centre in Media, Globalization and Risk, and co-director of the Collaborative Research Network in Human Rights, Security and the Media at Brunel University, UK. Curently he is Research Professor in the Department of Communication and Media, School of Design, Communication and

IT, University of Newcastle, New South Wales. His more recent books include: *Trevor Griffiths* (2007); *One Day in July: Experiencing 7/7* (2006); *Shakespeare and Chekhov in Production and Reception* (2005); *Risk and Everyday Life* (with Deborah Lupton, 2003); *Watching Television Audiences* (2000); *Performing Culture* (1999); *Television, Risk and AIDS* (1997); *Science Fiction Audiences: Watching Doctor Who and Star Trek* (with Henry Jenkins, 1995). Currently, with R. Warwick Blood, he is writing *Images of War, Terror and Risk.*

Howard Tumber is Professor of Journalism and Communication in the Graduate School of Journalism at City University London, UK. He has published widely in the field of the sociology of news and journalism and is the author, co-author/editor of eight books including: *Critical Concepts in Journalism* (4 vols, 2008), *Journalists under Fire* (2006), *Media at War: the Iraq Crisis* (2004), *Media Power, Policies and Professionals* (2000), *News: A Reader* (1999), *Reporting Crime – The Media Politics of Criminal Justice* (1994), *Journalists at War* (1988), *Television and Riots* (1982). He is a founder and co-editor of the journal *Journalism: Theory, Practice and Criticism.* His recent work concerns the role of journalists and the reporting of international conflict.

Silvio Waisbord is Assistant Professor in the School of Media and Public Affairs at George Washington University, USA. He is the Editor of the *International Journal of Press/Politics.* Previously, he was Associate Professor and Director of the Journalism Resources Institute at Rutgers University. He is the author and editor of four books, including *Watchdog Journalism in South America.* His current work focuses on journalism, civic society and social change. He was a fellow at the Annenberg School for Communication, the Kellogg Institute for International Studies, and the Media Studies Center.

Garry Whannel is Professor of Media Cultures at the University of Bedfordshire, UK. He has been writing on media and sport for 30 years. His published work includes *Culture, Politics and Sport* (2008), *Media Sport Stars: Masculinities and Moralities* (2001), *Fields in Vision* (1992) and *Blowing the Whistle* (1983). His current research interests include celebrity culture and the vortextuality process, journalism, politics and the Olympic Games, the growth of commercial sponsorship, and the roots of political humour.

Andrew Williams is the RCUK Research Fellow in Risk, Health and Science Communication in the School of Journalism, Media and Cultural Studies at Cardiff University, UK. He has authored (and co-authored) a number of book chapters, journal articles and reports on the relationship between public relations and the news, media representations of science and health, and the rise of digital journalism and participatory media.

Barbie Zelizer is the Raymond Williams Professor of Communication and Director of the Scholars Program in Culture and Communication at the University of Pennsylvania's Annenberg School for Communication, USA. A former journalist, she has authored or edited eight books, including the award-winning *Remembering to Forget: Holocaust Memory Through the Camera's Eye* (1998), *Covering the Body: The Kennedy Assassination, the Media, and the Shaping of Collective Memory* (1992), and *Taking Journalism Seriously* (2004). In 2008, she published *Explorations in Communication and History* (Routledge). She is a founder and co-editor of *Journalism: Theory, Practice and Criticism*. Currently President-Elect of the International Communication Association, she has just completed a book on about-to-die photographs and journalism.

INTRODUCTION: RECRAFTING NEWS AND JOURNALISM

Stuart Allan

'Imagine, if you will, sitting down to your morning coffee, turning on your home computer to read the day's newspaper. Well, it's not as far-fetched as it may seem.' So begins the news anchor's introduction to a story in a KRON-TV evening newscast, one concerning a novel initiative by two of San Francisco's newspapers to make their stories available on a fledgling 'computer network' set up between eight newspapers around the country. The year was 1981, a time when few of the viewers watching would have personal experience of computing, let alone this 'newest form of electronic journalism' as it was being called here. The story, presented by the station's science editor, Steve Newman, proceeds to describe 'the brand new system' by showing editors at the *San Francisco Examiner* 'programming' the day's edition of the newspaper into a computer connected over a telephone line to another one in Columbus, Ohio. 'This is an experiment,' David Cole of the *Examiner* is shown stating. 'We're trying to figure out what it's going to mean to us, as editors and reporters and what it means to the home user.' Rather tellingly, he then adds 'we're not in it to make money, we're probably not going to lose a lot, but we aren't going to make much either.'

Newman reports that the two-week-old service is aimed at the estimated two to three thousand home computer owners in the San Francisco Bay area. One such user, evidently excited by the potential of this 'electronic newspaper,' appears in the story. He states:

> With this system, we have the option not only of seeing the newspaper on the screen but also, optionally, we can copy it, so anything we are interested in we can go back in again and copy it on to paper and save it. Which I think is the [inaudible] future of the type of interrogation an individual will give to the newspapers (Richard Halloran, cited in KRON-TV, 1981).

In bringing the story to a close, Newman informs those watching: 'This is only the first step in newspapers by computer. Engineers now predict the day will come when we get all our newspapers and magazines by home computer, but that's a few years off.' The story then cuts to its final shot, showing a newspaper seller on the street with a customer, as the voice-over concludes – in a slightly sarcastic tone – 'So for the moment at least this fellow isn't worried about being out of a job.' Back in the studio, the news anchor rounds out the story, observing: 'Well, it takes over two hours to receive the entire text of the newspaper over the phone. And with an hourly use charge of five dollars, the new tele-paper won't be much competition for the twenty-cent street edition.'

Viewed from the vantage point of today, this news story seems remarkably prescient, which perhaps explains why it went viral when posted on YouTube under the title '1981 primitive Internet report on KRON' in early 2009.[1] It is impossible to say, of course, why it proved to be so popular. Perhaps it was due to a warm glow of nostalgia it elicits for journalism in a pre-internet era, or maybe it is the unsettling realisation it engenders that several of the issues identified continue to challenge us today. Five such issues, in my interpretation, revolve around the following:

Technology. Implicit throughout the news story is the premise that technological innovation is propelling journalism forward. The potential benefits of this 'brand new system' involving a modem and rotary telephone to connect newspapers with distant readers seems certain to deliver on this promise, however 'far-fetched … it may seem' to the sceptical viewer. Quite how long it will be before the news organisations 'figure out' the significance of this 'experiment' is a matter of speculation ('engineers now predict the day will come …'), the reporter concedes, but this is none the less a confident technology-led projection of the newspaper's future in the name of progress.

Profitability. While Cole's phrase 'we're not in it to make money' invites a wry response, it neatly pinpoints the absence of a viable business model to justify the reason why the newspapers involved are 'investing a lot of money' in this experiment. The alignment of journalism with commercial imperatives is taken for granted, with the cost to the consumer of the internet – five dollars per hour for the new 'tele-paper' as opposed to the twenty-cent paper and ink edition – being presented as a decisive factor. While the possible implications for the employment of the newspaper seller on the street are highlighted ('this fellow isn't worried about being out of a job'), no mention is made of the journalist's status in this regard.

Journalistic form. Little information is provided about the actual content of this 'newest form of electronic journalism' beyond the fact that it is, in effect, the same as the newspaper minus 'pictures, ads, and the comics.' Various screen shots indicate that the text is presented in standard computer type – e.g., flickering blue or green letters on an otherwise blank screen – without stylistic variation. In reportorial terms, this is the re-mediation of newspaper copy onto an online delivery platform. No conception of an emergent journalism of the internet (in contrast with journalism on the internet) is acknowledged; rather, current conventions define the limits of form and practice.

Consumption. The envisioned community of users is small – 'two to three thousand home computer owners' being a mere fraction of the city's population – where a link appears to be implied between technological access and personal wealth. The one user identified, Richard Halloran, is described as living in a 'fashionable North Beach apartment,' while presumably the slow speed of the electronic service would be prohibitive (cost-, but also time-wise) for most prospective users. Halloran himself is elderly, which opens up a further dimension to his presumed representative status. Similarly relevant is the view of consumption taking place in the private realm of the affluent household.

Interactivity. While various shots show Halloran sitting in front of his computer, virtually nothing is said about how prospective users are expected to relate to the 'electronic newspaper' other than simply reading it with their morning coffee. Except, that is, for Halloran himself, who describes a process of copying electronic text onto paper in order to save it before making the point that this capability makes possible new forms of 'interrogation' where the newspaper's coverage is concerned. Interrogation, in this sense, resonates with the type of critique provided by citizen journalists and bloggers today.

Further issues are apparent, of course, including the larger significance of such news stories for professional conceptions of the craft, amongst others. That is to say, the newscast's assignment of news value to an item about news reporting is interesting in its own right (television news reporting about newspapers, let alone a prospective electronic rival, typically having a certain edge), but from a current perspective

– almost thirty years after the initial broadcast – the story becomes a resource for tracing how the internet re-configures professional identities. Indeed, its status in this regard speaks to questions of reportorial tradition, values and memory, helping to illuminate otherwise tacit aspects of a collective sense of journalism as an 'interpretive community' (Zelizer, this volume) where self-definition based on precedents of form and practice is a priority.

In dwelling on this rather curious artefact of a seemingly bygone era, one can be forgiven for pausing to reminisce about a time when the future of journalism seemed confident, if not assured. In any case, though, I would like to suggest that the themes it illustrates continue to be deserving of our close attention. To the extent that a careful reading helps to disrupt our taken-for-granted, seemingly common-sensical assumptions about journalism – not least the evolving relationship between newspapers and the internet – such materials promise to spark creative thinking about familiar issues.

Such issues are becoming increasingly pressing in these troubled times as the news industry, paradoxically, finds itself subjected to intense journalistic scrutiny for all of the wrong reasons. Grim headlines document the agonising twists and turns of news organisations caught up in a desperate struggle to remain financially viable under severe, seemingly inexorable market pressures. Newspapers, in particular, are buckling under the strain. Some are collapsing altogether – their hard-won reputations for reportorial integrity, earned over generations, consigned to history's dustbin – while others dramatically refashion themselves with an unwavering eye to bottom-line profitability. While managers talk of 'reorganisation,' 'downsizing,' 'layoffs', 'cutbacks,' 'concessions' and the like (while striving to avoid the word 'bankruptcy'), news and editorial posts are being 'concentrated,' with remaining staff members compelled to 'multi-task' as they adopt greater 'flexibility' with regard to their salary and working conditions. 'Converged' content is being 'repackaged,' a polite way of saying that its quantity – and, too often, quality – is shrinking as 'efficiencies' are imposed. The closing of local news beats, like the foreign bureaus before them, is a price too high to pay for some, leading them to merge operations with former competitors in order to save revenue by sharing coverage. For others, forced to think the unthinkable, the decision has been made to abandon the print edition entirely, focusing remaining resources on transforming into internet-only news sources. Even here the language of 'innovation' and 'experimentation' can fail to conceal the unspoken fear that such a bold 'initiative' may soon prove to be too little, too late.

At a time when this ominous trend appears to be gathering momentum, it is readily apparent that the kind of optimism expressed in the KRON-TV news item described above is in short supply. And yet, some are convinced that a new business model for news organisations is in the process of emerging, one sufficiently robust to support high-quality coverage across a diverse range of delivery platforms. Declarations about the 'death of newspapers,' they contend, are wide of the mark. While decidedly anxious about the prospect of managing the changes ushered in by the internet, they nevertheless see a potential for new, enriched types of news reporting to flourish in the digital age. The imperatives transforming what counts as journalism present opportunities for progressive change, they believe, quite possibly in ways that will empower ordinary citizens to reassert their claim on it in the name of democratising media power.

Interesting in this regard are the views of Alan Rusbridger (2008), editor of the *Guardian* in London. In describing the 'new world order' of journalism, he recalled a definition of the newspaper offered by *Washington Post* columnist David Broder nearly three decades ago (around the time of the KRON-TV report) which, in his view, retains its value:

> I would like to see us say over and over until the point has been made ... that the newspaper that drops on your doorstep is a partial, hasty, incomplete, inevitably somewhat flawed and inaccurate rendering of some of the things we heard about in the past 24 hours ... distorted despite our best efforts to eliminate gross bias by the very process of compression that makes it possible for you ... to read it in about an hour. If we labeled the paper accurately then we would immediately add: But it's the best we could do under the circumstances, and we will be back tomorrow with a corrected updated version ... (Broder, cited in Rusbridger, 2008: 248).

For Rusbridger, who first read this description when he was a young reporter in Washington, its insight is still relevant today. 'The greater the speed required of us in the digital world – and speed does matter, but never at the expense of accuracy or fairness or anything which would imperil trust – the more we should be honest about the tentative nature of what is possible,' he observes. This type of self-reflexivity does not belie a lack of conviction, of course. Rather, it appears to signal Rusbridger's commitment to re-assessing what the 'conceptual shifts' occurring in the news industry will mean for the future of journalism and the value of the record it creates. Precisely how this process will unfold is anything but clear, but is certain to prove 'enormously difficult to manage' in his view, and involve 'quite painful re-engineering of traditional workforces and re-allocation of resources' (2008: 249). The option of standing still, to wait and see what will happen, is not sustainable; the 'revolutionary experiment' is already underway and gathering speed. And in 'a 24/7 world – which is what we're all moving to – it has to begin with a searching examination of what journalism is,' he believes, as challenging as this may prove to be.

Bearing this challenge in mind, our attention turns in the next section to consider a lively exchange of views regarding the nature of what constitutes journalism in the face of the threat – or the promise, in the eyes of some – posed by citizen journalism. The particular debate under scrutiny here has been transpiring over recent years against the backdrop of Columbia University's decision to rethink its journalism curriculum, a move which attracted press attention around the world due to the School of Journalism's prestige as a leading voice in journalism education (see also Adam's chapter, this volume). Questions about how best to prepare the next generation of journalists are proving particularly vexing in this climate of constant change, and go to the heart of this *Companion*'s aims and objectives.

Journalism and democracy

In a 1906 letter to one of his *Post-Dispatch* editors, newspaper proprietor Joseph Pulitzer explained how to ensure the title served its readers:

> Summing up in a nutshell: DON'T be afraid, but be sure that you are right. Don't go to the other extreme, but be exactly judicial and independent and always fair. Have nothing to do with politicians on either side. [...] [E]very issue of the paper presents an opportunity and duty to say something courageous and true; to rise above the mediocre and conventional; to say something that will command the respect of the intelligent, the educated, the independent part of the community; to rise above fear of partisanship and fear of popular prejudice (Cited in Seitz, 1924: 286; see also Ireland, 1938).

On the occasion of Pulitzer's death, five years later, this vision – together with opinions about the relative extent to which it was realized – figured prominently in assessments of his life and the impact his newspapers had on the 'new journalism' of the era. Shortly after, on 30 September 1912, the first cohort of students arrived to attend the School of Journalism at Columbia University in New York, a school made possible by Pulitzer's beneficence (see Boylan, 2003; Hohenberg, 1974).

In contrast with the legal or medical professions, which adopted strict procedures of entry, licensed codes of ethics, and formal methods of self-regulation, no such measures were thought to be consistent with the practice of journalism. None the less, Pulitzer steadfastly believed that journalism's status – its elevation in the eyes of readers, as well as for journalists themselves – deserved equal recognition. Professionalism would provide the guiding ethos to which all journalists should properly aspire. The factors shaping identity formation were to revolve around a declared commitment to the virtues of public-spiritedness. Precisely what the attendant 'standard of civic righteousness' would entail defied easy elucidation; meanwhile, Pulitzer only knew that a broad definition in relation to the 'character' was necessary to advance the public good. Moral courage, so vital for public service, needed to be taught; aptitude for its principles and determination to behave responsibly were not inborn. Here, Pulitzer's (1904) distinction between 'real journalists' and those whose newspaper work 'requires neither knowledge nor conviction' underscored the difference between the personal qualities to be engendered by journalism education and those derived from 'mere business training' (1904: 19).

More than a question of semantics, the nature of the proper identity to be affirmed by the journalist within a democracy continues to be hotly contested. Indeed, in recent years, nowhere have the tacit assumptions informing a collective sense of identity been more openly challenged than by the emergence of 'citizen journalism.' In championing the virtues of 'amateur' reporters – especially their freedom from 'professional' complicity in the gatekeeping machinations of Big Media – citizen journalism has succeeded in rattling the foundations of the craft. Reactions to it, both from within journalism's inner circles as well as from a wide range of journalism educators, have tended to range from the condemnatory to the dismissive. One such commentator is Samuel Freedman (2006), Professor of Journalism at Columbia University as well as an education columnist for the *New York Times*. Expressing his 'despair over the movement's current cachet,' he has argued that despite its wrapping in idealism, 'citizen journalism forms part of a larger attempt to degrade, even to disfranchise journalism as practiced by trained professionals.' At a time when, in his view, 'traditional, reportorial journalism seems so besieged', the threat posed by citizen journalism deserves much wider recognition:

> To treat an amateur as equally credible as a professional, to congratulate the wannabe with the title 'journalist,' is only to further erode the line between raw material and finished product. For those people who believe that editorial gate-keeping is a form of censorship, if not mind control, then I suppose the absence of any mediating intelligence is considered a good thing (Freedman, 2006).

For critics like Freedman, an appreciation of the differing capacities of 'the amateur, however well-meaning, and the pro' is in serious danger of being lost. The implications for traditional journalism, they fear, may well prove detrimental, hence their calls to shore up the crumbling defences of journalistic identity accordingly.

Freedman's colleague at Columbia, Dean Nicholas Lemann (2006), weighed into the controversy surrounding what some critics were calling 'journalism without journalists' by publishing a critique in *The New Yorker*. His essay, titled 'Amateur Hour,' spelt out what he considered to be the implications of amateurism for news reporting:

> Reporting – meaning the tradition by which a member of a distinct occupational category gets to cross the usual bounds of geography and class, to go where important things are happening, to ask powerful people blunt and impertinent questions, and to report back, reliably and in plain language, to a general audience – is a distinctive, fairly recent invention. [...] It is a powerful social tool, because it provides citizens with an independent source of information about the state and other holders of power. It sounds obvious, but reporting requires reporters. They don't have to be priests or gatekeepers or even paid professionals; they just have to go out and do the work (Lemann, 2006).

In the case of citizen reporting on the internet, he argued, there is a danger that this 'distinct occupational category' will become blurred to the point that journalism itself suffers as a result.

> The Internet is not unfriendly to reporting; potentially, it is the best reporting medium ever invented. A few places, like the site on Yahoo! operated by Kevin Sites, consistently offer good journalism that has a distinctly Internet,

rather than repurposed, feeling. To keep pushing in that direction, though, requires that we hold up original reporting as a virtue and use the Internet to find new ways of presenting fresh material – which, inescapably, will wind up being produced by people who do that full time, not 'citizens' with day jobs (Lemann, 2006).

This invocation of a stark dichotomy between the traditional journalist producing original reporting, on the one hand, and 'citizens' with 'day jobs', on the other, left little doubt about where Lemann believed journalistic identity was to be appropriately defined. The internet's 'cheerleaders,' he argued, 'have got the rhetorical upper hand; traditional journalists answering their challenges often sound either clueless or cowed and apologetic.' This when, in his view, 'there is not much relation between claims for the possibilities inherent in journalist-free journalism and what the people engaged in that pursuit are actually producing.'

Underlying Lemann's remarks was the conviction that the reportorial achievements of citizen journalism were too modest to warrant the 'soaring rhetoric' associated with them, a viewpoint which one presumes he knew was certain to ignite a powerful reaction in the blogosphere. This is precisely what happened, with a diverse array of ripostes swiftly registering from across the journalistic spectrum, including from citizen journalists cited in the essay. To the extent it is possible to generalize, the main points of dispute revolved around the claims made about amateur reporting replacing professional journalism (as opposed to complementing it, many remarked), the relative amount of original material being produced, and whether or not the movement was living up to its 'hype' (in the eyes of critics) or 'promise' (in the opinion of advocates). Moreover, Lemann's personal status as an elite member of the 'journalistic estab-lishment' frequently attracted comment, with some claiming to detect a 'patronizing attitude' in his comments. Amongst the more even-handed responses, in my reading, was a post by Mitch Ratcliffe on the blog ZDNet. In his appraisal of Lemann's thesis, he wrote:

> What must be embraced by the citizen journalists out there is the rigor and self-criticism that journalism represents. Where Nicholas Lemann's critique of citizen journalism falls down is his lack of critical reflection on journalism itself. Yes, most citizen journalism today looks like church newsletter writing [a claim made in the essay], but so does a lot of 'real' journalism. The celebrity-and-spin mechanism has taken such thorough hold of the mainstream that good journalism is the exception there, too (Ratcliffe, Blogs.ZDNet.com, 31 July 2006).

An angrier tone permeates Jeff Jarvis's post on his blog BuzzMachine, where he chastised Lemann for setting up 'easy straw men' in order to 'tear them down' with a 'lazy argument.' One particularly contentious point concerned journalism's standards. Taking issue with Lemann's view that they are set by professionals, he argued:

I'd say they are still being set by the public who have always decided every day whom to believe and whom to trust – only now, we get to hear their decision process. [Lemann] continues to try to define journalists as the professionals, to define the act by the person who performs it (and, implicitly, the training he [or she] has) rather than by the act itself (Jarvis, BuzzMachine, 31 July 2006).

Challenging Lemann for limiting 'journalism to journalists,' Jarvis called for professionals to engage in a partnership with their citizen counterparts. 'The implication is that until bloggers do what professional journalists do,' he added, 'then they are not doing journalism, not pulling their weight.' How much better it would be, Jarvis suggested, for new opportunities to be identified – within both journalism and journalism schools – for this partnership to be formalized into a collaborative, networked endeavour.

In considering the conceptual tensions implicit in Lemann's defence of what he terms the 'traditional journalist,' it is striking to note the extent of its reliance upon certain familiar assumptions about identity. That is to say, consistent with the broader discourse of journalism as an emergent profession is the conviction that the journalist will necessarily uphold at all times – even in the face of great personal sacrifice – proper reportorial standards when fulfilling his or her obligations. This when the evaluative criteria by which these standards are defined recurrently elude efforts to codify them (exceptions including the legal terms of libel or slander, for example), being regarded as self-evident in the main. Indeed, it is their perceived violation by the 'amateur' that is much more likely to render them visible; rules, as always, tending to be more clearly understood when they are broken. The correlative commitment to the strictures of 'objectivity' is similarly left unspoken, but is none the less discernible in the espousal of ostensibly dispassionate observation and detached transcription. The apparent subjectivity of the citizen journalist, it follows, warrants condemnation to the extent that it fails to separate out facts from values, let alone opinion. The skill to identify and sustain such differentiations, long-associated with the ascendancy of the 'quality' newspaper press, is thereby deemed to be a matter of personal integrity for the common good of the craft – and as such a key factor distinguishing the journalist from the aspirant (see also Allan, 2006, 2009).

One might be tempted to draw certain parallels between the 'raw' journalist 'knowing nothing of principles' in need of university education, as perceived by Pulitzer, and the 'citizens' with 'day jobs' rebuffed by Lemann. Indicative of both perspectives is a marked disdain for the apparent deviancy of the amateur, the pretensions of whom are perceived to represent an implied threat to the ideology of professionalism ideally associated with the performance of the craft. In the period when the Columbia school was founded, the tenets of this ideology were being hurriedly consolidated in the curriculum. Journalists at the time, as the late James W. Carey (1978, 2000) reminded us, were widely regarded as a 'ragtag collection,' most of whom were not educated in any formal sense of the term beyond their school years. Most assuredly, he observed, they were not 'men or women of letters'; rather:

They were an unlikely collection of itinerant scribblers, aspiring or more often failed novelists, ne'er-do-well sons or daughters of established families and, most importantly, the upwardly mobile children of immigrants with an inherited rather than an educated gift of language, without much education and certainly without much refinement.

They were often radical in their politics and unpredictable in their conduct. In fact, their behavior forms much of the folklore of the craft. They lived in and romanced the low life of the city and had no aversion to socialism or trade unions and little illusion about the motives of those for whom they worked (Carey, 2000: 16).

Rather provocatively, Carey proceeded to depart from the accustomed laudatory treatments of Pulitzer's ambition to launch the Columbia school by calling into question the motives behind the proprietor's initiative. Specifically, he contended, 'Pulitzer was probably not alone in believing that a university education might domesticate this unruly class, turn them into disciplined workers and end their flirtation with socialism and trade unions' (2000: 16). Journalism education, viewed from this angle, constitutes a form of social control. That is, it is seen to be a means of 'co-opting an undisciplined and contentious group and aligning them more closely with the aims of business enterprise.' Intertwined with discourses of 'the quest for knowledge' and 'professional standards,' it follows, is the desire 'to have a workforce that is moral, orderly, habitual, and conservative' (2000: 16).

Carey was suggesting, in effect, that greater attention needed to be devoted to the ways in which courses like Columbia's were intended to fulfill the objective of transforming 'irresponsible writers' into 'responsible journalists' for prospective employers, on the one hand, and for reasons that suited the university more generally, on the other. When considering the latter, he maintained, it becomes apparent that faculty advisors were aiming to design a course revolving around not only the essentials of the craft 'but a politics and ethics congenial to the needs of college presidents seeking, like all administrators, more order and docility' (2000: 19). This amounted to curbing the 'natural excess of students who wanted to be journalists,' especially where they had yet to learn 'the good habits of adults or the responsible commitments of capitalism' (2000: 19). To the extent that courses of this type were perceived to be successful in this regard, they were rewarded with institutional legitimacy – both in educational terms (where journalism's place in the academy was slowly being secured, albeit in less than comfortable circumstances), as well as in professional ones. 'The history of journalism education is, therefore, part of the story of the creation of a new social class invested with enormous power, and authority,' Carey concluded (1978: 848). And as such, 'without meeting the historic canons by which professions are identified, journalism has been made a profession by fiat' (1978: 850). It followed, in turn, that ensuing debates about the 'expert' identity to be assumed by the journalist – once cast within the terms of an 'ethical practitioners versus amoral hacks' continuum – would be in all likelihood effectively resolved before they had properly commenced. Much to the dismay, needless to say, of those who, like Carey, actively sought to resist the conflation of professionalism and morality.

Set against this of critique, Pulitzer's bold assessment of the normative criteria shaping his preferred configuration of journalistic identity nevertheless helps to illuminate some of the taken-for-granted assumptions informing current journalists' role perceptions. A certain mythology exists which celebrates this aspiration to democratic ideals (ranging from claims made by advocacy organisations to fictional portrayals of journalism in the entertainment media, and beyond), despite the recurrent scepticism expressed by many journalists themselves where such 'visions' of their craft are concerned. More often than not, however, these familiar discourses of identity, when read against the grain, reveal their dependence upon normalised – that is to say, professionalised – structures of social exclusion.

Critical researchers have documented the ways in which class differences can underpin hiring decisions within news organisations, for example, where informal considerations about family or personal connections, educational background, and financial resources (to offset the relatively low pay at entry levels) may come to bear in what is almost always a highly competitive process. Feminist researchers have examined the extent to which journalistic identity continues to be defined within the day-to-day 'macho culture' of the newsroom, where female journalists' perceptions of sexual discrimination typically vary sharply from those held by their male colleagues. Ethnic minority journalists, research suggests, may find themselves encountering inferential forms of racism, where pressures are placed upon them to 'write white' so as to conform to certain preconceptions about what constitutes proper, objective reporting for predominantly white audiences. It is in the course of deconstructing these types of factors – often subtle, seemingly 'common sensical' in their influence – that the gap between the rhetoric of journalistic identity and its lived materiality is rendered explicit. Pulitzer's intervention, in the end, was about enhancing the relevance of journalistic identity to democratic values, the intention being to ensure that in the making of journalists, citizens would be produced. As such, it continues to this day to represent a clarion call for change in both the newsroom and the journalism classroom.

One way to engage with citizen journalism, it follows, is to reinvigorate the journalist's identity as a citizen. 'The modern school of journalism begins its teaching from the premises of the profession it serves,' Carey (1978) observed some three decades ago. 'In transmitting the language of professionalism it makes available to students a "taken-for-granted world" of journalism that is rarely questioned or critically analyzed' (1978: 853). In considering the extent to which this holds true today, when long-established approaches to journalism education risk appearing anachronistic in the brave new world of the internet, it invites a welcome degree of self-reflexivity about all aspects of a university programme's provision. The pressures brought to bear upon journalism educators to make their curricula conform to the changing demands of the news industry must be met at a number of different levels, but especially with respect to the implications for teaching what counts as an appropriate identity – in both personal and collective terms – for tomorrow's journalist. When familiar pedagogical approaches are threatening to unravel, it is vital that a renewed commitment to experiment and exploration be sustained.

The prestigious role once held to be the exclusive provenance of the professional journalist is being rapidly rewritten by citizen journalism, a process as far-reaching in its implications as it is inevitable. Any sense of complacency, however ingrained in institutional norms and values, must be recast before viable alternatives will begin to find their purchase. For prospective journalists willing to participate in dialogue and debate about how best to define their identity in new, progressive ways, it may prove advantageous to begin not with the premises of a profession they seek to serve, but rather with their obligations to the diverse publics whose interests they will claim to represent. In the event that Carey (2007) was right in his contention that 'the age of independent journalism may be over after a successful hundred-year run,' then now is the time for journalists to be thinking afresh about the fraught relationship they share with their fellow citizens. And therein lies the reason why he believed that a better understanding of journalism's history matters, namely because it 'might help journalists grasp the significance of this moment and perhaps to see directions of growth and reform in the practice of this valuable craft' (2007: 5).

This volume

This is the critical juncture where *The Routledge Companion to News and Journalism* seeks to intervene. In light of these and related sorts of concerns, it is hardly surprising that the language of 'crisis' is being used by journalists and commentators alike as they struggle to make sense of the sweeping changes transpiring around them.

The *Companion* is organised to address a series of themes pertinent to the on-going theoretical and methodological development of news and journalism studies around the globe, with particular reference to work conducted in Britain and the United States. Each of the 60 chapters that follow, situated across seven subsections, promises to offer the reader a unique perspective in a manner at once theoretically grounded and yet alive to the prospects of futures unfolding apace. In other words, this volume is not intended as an academic treatment for its own sake. Rather, each chapter makes the case for the value of a critical, historically informed perspective in order to deepen and enrich ongoing dialogue and debate amongst all participants interested in testing familiar assumptions with a view to advancing alternative perspectives. It is in this evaluative capacity that academic researchers are especially well placed to contribute an array of insights into the underlying factors giving shape to current developments.

Accordingly, this *Companion* examines the reasons why we have ended up with the kind of news reporting we have today – its remarkable strengths as well as the formidable challenges it faces – with a view to exploring how we might improve upon it for tomorrow. While no one volume can be truly comprehensive, care has been taken to select topics which effectively blur the familiar 'theory' and 'practice' divide to advantage, thereby helping to ensure that they will be useful in a wide range of contexts. More specifically, in seeking to adopt a distinctive approach, the *Companion* presents the following features:

- It is inclusive in the scope of its scholarship, offering a multiplicity of perspectives which – taken together – provide a treatment of pressing concerns that is unique in breadth and depth. Given the shared commitment to reinvigorate current debates, a value has been placed on innovative thinking so as to encourage challenging, even counter-intuitive views to emerge.
- Each chapter's topic is problem-led, which is to say that it seeks to address a 'real world' concern that casts light on an important dimension of news and journalism to show why it matters. This type of approach, it is hoped, will ensure this volume is regarded as making a contribution in its own right to the conceptual and methodo-logical formalisation of this area of enquiry.
- A recurrent theme evident throughout the *Companion* concerns journalism's responsibilities in a democracy. In the course of elucidating pertinent debates – including questions of citizenship, for example, or social exclusion where age, class, gender, ethnicity and sexuality are concerned – the chapters draw upon a range of academic disciplines. This commitment to interdisciplinarity ensures that a range of social issues is encompassed that might otherwise fall outside of the domain of news or journalism studies more narrowly defined.
- The discussion revolves primarily around academic research conducted and published in the UK and the US in the main, although about one quarter of the volume is made up of contributions from other national contexts. This approach allows for international comparisons to be made, as well an array of global perspec-tives to be rehearsed – including those seeking to render problematic traditional, typically Western, assumptions.

The aim of this *Companion*, it follows, is not to set down the terms of debate, but rather to encourage new forms of dialogue. In the remaining portion of this intro-ductory chapter, I shall briefly outline the rationale for the selection of topics by offering a few words about the contents of each of the 60 chapters in turn. As will soon become apparent, alternative orderings present themselves, any one of which would engender positive advantages. It is hoped that the chosen structure will contribute to an over-arching narrative, however, one that speaks to the intellectual formation of news and journalism studies by elucidating key ideas, concepts, issues and debates while, at the same time, stressing the value of reinvigorating scholarship with a critical eye to developments in the professional realm.

Structure and contents

The opening section of the *Companion*, 'The Evolving Ideals of Journalism,' illuminates important dimensions of the guiding ethos of news reporting today by casting its features in historical terms. The first chapter, by Mark Hampton, traces the emergence of the idea of the press as a 'Fourth Estate,' that is, as a *de facto* – albeit unofficial – branch of government in British and US contexts. This idea, which has long figured as a normative vision to which journalists aspire, is shown to rest upon several rival (often overlapping) ideals concerning the relationship between the press and its readers. This relationship is approached from a different angle by John Hartley (Chapter 2), who introduces the premise that popular culture is the 'true seed-bed' of modern popular journalism. Over the course of his analysis, he examines the evolution of this type of journalism, paying particular attention to how spectacle, celebrity and entertainment underpin its shift from a 'radical-popular' ('we') press to the 'commercial-popular' ('they') press typically associated with modernity. In Chapter 3, Richard Kaplan offers a complementary perspective, focusing on the origins of objectivity as a defining ideal of journalism. For over a century, he points out, the US press has sought to align its core public mission with a professional code of studied impartiality and rigorous factuality, notwithstanding the difficulties in achieving this ethic of objectivity in practice over the years. Wolfgang Donsbach (Chapter 4) centres this issue of professionalism in his discussion, outlining three traditions of journalism – subjective, public service, and commercial – in order to highlight changing conceptions of journalistic identity. Of particular relevance in this regard is the institutionalisation of journalism as a profession equipped to fulfil its societal tasks, he argues, a process which entails a reconsideration of the competencies associated with the social responsibilities of the reporter.

Deborah Chambers and Linda Steiner (Chapter 5) similarly engage with the changing status of the reporter, pointing out that female journalists now appear well-established in a profession that for most of its history has been a male enclave. Over the course of this discussion, which ranges from women journalists during the colonial period to current efforts to shatter the glass ceilings in news organisations today, they highlight the extent to which journalism's ideals have been defined in ways beneficial to male privilege. In Stuart Allan's (Chapter 6) contribution, it is the idealised conception of the news media's role vis-à-vis the formation of public opinion that is under scrutiny. In the course of contrasting the differing views of the journalist Walter Lippmann and the philosopher John Dewey in the 1920s, a number of significant issues emerge regarding journalism's perceived obligations to the ordinary citizen in a democracy. Bonnie Brennen (Chapter 7) explores how certain ideals have informed the emergence and development of photojournalism as a medium of reporting. She devotes particular attention to its presumed ability to provide neutral records of 'objective reality,' that is, to render images of news events that are truthful, transparent and authentic. Differing claims about this capacity have evolved over the years, with the arrival of digital technologies providing a fresh impetus for rethinking photojournalism's claim on the real. In Donald Matheson's (Chapter 8) contribution, which rounds out the section, it is the changing forms of investigative reporting that are singled out for critique. Beginning with the Watergate ideal – still widely celebrated as a symbol of journalism's commitment to the public interest in the face of political power and corruption – he offers an evaluative assessment of the mythology surrounding investigative reporting.

In the *Companion's* second section, 'News and Social Agendas,' the chapters revolve around a shared interest in delving into journalism's responsibilities within public life. Herbert J. Gans (Chapter 9) gets the discussion underway with the observation that, while journalists in the US have long insisted that they are essential to democracy, insufficient attention has been given to specifying precisely what it is that they do for the country's representative government. Having first considered the roles journalists play in the polity, he proceeds to ask what they *could* do to further enhance their involvement in the democratic process. W. Lance Bennett (Chapter 10) adopts a related perspective in his exploration of the 'dilemmas of power and accountability' engendered by the press's over-reliance on official sources obsessed with 'spinning' information to strategic advantage. In showing why, in his view, press freedom is not a sufficient condition for the production of timely and useful public information, he examines press coverage of the Iraq War during the Bush administration. Douglas Kellner (Chapter 11) pursues a similar theme in his contribution. Using French theorist Guy Debord's notion of the 'society of the spectacle' as his point of departure, he embarks upon an analysis of how mainstream corporate media process news as a form of 'media spectacle.' The growing prevalence of spectacle-led reporting is undermining the quality of journalism, he argues, a transformation he analyses with regard to the coverage of the 2008 presidential campaign in the era of the 'Obama spectacle.'

Journalism's social agendas are considered in non-Western terms in the next four chapters. Lisbeth Clausen (Chapter 12) offers an assessment of scholarship concerned with international news agencies and their 'agenda setting effects,' beginning with the New World Information and Communication Order debates in the 1970s up to and including current research into global news. The flow of international news is an agent of globalisation and its ideological influence, she contends, with profound implications for how people perceive the world around them. In Chapter 13, Qing Cao examines the changing role of the news media with regard to political change in China. The prospect of democracy is set in relation to the gradual relaxation of control exercised by Party-controlled journalism as the latter undergoes a process of commercialisation. Silvio Waisbord (Chapter 14) focuses on development journalism (DJ) in order to situate it in relation to current debates about normative models of news reporting in a globalised world. In the course of considering DJ's relative strengths and limitations with respect to advancing democratic objectives, he draws particular attention to its capacity to promote citizens' voices – and thereby a politics of social justice. Tanja Bosch discusses radio news in developing context, namely South Africa, in Chapter 15. She offers insights based on case studies of local radio stations, where concrete strategies are being developed to recast Western notions of news values so as to secure forms of news reporting that directly support democratic initiatives. Finally, Chris Atton (Chapter 16) brings this section to a close by showing how practitioners of alternative forms of journalism seek to redress what they consider to be an imbalance of media power in mainstream media. In seeking to disrupt professionalised norms and values in ideological terms, he argues, these practitioners strive to refashion what counts as journalism in order to reverse the marginalisation of certain social groups and movements.

The chapters in Section Three, 'Newsmaking: Rules, Routines and Rituals,' unravel the seemingly common-sensical imperatives shaping everyday news reporting. Despite an array of changes unfolding over recent years, Barbie Zelizer (Chapter 17) argues that journalists continue to do what they have always done, namely craft 'adjustments to both their newsmaking routines and their interpretive strategies so as to keep the journalistic community intact.' In considering how journalists collectively made sense of a specific news event – the hanging of Iraqi leader Saddam Hussein – she shows how the ensuing news coverage helped to reaffirm a collective and authoritative voice amidst the evolving boundaries of newswork. In Chapter 18, Jackie Harrison provides a close critique of two crucial aspects of news production – gatekeeping and news selection – in order to further critical understandings of how journalism is driven by processes of symbolic mediation. Relevant here, she maintains, is a distinction between the 'background' and 'foreground' of this mediation process, the everyday negotiation of which is at the heart of what she terms 'newsroom subjectivity.' Bob Franklin, Justin Lewis and Andrew Williams (Chapter 19) extend a complementary critique of news production by examining the shifting 'editorial balance' between journalism and public relations. In assessing the impact of the latter on journalists' professional practices in both the national and local press, they reveal the intense pressures journalists are under to accept information subsidies as a substitute for their own independent reportorial inquiries. Dale Jacquette (Chapter 20) privileges journalistic ethics for consideration, specifically the journalist's moral commitment to truth-telling in the public interest and for the public good. In developing his line of argument in relation to a case study – where a CNN news story is subjected to critique – he highlights 'the troubled interface where ideal abstract moral philosophical theory meets realistic workaday professional practice.' Issues surrounding truth-telling similarly inform Roger Dickinson's (Chapter 21) contribution. He explores several examples of journalistic delinquency, beginning with the Jayson Blair scandal at The New York Times, with an eye to examining afresh familiar assumptions about social control in the newsroom. The implications for public trust in journalism, he points out, warranting a considered evaluation.

The remarkable growth of autobiographical, 'confessional' journalism is closely documented by Ros Coward (Chapter 22). In identifying the characteristics which make it a distinctive genre of reporting, she questions the reasons for its popularity, including the possibility that it constitutes evidence of a journalistic 'dumbing-down' of professional values. Similar tensions are discerned by Raymond Boyle, David Rowe and Garry Whannel (Chapter 23) in their analysis of sports news. In the light of criticisms made against this genre of reporting, namely that it is trivial, superficial and uninformative, they assess whether sports journalists have 'compromised their own occupational standing by failing to discharge their "fourth estate" duties of independence, inquiry and, where necessary, sustained critique.' In Chapter 24, Mats Ekström, Bengt Johansson and Larsåke Larsson investigate local news – in particular, political journalism at the community level – as a distinct genre of reporting, with its own forms and conventions. On the basis of findings from an empirical study they conducted of journalism and local politics in a Swedish context, they contend that the 'watchdog role' of the local press is deserving of particular attention in this regard. The next two chapters round out this section of the Companion by underscoring the ways in which digital technologies are reshaping everyday routines of newswork. In situating journalism within a larger 'convergence culture,' Mark Deuze (Chapter 25) points out that these technological processes are imbued with cultural logics requiring careful elucidation in their own right. In exploring both the 'top down' and 'bottom up' manifestations of convergence culture in newswork, he considers both the dangers and opportunities for recasting anew journalism and its priorities. Jane Singer (Chapter 26) extends a similar line of inquiry, placing an emphasis on how the internet invites a reconsideration of journalism in relation to the power of networks. Journalists, she argues, 'face a rapid, radical decline in their power to oversee the information flow,' which will necessarily entail a creative reappraisal of the reporting process. To help advance this discussion, she shares insights from three case studies of journalism in a networked environment.

The fourth section of the *Companion*, 'Truth, Facts and Values,' brings issues concerning representation to the fore of the discussion. James S. Ettema (Chapter 27) shows how a critical understanding of news as a cultural form helps to elucidate a number of tensions in familiar theoretical approaches. Too often, he argues, the relationship between culture and journalism is reduced to an array of object-like conceptions – narrative structures, archetypal figures, metaphoric images and so forth – when what is at stake is actually an active, dynamic process of mediation. In Chapter 28, Barry Richards attends to a further dimension of news that has not received the attention it deserves, namely its emotional impact or influence. He outlines a conception of the 'emotional public sphere' – the emotions involved in the political life of a nation – to pinpoint several of the ways in which news reporting shapes public mood. Questions raised here provide an appropriate context for Joseph Harker's (Chapter 29) examination of race and diversity in the news. Drawing upon his personal experience in newspaper reporting, he shares his perceptions of the ways in which news can all too often reaffirm – rather than challenge – entrenched inequalities based on discrimination and prejudice. This theme similarly informs Marguerite Moritz's (Chapter 30) critique of how the sexualities of lesbian, gay, bisexual and transgender people have been recurrently represented in news reports in hurtful ways. 'Journalists have an obligation to be informed as well as inclusive and impartial,' she argues. 'Perhaps most importantly, they need to appreciate the consequences of prejudice on the safety and civil rights of the people they portray.'

Questions of representation similarly figure in Martin Montgomery's (Chapter 31) analysis of the broadcast news interview as discourse. Specifically, he unravels typical sorts of assumptions about the dynamics of interviews with political figures in newscasts, usefully offering a typology of news interview types so as to help researchers attend to the tacit norms and values of these exchanges with greater analytical specificity. David Rowe (Chapter 32) similarly advances an alternative line of inquiry, centering 'tabloidisation' as a process of representation for purposes of investigation. In delving beneath bold rhetorical claims about 'the tabloid' – not least its use as a stigmatised label to describe the perceived erosion of journalistic integrity in newspaper reporting – he draws upon empirical evidence from a case study to try to determine what is actually happening in the Australian press. Daya Kishan Thussu shifts the focus to television news in Chapter 33, examining the growth of what has been termed 'infotainment' – that is, the convergence of information and entertainment – found to varying degrees in the editorial output from television newsrooms across the globe. It is his contention that this form of 'soft' news is contributing to the corporate colonisation of the public sphere, namely by helping to legitimise a neo-liberal ideology predicated on the perceived superiority of free-market democracy. Geoffrey Baym (Chapter 34) is similarly concerned with the blurring of news and entertainment, taking as his focus 'fake' news – such as *The Daily Show* (with comedian Jon Stewart) and its spin-off *The Colbert Report* (with comedian Stephen Colbert). He argues that the label 'fake' is misleading, not only because it neglects the serious role these programmes are playing in public political discourse, but also because it glosses over the potential of these programmes to reinvent public-interest journalism in progressive ways. In the final chapter in this section, Brian McNair (Chapter 35) explores the representation of journalism in one of the most important popular culture forms, cinema. Cinema is the conscience of the journalistic profession, he argues, a key location where its role and functions are held up to broad public inspection – a thesis he illustrates using an array of examples from different films over the years.

'Making Sense of the News,' the fifth section of the *Companion*, highlights the varied uses of news and journalism, that is, the ways in which they are rendered meaningful by diverse publics within the contexts of everyday life. The thorny issue of citizenship is grasped by Toby Miller in Chapter 36. He identifies three zones of citizenship, namely the political (covering the right to reside and vote), the economic (the right to work and prosper), and the cultural (the right to know and speak), in order to discern their impact on journalism. While each zone corresponds to a number of traditional news beats – broadly grouped under government, economics and cultural institutions, respectively – an assessment of their current relevance, he argues, reveals journalism's shortcomings in speaking to the concerns of ordinary citizens. Greg Philo (Chapter 37) examines the contribution of the Glasgow University Media Group to research concerned with the influence of media messages in relation to the development of social attitudes and beliefs. In taking issue with conceptions of the 'active audience' in certain strands of cultural and media studies research, he shows how the Group's findings underscore the importance of recognising the role of media power in constructing public knowledge. Chapter 38, by S. Elizabeth Bird, poses the question: 'what does news mean in everyday life?' In the course of exploring possible responses – including scholarship examining news consumption as a 'habit' as well as research into people's 'news talk' in their daily lives – she addresses how the new online environment may be changing certain longstanding assumptions about how news is negotiated, with significant implications for civic participation. Mirca Madianou (Chapter 39) focuses on the contribution ethnographies of news consumption can make to furthering understanding of news as a social phenomenon in everyday life. She devotes particular attention to how ethnography can uncover the practices surrounding news consumption, and the ways in which these daily rituals are implicated in wider processes of identity, citizenship and power.

In light of current debates surrounding international news broadcaster Al-Jazeera English's impact, Mohammed el-Nawawy and Shawn Powers (Chapter 40) report on their study of its influence amongst audiences across six countries. Their findings suggest that while Al-Jazeera English's news coverage exhibits a tendency to reinforce already existing opinions and attitudes regarding politically salient topics, watching it may be having 'a positive impact on facilitating less dogmatic and more open-minded thinking amongst its viewers.' The next chapter emerges from the recognition that debates about news audiences tend to prefigure the experiences of adult viewers, listeners and readers exclusively, especially where debates about citizenship are concerned. Kaitlynn Mendes, Cynthia Carter and Máire Messenger Davies (Chapter 41) offer an alternative perspective by privileging for investigation children and young people's engagement with news. In appraising the apparent disconnect between major news broadcasters and their younger audiences, the authors share findings from a study conducted with school children across the UK exploring their perceptions of children's news – specifically, the BBC programme *Newsround* – and its reporting of citizenship issues. Andrew Hoskins's (Chapter 42) contribution highlights key questions concerning news and memory: that is, the ways in which the 'unfolding details of everyday life – our personal biographies – intersect with larger society through the aperture of the news media.' It is by thinking through the concept of memory, he argues, that researchers can gain important insights into how news reports mediate ongoing experiences of the world by revivifying certain conceptions of the past over and above alternative ones. While television news is regarded as being especially powerful in shaping individual, social and cultural memory, digital media are proving increasingly salient in generating 'connective memories' today.

In Section Six, 'Crisis, Conflict and Controversy,' the *Companion* presents a range of contributions concerned with the news reporting of crisis events unfolding around the world. Simon Cottle (Chapter 43) begins by providing a conceptual map of several pressing issues, highlighting the extent to which the news media help to *constitute* crises in the course of *communicating* them to distant publics. His survey of several recent global crises enables him to discern three analytically distinguishable modalities of global crisis reporting – specifically, surveillance, focusing events and spectacle – within the world's news ecology today. Anabela Carvalho (Chapter 44) takes one global crisis as her principal concern, namely the news reporting of climate change. She focuses on the roles the mainstream news media have played over the last two decades in the social construction of climate change as an exigent problem, looking in particular at the relations between science, policy and public opinion formation. Journalism, she argues, needs to take greater responsibility for promoting the public accountability of the key stakeholders involved. The everyday crises of foreign affairs are the backdrop of Philip Seib's (Chapter 45) contribution. The news media are *de facto* players in this realm, he points out, helping to set the public's agenda in terms of what issues receive attention – and thereby affecting, to varying degrees, policymakers' decisions. In showing why it is the duty of the news media to maintain a 'constructively adversarial' relationship with government, he discusses several examples from the post-September 11 years. Increasingly apparent, he argues, is the extent to which new technologies are reshaping the news–foreign-policy nexus.

The focus of the next set of chapters in this section is placed directly on the news reporting of war and conflict. John Tulloch and R. Warwick Blood (Chapter 46) examine what they term 'iconic photojournalism,' that is, news images which have acquired an iconic status because of their perceived capacity to encapsulate – and thereby help to define – a particular historical moment. Alert to the complex ways in which such imagery circulates, the authors proceed to examine Huỳnh Công Út's (known as Nick Ut) Pulitzer Prize winning photograph, the 'napalm girl,' which appeared on the front page of newspapers around the world during the Vietnam War. Its appearance in a recent exhibition, titled *Bangladesh 1971*, provides an opportunity to assess its continuing symbolic power, and its importance for rethinking the tenets of photojournalism. Lilie Chouliaraki (Chapter 47) is similarly concerned with the visual politics of war and conflict. Her discussion revolves around two case studies – the 'shock and awe' bombardment of Baghdad in 2003 and the killing of a Greek-Cypriot in the green zone of Cyprus in 1996 – in order to show how news images contribute to the imagination of community, a process where the production of Otherness is of vital importance. Howard Tumber (Chapter 48), in examining the changing role of journalists – including photojournalists – covering conflict, pays particular attention to the relationship between these journalists and human rights workers. Questions of moral responsibility are acutely challenging under such circumstances, he points out, leading to a heightened reflexivity amongst war reporters concerning the implications of their actions, relationships with sources, the quality of their coverage, and their personal safety, amongst other concerns. Lastly in this section, Jake Lynch (Chapter 49) shifts the emphasis from war to peace journalism, introducing a counter-logic to familiar assumptions. He begins by exploring the origins of the concept of peace journalism, as well as some of the controversies it has generated, before moving to consider its contribution to specific conflicts over the years. Peace journalism, he argues, throws into sharp relief the limitations of the more traditional tenets of war reporting, thereby inviting a vigorous debate about ways to improve matters.

The final section of the *Companion* explores 'Journalism's Futures' with a series of forward-looking chapters. Natalie Fenton (Chapter 50) illuminates the features of current debates concerning what constitutes news in the digital age. She shows how the major themes that emerge – speed and space; multiplicity and polycentrality; interactivity and participation – can usefully pinpoint, in turn, a host of concerns deserving of careful consideration as journalism evolves across ever changing contexts. The business of news, she fears, is increasingly not the business of journalists. In Chapter 51, Henrik Örnebring looks to the distant past in order to better anticipate the future. Specifically, he scrutinises key elements generally thought to be important in the history of professionalisation of journalism in order to help assess the available evidence for bold claims made regarding the process of de-professionalisation arguably underway today. In discerning a basis to suggest that we are witnessing a simultaneous professionalisation / de-professionalisation of journalism, he signals his concern about its future viability. Current debates about professionalisation usefully set up Mark Glaser's (Chapter 52) elucidation of the factors giving rise to the citizen journalism movement. Tracing its emergence and development from pre-internet days up to the present scene, he identifies a number of tensions in competing views about who can claim the status of 'journalist' in order to 'contribute to the media conversation.' The rise of hyper-local news is shown to be of particular relevance to future directions in citizen reporting.

In the light of these and related developments, it is understandable why the very future of the newspaper is under consideration in James R. Compton's (Chapter 53) investigation. His assessment of the political economy underpinning the newspaper as a newsgathering institution leads him to situate a number of the problems currently facing the newspaper industry in the larger context of a broader restructuring of the global economy. Too often explanatory accounts are narrowly focused around technology, he contends, which can mean that other pressing issues – not least the restructuring of paid labour within newspapers – fail to receive adequate attention. Julian Petley (Chapter 54) moves the discussion on to news broadcasting, showing how the issue of 'impartiality' counterposes discourses of profitability against those of public service in the UK. Demands for impartiality commitments to be relaxed should not be heeded, he argues, namely because 'abolishing the impartiality rules could, paradoxically, result in *less* diversity of viewpoints in public service broadcasting.' Future efforts, it follows, should focus instead on actively re-interpreting these rules. In Chapter 55, Rodney Benson's contribution resonates with the themes of this section of the *Companion* by offering an appraisal of what comparative research can provide to related inquiries. Identifying similarities and contrasting differences between news media systems can usefully reveal issues otherwise obscured, a thesis he proceeds to demonstrate by comparing the French and US news media – including their relations to political and economic power, and in their journalistic professional traditions – so as to form a fresh basis for theory-building. It is with an eye to the future that he concludes by offering insight into the 'new frontiers' of research on non-Western media and internet journalism. G. Stuart Adam (Chapter 56) turns our attention to journalism education. Efforts to place journalism studies on a stable, intellectually-demanding foundation have struggled against formidable forces ever since the first university-level programmes emerged over 100 years ago, he observes, leading him to question what must be done to improve its quality for tomorrow. In seeking to provide an answer, he outlines an alternative approach to the development of a journalism curriculum in the years ahead. Based, in part, on the philosophy of the late James W. Carey, this approach – as Adam envisages it – would aim to prepare students not only in professional terms but also with regard to their potential role in shaping a common democratic culture.

In the first of the four new chapters for this edition of the *Companion*, Brian Baresch, Shih-Hsien Hsu and Stephen D. Reese (Chapter 57) examine the power of framing. News frames, they point out, 'highlight some aspects of the events behind a story and downplay others, often with the effect of supporting a certain way of looking at the world.' In assessing the relative merits of specific approaches to conceptualising this complex process over the years, the authors identify several pressing issues deserving careful reconsideration in relation to the new media ecosystem. Framing research, they contend, must develop innovative methods to explore how this evolving ecosystem influences the means by which 'we build our pictures of our world.'

Heidi Mau and Carolyn Kitch (Chapter 58) engage with a related set of challenges with specific reference to newsmagazines. Their analysis of the strategies adopted by different titles – such as *Time*, *Newsweek* and *US News & World Report* – striving to survive in the digital age pinpoints a number of dangers, as well as opportunities. Such are the pressures being brought to bear on the newsmagazine industry, certain longstanding rules of this genre of journalism are being actively rewritten with an eye to securing its future. In Chapter 59, Guy Starkey and Andrew Crisell investigate the impact of digital technologies on radio journalism. Precisely what counts as radio news, they proceed to show, is being transformed by a myriad of factors sometimes overlooked in sweeping claims made about multi-media convergence. In sifting through the rhetoric, the authors offer a fresh perspective on how radio journalism is recasting its relationship with its listening communities. Finally, Alfred Hermida (Chapter 60) draws the volume to a close by scrutinising how social media – with the social messaging technology Twitter at the fore – are changing the ways in which news is gathered, disseminated and consumed. In tracing how Twitter has developed into 'the default media network for real-time news,' he discerns important implications for the wider practice of journalism at a time when searching questions are being asked about its capacity to reinvent itself anew. A fitting note, then, to draw this *Companion's* discussion to a close.

Note

1 This video is easily found on a number of websites, including YouTube.com by searching for the title: '1981 primitive Internet report on KRON' or any of these keywords (e.g., '1981' and 'KRON' together): http://www.youtube.com/watch?v=5WCTn4FljUQ

References

Allan, S. (2006) *Online News: Journalism and the Internet*. Maidenhead and New York: Open University Press.

Allan, S. (2009) 'Journalism Without Journalists? Rethinking Questions of Professionalism,' in L. Steiner and C. Christians (eds) *Key Concepts in Critical Cultural Studies*. Urbana: University of Illinois Press, in press.

Boylan, J. (2003) *Pulitzer's School. Columbia University's School of Journalism, 1903–2003*. New York: Columbia University Press.

Carey, J.W. (1978) 'A Plea for the University Tradition,' *Journalism Quarterly*, Volume 55, Winter, 846–55.

Carey, J.W. (2000) 'Some Personal Notes on US Journalism Education,' *Journalism*, 1(1): 12–23.

Carey, J.W. (2007) 'A Short History of Journalism for Journalists: A Proposal and Essay,' *The International Journal of Press/Politics* 12(1): 3–16.

Freedman, S. (2006) 'Outside Voices,' *Public Eye*, CBSNews.com, 31 March.

Hohenberg, J. (1974) *The Pulitzer Prizes*. New York: Columbia University Press.

Ireland, A. (1938) *An Adventure with a Genius: Recollections of Joseph Pulitzer*. London: Lovat Dickson.

Lemann, N. (2006) 'Amateur Hour,' *The New Yorker*, 7 August.

Pulitzer, J. (1904) 'The School of Journalism in Columbia University,' 2006 facsimile reproduction, *The School of Journalism*. Seattle: Inkling Books.

Rusbridger, A. (2008) 'New World Order,' in J. Gibson (ed) *Media 08*. London: Guardian Books, 243–9.

Seitz, D.C. (1924) *Joseph Pulitzer: His Life & Letters*. New York: Simon & Schuster.

Part I

THE EVOLVING IDEALS
OF JOURNALISM

1

THE FOURTH ESTATE IDEAL IN JOURNALISM HISTORY

Mark Hampton

According to Thomas Carlyle (1840), Edmund Burke first applied the term "Fourth Estate" to the press gallery in the late eighteenth century, contrasting it with the three Estates of the Realm in France (Clergy, Aristocracy, and Commoners). In a British context, the first three estates might be regarded, instead, as King, Lords, and Commons. In either case, the idea of the Fourth Estate signifies that, whatever the formal constitution, genuine political power resides in the informal role of the press, which in turn derives from the relationship between the press and its readers. In Burke's usage the press's ability to mediate between formal politics and the "mob" beyond parliament did not recommend it, but as Britain subsequently democratized, the idea of the press as a "Fourth Estate" would become an important source of legitimization for an increasingly prominent and self-confident institution. Although in the United States the concept of "three Estates" had less relevance, the term "Fourth Estate" – and, more importantly, the underlying concept identified above – has enjoyed similar currency.

To be sure, the term "Fourth Estate" is often employed simply as a synonym for "the press," without necessarily including all of the connotations identified here. It is used ironically, as in the title of Jeffrey Archer's (1996) potboiler, to suggest that the institution is not living up to its lofty purpose. The present chapter concentrates on the concept of the press as a *de facto*, but not official, branch of government in British and American contexts, whether or not the term "Fourth Estate" is actually used. It will briefly examine the relationship between the press and its readers historically envisioned in the concept of the "Fourth Estate," before considering the challenges posed to this vision by the press's inclusion within a commercialized mass media and by the press's relationship to the state. Both factors call into question whether or not the press – and, more recently, broadcast journalism – enjoys the independent perspective required of the "Fourth Estate" ideal.

The press and its readers

The idea of the press as a "Fourth Estate" has rested upon rival (but often overlapping) ideals of the relationship between the press and its readers.[1] In nineteenth-century Britain, the predominant model, which may be called an "educational" ideal, suggested that the press serves as an agency of public discussion, in which rival ideas and interests compete with each other until, ideally, the "truth" or the "common good" prevail. This vision presumed rationality and open-mindedness on the part of readers and treated the press as a public sphere analogous to Parliament itself. In other words, the same debates about public affairs that took place within Parliament also took place among the wider political nation in the pages of daily newspapers and serious periodicals. Therefore, even if representative government operated at a level of distance from its constituents, the press allowed constituents and representatives to participate in the same conversation, or what might be called a "politics by public discussion." This idea of the press, which anticipated Jürgen Habermas's (1991 [1962]) idea of a bourgeois public sphere, is captured in R.A. Scott-James's 1913 likening the press to a "polis." That is, although modern democracies did not entail the face-to-face communication of ancient Athens, the press ensured that all citizens could communicate with each other, and with their parliamentary representatives. Simultaneously, at its most optimistic, this model suggested that working class readers could be integrated into the political nation and could participate in a common, unified public sphere. Confidence that the press was doing this job adequately underlay the abolition of the "Taxes on Knowledge" in Britain between 1853 and 1861, taxes on advertising, paper, and newspaper publication that collectively had prevented the emergence of an inexpensive daily press. In addition, it helped to justify the passage of the 1867 Reform Act, which significantly expanded the British electorate. A similar understanding of the press's informational role in the United States underlay the First Amendment and Congressional legislation throughout the nineteenth century in support of a free media, for example through post office subsidies (McChesney, 2004; Starr, 2004).

The second model, which may be called a "representative" model, focused less on *integrating* a mass readership into a common public sphere than on actually *constituting* readers' involvement in politics. Rather than facilitating a political discussion in which newspaper readers and politicians both addressed important "questions of the day," according to the "representative" model the press reflected readers' interests. More specifically, by publicizing corruption, scandal in high places, or the government's simple inattention to the needs of the people, the press could ensure that a nominally democratic government met its obligations to its constituents. W.T. Stead, a British radical whose editorial positions included the *Darlington Northern Echo* (1871–80) and the *Pall Mall Gazette* (1883–90), went so far as to refer to Parliament as the "Chamber of Initiative." As he wrote, "No measure ever gets itself into shape, as a rule, before being debated many times as a project in the columns of the newspapers" (Stead, 1886, 656). Stead's argument contains more than a hint of self-justification – he wrote it during a short prison term for kidnapping a young girl who he purchased as part of his campaign against underage prostitution or "white slavery" – but it exemplifies the prevailing understanding of the press's political role during the last two decades of the nineteenth century. Muhlmann (2008) has recently described a similar function, in the context of late nineteenth- and early twentieth-century American, British, and French journalism, as a "unifying" journalism based on the model of the journalist as a "witness-ambassador." For such figures as the French journalist Séverine, exposing the injustice of the Dreyfus Affair, or the American "muckraker" Lincoln Steffens, the role of journalism was to unify a nation's citizens through exposing the actions of malefactors who threatened the nation.

The Fourth Estate and journalistic "independence"

What both of these models have in common is that the press was to serve as an "indispensable link" between a representative government and its constituents (Boyce, 1978: 21). Whether to promote discussion and "educate" readers, or to "represent" them by publicizing abuses, any concept of the press as a "Fourth Estate" would seem, therefore, to require the accessible presentation of serious information and an independent perspective. For this reason, in the view of many critics (particularly on the Left), the concept of the press as a "Fourth Estate" has been threatened by the growing concentration of media ownership in the twentieth century, and the incorporation of media within diversified corporations that have various non-media interests. At the same time, twentieth-century British and American critics have noted the tendency of journalism to identify too closely with the perspective of the state. Both of these developments have threatened the notion of "independence" that is essential to the function of the press as a "Fourth Estate." Although the "Fourth Estate" ideal originally referred to newspapers, it has been extended since the early twentieth century to broadcast media and, more recently, to the Internet, so that questions concerning ownership, commercialization, and the role of the state apply to these more recent media as well (Barnett and Gaber, 2001, 1).

Boyce, in a stimulating examination of the "Fourth Estate" concept in Britain, points out that the nineteenth-century articulation of that "myth" rarely considered the financial underpinnings of the press, and that as late as the early twentieth century the elite papers on which the ideal relied – such as the *Manchester Guardian*, the *Daily Chronicle*, the *Daily News*, and the *Westminster Gazette* – remained heavily dependent on finance by political parties (1978, 28–9).[2] Rather than Stead's "government by journalism," therefore, the result was "government by politicians, with journalists acting as go-betweens, advisers, and, occasionally, opponents of the practising politicians." Not only did press finance contribute to this close relationship, but elite journalists themselves welcomed it as a means of gaining greater influence than they would through an adversarial role (Boyce, 1978, 29). Boyce highlights the irony that "press barons" such as Lord Northcliffe, Lord Beaverbrook, and Lord Rothermere, whose papers' huge circulations and resulting advertising revenues freed them from financial dependence on the politicians, were so fiercely denounced as a threat to an independent "Fourth Estate." Curran argues, likewise, that the difference between press barons and earlier newspaper owners was that the press barons "sought to use their papers, not as levers of power within the political parties, but as instruments of power against the political parties" (Curran 1997, 49). Indeed, while Stead had boasted of the press's ability to unseat parliaments, Northcliffe was widely perceived actually to have done so in 1916, having helped to replace Asquith's wartime Liberal Government with Lloyd George's Coalition Government (McEwen, 1978). In an example of even greater long-term importance, one of the great American press magnates, William Randolph Hearst, was credited with a large role in helping to engineer the 17th Amendment to the US Constitution (1912), providing for the direct election of Senators (Proctor 1998, 216). Hearst's campaign, namely the 1906 publication of David Graham Phillips' "The Treason of the Senate" in *Cosmopolitan*, centred on charges that numerous Senators were simply the hired guns of special interests, and had accordingly squashed populist reform that had been proposed by the more democratically responsive House of Representatives.

Such episodes would appear to stand as salutary examples of the power of the independent commercial press to perform a credible "watchdog" role. In the popular mythology, such episodes are joined by the *New York Times'* publication of The Pentagon Papers (1971), Edward Murrow's *See it Now* campaign against Senator McCarthy (1954), and Bob Woodward and Carl Bernstein's exposure of the Watergate break-in and cover-up (1973).[3] British media history perhaps lacks such iconic moments, but its tradition of investigative journalism is well-established, including such examples as John Pilger's campaigning journalism for the *Daily Mirror* in the 1960s and *The Sunday Times'* 1970s campaign against the government on behalf of thalidomide victims.[4] According to liberal scholars such examples provide evidence of commercial journalism's contribution to a democratic public sphere (e.g., McNair, 2000).

Yet if the press barons and corporate media have at times demonstrated a credible financial and political independence of government and have, on occasion, gone so far as to undermine corrupt or anti-democratic government policies, radical critics none the less remain sceptical about a commercial media's inability to perform a consistent "Fourth Estate" role as either a government "watchdog" or more ambitiously (to return to Stead's term) a "chamber of initiative." On the one hand, commercialization has its limits as a basis for journalistic independence; on the other hand, and not unrelated, twentieth century democratic governments have shown themselves quite capable of using commercial media for their own political ends.

Commercialization

In one sense, the term "commercialization" is misleading. Rather, what it entails, in a process normally dated to the 1830s in the United States and the 1850s in Britain, is newspapers' gradual shift away from financial dependence upon political parties to dependence upon circulation and advertising revenues. Yet whatever term one uses, a press whose finances are based on circulation and advertising revenues has, in practice, experienced several distinct threats to the independence and serious purpose required of a "Fourth Estate" role. First, technological innovations since the mid-nineteenth century have led to increasingly high entry costs, so that concentration of newspaper ownership increased dramatically during the early twentieth century, and ownership of broadcasting media outlets has been fairly tightly concentrated from their beginnings (initially, in large part, on grounds of spectrum scarcity). This concentration has taken different forms in Britain and the United States. In Britain, where mostly London-based papers had evolved into a national press by the early twentieth century, the issue was that a small number of owners controlled papers earning the lion's share of national circulation. Curran (1997, 78) shows, for example, that by 1947 the three leading corporations had attained circulation shares of 62% and 60%, respectively, for national daily and national Sunday circulation; the figure for total daily and Sunday circulation was somewhat more modest at 42%. By 1961 these respective figures were 89%, 84%, and 65%, though they fell off modestly in subsequent decades. In the United States, by contrast, where most readers remained loyal to local or regional newspapers, the issue was that fewer and fewer towns possessed competing papers, and papers were increasingly part of national chains such as Gannett or Scripps (McChesney, 2004; Hamilton, 2004). Such concentration of ownership has made the notion of a "marketplace of ideas" problematic. To be fair, it is not clear exactly how many newspapers or television news outlets are necessary for a healthy public sphere, but it is none the less clear that the idea that potential new entrants perpetually force existing players to remain responsive to democratic forces is, at best, far-fetched.

Second, and closely related, news outlets are increasingly part of non-media conglomerates, in many cases operating on an international basis. Given that international corporations play an ever-increasing role in making decisions that affect the lives of citizens, it would seem appropriate to expand the Fourth Estate's watchdog remit to include their activities as well as those of elected officials. Indeed, the extension of the concept to monitoring powerful corporations can be seen in popular culture, for example in the American film *The Insider* (2000), a dramatization of Lowell Bergman's *60 Minutes* exposé of the tobacco industry. Yet critics caution that it is unrealistic to expect NBC News or ABC News, for example, consistently to report critically on the activities of respective parent companies General Electric and Disney, while McChesney (1999, 53–4) points to examples of NBC and ABC using news programmes to promote (respectively) NBC television ratings and Disney films. Indeed even Bergman's tobacco story affirms the embattled crusading journalist only through highlighting his difficulty in overcoming the corporate censorship of his own employer, CBS, whose executives worried about the possibility of a lawsuit (Rich, 1999). Moreover, such worries go beyond simply whether individual companies will be reported from an independent and critical perspective. Rather, critics argue, corporate media have a built-in bias toward presenting news in such a way as to create an overall favourable environment for business, not least that of the media companies themselves (e.g., Moyers, 2008).

Third, for a century critics have argued that defining news values according to what would attain the circulation that would attract advertising revenues has led to the "dumbing down" of serious news (Engel, 1996; Sparks, 1991). Sometimes, such criticism smacks of elitist snobbery, and both liberal and populist scholars in different ways defend the compatibility of a democratic public sphere with a definition of news larger than the narrowly "political" (Conboy, 2004; McNair, 2000; Hamilton, 2004). Late nineteenth-century critics in Britain and the USA objected to shorter paragraphs and large headlines in place of long, unbroken columns, as well as to the prevalence of human interest stories that might, in fact, have had a political relevance. Nevertheless, it is difficult to discount Franklin's characterization of much late twentieth-century journalism, even in the "quality" papers, as "newszak," light, easily-digested stories that often have little apparent public use; he gives the example (1997, 9) of a 1997 *Guardian* column asking the question "Could you fancy a man who has had his penis surgically enlarged?" In both countries television news programmes frequently consist of celebrity interviews, while newspapers – especially the tabloids, but the "quality" press as well – give increasing attention to celebrity news as space for investigative and foreign news declines in proportion. Certainly scholars can argue about the *extent* to which such trends characterize recent journalism, and perhaps an argument can even be made that celebrity or human interest stories are useful ways of framing genuine public issues (Conboy, 2006). In addition, the exposé character of many celebrity stories owes at least a rhetorical debt to the informational and adversarial components of the Fourth Estate ideal – as does the "pseudo-controversy" paradigm implied in the penis enhancement story cited above. Yet it is difficult to dismiss evidence that much journalism has little relevance to a "Fourth Estate" function as it is historically understood.

Fourth, even where newspapers and television networks remain theoretically committed to serious investigative journalism, the relentless drive for profits has increasingly put pressure on the budgets allocated for newsgathering. Between 1969 and 1994, for example, the proportion of British journalists who worked as freelancers skyrocketed, from approximately 10% of the total to somewhere between one-fourth and one-third. Unlike dedicated "beat" journalists, these contract workers, generally paid only upon delivering copy, are not in a position to devote months to an investigative project that might never result in a story (Franklin, 1997). Meanwhile, even for journalists with full-time positions, the pressure to "do more with less" meant that budgets were generally not forthcoming for a patient, careful investigation that might not result in a story (McChesney, 2004, 81).[5]

Journalism and the state

Even while the commercial basis of news has proven at best an unreliable basis for the critical independence required of the "Fourth Estate" ideal, media critics have suggested that even journalism's independence from the state has been exaggerated. In contexts in which national security can plausibly be invoked, both the US and British states have legal mechanisms for restraining the publication of sensitive news. In the case of Britain, the Official Secrets Act and the Defence of the Realm Act provide legal cover for punishing journalists whose revelations go beyond the permissible, and the former was fairly effective until the 1980s (Seymour-Ure, 1996, 252–7). In the United States, a Supreme Court ruling shortly after World War I established the standard that First Amendment freedoms of the press could be restricted in the interests of national security only in the case of a "clear and present danger" (Siebert et al, 1963, 58–9). Despite this ruling, however, in particularly contentious periods the American state has remained willing to use a heavy hand. For example, so long as criticism of the Vietnam War remained the province of a small-circulation dissident press, readers of anti-war papers such as the *National Guardian* could be the victims of "intimidating phone calls and visits from FBI agents, resulting in hundreds of canceled subscriptions" (Streitmatter, 2001, 197).[6] Similarly, Milo Radulovich, the McCarthy victim discharged from the Air Force in 1953 as a security risk before being acquitted through the efforts of Murrow's *See it Now*, was targeted largely because his father and sister subscribed to a Serbian newspaper that was thought to support a Communist party. Although McCarthy's disgrace at the hands of Murrow is one of the signature moments within Fourth Estate discourse, the episode also reminds us that on occasion the state has used its power to intimidate readers of non-mainstream papers.

Even short of such drastic measures, both states and their variously governing parties have developed sophisticated apparatuses for getting their perspectives into independent news media, a practice that is sometimes called "spin." Moore (2006) locates the "origins of modern spin" in Britain in the efforts of the 1945–51 Labour government to combat the hostility of the predominantly conservative press to Labour's nationalizing and welfare programs.[7] Observers have argued that these efforts only intensified and grew more sophisticated in the 1980s and later, and built their effectiveness on an understanding of news cycles. For example, as Barnett and Gaber (2001, 7) argue, "It is now established practice to release relatively complex but important information close to reporters' deadlines. This ensures that journalists are increasingly dependent on sources not just for the information itself but for the interpretation – the 'spin'". This practice relies on an understanding of the speeded-up working conditions journalists face as a result of ever more stringent budget cuts (Franklin, 1997), as well as professional journalism's bias toward "official" sources and, in the US, the "on the one hand … on the other" style of "objectivity" (Schudson, 1978).[8] As McChesney (2004, 69) says of American journalists' dealings with politicians, journalists "discover that they cannot antagonize their sources or they might get cut off from all information." Such a deprivation of access would, of course, severely hamper a journalist's effectiveness, and by extension his or her career prospects. During the early stages of the 2003 Iraq War, the American government introduced the concept of "embedded" soldiers in an effort to manage journalistic access and thus ensure that the government's perspective predominated in media coverage (Tumber and Palmer, 2004). Herman and Chomsky (1988) have gone so far as to argue that in the United States the nexus between state interest and corporate media's economic incentives has produced a consistent propaganda model – a far cry from the Fourth Estate's putative critical and adversarial role.

Finally, even where corporate policy or professional survival do not demand subservience to the desired policies of the state, journalists tend to operate within a national frame, especially within times of crisis (Jamieson and Waldman, 2003, 131). Famous counter-examples such as the BBC's treating British and Argentine official statements as moral equivalents during the Falklands War stand out for their rarity, particularly in American journalism. According to American media scholars Jamieson and Waldman (2003, 14), although people often take for granted that the press plays an "adversarial role to those in power and is quick to unmask, debunk, and challenge," the press does so only very selectively. Particularly, in cases in which reporters assume that the nation "supports the person telling the story ... and opposing narratives are not being offered by competing players", the adversarial role is significantly reduced. Hallin (1989) offers a similar explanation of the American media's conduct during the Vietnam War, pointing out that, so long as the public (and especially the elites) remained broadly united in support of the war, mainstream media were fairly uncritical in their coverage; critical coverage followed, rather than led, the shift in public opinion. From a "Fourth Estate" perspective, this would seem to be precisely backwards. Similarly, although critical American media coverage of the Iraq War was common by 2006, when support for the war was being built in late 2002 and 2003 neither newspapers nor television news questioned key claims of the Bush administration. Not even the *New York Times*, widely regarded as the "paper of record," provided basic information about available evidence that Iraq had suspended its weapons programmes or that, according to international agreements to which the United States was a party, even the confirmation of a weapons programme would not have warranted a unilateral invasion (Friel and Falk, 2004).

Concluding remarks

The criticisms outlined above suggest that mainstream journalism has significant practical limitations as a Fourth Estate. It may be that "alternative" or "dissident" journalism is the most promising venue for a thoroughgoing "Fourth Estate" media (Atton, 2001; Streitmatter, 2001), and defenders of this position can point to examples of perspectives in alternative media that eventually made their way to mainstream media. Yet it is difficult to imagine that many opponents of the Vietnam War (for example) would take comfort from the fact that the early 1960s critique made its way into mainstream American newspaper and television coverage only after several more years of war. The Internet is similarly heralded by many as a potentially democratic "watchdog" that promises to break the hold of dominant corporations over the circulation of news; but even if the Internet is capable of decentralizing the *distribution* of news and opinion, which is no foregone conclusion, given that corporations control the search engines and portals (McChesney, 1999), it will not solve the problem of the costs of gathering news, particularly of investigative journalism (Hamilton, 2004).

Yet if media that are organized along commercial lines fail to provide a consistent critique of government and corporate institutions, we should perhaps not be surprised. The great contribution of the "Fourth Estate" ideal may well be that it provides a vision to which journalists often aspire, and an obligation that is met frequently enough to force governments and corporations at least to consider the public response to their actions.[9]

References

Archer, J. (1996) *The Fourth Estate*, London: HarperCollins.

Atton, C. (2001) *Alternative Media*, London: Sage.

Barnett, S. and Gaber, I. (2001) *Westminster Tales: The Twenty-First-Century Crisis in Political Journalism*, London: Continuum.

Boyce, G. (1978) "The Fourth Estate: the Reappraisal of a Concept," in George Boyce, James Curran, and Pauline Wingate, eds., *Newspaper History from the Seventeenth Century to the Present Day*, London: Constable.

Brown, D. (2009) "Morally Transforming the World or Spinning a Line? Politicians and the Newspaper Press in Mid-Victorian Britain," *Historical Research* (forthcoming).

Campbell, W. (2006) *The Year That Defined American Journalism: 1897 and the Clash of Paradigms*, New York: Routledge.

Carlyle, T. (1840) *The Hero as Man of Letters: Johnson, Rousseau, Burns* (Lecture V, May 19, 1840). <http://www.victorianweb.org/authors/carlyle/heroes/hero5.html> (accessed 19 October 2008).

Chalaby, J. (1998) *The Invention of Journalism*, Houndmills: Macmillan.

Conboy, M. (2004) *Journalism: A Critical History*, London: Sage.

——. (2006) *Tabloid Britain: Constructing a Community through Language*, London: Routledge.

Curran, J. (1997) "Press History", in J. Curran and J. Seaton, Power Without Responsibility: the Press and Broadcasting in Britain, 5th ed., London: Routledge.

Engel, M. (1996) *Tickle the Public: One Hundred Years of the Popular Press*, London: Victor Gollancz.

Erlich, M. (2006) *Journalism in the Movies*, Urbana and Chicago: University of Illinois Press.

Franklin, B. (1997) *Newszak & News Media*, London: Arnold.

Friel, H. and Falk R. (2004) *The Record of the Paper: How the New York Times Misreports US Foreign Policy*, London and New York: Verso.

Habermas, J. (1991) *The Structural Transformation of the Public Sphere: An Inquiry into a Category of Bourgeois Society*. Trans. by Thomas Burger. Cambridge, MA: The MIT Press.

Hallin, D. (1989) *The 'Uncensored War': The Media and Vietnam*, Berkeley and Los Angeles: University of California Press.

Hamilton (2004) *All the News that's Fit to Sell: How the Market Transforms Information into News*, Princeton, NJ: Princeton University Press.

Hampton, M. (2004) *Visions of the Press in Britain, 1850–1950*, Urbana, IL: University of Illinois Press.

Hampton, M. (2009) "Renewing the liberal tradition: the press and public discussion in twentieth-century Britain," in Michael Bailey (ed.), *Narrating Media History*, London: Routledge.

Herman, E. and Chomsky, N. (1988) *Manufacturing Consent: The Political Economy of the Mass Media*, New York, Pantheon Books.

Jamieson, K. and Waldman, P. (2003) *The Press Effect: Politicians, Journalists, and the Stories that Shape the Political World*, Oxford: Oxford University Press.

Keane, J. (1991) *The Media and Democracy*, Cambridge: Polity Press.

McChesney, R. (1999) *Rich Media, Poor Democracy: Communication Politics in Dubious Times*, Urbana, IL: University of Illinois Press.

——. (2004) *The Problem of the Media: U.S. Communication Politics in the Twenty-first Century*, New York: Monthly Review Press.

McEwen, J. (1978) "The Press and the Fall of Asquith." *Historical Journal* 21 (December): 863–83.

McNair, B. (2000) *Journalism and Democracy: An Evaluation of the Political Public Sphere*, London: Routledge.

Moore, M. (2006) *The Origins of Modern Spin: Democratic Government and the Media in Britain, 1945-51*, Basingstoke: Palgrave.

Moyers, B. (2008) "Is the Fourth Estate a Fifth Column? Corporate Media Colludes with Democracy's Demise," *In these Times*, 11 July. <http://www.inthesetimes.com/article/3790/is_the_fourth_estate_a_fifth_column> (accessed 20 October 2008).

Muhlmann, G. (2008) *A Political History of Journalism*, Cambridge: Polity.

Petley, J. (2004) "Fourth Rate Estate: Was Journalism Ever the Democratic Watchdog and Champion of Freedom its Advocates Claim?" *Index on Citizenship* 33 (April): 68–75.

Proctor, B. (1998) *William Randolph Hearst: the Early Years, 1863–1910*, New York: Oxford University Press.

Rich, F. (1999) "Journal: Is Mike Wallace Ready for his Closeup?" *New York Times*, 17 July. <http://query.nytimes.com/gst/fullpage.html?res=9F05E1DF123FF934A25754C0A96F958260&sec=&spon=&pagewanted=all> (accessed 19 October 2008).

Schudson, M. (1978) *Discovering the News: A Social History of American Newspapers*, New York: Basic Books.

Scott-James, R.A. (1913) *The Influence of the Press*. London: Partridge and Co.

Seymour-Ure, C. (1996) *The British Press and Broadcasting Since 1945*, 2nd ed., Oxford: Blackwell.

Siebert, F., Peterson, T., and Schramm, W. (1963) *Four Theories of the Press: The Authoritarian, Libertarian, Social Responsibility and Soviet Communist Concepts of what the Press Should Be and Do*, Urbana, IL: University of Illinois Press.

Sparks, C. (1991) 'Goodbye, Hildy Johnson: the vanishing "serious press"', in P. Dahlgren and C. Sparks (eds.) *Communication and Citizenship*, London: Routledge.

Starr, P. (2004) *The Creation of the Media*, New York: Basic Books.

Stead, W.T. (1886) "Government by Journalism," *Contemporary Review* 49 (May): 653–74.

Streitmatter, R. (2001) *Voices of Revolution: The Dissident Press in America*, New York: Columbia University Press.

Tumber, H. and Palmer, J. (2004) *The Media at War: The Iraq Crisis*, London: Sage.

Notes

1 This paragraph and the subsequent one draw liberally on Hampton, 2004, which discusses the "educational" and "representative" ideals in a British context. Campbell, 2006, provides an excellent, historically focused account of the clash between rival theories of journalism in late nineteenth century United States. In addition, for eloquent and erudite discussions of similar themes across national boundaries and centuries see Keane, 1991, 1–50 and Siebert et al., 1963, 39–71.

2 See also the excellent discussions in Conboy, 2004, 109–27; Petley, 2004.

3 For stimulating discussions of the popular image of journalism, see Erlich, 2006; Franklin, 1997, 25–32.

4 I am grateful to Tom O'Malley for his advice on this theme. In addition to these examples from a commercial press, Britain possesses an investigative tradition of public service broadcasting, notable examples including ITV's *World in Action* and BBC's *Panorama*.

5 This pressure to cut costs in order to deliver greater shareholder profits, in a contemporary American context, is one of the major plot-lines of the HBO TV programme *The Wire*, series 5.

6 Streitmatter (2001, 196) also points out that the *National Guardian* struggled financially because "few businesses were willing to buy advertisements in an anti-war newspaper," illustrating again the hazards of relying on the market to support a critical and independent press.

7 Yet if the extent of government efforts to shape media coverage has increased since World War II, they have a rich history. See, for example, Brown, 2009, for Lord Palmerston's ability to shape newspaper coverage in the 1850s.

8 Professional journalism's reliance on official sources is illustrated by the fact that even such celebrated examples of "Fourth Estate" journalism as the publication of the Pentagon Papers and the exposure of the Watergate break-in and cover-up relied on leaks from government officials at odds with their agencies or departments. The "adversarial" journalism in each case thus constituted, from one perspective, not so much journalists taking on the government as a dissenting position in the government employing the media against the dominant position.

9 See, for example, Hampton, 2009.

2

JOURNALISM, HISTORY AND THE POLITICS OF POPULAR CULTURE

John Hartley

In this chapter I show how the evolution of popular journalism from its beginnings in the early nineteenth century involved a shift from radical to commercial, 'subject' to 'object,' and substance to style. But it was not the popular press as such that effected this change. Rather it was the discovery – made by journalist Walter Bagehot – that celebrity journalism was a crucial component of the constitution, vital to the safety of a grudgingly democratised polity. Here is the origin of the use of spectacle to cloak the exercise of 'real rule' behind the scenes. The popular self-representation championed in the early 'pauper press' was inverted; now journalism was directed to the people, not from them. Only recently, with the growth of DIY digital media and online citizen journalism, has popular self-representation re-emerged. Journalism's polarity may be in process of inverting once again – from 'objective' to 'subjective.'

Liberty and libertinage

We are forced to ask ourselves how inflammatory language and mythologizing can offer a legitimate exegesis on the politics of the day.

(de Baecque, 1989: p. 168)

Popular culture is the true seed-bed of modern popular journalism. Although newspapers for the gentry and merchant classes had been around since the seventeenth century, it was only when the press achieved mass scale that it took on contemporary shape, and only with the radical 'pauper press' that journalism achieved its potential of communicating with entire populations regardless of their local class or status. In turn, journalism played a strong role in developing popular culture as a modern, urban, mediated experience, as opposed to the prevailing notion at the time of popular culture as craft-based rural folk art.

Popular journalism was born of the European Enlightenment, French Revolution, and British industrialisation and urbanisation during the period from the 1790s to the

1840s. In that half-century, motivated by a desire for political emancipation as well as an entrepreneurial bid for profit, radical journalists and publishers, from Tom Paine and William Cobbett to Richard Carlisle and Henry Hetherington (see Spartacus n.d.), perfected the means for secular, cross-demographic communication about public (and private) affairs to 'ordinary' readers numbering in the hundreds of thousands, reaching millions by the time the ultra-radical Sunday newspaper The *News of the World* came on to the scene in 1843. This was, as historian Robert K. Webb puts it, 'a pioneering effort to solve the problem of getting ideas across from one man, or one class, to another' (Webb 1955: p. 35; and see Hartley 1996: pp. 94–9). The 'pauper press' succeeded in creating the popular 'reading public'; an achievement won by activists without the vote, often poor, in the teeth of government suppressions, and with no established business infrastructure or market.

'Getting ideas across' was not a merely cerebral business, however. Modern political journalism was founded as much in scandal, gossip and sensationalism as it was in reason and truth. As the *ancien régime* was propelled against its will towards political modernisation via the French Revolution, salacious novels and pornographic pamphlets were the 'real sources from which political journalism originated in France,' according to the historian Robert Darnton (1982: 203). Sex and politics were coterminous; as the bedroom antics of *Thérèse philosophe* (Anon. 1748) and her many successors demonstrated by the simple narrative device of equating the achievement of orgasm with that of freedom. Sexual gossip, scandal and innuendo about the king, queen, courtiers and clerics were used to undermine deference towards royalty and aristocracy, while stories of sexual awakening and libertinage were grand metaphors for political self-realisation and philosophical freedom. The most celebrated writers of the Enlightenment – Diderot, Voltaire, Montesquieu, Mirabeau – wrote bawdy and pornographic works as well as political journalism and philosophy, without making a distinction between the personal (popular culture) and the political (journalism). On the contrary, the genre of publishing that gave birth to popular journalism in France, the *'livres philosophiques,'* lumped porn together with philosophy (Darnton & Roche 1989: pp. 27–49). In short, and not only in France but also in Britain (e.g. McCalman 1993), the radical underground was not squeamish about where journalism stopped and other forms of writing and representation began. 'Liberty' and 'libertinage' shared the same philosophical history (Grayling 2005: pp. 116–18).

Popular culture: subject or object?

> *The whole history of civilisation, is strewn with creeds and institutions which were invaluable at first, and deadly afterwards.*
>
> (Bagehot 1891)

By mid-century, the focus had shifted from 'radical-popular' to 'commercial-popular' press, and with that the emphasis changed from scandal to *expose* government towards spectacle to *cloak* government. This version of popular journalism was enshrined at the core of the nearest thing 'the English' (i.e. the British) have to a constitution.

Furthermore, the kind of journalism that was installed as a pillar of the state was not the 'journalism of record' of *The Times*. It was what we would now call celebrity or gossip news. This starring role for tabloid media was proposed by Walter Bagehot, the author of *The English Constitution* (1867), who was not a constitutional lawyer or political scientist, but a journalist. He was indeed no less than the editor of one of the greatest 'organs of enlightenment' of that time (or this), *The Economist*.

The main reason that Bagehot was interested in popular journalism was that he was afraid of popular insurrection. The 1867 Reform Act prompted him to write *The English Constitution*, as a way of demonstrating how unwritten but pragmatic arrangements, by this time well established – and good for the governance of a world empire as well as the home polity – were preferable to constitutional models like that of the USA, but in danger of imminent destruction. Bagehot was afraid that the extension of the franchise to property-less labourers would overwhelm the political process, such that 'ignorance' would expunge 'instruction,' and 'numbers' would overwhelm 'knowledge.' Given that this is the very fate predicted for democracy by those who queue up to denounce the tabloid media today, the fact that he turned to them to *avoid* such a fate clearly needs some explanation.

Bagehot was in fact proposing a new role for the press. He saw the popular press as a tool of government, not as a means of self-representation for the popular classes. He was certainly not advocating a constitutional role for the radical, insurrectionary, 'great unstamped' that had burgeoned with the rise of industrialisation (1790 to 1848). Under the slogan 'Knowledge is Power,' the 'pauper press' was one of the chief proponents of, and forces for, the 'creative destruction' of the political old regime; the royal and aristocratic monopoly over both the franchise and the government. This version of the popular press saw popular culture as the 'subject' – the *cause* – of political action, not as the 'object' or *effect* of political communication originating from a ruling elite, least of all one that claimed constitutional legitimacy for arrangements that sought to pacify the popular classes by means of a nineteenth-century version of showbiz.

Bagehot's 'English constitution' was at odds, then, with an earlier and hard-fought version of the press that sought to *speak for and as* 'the people.' He replaced it with one that sought to *speak to* them. He took the craze for political commentary that characterised British popular culture throughout the nineteenth century and converted it from *action* to *entertainment*. In the process, popular journalism's polarity was reversed – it turned from 'subjective' to 'objective.' While it might seem obvious that an 'objective' stance is preferable for journalism, the history of how popular culture was turned into an object suggests that this is by no means a reliable conclusion (Hartley 2009).

Walter Bagehot's innovative theorisation of the constitutional role of celebrity journalism should give pause to those who would dismiss the latter as a populist contagion, infecting the political process with sensationalist values and dumbing-down the public sphere to the disadvantage of democracy. Bagehot's contention was that the very reverse was the case. Thus, those who study news and journalism may need to be reminded of the historical development of popular journalism and its use for both emancipationist and governmental purposes. This is especially important now, when near-ubiquitous digital technologies allow for direct 'peer to peer' communication among the polity (social networks) and DIY or participatory media – a return, I will argue, to popular culture as 'subject.'

Representation – two models for 'two nations'

It was not easy to escape from politics in nineteenth-century Britain. It filled the newspapers; it was a principal means of mass entertainment.

(Webb 1955: p. 83)

During the early nineteenth century, when industrialisation took, hold first of all in Britain, only three men in a hundred and no women had the vote. There was a sharp divide between the working class and the political class: they were, in Disraeli's famous phrase, 'two nations.' The propertied, educated and enfranchised class, both conservative and liberal (as famously satirised in Gilbert & Sullivan's *Iolanthe*), followed public affairs in papers such as *The Times* and *The Economist*. These were dedicated to:

- politics (confidence or otherwise in the government of the day),
- public administration (e.g. campaigns for army reform, or against slavery or capital punishment), and
- the economy (e.g. promotion of or opposition to free trade).

Meanwhile, the other nation, the unenfranchised popular majority, developed their own press, both radical-popular (e.g. the *Republican, Poor Man's Guardian, Northern Star*) and, increasingly in and after the 1840s, commercial-popular (e.g. *Lloyd's Weekly News, Reynold's News, News of the World*). There was however a telling mismatch between scale of readership and degree of political influence. With a circulation in the low thousands, *The Times* could topple governments; with sales in the hundreds of thousands and multiple readers per copy (Webb 1955: pp. 33–4), the pauper presses were physically attacked by the government: their premises were raided, their property seized and their proprietors imprisoned.

Because of these asymmetric purposes and powers, the respectable and the radical press were expressions of different models of communication. *The Times* and *The Economist* developed journalism as professional expertise, to serve a readership with a stake in both economic and political questions. These papers connected the minority of emancipated citizens to each other. The pauper press, meanwhile, saw itself as part of the struggle against the current economic and political arrangements. Its mode was as much to accuse opponents as to address its own readers, because it spoke on behalf of – as the voice of – a class that had not attained citizenship. The poorest sections of that class weren't even *counted* in the census (Mayhew 1849: preface). Here already, then, there appeared the chalk and cheese distinction between professional journalism (*The Times*) and popular culture (*Poor Man's Guardian*), even though journalistic skills were to be found on both sides of the fence. The difference was founded on the status of popular culture itself. This was the basis for a divergence between journalism that saw popular culture as object (to be feared and controlled) and journalism that saw popular culture as subject; 'we the people.'

The early mass-circulation newspapers were produced by radicals among whom were also entrepreneurs, who had the 'ability to harness commercialism for the purposes of political dissent and cultural populism,' and who were proud to use the latest high-tech industrial inventions such as the steam-powered rotary press (Haywood 2004: p. 164) in order to reach a mass reading public. They pioneered the 'mass' media. However, as time unfolded the commitment to oppositional self-representation in these newspapers declined as their scale and profits increased. As the nineteenth century progressed, wages, leisure, literacy and the franchise were progressively increased and extended. The 'radical-popular' ('we') press began to give way to the 'commercial-popular' ('they') press.

A good example is the *News of the World*, launched as an unstamped 'ultra-radical' Sunday newspaper in 1843 (Maccoby 2001: p. 420). Eventually it became the newspaper with the largest circulation in the world, when it was widely known as the 'News of the Screws' because of its penchant for exposing sex scandals, in the honourable tradition of the *livres philosophiques* and in ample fulfilment of its own longstanding motto of 'All Human Life is There.' It was Rupert Murdoch's first Fleet Street acquisition in 1969. It remains the Sunday stablemate of News Corp's *Sun*. The *Sun's* own career followed the same route in the twentieth century. It began in 1911 as the *Daily Herald*, a strike-sheet published by printing unions as part of an industrial dispute. It was taken over by the Trades Union Congress and with the help of the publisher Odhams. It became the official mouthpiece of the union movement and the Labour Party. In its turn, during the 1930s, it too became the biggest-selling newspaper in the world, but suffered in brutal circulation wars with the *Daily Express*. When the Mirror Group took over Odhams in the 1960s they revamped the *Herald*, changed its name to the *Sun*, and then sold it to Rupert Murdoch in 1969 (see NMPFT 2000). Both papers were transformed from radical-popular agents of workers' self-representation to commercial popular mechanisms for turning them into a market; from 'subject' to 'object.'

By the turn of the twentieth century the popular press had largely fallen to conservative press barons, who launched commercial picture-tabloids like the *Daily Mail* and *Daily Mirror*. Their proprietors addressed the labouring classes and their families not as radical activists but as domestic consumers – and biddable voters. They boosted their circulation with stunts and prizes and pretty girls rather than firebrand politics, although the *Mirror* did a bit of both. During World War I they were fully incorporated into the purposes of the state, their proprietors becoming cabinet ministers. They ushered in the *Citizen Kane* era of press barons whose political clout was based on popular reach, exemplified on one side of the Atlantic by William Randolph Hearst ('you furnish the pictures, I'll furnish the war!'), and on the other by Lords Northcliffe, Rothermere, Beaverbrook, Kemsley, Camrose and Thomson.

Constitutional journalism – a 'certain charmed spectacle'

It is nice to trace how the actions of a retired widow [the Queen] *and an unemployed youth* [the Prince of Wales] *become of such importance.*

(Bagehot 1867)

In the process, the self-representative communication model of the radical press was recast into the sender-receiver model that still characterises journalism research. The latter model connects journalism to popular culture only indirectly. Journalism is seen as a production system that conveys news to the public, while popular culture is a consumption system of commercially purveyed entertainment (Hartley 2009). But despite the asymmetry, each side needs the other: no readers, no news; no entertainment, no readers. However, compared with the earlier radical-popular press upon which commercial-popular journalism is built, in this model 'representation' has shifted from the demand to the supply side.

It was here that Walter Bagehot entered the picture, making his famous distinction between those component parts of the constitution that excite 'the reverence of the population' and those 'by which it, in fact, works and rules' (Bagehot 1867). He called them the *'dignified'* and *'efficient'* parts respectively. The monarchy and aristocracy (House of Lords) were the 'dignified part'; the Cabinet and the House of Commons were the 'efficient part.' In point of historical fact, Bagehot was a little ahead of himself. The aristocracy did not collapse as a viable political force in Britain until World War II. But he saw clearly – and early – what the consequences of popular emancipation would be. Following the extension of the vote to unskilled male labourers in the 1867 Reform Act, he wrote, 'I am exceedingly afraid of the ignorant multitude of the new constituencies' in the industrialised cities. Bagehot feared what he called 'the supremacy of ignorance over instruction and of numbers over knowledge.'

To counter their numerical supremacy Bagehot made a less well-remembered distinction between *'deference'* and *'democracy.'* He preferred deference, where electors defer to wealth and rank, and thence to 'the higher qualities of which these are the rough symbols and the common accompaniments,' over democracy, which exalts the 'vacant many' over the 'inquiring few.' Bagehot felt, however, that the parliamentary system itself could be used 'to prevent or to mitigate the rule of uneducated numbers,' so long as deference was maintained. By deference he did not mean – or mean alone – forelock-tugging subservience. Bagehot had something much more modern in mind:

> In fact, the mass of the English people yield a deference rather to something else than to their rulers. They defer to what we may call the theatrical show of society. A certain state passes before them; a certain pomp of great men; a certain spectacle of beautiful women; a wonderful scene of wealth and enjoyment is displayed, and they are coerced by it. … Courts and aristocracies have the great quality which rules the multitude, though philosophers can see nothing in it – visibility.

(Bagehot 1867)

Bagehot is describing nothing less than the genesis of what is now more easily named as celebrity culture (Plunkett 2003). Rather than siding with those 'philosophers' who would 'deride this superstition,' he makes celebrity journalism central to the constitutional arrangements of what was at the time the most powerful empire on earth. He argued that the 'charmed spectacle' and human values of the royal and aristocratic families could succeed in preserving popular deference:

> What impresses men is not mind, but the result of mind. And the greatest of these results is this wonderful spectacle of society, which is ever new, and yet ever the same; in which accidents pass and essence remains; in which one generation dies and another succeeds.
>
> (Bagehot 1867)

Bagehot explains how the mundane business of government can continue unimpeded in anonymous but expert hands:

> The apparent rulers of the English nation are like the most imposing personages of a splendid procession: it is by them the mob are influenced; it is they whom the spectators cheer. The real rulers are secreted in second-rate carriages; no one cares for them or asks about them, but they are obeyed implicitly and unconsciously by reason of the splendour of those who eclipsed and preceded them.
>
> (Bagehot 1867: VIII)

This distinction between the dignified (deferential) and efficient (ruling) parts of the constitution is crucial to any consideration of the relationship between journalism and popular culture. It makes of the 'charmed spectacle,' and thus of the popular/media culture which is the stage for it, what may be called a ruse to rule. Journalism on both sides of this divide is part of the 'constitutional' mechanism for social order: there is journalism for efficiency (*The Times*, *The Economist*), and journalism for deference (celebrity spectacle). The overall system requires both parts for the ordered continuation of good government in a polity governed by fear of a democratic majority which has no direct role to play in rule. Bagehot's schema makes clear what subsequent familiarity may well have blurred; that the spectacle of 'wealth and enjoyment,' the celebrity of 'great men' and 'beautiful women,' and the 'theatrical show of society,' are all *an essential part of government*.

'Common human nature' and 'a universal fact'

> *'The paparazzi create the oxygen and the euphoria for fame. How are you going to make people famous without making them famous? And who makes them famous?'*
> (Darryn Lyons, in Aitkenhead 2008)

Popular culture is the domain of spectacle and celebrity. These are communicated to the 'mob' of 'spectators' via popular journalism. Therefore, in line with Bagehot's insight about the need for both rule and the spectacle of rule – and that these are distinct but equally necessary as the efficient and dignified parts of the constitution – journalism also has two essential 'constitutional' components: one that follows the 'real rulers secreted in second-rate carriages,' and another that follows the 'charmed spectacle' of 'high society.'

> No feeling could seem more childish than the enthusiasm of the English at the marriage of the Prince of Wales ... But no feeling could be more like common human nature as it is, and as it is likely to be ... A princely marriage is the brilliant edition of a universal fact, and, as such, it rivets mankind.

The 1867 Reform Act enfranchised over a million working men. Modern journalism (as part of Bagehot's constitution) is founded on fear of the newly sovereign demos. How then to 'rivet' the popular mind to a constitution in which 'real rule' might remain with those 'secreted in second-rate carriages'? The cultivation of deference via popular culture, using 'universal facts' and 'common human nature' to 'rivet mankind', was, however, not straightforward but a hazardous venture, not least because a 'princely marriage' may swiftly be followed by royal adultery and marital scandal – as has duly unfolded for not one but three Princes of Wales since then. Further, it was not necessarily the target populace who were most riveted. The people who really enjoyed that 'great quality' of visibility seemed to be the respectable classes themselves, along with the courtiers whose job it was to attract the attention of the press. As Lord McGregor (then chair of Reuters Trust) noted:

> At the time of the wedding of the Prince of Wales [1863], sales of *The Times* increased to 108,000 copies compared with its average of around 60–65,000 during the 1860s. In 1864, the Prince and Princess visited Denmark accompanied by Lord Spencer who ... went on to complain that court officials with their '*adulation of reporters* show great want of dignity.'
>
> (McGregor 1995, my emphasis)

In short, it was not by any means a case of the posh papers providing rational information for rulers while popular culture laid on celebrity, spectacle, spin and bread and circuses for the masses. It was if anything the other way around. Circulation of *The Times* nearly doubled on Royal Wedding day. For the have-nots, on the other hand, the spectacle was not always so welcome – it served to inflame 'the knockabout anti-monarchism of the popular press ... and ... the republican political rumblings in the 1860s and 1870s, some of which found a parliamentary voice opposing grants to the Queen's children on occasions such as royal marriages' (Thompson 2001, p. 75).

Similarly, it should not be assumed that the respectable press was always pro-*government*, even if it was always pro-*rule*. Thomas Barnes in *The Times* joined with Richard Carlile in the *Republican* in denouncing the Peterloo Massacre of 1819. *The Times* was in favour of the 1932 Reform Bill to extend the franchise, while the *Morning Chronicle* commissioned both Charles Dickens's 'sketches by Boz' and Henry Mayhew's reports on the condition of the labouring poor in England and Wales (Mayhew 1849). In other words, the top people's press was averse neither to spectacle and sensation nor to social reform. What really differentiated the two types of journalism discussed here was their *readership*, divided into 'two nations,' and still now not fully integrated into one public; politically, journalistically or culturally.

To counter the influence of the 'ignorant multitude,' Bagehot proposed not to educate the masses as to their 'real rulers,' (much less to rule themselves), but to put on a good show – 'not mind, but the result of mind.' In this endeavour he was aided and abetted by the 'efficient' papers, the conservative press barons, and the 'objective' model of communication. It is this model of communication that underlies commercial-popular journalism to this day, and this is also the model most widely taught to journalists.

Plus ça change?

The logic of the history I have been outlining . . . is for the industry to keep flogging the dead horse of its weary old formats until they lose their audience entirely. At that point, the networks can claim to have proved there is no market for current affairs programs any more, and replace them with a game show.

(Turner 2005: 159)

The current period is experiencing a return to self-representation or demand-led rather than supply-led journalism, via user-generated content, citizen journalism and self-made or DIY media of various kinds, all of which can be used for journalism as well as for self-expression and entertainment, including plenty of bawdy stuff that retreads the fuzzy line between liberty and licentiousness. These activities too are proving to be an energetic and surprising locus of innovation, as ideas and social networks form in the sphere of self-representation (daydreaming and mischief as well as freedom and comfort), and some are subsequently adopted in that of economic enterprise and professionalised production, crossing from culture to economy – subjective to objective – in the process.

Perhaps the model of communication established in the early pauper press is due for a revival. Certainly there are straws in the wind. One that blew by as I was thinking about this chapter was a newspaper story in *The Australian*, syndicated from *The Times* – both newspapers of record. It reported on the popularity of a YouTube video of model Amber Lee Ettinger 'prancing around New York in various stages of undress while lip-synching the words of a song declaring she had a crush on presidential candidate Barack Obama' (*Australian* 2007a). Among the lyrics quoted are these:

Baby I cannot wait
Till 2008,
Baby you're the best candidate. ...
You're into border security,
Let's break this border between you and me.
Universal healthcare reform,
Mmmm – it makes me warm.

(Obama Girl 2007)

Quite apart from the combination of humour, sexuality and politics, what links Obama Girl to self-representative journalism is the item's non-canonical provenance and its popular reach. It was published on the 'broadcast yourself' platform, where it has attracted over twelve million hits, nearly seventy thousand comments (as at December 2008), and the attention of 'over 200 TV stations around the world' (Obama Girl 2007). Although it appears to have been professionally made, it personifies the perspective of the citizen (whose part is performed by 'Obama Girl'), while using the resources of popular culture, including comedy, music, dance, and a pretty girl to say something that is serious, at least to the extent that it addresses a notoriously non-voting demographic in the name of anti-Bush politics.

Fusing sex and politics (and rock and roll) in the name of liberty has remained a well-trodden route to fame (and sometimes fortune) from the *livres philosophiques* onwards. It has been continued in the present era via such figures as Felix Dennis (from *Oz* to *Maxim*), Larry Flynt (*Hustler*) and Darryn Lyons (Big Picture paparazzi agency). An endless succession of scandals, from royal mistresses to Monica Lewinski, continually reminds us that sex remains one of the most potent elements of political journalism. The staples of popular culture – scandal, celebrity, bedroom antics – are the very propellant of modern journalism and therefore of modern ideas (Hartley 1996: pp. 114–20).

In a similar vein, during the Australian federal election campaign of 2007, the first YouTube election in that country, a 23-year-old law student at Sydney University named Hugh Atkin trumped the political professionals by uploading a self-made spoof called 'Kevin Rudd – Chinese Propaganda Video' (Atkin 2007). As Australian voters knew, this referred to Labour leader Kevin Rudd's fluency in Mandarin (he had previously served as a diplomat). It scored over 200,000 views and hundreds of comments, favourites, honours and responses. It was shown on *The 7.30 Report*, the ABC's flagship current affairs programme, and received copious coverage in the news media, most of which concurred with this assessment: 'The two main political parties, with their multi-million advertising budgets, are proving no match for the power and creativity of the guerilla videomakers of the internet' (*Sydney Morning Herald* 2007). While its qualities as satire were admired, its politics were ambivalent, as noted by a comment on the site:

> This is pure, absolute, unadulterated genius. But I can't figure out if it's pro-Liberal or pro-Labor. Can I get some help here??? WHAT SHOULD I THINK??!?
>
> (au.youtube.com/user/mpesce)

This was posted by Mark Pesce, a prominent new-media entrepreneur and writer (see markpesce.com/). In the conversational mode of social networks, his rhetorical question was answered by Atkin personally, among a long string of others debating the issues. Another comment recommended viewers to look at an 'even funnier' video by 'Cyrius01' (Stefan Sojka; see www.cyrius.com.au/), called 'Bennelong Time' (Bennelong is the name of the seat that Prime Minister John Howard lost at this election). It re-voiced a Led Zeppelin classic with apposite anti-Howard lyrics, ending with a call to vote for the Greens. This too went viral, attracted over 60,000 views and was featured on ABC TV. Sojka was interviewed on ABC Radio and in *The Australian*, where he said:

> For years and years you sit there looking at the television and screaming at it, trying to put your arguments across during all the political current affairs shows, and then I thought, well, there is a place where I can actually do it and say something and maybe be heard.
>
> (*Australian* 2007b)

The Australian commented: 'It's unofficial, unauthorised and may yet have an influence on the voting intentions of generations X and Y.' In the event, the politicians with the savviest YouTube following won, in both the USA and Australia. In terms of popular appeal, it seemed that these spoofs were upstaging not only the parties and advertising agencies, but also straight political journalism was reduced to making news stories out of popular self-representation that originated on YouTube.

Is this what has become of the tradition of popular culture as subject? Certainly popular culture is the ground on which new experiments in journalism are propagating. Developments in online media are a definite challenge to expert, top-down, producer-led, supply side 'objective' journalism, as is well recognised in industry and among the commentariat. The industrial-era model of one-way, one-to-many, read-only, mass communication that sees the populace as an object (of policy and campaigns) is now supplemented if not supplanted by two-way, peer-to-peer, read and write, networked communication where popular culture is once again the subject and agent of its own representation. The reading public is at last evolving into a writing public. Now, in principle, everyone can be a journalist; anyone can publish journalism (Hartley 2008). The tradition of self-representation has found a mechanism to cut out (or never cut in) the intermediary agency of the professional expert and the political activist alike. People can and do speak for themselves in an expectation of being heard, whether by a small group of peers or more widely. In short, the supply-chain model of journalism is again in conflict with the self-representation model, as was the case at the beginning of modern journalism in the period 1790–1830, although it may be that the self-representatives have learnt the lesson of Walter Bagehot and are now more attuned to the constitutional possibilities of spectacle, celebrity and entertainment. Are journalism and popular culture finally dissolving into each other? Is it possible to imagine both numbers and knowledge, radical and commercial, subject and object, in the rule and self-representation of (what's left of) modernity?

References

Aitkenhead, Decca (2008) 'Mr Paparazzi, I presume?' *The Guardian*, June 7. Accessible at: www.guardian.co.uk/media/2008/jun/07/privacy.pressandpublishing

Anonymous [Attributed to marquis Boyer d'Argens] (1748) *Thérèse Philosophe, ou Mémoires pour servir à l'histoire du père Dirrag et de mademoiselle Éradice*. Accessible at: du.laurens.free.fr/auteurs/Boyer_Argens-Therese_philo.htm

Atkin, Hugh (2007) 'Kevin Rudd – Chinese Propaganda Video,' *YouTube*. Accessible at: au.youtube.com/watch?v=ptccZze7VxQ

Australian, The (2007a) "Obama Girl' Highlights Senator's YouTube Dilemma,' *The Australian* June 19, p. 9. Accessible at: www.theaustralian.news.com.au/story/0,20867,21929093-2703,00.html

Australian, The (2007b) 'Political Ads Mocked on YouTube,' *The Australian* October 25. Accessible at: www.theaustralian.news.com.au/story/0,25197,22643204-26077,00.html

Baecque, Antoine De (1989) 'Pamphlets: Libel and Political Mythology,' In Darnton & Roche (eds), pp. 165–76.

Bagehot, Walter (1867). *The English Constitution*. Accessible at: www.gutenberg.org/etext/4351 (1872 revised edition).

Bagehot, Walter (1891) *Physics and Politics, or, Thoughts on the Application of the Principles of 'Natural Selection' and 'Inheritance' to Political Society* (No. II, The Use of Conflict). Accessible at: www.gutenberg.org/etext/4350

Cyrius01 (2007) 'John Howard 2007 Bennelong Time Since I Rock and Rolled,' *YouTube*. Accessible at: au.youtube.com/watch?v=8_zulGddP6o

Darnton, Robert (1982) *The Literary Underground of the Old Regime*, Cambridge, MA: Harvard University Press.

Darnton, Robert and Daniel Roche (eds) (1989) *Revolution in Print: The Press in France 1775–1800*, Berkeley: University of California Press.

Grayling, A. C. (2005) *Descartes: The Life of René Descartes and Its Place in his Times*, London: The Free Press/Pocket Books.

Hartley, John (1996) *Popular Reality: Journalism, Modernity, Popular Culture*, London: Arnold.

Hartley, John (2008) 'Journalism as a Human Right: the Cultural Approach to Journalism,' in Martin Löffelholz and David Weaver (eds) *Journalism Research in an Era of Globalization*, London: Routledge, pp. 40–50.

Hartley, John (2009) 'Journalism and popular culture,' in Karin Wahl-Jorgensen and Thomas Hanitzsch (eds) *The Handbook of Journalism Studies*, New York: Routledge, pp. 310–24.

Haywood, Ian (2004) *The Revolution in Popular Literature: Print, Politics and the People, 1790–1860*, Cambridge: Cambridge University Press.

Lanham, Richard A. (2006) *The Economics of Attention: Style and Substance in the Age of Information*, Chicago: Chicago University Press. Part accessible at: www.press.uchicago.edu/Misc/Chicago/468828.html

Maccoby, Simon (2001) *English Radicalism: 1832–1852*, London: Routledge.

Mayhew, Henry (1849) *London Labour and the London Poor*. Accessible at: etext.virginia.edu/toc/modeng/public/MayLond.html.

Mcgregor of Durris, Lord Oliver Ross (1995) 'Rights, Royals and Regulation: The British Experience,' Harold W. Andersen Lecture (World Press Freedom Committee). Accessible at: www.wpfc.org/AL1995.htm.

McCalman, Iain D. (1993) *Radical Underworld: Prophets, Revolutionaries and Pornographers in London, 1795–1840*, Oxford: Clarendon Press.

NMPFT (2000) 'The *Daily Herald* Newspaper and Archive,' Bradford: National Museum of Photography, Film & Television. Accessible at: nmpft.org.uk/insight/info/5.3.29.pdf

Obama Girl (2007) 'I Got a Crush … on Obama,' *YouTube*. Accessible at: www.youtube.com/watch?v=wKsoXHYICqU

Plunkett, John (2003) *Queen Victoria: First Media Monarch*, Oxford: Oxford University Press.

Spartacus (n.d.) (by John Simkin) 'Journalists,' *Spartacus Educational* website: Accessible at: www.spartacus.schoolnet.co.uk/journalists.htm

Sydney Morning Herald (2007) 'YouTube Revolutionaries Upstage the Party Machine,' *Sydney Morning Herald*, October 26 2007. Accessible at: www.smh.com.au/news/federalelection2007news/rudd-faces-youtube-revolution/2007/10/25/1192941243230.html?s_cid=rss_news

Thompson, Dorothy (2001) 'The English Republic,' *The Republic*, Issue 2 (*The Common Good*), pp. 72–80. Accessible at: www.republicjournal.com/02/contents002.html

Turner, Greame (2005) *Ending the Affair: The Decline of Current Affairs in Australia*, Sydney: UNSW Press.

Webb, Robert K. (1955) *The British Working Class Reader 1790–1848*, London: George Allen & Unwin.

3

THE ORIGINS OF OBJECTIVITY IN AMERICAN JOURNALISM

Richard Kaplan

For over a century, the US press has embraced the ethic of objectivity as defining its core public mission. This professional code of studied impartiality and rigorous factuality has been celebrated as American journalism's proudest, if most difficult to sustain, achievement. Considered a crucial tool for democracy, objectivity supposedly secures a space for neutral, factual information and public deliberation outside the corruption, rancor, and partisan spin that normally characterizes public discourse.

Practitioners of journalism in the United States and across the globe have often seen the American ethic of objectivity as a model to emulate. Backed by the prestige and power of the United States, reinforced by foundations and think-tanks, the professional ethic has appeared as an ideal commodity for export. When other national journalisms enter into crisis, as in the former communist countries, or grow tired of the passions of partisanship, objectivity is the proposed solution. Nevertheless, these domestic and foreign advocates of objectivity typically ignore the institutional conditions that first promoted its American creation and then sustained it. In this chapter, we explore the genesis of this ethic and its underlying political context.

Historiography, in fact, offers conflicting accounts of when and why the US press broke from a traditional ethic of avid partisanship and adopted the professional code of objectivity. Media scholars variously situate this transformation in the 1830s Jacksonian Revolution, the 1870s Mugwump revolt against party loyalty, a late-nineteenth-century shift in press economics, or the emergence of a new, distinct occupational identity in the 1920s (Schudson 1978; Schiller 1981; Baldasty and Rutenbeck 1988; Curl, Donald. *Murat Halstead and the Cincinnati Commercial*. Boca Raton: University Presses of Florida, 1983. Baldasty 1992). In contrast, we locate this transformation in the late nineteenth–early twentieth centuries and offer a political accounting of the origins of US objectivity.

It's our central contention, against all naturalistic and functional explanations of the origins of objectivity, that journalism's professional ethic reflects the overarching structure of the political field with all its contentions about who is a proper public speaker and what is proper public rhetoric. When these broader political institutions and cultural ideas shift, those changes are inevitably reflected and refracted in the public mission of the press.

The United States underwent a major recalibration in its political institutions in the late nineteenth–early twentieth centuries. In the critical election of 1896 and the political reforms of the Progressive Era, 1900–20, the policies and coalitions making up the two dominant parties were dramatically reshuffled, the parties were weakened, and voting turnout fell precipitously. Against this backdrop, American journalism broke from its past explicit, formal partisanship and adopted a new public ethic.

In what follows, we first consider two alternative historical perspectives on the origins of the United States' exceptional ethic. We then outline the theoretical logic of a political explanation of journalism's professional codes, before turning to a detailed narrative of US journalism's transformation from a partisan model of reporting to its modern ethic of independent, stringent objectivity during 1896–1920.

Objectivity, what is it?

Professional ethics and independence from external political control define many, although certainly not all, of the national media systems around the globe (Hallin and Mancini 2004). From England and Japan to Holland and Canada, professional journalists supposedly set the news agenda on the basis of their own judgment of topical importance and then factually report the news.

Objectivity, however, participates in a more austere regime of press ethics. As Michael Schudson (1978: pp. 5–7) explains, objectivity points to a radical doubt about the possibility of any straightforward empirical determination of the facts. Under objectivity, journalists adopt the pose of scientists and vow to eliminate their own beliefs and values as guides in ascertaining what was said and done. Supposedly avoiding all subjective judgments and analysis, the journalist strives to become a rigorously impartial, expert collector of information. More than just ending formal political alliances and external control, the objective press must eliminate any organizing philosophies or social commitments from influencing the news. In this fashion, the rarified ethic of objectivity seeks a high degree of differentiation from the polity, economy, and, as some have charged, from the general value commitments of the society.

The ethic of objectivity has long been seen, at least within the United States, as the single best ideal for the operation of media in modern democracy. Indeed, with its refusal of interpretation, its critical distance from all authorities, and its elevation of 'balance,' objectivity operates as something akin to the lifeblood of the US press. Certainly, there exist discordant strands, deviant models, and alternative practices in American journalism – from community papers and journals of opinion to trade publications, minority weeklies, and advertising puff sheets – but they form largely invisible, undiscussed, or else derided alternatives to the dominant paradigm.

Objectivity today stands as the unchallenged commonsense of journalists, politicians, and public. So much so that the remedy posed by critics and practitioners alike for any perceived deficiencies of the press is simply more objectivity: less bias, more facts. Even such openly partisan media outlets as the cable network Fox News feel compelled to pay lip service to the rhetoric of an impartial expert journalism. In its marketing slogans, Fox declares, 'We report, you decide.'

From our perspective, objectivity refers to a series of interconnected discourses, institutions, and practices (see Ryfe 2006). These encompass a political philosophy of the media's role in public life, journalism's professional code of ethics, the bureaucratic organization of the news corporation with its hierarchical division of labor, the organization of news-gathering into desks and beats (Sparrow 1990), standardized rhetoric justifying the journalist's choices and interpretations (Tuchman 1980: pp. 31–8), and the typical forms of visual presentation, narrative structuring, and literary emplotment of the news (Nerone and Barnhurst 2001).

Competing histories

Traditional historiographic accounts of the origins of the US press's professional ethic start from the assumption that objectivity is the media's natural and ideal public ethic. According to such standard accounts as those offered by Walter Lippman (1931), once the press gains its independence from the external control of corrupt politicians and profit-hungry capitalists, it can pursue its own natural, distinctive, independent mission. The development of a vigorous market purportedly breaks the hold of the politicians over journalism, while the emergence of professional ethical code insulates journalism from the corruptions of the market. An independent, objective press supposedly reflects the triumphal unfolding of modernity in general and American democracy in particular (Nerone 1995; Hallin and Mancini 2004: pp. 76–80).

From this insular and functional perspective, the role that power and culture plays in the development of alternative models of modern journalism is hidden from view. The ways in which the particular configuration of press institutions reflect and incorporate the broader social context are obscured. It is of course just such a provincial and naturalistic accounting of social institutions that is challenged by comparative history and also more robust historical understandings, as offered here (cf. Benson 2009).

An exceptional ethic?

In contrast to the traditional historiography, it is the particular merits of Michael Schudson's classic account, *Discovering the News* (1978), to offer a socially grounded account of the origins of objectivity. Far from operating with a triumphalist, teleological view of what is journalism's proper and natural ethic, Schudson details the deep paradigmatic features of the US press and connects these to particular political traits, which elsewhere have been labeled 'American exceptionalism.'

The United States has long been seen to possess a distinctively liberal culture. The country, claim historians like Louis Hartz and Richard Hofstadter, lacks the sharp cultural and economic divisions that marred the social order of old-world European societies. The United States has neither a conservative traditionalist movement nor a radical socialist movement because all citizens subscribed to a philosophy of liberal individualism with its desire for individual prosperity and property (Plotke 1996).

Neither polarized social divisions nor, in Schudson terms, conflicting communal political visions define the country's political culture. The press faces consensus instead of contention and, on the basis of shared social norms, can offer neutral, fact-based descriptive accounts of the day's events. Such reports take their implicit interpretations and salience from the overarching, shared social norms, which they help to thematize and reinforce (Alexander 1981). The prototypical news story here is one of scandal or crime.

Schudson located the emergence of this exceptional culture of liberal individualism (or in his terms a 'democratic market society') and likewise an independent and factual, news-oriented press in the 1830s Jacksonian revolution, which saw both the birth of mass political parties and an extended market economy (Nerone and Barnhurst 2001: pp. 58–67; Saxton 1990: chs 3–4). Despite the cogency and depth of his interpretation, however, no independent, factual press, much less an 'objective' journalism, emerged in the 1830s.

Later research has demonstrated that as mass political parties flourished, starting in the 1830s, so did a partisan press. Open, public partisan advocacy persisted as the dominant ethic of US journalism throughout the nineteenth century (Kaplan 2002; McGerr 1996). Only in the early twentieth century, did journalism break from a posture of public partisanship. A largely static account of American political culture and institutions, like Schudson's American exceptionalism, cannot account for the dynamic development of a new press ethics in the early twentieth century.

The dynamics of critical elections

In contrast to Schudson, the theory of critical realigning elections offers a more dynamic account of the essential political attributes of the United States. Realignment theory demarcates different political periods in US history and thus departs from Schudson's overly global and static perspective (Plotke 1996: ch. 2). According to this perspective, US political institutions go through periods of relative stasis and equilibrium punctuated by short periods of collective upheaval and change. At key elections, social groups and issues that were previously unrepresented in the formal polity break into the public arena. The entry of contentious issues like slavery or corporate monopolies typically upends the two parties' relative identities, power, and underpinning social coalitions. As leading historian Walter Dean Burnham states, a realigning election 'constitutes a political decision of the first magnitude and a turning point in ... national policy formation. Characteristically, the relationship among policymaking institutions, their relative power and decision-making capacity, and the policy outputs they produce are profoundly affected ...' (Burnham 1982: 101; Katznelson and Kesselman 1979: 241–58.)

It's the contention here that the critical election of 1896, the subsequent shifts in political institutions, and the flourishing of political reform movements in the early twentieth century are the decisive context behind the American press's break with formal public partisanship. Furthermore, this shift can be in many ways considered similar to the move toward 'catch-all' parties, with their pragmatism and focus on economics that increasingy defined much of Western Europe during the 1950s onward (Hallin and Mancini 2004: pp. 178–80, 263–73; Skocpol 1993).

Why politics?

What, however, explains the press's entanglement with the broader political culture? Why, despite their many protestations of political innocence, neutrality, and independence, do the media continue to remain embedded within the broader public sphere? What accounts for the continual, if subterranean, influence of the political field and its doctrines upon the forms and contents of journalism? Why isn't the fourth estate entirely free to pursue the facts as it judges right and appropriate according to its own professional criteria? Why, even with differentiation, do the broader cultural ideals and inequalities of public voice infiltrate the independent medium of the press?[1]

Certain dimensions of journalism render it susceptible to influence from its political environment. As a public narrative of collective social reality, the news cannot claim any exclusive jurisdiction for its pronouncements. In the democratic public sphere, the press lacks the proprietary power to stake out any special territory for its occupational expertise; it cannot exempt any part of the public domain from the democratic clamor of competing interpretations. Unlike other professions, journalism distinctively lacks those attributes that would allow it to exercise an exclusive franchise in defining the truth of its special domain, that is, narrating the social world. No specialized technical knowledge, no formal credentialed training, no esoteric occupational languages, nor the creation of a self-evidently socially useful product – none of these shields journalism from external criticisms. As Schudson (1978: pp. 7–9) remarks, journalism is a relatively 'uninsulated profession.' In the words of James Carey, it is a 'vernacular craft.'

As politicians are well aware, news reports possess important consequences for the conduct of government. These political officials, such as the president, often possess their own mandate, their own legitimacy to provide authoritative public interpretations of important national events (Cf. Blumler and Gurevitch, 1995). In addition, these alternative public voices know their own case might be enhanced by accusing the press of bias and distortion. Consequently, they challenge, criticize, and thereby seek to influence the media's reports. (So common is this practice in American politics that it has gained its own cliché and is known as 'softening up the referee.') In the end, no matter how the press strives to achieve 'objectivity,' its pronouncements remain permanently entangled in the political bickering of the public sphere. Reporters must continually assert the validity of their news descriptions and analyses against a host of contending views and alternative authorities.

Confronting a welter of critics and competing interpretive authorities, yet possessing only weak rationales for the importance and truth of their particular accounts, the press implicitly draws upon the broader political culture and refracts the existing constellations of public power to justify its prominence and authority in the public sphere. Given this underlying dependence of the press upon the broader constellations of political power and culture, when the overarching political institutions and culture change so does the press's dominant ethic or public philosophy.

Partisan journalism of the gilded age

Throughout the nineteenth century, American journalism was publicly and forthrightly partisan. What was the nature of this partisan news and how did it incorporate the overarching cultural and power assumptions of the broader political system?

Victorian-era America, as in late-nineteenth-century Western Europe, was the age of mass organizational parties (Barraclough 1964). Political parties had battered down the gates of liberal democracy and carried the (white, male) masses into the electoral arena, granting them political influence. In return, American voters rewarded their parties with strong bonds of affection and loyalty. Party identifications rapidly metamorphosed into family traditions and ethnic heritages, to be handed down from generation to generation (see McCormick 1986: chs 1, 3).

As historians, John Nerone (1987), Alexander Saxton (1990), and Schudson have underlined, the 1830s Jacksonian revolution, which democratized American politics and created mass political parties, also saw the first wave of a mass circulation daily press. No accident that, as parties reached out to incorporate the white male populace into the rites of democracy and elaborated competing, compelling visions of America and its prospects, the news media gained a readership. The press too viewed the world through partisan lens and fed its subscribers hyperbolic narratives of party conflict, triumph, and at times tragedy.

In addition to their hold on popular loyalty, parties controlled the machinery of government. In an epoch of a limited presidency and weak administrative bureaucracies, parties and courts constituted the sinews and ligaments of the US state. Parties took governmental policies and offices as their reward for election victories, and used these political spoils to reinforce their mandate as the exclusive representative of the American voter (Skocpol 1992; Skowronek 1981).

Given their public legitimacy and their extensive control of governmental resources, the two parties spoke as the dominant, if not exclusive, public voices on all issues of national import. In this context of parties' overweening power, newspapers too pledged allegiance to the Democrats or their opponent, be it Whig or Republican. Outside of the two parties, with their ceaseless polemics and wrangling, there appeared to be no neutral space from which journalists could comment upon and observe American social life (cf. Dickens-Garcia 1989: 49; McGerr 1986: 115–16). Neither journalistic traditions nor public culture supported the existence of an independent press.

As a loyal party organ, the newspaper was charged with a variety of political duties that demonstrated its commitment to the party (Kaplan 2002: ch. 1). First and foremost, a journal was obliged to endorse the party's 'men and measures' without expressing any qualms or quibbles. Indeed, any contravention of important policy positions might bring censure upon the newspaper, reader boycotts, or copies of the newspaper piled high into blazing bonfires (cf. Swanberg 1967: pp. 129–30). When the party announced its slate of candidates, the journal naturally printed and endorsed the nominees. However, this published list appeared not just once, but day in and day out for the entire election season. Reporting too was colored by political preferences. News reports persistently described party rallies around the state in a manifestly exaggerated fashion; the speeches were always deemed rousing, the crowds enthusiastic and overflowing. Furthermore, the journal reprinted verbatim the oratory of the party's leading stump speakers. And, the paper often spoke as a 'we,' including its readers in an intimate circle of party members, united in their opposition to the political enemy. Throughout, the organ demonstrated its support for the party and celebrated the partisan political community, thus making partisan identities natural and exciting (McGerr 1986: pp. 14–22).

The editorial page continued this simple, enthusiastic categorization of friends and foes. For the education of the readers, it published extended defenses of party policy. For their entertainment, the paper jeered the missteps and defects of its political opponent. Throughout the last half of the nineteenth century, the majority of American newspaper editorials, in election season and out, pleaded the party's cause and defended its policies (cf. Kaplan 1997). Even as they showcased public debate, partisan papers simplified it – stereotyping the issues and arguments. Journals spoke not as impartial or external commentators, but instead as representatives of the political community. Editorials became part of an extended dialogue, or more accurately diatribe, between local papers standing in for the two parties. In this two-sided debate, daily sheets tacitly implied that the Democrats and Republicans exhausted the relevant spectrum of political viewpoints. The press adopted the naturalizing assumptions of the broader political culture; parties were the only pertinent public speakers, the only true representatives of democracy's will.

In the political culture of the era, the daily paper was far from being an independent producer of information that was then dispensed to private consumers via the impersonal mechanism of the market. Instead, the partisan paper was part and parcel of a public political community. Journals therefore operated as more than neutral transmitters of information. They labored to build a shared partisan identity, either through democratic communication or through expressive rites of group loyalty. Such constructed ties of partisan solidarity were seen as enhancing the party's prospects in its strategic pursuit of electoral power.

Journalists were, not antagonists of politicians, but appendages, and, in general, newspapers were parasitic upon parties' larger mandate for public speech. The press's authority to narrate American social reality derived from its affiliation with a party. In fact, as they prosecuted their party's case before the bar of public opinion, journals often tried to assume the mantle of party authority. A share of a paper's prestige and power derived from its ability to present its own words as the official pronouncements of leading politicians. *The New York Tribune*, for instance, gained national prominence during 1876–1910 as the quasi-authorized organ of the Republican Party's reform wing. The line between journalist and politician blurred as the *Tribune's* staff often advised the president and its publisher was nominated for vice-president in 1892.

Given the partisan press's emphatic, evaluative voice, the news of the Gilded Age appeared irredeemably particular, plural, and political (cf. Nerone and Barnhurst 2001: p. 187). It emerged from a specific political community and stood opposed to the news of its political foes. American political culture with its emphatic ideal of partisanship offered little legitimating basis for an independent impartial journalism. Furthermore, this political culture was united with a complex set of economic and political mechanisms that reinforced the press's devotion to the 'manly' and open expression of political allegiances (Kaplan 2002: ch. 2). Most importantly, as an organization catering to a mass audience, the daily press was dependent upon the inclinations and belief of the mass of Americans, who preferred their news packed with a sharp partisan punch.

Declarations of press independence

What abrogated this journalistic regime? What ended avid partisanship as the press's professional ideal? What broke the hold of parties over the press? Throughout the nineteenth century, the daily press in its serious and its sensationalist versions remained largely partisan. However, at century's end the power of parties to dominate the American public sphere, to monopolize rights of public speech, began a precipitous decline. This overarching shift in American political culture and political institutions would fundamentally affect journalism's day-to-day reporting practices as well as its highest ideals.

Two key episodes marked the toppling of parties from their pride of place in the American public sphere: the critical election of 1896, and the antipartisan political reforms of the Progressive Era, 1900–20. Against this political backdrop, US newspapers broke from all party ties and reformulated their role in American public life. Drawing upon Progressive Era rhetoric of professional expertise, the press promulgated a new vision of journalism as independent and objective. Henceforth, the press declared it would be free from all encumbering political affiliations and would function as an impartial arbitrator of democracy's public debate.

At first, the presidential campaign of 1896 seemed to signal an upsurge in partisan fervor. William Jennings Bryan, already endorsed by the Populist Party, captured the Democratic presidential nomination and ushered new contentious issues into the political arena. The long-standing grievances of farmers – who were oppressed by inequitable railroad rates, declining prices for agricultural goods, and a deflationary currency – burst into the two-party system. Under the candidacy of Bryan, the Democratic Party emerged as the voice of protest and reform. The specific protest issues, however, were quickly overwhelmed by widespread hysteria. The *Nation* declared, 'Probably no man in civil life has succeeded in inspiring so much terror without taking life as Bryan.' The Democratic candidate was repeatedly reviled from the platform as well as the pulpit. Democratic papers deserted the party en masse (Baehr 1972: p. 255; Jensen 1971: pp. 272–5; Sarasohn 1989: pp. 10–11; Wiebe 1967: ch. 4). Conservative elite dailies like the *New York Times* and the *Detroit Free Press* issued 'declarations of independence.' Even liberal, sensationalist journals such as

Pulitzer's *World*, or Scripps' *Cincinnati Post* dumped the party. In New York City, only the heretical William Randolph Hearst trumpeted Bryan's candidacy. At the campaign's close, Bryan (quoted in Livingstone, 1904) remarked on the journalistic inequality between the two parties: 'With all the newspapers of the country against us, our 6,500,000 votes is a vindication of which we have a right to be proud.' Hallim and Mancini (1984) have argued that each country's 'structure of the public sphere deeply influences the form and content of its news'.

The press's flight from the Democrats was reinforced by the fallout from the election. The emotional issues of the campaign fundamentally reshuffled the social coalitions underlying the two parties and, thus, disrupted long-standing ties of party loyalty. Furthermore, the election so weakened the Democrats that at both the national level and in the North and West they were demoted to a minority party. Elections became uncompetitive. Deprived of a significant choice, voter participation dropped and continued to fall from 84% in 1896 until it reached its nadir in 1920 at 53% (Burnham 1970). From all-absorbing public drama, the fights and furies of the parties on Capitol Hill and in the pages of the press turned drab and unappealing.

Newspapers had bolted from parties before, notably in the exodus from the Republicans in 1872 and 1884. But after their momentary apostasy, journals had always returned home, usually humbled, to one political church or the other. And, in any case, bolting papers had maintained their right to express forcefully political opinions. In the early twentieth century, this public partisanship came to a permanent end. As party competition and polemics turned into an extraneous sideshow, the Progressive movement rose up to press the attack against parties and their public legitimacy.

Progressives harshly criticized 'corrupt' 'party machines,' and they initiated reforms that undermined parties' central role in political life: primary elections, direct election of senators, non-partisan ballots, and civil service reform (Burnham 1970, ch.4). By a variety of measures, parties had become distinctly weaker (Burnham 1991). In this context of electoral upheaval, fading party power, and an anti-partisan ideology purveyed by a movement of the middle classes, newspapers severed their links to the Democrats and Republicans.

A new news ethic

Given the fall of parties with their broad justifying rationales and mass support, how could journalism's role in the public sphere be stabilized? What authority would the press now possess in American public life, and what would be its strategic legitimating rationale? How could it justify its own public prominence and the necessary selectivity of its reporting? In what way could the news media insulate itself from the inevitable attacks and criticism of the powerful?

Publishers and editors drew upon the political rationales of Progressive reformers to reframe and reconstruct journalism's public role (Gans 1978; Hofstadter 1955: pp. 186–98; Kaplan 1997; Nord 1995). Progressive notions of 'public service' and professional expertise became the rhetorical mainstay of journalism's occupational ideals and a defense against all external criticisms. In the face of widespread fears over monopolies, the idea of public service denied that such concentrations of power advanced private interests (cf. Leach 1993: ch. 5).

The press asserted that its control over extensive powers of publicity (indeed, its monopolization of the public sphere) was not employed for private goals or partisan ends. As one publisher (Booth 1915) noted, 'Our policies in the conduct of the [*Detroit*] *News* are not private policies… We have no ulterior motive, no private axe to grind.' Journalism was purportedly devoted to the general community and was rewarded only for serving that public good. Furthermore, instead of personal judgments and political evaluations, Progressive-era publishers asserted that professional technical expertise would direct their news choices and interpretations. This new rhetoric was already widely accepted when the American Society of Newspaper Editors issued its 'Code of Ethics' in 1923 (1960). The Code's key terms were factuality, independence, impartiality, and public service.

Journalism's preference for 'objectivity' represented a fundamentally reformulated basis of legitimacy after the previous century's justifications of avid, public partisanship. Party papers had affirmed a right to political speech, but in the twentieth century, publishers no longer upheld their sheets' right to purvey an explicit point of view in opposition to other perspectives. Gradually, the press developed a claim to be above the wrangling of politics. The news, journalists asserted, is not part of the swirl of opinions and partisan biases, and it does not aspire to serve one particular segment of public opinion (Alexander 1981: pp. 23–39). Much in the manner of the modern presidency, the press abjured speaking for this or that political interest but, instead, claimed to be neutrally speaking for the entire commonweal.

Newspapers' new objectivity, which was designed to free the press from the ubiquitous contention of the public sphere, participated in a more general ideological movement of society. Journalism's claims of autonomy and technical expertise paralleled a general expansion of professional authority and decision-making by experts and managers. Progressive-era changes in American political culture and institutions encouraged a segmentation of society into specialized domains for technical decision-making. Progressive reformers believed that social problems were a question of facts and technical solutions best left to impartial, informed experts. The growth of such technical administrative procedures attacked the public expression of conflict among classes and diverse social interests. They aimed at eliminating the open, contentious, collective deliberations of politics, of which the decline of parties in American politics was the most prominent example (Burnham 1991; Haber 1964; Rogin 1967; Wiebe 1967).

In its new public impartiality, the press supposedly did not operate as a platform for one dominant public voice but, rather, as a 'channel' for a variety of speakers. Ideally, new voices could gain access to the press, and enter into democracy's public discussion. But the objective press did not mark a return to the republican notions that defined the early American press, with its openness to a plurality of public rational voices. Instead, the twentieth-century press served as technocratic, professional mediator of the public re. Following John Nerone (1995: 51–2), we might call this reconstituted press in onstructed public sphere 'neo-liberal.' All voices must be vetted and processed by the press before they can reach the mass public. Rights of participation are diminished, and rights of hearing accurate information reinforced (Schudson 2008).

Society, marked by new concentrations of economic power and the entrance of the masses into the public arena, supposedly requires a caretaker. Liberal society needs a new, technical, selfless elite to administer it. This press model depends crucially on professional notions of supplying impartial, ethical public service against the corruptions of the market and the state. The profession carves out an autonomous realm for the exercise of its disinterested expertise against those who would subject social life to more instrumental calculations.

However, guided by their technocratic ethic and typically conforming to pressures from the polity, the dailies did not so much expand their coverage of civil society's diverse opinions as continue to publicize the policies and pronouncements of 'important' legitimate speakers from formal political institutions. In contrast to the past, however, twentieth-century journals now balanced their coverage between the two major parties. They no longer exhibited a preference for one party over the other. Far from eliminating the influence of particular class interests in politics and publicity, journalism's technocratic ideals took for granted the established hierarchy of power. Governmental and corporate power-holders were taken as the embodiment of modern industrial society's functional rationality. Their pronouncements should be reported, their decisions respected, not probed, much less challenged (Sigal 1986, Tuchman 1980, Weddle et al. 1993).

To summarize, between the nineteenth and early twentieth centuries, the ideals and practices of American journalism fundamentally shifted. Reflecting more overarching transformations of the political field, journalism dispensed with its previous practices and ideals of forthright, emotional partisanship in its news and editorials. The daily press, instead, asserted a right to mediate the public sphere as impartial, expert professionals. This new twentieth-century journalistic regime was upheld by the dominant alignments of political culture and public authority and reinforced by technocratic occupational ideals, an increasingly monopolistic market structure, and corporate ownership of the press. While offering a justification for an independent professional news media, objectivity as a public philosophy offered only limited resources and rationale for the press to pursue its democratic mission in the face of other competing voices and concentrations of power (Kaplan 2002: conclusion; Rosen, 1992).

Note

1 Certainly, media analysts have documented the influence of the political field and its array of forces on the definition of the news. Most prominently, W. Lance Bennett (1990) points to the way dominant, legitimate, organized political groups influence the range of views presented in mainstream media. In his 'indexing hypothesis', he demonstrates how the news duplicates the limited conflict between the two parties. Molotch and Lester (1974) have posited that the news, far from publicizing unadorned facts, reflects issues first made into matters of public attention by the conflict of political forces. Other media research, notably the investigations of Leon Sigal (1986) and Weddle (1993), documents the power of legitimate political officials to frame the news through their dominance as news sources.

References

Alexander, J. 1981. 'The News Media in Systematic, Historical and Comparative Perspective.' In E. Katz and T. Szeczko (eds.) *Mass Media and Social Change*. Thousand Oaks, CA: Sage, pp. 17–51.

American Society of Newspaper Editors. 1960. 'Canons of Journalism.' In W. Schramm (ed.) *Mass Communications* (pp. 623–25). Urbana: University of Illinois Press.

Baehr Jr., H. 1972. *The New York Tribune since the Civil War*. New York: Octagon Books.

Baldasty, G. 1992. *The Commercialization of News in the Nineteenth Century*. Madison: University of Wisconsin Press.

Baldasty G. and J. Rutenbeck. 1988. 'Money, Politics and Newspapers: The Business Environment of Press Partisanship in the Late 19th Century.' *Journalism History*.

Barraclough, G. 1964. *An Introduction to Contemporary History*. New York: Penguin Books.

Bennett, W. 1990. 'Toward a Theory of Press-State Relations in the United States.' *Journal of Communication* 40:2, pp. 103–25.

Benson, R. 2009. 'Comparative History.' this volume.

Blumler J. and M. Gurevitch. 1995. *The Crisis of Public Communication*. New York: Routledge.

Booth, G. 1915. Letter to H. Chalmers. (dated 7 Nov. 1915). Bloomfield Hills. MI: Cranbrook Archives.

Burnham, W. 1970. *Critical Elections and the Mainsprings of American Politics*. New York: W. W. Norton.

——. 1982. *The Crisis in American Politics*. New York: Oxford University Press.

——. 1991. 'The System of 1896: An Analysis.' In P. Kleppner (ed.) *The Evolution of American Electoral Systems*. Westport CT: Greenwood Press.

Curl, D. 1980. *Murat Halstead and the Cincinnati Commercial*. Florida: Atlantic University Press.

Dickens-Garcia, H. 1989. *Journalistic Standards in Nineteenth-Century America*. Madison: University of Wisconsin Press.

Gans, H. 1978. *Deciding What's News*. New York: Vintage Books.

Haber, S. 1964. *Efficiency and Uplift: Scientific Management in the Progressive Era, 1908–1920*. Chicago: University of Chicago Press.

Hallin D. and P. Mancini. 2004. *Comparing Media Systems: Three Models of Media and Politics*. Cambridge: Cambridge University Press.

——. 1984. 'Speaking of the President. Political Structure and Representational Form in US and Italian Television News.' Theory and Society V. 13. pp. 829–50.

Hofstadter, R. 1955. *The Age of Reform*. New York: Vintage Books.

Jensen, R. 1971. *The Winning of the Midwest*. Chicago: University of Chicago Press.

Kaplan, R. 1997. 'The American Press and Political Community: Reporting in Detroit, 1865–1920.' *Media, Culture and Society* 19:3, pp. 331–55.

——. 2002. *Politics and the American Press: The Rise of Objectivity, 1865–1920*. Cambridge; Cambridge University Press.

Katznelson I. and M. Kesselman. 1979. *The Politics of Power*. New York: Thomson Learning.

Leach, W. 1993. *Land of Desire: Merchants, Power and the Rise of New American Culture*. New York: Vintage Books.

Lippmann, W. 1931. 'Two Revolutions in the American Press,' *Yale Review*, pp. 433–41.

Livingstone, W. 1904. *The Republican Party*. New York: G. P. Putnam's Sons, V. 2.

McGerr, M. 1986. *The Decline of Popular Politics: The American North, 1865–1928*. New York: Oxford University Press.

McCormick, R. 1986. *The Party Period and Public Policy*. New York: Oxford University Press.

Molotch, H. and Lester, N. 1974. 'Accidents, Scandals, and Routines: Resources for Insurgent Methodology.' In G. Tuchman (ed.) *The TV Establishment*. Englewood Cliffs, NJ: Prentice Hall.

Nerone, J. 1987. 'The Mythology of the Penny Press.' *Critical Studies in Mass Communication* 4:4

Nerone, J. (ed.) 1995. *Last Right: Revising Four Theories of the Press*. Chicago: University of Illinois Press.

Nerone, J and Barnhurst, K. (2001) *The Form of the News: A History*. New York: Guilford Press.

Nord, D. 1995. 'Reading the Newspaper: Strategies and Politics of Reader Response, Chicago, 1912–1917.' *Journal of Communication* 45: 3.

͘ke, D. 1996. *Building a Democratic Political Order: Reshaping American Liberalism in the 1930s and 1940s*. ͘bridge: Cambridge University Press.

Rogin, M. 1967. *McCarthy and the Intellectuals*. Cambridge, Mass.: MIT Press.

Rosen, J. 1992. 'Politics, Vision, and the Press,' in *The New News v. The Old News: the Press and Politics in the 1990s*, In J. Rosen and P. Taylor (eds.). New York: Twentieth Century Fund, pp. 1–33.

Ryfe, D. 2006. 'Introduction: New Institutionalism and the News,' *Political Communication* 23:2. pp. 135–44.

Sarasohn, D. 1989. *The Party of Reform: Democrats in the Progressive Era*. Jackson: University Press of Mississippi.

Saxton, A. 1990. *The Rise and Fall of the White Republic: Class, Politics and Mass Culture in Nineteenth-Century America*. New York: Verso.

Schiller, D. 1981. *Objectivity and the News: The Public and the Rise of Commercial Journalism*. Philadelphia: University of Pennsylvania Press.

Schudson, M. 1978. *Discovering the News: A Social History of American Newspapers*. New York: Basic Books.

Schudson, M. 2008. 'The "Lippmann–Dewey Debate." *International Journal of Communication* V. 2. pp. 1031–42.

Sigal, L. 1986. 'Who? Sources Make the News.' In M. Schudson and R. Manoff (eds.). *Reading the News*. New York: Vintage Books. pp. 9–37.

Skocpol, T. 1993. *Protecting Soldiers and Mothers: The Political Origins of Social Policy in the United States*. Cambridge, Mass.: Harvard University Press.

Skowronek, S. 1981. *Building A New American State: The Expansion of National Administrative Capacities, 1877–1920*. New York: Cambridge University Press.

Sparrow, B. 1999. *Uncertain Guardians: The News Media as a Political Institution*. Johns Hopkins University Press.

Swanberg, W. A. 1967. *Pulitzer*. New York: Scribner.

Tuchman, G., 1980. *Making News: A Study in the Construction of Reality*. New York: Free Press.

Weddle, J, Hallin, D., and R. Manoff. 1993. 'Sourcing Patterns of National Security Reporters.' *Journalism Quarterly* 70:4, pp. 753–66.

Wiebe, R. 1967. *The Search for Order, 1877–1920*. New York: Hill and Wang.

4

JOURNALISTS AND THEIR PROFESSIONAL IDENTITIES

Wolfgang Donsbach

The identity of journalism as a profession lives on the assumption "I know it when I see it". There is no other profession in our modern societies where the gap between its undisputed importance for the whole of society and the perception of its borders, structures and competencies is so large. This has always been the case throughout the history of this occupation. But over the last decades it has become an even more salient problem – not only to the occupation itself but also to its capability of fulfilling its societal function. Several developments in society and in the media business are challenging the professional identity of journalism and have rendered it even more blurring of boundaries than before. In this chapter, we will identify what these challenges are and how they might be overcome. First, though, we briefly describe what journalism is about, what role it plays in society and how journalists see their role themselves.

What is journalism about? The three traditions of the profession

In their entry "Journalism" in the International Encyclopedia of Communication, Barnhurst and Owens (2008: 2557) define journalism as follows: "(It) is a constellation of practices that have acquired special status within the larger domain of communication through a long history that separated out news-sharing from its origins in interpersonal communication." Thus, while sharing new information with others in one's social surroundings is a common and everyday human activity, it needed a social role that ascertains truth and distinguishes "intelligence from gossip". Therefore, "telling about events, supplying novelty, and, from the process, discerning factual truth are the main rudiments that came to define journalism as a cultural practice" (ibid.), a definition that can be best described as the *public service tradition*.

Schudson describes in an excellent way how this societal function developed in the US in the first half of the nineteenth century. The individualization of society and the loosening of traditional familial structures were part of a growing mobility that itself was caused by industrialization. The citizens in this new society asked for neutral and valuable information to cope with their changing environments – e.g. to know where the jobs and the markets are and who runs for office. This demand for a new quality of information stimulated a more neutral and factual reporting and eventually led to the professional norm of "objective journalism" and to the division of labour between reporters, editors, and commentators. "The revolution led to the triumph of the news over the editorial and facts over opinion, a change which was shaped by the expansion of democracy and the market, and which would lead, in time, to the journalist's uneasy allegiance to objectivity" (Schudson 1978: 14). Thus, probably the most important reason for the existence of journalism is a *professional service* whose unique selling proposition is the validation of assertions about reality with a high degree of responsibility. We should keep this in mind when talking about more recent developments and how they affect the identity of journalism.

However, this need for valid information as described in the definition by Barnhurst and Owens is historically not the first tradition of journalism. Another and earlier one is the occupation's, in a wider sense of the word, "political" role of individual actors (*"subjective tradition"*). Citizens who fought for specific goals (e.g. freedom of speech) or wanted to disseminate their ideas (e.g. about the church or the state) did this by employing technical media of multiplication and distribution. They thus contributed to the development of what Habermas called the "public sphere" (Habermas 1962, Nerone 2008).

Journalism has developed on the fundamentals of press freedom and the arguments with which philosophers from Milton to Mill in England, the founding fathers in the United States, or journalists like Joseph Görres in Germany fought for it. One of the core arguments of these protagonists was the assumption that only a free communication structure and the plurality of facts, arguments and values will lead to the best possible result for the whole society. The finding of truth is seen as a collective and cumulative process in which journalists as public communicators play a most crucial role. However, these ideas had their origin in a political context in which this freedom of speech and of the press were still absent, and therefore many journalists saw themselves (and rightly so) as freedom fighters. And this is in varying degrees still the case today. It is obvious that the later a country turned to a democracy and thus gained its civic rights the stronger is the persistence of this professional element in the journalistic tradition even today. Therefore, besides being a professional and detached trader of valid information (a "mediator"), a second tradition of journalism is the "communicator" in his own right who pursues subjective goals, however, most of the time by claiming to act for the sake of the *"volonté general"* (Rousseau) or public good.

Finally, a third stream in journalists' identity is the *economic tradition*. Journalists, nowadays most of them employed by large, often global companies, are hired to make profits by selling their products. This has always been the case throughout the development of the profession. Printer-editors were among the first to do this on a regular basis by gleaning material from all the sources that passed information through their hands (Briggs and Burke 2002). The advent of the mass or "penny press" for the first time pursued this goal openly. The *New York Sun*, first published in 1834, wanted "to lay before the public, at a price within the means of everyone all the news of the day, and at the same time afford an advantageous medium of advertising" (cited in Schudson 1978: 21).

Within the framework of this news ideology the media content became more and more a dependent variable of consumer needs with the consequence, for instance, that politics "became just a part of a larger universe of news" and the *Sun* would, for instance, not cover the proceedings of Congress if nothing interesting to their readers had happened (Schudson 1978: 22). Today, selling a "communication product" that meets the expectations and tastes of the widest public (or the best defined target group) has come even more to the forefront of the journalistic identity than ever before (Murdock and Wasko 2007).

Many authors have developed theoretical concepts for the journalistic identity, some as ideal types, some as normative standards, and some as empirical typologies. Interestingly, most of the more seasoned concepts neglect the economic dimension, perhaps because they are driven by the normatively more acceptable roles of the professional and the political journalist. For instance, Janowitz (1975) distinguished between the ideal types of the "gatekeeper" and "advocate" in journalists' role percep-tions. While the former would select the news according to professional standards such as news values, the latter would select it according to its instrumentality for the (deprived) social groups he or she supports. However, given the three-dimensional identity as described above, a proper theoretical concept would conceptualize journalists' roles in a more differentiated way (Deuze 2005; Donsbach 2008a).

All three major avenues of the journalistic history and identity have left their mark in the self-identification and role perception of journalists, at least in free societies. All journalists have acquired elements of all these dimensions from the available role models. Scholars can usually explain the differences between journalistic cultures when comparing countries or between individual journalists in a single country by examining which of the alternatives prevails. The table opposite summarizes these traditions and distinguishes between their different goals, relationships, prototypes, dominant values, the dominant content, and the role of the journalist.

Empirical evidence on these traditions

Many studies have investigated to what extent journalists "score" on each of these dimensions. International comparisons have been of particular value because they help to interpret the findings from a single country (see e.g. Deuze 2002). On the dimension of the subjective tradition studies have been primarily interested in the extent to which journalists make news decisions based on their own values, attitudes and opinions. Several of these have shown that the news value of an event or statement varies with its "instrumentality" for the journalist's own goals (Kepplinger et al. 1991, Patterson and Donsbach 1996). Another line of research along this avenue has been surveys on journalists' role perceptions and of the organization of the workflow in newsrooms (Gans 1979; Esser 1998). In all three areas – i.e. news decisions, role perceptions and work organization – the evidence shows rather considerable

	Subjective Tradition Pursuing individual goals	Public Service Tradition Supplying valid information	Commercial Tradition Give the people what they want
Goal	Self-actualization	Adaption of individual to reality and functioning of society	Economic interest of owners
Dominant Relationship	Journalist-Authorities	Medium-Society	Media-Markets/ Shareholders
Prototypes	John Milton	Joseph Pulitzer	Rupert Murdoch
Dominant Value	Subjectivity/ Freedom of expression	Objectivity/Plurality	Economic success/ shareholder value
Dominant Content	Opinions before facts	Facts before opinions	Whatever sells
Journalist's Role	Individual writer	Professional	Employee

Model of the three traditions of journalism

differences between the continental European and the British–American way of conducting news journalism, although some convergence due to the global trend towards commercialization can be observed. But still today, two-thirds of German news journalists say that "championing particular values and ideas" is an important aspect of their work as a journalist (Donsbach 2008b).

Research on the service tradition has been primarily interested in the professional norms and conduct of journalism. This includes studies on the degree of objectivity, neutrality, fairness and other norms as well as on the subjective importance of these norms to journalists. Again, this research has found remarkable differences even between countries of a similar media structure. Objectivity, for instance, has a slightly different meaning and a higher value for US American than for German journalists (Donsbach and Klett 1993). Journalists also differ in the degree of research and investigation as well as in the application of specific research methods (Löffelholz and Weaver 2008).

Lately the commercial tradition has come more into the focus of research. Almost all studies in several countries have shown that journalists' decisions on media content are more and more driven by the necessity to reach the widest audience and that therefore interventions by seniors and management become more prevalent than ever before. For instance, today three times more German news journalists than in the early 1990s say that news that they have prepared "has been changed by someone else in the newsroom in order to increase audience interest" (Donsbach 2008b). While the freedom of journalists in the newsroom has been a research topic for many decades the focus now has changed. In earlier times researchers were interested in their independence towards the editorial slant as set by the owners (see for instance, Breed 1955). Today the question is how independent journalists can be towards seniors and managers who impose soft news standards and features of tabloidization in order to reach the widest audience.

Challenges to journalism and its identity

Journalism is facing several challenges the salience of which can only be compared to the impact authoritarianism had on a free press. The problem is, however, that all of this happens in free societies and that there is no single power to be blamed for a development that can be detrimental for society, at least for the quality of its public discourse. Among the many problems that the profession is facing, four stand out.

First, there is a *declining audience for the news*. The traditional news media are losing audiences in almost all developed countries. This trend affects particularly the newspapers and here the younger age groups. For instance, in Germany the regular readership of newspapers among the 14 to 29-year-old young Germans was almost cut in half between 1980 and 2008. The declining exposure to the traditional news media is not yet counterbalanced by exposure to news sources on the Internet. According to a Pew Research Center (2006) survey in 2006 only 23 per cent of the population said they had seen news the previous day over the Internet. The latest corresponding figure in Germany is only 15 per cent. This declining exposure to news complies with a declining subjective interest in the news or what is called the civic "duty to keep informed". According to the same Pew Center study only 38 per cent of the age group between 18–29 years "enjoys keeping up with the news". In Germany, in only five years, between 2003 and 2008, the proportion of Germans under 30 years of age who said that they "want to be informed about what is going on in the world" declined from 45 to 37 per cent (Köcher 2008).

A second challenge to journalism is the increasing *market pressures* impacting news decisions. As already mentioned above, research results have shown several indicators for an increasing impact of commercial objectives on new decisions. According to a report by the Carnegie Corporation (2007, 3) "the quality of journalism is losing ground in the drive for profit, diminished objectivity and the spread of the 'entertainment virus.'" This economic impact comes from two sides. The need to attract large audiences affects the selection and presentation of topics. The need to attract advertisers jeopardizes the firmness of the firewall between the newsrooms and the advertising departments. According to a German study news media increasingly offer to print public relations articles in exchange for the placement of advertisements. Today two-thirds (68 per cent) of US journalists believe that increased "bottom-line pressure is hurting journalism". This figure is up from 41 per cent in 1995 (Pew

Center 2008). Only half of the respondents think that their news organization's top management gives higher priority to the public interest than to the organization's financial performance. As a consequence to all of these observations and experiences, about six in ten US journalists think that journalism is going "in the wrong direction".

A third challenge is the *declining reputation* of the profession. Journalists lose on almost all dimensions their public support. Longitudinal data in the US show that this declining reputation has been faster and more severe than for all other institutions. And it correlates with media use: "We have clear evidence that familiarity with the news product breeds a lack of confidence (if not contempt) with the press as an institution" (Cronke and Cook 2007, 270). In Germany only one third have trust in journalists (Donsbach et al. 2009). More Americans believe that they get an "accurate picture of the war in Iraq" by the military than by the press (Pew Research Center 2007).

Finally, a fourth challenge is *the loss of identity* that the journalistic occupation is facing. New technologies have offered a vast array of communication tools for everybody. Communicating with the public no longer requires the involvement of the traditional mass media. As exciting as these developments might be for the potential of a more grassroots communication structure, it has tremendously affected the distinctness of journalism in the perception of the public. One indicator is usage. We have already seen that the traditional news media are losing audiences. But more serious is the fact that even on the same media platform the news organizations are losing to their new competitors. According to a study by the Joan Shorenstein Center at Harvard University (2007), the audience of non-traditional news disseminators – such as news aggregators, bloggers, search engines, social-networking sites and service providers – has grown considerably faster than the audience of the websites of traditional news outlets. Younger people are increasingly using blogs, chatrooms or community networks such as Facebook or MySpace to receive what they think is "news". In addition, clever public-relations communications posing as journalism undermine the profession. The very definition of "journalism" and what it means to be a journalist is no longer as clearly defined as in the past when journalists were reporters and editors working for newspapers, the broadcast media or wire services. What we are observing is a declining appreciation for a specific product.

One could argue that in history occupations have come and gone – like many other social institutions and phenomena (except for the media, at least for the time being). So, why bother? The problem we are observing with journalism is not a disappearing occupation but a disappearing social function. If fewer and fewer citizens look for validated information that has been brought about by a sophisticated process of research, checks and professional handling (a product that we have been used to call "the news") and if this product is less valued than before, then journalism loses its core function. Consequently, it also loses its "brand", its distinctness. We would be thrown back to the times when every form of communication, personal or mediated, is perceived as being of the same quality and the same legitimacy of its assertions about reality.

There can be no question that journalism itself has contributed to its declining reputation by succumbing to sensationalism, tabloidization and public relations. The profession is not only a victim but an actor in this process. But the problem is that, in contrast to most other professions, challenges to journalism are challenges to democracy! When the public is less interested in civic news and when the quality of the news is on the decline, the basis for informed public discourse is undermined.

Journalism as the new knowledge profession

In light of all these challenges journalism today seems to be at a crossroad. The question is where to go from here. It can certainly not be the goal to just re-establish the occupation as it was up to about 20 years ago because it has proven not to be equipped for meeting the challenges – and it would no longer find its audiences. We must take the opportunity to rethink and perhaps re-define its identity. By doing so one must be aware that many developments are not and will not be in the hands of journalists or those who educate them. For instance, even the best-quality news needs an audience. To create this demand, the "duty to keep informed" (see p. 42) cannot be the task of journalism but is an educational goal that is more in the hands of the families and schools.

Despite these limitations we might think of journalism as the new "knowledge profession" of our age that replaces former professions in this role. Societies live on knowledge. In a technical sense, knowledge is important to enable humans to cope with the challenges of the environment, for example how to build fire, store water or fight diseases. In a sociological sense, knowledge is a basis for the functioning of societies because shared knowledge forms the basis for communication and common action in a society. Before Gutenberg's invention of the printing press it was the clergy and, to a lesser extent, the secular powers of the state. After Gutenberg the printers and librarians and – with the spread of compulsory education in the modern state – teachers and university professors assumed this role. Later, with the further dissemination of newspapers, journalists complemented the role of librarians and educators – the former being more in the business of storing knowledge and the latter in the business of conveying it. But journalism has focused primarily on gathering and conveying the news of the day and less – if at all – on connecting this information with other areas of knowledge.

It is possible that journalists have to widen their societal role for three reasons. First, with the fast acceleration of knowledge the educational system is less able to identify which subjects among a myriad of others need to be included in a relatively fixed school curriculum. Second, the quasi-monopoly of libraries as knowledge archives has ended through the internet that holds almost all information on almost everything. Third, the new information technology empowers the individual to take control of the knowledge-retrieval process. As a consequence, exposure to knowledge is more personalized, more selective and thus more fragmented. With the ready availability of hundreds of millions of websites, each catering to a tiny slice of society, people looking for information on exactly the same subject – a political candidate, for example – can find very different, even contradictory, things. As a consequence, communities risk disintegrating into many different units each of which has its own reality but very little shared reality and therefore lacks the capability to communicate with the others.

If we accept that in functioning societies people have to act (a) on valid and (b) on shared information and knowledge, the question arises: What occupation in today's situation can best adopt this role? The answer probably has to be "journalism". If trained in the right way and allowed to perform according to their professional standards, they can become the modern distillers and connectors of knowledge, the professionals who supply to society the best possible universal knowledge. Historian Stig Hjarvard wrote "In earlier societies, social institutions like family, school and church were the most important providers of information, tradition and moral orientation for the individual member of society. Today, these institutions have lost some of their former authority, and the media have to some extent taken over their role as providers of information and moral orientation, at the same time as the media have become society's most important storyteller about society itself" (Hjarvard 2008: 7).

The five competencies of journalism

If we do regard journalism as the "new knowledge profession," we have to define its specific competencies. This new role requires five basic fields of competence, all of which are not new to journalism education but rarely if ever exist in a single educational programme: journalists should (1) possess a keen awareness of relevant history, current affairs, and analytical thinking, (2) have expertise in the specific subjects about which he or she reports, (3) have a scientifically based knowledge about the communication process, (4) have mastered journalistic skills, and (5) conduct himself or herself within the norms of professional ethics.

General Competence simply means that journalists, in order to assess the salience of events and issues and to connect knowledge to context, need the broader, intellectual perspective that enables them to make sound news decisions. Furthermore, journalists need to know how to apply analytical thinking to all that they do, from challenging the veracity of information or news sources to understanding the behaviour patterns and motivations of people. As Scheuer put it: "Journalists, like scholars, formulate knowledge by knitting facts to contexts. They need analytical and critical as well as narrative skills and substantive knowledge. ... subject knowledge and practical skills will always jointly affect the quality of reporting, just as they jointly affect the quality of teaching" (Scheuer 2007a, e23; see also Scheuer 2007b).

Journalists also need a deeper knowledge of the subjects they are covering, i.e. *Subject Competence*. In all areas, only journalists with subject competence will be able to make sound judgments on the newsworthiness of events, only they can ask critical questions to the actors, find the right experts, and only they can resist infiltration of non-professional factors to their decision-making. While the level of this knowledge of journalists will rarely compare to the level that the experts in the respective field have, it has to be sufficiently deep so that the structure of the field is understood and the main actors are known.

Process Competence means knowledge about the communication process from the factors influencing a journalist's own news decisions to possible effects on the audience. If journalists know about, for instance, socio-psychological factors and group dynamics they might resist the drives of "pack journalism" better and its often irrational decision-making. If journalists know more about audience research they will be able to present their messages in a way that maximizes not only attention to news but also, if employed in a responsible way, it can also maximize its cognitive processing by the audience.

Journalistic Skills are what most journalists around the world will already bring to the job. Few of these skills are taught, however, based on scientific evidence. With the technological changes brought by digitalization, journalists must also learn to work across different media platforms to convey their messages to the audience.

Professional Values, the fifth area of competence, mean that journalists are aware of their general societal role and have clearly defined norms that guide their behaviour on the job. As lawyers are made aware of their role within the juridical system during their academic training, journalists must be made aware of the role they play for the democratic process. This includes knowledge about where the journalists' loyalties are (e.g. to the audience and not the advertiser or the owner) and what their rights are towards seniors and proprietors. But, at the same time, they must be aware of the limitations of their rights relative to the rights of others such as their sources or objects of their coverage, be it people or institutions, and their audience with its right to make up its own mind on all issues.

Further professionalization needed

Occupations operating in areas that are essential for the functioning of a society and that relate to important values, usually become "professionalized". Medicine and the law are prototypes of such professionalization processes. Professionalists enjoy both a high degree of autonomy and a high reputation in society and they rest upon a research-based education that entailed the teaching of ethical standards, select admission and a system of checks and sanctions in cases of malpractice. While journalism's constitutional underpinnings in most countries obviate the licensing of practitioners, a lot can be done to foster a *de facto*-professionalization. By "*de facto*-professionalization" we mean the development of an educational and behavioural standard in the profession without these standards being imposed and controlled by the authorities.

This requires the existence of educational programmes that combine the five competencies and teach the prerequisites for the new knowledge profession. It also requires the existence of a professional community that reinforces these standards and has the guts and the power to separate the wheat from the chaff. Professions have to accept only the guidelines imposed on them by their fellow professionals. Thus, such a professionalization process would also make journalists more independent of commercial influences and help to rebuild the firewall between the newsroom and the advert-isement department.

Historically journalists have avoided taking steps that would limit entry into the profession, such as through mandatory certification. But today, even practitioners themselves seem to re-think this issue. *Time Inc.* editor-in-chief Norman Pearlstine wondered "whether licensing is the opposite of everything journalism believes, or whether the idea of national standards or even a certification of some kind is worth considering … Medical licenses help give people faith in doctors … and although that's anathema to all of us in terms of our own training, there might be some kind of middle ground." (quoted in Carnegie Corporation 2006, 19).

Only by rethinking and reinvigorating journalism and journalism education will it be possible to institutionalize journalism as a profession that is equipped to fulfil its societal tasks. Other than the educational institutions of the established professions, journalism schools too often have been thought of as trade schools rather than modern professional schools. As the importance and the challenges of journalism grow, the occupation's task of explaining the world to the public becomes more complex and demanding. And this needs a response by journalism education and by the professional community. Such a redefinition of journalism would create this new role of the knowledge profession that will make journalism distinct again from other forms of communication – for the sake of the quality of the public discourse.

References

Barnhurst, K. G. and Owens, J. (2008): Journalism. In: Donsbach, W. (ed.): *The International Encyclopedia of Communication*. Vol. 6. Malden: Wiley-Blackwell, 2557–69.

Breed, W. (1955). Social control in the newsroom. A functional analysis. *Social Forces, vol. 33, 326–335.*

Breed, W. (1960). Social control in the news room. In: Schramm, W. (ed.), *Mass Communication: A Book of Readings*. Urbana, IL: University of Illinois Press, 178–194.

Briggs, A. and Burke, P. (2002): *A Social History of the Media*, Cambridge: Polity Press.

Carnegie Corporation of New York (2005): *Improving the Education of Tomorrow's Journalists*. New York: Carnegie Corporation.

——. (2006): *Journalism's Crisis of Confidence: A Challenge for the Next Generation*. New York: Carnegie Corporation.

Deuze, M. (2002): National news cultures: A comparison of Dutch, German, British, Australian, and U.S. journalists. *Journalism and Mass Communication Quarterly*, 79, 134–49.

——. (2005): What is journalism? Professional identity and ideology of journalists reconsidered. *Journalism*, 6, 442–64.

Donsbach, W. (2008a): Journalists' Role Perceptions. In: Donsbach, W. (ed.): *The International Encyclopedia of Communication*. Vol. 6. Malden: Wiley-Blackwell, 2605–10.

——. (2008b): Changing journalism. Second wave of the Media and Democracy international survey of news journalists. *International Communication Association Conference*. Montreal, Quebec, Canada – May 23 (www.donsbach.net).

Donsbach, W. and Klett, B. (1993): Subjective objectivity. How journalists in four countries define a key term of their profession. *Gazette*, 51, 53–83.

Donsbach, W., Degen, S., Rentsch, M., et al. (2009): Entzauberung eines Berufs. Was die Deutschen vom Journalisten erwarten und wie sie enttäuscht werden. Konstanz: UVK.

Esser, F. (1998): Editorial structures and work principles in British and German newsrooms. *European Journal of Communication*, vol. 13, No. 3, pp. 375–405.

Gans, H. J. (1979). *Deciding What's News: A Study of CBS Evening News, NBC Nightly News, Newsweek, and Time*. New York: Pantheon.

Gronke, P. and Cook, T. E. (2007): Disdaining the media: the American public's changing attitudes toward the news. *Political Communication*, 24, 259–81.

Habermas, J. (1962): *Strukturwandel der Öffentlichkeit*. Neuwied: Luchterhand. Engl. Habermas, J. (1989): *The Structural Transformation of the Public Sphere*. Cambridge, Mass.: MIT Press.

Hjarvard, S. (2008). The mediatization of religion: A theory of the media as agents of religious change. In: *Northern Lights 2008. Yearbook of Film & Media Studies*. Bristol: Intellect Press.

Janowitz, M. (1975): Professional Models in Journalism: The Gatekeeper and the Advocate. *Journalism Quarterly*, 52, 618–26, 662.

Joan Shorenstein Center for the Press, Politics, and Public Policy (2007): Creative Destruction: An Exploratory Look at News on the Internet. Cambridge, Mass.: Kennedy School of Government.

Kepplinger, H. M., Brosius, H.-B. and Staab, J. F. (1991): Instrumental actualization: A theory of mediated conflicts. *European Journal of Communication*, 6, 263–90.

Köcher, R. (2008): Schleichende Veränderung. Dokumentation des Beitrags in der *Frankfurter Allgemeinen Zeitung* Nr. 194 vom 20. August.

Löffelholz, M. and Weaver, D. (eds.) (2008): *Global Journalism Research. Theories, Methods, Findings, Future*. Malden, Oxford, Carlton: Blackwell Publishing.

Murdock, G. and Wasko, J. (2007): *Media in The Age of Marketisation*. Creskill, NJ: Hampton Press Inc.

Neron, Jon (2008): Journalism, History of. In, Donsbach, W. (ed.) *The International Encyclopedia of Communication*. Vol. 6, Malden: Wiley-Blackwell, 2579–85.

Patterson, T. E. and Donsbach, W. (1996): News decisions: Journalists as partisan actors. *Political Communication*, 13, 455–68.

Pew Research Center for the People and the Press (2006): *Maturing Internet News Audience – Broader Than Deep*. Washington, DC: Pew Research Center.

——. (2007): *Views of Press Values and Performance: 1985–2007. Internet Audience Highly Critical of News Organizations*. http://people-press.org/reports/pdf/348.pdf (accessed March 20, 2008).

——. (2008): *The Web: Alarming, Appealing and a Challenge to Journalistic Values. Financial vows now overshadow all other concerns for journalists*. http://people-press.org/reports/pdf/403.pdf (accessed March 20, 2008).

Scheuer, J. (2007a): Journalism and academia: How they can work together. *Nieman Reports*, 61, No. 3, e23-e25.

——. (2007b): *The Big Picture: Democracy and Journalistic Excellence*. Abingdon: Routledge.

Schudson, M. (1978): *Discovering the News: A Social history of American Newspapers*. New York: Basic Books.

5
THE CHANGING STATUS OF WOMEN JOURNALISTS

Deborah Chambers and Linda Steiner

Women journalists now appear well-established in a profession that, until two decades ago, was a male enclave. They played a significant role in redefining news to incorporate issues associated with the quotidian concerns of women as a whole. Yet at the very top rungs of the journalism hierarchy, the percentage of women remains small. They continue to be concentrated in areas considered to be low-status or 'soft news' sectors such as small-town or regional news organizations and community weeklies, and human interest stories and features. Prestige areas of news production remain largely dominated by men, particularly the high-status category of politics, as well as business, and sport.

Women's high visibility in television – through regular and often sexualised scrutiny of their bodies, hairstyles, fashion, and voices – is matched by their invisibility in top management and boardrooms. Despite demands to be treated as professional equals alongside their male counterparts, women's promotion to key decision-making positions in journalism is frequently blocked by a 'glass ceiling'. Some women still experience outright sexism in newsrooms. Working mothers are disadvantaged by a 'long hours' culture, coupled with insufficient childcare.

An impressive number of platforms are now offered to citizens to air their views in public, including blogging and twittering in the context of citizen journalism; this provides opportunities for democratising relations between men and women. However, while women dominate as both entertainers and consumers of *popular* media, they are less valued as professional producers of news (Thornham, 2007).

This chapter reviews key themes pertaining to women journalists, examining how women have contributed to changing news agendas, news values and definitions of 'news'.[1] We review the status, practices and views of women journalists, focusing on the United States and Britain. The chapter summarises women's entrance into the profession and their principal roles in generating new styles of journalism. How women experienced and changed newsroom cultures and values, and the establishment of women's alternative journalism are then examined. Women's participation in traditionally male-dominated fields is addressed, focusing on their experiences as war correspondents. A discussion of 'post-feminist journalism' deals with women's involvement in a market-led journalism characterised by human interest stories, celebrity journalism, confessional and therapy news. The chapter ends by speculating about the ongoing role of women in Internet news.

Early women journalists

In the United States and Britain, women began participating in journalism during the colonial period. Their entry into the profession was typically through husbands or fathers. The numbers of women journalists began to rise during the mid-nineteenth century. By the end of the century, their increasing presence began to alarm male editors and reporters. None the less, no one questioned the treatment of women as consumers rather than producers of 'news'. Male editors assumed that women could only write *as* women *for* and *about* women. Women entered a gendered public sphere, defined largely on men's terms. Despite claims to objectivity, 'news' conformed to a masculine discourse: the concerns and experiences of men were privileged over those of women. Journalists' attention to competition, war, and conflict essentially marginalised issues pertaining to the home, family and children's welfare.

A sub-category labelled 'women's news' evolved out of the need, in the late nineteenth and early twentieth century, to attract women readers. This prompted the creation of 'women's columns' and 'women's pages'. 'Women's news' was characterised by a restricted understanding of women's interests: domestic and family life, including society news, child-rearing and household duties. Women wishing to enter journalism therefore faced many challenges to overcome the ghettoisation of their work in 'women's news' and human interest stories. Yet in nineteenth and early twentieth-century America, journalism was viewed as a meaningful and even glamorous vocation for educated, middle-class women. It offered an exit from the confines of domesticity and was particularly attractive to unmarried women and middle-class women.

Access to a university degree in journalism, made available first in the US in the early twentieth century, provided women with opportunities to train as reporters alongside men. Ironically, since journalism schools never anticipated that women would apply, they had not thought to exclude them. Universities offered women more egalitarian contexts in which to develop journalistic skills than did sexist on-the-job training. Women faced the problem of journalism textbooks that either addressed men as the norm, or relegated 'women's writing' to a subcategory. Even the materials written by women generally discouraged women from regarding journalism as a serious career. Arguably, journalism curricula and textbooks continue to ignore gender issues. By contrast, in Britain, journalists trained on-the-job, within an apprenticeship system into the 1980s. The main challenge for British women was being recruited as an apprentice in the first place.

The late nineteenth-century establishment of women's pages and features in print media targeting women readers corresponded with the growth of advertising for department stores, products aimed at women, and 'new' newspapers produced for a wider and working-class readership. This trend required additional women journalists. Male writers were not perceived as capable of attracting the newly targeted women readers as consumers, especially young working women. Male reporters had little interest in writing for female readers. Issues that addressed the status and experiences of women such as fertility, childcare, and sexual violence were often ignored or rendered sensational. This form of 'women's journalism' addressed neither what we now call 'feminist politics' nor women's welfare. Women's concerns were understood as specifically 'women's interests' and treated as secondary. An additional way to attract women readers was to hire gossip columnists. Joseph Pulitzer and William Randolph Hearst hired women such as Nellie Bly and Winifred Black, whose pseudonym was 'Annie Laurie', to produce sensationalised ('yellow') and stunt journalism. Credited with inventing the first advice to the lovelorn column under the name Beatrice Fairfax, Marie Manning wrote the popular advice column for the *New York Evening Journal* from 1889 until 1945. Elizabeth Meriwether Gilmer began 'Dorothy Dix Talks' in 1895. At its height, it was read by almost 30 million people.

The First and Second World Wars gave women journalists opportunities to advance their careers by moving into 'serious' news. Military officials refused to accredit women war reporters. None the less, with men conscripted into the war effort, women took their newsroom jobs, at least until peace was restored, when women were usually evicted from newsrooms. Thus women's advances within journalism were largely temporary and unstable. Advantages in being a female reporter were rare. As a First Lady with her own press credentials (she wrote a syndicated column) Eleanor Roosevelt held over 300 press conferences specifically restricted to women journalists. She knew that news organisations all over the country would need to hire a woman in order to have access to the First Lady and the scoops she provided.

Notwithstanding the social constraints of gender difference at the time, some women carved out spectacularly successful careers. Despite being systematically barred from decision-making in newsrooms until the mid-twentieth century, there were exceptional women who found imaginative ways of evading obstacles and entering news 'beats'. *New York Herald Tribune* front page reporter Ishbel Ross compiled *Ladies of the Press* in 1936 to trace the history of women in the newspaper business from colonial times. Ross records that the famous editor Stanley Walker praised her for coming closer than any other female reporters to the man's idea of what a newspaperwoman should be (Ross, 1936). This back-handed compliment evokes men as the gold standard against which women's performance was to be measured.

Radio was launched in the 1920s, first in the United States, and soon after in Britain. In both countries, radio programming for women focused on their role as housewives, with a stress on fashion, beauty, and household tips. Male voices were preferred across programming formats, signifying the authority of male communicators. Women's voices were frequently assumed to be irritating to listeners. Women did, however, play critical administrative roles backstage. A small number of women reached senior positions, not as journalists but in a variety of other significant roles, exemplified by Hilda Matheson, who became BBC Head of Talks by 1927. In the United States, where commercial radio dominated, women enjoyed more opportunities to take on principal roles in an innovative environment. For example, Judith Cary Waller became manager of a radio station as early as 1922. The Second World War provided the chance for women to be radio anchors, reporters, and even war correspondents. Women headed educational and public services in all four US radio networks by the 1940s. Nevertheless, the notion that women's voices lacked conviction and were too high pitched for radio persisted for decades in both the USA and Britain. Women entering radio were largely confined to programmes targeting housewives.

British radio was restricted to public service broadcasting until 1973, when commercial radio was launched. This restricted the careers of women journalists, who were initially excluded from the BBC under the strict moral code of its director. The BBC did not hire women as regular newsreaders until the 1970s, when competition from commercial radio forced the BBC to reassess its attitude to women as newsreaders. Until then, men typically claimed radio's more varied, interesting and serious journalistic tasks such as foreign reporting and conflicts. Women were mainly consigned to human interest stories and light news.

Similarly, in television the United States was ahead of Britain in employing women in leading roles. Frieda Hennock was the first woman commissioner for the Federal Communications Commission as early as 1948. Women appeared as reporters and NBC boasted six women news anchors by 1971. In Britain, women were barred as television newsreaders until 1960, when Nan Winton was appointed. Even then, women were only sporadically used as newsreaders. News 'objectivity' and 'authority' were qualities associated with masculinity, with women confined mainly to lifestyle radio and TV programmes on cookery, fashion, and childcare. While older, greying men were – and continue to be – regularly employed for their journalistic skills, physical attractiveness remains a job requirement for women in television journalism. The demand for youthful and attractive but professional femininity of female newscasters has corresponded with shifts in news agendas, styles and topics.

Fierce competition between newspapers, radio and television from the 1970s prompted news organisations to increase the employment of women journalists for attracting larger audiences. By the 1970s, in the United States, every newscast had a woman co-anchor – expected to be blonde, beautiful and feminine but also able to read serious news. In some cases, women were pushed into the spotlight before they were ready, exemplified by the meteoric rise of Jessica Savitch. Savitch worked at various broadcast stations before being spotted in the early 1970s by a television talent scout. Savitch was recommended to a station searching for a pretty face to keep ahead of rival news stations. She negotiated an enhanced contract and gained access to influential friends. Less than a year after moving to Philadelphia, NBC hired Savitch to report on the US Senate (Savitch, 1982). As one of the most popular news anchors, Savitch was promoted to anchor NBC Nightly News. Critics claimed that she lacked qualifications for national network news, and the pressure apparently proved her personal and professional undoing.

The history of women's entrance into journalism is characterised, then, by confinement to a particular genre of 'women's news' from the late nineteenth century. By the early twentieth century, many women had stormed the gates of news genres once restricted to men. Some women escaped the women's 'news ghetto' early on; and some were never part of it. Some women continued to be restricted to writing women's news and thought this was appropriate, perceiving women to have distinct and separate interests. Others hated writing 'women's news'. Nevertheless, the broad journalistic constraints imposed on most early women journalists allowed them to spearhead a new kind of news: an innovative style addressing the personal lives of readers. Although the 'women's pages' of early newspapers were framed by a feminine discourse of domesticity, they opened a door for the feminist debates of the 1960s. Topics such as equal opportunities in employment, equal pay, divorce and abortion became regular features in women's sections. The personalised technique of human interest stories written by women proved to be flexible enough, in a new political era, to trigger new styles of reporting and writing news, ones that have become standard.

Women's contemporary status in journalism

Large-scale surveys of journalists reveal some differences between men's and women's career trajectories and work tasks but the statistics do not explain the reasons for these disparities (see Gallagher, 1995; Weaver and Wilhoit, 1996; Delano and Henningham, 1995; Henningham and Delano, 1998). Women have gradually gained critical mass in certain segments of the profession in the last two decades. More accommodating working arrangements have been introduced that benefit women, including flexible hours and job shares. None the less, the invisible barriers to promotion known as a 'glass ceiling' have yet to be shattered; men continue to dominate senior management positions. A 2002 study confirmed that women comprise one-third of all full-time journalists in US mainstream media (Weaver et al., 2003). Although more women are graduating from journalism schools and entering the profession, this figure remains constant, since 1982. The highest numbers of women work in news magazines (43.5 percent); the lowest for major wire services (20.3 percent) and radio (21.9 percent). Women comprise 37.4 percent of television journalists, 36.9 percent of weekly newspaper journalists, and 33 percent of daily newspaper journalists. Among journalists with less than five years of work experience, women outnumber men for the first time at 54.2 percent.

Perhaps the reason women journalists are generally younger than their male counterparts is that women leave the profession early – deterred by barriers to advancement, lack of childcare facilities, long hours, or masculine values within newsroom culture. Sexism in the newsroom persists: two-thirds of women report having experienced sexism (Henningham and Delano, 1998: 148; Ross, 2001). Through trade unions, guilds and press associations, gender discrimination and sexism have been challenged in recruitment and assignment decisions, salary differentials and promotion procedures. Women have also created their own associations and organisations, particularly in the United States, to advance their interests, since in recent years conventional unions have often been ineffective. However, job satisfaction in the profession as a whole is strong among both male and female journalists, at least among those who have chosen to remain (Weaver et al., 2003). Women tended to be less satisfied in 2002 than were men, with 71.7 percent of women journalists saying 'fairly' or 'very' satisfied compared to 86.6 percent of male journalists. According to 1990s data, women were concentrated in areas where they reported on women's lives and they tended to focus on personalities and personal views (Mills, 1997; Skidmore, 1998; Christmas, 1997).

Gendered newsroom cultures and values

While changes in news agendas and writing styles have been associated with women's growing presence in the newsroom, the impact of gender on newsroom culture and news agendas is not clear-cut. All journalists are subjected to the professional norms, daily routines and structures of news organisations. Nevertheless, newsrooms continue to be dominated by male editors and newsrooms may operate as male-ordered through macro structures and everyday routines (Ross, 2001). Yet more stories now address women's issues. Women journalists are more likely to draw on women as sources; insisting that 'ordinary citizens', not just those in positions of power, are newsworthy. Women journalists also focus more on social problems, sex crimes and protests than male counterparts. Over the decades, women have drawn attention to the political significance of issues associated with women such as reproductive rights, education, divorce, management of childcare and homes. This tendency may have triggered a more general shift from conventional government and crime news to human interest news with an accent on personalising issues. More controversial are claims that women have changed news agendas by introducing new postmodern, feature-oriented styles of writing that focus on confessional narratives and on the personal, including the writers' own feelings (Christmas, 1997; Mayes, 2000).

However, despite no conclusive evidence that women and men write differently, it *is* apparent that in the past, women were encouraged and pressured into reporting differently, for example, by writing with greater sentiment for women readers. Rather than women demonstrating distinct writing styles, recent changes in news values and practices are more likely to have been driven by commercial needs that confine women journalists to assignments on 'feminine' topics such as fashion and lifestyle. This implies that women audiences are uninterested in 'hard' news. Although constrained by commercial imperatives, women's rising visibility in journalism has allowed them to contest traditional masculine news genres.

Women's alternative journalism

The nineteenth-century feminist or radical press enabled women to take on ownership, decision-making and editorial roles, and to participate in the public sphere on their own terms. Most women who worked for alternative newspapers did so voluntarily, focusing on suffrage, abolition, professional rights, and celebration of lesbian sexuality. Suffrage newspapers were crucial channels for advocating women's right to vote and new ways of being women. Hundreds of women-run newspapers and magazines proposed new ideas about womanhood and provided a platform for women's activism in the public sphere (Steiner, 1983, 1991; DiCenzo, 2000; Tusan, 2005). Meanwhile, these women also experimented with distinctive ways of working through cooperative and collective management styles.

Alternative periodicals of the 1970s and 1980s contested the mainstream media's images of the 'superwoman': a bold, congratulatory discourse that promoted the myth of a highly aspirational, self-assertive woman who 'can have it all', with 'all' defined as family, career, and stylish clothes. The 1980s was also the era of popular feminist magazines such as *off our backs* and Ms. *Magazine* in the USA, and *Spare Rib* in the UK – independently produced magazines that contributed to the redefinition of women's news and politics. A distinctive feature of women's alternative news media is to treat the public as *citizens* rather than *consumers*, and 'the personal as political'.

The first two waves of the women's movement, and the news organisations that supported and sustained them, were mainly focused on the interests of white, middle-class, heterosexual, and educated Western women. More recently, and especially inspired by transnational work that the Internet encourages, feminists have launched experiments in activist journalism that critique how gender, race and ethnicity, sexuality are interrelated. These newer forms highlight Third World poverty, sex slavery, and female genocide. Alternative press, radio, cable, television and Internet newsgroups have empowered women, providing them with the confidence to change their lives and train women to exploit media technologies. They have advanced women's status in mainstream news by demanding changes in recruitment, new ways of working and reporting radical movements.

Some women's information networks challenge distinctions between professional and non-professional journalism, providing a crucial space for ordinary women citizens to speak directly for themselves and report on their concerns. Examples include *WomensNet*, *Women's International Network News* and *Aviva* (see Chambers *et al.*, 2004). Run by an international group of feminists, *Aviva* is a monthly webzine covering global news (www.aviva.org). *Aviva* also trains women in Internet design and publishing, and hosts other women's services. These independent news networks and 'webzines' allow women to produce information and foster networks, echoing the objectives of the women's suffrage press. They raise fundamental questions about the democratisation and feminisation of the public sphere. However, while women can now communicate speedily and globally on an equal footing, access remains a problem. The digital divide across First and Third World has a profound gender dimension. In developing nations, men have greater access to digital media than women.

Women in 'male bastions' of journalism

The Vietnam War of 1965–75 signalled a significant change for women war correspondents. In fighting a guerrilla war, the military imposed fewer, less rigid restrictions. Women could buy their own plane tickets to Vietnam. Once there, some military officials and soldiers enjoyed talking to women journalists such that some women even claimed to have an advantage over male competitors. Women certainly had much wider access than in previous military conflicts. Their ability to improvise was vital in dealing with unforeseen events. This was unlike the First and Second World Wars, when the military formally refused to grant women permission to cover the front, with the lame excuse that it lacked toilets for women. Nevertheless, some women covering the Vietnam War experienced anti-woman prejudices of bureau chiefs, fellow reporters and military officials.

By the 1980s, women war correspondents such as BBC reporter Kate Adie were achieving prominence and notoriety. Political and press critics accused Adie of being sympathetic to Colonal Gaddafi's regime in Libya after she reported on the1986 US bombing of Tripoli in which she referred briefly to the death of Gaddafi's adopted daughter. She was plagued with insults about her hair, forcing her to take curling tongs, and was accused of enlisting soldiers to search for jewellery lost in the desert during the first Iraq war. Women journalists continue to provoke controversy as objects of the public gaze. Their lives are recurrently scrutinised and criticised: for their single status, for risking their lives as mothers in conflict zones, and for their peculiarities in a male-dominated part of the profession. When Yvonne Ridley was captured by the Taliban at the Pakistani border after reporting on Afghanistan in 2000, she was accused of being reckless in taking on such a dangerous job and failing in her parental responsibilities to her daughter (Ridley, 2001). Ridley felt demonised by reporters who exposed in detail her three marriages, implying a dysfunctional femininity. This example demonstrates a classic double-bind that women face: they are often devalued either as 'proper professionals' or as negligent towards their families – or both.

Many scholars and women journalists claim women and men report on wars and regional conflicts in the same way. Yet others praise women for highlighting the human, non-military dimensions of war, including rape as an instrument of war (Rouvalis and Schackner, 2000; Sebba, 1994), and claim women have challenged the 'bullets and bombs' discourse dominating war reporting by personalising stories, even while providing an appropriate political and historical context. Orla Guerin, a BBC foreign correspondent who covered the Israeli–Palestinian conflict in 2001, says men and women journalists work differently; she says it is not merely 'women writing about refugees and men about tanks' but that women have different emphases in their coverage. (Guerin, interviewed on *Woman's Hour*, BBC Radio 4, October 4, 2001).

Women have participated in the emergence of a new style of war reporting highlighting issues such as civilian suffering, the systematic rape of women and the contribution of women as nurses to the war effort. But again, others insist that, since the Vietnam War, women and men do not write differently and that all good reporters provide full context. Importantly, some women journalists reject invitations to cover the 'women's angle' on various wars, fearing that this will deprive them of access to the top of the news hour or front page. In either case, newspapers have typically assigned fewer women correspondents to conflict zones than broadcasting media. Whether this is because broadcast journalism is more egalitarian than newspaper journalism or market forces are exploiting femininity is unclear (see Van Zoonen, 1998).

'Post-feminist' journalism

In the late nineteenth century, male reporters denigrated women as 'Sob Sisters' or 'agony aunts' for allegedly bringing readers to tears with their dramatic, personal, and emotional stories. Arguably, in addressing demands for good, relevant, story-telling, these women sparked a controversy that continues to resonate with the emergence of market-led, post-feminist efforts to attract female audiences (Whelehan, 2000). The construction of news as a commodity has promoted a post-feminist journalism claiming to advance women's issues. But, in its exploration of feminine identity, this commodified news often undermines women's claims to professionalism. Forged by the pressures of the market, this set of genres is configured by confessional and therapy news as well as celebrity reporting, gossip, and human interest stories aimed at women. 'Confessional journalism' and 'therapy news' emerged in the 1990s when female newspaper columnists started borrowing styles and themes from women's magazine and feature genres. The focus is on feelings, intimate thoughts, family and sex lives of victims and the rich and famous (Heller, 1999). Post-feminist journalism signifies human interest stories, consumer items and fashion tidbits, framed in a playful, clever, and amusing discourse (Mayes, 2000: 30).

One analysis of 'women's media' by a self-defined conservative woman who spent ten years as editor-in-chief of the *Ladies Home Journal*, alleges a collusion between public relations firms, celebrities, and women journalists to manufacture and sell news targeted at women. Myrna Blyth claims an institutionalised peddling of a misplaced liberal message characterising women as victims (Blyth, 2004). Despite this, the intimate link between PR, celebrity journalism and advertising may be said to undermine the concept of 'news' as impartial and, where necessary, as probing. Celebrity news has become conspicuous in the last decade, pressurising journalists to form cosy relations with public figures in the entertainment industry. The trend in post-feminist journalism echoes the representations of feminine individualism typical of earlier years. Under a liberal façade of choice, freedom and feminine autonomy, this tendency all too often represents a depoliticisation of women's issues. Led by an assertive consumer culture, post-feminist journalism arguably celebrates popular culture at the expense of hard-hitting investigative journalism on gendered issues.

Women and the Internet future

The Internet has influenced women's role and status in journalism in two key ways. First, within alternative news media, the Internet is a vital tool for promoting global networks between women and challenging mainstream news definitions. Second, the emergence of on-line reporting by more mainstream organisations has created an important niche for women. Yet how the rise of online journalism influences gender relations in mainstream news organisations is not yet known. In the late 1990s, online journalism copied conventional news formats. While some observers originally argued that the unique multimedia, hypertextual and interactive qualities of the Internet could lead to a unique on-line medium (Deuze, 1999), evidence suggests that on-line journalism has suffered from deskilling of the profession. Rather than leading to a male-dominated 'labour aristocracy' as once surmised, on-line journalism may trigger deskilling (Deuze, 2001) and a feminisation of the profession.

Thus, while the Internet opens up significant possibilities for women to participate in a more democratised public sphere, unequal access to information communication technology at a global level and the deskilling of the journalism profession may indicate continuing challenges for women. The potential for global communication is developing at the very moment that the journalism profession is undergoing serious difficulties. Transformations in an increasingly competitive media industry are characterised by instability, reduced profits, a shrinking workforce and deskilling. In this climate, the last-in and first-out principle may mean the firing of women. Nevertheless, citizens' deliberation in the public sphere has the potential to expose social inequalities. In the context of alternative Internet media, the possibilities are enormous.

Note

1 This chapter is based on a summary of the key debates addressed in the book *Women and Journalism* by Deborah Chambers, Linda Steiner and Carole Fleming (Routledge, 2004).

References

Blyth, M. (2004) *Spin Sisters: How the Women of the Media Sell Unhappiness – And Liberalism – To the Women of America*, New York: St Martins Press.

Chambers, D., Steiner, L. and Fleming, C. (2004) *Women and Journalism*, London: Routledge.

Christmas, L. (1997) *Chaps of Both Sexes? Women decision-makers in Newspapers: Do They make a Difference?*, London: BT Forum/Women in Journalism.

Deuze, M. (1999) 'Journalism and the Web: An analysis of skills and standards in an online enviroment', *Gazette* 61(5):373–90.

Deuze, M. (2007) 'Online journalism: modelling the first generation of news media on the World wide web', First Monday 6(10), on-line. Available http://www.first-monday.org/issues/issues6_10/deuze/index.html (accessed 22 May 2003).

Deuze, M. (2007) *Media Work*, Cambridge: Polity Press.

DiCenzo, M. (2000) 'Militant distribution: Votes for women and the public sphere', *Media History* 6(2): 115–28.

Delano, A. and Henningham, J. (1995) *The News Breed: British Journalists in the 1990s*, London: London Institute.

Gallagher, M. (1995) *An Unfinished Story: Gender Patterns in Media Employment*, Reports on Mass Communication, 110, Paris: UNESCO.

Heller, Z. (1999) 'Girl columns', in S. Glover (ed.) *Secrets of the Press: Journalists on journalism*, Harmondsworth: Penguin, pp. 10–17.

Henningham, J. and Delano, A. (1998) 'British journalists' in D.H. Weaver (ed.) *The Global Journalist: News People Around the World*, Cresskill, NJ: Hampton Press.

Mayes, T. (2000) 'Submerging in "Therapy News"', *British Journalism Review* 1(4): 30–5.

Mills, K. (1997) 'What difference do women journalists make?' in P. Norris (ed.) *Women, Media and Politics*, New York and Oxford: Oxford University Press.

Ridley, Y. (2001) *In the hands of the Taliban: Her extraordinary story*, London: Robson Books.

Ross, I. (1936) *Ladies of the Press*, New York: Harper.

Ross, K. (2001) 'Women at work: Journalism as en-gendered practice', *Journalism Studies* 2(4): 531–44.

Rouvalis, C. and Schackner, B. (2000) 'Female correspondents recall their historic role reporting from Vietnam', on-line. Available http://www.Post-Gazette.com/magazine/20000330namwomen2.asp (accessed 22 May 2003).

Savitch, J. (1982) *Anchorwoman*, New York: G.P. Putnam's Sons.

Sebba, A. (1994) *Battling for News: The Rise of the Woman Reporter*, London: Hodder and Stoughton.

Skidmore, P. (1998) 'Gender and the agenda: News reporting of child sex abuse', in C. Carter, G. Branston and S. Allan (eds) *News, Gender and Power*, London: Routledge, pp. 204–18.

Steiner, L. (1983) 'Finding community in nineteenth century suffrage periodicals', *American Journalism* 1(1): 1–16.

Steiner, L. (1991) 'Evolving rhetorical strategies/evolving identities', in M.M. Solomon (ed.) *A Voice of their Own: The Woman Suffrage Press*, 1840-1910, Tuscaloosa, Ala.: University of Alabama Press, pp. 183–97.

Thornham, S. (2007) *Women, Feminism and Media*, Edinburgh: Edinburgh University Press.

Tusan, M.E. (2005) *Women Making News: Gender and Journalism in Modern Britain*. Urbana and Chicago: University of Illinois Press.

Van Zoonen, E. (1998) 'One of the girls: The changing gender of journalism', in C. Carter, G. Branston and S. Allan (eds) *News, Gender and Power*, London: Routledge, pp. 33–46.

Walker, S. (1934) *City Editor*, New York: Frederick A. Stokes.

Weaver, D.H. and Wilhoit, G.C. (1996) *The American Journalist in the 1990s: U.S. News People at the End of an Era*, Mahwah, NJ: Erlbaum.

Weaver, D.H., Beam, R., Brownlee, B., Voakes, P. and Wilhoit, G.C. (2003) 'The American journalist in the 21st century: Key findings'. Available http://www.poynter.org.

Whelehan, I. (2000) *Overloaded: Popular Culture and the Future of Feminism*, London: The Women's Press.

6

JOURNALISM AND ITS PUBLICS: THE LIPPMANN–DEWEY DEBATE

Stuart Allan

'Merely to talk about the reporter in terms of his [or her] real importance to civilization will make newspaper men laugh,' Walter Lippmann (1920) wrote in *Liberty and the News*. 'Yet reporting is a post of peculiar honor. Observation must precede every other activity, and the public observer (that is, the reporter) is a man [or woman] of critical value' (1920: 79–80). At stake in this process is nothing less than the very health of democratic society itself, he believed. The 'objective information' required for governing institutions to operate effectively necessitates that the press supply 'trustworthy news', a role demanding that the 'newspaper enterprise' be transformed from 'a haphazard trade into a disciplined profession.' And, it follows from this premise, explains the reason why the relationship between journalism and its public warrants rigorous assessment and critique.

This chapter examines Lippmann's thinking about the nature of this relationship, paying particular attention to his writings in the 1920s. Over the course of this decade, he rapidly established himself as one of the foremost journalists and public commentators in the United States. To this day, his incisive treatment of searching questions regarding the press and public opinion continue to exercise a formative influence on news and journalism studies around the world. Indeed, read from a contemporary vantage point, the essays and books he published in this period represent a significant intervention, remarkable in its own right but also for the debating stance it provoked for one of his most perceptive critics, the philosopher John Dewey. In taking this intervention as its thematic focus, this chapter endeavours to contribute to efforts to reinvigorate ongoing discussion about journalism's place in democratic culture. The insights engendered by Lippmann and Dewey's respective positions resonate with current concerns in surprising ways, inviting challenging – perhaps even counter-intuitive – perspectives to emerge.

The 'modern news problem'

Critical assessments of journalism published in the immediate aftermath of the First World War tended to dwell on a number of common themes (see Angell, 1922; Hayword and Langdon-Davies, 1919; Sinclair, 1920). Particularly salient in this regard were concerns expressed regarding the extent to which popular disillusionment with wartime propaganda campaigns created a wariness of 'official' channels of information, a problem perceived by some commentators to be seriously compounded by 'press agents' and 'publicity' or 'promotion experts' (Allen, 1922; the *New York Times*, 1920). For those journalists alert to the danger of equating facts with officially-sanctioned definitions of truth, the need for more 'scientific' methods to process information accurately was increasingly recognised.

The publication in 1920 of Lippmann's book, *Liberty and the News*, represents his first sustained engagement with what he chose to call the 'modern news problem'. Writing with remarkable flair and conviction, he makes clear his belief that 'the present crisis of western democracy' is also, at the same time, 'a crisis in journalism'. He stresses the intrinsic value of facts, maintaining that they must be made available to members of the public so as to facilitate their efforts to engage with the pressing questions of the day. The reason people everywhere feel baffled and misled, he contends, is because they do not possess sufficient confidence in what they are being told. Journalism in its modern state, he is convinced, is complicit in this exigency. Several underlying causes are briefly rehearsed – such as the corruption of those who exercise 'moneyed control' over the 'so-called free press', their self-interested pettiness, and their tendency to make light of serious matters – before Lippmann offers his alternative explanation. Edification, he believes, is being privileged over and above veracity (a veiled criticism of the likes of Adolf Ochs in New York or Lord Northcliffe in London). 'The current theory of American newspaperdom is that an abstraction like the truth and a grace like fairness must be sacrificed whenever anyone thinks the necessities of civilization require the sacrifice' (1920: 8), he added with customary panache.

Reporters, it follows, have effectively assumed for themselves the work of 'preachers, revivalists, prophets and agitators'. In so doing, their 'idea of what is patriotic' is actually serving to temper the 'curiosity of their readers'. For Lippmann, the implications are dire:

> Just as the most poisonous form of disorder is the mob incited from high places, the most immoral act the immorality of a government, so the most destructive form of untruth is sophistry and propaganda by those whose profession it is to report the news. The news columns are common carriers. When those who control them arrogate to themselves the right to determine by their own consciences what shall be reported and for what purpose, democracy is unworkable. Public opinion is blockaded (1920: 10–11).

To the extent that the press fails to deliver factual information, offering in its place little more than the whims of personal opinion, the basis of government will be decisively undermined. He writes:

> All that the sharpest critics of democracy have alleged is true, if there is no supply of trustworthy and relevant news. Incompetence and aimlessness, corruption and disloyalty, panic and ultimate disaster, must come to any people which is denied an assured access to the facts. No one can manage anything on pap. Neither can a people (1920: 11).

The very future of popular government by consent is at risk, Lippmann warns, if what stand in its place are news organisations busily 'manufacturing consent' to suit their own self-interested purposes. The reporting of daily news must be wrested away from 'untrained and biased hands', and realigned with new standards of independence and integrity that signal a renewed commitment to 'reporting the facts'. It is on this note that *Liberty and the News* comes to a close, its final sentence neatly pinpointing the basis for Lippmann's reformist agenda. 'We shall advance,' he writes, 'when we have learned humility; when we have learned to seek the truth, to reveal it and publish it; when we care more for that than for the privilege of arguing about ideas in a fog of uncertainty' (1920: 104; see also Lippmann and Merz, 1920).

Truth and democracy

In a modern world so complicated that it defies the citizen's powers of understanding, it follows that the journalist will similarly struggle when trying to interpret the significance of events for their benefit. Lippmann's (1922) next book, *Public Opinion*, further elaborates upon this dilemma, boldly challenging the foundational ideals of democracy.

Representative government can be criticised for its apparent reliance on an unworkable fiction, Lippmann writes, namely that 'each of us must acquire a competent opinion about all public affairs' (1922: 19). An impossible demand, it should be abandoned for being untenable in practical terms. The idealised conception of community prefigured by such a doctrine bears little resemblance to life in modern society. Moreover, it would be unreasonable to expect the press to succeed in the task of furnishing the omnicompetent citizen with sufficient information to maintain this fiction in any case. The press may be the 'chief means of contact with the unseen environment', Lippmann argues, but it is incapable of assuming responsibility for presenting citizens with 'a true picture of all the outer world' to an adequate extent. The newspapers, it follows, are 'defective' in their organisation of public opinion (1922: 19).

In striving to reverse certain 'ancient beliefs' about truth and democracy, Lippmann contends that public opinion must be organised for the press, and not the other way around. 'We expect the newspaper to serve us with truth however unprofitable the truth may be,' he observes. 'For this difficult and often dangerous service, which we recognize as fundamental, we expected to pay until recently the smallest coin turned out by the mint' (1922: 203). The burden placed upon the press to fulfil its obligations thus stands in sharp contrast with the commitment – or, more to the point, lack thereof – displayed by the fickle citizen consumer to it in return. 'Somebody has said quite aptly,' Lippmann remarks, 'that the newspaper editor has to be re-elected every day' (1922: 203). In effect, the attention of the reader – as a member of the 'buying public' – becomes a commodity, the sale of which by the newspaper to the advertiser underwrites its viability. The point of view judged to be representative of the buying public, it follows, cannot be safely ignored. 'A newspaper which angers those whom it pays best to reach through advertisements is a bad medium for an advertiser,' Lippmann states. 'And since no one ever claimed that advertising was philanthropy, advertisers buy space in those publications which are fairly certain to reach their future customers' (1922: 205). At the same time, those readers with the most money to spend are likely to have their opinions recognised to a greater extent.

It is telling that Lippmann chooses to sidestep questions about the class politics giving shape to this notion of a 'buying public', or even the emergent tensions between competing conceptions of the reader – that is, as citizen or consumer – which might have been expected to follow in this line of critique. Instead, he emphasises the typical newspaper's struggle to turn what is a 'medley of catch-as-catch-can news stand buyers' into that most elusive of quarry, namely 'a devoted band of constant readers'. Given that no newspaper can depend on the unwavering support of its readers, every effort must be made to maintain their loyalty from one day to the next. 'A newspaper can flout an advertiser, it can attack a powerful banking or traction interest, but if it alienates the buying public, it loses the one indispensable asset of its existence', Lippmann remarks (1922: 205). And yet, to understand why the reader engages with the newspaper in the first place, it follows, the nature of news itself must be closely examined.

Standards of judgement

News is not a mirror of social conditions, Lippmann argues, nor is it simple collection of obvious facts spontaneously taking shape in knowable form. Contrary to a certain mythology, it is only in exceptional circumstances that news offers a first hand report of 'raw material' gathered by the journalist; rather, he or she is much more likely to encounter such material only once it has been 'stylized' by someone else (not least 'the publicity man') beforehand. 'All the reporters in the world working all the hours of the day could not witness all the happenings in the world,' Lippmann remarks. 'Reporters are not clairvoyant, they do not gaze into a crystal ball and see the world at will, they are not assisted by thought-transference' (1922: 214).

Certain everyday routines enable the reporter to watch over a small number of places – such as City Hall, Police Headquarters, the Coroner's office, or the White House for that matter – where occurrences likely to prove worthy of coverage can be assumed to be transpiring. Especially valued are those occurrences which represent overt departures from the ordinary, something specific that has 'obtruded itself' from the norm so as provide the reporter, in turn, with a peg for the ensuing story. In other words, unusual happenings which can be 'fixed, objectified, measured, and named' are much more likely to be considered newsworthy. 'The course of events must assume a certain definable shape,' Lippmann writes, 'and until it is in a phase where some aspect is an accomplished fact, news does not separate itself from the ocean of possible truth' (1922: 215).

Departing from his relatively imprecise formulation of this relationship in *Liberty and the News*, he proceeds to propose that a more realistic way forward is to better appreciate the constraints under which reporters operate. 'It is possible and necessary for journalists to bring home to people the uncertain character of the truth on which their opinions are founded,' he believes. More than that, however, the press can also direct 'criticism and agitation' in a manner which will prod both social scientists and state officials into establishing 'more visible institutions' to formulate useable social facts. In waging this fight for 'the extension of reportable truth', the press can help to ensure that these institutions – as opposed to newspapers alone – will adequately equip citizens with the information they require in a democratic society. The press, Lippmann writes, 'is too frail to carry the whole burden of popular sovereignty, to supply spontaneously the truth which democrats hoped was inborn. And when we expect it to supply such a body of truth we employ a misleading standard of judgment' (1922: 228). The entire democratic theory of public opinion needs to be reconsidered, he argues, because of its failure to understand the limited nature of news, the illimitable complexities of society, and the relative competence (including the presumed 'appetite for uninteresting truths') of ordinary citizens.

On this basis, Lippmann declares his break from the prescriptive role envisaged for the press as a vital organ of direct democracy. It is deemed an impractical alternative to those institutions that should rightly assume responsibility for making public life sufficiently intelligible for popular decisions. While the press may be likened to the beam of a searchlight that 'moves restlessly about, bringing one episode and then another out of darkness into vision', it is impossible for individuals to do 'the work of the world by this light alone. They cannot govern society by episodes, incidents, and eruptions. [Rather, they require] a steady light of their own' (1922: 229). Lippmann's recommendations for change are forthright. In suggesting that the trouble lies at a deeper level than the press, he points to a myriad of contributory factors which can be traced to a common source: 'the failure of self-governing people to transcend their casual experience and their prejudice, by inventing, creating, and organizing a machinery of knowledge' (1922: 229–30). Herein can be identified the remedy, namely that a 'system of intelligence' be set in motion to provide the means of analysis necessary to ensure the coordination of decision-making (and, in so doing, act as a check upon a wayward press). Until governments – and newspapers – have a 'reliable picture of the world' on which to act, little headway will be made 'against the more obvious failings of democracy, against violent prejudice, apathy, preference for the curious trivial as against the dull important, and the hunger for sideshows and three legged calves' (1922: 230).

While Lippmann does not dwell on how this 'system of intelligence' will be operationalised, he is convinced that real progress will be achieved once the theory of the 'omnicompetent citizen' is safely discarded. Citizens need not be presented with expert opinion on all social questions before them, he argues, for it is too great a burden to bear. The responsible administrator is better equipped to act on their behalf, making effective use of the intelligence system to assist representative government and administration (both in politics and in industry) from one day to the next. 'Only by insisting that problems shall not come up to him [or her] until they have passed through a procedure,' Lippmann writes, 'can the busy citizen of a modern state hope to deal with them in a form that is intelligible' (1922: 252).

Chasing phantoms

Public Opinion made a considerable splash. Looking across a range of reviews printed at the time of its publication, it soon becomes apparent that Lippmann's advocacy for an enhanced role for a 'system of intelligence' based on social science in public life attracted particular attention. Comments proffered by John Dewey (1922) in his review for *The New Republic* were especially noteworthy. One of the most eminent philosophers of the day, Dewey brought to bear in his engagement with the young journalist's writings a hard-won experience of progressive politics. His review of *Public Opinion* would prove to be an important step toward formalising his own counter-position in the years to come.

Dewey begins his assessment by revelling in the pleasures of the text. He finds inspiration in Lippmann's willingness to challenge those analysts who simply take the force of public opinion for granted, seeing much to admire in the way he goes about rendering problematic their most basic assumptions. Of particular import in this respect, Dewey points out, is the doctrine of 'the omnicompetent individual' demanded by democratic theory, and with it the idealised conception of public opinion arising in spontaneous fashion as a matter of political instinct. Broadly concurring with Lippmann's insights into the ways in which this 'problem of knowledge' impacts on journalism, Dewey turns to the possible remedies on offer. It is here where the two part company from one another. Specifically, he takes issue with Lippmann's reluctance to envisage newspapers as being capable of ever performing the role of enlightening and directing public opinion, as well as with his proposals regarding the organisation of expert intelligence. In his words:

> Mr. Lippmann seems to surrender the case for press too readily – to assume too easily that what the press is it must continue to be. It is true that news must deal with events rather than with conditions and forces. It is true that the latter, *taken by themselves*, are too remote and abstract to make an appeal. Their record will be too dull and unsensational to reach the mass of readers. But there remains the possibility of treating news events in the light of a continuing study and record of underlying conditions. The union of social science, access to facts, and the art of literary presentation is not an easy thing to achieve. But its attainment seems to me the only genuine solution of the problem of an intelligent direction of social life (Dewey, 1922: 288; emphasis in original).

A competent treatment of the day's events, he maintains, can be positively 'sensational' to the degree it reveals the underlying forces shaping events that otherwise appear to be 'casual and disjointed'. It is vital that the reporting of news sets facts in relation to one another so as to create, in turn, 'a picture of situations on which men [and women] can act intelligently'. Journalism, he is convinced, can be transformed so as to offer an objective record of the news, just as the types of expert organisations Lippmann envisages can be endorsed so long as they are closely aligned with the concerns of ordinary people. 'The enlightenment of public opinion still seems to me to have priority over the enlightenment of officials and directors,' he contends. Democracy, it follows, requires a 'thoroughgoing education' for each and every one of its citizens – and not just the privileged elite who meet with Lippmann's approval.

Dewey's passionate appeal to democratic theory thus appears to be almost romantic in its sentiments when counterpoised against Lippmann's scepticism, a contrast which became even starker following the publication of the latter's *The Phantom Public* in 1925. From the opening paragraphs of its first chapter, titled 'The Disenchanted Man', Lippmann provides a bleak appraisal of 'direct democracy's' apparent shortcomings:

> The private citizen today has come to feel rather like a deaf spectator in the back row, who ought to keep his mind on the mystery off there, but cannot quite manage to stay awake. He knows he is somehow affected by what is going on. Rules and regulations continually, taxes annually and wars occasionally remind him that he is being swept along by great drifts of circumstance (Lippmann, 1925: 3–4).

The failure of newspapers to report on the social environment in a way that will enable citizens to fully grasp it is painfully apparent, he argues. This 'disenchanted man' – and woman – has become painfully aware that their 'sovereignty is a fiction', that is, they know that while they reign in theory, they do not govern in practice. Lippmann contends that this is perfectly understandable because the part they play in public affairs appears to be inconsequential to them, despite its celebrated status within democratic rhetoric. The accepted ideal of the omnicompetent citizen is as familiar as it is unattainable. In other words, the belief that there exists a public capable of directing the course of events is profoundly misguided, in his view, for such a public is an abstraction – 'a mere phantom' – that is being falsely exalted.

Lippmann's stature ensured that *The Phantom Public* elicited a range of responses in the press. Once again, though, it is John Dewey's (1925) review that discerns an especially insightful line of critique. In contrast to those anxious to dismiss Lippmann's criticisms out of hand, he sees in them a 'statement of faith in a pruned and temperate democratic theory', one that will improve matters by refining claims made about the public and its powers. He concurs with Lippmann's plea for the 'ethical improvement' of the press so that it may better service, in turn, the scientific organisations Lippmann envisions guiding publicity in relation to the public. This to Dewey's way of thinking is both a technical question ('discovering, recording and interpreting' the conduct of insiders having a public bearing) as well as an aesthetic one (ensuring that the results of such enquiries are sufficiently interesting and weighty). 'I do not suppose that most persons buy sugar because of belief in its nutritive value; they buy from habit and to please the palate,' he writes. 'And so it must be with buying facts which would prepare various publics in particular and the wider public in general to see private activities in their public bearings and to deal with them on the basis of the public interest' (1925: 54).

'The public' versus 'publics'

Dewey's conception of 'the public', as this last point suggests, placed him at odds with Lippmann's pluralised notion of 'publics', albeit in a manner which he found richly suggestive. Inspired to prepare a methodical assessment of its implications (to the extent it represented a 'debate', it was somewhat one-sided), he published *The Public and Its Problems* two years later. At the heart of this book is Dewey's (1927) attempt to formulate an alternative trajectory, namely by marshalling sufficient evidence to support a defence of democratic ideals in the face of Lippmann's pessimism. While much could be gained from the latter's critique – Dewey appears to be in broad agreement with Lippmann's diagnosis of the modern condition – his own analysis produces sharply divergent conclusions.

'Optimism about democracy is to-day under a cloud,' Dewey observes as a starting point for his discussion of what he terms the 'eclipse' of the public. While a considerable portion of *The Public and Its Problems* is devoted to more abstract philosophical matters, there is little doubt in Dewey's mind that the current form of political democracy 'calls for adverse criticism in abundance'. Critics are confounded over what has become of 'the Public', he points out. It 'seems to be lost', existing in effect as a figure of language imputed by officials in justification of their behaviour. 'If a public exists,' he writes, 'it is surely as uncertain about its own whereabouts as philosophers since Hume have been about the residence and make-up of the self' (1927: 117). At a time when electoral statistics indicate that the number of voters exercising their 'majestic right' is steadily decreasing (the 'ratio of actual to eligible voters is now about one-half', he observes), difficult questions arise regarding the continued viability of democratic institutions in practical terms. The social idea of democracy will be 'barren and empty' unless it is 'incarnated in human relationships' that make it meaningful. These relationships encompass the state, but also extend beyond into the realms of family, school, industry and the like – 'all modes of human association' indicative of everyday communities. Indeed, he adds, democracy is in essence 'the idea of community life itself' (1927: 148).

This reappraisal of democracy casts journalism in a different light. The news media are to be regarded as intermediaries between a divisive political system – the very legitimacy of which is increasingly open to dispute by competing interests – and its distrustful citizens. Pressing social problems demand nothing less than an alternative form of journalism, namely one capable of ensuring that it contributes to the formation of a socially alert and informed public. Pausing to clarify his conception of news, Dewey writes:

> 'News' signifies something which has just happened, and which is new just because it deviates from the old and regular. But its *meaning* depends upon

relation to what it imports, to what its social consequences are. This import cannot be determined unless the new is placed in relation to the old, to what has happened and been integrated into the course of events. Without coordination and consecutiveness, events are not events, but mere occurrences, intrusions; an event implies that out of which a happening proceeds. Hence even if we discount the influence of private interests in procuring suppression, secrecy and misinterpretation, we have here an explanation of the triviality and 'sensational' quality of so much of what passes as news (Dewey, 1927: 179–80).

The event-centred priorities of news, together with a corresponding fascination with newness virtually for its own sake (so as to supply 'the element of shock' required), thus combine to isolate the 'catastrophic' – such as crime, accidents, personal conflicts and so forth – from its connections to the social world. That is to say, in recognising the extent to which news represents the exceptional, that is, the 'breaches of continuity', Dewey is suggesting that the unexceptional warrants greater attention than it would typically receive. Journalism must become more rigorous in its analyses and, at the same time, more compelling in its presentation of facts.

It is in thinking through the social consequences engendered by news reporting that Dewey reaffirms Lippmann's espousal of social science's contribution to public life. To reinvigorate the press along more scientific principles, such that social science is seen to give shape to its priorities to a much greater extent, is to instil in its daily reporting a new set of moral values. Precisely what should constitute a news event, it follows, needs to be reconsidered. In a more speculative turn, he prophesies that 'the assembling and reporting of news would be a very different thing if the genuine interests of reporters were permitted to work freely' (1927: 182). Although he does not elaborate on this point, it is apparent that Dewey is discerning in the press a capacity for social reform that Lippmann steadfastly refused to grant it. The journalist, like the social scientist, is charged with the responsibility of providing the information about pressing issues of the day – as well as interpretations of its significance – so as to enable members of the public to arrive at sound judgements. In grappling with what he perceives to be essentially an 'intellectual problem' rather than one of public policy, it seems apparent to Dewey that democracy must become more democratic, that is, more firmly rooted in everyday communities of interaction. To the extent that the journalist contributes to the organisation of the public – not least by facilitating lay participation in the rough and tumble of decision-making – the citizenry will be equipped to recognise, even challenge the authority exercised by powerful interests.

Dewey's conviction that the Great Society can be transformed into the Great Community rests, crucially, on his belief in the rationality of ordinary people to bring to life democratic ideals when provided with the opportunity to do so. 'Until secrecy, prejudice, bias, misrepresentation, and propaganda as well as sheer ignorance are replaced by inquiry and publicity,' Dewey explains, 'we have no way of telling how apt for judgement of social policies the existing intelligence of the masses may be' (1927: 209). This appeal to the citizenry's 'embodied knowledge' effectively underscores the basis for his opposition to the elitism of Lippmann's stance. 'A class of experts,' Dewey contends, 'is inevitably so removed from common interests as to become a class with private interests and private knowledge, which in social matters is not knowledge at all' (1927: 207). While he concedes that Lippmann is rightly critical of certain instances of foolishness engendered by majority rule, it is vital to recognise that it is the means by which a majority is established in the first place that is of paramount importance. The very process by which minorities contest one another with a view to becoming a majority must be preserved at all costs. 'No government by experts in which the masses do not have the chance to inform the experts as to their needs can be anything but an oligarchy managed in the interests of the few,' Dewey maintains (1927: 208).

It goes almost without saying, of course, that it is rather unlikely that the expert – or 'administrative specialist' – will take account of the needs of ordinary citizens by their own volition; rather, he or she will have to be compelled to act in this way. Although he acknowledges the necessarily conflictual nature of this dynamic, Dewey is reluctant to dwell on the social divisions permeating democratic politics. Like Lippmann, he does not engage with the issues raised by the women's movement (the right to vote having been finally achieved in the 1920s), nor comment on civil rights concerns, in a sustained way. Nor does he choose to elaborate on how journalism – alongside the arts and social sciences – might empower citizens to 'break through the crust of conventionalized and routine consciousness' (1927: 183). Nevertheless, he makes plain his personal alignment with 'the masses' in opposition to 'leaders and authorities', pointing out that the world has suffered more from the latter than from the former. 'The essential need,' he writes, 'is the improvement of the methods and conditions of debate, discussion and persuasion. That is *the* problem of the public' (1927: 208). How best to realise this agenda in strategic terms, however, would be left for others to determine.

Divergent visions

Various attempts have been made over the years to characterise Lippmann and Dewey as feisty opponents waging an impassioned, even acrimonious dispute. These efforts make for interesting reading, especially to the degree that legitimate points of contention are highlighted, but risk overstating the nature and intensity of their engagement. With the exception of an occasional footnote or citation, or possible veiled reference, there is little concrete evidence to indicate that either deliberately formulated their position as a debating stance. From the vantage point of today, it is apparent that they shared a considerable amount of common ground, yet their differences remain intriguing.

Lippmann's pessimistic appraisal of journalism's possibilities in an era where 'manufactured consent' passes for representative democracy may seem cold and distant compared with Dewey's heartfelt beliefs about participatory communication, yet it equally behoves the latter to make good the courage of his convictions and outline a radical form of alternative critique. Uniting the projects of both writers is a desire to effect social change, to contribute to efforts to improve upon the existing machinery of democracy, so long as it remains a question of reform. Neither of them advocated a structural transformation of the economic, political or cultural logics underpinning the inequalities endemic to public life at the time. Democracy and capitalism were effectively conflated in their respective interventions (although, in fairness, Dewey underscored the engendered tensions), making it virtually impossible to call for the recasting of the former without being seen to be reaffirming the preservation of the latter.

What may have seemed to be simply an interesting debate in its own right, albeit one effectively contained within narrow ideological parameters, suddenly looks acutely relevant in light of the changes confronting news organisations today, however. So many of the issues considered above assume an exigent quality when contextualised in relation to the imperatives re-writing familiar conventions, not least with regard to the impact of the protracted financial crisis, on the one hand, and the digital convergences ushered in by the Internet, on the other. The speed at which news organisations are moving to refashion their relationship with their publics – presciently anticipated by advocates of public or civic journalism (for whom Dewey's work has long provided intellectual sustenance) years ago – is truly breathtaking. Where Lippmann's ideas once seemed to hold sway, resonating with the cynicism of a postmodern relativism, now it is Dewey's conception of participatory initiatives rooted in everyday (virtual) communities of interaction that chimes with the ethos of citizen-led media. Time will tell how this debate will continue to evolve, of course, but there are grounds for cautious optimism that the promise of journalism so eloquently championed by Dewey may yet find its popular purchase in these troubled times.

References

Allen, E.W. (1922) 'The Social Value of a Code of Ethics for Journalists', The ANNALS of the American Academy of Political and Social Science, 101(1): 170–9.

Angell, N. (1922) The Press and the Organisation of Society. London: Labour Publishing Company.

Dewey, J. (1922) 'Review of Public Opinion', The New Republic, 3 May, 286–8.

Dewey, J. (1925) 'Practical Democracy', The New Republic, 2 December, 52–4.

Dewey, J. (1927) The Public and Its Problems. Athens, OH: Swallow Press.

Hayword, F.H. and Langdon-Davies, B.N. (1919) Democracy and the Press. Manchester: National Labour Press.

Lippmann, W. (1920) Liberty and the News. New York: Harcourt, Brace and Howe.

Lippmann, W. (1922) Public Opinion. New York: Free Press.

Lippmann, W. (1925) The Phantom Public. New York: Harcourt Brace.

Lippmann, W. and Merz, C. (1920) 'A Test of the News,' A Supplement to The New Republic, 4 August, 1–42.

Sinclair, U. (1920) The Brass Check: A Study of American Journalism. Pasadena, CA.

The New York Times (1920a) 'Press agents and public opinion,' 5 September, p. 3.

7

PHOTOJOURNALISM: HISTORICAL DIMENSIONS TO CONTEMPORARY DEBATES

Bonnie Brennen

This chapter offers a brief discussion of the historical context surrounding recent discussions of photography and focuses on the role of photojournalism in contemporary society. As such, it addresses the introduction of photography and its perceived ability to provide authentic documentation of "reality" and details the development of photojournalism during the twentieth century. This chapter then focuses on challenges to the documentary role of photography since the introduction of digital technologies and notes the changing role of photojournalists showcasing their current emphasis on illustrating emotional aspects of experience.

The pencil of nature

Photographs are a way of imprisoning reality, understood as recalcitrant, inaccessible; of making it stand still (Sontag 1977:163).

The introduction of the daguerreotype in 1839 showcased the ability of the new medium of communication to accurately represent material aspects of society in a truthful, transparent, and authentic manner. First heralded as an "extraordinary triumph of modern science," (Poe 1840/1980: 37) the history of photography has presented photographs as news items, documentary evidence, objective renderings of reality, and individual works of art.

The word photography has Greek origins and literally means "writing with light." Initially, photographic images were thought to be devoid of human agency and formed solely through a chemical process dependent on "recording light-based information onto a reactive surface" (Newton 2001: 6). Soon after the development of the daguerreotype in the late 1830s, photographs began to shape not only the way individuals saw themselves but also the way they envisioned the world. Photographs were thought to verify the existence of a subject and offer a "triumph – of reality over illusion, of accuracy over art" (Adatto 2008: 42). Described as "the pencil of nature," photographs were presumed to provide objective proof that something actually happened and individuals began to believe that photographs could provide a "more accurate relation to visible reality" (Sontag 1977: 5) than other artistic renderings of society.

Given that photographs were created from the effects of light on film and lenses, they maintained a level of authenticity that could be considered to bypass human agency. C.S. Peirce refers to photographs as "indicies," direct pointers of reality that provide an assumed guarantee of being closer to the truth than other types of communication (Messaris and Abraham 2001: 217). Cameras were thought to produce photographs that were extraordinarily realistic, offering an authentic representation of things that actually existed; it was generally thought that the world could truly be seen and known through the transparent representations found in photographs (Walton 1984: 251). As John Berger explains: "What the camera does, and what the eye can never do, is to fix the appearance of that event. The camera saves a set of appearances from the otherwise inevitable supersession of further appearances. It holds them unchanging. And before the invention of the camera nothing could do this, except in the mind's eye, the faculty of memory" (Berger 1980: 14).

Because of their envisioned ability to represent an external reality, photographs have been thought to possess the power to authenticate evidence, to identify truth, and to expose deception. Throughout their history, photographs have been used to document news events, provide evidence of criminal activity, and to showcase scientific discoveries. For Roland Barthes, it is impossible to deny the existence of an image because "Photography's inimitable feature is that someone has seen the referent *in flesh and blood*, or again *in person*" (Barthes 1981: 79). In other words, if a horse is shown in a photograph, it is generally assumed that a horse must have been positioned in front of a camera, and did not merely exist in a photographer's imagination. The public's faith in the documentary aspect of photographs was so strong that, when confronted with an image of a horse, people not only believed that it existed but that the photograph depicted what the horse actually looked like. For many years, photographs were readily accepted as authentic representations of the real.

Photographers were first conceptualized as scribes, neutral observers who recorded an objective reality without any attempt at interpretation. The first photographers were not considered artists or authors but instead were known as camera operators. During the nineteenth century, photographers were generally treated as "technicians who initially received no credit or byline for the work they produced" (Schwartz 1999: 173). But soon it became clear that different people took different pictures, even when they were photographing the same thing, and the idea that cameras created an objective image soon began to give way to an understanding that photographs provide "evidence not only of what's there but of what an individual sees, not just a record but an evaluation of the world" (Sontag 1977: 88). Researchers began to demonstrate that the choice of a subject and the framing of that subject, as well as lighting decisions and camera angles, printing strategies, retouching, cropping, and labeling, all influenced the way an image would be interpreted; yet, in their daily usage photographs continued to be seen as truthful depictions of an objective reality. Photographs catered to the public's desire for facts and on newspapers and magazines, editors treated images as objective representations of the news, "reinforcing the professional ideology of objectivity and becoming the site of reality" (Hardt 2000: 63).

Although the camera continued to hold the promise of capturing realistic renderings of society, it was also a technology that could deceive, blurring the line between representation and reality. For example, Mathew Brady's collection of Civil War images represents the first time in the history of photography that a war was covered in its entirety. Brady and his team of photographers including Alexander Gardner, Timothy O'Sullivan, and George Barnard compiled approximately 7,000 images of Civil War battlefields and encampments. The "grim photographic images of the carnage left on the great battlegrounds of Antietam, Fredericksburg, Gettysburg, Spotsylvania, Cold Harbor, Petersburg, and Richmond" (Griffin 1999: 132) were initially thought to illustrate the reality of an extremely gruesome war. And yet, contemporary historians now maintain that the single most famous image in the Brady collection, "Home of a Rebel Sharpshooter," taken by Gardner with the assistance of O'Sullivan, was actually staged.

The rise of photojournalism

Images are bearers of meanings, enduring carriers of ideals and myths (Adatto 2008: 243).

The field of photojournalism is generally considered to address the presentation of news and information primarily through visual images. Documenting relevant social and political issues, at its best photojournalism may provoke engagement with written news reports and may question the status quo. And sometimes it may be seen to "capture art in real life" (Winslow 2006: 2). Yet, Michael Griffin suggests that the term photojournalism was "superimposed on the history of photography in hindsight" (Griffin 1999: 122); although the term was coined in response to the development of picture magazines established during the 1920s and 1930s, the concept of photojournalism has actually been used to showcase a variety of photographic practices that began in the 1830s.

While photojournalism came of age during the early twentieth century, combining documentary conventions with news, opinion, publicity, and propaganda, its history is often traced to the development of the daguerreotype in the late 1830s. Historians have determined that by 1846 news photography became a regular aspect of the work done by daguerreotypists. Between 1885 and 1910, an extensive number of photographs printed in newspapers and magazines helped lead to a "visual reorientation" among the American public, which seemed to offer them direct access to reality. At the end of the nineteenth century, the mass production of smaller and easy to use photographic equipment combined with the development of flexible film and faster dry plates helped to fuel the use of photography in advertising and journalism. And yet, the documentary promise contained in the halftone photographs "coexisted with the dangers of distortion, fabrication and simplification" (Newton 2001: 121).

During the early twentieth century, the publication of magazines such as *Look* and *Life* emphasized a documentary style of photography, showcasing journalistic objectivity, a search for social truths, and an affinity with the real. By the 1930s, documentary photography went beyond reproducing visions of everyday life, to describe key social and economic conditions shaping public views on immigration, poverty, and farm labor and aiding in the construction of an American national identity. Press photographers reflected contemporary values of newsworthiness, confirming or questioning "the facts" and offering "a visual gestalt of the news, information, and entertainment" (Hardt and Brennen 1999a: 5) that soon came to characterize the modern press.

In 1947, four photographers – Robert Capa, Henri Cartier-Bresson, George Rodger, and David "Chim" Seymour – founded the Magnum photo agency in an effort to combine artistry with an emphasis on interpretation. The photographers sought to showcase the poetry in the reality of life and they wanted the flexibility to choose their own stories and the amount of time they spent documenting them. Cartier-Bresson rejected the notion of photojournalists as neutral observers and insisted that, "photographers had to have a point of view in their imagery that transcended any formulaic recording of contemporary events" (Magnum Photos 2008). Generally considered the premier photographic agency, to this day Magnum supplies images to news media outlets, advertising agencies, galleries and museums throughout the world.

Throughout its history, the field of photojournalism has responded to pressures to provide aesthetically pleasing images along with authentic and truthful information about the world. As photographs began to provide objective news accounts, bolstering the authority of journalism, they acquired an aura of reality, truth, and objectivity documenting important events for readers. For example, photojournalists' realistic and graphic depictions of the liberation of the concentration camps confirmed journalistic reports and offered "irrefutable evidence of Nazi degradation and brutality" (Zelizer 1999: 106), while during the Vietnam War, photojournalists' graphic documentary images called into question official policy and were used as evidence to challenge the legitimacy of the war (Ritchin 1990).

Yet others began to focus on another aspect of photography – its ability to provide surveillance for powerful people in government, business, and science. As John Tagg explains: "Like the state, the camera is never neutral. The representations it produces are highly coded, and the power it wields is never its own. As a means of record, it arrives on the scene vested with a particular authority to arrest, picture and transform daily life; a power to see and record; a power of surveillance …" (Tagg 1993: 63–4).

In the twenty-first century, while photographers still question how those with power might use or abuse their images, the focus on technical concerns regarding the construction of images seems less important than their ability to craft meaningful stories about important social concerns within their communities. As Paul Martin Lester explains, these days "A photojournalist is a mixture of a cool, detached professional and a sensitive, involved citizen. The taking of images is much more than f-stops, shutter speeds, white balances, and flak jackets" (Lester 2006: 144).

Challenging the veracity of the image

It seduces us by its proximity to the real and gives us the sensation of putting truth at our fingertips ... and then it throws a jug of cold water in our face (Meyer 1995: 7).

The development of new digital technologies near the end of the twentieth century signaled a series of challenges to the field of photojournalism. Questions were quickly raised about the authenticity of images, the responsibility for the content of photographs, and the role of photojournalists in contemporary society, which raised concerns that in the long run the new technologies might diminish the public's trust in journalism.

With digital imaging, elements of a photograph can easily be added, subtracted, and modified without detection. Critics invariably questioned the reliability of photographs to authentically document news and provide realistic information, and some began to wonder about the potential for digital images "to subvert reality" (Adatto 2008: 65).

Researchers and critics contend that because the manipulation of digital images can be impossible to detect, the new technology has compromised the perceived reliability, objectivity, and facticity of the photographic image. Given that photographers are now able to create images of things that do not exist, it is no longer possible to claim photography as an authentic "index of reality" (Mirzoeff 1999: 88). The Mexican poet Veronica Volkow suggests that because of the digital revolution, "the photograph breaks its loyalty with what is real, that unique marriage between the arts, only to fall into the infinite temptations of the imagination. It is now more the sister of fantasy and dreams than presence" (Volkow, in Meyer 1995: 78).

Digital images can be repositioned, reshaped or removed, blended with images from different sources, altered, deleted, or recorded over immediately or years later, which tends to lessen the authenticity of images because there is no longer an "equivalent to an original, archivally permanent negative" (Richin 1990: 65). In addition, there are fundamental differences between photographs and digital images particularly as it relates to the processes of enlargement and reproduction. The information in photographs is unending and the images can be continually enlarged to showcase greater detail. However, digital images can only be enlarged to a certain point, and beyond that point no additional information can be ascertained (Savedoff 1997: 210).

In digital imaging, "light is translated into a digital code read by a computer. Not only can that digital code be altered easily, but its alteration can be done in such a way as to be undetectable" (Newton 2001: 6). While the photographic process focuses on the recording of light, in the case of digital imaging, light is converted. Newton suggests that the words recorded and converted may help to explain the public's original trust in photography and their current distrust in digital imaging.

As William J. Mitchell notes, with digital imaging, "the referent has become unstuck" (Mitchell 1992: 31) and photographs no longer have the power to convince people that the evidence they provide is authentic and real. In his research, Mitchell draws on George Orwell's 1984, specifically referencing the novel's records department, which specialized in faking photographs. He suggests that with the development of personal computers, such a department is no longer necessary because now it is possible for anyone to fake photographs. Contemporary examples of digital abuse support Mitchell's concerns. For example, National Geographic's cover image of the pyramids of Giza was created by digitally moving the pyramids closer together so that the photograph would fit the magazine's vertical format. Newsweek combined separate images of Tom Cruise and Dustin Hoffman into what appears as an image of the two actors together; while the Los Angeles Times and its sister publications the Chicago Tribune and the Hartford Courant ran a front page news photograph of Iraqi citizens sitting on the ground, as an armed American soldier stands in the foreground which was actually a digital image created from two distinct photographs.

While digitally altered images currently "trade on the documentary aura" (Savedoff 1997: 213) of traditional photography, some fear that, as the digital manipulation of images becomes more widespread, all photography will lose its documentary function and the public will no longer consider it to represent the real. However, Mexican photographer Pedro Meyer challenges the public to avoid the hypocrisy associated with concerns over the manipulation of digital images, and he insists that "all photographs are manipulated" (Meyer 1995: 12). Meyer maintains that, through the choice of subject matter, the focus and framing of images, all photographers manipulate images. However, for Meyer, what is important to consider is the criteria or the intentions that are applied to the manipulation.

Some critics speculate that because of the inability to distinguish between an authentic image and one that has been electronically manipulated, in the future, media outlets will no longer use photographs to document events but will instead use photographs as illustrations. "Photographs will appear less like facts and more like factoids – as a kind of unsettled and unsettling hybrid imagery based not so much on observable reality and actual events as on the imagination" (Grundberg 1990: 1).

Yet others like New York Times reporter Andy Grundberg argue that photojournalism's loss of documentary authority may have more to do with the "superabundance and stereotypicality" (Grundberg 1990: 5) of images that populate the contemporary media landscape than with any specific challenges of digital imaging technology. Similarly, John Hartley suggests that photographs have become so ubiquitous and the media landscape now littered with images, that there is no longer much room for analysis or commentary (Hartley 2007: 556).

However, Kiku Adatto suggests that even with their ability to falsify information that the documentary power of the camera remains a significant feature in contemporary society. "We still want the camera to fulfill its documentary promise, to provide us with insight, and to be a record of our lives and the world around us" (Adatto 2008: 8).

Adatto offers the example of the images of Abu Ghraib to illustrate the current documentary power of photographs and insists that without photographs there would have been no understanding of this issue and no investigation of the prison abuses.

Responding to concerns regarding the potential for the manipulation of digital imagery, newspaper executives have enacted strict guidelines against digitally altering news images and have disciplined photojournalists who have been caught changing images. Clearly maintaining a belief in the ability of photographs to document reality, in 1997 *The Minneapolis Star Tribune* suspended its photographer Stormi Greener, for digitally eliminating power lines from a photograph in violation of the newspaper's policy regarding the digital manipulation of images. It has been suggested that the newspaper's action of "publically excoriating Greener demonstrated to readers that the *Star Tribune* makes good on its claim to present only unmanipulated photographs" (Schwartz 1999: 159). More recently, in the 2003 example mentioned earlier, *Los Angeles Times* photographer Brian Walski was fired after the newspaper discovered that he had digitally combined two images to create a new photograph of the Iraq War, while in 2006, *Charlotte Observer* photojournalist Patrick Schneider was also fired for digitally altering the color of the sky in a picture of a Charlotte firefighter. The newspaper reported that Schneider violated its photo policy, which states: "No colors will be altered from the original scene photographed" (Winslow 2006: 1).

In an effort to quell concerns regarding the potential to manipulate digital images as well as to strengthen public perception of photojournalism, the National Press Photographers Association (NPPA) recently updated its Code of Ethics. Affirming a primary goal of the "faithful and comprehensive depiction" of society, the ethics code warns photojournalists not to manipulate images and to avoid presenting their own "biases" in their work (NPPA 2008). John Long, chairperson of NPPA's Ethics and Standards Committee insists that all documentary news photographs are expected to be real and that if a news image looks real, "it better be real" (Long, quoted in Winslow 2006: 4).

From documentary to emotional photojournalism

Photography is subversive not when it frightens, repels, or even stigmatizes, but when it is pensive, when it thinks (Barthes 1981: 38)

By the mid-twentieth century, photojournalists were expected to provide technically perfect photographs, which were thought to portray an unbiased objective reality. For contemporary photojournalists, the emphasis is less on the physical process and photojournalists now focus on a more interpretive role, providing representations, persuasions, and understandings of larger issues in society.

Fred Richin suggests that new technologies have forced photojournalists to redefine their relationship to images; he urges photographers to stop overestimating the power of technology and to instead embrace the subjectivity of images. Ritchin draws on photographer Pedro Meyer's story of a nail on a wall to illustrate the capacity of photographs to engage in "subtle ambiguity, in soaring metaphor, in questioning the nature of reality rather than delineating conventional responses" (Ritchin 1990: 143). Meyer tells of a Peruvian experiment with Indian children who took pictures illustrating the concept of exploitation. One child took a picture of a nail on a wall. At first the instructors thought the child did not understand the assignment. However, they soon learned that a group of children lived in a poor town outside of Lima and each day they walked several miles into town to shine shoes. The children rented nails on a wall from a man who lived in town so that they did not have to carry the heavy shoeboxes back and forth each day. The man charged the children half of what they earned each day for rental of the nails. "As you can see, sometimes a picture of a nail on the wall means much more than just a nail on the wall" (Meyer, in Ritchin 1990: 100).

However, John Tagg warns that, although documentary photography has rejected the notion of objective evidence in favor of an emphasis on the emotion of experience, structures of power remain inscribed into photographic images. Tagg takes issue with the ways photojournalists position their subjects "as the 'feminised' Other, as passive but pathetic objects capable only of offering themselves up to a benevolent, transcendent gaze – the gaze of the camera and the gaze of the paternal state" (Tagg 1993: 12).

Because of their emotional power to entertain, educate, and persuade, media ethicists suggest that great care should be taken with all images that are published in order to insure that the representations do no harm. "The best reasons, ethically speaking, to show any news image are that it moves people to care and that it helps people to safely navigate through their daily lives" (Lester 2006: 141).

Photojournalist Marco Vernaschi suggests that contemporary photojournalism is shifting from an explicit documentary style to an emotional documentary style which goes beyond illustrating ideas and concepts found in news articles to help readers "feel the intensity of what they read" in journalistic reports (Vernaschi 2008) . By visually representing emotions, documentary photographs present a specific world view and attempt to connect with the public on an intimate level encouraging the "sympathetic experience and action" of a diverse audience (Starrett 2003: 418). Contemporary photographs offer life stories of newsworthy individuals, illustrating their joy and pain, as well as their conflicts, challenges, and struggles, in an attempt to move readers on a personal and emotional level. Images that are not only aesthetically pleasing but also capture readers' attention emotionally are thought to help to foster understanding and create a sense of community (Rees 2004).

From this perspective, the photojournalist may be seen to inhabit the space of a "covert artist with an acute social conscience, intent on naming the nameless, revealing the contradictions of life, and exposing the emotions people would rather ignore or suppress beneath our supposedly rational culture" (Newton 2001: 50). As bell hooks suggests, readers' interpretations of photographs are based on their specific experiences and their emotional engagement with the images. Photographs can embrace, captivate, and seduce: "Such is the power of the photograph, of the image, that it can give back and take away, that it can bind" (hooks 1995: 56).

Some photographic images offer such a strong emotional response or identification that they have reached iconic status and are reproduced and used within a variety of media to represent key historic events and issues. Lewis Hine's 1911 image "Breaker Boys," Dorothea Lange's 1936 photograph "Migrant Mother," Joe Rosenthal's 1945 image, "Flag Raising on Iwo Jima," and Eddie Adams' 1968 photograph of the shooting of an alleged Vietnamese terrorist are all powerful ideological constructions that have contributed to widely accepted interpretations of history which have helped to build a socially constructed national identity (Hardt and Brennen 1999b: 15). More recently, the image of three Ground Zero firefighters standing on a pile of rubble and raising the American flag has "lodged in the public consciousness" (Franklin 2002: 64), becoming a powerful iconic image. Tom Franklin, the photographer who took the image, notes that his photograph has been reprinted extensively in the press and has been reproduced without authorization on plaques, figurines, coins, jewelry, T-shirts, Christmas tree ornaments, and country barns and used to represent Americans' courage, strength, and resilience following September 11.

According to Barbie Zelizer, after September 11, photography "rose to fill the space of chaos and confusion that journalism was expected to render orderly" (Zelizer 2002: 48). Images recycled in newspapers, news magazines, as well as in commemorative volumes became an integral aspect of journalism, creating a realm of contemplation within the documentary record, helping citizens to bear witness to the events, and providing public support for future political and military activities. The recycling of September 11 images also served in a phenomenological role, providing realistic representations and also mementos of the actual experience for people to purchase, save, share, critique, and revisit (Anden-Papadopoulus 2003: 102). Iconic photographs that are infused with memory and history may ultimately provide representations of historically based "truths" that help to create a socially constructed collective identity in contemporary societies.

Finally, in a media saturated environment when everyone who owns a cell phone may be considered a member of the press, and when any image may be posted on line and become a part of the public record, it seems important to consider, who is a photojournalist?

In 2009, newspapers and magazines employ a limited number of staff photographers – the majority of the images used now come from freelance photographers, photo-agencies like Magnum, and archives. Media outlets are provided with a large number of images from which they are able to select, revise, and change the photographs at will. Such a system provides editors with the images they desire as well as a great degree of visual flexibility, without the need to "maintain a waged workforce of photojournalists" (Hartley 2007: 557). The emphasis on freelance photographers has helped to reduce the power of photojournalists who, in one sense, may now be seen as "a vulnerable and often passive cog in a well-oiled machine" (Ritchin 1990: 110).

While photographs may be seen as visual constructions of a social reality, it may be particularly important to heed John Hartley's warning that, in late industrial capitalist societies, "the democratization and monetization of photojournalism has reached its logical conclusion: now we're all paparazzi" (Hartley 2007: 561).

References

Adatto, K. (2008) *Picture Perfect. Life in the Age of the Photo Op*. Princeton: Princeton University Press.

Anden-Papadopoulus, K. (2003) "The Trauma of Representation. Visual Culture, Photojournalism and the September 11 Terrorist Attack," *Nordicom Review*, 24: 89–104.

Barthes, R. (1981) *Camera Lucida. Reflections on Photography*. New York: Hill and Wang.

Berger, J. (1980) *About Looking*. New York: Pantheon Books.

Franklin, T. (2002) "The After-Life of a Photo That Touched a Nation," *Columbia Journalism Review*, March/April: 64–5.

Griffin, M. (1999) "The Great War Photographs," pp. 122–57, in B. Brennen and H. Hardt, (eds.) *Picturing the Past. Media, History and Photography*, Urbana: University of Illinois Press.

Grundberg, A. (1990) "Photography View; Ask It No Questions: The Camera Can Lie," *New York Times*. Online. Available: http://query.nytimes.com/gst/fullpage.html?res=9C0CE7DC163CF931A2575BC0 A966958260 (accessed 17 October 2008).

Hardt, H. (2000) *In the Company of Media. Cultural Constructions of Communication, 1920s-1930s*. Boulder, CO: Westview.

Hardt, H. and Brennen, B. (1999a) "Introduction," pp. 1–10, in B. Brennen and H. Hardt, (eds.) *Picturing the Past. Media, History and Photography*, Urbana: University of Illinois Press.

Hardt, H. and Brennen, B. (1999b) "Newswork, History, and Photographic Evidence: A Visual Analysis of a 1930s Newsroom," pp. 11–35, in B. Brennen and H. Hardt (eds.) *Picturing the Past. Media, History and Photography*, Urbana: University of Illinois Press.

Hartley, J. (2007) "Documenting Kate Moss. Fashion Photography and the Persistence of Photojournalism," *Journalism Studies*, 8: 555–65.

hooks, b. (1995) *Art On My Mind. Visual Politics*. New York: New Press.

Lester, P.M. (2006) "On Mentors, Ethics, and Weapons," *Visual Communication Quarterly*, 12: 136–45.

Magnum Photos. (2008) "History of Magnum," Online. Available: http://agency.magnumphotos.com/print/node/50 (accessed 4 September 2008).

Messaris, P. and Abraham, L. (2001) "The Role of Images in Framing News Stories," pp. 215–26, in S. Reese, O. Gandy, Jr., and A. Grant (eds.) *Framing Public Life: Perspectives on Media and Our Understanding of the Social World*, Mahwah, NJ: Erlbaum.

Meyer, P. (1995) *Truths and Fictions: A Journey from Documentary to Digital Photography*. New York: Aperture.

Mirzoeff, N. (1999) *An Introduction to Visual Culture*. London: Routledge.

Mitchell, W.J. (1992) *The Reconfigured Eye. Visual Truth in the Post-Photographic Era*. Cambridge, MA: The MIT Press.

NPPA Code of Ethics (2008). Online. Available: http://www.nppa.org/professional_development/business_practices/ethics/html (accessed 2 October 2008).

Newton, J.H. (2001) *The Burden of Visual Truth. The Role of Photojournalism in Mediating Reality*. Mahwah, NJ: Erlbaum.

Poe, E.A. (1840/1980) "The Daguerreotype," pp. 37–38, in A. Trachtenberg, (ed.) *Classic Essays on Photography*. New Haven, CN: Leete's Island Books.

Rees, D. (2004) "Picturing a Free Press. Photographs Have the Power to Bring the Truth to Life," *IPI Global Journalist*, 3rd quarter: 16.

Ritchin, F. (1990) *In Our Own Image. The Coming Revolution in Photography*. New York, Aperture.

Savedoff, B. (1997) "Escaping Reality: Digital Imagery and the Resources of Photography," *The Journal of Aesthetics and Art Criticism*, 55: 201–14.

Schwartz, D. (1999) "Objective Representation: Photographs as Facts," pp. 158–81, in B. Brennen and H. Hardt (eds.) *Picturing the Past. Media, History and Photography*, Urbana: University of Illinois Press

Sontag, S. (1977) *On Photography*. New York: Farrar, Straus and Giroux.

Starrett, G. (2003) "Violence and the Rhetoric of Images," *Cultural Anthropology*, 18: 398–428.

Tagg, J. (1993) *The Burden of Representation. Essays on Photographies and Histories*. Minneapolis: University of Minnesota Press.

Vernaschi, M. (2008) "An Interview With Photojournalist Marco Vernaschi." Online. Available: <http://www.magicalplacesfineart.com/blog/2007/10/an-interview-with-photojournalist-marco-vernaschi/ (accessed 3 October 2008).

Walton, K.L. (1984) "Transparent Pictures: On the Nature of Photographic Realism," *Critical Inquiry*, 11: 246–77.

Winslow, D.R. (2006) "A Question of Truth: Photojournalism and Visual Ethics," National Press Photographers Association. Online. Available: http://www.nppa.org/news_and_events/news/2006/08/ethics.html (accessed 12 October 2008).

Zelizer, B. (2002) "Photography, Journalism, and Trauma," pp. 48–68, in B. Zelizer and S. Allan (eds.) *Journalism After September 11*, London: Routledge.

Zelizer, B. (1999). "From the Image of Record to the Image of Memory: Holocaust Photography Then and Now," pp. 98–121, in B. Brennen and H. Hardt (eds.) *Picturing the Past. Media, History and Photography*, Urbana: University of Illinois Press.

8

THE WATCHDOG'S NEW BARK: CHANGING FORMS OF INVESTIGATIVE REPORTING

Donald Matheson

Investigative reporting's importance to journalism lies primarily in its symbolic role: investigations, while rare, represent the practice at its best. Here journalism can be seen, often spectacularly, to be carrying out the fourth estate role described in the Anglo-American liberal tradition. The Watergate scandal, although a significant moment in 1970s US politics, still has enormous resonance around the world more than 30 years later perhaps largely for this reason. It symbolises so successfully (particularly in the glamorous film version) the good that reporting can do, independently monitoring power and aligning itself with the interests of the people. Spectacular investigations can also be read as markers of significant change in the position of journalists within the political domain. The British *Guardian*'s 'cash for questions' investigations and a raft of other 'sleaze' exposés in the British media symbolised both the end of Conservative dominance in UK politics in the mid-1990s and the reinvigoration of a profession whose power of self-determination had been severely shaken by a coalition between the Thatcher Government and corporate media owners (Doig 1997).

The importance of these narratives is widely recognised in journalism studies – indeed Zelizer's classic study of journalism as an interpretive community uses as one of its key examples the reception by US journalists of the Watergate scandal (Zelizer 1993). Yet scholars and journalists have become increasingly sceptical of the way journalism culture has told the story, particularly in relation to politics. This is only partly a matter of a weakening in the actual numbers of high-profile exposés of political malfeasance. More significantly, studies of journalism and politics suggest that the media's role in battles against the abuse of political power can no longer be made to fit very well the stories told of reporters conducting independent investigations of political power.

This chapter explores, then, a weakening of the symbolic power of the figure of the dogged, lone, investigative reporter in Western democracies. It suggests, firstly, that the critical literature concentrates too much on fears of a decline in journalistic investigation, defining the practice in terms of mythic exemplars such as Watergate. The argument, secondly, proposes that the heroic figure of the investigative reporter makes a little less sense in a world where the media are themselves so powerful that they, in some estimations, form the stage on which much politics is carried out. Indeed, the Watergate story itself can be re-read as part of the rise of scandal politics and the rise of an audit culture in public life, in which other actors play a more powerful role than journalists. Consequently, this chapter will emphasise less a story of decline in investigative reporting than one of such significant change that the dominant narrative of the investigative is losing some purchase. Indeed, as will be discussed in the final section, other narratives of investigation are gaining some prominence among journalists.

The question of decline

The analysis of a decline in the number of investigations of political power by journalists in Western democracies undoubtedly has much to recommend it. The pressures on this kind of reporting have always been intense, but an economic downturn in the news business, combined with the tightening in a number of countries of laws limiting journalists' access to information, often on the grounds of national security, has arguably tipped the scales. The former head of the US Center for Public Integrity, Charles Lewis (2007), notes that the 'landscape looks precarious' for serious, well-resourced journalism, citing research showing a drop in the volume and the quality of journalism in newspapers in the US. In what some called the 'midsummer massacre', 4000 newspaper jobs disappeared there in July and August, 2008. In all Western countries, news consumption is trending downwards (a drop of two million readers for British national newspapers in 10 years; Tumber & Waisbord 2004b). Consequently, the resources for long investigations in the public interest are tight. Davies (2008) argues that, partly because of those financial pressures, much UK journalism is becoming 'churnalism', or low-quality material largely dependent on press releases and media minders.

Investigative reporting has, it should be pointed out, risen and fallen in the past. Weinberg (1996: 283) notes that the sudden explosion of 'muckraking' onto the US political scene at the turn of the twentieth century was followed by 30 years of decline in quantity and quality. Doig (1997) charts the rise of modern investigative reporting in the 1970s in the UK, when the *Sunday Times* launched its highly successful 'Insight' team, followed by a decline in the 1980s. Waisbord (1996) describes a sudden increase in newspaper and television news investigations of politicians in South America in the 1990s, leading to the fall of the Brazilian and Venezuelan presidents and other officials. The reasons behind these patterns are contested – Waisbord, for example, argues that investigative reporting does not simply reflect changes in press freedoms or democratic processes, but also a complex mix of factors, ranging from the economic to the professional and the political. It should also be noted that the number of investigations at any one time is small, and that therefore a few high profile cases, whether it is the success of the Watergate investigation or indeed the alleged punishment of Thames Television by the Thatcher Government through regulatory reform after its investigation into its shooting by British Agents of unarmed IRA activists, are often read as symptomatic of the wider state of investigative journalism, if not of journalism in general (Doig 1997: 204–5).

Molloy notes that journalism is also prone to a golden age-ism, by which the state of journalism a generation earlier is invariably romanticised and the present state lamented (cited in Thomas 2000). Particularly in the case of investigative reporting, because of its resonance in the interpretive community of journalism, there is some risk that changes in practice will be read as decline. Mair (2008) makes just this point, suggesting that Davies' lament overstates the problem, and concluding that: 'The watchdog that is the British national press is now barking in different ways' (2008: 48). As explored in the remainder of this chapter, this view gains some support if we look beyond the dominant model of investigative reporting. Lewis (2007), whose concern at the ailing US newspaper business is cited above, points to the rise of other ways of funding and conducting investigative journalism, including journalists working with non-profit institutes rather than relying on corporate-owned news. While Lewis focuses on business models, the question is perhaps at heart one of the stories and definitions that journalists and critics use to discuss the investigation and critique of power.

Definitional stories

There has been considerable homogeneity in the idea of investigative reporting, certainly within the Anglo-American tradition. From W.T. Stead's undercover exposé of child sex slavery in 1880s London, which brought crowds onto the streets protesting for reform, to William Howard Russell's exposure of conditions within the British Army in the Crimea, to the Watergate case, most stories told of this kind of reporting are similar. A model is discernible in which independent journalists investigate the moral lapses of politicians, triumphing despite intimidation, legal barriers and a shortage of money because of the support of editors and their careful accumulation of factual evidence. In the end they stimulate public indignation and force the resignation or overthrow of those politicians. These stories solidify into slightly different definitions in different accounts. Blevens (1997) cites a number of journalists and critics who define the practice as involving the uncovering of secret or concealed information, others who emphasise the skills required, and others who emphasise the independence of journalists from power. As the gloss often used in the US, 'enterprise reporting', suggests, all seem to agree that investigations are moments when journalism steps outside its usual practices of tracking the debates amongst society's dominant voices or reproducing the material pre-produced for it by public relations. In this process of setting independent agendas and deploying greater detective skills, journalists seek out difficult to access sources, analyse original documents and confront the powerful with alternative accounts. Investigative reporting therefore allows journalists to feel their craft at least sometimes lives up to the highest expectations of it. It is a term particularly associated with Anglo-American liberal journalism, where facticity and impartiality are what Zelizer (2004) calls 'god-terms', and perhaps less clearly identifiable in places where the line between reporting and opinion is less clear (Waisbord 1996). In the United States in particular, investigative reporting allows journalism, at least for brief moments, to reconcile its somewhat contradictory notion of itself as both an objective recorder of fact and a crusader for justice. Ettema and Glasser (1998), in the major study of US investigative reporting, talk of the combination of the 'fiercest of indignation' with the 'hardest of fact' (1998: 3).

At the centre of the idea of investigative journalism lies Watergate, the story of two junior reporters at the *Washington Post*, Bob Woodward and Carl Bernstein, who from 1972 to 1974 doggedly pursued electoral espionage and subsequent cover-up by officials of the Republican Party, a story which finally engulfed President Nixon. Schudson (1995, 2004) calls it the archetype of investigative journalism and a moment which 'overwhelms modern American journalism'. Weinberg (1996) uses it as the paradigmatic case by which to distinguish investigations from other struggles to hold politics to account. From Irangate to minor scandals such as Cheriegate, it defines political crisis brought on by journalistic investigation.[1] The story is used both as a model and to castigate journalism which falls short. As Schudson (1995) notes, Watergate has this power because, at least as told by the reporters in their book and the 1975 film, 'All the President's Men', it confirmed and gave new form so tidily to journalistic ideals of its independence, public interest and political power.

Watergate and similar stories told within journalism are mythic, in Barthes' (1973) sense of structures which make sense of and organise other occurrences. They are also mythic, however, in the related sense of being idealised tellings that over-emphasise journalism's heroism. For, Schudson also notes, most of what the reporters found out was also known already to the FBI and other agencies investigating the break-in and related issues. Indeed it was brave officials who leaked much of this to the reporters and the campaigning judge John Sirica who pushed the small players in the story to implicate those above them. In addition, very few of the 400 Washington correspondents at the time worked on the story, at least while it remained controversial. Watergate does not live up well to its own myth. But it is a powerful mobilising force. The 'kernel of truth' in the tale sustains a larger truth of 'what we may have been once, what we might again become, what we would like to be "if"' (Schudson, 1995: 123). In doing so, of course, the risk is that it becomes a comfortable credo, which journalists can recite to buttress their sense that what they do is more than a commercial product or in the service of elites. Rosen (2005) charges that it is a credo which does not prepare journalists particularly well for a world where reporting is rewarded much more poorly than punditry, where the truth rarely wins out by itself and where journalism does not stand outside politics, looking in, but is often closely tied to power.

Reinterpreting investigations as scandals

Another version of the Watergate story, told by political scientists and journalism scholars, is that it was an early moment in the wave of scandals which has washed over late twentieth-century Western political life. In one of the few long-term studies in this area, Benson and Hallin (2005) find that in both France and the US, the number of media scandals roughly doubled between the 1960s and the 1990s. Tumber and Waisbord note that many countries, from the United States to South Korea to India, appear to be in a state of 'permanent scandal' (Tumber & Waisbord 2004a: 1031). Castells describes a market for damaging political information which emerges once corruption of one kind or another becomes a public topic, leading to more and more stories of this kind (Castells 1996: 338, cited in Tumber & Waisbord 2004a: 1034). In Thompson's (2000) influential analysis, the various kinds of political scandal (about the abuse of power, finances, or the personal lives of politicians) can be traced back to the growing importance of the media as a site of political power, and the importance of reputation in this form of power. Sanders and Canel (2007: 457) write:

> Reputation is a kind of resource, a symbolic capital, allowing politicians to build up legitimacy, to develop trust among several publics including fellow politicians, the electorate and media professionals. Politicians must constantly use 'symbolic power' to persuade, confront, influence actions and beliefs (Thompson 2000: 262). Scandal is important because it can destroy this resource.

Much of the investigative reporting surrounding politics in recent years, including the 'sleaze' stories on the infidelities and sexual preferences of British Conservative MPs, makes sense in terms of this contest for symbolic capital.

Media scandal also, then, goes hand in hand with the growth of promotional politics. As politics becomes ever more a matter of visibility and less one of policies or ideological alignments (Bennett 2001; Thompson 2000), political actors grow ever more sophisticated in managing their symbolic selves. The scandal that disrupts that management by bringing secret or backstage information onto the front stage – recordings of private conversations that contradict stated policy, for example – becomes significant. For politicians, it is a way to damage their opponents; for journalists, scandals are a display of their independence in the face of increased media management, as well as being good for ratings.

The importance of personal reputation in political power also has a cultural dimension. Thompson (2000) suggests that scandals are part of a cultural change in which social distance is being compressed, so that politicians become judged in terms of everyday and interpersonal relations, and particularly in terms of trust. Seen in this wider frame, scandals may be viewed not so much as debased journalism but as part of the way power is contested in mediated politics. El Gody (2007) describes something of this sort taking place in the pan-Arabic public space. Al Jazeera's approach to critiquing Arab political leaders, he argues, is 'politainment', which works to delegitimise

Arab governments through discussion of financial and power scandals on its talk show and interview programmes. The US comedy current affairs programme, 'The Daily Show', is discussed in similar terms by a number of scholars as an enormously influential site where the political legitimacy of political and media elites is contested by exposing duplicity and dissembling.

Scholarship has, then, steadily undermined the heroic myth of the individual journalist's morally charged exposure of hidden facts. Not only is the journalist no longer the driving force behind the exposure of wrongs, for in these analyses changes in politics and culture are more important drivers, but the media's role changes from one of setting the agenda to providing the stage for scandal. Liebes and Blum-Kulka (2007) argue that journalists are relatively weak in uncovering scandals, which depend more on whistle-blowers or sources with their own agendas. Feldstein (2007) similarly describes journalists as 'ventriloquists' much of the time, amplifying stories seeded by sources with particular agendas. 'Often the journalist is merely the conduit, a nearly interchangeable vessel selected as the vehicle for furthering the informant's objectives' (2007: 505). Spanish reporter Fernando Garea told researchers that, even in investigative reporting, much of the material comes from unsolicited phone calls or letters: 'the myths about investigative journalism should be exploded because it's really much more simple' (Sanders & Canel 2006: 463). Williams and Delli Carpini (2004) go as far as to say that the mainstream press has virtually lost its gatekeeping role in this kind of story, with its emphasis less on the uncovering of factual details of events and more on the individual's reputation, for that kind of reporting takes place as easily on satellite and cable television comedy shows, the Internet and talk shows. They conclude that the traditional faces of the elite – journalists, policy experts and public officials – have lost power in this new media system, but that overall political elites, transformed into celebrities and therefore able to move between news, sports and entertainment media with ease, have maintained power. In that scenario, journalism's independence as an arbiter of public affairs is severely diminished, a point they explore by examining the Clinton–Lewinsky scandal of the late 1990s. Not only was the story of the president's sexual activities broken by Matt Drudge on his website, but the story spread though talk radio and comedy shows as much as through news journalism. One could spend 24 hours a day hearing about the scandal in the US and 'tellingly, one could do so without ever tuning in or picking up a traditional news source' (Williams & Delli Carpini 2004: 1221).

In addition, there is some consensus that other actors have taken over the investigative function that the Watergate story expects journalism to perform in relation to a scandal. In the Clinton–Lewinsky case, it was well organised right-wing groups. Williams and Delli Carpini (2004: 1226) talk of an 'insurgency movement by the far right' that was able to make most effective use of talk radio and other emergent media. In Germany, journalism appears to have played a minor role in uncovering the immense political scandal that has brewed for nearly 10 years over corruption within the CDU, ultimately implicating its former leader Helmut Kohl, when compared to the efforts of public prosecutors and CDU insiders (Esser & Hartung 2004: 1056). The audit culture (O'Neill 2002) which has swept over Western public life provides a multitude of such agencies doing what muckraking or investigative journalists might have done in the past, but in far greater thoroughness and with better resources.

Journalism as a stage

These points converge in the observation made by a number of critics that investigative journalism, where the reporter goes undercover or vouches for what he or she has found out from documents or sources, has been eclipsed to an extent by journalism which provides a stage on which others act out the norms and limits of acceptable political behaviour. As Gaines (2007) puts it in his nostalgic account of the demise of stings and undercover reporting, television cameras eliminate the need for the first-person account by the reporter, for they work by displaying people talking deceitfully. This kind of journalism is by no means passive but it has more of what Cottle (2006) calls a ritual power of bringing people together in a mediated moment that symbolises and restates ideas of how society should be. It is performative, an act of speech, like a promise or accusation or christening, that does not describe something outside itself but performs its own meaning. Ekström and Johansson (2008: 65) write that news media:

> put a great deal of work into creating conditions in which such scandals could occur, preferably in front of the photographers' cameras so that they can be shown live. The central focus of the media's involvement changes from the revelation to the staging of transgressions.

A political scandal, in this sense, is largely a matter of talk (ibid.: 72). In staging politics in this way, journalists ask interview questions with the goal of causing politicians themselves to reveal what lies behind their pre-planned actions, or they juxtapose previous statements with contemporary ones as ironic devices to demonstrate the less than truthful nature of the latest utterances.

While we might lament these changes, they do also give weight to Schudson's (2005) argument that journalism's stories of its independence and mobilisation of the population may be exaggerated. Feldstein (2007) proposes a model in which journalistic investigations belong to a relatively closed world of elites. In simulating rather than stimulating public outrage, journalists become in effect collaborators with the elites whom they are claiming to hold to account. From nineteenth-century 'Tammany Hall' graft to the Enron and Arthur Andersen accounting scandal in 2001, journalists have been much less independent fact-gatherers, and much more dependent on elite whistleblowers or informants, than they might claim. Rosen (2005) accuses journalism of deluding itself, implying it needs to live in the light of fact not myth. An alternative approach would be to give space to a wider range of stories to imagine – and model – journalism in an evolving political and cultural context. Such work requires sustained analysis of journalism culture, but some suggestions are made below of emergent alternative models of investigative journalism.

Collaborative investigations

If the literature suggests the notion of journalism as uniquely positioned to independently investigate political life is overstated, there is perhaps value in exploring forms of investigative journalism in which reporters consciously work with others. In the mid-nineteenth century, when *The Times* thundered against British military incompetence in the Crimea, the liberal creed that 'a free press able and willing to expose corruption' lay at the heart of political accountability carried some weight (Diamond & Plattner 1993: 101; cited in Tumber & Waisbord 2004a: 1035). If public life is now crowded with organisations auditing the state sector, producing analyses, mobilising public opinion and investigating problems, other stories than the reporter-centred Watergate myth might make more sense of journalism's best work. Heroes in this other kind of story might include organisations such as the Institute for War and Peace Reporting, founded by four British, US and Serbian journalists during the 1990s Balkans wars. The IWPR has exposed war crimes, injustices and systematic problems not so much through the reports by its staff as through training local journalists in many war-torn countries and disseminating their reports. These include reports detailing war crimes and the rule of vigilante law in parts of Kosovo. Lewis (2008) points to many such NGOs and non-profits involved in investigative journalism, from the mundane level of consumer lobby groups, many of whose high quality consumer reports shape news agendas, to groups such as the Fund for Investigative Journalism, which part-funded Seymour Hersh's reporting in 1969 of the My Lai massacre in Vietnam. He sees this broadening of the investigatory effort as a 'way to rejuvenate and sustain the soul of journalism' (36).

There are risks to journalism's independence in these ventures. State aid money from the West, for example, funds investigative centres in some countries. Worse, some of these organisations have been tentatively linked to security services. The rise of OhmyNews in South Korea, in which journalist Oh Yeon-Ho was joined by tens of thousands of citizen journalists in what he called 'guerrilla warfare' against the country's conservative media and the conservative government it supported (Hauben 2005), would trouble many journalists. The line between campaigning journalism and a political campaign was weak here – indeed rather than bring down a politician, OhmyNews's claim to fame is that it helped bring reformist president Roh Moo-hyun into power. There is perhaps value in journalism acknowledging that the ideals of objectivity do not always further it in calling power to account (see also Waisbord 1996, Ettema & Glasser 1998, Benson & Hallin 2005). Regardless of which version of the collaboration story is emphasised, however, what is important is that journalism foregrounds and therefore takes responsibility for how and with whom it collaborates in these tales of the institution of the news responding to powerful sources through planned and sustained collaborations, often with otherwise weak or even unheard sources, to cast fresh light on the workings of power.

A journalism of connections

The second, and related, model involves less of an emphasis on journalism which exposes corruption and more on connecting up information on the workings of power and therefore fostering greater transparency. Contemporary Western journalism operates in an information-saturated society, what Castells (1996) terms information-alism, in which power lies not so much in having information as in being able to deploy it quickly. This is true of financial markets, but also of the struggle against dictatorship. In Zimbabwe, for example, a key part of the story of struggle is the use made of digital media by groups such as Sokwanele Civic Action Support Group,[2] which gathered the results of the 2008 presidential and parliamentary ballots, posted outside each polling booth, making it harder for the Harare-based electoral commission to massage the final figures. During the subsequent political turmoil its website also featured a 'mash-up', or combination of media forms, in which a map of Zimbabwe was overlaid with clickable icons representing political murders and acts of intimidation. This information, available in fragmented form elsewhere, became a powerful indictment when gathered together. A similar role is performed by 'Iraq Body Count', a website which gathers media accounts of the deaths of civilians since the US-led invasion of Iraq, as a pointed reminder to the US and UK governments of the civilian casualty figures they have themselves refused to make available. Many current experiments in US political investigative reporting are of this kind, from the Sunlight Foundation's digitising of US official documents (Allison 2008), to blogger Josh Marshall's use of his readers to plough through enormous piles of documents released during the Gonzalez scandal (Niles 2007). The information here is not the dramatic disclosure of previously hidden wrong behaviour which mobilises public sentiment. Journalism is not operating as a check on power but as an actor. Instead, the information makes sense in terms of the contemporary value placed on deliberative democracy (e.g. Giddens 1984: 114ff), where decision-making must be transparent, conducted on the public stage which the media themselves construct and call people to, in order to be legitimate. Because of the power of Sokwanele to link up voting information in near real time, the Zimbabwe elections happened partly through its investigations, and its website became one of the stages on which politics took place.

Final thoughts

Such stories are beginning to appear in fora such as the Investigative Reporters and Editors journal and at the many conferences now being hosted by the growing global networks of investigative reporters (see Aucoin 2008). They suggest two things. Firstly, when it is forced to change by external pressures, whether economic or cultural, journalism does not necessarily simply get worse. In some aspects it changes, and out of that change comes some realignment of journalism with its context. In a world where political groups strategise their use of the media and where media act as the central stage of political life, a journalism of radical independence is perhaps less tenable at times than one which enters into strategic partnerships to open up access to other voices. In a media-saturated, always-on world, media which are used as a stage on which information is linked up at speed, allow journalists and activists to make powerful claims to enact a more deliberative democracy. Secondly, these stories suggest there are many ways to do investigative journalism. There is some merit in the scepticism from some journalists of the hype over its investigative branch. The late Paul Foot, for example, has argued: 'all journalism worthy of the name carries with it a duty to ask questions, check facts, investigate' (Foot 1998: 81; cited in Sanders & Canel 2006: 454). The dominance of one mythic ideal of investigation is a limiting force within journalism. To close, while one would not want to celebrate the enormous economic pressures on news practice which are weakening the purchase of the Watergate ideal, there are other stories to tell.

Notes

1 See Wikipedia for a list of around 50 such '-gate' scandals: http://en.wikipedia.org/wiki/List_of_scandals_with_%22-gate%22_suffix.
2 Sokwanele is a Shona phrase that apparently translates as 'enough is enough'.

References

Allison, B. (2008) 'Real-time watchdogs: Sunlight Foundation bloggers chip away at government secrets', *IRE Journal*, 31(2): 20–22.
Aucoin, J.L. (2008) 'Investigative reporting', in W. Donsbach (ed.), *The International Encyclopedia of Communication*, Cambridge: Blackwell Reference Online.
Barthes, R. (1973) *Mythologies*, London: Granada.
Bennett, W.L. (2001) *News: the Politics of Illusion*, New York: Addison Wesley Longman.
Benson, R. and Hallin, D.C. (2005) 'How states, markets and globalization shape the news: French and American national political journalism, 1965-1997'. Paper presented at International Communication Association conference, New York City, 26–30 May.
Blevens, F. (1997) 'The shifting paradigms of investigative journalism in the 20th century', *American Journalism*, 14(3/4): 257–61.
Castells, M. (1996) *The Rise of the Network Society*, Oxford: Blackwell.
Cottle, S. (2006) 'Mediatized rituals: beyond manufacturing consent', *Media, Culture and Society*, 28(3): 411–32.
Davies, N. (2008) *Flat Earth News: an award-winning reporter exposes falsehood, distortion and propaganda in the global media*, London: Chatto & Windus.
Diamond, L. and Plattner, M.F. (1993) *The Global Resurgence of Democracy*, Baltimore: Johns Hopkins University Press.
Doig, A. (1997) 'The decline of investigatory journalism', in M. Bromley and T. O'Malley (eds) *Journalism: a reader*, London: Routledge, pp. 189–213.
Ekström, M. and Johansson, B. (2008) 'Talk scandals', *Media, Culture and Society*, 30(1): 61–79.
El Gody, A. (2007) 'Al Jazeera and the power of political scandal in Arab democratization process'. Paper presented at International Communication Association conference, San Francisco, 24–28 May.
Esser, F. and Hartung, U. (2004) 'Nazis, pollution, and no sex: political scandals as a reflection of political culture in Germany', *American Behavioral Scientist*, 47(8): 1040–71.
Ettema, J. S. and Glasser, T.L. (1998) *Custodians of Conscience: investigative journalism and public virtue*, New York: Columbia University Press.
Feldstein, M. (2007) 'Dummies and ventriloquists: models of how sources set the investigative agenda', *Journalism*, 8(5): 499–509.

Foot, P. (1998) 'The slow death of investigative journalism', in S. Glover (ed.) *Secrets of the Press: journalists on journalism*, London: Allen Lane: pp. 79–89.

Gaines, W. (2007) 'Lost art of infiltration', *Journalism*, 8(5): 495–98.

Giddens, A. (1984) *The Constitution of Society: outline of the theory of structuration*, Cambridge: Polity.

Hauben, R. (2005) 'OhmyNews and 21st-century journalism', *OhmyNews (International)*, 9 September. Online. Available: http://english.ohmynews.com/articleview/article_view.asp?menu=c10400&no=2467 87&rel_no=1 (accessed 29 August, 2008).

Lewis, C. (2007) 'The non-profit road', *Columbia Journalism Review*, 46(3): 32–36.

Liebes, T. and Blum-Kulka, S. (2004) 'It takes two to blow the whistle: do journalists control the outbreak of scandal?' *American Behavioral Scientist*, 47(9): 1153–70.

Mair, J. (2008) 'Review: *Flat Earth News*', Ethical Space, 5(2): 47–8.

Niles, R. (2007) 'Lessons from "Talking Points Memo" and the U.S. attorney scandal', *Online Journalism Review*, 20 March. Online. Available: http://www.ojr.org/ojr/stories/070320niles/ (accessed 1 September).

O'Neill, O. (2002) *Autonomy and Trust in Bioethics*, Cambridge: Cambridge University Press.

Rosen, J. (2005) 'Deep Throat, j-school and newsroom religion', *PressThink*, 5 June. Online. Available: http://journalism.nyu.edu/pubzone/weblogs/pressthink/2005/06/05/wtrg_js.html (accessed 28 August 2008).

Sanders, K. and Canel, M.J. (2006) 'A scribbling tribe: reporting political scandal in Britain and Spain', *Journalism*, 7(4): 453–76.

Schudson, M. (1995) *The Power of News*, London: Harvard University Press.

Schudson, M. (2004) 'Notes on scandal and the Watergate legacy', *American Behavioral Scientist*, 47(9): 1231–38.

Thomas, J. (2000) 'The Daily Mirror and the popular press in the twentieth century', *Media History*, 6(2): 207–8.

Thompson, J.B. (2000) *Political Scandal: power and visibility in the media age*, Cambridge: Polity Press.

Tumber, H. and Waisbord, S.R. (2004a) 'Introduction: political scandals and media across democracies, volume I', *American Behavioral Scientist*, 47(8): 1031–39.

Tumber, H. and Waisbord, S.R. (2004b) 'Introduction: political scandals and media across democracies, volume II', *American Behavioral Scientist*, 47(9): 1143–52.

Waisbord, S. (1996) 'Investigative journalism and political accountability in South American democracies', *Critical Studies in Mass Communication*, 13(4): 343–72.

Weinberg, S. (1996) *The Reporter's Handbook: an investigator's guide to documents and techniques*, New York: St Martin's Press.

Williams, B.A. and Delli Carpini, M.X. (2004) 'Monica and Bill all the time and everywhere: the collapse of gatekeeping and agenda setting in the new media environment', *American Behavioral Scientist*, 47(9): 1208–30.

Zelizer, B. (1993) 'Journalists as interpretive communities', *Critical Studies in Mass Communication*, 10(2): 219–37.

Zelizer, B. (2004) 'When facts, truth, and reality are God-terms: on journalism's uneasy place in cultural studies', *Communication and Critical/Cultural Studies*, 1(1): 100–19.

Part II
NEWS AND SOCIAL AGENDAS

9

NEWS AND DEMOCRACY IN THE UNITED STATES: CURRENT PROBLEMS, FUTURE POSSIBILITIES

Herbert J. Gans

American journalists have long insisted that they are essential to the persistence of American democracy, but they have not devoted much thought to what exactly they do for the country's representative democracy. I asked this question and a second one, what they *could* do, in a book published in 2003, *Democracy and the News*, but enough change has taken place in the news media since then to consider both questions once more.

This chapter asks first what the news media can do, looking at the roles they and journalists play in the polity. Then it reviews current and likely future changes in the news media and concludes by asking what else the news media and the journalists could do in support of representative democracy.

Political roles of the news media

If the truth be told, America's journalists have done less on behalf of the country's democracy than they believe. However, they operate with a theory of democracy and a conception of their own responsibility which only require them to present as much political and, when relevant, economic and other news as is logically feasible. If citizens pay proper attention to the news they receive, the theory claims, they will become informed citizens and will then be able to carry out their political responsibilities as citizens, which will in turn preserve and strengthen American democracy.

This theory remains unwritten and is therefore not discussed or debated. Nevertheless, it is dubious on many grounds. While it seems clear that without news media of some kind, democracy cannot survive, all societies with formal political institutions, democratic or non-democratic, have news media. Even totalitarian polities could not long continue without them. Still, the presence of functioning news media does not automatically result either in a population of informed citizens or in a democratic society.

Still, because a considerable proportion of the news is about government and politics, the news media clearly play some roles in, and have some effects on democracy. Four such roles strike me as most important although there are several others which surface from time to time:

1. *Messengers for the political elites.* Probably the most important role of the news media, especially the major ones reaching the largest number of people, is to report what they think are the most important new political and politically relevant happenings. Sometimes, they are reporting democracy in action or democracy in harm's way, although the stories are not necessarily framed explicitly in that way.

Given the limited number of words and minutes that most news media can allocate to individual news stories, they mainly report the actions and statements of the highest government officials. Since they generally pass on the stories these officials tell them, their reportage may be described as *passive*, and so much so that journalists are sometimes criticized as stenographers for the top political leaders they consider newsworthy. Passive reporting offers visibility and publicity to the public officials who get into the news most often, but keeps invisible those officials without the publicity apparatus and the ability to make news available to the public.

When leaders disagree on issues journalists consider important, the news media report the disagreements between and conflicts among them. These are usually constructed as being between two sides, with the reporters distancing themselves sufficiently so that they do not consciously favor either side. Then the reporting can become *active*, with journalists interviewing other sources, ostensibly to help the news audience inform itself about the conflict and to decide which side they support.

American journalists do their most active political reporting around election campaign news, however, and since American election campaigns are so long, a great deal of domestic news is pegged to the next national election. In recent years, reporters have been supplemented by the commentators, columnists and other pundits who offer analyses and opinions on cable television news channels and the principal political web sites. When there is time or space to fill, they minutely describe, analyze and evaluate every new campaign activity or statement, but almost always to judge whose electoral chances will be helped or hurt this time. The horse race trumps issues and all other electoral news.

2. *Messengers for the citizenry.* From time to time, the news media also report on the political involvements of the citizenry, although such news is usually limited to their attitudes as reported by pollsters and to their voting decisions. In addition, the news media report major demonstrations, protest marches and the like, though mainly to indicate whether they were accompanied by "trouble" for the police or the targets of the demonstrations. Occasionally, the activities of the more important lobbies that speak for citizens make it into the news.

3. *Disaster messengers.* The news media regularly report on disasters, especially those with large losses of American life or property, but also events that upset people, such as dramatic increases in gasoline prices. Disasters are in the news for several reasons but the resulting stories are relevant to democracy because they have or are expected to have political consequences. Disasters that typically play a political role include major hurricanes and other destructive acts of nature, manmade accidents, terrorist attacks, as well as the foreign atrocities, genocides and other incidents of political violence that can have domestic political effects. At the time of this writing in the fall of 2008, the worldwide economic crisis has joined the list of politically relevant disasters, but sizable declines in the stock market have always been important disaster news.

4. *Watchdogs.* The news media function as watchdogs or guardians on behalf of several politically relevant American values, and see it as their role to expose corruption, malfeasance, dishonesty, hypocrisy, scandal and the violation of other mainstream rules of behavior.

Most watchdog journalism appears in everyday reporting, whenever journalists spot or are told about deviant political behavior, although the watchdog role is usually associated with investigative reporting that results in individual wrongdoing or systemic malfeasance being exposed. In fact, sometimes journalists function as watchdogs by their mere presence, for politicians do not curse when reporters are around and the US military does not commit atrocities when video cameras are there to record them. In this role, as in some others, journalists are representing the country's political and other norms, and, thereby, the citizenry itself.

Most politically relevant watchdog reporting takes place on behalf of what I have described as altruistic democracy, in which politicians are expected to be honest, efficient, meritocratic, respectful of the Constitution and other official values, and devoted to a selfless pursuit of the public interest.

Although the news media make the conventional American separation of polity and economy, altruistic democracy goes hand in hand with what I call responsible capitalism, in which firms compete with each other in order to create economic growth and prosperity for all, in the process refraining from unreasonable profits, gross exploitation of workers and customers and dishonest ways of doing business.

Journalists attach great importance to their watchdog role, and investigative reporting is a highly rewarded activity. The profession's most prestigious prizes are regularly presented to those who have produced successful exposés, such as the identification of public officials who can be removed from office or sent to jail. Sometimes exposés can bring about political or social reform, including lasting structural change that reduces the chance that new villains will replace old ones.

Even what I have called everyday watchdog journalism and its reporting of deviant behavior can have major consequences. For example, "Watergate" and the eventual abdication of President Nixon began with the investigation of an unusual burglary. More recently, Katie Couric's determined followup questioning of 2008 Vice Presidential candidate Sarah Palin revealed her meager lack of politically relevant knowledge. Had her handlers been successful in keeping her away from the news media, Governor Palin's shortcomings might not have become known in time.

Both kinds of watchdog journalism enable the news media to make direct contributions to democracy. However, such contributions are rare and unpredictable, often accidental, and usually dependent on forces and agents other than the news media alone.

The four roles I have described and the values associated with them are implicit in the detached or objective reporting still practiced by most reporters. In addition, the values often become explicit in some of the commentary that accompanies the news, whether as editorials, op eds, columns, letters and their cable television and web equivalents, or in the so called fake news of comedians like Jon Stewart, Stephen Colbert and Bill Maher. In fact, cable television and digital news media often emphasize commentary, which requires only a set of professional or amateur pundits and can therefore avoid the costs of a fully staffed professional news organization. Pundits can state many opinions on politically relevant topics inside the ideological boundaries in which mainstream news exists, but they are usually expected to abide by the values defended by watchdogs and those implicit in the other main types of watchdog journalism.

The changing news media

The changes that have taken place in the news media in the last decade and that are expected in the next one are by now familiar: continuing shrinkages in the old print and electronic news media combined with growth in the number and content of the websites that constitute the new digital news media. In fact, the old news media are shrinking in every way, in size of staffs, audience, advertising, profits, and, in the print media at least, in the size of the newshole as well, while the digital news media are growing in every respect. We are now involved in a technological and economic transition from old to new news media.

Technological transitions rarely put an end to the old, and predictions that newspapers, magazines and radio and television news will soon be extinct are not credible. Most observers of the news business agree that there will be fewer daily newspapers ten years hence, and today's weekly news magazines may be reduced to one. Perhaps the three commercial network television evening news programs will decrease in number too, although it is hard to imagine that any network will want to be the first to give up its most visible news program.

Even so, the shrinkage is not complete; when the news is especially newsworthy, at least in the eyes of the audience, even the news media with budgetary problems expand their coverage to meet audience demand.

Concurrently, the growth of digital news is in some respects deceptive because websites that obtain their content from their own news organizations are still rare. Most digital news is still supplied by the journalists who also gather and report news for the print and electronic news media although the websites now usually report it first. Only the political blogs, the web's equivalent of the print media journals of opinion, feature their own staffs, although by no means all are paid.

Eventually, the news websites will be choosing the news staffs, although they may still spend part of their worktime supplying their employers' electronic and print media. Most of the web news audience will probably have gravitated to a small number of primary news websites, the digital equivalent of today's television networks and national newspapers and news magazines. In addition, the primary news websites are likely to be run by a handful of major news firms, perhaps some of the same ones now supplying the news. The mainstream news media will just have moved to cyberspace.

The news audience is also moving to the web, but audiences are harder to count, and understand, than websites. We know that the audiences for the print and electronic news media are also continuing to shrink, but that may be partly a result of the audience's fragmentation – its access to so many more news sources. Also, since most electronic and digital news media repeat their major news stories all day long, it is possible that today's audiences – other than those addicted to the news – are less likely or perhaps less willing than earlier ones to pay attention to the same stories several times a day.

In addition, the actual consumption of news remains a mystery. Circulation and ratings figures cannot reveal how much actual reading, listening and viewing is going on. Even the costly audience studies undertaken in flush times could not measure these accurately – or how well the news audience comprehends what it receives and how much it absorbs. Equivalent doubts can be raised about the digital news audience, at least until audience researchers learn more about the meaning of "hits" and how much attention to the news is involved in the hitting process.

Some political effects of news media changes

The new technology will have a number of other effects on the news, but three seem to have the greatest implications for the relation between the news and democracy.

First, the digital news media have added several new players that will be important to the future of news. One is a new set of rumor mongers, messengers of fake facts and creators of hateful images. Although they have always existed, they have been largely ignored or filtered out by the print and electronic news media so that they survived only in interpersonal communication. Now, there are endless websites on which they can flourish.

The two other newcomers are likely to have more positive effects. One is the ever larger set of bloggers and their commenters. Whether they are ordinary people or experts, they vastly expand the supply of columns, op eds and letters to the editor. Moreover, they help to enlarge the so called public sphere and they add many voices to the democratic "conversation" which some theorists believe is necessary for the health of democracy. Indeed, the bloggers and their respondents already offer a test to determine what role, if any, that conversation plays in democracy. Perhaps more important, groups of bloggers are creating citizen websites which, if they and their audiences are numerous enough, have political potential and could someday act as mobilizers for particular causes. Remember that MoveOn began as a citizen website.

The other new arrivals are the people, mostly amateurs but some with journalistic training, who contribute usable news, photos, videos and tips to the news media as well as nonjournalistic websites with huge audiences such as YouTube. Currently they are called citizen-journalists, even though they do not make their contributions as citizens and they are not journalists.

Whether people could function both as citizens and journalists at the same time raises provocative issues in both democratic and journalistic theory. These deserve discussion, but the people now labeled citizen-journalists should be called amateur reporters or contributors. Some will undoubtedly become regular enough to turn into stringers, the paid and unpaid part-timers who have always submitted stories and tips, and some might eventually become professional journalists.

These digital contributors have arrived at an appropriate time because the shrinkage of news media and staffs has reduced the journalists' ability to monitor the entire society. In addition, some contributors are located in places which journalists do not normally monitor or from which they are barred. When such places suddenly produce newsworthy events, the amateur contributors can be replaced or complemented by trained reporters.

Admittedly, contributors and even stringers are cheap, creating the danger that they may replace some professional journalists if news firms continue to slash budgets. Moreover, untrained contributors can make serious mistakes that impair the credibility of the news media, and if their role becomes significant enough, they ought to receive some basic training and supervision by professional journalists. Otherwise, unsupervised amateurs can easily become rumor mongers.

A second effect of the arrival of digital news is the lower visibility of the news. Newspapers, magazines and television create a dominating presence that websites have not, or at least not yet, achieved. Someday that low visibility could affect the political influence and status of the news media in general, especially during periods when world and national happenings do not attract widespread audience interest.

A third effect is the overall reduction in the number of journalists, and thus of professionals trained to inform society about itself. We should be collecting data on how well societies inform themselves, including the number of trained journalists per capita.

Because news supply always exceeds demand, most of the news audience may not have noticed, or cared about, the reduction of news bureaus and journalists, but the reductions affect the roles that journalists play in democracy. Everyday watchdogging and investigative reporting may be affected the most. If elected officials know that fewer journalists are monitoring them, they may also be somewhat freer to ignore the electorate, for bad and good.

Needless to say, the decline in the number of journalists resulted mainly from the economic slowdown of the last decade, and from the shift of advertising from the traditional news media to the internet. However, digital news may require fewer journalists than the print and electronic news media. At least now, digital news is shorter; websites do not often present 40-paragraph stories or hour-long documentaries.

Ultimately, the fate of the news media depends on the health of the economy: how much spending money the news audience has in its pockets, and therefore how much advertising the news media will receive and most important, how much news websites can charge for it. In addition that fate depends on the audience's need and desire for news; and its need depends on what happens in the world that is relevant to the audience's lives. For example, if the country's economy remains fragile and if government intervenes more extensively in the economy, I imagine the audience demand for economic news could increase. However, should people ever be fully satisfied with the economy and polity, they may reduce their need to know what is going on. Conversely, they could also be so disgusted with and alienated from their society that they may reduce their desire to know what is going on.

The likely changes in future news media and audiences will have effects on the four roles of the news media described above. The elite messenger function would surely remain; as long as elected and appointed officials need to get their message out, they will also need news media and journalists who can function as their stenographers. Moreover, the journalists need public officials, because they can be counted on to produce the speeches, actions, events, as well as drama and conflict, with which journalists fill up their newsholes.

News about the citizenry is also likely to survive. It may not be frequent and politically important enough to attract the major news media, including the web's most popular news sites. However, politically inclined bloggers and perhaps literal citizen-journalists who are interested in reporting and encouraging citizen political activity may be keen contributors.

Disaster news always draws journalists and attracts audiences and will therefore also survive. Amateurs with video cameras are already supplying such news when they are on the scene before the professionals arrive and they will surely continue to do so.

Everyday watchdog news will continue too, at least as long as there is room and money in news organizations for reporters who are more than passive stenographers. Investigative reporting, being expensive, would suffer, especially if there are cheaper ways to website "hits". Journalism as a profession feels strongly about its watchdog function, but whether economically fragile or politically nervous news firms will be able to do so is another question.

Implications for democracy

What might these changes in the news mean for American democracy? Since elected officials need journalists as much as the latter need elected officials as news story sources, the news media are here to stay.

Much depends on how the digital news media adapt to their sources and audiences. Presumably, someday the stories that lead the websites of the national news media will obtain the same kind of initial attention as the first page of today's *New York Times*. If the digital news media are willing and able to compete with each other in covering important stories, obtaining exclusives and producing exposés, the main roles that the news media play in democracy may be unchanged.

Moreover, if the bloggers and their websites continue to increase the amount of opinion available to the news audience, they could, in the future, reduce the pluralistic ignorance in which most Americans are embedded and increase people's knowledge of what others think. If and when sizable populations discover that they hold the same opinions and with the same intensity, their elected representatives will surely take notice.

However, if most of the web's news audience will eventually choose the same handful of mainstream sites that they do today on network and cable television, the national conversation could be limited, and dominated by many of the same voices that are heard today. What will happen probably depends less on the news media than on the country's economic and political conditions and on the polity that deals with them.

Today, most citizens have little to do with government other than during election campaigns – in fact, government has little use for them – and it is not clear how much election campaign news affects potential voters. In 2008, a record amount of campaign spending had the net result of increasing voting only up to 57 percent. Moreover, every election is different, even if the news media continue to cover it as a horse race and play down the issues. Besides, many people seem to prefer news and opinion that support their own stands on the issues. Facts do not always alter opinions and far more people get their opinions from each other than from the news media.

Consequently, one should not expect that the news media, even in a digital era in which news and opinion websites abound and everyone is linked to every other one, can have a greater effect on democracy than they do now.

Increasing the journalistic contribution to democracy

What, then, might be done to increase the journalistic contribution to America's representative democracy. Such a contribution would have to come from all the major players: news firms, advertisers, journalists and the audience.

The prime task for today's news firms is to find ways of restoring their economic health; only then could they consider whether to risk greater involvement in the polity that would probably be required by further democratization of the country. However, the firms' economic health depends on both the advertisers and the audience, and thus on that of the country. If it has money in its pocket, a growing audience is likely to increase advertiser interest, even in the print and electronic news media, if these move goods and services more effectively than the internet.

But how to increase the audience? Before such a question can be answered, much more must be learned about it and the roles the news plays in its life. Few industries now know as little about their audiences as the news media.

Researchers appear to agree that young people are paying less interest than in the past, although old people have constituted the majority or plurality of the news audience for a long time. We should ask more about the young: how much news they believe they actually need – and why or whether they are shorter of time these days than young people in the past. Perhaps they believe that their everyday lives do not require keeping up with the news – or only with certain news subjects – and maybe they are unwilling to pay attention to the old people who are the major newsmakers.

Adequate information about the news audience may provide clues about how to enlarge the audience, but meanwhile, two ways suggest themselves. One is to rethink the language of the news, making it less technical and more comprehensible so as to attract new people. Comprehension data is hard to come by but sizable portions of the present news audience do not understand everything in even the major stories and a significant number who are not in the news audience might join or rejoin it if the news were easier to understand.

Perhaps parts of the audience would like the news to be more anecdotal than it already is, or less so, or more conversational, a change already apparent in texting and other forms of digital communication. In addition, professionals might learn from what I call everyday newswork; from how ordinary people tell their families about the day's activities and report what they consider to be newsworthy information to friends and workmates.

The second way of enlarging the audience, already suggested, is to increase people's need for news. If everyday life depended on information available only from the news media, more people would have to turn to the news. Alternatively, if government and politics were reorganized to require greater citizen involvement, the news audience would undoubtedly increase.

A larger audience should attract more advertisers who will help to revitalize news firms. However, if commercially supplied news cannot be made economically viable, at least some news organizations would have to be funded from governmental or nonprofit sector monies. Some media thinkers have even suggested bringing back the party press and letting parties own newspapers and sponsor TV news programs.

Alternatively, the news media could be reorganized as utilities which would be regulated to supply a steadier but lower profit. Even some form of the European licensing system could be explored, even though it has not found favor in America in the past. Moreover, declining commercial ventures do not often attract nonprofit or public funding.

Meanwhile, outside funding sources should be encouraged to pay for, or help to pay for investigative reporting that news organizations would otherwise be unable to afford. "The Nation" and other small news organizations already draw on such sources from small foundations. Some of the big foundations should be able and willing to pay for larger investigative reporting projects for the mainstream news media. However, funding such reporting can be politically risky, and the foundations will need protection, perhaps through an equivalent form of the shield laws that protect journalists.

Journalists have a task as well: to rethink their professional role. In an interdependent world, the conception of newsworthiness – what makes a story important and to whom – needs to be rethought. More journalists need to be analytic more frequently, going beyond description and adding interpretation as well as explanation, especially about topics that many people find confusing. Currently, the need for more journalists knowledgeable about the economy and not just business should be obvious.

In addition, beat reporters and others who have covered an important happening exhaustively should be encouraged to use their fact gathering to draw conclusions and offer evaluations and opinions, using what they have learned to enable the news audience to make up its mind about the happening. General reporters can continue to stick to "the facts" and the distancing called objectivity. But journalists generally need to be more active and to minimize passive or stenographic journalism.

Although journalists cannot make this and other changes on their own, rethinking the obligations and goals of the profession will put some pressure on news organizations and news firms to make them when economic conditions are conducive.

The news media: necessary but insufficient

Journalists like to claim that, because knowledge is power, their knowledge is powerful. More often, however, the opposite is true; power determines what knowledge is relevant to effective political participation. Almost all of the knowledge transmitted by the news media fails this test, and even news buffs who are addicted to the news are not empowered politically by reading, viewing or listening to everything they can get their hands on. Citizens must turn elsewhere and for other kinds of information if they want to intervene in the political process. Moreover, the news media are not political institutions that can enhance or prevent threats to democracy. For example, they could do nothing to discourage the Bush administration from centralizing more power in the executive branch. The news media are messengers; change agents must come from elsewhere.

In the final chapter of *Democracy and the News* I suggested some of the kinds of structural change needed for further democratization in America; among them, a growth of citizen lobbies to counter the corporate lobbies and their professional and other allies; restructuring the Senate, the Electoral College and other governmental and political bodies that now prevent majority rule; as well as a reduction of economic inequality so that economic power holders cannot wield an unfair share of political power.

During the 2008 presidential election campaign, the two candidates divided America into "Wall Street" and "Main Street". Both are imaginaries that should not be taken too literally, but if America were ready for further democratization, it would have to mainly benefit "the middle class" and others associated with Main Street. In that case, the national news media would have to find ways of further distancing themselves from the corporate commercial world represented by Wall Street.

Commercial news firms cannot stop being commercial news firms, but journalists can be more than messengers from the top of the polity and the economy and detached reporters of the policies proposed and legislated at the top. Although it is dangerous to project current ideals on to the newest technology, perhaps the coming digital age will make it possible, somehow, for the news media to become more pluralistic, and among other things to become effective messengers from, as well as, to Main Street.

10
THE PRESS, POWER AND PUBLIC ACCOUNTABILITY*

W. Lance Bennett

Two interesting dimensions emerge from investigations of press–state relationships in the Western democratic nations: consistently strong norms favoring press freedom and journalistic independence, contrasted with markedly different media cultures defining the social responsibility of the press vis-à-vis audiences and public officials (Hallin & Mancini, 2004; Hanitzsch, 2007). As McQuail (2003) has pointed out, these dimensions of press freedom and public accountability are curiously independent and poorly articulated ideals in democratic life. Without freedom, accountability is jeopardized, yet freedom does not guarantee that media organizations will advance the public interest or take adversarial and independent stances toward government, business, and other centers of power in society. Even when accountability standards are imposed, the press may resist for various reasons ranging from a misplaced sense of autonomy to commercial pressures favoring sensational content. The relationship between freedom and accountability is further vexed when the politicians who create and enforce accountability standards do not see the public interest as separate from their own partisan goals. The result is an enduring democratic dilemma that often turns press freedom into a political shield against imposed standards of public accountability.

This chapter explores the dilemmas of power and accountability that results from press dependence on official sources that offer spin instead of transparent information about their activities and motives. This dilemma goes to the core of the quality of public information in democracies, and illustrates why press freedom is a necessary but not sufficient guardian of the public interest. The argument proceeds in several parts, beginning with an explanation of why press freedom is not a sufficient condition for the production of timely and useful public information, even by the best news organizations. The next step of the argument is to examine how press organizations that become overly dependent on official sources for their raw material can end up being spun into communication branches of the state. This argument is then illustrated by an analysis of press coverage of the Iraq War during the Bush administration. The conclusion offers a few modest proposals for developing a more independent press.

Why press freedom does not guarantee quality public information

The United States offers an example of why guarantees of press freedom do not routinely produce content diversity or journalistic independence from political spin. Protections for the press in the United States are among the most developed in the world. A survey of journalists in five nations (Britain, Italy, Germany, Sweden and the United States) conducted by Donsbach and Patterson (2004) revealed that US journalists claimed fewer restrictions on their approaches to hypothetical stories, yet US journalists also employed a narrower range of sources and story frames than those in other countries (Patterson, 1992). Indeed, content analyses indicate this oft-proclaimed "world's freest press" produces great homogeneity in the range of sources and viewpoints in policy and events coverage (Political Communication, 2006; Bennett, Lawrence, and Livingston, 2007). This uniformity of output in the US press system does not mean that there is a consistent lack of controversy or debate. For example, a study of discourses on abortion in US and German media found that the range of voices and viewpoints was considerably greater and more prominent in the US media than in Germany (Feree et al., 2002). Thus, most mainstream US news organizations may display similar content, but the range of sources and views in that news content expands when there is broad institutional debate on issues such as abortion, and shrinks when institutional debate narrows on issues such as the decision to invade Iraq. As a result, the news often seems more a record of the ebb and flow of political power than a steady or independent discussion of the issues over which those power struggles are waged.

A prolonged deregulatory trend favoring commercialization of the news product is often associated with deteriorating news quality and capacity to challenge dubious government policies and actions (McChesney, 2004). The pressures of market forces on the quality of journalism are not new. Habermas (1989) traced the erosion of an independent media sphere to the rise of commercial media and advertising in the nineteenth century. Indeed, the dilemmas of press independence led to the creation of public service broadcasting systems in most democracies. Yet public service channels increasingly compete for audiences attracted to commercial alternatives, and they are no less immune from dependence on official sources competing for daily stories. Given these trends, the problem of how to engineer a vital public sphere from the standpoint of public accountability is far from obvious.

How political power can impose limits on public accountability

The most obvious answer to the question of when public accountability in the press is achieved is that it most often occurs when the formal institutions of politics (elected parties, legislatures, executives, courts) publicly engage in open debates over policy issues. When parties or factions are in public conflict, the news is more likely to contain a richer range of information and ideas. Although it is often alleged (by both politicians and academics) that the press sets the public agenda, the opposite may more often be true, as outlined in what I have called the *indexing theory* (Bennett, 1990):

a) Officials in institutions of government generally make the news

and

b) Journalists in various national press systems rely on established norms that implicitly filter or "index" the sources and viewpoints in the news according to perceived power balances among factions within political institutions.

The close alignment of a democratic press system to official institutional outputs makes a certain amount of sense at one level because reporting to the people on the governments they have elected is what publics generally expect the press do. In this process of providing daily updates on what politicians are doing, journalists become routinely exposed to officials and press handlers trying to get their daily spin into the news. Press coverage is crucial for politicians' capacity to dominate public debate, which makes the press an important institution of governing, although not in the sense that most democratic theorists think of it (Cook, 1998). The question is: How do different news systems manage and negotiate this proximity of journalists to power?

It is tempting to conclude, as McQuail (2003) does, that, despite the many different solutions for addressing the freedom–accountability dilemma, most press systems in advanced democracies seem to be doing a reasonably good job. But what does it mean for the press to be doing a good job in routine times? When governments are pursuing their electoral mandates in relatively transparent fashion and the opposition is holding governing coalitions accountable on performance measures, the tendency of the press to filter and repackage the range of official (government and opposition) spin may offer a reasonably good public account of issues and events.

However, periods when democracy is functioning reasonably well do not really test the qualities of an independent press. The key question about the press and the state is what happens when governing institutions fall to corruption, incompetence, political intimidation, deception, or deal making, and the range of official spin becomes a poor or misleading account of the events and issues in the news? What happens in these moments when an official opposition fails to arise to hold government accountable?

The Bush administration revealed a good deal about the precarious dependence of the US press on the commitment of public officials, themselves, to democratic values such as public accountability and honesty. Consider, for example, an interview between a senior Bush advisor and Ron Suskind, a prominent journalist who was concerned about the truthfulness of administration claims about the war. The advisor, as if stepping from the pages of Baudrillard, dismissed the journalist and his colleagues as belonging to the "reality-based community." While journalists and academics were preoccupied with nagging matters of truth, the government was using its powers to create reality:

> We're an empire now, and when we act, we create our own reality. And while you're studying that reality – judiciously, as you will – we'll act again, creating other new realities, which you can study too, and that's how things will sort

out. We're history's actors ... and you, all of you, will be left to just study what we do. (Bennett, Lawrence & Livingston, 2007: 138)

Happily for democracy, not all governments are as willing to sacrifice accountability for hegemonic power as the Bush administration was, but the critical question for thinking about public accountability is: How does the press behave when governments do operate like this? In many cases, in their efforts to get the inside story about what the government is doing, journalists end up reporting the government spin intended to advance its projections of power (Entman, 2004). The result is that the press (in this case, the US press) becomes particularly vulnerable to not reporting other sides of big stories simply because an official opposition seems ineffective or nonexistent. In other words, the press becomes a communication arm of government – albeit one that may compete fiercely for getting inside interviews with the top sources spinning the story, as happened repeatedly during coverage of Bush administration Iraq policies.

The case of Iraq

Even though poorly documented Bush administration stories about weapons of mass destruction were directly contradicted by United Nations weapons inspectors' accounts from inside Iraq, the headlines of the leading US newspapers such as the *New York Times* and the *Washington Post* (and most of the thousands of daily television programs and local papers that those elite organizations influence) primarily contained Bush administration spin (Bennett, Lawrence and Livingston, 2007).

Following the invasion of Iraq and the failure of Bush administration claims to correspond to observable realities, both the *Washington Post* (Kurtz, 2004) and the *New York Times* (2004) responded to reader pressure by issuing unusual apologies for letting the story become so dominated by administration sources that in retrospect seemed unreliable.

Following these revealing apologies, one might expect these prestigious news organizations to correct their mistakes and cover the next big story differently. Yet the indexing theory predicts that, under the same conditions, the press will behave in the same way. The next big story came shortly after these moments of journalistic self-reflection about failures in their coverage, providing something of a natural experiment through which to test the predictive capacity of the indexing theory.

The press and Abu Ghraib

By any measure, the Abu Ghraib prison story that broke at the end of March 2004 was among the biggest international news events of the war. The shocking photos of cruelty to Iraqi prisoners being held by the US in one of Saddam's worst prisons created volumes of coverage and protest around the world. The images included a hooded man standing on a box with electrical wires coming from his body, dogs menacing naked prisoners, and scenes of sexual humiliation. US news organizations, led by CBS television, and then the *Washington Post*, ran thousands of stories as congressional investigations kept the situation in the news through the summer of 2004, just months before the presidential and congressional elections in November.

The Bush administration labeled the scenes as a case of unfortunate but isolated *abuse* of prisoners by low-level personnel who would be punished. Yet evidence existed from the Red Cross and other human rights organizations that a more systematic pattern of cruelty, and perhaps even torture, was occurring in US detention facilities in Iraq, Afghanistan, Guantanamo, Cuba, and elsewhere. In addition, memos surfaced indicating that the White House legal counsel (later US Attorney General) Alberto Gonzalez had participated in constructing a legal cover to exempt interrogation practices in the war against terror from domestic and international laws against torture. The fascinating question then became how would the press frame these various elements of the situation.

Recall that the key factor for making a prediction based on indexing theory is the power balance among factions involved in key policy debates in the political institutions. In the case of Abu Ghraib, the political calculations of the opposition party resembled the same position they took before the war: for a weak Democratic party, torture seemed a volatile issue to present to American voters on the eve of an election. Even critics who would emerge later from within the Republican Party (e.g., Senator John McCain) remained quiet until after the election. The prediction under these circumstances is that the administration framing of a regrettable but isolated case of abuse (i.e., an isolated incident involving bad treatment) would dominate the news.

Along with colleagues Regina Lawrence and Steven Livingston, I gathered all *Washington Post* news articles and editorials on the scandal between 1 April (ahead of when the first photos appeared) and 31 August 2004 (when the official investigations and congressional hearings finished and the parties turned toward the election). This produced a sample of 242 news articles and 52 editorials, which were then coded for the news frames (torture, abuse, mistreatment, and scandal) used to describe the situation depicted in the photographs. The coding was done by trained coders and tested for reliability as reported in Bennett, Lawrence and Livingston (2007).[1] In addition, we gathered a LexisNexis sample of 895 articles and editorials from ten national newspapers,[2] and 54 CBS News reports over the same time period. The latter two samples were machine coded based on confidence that the hand coded *Washington Post* sample produced reliable and meaningful results. The general findings from all samples indicated that the administration framing of the story overwhelmingly dominated news coverage.

The results of the analysis in Table 10.01 (overleaf) of *Washington Post* news reports and editorials show that the administration frame of abuse dominated the news reports, accounting for fully 81 per cent of primary story frames (appearing in headlines and opening paragraphs of items), compared to just 3 per cent for the torture frame. Filling out the news plots were the terms "mistreatment" and "scandal." Together, these four frames accounted for 99 per cent of the leading frames found in all the news stories and editorials. While torture was more commonly introduced in editorials, even there, abuse was by far the dominant news theme. We also coded the news and editorials to allow for secondary frames to cover the possibility that torture might appear later in stories. Although the incidence of torture was slightly higher when multiple codes were permitted for each item, the administration spin still dominated the news (Bennett, Lawrence and Livingston, 2007: ch. 3).

Table 10.1 Primary labels used to describe Abu Ghraib, by type, *Washington Post*, 1 April 2004–31 August 2004

	"Abuse"	*"Torture"*	*"Mistreatment"*	*"Scandal"*
News (n = 242)	81% (188)	3% (9)	3% (7)	12% (29)
Editorials (n = 52)	61% (32)	17% (9)	3% (2)	13% (7)

*These data are based on the *first* label used in each article. Numbers in parentheses are the counts for each cell; percentages are not rounded.

Our national sample of big-city papers shown in Fgiure 10.1 indicates that the same pattern appeared. The pattern was also the same for television news, including CBS, the news organization that broke the story. Of the 54 CBS stories on Abu Ghraib over the summer of 2004, abuse was either the first or the second label used in 50 (92 per cent) of the stories, compared to torture appearing as either the first or second theme in just 10 (18 per cent) of the stories.

Our data indicate that, despite thousands of news stories and repeated showing of disturbing photographs, the Bush administration succeeded in spinning the story as a case of isolated abuse. Only after the election did a credible opposing perspective emerge. Ironically, it came from within the president's own party. Republican Senator John McCain – himself a prisoner of war in Vietnam, and a victim of torture – organized enough votes in the Senate to require the president to conform to the law and abandon practices known to be occurring in various US detention facilities. With this power shift in official decision circles, the news framing also shifted, and the term torture for the first time became more dominant than abuse.

The indexing theory thus explains how the mainstream US press missed almost entirely some very important sides to the Iraq story. It missed those sides of the story not because they were hard to see. To the contrary, they were plainly visible, and connected to credible sources. Indeed, several publications outside of the mainstream press (such as *The New Yorker* and the *New York Review of Books*) carried well-documented reports from journalists such as Seymour Hersh and Mark Danner. One suspects that most members of the national press read these reports. They simply could not follow them up in their own papers and broadcasts. Thus, the majority of the (generally inattentive) public was deprived of hearing much beyond administration spin. Not surprisingly, public opinion reflected this daily flow of official spin from a mainstream media that had become an unwitting propaganda arm of government. Well into 2006, majorities or large pluralities continued to echo Bush administration claims about reality (belief that weapons of mass destruction had been found in Iraq, that Saddam Hussein was involved in the 9/11 attacks, etc.). When the Democrats

Figure 10.1 Mentions of "torture" and other labels in connection with Abu Ghraib in news and editorial items, US national newspaper sample, 1 April 2004– 19 January 2005.

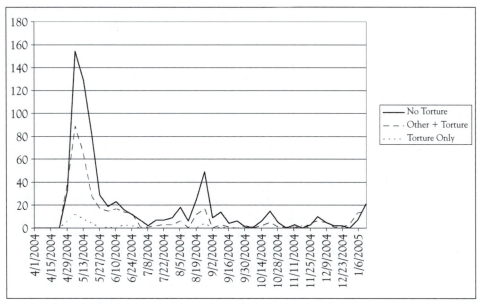

finally won narrow control of Congress in the 2006 elections and used that power position to begin mounting challenges to the administration on the war, the news began to expand to include other points of view (for example, calling the situation in Iraq a civil war, which the administration had long denied).

Indexing in other press systems

The US press system may be unusually prone to the collapse of political oppositions due to the lack of proportional representation and the difficulty of maintaining party positions and discipline in an unwieldy two party system. However, many press systems in the advanced democracies involve both highly professionalized official spin operations and the capacity of governments to reward and punish journalists and news organizations that are more or less cooperative. Add to this the growing dependence of public service broadcasting on government funding in increasingly market-oriented media environments, and the conditions seem ripe for some sort of political indexing to operate in different democracies.[3] Preliminary evidence suggests that variations on indexing may exist in different nations.

Indeed, news content across the mainstream press in many nations may be more similar than one might expect given seemingly substantial differences in media markets and the spectrum of partisan newspapers. For example, a study of British press coverage of several national policy issues showed that the mainstream press tended to follow the lines of party differences and cover party positions as the rough guide

111

to the range of content in the news (Bennett & Alexseev, 1995). In addition, the UK tradition of the "question time" ensures that some opposition voice is raised in public on most policy issues, providing news organizations with some range of story diversity as a result of routine newsgathering. Thus, even in the case of a political system with a relatively diverse press mixture (public service broadcasting, commercial broadcasting and papers, and a foundation operated partisan newspaper in the case of the *Guardian*), the basic news agenda still derives largely from official government activities and spin. For example, the party finance scandal that rocked the Brown government in 2007 was largely the result of an official investigation of party records, and spin from the opposition party (and, one suspects, the remaining Blair faction in the labour party) that kept the story in the news.

A similar party-based form of indexing appears to operate in the German press system (Vogelsang and Fretwurst, 2005; Maurer, 2005; Weiss and Trebbe, 2005). A study of two leading German papers with pronounced political differences (*Frankfurter Allgemeine Zeitung, Suddeutsche Zeitung*) on coverage of German involvement in three wars – Kosovo, Afghanistan, and Iraq – showed that both papers tended to co-vary in volume and direction with official views favoring or opposing involvement in the wars. The authors concluded that: "The general political orientation of German newspapers had no influence on their evaluations of the three wars" (Maurer *et al.*, 2008, 161).

Since it is unlikely that wars inherently tell journalists how to cover them, the likely intervening factor is how government and opposition line up in different cases. This is precisely what Weiss and Weiss (2005) concluded from their analysis of political positions on the three wars: "... media coverage of international crises and wars ... is closely linked to official national positions toward the respective wars." They note that Kosovo was supported across the entire political spectrum and that differences were resolved before military involvement began. As indexing would predict, Kosovo received the highest levels of positive (or pro-government) news content both on TV and across the spectrum of mainstream papers. Afghanistan was in the middle of the critical content spectrum, reflecting divisions in government (many Greens and leftist Social Democrats expressed reservations) about military involvement. Finally, involvement in Iraq was opposed across the political spectrum, and news content reflected this generally negative view of the war across television and different papers. Thus, the conventional wisdom that a more diverse press system (measured in these studies by public vs. private television, and politically left and right papers) would reflect greater differences across news organizations did not prove true. Different news organizations were more similar than different because they reflected more the range of official positions in political institutions. Weiss and Weiss (2008) conclude that the indexing hypothesis "can be extended beyond its initial focus on press state relations in the U.S." Vowe and Dohle (2007) cite other studies supporting a similar conclusion.

Conclusion

Does this mean that there are no differences among press systems when it comes to holding governments independently accountable for policy decisions? Such a broad claim seems unwarranted based on the evidence offered here. The tentative conclusion here is that high levels of political consensus (reached for whatever reason) may narrow the outputs of otherwise diverse press systems. At the same time, the routine daily news output of different systems may diverge along a number of important dimensions. For example, strong public service systems may offer more detailed coverage of more policy issues than commercial systems. On another dimension, press systems arrayed along general party or ideological lines may cover more issue positions from more diverse points of view (at least until the point that power distributions in official policy circles seem clear). Politically diverse press systems may also introduce more opinion and analysis into routine reporting than homogeneous systems such as the US that emphasize norms of neutrality and balance. Such differences may be important for generating interest and knowledge among citizens, and in making politicians aware that their everyday actions are subject to public scrutiny. Thus, public accountability may have multiple dimensions, and an important task is to identify more of them so that press systems can be observed in more refined ways.

This suggests that we may want to classify press systems less in terms of professional journalism norms or surface differences such as degree of commercialization vs. public service. Yet, scholars continue to analyze these surface qualities both because they are readily observable and because they offer an obvious means of categorizing different systems in formal terms. When comparing different systems, different types of political indexing are likely to be observed. Few democracies are as likely to marginalize opposition voices in policy debates (and, consequently, in the press) as in the US. More common, as the above cases of Germany and the UK indicate, are parliamentary systems in which opposition parties routinely take positions on issues. The range of viewpoints in news coverage generally reflects the degree and intensity of that parliamentary opposition.

In sum, the mixture of public service, commercial, and partisan organizations in a press system may contribute to the diversity of content. However, as the German studies reported above suggest, the organizational diversity within a press system may not make as much difference as common sense would suggest. Indeed, it is more the diversity of views among parties and public officials than in the press that determines the balance of viewpoints in the news. This is why it is important to try to determine how news organizations locate themselves in relation to political power rather than simply focus on the more explicit norms that define the journalistic profession. This capacity of political power to shape journalistic content is important to monitor as the *realpolitik* in every democratic system.

Is there a solution for the corrupting effects of power on public information? The obvious solution is for news organizations to temper the spin and the breathless 24/7 updates with old-fashioned investigative reporting. However, in the contemporary media environment where corporate pressures diminish the capacity of journalists to pursue the best traditions of their craft, this scenario does not seem promising. Perhaps the loss of public confidence in the press in nations such as the US, along with the rise of new digital information channels, will change the ways in which information is produced and consumed. Indeed, signs of change are evident in the large-scale participation of voters in the 2008 US election campaign through *youtube.com*, *myspace.com*, and candidate information/action networks such as *mybarackobama. com*. These digital platforms, along with the rise of numerous citizen journalism experiments, suggest that change is occurring. However, when it comes to informing large numbers of citizens about what government is doing, there still seems to be a need for something like independent journalism. Perhaps the pressures from large publics joined in independent digital networks will challenge news organizations to reposition themselves in the marketplace of ideas.

Note

* Portions of this chapter appear in *Politischen Vierteljarhesschrift* 42 (2008).

Notes

1 For a detailed discussion of the coding methods and reliability statistics see Bennett, Lawrence & Livingston (2007), pp. 89–92 and 208–209.
2 *Atlanta Journal and Constitution, Boston Globe, Chicago Sun-Times, Los Angeles Times, New York Times, Cleveland Plain Dealer, San Francisco Chronicle, Seattle Times, St. Petersburg Times, USA Today.*
3 Even the venerable BBC was severely disciplined by the Blair government for a story that accurately reported government intelligence spinning activities, but failed to report it properly.

References

Bennett, W.L. (1990) Toward a Theory of Press-State Relations. *Journal of Communication* 40 (2): 103–125.

Bennett, W.L. and Alexseev, M. (1995) For Whom the Gates Open: News Reporting and Government Source Patterns in the United States, Great Britain, and Russia. *Political Comunication*. 12: 395–412.

Bennett, W.L., Lawrence, R.G., and Livingston, S. (2007) *When the Press Fails: Political Power and the News Media from Iraq to Katrina*. Chicago: University of Chicago Press.

Cook, T. (1998) *Governing with the News: The News Media as a Political Institution*. Chicago: University of Chicago Press.

Donsbach, W. and Patterson, T. (2004) Political News Journalists: Partisanship, Professionalism, and Political Roles in Five Countries. In F. Esser and B. Pfetsch (eds.), *Comparing Political Communication: Theories, Cases, and Challenges* (pp. 251–270). New York: Cambridge University Press.

Entman, R.M. (2004) *Projections of Power: Framing News, Public Opinion and U.S. Foreign Policy*. Chicago: University of Chicago Press.

Feree, M.M., Gamson, W.A., Gerhards, J., and Rucht, D. (2002) *Shaping Abortion Discourse: Democracy and the Public Sphere in Germany and the United States*. New York: Cambridge University Press.

Habermas, J. (1989) *The Structural Transformation of the Public Sphere: An Inquiry into a Category of Bourgeois Society*. Cambridge: Polity Press.

Hallin, D. and Mancini, P. (2004) *Comparing Media Systems: Three Models of Media and Politics*. New York: Cambridge University Press.

Hanitzsch, T. (2007) Deconstructing Journalism Culture: Toward a Universal Theory. *Journal of Communication*. 17: 367–385.

Kurtz, H. (2004) The Post on WMDs: An Inside Story: Prewar Articles Questioning Threat Often Didn't Make Front Page. *Washington Post*, August 12, A1.

Maurer, T. (2005) 'Political Biases in German TV Coverage of Three Wars,' paper presented at the annual Meeting of the International Communication Association, in New York, May 2005.

Maurer, T., Vogelgesang, J., Weiss M., and Weiss, J. (2005) Aktive oder passive Berichterstatter? Die Rolle der Massenmedien während des Kosovo-, Afghanistan- und Irakkriegs. In: Pfetsch, Barbara & Adam, Silke (eds) Massenmedien als politische Akteure. Wiesbaden: VS, 2008, 144–167.

McChesney. R. (2004) *The Problem of the Media: U.S. Communication Politics in the 21st Century*. New York: Monthly Review Press.

McQuail, D. (2003) *Media Accountability and Freedom of Publication*. New York: Oxford University Press.

New York Times. (2004) The Times and Iraq. May 26. http://www.nytimes.com/2004/05/26/international/middleeast/26FTE_NOTE.html?ex=1400990400&en=94c17fcffad92ca9&ei=5007&partner=USERLAND

Patterson, T. (1992) 'Irony of the Free Press: Professional Journalism and News Diversity,' in paper presented at the annual Meeting of the American Political Science Association in Chicago, September 1992.

Political Communication. (2006) Special Issue: New Institutionalism and the News. Vol. 23, No. 2. April–June.

Vogelsang, J. and Fretwurst, B. (2005) 'Political Biases in German Press Coverage of Three Wars: Kosovo 1999, Afghanistan 2001, Iraq 2003,' in paper presented at the annual Meeting of the International Communication Association in New York, May 2005.

Vowe, D. and Dohle, M. (2007) Politische kommunikation im Umbruch – neue Forschung zu Akteuren, Medieninhalten und Wirkungen. *Politische Vierteljahrensschrift*. 48(2): 338–359.

Weiss, H. and Trebbe, J. (2005) 'Implicit vs. Explicit Editorial Commentary: Political Biases of German TV Coverage of the Iraq War,' paper presented at the annual Meeting of the International Communication Association in New York, May 2005.

Weiss, M. and Weiss, H. (2005) 'Indexing: A General Approach for Explaining Political Biases in War Coverage,' paper presented at the annual Meeting of the International Communication Association in New York, May 2005.

11

MEDIA SPECTACLE, PRESIDENTIAL POLITICS, AND THE TRANSFORMATION OF JOURNALISM

Douglas Kellner

The mainstream corporate media today in the United States increasingly process events, news, and information in the form of media spectacle (see Kellner 2001; 2003a, 2003b, 2005, 2008). In an arena of intense competition with 24/7 cable TV networks, talk radio, Internet sites and blogs, and ever proliferating new media like Facebook, MySpace, Twitter and YouTube, competition for attention is ever more intense leading the corporate media to go to sensationalistic tabloidized stories which they construct in the forms of media spectacle that attempt to attract maximum audiences for as much time as possible, until the next spectacle emerges.

By spectacle, I mean media constructs that are out of the ordinary and habitual daily routine which become special media spectacles. They involve an aesthetic dimension and often are dramatic, bound up with competition like the Olympics or Oscars. Media spectacle refers to technologically mediated events, in which media forms like broadcasting, print media, or the Internet process events in a spectacular form. Examples of political events that became media spectacles would include the Clinton sex and impeachment scandal in the late 1990s, the death of Princess Diana, the 9/11 terror attacks, and, currently, the meltdown of the US and perhaps global financial system. For instance, the September 11, 2001 terrorist attacks on the World Trade Center and the Pentagon became global media spectacles that dominated the news for days. Henceforth, with terrorist attacks on London, Madrid, Bali, and other places in the world, daily news would be interpreted by "Breaking News" bulletins on the terrorist attacks which would then dominate journalism for days.

In this chapter, I will theorize media spectacle as becoming a major form of journalism in today's commercialized media milieu dominated by corporate media, and then illustrate my theory with an analysis of the 2008 presidential campaign. My argument is that news and information in situations controlled by corporate media are increasingly dominated by the forms of media spectacle which are changing the nature of journalism in an era increasingly marked by image, sensationalism, and spectacle.

Guy Debord's society of the spectacle and media spectacles: some conceptual distinctions

The concept of the "society of the spectacle" developed by French theorist Guy Debord (in his book *Society of the Spectacle*) and his comrades in the Situationist International has had a major impact on a variety of contemporary theories of society and culture. My notion of media spectacle builds on Debord's conception of the society of spectacle, but differs significantly. For Debord, "spectacle" constituted the overarching concept to describe the media and consumer society, including the packaging, promotion, and display of commodities and the production and effects of all media. Using the term "media spectacle," I am largely focusing on various forms of technologically-constructed media productions that are produced and disseminated through the so-called mass media, ranging from radio and television to the Internet and latest wireless gadgets.

Further, while Debord presents a rather generalized and abstract notion of spectacle, I engage specific examples of media spectacle and how they are produced, constructed, circulated, and function in the present era. In this chapter, I am also arguing that media spectacle is colonizing news and information, especially on the cable news networks, but also increasingly in print and Internet media, especially commercialized forms controlled by corporate media. I also want to argue in this chapter that media spectacle has become the form of political contestation, especially in the United States, but increasingly globally as well. Thus, in contrast to Debord's notion of a monolithic spectacle that constitutes the media and consumer society as a whole and thus is a potent agent for advanced capitalism, I see the spectacle as contested and have a notion of the reversal of the spectacle. In my conception, the spectacle is a *contested terrain* in which different forces use the spectacle to push their interests (Kellner 2003a, 2003b, 2005, 2008).

Indeed, politics and journalism are increasingly mediated by media spectacle. Political conflicts, campaigns, and those attention-grabbing occurrences that we call "news" have all been subjected to the logic of spectacle and tabloidization in the era of the media sensationalism, infotainment, political scandal and contestation, seemingly unending cultural war, the on-going phenomenon of Terror War, and now the emergent era of the Obama spectacle.

Media spectacles are thus becoming the form in which news, information, and the events of the era are processed by media corporations, the state and political groups, and institutions and individuals who have the power to construct political and social realities. In an earlier era of broadcasting, media events were the major form in which the media and the state constructed significant social rituals that reproduced the existing society. Media events tended to be temporally regular, discrete, short-termed, and relatively predictable (Dayan and Katz 1992). In the early era of television, as Lang and Lang have argued (1992 [1984]), media events became key markers and constitutents of the political and social reality of the day, although as Boorstin (1961) warned, they could also be constructed as pseudo-events.

Media spectacles, by contrast, are more diffuse, variable, unpredictable, and contestable. Media spectacles emerged as a dominant form of defining and contesting existing social and political realities during the era of cable and satellite television and the metaphysical event of the Internet, which changed everything. Whereas media events tended to be national, media spectacles are often global. In what McLuhan (1964) foresaw as a "global village," a networked and wired world can experience the same events simultaneously and in real time as during September 2008, when the entire world suffered through the Chinese milk poisoning and then the meltdown of US financial institutions, which threatened the global economy, or the November 2008 terror attacks on Mumbai.

Media spectacles are orchestrated by the state in the case of wars, governing, or political elections, while media corporations on a daily basis constructed media spectacles out of "breaking news" and what are defined as the major events of the day. Media corporations want to hook consumers into big stories so that they will stay tuned, logged on, or keep their eyes and attention on the big events of the day that are increasingly orchestrated as media spectacles. This was the case in the United States and to some extent globally, with the 2008 US presidential election whose outcome defined a new historical era.

Cultural studies and political spectacle: the case of the 2008 US presidential election

Looking at the 2008 Democratic Party primaries we saw exhibited once again the triumph of the spectacle. In this case, the spectacle of Barack Obama and Hillary Clinton, the first serious African-American candidate vs. the first serious woman candidate, brought on a compelling spectacle of race and gender, as well as a campaign spectacle in incredibly hard-fought and unpredictable primaries. From the first primary in Iowa where in January he won a startling victory, it was the Obama spectacle, a spectacle of Hope, of Change, of Color, and of Youth. In addition to his daily campaign speeches on the stump which mobilized record crowds, after every primary election, Obama made a spirited speech, even after his loss in New Hampshire and other primaries. He gave a magnificent Super Tuesday victory speech that could have been the most watched event of the primary season and was probably the most circulated speech on the Internet that week, in which Obama pulled slightly ahead in a multi-state primary night. Obama then won 11 primaries in a row, made another magnificent speech after the Wisconsin primary where Obama took over airways for about an hour, providing a vision of the US coming together, mobilizing people for change, carrying out a progressive agenda, getting out of Iraq, using the money spent there to rebuild the infrastructure, schools, health system, and so on. Even when he lost primaries, he gave inspiring and impassioned speeches.

Following Obama's impressive performance on the stump in the Democratic Party primaries, coverage of both the party primaries and general election were dominated by the form of media spectacle. In terms of stagecraft and spectacle, in Obama's daily stump speeches on the campaign trial, his post-victory and even defeat speeches in the Democratic primaries, and his grassroots Internet and cultural support have shown that Obama is a master of the spectacle. Hence Obama eventually secured the Democratic presidential nomination setting himself to run against John McCain as the Republican party candidate. Since Obama is the master of the spectacle, McCain presumably had to produce good media spectacle himself, or anti-Obama spectacles. From the time Obama clinched the nomination, McCain largely attempted to create an anti-Obama spectacle through TV ads, planting anti-Obama stories in the press and circulating them through the Internet, and eventually savagely attacking Obama every day on the campaign trial.

While the McCain camp engaged in petty anti-Obama ads and attacks in summer 2008, Obama went on a Global Tour that itself became a major media spectacle as he traveled from Afghanistan and Iraq to Europe. Obama gave a rousing speech in Berlin that attracted hundreds and thousands of spectators and a global TV audience, and was shown meeting with leaders in all of these countries, as if he were the presumptive president.

As the campaigns neared their party conventions, traditionally a great TV spectacle, the presidential race established once again the primacy of TV democracy whereby the election is battled out on television – although print media, Internet, and new media are also significant, as I have been suggesting. Following the great spectacle of the Democratic convention in late August with memorable speeches by Obama, Al Gore, Bill and Hillary Clinton, and a moving appearance by Senator Ted Kennedy, McCain desperately needed some spectacle and got it in spades when he announced and presented his Vice-President candidate, who generated the Sarah Palin spectacle, one of the more astounding media spectacles in US political history.

Palin, a short-term Governor of Alaska and former small-town mayor who few knew when McCain introduced her, became one of the most controversial figures in US politics. It was immediately clear that Palin created compelling spectacle: images the opening day of her campaign revealed that she was a gun owner and NRA activist, and footage all day showed her shooting guns. She was also a high school basketball star so there was good spectacle of her playing basketball (although Obama could probably beat her one on one). Palin's husband was a snowmobile champion so you got more good sports spectacle and Sarah's a beauty contest winner, winning local contests and coming runner up as Miss Alaska, so there were images of her as pin-up girl that first day which introduced her to the American public. Gov. Palin's a mother with five children, so you had great family pictures, including a newborn baby with Down's syndrome. After her initial speech with McCain introducing her, her family and the McCains went shopping and she was shown as an enthusiastic shopper marking her as a typical American.

Then on Labor Day, September 1 the public learned that Palin's 17-year-old daughter was pregnant and unmarried so we had sex scandal spectacle all day and debates whether a mother with all these problems should run for Vice President and submit her family to media scrutiny; many other scandals about Palin herself came out: she had fired state employees who would not do her bidding and had appointed unqualified high school friends and cronies to state jobs; she had supported corrupt politicians, had lied about her record, and had consistently taken positions to the right of Dick Cheney. So Sarah Palin suddenly became a spectacle of scandal, as well as adulation by the Christian and Republican Right.

The Republicans were forced to postpone their convention because of another spectacle, the Hurricane Gustav spectacle that was said to be twice as dangerous as Katrina, but turned out to be only half as bad. Once the Republicans got their convention started, Sarah Palin gave an electrifying speech that mobilized the rightwing Republican base and a new star was born. For a couple of weeks after the Republican convention Sarah Palin was the spectacle of the day and the media buzzed around the clock about her past and her record, her qualifications or lack of them, and her effect on the election.

The Stupid Season in the campaign was over, however, on Monday September 15, 2008 when the collapse of the Lehman Brothers investment company helped trigger what appeared to be one of the great US and global financial crises in history. Suddenly, the election was caught up in the spectacle of the possible collapse of the US and global economy so economics took front and center stage. In two wild weeks of campaigning, McCain first insisted that the "fundamentals" of the US economy were sound, and when everyone ridiculed him, he recognized the significance of the crisis and said that as president he would fire the head of the SEC (Security Exchange Commission), although this official does not serve directly under the president, and everyone from the *Wall Street Journal* to the television networks admonished McCain for trying to scapegoat someone who experts knew was not responsible for the crisis.

Obama seemed to gain the initiative during the economic crisis as he made measured and intelligent statements on the economy, and so the Republicans desperately began a strategy of the Big Lie, endlessly distorting his tax proposals, accusing him of crony relations with disgraced federal officials who he hardly knew, and making ridiculous claims about Obama's responsibility for the economic mess. It was becoming apparent that the Republicans were pursuing the Karl Rove/George W. Bush strategy of simply lying about their opponents, trying to create an alternative reality. It was becoming clear that Sarah Palin's candidacy was based on Big Lies, as McCain introduced her as the woman who had stopped the Bridge to Nowhere in Alaska and was a champion of cutting "earmarks," pork barrel legislation to benefit special interests in one's district. Palin repeated these claims day after day, but research revealed that she had supported the Bridge to Nowhere from the beginning, had hired a public relations firm to get earmarks for her district and her state, and had in fact received more earmarks per capita than almost anyone in the country.

With the September 22, 2008 economic meltdown, however, when it looked like the US economy was in a freefall collapse and the Bush–Cheney administration proposed a multibillion dollar bailout package, John McCain embarked on one of the truly incredible political spectacles in US history, trying to position himself as the savior of the economic system and then making an utter fool of himself as day after day he engaged in increasingly bizarre and erratic behavior. Just before the first presidential debate on September 26, McCain announced he was suspending his campaign, was going to Washington to resolve the financial crisis and would stay until it was resolved, threatening to miss the presidential debate. After a lot of negative publicity, he showed up for the debate, viciously attacked Barack Obama in probably the most thuggish debate performance in US political history, with his website declaring him the winner before the debate even took place (subsequent polls showed that Obama got a bounce from the debate and the candidate's performances in response to the financial crisis).

Over the weekend, McCain came to Washington, claiming he was bringing together Congressmen to resolve the financial crisis and attacked Obama for staying on the campaign trial. The morning of the Congressional vote on the debate, McCain and his surrogates claimed it was John McCain alone who had brought Democrats and Republicans together to resolve the financial crisis and continued vicious attacks on Obama. When, hours later, it was revealed that the bailout package pushed by the Bush–Cheney administration and supported by McCain, Obama and the Democratic and Republican party house leaders, failed because two-thirds of the Republicans, who McCain was supposed to be leading, voted against it, McCain had more than a little egg on his face as the stock market plunged in the biggest one-day drop in history.

Hence, following the logic of spectacle that is coming to dominate US journalism, especially presidential campaigns, McCain attempted to create a spectacle of himself as a maverick and active leader rather than cogently arguing his positions on the economic crisis and how they differed from Obama and the Democrats, and his performance was generally rated as erratic and chaotic. By contrast, Palin's conservative base loved her down-home hockey-mom performance and so Palin was unleashed as the attack dog on the campaign trail, as a desperate McCain, with polls indicating that votes were going Obama's way in key states, decided to attack Obama's personal character as a last-ditch way to try to win votes. After the *New York Times* published an article on Obama and former Weather-underground member Bill Ayers, Palin started referring daily to "Obama's pallin' around with terrorists," and John McCain began personally attacking Obama, raising the question "who is the real Barack Obama," with the audience screaming "terrorist!"

Throughout the second week of October, Palin and McCain continued to make the Ayers connection in their campaign rallies, media interviews, and TV ads, personally attacking Obama, and the frenzied Republican mob would scream "Kill him!," "Traitor!," "Bomb Obama!" When one confused woman in the Republican mob told McCain that she "didn't trust Obama" because of things she'd been hearing about him, stammering "he's an Arab!," it was clear that the Republicans lies and demagoguery had led their rabid rightwing base to believe that Obama was an Arab, a Muslim, a terrorist, and not an American. It was also clear that Palin and McCain had stirred up significant levels of mob fear, ignorance, and violence that were becoming extremely volatile and dangerous.

Investigative reporters indicated that Obama had only a casual relation with Ayers, whereas Palin and her husband were involved in an Alaskan secessionist party whose rightwing and anti-Semitic founder had a long history of outrageous anti-American ranting, racist ramblings, and ultra-right politics: Palin's husband had belonged to that party and just this year Sarah Palin addressed their party convention wishing them "good luck." Another investigative report linked Palin to a number of extreme rightwing groups and individuals who had promoted her career (McCain, too, it was revealed, had been associated with an unsavory lot). But Palin's week of infamy came to a proper conclusion when the Alaskan Supreme Court ruled on October 10 that a report into the "Troopergate" scandal could be released and the report itself pointed out that Palin had "abused her authority as governor" and violated Alaska's ethics regulations. Thrown off her moralistic high horse, Palin none the less continued to be McCain's attack dog and raise controversy on the campaign trail.

It was clear that Republicans were playing a politics of association to feed their media spectacles, just as the Bush–Cheney administration had associated Iraq with 9/11, Al Qaeda, and "weapons of mass destruction," connections that were obviously false, but the associations worked to sell the war to their base, gullible Democrats, and the media. Republicans had long sold their rightwing corporate class politics to voters by associating the Democrats with gay marriage, abortion, and secularism. Would the public and media wake up to the Republicans' politics of lying and manipulation or would they continue to get away with their decades of misrule and mendaciousness?

The major theme of the final debate pushed by McCain that remained a touchstone of his campaign was how Obama's answer to Joe the Plumber proved that he was going to raise taxes on small business. In an Obama campaign event the previous weekend, the man who McCain referred to as Joe the Plumber told Obama that he had been a plumber for fifteen years and was trying to buy the business he worked for – and since it cost over $250,000, he would be forced to pay higher taxes since Obama's tax reform proposal would increase taxes on those making over $250,000 and lower those making less. It turned out Joe wasn't the dude's first name, whose real name was Samuel J. Wurzelbacher; that he was not a licensed plumber; that his income the previous year was around $40,000; and that he owed over $1,000 in back unpaid taxes. These paltry facts did not stop McCain and Palin who continued to raise Joe the Plumber in every campaign stop and making it the major theme of their campaign to generate an opposition between Obama the tax-and-spend liberal who would raise your taxes and McCain and Palin who took the side of Joe the Plumber, Ted the Carpenter, and a daily array of allegedly working class people who opposed Obama.

As the two campaigns entered their last week of campaigning before the November 4 election, Obama made speeches with his "closing arguments" hoping to "seal the deal." During September, Obama raised an unprecedented $150 million, much of it from small Internet and personal donations, and also was getting soaring poll numbers, showing him pulling ahead nationally and in the significant battleground states. As he entered the last week of the campaign, Obama presented the spectacle of a young, energetic, articulate candidate who had run what many considered an almost flawless campaign and attempted during the election's final days to project images of hope, change, and bringing the country together to address its growing problems and divisions – exactly the message that Obama started off his campaign with.

The McCain–Palin camp seemed to close with the same basic argument with which most Republican candidates end their campaign: the Democrats want to raise taxes and spread around the wealth, an accusation increasingly hyped by the rightwing base and McCain and Palin themselves that Obama was really a "socialist." McCain continued to raise questions about Obama's experience and the risk that the country would undergo with an untried president, while Obama retorted that the real risk was continuing with more of the last eight years of catastrophic economic policies and a failed foreign policy.

As the campaign came to a close, Obama tried to seal the deal with a multi-million dollar infomercial played on major networks during prime-time just before the World Series game on October 29. In a Hollywoodesque production, the Obama spectacle came together with "American stories" about hard times and struggles and how Obama would deal with these problems and help people. The Obama TV spectacle also contained a rare acknowledgment of the seriousness of the economic problems and what Obama would do to deal with the crisis; a reprise of his story, highlighting his biracial heritage and close relations to his white mother and grandparents; testimonies from a variety of individuals concerning Obama's experience in community, state politics, and the national level; and highlights from some of Obama's greatest moments of his speeches.

This event was followed by a live appearance with President Bill Clinton in a midnight campaign rally in Florida, his first campaign event with the former president and husband of his primary campaign rival Hillary Clinton. Bill enthusiastically endorsed Obama, indicating that Obama was regularly calling him for advice concerning the economic crisis and praising Obama's reaching out for experts on the issue and that the Clintons and Obama had made up, at least for the present. Obama returned the compliments with praise of Clinton's presidency and a comparison between good times under Clinton and the Democrats contrasted with the messes of the past years under the Republican Bush–Cheney regime, which Clinton and Obama both claimed John McCain would basically continue.

Barack Obama continued to draw large and adoring crowds throughout his fall campaign, but consistently tried to present an image of himself as cool, calm, competent, and presidential on the campaign trail and during media interviews and the presidential debates. Unlike the McCain–Palin campaign, he avoided dramatic daily shifts and attention-grabbing stunts to try to present an image of a mature and intelligent leader who is able to rationally deal with crises and respond to attacks in a measured and cool manner, giving him the current moniker "No drama, Obama."

Election night on November 4, 2008 started slowly with Obama getting the predictable Democratic Party states in the Northeast and McCain getting predictable Republican Southern states. Excitement mounted when Obama was awarded the plum of Pennsylvania, which McCain and Palin had campaigned hard for, and when an hour or so later Obama was given Ohio it was clear that he was on the way to victory. At 11:00 pm, the networks opened the hour with the banner heading "Barack Obama Elected 44th President of the United States," or just "Obama Elected President." His sweep of the west coast states of California, Oregon, and Washington, plus the bonus of Hawaii and the hard-fought southern state of Virginia sealed it for Obama who was on his way to a big win.

Meanwhile, in Grant Park in Chicago, the scene of the spectacle "The Whole World is Watching" during the Democratic convention in 1968, when the police tear-gassed antiwar spectators, and the site a year later of the Weather Underground abortive "Days of Rage" spectacle, this time a peaceful assembly of a couple of hundred thousand spectators, mostly young and of many colors, had assembled to celebrate Obama's historical victory. In the crowd, close-ups appeared of celebrities like Jessie Jackson, tears streaming down his face, a jubilant Spike Lee, a solemn and smiling Oprah Winfrey, and other celebrities who joined the mostly young crowd to hear Barack Obama's victory speech. The park hushed into silence as John McCain gave his concession speech and the audience nodded and applauded respectfully, suggesting that the country could come together.

When Obama, his wife Michelle, and their two beautiful girls took stage the place went wild and the eyes of the world were watching the spectacle of Barack Obama becoming president of the United States. Television networks showed the spectacle of people celebrating throughout the United States, from Times Square to Atlanta, Georgia, and even throughout the world. There were special celebrations in countries like Kenya and Indonesia where Obama had lived and his former residences in these countries were becoming national shrines that would be tourist destinations. Obama was indeed a *global spectacle* and his stunning victory would make him a world superstar of global politics.

Deconstructing the spectacle

In this chapter, I have focused on the dimension of presidential campaigns as media spectacle and have described the spectacles of the 2008 presidential election, arguing that media spectacles are coming to dominate journalism and political campaigns. While I have argued that presidential campaigns in the US and elsewhere are primarily orchestrated as media spectacles, I do not want to suggest that this is the most important aspect of determining who wins an election, or the master key to victory. Obviously, money plays a major part in presidential elections and often, whoever raises the most money wins. In a media age, money allows candidates to produce their own spectacles in the form of TV ads and they need millions to raise money to orchestrate campaign events and produce an organization. Obama had raised an unprecedented amount of money, including record donations from small contributions and a record amount of money raised through the Internet.

People also vote because of political affiliations and ideology, their economic interests, and sometimes even because of issues and substance, no matter what the spectacle of the day has to offer. Yet while I write this shortly after the election and see that serious scholars have not yet fully explained Obama's victory, I would suggest that certain resonant images and media spectacles contributed to Obama's victory. People obviously wanted change and hope and Obama offered a spectacle of both since he was the first candidate of color and also represented generational change. The Obama campaign pushed daily the spectacle of the connections of John McCain with the Bush administration, in TV ads, daily rallies, the debates, and other forums with TV news playing endlessly pictures of Bush and McCain embracing and graphics showing that McCain had voted with the most unpopular and failed president of recent history 90% of the time.

The global collapse of the financial markets and crisis of the US and global economy produced one of the major media spectacles of the campaign and the McCain spectacle of erratic pronouncements and daily stunts to exploit the crisis appeared to have turned voters off, while Obama remained cool and rational during this spectacle and time of danger, showing he was more presidential and better able to deal with crises.

During this difficult period in US and global history, voters obviously reacted against the politics of distraction with the Republican spectacles of daily attacks on Obama backfiring and the negative spectacle of Republican crowds screaming "terrorist," "traitor," "kill him!" and the like produced an extremely negative spectacle of a Republican mob, stirred up by McCain and Palin and seeming to inspire rational voters to line up, for hours if necessary, to vote for Obama and a new politics. Thus campaign spectacles can backfire and while the Sarah Palin spectacle did not alone destroy the Republican campaign it certainly did not help recruit voters, although it made Palin a darling of the Republican extreme right and a media superstar.

No doubt other factors will become part of the story of how Barack Obama emerged from relative obscurity to beat Hillary Clinton in a hard fought Democratic Party primary, and then whipped John McCain in one of the wildest and most spectacular elections in US history, one that is transformative and will be pondered for years to come both in terms of its form as media spectacle and its outcome in producing the first African-American president of the United States.

Finally, to be a literate reader of US presidential campaigns, one needs to see how the opposing parties construct narratives, media spectacle, and spin to try to produce a positive image of their candidate to sell to the American public. In presidential campaigns, there are daily photo opportunities and media events, themes and points of the day that candidates want to highlight, and narratives about the candidates that will win support for the public. Obama's narrative from the beginning was bound up with the Obama spectacle, a new kind of politician representing change and bringing together people of different colors and ethnicities, ages, parts of the nation, and political views. He has effectively used media spectacle and Internet spectacle to promote his candidacy and has generally been consistent in his major themes and story-lines, although the Republicans tried to subvert his story with allegations of close connections with radicals like the Rev. Jeremiah Wright and Bill Ayers.

An informed and intelligent public thus needs to learn to deconstruct the spectacle to see what are the real issues behind the election, what interests and ideology do the candidates represent, and what sort of spin, narrative, and media spectacles are they using to sell their candidates. This chapter limited itself to describing the media spectacle dimension of the campaign. I do not want to claim that this is the key to or essence of presidential campaigns as they also depend on traditional organizing, campaign literature, debate, and getting out the vote, the so-called "ground game." But I would argue that media spectacle is becoming an increasingly salient feature of presidential and other elections in the United States and many other countries today.

References

Boorstin, D. (1961) *The Image: A Guide to Pseudo-Events in America*. New York: Harper and Row.

Debord, G. (1967) *Society of the Spectacle*. Detroit: Black and Red.

Katz, E. and Dayan, D. (1992) *Media Events: The Live broadcasting of History*. Cambridge, Mass: Harvard University Press.

Kellner, D. (1995) *Media Culture*. London and New York: Routledge.

——. (2001) *Grand Theft 2000*. Lanham, Md.: Rowman and Littlefield.

——. (2003a) *Media Spectacle*. London and New York: Routledge.

——. (2003b) *From September 11 to Terror War: The Dangers of the Bush Legacy*. Lanham, Md.: Rowman and Littlefield.

——. (2005) *Media Spectacle and the Crisis of Democracy*. Boulder, CO: Paradigm Press.

——. (2008) *Guys and Guns Amok: Domestic Terrorism and School Shootings from the Oklahoma City Bombings to the Virginia Tech Massacre*. Boulder, Col.: Paradigm Press.

Lang, G. and Lang, K. (1992 [1984]) *Politics and Television*. Edison, NJ: Transaction Publishers.

McLuhan, M. (1964) *Understanding Media*. New York: McGraw-Hill

Wolfe, R. (2009) *Renegade. The Making of a President*. New York: Crown Publishers.

12

INTERNATIONAL NEWS FLOW

Lisbeth Clausen

Television and internet news programmes provide a mosaic of international images. A world information order – an international system of the production, distribution and consumption of informational goods – has come into being (Giddens, 1989). Since the advent of television in the middle of the twentieth century, one of its earliest content genres has been news. News has become a global phenomenon (van Ginneken, 1998). Its format, content and style are recognised worldwide.

And yet, the fact that we are presented with world events and historical handshakes may give us a sense of inhabiting one world. In this way, McLuhan's vision from the 1960s of a 'global village' has come true. However, while the effect of international news communication may include homogenising elements, global events are *also* mediated according to national, organisational and professional strategies (Clausen, 2004) The complexity of news systems production and reception may render the plural term 'global villages' more appropriate, especially when we remember the diaspora television programming existing in parallel to mainstream programmes at national, regional and global levels. Considering these complex systems of international supply and demand, the common experience may still be sporadic and indirect. Journalism studies research has shown that exposure to international news has an impact in setting at least part of the public agenda and on attitudes towards foreign countries (Jensen, 1998; Semetko, Brzinski, Weaver & Willnat, 1992). News media use is a catalyst to conversation about politics and participation in democratic systems (Kim, Wyatt & Katz, 1999)

Situated against the backdrop of the increasing globalization of news organizations (Chalaby, 2005) in the context of greater political and economic interdependence among nations, the role of foreign news seems to be gaining increased importance. The 'CNN Effect' on global politics (Robinson, 2002; Volkmer, 1999) is being hotly debated (Gilboa, 2005). And while the formats of television newscasts have developed over the years with variability in public service and commercial styles, there are recognized commonalities in news values from one broadcasting system to the next (Dahlgren, 1995; Cottle, 2000).

Accordingly, in this chapter I shall provide an overview of several issues central to the international news flow studies. Particular attention will be given to the international news agencies and their agenda setting effects, highlighting the ways in which an array of factors – such as technological development, formats, production and reception of international or foreign news – give shape to what is reported, how and why.

International news flow studies

The first international news flow study was conducted in 1978. Its insights led to a call for a redefinition of news, which was flowing predominantly from the northern to the southern hemisphere. The ensuing debate, over what became known as the New World Information and Communication Order (NWICO), was informed by research funded by UNESCO to cover 29 countries (Sreberny-Mohammadi *et al.*, 1985). A key finding was the prominence of *regionalism*. Every national system devoted most attention to events happening within its immediate geographical region. Secondly, it was found that *politics* dominated international news reporting everywhere. 'Hard' news was presented by two political categories, namely political international and domestic news, followed by military, defence and economics, which accounted for the main news stories. Similarly, it was found that *political figures* dominated participation in news, comprising 25 to 60 per cent of all actors in international news; few other categories of actors received significant mention. Not surprisingly, the United States and Western Europe came out in the study as the consistent newsmakers in all parts of the world. It was found that international news would focus on spectacular singular happenings, drawing attention for a short intense period of time. News from the developing world, this research demonstrated, was relatively scarce.

The complicity of the media in 'cultural imperialism' has been a recurring issue, one similarly raised by the news flow studies of the 1970s (Stevenson & Shawn, 1984). These studies established that, while information flowed from first world countries in the North to developing countries in the South, very little information flowed in the reverse direction. A similar pattern was found to exist between the Western countries of North America and Europe and the Eastern countries of Asia. In 1970, UNESCO promoted the idea of a 'New World Information Order' that would provide more impartial (and more positive) information on non-Western countries. More recently, there has been a debate within the context of the GATT (now the WTO), in which some countries such as France and China have sought to defend their cultural integrity by banning imports of foreign media products (De Burgh, 2000).

Much of this research has shown that the international media environment is far more complex than has been suggested by the Western 'cultural imperialism' model. The depiction of a hegemonic media system leading the global media may have seemed appropriate in the 1970s, but has since become increasingly open to challenge (Sreberny-Mohammadhi, 1995: 180). The conventional categories of 'imbalances' and 'expansion' did not suffice to explain the global communication flow. Relevant here is Kaarle Nordenstreng et al.'s (1985) argument that more sophisticated methodological frameworks were required to document news flow, namely to ensure that the qualitative sphere of image building would be addressed (instead of relying entirely upon conventional categories of content analysis, such as topics/types of news, countries/ regions, etc.). In other words, an understanding of foreign countries as reflected in news coverage required a much more nuanced approach than the simple counting of how much attention was being devoted to such categories (in topical terms) as politics, natural catastrophes, and so forth. The fact that certain aspects of reality lend themselves to convenient measurement does not mean that those aspects are necessarily the most essential to our understanding of reality (1985: 634). New parameters of international news communication, revealing the parallelism of 'universal'/'global' and 'particular'/'local' elements, were needed.

Proposals for the study of *meaning*, rather than a merely topical approach to news, came from a number of directions. They helped to inspire a follow up study, entitled 'The Corporate Study of Foreign News and International News Flow in the 1990s,' more widely referred to as the 'News Flow Study.'[1] Approximately 40 countries participated in the study, the goal of which was to map the emerging global news geography, in terms of the major suppliers of news, the geographic and cultural maps that news coverage represents, and the discourses and images of 'otherness' that define 'foreign' news (see also Stevenson, 1995).

Here it is worth noting, however, that this study still assumed a linear notion of news flow among nations. Its conception of one-way news flow, implying a top-down imposition of 'news flows' from the 'centre' (North and West) to the periphery, provided little insight into the dynamics of globalisation processes. That is to say, it did not take into account the interpenetrating and overlapping influences in local production contexts. Macro-level analysis, based on quantitative data (number of newspapers, TV channels in the countries monitored), overlooked micro-level processes. Critics such as Hjarvard (1995) argued that a new perspective was required, one encompassing a middle level of analysis focusing on *interaction* so as to give proper attention to the inter-relatedness between social actors and between different factors in the news *process*. However, the resources needed to pursue this line of enquiry, together with difficulties in accessing newsrooms, made the practical implementation of his proposal impossible in all but a few countries.

Since the spring of 2008, a study led by Professor Akiba Cohen of Tel Aviv University, titled 'Foreign News on TV,' has been underway. In aiming to investigate the way foreign news is presented on broadcast television, it is currently drawing together data from 20 countries. While still employing a mainly quantitative methodology in the analysis of news content, it also seeks to examine qualitative aspects, namely through in-depth interviews with news producers and audiences. The framework for this international news flow study is referred to as 'start to finish research' (Braman & Cohen, 1990) – that is, media research which examines the production of the news, the content itself and the consumption or reception of the news content. Its principal findings will include a new mapping of the complexity of international news flow, including the influence of international news suppliers, the editorial processes in the national news rooms and the reception by national audiences.

International news agencies

The leading Western agencies of the 1990s were generally acknowledged to be Agence France-Presse (AFP), Associated Press (AP), and Reuters. Two of these organisations, AP and Reuters (formerly Visnews), were involved in print news for newspapers and audio-visual news (APTV and Reuters Television) for broadcasters. Here it is also necessary to add World Television News (WTN) to the list of major agencies. WTN, the successor of UPITN (owned by UPI in the US and ITN in the UK), was bought by Reuters TV in 1998. Although these agencies are 'global' in the scope of their activities, they each retain significant associations with particular nations, namely France (AFP), the United States (AP) and the UK (Reuters). News agencies in the Soviet Union (Tass, now Itar-Tass) and China (Xinhau) are non-commercial, and as such function as government departments. These sources continue to be influential for the information they provide about Russia and China, respectively, but not as sources of news about other countries. This is similar to the situation with the Japanese national news agencies, Jiji Press and Kyodo News Service. They operate, in effect, as national news services (Ito, 1990).

The above news agencies – together with international broadcasters such as the BBC, CNNI and World Service Television (WSTV) and the US networks ABC, CBS, NBC, and Fox, among others – have established extensive linkages with broadcasters throughout the world for news feeds, specialised information services and video footage. These linkages represent an exchange-based co-operative system, albeit one that is a hierarchically organised in the interests of US and European-based organisations (Paterson, 1996, 1998). Malik's (1992) news agenda survey was one of the first to suggest that a worldwide convergence in international television news coverage was underway. On the basis of his data, he warned that the power of these exchange systems, when set in relation to the news agencies, was much greater than members of the public tended to realise (1992: 37–41).

Since this pioneering study appeared, several scholars have contended that the international news agencies are working to standardise television news programmes across the globe. This is occurring primarily through shared conventions in production: that is, the similarity in resource allocation, news values and journalistic routines, but also certain competitive pressures to duplicate coverage provided by one another. These shared foci on standard frames or themes in news coverage engender a certain homogenisation of international news. Paterson describes the strategies of the news agencies as follows:

> The international news agencies go to great length, and take great pride in their ability, to provide a 'balanced', 'objective' view of the world in their news feeds. They generally admit, however, that their news feeds concentrate upon news of the industrialised world, but insist that the reason is that these countries established them and (mostly) pay for them. They also historically claim to provide 'raw' pictures and sounds, which enable broadcasters to construct their own international news stories (Paterson, 1998: 84).

Professional norms such as balance or objectivity have historically served the agencies well in their promotion of news as a product. National broadcasters have been encouraged, in turn, to rely on international news material supplied by these agencies, and yet they continue to downplay their significance (Hjarvard, 1995a; Malik, 1992). Rather, they tend to argue that the agencies only provide supplementary illustration to stories – sometimes derisively called 'video wallpaper' – when, in reality, 'agency material often constitutes the bulk of a story, including the "spin" of the story' (Paterson, 1998: 85). Moreover, concern has been expressed by critics that this material tends to reinforce a Western news tradition as a journalistic ideal, thereby limiting the diversity of alternative approaches to news gathering and presentation.

Technological development

Since the 1990s, the term 'global' has been widely used in connection with the communications industry, primarily to refer to the sheer volume of coverage around the world. The popularity of satellite television, in particular, is evidence of the globalisation of communications. CNN, for example, is available in over 150 countries. Recent studies, especially trade reports, also point to the growing use of the internet for news, mainly by people in their place of work who have regular access to computers. The so-called 'YouTube presidential election' in the US, where Barack Obama's campaign made every advantage of the internet to mobilise its messages around the planet, is a case in point. Nevertheless, any notion of the 'global' must acknowledge the extent to which globalisation is an uneven process. Researchers routinely point out that it has only truly penetrated the OECD and G8 member countries, which together constitute just one third of the world's population.

Communication technology has created the opportunity for media organisations to become global in their reach. However, the logic of the global marketplace, when it encounters local customs, laws and traditions, will necessarily risk fragmentation. Questions thus arise regarding issues of representation – that is, the ways in which global media report on the cultures of the different countries that they cover. These are not just questions of cultural diversity, but also questions about how politics, law and economics are intertwined.

Media organisations, when dispersing correspondents and stringers in different countries, need to ensure that they are managed in a way which attends to this cultural diversity. CNN has announced a major investment in international newsgathering, with new operations planned for Afghanistan, Belgium, India, Kenya, Malaysia, Nigeria, the Philippines, Poland and Vietnam. The BBC World Service has started programme production in India, while Rupert Murdoch's Star TV is now targeting regional-language audiences within Asia (primarily those speaking Chinese, Malay, and certain Indian languages). Indeed, within a changing geo-linguistic media landscape, Singapore and Hong Kong have become the centres for Asian satellite TV services. Satellite sub-regions have been formed based on cultural similarities. For example, there are Chinese and Indian language sub-regions, and an ASEAN sub-region has been formed as a result of the ten members of ASEAN launching satellites for domestic services together with neighbouring countries (Goonasekera, 2000).

Nevertheless, despite this ongoing evolution, it is important to recognise that trans-national communicative interactions are not limited to commercial concerns. The use of new technologies to facilitate the flow of news and information also shapes politics, both amongst governments and non-governmental organisations (NGOs) alike. For instance, public relations agencies of large organisations such as the UN, which currently has three departments (UNESCO TV, UNRWA TV and EPTV), and the European Parliament Public Relations Division, produce programmes carried by CNN.

News routines

Today, news agencies have become global forces of information circulation (Boyd-Barrett, 1980, 1998), and yet foreign correspondents do not always know the local language, let alone have a deep cultural understanding of the events they are responsible for covering. There is a marked tendency for the ensuing news coverage to portray issues from Western perspectives, that is, in terms of the potential impact such events may have on the political or economic interests of the US or UK (De Burgh, 2000: 311). Cultural bias in journalism is an ongoing issue. While objectivity, fairness and balance are widely shared news criteria (Tuchman, 1972; Soloski, 1989), several factors shaping the cultural specificity of foreign reporting require careful attention (Bantz et al., 1981).

News producers, in deciding what counts as news, play a decisive role in shaping coverage. Many of the decisions made throughout the day may seem to be arbitrary, but are actually conditioned by structural factors influencing their work strategies as they struggle to commission assignments and secure airtime for reports. International stories go through processes of 'domestication' with a view to the perceived interests and inclinations of local audiences (Gurevitch et al., 1991; Cohen et al., 1996). 'Domestication' is understood as a process of framing: recognising, defining, selecting and organising news in a way judged to be appropriate for the intended audiences. Moreover, some news items are produced as 'hybrids,' including both domestic and international components (Nossek, 2004). 'Hybrid' news may deal with an event or issue in a foreign country but also point out issues within the same news item that have direct relevance to the country of broadcast.

Comparative research suggests that the strategies adopted by news producers differ not only in terms of the agendas of national broadcast media, but also in terms of the organisational and professional presentation practices of public service and commercial stations (Helland, 1993; Clausen, 2003). The logic of commerce, and with it the commodification of entertainment-driven news values, has led to the proliferation of 'infotainment' and 'tabloid news' formats. The relentless demand for a 24/7 news supply has led to a convergence of styles between commercial broadcasters and public service stations. Subjective, 'soft' news is valued over and above objective, 'hard' news for two reasons: the former is perceived to be more popular with audiences, and because it is much cheaper to produce.

A further factor worthy of attention in this regard is the rise of the public relations industry as exemplified above. Governments and corporations, and even new social movements, employ professional media spokespersons skilled in 'spinning' the news message to the advantage of their view. A 'spin' with international implications, for instance, is the broadcast of US Secretary of State Hillary Clinton shaking hands with Chinese Prime Minister Wen Jiabao on her first international visit. This signifies the priority of US foreign relations with China and the dissemination of this symbolic event again and again helps recreate and maintain the present political world order. In this sense, news is a means to constitute the rituals of public life and political performance (Carey, 1989; Dayan & Katz, 1992).

New forms of journalism

Any survey of international news coverage will quickly discern the extent to which the reporting of political conflict and war predominates. To pass the editorial threshold of newsworthiness, a foreign crisis must usually be perceived to be more complex and/ or more intense and/or more difficult to solve than a domestic conflict (Cohen, Adoni & Bantz, 1990). Since the attacks of September 11, 2001, the nature of this threshold has changed however (see also Zelizer & Allan, 2002). For better or for worse, news producers have regained an overarching framework for reporting on world affairs, something which had been missing since the fall of the Berlin Wall.

For decades following the Second World War, the Cold War between the Soviet Union and the US served as a framework for the interpretation of international affairs. The events of 9/11, followed by the US-led invasions of Afghanistan and Iraq, have provided a new global framework for a political interpretation of news events (see also Allan & Zelizer, 2004). This has meant that the relationship between the global and the local (and thereby distinctions between 'foreign' and 'domestic' affairs) has blurred in international newsrooms. News coverage and political commentary are no longer strictly defined in relation to one or the other, but rather interweave a mix of both (Volkmer, 2002). News frames have moved from the perceived communist threat to one revolving around religious extremism, one that risks reifying a narrative binarism between Christians and Muslims that is dangerous.

Significantly, however, the events of 9/11 and their aftermath also attracted world attention to a new player in the international news arena, namely the Arab-owned Al-Jazeera, headquartered in Doha, Qatar. Al-Jazeera is now the world's third largest English news broadcaster after the CNNI and BBC World Service. It is also a news agency and supplier of news material. Its rise as an important player in the global news supply system previously dominated by the West has been remarkable.

Yet another new player in this arena, so to speak, is the ordinary citizen turned citizen journalist. Recent crises have shown the extent to which individuals with access to the internet have been able to contribute to the news reporting of events. Citizen journalism enables firsthand reporting, as well as political commentary, concerning breaking news events by individuals on personal internet weblogs or 'blogs'. However, as English is the lingua franca in Western world blogging, the use of local language in most countries still creates barriers to a truly global flow of news between individuals.

'Global consciousness'

In one hour of television watching (zapping from one channel to the next), viewers are likely to be confronted with an astonishing array of visual impressions from around the world. And yet, some research studies have found that television news is difficult to process and comprehend by many people. This appears to be the case for a variety of reasons, including the nature of the informational content, the format of presentation, and the limited knowledge base many viewers possess (Jensen, 1998). Television journalists, it seems, may be unaware of these cognitive limitations. Often international news items lack the necessary background information or contextual details needed to understand items in their complexity. The drive to be first with the story, to accentuate the immediacy effect for its news value, sometimes means that events are portrayed without adequate analysis or interpretation.

This is a significant concern, not least when audience research shows that, for the vast majority of citizens, television news broadcasts remain a prime source of information about the outside world (Cohen & Shoemaker, 2006). News media link together people across vast areas of geographical space, creating new relationships of social, communicative and cultural interaction. As such, they provide an ever more important forum for the enactment of international as well as domestic politics on a day to day basis. The process of globalisation, therefore, is as much a psychological phenomenon as it is an economic or political reality. Owing to the dynamic flows of media images, texts, sounds and graphics across countries, globalisation entails an increased awareness of other cultures, and thereby a deeper understanding of one's own local culture. The flow of international news, it follows, is both affected by globalisation trends and is itself an agent of their ideological influence.

Notes

1 http//sunsite.unc.edu/newsflow/

References

Allan, S. and Zelizer, B. (eds) (2004) *Reporting War: Journalism in Wartime.* London and New York: Routledge.

Anura Goonasekera (2000) "Media in the Information Highway. Representing different cultures in the age of global communication", in *The New Communications Landscape. Demystifying Media Globalization*, Georgette Wang, Jan Servaes and Anura Goonasekera. London and New York: Routledge.

Bantz, C. R., McCorkle, S., Baade, R.C. (1981) The news factory. In G.C. Wilhoit & H. deBodk (eds.) *Mass Communication Review Yearbook.* Vol. 2, pp. 366–389. Newbury Park: Sage.

Boyd-Barrett, O. (1980). *The International News Agencies.* London: Constable.

Boyd-Barrett, O. (1998) Global News Agencies, in Boyd-Barett, Oliver & Rantanen, Terry (eds.) *The Globalization of News.* London: Sage.

Braman, S. and Cohen, A. A. (1990). 'Research from start to finish.' In J. A. Anderson (ed.), *Communication Yearbook 13*. Newbury Park, CA: Sage (pp. 511–518).

Burgh, Hugo de (ed) (2000) *Investigative journalism: context and practice*, London: Routledge.

Carey, J. (1989) *Communication as Cuture*. London: Unwin Hyman.

Chalaby, J. K. (2005). Towards an understanding of media transnationalism. In J. K. Chalaby (ed.), *Transnational Television Worldwide: Towards a new media order*. London: I. B. Tauris (pp. 1–13).

Clausen, Lisbeth (1997) 'International news in Japan. A reception analysis', *Keio Communication Review*. No. 19: 39–67.

Clausen, Lisbeth (2003) *Global News Production*. Copenhagen: CBS Press.

Clausen, Lisbeth (2004) 'Localising the Global. "Domestication" Processes in the Production of International news', *Media Culture and Society*. London: Sage Publications, vol. 26 issue 1: 25–45.

Cohen, Akiba Adoni, Hanna, Bantz, Charles (eds) (1990) *Social Conflict and Television News: A Cross-National Study of Content and Perception*, London: Sage.

Cohen, A. A. (2002). 'Globalization Ltd.: Domestication on the boundaries of television news.' In J. M. Chan and B. T. McIntyre (eds.), *In Search of Boundaries: Communication, Nation-States and Cultural Identities*. Westport, CT: Ablex, pp. 167–180.

Cohen, A. A., Levy, M. R., Roeh, I., and Gurevitch, M. (1996). *Global Newsrooms, Local Audiences: A Study of the Eurovision News Exchange*. London: John Libbey.

Cottle, Simon (2000) New(s) Times. Towards a 'Second Wave' of News Ethnography, *The European Journal of Communications Research* 25 (1) P. 19–41.

Dahlgren, Peter (1995) *Television and the Public Sphere – Citizenship, Democracy and the Media*. London: Sage.

Dayan, D. and Katz, E. (1992) *Media Event: The Live Broadcasting of History*. Cambridge, Massachusetts: Harvard University Press.

Galtung, J. and Ruge, M. (1965). The structure of foreign news: The presentation of the Congo, Cuba and Cypress crises in four Norwegian newspapers. *Journal of Peace Research*, 1, 64–91.

Giddens, Anthony (1989) *Sociology*. Cambridge: Cambridge University Press.

Gilboa, E. (2005). 'Global television news and foreign policy: Debating the CNN effect.' *International Studies Perspectives*, 6, 325–341.

Ginneken, Jaap van (1998) *Understanding global news*. London: Sage.

Goonasekera, Anura (2000) 'Freedom of expression in the information age: Access to information'. Media Asia vol. 27, no. 2: 75–84.

Gurevitch M., Levy, M., Roeh, I, (1991) 'The Global Newsroom: Convergences and diversities in the globalisation of television news,' in P. and C. Sparks (eds.) *Communications and Citizenship: Journalism and the Public Sphere in the New Media Age*, London: Routledge.

Hjarvard, Stig (1995) 'TV News Flow Studies Revisited', Electronic Journal of Communication, vol. 5, nos. 2 & 3, http://www.cios.org/EJCPUBLIC/005/2/005214.html

Hannerz, U. (2004) *Foreign News. Exploring the World of Foreign Correspondents*. Chicago and London: University of Chicago Press.

Helland, K. (1993) *Public Service and Commercial News: Contexts of Production, Genre Conventions and Textual Claims in Television*. Bergen: University of Bergen (Report No. 18).

Hjarvard, Stig (1995a) – please use the same ref above and turn the 1995a into 1995

Hjarvard, S. (2001) *News in a Globalised Society*. Göteborg: Nordicom.

Hugo de Burg (ed.) (2000) Investigative Journalism. Context and Practice. London and New York: Routledge.

Ito, Youichi (1998) The Pattern and Determinant Factors of International News. Paper presented to the IAMCR, Glasgow.

Jakubowics, A. (1995) "Media in Multicultural Nations: Some Comparisons," in Downing, John, Mohammadi, Ali, and Sreberny-Mohammadi, Annabelle (eds), *Questioning the media: A critical introduction*, Thousand Oaks, CA: Sage, pp. 165-183.

Jensen, Klaus Bruhn (ed.) (1998) *News of the World: World Cultures Look at Television News*. London: Routledge.

Kim, J., Wyatt, R. O., and Katz, E. (1999). News, talk, opinion, participation: The part played by conversation in deliberative democracy. *Political Communication*, 16(4) 361–385.

Lull, J. (ed.) (1988) *World Families Watch Television*, California: Sage Publications.

Malik, R. (1992). 'The global news agenda.' *Intermedia*, 20(1), 8–70.

McCormick Barrett L. and Qing Liu. (2003) 'Globalization and the Chinese Media: technologies, content, commerce and the prospects for the public sphere.' Chinese Media Global Contexts. Chin-Chuan Lee ed. London and New York, RoutledgeCurzon.

McLuhan, M. (1960) *Understanding Media: The Extensions of Man*, New York: McGraw-Hill.

Morley, David (1986) *Family Television: Cultural Power and Domestic Leisure*, London: Comedia.

Nordenstreng, K. with Sreberny-Mohammadi, A. Stevenson, R. and Ugboajah F. (eds.) (1985) *Foreign News in the Media: International Reporting in 29 Countries*, Paris: UNESCO.

Nossek, H. (2004). Our news and their news: The role of national identity in the coverage of foreign news. *Journalism*, 5(3), 343–368.

Paterson, Christopher (1996) New Production at Worldwide Television News (WTN): An analysis of Television News Agency coverage of Developing Countries, PhD Dissertation.

Paterson, Christopher (1998) 'Global Battlefields,' in Boyd-Barrett, Oliver & Rantanen, Terhi (eds.) *The Globalisation of News*. London: Sage.

Perry, D. K. (1990). 'News reading, knowledge about, and attitudes toward foreign countries.' *Journalism Quarterly*, 67(2), 353–358.

Philo, G. (2004). The mass production of ignorance: News content and audience. In C. Paterson and A. Sreberny (eds.), *International News in the Twenty-first Century*. Eastleigh, UK: John Libbey (pp. 199–224).

Robinson, P. (2002). *The CNN Effect: The myth of news, foreign policy and intervention*. London: Routledge.

Semetko, H. A., Brzinski, J. B., Weaver, D., and Willnat, L. (1992). 'TV news and U.S. public opinion about foreign countries: The impact of exposure and attention.' *International Journal of Public Opinion Research*, 4(1), 18–36.

Shoemaker, P. J. & Cohen, A. A. (2006) *News Around the World: Content, practitioners and the public*. New York: Routledge.

Soloski, J. (1989) 'News reporting and professionalism: some constraints on the reporting of news.' *Media, Culture and Society*. 11: 207–228.

Sreberny-Mohammadi, A., K. Nordenstreng, R. Stevenson, & F. Ugboajah (eds.) (1985) *Foreign News in the Media: International Reporting in 29 countries*, Paris: UNESCO.

Sreberny-Mohammadi, A. (1996) 'The global and the local in International Communications', in Curran J. and Gurevitch M. (eds.) *Mass Media and Society*. London: Arnold.

Stevenson, Robert L. and Shawn, D. L. (eds.) (1984) Foreign News and the New World Information Order. Ames: The Iowa State University Press.

Stevenson, Robert (1995) 'Project Proposal: Corporate Study of Foreign News and International News Flow in the 1990s', http//sunsite.unc.edu/newsflow/.

Tuchman, G. (1972) 'Objectivity as strategic ritual: an examination of newsmen's notions of objectivity', *American Journal of Sociology*. No 77: 660–679.

Volkmer, I. (1999) *News in the Global Sphere: A study of CNN and its impact on global communication*. Luton: University of Luton Press.

Volkmer, Ingrid (2002) 'Journalism and Political Crises,' in Allan, S. and Zelizer, B. (eds.) *Journalism after September 11*. London and New York: Routledge.

Zelizer, B. and Allan S. (eds.) (2002) *Journalism after September 11*. London and New York: Routledge.

13

JOURNALISM AND POLITICAL CHANGE: THE CASE OF CHINA

Qing Cao

When democratisation swept across the world in late twentieth century, China remained largely untouched by this 'wind of change' (Huntington, 1993).[1] Three decades of reform since 1978 had witnessed phenomenal economic growth, but not fundamental changes in the political terrain. Pye (1997) captures a central question that many ask, namely: 'Can the Chinese remain almost alone in the world in resisting the apparently inexorable trend of democratisation?' (1997: 205). The question is straightforward but complex, defying any simplistic answers. In the growing literature concerning democratisation in China, some researchers apply Western concepts and categories in measuring democratic progress (Nathan, 1985; Friedman, 1995; and Pye, 1997). Others highlight Asian values to argue China is pursuing a different road to modernity and therefore an alternative political future (He, 1996; He and Guo, 2000; Pan, 2003). As China's global integration becomes deeper, however, there is a general assumption that China's opening up of its domestic markets will undermine its one-party rule and contribute to democratic changes, at least in the area of communication. Political change is thus being linked to the mass media, even though scepticism exists about a direct link between a free market press and progressive reform (Curran, 2000) or even between press freedom and democracy (Merrill, 2000).

This chapter provides an overview of the trajectory of the party-controlled journalism in contemporary China. It discusses the dynamic relationship between journalism, political changes and prospects for democracy under an authoritarian state. It first examines the idea of democracy as understood in China through its *minben* tradition, and then moves on to relate this political culture to key functions of Chinese journalism as part of state apparatus, followed by an analysis of the impact of media commercialisation on journalism. The chapter concludes with an evaluation of Chinese journalism in a complex matrix of economic and political transformations.

Minben and democracy in China

The Chinese understanding of democracy, to the extent it is possible to generalise, is deeply rooted in the Chinese traditional political culture and its struggle to construct a new cultural and political identity in the modern world. The practice of journalism is just one part of this complex process of nation and state-building and an intense search for a Chinese road to modernity. Journalism in China therefore shows significant differences from that in the West and other parts of the world. Before Western ideas of democracy were introduced into China around the start of the twentieth century, the Chinese concept '*minben*' (people as basis) had existed for over two millennia. *Minben* as a coherent political idea originated from the Chinese classic *Shang Shu*, but was elaborated by Mencius (371–289BC) and in other early historical writings such as *Zhan Guo Ce* (Chronicles of Warring States). It emphasises people as the source of political authority and basis for an ethical political order. The ruler is a facilitator selected by Heaven to provide welfare for his people. To Mencius, the primary function of the king is to provide for the people: a good economy sustains a content population. *Minben* encapsulates core Classical Confucian values representing an ideal form of good governance. Though Imperial Confucianism[2] that emerged in West Han dynasty (206BC–23AD) shifted the emphasis of power to the ruler, *minben* as an ideal of Confucian governance, has a deep and lasting impact (Wang and Titunik, 2000). This welfare-based legitimacy to rule has increasingly been used to justify the one-party system in post-Mao China. In the early 2000s, the Hu–Wen (President Hu Jintao and Premier Wen Jiabao) leadership refocused on the *minben* tradition as the Chinese approach to democracy, placing an emphasis on people-centred (*yi ren wei ben*) governance through the promotion of a 'harmonious society'.

When 'democracy' was introduced into China, it was translated as *minzhu* (literally 'people master'), a term that first appeared in *Shang Shu*, meaning 'people's master' or 'people's king'. Obviously, the translator meant it to be 'people as master'. The multiple meanings derive from the combination of two Chinese characters, *min* and *zhu*; each has different meanings in different contexts (Guang, 1996). However, the semantic confusion belies a deeper chasm between Western democratic principles and Chinese interpretations of the term imbedded in a *minben* tradition and complex political realities. First, 'people' as assumed in the paternalistic, elitist and non-participatory notion of *minben* is fundamentally different from 'people' understood in 'democracy' as sovereign subjects exercising political right through elections and freedom of speech. Second, contrary to *minben* as a traditional ideology sanctioning the deposing of a corrupt ruler through a divine power, democracy relies crucially on the checks and balances of a tripartite political system. Furthermore, the historical legacy of China's resistance to Western colonial encroachment means that 'democracy' as a Western idea was largely seen as an instrument to serve the Chinese nationalist goal of achieving political independence and wealth and power.

Rooted in this cultural and historical heritage, various formulations of 'democracy' were shaped by different political objectives, from imperial constitutional reform to Maoist 'new people's democracy' (1949–1976) and Dengist 'socialist democracy' (post-1978). It was employed to seek to reinvigorate the imperial state, to establish a communist political power and to consolidate a one-party system. Few accepted liberal democratic assumptions like competition for public office, participation in the political leader selection, and civil and political liberties. The inherited *minben* elements in 'democracy' bestow people with nominal power that is difficult to exercise and therefore intangible, in contrast to liberal democracy that focuses on procedural mechanisms in the exercise of political power by individuals. In addition, *minben* sees the state as a moral organisation where the head of it, the ruler, naturally assumes moral authority. Consequently, Chinese journalism from its birth in the nineteenth century assumed an elitist, though dependent, role in the service of a political force either to bring about a revolution or to consolidate a political power. Like the concept of democracy that is complicated by a *minben* legacy, journalism in China is also embedded in a Confucian as well as a revolutionary tradition.

Journalism as a 'mouthpiece'

Mao famously concluded that the success of the Chinese revolution relies crucially on 'the barrel of the gun (the military) and the pen (propaganda)'. For the Chinese Communist Party (CCP), to seize power is only part of the political function of journalism. After the CCP came to power in 1949 journalism was imbued with a range of new roles – to consolidate power and transform people's consciousness through moulding a uniform thinking in the image of the Party. Under the Leninist 'democratic centralism', democracy came to mean selective consultation within internal organisations, the right of decision-making remaining the exclusive reserve of the CCP elites. Similar to traditional *minben*, the paternalistic democratic centralism sees people as incapable of articulating their true interests and involves them only as a source of political power. Indeed, democratic centralism as an organisational principle is part of the Maoist 'people's democratic dictatorship', in which democracy takes a more abstract form of 'dictatorship' by the people over class enemies. In the redefined Party–people relationship the former assumes an autocratic power on behalf of the latter it rules. The post-1949 journalism thus became an integral part of the state apparatus of the People's Republic of China (PRC) and is officially defined as the 'throat and tongue' (*hou she*) of the Party. The '*hou she*' theory, or mouthpiece journalism, derived from a wartime propaganda ethos in the 1940s when the CCP used the mass media as its powerful weapon. The idea of press freedom associated with liberal democracy is alien to the Communist state and theoretically refuted as a hypocritical pretence of a Western bourgeois state in the service of the capitalist class. In the creation of a utopian communist society with ideological indoctrination and thought control, journalism is seen to be a political tool.

A key feature of Chinese journalism is its 'Party character'; that is, all journalists must consciously toe the Party lines and identify actively with the Party's political stand as an *absolute* guiding principle. The Party character derives from Leninist journalism of mass mobilisation. Mao calls this practice 'politics takes command' – the subjugation of journalism to political imperatives. In theory, however, there also exists 'people's character' of journalism; namely journalists should put people's interests above anything else, to follow Mao's call to 'serve the people'. However, like 'people' in *minben*, it remains an abstract, empty and sometimes meaningless category. According to CCP journalism orthodoxy, since the Party represents the best interests of the people the Party's character *equates* the people's character. Nevertheless, the Party vs. people tension has never ceased and often surfaces when liberal-minded editors and journalists seek more freedom from the CCP ideologues in the name of the latter, as shown in the extraordinary outburst of support by journalists for the 1989 popular pro-democracy protests. 'Speak out for the people' is the rallying cry for journalists who took to the street to demand press freedom.

One primary responsibility of Chinese journalism is to 'guide public opinions' – to lead the public to think 'correctly' on matters of importance, to distinguish 'right' from 'wrong' and to 'elevate' people's political consciousness. Mao believes that 'correct thought' determines 'correct actions'. If the broad masses develop 'correct' thought or attitude, they will act 'correctly'. 'Guide public opinions' has been re-emphasised in recent years when social unrest has grown considerably as the gap between rich and poor is widening, despite the CCP's policies of promoting a 'harmonious society' since the early 2000s. The role of journalism is to foster an atmosphere of harmony and to create maximum social impact by relating to the CCP's ideology of the day and its specific policy 'lines', though not to the political and socio-economic realities. The moralist role of guiding the public assumed by the CCP is part rooted in the Confucian tradition of cultivating a good morality among the people. Confucius believed that a good king needs to educate his people and cultivates in them a strong sense of moral values, defined mainly in conducting appropriate human relations. Propriety is the key to any successful execution of such relationships. A sense of honour and shame is central to the cultivation of inner excellence and essential to perform the prescribed role appropriate to one's position in the society. The CCP mouthpiece of journalism aims not only to engineer a socialist morality, which is increasingly difficult in a capitalist economy, but to 'correct' public opinions. However, rather than using a Confucian moral persuasion, it wields the state coercive power that can speak the language of terror, if necessary, in a time of radical political campaigns such as the Cultural Revolution.

Journalism between the state and market

Rueschemeyer *et al.* (1992) believed that capitalist development is associated with democracy because such development transforms class structures. Others, such as Berger (1986), maintain that liberal capitalism will not provide sufficient conditions for democracy. Media development in China complicates these assumptions, and calls for a more sophisticated account of the relationship between democracy and capitalism.

After three decades of reform, China has been transformed from one of the poorest countries to the world's third largest economy. However, it remains an unending series of contradictions. Central to these contradictions is the coexistence of a liberal economy and Leninist politics. Nowhere is this contradiction more evident than in the mass media that have embraced the market for a profit while retaining its mouthpiece function, despite the general assumption that a capitalist market is instrumental to liberal democracy. Indeed, market economy in China has never been a natural process of development but part of state capitalism sponsored by the CCP. Under Deng Xiaoping's pragmatic policies, capitalist institutions are borrowed as an instrument to salvage a bankrupt Maoist socialist economy. The suppression of liberal and democratic forces in the 1980s, culminating in the 1989 Tiananmen crackdown, left many in China with no illusion that a genuine political reform was on the agenda. The rebellious media in the 1989 popular protest, including the CCP's flagship paper *People's Daily* (Tan, 1990), was quickly brought back to the Party's orbit in singing the official tune of promoting the ideology of developmentalism in a new wave of all-out marketisation in the 1990s. The deepening of market reforms was carried out at the cost of relentless extraction of rural surplus labour and large-scale laid-off urban workers in state-owned enterprises. Wang Hui observes that 'after the armed crackdown on the June Fourth Movement people lost their chance to protest and the price reform introduced at gunpoint became a success' (2000: 80). Though the Maoist totalitarianism was replaced by the Dengist technocratic authoritarianism, the repressive nature of the Party-state remained unchanged. Neither the mass media nor the public are able to play any meaningful democratic role in the nation's political life. Official corruption quickly became rampant in the booming economy which, ironically, extended into the mass media which should act as a watchdog to expose precisely such social ills (Zhao, 1998).

Under the new Party-state capitalism (Meisner, 1996), massive commercialisation moves were introduced in the media industry. After 1992, the media were expected to survive financially in the market on their own when state subsidies were cut off. Meanwhile, non-Party organs such as the evening and metropolitan press are no longer required to carry Party propaganda and therefore plunged fully into profit-making operations (Huang, 2001). The sharp rise of advertising demands, coupled with a proliferation of market-oriented papers and TV channels, provide the media with golden opportunities to make a fortune with their state-protected monopolistic status. China's first press group, the *Guangzhou Daily*, was designated by the Party in 1996 as a pilot socialist press group. By 1998, it achieved an impressive revenue of 1.72 billion yuan (£130 million) with a profit of 349 million yuan (£26.66 million), and even became one of Guangzhou's top ten state enterprises. In anticipation of an intense, perhaps exaggerated, commercial competition from global media giants with an imminent TWO membership, Chinese media organisations rushed to form conglomerates in the second half of the 1990s. By 2004, China had already set up 38 press groups, eight radio and television groups, six publishing groups and three motion pictures groups. Many of these groups were formed through initial internal diversification operations, in particular within major Party newspapers. The media quickly developed into a major highly profitable industry. *China Central Television*, the only TV station allowed to cover the entire China, generated 10 billion yuan (£758 million) revenue from advertising alone in 2007. The media industry now contributes 2.1%–2.2% of China's GDP growth.

With the CCP-sponsored but state-protected commercialisation drive, the Chinese media have been transformed from a pure Leninist propaganda machine into a 'Party Publicity Inc.' (He, 2000) that operates to generate profit while continuing to act as a reformed mouthpiece. The new 'Inc.' is oriented more toward political publicity than ideological brainwashing and conversion. It focuses on promoting the image of the Party and justifying its legitimacy. However, as it is financially responsible for its survival it is subject as much to economic pressure as political influence. In this 'marketisation of political management' (Berger, 1986), the media have two masters to serve: the Party and the market. One unintended consequence of commercialisation is the depoliticising of large sections of the media that are more responsive to market demands in a cutthroat competition for ratings and audience share. The abstract 'people' in Party journalism is thus transformed into practical 'consumers'. The 'Party Publicity Inc.' became attuned to pleasing both masters in a shrewd operation that sells news and other media products as appealing commodities, though under no circumstances did they undermine the Party-state ideological premises.

One way this is executed is through a dual operation within one press group. That is, the parent papers strive to meet their political obligations by following the Party demands, while the subsidiary papers cater for readers' interests – a strategy dubbed as 'the big paper (Party broadsheet) manages ideological directions, the small paper (tabloids) manages the market' (*dabao guan fangxiang, xiaobao guan shichang*). This institutional innovation is characteristic of bureaucratic state capitalism – the convenience marriage of money and power. The Party-state, as the largest capitalist stakeholder, monopolises major resources and only grants media conglomerates economic privileges when they meet its ideological and political imperatives (Lee *et al.*, 2006). The dual money-mouthpiece function is guaranteed, along with others, by the CCP-appointed senior media managers as loyal propagandists and shrewd business executives. However, the dual-track journalism is not always an easy one. In competing for readers, the market-oriented press constantly pushes the boundary and exploits ideologically grey areas for a profit. This can create unforeseen consequences. For example, the *idealist* world order promoted by the *People's Daily* contrasts sharply with the *realist* jungle world portrayed by its subsidiary *Global Times*. The former reflects official pragmatic foreign policies while the latter expresses popular nationalistic feelings (Cao, 2007). Adopting market strategies in the popular press results in different styles of journalism as shown in Table 13.1.

Democracy and the commercialised media

Deeply entrenched in the new political economic order, the Chinese media have profited from the inroad of capitalism as a state-protected sector. Capitalist acceleration in China witnessed the retreat of the media from its role as an agent for a progressive political change. Hopes for press freedom pushed by aspirant editors, liberal-minded intellectuals and government officials in the 1980s were dashed in the 1989 crackdown of pro-democracy protests. In its place came the economic pragmatism of the 1990s. Without an independent status, the media have limited

Table 13.1 Two types of journalism

Features	The Party press	Market-oriented press
Perspectives	Moralist Abstract Party-state	Practical Specific Consumer
Contents	Leader and government activities Principles/rationales/expositions Problems in the background High politics	Human interest stories Hard facts Problems highlighted Everyday life
Style	Preaching Sterile Formal Dry headlines	Informing Lively Informal Eye-catching/sensationalist headlines
Readership	Party/government officials	People in the street
Circulation	Small	Large

democratic potentials even with a capitalist economy. The inclusion of the journalist profession to the new middle class club gives them more incentives to work with, rather than against, the established power. Just as a democratic state and the private media could at times collaborate for mutual benefits (Curran, 2000), an authoritarian state can use capitalist development in its favour.

With 'socialist press freedom' fading away as a distant dream of the last century, the 'watchdog' role has become a new theoretical and practical focus in the Chinese media since the mid-1990s. The *China Central Television* primetime investigative programme *Focus* has been used as an example of the media as a 'watchdog' on the government, because the programme galvanised the audience for its exposure of corruption cases since its launch in mid-1990s. The party media's watchdog role is a strong claim as the watchdog function is related closely to the democratic function of the media. Curran (2000: 121) concludes that 'the principal democratic role of the media, according to liberal theory, is to act as a check on the state. The media should monitor the full range of state activities and fearlessly expose abuses of official authority'. However, engineered by the Party-state, the watchdog role for the Chinese media was a rhetoric designed to cement the tie between the Party and the alienated people, and to bring dysfunctional local bureaucracies under central control. The Party television only 'swats small flies, but not to beat the big tiger'. Invoking discourse of accountability and liberal notions of checks and balances, the watchdog claim creates an illusion of the Party-state 'speaking' for the people – a *minben*-styled central authority to deliver the promise of a benevolent 'good governance'. Ultimately, 'the watchdog on Party leashes' (Zhao, 2000) serves primarily the CCP's imperative of legitimacy, and therefore reflects the 'Party's character' of journalism, rather than the 'democratic function' of the media described in liberal theory.

There is also a general assumption, particularly in the US, that 'ideological incompatibility' exists between China's state-controlled communications system and the global communications market, and that transnational media operations have an 'inherently democratising impact' (Zhao, 2003: 57). This assumption, at best, is thinly supported by empirical evidence. Though the Western media apply democracy and human rights as a dominant frame in covering post-Tiananmen China (Cao, 2006), transnational media operations are often more concerned with their business advances than with democratic changes in China. For example, to protect his business interests in China, Rupert Murdoch removed his BBC World News service from his Asian Star satellite system in the mid-1990s and later blocked the publication of Chris Patten's memoirs by his publishers HarperCollins out of fear of offending the Beijing leadership. A casual connection between market liberalisation, pluralism and civil society proves to be a flawed framework for analysing the political implications of China's WTO membership (Keane, 2002). Furthermore, the democratising assumption of transnational media underestimates the Chinese state's capacity to negotiate with global capital over the terms of its entry into the Chinese market and its determination to censor sensitive information. US global media companies Yahoo!, Google and Microsoft were all accused of cooperating with the Chinese state for censorship.

None the less, most liberal critics share the broad assessment that media commercialisation in China is, overall, a positive development. It has been linked to what Lee (2000) calls 'demobilised liberalisation' of the post-Mao political economy. Economic momentum has helped the media to expand 'negative freedom' (Berlin, 1969) in many non-political areas, and progressively depoliticised the state, the economy and culture, resulting in considerable media liberalisation in social, though not political, fields (Lee, 2001). The explosive growth of popular media unleashed by the market forces contrasts with the decline of Party paper circulations. Though the stern-faced propaganda has been softened in the 'Party Publicity Inc.', the ritualistic chanting of official ideology can hardly compete with mass-appeal media. Furthermore, young, urban and well-educated people have largely turned away from 'mainstream' Party papers and TV channels, and instead use the internet to search for information they need. By March 2009, the number of internet users in China reached 316 million, the largest group in the world. Fully aware of such problems, propagandists resolve to adopt a range of strategies, including packaging soft messages in non-political media products such as period dramas. Still, its effectiveness is questionable. These developments have inevitably eroded the media's mouthpiece function, and demonstrated the limits to what the CCP can do in the commercialised media environment. The Chinese Party-state is thus caught between unleashing market forces for economic growth and retaining its grip on power. This is a contradiction that has yet to be resolved. It prompts a veteran China-watcher to predict: '... just as the pressure of one geologic plate against another creates earthquakes, it is possible that China's increasingly market-driven media will ultimately collide with its stubbornly resistant, Leninist state in a politically tectonic way' (Schell, 1998: 35).

Conclusions

Journalism has been central to the turbulent political developments in modern China. It has been employed as a weapon by progressive reformers such as Liang Qichao, Sun Yatsen and Zhang Taiyan for a democratic change, and by communist propagandists for seizing political power in the name of democracy. In the treacherous road to democracy, from Qing constitutional reform to the 1919 May Fourth and 1989 June Fourth movements, high hopes were raised but democracy failed to take root and lead to a constitutional state. The *minben* tradition complicates the discourse and practice of democracy, and even contributes to an authoritarian tendency.

Under the one-party rule, Chinese journalism is still largely locked into the logic of 'Party character' and mouthpiece function, though their effectiveness is being weakened. However, as Lowenstein and Merrill (1990: 158) contend, 'media systems are supportive, not directive; they are considered more as extensions of a nation's political philosophy than as determiners of its philosophy'. The CCP-sponsored capitalism aimed at salvaging its legitimacy, not undermining it. State monopoly and absence of private media ownership mean that media commercialisation in China is not a fully-fledged free market operation. Furthermore, there is little historical evidence to suggest a journalist/media-led democratic political revolution without a credible oppositional political force (as in former Eastern Europe) or political division at the very top (as in China in the 1980s) that either uses or supports it. Media systems are ultimately shaped by the political and economic institutions of society, not the other way round. It is for this reason that Lee (2001) emphasises the importance of critiquing the state with a liberal-pluralist approach in the study of Chinese media, though a critique of the capital has become relevant in China with a radical-Marxist approach, which is often associated with analysing free market media systems in the West.

Nevertheless, Chinese society has become substantially more liberal in the post-Mao era. There has been considerable expansion of non-political space as the CCP has retreated from its intrusive control of people's private life, and concentrated on protecting its core interests, mainly its continued legitimacy to rule. The rapid growth of the mass media, for most consumers, simply means that the media have become more accessible, participatory and enjoyable. To better account for these multidimensional developments, Huang (2007: 403) proposes a 'from control to negotiation' model to complement the 'media-democracy link-up' approach. According to this model, the Party-state has become less hegemonic in dealing with the media, and started to engage in a bargaining process participated by the media, the market and the society. Though highly uneven in power relations, the four-party bargaining means at least that the media development is no longer a pure 'one-power game' and control has to be exercised through negotiation, rather than imposition. Despite the CCP's tight control, the market has generated a liberating and subversive potential to undermine the official ideology in ways unforeseen by the Party-state. After all, freer information and a more informed public are conditions for democracy. Such conditions have started to emerge, though still in a limited way. It is difficult to predict what the future holds for democracy in China, but one thing is certain: journalism will make it more difficult for the party-state to control the flow of information and to ignore the popular aspiration for a Democratic change.

Notes

1 The author wishes to thank the British Academy for the production of this chapter with a research grant that enabled the author to conduct interviews with media and government officials and collect primary data in Beijing and Shanghai in the summer of 2007.
2 Classical (or Cultural) Confucianism refers to early writings by Confucius (551–479BC) and Mencius before China was first unified under Qin Shihuang. Imperial (or State) Confucianism refers to Confucian ideology adopted by Han Wu Di (reign during 156–87BC).

References

Berger, P.L. (1986) *The Capitalist Development: fifty propositions about prosperity, equality and liberty*, New York: Basic.

Berlin, I. (1969) *Four Essays on Liberty*, Oxford: Oxford University Press.

Cao, Q. (2006) 'Western representation of the Other', pp. 105–122, in X Shi (ed.) *Discourse as Cultural Struggle*, Hong Kong: Hong Kong University Press.

Cao, Q. (2007) 'Confucian vision of a new world order? Culturalist discourse, foreign policy and the press in contemporary China', *Gazette*, 69(5):431–450.

Curran, J. (2000) 'Rethinking media and democracy', pp. 120–154 in J. Curran and M. Gurevitch (eds.) *Mass Media and Society*, London: Arnold.

Guang, L. (1996) 'Elusive democracy: conceptual change and the Chinese democracy movement, 1979/79–1989', *Modern China*, 22, 4:417–447.

Friedman, E. (1995) *National Identity and Democratic Prospects in Socialist China*, New York and London: M.E. Sharpe.

He, B.G. (1996) *The Democratisation of China*, London and New York: Routledge.

He, B.G. and Guo, Y.J. (2000) *Nationalism, National Identity and Democratisation in China*, Hants and Vermont: Ashgate.

He, Z. (2000) 'Chinese Communist Party press in a tug of war: a political economy analysis of Shenzhen Special Zone press', pp. 112–151 in C.C. Lee (ed.) *Power, Money and Media: Communication Patterns and Bureaucratic Control in Cultural China*. Evanston, IL: Northwestern University Press.

Huang, C.J. (2001) 'China's state-run tabloids: the rise of "city newspapers"', *Gazette*, 63(5):435–450.

Huang, C.J. (2007) 'From control to negotiation: Chinese media in the 2000s', *Gazette*, 69(5):402–412.

Huntington, S.P. (1993) *The Third Wave: Democratization in the Late Twentieth Century*, Norman, OK: University of Oklahoma Press.

Keane, M. (2002) 'Facing off on the final frontier: the WTO accession and the rebranding of China's national champions', *Media International Australia*, 105, 130–147.

Lee, C.C. (2000) 'China's journalism: the emancipatory potential of society theory', *Journalism Studies*, 1(4):559–575.

Lee, C.C. (2001) 'Rethinking the political economy: implications for media and democracy in Greater China', *The Public*, 8(3):1–22.

Lee, C.C., He, Z., and Huang, Y. (2006) '"Chinese Party Publicity Inc." conglomerated: the case of the Shenzhen Press Group', *Media, Culture & Society*, 28(4):581–602.

Lowenstein, R. L. and M. J. C. (1990) *Macromedia: mission message and morality*, New York and London: Longman.

Merrill, J.C. (2000) 'Democracy and the press: the reality and the myth', *Media Asia*, 27(4):197–199.

Meisner, M. (1996) *The Deng Xiaoping Era: an inquiry into the fate of Chinese socialism, 1978-1994*, New York: Hill and Wang.

Nathan, A.J. (1985) *Chinese Democracy*, Berkeley and Los Angeles: University of California Press.

Pan, W. (2003) 'Toward a consultative rule of law regime in China', *Journal of Contemporary China*, 12(34):3–44.

Pye, W.P. (1997) 'Chinese democracy and constitutional development', pp. 205–218 in F. Itoh (ed.) *China in the Twenty-first Century: politics, economy and society*, Tokyo and New York: United Nations University Press.

Rueschemeyer, D., Stephens, E.H. and Stephens, J.D. (1992) *Capitalist Development and Democracy*, Chicago: Chicago University Press.

Schell, O. (1998) 'Maoism vs. media in the marketplace', pp. 35–42 in E.E. Dennis and R.W. Snyder (eds.) *Media & Democracy*, New Brunswick and London: Transaction Publishers.

Tan, F. (1990) 'The People's Daily: politics and popular will – journalistic defiance in China during the spring of 1989', *Pacific Affairs*, 63(2):151–169.

Wang, E.B. and Titunik, R.F. (2000) 'Democracy in China: the theory and practice of minben', pp. 55–72 in S.S. Zhao (ed.) *China and Democracy: the prospects for a democratic China*, New York and London: Routledge.

Wang, H. (2000) 'Fire at the castle gate', *New Left Review*, 6:69–99.

Zhao, Y.Z. (1998) *Media, Market and Democracy in China: between the party line and bottom line*, Urbana: University of Illinois Press.

Zhao, Y.Z. (2000) 'Watchdog on party leashes? Contexts and implications of investigative journalism in post-Deng China', *Journalism Studies*, 1(2):577–597.

Zhao, Y.Z. (2003) 'Transnational capital, the Chinese state, and China's Communication Industries in a fractured society', *The Public/Javnost*, 10(4):53–74.

14
RETHINKING "DEVELOPMENT" JOURNALISM

Silvio Waisbord

In this chapter, I discuss the concept of development journalism (DJ), and its relevance to contemporary debates about press and democracy around the world. The first section discusses competing interpretations of DJ. The second section examines defenses and critiques of DJ amidst broad debates about communication and development. The third and fourth sections examine the problems of using "development" to identify core ideals of democratic journalism. The chapter concludes with a call to approach the idea of DJ critically in the context of discussions about normative models of journalism.

Competing definitions of development journalism

The concept of DJ was born at a time when political, economic, and social development in Africa, Asia, and Latin America dominated policy and academic debates in the post-World War II period. Early efforts to theorize DJ were linked to debates about the role of communication and media in development.

Filipino academics and journalists and the Press Foundation of Asia have been credited with coining the term "development journalism" and pioneering education in DJ in the mid-1960s (Encanto 1982; Lent 1977). Subsequently, the concept became adopted particularly in Asia and Africa. Newspapers in Bangladesh, India, Indonesia, Kenya, and Tanzania, among other countries, embraced DJ. Training institutes and academic curricula specializing in DJ blossomed. Government units and foundations launched DJ programs (Manyozo 2008). Since then, DJ has been a matter of continuous debate and analysis, as well as a flashpoint amidst discussions about global press freedom and the linkages between communication and development.

Two approaches need to be distinguished in definition of DJ (McQuail 1991; Romano 1998). One set of studies has identified it with social and communitarian reporting of news about rural, education, health, and economic issues that affect the majority of people in the "global South" (Haque 1986; Shah 1989; Vilanilam 1975).

DJ is primarily concerned with news about social circumstances, challenges, and interventions related to the lives of the non-elites, the vast number of dispossessed and impoverished people. A focus on development issues also demands that the press examines critically the reality of post-colonial societies, domestic and international programs aimed to redress social conditions, and the obstacles to the improvement of people's lives. DJ also refers to reporting that brings out popular voices in the identification of problems and solutions (Aggarwala 1979; Golding 1974; Ogan 1982).

These goals require a major reshuffling of the priorities of journalism. Instead of providing entertainment, journalism should educate people about issues of significant public interest. A focus on ordinary people should be prioritized over elite information. Coverage of recent events should be replaced by reporting long-term, structural processes underlying vital issues in people's lives. Public goals should prevail over commercial principles. DJ is expected to influence development policies by indicating issues that need attention, offering perspectives and solutions, and monitoring policies and programs (McKay 1993). More recently, DJ has been redefined in terms of journalism that promotes human emancipation and citizen participation. The press should facilitate citizens' empowerment in connection to social movements and others forms of political involvement (Shah 1996).

A second set of definitions has emphasized the notion of DJ as a nation-state building instrument (Hachten 1993). Here the emphasis is put on the idea that journalists should be part of broad political and social efforts towards development, national integration, and internal cooperation. This includes supporting government policies and programs designed to build integrated, stable, and economically "developed" societies. In the context of countries with deep divisions in terms of religion, ethnicity, language, and tribal identities, the press should play a crucial role in national integration. Statist approaches to DJ believed that, just as it did during anti-imperialist struggles, the press should support political efforts towards national unity and modernization. Such a proposal expressed concerns about the danger of disintegration and violence in post-colonial societies. A press that fostered criticism, as proposed by the Western liberal model, was deemed dangerous in the context of politically frail and culturally divided countries. "Development" goals should take priority over political conflict and divergent opinions. Former colonies could afford neither a "free, adversarial press" nor a journalism focused on controversy, "spot news," and competition. Because it can potentially sharpen divisions and derail development efforts, such a model of journalism is negative for countries with different priorities, socio-economic structures, and political history (Dare 2000).

Such a view of DJ was particularly widespread among many political leaders of independent countries in Africa and Asia in the 1960s and 1970s. Not only did they frequently appeal to the press to aid "development" efforts and refrain from fueling divisions. They also created government bodies to control the press and promote journalism education. In Malaysia and Singapore, for example, the government supported the creation of journalism programs as part of its overall efforts to gain support for "development policies" and national integration (Anuar 2005; Richstad 2000). Their legacy still survives in the existence of DJ programs established in the 1960s and 1970s under the impetus of development policies (Wimmer and Wolf 2005).

The co-existence of communitarian and statist approaches turned DJ into a complex and contradictory notion. This tension is rooted in the fact that DJ expressed the wishes and expectations of a broad set of interests in the "global South." From political leaders who promoted a mix of nationalistic, socialistic, and authoritarian policies to grassroots activists, a disparate coalition endorsed DJ. DJ represented different ideals to many constituencies, who became accidental allies in efforts to outline an alternative model to the liberal and the communist models of the press. Not surprisingly, then, DJ comprised a long list of aspirations that neither ideologically nor theoretically fit together. Various principles attributed to DJ were in direct contradiction with each other. For example, the ideal of "positive news" showing the achievements of government programs was antithetical to the aspirations that journalism should report "non-elites" news about the concerns and demands of ordinary folks. Dialogic and critical journalism wasn't congruent with calls for the press to promote social harmony and integration. What held together different strands of DJ was their categorical opposition to the liberal model of the press, and more broadly, to any communication paradigm rooted in "Western" ideas.

Such consensus has been neither sufficient to delineate a normative model of social responsibility of the press nor to ground the claims that the "global South" requires a type of journalism different from the West. While many of the ideals of DJ are still commendable, "development" is a worn-out adjective. Many DJ advocates rightly suggested that democracies need a journalism that provides a wide range of views on significant public issues, focuses on the lives and demands of regular citizens, provides opportunities for the expression of citizens' voices, covers long-term processes, and scrutinizes the actions of the powerful. Continuing to call that journalism "development," however, is misguided. It neither clarifies the mission of journalism nor provides guidelines about how it is feasible.

DJ and the debate about development communication

Early definitions of DJ were critical of "modernization" positions that argued that the mass media positively contribute to the development of "traditional," non-Western societies through the dissemination of "modern" values (Sparks 2007; Waisbord 2000b). Such argument was anchored in idealist premises, according to which specific cultural values were drivers of modernity. Political and economic modernization were possible when modern, Western values (e.g. individualism, secularism), existed. Exposure to modern values transmitted through radio and newspapers was assumed to contribute to shaping a modern mindset.

On the one hand, DJ clearly diverged from the "modernization" argument. Instead of seeing local culture as obstacle to development, its proponents believed that the press needs to tap into historical and cultural traditions. Local knowledge was not an impediment, but rather, a boon to development. Further, DJ was seen as promoting public dialogue to discuss matters of local interest. Underlying this vision was a model of horizontal, grassroots communication that differed from the top-down model of communication promoted by "modernization" theory. On the other hand, the notion that DJ should play a key role in process of national integration echoed similar arguments made by modernization theorists. They also viewed the "modern" media as having a critical role in fostering national cohesion and development in traditional societies with deep cultural and political divisions.

DJ was placed in the "social responsibility" tradition of model of press systems. DJ opposed key values of the liberal canon of the press, basically because it considered them unfitting for "developing" societies. The question of press freedom, a cornerstone of classic liberalism, was not central to DJ. It was either ignored or dismissed on the account that post-colonial societies require press systems and journalistic practices that are different from the West. The idea that governments are untrustworthy and secretive was not a central preoccupation to DJ. Nor were other core notions of the liberal model such as "the press as Fourth Estate," truth-telling, and objectivity.

Although DJ rejected liberal principles, it did not embrace the totalitarian/agitprop model of the press. While they were concerned about the political consequences of unrestricted press criticism, proponents of DJ didn't task the press with ideological indoctrination or mass mobilization along the lines of the communist model. They were more concerned with the tendency of the dominant, Western-influenced press to ignore social ills and economic development. Certainly, "statist" advocates of DJ called the press to support national integration and government goals, a view that reflected the appeal of socialist and nationalist policies in many independent countries, particularly in Africa, in the 1960s and 1970s (Odhiambo 1991).

That position became the target of liberal and conservative critics, who accused DJ of proposing an anti-democratic model of the press (Stevenson 1994; Sussman 1977, 1978). In their view, DJ embodied the communist ideals of putting the media in the service of ideological domination by the government. "Development journalism" was an attempt to redress communist ideology in a different package. Certainly, in the name of DJ, many governments exercised discretionary control of the press. The adoption of DJ in the context of authoritarian regimes in several African and Asian countries in the 1960s and 1970s validated the critics. The collusion between government and the press created "ethical dilemmas" for journalists who, although they supported nationalistic causes, also believed that the press should be separated from the government (Ebo 1994). Because post-colonial governments generally failed to create democratic mechanisms of control and accountability, DJ became integrated into authoritarian structures. Official manipulation eviscerated its radical democratic premises, and turned DJ into an instrument of political control (Gunaratne 1990; Lent 1981; Reeves 1993).

During the 1970s and 1980s, the debate about DJ became engulfed in Cold War politics. Debates about press models were dominated by dichotomous views that reduced alternatives to liberal-democratic and authoritarian/communist models. Journalists and scholars who supported the orthodox model of the Western press were hostile to both DJ and UNESCO's proposals for a New World Information and Communication Order (NWICO). The NWICO debates were based on the conclusion that Western control of global flows of information had pernicious effects for freedom of expression and information worldwide. Like DJ, NWICO advocates considered that the Western, market-based model of the press was antithetical to the development and democracy in the global South. A diversity of positions converged in both DJ and NWICO, including authoritarian and communitarian, liberal and communist, progressive and conservative. Some didn't see government necessarily as an enemy of the press, but rather, as a potential ally. Others, instead, were primarily interested in a journalism that facilitates local participation and raises awareness about the social conditions affecting the majority of the population in post-colonial settings. Such differences, however, got lost amidst the polarized politics of the Cold War. While critics accused NWICO and DJ of promoting communist ideals, their supporters condemned Western domination of international news flows and the global imposition of the liberal model of the press. Caught in the bipolar global politics of the time, the debate offered little room for nuanced, alternative positions that sought to carve out a "third way" for journalism.

"Development" and its conceptual problems

Despite a voluminous academic literature, DJ continues to lack a unified set of theoretical principles. It blended various ideological and political traditions. It has served as a unifying idea for various political and intellectual positions intended to outline a press model for "developing" countries that diverged from the canon of Anglo–American liberalism. Because DJ has functioned as a screen on which various expectations were projected, it has remained conceptually ambiguous.

The ambivalent meaning of "development" also contributed to the conceptual fuzziness of DJ. For decades, "development" has been liberally used to refer to a diversity of social processes. It has been used to refer to a multifaceted process of social change, a specific theory, as well as an ideological framework. It alludes to "modern" forms of economic and political organization, community participation and empowerment, national integration, social emancipation, industrialization, "social progress," and so on. From modernization to post-development theories, a variety of intellectual approaches have offered wide-ranging and opposite definitions of development. For some, development was synonymous with the historical evolution of Western societies towards industrialized, capitalist democracy. For others, it refers to the expansion of political and social participation in local decision-making. For critical perspectives, "development" became the normative ideal constructed on a selective interpretation of the modern Western experience. As both intellectual enterprise and policy recom- mendations, "developmentalism" embodied Western-centric, patronizing attitudes, and essentialist assumptions (Escobar 2000). These criticisms have animated efforts to sketch out ideas for "alternative development" grounded on local forms of actions and linked to grassroots participation (Matthews 2004).

Despite its knotty intellectual genealogy, the concept of "development" survives in contemporary academic and political debates. Although it is hardly the buzzword it was during the post-World War II years, development remains widely used to refer to global policies and programs that address education, environmental, health, poverty, economic, and political issues. "Development" prominently figures in the mandate of United Nations agencies, multilateral financial institutions, and international aid programs. It is also extensively used by "post-development" advocates who criticize the "developmentalist" mindset underpinning international aid and "globalizing" policies promoted by Western financial institutions and governments. Advocates continue to use "development" to designate actions towards the improvement of political, economic and social conditions; critics, instead, find it irremediably loaded with authoritarian implications and embedded in Western thinking.

Is "development journalism" still a useful category?

The reality of DJ is more complex than when it emerged. DJ has been institutionalized in university programs, including prestigious journalism schools in the global South such as the University of Philippines-Los Banos. A generation of Asian and African journalists has been trained under the principles of "DJ." Core concepts of DJ are upheld as desirable, professional values among contemporary journalists in Malaysia, Singapore, and Tanzania (Ramaprasad 2001). DJ still grips the imagination of scores of journalists around the world. It stands as the alternative to the libertarian model of the press, a tradition that it is still viewed skeptically on the grounds that it is not fully applicable to the "developing" world (Dixon 1997).

DJ is in trouble, however, both practically and conceptually. In terms of actual practice, several problems undermine the implementation of DJ. Rampant commercialism, government control, and weak commitment of news organizations to covering public issues run against the ideals of DJ (Bhattarcharjea 1994; Cenite et al. 2008; Edeani 1993). Conceptually, development doesn't describe the original ideals of DJ. Confusion around the idea of development as well as its assumptions embedded in a flawed model of social change raises questions about its usefulness to define the ideals of journalism in the global South. "Development" continues to overburden journalism with a long list of normative and contradictory ideals. Half a century later, linking development to journalism seems questionable. The biting critique of "developmentalism" coupled with the passing of "development" policies embraced by many "Third World" countries in the 1960s and 1970s have rendered "development" a hollowed-out and anachronistic concept. As an adjective, it hardly adds much to describe either journalistic ideals in the "global South" or the public mission and social commitment of journalism.

My intention is not to reignite a debate about appropriate labels or propose possible successors to DJ. I am not sure a replacement or a new paradigm is necessary. Engaging in discussions about what to call "the good journalism" is a potentially stimulating theoretical exercise, but unfortunately, it has often been bogged down by long semantic squabbles with few implications for journalistic practice. Key elements of DJ are well captured by various models that emphasize the role of journalism in support of participatory democracy and social justice. The core ideals of DJ overlap with "civic journalism" (Gunaratne 1996), "emancipatory journalism" (Shah 1996), "watchdog journalism" (Waisbord 2000a), and "peace journalism" (Galtung and Vincent 1992).

My aim is to interrogate a key notion underlying DJ: The idea that the "global South" requires a specific kind of journalism. DJ offered to report the news from "a Third World perspective" (Aggarwala 1978). DJ was originally animated by the idea that "poor" countries shared common traits given their political and economic history and position in world development. In his taxonomy of press theories, Denis McQuail (1991: 120) correctly points out, "the starting point for a separate 'development theory' of mass media is the fact of some common circumstance of developing countries that limit the application of other theories or that reduce their potential benefits." The problem is that development theory originally did not recognize significant differences within the "periphery" as well as overlapping challenges between the "West" and the "Rest." Stark dichotomies paved over important differences among non-Western countries. Both "development" and "journalism" were more complex than what those dyadic options allowed for. Neither post-colonial histories have followed similar paths in the global South nor was the evolution of journalism identical or completely different from the global North.

The idea that "developing" societies require a unique press is embedded in an essentialist vision about the "global South." Just to cluster countries as "poor" (or "wealthy" for that matter) says little about supposed common demands for a certain model of journalism. One could argue that a journalism that contributes to participation, citizens' expression and social justice, as many champions of DJ have advocated (Galtung and Vincent 1992), is not linked to the position of countries in the "Human Development" index. Rather, it is a requirement for democracy without adjectives and geographical boundaries. Why should citizens' participation or the accountability of powerful actors be limited to the global South? Why should certain journalistic principles be only applicable to countries with abysmal social disparities? Why should news coverage about social distribution of wealth, linkages between rich and poor countries, and long-term structural processes be desirable only in some countries? Why should the ideals of DJ be unique to "developing" countries, considering that some of its basic principles (e.g. promotion of local concerns, horizontal communication) are not applicable but are also found in news organizations in "developed" countries? (Bowd 2003)? Shouldn't journalism pursue those ideals regardless of locale? If not, upon what grounds can such argument be justified?

No doubt, one cannot ignore that the challenges for democracy and social justice are profoundly different across the world. In the last decades, the deepening divide between "poor" and "rich" countries has intensified political, social, and economic challenges in the "global South." Any model of journalism needs to be historically grounded and sensitive to local conditions. This does not exclude the desirability of democratic, civic-minded journalism adjusted to unique circumstances of local settings.

Such ideal of journalism faces similar challenges worldwide. Doubtless, problems such as arbitrary government censorship, draconian press laws, and other threats on journalistic autonomy and media pluralism are particularly grave in new democracies and authoritarian and monarchical regimes. A whole set of problems, however, undermines the goals of DJ. Just to mention some examples, cozy relations between the press and powerful political and business interests, the domination of elite-centered news and sensationalist coverage, and the overwhelming presence of official views are some of the challenges that narrow the scope of journalism globally.

Conclusion

A sober reassessment of DJ is necessary to determine both its theoretical and its pragmatic validity. From a perspective that considers that the press plays key roles in strengthening democracy and social justice, some of its goals are still pertinent and desirable. Other ideals, however, are troubling and unjustifiable.

A civic-minded journalism guided by many values that had been ascribed to DJ seems as necessary as ever across the "global South." Participation, debate, and criticism are needed to identify and discuss priorities and courses of action. Reporting needs and demands of socially excluded populations is important to raise and maintain attention on problems. Promoting citizens' voices through community media and the diversification of information sources is necessary to capture a variety of concerns. Scrutiny and constructive criticism of programs and policies aimed to address social conditions are fundamental. Calling such journalism "development," however, doesn't help to address the perennial problems of theoretical rigor that have plagued DJ.

It is also necessary to recognize that some ideals identified with DJ are antithetical to democratic governance and civic life. One is the idea that journalism should uncritically support government policies in the name of national security and integration. At this point, that seems to be a bogus justification for official discretionary control of the press, a request for journalism to give carte blanche to power. Often, the ideals of DJ have been twisted to silence criticism or launch xenophobic attacks against dissident journalists. No doubt, journalism needs to be responsible and exercise careful judgment in situations of heightened sensitivities amidst ethnic and religious tensions. Fanning the flames during conflictive moments neither serves goals of peace nor helps democracy in multicultural settings. Such expectation does not entail that the press should act as a lackey of governments. Efforts to recruit the press to serve in the interest of the people, the government and/or the nation smack of repressive, anti-liberal policies to suppress diversity and dissidence.

The other principle to be critically considered is the notion that journalism should embody unique local values. Certainly, particular traditions infuse journalism with specific characteristics. Local cultures ground ethical principles underpinning both the theory and the practice of journalism. The danger is to fall into essentialist and relativist positions that romantically view local models and ethical prescriptions as inherently good. Such positions easily provide justification for curtailing debate and critical reflexivity on the grounds that they threaten values such as "respect for authority" and "local morals" (Tomaselli 2003). Continuous pleas for journalism to be imbued by "Asian" and "African" values raise questions about the applicability of foreign models to local realities. Such arguments, however, easily fall into cultural essentialism as they assume the immanent existence of certain values across countries and communities, and are prone to uncritically defend local cultures, distrust "foreign" ideas, and curtail basic press rights (Massey and Li-jing 2006; Wong 2004).

More importantly, those arguments reveal the significance of discussions about universalistic and particularistic ethics in a globalized world. This is a critical point that underlined debates about DJ, such as questions about the appropriateness of Western models of communication and journalism and the justification of distinct ideals given cultural, economic, and political reasons. This question has recently moved center stage in journalism studies (Musa and Domatob 2007; Rao and Wasserman 2007). It is the axis of current discussions about the global validity of normative journalistic principles. Are there journalistic principles that are valid irrespective of local differences? Is any attempt to wish for certain press ideals such as autonomy and diversity necessarily suspect of ethnocentrism? Under the thrust of post-modern, post-colonial positions in academia, the intensification of global movements of people and cultures, and the currency of multi-culturalist politics in the contemporary world, the problem of "universal" and "particular" ethics has become central. In the past, and driven by different academic and political preoccupations, this tension was central to debates about DJ. Promoting a monolithic model of press and journalistic practices globally or vindicating a local/regional model based on cultural distinctiveness is equally problematic for democracy and social justice. One ignores particular histories, cultural trajectories and unique realities; the other easily becomes a rationalization for uncritical celebration of localism and difference.

We need to reconsider the validity of DJ in light of new intellectual debates and the problems of dividing the world into developed/developing regions. Economic, political, and cultural differences as well as distinct media traditions are present across the "global South." Certainly, some ideals of DJ, such as the need to report the concerns of ordinary citizens and diversify news issues and voices, remain relevant for democracy and social change. However, the overall relevance of DJ as a response to specific concerns during the period of decolonization may have passed. Although some of its components and aspirations are still significant, its currency as an intellectual and political enterprise is questionable.

Even as I remain skeptical about its usefulness, I don't have high hopes that DJ would fall out of favor anytime soon. "Development" is a resilient concept that has proven to survive intellectual and policy fads. It remains solidly entrenched in global technical and financial institutions as well as in government departments dealing with international affairs and aid. It is commonly used as a catchword to refer to a better future, human emancipation, progress, and other lofty ideals. Also, DJ is the focus of training centers and university programs in dozens of countries in the global South, a convenient shortcut to designate a journalism that contributes to the improvement of human conditions. Even if DJ remains a semantic leftover of bygone times, it is imperative to approach it critically and integrate it in current debates about normative models of journalism in a globalized world.

References

Aggarwala, Narinder K. 1978. News with Third World perspectives: A practical suggestion, In Philip C. Horton Ed., *The Third World and Press Freedom*, 197–209. New York: Praeger.

Aggarwala, Narinder K. 1979. What is development news? *Journal of Communication* 29, 2:181–82.

Anuar, Mustafa. 2005. Journalism, national development and social justice in Malaysia, *Asia Pacific Media Educator* 16.

Bhattacharjea, Arun. 1994. Constraints in development reporting, in M.R. Dua and V.S. Gupta Eds., *Media and Development: Themes in communication and extension*, 46–53. New Delhi: Har-Anand Publications.

Bowd, Kathryn. 2003. How different is 'different'? Australian country newspapers and development journalism, *Asia Pacific Media Educator* 14: 117–30.

Cenite, Mark, Shing Yee, Chong; Teck Juan, Han; Li Qin, Lim; Xian Lin, Tan. 2008. Perpetual development journalism? Balance and framing in the 2006 Singapore election coverage, *Asian Journal of Communication*, 18 (3): 280–95.

Dare, Olatunji. 2000. Development journalism, in Andrew A. Moemeka Ed., *Development Communication in Action: Building understanding and creating participation*, 161–78. Lanham, MD: University Press of America.

Dixon, David N. 1997. Press law debate in Kenya: Ethics as political power. *Journal of Mass Media Ethics* 12, 3: 171–82.

Ebo, Bosah L. 1994. The ethical dilemma of African journalists: A Nigerian perspective, *Journal of Mass Media Ethics*, 9: 84–93.

Edeani, David. 1993. Role of development journalism in Nigeria's development, *International Communication Gazette*.52: 123–43.

Encanto, G. R. 1982. Development journalism in the Philippines. In L. Erwin Atwood, Stuart J. Bullion and Sharon M. Murphy Eds., *International Perspectives on News*. Carbondale, IL: Southern Illinois University Press.

Escobar, Arturo. 2000. Beyond the search for a paradigm? *Post-development* and beyond, *Development*, 43 (4): 11–15.

Galtung, Johan and Richard Vincent. 1992. *Global Glasnost: Toward a New World Information/Communication Order*. Cresskill, NJ: Hampton Press.

Golding, Peter. 1974. Media role in national development: Critique of a theoretical orthodoxy, *Journal of Communication* 24: 39–53.

Gunaratne, Shelton. 1990. Media subservience and development journalism, in L. John Martin and Ray Eldon Hiebert Eds., *Current Issues in International Communication*, 352–54. White Plains, NY: Longman.

Gunaratne, Sheldon. 1996. Old wine in a new bottle: Public journalism movement in the United States and the erstwhile NWICO debate. *Asia Pacific Media Educator*, 1, 1: 64–75.

Hachten, William A. 1993. *The Growth of Media in the Third World: African failures, Asian successes*. Ames: Iowa State University Press.

Haque, Mazharaul. 1986. Is development news more salient than human interest stories in the Indian elites press? *Gazette* 38: 83–99.

Lent, John A. 1977. A Third World news deal? Part One: The Guiding Light., *Index on Censorship* 6, 5: 17–26.

Lent, John A. 1981. The perpetual see-saw: Press freedom in the ASEAN countries, *Human Rights Quarterly* 3: 62–77.

Manyozo, Linje. 2008. Communication for development: An historical overview, in UNESCO, *Media, Communication, Information: Celebrating 50 years of theories and practice*, 31–53.

Massey, Brian and Li-jing Arthur Chang. 2006. Locating Asian Values in Asian Journalism: A Content Analysis of Web Newspapers, *Journal of Communication* 52, 4: 987–1003.

Matthews, Sally. 2004. Post-development theory and the question of alternatives: A view from Africa, *Third World Quarterly* 25, 2: 373–84.

McKay, Floyd J. 1993. Development journalism in an Asian setting: A study of Depth news, *International Communication Gazette* 51, 3: 237–51.

McQuail, Denis. 1991. *Mass Communication Theory: An Introduction*. London: Sage.

Musa, Bala, and Domatob, Jerry. 2007. Who is a development journalist? Perspectives on media ethics and professionalism in post-colonial societies. *Journal of Mass Media Ethics* 22, 4: 315–31.

Odhiambo, Lewis. 1991. Development journalism in Africa: Capitulation of the Fourth Estate?, *African Media Review* 5, 2: 17–30.

Ogan, Christine. 1982. Development journalism/communication: The status of the concept, *International Communication Gazette* 29 (1-2): 3–13.

Ramaprasad, Jyotika. 2001. A profile of journalists in post-independence Tanzania, *International Communication Gazette*, 63, 6: 539–55.

Rao, Shakuntala, and Herman Wasserman. 2007. Global media ethics revisited: A postcolonial critique, *Global Media and Communication*, 3, 1: 29–50.

Reeves, Geoffrey. 1993. *Communications and the "Third World"*. London: Routledge.

Richstad, Jim. 2000. Asian journalism in the twentieth century, *Journalism Studies*, 1, 2: 273–84.

Romano, Angela. 1998. Normative theories of development journalism: State versus practitioner perspectives in Indonesia, *Australian Journalism Review*, 20: 2, 60–87.

Shah, Hemant. 1989. Some methodological considerations for the study of development news: An examination of three Indian daily newspapers, *Gazette* 45: 33–48.

Shah, Hemant. 1996. Modernization, Marginalization, and Emancipation: Toward a Normative Model of Journalism and National Development, *Communication Theory* 6, 2: 143–66.

Sparks, Colin. 2007. *Globalization, Development and the Mass Media*. London: sage.

Stevenson, Robert L. 1994. *Global Communication in the Twentieth-first Century*. New York: Longman.

Sussman, Leonard R. 1978. Development journalism: The ideological factor, in P. C. Horton Ed., *The Third World and Press Freedom*, 74–92. New York: Praeger.

Sussman, Leonard. 1977. *Mass News Media and the Third World Challenge*. Beverly Hills: Sage.

Tomaselli, Keyan G. 2003. 'Our Culture' vs 'Foreign Culture': An essay on ontological and professional issues in African journalism, *Gazette*, 65, 6: 427–41.

Vilanilam, J. 1975. Developmental news in two leading Indian newspapers, *Media Asia* 2: 37–40.

Waisbord, Silvio. 2000a. *Watchdog Journalism in South America*. New York: Columbia University Press.

Waisbord, Silvio. 2000b. Family tree of theories and approaches in development communication, available online at http://www.comminit.org

Wimmer, Jeffrey and Suzanne Wolf. 2005. Development journalism: Out of date? Available at http://epub.ub.uni-muenchen.de/647/1/mbk_3.pdf

Wong, Kokkeong. 2004. Asian-based development journalism and political elections, *Gazette: International Journal of Communication Studies*, 66, 1: 25–40.

15

RADIO NEWS: RE-IMAGINING THE COMMUNITY

Tanja Bosch

The newsroom at community station Bush Radio in Cape Town is usually bustling with activity. Locally trained news producers, activists, student interns and citizen journalists edit tape and write news copy – in English and two local languages – for the half-hourly news bulletins. The audience, many of whom live in informal settlements and low-income housing spread across the Cape Flats, a sandy stretch of land on the outskirts of the city of Cape Town, listen on battery operated or wind-up radio sets. For many of these marginalized communities, this is their only access to local news. These newscasts tend to provide positive representations of a community that, much more typically, makes front-page news in the mainstream press with negative news items related to crime and gang crime.

The widespread, pervasive nature of radio, particularly in these kinds of developing context, makes it a logical choice for the promotion of democracy. Especially for small, marginalized or rural communities, radio offers programming in indigenous languages, local perspectives and easy access to news due to low production and distribution costs (Girard, 1999). Radio news, in particular, is often of paramount importance in this regard. For radio stations, the 'quality' of broadcasts is often judged by the 'quality' of the news broadcasts, including content as well as delivery and presentation style. Moreover, news is often considered to be an agent of representative democracy (Allan, 2004). News is important to everyday life and culture (Hartley, 1988), as a central element of human communication, keeping people connected to the world around them (Halberstam, 1992).

This chapter discusses the role of radio news in developing contexts, taking into account a number of theoretical perspectives on journalism.[1] First, having situated radio as a medium in its own right, we explore radio forms and practices of civic journalism, as well as talk radio's potential to create deliberative public spheres. These two examples will be shown to highlight important links between radio news and democracy. The main focus of the chapter, however, is on two local radio stations in South Africa, namely Bush Radio, mentioned above, and MFM, a campus based station. Through an exploration of their day-to-day operation, the chapter demonstrates how radio news in developing contexts moves beyond traditional Western notions of news values toward a news journalism that directly supports development and democracy.

Radio in developing societies

The norms and values of news have always been contested in democratic societies, with journalists in newly democratic societies grappling with their roles in the agenda-setting process (Graber *et al.*, 1998). The news media not only inform, but also identify and consolidate community, orchestrate public conversation, and play an important role in reforming the political system (Shudson, 2003). In post-apartheid South Africa, journalists are effecting a transition from state-owned media and biased news propaganda to a more progressive nation-building role. The power of news broadcasts, either as state propaganda or anti-propaganda, thus emerges as a clear issue in the consideration of radio news in developing contexts.

In general, radio remains the most pervasive medium with the greatest potential for participatory communication strategies. This is primarily due to its low cost and accessibility to illiterate populations, particularly in rural areas. Radio has been described as being the most democratic of all media because of its ability to reach people isolated by geography or illiteracy (Van der Veur, 2002). Community radio has provided groups with access to media and an opportunity to articulate their views through direct and indirect participation. The rise of radio as a vehicle for popular, participatory communication began with the Bolivian miners' radios in the 1940s (O'Connor, 1990), but extended beyond its Latin American origins to the Caribbean, Asia, Australia, Europe and Africa. In South Africa, over 80 community radio stations were granted broadcast licenses in 1994, and in 2009 there are over 100 such stations operating.[2]

Around the developing world, small-scale, locally owned media have developed to counter the spread of global media corporations. Citizens' groups in these countries express their opinions and needs by using modern technologies to gain participation in the public sphere (Mowlana, 1998). Alternative media or citizen's media – and community radio in particular – resist the homogenizing tendencies of mainstream media in order to provide alternative international news, as well as more localized forms of news than commercial channels. The notion of counter-publics (articulated by Fraser, 1992) comes into sharp focus here, as audiences have the possibility to embrace multiple identities within the context of counter-hegemonic political discourse. In other ways, community radio provides alternative public spheres in their local communities, creating opportunities for citizens to exercise their communicative agency as media producers, in response to the trend of concentrated media ownership (Schiller, 2007).[3]

In South Africa, alternative media outlets increasingly use the term 'people's media' to deliberately contextualize the unstable notions of 'citizen' and 'community'. News broadcasts are usually one of the ways these radio stations differentiate their programming from the mainstream. Community stations generate more local news, choosing to place on the agenda the kinds of stories that might never cross the threshold of newsworthiness in national or commercial stations; in addition, they often frame these stories from a communication for development perspective. One example is the deliberate selection of 'good' news stories, selecting these kinds of human-interest stories over those focusing on crime and violence, which might be seen to portray the target audience negatively. These local radio stations are often acutely aware of the challenges presented by the increasing globalization of news, particularly as international news agencies already tend to shape national print news agendas. This is increasingly the case with local radio news, where limited resources sometimes mean that they are overly dependent on print media as a major source of news.

Community stations often exert a form of cultural resistance in deliberately seeking to prioritize local events in their news bulletins, even when these stories sometimes do not meet news values of immediacy or controversy. Of course, community journalists need to strike a balance between nation-building or 'sunshine' journalism and reporting 'bad news' stories, particularly with regard to HIV/AIDS, but at the same time, it remains important to challenge stereotypical reporting of Africa by the Western media (Hunter-Gault, 2006). Perhaps this is most easily defined as a kind of civic or public journalism, which is increasingly characterizing news in developing contexts, where citizens become the new agenda-setters.

Civic journalism and local radio

In the 1970s, UNESCO launched the debate over the dominance of Western influence in world news flow, resulting in the New World Information Order. Several Third World nations argued for their right to restrict the free flow of news across their borders, prioritizing instead the development of their own national news agencies. This included the Non-Aligned News Agencies Pool, dedicated to a journalism of national development (Stevenson, 1988).

It may be argued that the ultimate goal of socially responsible journalism falls within the domain of the community media model. In some way, this has been an attempt to counter Schramm's (1964) argument that there is little news flow between developing nations; that undue attention is given in newscasts to the more developed nations; and that reality is distorted as a result. Furthermore, the discipline of journalism lends itself to civic engagement. With an increased global emphasis on civic journalism, the role of the trainee community journalist has become progressively more important. Alternative and community media projects represent a small but growing resistance to mainstream media and the conglomeration of media ownership. In addition, mainstream media are being increasingly driven by commercial interests, leaving little room for the use of media as a vehicle for social change.

Civic or public journalism is here understood as a kind of journalism that emphasizes service to the community. This is achieved, in part, by identifying important social issues and focusing on them, thereby framing news in a way that facilitates collective efforts to find solutions, not just problems and conflict (Shepherd, 1994). It may also entail journalists being involved in attempts to help create and sustain public discussion to ensure that communities face their problems, with a wide-ranging exploration of conflicting perspectives and sources of information aired and discussed. This approach encourages journalists to put citizens first and to share with them the task of setting the news agenda (Graber et al., 1998).

Traditionally, the media have been cast in a watchdog role, but increasingly scholars concerned with developing countries agree that media institutions have much wider social and political responsibilities to perform (Meijer, 2001). This is in line with the growth of a new journalism that increasingly challenges classical notions of objectivity in news – that is, that the journalist exists merely to report on 'the facts' in a dispassionate manner. In other words, the assumption that journalism can be divorced from the society in which it operates is being openly questioned. In its place is a new emphasis on journalism's role in fostering discussion and debate about social transformation, which necessarily situates it at the heart of political change.

Community radio news in Cape Town, South Africa

Bush Radio is the oldest community radio project in South Africa, based in the city of Cape Town. The station was set up to serve the black communities who were forcibly removed from the city and relocated to a vast sandy area known as the Cape Flats. Today, more than a decade after the legislated racism of apartheid, the station still prides itself on its alternative talk-based programming. The music–talk ratio is about 40%–60%, with music programmes often focusing on music education, and highlighting genres of music such as kwaito, jazz and blues, which do not regularly receive airplay on commercial radio. The talk-based content includes locally produced news, talk shows and documentaries on a range of issues, all centred around local politics and economics. There is also a strong focus on socially conscious programming intended to increase knowledge and change behaviour around various health issues, including HIV and AIDS.

Here at Bush Radio in South Africa, international students from various destinations visit the station for periods ranging from 4 to 12 weeks and participate in various programming tasks. In 2005 students from the University of Southern California, Emory University, Syracuse and Marquette University in the United States participated, as well as students from several Irish, Dutch and German campuses. The students are fully integrated into daily activities and carry out administrative tasks, participate in the production of local news bulletins, liaise with NGOs and interest groups in the production of programmes, and visit various Cape Flats townships to assist with field broadcasts. This experience of living and working with people from diverse backgrounds can yield a kind of expertise and knowledge that is particularly useful for effective moral and civic engagement (Erlich, 2000).

For many of these students from the North, this is often their first interaction with local cultural and economic minorities and communities; and likewise, for the community radio station, local staff members are afforded the opportunity to learn more about various international destinations and cultures they may otherwise not have had the opportunity to explore. Local staff, when interviewed, pointed out that their interaction with these international interns demystified European or North American culture, and inspired a greater interest in global political events. Similarly, the foreign interns expressed a new understanding of the continent and its people. In several instances, the foreign students indicated that their involvement in impoverished communities in Cape Town had inspired them to be more aware of similar social problems in their own countries.

Several research studies have shown, in Erlich's (2000) words, that 'the long-term impact of youth service experience on later political and community involvement can best be explained by the contribution these service experiences make to the creation of an enduring sense of oneself as a politically engaged and socially conscious person' (2000, p. 6). In concurring with this view, I would point out that, through participation in outside broadcasts, even the local interns indicated that they were afforded the opportunity to enter areas they otherwise may not have, either through lack of opportunity or unwarranted fear of crime. Local interns from the Cape Peninsula University of Technology spend a full year at the station before returning to their diploma programme for one more semester before graduation. Their first two years provide them with a firm grasp of journalism theory, while this one-year internship is meant to provide practical experience.

Similarly, MFM (previously Matie FM) is a campus-based community radio station located at Stellenbosch University in the Western Cape. 'Matie' is the colloquial term used to refer to a student at the university. The radio station serves university students, as well as the surrounding communities of Stellenbosch, many of which are impoverished township areas. The radio station has had a partnership with the university's journalism department, where students produce daily local news as part of their curriculum.

At MFM, fourth-year journalism students are compelled to engage with news from the local community, providing a similar experience. As part of their one-year postgraduate programme, they produce daily news bulletins for the radio station, with an emphasis on local news and angles. Participating in political or community service activities often entails facing moral challenges, and can expand the range of people for whom one feels empathy and responsibility, as well as fostering the capacity to understand others' perspectives. It is hoped that this will lead, in turn, to a change in the ways students see themselves, generating a willingness to take action on moral and civic issues (Erlich, 2000).

For students at Bush Radio and MFM, learning to produce news in ways that differ from their usual experiences of the mainstream is often challenging. Furthermore, their day-to-day work activities not only teach them the nuts and bolts of radio production, but also immerse them in the realities of communities they might otherwise not have known. Instead of merely producing programming, students become involved with community members in various ways. Often these community members are volunteers at the station, but sometimes the students are also required to hold focus group discussions as part of formative research for communication campaigns, or simply find themselves chatting with community members at community events.

For those students who are from the station's target communities, their work activities allow them to realize a sense of self and group efficacy. As they progressed through their stay at the station, the students who formed part of this study indicated an increased understanding of how these communities operate and the richness of their diversity, and expressed a willingness to continue this kind of work in the future. Most journalism students undertake some form of internship or field experience. However, those who are placed at community radio stations are usually more likely to encounter civic journalism in the form of communication for development and social change. It is their production of news, in particular, which allows them to challenge the mainstream in ways that they might previously not have had the opportunity to consider.

From civic journalism to citizen journalism

Developing contexts can vary widely, and as such, precise definitions of radio news may also vary widely from location to location. At the same time, the growth of local forms of community radio within development journalism has led to changes in the role of the audience as well. Traditionally, news producers addressed what they perceived to be a relatively passive audience. These perceptions are being dramatically altered, however, by a greater recognition of audiences' capacity for participatory involvement. Radio stations are becoming increasingly inclined to engage in forms of citizen journalism (sometimes called 'democratic journalism'), where non-professionals play an active role in collecting, reporting and disseminating the news (Bowman & Willis, 2003). At local radio stations, this often means that community members call into the station with news items, agree to be drawn upon as sources, and even help to staff newsrooms or generate citizen-based forms of first-hand reporting. In so doing, members of community audiences are helping to drive news agendas in sometimes unexpected directions.

Here we see how familiar strictures of professionalism, codified in a number of different ways in the West, are being challenged in developing contexts. Citizen journalism invites an exploration of the existing ecology of radio news. Audience-driven news content is often associated with a 'tabloidization' of the news agenda (see Allan, 2004). Here the term tabloidization refers to a particular style of human interest reporting, often negatively associated with a disregard for the truth in favour of sensationalism, gossip, celebrity and sex. Human interest is seen to engender a harmful influence on proper reporting, a dangerous distraction. However, in developing contexts, more human-centred conceptions of newsworthiness are more likely to be valued, being allied to notions of progressive social change and democracy.

Pressing issues surrounding the impact of technology on news are similarly linked to audience involvement. Listeners often use their mobile phones to interact directly with their community radio stations, for example. Moreover, radio stations are increasingly adopting multimedia approaches, sometimes making use of blogs or online social networking sites to engage listeners and solicit feedback. Bush Radio, for example, uploads its community news to www.bushradionews.blogspot.com, while commercial talk station, Cape Talk 567, engages with listeners via a Facebook group.

Talk radio and educational radio

Despite the challenges posed by market-driven imperatives for local radio, commercial talk radio provides a further example of the intersection of radio news and democracy in a South African context. When one considers the forms and conventions of talk radio, its potential to be instrumental in the development and maintenance of a discursive public sphere comes into sharp focus.

The Habermasian (Habermas, 1989) notion of the public sphere builds on the premise of citizens being able to enter into public discussion on an equal basis. Here it may be argued that talk radio, to some extent, plays a role in promoting rational – critical debate, the lifeblood of the public sphere. But talk radio is bound by its commercial imperatives, depending as it does on advertising for its survival. This dependency means that talk stations such as 567MW in Cape Town are continually caught between competing pressures, namely between these 'laws of the market,' on the one hand, and those of press freedom (where diversity in news and views are valued for their enrichment of public dialogue), on the other (Benson & Neveu, 2005). For a station to enjoy greater flexibility in experimenting with formats, presenters or content, and to be free to make the most of citizen journalism, an alternative economic model would be necessary. For Cape Talk, their audience members are consumers first, and citizens second. Here we see how talk radio reconfigures the public sphere in commodified terms as an 'unseen market place' (Allan, 2004: 31).

Nevertheless, news is of paramount importance to the station, which describes itself as the Cape's 'Number 1 news and talk station.' And in some ways, the news is positioned in such a way as to build national identity. The strong commitment to local news items – which sometimes takes the form of a 'glocalization' of international news items – means that news is used to enrich a local public sphere. The station's news is billed as being based upon 'eyewitness' reporting, where an emphasis is placed upon local sources and firsthand accounts of events. What is especially interesting here, in my view, is the extent to which this rendering of news resists the trends in other places, where increased competition has led to more entertainment-centred news.

Radio has also been used in developing countries for various kinds of education, including voter education and pro-social campaigning. There are numerous examples of this, including the use of radio to teach mathematics to schoolchildren in Thailand (Galda, 1984), for literacy training in Mexico (Ginsburg & Arias-Goding, 1984), among others. One of the most widespread examples of radio for education is the *Farm Radio Forum*, a project that started in Canada in 1941, but which has since spread to many other countries, particularly in Africa. The programmes focus on problems of agriculture, rural development, education, innovation, self-government and literacy (Nwaerondu & Thompson, 1987). Here we see the expansion of the concept of 'news' to include items that are not necessarily 'newsworthy', but that contribute to media-driven campaigns for social development. At stake is the need to build local identity while, at the same time, promote the advancement of marginalized groups.

Conclusions

This chapter has explored the role of radio news in developing contexts through the selection of the cases of Bush Radio and MFM, two local radio stations in South Africa. Through their focus on community journalism, both stations exercise cultural resistance in prioritizing local news and promoting audience-driven news content. Similarly, talk radio's strong emphasis on local news items has been shown to possess the potential to contribute to the enhancement of a discursive public sphere.

The constraints on radio news in developing contexts include rapid technological development, increasing competition for fragmenting news audiences, and the development of a global news market (Harrison, 2006; Van der Veur, 2002). Compounding matters are fears about the loss of journalistic independence and trends towards media 'tabloidization'. The convergence of globalized news flows similarly impacts on radio news in developing contexts. However, the rise of localized forms of news reporting, including citizen journalism, brings with it new media ecologies intrinsically tied to development. While it is difficult to draw definitive conclusions about the links between radio news and development in a region as vast as the global South, there are grounds for cautious optimism. Positive initiatives are underway, including those discussed above, which together signal ways forward in thinking about how best radio news might fulfil its democratic potential.

There is a widespread view that the media in new democracies should serve the state by giving a positive spin to news and analysis; or play a constructive role in development by strengthening the new government's ability to rule effectively. The alternate view (more often than not emanating from the media themselves) is that the media's primary role should be that of a watchdog on the lookout for bad behaviour, revealing abuses in the exercise of state authority (Curran, 1997). However, as I have sought to show in this chapter, radio news needs to serve the public interest by design, rather than simply by chance. Radio news in a South African context, I believe, needs to move beyond Western journalism's norms and values in order to embrace community-centred priorities. For its capacity to promote democracy to be realized, however, it will have to envisage afresh its social roles and responsibilities.

Notes

1 Various theoretical approaches have been used to study news, alternately focusing on production, content or consumption. Political economy approaches explore the structure of ownership and control, often arguing that this results in content shaped by dominant power relations (see Tumber, 1999 for an overview). Culturalist approaches tend to draw upon a neo-Marxist model, which analyses the role of institutions, social processes and cultural forms, arguing that the news media align hegemonic views with 'common sense' (Hall, 1980; Williams, 1974). Organizational approaches concentrate on the production of news, taking into account the constraints imposed upon journalists by their work routines, often seeing news as the social construction of reality (Harrison, 2006). New media theory takes into account new technologies and globalization, examining the use of technology to disseminate news, as well as trends towards international flows of news (Williams, 2003).

2 Community radio in the developing world emerged within the context of participatory communication projects in Latin America in the 1960s, following the criticisms of the failures of the dominant, capitalist paradigm of the West and the Marxist/socialist paradigm of the East (Nwosu et al., 1995).

Led by Third World scholars and activists, such as Paulo Freire, these critics pointed out that mass media agendas were irrelevant to Third World citizens. Scholars and activists searched for alternatives, leading to the global rise of participatory communication initiatives, which include community radio (Rodriguez, 2000).

3 Predominantly referred to as community radio in Africa and the Caribbean, the term alternative radio is used in Latin America and the United States. In Europe it is more likely to be known as free or association radio, and in Australia it is often called ethnic or aboriginal radio. More recently, Rodriguez (2000) coined the term citizens' media in an attempt to overcome binary categories traditionally used to theorize alternative media. While used widely, the term 'alternative' suggests its own lesser relationship to dominant media. British theorist John Downing (2001) prefers the term radical media to refer to any small-scale media that express views alternative to hegemonic perspectives.

References

Allan, S. (2004). *News culture*. Maidenhead and New York: Open University Press.

Benson, R. and Neveu, E. (eds) (2005). *Bourdieu and the journalistic field*. Cambridge: Polity Press.

Bosch, T. (2005). *Service learning and civic journalism: Social responsibility and the role of community radio internships in building citizenship*. Unpublished conference paper presented to the International Symposium on Service Learning – Models for the 21st Century, Stellenbosch University, 20–22 November 2005.

Bourdieu, P. (1991). *Language and symbolic power*. Cambridge: Polity Press.

Bourdieu, P and Passeron, J. (1990). *Reproduction in education, society and culture*. Translated by Richard Nice. London: Sage Publications.

Bowman, S. and Willis, C. (2003). *We media: How audiences are shaping the future of news and information*. The Media Centre at the American Press Institute.

Coleman, Stephen (1998). BBC Radio Ulster's Talkback phone-in: Public feedback in a divided public space. *The Public* 5 (2): 7–19.

Curran, J. (2002). *Media and power*. Routledge: London.

Downing, J. (2001). *Radical media: Rebellious communication and social movements*. London: Sage Publications, Inc.

Erlich, Thomas (ed.) (2000). *Civic responsibility and higher education*. Phoenix: Oryx Press.

Foucault, Michel (1980). *Power/knowledge: Selected interviews & other writings 1972-1977*. Ed. Colin Gordon. New York: Pantheon Books.

Fraser, N. (1992). Rethinking the public sphere: A contribution to the critique of actually existing democracy. In Calhoun, C. (ed.) *Habermas and the public sphere*. Cambridge, MA: MIT Press: 109–42.

Freire, Paulo (1970). The Pedagogy of the Oppressed. London: Continium.

——. (1985). The Polits of Education, Culture, Power and Liberation. New York: Bergin & Garvey.

Galda, L. (1984). Learning maths by radio. *Media in education and development* 17(1) 40–42.

Girard, B. (1999). Radio Broadcasting and the Internet: Converging for development and democracy. *Voices*, 3(3), December 1999.

Graber, D., Mcquail, D. and Norris, P. (1998). *The politics of news: The news of politics*. Washington, DC: CQ Press.

Habermas, J. (1989). *The structural transformation of the public sphere*. Cambridge, MA: MIT Press. Translated by Thomas Burger and Frederick Lawrence.

Halberstam, J. (1992) 'A prolegomenon for a theory of news', E. D. Cohen (ed.) *Philosophical issues in journalism*. Oxford: Oxford University Press: 11–21.

Hall, S. (1993). Encoding/decoding, in S. During (ed.). *The cultural studies reader*. London: Routledge: 90–103.

Hartley, J. (1988). *Understanding news*. London: Routledge.

Harrison, J. (2006). *News*. New York: Taylor & Francis.

Herbst, Susan (1995). On electronic public space: Talk shows in theoretical perspective. *Political Communication* 12: 263–74.

Hunter-Gault, Charlayne (2006). *New news out of Africa: Uncovering Africa's Renaissance*. New York: Oxford University Press.

Hyden, G. *et al.* (eds.). (2002). *Media and democracy in Africa*. New Brunswick, NJ: Transaction Publishers.

Kuper, A. and Kuper, J. (2001). Serving a new democracy: Must the media speak softly? Learning from South Africa. International Journal of Public Opinion Research. 13 (4).

Meijer, I. (2001). The public quality of popular journalism: Developing a normative framework. *Journalism Studies* 2(2): 189–205.

Mowlana, H. (1998). *Communication technology and development*. Paris: UNESCO.

Nightingale, K. (2008). Pod-ready: Podcasting for the developing world. Available online at http://www.scidev.net/en/features/pod-ready-podcasting-for-the-developing-world.html. Accessed 9/9/2008.

Nwaerondu, N. and Thompson, G. (1987). The use of educational radio in developing countries: Lessons from the past. *Journal of Distance Education*, Fall, 1987, 2(2): 43–54.

Nwosu, P., Onwumechili, C., and M'Bayo, R. (eds). (1995). *Communication and the transformation of society*. Lanham, ML: University Press of America.

O'Connor, A. (1990). The miners' radio station in Bolivia: A culture of resistance. *Journal of Communication* 40(1): 102-110.

Rodriguez, C. (2000). Civil society and citizen's media: Peace architects for the new millenium. In Wilkins, K. *Redeveloping communication for social change: Theory, practice and power*. Rowman & Littlefield Publishers, Inc.: Boulder, CO.

Schiller, J. (2007). On becoming the media: Low power FM and the alternative public sphere. In Butsch, R. (ed.). *Media and public spheres*. New York, NY: Palgrave Macmillan: 122–35.

Schramm, W. (1964). *Mass media and national development*. Stanford, CA: Stanford University Press.

Shudson, Michael. (2003). *The sociology of news*. New York, London: W. W. Norton and Company.

Stevenson, R. (1988). *Communication, development and the Third World: The global politics of information*. New York: Longman.

Strelitz, L. Towards a philosophy of African journalism. Online at http://www.highwayafrica.ru.ac.za/presentations/Introductory%20Remarks%20to%20First%20Session%20-%20Larry%20Strelitz.doc (Accessed 10 September 2008).

Tumber, H. (1999). *News: A reader*. Oxford: Oxford University Press.

Van der Veur, P. (2002). Broadcasting and political reform. In *Media and Democracy in Africa*. (eds), Goran Hyden, Michael Leslie and Folu Ogundimu. New Brunswick, NJ: Transaction Publishers.

Williams, K. (2003). *Understanding media theory*. London: Arnold.

Williams, R. (1974). *Television, technology and cultural form*. New York: Schocken Books.

16
ALTERNATIVE JOURNALISM: IDEOLOGY AND PRACTICE

Chris Atton

What Stuart Hall (1977) once termed the 'ideological effect' of the mass media is now an accepted foundation of critical media studies. Hebdige (1979) summarised this effect as 'the role the media play in shaping and maintaining consent' (1979: 156). This dominant ideology is effected through the practices of professionalised journalism: the conventions of news sourcing and representation; the hierarchical and capitalised economy of commercial journalism; the professional, elite basis of journalism as a practice; the professional norm of objectivity; and the passive role of audience as receiver.

The present chapter explores journalistic practices that spring from an ideology that presents a direct challenge to the mass media's 'dominant discourses about reality ... the interests of the dominant groups in society' (Hebdige, 1979: 15). The ideology of alternative journalism embodies a critique of the ideological effect of the mass media through developing practices that challenge the dominant practices of professionalised journalism. Consequently, in its ideal form alternative journalism is produced outside mainstream media institutions and networks. It 'can include the media of protest groups, dissidents, fringe political organisations, even fans and hobbyists' (Atton, 2004: 3). It tends to be produced not by professionals, but by amateurs who typically have little or no training or professional qualifications as journalists: they write and report from their position as citizens, as members of communities, as activists or as fans. (Though as we shall see, there are examples of alternative journalism where professional journalists and professional techniques are employed, often in radically different ways from their conventional uses.) The ideological work of alternative journalism is not only concerned with who is able to be a journalist, but also with representing the interests, views and needs of under-represented groups in society. As well as being homes for radical content, projects of alternative journalism also tend to be organised in non-mainstream ways, often non-hierarchically or collectively, and almost always on a non-commercial basis. They hope to be independent of the market and immune to institutionalisation.

Practitioners of alternative journalism also seek to redress what they consider an imbalance of media power in mainstream media, which can result in the marginalisation of certain social and cultural groups and movements. It is this emphasis on media power that lies at the heart of alternative journalism. The term 'alternative journalism' functions as a comparative term to indicate that 'whether indirectly or directly, media power is what is at stake' (Couldry and Curran, 2003: 7). This perspective is able to accommodate a range of theories that have been put forward to make sense of alternative media production. These include John Downing's theory of radical media (Downing, 1984; Downing et al., 2001); Clemencia Rodriguez's 'citizen's media' (2000) and Hackett and Carroll's (2006) notion of democratic media activism, all of which share a common assumption that alternative media are primarily concerned with radical politics and social empowerment, with what Pippa Norris has called 'critical citizens' (Norris, 1999). By contrast, Couldry and Curran (2003: 7) find broader aims in alternative media, aims that 'may or may not be politically radical or socially empowering'.

Alternative journalism, then, becomes both a comparative term and a broader term. Within it we may place not only the journalism of politics and empowerment, but also those of popular culture and the everyday. Alternative journalism may be home to explorations of individual enthusiasm and subcultural identity just as much as it may be home to radical visions of society and the polity. If media power is indeed at stake in its varied principles and practices, we must also ask such questions as: how does it relate to the dominant ideology and practices of journalism? How is it culturally and socially significant? What is the status of this journalism? Should we think of it as a fifth estate (to borrow the title of a long-standing US anarchist newspaper), distinct from the mainstream media in its ideology, practices and audiences? Or should we consider it an adjunct or extension of existing practices, enhancing conventional news reporting, comment and opinion by drawing on the experiences of 'ordinary people', presenting their versions of reality in their own, deprofessionalised discourses?

This chapter presents an understanding of alternative journalism that proceeds neither from the separatist vision of alternative journalism that remains forever on the outside, marginal and antagonistic, nor from the neutered and incorporated notion that treats citizen journalism as user-generated content to add occasional colour to professional news reports. There are occasions, of course, where user-generated content has proved invaluable to the mainstream media, where amateur photographers have captured images on mobile phones and camcorders in the absence of the professional camera crew (Thurman, 2008). The value of these contributions is inevitably circumscribed by the dominant news values of the mainstream. Such contributions do not present the 'citizen' as active participant in democratic discourse; the citizen is merely the amateur advance guard of the camera crew. As soon as the latter are present, the amateur's work is done.

A more nuanced approach, neither separatist nor incorporated, can illuminate the relationship between an alternative model of journalism and the dominant, professional model of journalism. This approach can also inform the continuing debates about the role of professional journalism in society.

Theorising alternative media

Little attention has been paid to alternative journalism in terms of its practices: Atton and Hamilton (2008) provide the first book-length examination of the subject (though there are useful case studies, such as those in Harcup, 1994, 2003 and 2006). Most often the subject is approached through studies of its parent subject, alternative media (even here the coverage of alternative journalism is uneven). It is necessary, therefore, to turn first to this wider landscape. There is not the space here to examine all relevant studies of alternative media in depth. Instead, a recent synthesis of alternative media by Bailey, Cammaerts and Carpentier (2008) offers a useful, fourfold typology of alternative media in which to place alternative journalism in a broader context.

First, alternative media may serve specific communities and enable participation by those communities in media production. The primary aim of this type is to present representations of communities that challenge the dominant forms of representation that, for instance, might be found in the local commercial press. Second, there are media that provide more autonomous alternatives to mainstream media, whether in their organisation, the forms of representation they use in their journalism or their methods of distribution. If community media are complementary to the mainstream, then autonomous or 'essentialist' media tend to be actively constructed in opposition to mainstream media practices. For Bailey, Cammaerts and Carpentier these first two types are centred on media production: both offer participants a means to represent their lives and interests in ways that differ significantly from the representations of the mainstream media.

The third and fourth types are centred not on media but on society: both use the possibilities of participation in media production to effect social and political change, or at least to attempt it. The third type, civil society media, achieve this through organisation that is teleological, with more or less fixed aims and objectives. The fourth type is 'rhizomatic media' (a metaphor taken from Deleuze and Guattari) that tend to be interconnected, often on a global scale; the network is key to these media, where organisation is fluid and often transient. Rhizomatic media are able to mutate as social or political conditions change. To theorise alternative media we need to take account of all four types, to examine how they work with or against each other in different political, social, cultural and geographical contexts. In other words, these four approaches are not exclusive: community media may be rhizomatic; autonomous media may have a civil society function.

Theorised in this way, the practices of alternative media highlight challenges to dominant media practices in respect of structure (the market and the state), agency (participation, the network) and the ideology of journalistic practices (representation). However, in common with earlier work on alternative media (such as Atton, 2002; Downing et al., 2001; and Rodriguez, 2000), these arguments are developed from considerations of structure and agency.

The historical roots of alternative journalism

It is common for arguments such as those of Bailey, Cammaerts and Carpentier to be demonstrated through contemporary examples. However, the roots of alternative media and alternative journalism lie much further back in history (as Hamilton and Atton, 2001, and Hamilton, 2003 have shown). Moreover, the roots of professional journalism also lie in the precursors of contemporary journalism. In Britain the two forms of journalism share common ancestors in (at least) the unstamped Radical or 'pauper press' of the late eighteenth and early nineteenth centuries (Boyce, Curran and Wingate, 1978; Hollis, 1970; Lee, 1976; Thompson, 1966).

This is not the beginning of journalism itself (for example, the London *Times* predates this period), but it marks the beginning of the commercial-popular journalism that has dominated the media market for over a hundred years. The foundations of this dominant journalism lie not in notions of professional expertise and institutions but in the mobilisation of working people: '[h]istorically, journalism is a creature of the popular classes' (Hartley, 2009: 310). Popular journalism was born of the need to organise within the emerging working class, to educate readers and to mobilize them politically – in short, to 'struggle *against* the social leadership of their day' (p. 322, original emphasis). In this context, journalism was the result of political engagement that needed to speak the language of its readers. The readers included its writers, for this was a resolutely grassroots undertaking, where lived experience and the ability to convey that experience in writing to a wide audience were inseparable. In this sense the early popular journalism was amateur; for it to be anything else would disconnect it from its aims and its audience.

There is not space here to trace the development of journalism from these roots to the present. What is more important is to recognise the affinities between the Radical press two centuries ago and the alternative journalism of the present, and to emphasise the fundamental difference between the norms of alternative journalism and those of professional journalism. Hartley distinguishes the two by their location in society and their public function. Alternative journalism 'belongs to the public': it is concerned with 'emancipationist self-representation' (Hartley, 2009: 322 and 310). By contrast, professional journalism is 'top down', 'expert and representative' (ibid.). This positioning is in line with strong currents in alternative media research: alternative media comprise political projects of an emancipatory nature, where those engaged in political struggle are able to represent themselves and their communities through media of their own making (Downing *et al.*, 2001; Rodriguez, 2000).

Hackett and Carroll (2006) argue that, in terms of journalism practice, these projects present a direct challenge to the 'regime of objectivity' that dominates professionalised journalism (2006: 33). This challenge has both a normative and an epistemological aspect. The normative ideal of professionalised journalism emphasises the factual nature of news. It is based on the empiricist assumption that there exist 'facts' in the world and that it is possible to identify these facts accurately and without bias (the journalistic norm of detachment). The normative ideal of alternative journalism argues the opposite: that reporting is always bound up with values (personal, professional, institutional) and that it is therefore never possible to separate facts from values. This leads to the epistemological challenge: that different forms of knowledge may be produced, which themselves present different and multiple versions of 'reality' from those of mainstream media. What forms do these representations take? What practices characterise alternative journalism?

Ideology and practice in alternative journalism

If it is possible to speak of a single ideology of alternative journalism, it lies in the belief that journalism should enable, not restrict, the circulation of information and views to enable citizens to make their own assessments (Carlson, 2007). Therefore, a key aim of alternative journalism is to 'turn journalism from a lecture into a conversation' (Gerlis, 2008: 126), by democratising the notion of journalism and by encouraging consumers of news to become creators of news. Many alternative journalists consequently use a significantly 'different cast of voices' in their stories (Harcup, 2003: 360) that treat non-official sources (such as factory or shop workers, minor government officials, pensioners, working mothers, the unemployed, the homeless, even school children) as primary definers in their stories. This sourcing practice overturns the professionally-routinised hierarchy of access to the media (Glasgow University Media Group, 1976) that typically uses 'ordinary' people as material for superficial 'vox pop' interviews (Ross, 2006). The strategy of self-representation in alternative journalism actively seeks out 'ordinary' people as expert sources in their own lives and experiences. Alternative journalism reports

> from their perspective, presenting stories where they are the main actors, where they are permitted to speak with authority in those stories, as counters to the mainstream's regularised interest in public figures as the only authoritative voices, the predominant sources of 'validating information' (Atton, 2002: 116).

Harcup calls this kind of alternative journalism the 'parish magazines of the dispossessed' (Harcup, 1994: 3) and identifies the local alternative press that flourished in 1970s Britain as an exemplary form. Papers such as *Leeds Other Paper* and the *Northern Star* (which borrowed its name from its pauper press predecessor) used the practices of non-official sourcing and community-based self-representation to generate radical investigative journalism – what Franklin and Murphy (1991) referred to as 'the production of revelatory news' (p. 106) – of topics that directly affected the lives of working people in their communities. The reports could be significant to the local community, often bypassing the event-driven routines of mainstream news practices. Harcup shows how '[w]hereas mainstream media tended to notice health and safety stories only when there was a disaster ... [*Leeds Other Paper*] exposed potential health risks before even the workers or their trade unions were aware of them' (Harcup, 2006: 133).

This 'investigative journalism from the grassroots' (p. 132) demonstrated that it was possible to produce news that was relevant and useful to a local public, but that did not need to follow the conventions of professional journalism. Nevertheless, it did not break entirely with the norms of professional journalism. The reporting style was conventional, emulating the conventions of the popular, 'serious' tabloid papers – a style that, as we have seen, links papers like *Leeds Other Paper* directly to its pauper press roots. The investigative reporting of the local alternative press also resembled its mainstream counterparts in its pursuit of accuracy. This was not to subscribe to the 'regime of objectivity', however. The local alternative press did not attempt to separate facts from values, or to detach itself from the subjects of its reports. However, to argue for a journalism of commitment, where 'facts' and 'values' are considered inseparable, it was necessary to maintain a high standard of accuracy. The more partisan journalism becomes, the more it needs to convince – particularly if its reporting is striving for political or social change.

This concern with accuracy remains a feature of much alternative journalism. The British activist newspaper *Squall* (mostly active during the 1990s) prided itself on its accuracy, as well as the clarity of its writing. A number of its volunteer staff chose to take night classes in journalism to achieve this (Atton, 2002). This enabled the paper to communicate to two distinct audiences. The paper's primary audience was – it was hoped – supplied with comprehensible and accurate information and analyses that would enhance their participation in civil society (*Squall*'s primary audience comprised squatters, the homeless and 'travellers', three marginalised groups that were often in need of information, particularly to do with welfare benefits, housing and human rights). The secondary audience entailed what one of the paper's editors called 'writing to the bridge' (cited in Atton, 2002: 92), that is to say, reaching those with political and economic power: politicians, local councilors and even professional journalists. One of *Squall*'s editors, Jim Carey, has argued that alternative journalists need to be as accountable as their professional counterparts: 'we seek to make sure that the facts used in investigations are accurate, because the truth is more irrefutable than opinion' (quoted in Wasley, 2002: 62–63). What we find in the journalism of papers like *Leeds Other Paper* and *Squall* is an adherence to principles already familiar to us from mainstream journalism: chief amongst these are accuracy and veracity, practised through a journalism whose style might not break with historical practices, but which reworks them for an audience who are able to participate in the making of 'their' news. This form of alternative journalism presents a direct challenge to its professionalised counterpart by taking advantage of vulnerabilities in professional journalism.

Challenges to professional journalism

Lowrey (2006) identifies a number of features of professional journalism that make it vulnerable to 'jurisdictional encroachment' by non-professionals. Among these, three are particularly important. First, the need to serve 'every client' (2006: 492) in the interests of maximising circulation or audiences tends to restrict the range of stories and the degree of specialist content available in the commercial media.

Second, the powerful and institutionalised relationships between media organisations and source institutions (such as government, corporations and public relations
agencies) encourage a reliance on a narrow range of official and elite sources. Third,
the practice of journalism is not difficult to learn; the process of news reporting is
based on the sequence of investigation (data collection), making sense (analysing and
organising data) and treatment (presentation of data). Lowrey calls this the 'inference
process' (2006: 492) and argues that its routinisation in professional journalism makes
it easily recognisable and available to anyone wishing to work journalistically. More
generally, the occupational boundaries of journalism and its jurisdiction are far from
clear (Carlson, 2007; Gerlis, 2008; Knight, 2008). There is no obligatory licensure or
membership of a professional organisation; despite the growth of journalism schools
many journalists are hired without professional qualifications. Given the 'porous' nature
of the occupation (Lowrey, 2006: 485), it is no surprise that 'anyone and everyone can
be a journalist' (Gerlis, 2008: 126). When we turn from the production of news to
the generation of comment and opinion, the potential for democratising journalism
is even greater. In addition to principles of accuracy and truthfulness, comment and
opinion introduce questions of authority and credibility. These questions particularly
gather around the status of blogging as journalism.

Rethinking authority and credibility

The blog is distinguished from the reporting in papers like *Leeds Other Paper* and *Squall*
by its emphasis on comment and opinion. This is not to say that 'revelatory news' is
entirely absent from the blog (as Allan, 2006 shows), but in general bloggers present
themselves as commentators on events that have already been reported by mainstream
news organisations. This poses problems for professional journalists, not least because
bloggers represent a direct challenge to the authority and credibility of the professional
journalist. The roles of commentator and opinion writer in professional journalism
carry much cultural status; they are rarely the province of the tyro journalist. These
hard-won positions demonstrate an institutional acknowledgement of the writer's
expertise: they signify authority and seniority. Bloggers, on the other hand, are
unconstrained by institutional and professional norms; they can adopt anonymous or
pseudonymous personae; their motives are obscured by their independence from any
formal media organisation; they are free to roam where they please in the pursuit of
novelty; they can be 'unreliable or faddish' (Carlson, 2007: 272). They do not need
sources, bylines or ethics to produce their journalism, if it may be called journalism at
all (Knight, 2008).

This critique establishes a crude binary opposition between alternative and
professional journalists. It ignores the practice of anonymous leader writing in the
mainstream media. It has nothing to say about the often-unsourced professional
commentary or opinion piece. It passes over the promotion of the blog by professional
journalists: by the compilation of 'top ten' lists of the 'best blogs'; through the use of
blogs as sources by professional journalists and by the incorporation of the blog into
professional practice.

The use of the blog by the professional journalist tells us much about the practices of alternative journalism. This is not because it opposes these practices but, perhaps surprisingly, because the professional blog offers similar challenges to the profession at large as does the amateur blog, especially concerning notions of credibility, trustworthiness and authority. Matheson and Allan's (2007) study of bloggers during the war in Iraq included professional journalists as well as military personnel and Iraqi citizens. The study found that even blogs written by professional reporters tended to eschew the established standards of objectivity and impartiality, preferring instead a style of address that has more in common with eyewitness reporting. That is to say, the professional journalists wrote from direct, personal experience and emphasised their independence from organisational or administrative constraints. From their interviews with professional journalists who maintained blogs during the last Gulf War, Matheson and Allan found that it was these aspects that the reporters believed resonated with their readers. Bloggers were trusted because their methods were transparently subjective. Readers did not consider the blogs as absolute truth; instead they understood the war blogs as a set of accounts told from different perspectives. Journalists did not appear to present their eyewitness reports as 'fact', nor use their professional authority to present a definitive version of events. Instead, they used an alternative form of representation in a reflexive manner, developing their own practice as a result (Lowrey, 2006).

Nevertheless, doubts remain within the profession, especially where bloggers go beyond the personal and attempt a journalistic authority in competition with professional journalists. Journalists have accused blogs of 'sacrificing verification ... [and] lessen[ing] the gatekeeping function central to journalism's societal role' (Carlson, 2007: 274). Others believe that professional journalists must differentiate themselves from alternative journalists by maintaining 'proper ethical standards' (Gerlis, 2008: 125). Yet, as George (2008) points out, though alternative journalists may well be 'idiosyncratic' by comparison to their professional counterparts, this does not prevent them from being 'morally engaged' (p. 131).

George's description of the alternative journalist suggests a way of working that is neither careless nor irresponsible, but is ethically informed. Ethical journalism does not need to be the sole province of the professional: Harcup (2007) has argued for the centrality of ethics in all forms – and at all stages – of journalism practice. Ethical practice should form the basis of what it means to be a reflective practitioner, wherever the practice takes place.

Furthermore, a number of recent online journalism projects have shown how professionals and amateurs are able to work together, with the latter far more than mere suppliers of user-generated content to be embedded into existing media output. The South Korean online citizens' media project *OhmyNews* comprises an editorial hub staffed by 60 professionals (of whom 35 are reporters), who advise on and edit the contributions of thousands of citizen reporters (Kim and Hamilton, 2006). The online news and comment magazine *openDemocracy* shows how it is possible to conceive of an alternative journalism project with roots in the profession. The project was founded by a journalist from the left-of-centre, British political weekly *New Statesman*, and is mostly written by professional journalists and public intellectuals on the left. While we might still consider *openDemocracy* as a type of alternative journalism, it represents a diverse forum for a dissenting elite: 'a forum of debate for activist, academics, journalists, businesspeople, politicians and international civil servants' (Curran, 2003: 238).

Conclusion

The challenges raised by alternative journalism should be clear: authority does not need to be located institutionally or professionally; credibility and trustworthiness can be derived from accounts of lived experience, not only from objectively detached reporting; there is no moral imperative to separate facts from values. It is possible to find expert cultures beyond an institutionalised framework where expertise is exclusionary. We must remember that these challenges are not new: what was the journalism of the pauper press if not a display of inclusionary expertise?

In Matheson and Allan's study, as in Harcup's studies of the alternative local press, we see evidence of the practices of 'informed, embodied self-representation' (Hartley, 2009: 317) in opposition to the 'unembodied discourse that marks much of traditional journalism' (Carlson, 2007: 267). Moreover, while embodied discourse has its origins in the engaged, amateur journalism of the pauper press – and has been sustained through generations of alternative media – it need not be the sole preserve of the amateur journalist, as the use of blogs by professional journalists shows.

Nevertheless, it is in the practices of alternative journalism where we should look most closely. There are too few studies that deal with the everyday routines and processes of reporting and writing. Instead, most research places emphasis on conceptualising the democratisation of the media and the participation of citizens; it considers these matters at a distance from the processes of reporting, and has almost nothing to say about the product of that reporting, the stories that are central to any attempt at representation. Given the wealth of studies that have explored the reporting processes of mainstream journalism this might seem surprising, for without comparable studies how is it possible to understand fully the nature and outcomes of the discursive practices of alternative journalism?

References

Allan, Stuart (2006) *Online News: Journalism and the Internet*. Maidenhead and New York: Open University Press.

Atton, Chris (2002) *Alternative Media*. London: Sage.

Atton, Chris (2004) *An Alternative Internet: Radical Media, Politics and Creativity*. Edinburgh: Edinburgh University Press; and New York: Columbia University Press.

Atton, Chris and Hamilton, James F. (2008) *Alternative Journalism*. London: Sage.

Bailey, Olga Guedes, Cammaerts, Bart and Carpentier, Nico (2008) *Understanding Alternative Media*. Maidenhead: Open University Press.

Boyce, George, Curran, James and Wingate, Pauline (eds) (1978) *Newspaper History from the Seventeenth Century to the Present Day*. London: Constable.

Carlson, Matt (2007) 'Blogs and Journalistic Authority: The Role of Blogs in US Election Day 2004 Coverage', *Journalism Studies* 8(2): 264–279.

Couldry, Nick and Curran, James (2003) 'The Paradox of Media Power.' In Nick Couldry and James Curran (eds), *Contesting Media Power: Alternative Media in a Networked World*. Lanham: Rowman and Littlefield, pp. 3–15.

Curran, James (2003) 'Global Journalism: A Case Study of the Internet.' In Nick Couldry and James Curran (eds), *Contesting Media Power: Alternative Media in a Networked World*. Lanham: Rowman and Littlefield, pp. 227–241.

Downing, John (1984) *Radical Media: The Political Experience of Alternative Communication*. Boston, Mass.: South End Press.

Downing, John, Ford, Tamara Villareal, Gil, Geneve and Stein, Laura (2001) *Radical Media: Rebellious Communication and Social Movement*. Thousand Oaks: Sage.

Franklin, Bob and Murphy, David (1991) *What News? The Market, Politics and the Local Press*. London: Routledge.

Gerlis, Alex (2008) 'Who is a Journalist?', *Journalism Studies* 9(1): 125–128.

George, Cherian (2008) 'Value-driven Journalism', *Journalism Studies* 9(1): 128–131.

Glasgow University Media Group (1976) *Bad News*. London: Routledge and Kegan Paul.

Hackett, Robert A. and Carroll, William K. (2006) *Remaking Media: The Struggle to Democratize Public Communication*. New York and London: Routledge.

Hall, Stuart (1977) 'Culture, the Media and the "Ideological Effect".' In James Curran, Michael Gurevitch and Janet Woollacott (eds), *Mass Communication and Society*. London: Arnold, pp. 315–348.

Hamilton, James F. (2003) 'Remaking Media Participation in Early Modern England,' *Journalism: Theory, Practice, Criticism* 4(3): 293–313.

Hamilton, James F. and Atton, Chris (2001) 'Theorizing Anglo-American Alternative Media: Toward a Contextual History and Analysis of US and UK Scholarship', *Media History* 7(2): 119–135.

Harcup, Tony (1994) *A Northern Star: Leeds Other Paper and the Alternative Press 1974-1994*. London and Pontefract: Campaign for Press and Broadcasting Freedom.

Harcup, Tony (2003) '"The Unspoken – Said": The Journalism of Alternative Media', *Journalism: Theory, Practice, Criticism* 4(3): 356–376.

Harcup, Tony (2006) 'The Alternative Local Press.' In Bob Franklin (ed.), *Local Journalism and Local Media: Making the Local News*. London: Routledge, pp. 129–139.

Harcup, Tony (2007) *The Ethical Journalist*. London: Sage.

Hartley, John (2009) 'Journalism and Popular Culture.' In Karin Wahl-Jorgensen and Thomas Hanitzsch (eds), *Handbook of Journalism Studies*. New York and London: Routledge, pp. 310–324.

Hebdige, Dick (1979) *Subculture: The Meaning of Style*. London: Methuen.

Hollis, Patricia (1970) *The Pauper Press*. London: Oxford University Press.

Kim, Eun-Gyoo and Hamilton, James (2006) 'Capitulation to Capital? *OhmyNews* as Alternative Media', *Media, Culture and Society* 28(4): 541–560.

Knight, Alan (2008) 'Journalism in the Age of Blogging', *Journalism Studies* 9(1): 117–124.

Lee, Alan (1976) *The Origins of the Popular Press in England: 1855–1914*. London: Croom Helm.

Lowrey, Wilson (2006) 'Mapping the Journalism-blogging Relationship', *Journalism: Theory, Practice, Criticism* 7(4): 477–500.

Matheson, Donald and Allan, Stuart (2007) 'Truth in a War Zone: The Role of Warblogs in Iraq.' In Sarah Maltby and Richard Keeble (eds), *Communicating War: Memory, Media and Military*. Bury St. Edmunds: Arima, pp. 75–89.

Norris, Pippa (1999) *Critical Citizens: Global Support for Democratic Governance*. Oxford: Oxford University Press.

Rodriguez, Clemencia (2000) *Fissures in the Mediascape: An International Study of Citizens' Media*. Cresskill: Hampton Press.

Ross, Karen (2006) 'Open Source? Hearing Voices in the Local Press.' In Bob Franklin (ed.), *Local Journalism and Local Media: Making the Local News*. London: Routledge, pp. 232–244.

Thompson, E.P. (1966) *The Making of the English Working Class*. New York: Vintage.

Thurman, Neil (2008) 'Forums for Citizen Journalists? Adoption of User Generated Content Initiatives by Online News Media', *New Media and Society* 10(1): 139–157.

Wasley, Andrew (2002) 'Indy Journalism: Facts are Free, Opinion is Sacred?', *British Journalism Review* 13(3): 58–64.

Part III

NEWSMAKING: RULES, ROUTINES AND RITUALS

17
JOURNALISTS AS INTERPRETIVE COMMUNITIES, REVISITED

Barbie Zelizer

What does it take to make and keep a community? Since journalists were first concep-tualized as an interpretive community (Zelizer, 1992, 1993), journalism has undergone multiple changes. It has become more financially unstable, more open to alternative modes of newsgathering, more diversified across task, news organization and medium, more global, more responsive to the involvement of private citizens. What impact have these changes in journalism and the larger information environment had on the establishment of journalists as interpretive communities? Have they undermined or supported journalists' interpretive powers as we have considered them up until now?

This chapter suggests that journalists have responded to their changing circum-stances by doing what they have always done – crafting adjustments to both their newsmaking routines and their interpretive strategies so as to keep the journalistic community intact. Doing so maintains the relevance of collective interpretation in shaping what journalists do, the salience of their discourse, narratives and storytelling in doing so, and the impact of their informal contacts, even as their centrality, exclu-sivity, singularity and professional certainty have diminished. Interpretive strategies and the communities they legitimate continue to underscore how central collective interpretation remains in uniting reporters in their work and lending meaning and authority to journalism.

This chapter fast-forwards earlier discussions of journalists as interpretive commu-nities and applies them to the U.S. mainstream coverage of one recent public event – the hanging of Iraqi leader Saddam Hussein in December 2006. In considering how U.S. journalists collectively made sense of that event, it shows that they not only use journalistic coverage to generate meaning about journalism but also to retain a collective and authoritative voice amidst the changing – and often unpredictable – boundaries of newswork and a continually evolving information environment.

Journalists as members of interpretive communities

The idea of conceptualizing journalists as members of interpretive communities draws from anthropology, folklore and literary studies. Defined by Dell Hymes as a group united by its shared interpretations of reality (Hymes, 1980, p. 2) and by Stanley Fish as those who produce texts and "determine the shape of what is read" (Fish, 1980, p. 171), the interpretive community is a group that develops shared interpretive strategies for making sense of the world. First invoked in audience studies, where local understandings of a given text were arrived at differently by multiple audiences (i.e., Morley, 1980; Radway, 1984; Lindlof, 1987), communicators have since come to be seen themselves as interpretive communities (Zelizer, 1992, 1993, 2004; Berkowitz and TerKeurst, 1999; Lindlof, 2002; Traquina, 2004). This has had particular resonance for understanding journalists, because journalistic collectivity has long had its own place in scholarship on journalism: Park's view of news as a form of knowledge (Park, 1940), Carey's suggestions about communication as ritual and a shared frame for understanding (Carey, 1975), O'Brien's ideas about news as a pseudo-environment (O'Brien, 1983), and Schudson's studies of how journalists construct knowledge about themselves (Schudson, 1988; 1992) all suggested early on the importance of generating an understanding of journalism through their shared discourse and interpretation. Viewing journalists as an interpretive community thus draws from that scholarship, positioning journalists as a group united through its collective interpretations, where, using channels like news coverage, informal talks, professional and trade reviews, professional meetings, autobiographies and memoirs, interviews on talk shows and media retrospectives, they create a community that reflects what matters to them in the making of news.

Since the idea of journalists as interpretive communities was first broached, scholars have fruitfully used it to explain news practice. This is because journalism's interpretive communities assert their presence in multiple ways. First, journalists come together through discussions of critical incidents in the annals of journalism, what Levi-Strauss once called "hot moments" – phenomena or events through which a society or culture assesses its own significance (Levi-Strauss, 1966, p. 259): Covering the Kennedy assassination represents problems associated with live televised journalism (Zelizer, 1992), the emergence of public journalism is positioned as a rehabilitation of traditional U.S. journalistic ideology (Brewin, 1999), contemporary atrocity is seen through its earlier visualization when the Nazi concentration camps were liberated (Zelizer, 1998), and U.S. trade publications reveal a militarized and masculine tone in journalism's post-coverage address to 9/11 (Parameswaran, 2006). Second, journalists create community by correcting and temporally recontextualizing journalistic practice beyond news relay, using double-time to repair their earlier treatment of Watergate and McCarthyism (Zelizer, 1993), countering defensive journalism in response to doomsday scenarios (Huxford, 2006), and invoking memorializing discourse to reference key societal roles for journalists (Carlson, 2007). Third, journalists consolidate themselves collectively when discussing everyday work, such as politics or the police beat: Boundaries of appropriate practice are addressed by marginalizing a community outlier in Israeli journalism (Meyers, 2003), by repairing to an ideology of eyewitness authenticity regardless of how much reporters see (Zelizer, 2007), and by setting forth a model of cultural intermediaries for Arab journalists to follow (Mellor, 2008). Fourth, journalists use collective interpretations to guide them in actual practice, with guidelines about crisis journalism regularly used to direct stories on natural disaster and terrorism (i.e., American Press Institute, 2001), and the incorporation of interpretive strategies called for as an instrumental part of journalism education in South Africa (Garman, 2005). In each case, reporters and their news organizations have been able to espouse their appropriate and preferred standards of action through discourse and interpretation, and through them the agreed-upon boundaries of their own community. Through each of these practices, journalists make their collective lives meaningful and establish what is significant about their work in shared ways.

What happens, however, when interpreting newswork does not readily create a clear interpretive voice? The boundaries of journalism's interpretive communities shift and require adjustment when bumps on the road to interpretation obscure, challenge or otherwise undermine the capacity to form community.

The hanging of Saddam Hussein

Perhaps nowhere was a clear interpretive voice as necessary as in the U.S. mainstream coverage of Iraqi leader Saddam Hussein's execution. Though Hussein's hanging was expected to bring closure to many issues left open to interpretation during the early stages of the "war on terror," the divided sentiments on the war made such closure tenuous. How the hanging was interpreted had direct bearing on the meanings that prevailed, and journalism's role in crafting those meanings was central.

Hussein's hanging on December 30, 2006 came at a heightened point of U.S. dissonance about the war in Iraq, exacerbated by the images of Abu Ghraib. Those supporting the war's prosecution looked to the execution's coverage to assail public qualms, while those against the war voiced their hopes that it would generate greater opposition. Confronting competitive messages of the execution's appropriateness and brutality, journalists found themselves in an interpretive quandary before coverage even began.

In that the actual execution was anticipated, U.S. news organizations had time to set in place provisional guidelines for how to cover the goriness that would come, and, announcing what they hoped would be "tasteful" coverage, they held marathon meetings to debate the shape of the ensuing coverage. At first, ABC and CBS said that they would not air the full execution, noting that "we have very, very strict guidelines with how to deal with that" (Gough, 2006).

And yet such guidelines were not clear across the board. Recognizing that journalists faced what the Poynter Institute called "tough decisions about how best to present the news," helper feeds offered them ways to think about the impending story (Thompkins, 2006; Walters, 2006). Online seminars under catchy titles like "Displaying Death with Dignity" and "Saddam Hussein Death: Resources for Journalists" advised journalists

and news organizations to maintain "taste and compassion" and suggested a repertoire of tools – cropping, sequencing, changing placement and size, selective toning,
blurring, adding black bars and text, and offering disclosure – as ways to do so (Irby,
2006). Images were at the core of these discussions, in that they embodied what was
most graphic, brutal and final about the execution.

U.S. news organizations appeared to have many choices: whether to publish the
images or link to them through websites, whether to show Hussein being prepared
for hanging, whether to show the execution, whether to include graphic images on
the front page, on inside pages or not at all, whether to include verbal warning about
the images, and whether to respond if other news organizations and non-journalistic
websites decided to do things differently. Most news organizations set the full
execution off-limits, deciding to keep the actual moment of death off camera and
leaving the public to imagine, not see, Hussein's death and by implication the end of
his regime. As CNN's Anderson Cooper noted, "We are not going to just get these
images and slap them on TV" (Walters, 2006). As late as the day before the hanging,
executives for all three of the main U.S. networks insisted that even if an execution
video were distributed on the internet, they would not soften their resistance to
airing graphic images. News organizations set up forums for evaluating the decisions
they would take, and discussions of editorial decision-making which ran in *Editor
and Publisher* were widely circulated by the AP and Reuters (McBride, 2006; Gough,
2006). Journalists were somberly advised by the journalism think-tank, the Poynter
Institute, that "images leading up to the moment of death [could] be shown, but not
the actual death" (Irby, 2006).

However, once the hanging occurred, decision-making about coverage – embodied
in which images to show and in which method – was quickly complicated because
two visual records of Hussein's death emerged. The official video of Hussein's hanging,
made available shortly after the event to "head off skeptics who might not believe
Hussein was dead" (Zavis, 2007), showed a soundless sequence of him being guided
onto the steps of the gallows, a scarf put around his neck and a noose placed over his
head and tightened. One minute long, the video stopped short of his actual death.
It played repeatedly on the state-run Iraqi channel, Iraqia, and was quickly broadcast
around the world. Later that evening an independent camera phone video – with
audio – surfaced on al-Jazeera and al-Arabiya that showed Hussein being taunted as he
mounted the gallows. Shot from below, the video showed Hussein being led onto the
trapdoor by a group of masked men. As the noose was placed around his neck,
the crowd below became audibly abusive. Just after Hussein responded, the trapdoor
opened and he plunged to his death. The camera swung erratically and then
rested on a close-up of his wide-eyed lifeless corpse. No image was provided of the
actual execution.

The contrast between the videos was marked. As one news organization noted,
"unlike the silent, official film showing a subdued Saddam Hussein, the execution [in
the mobile phone version was] a charged, angry scene." From the independent video
it became clear "that the seemingly quiet, dignified send-off portrayed on the official
video [did] not tell the whole story" ("Video shows..." 2006).

News organizations faced a critical quandary. The second video changed circumstances from a choice involving duty, propriety and decency to raising the possibility that they would get the story wrong. What had been codified as an exercise in taste became a clear journalistic challenge, made acute by the fact that the independent video had a suspect form: journalists did not know who had made it, who had released it, and whether or not the Iraqi government could confirm what it showed.

At first, broadcast news organizations varied in their visual treatment of the story. While CNN showed parts of the independent video with subtitles revealing the insults leading up to the hanging, other news organizations showed even less of the independent video, with ABC offering a few brief clips and CBS and MSNBC showing none at all. CNN's Larry King devoted a full hour to the clock ticking on Hussein, at which point he asked, "is there something ghoulish about this?" One reporter later noted that "Mr. King looked a little let down when he had to sign off before the execution, promising viewers, 'It is really imminent now' ("He Couldn't..." 2006; Stanley, 2006). By contrast, Fox News offered full disclosure of the independent footage, connecting to the video on its website and providing links to three additional videos that traced the moments before, during and after the hanging. It also ran side-by-side still images of Hussein, one a file photo titled "Alive" and the other taken after the execution and labeled "Dead" (Bauder, 2006). Fox's treatment was telling, in that the news organization most aligned with those prosecuting the war opted to show the fullest visualization of Hussein's death, even if the video it showed raised interpretations of the hanging at odds with the Iraqi government's gloss on what had happened.

Variance in interpretation was not incidental, for the meaning of the event changed dramatically depending on which video one believed. Each video linked to a different mindset about whether the hanging was justified, necessary or appropriate. In one, Hussein was thought to be submissive and fearful, his handlers silent and reverent, the hanging a considered meting-out of justice. In the other, Hussein was thought to be defiant and scornful, his handlers derisive, the hanging a hastily organized event motivated by revenge. Some saw both videos as too graphic, and worried about responses concerning snuff photography and bad judgment, while others remarked that the images were not graphic enough, for they left open the possibility that Hussein was still alive (Rutten, 2007; "What did..." 2007).

Significantly, the role played by new media was central, as journalists tackled the question of who was to make decisions about which images to show. Called by media critic Jeff Jarvis "news served raw" and labeled by the *Los Angeles Times* a "perfect new media event," the new media involvement marked a critical transition in journalistic practice. It showed that "one man's citizen journalist is another's spy" and displayed an "era of wrenching journalistic transition" between old and new media (Rutten, 2007). The independent video's jerkiness and odd lighting enhanced its authenticity, making it the preferred documentation for many, and mainstream reporters were quick to note the challenge: Offering a somber note about the changing parameters of journalism, a *Wall Street Journal* columnist cautioned that "we better get used to living without visual boundaries – and with the curiosity and flexible morality of the viewer as the only limit on what we can see – from now on" (cited in Helmore, 2007).

The videos thus produced a range of contrasting responses, which alternately focused on propriety, evidence, inconsistencies and larger questions about new boundaries of journalistic practice in an alternative media age. In that the display of either video was only partly responsive to those who saw it, finding a visual that could accommodate the various impulses at play became important not only for public reasons but for journalistic ones too. In order to establish a clear interpretive voice, journalists needed to find a middle ground between the competitive interpretive impulses.

It was here that an about-to-die image – a still photo of Hussein facing his death – became relevant (Zelizer, forthcoming). Like other about-to-die pictures, the still image functioned in ways that the moving sequence of his hanging could not. Static, frozen and memorable, the still photo of Hussein facing death – instead of videos which offered conflicting interpretations of how he died – offered a visualization that neutralized the interpretive flux generated by the two videos. Sidestepping journalism's need to be accountable for one version of the event over another, the still image allowed for coverage of the hanging that supported a unified U.S. mainstream journalistic voice in telling its story.

The still image of Hussein was arresting: Frame-grabbed from the official video and circulated primarily by the Associated Press, the shot showed Hussein, his face stoic and hard, facing sideways as the hangman placed a noose around his neck. Coarse ropes crossed the forefront of the frame, heralding the bodily drop that they would facilitate. There was no context, environment or additional actions to complicate the frame. All that viewers saw was a moment frozen on Hussein's visage as he was about to die. Human anguish thus filled the frame.

This image of Hussein facing death appeared widely across the United States – on front pages, magazine covers, internal pages, at the top of websites, as the illustration for cover stories. On December 31, multiple newspapers featured the about-to-die image without a corresponding image of Hussein dead on their front pages – the *Washington Post*, the *Chicago Tribune*, the *Philadelphia Inquirer*, the *Los Angeles Times*, *Newsday*, the *Boston Globe*, the *Atlanta Journal-Constitution*, the *Dallas Morning News*, the *Charlotte Observer*, the *Hartford Courant*, the *San Jose Mercury News*, the *Pittsburgh Post-Gazette*, the *Sacramento Bee* and the *Detroit Free Press*, and the websites of the *New York Times*, *Los Angeles Times* and *Washington Post*. The image also illustrated the cover story of *Newsweek*. Sometimes it appeared multiple times in one newspaper, as when the *Denver Post* ran four front-page images of Hussein facing death alongside one of his corpse or the *Birmingham News* featured three about-to-die images side by side. Often positioned under mastheads and highlighted with the topicality of impending death, the image's titles proclaimed Hussein's "final moments" or "last minutes." Though not every U.S. newspaper chose to use visuals to illustrate the story, when they did the choice rested overwhelmingly with the about-to-die image. Each time the image surfaced, its accompanying texts confirmed that Hussein was dead, though journalists anticipated active public response and appended statements of disclosure and qualification across the board: The *Philadelphia Inquirer*, for instance, offered a boxed-in statement under the bold title "Graphic Pictures Inside" that read:

> To Our Readers: A sequence of photos of Saddam Hussein at the gallows appears on A11. *The Inquirer* has chosen to publish these photos because of their news value. Readers should be aware that the photos are of a graphic nature ("Graphic Photos Inside" 2006).

The *Atlanta Journal-Constitution* directed readers to an inside page where it displayed, in the newspaper's words, "photos of him on the gallows but not of the actual hanging" ("Newspapers, Online Editors..." 2006; Bauder, 2006). No surprise, then, that the photo remained the signal image of the execution even when news organizations also showed pictures of Hussein dead. The *New York Times* front-paged four shots, three of which showed Hussein about to die and a fourth which showed his corpse wrapped in a shroud (Santora, 2006). *USA Today*, the *Washington Post*, the *Philadelphia Inquirer* and the *Los Angeles Times* included a frame-grabbed image from the independent cellphone video on an inside page, which showed Hussein dead, but the primary image of Hussein facing death was seen first on the front page. Though readers' letters poured in responding to the hanging and its images, no discussion addressed the fact that in the move from video to still photo, U.S. mainstream journalism gravitated almost unanimously toward the more sanitized depiction of Hussein facing death instead of showing him dead in either moving or still form.

Because competitive interpretations do not disappear at will, the accompanying captions showed how resonant they remained: Headlined with competitive interpretations like "Saddam Video Outrage" or "The Tyrant Has Fallen," captions to the same image alternately described Hussein's final moments as dignified, calm, compliant and muted, on the one hand, and unrepentant, defiant, contemptuous and feisty, on the other ("Final minutes" 2006; Hurst, 2006). When noting Hussein's response to what was happening, captions said Hussein "was subdued and unresisting," "was scornful of his captors and exchanged angry words with the onlookers," "smiled at taunting onlookers" or "waited with dignity" ("Saddam meeting his fate," 2006; Hurst, 2006; "Saddam's last moments," 2006). In both mindsets, the picture of Hussein facing death prevailed.

What do the patterns in this collective display of Hussein's execution tell us? The about-to-die photo – and its reliance on suggestion rather than evidentiary force – was useful to journalists seeking to establish a unified interpretive voice in covering the hanging. It was useful for multiple reasons. First, it acted as a lowest common denominator: common to both videos, it did not force journalists to side with either the official or unofficial versions of the hanging and thus bolster one interpretation over the other. Second, it did not force journalists to violate their initial reluctance about showing graphic images. And third, it diminished the role played by new media, sidestepping mainstream journalists' ambivalence over the videos, skirting the critical questions that new media and the involvement of non-journalists raised about their own coverage of the hanging, and reducing new media's threat to traditional news organizations.

Thus, in converging on one open and suggestive still image as the core of their coverage, journalists were able to entertain variant and often contradictory accounts of what had transpired in ways that the videos did not make possible. Though many variations of the hanging were available in both forms – still image versus video, with or without sound – and in content – pre-hanging or hanging, hanging without the drop or the full unedited cut – journalists across the news media gravitated toward the one image that allowed all the dissonance to be simultaneously entertained rather than clarified – the still picture of Hussein facing his death. Doing so kept the interpretive community intact, reinstating interpretive control of a story which had momentarily slipped its grasp.

At the same time, gravitating toward the about-to-die image undermined journalistic accountability for the event's coverage. Because portraying Hussein about to die allowed journalists to accommodate multiple contradictory stances about the necessity, justification and appropriateness of the hanging; it also enabled them to stop short of telling the full story that the hanging suggested about the "war on terror" – its incomplete prosecution, unrealized aims and misjudged rationale. This suggests that, thanks to the force of journalists' interpretive strategies and their need to establish themselves as a unified interpretive community, journalists were able to consolidate an authoritative response to the hanging, even when doing so meant that they stopped short of providing its full documentation.

Discourse and journalism's interpretive communities

What does this suggest about journalism's interpretive communities? Reporters use discourse and interpretation to discuss, consider, and at times challenge the reigning consensus surrounding journalistic practice, facilitating their collective adaptation to changing technologies, changing circumstances, and the changing stature of newswork. Such is as it should be, for as Daniel Schorr once remarked, reporting is "not only a livelihood, but a frame of mind" (Schorr, 1977, p. vii).

But this discussion has shown that journalists' interpretive strategies do not always work in the direction of full and complete relay of information. Sometimes they work in the aid of journalistic empowerment. And understanding that empowerment may help us better understand how and why the interpretive communities of journalism keep coming out on top of circumstances that energetically work to diminish their authority.

Note

Thanks to Keren Tenenboim-Weinblatt for helping collect material on the U.S. coverage of the Saddam Hussein hanging and to Karin Becker and Kari Anden-Papadapolous for organizing an ICA session on amateur newswork that encouraged me to develop this paper. Parts of this chapter are drawn from Barbie Zelizer, "Journalists as interpretive communities," *Critical Studies in Mass Communication* 10 (1993, September), 219–237. Parts also appear in Barbie Zelizer, "*About to die*": *How news images move the public* (Chicago: University of Chicago Press, forthcoming).

References

American Press Institute (2001, October 2). *Crisis Journalism: A Handbook for Media Response.*

Bauder, D. (2006, December 31). "TV: Few tough decisions on Saddam pictures," Associated Press.

Berkowitz, D. and J.V. Terkeurst (1999, Summer). "Community as interpretive community: Rethinking the journalist-source relationship," *Journal of Communication* 49 (3), 125–136.

Brewin, M. (1999, July). "The interpretive community and reform: Public journalism plays out in North Carolina," *Journal of Communication Inquiry* 23 (3), 222–238.

Carey, J. (1975). "A cultural approach to communication," *Communication* 2, 1–22.

Carlson, M. (2007, May). "Making memories matter: Journalistic discourse and the memorializing discourse around Mary McGrory and David Brinkley," *Journalism* 8(2), 165–183.

"Final minutes: ex-dictator appeared confident, calm." (2006, December 31). *Philadelphia Inquirer*, 1.

Fish, S. (1980). *Is there a text in this class?* (Cambridge: Harvard University Press).

Garman, A. (2005). "Teaching journalism to produce 'interpretive communities' rather than just 'professionals,' Ecquid Novi: AJS, 26, 199–211.

Gough, P. (2006, December 19). "TV plans tasteful coverage of Saddam execution," Reuters.

"He Couldn't Die Fast Enough for Cable News." (2006, December 31). *Philadelphia Inquirer*, A11.

"Graphic Photos Inside." (2006, December 31). *Philadelphia Inquirer*, 1.

Helmore, E. (2007, January 7). "Saddam's 'snuff video' signals the end of editorial control," *The Observer*, 10.

Hurst, S. (2006, December 31). "Saddam defiant to the end," *Buffalo News*, A1.

Huxford, J. (2006, December). "Crying wolf: Scientific false alarms and defensive journalism in coverage of 'doomsday asteroids'," *Communication Review* 9(4), 269–295.

Hymes, D. (1980). "Functions of speech," in *Language in education* (Washington, DC: Center for Applied Linguistics), 1–18.

Irby, K. (2006, December 31). "Displaying death with dignity," *Poynteronline.*

Levi-Strauss, C. (1966). *The Savage Mind* (Chicago: University of Chicago Press).

Lindlof, T.R. (ed.). (1987). *Natural Audiences* (Norwood, New Jersey: Ablex).

Lindlof, T.R. (2002). "*Interpretive Community*: An approach to media and religion. *Journal of Media and Religion*, 1(1), 63–76.

McBride, K. (2006, December 29). "Weekend update: Coverage of the execution and its aftermath," *Poynteronline.*

Mellor, N. (2008). "Arab journalists as cultural intermediaries," *International Journal of Press/Politics*, 13(4), 465–483.

Meyers, O. (2003) "Israeli *journalists* as an *interpretive* memory *community*: The case study of Haolam Hazeh", unpublished PhD thesis, The Annenberg School for Communication, University of Pennsylvania.

Morley, D. (1980). "Texts, readers, subjects," in S. Hall *et al.* (eds.), *Culture, Media, Language* (London: Hutchinson).

"Newspapers, Online editors, TV show images of Saddam hanging." (2006, December 30). *EditorandPublisher. com.*

O'Brien, D. (1983). "The news as environment." *Journalism Monographs* 85.

Parameswaran, R. (2006, January). "Military metaphors, masculine modes and critical commentary: Deconstructing journalists' inner tales of September 11," *Journal of Communication Inquiry* 30 (1), 42–64.

Park, R.E. (1940). "News as a form of knowledge," *American Journal of Sociology* 45, 669–686.

Radway, J. (1984). *Reading the romance* (Chapel Hill: University of North Carolina Press).

Rutten, T. (2007, January 6). "Regarding media," *Los Angeles Times*, E1.

"Saddam meeting his fate." (2006, December 31). *Charlotte Observer*," 1A.

"Saddam's last moments." (2006, December 31). *Colorado Springs Gazette*, A1.

Santora, M. (2006, December 31). "As attacks go on, Iraqis are riveted by Hussein video," *New York Times.*

Schorr, D. (1977). *Clearing the Air* (New York: Berkley).

Schudson, M. (1988). "What is a reporter: The private face of public journalism," in J. Carey (ed.), *Media, Myths and Narratives* (Beverly Hills: Sage), 228–245.

Schudson, M. (1992). *Watergate in American Memory: How we remember, forget and reconstruct the past* (New York: Basic Books).

Stanley, A. (2006, December 31). "An overnight death watch, and then images of the hangman's noose," *New York Times*, 14.

Thompkins, A. (2006, December 29). "Saddam Hussein death: Resources for journalists," *Poynteronline*.

Traquina, N. (2004, February). "Theory consolidation in the study of journalism: A comparative analysis of the news coverage of the HIV/AIDS issue in four countries," *Journalism* 5(1). 97–116.

"Video shows taunts at execution." (2006, December 31). BBC News.

Walters, P. (2006, December 29). "Weekend update: Coverage of the execution and its aftermath," *Poynteronline*.

"What did Hussein's execution accomplish? (Readers Letters)," (2007, January 1). *New York Times*, 18.

Zavis, A. (2007, January 1). "The conflict in Iraq," *Los Angeles Times*, A1.

Zelizer, B. (1992). *Covering the Body: The Kennedy assassination, the media, and the shaping of collective memory* (Chicago: University of Chicago Press).

Zelizer, B. (1993, September). "Journalists as interpretive communities," *Critical Studies in Mass Communication* 10, 219–237.

Zelizer, B. (1998). *Remembering to Forget: Holocaust memory through the camera's eye* (Chicago: University of Chicago Press).

Zelizer, B. (2004). *Taking Journalism Seriously: News and the academy* (Thousand Oaks, CA: Sage).

Zelizer, B. (2007, December). "On 'having been there': 'Eyewitnessing' as a journalistic key word," *Critical Studies in Media Communication* 24(5), 408–428.

Zelizer, B. (forthcoming). *"About to die": How news images move the public* (Chicago: University of Chicago Press).

18

GATEKEEPING AND NEWS SELECTION AS SYMBOLIC MEDIATION

Jackie Harrison

This chapter argues that gatekeeping and news selection – news chosen for acceptance or rejection – operates according to the relationship between the 'background' and 'foreground' of the newsroom. In terms of the background, there are two related but contrastable views of news, which I shall call *informed public opinion* and *homogeneity*. The foreground is the mundane setting of gatekeeping and newsroom selection as it actually occurs in the newsroom. Here gatekeeping and news selection is the application of the background through daily journalistic rules, rhetoric and practices.

Having outlined these concepts, I will then argue that by combining an understanding of the background and foreground to gatekeeping and news selection we can better understand them as a form of newsroom subjectivity maintained and driven by a circular process of symbolic mediation. In other words, what is appropriate and what is inappropriate news (for a particular newsroom) is selected through the circular relationship between background and foreground. I contend that this is how gatekeeping and news selection works as symbolic mediation.

Newsroom background: the two symbolic models of news – informed public opinion and homogeneity

It is reasonable to form the view from the contemporary literature on news that there are two related but distinct versions of the news. They are either that news is located in and positively contributes to the world of informed public opinion, or it is located as part of a modern social imaginary dominated by homogeneity. The former is symbolised in terms of a participatory civil and public space, the later symbolised as a public space characterised by ideological (throughout this chapter meaning the un-reflexive conformity to a set of dominant ideas) rectitude and ultimately distortion.

To begin, we turn to C.W. Mills (1970: 21), who wrote:

The sociological imagination is becoming ... the major common denominator of our cultural life and its signal feature. This quality of mind is found
in the social and psychological sciences, but it goes far beyond these studies as
we now know them ... Yet in factual and moral concerns, in literary work and
in political analysis, the qualities of this imagination are regularly demanded.
In a great variety of expressions, they have become central features of intellectual endeavour and cultural sensibility. Leading critics exemplify these
qualities as do serious journalists – in fact, the work of both is often judged
in these terms.

Max Weber (1918) put it this way:

Not everybody realizes that a really good journalistic accomplishment requires
at least as much 'genius' as any scholarly accomplishment, especially because
of the necessity of producing at once and 'on order,' and because of the
necessity of being effective, to be sure, under quite different conditions
of production. It is almost never acknowledged that the responsibility of
the journalist is far greater, and that the sense of responsibility of every
honourable journalist is, on the average, not a bit lower than that of the
scholar, but rather, as the war has shown, higher. This is because, in the very
nature of the case, irresponsible journalistic accomplishments and their often
terrible effects are remembered.

Fred Inglis (2006: 13), following the American journalist Fred Hirsch, puts it this way:

[T]he journalist discovers what we could not possibly discover for ourselves,
and tells us what it is. He is faithful to his science, which is the history of
the present.

For these writers serious news journalism is a matter of intellectual endeavour,
scholarship and critique, and fidelity to a truth demanding science: 'the history
of the present'. The social and cultural context is one of informed and intelligent
public discourse. This is news journalism located in the public sphere of an active
civil society contributing to a participatory social and cultural way of independently
relating to the political order. It is ultimately and symbolically the news journalism
of free men and women who demand that public bodies, organisations and political
authorities are subject to the principle of informed public opinion and scrutiny. On
this Habermas (2003: 94–5) cites Edmund Burke:

... every man thinks he has a concern in all public matters; that he has a
right to deliver an opinion on them. They sift, examine and discuss them ...
In free countries, there is often found more real public wisdom and sagacity

in shops and manufactories than in the cabinet of princes in countries where none dare to have an opinion until he comes into them.

Habermas (2003: 95) also notes that by 1781 the terms 'general opinion' parallel with the term 'public spirit' received the name public opinion. Accordingly the first symbolic model of news is that of informing public opinion.

Now contrast the above with the second symbolic model of news; the world of a modern social imaginary dominated by homogeneity and limit. Charles Taylor (2007: 171) writes that a social imaginary is best understood as:

> ... something much broader and deeper than the intellectual scheme people may entertain when they think about social reality in a disengaged mode. I am thinking rather of the ways in which they imagine their social existence, how they fit together with others, how things go on between them and their fellows, the expectations which are normally met, and the deeper normative notions and images which underlie these expectations.

And following that, Taylor notes that such 'social self understanding' has three dimensions, of which only the second will concern us here. These are first the economy, second the public sphere and third the practices and outlooks of democratic self-rule (2007: 176). He has this to say: the public sphere is a central feature of modern society, even in repressive societies 'it has to be faked', it is independent from the polity, it is a common space in which the members of society are 'deemed to meet through a variety of media' and communicate with one another (2007: 185). Taylor (2007: 189) also cites Habermas on Burke (see opposite) before concluding that what the public sphere is supposed to do 'is enable society to come to a common mind, without the mediation of the political sphere, in a discourse of reason outside power' (2007: 191).

While this sounds very much like the first symbolic model of news described above, there is for Taylor (2007: 195) a particular modern aspect of the public sphere that we need to be very much aware of:

> The modern notion of simultaneity comes to be, in which events utterly unrelated in cause or meaning are held together simply by their co-occurrence at the same point in this single profane time line. Modern literature, as well as news media, seconded by social science, has accustomed us to think of society in terms of vertical time slices, holding together myriad happenings, related and unrelated.

In essence, the modern relation of simultaneity (due, according to Taylor, to a modern version of time consciousness) carries with it 'a presumption of homogeneity' (2007: 195). A 'presumption' that before Taylor, Heidegger (1977) had also noted when arguing that one particular feature of modernity was the extent to which the study of history was becoming a form of news journalism with its concern for 'the ordinary and the average' (1977: 123). It is this 'presumption of homogeneity' that critics of the first version of news journalism's symbolic significance rely on to show the ultimately ideological effects of news journalism.

Pierre Bourdieu (1998: 46) writes in this regard:

> Journalists – we should really say the journalism field – owe their importance in society to their de facto monopoly on the large-scale informational instruments of production and diffusion of information. Through these they control the access of ordinary citizens but also of other cultural producers such as scholars, artists and writers to what is sometimes called 'public space,' that is the space of mass circulation ... journalists exercise a very particular form of domination, since they control the means of public expression ... it remains true that, like other fields, the journalistic field is based on a set of shared assumptions and beliefs, which reach beyond differences of position and opinion.

And as a consequence of these assumptions and beliefs:

> There is no discourse (scientific analysis, political manifesto, whatever) and no action (demonstration, strike) that doesn't have to face this trial of journalistic selection in order to catch the public eye. The effect is *censorship*, which journalists practice without being aware of it. They retain only things capable of interesting them and "keeping their attention," which means things that fit their categories and mental grid; and they reject as insignificant or remain indifferent to symbolic expressions that ought to reach the population as a whole (1998: 47).

For Bourdieu news journalists are symbolic mediators who undertake their role in both an unreflexive and a harmful manner, and the way they contribute to a public sphere (within a modern social imaginary) is to mislead. Essentially, they contribute to the vulgarity of the modern world by uncritically accepting and circulating 'narrow particularisms' which undergo 'endless media repetition' to emerge as a new 'global common sense, a new vacuous kind of universalism' (McLennan and Osborne 2004: 57 following Bourdieu 1998). In short, news journalism distorts the public sphere by actively contributing to its intellectual limitations, its ordinariness and ultimately to its homogeneous character, while at the same time maintaining the myth of public participation. All in all this is a long way from Weber's conception of public journalism.

Essentially these two symbolic models of news, informed public opinion and homogeneity, provide the context for beginning to understand gatekeeping and news selection. Both appear to imply the constitution of a form and particular version of gatekeeping and news selection. The former sees gatekeeping and news selection in the iconic form of the journalist as a vigilant watchdog that only sponsors news on the basis of informing public opinion. The latter sees gatekeeping and news selection in the equally iconic form of the journalist as a compliant lap dog that unreflexively and recursively contributes to the homogenisation of the contemporary public sphere by uncritically serving particular dominant political ideas and partisan and sectarian worldviews (a view reinforced by the current over-reliance on news agency copy, particular sources and increased repurposing of news across platforms in modern Western converged newsrooms).

This deliberately bi-cameral (and so far stylised) understanding of gatekeeping and news selection comes down to this. It is practised either self consciously and knowingly, as something on behalf of a recognisably beneficial public purpose, or it is experienced as an activity in which the mediated representations of the world are simplified or misrepresented through the unreflexive and passive acceptance of a particular form of news status quo. The former is a view of news and news journalism as critical, the latter a view of news and news journalism as ideological. Both views rest upon the assumptions that gatekeeping and news selection are either an exercise in free and responsible journalism, or an exercise in a compliant and informal form of censorship. In reality gatekeeping and news selection are neither and, to understand this further, we must combine the above with an understanding of gatekeeping and news selection at the level of how it is experienced, at the level of its mundanity, and ultimately in relationship to these two symbolic models of news.

Newsroom foreground: gatekeeping and news selection as a form of newsroom subjectivity

To clarify, by gatekeeping and news selection I mean bestowing or withdrawing a form of news journalism legitimacy. In short, news content is approved or rejected according to its perceived ability to inform, or its perceived ability to conform. Thus failure to inform public opinion from the point of view of the first symbolic model of news, informed public opinion, results in rejection. Equally, failure to conform to a particular version of a news status quo from the point of view of the second symbolic model of news, homogeneity, will also result in rejection. Accordingly, I argue that gatekeeping and news selection are a form of newsroom subjectivity centred on the constant assessment of rejection and acceptance rules applied to news stories, and as such are an exercise both in quotidian authority and in the wider legitimation of a certain kind of commitment to the above two symbolic models of news. More precisely, as we shall see below, typically there is no 'either–or' attachment to one symbolic model or the other, there is in fact a mixture of commitments to both in the same newsroom.

My approach is therefore different from that advocated by Shoemaker (1991) whose account of gatekeeping still remains the most lucid and comprehensive. Shoemaker argued that there are five levels of analysis that should be applied to the study of gatekeeping. These are: the individual communication worker; the routines or practices of communication work; the organisational level; the social and institutional level; and the social system level (1991: 33). These five levels provide a model of gatekeeping that range, from individual psychological agency, to the extra media factors of the social, cultural and historical setting of the media themselves. In this, Shoemaker is advocating a systematic social psychological approach which, informed by organisational theory, provides an analysis of a process of gatekeeping, which occurs in the synthetic interplay and context of these levels. In this way Shoemaker seeks to provide an account of the reasons for and the mechanics of gatekeeping. From many points of view she is correct in both her identification of levels and her reasons for advocating their analysis. However, I do not wish to adopt a systematic social psychological (and organisational) approach, since it over-emphasises invariant structures, processes and forces which ultimately seem to imply a form of technical reductionism. Rather I wish to adopt a less systematic (and technical) approach and focus on the activity of gatekeeping and news selection as the work of conceiving the value of news itself, by which I mean that gatekeeping and news selection is a form of labour, which is more than instrumental action, and is certainly not alienated, since it involves judging and interpreting what constitutes news. Work understood this way is (following Habermas) a form of 'communicative action,' where the news is not something transcendental but materially experiential and mundane and yet is deemed worthy of a certain kind of public form.

To some extent I am returning to the type of work undertaken by David Manning White (1950) whose original study of gatekeeping involved the ironically named Mr Gates, a wire editor in a small newspaper, the *Peoria Star*. Mr Gates was asked to provide an explanation of why 90 percent of news stories from the wire services were rejected. As White notes, Mr Gates's judgements revealed how 'highly subjective, how reliant upon value-judgements based on the gatekeepers' own set of experiences, attitudes and expectations the communication of news really is' (1950: 386). In other words White was the first to describe gatekeeping as a form of experiential newsroom subjectivity whose rhetorical and discursive rationalisations for the rejection of news stories – these included 'lack of space,' 'waiting for more information,' 'style,' 'BS,' 'propaganda,' 'clarity, conciseness and angle' and on one occasion news stories 'slanted to conform to our editorial policies, (1950: 390) – were significant for understanding the link between a form of newsroom subjectivity and the subsequent public form of news. Following his lead I now wish to explore this version of gatekeeping and news selection.

In two previous studies (Harrison 2000 and 2006), I gave a list of reasons that was compiled from comments which were collected over several months' observation in a variety of newsrooms and which a variety of news journalists and editors had given to me to explain why some news stories were rejected and did not feature as news and some were selected and did. In 2007 I undertook another study, this time of 'User Generated Content' (UGC) at the BBC and again I saw that the same reasons for the rejection and acceptance of news stories were still being used, though with different levels of frequency due to changes in mobile technology. Both lists are worth repeating; first rejection, followed by selection.

Rejection:

- 'We've already done that';
- 'It's not our kind of story';
- 'It's too expensive';

- 'It's too late, my programme is full';
- 'It's too tacky, too down-market';
- 'It's boring';
- 'It's yesterday's news';
- 'We've not got any pics';
- 'It doesn't happen in our time';
- 'It doesn't move the story on';
- 'We've not got cameras there';
- 'Not enough dead';
- 'Too samey';
- 'It can wait'. (This story could be told any time, and does not have a particular 'peg' at the moment);
- 'Everyone's packages have come in over-long so something will have to go'. (This occurs when correspondents disobey the programme editor and squeeze a few extra seconds by making their package longer than the allocated time. If several correspondents do this on the same day it can result in a piece being dropped);
- 'It would take too much telling'. (The story is too complicated for the medium and for the time allocated to it).

Selection:

- there are pictures or film available (television news);
- they contain short, dramatic occurrences which can be sensationalised;
- they have novelty value;
- they are open to simple reporting;
- they occur on a grand scale;
- they are negative or contain violence, crime, confrontation or catastrophe;
- they are highly unexpected;
- they contain things which one would expect to happen;
- the events have meaning and relevance to the audience;
- similar events are already in the news;
- they provide a balanced programme;
- they contain elite people or nations;
- they allow an event to be reported in personal or human interest terms.

These rhetorical and discursive rationalisations reveal gatekeeping as the apparently self conscious control of a practical outcome, in which the practical outcome links the individual journalist and the institutional newsroom together in accepting or rejecting a story. In other words these rhetorical and discursive devices can be read at one level (there are, of course, others) as the invocation of a set of both substantive and procedural rules which describe a pattern of agreements about newsworthiness. That is, rejection and acceptance can be read from these rules as a matter of following a particular rule-adhering orthodoxy which is nothing other than a conventional and agreed way of providing reasons for rejecting or accepting news stories in the newsroom.

These rules appear unambiguous and seem to confirm in their conciseness the view that dealing with the news is conducted at a rapid tempo and requires direct and swift, if sometimes to outsiders, brutal or insensitive, judgements. They also appear narrow in range, uncomplicated and easily learnt, easy to apply and a way of dealing with the obvious, such as judgements about time, money, resources, appropriateness etc. In fact these rules seem to exist as a form of consent between people in the newsroom and, as Randall explains, ground the modus operandi of a journalistic culture which 'sets what editors and their executives regard as a good story or dismiss as "boring" and determines the subjects they think of as "sexy" and those that are not'; they also 'create the moral atmosphere of a paper [or newsroom]' (Randall 2000: 16).

And yet it is important, at this stage, to note that the mere existence of a rule-adhering orthodoxy in any given newsroom alone does not explain an adherence to either of the two symbolic models of news: informing public opinion or contributing to homogeneity. This is so because both symbolic models appear to be equally evoked by the same orthodox application of these rules. In short, the existence of these rules does little to explain any differences in their application that might exist between them and particular newsrooms with their different styles of news. Or in Randall's terms these rules alone do not set the 'moral atmosphere of the newspaper [or newsroom]'. Consequently, in order to understand the rationale for the application of these rules we need to go down a level and look at what dwells beneath them and what guides their application. That is, we must understand that, while the activity of applying these gatekeeping and news selection rules is made in a quotidian fashion and represents the common, mundane and daily setting which occurs in the foreground of the newsroom, we as yet do not know what this foreground relates to or to what extent there exists variant applications of these rules in different newsrooms.

The insights of two philosophers help to clarify this process. Wittgenstein (1969: 15e S94) wrote:

> ... I did not get my picture of the world by satisfying myself of its correctness; nor do I have it because I am satisfied of its correctness. No: it is the inherited background against which I distinguish between true and false.

Developing this concept of 'background', Taylor (2007: 13) observes:

> ... all beliefs are held within a context or framework of the taken-for-granted, which usually remains tacit, and may even be as yet unacknowledged by the agent, because never formulated.

By citing these two philosophers I am suggesting that the application of gatekeeping and news selection rules also occurs within the background setting of the above two symbolic models of news. Although these two symbolic models of news are very different, they are nevertheless related to each other and cannot, in any sensible analytic or empirical study of gatekeeping and news selection in the newsroom, be separated from each other. Indeed what recent empirical studies of modern Western newsrooms reveal is in fact that these symbolic models of news overlap. Judged from the vantage point of these studies, newsrooms are neither exclusive nor singular in their commitment to one or the other and talk of extremes is misplaced since they demonstrate that newsrooms are in fact committed to both symbolic models of news simultaneously, although in varying combinations.

In other words, news is best understood as Janus-faced in nature since it always carries within itself the capacity to be used both critically and ideologically, both to generate debate and to produce homogeneity. Nor does this alter much whether this Janus-faced nature of news journalism is acknowledged or unacknowledged, explicit or tacit. Ultimately, different newsrooms operate according to how the two symbolic models of news combine to form their own particular background; combinations that will be in different ratios and with different levels of commitment across different newsrooms. Indeed today it seems as if most newsrooms are capable of producing both types of news and that conventionally these are the newsrooms which are regarded as increasingly acceptable in liberal democratic societies. Newsrooms which are exclusively about informing public opinion or conforming to a fixed news status quo are increasingly regarded as extreme since either they require unwarranted public funding, or they are self evidently tendentious and, in spite of their popularity, are usually dismissed as 'not doing news.' Thus, only newsrooms that use both types of symbolic repertoire for their news journalism are generally regarded as the norm from the point of view of an emerging liberal democratic news consensus. And this is reflected in the way newsrooms regard their particular mixture of the 'back-grounded' and the 'fore-grounded' application of gatekeeping and news selection rules. The study of this often reveals them to be operating from an increasingly consensual view about what constitutes news.

In effect the following relationship is established. Gatekeeping and news selection are contextualised by the newsroom background from which the fore-grounded application of rules is applied in a mundane and daily fashion according to how news stories are judged to fit into that background. Consequently gatekeeping and news selection is always situated in a newsroom as the fore-grounded practical application of these rules, which in turn is guided by the background provided to their application. However, this description does not explain what activity drives and maintains the relationship between background and foreground, only that they provide the context from within which gatekeeping and news selection operate. I want to suggest that the relationship between the background and foreground is driven and maintained by the symbolic mediation of news and it is this which constitutes a form of newsroom subjectivity which holds them both together usually under the guise of 'objectivity norms' which enable news journalists to claim that selection criteria are neutral, balanced and fair.

Above (pp. 192–3) I suggested that gatekeeping and newsroom selection is work that (following Habermas) we can call a form of 'communicative action' which operates in the interpersonal communicative setting of both the ideational and symbolic background and the material foreground of the newsroom. This communicative action amounts to the application of the above rules and yet the application of rules requires judgement and interpretation about what constitutes news. This is judgement that matches news stories to a particular newsroom background through the interpretive application of these rules. Two things are here required to unify judgement and interpretation: first, knowledge of the background, and second, an understanding of the rules in terms of their relationship to the background. Both are acquired as a result of culturally learned behaviour and the attendant acquisition of the ability to undertake interpretive mediation. With regard to the foreground, this is well understood and documented in the numerous studies of newsroom acculturation. With regard to the background, matters are more confused. Here we are talking about the degree of free agency news journalists have to exercise their own interpretation of the relationship between background and rules (i.e. their applicability), and the extent to which such degrees of agency are exercised by journalists in modern newsrooms is subject to debate. However, what we can say is that both newsroom acculturation and the common practice which allows news journalists to identify what is and is not a good story is producing a greater news consensus. The reason for this is the range of judgements that match news stories to a particular background through the interpretive application of gatekeeping and news selection rules only uses a few of the many possible fundamental symbols located in either of the two symbolic models of news. For example the two symbolic models of news contain within them many diverse symbolic representations of various aspects of the news: positively these are freedom, citizenship, participatory republics, the public sphere of diversity, responsible public interest; or negatively, homogeneity, ordinariness, celebrity, partisanship, 'interesting the public,' attack journalism, witch hunts. Modern news journalism operates mainly according to an increasingly overlapping and narrow range of symbolic representations derived from both symbolic models of news.

Indeed it is as a result of the mixing of these two symbolic models that we now have an increasingly limited range of different types of news available. And this is in spite of the libertarian claims made on behalf of ICTs, user generated content and citizen journalism.

To put the matter another way, according to Geertz (1993: 214):

> Thinking, conceptualisation, formulation, comprehension, understanding, or what-have-you, consists not of ghostly happenstance in the head but of a matching of the states and processes of symbolic models against the states and process of the wider world.

The net result in the case of news is that the public form of news is limited and by and large operates according to unimaginatively and self justifying news agendas. A form of newsroom subjectivity based upon this mixing of the two symbolic models of news may appear an exercise in tolerance, but the resultant symbolic mediation of this mix, undertaken through the daily application of gatekeeping and news selection criteria, generates an increasingly narrow base from which diverse and divergent news and news forms can emerge. In effect a news consensus is achieved because the symbolic mediation of the news is being increasingly limited with the net result that gatekeeping and news selection, while a self-conscious activity, is in danger of becoming increasingly banal.

References

Bourdieu, P. (1998) *On Television and Journalism*, London: Pluto Press.

Geertz, C. (1993) *The Interpretation of Cultures*, London: Fontana Press.

Habermas, J. (2003 [1989]) *The Structural Transformation of the Public Sphere: An Inquiry into a Category of Bourgeois Society*, trans. T. Burger assisted by F. Lawrence, Cambridge: Polity Press.

Harrison, J. (2000) *Terrestrial Television News in Britain: The Culture of Production*, Manchester: Manchester University Press.

Harrison, J. (2006) *News*, London: Routledge.

Heidegger, M. (1977) 'The Age of the World Picture' in *The Question Concerning Technology and Other Essay*, trans. and ed., W. Lovitt, New York: Harper Torchbooks.

Inglis, F. (2006) *Letter from England: Journalism, Democracy, and American Popular Sentiment*, http://nick-jones.com/fred/journalism_and_democracy.pdf, Willard Thorp Lecture, University of Princeton, April 2006 (accessed 1 December 2007).

McLennan, G. and Osborne, T. (2004) 'Contemporary "Vehicularity" and "Romanticism": Debating the Status of Ideas and Intellectuals' in D. Cummings (ed.) *The Changing Role of the Public Intellectual*, London: Routledge.

Mills, C.W. (1970) *The Sociological Imagination*, Harmondsworth: Penguin.

Randall, D. (2000) *The Universal Journalist*, 2nd edn, London: Pluto Press.

Shoemaker, P. J. (1991) *Gatekeeping*, London: Sage Publications.

Taylor, C. (2007) *A Secular Age*, Cambridge, MA: The Belknap Press of Harvard University Press.

Weber, M. (1918) *Politics as a Vocation*, http://socialpolicy.ucc.ie/weber_Politics_as_Vocation.htm, (accessed 10 June 2007).

White, D. M. (1950) 'The gatekeeper: a case study in the selection of news', *Journalism Quarterly*, 27: 383–390.

Wittgenstein, L. (1969) *On Certainty* [*Uber Gewissheit*], trans. D. Paul and G.E.M. Anscombe, Oxford: Basil Blackwell.

19
JOURNALISM, NEWS SOURCES AND PUBLIC RELATIONS

Bob Franklin, Justin Lewis and Andrew Williams

The manufacture of news, unlike other forms of production, relies on inputs from individuals and organisations located outside the formal news organisation in which production takes place (Franklin 1997, pp. 19–21). They are not paid in the usual sense of that word for their contribution and they are not subject to managerial authority. And yet they are vital to the news production process. Their cooperation and participation in the processes of news gathering and reporting is the outcome of negotiations and bargains struck implicitly or explicitly between them and journalists. They are the news sources on which all journalists rely for their livelihood. The relationship between the two groups is complex, shifts across time and particular settings and has been the subject of considerable scholarly attention (Ericson *et al.* 1989; Gans 1979; Larsson 2002). An understanding of the relationship between journalists and their sources sits at the heart of journalism studies.

In the UK, the expansive public relations sector has become an increasingly significant source of news-serving not only as an agenda setter but actually providing stories which inform journalists' copy. Declining newspaper circulations and falling advertising revenues have prompted a crisis of profitability, job cuts within journalism and journalists' growing reliance on public relations materials to fill newspapers' editorial pages (Lewis, Williams and Franklin 2008a and 2008b). Davies describes PR as one of the two "primary conveyor belts" (the other being news agencies) feeding "the assembly line in the news factory" with the "raw materials" which journalists use to construct the national news (2008, p.74). This recent recognition of the resulting "*Flat Earth News*" has scholarly precedents. Thirty years ago Cutlip (1976) claimed 45% of newspaper stories originated in PR materials, while Golding and Elliot's (1979) classic study identified broadcast news as little more than "a passive reflection of the information provided by the information producing strata" (1979, p.169). But the argument here is that the recent rapid growth in public relations across the 1990s, in tandem with the stasis in the number of journalists engaged in news production, has impacted on journalists' news room practice, transforming them into mere *processors* rather than *originators* of news. This increasingly significant role for PR in shaping news agendas has triggered what has variously been described as 'churnalism' (Davies 2008), 'McJournalism' (Franklin 2005) and 'newszak' (Franklin 1997).

This chapter examines the shifting 'editorial balance' between journalism and public relations and the impact of the latter on journalists' products and professional practices in both the national and local press. We begin by considering briefly how scholars have understood the relationships between journalists and public relations.

Who leads the merry dance? Journalism and public relations in the UK

Two theoretical 'take off' points inform the subsequent analysis. The first acknowledges the importance of Gans' influential dance metaphor in identifying the cooperative, but not necessarily equal, character of relationships between journalists and sources. "It takes two to tango" he suggests, but "sources usually lead" (Gans 1979). More recently, Reich has argued that which partner becomes dominant and 'leads' varies at different stages in the cycle of news gathering and reporting (2006, pp. 497–515), while White and Hobsbawm identify a "love-hate relationship" (2007, pp. 284–5) which acknowledges the potential conflict inherent in these relations, which is typically trumped by a requirement for "mutal reciprocity" and cooperative ways of working if both journalists and PR sources are to achieve their professional objectives (Blumler and Gurevitch 1995). Some observers believe that such mutual reciprocity means that any "distinct professional identities" or "boundaries" between journalists and PR professionals are blurring, if not "vanishing" (Deuze 2007, p. 141).

Journalists typically object to this characterisation, arguing that it implies a too dominant role for sources. "Getting too close" to sources offends a key professional principle, and risks blunting journalists' critical edge transforming the journalistic watchdog into a public relations lapdog. This more conflictual account of the relationship is articulated in near caricature form by columnist Richard Littlejohn during his days at the *Sun*. "The job of someone like me", he claims, "is to sit at the back and throw bottles." Politicians and their PR advisers are among his favourite targets. "Politicians employ an entire industry," he suggests, "often using public money, to present themselves as favourably as possible and I certainly don't see it as my job to inflate the egos of little men" (Franklin, 1994, 15).

But the belief that public relations is influential in shaping news and editorial contents in newspapers has become increasingly commonplace among academics (Maloney 2006), journalists (Marr 2004) and public relations professionals (White and Hobsbawm 2007).

Financial Times journalist John Lloyd makes this dependence explicit.

> The normal journalistic approach to PRs ... is grossly self serving ... It glosses over, ignores or even denies the fact that much of current journalism ... is public relations in the sense that stories, ideas, features and interviews are

either suggested, or in the extreme actually written by public relations people. Until that becomes open and debated ... we will continue to have this artificially wide gulf where journalists pose as fearless seekers of truth and PRs are slimy creatures trying to put one over on us. It is not remotely like that (*Guardian* 10 April 2006, p. 3).

A second theoretical starting point is provided by Oscar Gandy's notion of an information subsidy, understood as "efforts by policy actors to increase the consumption of persuasive messages by reducing their costs" (1982). Gandy argues that PR practitioners offer a form of subsidy to news organisations via press releases, press conferences, VNRs (Video News Release), press briefings and lobbying. This enables them to reduce the costs of newsgathering and hence to maintain profitability in the context of declining circulations and advertising revenues for newspapers. News subsidies offer the prospect of not merely "cheap news" but "free news". They allow news organisations opportunities to "square the circle" between cost cutting (by reducing journalists' wages and the numbers of journalists employed) and sustaining, if not substantially increasing, news output (which has occurred in the context of UK newspapers), in order to maintain profitability in the highly competitive market in which news media are obliged to operate. But these subsidies exact their own demanding price. As news gathering and news reporting is increasingly "outsourced" to public relations professionals, journalists assume the role of desk-bound, office-based recipients and processors of the news gathering activities of those "outside the newsroom": the growing army of "journalism literate PR professionals" (Franklin 1997, Ch 1).

A recent study of trends in the employment of newspaper journalists in the UK offers empirical endorsement of Gandy's claims and signals the potential for PR practitioners to colonise the editorial ground "vacated" by journalists (Lewis *et al.* 2006). Detailed scrutiny of the annual reports and accounts of nine leading UK newspaper groups between 1985–2004 suggested that "throughout the 1990s, the total number of employees in these groups remained at a fairly stable average of 1000 employees per group with average editorial employees also being fairly constant at around 500 employees per group"[1] (Lewis *et al.* 2006, p. 7). The average number of editorial staff employed in each group in 1985 was 786, falling to a low of 427 in 1987 following News International's move to Wapping, but rising again through the 1990s to an average 741 in 2005, a figure very close to the number of journalist employed twenty years earlier. The study identified considerable variations between newspaper groups with Express Newspapers reducing journalist numbers from 968 to 532 between 1996 and 2004, while the total number of *Guardian* employees (editorial and other staffs) effectively doubled from 725 to 1429 between 1991 and 2000, reflecting commitments to online publication (ibid, pp. 7–8).

But significantly, while the number of working journalists has remained fairly static, the study identified "a very substantial increase in the overall size of ... national daily newspapers" with the average number of pages devoted to news and other editorial increasing virtually threefold from "a 14.6 page average in 1985 to 41 pages by 2006" (ibid. pp. 10–11). This expansion in newspapers' news sections, moreover, occurred alongside a marked growth in the number and pagination of supplements and the development of online editions. The study concludes that journalists' productivity increased significantly across the period signalling a "relative decline" in staffing compared with the 1980s up to the mid-1990s.

Across the same period, but in striking contrast, UK public relations has experienced explosive growth in the corporate private sector measured by the number of consultancies, their employees, revenues and profitability. During the 1980s and 1990s, for example, "growth rates for the medium and large British consultancies typically reached 20-40 per cent per annum" (Miller and Dinan 2000, p. 5). The public sector of PR has also enjoyed rapid expansion reflecting the tendency of central and local government information services – along with voluntary organisations and charities – to appoint increasing numbers of press and information officers, special advisers (spin doctors) and marketing specialists to meet politicians' growing commitments to public information campaigns and management of news agendas (Davis 2008, p. 274; Franklin 2004, pp. 103–106). Summarising this growth in agencies, practitioners, income and profits in UK public relations, Davis argued that "there are 2,500 agencies and 47,800 people working in the public relations profession in the UK. This figure excludes the 125,000 people working in the associated advertising and marketing industries, those working in PR support industries (e.g., press cutting, media evaluation, news distribution services), and the many professionals who have had media training. The estimated total turnover of the industry in 2005, consultancy and in-house, was £6.6 billion" (Davis 2008, p. 273). When estimates of the numbers of journalists across all media platforms oscillate between 40,000 (Franklin 1997, p. 51–53) and "between 60,000 and 70,000" (Journalism Training Forum 2002, p. 17), it is easy to appreciate the increasing potential for PR practitioners to influence and shape news agendas. We now assess whether this potential has been achieved in the UK.

Setting the news agenda: UK "quality" newspapers and public relations

A study of 2207 domestic news reports in a structured sample of UK 'quality' (*Guardian*, *The Times*, *Independent* and the *Telegraph*) and mid-market (*Daily Mail*) newspapers, during March and April 2005, generated unequivocal evidence confirming journalists' extensive use of information subsidies from public relations sources (Lewis *et al.* 2006). Researchers analysed each news story to establish and quantify any element of public relations material employed. Internet searches were conducted to trace relevant press releases which were then compared directly with published newspaper text to establish the extent of journalists' reliance on PR sources. This procedure necessarily delivered conservative estimates since news stories were coded as deriving from PR materials *only* when conclusive evidence, resulting from direct textual comparison of a press release with a published story, could be established.

The great majority of the 2207 newspaper stories analysed comprised main page articles of variable length (1564 – 71% of sample), with 561 (25.5%) shorter news in brief items (nibs), while the remainder were 'picture only' stories (0.5%) or opinion pieces (3%). These news items focused on eight key subject areas. The most popular was 'Crime' (20%), followed by 'Domestic issues' (15%) which included the NHS, education, the environment and immigration. Other editorial foci embraced 'Politics' (15%), 'Business/Consumer' news (12%), 'Health/natural world' (10%), 'Entertainment and Sport' (10%), 'Accidents/disasters' (5%), 'Defence/Foreign policy' (2%) and 'Other (11%) (Lewis *et al.* 2006, pp. 13–14).

The great majority of articles were attributed to a by-lined reporter (72%), with only 1% of stories attributed to the Press Association (PA) or another wire service, as well as a small proportion (2%) to a generalised identity such as an 'Independent Reporter'; approximately a quarter (24.5%) carried no by-line but these were typically the shorter nibs. By identifying journalists in this way newspapers suggested that articles represented the work of independent in-house reporters. But the appropriateness of such attribution is perhaps questionable when analysis revealed that almost a fifth (19%) of the sample stories derived 'wholly' (10%) or 'mainly' (9%) from PR sources. A further quarter (22%) were either a 'mix of PR with other materials' (11%) or 'PR but mainly other information' (11%) while a further 13% of stories strongly suggested a PR source which could not be identified and were therefore discounted; there was no identifiable PR source in only 46% of reports. Stories which offered near verbatim replication of source materials were found. *The Times* report, for example, "George Cross for Iraq War Hero" on 24 March 2006, which carried Michael Evans' by-line, reproduces almost exactly a Ministry of Defence press release. Similarly, a story about a new hay fever vaccine published in the *Daily Mail* reproduced a press release from the drug company Cytos without reporting any additional information reflecting independent journalistic inquiry (ibid., p. 17).

This reliance on public relations is not wholly negative, however, since public relations professionals may generate factually well informed and newsworthy stories which potentially enhance the plurality of sources of news from which journalists and editors can select and construct stories. But examination of the origins of PR materials reveals a fairly limited range of established and powerful elite groups and communities as sources. The corporate sector dominates with 38% of PR materials referenced in press coverage deriving from the 'business/corporate' world. Other contributors to press reports via pubic relations include 'public bodies' (the police, NHS, universities – 23%), 'Government and politicians' (21%), NGO/Charities (11%) and 'professional associations' (5%). The voice of ordinary citizens, however, remains almost mute; the opinions of ordinary men and women informed only 2% of stories (ibid. pp. 21–23). One consequence of journalists' increased reliance on public relations subsidies is that corporate and governmental voices enjoy extensive and unrepresentative access to the public debating chamber which newspapers provide. Press articulations of the public interest, which journalists so frequently claim to champion, amount to little more than a barely perceptible pip squeak above the deafening din of corporate and governmental interests.

The same sample of news items was also analysed to establish the extent of journalists' reliance on pre-packaged stories from news agencies, especially the PA; the same research protocols generated even more striking outcomes. Approximately half

(49%) the news stories published in the quality press were wholly (30%) or mainly (19%) dependent on materials produced and distributed by wire services with a further fifth (21%) of stories containing some element of agency copy (ibid., p. 15). Again, newspapers make little acknowledgement of this reliance on agency copy even when it is published virtually verbatim. On 24 March 2006, for example, the *Daily Mail* attributed its front-page story about the health risks of eating oily fish ("Why oily fish might not be so good for your health after all") to a *Daily Mail* reporter, even though it directly replicates quotations and factual materials from PA and Mercury news wire stories (ibid., pp. 35–38).

When quality press uses of both public relations and agency copy are examined, only 12% of published stories are without pre-packaged news content sourced from outside the newsroom; 60% of published stories rely wholly or mainly on external news sources (See Table 19.1).

The significance of these high levels of journalistic dependency on both PR and news agency materials is that they exercise a mutually reinforcing effect on newspapers' editorial contents. Our study revealed that journalists use PR subsidies directly, but PR text is also encoded in the agency copy which journalists use so routinely in news production. Forty-seven per cent of press stories which were based 'wholly' around PR materials closely replicated agency copy, suggesting the existence of a "multi-staged" process of news sourcing in which PR materials initially generate agency stories which in turn promote coverage in newspapers. Consequently, news agency copy serves as a Trojan horse for PR materials and must be analysed carefully if the full impact of PR on editorial agendas is to be established.

The opinions of 42 journalists working on national newspapers, the PA and PR companies were canvassed via (emailed) qualitative survey and follow-up interviews. Respondents confirmed this covert editorial role for public relations subsidies but, significantly, journalists also suggest it is increasing – and as a result of their increasing workload. The majority (28 of 42) of survey respondents claimed that PR informs their stories "sometimes" with the remainder suggesting they use it "often". The

Table 19.1 Newspaper stories with content derived from PR and Agencies

Sources of Editorial Content	%
All from PR/Wires	38
Mainly from PR/Wires	22
Mix of PR/Wires with other information	13
Mainly other information	7
All other information	12
Unclear	8

Source: Lewis *et al.* 2006, p. 25.

substantive majority (38 of 42) suggested that the use of PR for editorial purpose had increased over the last decade (ibid., p. 47). *The Times'* Health Editor suggested:

> There is much more PR these days. I get hundreds of press releases in my mailbox every day … It's become a lot easier to use PR because of the technology. It's very easy and convenient, and as we're producing so many more stories, we use it … if you're not feeling too energetic it's almost as if you could surf this great tidal wave of PR all the way in to the shore and not come up with any original material all day. (Personal interview cited in Lewis et al 2006, p. 48).

Two final points about journalists' uses of PR for editorial. First, most of the stories analysed (87%) were based on a single source but only a half (50%) of these made an attempt to contextualise the published information; in less than a fifth of cases (19%) was this done meaningfully. Second, when stories were based on specific factual claims we discovered that on 70% of occasions these claims were entirely uncorroborated and in only 12% of cases were they corroborated completely. Two-thirds of surveyed journalists confirmed that the number of checks on source material had declined. A journalist on a national paper confided: "newspapers have turned into copy factories … The arrival of online has also increased demand for quick copy reducing the time available for checking the facts" (ibid., 47). The fundamental journalistic practices necessary to produce accurate, well informed and reliable journalism are being ignored in the newsrooms of the national quality press. Research studies suggest the same observation is relevant in the context of local journalism.

Setting the local agenda; local and regional journalism and public relations

The impact of public relations on local journalists' working practices, as well as news agendas in the local press, has enjoyed sustained scholarly attention since the mid-1980s (Davis 2002; Franklin 1986, Franklin and VanSlyke Turk 1988; Harrison 2006; O'Neill and O'Connor 2008). The consensual conclusion of these studies is that the influence of public relations has been extensive, longstanding and expansive, with Harrison arguing – with a liberal measure of irony – that journalists' dependence on "the carefully prepared material provided by professional local government PROs" has become "so extensive" that "the town hall is becoming the last bastion of good municipal journalism" (Harrison 1998, p. 168).

An early study of local government public relations influence on local newspapers in the county of Northumberland, in the north east of the UK, concluded that 96% of press releases issued by the local authority generated stories in the local press. Significantly, most releases triggered stories in three or four newspapers; one story was published in 11 newspapers. The local press appeared to be recycling the same news around the county. Editing the press releases, including any additional information beyond that contained within the release, or telephoning the contact person named at the bottom of the release, was rare. When there was evidence of 'original' journalism, it was minimal (Franklin 1986, pp. 25–33). The great majority of these news releases were swallowed wholesale by a news-hungry local press. In a subsequent national study of local government public relations, 82% of responding press officers confirmed that "more than three-quarters of press releases" generated stories in the local press (Franklin 1988, p. 81). This very high 'strike rate' was less noticeable in a comparative study of similar state public relations practices in Louisiana (Franklin and VanSlyke Turk 1988, pp. 29–42).

Local papers' willingness to accept these public relations 'subsidies' related directly to the newspaper's size and resources but especially to the number of journalists employed by the paper and their areas of professional specialism. At daily papers with larger editorial staffs including a specialist municipal correspondent, press releases were extensively edited, while at the weeklies with leaner editorial resources, press releases were typically reproduced verbatim or edited by removing complete paragraphs or changing their order; in weekly free papers, editing of releases was non-existent, (Franklin 1986). Consequently, newspapers' variable journalism staffs constitute a hierarchy of dependence on PR subsidies in local communication networks, with 42% of press officers identifying free weekly papers as "most likely to use a press release", compared to 30% for paid weeklies, 22% evening and 5% for daily newspapers (Franklin 1988, p. 82). Davis confirms the close tie between reliance on PR and the size of journalism staffs. The increasing influence for public relations on local agenda setting" he claims, "is not the "result of powerful spin doctor pressure ... but because working news journalists have become increasingly stretched ... [and] public relations professionals with their increased resources have thus been ideally placed to make good the short fall in news-producing industries" (Davis 2002, p. 17).

The value of the information subsidy which PR offers to local newspapers is substantial. One press officer calculated an illustrative exemplar. "I estimate at Westminster" he suggested, that "we spend at least 30% of our time, equivalent to one and a half press officers costing £50,000 on servicing the local media ... Many of the requests from local papers are ... pleas for letters and press releases to fill the gaps in pages. In this sense media officers are simply filling the gaps in the newsroom staff" (cited in Harrison 2006, p. 188). Newspapers' reliance on these subsidies encourages local government PROs to view local newspapers as ready outlets, mere noticeboards for stories about local politics and government which are predictably uncritical and tend to stress the positive aspects of local government activities. The challenge to the independence and quality of local journalism is evident; not least to journalists. One journalist suggested that "If we are getting more copy for free from PR agencies, and we are, this raises lots of questions about journalistic independence and journalistic integrity" (Williams and Franklin 2007, p. 39).

Indeed, local journalists routinely complain about the pressure of time constraints, staff cuts, and lack of investment which obliges them increasingly to resort to using the convenient, cost effective, pre-packaged sources of news which PR delivers. They are also aware of the changes to their working practices which PR imposes: not least that journalism has increasingly become a desk-based job. "For most reporters," a journalist claimed, "there's not the time to go out as much as they should. The job is done more and more by cutting and pasting press releases because they're under pressure and there's space to be filled" (cited in Williams and Franklin 2007, p. 39). Recently this editorial dependence on PR has grown with 92% of journalists responding to an email survey claiming the use of PR had increased across the last decade, while only 6% suggested it had remained constant, with a further 2% claiming a reduction (Williams and Franklin 2007, p. 39).

The most recent study of local journalism and sources confirms this increasing influence for PR but, significantly, noted a growing tendency for journalists to rely on a single source for local news stories. Analysis of a sample of 2979 stories in four Yorkshire-based regional dailies, owned by three of the largest local and regional newspaper groups (Johnston Press, Newsquest Media Group and Trinity Mirror) and published during February 2007 revealed that 76% (2264 stories) cited only a single source (O'Neill and O'Connor 2008, pp. 487-500). Public relations materials, of course, seek to persuade more than inform, to win hearts and minds rather than hold the ring in a rational, pluralistic debate between competing voices; in press releases a loud harmonious chorus is preferred to the discordant voices which typify debate. Local journalists' reliance on such editorially narrow press releases makes them accomplices in such closure of discussion. The study concludes that this new generation of "passive journalists" are becoming "mere processors of one-sided information or bland copy dictated by sources. These trends indicate poor journalistic standards and may be exacerbating declining local newspaper sales" (*ibid.*).

This reliance on public relations has also changed radically the processes of journalistic verification of stories. As in national newsrooms, local journalists find little time for checking stories, to be sure their claims "stand up". A recent and extensive ethnographic study of 235 journalists' working practices across newspaper, radio, television and online media platforms in Germany found that across each working shift journalists "only spend about eleven minutes per day checking sources and information in terms of plausibility or correctness" (Machill and Beiler 2009). In the newsrooms of the 1304 newspapers which constitute the local and regional press in the UK, the fundamental journalistic practices necessary to produce accurate, well informed and reliable journalism are being ignored. Journalists believe such revised professional practices corrode the integrity of local journalism. "I think it's inevitable that the quality of the news has suffered" a journalist confided. "Sometimes we're in a state of desperation just to fill the paper and that means the quality can't possibly be the same as it would be if we spent the time doing the job and developing stories" (cited in Williams and Franklin 2007, pp. 39–40).

Conclusion

The current business strategy of national and local newspaper groups which stresses cost cutting, by reducing journalists' employment while simultaneously increasing pagination, supplements and newspaper sections to attract more readers and advertisers, demands that fewer journalists with reduced resources produce bigger newspapers with more supplements and sections, in both print and online editions. To reconcile these conflicting ambitions and fill the increasingly gaping news hole requires that journalists accept news subsidies from public relations professionals as a substitute for their own independent journalistic enquiries. This process imposes changes on journalists' working practices, revises editorial priorities and reduces markedly both the independence and the integrity of journalism. Newspaper groups believe they are seeking to resolve a "crisis of profitability" but in truth their strategy is creating a "crisis of journalistic integrity". The fourth estate risks being overwhelmed, by the fifth estate of public relations.[2]

Note

1 The study included the following newspaper groups: (1) Express Newspapers Ltd; (2) The Financial Times Ltd; (3) MGN Ltd; (4) News Group Newspapers Ltd; (5) Telegraph Group Ltd; (6) Guardian Newspapers Ltd; (7) Independent News and Media Ltd; (8) Times Newspapers Ltd; (9) Associated Newspapers Ltd.

2 This phrase was first coined by Tom Baistow in his classic study of Fleet Street titled *Fourth Rate estate*.

References

Baistow, T. *The Fourth Rate Estate: An Anatomy of Fleet Street*, London: Comedia 1985.

Blumler, J. and Gurevitch, M. (1995) *The Crisis of Public Communication*, New York: Routledge.

Cutlip, S. M. (1976) "Public Relations in the Government", *Public Relations Review*, 2(2), 19–21.

Davies, N. (2008) *Flat Earth News; An award wining reporter exposes falsehood, distortion and propaganda in the global media*, London: Chatto and Windus.

Davis, A. (2002) *Public Relations Democracy: Public Relations, Politics and the Mass Media in Britain*, Manchester: Manchester University Press.

Davis, A. (2008) "Public Relations in the News" in Franklin, B. (ed.) *Pulling Newspapers Apart; Analysing Print Journalism*, London: Routledge, pp. 272–281.

Deuze, M. (2007) *Mediawork*, Cambridge: Polity Press.

Ericson, R.V., Baranek, P. and Chan, J. (1989) *Negotiating Control*, Milton Keynes: Open University Press.

Franklin, B. (1986) "Public Relations, the Local Press and the Coverage of Local Government", *Local Government Studies*, Summer, 25–33.

Franklin, B. (1988) *Public Relations Activities in Local Government*, London: Charles Knight.

Franklin, B. (1997) *Newszak and News Media*, London: Arnold.

Franklin, B. (2004) *Packaging Politics; Political Communication in Britain's media democracy*, London: Arnold.

Franklin, B. (2005) "McJournalism? The McDonaldization Thesis, Local Newspapers and Local Journalism in the UK" in Allan, S. (ed.) *Journalism Studies: Critical Essays*, Milton Keynes: Open University Press, pp. 137–150.

Franklin, B. (2006) *Local Journalism and Local Media; Making the Local News*, London: Routledge.

Franklin, B. and Vanslyke Turk, J. (1988) "Information Subsidies: Agenda setting traditions", *Public Relations Review*, Spring, 29–41.

Gandy, O. (1982) *Beyond Agenda Setting: Information subsidies and public policy*, New York: Ablex.

Gans, H. (1979) *Deciding What's News*, New York: Pantheon.

Golding, P. and Elliott, P. (1979) *Making the News*, New York: Longman.

Harrison, S (1998) "The Local Government Agenda; News from the Town Hall" in Franklin, B and Murphy D (Eds) *Making the Local News; Local Journalism in Context*, London: Routledge

Harrison, S. (2006) "Local Government Public Relations and the Local Press" in Franklin, B., *Local Journalism and Local Media; making the Local News*, London: Routledge, pp. 175–188.

Journalism Training Forum (2002) *Journalists at Work: Their views on training, recruitment and conditions*, London: NTO/Skillset

Larsson, L. (2002) "Journalists and Politicians: A relationship requiring manoeuvring space", *Journalism Studies* 3(1), 21–33.

Lewis, J. Williams, A. and Franklin B. (2008a) "A Compromised Fourth Estate? UK News Journalism, Public Relations and News Sources", *Journalism Studies*, 9(1), 1–20.

Lewis, J., Williams, A. and Franklin, B. (2008b) "Four Rumours and an Explanation; A political economic account of journalists' changing news gathering and reporting practices", *Journalism Practice*, 2(1), 27–45.L

Lewis, J., Williams, A. Franklin, B., Thomas, J. and Mosdell, N. (2006) *The Quality and Independence of British Journalism*, commissioned report for the Joseph Rowntree Charitable Trust.

Lloyd, John. 'Press and PR Partnership-- networking or not working?' *Guardian*, 10th April, 2006, page 3.

Machill, M. and Beiler, M. (2009) "The Importance of the Internet for Journalistic Research", *Journalism Studies*, 10(2): 178-203, April.

Maloney, K. (2006) *Rethinking Public Relations: PR, propaganda and democracy*, Routledge: New York.

Miller, D. and Dinan, W. (2000) "The Rise of the PR Industry in Britain, 1979–1998", *European Journal of Communication* 15(1), 5–35.

Marr, A. (2004) *My Trade: A Short History of British Journalism*, Basingstoke: Macmillan.

O'Neill, D. and O'Connor, C. (2008) "The Passive Journalist; How Sources Dominate Local News", *Journalism Practice*, 2(3): 487-500, October.

Reich, Z. (2006) "The Process Model of News Initiative: Sources Lead First, Reporters Thereafter", *Journalism Studies*, 7(4), 497–514.

White, J. and Hobsbawm, J. (2007) "Public Relations and Journalism: The unquiet relationship – a view from the United Kingdom", *Journalism Practice*, 1(2), 283–92.

Williams, A. and Franklin, B. (2007) *Turning Around the Tanker; Implementing Trinity Mirror's Online Strategy*, Cardiff: Cardiff University.

20

JOURNALISM ETHICS AS TRUTH-TELLING IN THE PUBLIC INTEREST

Dale Jacquette

We look to journalists to be our eyes and ears about important events. We avail ourselves of journalistic expertise in collecting and interpreting facts that are vital to our own decision-making or that inspire our interest. The information presented by journalists is generally so important to our lives that we expect journalists to the best of their abilities to write and speak the truth. Journalism, like science and history, is about truth-telling, although not all truth-telling is newsworthy. The fact that readers and audiences depend on the accuracy of news reporting in deciding what to do is the source of moral obligation in journalistic ethics.

The enterprise of gathering and presenting the news is pervaded by experienced judgment in which professional, moral and market considerations mostly coincide but sometimes collide. As in any sphere in which individual or collective human judgment is called upon to decide the merits of specific actions and general policy, journalism like other professions out of necessity has developed a particular ethics. As Alia, Brennan, and Hoffmaster (1996) emphasize, journalistic ethics, whether implicit or encoded, guides the decisions that journalists and consumers of the news must make. There are conflicts of interest that arise daily for practicing journalists, and these conflicts, between the facts the public needs and wants to know, and the profit motive, reporters' personal, political, religious, and other biases, create tensions that are reflected in the moral choices about whether and how to report certain facts as news that journalists must repeatedly make. The problems affecting practicing journalists in this respect are well-documented in the recent literature especially by Seib (1997), Olen (1988), Knowlton and Parsons (1995), and Fink (1995).

The problems to be explored in the discussion to follow feature the question of a general principle of journalistic ethics in the unifying expression of a professional moral imperative, explaining the moral rights and responsibilities of working journalists. Directly associated topics ranged around this central theme in turn emphasize the challenges of maximally relevant truth-telling in the public interest and for the public good, and hence of avoiding deliberate and unintentional falsehoods and of responding appropriately when these occur in reporting the news. The difficulty of properly judging relevance and of the sorts of information that are or are not in the public interest for journalists to convey to their readers and audiences is illustrated and critically examined in light of a particular recent case study in developing the general theme of the relation between abstract moral journalistic ideals and the concrete realities of actual journalistic practice.

Professional journalistic moral imperative

An effort to explicate professional journalistic ethics might be presented as a 'fundamental justificatory principle and moral mandate for professional journalism' (see also Jacquette, 2007: 19–22). The principle articulates the equivalent of a descriptive scientific hypothesis about what it is that journalists do, together with a normative ideal of what they should try to the utmost of their abilities to do as professionals in their respective fields. The principle is meant to be conceptually accessible, and yet far-reaching in its implications and potential applications as a moral imperative of professional journalistic practice:

> Journalists are morally committed to maximally relevant truth-telling in the public interest and for the public good (Jacquette, 2007: 19).

The principle is designed to serve as a unifying foundation for all standard moral precepts in journalistic ethics. The standard topics of dispute within journalistic ethics find their place within the general framework provided by the principle. These include but are not limited to such essential problems as journalistic rights and responsibilities, plagiarism, freedom of the press and problems of censorship and withholding information for the greater public good, journalistic respect for privacy, protection of confidential sources, objectivity, news reporting perspective and bias, and editorial license and obligations.[1]

The fundamental principle of journalistic ethics is also meant to do justice to shifting conceptions of journalism, as a vocation, trade, craft, and profession in the most general sense. It embodies a vision of journalistic ethics that does not try to stipulate, like a Ten Commandments for professional journalists to follow, a set of moral dos and don'ts, but to support an ideal of journalism as a noble profession that has the potential at every level of participation to serve as a force for social good. The principle invites difficult questions about what exactly is meant by the concept of truth and maximally relevant truth-telling, whether it is possible for imperfect beings like ourselves to arrive at and communicate truth, and, of course, concerning what is and what is not in the public interest, and what is and what is not for the public good.

The problem of deciding what constitutes the public interest and the nature of the public good in particular is a much larger issue that belongs properly to a general discussion of ethics, political philosophy and social theory. Some of the most important difficulties in properly defining the concept of public interest are indicated by Iggers (1998). Also relevant in this context are Merrill (1997) and Pritchard (2000). The public good, we can nevertheless say, is related to what a majority of people need or want in order to survive, thrive, and attain whatever they deem to constitute happiness, among other values. The public interest can then be regarded as whatever potentially contributes to or detracts from the public good. The public, in this sense, just like an individual, does not always necessarily know what is or is not in its own interest. Journalists, equally, do not necessarily have any special insight into what constitutes the public interest or public good, even when it is sometimes clear that they have acted either with respect or in blatant disregard for what is deemed to be the interests of any of a variety of overlapping social collectivities.

Journalists are themselves active participants in social communities. Whereas facts are categorically distinct from values, and journalists are often held to a standard by which the discovery and reporting of facts is supposed to be independent of their personal subjective interests, the truth is that a reporter's own values and those of the nebulous public that journalists serve pervade in many ways the perceptions of facts and the determination of choices about which facts to report, how they are to be reported, with what sort of emphasis, and the like. The same is true concerning values on the receiving side of the journalistic enterprise, affecting the response to news items by an assortment of readers and audiences. As such, journalists are answerable for the quality of their reporting not simply to society or the public as a mysterious abstract social entity, but to multiple diverse publics, in a variety of guises, including but not limited to clientele, citizens, consumers, politicians, policy makers, social critics, the scientific community, religious leaders and followers, and many other identifiable groups affected by the news and sufficiently motivated to express their reactions to the content of news reporting. We find this perspective astutely defended by Merritt (1998).

The twofold division of responsibilities proposed by the fundamental principle of journalistic ethics makes it possible to organize the following discussion into two main parts, now to be taken up in the same order: (1) maximally relevant truth-telling; (2) in the public interest and for the public good.

The little matter of truth

Truth-telling in the public interest and for the public good is not an exaggerated, unattainable ideal, but one that, within the limits of practical affairs to which news reporting belongs, journalists can responsibly try to respect and observe. If we do not desire truthful news reporting, then we can occupy our time instead with fiction, sports, and similar entertainments.

Philosophers and other people with too much time on their hands sometimes try to make heavy weather of what is meant by the truth and the possibility of arriving at the truth. In some areas, the epistemology of truth discovery is more problematic than in others, and in the most abstract conceptual terms there can be serious diffi-culties surrounding the nature of truth and the attainability of knowledge that need to be competently addressed. Where practical affairs, including news reporting, are concerned, however, the situation is far less daunting. What we mean by truth and truthful journalistic reporting is not something inexplicable or impossible. It entails practical challenges, to be sure, for the truth is not always easy to discover or communicate to others.

Truth is the gold standard by which journalists are judged. When a reporter says that there was a bank robbery in downtown Manhattan and there was in fact a bank robbery there, then the reporter has told the truth; otherwise, the report is false. Truth-telling is a positive correspondence with the state of the world, with the facts, events and states of affairs that an effort at truth-telling is supposed to describe. The measure of truth-telling in journalism is commonsensical; it represents the same rough and ready criterion by which we teach our children the value of honesty, and by which we determine the accuracy and reliability of information we put to use in conducting our everyday affairs. The importance of truth-telling among related virtues is discussed at length by Fuller (1996) in his invaluable inquiry about future directions in journalism.

Falsehoods appear as a result of careless use of unreliable sources, and from countless deliberate and inadvertent practices. The truth value quality of news reporting is as important to our personal and political decision making as is the quality of our food, water, air and pharmaceuticals, and in all such areas no compromises should be tolerated. Deliberate falsehood in news reporting is the work of rogue reporters whose professional misconduct is considered within the profession and by reflective news consumers to be morally intolerable. The recent spectacular cases of fraudulent fabricating of news reports by Jayson Blair at the *New York Times* and Stephen Glass at *The New Republic* remind journalistic watchdogs not to be distracted from vigilance in exposing and addressing deliberate false news reporting.

Inadvertent falsehoods can also creep into the news in different ways. All such instances amount to saying that something has happened that did not in fact happen. Whether and how the inadvertent occurrence of false reporting can be discovered and whether and how it should then be revealed is always another issue. News organizations take great pains to root out mistakes and inaccuracies in their reporting, and to act decisively thereafter by reporting mistakes and acting to correct the damage their erroneous reporting may have caused by publicly and conspicuously setting the record straight. Moral censure can still be justified even in such cases when news organizations do not act quickly enough on their own initiative or with insufficient publicity for mistakes in the reporting for which they are responsible.

Although journalists by avocation and professional training may have special motivations and skills to help them minimize the extent of their inadvertent inaccuracies, including independent fact-checking, they are by no means exceptions to the general rule that human beings are epistemically fallible. Professional journalistic ethical responsibility in such cases includes a provision to try to avoid all error in the first place, to actively seek out errors in the news and expose and correct them, and to take appropriate action to mitigate the damage caused by inadvertent falsehoods in the news. As with other virtues, education for truth-telling generally begins at an early age, and, in the case of journalists, must be reinforced especially as students and during on the job training. The need for journalists to be encultured in a work ethic that emphasizes professional integrity is examined in a Hastings Center, Institute for Society, Ethics and the Life Sciences report by Christians and Covert (1980).

The further qualification of truth-telling as maximally relevant is also a matter of practical judgment. Not all true propositions that might be reported are newsworthy. Truths must be relevant to a specific group of readers, viewers or listeners, as understood within a particular historical and cultural context and against a background of particular issues of current social concern. It is true that Abraham Lincoln was assassinated in 1865, but it hardly makes news to report the fact in 2009, except perhaps in reference to topics of more contemporary interest. Similarly, for such trivial inconsequential facts, other things being equal, of the exact shoe size of the judge in an important murder trial. True, but not relevant, is a consideration that must exclude many otherwise correct facts from the journalist's moral responsibility to report the news. Where, precisely, to draw the line on what is and what is not relevant is always one of the most difficult challenges in journalistic practice. The difficulty of making such judgment calls does not detract in any way from the validity of the principle that journalists are morally obligated to provide their clientele with as many relevant truths as they and their editors in their professional judgment can discover and communicate.

It is in relation to the fundamental principle and moral mandate for journalistic ethics that we can now ask: Why is it morally objectionable for professional journalists to plagiarize? There are two reasons. The first is that plagiarism amounts to a violation of the intellectual property rights of others, which in the case of plagiarism effectively constitutes theft. It is taking public credit for someone else's ideas and someone else's work. The plagiarist illegally appropriates another person's efforts without the original author's consent and without compensating the original author for his or her efforts. The second reason, more germane to the present discussion of truth-telling in journalism, is that plagiarism constitutes a deliberate inaccuracy and misrepresentation of facts. This is the logical implication even when the content of the plagiarized news report itself happens to be 100% truthful. If a journalist signs an article or presents a news story on the air as though it were the fruit of his or her labor, as something he or she has researched and whose facts he or she has personally verified, when in fact the content of the material has been plagiarized from another author, then the reader or audience is misled as to the source, originality, and credibility of the information conveyed. A plagiarist, as a result, lies to the public about the authority of a news item, even when the item itself contains no falsehoods (see Kovach, 2001).

The profession in its self-regulation is obligated to try its best to identify such offenders, to publicize the wrong they have done, and to correct whatever damage may have occurred by making the public generally aware of the specific falsehoods or unsupported content of bogus reporting. Those in authority within the profession may also be justified in taking further punitive actions within their power, such as ostracizing rogue reporters, refusing them further employment or recommendations for employment, and, in some cases, depending on the severity of the offense and the applicable laws, having them remanded for criminal prosecution. These instances, fortunately, are outstanding exceptions among what for the most part are persons of exceptional integrity who want to tell the truth about the events on which they report. A useful resource for further discussions of these and related topics is Lambeth, Meyer, and Thorson (1998).

In the Public Interest and for the Public Good

The second key component of the fundamental principle of journalistic ethics is that maximally relevant truth-telling be directed toward the public interest and in the public good. There is fertile ground aplenty here for nuanced interpretation of what is and what is not socially responsible and socially beneficial, with the possibility for many misgivings and sincere as well as more deviously expedient spins on whether and how the obligations of journalistic ethics have been satisfied.

To illustrate the problem, we consider a case study involving a recent exclusive report from the CNN Special Investigations Unit by Drew Griffin, Kathleen Johnston and Todd Schwarzschild, titled "Sources: Air Marshals Missing From Almost All Flights". Dated 25 March 2008, and offered both in broadcast and on-line internet formats, the report cites official statistics and anecdotal evidence collected from interviews with both named and anonymous sources about the surprising paucity of armed air marshals accompanying passenger flights in the United States in the wake of the terrorist hi-jacked airplane strikes against the World Trade Center in Manhattan and the Pentagon in Washington, DC, on 11 September 2001. Here are some of the report's highlights from the network's website:

> (CNN) – Of the 28,000 commercial airline flights that take to the skies on an average day in the United States, fewer than 1 percent are protected by on-board, armed federal air marshals, a nationwide CNN investigation has found ... That means that a terrorist or other criminal bent on taking over an aircraft would be confronted by a trained air marshal on as few as 280 daily flights, according to more than a dozen federal air marshals and pilots interviewed by CNN ... The investigation found those low numbers even as the Transportation Security Administration in recent months has conducted tests in which it has been able to smuggle guns and bomb-making materials past airport security screeners (available on-line at: http://www.cnn.com/2008/TRAVEL/03/25/siu.air.marshals/).

This is attention-getting journalism. It touches a nerve for all people who travel by air or have friends and relatives who fly. We who deplore the acts of terrorists targeting innocent civilians are rightly concerned about airline safety, and one important component of the effort to make the skies safer is to have air marshals, armed and well-trained guards discreetly in disguise on commercial flights, ready to disable any bad guys who might threaten passengers or crew. What CNN informs us, and with apparently solid justification, is the startling fact that there are actually very few air marshals aboard US flights. Where we thought that in flying within the United States we were being protected by one essential plank of homeland security, the truth appears to be that we are not.

The public's right to know whether and to what extent they are protected when they fly is undisputed. The difficulty is that by releasing such information there is a potential for encouraging terrorists to think that security may be sufficiently lax for them to succeed in undertaking further acts of violence. The anecdotal evidence assembled by the CNN special documentary is as compelling as it is chilling. Here is a further and final representative quotation from the same report:

> Air marshals told CNN that while the TSA tells the public it cannot divulge numbers because they are classified, the agency tells its own agents that at least 5 percent of all flights are covered. But marshals across the country – all of whom spoke with CNN on the condition they not be identified for fear of losing their jobs – said the 5 percent figure quoted to them by their TSA bosses is not possible. One marshal said that while security is certainly one reason the numbers are kept secret, he believes the agency simply doesn't want taxpayers to know the truth … "The American public would be shocked. … I think the average person understands there's no physical way to protect every single flight everywhere," the air marshal said. "But it's such a small percentage. It's just very aggravating for us."

The controversy is that by informing the public that there are far fewer air marshals patrolling the skies than may have been reported and expected, the journalists offering the report may also be giving extra confidence, aid and comfort in the form of otherwise unavailable information, to prospective wrongdoers. The dilemma for journalistic ethics dramatized by this investigative news item is whether revealing or concealing the information is more in keeping with the principle that journalists have a moral obligation to provide maximally relevant truth-telling in the public interest and for the public good.

We shall assume for the sake of argument that the CNN report is correct and accurate. There is no doubt that it is relevant to the issues and concerns of the day as well, so that the story can be regarded as satisfying the first part of the principle by virtue of constituting an exercise in maximally relevant journalistic truth-telling. The point of difficulty is whether reporting on a shortfall of air marshals accompanying domestic commercial flights is truly in the public interest and for the public good. Were the CNN watchdog reporters who blew the whistle on the Transportation Security Administration (TSA) under the auspices of the Department of Homeland Security truly acting in the public interest and for the public good? Or would they have better served this element of the principle of journalistic ethics if they had withheld such information, at least, perhaps, until the problem had been addressed?

That there is room for heated dispute about the matter is demonstrated by the enormous outpouring of public opinion voiced on the network's internet blog site immediately after the CNN Special Report aired. As one might easily predict, viewers were sharply divided between those defending the public's right to know and those deploring the risks of informing terrorists about possible weaknesses in the nation's air security network. Typical reactions included the following two, chosen from the first write-in comments covering more than 25 virtual pages.

> Come on CNN!!! Enough of this reporting of security lapses/loopholes in our country for the terrorists to see. Which side are you on anyway? ... [How] about having some responsibility and quit using the excuse of 'the public needs to know'.

> If we don't talk about it, then the Air Marshals are surely not going to fix it. You are assuming, incorrectly, that by keeping this information hidden the terrorists will not attack us. That is false logic. Better for us to discover [the] problem in advance then [sic.] find out after another 9[/]11 don't you agree??

Assuming that both persons supporting and others opposed to CNN's broadcasting of its Special Report on the dearth of air marshals in service share the common goal of thwarting and finally defeating terrorism, it remains an open question as to whether making such information known ultimately contributes to or impedes the course of terrorism. I think that both sides of this emotionally charged quarrel represent reasonable reactions to the report, but I also believe that in the end CNN was right to broadcast the story and to disclose what they had discovered about the surprisingly low numbers of air marshals protecting commercial flights. By revealing rather than withholding the information I suggest that the reporters better served the journalistic mandate of acting in the public interest and for the public good. By notifying the public of the problem there seems to be a greater possibility that the deficiency will be corrected than that increasing numbers of terrorists will attempt criminal acts against airline passengers.

Not only does the public have the moral right to know whether the levels of protection publicized by security agencies are actually in place, but by announcing the fact that there are deficiencies in the air marshal program the reporters stand to create a popular demand that the problem be solved. Government administrators in a democracy can only be brought to task if there is a constant public monitoring of their conduct, including their successes, failures, and lax performance, which in turn requires a continuous effort to verify or disconfirm the truth of what they promise and claim to have delivered in the course of fulfilling their sworn duties. If air safety demands that there be a certain number of air marshals accompanying domestic commercial flights, and if that priority is not being met, contrary to public relations misinformation, then the public good dictates that it is not only morally permissible but morally obligatory for journalists in possession of the facts to make that information known. It is acting in the public interest and for the public good to do so, if I am right, because society has more to gain in combating terrorism by improving air marshal patrols than it stands to lose in terms of possibly encouraging some would-be terrorists to act, and because the best and perhaps even the only way to make sure that air marshal numbers are brought up to more acceptable numbers is by making the public aware that improvements are needed. The new breed of terrorists, many of whom are bent on martyrdom anyway, are not necessarily intimidated by the presence of air marshals, and many are no doubt prepared to risk the odds of encountering air marshals if they succeed again in bringing weapons on board a plane. The only meaningful deterrent where pre-boarding screening fails is to have multiple air marshals on every flight, which is a logistical impracticality for all the obvious reasons.

Moral ideals and journalistic practice

The problem of the air marshals report nevertheless brings home an important lesson about the complexities of journalistic ethics. It is one thing to agree in principle and in the abstract about how to characterize the moral rights and responsibilities of journalists, and quite another to apply the principle with confidence to real life situations that journalists face when investigating and reporting the news.

The moral dilemmas confronting practicing journalists are not mere intellectual challenges, but sometimes life or death predicaments. Often it is necessary not only to have a textbook understanding of what may be morally obligatory for a news reporter to do, but to exercise sound judgment based on years of experience and a solid grounding in the values of the culture for which the news is intended. Truth and accuracy, cross-checking of sources and other standard tools of responsible journalism, assessment of relevance, and the like, can be acquired as a matter of professional training. What is further required as an essential ingredient in fulfilling the moral requirements of journalistic ethics is something that is less easily taught. It is a matter of a journalist's understanding matters of value and having a moral outlook from which standpoint it is possible to make difficult choices about what is and what is not in the public interest and for the public good. Among the most informative recent discussions of this topic from a similar case studies approach should be included Foerstel (2001) and Day (2003).

Arguably, CNN made exactly the right decision in reporting the air marshals' story. In many circumstances, however, the moral choices working journalists encounter are even less clear-cut and even more ethically equivocal. Nor should we imagine that the final arbiter of whether or not a journalist or news agency has made the right decision is ultimately determined by its popular acceptance or approval rating. Journalists must be prepared when necessary to make unpopular and even strongly disapproved decisions when with good judgment and sound reasoning they sincerely believe that they are reporting relevant truths in the public interest and for the sake of the public good. The CNN air marshals' story illustrates how difficult and controversial such journalistic ethical judgment calls can sometimes be. It highlights the troubled interface where ideal abstract moral philosophical theory meets realistic workaday professional practice.

Note

1 Related problems of journalistic ethics in connection with this study are also discussed on Stanford University's philosophy radio talk program during a live broadcast and media stream discussion between Jacquette and Stanford University's John Perry and Ken Taylor on 29 April 2007, and available for mp3 download at http://www.philosophytalk.org/pastShows/EthicsinJournalism.html. Worthwhile resources discussing these interconnected difficulties prominently include Black, *et al.* (1995), Knowlton (1997), and what has today become a classic treatment of the subject, Crawford (1924; rpt. 1969).

References

Alia, V., Brennan, B. and Hoffmaster, B. (eds) *Deadlines and Diversity: Journalism Ethics in a Changing World* (Nova Scotia: Fernwood Publishing, 1996).

Black, J., Steele, B. and Barney, R. *Doing Ethics in Journalism: A Handbook With Case Studies* (Boston: Allyn and Bacon, 1995).

Christians, C.G. and Covert, C.L. *Teaching Ethics in Journalism Education* (Garrison: Hastings Center, Institute for Society, Ethics and the Life Sciences, 1980).

Crawford, N.A. *The Ethics of Journalism* (New York: A.A. Knopf, 1924; 1969).

Day, L.A., *Ethics in Media Communications: Cases and Controversies*, 4th edition (Belmont: Wadsworth Publishing, 2003).

Fink, C.C. *Media Ethics* (Boston: Allyn and Bacon, 1995).

Foerstel, H.N. *From Watergate to Monicagate: Ten Controversies in Modern Journalism and Media* (Westport: Greenwood Press, 2001).

Fuller, J. *News Values: Ideas for an Information Age* (Chicago: University of Chicago Press, 1996).

Iggers, J. *Good News, Bad News: Journalism Ethics and the Public Interest* (Boulder: Westview Press, 1998).

Jacquette, D. *Journalistic Ethics: Moral Responsibility in the Media* (Upper Saddle River: Pearson / Prentice Hall, 2007).

Knowlton, S.R. and Parsons, P.R. (eds), *The Journalist's Moral Compass: Basic Principles* (New York: Praeger, 1995).

Knowlton, S.R. *Moral Reasoning for Journalists: Cases and Commentary* (New York: Praeger, 1997).

Kovach, B. *The Elements of Journalism: What News People Should Know and the Public Should Expect* (New York: Crown Publishing Group (Random House), 2001).

Lambeth, E.B., Meyer, P.E., and Thorson, E. (eds) *Assessing Public Journalism* (Columbia: University of Missouri Press, 1998).

Merrill, J.C. *Journalism Ethics: Philosophical Foundations for News Media* (New York: St. Martin's Press, 1997).

Merritt, D. *Public Journalism and Public Life: Why Telling the News is Not Enough*, 2nd edition (Philadelphia: Lawrence Erlbaum Associates, 1998).

Olen, J. *Ethics in Journalism* (Englewood Cliffs: Prentice-Hall, 1988).

Pritchard, D. (ed.) *Holding the Media Accountable: Citizens, Ethics, and the Law* (Bloomington: Indiana University Press, 2000).

Seib, P.M. *Journalism Ethics* (Fort Worth: Harcourt Brace College Publishers, 1997).

21

MAKING UP THE NEWS: JOURNALISTS, DEVIANCE AND SOCIAL CONTROL IN NEWS PRODUCTION

Roger Dickinson

In May 2003 the *New York Times* revealed to its readers in a front-page article how one of its most promising and prolific reporters had over several years at the paper broken the fundamental rules of journalism. Jayson Blair, who had been working for *The Times'* national news desk, had falsely claimed to be reporting from places he had never visited, to have interviewed people he had never spoken to and to have written reports that were in fact the work of others. *The Times* article described Blair's increasingly audacious output as the work of a 'troubled young man veering toward professional self-destruction' (Barry, *et al.*, 2003). The scandal not only ended Blair's career as a journalist, but also led to the resignations of the newspaper's executive editor, Howell Raines, and its managing editor, Gerald Boyd.

This chapter is concerned with journalistic delinquency, an aspect of news work that has so far received relatively little academic attention. The topic is important not least because a firmer grasp of it would contribute to a deeper understanding of the formation of journalists' occupational identity and thus the production of news. But there is another, perhaps more pressing, reason for taking it seriously: journalists' behaviour has a bearing on the credibility of news as a source of public knowledge.

Journalists have never been held in very high esteem by the British public, but a national opinion survey conducted in early 2008 showed that their reputation had reached a new low. Alongside diminishing public trust in a number of professions ranging from family doctors to head teachers, politicians, and senior police officers over the previous three years, there was a dramatic decline in trust for journalists, especially those working in print, and an even more dramatic one for those working in the popular press. In a commentary on the survey findings, Barnett suggests that this was a result of the 'catalogue of disasters' that had befallen the British media industry in the months prior to the survey (Barnett, 2008: 7). His list includes the imprisonment of a *News of the World* reporter for using intercepted mobile telephone messages (among them those of three members of the British Royal Family) and the subsequent resignation of that newspaper's editor; the revelation in a report to British parliament that the use of illegally obtained information in the pursuit of stories was widespread across the British news industry (Thomas, 2006); the exposure of several 'media scams' (e.g. using video edited misleadingly in television transmissions) and apparently endemic dishonesty in the use of phone voting in television. Barnett argues that these events have all had an influence on the public's feelings of trust – or rather mistrust – in journalists.

In an era of rampant media competition, says Barnett, dishonest behaviour among some journalists can, via a sequence of reporting, public condemnation and further reporting, have quite significant effects on public perceptions. He suggests that the over-reporting of misconduct, whether it is perpetrated inside or outside the media, can easily turn public scepticism for officialdom (which is healthy for democracy), into cynicism (which is less healthy for democracy). While the consequences of widespread cynicism for society at large may be damaging enough, wholesale mistrust of journalism, says Barnett, may lead ultimately to its destruction. He concludes that, unless trust can be restored, journalism will cease to make its proper contribution to democracy.

Based on this analysis, one might have thought that journalists' conduct would be regarded as an important topic for academic study, yet, surprisingly, the subject has attracted little scholarly attention. The way the news is shaped and controlled by the organizational context of news work has of course been the subject of sociological research for many years and has been an explicit focus since the earliest newsroom studies of the 1940s and 1950s, but misconduct and malpractice – what we might call 'newsroom deviance' – has not been studied in detail.

In what follows I offer a brief review of some relevant research and discuss some of the ways the topic of deviance in journalism might be investigated in the future. I begin by examining both recent and very much earlier research on the social control of journalists and ask whether, in changing times and under changing conditions, the social practices and organizational mechanisms that help to regulate journalists' behaviour should now be examined more carefully than they have been in the past. I suggest that the approaches of sociologists of an earlier era who were concerned with deviance in the workplace might help us to do this. If Barnett's judgement is correct, and journalism is indeed on the brink of self-destruction, such work could have renewed significance.

Deception in journalism

As the case of Jayson Blair illustrates, journalistic misconduct is not unique to the British media. Indeed in recent years the instances of deviance among journalists that have earned most notoriety have in fact occurred in the US. Lasorsa and Dai (2007) report that between 1998 and 2004 around 50 journalists working for leading US news organizations were found to have indulged in 'journalistic deception', defined, after Elliot and Culver (1992), as 'an act of communicating messages not only by lying but also by withholding information, so as to lead someone to have a false belief' (p160). This type of deviance is rather different from the sometimes plainly criminal acts of British journalists mentioned earlier, but because the consequences of both are quite similar, the responses to deception are instructive for our understanding of all manner of journalistic deviance.

In 2004 Jayson Blair published a book-length account of his story (Blair, 2004). In this he offered as a partial explanation for his behaviour the pressure he felt he was under as a young reporter expected to produce vivid and hard-hitting 'people stories' week in, week out. The exposure of his misdeeds placed him in a notorious group of US journalists who had been caught 'violating professional ethics' and 'breaching the trust' of their readers by plagiarising, fabricating or embellishing stories. Each of these told similar stories to Blair's in their accounts of their own delinquency, showing how they had avoided the routine checks and controls of the workplace in their efforts to meet their managers' and colleagues' expectations.[1]

These cases raised questions inside the occupation and some discussion in the US press itself about employment practices in the news media and the changing traditions of journalism and news reporting. There are divisions in the debate over where blame should lie in individual cases, but whatever the contradictions between the urge for attention-grabbing reporting and the realities of increasingly competitive working environments, most outrage at these events centres on the carelessness with which delinquent journalists seemed to regard their duty to report the facts and to do so truthfully. Respect for facts and for 'the truth' continues to symbolise all that is positive about journalism in professional accounts of these events. Again, evidence that these values are treated casually by their colleagues leads members of the occupation to fear for its (and their) future status and credibility.

Some discussions of these cases from the academic field of journalism studies have taken an avowedly normative stance in their summing up of the issues they raise. There is much writing in broad terms of public trust, the social responsibility of the press, the obligations of managers and editors to establish strong professional/ethical norms, and so on. Lasorsa and Dai (2007), for example, account for journalistic deception in terms of 'newsroom culture'. Drawing on Patterson and Urbanski's analysis (Patterson and Urbanski, 2006) this culture is for them a 'toxic environment' in which journalists abandon sacred occupational norms in pursuit of award-winning stories that can help maintain the profile of their newspapers in their struggle to survive in the hyper-competitive news marketplace. You might expect scholars of journalism to be interested in exploring the culture and environment in which these things happen, but instead of offering an analysis of that culture and the social actors who create it, Lasorsa and Dai examine the characteristics of the deception stories themselves. They search for these stories' distinguishing characteristics in order that in the future they might be identified – and spiked – by vigilant editors who must now renew their commitment to a way of thinking seemingly not yet fully absorbed by new recruits and in danger of being forgotten by their colleagues.

While there are clearly practical benefits from such an approach, it seems to me to dodge some important questions about rule-breaking in journalism: if Jayson Blair was 'out of control', what keeps his fellow reporters at the *New York Times* and elsewhere 'under control'? Are the delinquent journalists who hit the headlines merely aberrant isolates, instances of a few bad apples in the barrel of otherwise orderly and conscientious professionals? In short, what do we know about the social control of news workers? Might the mechanisms that regulate their behaviour be changing and, if they are, how are they being shaped?

Social control in the newsroom – Breed and beyond

Although his was not an investigation of deviance in the sense that I have been discussing, the starting point for thinking about the regulation of news workers is inevitably – as it has been for many explorations of newsroom sociology – Warren Breed's study of the social control of journalists (Breed, 1955). Breed's conclusions from his interviews with newspaper reporters, as well as his observations as a journalist, were not that journalistic delinquency was rife in the US newspapers of the 1950s. Instead, his functionalist analysis of news workers' behaviour and motivations, which he described in terms of social norms and roles, explained how newspapers' policies seemed to be followed a great deal more often than they were flouted.[2] His curiosity was stimulated primarily by a broader sociological interest in the concept of conformity rather than a concern with journalists' delinquency, but for Breed a compelling feature of the social realm of news work was that the control of journalists could not be taken for granted, a) because journalistic ethical norms – responsibility, impartiality, accuracy, fair play and objectivity – helped to legitimize journalists' desire for independence from organizational goals; b) because journalists tended to have more liberal attitudes than publishers and owners; and c) because it was taboo for publishers and owners to make overt demands on their staff to follow policy.

Breed was among the first to point out a key feature of the occupation (one that successive newsroom studies confirmed), namely that journalists are not trained in their newspapers' policies or told how to slant stories by 'executives'; he found that all but the most inexperienced knew – 'by osmosis' (Breed, 1955: 328) – what their newspaper's policy was. But, given the factors that would seem to prevent it, why, he asked, do newsmen conform to a newspaper's policy? What prevents their deviance?

Conformity, Breed discovered, was the result of several factors. In rare cases of non-conformity employers could apply sanctions – by sacking rule-breakers or by reassigning them to less desirable reporting jobs – but the most powerful controls over journalists' behaviour were the sharing of norms between junior and more experienced, senior staff, a sense of obligation to and a need to get on with colleagues, and the 'continuous challenge' – shared by all – of 'getting the news' (Breed, 1955: 331). The news itself was the main source of reward in terms of esteem and it was the main criterion of performance. In other words, in the language of much later newsroom studies, getting the news was the central element of an *occupational ideology* (see, for example, Golding and Elliott, 1979). Breed concluded that it therefore exercised the main form of control over what journalists – the 'staffers' in his newsrooms – did every day:

> The process of learning policy crystallizes into a process of social control, in which deviations are punished (usually gently) by reprimand, cutting one's story, the withholding of friendly comment by an executive, etc. [...] [W]hen an executive sees a clearly anti-policy item, he blue-pencils it, and this constitutes a lesson for the staffer. Rarely does the staffer persist in violating policy (Breed, 1955: 332).

Breed observed that the need for speed and the demands of competition between media meant that journalists gave first priority to getting the news even when their concern over issues of ethics and objectivity over a given story might have been in conflict with their newspaper's policy. This is a significant point for, as we shall see, it is precisely this element of the journalist's outlook that we need to consider more carefully.

So, when did deviance happen in Breed's newsrooms? He found that journalists' feelings of obligation and esteem towards superiors varied between newspapers and where executives and older staff members were less respected there was increased staff turnover, lower morale, less enthusiasm, and a discernible hostility to policy. Elsewhere occasionally an 'anti-policy' story would be printed, Breed found, when policy was unclear; when the superior knowledge of journalists enabled them to subvert it; when journalists were able to 'plant' stories in a rival outlet and then plead that it was too big a story for their own paper to ignore; when a story was from a recognised news beat or when it was self-initiated. Breed also found that journalists with star status could transgress policy more readily than newcomers, but his overall conclusion was that such transgressions were the exception and journalistic deviance was rare:

> Thus we conclude that the publisher's policy, when established in a given subject area, is usually followed, and that a description of the dynamic socio-cultural situation of the newsroom will suggest explanations for this conformity. The newsman's source of rewards is located not among the readers, who are manifestly his clients, but among his colleagues and superiors. Instead of adhering to societal and professional ideals, he re-defines his values to the more pragmatic level of the newsroom group. He thereby gains not only status rewards, but also acceptance in a solidary group engaged in interesting, varied and sometimes important work.
>
> (Breed, 1955: 335)

Breed went on to speculate on the implications of this for the broader concerns about press freedom and diversity that have endured and are threaded through the body of literature on news production published since his study. Curiously, Breed's early emphasis on conformity appears to have had the effect of deflecting academic attention away from journalistic deviance. Nearly thirty-five years later in a widely quoted article Soloski (1989) reinforced the prevailing assumption of control and conformity in newsrooms arguing that journalists' adherence to the norms of 'news professionalism' helps them to progress in their careers and earn greater rewards. This, together with what Soloski calls the 'intra-organizational' control of an organisation's news policy, almost completely directs the actions of journalists: 'Like a game, professional norms and news policies are rules that everyone has learned to play by; only rarely are these rules made explicit, and only rarely are the rules called into question' (Soloski, 1989: 218).[3]

In the intervening years the mechanisms of social control in newsrooms seem to have been taken for granted, assumed as a constant factor while other features of news work have altered with changing production practices and the wider media environment. Although Breed's and Soloski's interest in conformity was centred on editorial policy rather than the routines of news reporting, it may be that their conclusions have been widely interpreted as applying to journalistic practice in general, that for the same reasons that they conform to editorial policy, journalists generally conform to other production norms as well, and that this need be given little scholarly attention.

This is not to say, however, that there has been no research exploring the topic of deviance since Breed's study. In recent work Lee (2004, 2005) has taken a very specific focus and explored the nature of *deception* in journalism and journalists' attitudes towards it. Her findings suggest, intriguingly, that deception is a routine part of much news work. This does not necessarily contradict Breed's conclusions about the conformist character of the newsroom in terms of adherence to policy, but picking up the theme he identified of the centrality of the news as the top priority over all regardless of ethical concerns, Lee offers an insight into the way a sort of dishonesty appears to be firmly embedded in the practices followed there.

Lee (2004) interviewed 20 journalists to explore their attitudes to deception in news gathering, processing, and presentation. She found that deception was a function of a 'negotiated occupational order' (Hunt and Manning, 1991, cited in Lee, 2004: 109) in which types of deception were woven into occupational practice. The journalists she interviewed tended to follow three unspoken rules that determined what was acceptable. First, that it is better to deceive news sources than to deceive the audience. Using hidden cameras and lying to sources could be acceptable on certain occasions (in order, say, to expose poor standards of hygiene in food preparation in a restaurant), but fabricating stories could not. Second, that it is better to deceive 'bad' people than 'good' people in the course of news gathering (concealing one's identity by getting a job as a waitress in order to investigate the restaurant-owner's attitudes to food hygiene regulations, for example). In this journalists claim some moral authority, distinguishing the bad from the good in the name of what is in the public interest. The third rule that Lee identified is that it is better to deceive by omission than by commission. Not disclosing that one is a journalist, for example, can sometimes be an acceptable way of facilitating the gathering of information from wary sources. Making up quotes, manipulating still or moving images, or staging events in order to get better pictures, however, are more difficult practices to justify. As Lee writes, this distinction is consistent with other studies in which passive deception was felt to be morally less problematic than active deception (Goodwin and Smith, 1994, cited in Lee, 2004). Lee concludes that deception is part and parcel of the journalist's craft.[4] As she puts it: 'Because the subtleties and tacit rules that journalists use to evaluate what is acceptable deception and what is not are derived from a negotiated meaning from within an occupation, journalistic deception becomes a criterion as well as an outcome of group membership' (Lee, 2004: 116).[5]

This point is well illustrated by the case of Martin Bashir, the British journalist who came to prominence in 1995 through his interview on BBC television with the Princess of Wales (in which she spoke for first time in public of her 'crowded' marriage and her desire to become the 'Queen of Hearts'). In February 2004 Bashir was reported to have been offered $1m to join ABC network television in the US as its chief current affairs reporter. This news gave the British press the opportunity to review his record and reflect on his success. His interview with the Princess and the 2003 exclusive Channel 4 documentary on the singer Michael Jackson (which subsequently led to Jackson's career-devastating court case) earned Bashir a reputation as a determined and, some say, ruthless and unprincipled operator who wins the confidence of his subjects by promising an easy ride and then exposing rather more of them than they had bargained for. Jackson complained after the documentary was screened that Bashir had betrayed him. According to the *Guardian* newspaper, after Jackson's account of the relationship was made public, the *New York Times* accused Bashir of 'callous self-interest masked as sympathy' (Branigan, 2004: 16).

We have already seen how the pursuit of truth is venerated within the occupation. But taking this beyond what some would argue is acceptable may also be seen as a positive attribute. In its profile of Martin Bashir, the *Guardian* quoted the PR consultant Max Clifford (who has a number of high profile celebrity clients) as saying, 'You wouldn't want Martin Bashir getting close to your star because you know you would be putting them in jeopardy ... Could you trust him? Of course you couldn't. *But that doesn't make him anything other than a professional*' (Branigan, 2004: 16, my emphasis).

Lee's work, then, takes us in a potentially more fruitful direction than Breed's could, for if deception is part of what being a journalist is, a defining feature as important as independence and autonomy, perhaps we should not be surprised to learn that some journalists will, on occasion, cross the line into full-blown delinquency. This may well happen more frequently than we might at first think. In Jayson Blair's account of his misdeeds he implies strongly that he was not alone in producing fraudulent reports at the *New York Times*. His case and those of others like him represent a challenge to media sociology that should be taken seriously. For want of such research and in order to begin to understand this behaviour more fully it may be best to turn to research from other branches of sociology for inspiration. Much of this work will be regarded by many as old-fashioned, ill-suited to an examination of the complexities of any contemporary workplace, let alone the modern newsroom, but if we want a deeper understanding of what goes on in contemporary newsrooms, this, I want to suggest, is a very good place to begin.

Breaking rules at work

In the well-known anthology of his early work on deviance Howard Becker (Becker, 1963) devotes a chapter to a discussion of research on 'rules and their enforcement'. In this he develops the argument that rules are enforced only when someone is motivated enough – by personal interest, say – to want them to be. If there are no interests to be served by enforcing a rule, Becker argues, then that rule will continue to be broken. For Becker this is significant because he wants to go on to explain how certain forms of deviance receive a disproportionate degree of public disapprobation, police reaction, and so on, but he illustrates this principle by referring to studies of workplace deviance in which the failure to enforce rules benefits both management and workers. If one understands journalism principally as an occupation – a form of work – then Becker's examples are useful to illustrate some general points that might be applied to cases of journalistic delinquency.

Citing Dalton (1959), Becker describes examples of workplace rules that workers break systematically. These include the 'appropriation' of an organization's services and materials for the employee's personal use – acts that would ordinarily be regarded as theft. Cases discussed by Dalton range from a factory foreman who equipped his home workshop with expensive machinery taken from work, to an office worker who conducted all her private correspondence at work using company stationery and stamps. Dalton argues that to consider these acts merely as theft is to misunderstand them. Management generally conspires in the appropriation of an employer's services and materials. Their use serves as a reward for an employee's contribution to the enterprise when other rewards are limited or unavailable.

Breaking rules can have further benefits. Becker describes a study by Roy (1954) which examined routines in a factory workshop and the efforts of machinists to 'make out' (i.e. earn more than they would normally be able to by increasing their rate of output). Roy found that if a rule prevented machinists from making out and disrupted the routines of their co-workers, it would be evaded. All workers would participate in the evasion so that work could be completed with the minimum of disruption. Rule breaking was thus a way of making things go more smoothly, and, most importantly, as a way of keeping control over work that all employees tacitly accepted and took part in.

Later research in this vein by Eliot Freidson showed that deviance was by no means confined to the realms of manual or clerical labour (Freidson, 1975). Freidson studied a group of medical doctors working in a group practice financed by medical insurance and administered by a bureaucracy. He wondered how an historically powerful occupation would respond to bureaucratic control and whether the informal social control processes of the workgroup evident in other occupational settings would prevail. He found that they did. Professional etiquette and group loyalty meant that bad medical practice was covered up or, most often, ignored. The key principle of discretion in applying expertise helped to protect doctors from external constraints; their status as medical doctors effectively gave them control over their work. Group membership was based on a reluctance to criticize colleagues' decisions and a respect for individualism. Administrative schemes of control were ineffective because they either threatened to destroy the scope for the exercise of professional discretion or they threatened to drive it underground. Either way, doctors were in control and delinquent acts – mistakes, bad practice – helped to strengthen the bonds of the workgroup. Freidson concluded that the doctors he studied could be described accurately as a 'delinquent community'.

Conclusions

How does this work help us understand the social control of journalists? Given what we know of journalistic practice and the attitudes of journalists to deception, can they similarly be described as a delinquent community? Before reaching a conclusion, a brief summary of the argument so far may be helpful.

In recent years several examples of misconduct and bad journalistic practice have been exposed and, arguably, have contributed to a decline in public trust in journalism. Academic understanding of journalistic malpractice and the social control of journalists is surprisingly sparse. The conventional view of news work – based on the findings of one of the earliest newsroom studies – is that journalists tend to conform to the policies of their employing organizations. While the evidence for this is persuasive, the related but perhaps over-generalized conclusion that journalistic deviance is rare appears to have deflected scholarly attention away from the less seemly journalistic practices that are apparently so damaging to public perceptions. More recent research shows that deception in journalism is routine and is in fact a defining characteristic of the occupation, but whether this betrays a tendency to dishonesty of a more general sort is so far unclear. A potentially fruitful way of improving our understanding of journalistic deviance is to examine research on workplace deviance in other occupations. This research shows that rule-breaking is common, helps employees keep control over their work, and is accepted by employers. Given the benefits that breaking rules at work brings, we can expect to find evidence of it in most occupations. In occupations where group loyalty and professional norms, autonomy and discretion are strong, problems and errors are often covered up. Newsroom research has shown that group loyalty is strong among journalists, that they resist regulation and are protective of their autonomy. This suggests that similar attitudes to errors and problems in work found among members of other occupations might be found among journalists.

So, is the community of journalists delinquent? At present too little research has been done and too little evidence collected to lead us to that conclusion. If deception lies at the core of journalism's culture, it would not be surprising to learn that journalists resist the control and regulation of their practices. How this resistance is enacted and precisely how the rules of deception are learnt and passed on remain important empirical questions. It may well be the case that a tendency towards deception and dishonesty is reinforced by the working conditions and employment practices in the news industry's current climate of competitiveness, but at present we understand too little of the interplay between these factors to reach any firm conclusions.

I look forward to the prospect of further research on this topic of the sort discussed in the previous section of this chapter for this will not only enhance our understanding of the more spectacular cases of deviance such as Jayson Blair's, but it will also contribute to the larger project of improving understanding of the complex of processes through which journalists accomplish, and maintain, their occupational identity. If Barnett's fear of a looming crisis in public trust in journalism is justified, such an understanding may be the first step towards ensuring journalism's survival.

Notes

1 These phrases are typical of much of the media coverage of these episodes. Among the most well-known cases of fakery and fabrication are those of Blair and, soon after his exposure, Rick Bragg, both of the *New York Times*, Janet Cooke, of the *Washington Post* (see Eason, 1986) and Stephen Glass of the *New Republic*. Fittingly, after his fall from grace, Glass published an account of his exploits in the form of a novel, casting himself as the central character (Glass, 2003).

2 Breed defined 'policy' as the 'more or less consistent orientation shown by the paper, not only in its editorial but in its news columns and headlines as well, concerning selected issues and events.' (Breed, 1955: 327).

3 The essence of Soloski's point (and that of the sociologists of the professions on which he draws) has resurfaced in research on the wider sociology of occupations and in a slightly wider, and more encompassing, sense. Several studies have drawn on the work of Michel Foucault to examine how occupational ideologies – in particular the 'discourse of professionalism' – can have the effect of controlling employees' behaviour by fostering self-discipline (Fournier, 1999; Casey & Allen, 2004). Discussions of the professional status of journalists and other media workers in the face of changes in the industry (de-regulation; altered employment practices; the introduction of new production technologies) have taken up this line of reasoning (Aldridge & Evetts, 2003; Ursell, 2000, 2003) to explain why media workers appear to be relatively docile as a workforce. What this work lacks, however, is a sufficiently detailed understanding of how working environments and 'workplace discourses' are experienced by media workers themselves. Without this, it is difficult to make sense of the behaviour of Jayson Blair, for example, who seemed immune to his employer's controlling discourse.

4 Conboy suggests that the clandestine nature of journalistic practice was characteristic of its earliest manifestation in mid-seventeenth century England and was, to a large extent, important for its survival (Conboy, 2004: 42–43).

5 One way of interpreting the journalists' accounts of deception in Lee's research is to see them as attempts to reduce or neutralise the disruption that deviance represents to the stability of their occupational identity and thus their professional project. In other words, journalists may find ways to justify their less dignified practices in order to maintain a sense of their work as overwhelmingly just and honourable. Lee stops short of such a conclusion, but further exploration along these lines may help to illuminate this aspect of journalistic practice.

References

Aldridge, Meryl and Evetts, Julia (2003) Rethinking the concept of professionalism: the case of journalism. *British Journal of Sociology* 54 (4) 547–564.

Barnett, Steven (2008) On the road to self-destruction. *British Journalism Review* 19 (2) 5–13.

Barry, Dan, Barstow, David, Glater, Jonathan D., Liptak, Adam and Steinberg, Jacques (2003) 'Correcting the record; Times reporter who resigned leaves long trail of deception.' The *New York Times* 11 May, p1.

Becker, Howard, S. (1963) *Outsiders. Studies in the sociology of deviance*. New York: Glencoe.

Blair, Jayson (2004) *Burning down my master's house. My life at the New York Times*. Beverly Hills, CA: New Millenium Press.

Branigan, Tania (2004) *The Guardian* profile: Martin Bashir, The *Guardian*, 27 February 2004 p16.

Breed, Warren (1955) Social control in the newsroom: a functional analysis. *Social Forces* 33 326–355

Casey, Rionach and Allen, Chris (2004) Social housing managers and the performance ethos. Towards a 'professional project of the self'. *Work, Emplyment and Society* 18 (2) 395–412.

Conboy, Martin (2004) *Journalism: a critical history*. London: Sage Publications.

Dalton, Melville (1959) *Men who manage: fusions of feeling and theory in administration*. New York: John Wiley and Sons.

Eason, David, L. (1986) On journalistic authority: the Janet Cooke scandal. *Critical Studies in Mass Communication* 3 (4) 429–447.

Elliot, Deni and Culver, Charles (1992) Defining and analyzing journalistic deception. *Journal of Mass Media Ethics* 7(2) 69–84.

Fournier, Valerie (1999) The appeal to 'professionalism' as a disciplinary mechanism. *The Sociological Review* 47 (2) 280-307.

Freidson, Elliott (1975) *Doctoring together. A study of professional social control*. Oxford: Elsevier.

Hunt, Jennifer and Manning, Peter K. (1991) The social context of police lying. *Symbolic Interaction* 14 (1) 51–70.

Glass, Stephen (2003) *The fabulist. A novel*. New York: Simon and Schuster.

Golding, Peter and Elliott, Philip (1979) *Making the news*. London: Longman.

Goodwin, H. Eugene and Smith, Ron F. (1994) *Groping for ethics in journalism* (3rd ed.). Ames: Iowa State University Press.

Lasorsa, Dominic L. and Dai, Jia (2007) Newsroom's normal accident? *Journalism Practice* 1 (2)159–174.

Lee, Seow Ting (2004) Lying to tell the truth: journalists and social context of deception. *Mass Communication & Society* 7 (1) 97–120.

Lee, Seow Ting (2005) 'The ethics of journalistic deception'. In Wilkins, Lee and Coleman, Renita *The moral media: how journalists reason about ethics*. London: Routledge, pp. 92–113.

Patterson, Maggie Jones and Urbanski, Steve (2006) What Jayson Blair and Janet Cooke say about the press and the erosion of public trust. *Journalism Studies* 7 (6) 828–850.

Roy, Donald F. (1954) Efficiency and 'the fix': informal inter-group relations in a piecework machine shop. *American Journal of Sociology*. 60, 255–266.

Soloski, John (1989) News reporting and professionalism: some constraints on the reporting of news. *Media Culture and Society* 11 (2) 207–228.

Thomas, Richard (2006) *What price privacy? The unlawful trade in confidential personal information. Information Commission report to parliament*. London: The Stationery Office.

Ursell, Gillian (2000) Television production: issues of exploitation, commodification and subjectivity in UK television. *Media Culture and Society* 22 (6) 805–826.

Ursell, Gillian (2003) Creating value and valuing creation in contemporary television or 'dumbing down' the workforce. *Journalism Studies* 4 (1) 31–46.

22
ME, ME, ME: THE RISE AND RISE OF AUTOBIOGRAPHICAL JOURNALISM

Ros Coward

The growth of autobiographical, 'confessional' journalism is one of the most striking elements in contemporary journalism. This is journalism given over to the intimate details of writers' personal and emotional lives. Some articles are 'one-offs', writers talking about particular events in their lives. Some are barely distinguishable from diaries or blogs, ongoing accounts of the writers' daily existence. Some are ongoing but focused on problems in the writers' life, such as divorce or cancer. No subject is off-limits nor are there many limits to the intimacies which writers are now prepared to share.

Thirty years ago such columns were almost non-existent, especially in serious newspapers. Now they are a staple element of features sections and weekend supplements, even recognised as a distinctive genre. "This genre" writes Bendorf, is "a flexible form of personal essay" which "is a way to share life's defining events and relationships in a form that connects with your readers."

Where has the phenomenon of autobiographical, confessional journalism come from? Why has it taken hold in a practice whose professional values were previously more concerned with providing a record of events, with objectivity and impartiality? Indeed not only why has it taken hold but why has it become so prevalent? Is this evidence of journalistic dumbing-down?

The rise and rise of autobiographical journalism

These changes in journalistic content are of particular interest to myself, not just academically, but also in professional practice, since my own journalism has mirrored this, moving from general features to, more recently, writing an autobiographical column about looking after my mother with dementia.[1]

Although I had often used events in my life as a source in features and even to some extent when writing political and social commentary on Op Ed pages,[2] I had never written like this before, a personal column exposing intimate aspects of my life and my mother's memory problems.

When I first started feature writing in the 1980s I had been more concerned about *avoiding* being too anecdotal or personal. Conscious that I had missed out on formal journalism training, I worried my writing might not be *"reporterly"* enough, by which I meant embodying the values of objective recording of first hand observations. Yet in the intervening years values had changed sufficiently for these inhibitions to be abandoned. It no longer seemed "un-journalistic" to bare all even in quality broadsheets.

The rise and rise of autobiographical journalism (experiential first person writing) is one of the most dramatic changes in print journalism in recent years. This genre is now ubiquitous, taken for granted even in serious broadsheets. Many newspapers include sections called "Real Lives", "First Person", or "Relative Values". Most are first person accounts of personal, emotional difficulties like Sophie McKimm on how "her grandmother has fallen in love with a 25 year old man from the Gambia" (The *Guardian*'s Real Lives (in G2) or "Domestic violence destroyed my family" (*Guardian Weekend*), or Marjorie Wallace who "for the first time ... reveals her own battle with depression" (*Daily Mail*).

Weekend supplements of many mid-market tabloids and broadsheets carry columns which are pretty much personal diaries like Euan Ferguson (*Observer*), John Ronson, Tim Dowling, Zoe Williams, and Lucy Mangan (*Guardian*), Alison Pearson, (*Daily Mail*) and Barbara Ellen (*Observer*). Sometimes these are about little more than the writers loafing about all day, their interest dependent on journalists making themselves "amusing".

Increasingly, however, this writing is just as likely to emanate from journalists known for "serious" journalism. Several memorable pieces – all in the *Guardian* – include Decca Aitkenhead writing about her mother's death, Matthew Engel writing about the death of his son (in an article called "The day the sky fell in"), or even the editor Alan Rusbridger writing about the death of his own father.

Many autobiographical columns – like my own or the anonymous *Living with Teenagers* – emulate diaries. The most extreme and raw examples of these autobiographical diaries have been cancer diaries written by established journalists. Journalist Ruth Picardie started writing a column for the *Observer* when she was diagnosed with breast cancer – aged 32 and the mother of one-year-old twins. She only wrote seven columns before she died, but had an enormous impact because of her unflinching account. Others include John Diamond in *The Times*, Ivan Noble the BBC's science correspondent who wrote an online diary, and Dana Rabinowitz who wrote occasional columns for the *Guardian* prior to her death early in 2008.

These first person pieces might seem at first glance to belong to a trend described by some media theorists as 'dumbing down' (Conboy etc). These theorists suggest that 'hard news' and serious journalism – which require investigation, research and verification – are being driven out by a proliferation of 'soft' features. These are defined as dealing with less serious subjects – family relationships and feelings – rather than economics, politics and world affairs. 'Soft journalism' is also defined as more subjective, less well-researched, more opinionated, more personal.

But it is not necessarily the case that this writing crowds out other more substantial, serious journalism. In broadsheets like the *Guardian*, *The Times*, the *Independent*, it co-exists alongside – rather than drives out – news, comment and analysis. First person, experiential, writing is a sub-section of a more general expansion of feature writing, especially the expansion of column inches devoted to lifestyle, life dilemmas, intimate issues and the emotional realm. Nor, given the subjects covered – cancer, death, rape, sex abuse – would it be fair to describe the subjects as trivial. But if this is not dumbing-down, what else might explain the explosion of this kind of writing in a profession still defined by other apparently contradictory values?

Traditionally, journalism has been associated with researching the outside world – the other – and reporting this back to its readership. Even though naïve understandings of this have been challenged by academics it remains a commonly held belief among practitioners about what 'proper' journalism is. "Journalists", says Andrew Marr (2004: 5) "are people who attempt to search out the truths of the world around them, and then inform the societies they inhabit." The journalist in this account is the one who experiences first hand what the reader does not, and reports back – at best with objectivity, accuracy and balance. Even after critical interrogation about bias (conscious and otherwise), these remain the core values most serious journalists aspire to and which are still taught on most vocational journalism courses.

Given these values still prevail, how has the interior world found a place in serious journalism, a place almost as significant as the external world? When and why did the self (ME) become a legitimate subject of reportage? Why has journalism started reporting back from the front line of the emotional life?

The autobiographical society

Journalism is not an isolated phenomenon. There is an underlying preoccupation across most areas of cultural life, both popular and 'high' culture, with self, subjectivity and identity, with who we are, where we come from, and especially what we feel. These preoccupations appear in many different places and take many different forms. Popular culture, for example, is infused with questions about identity and subjectivity: magazines, books and TV programmes explore how to improve, alter or come to terms with both our characters and our bodies. Self-preoccupation is also at the heart of the current passion for family history or finding out our ethnic make-up from DNA testing. At the other cultural extreme, it has been said that one of the strongest themes of contemporary art are the artists themselves – a subject to which I will return.

This preoccupation with the self is not just with our own selves. We want to witness others finding out who they are, what they are made of, and if they can change. This is the stuff of "true life" magazines and reality television, for which there is an insatiable appetite.

Nor do we discriminate. Autobiography and self-revelation are no longer the preserve of the "great" but have been democratised. Programmes like *Oprah* are based around the confessions of ordinary people: everyone has a story to tell now. But we are especially keen to hear from people who have had difficult and extreme experiences. Dave Pelzer's "A Boy Called It" started a publishing avalanche of ever more harrowing real life stories. Recent hits include *Ugly* by QC Constance Briscoe, *Just A Boy*, the story of Richard McCann, whose mother was the first victim of the Yorkshire Ripper, and *The Little Prisoner*, the tale of Jane Elliott, confined in a fortress-like house and subjected to ritual abuse by her sadistic stepfather.

According to Plummer (2001) the start of the twentieth century was characterised by an unprecedented obsession with telling, witnessing and (importantly) recording life stories. It has "become such a voluminous business that we could even start to talk of something like an 'auto/biographical society': life stories are everywhere" (2001: 78). He locates this phenomenon within "historical shifts brought about through accelerated industrialisation. The realisation of a 'possessed' individual, in a movement away from other structures of organisations and government means that such personal narratives take on new meaning."

Although the autobiographical confessional society may have origins earlier in the twentieth century, the 1980s witnessed a quantum leap. It was this shift which eventually eroded the traditional journalistic values which had regarded personal and emotional accounts as beyond the proper business of journalism.

These changes have been part of my own intellectual journey. It was from within feminism in the 1970s and 1980s that some of this pressure on the cultural institutions towards including personal experiences and concomitant "democratisation" took place. Feminists challenged conventions about appropriate subjects and authors of biographies and autobiographies. Amongst other things, feminism "recovered" lost diaries and autobiographies of women who had been "hidden from history" challenging the hierarchy of what had previously been considered historically important or significant. It asked why the life stories of the Match Girls should not be as interesting and valuable as those of the Rear Admirals and official versions of history? "Autobiography" says Laura Marcus (1994: 1), "was a central case for feminist criticism in the 1980's exposing processes of exclusion and marginalisation in the construction of literary canons ... The extensive feminist literature on women's autobiography over the last decade or so introduces many writers previously excluded from discussion, while revealing how androcentric the autobiographical tradition and autobiographical criticism have been."

Feminism's assault on orthodoxies was part of a more general challenge to old certainties about authoritative history and opinion. It was no longer possible to accept the old hierarchies about which lives were most important or the pretence that an author's own values were not affecting their views. Instead it was recognised that authors' identities, and cultural formations, affected the position from which they spoke and should be acknowledged.

This critique – both symptom and cause – had a major impact within academia, undermining the authoritative voice of "truth". Academics had to become conscious of their own cultural formation. "Many of us" writes Bleich (2004: 41) "want to speak more deeply from personal experience, to add this dimension to the habits of scholarly citation and critical interpretation."

In journalism too feminism played a hand in shifting boundaries about what was and was not relevant subject matter and the inclusion of "personal" perspectives. To say this, is not to attribute to feminism too much significance, or to overlook other previous developments in this direction. The writers associated with the phenomenon of "New Journalism" – Tom Wolfe, Hunter S Thompson and Truman Capote – all foregrounded their experiences and responses, and extended the range of subject matter. "The tone was resoundingly colourful and experimental and horror of horrors, the writer's own feelings and experiences often formed a cohesive part of the story."[3] However, the routine inclusion of personal confessional in mainstream journalism is a relatively new phenomenon.

Feminism's challenges to the orthodoxies, while not solely responsible for these developments, certainly assisted them. When I first wrote for the *Guardian* it was as a new author of the book *Female Desire* (1984). That book was very much of its moment, when the personal and everyday began to be considered important for revealing deeper aspects of how male dominated society worked – ideas embodied in feminism's slogan: "the personal is political".

Simultaneously however, the subjects women tackled were still definitely demarcated. Subjects like domestic violence, rape, pregnancy and childcare – all the personal, family stuff – were still marginal, confined to the women's page. It was only gradually that boundaries crumbled and these subjects became legitimate in mainstream journalism.

These changes within journalism have been very important in widening access and bringing previously marginalised issues into the mainstream: health, lifestyle, leisure, the domestic. Linda Christmas (1997) argues they are evidence of women exercising greater influence over content and style within the profession, a positive process of "feminisation". "Women have already made a difference, particularly on the magazine and feature side of newspapers ... the features content of all national daily and Sunday newspapers has increased in the last 15 years. There has been a huge increase in human interest stories."

Christmas emphasises the positive side of these developments including enabling discussions about previously neglected emotional and domestic issues. However, much of this writing far exceeds this, appearing instead to make self revelation an end in itself, revealing the writer and the writer's personality rather than the writer's experience illustrating some wider social problem. Typically, Ariel Leve (2008) tells us "I've just turned 40. As my birthday approached I was filled with dread. But now that it's happened I feel relieved ..." (*Guardian*). Much of this journalism is more about the spectacle of the writer than the issues, such as Liz Jones' staggeringly self-exposing diary in the *Mail on Sunday*.

Such examples would fuel Lasch's (1979) harsh condemnation of the culture of narcissism, "individuality has now gone so far as to create a narcissistic culture of self - absorbed individuals with no sense of public life, shared morality or outer control", giving ammunition to those who view Christmas' perspective as far too positive.

While questions about the pros and cons of this writing are important, more pressing here is: why has it found a place in journalism let alone come to such prominence? To answer that question I must first explore some of the hidden values in this wider cultural fascination with self-revelation.

The confessional society

Across all this writing about the self, what is striking is that identity is seen as something not fixed but fluid and changeable. Much "confessional" writing is dominated by narratives of transformation, describing journeys from one state of being to another, often journeys of self-discovery or struggles to triumphant changes. "What lies at the heart of this enormous outpouring of writing … is the idea that a highly individuated, self-conscious and unstable identity is replacing the old, stable, unitary self of traditional communities … The new selves are 'constructed' through shifts and changes in the modern world, and partly create a new sense of permanent identity crisis" (Plummer 2001: 83).

Secondly, great value is placed on having lived through *actual* experiences, on the accounts of those who have experienced things directly. Real is the word of the moment – real lives, real experiences as witnessed in the explosion of "reality TV". "What is key in this" (Ellis, 2007) "is the observation of so-called real/ordinary people reacting to different situations." Reality has been fetishised, far greater value being put on descriptions given by people who have lived through experiences than on imagined fictional scenarios or reports based on research and canvassed opinion, as in conventional feature writing.

There is a further value connected to this: *voyeurism*. It is a two-way process. As much as we want to explore or reveal ourselves, we hunger for seeing other people doing it too. Reality television operates in this space, putting people into real life difficult situations so they live through them but also catering to our voyeurism of wanting to see how they react. Reality TV asks: how would celebrities react in fat camps, or love islands or big brother households? How would ordinary people react to 1950s schooling, or a wartime diet or life in the Bronze Age?

These values illuminate deeper impulses behind the widespread cultural pre-occupations. More than a simple recognition of the emotional realm's importance, more than political interrogation of positions from which judgements are made, we have a culture preoccupied with witnessing how individuals react to, deal with, and feel about experiences, especially difficult ones. There has been discussion of this within television studies around the concept of witnessing (Frosch and Pinchevski 2008) but here what is most relevant is the wider cultural imperative. It is as if in a culture which is no longer under strict moral instructions from established authorities – the church, parents, the state – has begun to ask not how *should* we react, but how *would* we react? We need real life stories to witness and thereby to test ourselves.

Authenticity and autobiography

So why has mainstream – serious – journalism become such an important place for these real life revelations? The answer, ironically, returns us to the antithetical values of traditional journalism: accuracy, truthfulness, reporting reality as it is. But to understand this will entail detouring into the blogosphere.

Blogging could be seen as the apotheosis of democratising self-revelation and fetishising of direct experience. The blogosphere is dominated by personal, 'me, me, me' experience, what Andrew Keen (2007) has called "digital narcissism". The defining characteristic of the blog is that anyone can do it. In the world of blogs, the revelations of the blogger in his bedroom can be as interesting as a President.

Guardian editor, Alan Rusbridger (Rusbridger, A. 2006) has described the dramatic effect of this explosion of citizen voices on newspapers which have had to either incorporate, change, or both. In the spirit of incorporation, the *Guardian* ran two pages entitled "Public service bloggers special" (11 April 2007). They had trawled internet blogs by public service workers (like a mental health nurse and a university registrar) who can tell "in their own words, no holds barred," what is really going on. Here is citizen journalism apparently at its best, the authentic account from the coal face of life, unmediated by professional values or media organisations.

At the bottom of the page, however, there's an article about another social services blog, by someone called "Wandering Scribe". She writes about being homeless, living in a car, dealing with social services and dreaming of writing a book – which she is now doing. Her blog attracted an agent's attentions doubtless recognising a potential 'misery memoir' writer. The *Guardian* didn't reproduce this blog verbatim, instead contextualising it and warning that something about Wandering Scribe's account just wasn't ringing true.

Authenticity is at the heart of the issue. Across the different discourses promoting autobiographical revelations by real people, falls the shadow of inauthenticity, fakery. Nowhere more so than in the blogosphere. How can we know these self-revealers are telling the truth?

The answer is: we can't, something which has caused book publishers considerable embarrassment. Both Constance Briscoe's *Ugly* and Kathy O'Beirne's *Don't Ever Tell* about abusive childhoods have been disputed by their families. Briscoe's sister described her as "devious and dangerous". Her mother recently unsuccessfully sued her for defamation. James Frey's *A Million Little Pieces*, told of drug addiction, criminality, imprisonment and a struggle to personal redemption. It was Oprah's book choice and sold millions until exposed as a fake by a group of investigative journalists. Frey claimed he had been arrested while high on drugs. He'd hit a police officer with his car, reacted violently to arrest, and ended up charged with assault and given an 87-day jail sentence. The journalists found Frey had been issued with two traffic tickets, one for driving under the influence and one for driving without a licence, and had received a misdemeanour criminal summons for having an open beer bottle in his vehicle. He had been in police custody a mere five hours.

There is plenty more of what journalist Catherine Bennett has called this "flourishing sub-genre: miserable true-life memoirs of questionable or contested veracity" ('Oh, no, not another psychopathic nun' *Observer*, 9 March 2008). Authenticity haunts all this autobiographical writing like its shadow. Only "authenticity", "truthfulness", an ability to "reconstruct the facts" make these accounts autobiography rather than fiction.

Authenticity is therefore the holy grail of a culture needing to see how real people react to real difficulties. Yet in most of the places where these real life tales are told – in magazines, on Jerry Springer, on reality TV – authenticity cannot be guaranteed.

This is where journalism comes in. Journalism at its best is associated with giving us facts, not making things up. Journalism brings an aura of authenticity: journalists are meant to be truthful and operate within a profession which values veracity more highly than almost anything else.

Given recent press scandals such as huge payouts awarded to the McCanns (the parents of an abducted child) for the false stories circulated by the *Daily Express* it would be foolish to suggest the British press is a model of probity and constant truthfulness. Yet it is noteworthy that many scandals hitting the British press (phone tapping, single sources, entrapment) are connected with unethical practices involved in uncovering stories and not, by and large, scandals of fakery.

This is the clue to why journalism is so well-adapted for this confessional genre. In a culture hungry for real experiences, for personal, intimate self-revelation, journalism's professional values appear to guarantee authenticity. A recent article by Martin Townsend, a well respected *Guardian* writer, opens a piece on how for thirty years "lived with and around my manic depressive father" by first establishing these professional values: "As a journalist and editor for nearly 30 years, I have come across countless depressing stories about mental illness" (*Observer*, 16 April 2007). Newspapers draw on expectations of truthfulness, putting them in a prime position to carry this kind of writing while established journalists become particularly desirable to do it.

Conventions of autobiographical journalism

Does this mean that this journalistic genre is telling the truth, is free from conventions, or construction? You might think so from reactions to this kind of autobiographical writing as literal records of events. Actually, this kind of autobiographical writing – for all its guarantees of truthfulness – is as bounded by conventions as any other genre of writing.

In my column I elide many occasions and I leave a lot out. There are members of my family who would rather I wasn't writing this, so I use circumlocutions to avoid mentioning them. I cherry pick what goes in and what gets left out. I create voices and personalities who are strong enough to carry a "story". This is a parallel self, truthful to the issues and difficulties surrounding caring for someone with dementia and truthful also about my reactions, but not absolutely faithful to reality and certainly not without artifice. Philip Roth (cited in Benn, 2008) once wrote, "to suggest my writing

241

is autobiographical is not only to slight the suppositional nature of my writing but also to slight the art that goes into making it seem autobiographical."

John Diamond (1998) foregrounded this in a particularly dramatic column. "The me you meet here" he wrote on one important occasion "isn't the real me. He looks much the same as the real me, has the same number of wives and children, combines wit and witlessness in roughly the same proportions, has lived much the same life in many of the same places, but you will understand that if each week I were to deliver to you my life unpasteurised and absolutely as I experience it then that life would be unliveable. ... The me you see here is a sort of parallel me, picking and choosing the details which will best make the point, changing names or job titles out of a sense of propriety or social cowardice."

"Until last week", he added. Diamond had just been diagnosed with cancer. He went on to reflect on his hubris for having previously mentioned the lump "imagining that the following week he could casually tell his readers there had in fact been nothing to worry about." "What do you know?" he continued. "I had cancer all along. And have it still. The hubris-hating gods, it seems, read *The Times* too."

Diamond ponders the dilemmas: "So here's my problem. Well, not my real problem, which is that I have cancer and may expire before the date printed on the packet, but my columnar problem." Should he write about cancer in a "jaunty weekend column", can he continue to be jaunty if the treatment makes him sick? Should he? If he recovers, won't he sound "smugger than ever?" "Normally I try to address any qualms I have about what I'm about to write before I sit down to write it. This time, I'm sorry, I can't. There you are: the truth, at last."

Diamond's comments expose how, although autobiographical journalism promises authenticity, it is laden with conventions, narrative themes and expectations. His "domestic" pre-cancer column required jaunty self-revelation, his diagnosis forced him into a different genre. Diamond describes the shift as the intrusion of "truth" but the dilemmas he describes are also those of genre. "Illness narratives" are also convention-laden (Frank 2002), infected by desire for positive narrative outcomes, devoted to narratives of difficulties and charting journeys of change or redemption usually the result of personal will power. John Diamond's "columnar" problem is that either outcome awaiting him will be difficult in relation to the readers' narrative expectations. Even while exploring enormously important "life and death issues" there are powerful narrative conventions (about self and subjectivity) at the heart of autobiographical journalism.

Earlier I mentioned how self, and identity, are central preoccupations of contemporary art. Indeed, critic Isabelle de Maison Rouge (2004) claims the diverse artists and practices of contemporary art, are united by their pre-occupation with "personal mythologies". The language is striking: "personal mythologies". Not real lives, or autobiography, or true stories, but "personal mythologies". Contemporary art is on the same terrain as popular culture, concerned with issues of autobiography, identity, and the body – including pain, sex, death – but is far removed from popular culture's (and to some extent, journalism's) narratives of self-transformation and personal redemption. The self in contemporary art is not quite fiction, not quite fact, but a space of exploration for asking what is the body, what is identity, whether it is Cindy Sherman creating herself in multiple identities, Tracey Emin displaying her dishevelled bed, or Sophie Calle's extraordinary "scenarios" from her life.

One example highlights the gulf between the "me" of journalism and the "Me, myself and I" of contemporary art. Plastic surgery is a favourite topic for real life confessional journalism, sometimes by journalists who themselves have gone under the knife: "Confessions of a Botox convert" (*Daily Mail*) or "My whole family had plastic surgery" (*Sunday Mirror*) are typical.

By contrast the French artist Orlan has, since the age of 17, been exploring themes of the self, the body, identity and representation itself using plastic surgery not as means of self-improvement but to open debate. Orlan has done seven 'surgical performances' (her 'carnal art') which are given from operating theatres redesigned as artists' studios. Using only local anaesthetic, she directs the surgeon throughout, changes costume, reads poetry and plays music using props from art history to foreground ideals and conventions through which the female body is viewed.

In her final performance, Orlan asked the surgeon to put implants, normally used to make cheekbones more prominent, on her forehead, which she now wears permanently. "Orlan," says de Maison Rouge (2004), "diverts [plastic surgery] from its aim of improvement and rejuvenation and transforms it into an exhibitionist performance which challenges those watching to think about what is the real self and what are the limitations of the body."

There are many contemporary artists working with this richer, more suggestive discourse and almost no journalism that interrogates identity or foregrounds our own voyeuristic interest in scenarios of making, testing and changing identity. Accidentally Liz Jones' diary in the *Mail on Sunday* is so dizzyingly and narcissistically self-referential – even using the column to communicate with her estranged husband, Nirpal Dahliwal, who sometimes answers via his own column in the *Evening Standard* – that along with the cancer diaries, it's the nearest journalism comes to reflecting on its own practice and making the reader question their own voyeurism.

Conclusion

Autobiographical confessional journalism cannot be dismissed as dumbing-down. Often it appears excessively narcissistic and, by comparison with contemporary art, is often more about self-revelation than self-reflection. However, it is part of a wider cultural phenomenon concerned with investigating and assimilating the emotional and experiential, into the range of social and political concerns and is an important part of the culture's development of a more inclusive and emotionally intelligent approach to human experience.

Nevertheless, the self of autobiographical journalism is also a fabrication, a convention. These "Me, Me, Me" columns are convention-ridden. There are what Diamond called the "jaunty weekend columns" requiring faux self-deprecation and tales of incompetence. There are the cancer diaries, requiring if not always success against the disease, at least fortitude and the arrival at states of wisdom. And there are

243

domestic narrative columns which need personalities and tell selective stories. The effect – and the ethics – of these columns can sometimes be debateable[4] and as yet relatively un-debated. Medics for example are divided as to whether cancer sufferers find these blow-by-blow accounts helpful or scary.[5]

Journalism has an important role in a confessional society of providing an ambience and ethos of authenticity and veracity. The self of autobiographical journalism is restrained from excessive fabrication by the conventions of the profession. Yet the authenticity effect can mean that these conventions are even more difficult to detect than in less scrupulous discourses.

Notes

1 "Looking After Mother" was published fortnightly in the Family section of *Saturday Guardian* (January 2006–November 2008).
2 Between 1995–2004 I wrote a regular column for the *Guardian* comment pages.
3 Andrew Walker "Bedtime for Gonzo". BBC website http://news.bbc.co.uk/1/hi/magazine/4291311.stm
4 In May 2008 the anonymous author of "Living with Teenagers", a column in *Guardian Weekend* family section revealed how her children had "found out" about the column and their anger at having had their lives exposed in this way.
5 These issues were raised in "The impact of cancer diaries". By Jane Elliott: http://news.bbc.co.uk/1/hi/health/4243257.stm

References

Bleich, David "Finding the Right Word" in ed. Freeman, D. and Frey, O. *Autobiographical Writing Across the Disciplines*. 2004 Durham, NC: Duke University Press.
Briscoe, Constance, *Ugly*, 2006. London: Hodder and Stoughton.
Christmas, L., *Chaps of Both Sexes? Women decision-makers in newspapers: Do they make a Difference?*, 1997. London: The BT Forum.
Coward, Rosalind, *Female Desire*, 1984. London: HarperCollins.
De Maison Rouge, Isabelle, *Mythologies Personnelles. L'Art Contemporain et L'Intime*, 2004, Paris: Editions Scala.
Ellis, John, *Seeing Things: Television in the Age Of Uncertainty* 2001. London: I.B.Tauris, London.
Ellis, John, *TV FAQ*, 2007. London: IB Taurus.
Frank, Arthurs, "The Extrospection of Suffering: First-Person Illness Narratives", in ed Patterson, W., *Strategic Narrative*, 2002. Lanham, MD and Oxford: Lexington Books.
Frey, James, *A Million Little Pieces*, 2003. New York: Doubleday.
Frosch, P. 2008, 'Telling Presences: Witnessing, Mass Media, and the Imagined Lives of Strangers', in Frosch, P. and Pinchevski, A., Eds, Media Witnessing: Testimony in the Age of Mass Communication, London: Palgrave Macmillan.
Frosch, Paul and Pinchevski, Amit, Eds *Media Witnessing: Testimony in the Age of Mass Communication*, 2008. London: Palgrave Macmillan.
Keen, Andrew, *The Cult of the Amateur: How Today's Internet is Killing Our Culture*, 2007. New York: Doubleday.
Lasch, Christopher, *Culture of Narcissism: American Life in an Age of Diminishing Expectations*, 1979. London: W.W. Norton & Co.
Marcus, Laura, *Auto/biographical discourses. Theory. Criticism. Practice*, 1994. Manchester: University of Manchester Press.
Marr, Andrew (2004), *My Trade: A short, History of, British Journalism*, London: Palgrave Macmillan.
O'Beirne, Kathy, *Don't Ever Tell*, 2006. Edinburgh: Mainstream Publishing.
Rusbridger, Alan *Newspapers in the Age of Blogs* May 2006: www.thersa.org/acrobat/rusbridger_160306.pdf.
Plummer, Ken, *Documents of Life: An Invitation to a Critical Humanism*, 2001. London: Sage.

23

'DELIGHT IN TRIVIAL CONTROVERSY'? QUESTIONS FOR SPORTS JOURNALISM

Raymond Boyle, David Rowe and Garry Whannel

We are too quick to look at the finish line, instead of studying or enjoying the race. We want winners, even if the losers have better tales to tell. We want controversy instead of wisdom. We live in the era of breaking news. Too much, too quick, all the time.

Irish Times Sportswriter, Tom Humphries (2003: 371).

The sports section is not generally seen as prestigious within the culture of news and journalism. In an early attempt to articulate a critique of the politics of sport, Whannel (2008) notes that in England:

Varied and rich cultures surround different sports. But there is little public discussion of sport and society. This country has produced no reflective philosophy of sport. Everything about sporting activity is taken for granted. The media report sport with great professional skill but discuss it with a crass lack of seriousness. Newspapers relay results efficiently and delight in trivial controversy, but are timid and uninformative about the organisation of sport. Television sport takes up as much as one-sixth of air time and is for the vast majority of the population the public face of sport. The technical sophistication of living colour and slow-motion replay is remarkable. So is its failure to produce informative sport journalism. (2008: 112; first published in 1983)

Over a quarter of a century later, it is useful to reconsider this condemnation of the role and standing of sports journalism, and not only in England. This is a familiar critique that can be applied across the globe. A recent international survey of the sports press, analysing over 10,000 sports articles in 37 newspapers in Australia, Austria, Denmark, England, Germany, Norway, Romania, Scotland, Switzerland and the USA, was no more complimentary about what it dismissed as the 'world's best advertising agency'. While only ten countries out of the over 200 that play sport were covered by the survey, the 'formula' that it describes as shaping the economy of sport – close cooperation between sports business and media – has undoubted global significance. Schultz-Jorgensen (2005) argues:

> Here is the potent formula behind the booming sports economy: A global business partnership between the sports industry and the sports press. Together they have created an industry that excites and involves young and old all over the world and in Europe has an estimated turnover of 165 billion Euro (1.6 per cent of Europe's total GNP) and a turnover of 213 billion dollars in the US – annually.
>
> But the most extensive survey of the global sports press so far, the "International Sports Press Survey 2005", now documents that the powerful co-operation has some deeply problematic consequences for sports journalism. Sports editors of daily newspapers allow the sports industry to set the agenda and the priorities for coverage of sports events ...
>
> ... The survey shows that the sports pages in daily newspapers are dominated by the particular types of sport, sports stars and international events which create the biggest turnovers on parameters such as advertising, sponsorship, numbers of television viewers and spectators in the stadium. Conversely, the sports press has great difficulties reporting anything that takes place outside the angle of television cameras and after the stadium spotlights have been turned off. (Schultz-Jorgensen, 2005: 1)

Despite the vast amount of print, broadcast and online space dedicated to sport, and the considerable resources devoted to representing and reporting it, the sports desk has often been derided as 'the toy department of the news media'. That this typification is a corruption of a self-deprecating comment by a famous American sports broadcaster, the late Howard Cosell, that 'sports is the toy department of human life', reveals the extent to which the low professional status of sports journalism corresponds to an elite disdain for sport as corporeally-based popular culture among many intellectuals and arbiters of cultural taste (Rowe, 2007). It is not surprising, therefore, that within social science and the humanities, the sustained, serious analysis of sport and sports journalism has been rather less well regarded than that devoted to more 'serious' social domains and journalistic rounds (such as politics or business).

This chapter challenges unexamined, inherited prejudices towards sport and sports journalism while also being duly critical of the latter. The key questions that we address concern not only the professional or craft status of sports journalism (we do not propose here to dwell on the 'journalism as profession versus craft' debate because it applies to journalism in general, rather than to the sub-discipline of sport), but the extent to which sports journalists have compromised their own occupational standing by failing to discharge their 'fourth estate' duties of independence, inquiry and, where necessary, sustained critique. The main questions we raise are:

- Have sports journalists tended to confuse the roles of reporter and fan?
- Is sports journalism now an arm of the sports industry?
- Has the sports desk been 'ghettoized', insulating itself from the wider concerns and contexts with which it should be engaged?
- Is the sheer volume of sports journalism content saturating cultural space and impeding critical reflection?
- Are new media, user generated content and 'citizen sports journalism' contributing to the de-professionalization of sports journalism?

Before engaging with these questions it is necessary briefly to review the unfolding history of research and scholarship concerning sports journalism, drawing out the main concerns, analyses and critiques of academe and also those emanating from self-reflective contributions from within sports journalism itself.

Sports journalism: the state of textual play

Despite the growth of the study of journalism in the UK over the last decade, sustained academic engagement with the culture and practice of those working in sports journalism remains uneven. Within media and cultural studies, critical engagements with sports journalism were originally part of a broader investigation of the relationship between media and sport. There is no shortage of material that examines the representation of sport, either print or broadcast, and by implication these texts have involved an analysis of forms of sports journalism and the role that it plays in the mediation of sporting discourse. Sustained analysis of sports journalism gathered momentum in the early 1990s, with Whannel's (1992) study of television sport and Rowe's (1992) analysis of modes of sports writing beginning to elaborate a research agenda around journalism and sport. Blain et al.'s (1993) focus on the print media and national identity and Rowe's (2004) engagement with sports photojournalism helped to place sports journalism as a key site for the mediation of sport and its representation of a range of identities (see also Boyle and Haynes, 2000; Brookes, 2002; Crolley and Hand, 2002, 2006), while also highlighting the increasing importance of sport to the wider sphere of journalism and media.

However, there has been less analysis of the institutional and industrial context, and political economy of sport journalism. One early contribution to the field was Theberge and Cronk's (1986) study of sport newsroom routines. Whilst journalists all too readily aid in the publicizing of major sporting events, they will, Knoppers and Elling (2004) argue in their study of Dutch sport journalists, account for their poor coverage of women's sports by proclaiming that they do not indulge in promotional journalism. Later work by Mark Lowes (2004) on print and Michael Silk et al. (2004)

on broadcasting addressed the organizational routines of the sports rounds, but the corpus of such work is not substantial.

Rowe's work (2004, 2005), with its empirical focus, offered a contemporary updating of aspects of Tunstall's (1971) pioneering work on specialist journalists. Tunstall devotes a chapter to football journalists based on interviews carried out in the 1960s. He recognized that systematic study of the institutional position of journalism in the UK would seem incomplete without paying due attention to those plying their trade at what was seen then as 'the back of the book'. His interest in the professional ideologies that shaped and constrained these print football journalists offers a fascinating insight into an occupation that, in retrospect, was on the cusp of change as television coverage of the sport began to challenge the status of print journalism. It is instructive to note that Tunstall identifies 'football', rather than 'sport', as one of his specialist areas. There is indeed a logic in evidence here. In the UK it is perfectly possible to be a national press journalist specialist in football, or in horse racing. Most other sports do not get enough consistent coverage throughout the year for it to be so easy to be a full-time expert. Most other non-football sport journalists choose either to be 'experts' in a number of sports, or to specialise in one, and combine a range of magazine, television, radio and book outlets for their work.

This is not to argue that sports journalism has been ignored in mainstream Journalism Studies. Campbell (2004) looks at sports journalism as part of his examination of the entertainment journalism landscape, while Sugden and Tomlinson (2007) apply the theory of source-relations in Journalism Studies to their grounded empirical work that, over the years, has always been interested in sport and the journalists who report it. Several works with a more practice-focused approach to sports journalism, media and management have also been recently published (for example, Andrews, 2005; Nicholson, 2007; Fuller, 2008). However, given the scale of journalism about sport, its treatment within the field has remained fairly marginal.

None the less, within Media and Journalism Studies recent work opens up the range of ways in which the study of sports journalism connects with wider issues. Boyle and Haynes (2004), Boyle (2006) and Steen (2008) offer a broader canvas on which to locate the status, position and working practices of sports journalism in the digital age. One significant issue is whether a commercializing broadcasting system engages in *journalism about sport* or *broadcasting sport*, itself a very particular form of 'live' journalism. Other key subjects addressed and explored include the growing influence of public relations, commercial and marketing brokers on the environment within which sport journalists operate, as entertainment industry practice and management techniques are transferred into the sporting arena (Andrews and Jackson, 2001).

The issue of whether sports journalists occupy a distinct niche from other journalists has a long history. Certainly, Boyle (2006) has been struck by the increasingly generic constraints on all journalists working in a 24/7 news culture, suggesting that sport journalists have more in common with those in other fields than is often recognized. Political journalist Andrew Marr's (2004) history of British journalism, for example, reveals striking parallels between the 'pack' mentality among political journalists in Westminster and that of the sport reporting fraternity (the gendered term is used advisedly given its domination by men). He notes how most political media conferences end with a huddle between journalists keen to make sure that they have 'got the right line' on what has been said. Similarly, in an excellent and neglected book, Tim Crouse (1973) reveals the pack journalism tendencies inherent in American political journalism also so readily apparent among sports reporters.

There are, however, a growing number of published accounts from journalists on the culture of sports writing. Among the most insightful accounts of front-line sports journalism is Tom Humphries's (2003) account of a year in the life of a sportswriter working for the *Irish Times* in Dublin. Others offering insight as well as humour about their daily professional or craft practice include the *Daily Telegraph*'s Andrew Baker (2004) and Simon Hughes's (2005) reflections on switching between broadcast sports journalism for Channel 4 and the print media sector. Daniel Taylor's (2008) diary of following Manchester United for two seasons for the *Guardian* newspaper is a fascinating account of the pleasure and pain of being a contemporary 'beat' football journalist. He documents the relationships and pressures that front-line news journalists work within, contrasted with more distant and freewheeling sportswriters, often employed for their comment on, rather than reporting of, the events in question.

The work of Andrew Jennings (2007) is distinctive within sports journalism for his unflinching investigative drive to expose the corrupt underbelly of sport that television, in particular, chooses mostly to ignore. The late American sportswriter Leonard Koppett's (2003) history, completed just before his death, of his fifty years as a sportswriter remains one of the most insightful and compelling accounts of the changes wrought by television and the internet. In the UK, sports journalist Jeremy Whittle's (2008) exposé of the collusion involved in reporting cycling in general, and the Tour de France in particular, reminds us that for all the importance placed on the television coverage of sport, a perception remains that it is print journalism (either on the printed page or online) that remains the engine room of sports journalism. His work also highlights that different sports often have differing journalism cultures, but ultimately all journalism, in any form, revolves around relationships between journalists and sources. Whittle notes in covering professional cycling the ethics of 'crossing the line' between acquaintance, friendship and professional distance:

> Journalists develop an intimacy with the riders that is rare in other sports. They catch the same flights as they shuttle from race to race; they stay in the same hotels; they bump into them in lifts or at breakfast buffets, exchanging greetings and a word or two of encouragement. They share their success and failures, wince at their injuries, develop friendships with their families and – in one case I know of – transport their drugs for them. (Whittle, 2008: 5)

This discussion of sports journalism from within raises one of its most enduring issues – the distinction between the role of the critical, fourth estate watch dog and that of the 'star struck', even sycophantic fan. For Whittle such 'intimacy' between sportspeople and journalist is 'rare' – but similar comments have been made by many other commentators (for example, by Jennings (1996, 2007) with regard to journalists who cover the Olympics and association football). Such instances of the pathologization of sports journalism – from both within and outside its ranks – requires further interrogation, not least because it is unhealthy in any democracy for sport, a pivotal component of contemporary society, economics, politics and culture, to be a neglected subject of critical media scrutiny.

Issues and debates

Three questions in particular are evident: what is sports journalism; how is it changing; and what should it be doing? For much of the last century, 'sport' was constructed as a very specific form of news, with its own section of newspapers, and radio and television news programmes, and its own hierarchies and agendas. Sport is constructed as a world apart from the political, economic and social concerns that shape the rest of 'news'. But are these boundaries as fixed and impermeable as they might appear? With the growth of a 'surveillance society', scandals involving sport become front-page news. The rise of celebrity culture means that sport stars appear more often in other sections of the media – in fashion shoots, gossip columns, show business, celebrity profiles, chat and game shows. The sheer scale of the sports business has made it a subject for the financial and business sections of the print media. The intense focus on mega events such as the World Cup and the Olympic Games transcends the narrow boundaries of the sports section. Sport as a subject has found itself spreading beyond the confines of sports journalism and, indeed, often beyond the territory of sports journalists themselves.

Some of the best writing about sport has emerged in magazine journalism and in the interface between journalism and other forms of writing, such as novels and book–length non-fiction. This phenomenon has been especially evident in the USA, where the low status of sports journalism is not such a barrier to publication or critical approval. Some of America's most admired male writers – Paul Gallico, Ernest Hemingway, A.J. Liebling, Budd Schulberg, Norman Mailer, George Plimpton – have written on sport as reporters and essayists. Tom Wolfe's (Wolfe and Johnson 1973) influential anthology, *New Journalism*, included contributions on the Kentucky Derby (Hunter S. Thompson) and American Football (George Plimpton).

This form of writing on sport was less significant in the UK until the appearance of Nick Hornby's (1992) *Fever Pitch: A Fan's Life*. This highly successful autobiographical account of Hornby discovering football and becoming an Arsenal supporter triggered the emergence of a new culture of sports writing, encouraged and fostered in such locations as *Esquire* magazine and, until a change of editorship, *Observer Sport Monthly*. Both engaged and experiential, this new sports writing offered a rather different perspective on the cultures of sport than that typically provided by more mainstream sports journalism. It was influenced by the participant observation journalism of George Plimpton and the 'gonzo' journalism of Hunter S. Thompson which often offered a critical view of the conventional practices of sports journalism. In his account of the Superbowl, Thompson (1974) recounts with distaste the lack of interest of sports reporters in anything outside sport, routinely dumping, unread, all but the sports section of American newspapers. Plimpton (1978) noted that journalists were unable to respond to boxer Muhammad Ali's (Cassius Clay's) disruption of the normal clichéd exchanges at press conferences:

> The challenger's press conferences were tumultuous affairs. The old sportswriting hands disapproved of them; certainly they sat through them with disapproving frowns, sniffing slightly, as if tradition and decorum were being flouted. In the past they had put the required questions to the fighters ("how's your weight? What did you have for breakfast?") and they would write WT GD, 6 EGGS, 1 STEAK on a pad with a sense of accomplishment. Now the same sort of questions served only to unleash an hysterical monologue of self-assertion – snatches of poetry, home-grown aphorisms, punctuated with a brandishing of canes, cries of "rumble, man, rumble" – which might have been interesting the first time, but certainly wasn't the third time around. Still I was always surprised the writers couldn't get any fun out of it at all. They stared down at their pads, and sometimes they said under their breaths, "Aw, come off it, Clay". They rarely looked up at the fighter (Plimpton, 1978: 86–87).

Plimpton captures an unspoken consensus in the press not to get drawn into Ali's game. Their lack of a sense of absurdity – 'It seemed incredible that a smile or two wouldn't show up on a writer's face' (p. 87) – contrasts with today's tendency for a degree of postmodern irony to permeate much journalism. Plimpton's own distinctive method – training and playing in a professional sport in order to write about it (1961, 1964, 1968, 1978, 1985) – has recently been emulated by *Wall Street Journal* reporter Stefan Fatsis (2008), who spent three months learning to be a place-kicker with the Denver Broncos in order to write an insider account about American football.

Although the mainstream practices of sports journalism have not shifted in the direction of new journalism and the new sports writing, they are nevertheless being forced to adjust to the new multi-platform media environment. Sports journalism underwent a major transformation with the rise of television. The focus of print journalism had to shift from sport reporting to the discussion of sport, especially where rival players and managers could be induced to offer competing accounts of the same incident. With this development came the rise of the 'quote culture' in sports journalism and a fixation with comment and opinion – as opposed to straight reporting – which dominates so much of contemporary journalistic culture from sports to political coverage. There is some evidence that print-based sports journalists commonly resent the impact of broadcast sport upon their status (see Salwen and Garrison, 1998).

By contrast, television sports reporters have had limited scope to offer critical perspectives on events for which their employing institution has spent extensive sums to acquire the rights. Sports journalism is now undergoing a similar adjustment to the impact of the internet, digitalization, and the emergence of so-called 'citizen journalism'. There is far more information about sport than ever before, and advertising has grown in significance, supporting free newspapers and websites. The latter, when established by sport organizations, offer a competing and alternative source of information to that of newspapers and television. Deregulation and digitalization have led to a proliferation of electronic media channels with a voracious appetite for material, and a consequent growth of what Eco (1986) called 'sports chatter'. Much of this chatter is able to draw upon its audience for material in the form of football phone-in (or 'talkback') programmes. Postmodern irony and a post-fandom sensibility have contributed to the emergence of self-reflexive programmes that mock the conventions of sports journalism, examples of which in the UK include *Fantasy League Football* (BBC2), *They Think Its all Over* (BBC1), and *Fighting Talk* (BBC Radio 5). Similarly, several newspapers now include, during major events, elements of parody of the event that they are covering. Has this assembled volume of sports chatter displaced the centrality of the traditional 'sports section'?

Conclusion: 'Your Days are Numbered'.

What, in the light of this chapter's discussion, should sports journalists be doing anyway? Since their transformation by television, the major sports have acquired a globalized exposure, stimulating a lucrative merchandise, advertising and sponsorship-based economy. The business dealings of sport are not transparent, and sport institutions are prone to secretive, protective and defensive reactions to any probing of the financial dimensions of sport. There is little or no accountability to the fans. In such circumstances there is a pressing need for sports journalists to fulfil one of the long established functions of journalism – to act as a break on powerful institutions, to ask questions on behalf of their audience and to seek to hold institutions and individuals accountable for malpractice. Other disciplines of journalism, albeit in patchy and inconsistent fashion, challenge and expose corrupt or questionable practices. The influence of the Watergate affair in 1970s America was so great that now all scandal and exposure stories tend to be labelled with the suffix '-gate'. By contrast sports journalism has rarely pursued the disturbing instances of dubious activities within sport institutions regularly documented in the websites *Transparency in Sport* (run by Andrew Jennings, http://www.transparencyinsport.org/) or *Play the Game* (http://www.playthegame.org/). As has been argued above, television sport (especially commercial TV) is in most cases too intimately connected to its providers to pursue such issues.

Sport continues to offer a range of compelling narratives for the 21st century, and despite the rise of television sport, print sports journalists remain key cultural narrators. In short, sports journalism should be about reporting, enquiring, entertaining, explaining and, at times, holding sports to account on behalf of the fans. As sport becomes an increasingly central aspect of contemporary popular culture, the commercial value of sports journalism and of selected sports journalists will continue to escalate. The challenge for sports journalists is to offer uncompromised, informative and entertaining journalism against the backdrop of an increasingly commercial and privatized media system.

The above analysis has made clear that print sports journalism is regarded as a key area given the traditional opportunity that the print medium provides (although mostly, as we have noted, discarded by sports journalists) to reflect on its subject in depth rather than to concentrate on its immediate depiction. The role of television is particularly important in this regard, with its combination of instantaneity, audience reach and crucial rights revenue for sport establishing its domination across sports media. It is also worth reminding ourselves that, more than ever in the market-driven digital age of media development, the media institutions within which journalists (sporting or otherwise) work always shape their journalistic practice and culture. The media marketplace plays an increasingly key role in shaping the scale and scope of the type of journalism that appears in print, on television or on the web. Recent damning critiques of the state of journalism in the UK by Alastair Campbell (2008), the journalist and former communications advisor to Prime Minister Tony Blair, and by investigative journalist Nick Davies (2008), both cite the commercial constraints within which news organizations operate as having a negative impact on journalistic standards. While there are generic issues faced by all sports journalists there are particular constraints dictated by the specific medium within which journalists work.

As Sir Alex Ferguson, manager of the renowned Manchester United Football Club, stated to print sports journalists, 'Your days are numbered. Television gets everything now. All you lot can hope for is the crumbs that remain when television has had its fill' (quoted in Taylor, 2008: xxii). The hostile tone of this remark suggests, though, that Ferguson is relieved that he will not have to be exposed to persistent and perhaps unwelcoming questioning by print sports journalists, being subject only to the ritual, banal post-match enquiries by broadcast rights holders. Television's 'fill' may encourage the creation of a 'vacuum' within sports journalism, but how well positioned is it, in print or any other form, to challenge the institutional hierarchies of sport in the interests of open public debate about issues of power, equity and democracy within sport itself? Or are audiences too busy being entertained by the soap opera narratives that surround so much current media sport discourse about sport? It is no exaggeration to state that the future of sports journalism lies in the answers to these questions.

References

Andrews, D. L. and Jackson, S. J. (eds) (2001) *Sport Stars: The Cultural Politics of Sporting Celebrity*, London and New York: Routledge.

Andrews, P. (2005) *Sports Journalism: A Practical Guide*, London: Sage.

Baker, A. (2004) *Where Am I & Who's Winning?* London: Yellow Jersey Press.

Blain, N., Boyle, R. and O'Donnell, H. (1993) *Sport and National Identity in the European Media*, Leicester: Leicester University Press.

Boyle, R. (2006) *Sports Journalism: Context and Issues*, London: Sage.

Boyle, R. and Haynes, R. (2000) *Power Play: Sport, the Media & Popular Culture*, Harlow, UK: Pearson Education.

Boyle, R. and Haynes, R. (2004) *Football in the New Media Age*, London: Routledge.

Brookes, R. (2002) *Representing Sport*, London: Arnold.

Campbell, V. (2004) *Information Age Journalism*, London: Arnold.

Campbell, A. (2008) *The 2008 Cudlipp Lecture: Journalism, a Growth in Scale, alas, not in Stature*, 28 January, London.

Crolley, L. and Hand, D. (2002) *Football, Europe and the Press*, London: Frank Cass.

Crolley, L. and Hand, D. (2006) *Football and European Identity*, London: Routledge.

Crouse, T. (1973) *The Boys on the Bus*, New York, Random House.

Davies, N. (2008) *Flat Earth News*, London: Chatto and Windus.

Eco, U. (1986) *Travels in Hyperreality: Essays*, London: Picador.

Fatsis, S. (2008) *A Few Seconds of Panic: A 5-Foot-8, 170-Pound, 43-Year-Old Sportswriter Plays in the NFL*, New York: Penguin.

Fuller, L. (2008) *Sportscasters/Sportscasting: Principles and Practices*, New York: Routledge.

Hornby, N. (1992) *Fever Pitch: A Fan's Life*, London: Gollancz.

Hughes, S. (2005) *Morning Everyone: A Sportswriter's Life*, London: Orion.

Humphries, T. (2003) *Lap Dancing and the Nanny Goat Mambo: A Sports Writer's Year*, London: Pocket Books.

Jennings, A. (1996) *The New Lords of the Rings: Olympic Corruption and How to Buy Gold Medals*, London: Simon and Schuster.

Jennings, A. (2007) *Foul: The Secret World of FIFA: Bribes, Vote Rigging and Ticket Scandals*, London: Harper Collins/Willow.

Knoppers, A. and Elling, A. (2004) '"We Do Not Engage in Promotional Journalism": Discursive Strategies used by Sport Journalists to Describe the Selection Process', *International Review for the Sociology of Sport*, 39(1): 57–73.

Koppett, L. (2003) *The Rise and Fall of the Press Box*, Toronto: Sport Media.

Lowes, M.D. (2004) 'Sports Page: A Case Study in the Manufacture of Sports News for the Daily Press', in D. Rowe (ed.) *Critical Readings: Sport, Culture and the Media*. Maidenhead: Open University Press: 129–45.

Marr, Andrew, *My Trade: A short History of British Journalism*, 2004. London: Macmillan.

Nicholson, M. (2007) *Sport and the Media: Managing the Nexus*. Sydney: Elsevier.

Plimpton, G. (1961) *Out of My League*, New York: Harper and Row.

Plimpton, G. (1964) *Paper Lion*, New York: Harper and Row.

Plimpton, G. (1968) *The Bogey Man*, New York: Harper and Row.

Plimpton, G. (1978) *Shadow Box*, London: Simon and Schuster.

Plimpton, G. (1985) *Open Net*, New York: W. W. Norton.

Rowe, D. (1992) 'Modes of Sports Writing' in P. Dahlgren and C. Sparks (eds) *Journalism and Popular Culture*, London: Sage: 96–112.

Rowe, D. (2004) *Sport, Culture and the Media: The Unruly Trinity* (second edition; first edition, 1999), Maidenhead: Open University Press.

Rowe, D. (2005) 'Fourth Estate or Fan Club? Sports Journalism Engages the Popular', in S. Allan (ed.) *Journalism: Critical Issues*, Maidenhead: Open University Press: 125–36.

Rowe, D. (2007) 'Sports Journalism: Still the "Toy Department" of the News Media?', *Journalism*, 8(4): 385–405.

Salwen, M. B. and Garrison, B. (1998) 'Finding their Place in Journalism: Newspaper Sports Journalists Professional "Problems"', *Journal of Sport and Social Issues*, 22(1): 88–102

Schultz-Jorgensen, S. (2005) 'The World's Best Advertising Agency: The Sports Press', *International Sports Press Survey 2005*. Copenhagen: House of Monday Morning: Play the Game. http://www.playthegame.org/upload/sport_press_survey_english.pdf (accessed 31 August 2008).

Silk, M., Slack, T. and Amis, J. (2004) 'Bread, Butter and Gravy: An Institutional Approach to Televised Sport Production' in D. Rowe (ed.) *op cit*: 146–64.

Steen, R. (2008) *Sports Journalism: A Multimedia Primer*, London: Routledge.

Sugden, J. and Tomlinson, A. (2007) 'Stories from Planet Football and Sportsworld: Source Relations and Collusion in Sport Journalism, *Journalism Practice*, 1(1): 44–61.

Taylor, D. (2008) *This is the One: Sir Alex Ferguson: The Uncut Story of a Football Genius*, London: Aurum Press.

Theberge, N. and Cronk, A. (1986) 'Work Routines in Newspaper Sports Departments and the Coverage of Women's Sports', *Sociology of Sport Journal*, 3:195–203.

Thompson, H. S. (1974) 'Fear and Loathing at the Super Bowl', *Rolling Stone*, 28/2/74, and reprinted in *The Great Shark Hunt* (1980), London: Picador: 51–84.

Tunstall, J. (1971) *Journalists at Work*, London: Constable.

Whannel, G. (1992) *Fields in Vision: Television and Sport and Cultural Transformation*, London: Routledge.

Whannel, G. (2008) *Culture, Politics and Sport: Blowing the Whistle, Revisited*, London: Routledge.

Whittle, J. (2008) *Bad Blood: The Secret Life of the Tour de France*, London: Yellow Jersey Press.

Wolfe, T. and Johnson, E. W. (eds) (1973) *The New Journalism*, New York: Harper and Row.

24

JOURNALISM AND LOCAL POLITICS

Mats Ekström, Bengt Johansson and Larsåke Larsson

Over recent decades, scholarship concerned with exploring the relationship between journalism and politics has been extensive. Studies have tended to focus on this relationship as it evolves on national or international levels, however. That is to say, researchers interested in the news reporting of political affairs have tended to disregard the significance of local contexts, although there are exceptions (Arnold 2004; Neveu 2002; Kaniss 1991; Franklin & Murphy 1991; Larsson 2002). In this chapter, we will argue that local contexts create specific preconditions for distinctive types of political journalism that are worthy of investigation in their own right.

Political journalism at the local level, we intend to show here, exhibits its own forms and conventions, rather than simply mirroring those consistent with reporting at other levels. Our discussion begins with a brief assessment of the concept of 'the local', paying particular attention to how it has been used in journalism research. We then proceed to examine changing aspects of the relationship between journalism and local politics, not least the 'watchdog role' of the press. Against this backdrop, we present findings from an empirical study of journalism and local politics in a Swedish context in order to discern a basis for future research into this oft-neglected area of enquiry.

'The local'

The local level of politics is typically understood in relation to the political-administrative organization of local communities, and their institutionalized relations between different levels of state bureaucracy. News production, not surprisingly, tends to be structured in relation to such local political structures. However, what counts as local politics (and thereby the local political agenda) is in many ways also formed by the local news media themselves. In her book *Making Local News*, Phyllis Kaniss (1991) shows how local journalists define what should be understood as local, namely by emphasizing issues which can be regarded as symbols of local identity. For example, by giving media attention to central city development projects, such as public transportation systems or the construction of a new opera house or a sports arena, local news gives shape to the cognitive maps that citizens use to understand their communities.

In news reporting, spatial proximity represents an important news value, and as such is part of the standard repertoire employed in order to frame stories in ways that attract and hold the interest of diverse audiences. In local journalism, it follows that events covered in national news are routinely transformed into local news stories by pursuing a specific angle or hook. In the case of a national government's decisions, for example, the ensuing effects will be viewed from a local perspective, with the news organization explicitly positioning itself as the voice – if not the forthright champion – of the community and its interests (Neveu 2002; Johansson & Berglie 2007).

Significant aspects of the social integration function of local media with the community were first identified, in scholarly terms, by Janowitz (1952) in *The Community Press in an Urban Setting*. Janowitz showed how local newspapers contributed to the maintenance and operation of local urban communities over time. His study has proven to be a highly useful point of departure for many studies of local media and local news over the years (Stamm 1985; Kaniss 1991). Several studies have also indicated how this social integration role attributed to the media works to influence political participation. By consuming local news, it seems, people tend to be more inclined to take part in political processes (McLeod *et al.* 1996; Johansson 1998; Paek *et al.* 2005).

Local news and local media are not necessarily the same thing, however. In Sweden, for example, historical research suggests that when local newspapers emerged, they often did not contain much by way of local news. Indeed, related enquiries suggest that it would take until the 1960s before such news was deemed to be of central significance in the local press. Local news, especially local political news, was not regarded as being sufficiently interesting or worthwhile in comparison with national and international news. However, more recent decades have witnessed a growing tendency to devote ever greater attention to local news (Jacobsson 2008).

Similarly relevant here is the view that local news is worthy of study from a democratic normative perspective, where questions of diversity and informativeness are emphasized. Local media – sometimes just a single newspaper – can be shown to be highly influential in defining local politics in relation to citizenship. Findings from such studies indicate that in the case of local newspapers enjoying a monopolistic position, for example, they are likely to exhibit a decisive degree of influence over popular perceptions of politics within their area (Franklin & Murphy 1991). That said, though, research on media effects sometimes questions the impact of local news for a number of reasons, including people's personal experiences of life in the community and/or their interpersonal communication with one another on local issues (Zucker 1978; Demers 1996; Johansson 1998).

A symbiotic relationship

When it comes to the legitimacy of journalism as a relatively autonomous institution with a key role to perform in a democratic society, its perceived independence in relation to political institutions and power is essential. In everyday news reporting, journalists are supposed to be independent in relation to political pressure and public relation activities, in deciding and evaluating news sources, in the process of news selection, and in the construction of frames and angles. The norm of independency is also expressed in the idea that good journalism implies scrutinizing, digging up and exposing wrongdoings in politics as well as in the related areas of responsibilities assigned to public authorities (see e.g. de Burgh 2000; Ekström, Johansson & Larsson 2006a; Protess et al. 1991).

Nevertheless, however, research into the relationship between journalists and politicians has regularly highlighted what is often a close degree of co-operation and co-ordination between supposedly independent actors. Here attention has focused on the mutually adaptive, even dependent, roles they perform in what is a shared culture – that is, a culture where divergent objectives are usually held in delicate balance. Both sides of this equation seek relative advantage in symbiotic terms, such as where official actors provide information in exchange for media 'space' or even positive coverage (Blumler & Gurevitch 1981; Gans 1979; Sigal 1973).

For their part in this symbiotic relationship, reporters actively seek to establish regular connections with officials participating in the local governmental and administrative environment (Ericson et al. 1989). Officials, as news sources, present newsworthy material, but also partly take over the journalistic role of collecting this material in the first place, thereby becoming 'surrogate observers' (Roshco 1975: 84). Just as journalists report on municipal matters, Fishman (1980: 30) notes in his study of the local media-municipal relation, officials 'participate in the activities that they report' to journalists. Gieber and Johnson (1961), in their classic article 'The City Hall Beat', identify several characteristics of this local media-municipality relation. In addition to the degree of mutual dependence noted above, these include: assimilation of reporters in the municipal life, the holding of similar views about what represents news, shared programmatic ideas about municipal work, consensual ambitions about local society and close personal contacts, amongst others.

More recent research into journalism and local politics has called into question whether the principle of independency really works in practice on a local level (Franklin 2006). Counteracting circumstances have been observed which challenge perceptions of such an independency. There seems to be two general arguments in relation to these tensions. The first argument concerns the *structural conditions* of political journalism on a local level, while the second is about *current changes* in journalism in relation to the local media landscape.

In several aspects the structural conditions of local journalism seem to support close relations – and thereby mutual dependency – between journalism and local politics, rather than the other way around. Four interrelated aspects can be distinguished (see e.g. Neveu 2002; Larsson 1998; 2002):

(1) Social anchorage: Journalists working on local news media are often embedded in the community they have to report on. They share the same circumstances, life conditions and values. Social anchoring in a local context creates familiarity and shared points of identification, making it hard to keep a critical distance.

(2) Closeness to sources: On a local level journalists regularly meet people responsible for politics (as well as social services, etc.) in different contexts, not only in the job as a reporter but in the civil society in general and presumably also in private life. This might contribute to interdependencies, loyalties and an unwillingness to criticize and scrutinize.

(3) Closeness to the readers: Journalists also have to be prepared to be held accountable for their reports in regular meetings with readers. In many situations critical news reports into local politics, scrutinizing agencies and activities, will be widely appreciated, of course. However, watchdog journalism can also prove to be very provocative. Maintaining sufficient distance in these situations is consistent with professionalism. Though, as Larsson (1998; 2002) shows, taking a critical stance and keeping professional distance in small communities, where most people encounter one another on a regular basis in different local activities, can be a real challenge.

(4) The identity of the newspaper: Local newspapers, to a large extent, work as a voice of the community in relation to other communities (as well as at the national level of government). This is a structural factor counteracting the critical stance of journalism. In other words, the newspaper endeavouring to represent the local community's point of view in relation to the outside world will often take care to avoid local criticism. By this logic, the local press can be described as both an advocate for the municipality and a guard against external threats, and as such more of a guard-dog for local interests than a watchdog (Tichenor et al. 1980/1995; Donohue et al. 1995).

Bearing these and related points in mind, it is perhaps not too surprising that researchers often suggest that the glory days of the local press are over. Various studies have documented a decline in the number of local newspapers in several Western countries (Engblom 2002; Franklin 2006), a trend which may have negative effects on the plurality of voices in the public sphere. There is also a decrease in the number of journalists being employed, as resources for local news reporting continue to shrink. Fewer journalists being available to fill the pages with proper content means, in turn, that there is an obvious risk that news production will be entailing an ever greater reliance upon re-written copy from outside sources (press releases and other forms of prepared material), as well as articles produced by news agencies. There will be less time to conduct independent investigations, and thereby an increased vulnerability to news manipulation via information subsidies (see also Gandy 1992; Pfetsch 1998). A number of studies support a conclusion that local journalism has lost considerable control over the news agenda, effectively transforming the role of watchdog into lapdog (see Franklin 2006).

Also worthy of attention in this regard are changes in local politics. Harrison (2006) argues that 'local authorities are becoming more strategic, more focused, more professional in the development of their relations with the local media' (2006: 187). Public relations (PR) officers working on strategic communication and media relations have become increasingly prominent. This development can be understood partly as a way of coping with a situation in which local authorities have to justify what they are doing, and why, to members of the community. Extensive PR or 'spin' activities lead, in turn, to journalists being offered a lot of information. On the one hand, it is an important resource, but on the other hand, it may succeed in undermining local media's independence. Garner (2006) argues that the real competition over the news agenda is not between journalists and political actors, but rather between PR spokespeople offering contending types of news.

To summarize, there seems to be a general argument in the research literature indicating that journalism has become less independent in relation to local politics over the last two decades. What is implied in some research is a trend towards a more politicized media, a situation in which PR and related communication staff produce much of the news published in the local press, albeit with minor editorial changes (Franklin 2006). The watchdog has become increasingly muzzled, while political marketing more vociferous. This imbalance has been described as a general trend in journalism (Corner & Pels 2003). However, the role of journalism as an independent agency seems to be especially challenged at the local level.

Current research has produced empirical data about the nature of journalism and local politics, but there is a lack of studies designed to empirically test such hypotheses about changes in independence, in the balance between media and politics, in the power to set the news agenda, and the watchdog role of local journalism. In the next part of this chapter, we consider whether these apparent trends can be traced in local journalism from the early 1960s to the new millennium (2001).

Scrutiny, accountability and independence

In order to investigate trends in the relations between journalism and local politics, our study was designed to focus on the press in three Swedish municipalities in the years 1961, 1981 and 2001 (Ekström, Johansson & Larsson 2006a; 2006b). The study consists of a thorough textual analysis, based on a discourse-analytical approach. In total, some 1,500 articles – appearing in five local newspapers for two months of each year – have been analysed.

Two questions, in particular, will be focused on here. The first deals with the central democratic function of the media to investigate and scrutinize the operation of political power. The question is to see if the degree of scrutiny has increased or decreased. The second deals with the position of journalism in relation to its sources and the municipal agenda. The question is whether journalism has become more dependent on or independent of its sources.

Scrutiny, in journalistic terms, normally stands for investigative journalism. That is to say, it represents exhaustive enquiries intent on uncovering the reality otherwise hidden behind official descriptions. In scientific terms, scrutiny often signals a commitment to open, independent investigation as well as a transparent presentation of methods and sources. Bearing this in mind, and given that journalism's monitoring of political life is mostly performed in other, more everyday routines than those considered to be indicative of investigatory reporting, we believe that a broader concept is needed.

Consequently, we introduce a scrutiny concept that takes into consideration different forms and practices of journalistic evaluation. In this conceptualization, scrutinizing is about testing if and how local political institutions work, and whether or not their responsibilities are fulfilled. On this basis, we have identified seven different types of scrutiny:

1. Digging and revealing journalism – investigative news.
2. Quality tests, e.g. testing how specific municipal service work.
3. Closer observation of a service area, through overviews or interviews.
4. Investigation of a local issue, focusing on a specific controversy.
5. Presentation of other authorities/organization's scrutiny and revision.
6. Reporting criticism, where a newspaper encounters contrary views.
7. Reporting positive results.

Our findings indicate that 28 percent of all articles examined exhibited a scrutinizing frame linked to one or more of these seven categories. Correspondingly, 72 percent were not categorized as scrutinizing. Seen with the different types, *Reporting (others) criticism* proved to be the highest share with 11 percent, followed by the type *Closer observation of a service area* with nearly 8 percent. The other scrutinizing categories were found in a very limited degree, lowest for *Digging/revealing* articles (1 percent) and *Quality tests* (almost zero).

More scrutinizing

Over the 40-year-long period surveyed, the scrutinizing share in local news reports increased from the 1960s to the millennium, especially in the first half of this period. In 1961, the scrutinizing share was 15 percent, which increased to almost 29 percent in 1981. Twenty years later the share slowly increased to 31 percent (see Table 24.1 on p. 262).

In analysing the local news reportage from a normative perspective, it can be argued that accountability constitutes an important aspect of journalistic scrutiny of politics. A regulatory principle in a democratic society rests on citizens' control over political power, not least in the meaning of accountability – that is, who will hold whom accountable for what and in what context. The link between scrutiny and accountability is to be understood both from a normative perspective – the ideology of democratic journalism – and in relation to the discursive construction of news

Table 24.1 Scrutiny, problem-orientation and accountability claims in local reporting 1961, 1981 and 2001 (percent)

	1961	1981	2001	Total
Scrutiny	15.5	28.7	31.3	28.1
Problem-focusing[1]	8.0	21.5	24.2	20.9
Accountability-claiming[2]	6.9	19.7	22.2	19.2
Number of articles	188	661	654	1503

1) Includes those scrutinizing articles that identify and attend to problems in politics.
2) Includes those problem-focusing articles that explicitly call somebody to account for the problem.

reports. Scrutiny is thus a way of fulfilling the democratic obligations of journalism as a profession. It gives people the information they need to put pressure upon politicians and to hold them accountable for their actions.

In this study, we define accountability in terms of journalism committed to pointing out problems and to holding somebody responsible for them. The question is: To what extent and in what forms has accountability been integrated into journalistic scrutiny of local politics? The analysis is based on a distinction between (a) articles including scrutiny, (b) articles also locating problems, and (c) articles also claiming accountability.

As mentioned above, journalism developed towards a more scrutinizing frame between 1961 and 2001. A further question thus arises as to whether this is also true when it concerns problem-focusing and accountability-claiming. As documented in Table 24.1 this appears to be the case; local journalism in Sweden did become more inclined to scrutinize, but also more focused on problems and accountability claiming.

Although the scrutiny level was nearly the same in 2001 compared to 1981, a closer examination of the related articles unmasks a picture where accountability-claiming became more pronounced over time. We identified three forms of accountability illustrating such a radicalization. The first form (*Formal accountability is reported*) indicates that the text only states who or what institution is formally accountable for the issue at hand. The second form (*Critical exposure*) presents criticism and identifies the person(s) accountable. In the third form (*Public accusation*) the criticized actor(s) was asked to defend themselves. The study shows that formal accountability has decreased over the time period, while public accusations have increased.

Moreover, the study indicates that individual politicians and officials are increasingly held accountable in local news. Some 47 percent of the articles with accountability-claiming content were directed against individual persons in 1981 (and the rest directed to collectives, such as the municipality or a board). Two decades later, 59 percent of these accountability articles were directed to individuals. As a result, a certain personification of local politics can be verified during the period. This development goes hand-in-hand with an increased use of interviews as a method of journalistic news gathering.

In this study it was also possible to test the claim that there is a strongly positive correlation between the resources of the newspaper and the priority given to scrutinizing local politics. Two newspapers in the same municipality were compared during the period from 1961 to 2001. One is a large newspaper with significant editorial and financial resources, while the other is much smaller, with limited resources. The correlation assumption was not verified by the data. On the contrary, the newspaper with limited recourses gave higher priority to scrutiny articles. In 2001, this newspaper (when its resources had declined considerably) published more scrutiny articles, even in absolute numbers, compared to its much stronger local competitor.

A more independent local journalism

Independence in relation to municipal influence was studied in two ways. The first concerned whether news reporting is being done in line with the municipal agenda or not; the second whether news reports appear before or after decisions were announced by municipal bodies. Reporting before decisions would indicate a more independent journalism, while reporting after decisions means less independent work.

The study shows that media-reporting has become more independent from the municipal agenda since 1961. In that year, 42 percent of the articles are categorized as written in line with the agenda in town hall and other local political forums. The level of municipal-following reporting is found to be almost the same 20 years later, but compared with the situation in 2001 the level decreased – 33 percent of the articles were in line with the municipal agenda. We can say, therefore, that local journalism appears to have reduced its dependence on the municipality during this period.

Regarding the question whether the media reports before or after decisions in municipal bodies, the study shows that reporting-before increased from 29 percent of all articles in 1961, to 42 percent in 1981, and 49 percent in 2001. Correspondingly, reporting after decreased from 71 percent to 51 percent between the 1960s and the millennium. A more independent journalism is therefore to be noted during the period.

The second form of independence from the municipal organization and process concerns which type of sources journalists turn to, and if they use municipal sources or other sources in their reporting. The results show that the relative prominence of municipal sources has decreased during the period 1961–2001, as shown in Table 24.2.

The table shows that the newspapers in 1961 relied upon municipal sources to a considerable degree; nearly three out of four articles are built on such sources. This type of source use decreases by 10 percent in 1981, and by a further 10 percent in 2001.

Table 24.2 Municipal sources in municipal news 1961, 1981, 2001 (percent).

	1961	1981	2001	Total
Articles with only municipal sources	73	63	54	60
Articles with both municipal and other sources	13	18	26	21
Articles without municipal sources	14	19	20	19
Total percent	100	100	100	100
Number of articles	172	608	626	1406

The table similarly shows that the use of both sorts of sources increased, as did the use of non-municipal sources. Earlier research, conducted by Johansson (1998), has also suggested that the degree of news dependence on municipal sources declined during the 1980s and 1990s. Our research shows that this trend has a longer history.

This data suggest that the dominance of municipal sources has been eroded by other sources during the period 1961–2001. When these results are placed in a broader perspective, however, our study shows that local news continues to rely heavily on municipal sources, and this dependence necessarily shapes the reporting of local politics to a significant extent.

Conclusions

A key aim of the study was to trace the relative independence of local journalism over time. Against the backdrop of structural conditions and changes in the journalism/media landscape, as well as in local politics, some commentators are suggesting that there is a growing tendency towards a more source-dependent form of local journalism. However, the empirical results from our study call this claim into question.

Over the time period examined, local journalism appears to be increasingly independent. That is to say, it gradually becomes more scrutinizing, problem-oriented, and inclined to hold politicians and officials responsible for their actions. Additional aspects measuring independence also support the perception that independence is growing, since local news is less likely to follow the municipal agenda or to rely upon municipal sources.

The question remains, though: how can these results be understood in relation to what was said earlier concerning the changing structural conditions in both the media landscape and local politics? Here we need to state that even though the results indicate a tendency towards a more independent local journalism, the relationship between journalists and politicians remains quite strong. The study shows a decreasing portion of attention devoted to municipal sources over time, but a majority of the news articles still only use municipal sources in 2001. Still, there is a noticeable trend towards more independent local journalism. We suggest three possible explanations why the conclusions drawn from our study are quite different from those found in previous research.

The first explanation relates to the different case studies used to draw conclusions about the relationship. Most of the previous studies indicating a poorer quality of local journalism are based on studies in an Anglo-American setting. The results presented in this chapter from the Swedish context suggest that there are certainly similarities between the countries, but one should be aware of differences as well. A significant dissimilarity is the rather strong local press in Sweden, at least compared to both the UK and the US. Strong newspaper companies with extensive resources are likely to become more independent of their sources, and this might affect the conclusions accordingly. Another aspect concerns the apparent differences in journalism education, where a larger portion of journalists in Sweden have a degree in journalism compared to many other countries (Melin-Higgins 2008). This higher level of professionalization may help to explain the apparent increase in the relative independence of local journalism in Sweden compared to other countries.

A second explanation pertains to the study's time-frame. The empirical results compare and contrast local journalism over 40 years. This is a much longer time-span than that adopted in previous studies. Further differences in research design might similarly help to explain why different conclusions are drawn. A third explanation raises questions about whether the empirical results indicate real independence or just an imaginary independence. While we believe that our study highlights the many ways local journalism marks its independence, perhaps it more reflects what in the literature is called 'mediatization', that is, where political and other social actors not only adapt to the media logic, but internalize it so that it becomes a built-in part of the governing processes.

To conclude, then, the results of our longitudinal study display an image of a more robustly independent form of local journalism emerging, but it is not self-evident that this apparent trend will translate into better quality news. Indeed, we find ourselves wondering whether what we are really seeing reflects a growing influence of public relations, where what counts as 'local news' is being redefined in ways which better suit the interests of politicians and officials.

References

Arnold, Douglas (2004) 'Congress, the Press, and Political Accountability'. New York: Russell Sage Foundation.

Blumler, Jay G. & Gurevitch, Michael (1981) Politicians and the Press. An Essay on Role Relationships, in Nimmo & Sanders (eds) 'Handbook of Political Communication'. London: Sage.

Corner, John and Pels, Dick (2003) 'Introduction: The restyling of politics', in John Corner & Dick Pels (eds) 'Media and the restyling of Politics'. London: Sage.

de Burgh, Hugo (2000) (ed.) 'Investigative Journalism. Context and practice', London: Routledge.

Demers, David P. (1996) 'Does Personal Experience in a Community Increase or Decrease Newspaper Reading?', 'Journalism and Mass Communication Quarterly', 73:304–318.

Donohue, George; Tichenor, Philip & Olien, Clarice (1995): A Guard Dog Perspective on the Role of Media, Journal of Communication 45/2:115–132.

Ekström, Mats, Johansson, Bengt & Larsson, Larsåke (2006a) Journalism and the Scrutiny of Local Politics. A Study of Scrutiny and Accountability in Swedish Journalism. 'Journalism Studies' 7:2:292–311.

Ekström, Mats, Johansson, Bengt & Larsson, Larsåke (2006b) Mot en mer oberoende kommunal journalistik/Towards a more independent local journalism?/ *Nordicom Information* 28:4:37–54.

Engblom, Lars-Åke (2002) *Den 'svenska pressens historia IV /The Swedish Press History/'*. Stockholm: Ekelids.

Ericson, R., Baranek, P. & Chan, J. (1989) *'Negotiating Control. A Study of News Sources'*. Milton Keynes/London: Open University Press.

Fishman, Mark (1980) *'Manufacturing the News'*. Austin: University of Texas Press.

Franklin, Bob (2006) (ed.) *'Local Journalism and Local Media. Making the local news'*. London: Routledge.

Franklin, Bob & Murphy, David (1991) *'What News? The Market, Politics and the Local Press'*. London: Routledge.

Gandy, Oscar (1992) Public Relations and Public Policy, Toth & Heath (eds) *'Rhetorical and Critical Approaches to Public Relations'*. Hillsdale, J.J.: Lawrence Erlbaum.

Gans, Herbert J. (1979) *'Deciding What's News'*. New York: Pantheon.

Garner, Brent (2006): Hungry media need fast food: the role of the Central Office of Information, in Franklin, Bob (ed.): Local journalism and Local Media. London: Routledge.

Gieber, Walter & Johnson, Walter (1961): The City Hall 'Beat'. A Study of Reporter and Source Roles, Journalism Quarterly 38:289-297.

Harrison, Shirley (2006) Local government public relations and the local press, in Franklin (ed.) *'Local Journalism and Local Media. Making the Local News'*. London: Routledge.

Jacobsson, Diana (2008) Från politisk arena till lokal marknadsplats. En studie av innehållet i den borgerliga landsortspressen 1927-2007. Göteborgs universitet: JMG.

Janowitz, Morris (1952) *'The Community Press in an Urban Setting'*. Chicago: University of Chicago Press.

Johansson, Bengt (1998) Nyheter mitt ibland oss. Kommunala nyheter, personlig erfarenhet och lokal opinionsbildning /News among us .../ Göteborgs universitet: JMG.

Johansson, Bengt & Eva Berglie (2007) Att bevaka en region. University of Gothenburg: JMG.

Kaniss, Phyllis (1991) *'Making Local News'*. Chicago: University of Chicago Press.

Larsson, Larsåke (1998) *'Nyheter i samspel /News and co-operation'*. Göteborg: Göteborg University.

Larsson, Larsåke (2002) Journalists and Politicians: A Relationship Requiring Manoeuvring Space, in *'Journalism Studies'* 3:1:21–33.

McLeod, Jack M., Daily, Katie, Guo, Zhongshi, Eveland, William P. Jr., Yang, Seungchan & Wang, Hsu (1996) 'Community Integration, Local Media Use, and Democratic Processes', *'Communication Research'*, 23:179–209.

Melin-Higgins, Margareta (2008) *'Gendered Journalism Cultures. Strategies and tactics in the fields of journalism in Britain and Sweden'*. University of Gothenburg: JMG.

Neveu, Erik (2002) The Local Press and Farmers' Protests in Brittany: proximity and distance in the local newspaper coverage of a social movement, in *'Journalism Studies'* pp. 53–67(15).

Paek, Hye-Jin, Yoon, So-Huyang & Shah, Dahvan V. (2005) Local News, Social Integration and Community Participation. Hierarchical Linear Modeling of Contexual Cross-Level Effects, in *'Journalism & Mass Communication Quaterly'*, 82:3: 587–606.

Pfetsch, Barbara (1998) Government News Management, Graber, McQuail & Norris (eds) *'The Politics of News, The News of Politics'*. Washington: Congressional Quarterly.

Protess, David et al. (1991) *'The Journalism of Outrage'*. New York: The Guilford Press.

Roshco, Bernard (1975): Newsmaking. Chicago: University of Chicago.

Sigal, Leon (1973) *'Reporters and Officials. The Organization and Politics of Newsmaking'*. Lexington, MA: D.C. Heath and Company.

Stamm, Keith R. (1985) *'Newspaper Use and Communities. Toward a Dynamic Theory'*. Norwood, NJ: Ablex Publishing Corporation.

Tichenor, Philip J.; Donohue, George & Olien, Clarice N. (1980): Community Conflict & the Press. London: Sage.

Zucker, Harold G. (1978) 'The Variable Nature of News Media Influence', in Ruben, B. D. (ed.) *'Communication Yearbook 2'*. New Brunswick, NJ: Transaction.

25

JOURNALISM AND CONVERGENCE CULTURE

Mark Deuze

Convergence is not just a buzzword, it is a key identifier of many different trends in today's digital culture. In this chapter, I explore the context and consequences of media convergence for a professional identity of media workers in general, and journalists in particular. In today's digital culture, media work can be seen as a stomping ground for the forces of differentiated production and innovation processes, and the complex interaction and integration between work, life, and play, all of which are expressed in, and are facilitated by, the rapid development of new information and communication technologies. The new human condition, when seen through the lens of those in the forefront of changes in the way work and life are implicated in a participatory media culture, is convergent. This convergence is not just a technological process. Media convergence must also be seen as having a cultural logic of its own, blurring the lines between different channels, forms and formats, between different parts of the media enterprise, between the acts of production and consumption, between making media and using media, and between active or passive spectatorship of mediated culture. Although many of these developments have been addressed in recent scholarship, little theorizing has taken place on the level of the work environment and professional context of journalists, reporters, and editors.

My understanding of convergence in the context of professional media work as used in this chapter is based on the assumption that it contains two interdependent trends at the same time:

- the convergence of media industries, which in journalism means the establishment of multimedia newsrooms and integrated news companies;
- the convergence of media production and consumption, which in journalism refers to the increased use of the citizen-consumer as a source or co-creator of news reports, opinion and analysis.

Together, these trends are part of what Jenkins (2004) has described as the emergence of a "convergence culture", increasingly determining the business policies and managerial processes within the creative industries (Deuze 2007). In what follows, I will outline the basic premise of convergence culture, explore its top down and bottom up manifestations for newswork, and conclude with a discussion on how these developments are articulated with the literature on the professional identity of journalists.

Convergence culture

The ongoing merger of media enterprises as well as between media production and consumption signals the emergence of a global convergence culture, based on an increasingly participatory and interactive engagement between people and their media, within media as a business, as well as between professional and amateur media makers (Jenkins 2006). "Convergence is both a top-down corporate-driven process and a bottom-up consumer-driven process. Media companies are learning how to accelerate the flow of media content across delivery channels to expand revenue opportunities, broaden markets and reinforce viewer commitments. Consumers are learning how to use these different media technologies to bring the flow of media more fully under their control and to interact with other users" (Jenkins 2004: 37). For a holistic understanding of convergence culture it is therefore crucial to see the shift towards multimedia integration next to, and correlated with, the increased inclusion of the consumer in the production and product-innovation process of media companies.

In journalism, convergence culture gets expressed by two interdependent developments affecting life in the newsroom and on the work floor. First, news organizations increasingly shift their formerly distinct operations to more integrated, convergent, or all-in-one multimedia journalism units, where competitor-colleagues are now expected to collaborate in order to produce news across different media channels (print, broadcast, online), formats (information, opinion), and genres (breaking news, feature reporting, blogging, podcasting, and so on). From the bottom up, we see convergence culture occurring by editors of news publications actively considering adding so-called "citizen journalism" to their websites, allowing members of the audience to respond, comment, and submit their own news in text, audio and video (Outing 2005). Of course, citizen journalism takes place on different levels, and efforts to implement user-generated content (UGC) at news organization come in many different shapes and sizes. Two fundamental issues tend to determine the scope and implementation of UGC in professional news organizations (Deuze 2003):

- the balance between *content* and *connectivity* to what extent is UGC considered to *add* to existing, professionally created content (as in: comments, feedback, interaction with editors/reporters, article ratings, such as the *Opinio* site operated by German newspaper *Rheinische Post*), or to function as producing original content next to the materials produced by the newsroom (as in offering citizens blogspace on the company website, such as at *Le Monde* in France or the *Mail & Guardian* in

South Africa), and perhaps even in the workplace of journalists (as in the case of *YouNews* TV in the United States for example);

- a balance between *open* and *closed* news systems: to what extent UGC gets moderated, filtered, edited or otherwise forced through a more or less traditional (that is: centralized and professionally controlled) gatekeeping process rather than what Bruns (2005) has called "gatewatching", where journalists as gatewatchers fundamentally publicize news (by pointing to sources, including material offered by citizens) rather than publish it (by compiling a report from the available sources).

Multimedia news

A structure of convergent multimedia news organizations has been emerging since the mid-1990s, with companies all over the world opting for at least some form of cross-media cooperation or synergy between formerly separate staffers, newsrooms, and departments. According to a survey commissioned by the World Association of Newspapers (WAN) among 200 news executives worldwide in 2001, in almost three-quarters of these companies integration strategies were planned or implemented at that time. Perhaps the pioneering example is US-based Tampa Bay Online (TBO), a convergent news operation combining WFLA-TV (an NBC affiliate station), *The Tampa Tribune*, and a news website that provides original content plus material from print and television. The three media are housed in a special building called The News Center, where the different departments work together through a central multimedia news desk. After a couple of years of planning and development, in 2000 the reporters and editors of all the different media started moving in. Jane Stevens covered the transition for the *Online Journalism Review* and noted (2002) that the gathering of breaking and daily news on all three platforms did not happen "without a lot of angst, complaints, missteps and aggravation. Some employees quit rather than change their way of doing journalism. Many more grumbled and went along. And a few rode the bull into the ring with equal parts fear and exhilaration." The work at the Florida-based news organization is not completely integrated, but rather must be seen as an ongoing process of inter-firm collaborations. Michael Dupagne and Bruce Garrison (2006) for example note that the business and management operations of TBO remain separate, with staffs cooperating rather than working for a single converged organization.

After spending a week at the News Center in 2003, Jane B. Singer (2004) found that although they were not universally enthusiastic, most journalists at TBO perceived convergence as having a number of advantages relative to the long-standing system in which each news organization is independent and, in the case of the newspaper and television station, competitive. At a personal level, the journalists seemed to agree that the ability to work in more than one medium can be seen as a career booster or at least a useful addition to their resumé. William Silcock and Susan Keith (2006) also spent some time interviewing journalists at TBO (in 2002), focusing on the problems and challenges of convergence for everyday news work. One of the issues they found was the lack of a common language in which to discuss, negotiate and carry out more or less integrated news coverage. Instead, the journalists of the different media simply adopted a few words of each other's jargon, with print news workers (of whom there are 300+ in the newsroom on any given day) feeling in particular that they had to learn more about their ten or so colleagues in television than vice versa. "As a result, having a TV journalist write for one of the newspapers usually was, with a few exceptions, considered a waste of resources. So there was little need for TV reporters to learn the lingo of print journalism. However, in cases where print offered a dominant action, print terminology prevailed [...] The few television reporters who did write for print also had to adopt print's style conventions" (2006, p.617).

All the researchers involved in studying and observing the ongoing operations at TBO and other similar convergence journalism ventures around the world note how the biggest obstacles to seamless integration always boil down to cultural clashes. This goes especially for the print reporters, citing their deep distrust of broadcast journalists' work routines, being skeptical about the quality of news work if they are forced to do stand-ups for television or to write blurbs for the Web, and expressing a critical view on the quality and level of experience of their television and online counterparts. On the other side, television people reportedly feel their print colleagues to be conservative, slow, and oblivious to the wants and needs of their audiences (for instance as expressed through market research, sales figures and daily ratings). Killebrew (2004) even reports how news managers charged with implementing the convergence processes often seem unready, skeptical and untrained for the job. These kinds of mutual stereotypes are not just the products of a stressful and confusing convergence experience, but are exponents of the historical separation of different professional identities and work cultures – which also suggests that interpersonal relationships and communication across the different media may resolve some of these clashes. As recently as 2007, TBO.com announced cutting newsroom staff and embracing a more "hyperlocal" style of news coverage, suggesting the use of volunteer citizens (rather than professional correspondents) to report on local news.

Participatory journalism

The rise of what has been most generally described as "citizen journalism" provides a new challenge to a news industry, which in many developed nations faces significant problems. Readership for newspapers and viewership of television news is declining, especially among younger generations (see for the US, Mindich 2005; for The Netherlands: Costera Meijer 2006). The other market news companies serve – advertisers – is also retreating from the field of journalism, gradually shifting its attention to online or non-news channels. These long-term structural trends coincide with two co-determinant developments affecting journalists: a changing nature of work towards increasingly contingent, non-standard and otherwise "atypical" employment (IFJ, 2006); and a steady outsourcing of production work to "produsers" (the consumer-turned-producer) (Bruns 2005) or, as Rosen (2006) states, "the people formerly known as the audience."

Participatory news, citizen media, or what Jarvis (2006) defines as *networked journalism* "takes into account the collaborative nature of journalism now: professionals and amateurs working together to get the real story, linking to each other across brands and old boundaries to share facts, questions, answers, ideas, perspectives. It recognizes the complex relationships that will make news. And it focuses on the process more than the product." In earlier work, *network* journalism has been defined as a convergence between the core competences and functions of journalists and the civic potential of online interactive communication (Bardoel & Deuze 2001). Bardoel and Deuze predicted a new form of journalism that would embrace the previously mentioned cross-media functionality – publishing news across multiple media platforms – as well as an interactive relationship with audiences – acknowledging the lowered threshold for citizens to enter the public sphere. Ultimately, digital and networked journalism in whatever shape or form must be seen as a practice that is not exclusively tied to salaried work or professional institutions anymore.

Participatory journalism is any kind of news work at the hands of professionals and amateurs, of journalists and citizens, and of users and producers benchmarked by what Benkler calls commons-based peer production: "the networked environment makes possible a new modality of organizing production: radically decentralized, collaborative, and nonproprietary; based on sharing resources and outputs among widely distributed, loosely connected individuals who cooperate with each other without relying on either market signals or managerial commands" (2006: 60). Uricchio (2004: 86) describes the key to understanding the new media ecosystem as based on networked technologies that are P2P ("peer-to-peer") in organization and collaborative in principle. As such, an embrace of this networked environment by journalism challenges news organizations to extend the level of their direct engagement with audiences as participants in the processes of gathering, selecting, editing, producing, and communicating news.

Participatory journalism websites initially appeared in direct response to what were perceived as significant shortcomings in mainstream news media coverage – this is true for the rise of *Indymedia* as a means of covering the protests surrounding the 1999 World Trade Organization meeting in Seattle, for the development of *OhmyNews* as an alternative to the highly conservative mainstream press in South Korea (Kahney 2003), as well as for the myriad of news-related blogs in the wider blogosphere. Recent years have seen a further fine-tuning of the various models under which such sites are produced, employing various degrees of balance between enabling the open and direct participation of citizen journalist contributors in publicizing and discussing the news, and some level of editorial oversight by the operators or communities of participatory journalism sites (Deuze, Neuberger & Paulussen 2007). As argued earlier, there are significant differences in approach between the various participatory news formats currently in operation. In spite of the involvement of citizens as contributors, most news organizations retain a degree of conventional editorial control over what is eventually published, while others publish a list of submitted content immediately, or allow registered users to vote on what passes through the publication's gates; similarly, some sites harness their communities as content contributors mainly at the response and discussion stage, while others rely more immediately on users as contributors of original stories.

In online journalism as it is produced by professional/commercial news organizations, initiatives to implement interactive features are increasing – but journalists find it difficult to navigate the challenges this brings to established notions of professional identity and gatekeeping (Chung 2007). Additionally, although people may express a general preference for more interactivity on news websites, when confronted with increasingly elaborate interactive options users seem confused, and indeed are less likely to be able to effectively digest or follow the news on offer (Bucy 2004). It must be clear, then, that a more interactive, dialogical or participatory style of news work is currently very much "under construction"; that it occurs in its most advanced forms on Net-native and generally non-mainstream online platforms; and that more or less traditional makers and users of news are cautiously embracing its potential – an embrace which is not without problems for both the producers and the consumers involved.

Professional identity and convergence culture

The literature on the factors of influence on media production consistently suggests journalists are both "steered" by changing external factors, and "guided" by their own individual, personal particularities (see comprehensive overviews in: Berkowitz 1997; Weaver 1998; Tumber 1999; Loeffelholz 2000). Most authors maintain that the interplay between media organizational and actor variables most powerfully explains the behavior of professional journalists. Yet surveys among journalists in different countries suggest reporters and editors tend to be pluralistic in their self-perceptions, as most journalists see themselves as serving seemingly contradictory functions in society (Deuze 2002). As journalists can be seen both as actors guided by discursive structural factors – society, economy, culture, media system and history – and as influenced by personal characteristics (or subjectivities) – background, upbringing, commitment, involvement, gender, ethnicity, age – the way to analyze the impact of the developments sketched in this essay should take into account the apparent tensions between these principles. One should therefore stress the continuous negotiation between individual and collective level variables as shaping the behavior of "the people behind the keyboards", as van Zoonen puts it (1998: 123). Although Weischenberg for example also acknowledges the relative autonomy of individual news workers, he argues that their actions are to a certain extent shaped by media systemic, organizational and production variables (Weischenberg 1995: 69). Others have argued that all influences from "the outside" on journalists and mass media decision-making are predominantly moderated by self-organization and self-referential processes within journalism (Marcinowski 1993; Huber 1998: 49). The key to understanding this tension between individual and collective-level interpretations in a context of disruptive and technology-driven change, is to look at recent trends in journalism regarding labor relationships.

The production arrangements and management of creativity in the news industry are facilitated by technology. Yet technology is not an independent factor influencing the work of journalists from the outside, but must be seen in terms of its implementation, and therefore how it extends and amplifies previous ways of doing things. "The new technologies make possible changes in news production and news outputs, but there is no reason to expect that the impact of the new technologies will be uniform across all news providers. Rather we might expect to find that there are differing impacts, contingent upon different technological applications which in turn are contingent upon the goals and judgments of executive personnel and any political regulators" (Ursell 2001, p.178). I would like to extend Ursell's argument to include any and all workplace actors in the process of adopting and adapting to (the consequences of) new technologies – including those who do not work physically in the newsroom and who are quickly becoming the majority in the field of news work: freelancers, stringers, correspondents, and other non-permanently employed journalists (see the earlier mentioned 2006 report of the IFJ). Journalists are thus increasingly forced to give meaning to their work and thus construct their own professional identity in the context of rapidly changing and often overlapping work contexts. The impact of convergence culture on the professional identity of journalists therefore should emphasize the continuous negotiation processes going on regarding the individual media actor – a negotiation between the dynamics of the journalist as a person and as a professional, each of which functions with its own characteristics, conditions, perceptions and (thus) factors of influence on news decision-making and media production. In this respect van Zoonen (1998) and others tend to refer to issues of "organizational identity" in journalism, which refers to the agency of journalists as shaped by the constant interplay between structural constraints of the media production process on the one hand, and the influence of a wide array of of subjective personal aspects that journalists bring to the job. Beam (1990) has argued that the process of professionalism in journalism can be defined by looking at the identity of journalists as an organizational-level concept; as in the success of journalists in gaining control over the products and production processes within their organization.

The rich literature on social identity, organizational identity and corporate identity in companies tends to draw distinctions between different levels of analysis: the "individual (relating to people's personal sense of self within the organization), group (relating to the shared identity of teams and sections within an organization), organizational (relating to the identity of the organization as a whole) and cultural (relating to commonalities in identity across organizations and within a society as a whole)" (Cornelissen, Haslam & Balmer 2007: S2-3). A more singular view of professional identity is warranted when assessing contemporary changes and challenges to media work in general and journalism in particular, since it does not assume that a professional is necessarily situated within a given medium-specific organizational context. Such an assumption is hard to maintain in the current context where journalists can be seen as having multiple organizational identities – through working for different realms within one or more organization(s), windowing content cross-media, freelancing or producing content independent from organizational constructs for example as bloggers or copywriters, and not in the least by competing for editorial space with consumers as co-creators of (news) content.

Convergence culture particularly impacts on both sides – structure and subjectivity – of the professional identity of journalists. Elements of structure are the status and protection (by law) of the profession, ethical guidelines of one's organization (if any), budgets, preferred sources (every news organization has its own range of experts), market characteristics, set routines and rituals on the work floor, ownership, and so on. Subjectivities are those things that an individual journalist brings to the job: socio-demographic background, motivation and commitment, family situation, lifecycle, political views, role models, and so on (see Deuze 2002: 41–3). In terms of subjectivities, convergence culture adds a new type of media worker to the agency equation: the "produser" (Bruns 2005). This is someone with whom professionals now have to compete for a chance to create content, and to get the attention of consumers, competitor-colleagues, and advertisers. As the produser is generally someone who does not get paid, and he or she contributes unpredictably (and often using anonymous aliases or avatars), this new entry into the media production sphere is both ubiquitous and imperceptible. On the structural side, convergence culture introduces a constantly changing mix of features, contexts, processes and ideas to the work of individual news workers as their employers, organizations and newsrooms get reshuffled under the managerial impetus of integration and expectation of synergy. This, in combination with changes in (international) media law – making it easier for transnational corporations to own, sell, or integrate their holdings while still controlling all copyrights and intellectual property – and a gradual erosion of union or trade association membership and protection, certainly amplifies the precariousness of media work today (Deuze 2007).

Discussion

The key to understanding the currently evolving and to some extent emergent system of converged and participatory journalism is to see its function as a corrective to traditional or otherwise entrenched notions of what it means to be a journalist. The promises and challenges of a more participatory news gathering and distribution system cannot be understood without factoring the industry side of the equation: the tendency of institutions to adapt to innovation and change in ways to primarily reproduce what came before, and the dominant managerial reply to (real or perceived) economic decline: redistributing risk away from the company (to the employee) and increasing the cost-effectiveness of production away from labor (to the audience). Furthermore, convergence culture and media participation operate in a broader social context of a shift from expert intelligence to collective intelligence (Levy 1997), from solid modernity to liquid modernity (Bauman 2000), and from national/ethnic/religious essentialism to a post-national constellation – all transitions grounded in an increasing impotence of people in their identities as citizens, consumers and workers "to shape their own social environment and [to] develop the capacity for action necessary for such interventions to succeed" (Habermas 2001: p.60). Admittedly, these are general observations that need much more elaboration and detail to be explored effectively. However, such thematic considerations are introduced here to point towards a crucial conclusion: the changes underway in the social, technological and cultural domains of everyday life are beyond anyone's distinct control, yet affect each and every one of us distinctly. In this context, the fundamental role of professional journalism as providing society with some form of social cement, guidance and benchmarks is essential. Overseeing the currently available scholarly evidence on the implications of convergence and participation for the work that reporters and editors do, one could state conclusively that for different reasons their professional autonomy gets significantly undermined. What remains unclear is how increased collaboration with citizen-consumers, or integration with competitor-colleagues, can indeed lead to higher quality journalism. Of course, idealistically, cross-media production and crowd sourcing offer tremendous opportunities for comprehensive and multi-perspectival reporting. Yet, realistically, this is not what tends to happen. Media professionals are more likely to respond nostalgically and defensively to disruptive change, media management tend to interpret such changes primarily in terms of their potential to "depopulate" the profession, and audiences seem to embrace these developments more as a way to bypass and disintermediate journalism altogether rather than as a mechanism to foster closer ties.

Note

The material in this chapter is based on earlier work and published research, in part through collaborations with colleagues Axel Bruns and Christopher Neuberger. An earlier version of this work was published in 2008 as: Deuze, M. 'Professional Identity in a Participatory Media Culture' in: Quandt, Thorsten, Schweiger, Wolfgang (eds), *Journalismus online: Partizipation oder Profession?*, pp.251–262 (Wiesbaden: Verlag für Sozialwissenschaften).

References

Bardoel, Jo, Deuze, Mark (2001) ' Network Journalism': Converging Competencies of Old and New Media Professionals. *Australian Journalism Review* 23(3), pp.91–103.

Bauman, Zygmunt (2000) *Liquid Modernity*. Cambridge: Polity Press.

Beam, Randall (1990) 'Journalism professionalism as an organizational-level concept', *22Journalism Monographs* 121. Columbia: Association for Education in Journalism and Mass Communication.

Benkler, Yochai (2006) *The Wealth of Networks*. New Haven: Yale University Press.

Berkowitz, D. (1997) *The Social Meanings of News*. Thousand Oaks: Sage.

Bruns. Axel (2005) *Gatewatching: Collaborative Online News Production*. New York: Peter Lang.

Bucy, Eric (2004) "The interactivity paradox: closer to the news but confused", in: E. P. Bucy, J. E. Newhagen (Eds.), *Media Access: Social and Psychological Dimensions of New Technology*, pp. 47–72. Mahwah, NJ: Lawrence Erlbaum.

Chung, Deborah Soun (2007). Profits and Perils: Online News Producers' Perceptions of Interactivity and Uses of Interactive Features. *Convergence* 13(1): 43–61.

Cornelissen, Joep P., Haslam, S. Alexander, Balmer, John M.T. (2007) Social Identity, Organizational Identity and Corporate Identity: Towards an Integrated Understanding of Processes, Patternings and Products. *British Journal of Management* 18, S1–S16.

Costera Meijer, Irene (2006) *De toekomst van het nieuws*. Amsterdam: Otto Cramwinckel.

Deuze, Mark (2002) *Journalists in the Netherlands*. Amsterdam: Aksant.

Deuze, Mark (2003) The Web and its Journalisms: Considering the Consequences of Different Types of News Media Online. *New Media & Society* 5(2) 203–230.

Deuze, Mark (2007) *Media Work*. Cambridge: Polity Press.

Deuze, M., Neuberger, C., Paulussen, S. (2004) 'Journalism Education and Online Journalists in Belgium, Germany, and The Netherlands', *Journalism Studies* 5(1) 19–29.

Deuze, M., Bruns, A., Neuberger, C. (2007). Preparing for an Age of Participatory News. *'Journalism Practice'* 1(4), pp.322-338

Dupagne, Michel, Garrison, Bruce (2006) The meaning and influence of convergence: a qualitative case study of newsroom work at the Tampa News Center. *Journalism Studies* 3875 7(2) 237–255.

Habermas, Jurgen (2001) *The Postnational Constellation*. Boston: MIT Press.

Huber, C. (1998) Das Journalismus-Netzwerk. Innsbrueck: Studien-Verlag.

IF J (2006) *The changing nature of work: a global survey and case study of atypical work in the media industry.* International Federation of Journalists research report. URL: http://www.ifj.org/pdfs/ILOReport070606. pdf nstarts0.

Jarvis, Jeff (2006) *Networked Journalism.* Buzzmachine weblog post. URL: http://www.buzzmachine. com/2006/07/05/networked-journalism (accessed 5 July 2006).

Jenkins, Henry (2004) The cultural logic of media convergence. *International Journal of Cultural Studies* 7(1) 33–43.

Jenkins, Henry (2006) *Convergence Culture – Where Old and New Media Collide.* New York: New York University Press.

Kahney, Leander (2003) "Citizen Reporters Make the News", in: *Wired News* 17 May 2003. URL: http:// www.wired.com/news/culture/0,1284,58856,00.html.

Killebrew, Kenneth (2004) *Managing Media Convergence: Pathways to Journalistic Cooperation.* Malden: Blackwell.

Levy, Pierre (1997) *Collective Intelligence: Mankind's Emerging World in Cyberspace.* New York: Perseus.

Loeffelholz, M. (ed.) (2000) Theorien des Journalismus. Opladen: Westdeutscher Verlag.

Marcinowski, F. (1993) Publizistik als autopoietisches System. Opladen: Westdeutscher Verlag.

Mindich, David (2005) *Tuned Out: Why Americans Under 40 Don't Follow the News.* Oxford: Oxford University Press.

Outing, Steve (2005) The 11 Layers of Citizen Journalism. A resource guide to help you figure out how to put this industry trend to work for you and your newsroom. Posted: June 13, 2005. Updated: June 15, 2005. http://www.poynter.org/content/content_view.asp?id=83126 708 (accessed 7 December 2006)

Silcock, William, Keith, Susan (2006) Translating the tower of Babel? Issues of definition, language, and culture in converged newsrooms. *Journalism Studies* 7(4) 610–627.

Singer, J.B. (2004) 'Strange bedfellows: the diffusion of convergence in four news organizations', *Journalism Studies* 5(1) 3–18.

Stevens, J. (2002) TBO.com: Faces of Convergence. *Online Journalism Review*, April 3. URL: http://www. ojr.org/ojr/workplace/10178 58783.php.

Tumber, H. (ed.) (1999) *News: a reader*, Oxford: Oxford University Press.

Uricchio, William (2004). Beyond the great divide: collaborative networks and the challenge to dominant conceptions of creative industries. *International Journal of Cultural Studies* 7(1) 79–90.

Ursell, Gillian (2001) Dumbing down or shaping up? New technologies, new media, new journalism. *Journalism* 2(2) 175–196.

Weaver, D.H. (ed.) (1998). *The Global Journalist: News People Around the World.* Cresskill, New Jersey: Hampton Press.

Weischenberg, S. (1995). Journalistik: Theorie und Praxis aktueller Medienkommunikation. Band 2: Medientechnik, Medien funktionen, Medienakteure. Opladen: Westdeutscher Verlag.

Zoonen, L. van (1998). A professional, unreliable, heroic marionette (M/F): structure, agency and subjectivity in contemporary journalisms. *European Journal of Cultural Studies* 1(1) 123–143.

26

JOURNALISM IN THE NETWORK

Jane B. Singer

Journalists spent much of their first decade online learning to make use of one of the key characteristics of the internet: the fact that it is digital.

Being digital, as Negroponte (1995) put it in the early days of the Web, means all forms of content are just bits and bytes available to be seamlessly combined. For journalists, this creates an ability to accommodate 'multimedia' content – digital text, photos, video, audio, animation and more, blended in ways impossible in any single medium. Producing such content requires new technical and journalistic skills, as well as cultural adaptation. Newsroom processes and perceptions have had to change along with storytelling techniques (Boczkowski 2005; Singer 2004).

Yet, significant and sometimes stressful though it continues to be, that transition is much simpler than the one on which this chapter focuses. Multimedia content draws on complex and perhaps unfamiliar formats, but it still consists of stories produced and controlled by journalists.

In the Web's second decade, a different characteristic of the internet has become central: the fact that it is not just digital but also a network. In a network, all communicators and all communication are connected. The media space and control over what it contains are shared. This means a dramatic conceptual and practical shift for journalists, who face a rapid, radical decline in their power to oversee the information flow (Bruns 2005; Deuze 2005). Professional and cultural consequences are likely to be even more significant than those stemming from the medium's digital nature (Deuze 2007; Robinson 2007; Lowrey 2006).

The following pages briefly highlight three studies of what working in a shared space means for journalists. They offer successively wider scopes, from a national newspaper website, to one with a more global outlook and reach, and finally to a project encompassing two dozen websites in ten countries. Taken together, they indicate that journalists continue to see what they do and how they do it as clearly distinct – and relatively little changed from journalism in a more walled-off past. The chapter concludes with a suggestion about the opportunity that this networked environment offers for fresh thinking about what journalism is and does.

Scotsman.com: Democratic discourse in the 2007 Scottish election

In May 2007, Scotland held only its third national election in modern history. Although part of the United Kingdom, Scotland also has its own national parliament, created in the late 1990s and empowered to set laws governing Scots but not those who live elsewhere in Britain.

In the 2007 election, a big issue was a pledge by the Scottish National Party (SNP) leader that if elected First Minister – which he ultimately was, by a one-seat margin – he would call a national referendum on independence within four years. Users flocked to the shared website of three Edinburgh-based newspapers – *The Scotsman*, *Scotland on Sunday* and the *Edinburgh Evening News* – to talk through the implications. I focused on a section devoted to the election and offering 428 stories in the study period, two months surrounding the May 3 voting day (Singer 2009). Those stories attracted 39,300 comments from every continent except Antarctica.

The study relied on a sample of about 12 percent of the comments. More than 70 percent of these comments came from people claiming to reside in Scotland, and a majority were directly related to the election, politics and civic issues. While SNP and pro-independence voices were dominant, views were expressed from every point along the political spectrum. There were energetic debates about candidate positions, government policy, the viability of splitting from the United Kingdom and more.

How did journalists support, encourage and share in this robust discourse about the future of the country? They didn't. In a total of roughly 4,800 comments in the sample, only two were from newspaper employees. The only other evidence that anyone in the newsroom was even aware that a conversation was going on was the occasional removal of a comment flagged by users as 'unsuitable'. Approximately 1.5 percent of comments in the sample were removed.

The newspapers, then, provided a wide range of election stories that in turn formed the starting point for a robust online conversation, offering evidence of the sort of 'virtual public sphere' (Papacharissi 2002) that scholars have suggested is possible. Thousands of people from all over the world – but, importantly to the national papers, mostly from Scotland – gravitated to the scotsman.com website to form a thriving online community, with the explicit purpose of talking about politics, elections and the country's future. That is what democracy is all about, and the fact that they chose the newspaper site, from among plenty of other options, suggests they still see information provided by the media as central to the process.

But having created the space for that community to exist, the newspapers as an institution then chose to remain outside it. The online activities of journalists and users moved on parallel tracks. Journalists provided the stories, but nothing more. Users provided the commentary, but they talked only amongst themselves. An opportunity for the media company to strengthen its relationship with those users was thus ignored.

Things may be entirely different next time around. Much has changed at *The Scotsman* since this study; the website has a new editor, other new staff, new formats and new approaches. In 2007, though, the papers stuck to their traditional role, staying in a comfort zone that involved seeding the conversation with information –

but then steering clear. Perhaps the political nature of the discourse made journalists uncomfortable. Perhaps they wrote the users off as a pack of rabid nationalists. Perhaps they were just too busy or had no guidance in the task of interacting. Quite likely, all those things and more came into play.

It can be argued that creating separate zones is appropriate. Yet I would suggest that the internet is not an environment that tolerates boundaries of the sort that have become routine in older media. It is a space characterized, again, by interconnections – including between journalists and audiences, who must make mutual adjustments within the space they share.

Guardian.co.uk: Norms and the network

One intriguing aspect of this adjustment to a network is how journalists see it affecting their norms and ethical practices (Hermida and Thurman 2008). Britain's *Guardian* newspaper is especially interesting in this context both because it has been a UK leader in engaging online readers and because of its unusual ownership structure. The *Guardian* is owned by the Scott Trust, which provides an explicitly normative framework for how the paper and its employees are to operate. Comment is free, then-editor CP Scott wrote in 1921, but facts are sacred. He outlined a set of norms to go along with that proposition, including the mandate that the newspaper should be a platform for a diversity of voices to be heard – friends as well as foes.

Current executives love the 'comment is free' mantra so much that they named the main commentary section of their website just that. Comment Is Free, launched in 2006, is home to *Guardian* columnists, commissioned writers and bloggers – and, mostly in the form of comments, to users from all over the world.

Singer and Ashman (2009) talked with 33 *Guardian* journalists, focusing on three key norms:

- *Authenticity*, a set of related constructs centred on credibility;
- *Autonomy*, or journalistic independence;
- *Accountability*, closely akin to responsibility.

Of these, *authenticity* is probably the most complex. For journalists, it seems closely connected with credibility, journalistic authority and accuracy.

Guardian journalists were concerned about user contributions potentially jeopardizing credibility. Interviewees felt that, while they took adequate steps to ensure what they wrote was credible, they could neither assess nor affect the credibility of what users provided. They worried about how such material might reflect on the *Guardian* and on them personally.

Closely connected were concerns about challenges to their authority. Some saw a democratization of discourse as inherently healthy, viewing their own role as enabling robust debate rather than providing what one editor called 'definitive answers'. But others saw a crucial ongoing role for, quoting another editor, 'the expert journalist who can interrogate and understand and all those sorts of things in a way that the citizen reporter just can't'.

Users also confront journalistic authority in a direct way: through personal attacks, disagreement over opinions and disputes about facts.

Personal attacks were both easiest and hardest to deal with. They were easiest because just ignoring them was seen as the optimal response. But they were also hardest because ignoring a personal attack takes a lot of self-restraint – more, some confessed, than they possessed.

Differences of opinion drew mixed reaction. Most journalists said they appreciated cogent disagreement, and several said it nudged them out of complacency. But how the disagreement was expressed mattered. 'When users are just saying "I think this is crap", what can you say to that?' an editor asked. '"Sorry, but I don't"?'

Challenges to factual statements – to journalistic accuracy – generally were valued: interviewees said they were more careful about what they published because they knew they would get publicly slammed if it was wrong. But some veterans expressed concern that users were challenging what one called 'basic assumptions'; responding was tedious and time-consuming. Users do not necessarily see the world in ways that journalists take for granted.

In challenging those basic assumptions, users are taking on professional *autonomy* as well as authority. Hit logs and comment counts show which stories interest users. But most journalists were adamant that such information should not dictate news judgement, both because they feared becoming what one called 'traffic whores' and because they saw a potential threat to the *Guardian* brand. Celebrity gossip and weird animals were OK for the cheesy tabloids, but not for the *Guardian* – no matter how many hits such material might generate.

Our third ethical concept was *accountability*. Interviewees highlighted the quality of the content they provided – 'my responsibility to the community is to put up good quality stuff that is interesting and accurate', one said – and the quality of discourse about that content. 'There's a responsibility to maintain civilized discourse', said another. 'It's a problem for everyone.'

They also felt their willingness to publicly admit they had made a mistake was not just vital but in fact differentiated them from users who had few if any such obligations. 'With citizen journalists, it's all rights and no responsibilities', one writer said. They highlighted attributes such as honesty and transparency in this context. Users expect them to step out from behind their articles in order to discuss and defend their own ideas.

Anonymity also was an issue: users can be anonymous but journalists cannot. In particular, journalists saw anonymity as enabling users to be abusive. 'People feel licensed to say things, in content and style, that they wouldn't own if publishing as themselves', an editor said.

In general, new relationships between users and journalists seemed valuable as an abstract concept but often proved difficult in real life. The open discourse invited by a 'comment is free' philosophy sounds great in theory – all that good democracy-in-action stuff. But the reality was rougher, and many journalists expressed dismay over the disturbingly confrontational nature of user contributions to the conversation.

Unlike the people at *The Scotsman* in 2007, however, these journalists *were* wading into that conversation. Although at the time of this study, the *Guardian* had no set policy for how engagement should work, what seemed to be emerging was a sense that the best approach was essentially a carrot rather than a stick: finding ways to encourage the more cogent contributors rather than trying, futilely, to discourage the hostile ones.

That said, adjusting to life in a network takes time and considerable trial and error, leaving some bruised egos along the way. Journalism is no longer simply about informing or entertaining but also about engaging and interacting with an enormously diverse range of unseen (but not unheard) people. There are strains as longstanding norms related to the exercise of power and control over content are stretched in new directions and as journalists negotiate what one interviewee called the transition from a professional discourse to a far more personal one.

Multi-national perspective: Participatory journalism

The last study involves joint exploration by eight researchers into how leading papers in ten Western democracies are handling user-generated content, and the rationales behind their approaches. It is a rapidly moving topic, with innovations appearing constantly. We started by dividing the process of news production into five stages and looking at how open the stage was to user participation at each newspaper (Domingo et al. 2008):

- *The access or observation stage.* Can users report stories themselves or serve as sources?
- *The selection or filtering stage.* Can users decide what journalists are to cover?
- *The processing or editing stage.* Can users contribute content to the website?
- *The distribution stage.* Can users disseminate stories produced by journalists?
- *The interpretation stage.* Can users discuss journalists' stories after publication?

This last stage is where most of the action was at the time of our content analysis in late 2007 and interviews with editors in 2008. The *Guardian*'s innovations, for instance, were largely at this *interpretation* stage. Indeed, comments are nearly universal; most journalists see them as serving a democratic function and as fitting nicely into the journalistic mission to provide a forum for civic discourse (Glasser 1999). As a Finnish editor put it: 'What could be more proper journalistic work than acting as a medium for social debate?'

On these major newspaper sites, most of that debate is about big national or international topics: war, climate change, immigration. Both the volume and, as at the *Guardian*, the nature of the comments raise issues for editors. 'The problems with forums are the same as with letters to the editor', said a Belgian editor. 'But while we used to receive about 50 letters a day, we now host debates with 5,000 reactions per day'.

One question is whether to pre-moderate the conversation – to read everything before it is published – or publish first and see if anyone objects. The latter option terrified some journalists, such as the German editor who described un-moderated forums as 'like a seven-headed snake that cannot be tamed'. Still, many media organizations are counting on users to help police their own contributions, primarily by flagging problematic posts.

User contributions in other stages were more sporadic during the period of our iterviews, though now increasingly widespread. Can users serve as sources for stories, part of our *access and observation* stage? Yes, journalists did talk about scanning user material and contacting individuals for additional information. But is that giving users more control, or just expanding the journalist's source file? Probably the latter.

Users also can report information, though most of what they report has a personal and/or local focus: my friends, my wedding, my cat. Again, this contrasts with the bulk of user input at the interpretation stage, where discussion centres on national or international topics covered in stories written by journalists. Few users are able to provide first-hand information on those topics. They are, however, able to contribute information that is *not* easily available to the journalists: information close, sometimes very close, to home.

The related *processing and editing* stage, in which users can submit their own items, is another rapidly changing area. National papers are increasingly likely to offer sections of their websites as user publishing platforms, for instance by hosting user blogs. But there are more opportunities to contribute 'news' about topics such as travel destinations – places I visited, restaurants I liked – than to cover events of general civic importance, a core journalistic franchise.

That said, there is a growing trend toward relying on users for local news and sports, a development likely to continue as tools such as Twitter gain popularity. Local residents can cover things the nationals do not have the resources to handle with comparable depth. For the 2008 French municipal elections, for example, lefigaro.fr created 38,000 pages, one for each of the nation's local *communes*. Citizens and candidates contributed, and a series of debates spanning two months became mini-forums for every town in France. Users thus enabled Paris-based *Le Figaro* to cover elections at a hyper-local level – and to compete with the strong regional press on a story normally out of its reach.

User participation also is rapidly increasing in our *distribution* stage. Many newspaper sites offer widgets for recommendation sites such as digg.com, and use of internal recommendation systems is growing. Formatted usage data provide at-a-glance updates about stories that are most popular, most frequently e-mailed or most commented-upon. Newspapers also are developing their presence on social media sites such as Facebook, which enable user communities to form around the media outlet or particular content components.

Our final stage involved *selection* or *filtering*: Can users decide what journalists cover? The answer to date is 'no'. As we saw at the *Guardian*, journalists are very protective of their autonomous news judgement. It is OK for users to comment on what journalists have written or to provide coverage in areas journalists cannot reach. But telling journalists how to do their jobs? No, thanks. That central role of journalists in a traditional media environment – guarding the gate, deciding what is and is not news (Shoemaker 1991) – is one they are not letting go of easily.

For the moment, then, the largest chunk of content from users comes after the fact – comments generated about information gathered, structured and published by journalists. The other stages remain largely controlled by journalists and closed to users, who have little input into determining what is covered and published. While some websites are giving users tools and space to create content, much of it remains in separate 'ring-fenced' areas. Despite exceptions such as our municipal elections example from *Le Figaro*, few of these areas are ones on which the newspaper is staking its own brand or reputation, such as hard national or international news.

In the meantime, users are gaining a louder voice at the hyper-local and hyper-personal level, with contributions about things important to the individual but not a more broadly conceptualized public. This may gratify a user's ego, and it may benefit the newspaper by creating a local presence it otherwise couldn't have. But it is a considerable distance from the 'pro-am' collaboration that some prognosticators have envisioned (Rosen 2008).

Barbarians at the Gate or Liberators in Disguise?

These studies suggest that although much is changing rapidly, many journalists still see users as somewhat akin to invading barbarian hordes. As individual voices separate themselves from the aggregate numbers of a Web 1.0 world, a lot of those voices are proving pretty rowdy. And many that aren't rowdy do not have anything to say that journalists consider especially interesting. Users, it turns out, don't talk the same way or about the same things as journalists.

In theory, most journalists value the presence of more voices in the mix. But coping with the reality is harder than they perhaps envisioned. We're all for an open market-place of ideas when we're the ones selling the goods in that marketplace. A truly open market is scarier. If the gates are open and anyone can enter – anyone can trade in this marketplace – new relationships with different kinds of people will be necessary. We are seeing tentative steps in that direction.

But let me offer a different interpretation: newly opened channels are a tremendous opportunity for journalists and the media industry.

What do reporters and photographers spend way too much time doing? Covering routine meetings, checking police logs, rewriting press releases and maybe covering events those releases announce (Lewis et al. 2008). Such relatively trivial tasks waste journalists' time and their employers' money, not to mention that of their readers.

Users can and should do a great many of those things – with newsroom guidance, perhaps from novice journalists. Media companies have a huge opportunity to free up their expensive resources, the veteran journalists on their staffs, to do what they should be doing, which is what they – and not, by and large, these users – have the time, training and talent to do. Investigating stories that need investigating. Pursuing leads, following up tips and ideas. Telling stories well and fully, in the multiple formats that the digital medium facilitates.

283

Journalists should be providing not just basic information but also the context, the analysis, the explanations and the sense-making that the community or the nation needs to make sound decisions about how it is to work, how it is to move forward, how it is to be governed. That, after all, is what journalism is for in a democracy (Kovach & Rosenstiel 2001).

It is frustrating, to journalists and to readers, to see newspapers filled with unimportant items taken straight from press releases or official pronouncements – and that are old news by the time they appear in print. It is frustrating, too, to know that people who might provide a much more valuable service cannot do so because all their time and energy goes into processing this junk food and feeding it to a beast with multiplying, incessantly demanding mouths: a print mouth, an online one, maybe a mobile one.

Not only do we as members of the public derive little sustenance from these filling but not very nutritious titbits, but media companies don't, either. Revenues are plummeting, as are readerships, ad lineage and stock prices. All are in free fall in America, and heading that way elsewhere. Newsroom staff sizes are following, making it harder still for journalists to continue to focus on quality rather than quantity of output, what Davies (2008) calls 'churnalism'.

Nor is this downturn wholly cyclical in nature. The economy will improve, but the media market will remain irreversibly fluid and fickle, creating unprecedented pressures for a centuries-old revenue model based on advertising. That model requires media companies to deliver to advertisers a stable audience that wants – or at least is willing – to see advertising within a media product. But neither stability nor advertising receptiveness characterise the typical website user. This open, networked environment is well on its way to destroying the industrial-age business model, in which news media stood at a pivotal point on the information conveyor belt.

Media companies must be open to major, not just incremental, change. Amid various desperate efforts, I see only rare glimpses of the one approach that I think will work: recommitting resources to the unique thing these companies can provide better than anyone else.

That unique thing is solid, valuable – difficult and gutsy – journalism.

A business strategy based on this sort of journalism involves considerable risk. Newspapers have been described as simultaneously a traditional enterprise – a mature industry, producing and delivering information as they have done for centuries – and an innovative enterprise, an emerging industry needing and trying to do something new, or at least to do it in new ways (Rosenstiel 2007). It is hard to succeed at both at the same time. A mature industry requires different approaches, behaviours and world views from an emerging one. But some degree of risk tolerance is necessary by media managers and, importantly, by shareholders whose newspaper stock once consistently delivered a safe, and high, return.

I believe recommitting to journalism is potentially profitable – though less so than the old newspaper business was. But then, 30 percent profit margins are gone anyway, and I do not think they will come back when the overall economy recovers. The journalism I am talking about is not cheap to produce. Good journalists, unlike bloggers or users, don't work for free. Besides, this kind of journalism is likely to appeal to a smaller audience than the truly massive one of a traditional, limited media environment. But that smaller audience is likely to be relatively loyal, relatively well-educated and with relatively decent money to spend on the newspaper and on advertiser offerings.

Of course, many people love fast food, in news as at mealtimes. But again, here's where the user contributions come in. Users can take on a huge chunk of what is now the journalist's workload and beef up the media outlet's website with it, creating a portal for both the strong journalism and the press releases, as well as the hyper-local, hyper-personal content they are already beginning to provide. Users can contribute to timely spot news, event listings and coverage, much of the sports (including youth events), traffic and weather reports, and celebrity spottings. The basic crime stories? The police can provide most of them – as they do now, but through the media. The upbeat business stories that make advertisers smile? Press releases – same as now. The local council meetings? City councils have their own websites anyway, not to mention their own PR spokespeople.

Even better, users will provide that information for free. Create a space that feels like a community, and people will want to belong. Give those with an agenda a place to promote it, and they will. What's wrong with that? Nothing, as long as the source is clearly labelled – which, at the moment, the press releases that too often run almost verbatim are not.

All this content currently is costing media outlets money because they are paying journalists to churn it out. A rethink is needed about what they bring to the party and, more fundamentally, what the job of the journalist is all about.

The journalist's job is to keep the cops and the councillors honest. The journalist's job is to look out for the consumer who will frequent those businesses. The journalist's job is to keep an eye on all those volunteer sources, too, because while a few may be a bit unhinged, others are not only sane but actually know what they're talking about. Those in the second category provide a readily accessible database of fresh sources to supplement the old standbys. Importantly, including them also enables people to feel a part of media investigations that benefit them and their neighbours.

So yes, I do see this growth in user-generated content not just as a democratic vehicle but also as a practical opportunity on two fronts. The first is that, again, these are people who can take on mundane parts of the journalist's job that currently waste the most precious resource: the human beings in the newsrooms. The second is that it offers innumerable ways to bring new voices into journalists' work, from using them as sources to incorporating their contributions, including multimedia ones, in larger stories that reporters are pursuing. Users even can work collaboratively with journalists on 'crowd-sourced' investigations.

If Web 2.0 is about social networks and about the power of ubiquitous communication and connection, then Web 3.0 will be about cutting through the clutter. The medium's next iteration will emphasize the tools, processes and people to help us grasp what is meaningful, important and trustworthy amid all the noise (Jensen 2007). That sounds to me like the job of a journalist in the network that we all inhabit.

Note

Material in this chapter derives from the author's presentation at 'Journalismo: Mudanças na Profissão, Mudanças na Formação', a symposium held at the Universidade do Minho in Braga, Portugal, in September 2008. A version of the presentation appears in the proceedings, published online at URL TK (http://www.lasics.uminho. pt./ojs/index.php/jornalism08).

References

Boczkowski, Pablo J. (2005) *Digitizing the News: Innovation in Online Newspapers*. Cambridge, MA: MIT Press.

Bruns, Axel (2005) *Gatewatching: Collaborative Online News Production*. New York; Peter Lang.

Davies, Nick (2008) *Flat Earth News*. London: Chatto & Windus.

Deuze, Mark (2005) 'What is Journalism? Professional Identity and Ideology of Journalists Reconsidered', *Journalism* 6 (4): 442–464.

Deuze, Mark (2007) *Media Work*. Boston: Polity.

Domingo, David, Thorsten Quandt, Ari Heinonen, Steve Paulussen, Jane B. Singer and Marina Vujnovic (2008) 'Participatory Journalism Practices in the Media and Beyond: An International Comparative Study of Initiatives in Online Newspapers', *Journalism Practice* 2 (3): 326–342.

Glasser, Theodore Lewis (1999) *The Idea of Public Journalism*. New York: Guilford Press.

Hermida, Alfred and Neil Thurman (2008) 'A Clash of Cultures: The Integration of User-Generated Content within Professional Journalistic Frameworks at British Newspaper Websites', *Journalism Practice* 2 (3): 343–358.

Jensen, Michael (2007, June 15) 'The New Metrics of Scholarly Authority', *The Chronicle of Higher Education* 53 (41): B6.

Kovach, Bill and Tom Rosenstiel (2001) *The Elements of Journalism: What Newspeople Should Know and the Public Should Expect*. New York: Crown Books.

Lewis, Justin, Andrew Williams, Bob Franklin, James Thomas and Nick Mosdell (2008) 'The Quality and Independence of British Journalism: Tracking the Changes over 20 Years', report prepared for MediaWise: Journalism and Public Trust Project. Accessed 2 November 2008 from: http://www.mediawise. org.uk/display_page.php?id=999

Lowrey, Wilson (2006) 'Mapping the Journalism-Blogging Relationship', *Journalism* 7 (4): 477–500.

Negroponte, Nicholas (1995) *Being Digital*. New York: Vintage Books.

Papacharissi, Zizi (2002) 'The Virtual Sphere: The Internet as a Public Sphere', *New Media & Society* 4 (1): 9–27.

Robinson, Sue (2007) '"Someone's Gotta Be in Control Here": The Institutionalization of Online News and the Creation of a Shared Journalistic Authority', *Journalism Practice* 1 (3): 305–321.

Rosen, Jay (2008, 14 July) 'A Most Useful Definition of Citizen Journalism', PressThink. Accessed 3 October 2008 from: http://journalism.nyu.edu/pubzone/weblogs/pressthink/ 2008/07/14/a_most_ useful_d.html

Rosenstiel, Tom (2007, August) 'The Future of News', panel discussion, annual convention of the Association for Education in Journalism and Mass Communication; Washington, DC.

Shoemaker, Pamela J. (1991) *Gatekeeping*. Thousand Oaks: Sage.

Singer, Jane B. (2004) 'More Than Ink-Stained Wretches: The Resocialization of Print Journalists in Converged Newsrooms', *Journalism & Mass Communication Quarterly* 81 (4): 838–856.

Singer, Jane B. (2008) 'Hearts in the Highlands, Fingers on the Keys: Online Discourse and the 2007 Scottish Elections', paper presented to the annual convention of the International Communication Association; Montreal.

Singer, Jane B. and Ian Ashman (2009) '"Comment Is Free, but Facts Are Sacred": User-Generated Content and Ethical Constructs at the *Guardian*'. *Journal of Mass Media Ethics* 24 (1):3–21.

PART IV

TRUTHS, FACTS AND VALUES

27

NEWS AS CULTURE

James S. Ettema

News is a cultural form no less than it is an organizational product, an economic commodity or a political institution. Summarizing the role of culture in the making of news, Michael Schudson (2007: 254) wrote that 'journalists handle the anarchy of events by depending on available cultural resources, the treasure house of tropes, narrative forms, resonant mythic forms and frames of their culture. They assimilate the new, apparently novel, unique, unprecedented event to the familiar old ways of understanding the world.' To Schudson's list of cultural resources we must certainly add the concepts of media ritual and public memory. The goal of this chapter, however, is not to log a comprehensive inventory of the cultural resources employed by journalists but rather to highlight a few of the key issues encountered in the scholarship on news as a cultural form.

The culturological approach, as Schudson (1989) once tagged the perspective on news taken here, is now common in journalism studies. James W. Carey's call for a ritual view of communication which has been particularly influential among scholars in the United States has helped motivate development of theoretical alternatives to the transmission view that emphasizes the social psychology of media effects. 'If the archetypal case of communication under a transmission view is the extension of messages across geography for the purpose of control,' Carey wrote (1989 [1975]: 18), 'the archetypal case under a ritual view is the sacred ceremony that draws persons together in fellowship and communality.' A generation of scholars has both elaborated and critiqued this Durkheimian-inflected celebration of 'communion, community, and communication.' The result is a theoretically sophisticated body of literature that simultaneously challenges and complements media effects research. Of course this is not say that all – or for that matter *any* – of the key conceptual issues are settled. Indeed this scholarship can be characterized in terms of interlocking conceptual tensions with which cultural and critical analysts of journalism must grapple. We begin with the notion of 'cultural resources' itself which, given its emphasis on maintenance of society in time, stands in tension with processes of cultural and social change. This, in turn, suggests other tensions to be explored such as the universally human versus the politically contingent.

Cultural resources/cultural processes

In his important book *Daily News, Eternal Stories* Jack Lule (2001) captured the sense of culture as a vast store of materials from which journalists may acquire tropes, forms and frames to employ in their reports on current events. He began with an anecdote from his own reporting career as he struggled with an assignment for a Sunday magazine feature about how a murder victim sparked an urban neighborhood to take action against drug traffickers. After considering the facts of the case and the problem of making those facts interesting to the million or more readers in the city and suburbs, the reporter realized that the facts did indeed lend themselves to a certain kind of *story*. And in telling that story, as he later came to understand, he drew upon an archetype: 'unheralded in life, sanctified in death, an innocent victim whose sacrifice and death brought a people together' (p. 13). An implication of this account is that even scholars who understand the meaning of journalism primarily in terms of organizational, political or economic processes, must acknowledge that, in cultural terms, 'reporters and editors draw upon a fundamental story of earthly existence, a universal and shared story of mankind' in the course of enacting those processes (p. 18).

Lule's approach comports well with Ann Swidler's (1986: 273) 'image of culture as a "tool kit" of symbols, stories, rituals, and world-views, which people may use in varying configurations to solve different kinds of problems' thereby contributing to the 'strategies of action' by which groups and individuals pursue their goals. Swidler's emphasis on human agency reminds us, however, that those 'familiar old ways of understanding the world,' noted by Schudson, are often radically revised in the on-going course of human affairs, particularly in unsettled times when established relationships and longstanding goals may be overturned as new meaning systems, whether political or religious, emerge to organize action. In such times, Swidler argued, 'People developing new strategies of action depend on cultural models to learn styles of self, relationship, cooperation, authority ...' (p. 279). And in such times cultural systems are often highly coherent (i.e. explicitly ideological), she concluded, because 'they must battle to dominate the world views, assumptions, and habits of their members.' Culture therefore offers not merely a set of resources in the form of well-worn tools for story-telling but procedures for *re-tooling* strategies of action.

An instructive example comes from Serbian public discourse with regard to the status of Kosovo. Of the very unsettled period in 2006, Erjavec and Volčič (2007: 67) observed that 'newspapers continuously reproduce the dominant Serbian nationalism that focuses on the myth of Greater Serbia.' Among elements of the myth re-tooled for a new political application was the conception of Kosovo as the 'Serbian Jerusalem' that invoked the cultural memory of the battle between Serbs and Turks fought in 1389. This, in turn, framed Serbia as the ancient defender of Europe and Christendom and by metonymic extension as a contemporary warrior against terrorism and crime. 'From the past discourses,' the authors concluded, 'the newspapers have reproduced a particular type of religious discourse, and they have borrowed a European war on terrorism and crime discourse, and appropriated them both into the Serbian national political context' (p. 81). These acts of ideological appropriation – 'recontextualization' in Fairclough's (2003) terms – nicely illustrate Mihai Coman's (2005: 54) contention that even though myth (and ritual too) have atrophied in complex societies the on-going processes of mythification (and ritualization) continue to push media accounts of current events, especially crises, toward 'epic constructions that, though permanently unstable, provide accessible systems of interpretation.'

Media text/public performance

The mention of ritual together with myth points to another crucial analytic tension. With the conceptualization of news as culture in recent years, the work of journalists has quickly come to be understood not merely as stimuli for media effects but as textual and visual artifacts in which bits and pieces of myth can be identified. More difficult to grasp, however, has been the role of news and informational media as a venue for performance of socially sanctioned rituals. Indeed Carey's essay articulating a ritual view of communication seemed to emphasize reception of text by readers more than performance in, or by, media. Newspaper reading is a ritual much like the Mass, he argued (1989: 20), because it is 'a situation in which nothing new is learned but in which a particular view of the world is portrayed and confirmed.' With the publication of Daniel Dayan and Elihu Katz's landmark book *Media Events: The Live Broadcast History* (1992), however, efforts to theorize mass-mediated rituals as *performances* were moved to intellectual center stage. And there they remain. Dayan and Katz defined media events as preplanned but live broadcasts such as major sporting contests that do not merely present the event but rather re-imagine it in a form that could not exist without electronic media. 'Instead of a pale equivalent of the ceremonial experience,' wrote Dayan and Katz, such ritual 'offers the "uniquely televisual experience of not being there"' (1992: 100). Television thus offers viewers new modes of contact with the 'ceremonial center' where they may join the like-minded community of believers in a reaffirmation of shared meanings and values.

Despite Dayan and Katz's compelling analysis of live performance, the notion of mass-mediated ritual is still often understood as media production and audience reception of texts rather than as public performance. For example Carolyn Kitch (2003: 214) averred that in the wake of the terrorist attacks in New York and Washington the American news media covered religious ceremonies and sentiments but also 'themselves *enacted* such ceremonies and expressed such sentiments.' She characterized news weeklies as conducting 'a public funeral ceremony conforming to what anthropologists identify as the three stages of "transition rituals": separation, transformation (or liminality), and aggregation' (p. 215). Along with other national media, news magazines 'allowed their audiences to witness the scenes of disaster, to hear survivors' testimony and leaders' consolation, and to see their own representation as mourners.' But more than presiding at the burial of the dead, journalists helped transform and re-aggregate American society, Kitch concluded (p. 222), with a narrative that ultimately 'was not one of terror, death, and destruction but one of courage, redemption and patriotic pride.'

To raise the question of whether this 'enactment' qualifies as a funeral or more generally as a ritual performance is certainly not to deny the cultural moorings of such richly narrativized reporting. In another article Kitch (2002) found that since the 'real world' mourning rituals for John F. Kennedy Jr., unlike his father, were minimal (a private memorial and scattering of ashes at sea) the news media had a relatively blank slate upon which to devise an elegiac liturgy. 'From the beginning he belonged to us,' wrote *People Weekly* (cited in Kitch 2002: 300). 'It was terribly important that he be adventurous and modest and funny and self-deprecating and charitable to strangers and graceful and full of life, and we believed he was, and never cared to hear otherwise,' stated a well known writer in *Time*. 'He was what we needed him to be' (cited in Kitch 2002: 304). From passages such as these Kitch concluded, 'Given his chronological position in the Kennedy family story and in American history, JFK Jr. symbolized a collective sense of something lost in the late twentieth century as well as something that might have been, and still might be, gained in the twenty-first century' (p. 304). Even if these stories taken together do not constitute a ritual performance, the argument that at least they affirm values and promote social solidarity certainly remains plausible. And even if not fully a ritual, this journalism none the less responds to the constant tug of both mass-mediated mythification and ritualization.

Solidarity and continuity/conflict and change

Most analysts agree that ritual requires the coordinated engagement of audiences and elites, if not entire institutions, in formalized sequences of actions. Rituals are always more than they seem to the uninitiated in that they invoke transcendent values – 'the serious life' in Eric Rothenbuhler's (1998) phrase. But rituals are always more than private thoughts or feelings; they are public enactments. Rituals do necessarily express 'a hidden essence in which the performers explicitly believe,' as Nick Couldry argued (2003: 24). Indeed, 'rituals by their repetitive form reproduce categories and patterns of thought in a way that bypasses explicit belief.' A highly charged example of this paradox is offered in Carolyn Marvin and David W. Ingle's book *Blood Sacrifice and the Nation* (1999) which maintains that nationhood is constituted less in texts as some would maintain than in the memory of blood sacrifice. 'At the behest of the group, the lifeblood of community members must be shed,' the authors argued (1999: 4). 'Group solidarity, or sentiment, flows from the value of this sacrifice.' Blood sacrifice is not only made necessary by attack from the outside but is actually desired by the group within because it is the process that assures the 'construction of the social out of the flesh and blood of the group members' (p. 7). Thus the group seeks the death of its members even as it denies doing so. While the nation may experience dread at this taking of life the effect is to direct violence outward from the generative center of the community to its borders. 'Renouncing blood lust,' Marvin and Ingle wrote, 'convinces us we deplore violence so that our embrace of some future call for blood will seem both necessary and exceptional. We have not wished for the death of our own; we have resisted it to the last' (p. 154).

From classical poets to cable news, 'the media' have been instrumental to the articulation and perpetuation of memorials to blood sacrifice. Thus Marvin and Ingle's work can be read as an account of mediated rituals that fulfill the function not merely affirming but actually creating the social center and defining the perimeter. But this, it turns out, is exactly what Couldry (2003) argued media rituals do not do. For him the notion of any such center in contemporary society is itself a media myth. He defined 'the myth of the mediated centre' as the belief that 'there is a centre to the social world, and that, in some sense, the media speaks "for" that centre' (p. 2). The argument turns on the idea that social order has been radically destabilized although the desire to believe in order or at least its possibility remains strong. In a critique of Dayan and Katz, Couldry concluded, 'Once we drop the assumption that society has a core of "true" social values waiting to be "expressed," then we are free to reread contemporary processes of social and cultural definition for the open-ended conflicts that they really are' (p. 42).

The implication of this position is that no real generative center can be defined by blood and no basic order is maintained by sacrifice. Thus no deep truths exist to be revealed by or about blood sacrifice or any other ritual. There are, however, institutions of power and sites of conflict in which mediated rituals are implicated. 'The media do not act alone in the performance of political ritual but in concert with other political and social institutions,' wrote Phillip Elliot (1982: 606). 'Concert suggests harmony and this appears to be the more usual case but discordant press reporting may also be one of the instigators of ritual performance by other institutions.' This observation served as the point of departure for my own case study (Ettema 1990) of discordant press reporting that provoked a series of public rituals (e.g. public apologia and other attempts at closure) all structured by Turner's (1969) social drama sequence of breach, crisis, redress and reintegration (or separation). These events, I argued, 'show us how social life – complete with its grinding contradictions as well as its orderly sequences – can be produced within and through the process of mass-mediated ritual' (p. 328). Couldry (2003: 37) nicely captured this solidarity/conflict tension by posing a 'choice to be made between seeing rituals as the expression of something permanent and universal and seeing them as the articulation of contingent and historically specific (even if persistent) patterns of power.' And this passage nicely segues into the discussion of another tension – or perhaps another perspective on the same tension.

Universally human/politically contingent

Analysts who view news as culture are always on the watch for 'signs of the eruption of another story through the text of an existing one,' observed Robert Manoff (1986: 225). Similarly for Coman (2005: 114) the aim is to 'find the hidden text, the (narrative and possibly mythic) schema over which the various accounts of a particular event were built (independent of the journalist's immediate intentions).' It is easily supposed that such narrative and possibly mythic schemas, in Lule's terms (2001: 18), tell a 'fundamental story of earthly existence, a universal and shared story of mankind.' Broadcast coverage of air crashes, for example, can be read as a meditation on 'the role of fate in our lives ... which remains one of the eternal questions of human existence,' according to Vincent, Crow and Davis (1989: 15). Although no one is beyond the reach of the fate, the progression of the story – the retrieval of the 'black box' data recorder, the announcement of a technical explanation, the close of the investigation – offers reassurance that the disaster was, after all, 'an isolated, random instance of fate intervening in daily life and not evidence of a systematic spreading breakdown in technology (or society, or nature) which is likely to tragically disrupt the lives of average viewers' (p. 23). Thus the eternal and mythic are at the service of the contemporary and socio-political.

To qualify as mythic, however, narratives need not lay claim to the universal and eternal. This is demonstrated in Richard Campbell's (1987) analysis of the long running and highly rated American television series, 60 Minutes. Campbell described the program with its mix of investigative reporting, celebrity interviews and other features as 'a myth maker' (p. 326). The investigative segments typically follow the genre conventions of such reporting by narrating the travails of one or more sympathetic victims who have been wronged by a socio-political system in disarray (see Ettema and Glasser, 1998). In these segments, according to Campbell, 'The reporter receives metaphoric status as a heroic detective who champions Middle American individualism and integrity in the face of heartless bureaucracy' (1987: 333.) Thus the honor-bound hero affirms the distinctly, if not uniquely, American core value of individualism. Campbell seems to have anticipated Couldry's arguments when he underscored 'the formulaic and metaphoric power of news to provide a *center*, a cultural forum for discussion, that transforms complexity and contradiction through the narrative process' (p. 346). While he went on to note the economic value to CBS Television of that formulaic and metaphoric power, he also suggested that the 'center' generated by that power is, in some sense, real rather than imagined as Couldry would argue. Indeed Campbell concludes that within this television program Americans can 'discover once again *who we are*' (p. 347, emphasis in original).

Whatever the center is taken to be, for Campbell 60 Minutes provides an American – not a universal – center. If, as analysts of news-as-culture, we are dealing with historically contingent rather than essentially human meanings and values then we should inquire further about when and how that treasure house of tropes, forms and frames is restocked with cultural valuables. Erjavec and Volčič's (2007) analysis of Serbian discourse about Kosovo illustrates well that the answer must include the ability of powerful economic and political institutions to secure the resources and manage the processes needed to execute their strategies of action. As scholars of cultural memory maintain, remembered narratives are always open to revision and re-use – although, as Schudson (1992) maintained, not entirely open. Moreover, as researchers of media frames recognize, strategies of action are likely to entail the direction of public attention toward certain meanings and values and away from others. In another example from Kitch's (Kitch & Hume 2008) work, she found that coverage of a mine disaster became an ode to working class perseverance rather than the obvious story about mine safety. Similarly Barbara Barnett's (2006) analysis of reporting on mothers who killed their children revealed the social construction of '"bad" and "mad" mothers' (p. 417). Her interest was in all the issues *not raised* by journalists due to the public's fascination with these Dark Others of Lule's archetypal Good Mother. Such issues might include postpartum psychosis, teen pregnancy and spouse abuse. '[C]asting mothers who kill their children as insane or evil was a narrative device that helped journalists simplify their stories,' Barnett concludes (p. 425). 'However, demonization allowed reporters to ignore a central paradox in western culture: we idealize motherhood but offer little social support for women engaged in the day-to-day tasks of child care.' In this instance, apparently, the glittering treasures of culture have blinded the journalistic eye.

Form of the content/content of the form

Historiographer Hayden White (1978) maintained that human events do not, in themselves, constitute coherent stories. He identified 'two levels of interpretation in every historical work: one in which the historian constitutes a story out of the chronicle of events and another in which, by a more fundamental narrative technique, [the historian] progressively identifies the kind of story he is telling – comedy, tragedy, romance, epic or satire as the case might be' (p. 59). White went on to argue, 'It would be on the second level of interpretation that the mythic consciousness would operate most clearly.' That is to say, culture provides story forms within which events can be organized, recounted and understood. 'News in a newspaper or on television has a relationship to the "real world," not only in content but in form;' wrote Schudson (1995: 54) applying this insight to journalism, 'that is, in the way the world is incorporated into unquestioned and unnoticed conventions of narration, and then transfigured, no longer a subject for discussion but a premise of any conversation at all.' From this perspective Ettema and Glasser (1998) examined the discursive strategies employed by investigative reporters to define the guilt of villains and the (relative) innocence of their victims within a melodramatic narrative that is part tragedy and part ironic satire of bureaucratic failure and hypocrisy. In this application irony incorporates the facts into unquestioned premises by appropriating the forms of objective journalism for purposes of moral condemnation. Irony, we argued, 'does not merely operate within the constraints imposed by the conventions of journalistic objectivity; it *transfigures* those conventions into a moralistic vocabulary for condemnation of the villains to whom we have foolishly entrusted our public affairs' (p. 87).

And yet limits do exist on the freedom of 'mythic consciousness' to impose form on content. Schudson (2007) took to task the idea that the relationship between form and content is largely a matter of journalistic free choice in his critique of an author who characterized Al Qaeda's attack on New York and Washington as, in his paraphrasing, 'an entirely neutral or ambiguous event that Fox News prematurely turned to melodrama' (p. 255). Schudson's contention was that news cannot be fully tamed by culturally-given forms because, according to bumper sticker wisdom, 'shit happens' and that makes news less subject to the discipline of government or marketplace. 'Because shit happens, journalists gain some freedom from official opinion, professional routines, and conventional wisdom,' he wrote (p. 254). 'Journalists make their own stories but not from materials they have personally selected. Materials are thrust upon them.' But as noted at the very beginning of this chapter, Schudson did recognize that journalists 'make choices from a variety of narrative forms and conventions.' He did not attempt to resolve the tension between form and content, concluding only, 'The next question is to understand how they make these choices' (p. 257).

In some situations such as the coronations and contests studied by Dayan and Katz the connection between form and content does seem rather closely coupled. Here rituals provide well established molds into which specific visual and verbal content can be poured. For other events the connection may not be a necessary one but none the less strongly implied. The 'horse race' coverage of American electoral campaigns, a framework for choosing and organizing facts that emphasizes strategy over policy, comes readily to mind. Referring to this form of journalism as the 'strategic frame' Jamieson and Waldman (2003: 168) argued that a consequence of the form is the cynical implication that 'the substance of a speech or a policy is less important for citizens to know than the real (strategic) motive behind it.' This strategic frame is actually a meta-frame within which various tropes and narratives can be deployed. The *New York Times*, for example, reviewed the doomed struggle of John McCain's 2008 US presidential campaign in terms of what it took to be a progression of 'backfiring narratives' including 'Country First Deal Maker vs. the Nonpartisan Pretender' and 'The Team of Mavericks vs. Old-Style Washington' (Draper 2008: 57–8). This article was, then, the narrativization of failed narratives.

For still other events, such as those covered in Lule's feature reporting, journalists may have still more discretion in choosing the archetypes and other cultural resources used to form the facts into a story. All of these examples, however, demonstrate that form itself does convey meaning with regard to such considerations as agency, coherence, causality and closure. Indeed the mere presence of the media, especially television, conveys meaning in such situations as those characterized by Leibes (1998) as 'disaster marathons.' (See also Zelizer and Allan 2002.) Reviewing several instances of crisis journalism on Swedish television Riegert and Olsson (2007: 150) observed that 'the way the media performs will be part of the way audiences remember the event itself.' Moreover news managers are quite aware of this as they make 'decisions during these crises in terms of "being there," reassuring audiences and helping to "work through" events.'

As Riegert and Olsson's analysis suggests the formal features of news, as much as (or more than) its content, are a source of whatever socio-cultural authority that journalism retains. Continuous live coverage, according to one news manager they interviewed, is important as a way of 'demonstrating one's respect for the impact of the event.' Another manager said simply, '[T]here is the need just to be present for the audience' (p. 153). But even this mere presence can bear insidious as well as comforting meanings. Examining television coverage of the violent events in 1992 that followed the not-guilty verdict in the trial of police officers who beat Los Angeles motorist Rodney King, John Thornton Caldwell (1995) analyzed such mundane formal features as split screen images. In one instance King's attorney paraphrases his client's now-famous plea for everyone to 'just get along' as another image is juxtaposed. Of this image Caldwell observed: 'Even as the audience hears and views these pleas screen-right, the left side of the screen simultaneously shows armed Army National Guard troops storming off the back of a military truck in South Central [Los Angeles]' (pp. 313–14). He concluded of this visual editorializing that what was 'dangerous in televisuality's crisis management during the rebellion was not its high-tech stylization of the event, but rather the use of those modes to bolster old-style class and racial politics' (p. 334).

Framing as schematization/framing as categorization

Mapping an answer to the question posed by Schudson about how journalists make the choices that they do compasses a vast conceptual territory in which the idea of framing is a prominent landmark. Understood as a process in which cognition engages culture and vice versa, framing accomplishes at least two basic tasks. One such task can be metaphorically characterized as the framing of a building under construction. That is to say, framing organizes the facts into a meaningful conceptual structure such as a recognizable sequence of events that emphasizes agents, motives and contexts as well as actions. An especially important conceptual structure can be called 'the social problem schema' which entails problem, cause, responsible agent and proposed solution. Robert Entman has incorporated this conception into a definition that serves as the default meaning of framing in journalism studies. 'To frame,' he wrote (Entman 1993: 52), 'is to select some aspects of perceived reality and make them more salient in a communicating text in such a way as to promote a particular problem definition, causal interpretation, moral evaluation and/or treatment recommendation.' The social problem schema, however, is not the only schema to be found in that treasure house of culture. Some others presented in their simplest – that is to say, in the most schematic – terms include the Manichean struggle of good and evil evoked in wartime, tribulation and triumph often evoked for reporting natural disasters, hubris and comeuppance which is the essential mechanism of situational irony, as well as action and reaction which is the fundamental schema of journalistic balance. Of course not all schemata are reducible to neat pairs as demonstrated by Turner's four-phase social drama paradigm or the three-phase mourning process observed by Kitch. So central are schema to human thought that Paul DiMaggio (1997: 272) has argued that 'it may be useful to treat schema as a basic unit of analysis for the study of culture.'

Among the schematic pairs enumerated above, good/evil and its variants (right/wrong, sacred/profane, us/them) is perhaps more commonly understood as a set of social classifications or categories rather than as a rudimentary narrative structure. This, in turn, points to another essential task of the framing process: the classification of social actors and actions through the rendering of some facts about them more salient than others. In Entman's (1993: 54) terms, 'frames exert their power through the selective description and omission of the features of a situation.' A well-studied example is categorization of politically engaged groups as 'radicals' which is a label, according to Boyle and colleagues (2005: 638), that translates into either less media attention ('selection bias') or harsher attention ('description bias'). Entman (2004) provides a brilliant example of this metaphorical framing of the moving images created by newsworthy events in his analysis of reporting on the intentional, if mistaken, destruction of two airliners in mid-flight. One was a South Korean plane shot down by the Soviet Union; the other an Iranian plane shot down by the United States. In the pages of US newspapers and magazines the former event was typically framed as an 'attack' while the latter was a 'tragedy' (p. 40). This, together with the greater attention to the victims on the South Korean plane, Entman argued, helped classify one incident as a moral outrage and the other as merely a technical problem. A system of categories need not be limited to pairs, of course, but anthropologists, cultural sociologists and literary theorists would certainly recognize the cultural ubiquity of such binary opposi-tions. Post-structuralism has taught us that these oppositions are socially constructed rather than essentially human. But whatever their ontology they are central to the culturally-sanctioned common sense upon which journalism depends.

The social/the cultural: a conclusion

The first conceptual tension reviewed above – cultural resources/cultural processes – raises the most fundamental issue for scholarship on news-as-culture. With a few exceptions such as the major works on media ritual, the relationship between culture and journalism is theorized too often and too simplistically as merely an array of object-like cultural conceptions – narrative structures, archetypal figures, metaphoric images, and so on. To transcend (but incorporate) the cultural treasure house notion of news-as-culture, journalism studies might well pursue Coman's argument that, even if myth and ritual now survive in only a withered state, the processes of *mythification* and *ritualization* are still at work in a range of media forms including news. To these we might add a process of *narrativization*. As noted above not all narrative is mythic, but the public casting up of events and experiences in story form is evermore pervasive in the digital and multichannel media environment. We can also add *recontextualization* and public *memorialization* as well as *schematization* and *categorization* (i.e. framing as formulated above).

The analysis of these processes can contribute importantly to an understanding of the master process of *mediation*. Drawing upon Silverstone (2005), Couldry (2008) formulates mediation as the dialectical process involving media and other powerful institutions by which social and cultural environments are constantly shaped as these institutions react and adjust, each to the others. The analysis of news-as-culture adds still more complexity to the concept by insisting that the cultural environment is itself constitutive of, as well as a response to, mediation. Citing Geertz (1973), anthro-pologist Sherri Ortner (2006: 15) observes that 'without culture – external systems of symbols and meanings – people would not be able to think at all.' And yet cultural systems can be reshaped, as Swidler would certainly agree, just as social structures can be. Indeed, as Ortner argues, the latter requires the former. '[S]ocial transformation works in part through the constant production, contestation, and transformation of public culture, of media and other representations of all kinds, embodying and seeking to shape old and new thoughts, feelings and ideologies.' She concludes, 'social trans-formation must also be cultural transformation or it will be nothing at all' (p. 18). The pursuit of scholarship on news-as-culture provides an excellent opportunity to sort out and understand these dynamic interconnections.

References

Bennett, B. (2006) 'Medea in the Media: Narrative and Myth in Newspaper Coverage of Women Who Kill Their Children,' *Journalism*, 7: 411–432.

Boyle, M., McCluskey, M.R., McLeod, D.E. and Stein, S.E. (2005) 'Newspapers and Protest: An Examination of Protest Coverage from 1960 to 1999,' *Journalism and Mass Communication Quarterly*, 82: 638–653.

Caldwell, J.T. (1995) *Televisuality: Style, Crisis, and Authority in American Television*, New Brunswick, NJ: Rutgers University Press.

Campbell, R. (1987) 'Securing the Middle Ground: Reporter Formulas in *60 Minutes*,' *Critical Studies in Mass Communication*, 4: 325–350.

Carey, J.W. (1989 [1975]) *Communication as Culture: Essays on Media and Society*, Winchester, MA: Unwin Hyman.

Coman, M. (2005) 'Cultural Anthropology and Mass Media: A Processual Approach,' in Eric C. Rothenbuhler and Mihai Coman (eds.), *Media Anthropology*, Thousand Oaks, CA: Sage Publications.

Couldry, N. (2003) *Media Rituals: A Critical Approach*, London: Routledge.

Couldry, N. (2008) 'Mediatization or Mediation? Alternative Understandings of the Emergent Space of Digital Storytelling,' *New Media & Society*, 10: 373–391.

Dayan, D. and Katz, E. (1992) *Media Events: The Live Broadcast of History*, Cambridge, MA: Harvard University Press.

DiMaggio, P. (1997) 'Culture and Cognition,' *Annual Review of Sociology*, 23: 263–287.

Draper, R. (2008) 'The Making (and Remaking and Remaking) of the Candidate,' The *New York Times Magazine*, October 26: 52–59, 74, 112.

Elliot, P. (1982) 'Press Performance as Political Ritual,' in D.C. Whitney, E.A. Wartella and S. Windahl (eds.), *Mass Communication Review Yearbook Volume 3*, Beverly Hills, CA: Sage Publications.

Entman, R.M. (1993) 'Framing: Toward Clarification of Fractured Paradigm,' *Journal of Communication*, 43: 51–58.

Entman, R.M. (2004) *Projections of Power: Framing News, Public Opinion and U.S. Foreign Policy*, Chicago: University of Chicago Press.

Erjavec, K. and Volčič, Z. (2007) 'The Kosovo Battle: Media's Recontextualization of the Serbian Nationalistic Discourses,' *Press/Politics*, 12: 67–86.

Ettema, J.S. (1990) 'Press Rites and Race Relations: A Study of Mass-Mediated Ritual, *Critical Studies in Mass Communication*, 7: 309–331.

Ettema, J.S. and Glasser, T.L. (1998) *Custodians of Conscience: Investigative Journalism and Public Virtue*, New York: Columbia University Press.

Fairclough, N. (2003) *Analyzing Discourse: Textual Analysis for Social Research*, London: Routledge.

Geertz, C. (1973 [1962]) *The Interpretation of Cultures*, New York: Basic Books.

Jamieson, K.H. and Waldman, P. (2003) *The Press Effect: Politicians, Journalists, and the Stories that Shape the Political World*, Oxford: Oxford University Press.

Kitch, C. (2002) '"A Death in the American Family": Myth, Memory, and National Values in the Media Mourning of John F. Kennedy Jr," *Journalism and Mass Communication Quarterly*, 79: 294–309.

Kitch C. (2003) '"Mourning in America": Ritual, Redemption, and Recovery in News Narrative after September 11,' *Journalism Studies*, 4: 213–224.

Kitch, C. and Hume, J. (2008) *Journalism in a Culture of Grief*, New York: Routledge.

Leibes, T. (1998) 'Television's Disaster Marathons: A Danger for Democratic Processes,' in T. Leibes and J. Curran (eds.), *Media, Ritual and Identity*, London: Routledge.

Lule, J. (2001) *Daily News, Eternal Stories: The Mythological Role of Journalism*, New York: Guilford Press.

Manoff, R.K. (1986) 'Reading the News – By Telling the Story,' in R.K. Manoff and M. Schudson (eds.), *Reading the News*, New York: Pantheon Books.

Marvin, C. and Ingle, D.W. (1999) *Blood Sacrifice and the Nation*, Cambridge: Cambridge University Press.

Ortner, S.B. (2006) *Anthropology and Social Theory: Culture, Power, and the Acting Subject*, Durham, NC: Duke University Press.

Riegert, K. and Olsson, E. (2007), 'The Importance of Ritual in Crisis Journalism,' *Journalism Practice*, 1: 143–158.

Rothenbuhler, E. (1998) *Ritual Communication*, Thousand Oaks, CA: Sage Publications.

Schudson, M. (1989) 'The Sociology of News Production,' *Media, Culture and Society*, 11: 263–282.

Schudson, M. (1992) *Watergate in American Memory: How We Remember, Forget, and Reconstruct the Past*, New York: Basic Books.

Schudson, M. (1995) *The Power of News*. Cambridge, MA: Harvard University Press.

Schudson, M. (2007) 'The Anarchy of Events and the Anxiety of Story Telling,' *Political Communication*, 24: 253–257.

Silverstone, R. (2005) 'Mediation and Communication,' in C. Calhoun, C. Rojek and B, Turner (eds.), *The International Handbook of Sociology*, London: Sage Publications.

Swidler, A. (1986) 'Culture in Action: Symbols and Strategies,' *American Sociological Review* 51: 273–286.

Turner, V. (1969) *The Ritual Process: Structure and Anti-Structure*, Chicago: Aldine.

Vincent, R.C., Crow, B.K. and Davis, D.K. (1989) 'When Technology Fails: The Drama of Airline Crashes in Network Television News,' *Journalism Monographs No. 117*.

White, H. (1978) *Tropics of Discourse: Essays in Cultural Criticism*, Baltimore: Johns Hopkins University Press.

Zelizer, B. and Allan, S. (eds.) (2002) *Journalism After September 11*, London: Routledge.

28
NEWS AND THE EMOTIONAL PUBLIC SPHERE

Barry Richards

This chapter argues that studying the emotional dimensions of news is essential to understanding its political and cultural influence, and can bring new perspectives to some long-standing debates about the place of news and journalism in democracy and everyday life. It is divided into four parts. The first offers a concept of the 'emotional public sphere' and its relevance to the study of news. The second situates this concept in relation to the sociological theory of the 'public sphere', and to linked concepts such as public, audience, and civic culture. The third considers some of the main contemporary contributions of news to the emotional public sphere. In the fourth section there is some discussion of how news might contribute to a healthier emotional public sphere and thereby to a stronger democracy.

The importance of the emotional public sphere

The 'emotional public sphere' will be defined in this chapter as the emotional dimension of the political public sphere, that is, as the emotions which are involved in the political life of a nation. This definition is elaborated, and compared to other possible definitions, in the next section. But before we get into the finer points of that discussion, we need to establish why we might bother to do so. Why is understanding the emotional public sphere important? The answer is simple. Our understanding of how democracies today work, and our capacity to defend and enhance them, both depend on developing a better understanding of the essential and ongoing power of emotion within the democratic process. Crudely put, the emotions of the public are the key factor in most elections, and in many legislative outcomes. And this topic belongs in this book because news is by far the largest single influence on the shaping and strength of emotions in the political public sphere.

At the time of writing (October 2008) the global credit crisis is reminding us of another urgent reason for taking the study of public emotion very seriously. While there may be genuine *economic* reasons for economic crises, such as unsustainable levels of corporate or national debt, all analysis and commentary seems to agree that 'market sentiment' in one form or another is crucial in triggering and in ending economic crises. A complex of feelings, including confidence, anxiety, optimism, despair, trust, suspicion and recklessness, is always flowing through the finance and stock markets, while 'consumer confidence' amongst the general public is an ever-present factor in analyses of economic performance and prospects. These emotional dimensions of the commercial sphere are interwoven with the emotional aspects of politics, not least because national political leaders are looked to for measures which can manage the emotional volatility of markets. Here again, there can be no doubting the importance of news as an influence in shaping public emotions.

Of course the news is one of a number of such influences. In both politics and business there are dense interpersonal networks and word-of-mouth influences, especially amongst the political and business elites and other main actors involved, which may be paramount. Critics of 'media effects' theory may argue that even amongst the wider public the formative influence of the mass media on opinion and feeling cannot be assumed. Moreover the long-term impact of the web on the public sphere has yet to be clarified. While the rise of blogging and the growth of 'citizen journalism' do not seem likely to displace the professional journalist, nor to dissolve the dominance of major news channels and print titles, they clearly complicate the picture. Here, it will be assumed that the mainstream news media are and will remain crucial in shaping the emotional public, albeit in ways that are often complex and not yet fully understood.

Defining the emotional public sphere

The term 'emotional public sphere' is sometimes understood to refer to the display of emotion in the public sphere, to those occasions when, or places where, people emote in public. This shifts the focus away from news, which, although its content is often very emotive, is usually presented dispassionately. Other media genres are, in contrast, based on the staging of emotional performances. This is particularly true of many examples of reality television. Here the expression of raw and often negative emotions, with anger frequently centre stage, is typical. This has led to the suggestion that an 'emotional public sphere' is being created (Lunt and Stenner 2005; Lorenzo-Dus 2008) as a particular site in popular culture. This may be seen as a part of a broader and multi-faceted development which may be described as the 'emotionalisation' of contemporary culture, or as the emergence of 'therapeutic culture'.

There is no space here to go into the debates about the scale and significance of this cultural trend, although these debates (e.g. Anderson and Mullen 1998; Richards and Brown 2002; Furedi 2003) are certainly relevant to analyses of contemporary news and its impact. The aim of this chapter is to foreground a definition of the emotional public sphere which is not tied to a notion of explicitly emotionalised performance, but which sees it as an ever-present dimension of all public discourse. This emotional dimension of the political public sphere is in itself neither good nor bad.

Reflecting human nature, it includes the toxic and destructive as well as the prosocial and reparative.

It comprises the emotions of the public as they bear upon matters of public interest, though some of these emotions will only ever be expressed in private, and some not even there. In practical reality this emotional public sphere is always intertwined with the substance of the debates about values, policies, procedures and so forth which constitute the public sphere of would-be rational discussion. But in the pursuit of analysis and understanding, it can be described as a distinctive component of a society. Debates about public service broadcasting, for example, have their detailed socio-economic content concerning funding, audiences, regulation and so on, but also have powerful emotional resonance primarily around images of the state (as oppressor/benefactor) and of the market (as destroyer/facilitator). These images are typically non-empirical – that is to say, they are based on deep preconception, often unknowingly (psychoanalysts would call this unconscious fantasy or phantasy), rather than on experience.

To many commonsense observers this point may seem obvious and scarcely needing restatement. Yet the rationalistic bias of much political and social science has meant that it does need to be stated, and the case needs to be made for the systematic study of the emotional public sphere. The hugely influential way in which the concept of the public sphere was formulated, by the German sociologist Jurgen Habermas, has militated against scholarly attention to its emotional dimension. Habermas (1962: 27) defined it as people's public use of their reason, and so inserted it into one side of the dichotomy between reason and emotion which has distorted much post-Enlightenment thought. In the large literature on Habermas's work there is very little direct reference to its emotional nature. Two key texts, for example Calhoun (1992) and McCarthy (1981), make no reference to it, though McCarthy discusses in detail the links between the Habermasian concept of the public sphere and Freud's psychoanalytic theory, with which Habermas (as a graduate of the Frankfurt School of social thought) was of course very familiar.

We might have thought that a social theory so closely linked in its lineage to this theory of the human passions, and their centrality to psychological life, would have reflected this in how it saw their place in social life. Yet in the normative model of the public sphere there is little or no place for passion or emotion. Crossley (2004) notes the influence on Habermas of an early Freudian model (one left behind in later developments of psychoanalysis, and anyway arguably never typical of Freud's own thought) in which a rational ego is assailed from outside of itself by irrational symptoms originating elsewhere in the psyche. Similarly the public sphere of rational debate is contaminated by 'distorted communications' of which it can in theory be purged. The presence of emotion in the fundamental constitution of both ego and public sphere is obscured by this model.

In recent decades an 'affective turn' in the social sciences has challenged both this dichotomy and the marginalisation of emotion in the study of many areas of social life. This turn was becoming established in sociology in the 1990s (Bendelow and Williams 1998; Lupton 1998), had reached geography by 2001 (Anderson and Smith 2001), and has moved into politics in a variety of work which has in different ways argued for the necessity of placing emotion at the heart of our understanding of politics (Goodwin, Jasper and Polletta 2001; Rustin 2001; Marcus 2002; Clarke et al. 2006). One key theme explicit or implicit in much of this work is that our commitment to reason is an emotional one, in that we invest it with hope, trust and a sense of goodness. Another is that, moreover, our very exercise of reason rests on underlying beliefs in the world as knowable and relationships as negotiable, which themselves depend on certain benign qualities having been present in the early emotional experience of significant others. So in both individuals and societies, strong reserves of emotional capital are necessary for mature and reasoning modes of conduct to prevail. This is simply the obverse of the easily-accepted maxim that the emotional impoverishment or perversion of a society is the underpinning for destructive forces to prevail in national politics.

However this turn in social thought, which sees emotion as omnipresent and multivalent, has yet to have much influence in many areas of political science, and in journalism studies. This is perhaps surprising when we consider that journalism studies is an area within media studies, and it is through the intensifying mediatisation of politics that the emotional public sphere is brought more into view. For example, ever closer scrutiny of the *person* and the emotions of the politician is demanded by our culture, because that culture is both increasingly psychologically-minded and celebrity-oriented. This scrutiny is made possible by television, and by the efforts of political journalists.

For some, this kind of development is worrying because it turns the *public* into an *audience*, and so degrades the active citizenry into a passive entity, an aggregate of individuals who consume entertainment rather than seek constructive participation. However, as Livingstone (2005) argues, a sharp opposition between publics and audiences cannot be sustained; along with others (e.g. Corner 1995; Dahlgren 2003; van Zoonen 2004), she argues for a more fluid and contingent assessment in which some contemporary 'audiences' can be seen to be thinking, deliberating and even participating, i.e. behaving as 'publics', or at least as contributing to the domain of 'civic culture' as a resource on which the political public sphere can draw. In seeing the civic as a kind of pre-political sphere, Livingstone (2005, p.32) finds in it diverse examples approximating to the emotional public sphere both as emotion in public and as the emotional dimension of politics.

To emphasise the importance of emotion in the public sphere, then, does not tie us to any evaluative judgement about what has happened or is happening to the quality of public life and democratic discourse. As it happens, this chapter is written from a basically positive standpoint, in the belief that the 'therapeutic' trend, while dissolving some aspects of the previous mode of political discourse, not least its formality (Wouters 2007), carries the potential for a deepening of democracy by opening up new modes of engagement. Moreover, the emotional public sphere has never been just a site for manipulation or alienation. Admittedly, suspicion and distrust are major and central problems for many polities today. Still, the overall degradation of the public sphere feared by some critics of recent trends such as the rise of global news corporations, the intensifying use of news management techniques by governments and political parties, and changes in public service broadcasting, has not yet fully arrived.

So the emotional public sphere has always been there, and will remain. The important questions are about its content: what are its prevalent dynamics, and how can we influence them? In particular, what are the powers and responsibilities of journalism in relation to it?

The contributions of news to the emotional public sphere

1. Containment and emotional labour[1]

The emotional public sphere is a highly complex field of emotional forces. The disposition of these emotions at any given time will shape the contours of public opinion, will broadly determine the range of political alternatives which are on offer, and will set parameters and probabilities for the kinds of participation which people will engage in. What is the role of the news in this complex force-field of collective, public emotions? Very briefly, we can see this role normatively as one of *containment*. The world is full of alarming, confusing and anger-inducing events, and the task of news is to bring these to us in ways that do not spare us the realities but that enable us, as far as possible, to tolerate (rather than to escape or deny) the painful feelings that may be involved, and to develop our capacities for understanding the world (rather than assuming we already know everything, or can know nothing).[2] In the terms of psychodynamic theory, this is containment, and is about building capacities to feel and to think. Of course this requirement of news is a much higher demand than most journalists would be likely to make of themselves. It posits journalists as engaged in a kind of *emotional labour* (Hochschild 1983) that is in a professional practice with emotional effects on others which they have a responsibility to consider and to manage.

2. The dramatic and the dull

There is something of a paradox in the overall emotional impact of the news. On the one hand, if we look at the less political zones of the public sphere, the news provides us with many of the most powerful stimulants to, and templates for, feelings of the deepest kinds which we encounter in everyday life. This is the territory of reporting on crime, disaster, accident and other tragedies, which along with the creative outputs of popular culture (television drama, film and music) provides the main vehicles for public acknowledgement of and engagement with a wide range of feelings including anger, guilt, sympathy, pity, indignation, and remorse. While the popular press (extravagantly represented by the UK 'tabloid' or 'redtop' titles) typically offers the noisiest emotional register here, all the news media, if only by their visual content, serve to elicit these feelings. The ways in which they do this vary greatly, and there are many long-running debates about the social and moral effects involved. Social science, in keeping with its broadly critical mission, has tended to focus on the negative effects. The analyses of the 'moral panics' sometimes generated entirely, it seems, by editorial agendas (Critcher 2003) offer some of the closest examinations of how particular kinds of turbulence, often with strong punitive and paranoid content, enter into and persist in the emotional public sphere.

On the other hand, there is a tradition of emotional inhibition in much political reporting. It could be argued that in recent years the informalising trend has changed the picture somewhat, especially in broadcast coverage, with correspondents feeling more free to indulge in ironic or humorous asides, or to reach for amusement in the way that an item is introduced or framed, and thereby on occasions to open up a topic to some reflection on its emotional significance.[3] This is particularly likely where the topic is some aspect of the interpersonal relations of political leaders. There is invariably great resistance from politicians themselves to this kind of presentation. This stems partly from an understandable wish for politics not to be seen as driven by personal feuds, but also from a broader principle that politics is not about individual people at all, but about 'policies'. Here the hyperrationalism of some political science has its counterpart in the everyday rhetoric of politicians, in the insistence that they should be judged on their policies alone, as if the electorate's choice was a simple, evidence-based computation. Of course there is a major contradiction between this kind of rhetoric and another staple of political communication, which is the (would-be) leader's claim that s/he has the personal qualities to lead. Moreover, positing the electorate as driven by calculative rationality and good sense, while such flattery may be seen as electorally necessary, does not square with the acknowledged importance of passion in electoral contests, with the need for voters to be emotionally mobilised. Still, the tendency is for many politicians in their mediated communications to present themselves impersonally or at most with stereotypical, one-dimensional expressions of affect.

The reasons for this are complex, and cannot be gone into here fully since our focus is on news and journalism not on politicians. However, political journalism has to a considerable extent reflected the emotionally constricted nature of the statements made by politicians, and so served to maintain an emotional public sphere which, around the core business of democratic politics in policy debates and electoral contests, is often impoverished or artificial. The resulting 'emotional deficit' (Richards 2004) has been implicated in many studies of falling turnout and of political disengagement, especially amongst the young, in which the failure of political discourse to make emotional connection with younger citizens has been a recurrent underlying theme (Corner and Pels 2003; Meijer 2007) The 'boring' nature of politics stems at least in part from its difference and distance from the increasingly emotionalised forms of popular culture, where opportunities for the expression of, reflection upon and management of emotions have proliferated in recent decades.

3. Conflicts within and without

Nor has the news media's role in this been just a process of passive reflection and transmission by them of a malaise located elsewhere. In some respects the media have contributed very actively to this deficit. There is a striking illustration of the difficulty a leading politician would have if s/he engaged in public reflection on any mixed feelings they might have had about supporting a particular measure. Accusations of indecision, confusion or weakness from the media as well as opposing politicians would be likely to drown the confessor's career in a wave of bad publicity.

The constant media probing for hesitations, doubts, or cracks of any sort in a politician's or party's position can be seen as an intolerance of emotional complexity. One effect of it must be to limit the extent to which the conflicts people have within themselves are discussed and explored in the emotional public sphere, and so to limit the honesty and depth as well as the sophistication of exchanges within that sphere. This penchant of the political journalist is related to another approach taken by the news media towards politicians, one widely documented and intensively debated in the US and the UK for over two decades. Here we come to what is arguably the most prominent current contribution of the news to the emotional public sphere, at least in those two countries, which is in the generation of feeling by confrontational inter-viewing styles. The meanings and merits of these cross-examinations have been the subject of the debates. On the view taken here, their main impact is in the promotion of an ethos of adversariality, suspicion, and cynical pessimism about politics (see also Chapter 6 of Richards 2007). This assertion would of course be rejected by many journalists and academics, and so takes us into a territory of debate rather than of pure scholarly dispute. The position taken here is broadly that of, for example, Paterson (1994), Fallows (1996), Barnett (2002) and Lloyd (2004), in their analyses of 'attack' journalism and politics in the US and UK. On this view the fractious confrontation-alism of today's journalists adds to the likelihood that some members of the public will feel alienated from the democratic process, as they withdraw from what they believe to be the intrinsically negative and repetitive content of public conversations about it.[4]

Of course many readers of this piece may disagree with these analyses, but the disagreements are more about the meanings of behaviours rather than the fact of their occurrence. Whatever our interpretation of these meanings, political journalism has a prominent position in the emotional public sphere. The predominant style amongst political journalists in their examination of politicians and other public authorities, and in their modelling of attitudes towards politics, will therefore be a major influence on the mood of the emotional public sphere.

4. Detachment and the gut feeling

There is a paradox in the relationships between the news and the emotions that occurs 'behind the scenes', in the production of news, though it is relevant to under-standing journalism's contribution to the emotional public sphere. There is a major discrepancy between two of the core values of journalism, specifically between, on the one hand, the celebrated value of 'objectivity' and, on the other, the belief that there is a 'gut feeling' which journalists have about the strength and importance of a story. It is perhaps surprising that a profession which rightly places great value on its capacity for sober, evidence-based even-handedness, and which in its core everyday activity is about bringing things to light, and seeking transparency and justification, should when describing itself have such frequent recourse to a notion of 'instinctive' or 'intuitive' judgement, for which no systematic evidence is adduced. Schultz (2007) suggests that the 'journalistic gut feeling' can be analysed in terms of various criteria of newsworthiness, but her research shows that these criteria (such as timeliness, relevance, audience identification) are not applied in a systematic or rational way to choose between stories or angles. On the contrary, her respondents spoke of the basis of their judgements about newsworthiness being in, for example, 'your spinal cord', 'the back of your head' or 'something like a feeling', as if, Schultz observes, 'newsworthiness is an integral part of the editor himself' (p.198) – and moreover, we might note, an integral part of the editor as emotionally sentient being, not as detached and rational observer. Furthermore, some of the criteria are not even part of the universe of explicit discourse about journalistic judgement, but belong in the taken-for-granted background of the undiscussed and undisputed (what Schultz, following Bourdieu, calls the 'doxa' of the profession). A similar understanding can be found amongst journalists of their capacity to identify '*the story*' (Rees and Richards, forthcoming), a term for conveying news values and newsworthiness around which a mystique of intuitive certainty can be found.

An awareness of these journalistic mythologies does not tell us much about the specific emotional content of the news and its contribution to the emotional public sphere. It does however enable us to see that in its mode of information production, as much as in its consumption by audiences, the news is an emotional business. The way in which professional values and practices shape the emotional investments which individual journalists have in their work is little understood, but is an important part of understanding how the emotional public sphere is shaped.

5. Re-emotionalising the public sphere?

Emotionally, the content of political news is of course not all constricted or cynically negative. Two major illustrations of this are in the role of news in generating public conscience about global suffering, and in the increasing personalisation of leadership. For both, it is television news in particular which has led the way, in a combination of technological and social factors. The introduction of television itself, then of colour, and images of ever-improving quality, has brought distant peoples and domestic politicians to us in vivid, near-palpable ways. This facility has meshed with two broad socio-cultural trends, one towards the emergence of a world public, or at least of national publics open to mobilisation on international issues, and the other being the growth of therapeutic culture with its emphases on individuals as persons. The fact that these phenomena have all occurred in recent decades perhaps enables us to suggest that there has been a *re*-emotionalisation of the public sphere, after a phase in the post-WW2 period when, at least in the UK, the cultural changes brought by the consumer society and by de-industrialisation left the discourse of politics behind, so that, as described above, it was increasingly out of touch with the public and unable to make much emotional connection with it. Now, a partially de-traditionalised politics is potentially more in tune with the public, and the emotional dimensions of the public sphere are more evident.

One example of this is the role of the reporting of famine in underpinning the success from the 1980s onwards of new initiatives to encourage charitable giving, which required new levels of public awareness and compassionate feeling (whether based primarily on empathy, guilt or anger). A second is the intensifying scrutiny of political leaders as persons. Audiences now have much more opportunity than in the past to do this directly themselves, by watching close-ups of them performing in interviews and meetings, but also there is abundant media commentary on and analysis of their temperaments, relationships and qualities. There is a large debate around this trend, with many decrying it as the debasement of politics to soap opera, while others see in it potential for re-engaging citizens and re-establishing trust in new ways based on emotional connection and judgements of authenticity.

How might news contribute to a healthier emotional public sphere?

How we answer this question will depend on what model of the public sphere we are working with, or would prefer to see in existence, and the role of journalism within that. Following Ferree at al.'s (2002) typology, we could say that two models (the elite/representative and the discursive/deliberative) have more stringent requirements of the emotional public sphere than do the other two – the participatory/liberal model and the 'constructionist' model (which they see as the expression of feminist/Foucauldian thinking). The latter two value inclusion and empowerment above all, and so permit, maybe even encourage, confrontation and fractiousness, as necessary components of continuous contestation in which all voices must be heard. Civility and deference to expertise can be seen in these models as oppressive censorship, a view which carries the risk of leading to an uncontained emotional free-for-all.

The discursive/deliberative and elite/representative models allow for strong feeling but value civility. Deliberators in particular seek consensus, and some closure of an issue once a direction has been decided. The risk here, in the emotional public sphere, is of certain feelings being unrecognised or delegitimated, in favour of an idealised image of harmony or integration which would not be emotionally realistic. But on balance a deliberative model is closest to the principles of containment and emotional realism which underlie the analysis offered in this chapter. We will conclude with a statement of two broad ways in which the news can be steered to follow those principles and thereby to optimise its contribution to the emotional public sphere.

1. The news should prioritise the construction of an emotional world public oriented towards mass threats to the wellbeing or lives of others (situations often referred to awkwardly as 'humanitarian disasters'), thus ensuring that the fundamentals of emotional life – feelings around security and death – are explicitly at the heart of public discourse. There are major difficulties here around the legitimate needs of audiences for domestically-focused news, and around 'compassion fatigue'. However news can take the lead in educating publics towards a more actively compassionate and more inquiring awareness of suffering.

2. The news should move attack journalism to its margins, and aim to build civility and open-mindedness into the foundations of political debate. In particular it should desist from attacking the politician who deviates from a rigid fixity of mind, allowing space for the examination of mixed feelings and so cultivating greater emotional realism. Again, there is an important role in enhancing political culture awaiting the political journalists who could make a significant break with the present constricting orthodoxies and work to undercut the self-absorbed ritual exchanges of party politics.

Overall, a focus on journalism's contributions to the emotional public sphere should at least lead to more reflection on how the news shapes public mood, and on how this could be done differently. This is no small task, but is needed to enable journalism, and training for journalism, to keep pace with cultural change and to meet their responsibilities. The news, as a foundation of civic and political culture, and as a key source of critical commentary on society, is an emotional matter.

Notes

1 The socio-psychodynamic theory of the news briefly outlined in this section is developed at length in Chapter 5 of the author's *Emotional Governance: Politics, Media and Terror* (2007).
2 Silverstone's (1994) concept of the news as a key site for anxiety-management is a closely related, though probably less extensive, concept.
3 For example, in a September 2008 BBC2 item on an impending Cabinet reshuffle the correspondent is standing in a modest living room, with photographs on the mantelpiece of Cabinet members as if they were family members. As the photos are moved around in a visual accompaniment to the spoken analysis of the Prime Minister's options, the audience is tacitly encouraged to view the reshuffle as determined by relationships of attachment, (dis)trust and rivalry, on the model of family dynamics. Perhaps typical of a problem for these more whimsical kinds of packaging, this item hovered between the engaging and the trite.
4 On Lloyd's analysis a central component of this journalistic strategy is the axiom that most issues can be reduced to an insoluble conflict. If this is so it makes for an interesting contrast with the intolerance of emotional complexity, noted earlier, and the implicit contempt for the individual who experiences internal conflict. Psychodynamically, we could see this contrast as making sense. Persons who are uncomfortable with inner conflict, and unconfident of resolving it, see it as weakness. Their own inner conflicts are then defensively projected onto the external world, in which accordingly they can see little scope for workable compromises and creative resolutions.

References

Anderson, D. and Mullen, P. (1998) *Faking It. The Sentimentalisation of Society*, London: The Social Affairs Unit.
Anderson, K. and Smith, S. (2001) 'Emotional geographies', *Transactions of the Institute of British Geographers*, 26(1), 7-10.
Barnett, S. (2002) 'Will a crisis in journalism provoke a crisis in democracy?', *Political Quarterly*, 73 (4): 400-8.
Bendelow, G. and Williams, S. (eds.) (1998) *Emotions in Social Life. Crirtcal Themes and Contemporary Issues*, London: Routledge.
Calhoun, C., (ed.) (1992) *Habermas and the Public Sphere*, Cambridge, MA: MIT Press.

Clarke, S., Hoggett, P. and Thompson, S. (eds.) (2006) *Emotion, Politics and Society*, Basingstoke: Palgrave Macmillan.

Corner, J. (1995) *Television Form and Public Address*, London: Edward Arnold.

Corner, J. and Pels, D. (eds.) (2003) *Media and the Restyling of Politics*, London: Sage.

Critcher, C. (2003) *Moral Panics and the Media*, Maidenhead: Open University Press.

Crossley, N. (2004) 'On systematically distorted communication: Bourdieu and the socio-analysis of publics', in Crossley, N. & Roberts, J. (eds.) *After Habermas: New Perspectives on the Public Sphere*, Oxford: Blackwell.

Dahlgren, P. (2003) 'Reconfiguring civic culture in the new media milieu', in Corner, J. and Pels, D. (eds.) *Media and the Restyling of Politics*, London: Sage.

Fallows, J. (1997) *Breaking the News: How the Media Undermine American Democracy*, New York: Vintage.

Ferree, M., Gamson, W., Gerhard, J. and Rucht, D. (2002) 'Four models of the public sphere in modern democracies', *Theory and Society* 31(3), 289-324.

Furedi, F. (2003) *Therapy Culture: Cultivating Vulnerability in an Uncertain Age*, London: Routledge.

Habermas, J. (1962) *The Structural Transformation of the Public Sphere*, Cambridge: Polity.

Hochschild, A. (1983) *The Managed Heart: The Commercialization of Human Feeling*, Berkeley: University of California Press.

Goodwin, J., Jasper, J. and Polletta, F. (eds.) (2001) *Passionate Politics: Emotions and Social Movements*, Chicago: University of Chicago Press.

Livingstone, S. (2005) 'On the relation between audiences and publics', in *Changing Media – Changing Europe*, Bristol: Intellect Books.

Lloyd, J. (2004) *What the Media are Doing to our Politics*, London: Constable.

Lorenzo-Dus, N. (2008) 'Real disorder in the court: an investigation of conflict talk in US television courtroom shows', *Media, Culture and Society*, 30 (1), 81-107.

Lunt, P. and Stenner, P. (2005) 'The Jerry Springer Show as an emotional public sphere', *Media, Culture and Society* 27, 59-81.

Lupton, D. (1998) *The Emotional Self: A Sociocultural Exploration*, London: Sage.

Marcus, G. (2002) *The Sentimental Citizen: Emotion in Democratic Politics*, University Park, PA: University of Pennsylvania Press.

McCarthy, T. (1981) *The Critical Theory of Jurgen Habermas*, Cambridge, MA: MIT Press.

Meijer, I. (2007) 'The paradox of popularity', *Journalism Studies*, 8(1), 96-116.

Patterson, T. (1994) *Out of Order*, New York: Vintage.

Rees, G. and Richards, B. (forthcoming) 'Journalism and emotional literacy'.

Richards, B. (2004) 'The emotional deficit in political communication', *Political Communication*, 21(3), 339-352.

Richards, B. (2007) *Emotional Governance: Politics, Media and Terror*, Basingstoke: Palgrave Macmilllan.

Richards, B. and Brown, J. (2002) 'The therapeutic culture hypothesis', in Johansson, T. and Sernhede, O. (eds.) *Lifestyle, Desire and Politics: Contemporary Identities*, Goteborg: Daedalos.

Rustin, M. (2001) *Reason and Unreason: Psychoanalysis, Science and Politics*, London: Continuum.

Schultz, I. (2007) 'The journalistic gut feeling', *Journalism Practice*, 1(2) 190-207.

Silverstone, R. (1994) *Television and Everyday Life*, London: Routledge.

Van Zoonen, L. (2004) *Entertaining the Citizen: When Politics and Popular Culture Converge*, Lanham, MD: Rowman & Littlefield.

Wouters, C. (2007) *Informalization: Manners and Emotions Since 1890*, London: Sage/Theory, Culture and Society.

29

RACE AND DIVERSITY IN THE NEWS

Joseph Harker

The historic election of Barack Obama as the United States' first black president produced a wealth of comment in the British press about the possibility of a black British prime minister. Could it happen here? Is Britain as racist as America? Are there any home-grown black politicians of Obama's calibre? Much of this involved much wild speculation and many gross generalisations. They might instead have used the occasion to make more informed comments about matters closer connected to their field of experience: namely, are we likely to see a black British national newspaper editor in our lifetime?

In late 2007 Kamal Ahmed, the *Observer*'s executive editor, left the paper to join the UK's Equality and Human Rights Commission. With him went probably the best chance we'll have in a long time to see such a breakthrough (ironically, the *Observer*'s editor, Roger Alton, stood down just a month later). Just as with Obama, for the British press the appointment of the first black editor, if it ever happens, will also be hugely symbolic.

Ahmed was a former *Observer* political editor, as well as media editor on his previous newspaper, the *Guardian* – positions never before or since held by a person of colour on any national newspaper. Indeed, the number of racial minorities in editing positions across all Fleet Street is tiny. One thinks of Peter Victor, who news-edits the *Independent on Sunday*, or Malik Meer on the *Guardian*'s Saturday Guide, as possibly the only two, at the time of writing, who run significant departments. Aside from that, most of the main desks on the nationals – home news, foreign, city, features, sports – are run by entirely white teams. One may find the occasional black or Asian journalist in a junior role on the commissioning desk, but rarely, if ever, in a position where they can make a decision on what goes into the next day's paper, let alone have any major long-term impact.

Don't get me wrong. Things have improved. I entered journalism, working within the black press, in the late 1980s. Within the nationals, this was the era of "black crime shock" headlines emblazoned across the tabloids and long before any industry codes on race reporting. Almost without exception, black people were only reported when crime statistics came out, or when there were riots on the streets. Asian people were invisible.

I worked with several very good journalists in a niche sector that was thriving; but as my colleagues moved on to new challenges, just one of them gained a staff job on a national newspaper – the rest went into television. The national press was effectively a closed shop: jobs were, proudly, never advertised and only those moving within established media circles stood any chance of getting one. This did not include black or Asian people.

Now things have changed a little and some newspapers have accepted the unfairness of the old system. There are ethnic minority reporters and/or sub-editors on most papers, though mostly in very small numbers. But progress has been slow. Of those editors who recognised this as a problem, many initially believed – and some still do – that they could change their mix of staff without changing traditional methods of recruitment. Earlier, this had, after all, been sufficient to bring women into the ranks. Nepotism could be extended to female family and friends, and the dinner-party circuit gave women guests a chance to impress. With racial minorities, though, both routes were non-starters. They were raised a long way from the privileged and often public-school backgrounds of many Fleet Street editors and their associates.

Further, it's now more than 50 years since sections devoted to women's issues – written by women, for women – began to appear in the British press. Through their pages have emerged many top women writers, seizing the available space to hone their skills, to prove their ability, and to demonstrate incontrovertibly that their voice is valid, product-enhancing, and impossible to ignore. There has, however, been no equivalent outlet for any minority-race coverage, despite the potential benefits – although some of the regional press, covering areas with significant minority populations, have run dedicated sections.

Entrenched inequality

A few national newspapers have made some positive efforts to redress the imbalance, occasionally offering traineeships specifically for black and Asian starters. At the *Guardian* – a daily paper which along with its stablemate the *Observer* and website guardian.co.uk forms Britain's leading liberal media organisation – we have been running a positive-action work placement programme, targeting racial minorities. The large numbers of intelligent, enthusiastic, hardworking and motivated young men and women we've been able to bring into our office (and, yes, Muslim women too) have given the lie to that old media mantra, "but they don't apply".

In 2007 the editor Alan Rusbridger introduced a plan of action to redress inequality. This includes interview, recruitment and management training for editors and section heads; consultations with minority staff; advertising all entry-level jobs externally; and alerting minority journalists on our database when vacancies arise.

This plan is backed up by ethnic monitoring, so we can measure the progress we're making. But the *Guardian* apart, most papers seem to believe the small steps they've already taken are enough to level the playing field. I contacted four other national newspaper groups, and all were quick to claim that they do not discriminate, yet none had even a rough idea of the numbers of minority staff they employ. This despite the fact that diversity organisations see monitoring – now common in many industries such as banking and manufacturing – as a crucial step in tackling institutional inequality.

Monitoring "is not something I regard as significant", *Sunday Times* managing editor Richard Caseby told me. "The overriding factor when employing people is: if someone can do the job well, they get the job. Performance is the only issue we consider." But without any supporting information, can newspapers really be sure that their recruitment is unbiased and that their editors see beyond the indeterminate cultural factors that so often lie behind selection decisions, such as: "Do I feel comfortable with him?" "Would she be a good laugh down the pub?" "Would they fit in with our reporting team?" Journalists I contacted who work in some of these newsrooms reported that they are very white places indeed.

Of course, though, representation is more than just a recruitment issue. The internal culture of a media organisation is a major influence on its external output, which in turn can have a significant impact on the wider public and its attitudes. The negative and imbalanced reporting of 20 years ago generally gave way to a more measured approach during the 1990s – most notably in the reporting of the racist murder of black teenager Stephen Lawrence and its aftermath, with even the conservative *Daily Mail* weighing in heavily on the side of the victim's family. And when the Macpherson report into the Metropolitan Police's investigation of his killing was published in February 1999, there was a real sense that papers should in some way reflect the communities they served. The inquiry's central finding was that the police were guilty of "institutional racism"; but any journalist who wanted to join the criticism need only have looked at the faces in his or her newsroom to see that the accusation did not apply only to the police.

A little fewer than 1,000 days after the report, however, came 9/11 – and a new form of scapegoating was unleashed, with Muslims bearing the brunt. Space prohibits examining this issue in detail, but I will just ask why is it that picture editors so often choose pictures of niqab-wearing women to accompany articles on Islam? For the most part, this veil has no relevance to the piece and, in any case, it is worn by only a tiny number of Muslim women. In effect, this image has become the modern equivalent of the notorious police mugshot of Winston Silcott (the man wrongly convicted of killing a policeman during riots in Tottenham in 1985) – a face of menace that demonised a whole community.

What do Britain's ethnic minorities think about this? At about 9 per cent of the national population, and 30 per cent of London's – where most of the media is based – they are now an established part of the country and play an increasingly important role. Despite this, our newspapers have made little or no effort to attract them as potential readers. Marketing executives tend to think in terms of social status (A, B, C1, C2, D, E: the former deemed readers of quality broadsheets; the latter of red-top tabloids) or job type (public sector, the *Guardian*; lawyers, *The Times*; business, the *Daily Telegraph*). Promotions departments then put their efforts into shoring up their own traditional group, or launching advertising campaigns in attempts to reach out to others. They assume that racial minorities fit wholly into this matrix – they buy the dailies just like the rest of the population, so surely they're no different to any other readers?

In 2004 at the *Guardian* we carried out what was possibly the first focus-group research aimed purely at minority readers. Talking to black and Asian broadsheet buyers, we found that they had markedly negative views about the coverage of minorities – both in terms of the space given and of the issues reported. And this was true for all papers, regardless of political stance. In another focus group, one member said he believed that black people were only ever reported as "victims, villains, or village idiots".

To find out if there was any basis in fact for these perceptions, we carried out some analysis of content from a fortnight's papers. Obviously this has to be viewed with caution – we weren't using established scientific methods – but it was interesting anecdotally nevertheless. It should also be noted that this was before Barack Obama's election campaign and presidency, which has provided the front pages with numerous positive black stories. The underlying problems persist, though.

(Im)balanced coverage

Outside the foreign pages, we found that a tiny amount of space was allocated to minorities. And within the overall coverage, white people were reported overwhelmingly positively; Asian people were reported overwhelmingly negatively (half the stories were about Muslim terrorism); and, although black people's coverage was equally balanced between positive and negative, almost all the positive stories were, stereotypically, either entertainment- or sports-related. So it seems that the black and Asian readers were not paranoid – the media really have got it in for them.

Editors would no doubt counter that we're in the middle of a major Islamic terrorist threat, so this is bound to affect coverage. I accept this point. But the issue is balance. For every story about a (white) politician who's been exposed as incompetent, there's another of (white) human achievement, or act of selfless charity, or miracle birth, or whatever – and, let's face it, even stories of white criminals, for example, are offset by the appearance of a prominent, responsible, white authority figure, be it a judge, barrister or police chief. With black and Asian coverage, such counterbalance is rare. It has to be significant that almost every story which is published in the national press has to have the approval of a white desk editor – most of whom have had little or no contact with any of Britain's minority communities. This means that a story which might be of great importance to, say, a person of Indian or Caribbean origin is far less likely to arouse the interest of the man or woman deciding the news list.

In 2006, the then Metropolitan Police Commissioner for London, Sir Ian Blair, accused the British media of institutional racism over their coverage of white murders compared with black – the latter victims, he said, gained far fewer column inches. Leader articles and columnists swiftly and roundly condemned him: this was a ridiculous and unfounded allegation, they declared in united outrage. The facts, though, were with Blair. In 2008 knife crime became a burning media issue, with 27 teenagers murdered in London alone by September. Only three of these victims were white. I did an analysis of press coverage and discovered that the 24 black and Asian victims had generated about 50 stories each – apart from one which, because the investigation threw up several leads and the alleged killers were quickly caught, created just over 100 articles. The three white victims had received between 200 and 350 articles. On average, therefore, the loss of a white life gained five to six times more coverage than that of a non-white.

Around that time, I appeared on the panel for a BBC Radio 4 media show. When I pointed this out, I was told by a senior and well-respected journalist from another paper that this was because the white murders were "random", and hence were especially shocking because they could happen to any reader's child. This, to me, epitomises the lingering stereotypes which infect media coverage of minority issues. Somehow a black murder isn't due to some random attack; in all 24 cases, this journalist would have us believe, the victim – either through their circle of associates or by their behaviour – must have contributed in some way to their own murder. In other words, a non-white victim's innocence must always be suspect.

I am certain that this person is not alone in her thinking. Think of the commonly-used phrase "black-on-black", always in the context of violence. This is a term which dehumanises those to whom it refers. It's shorthand for saying: there's no need for further explanation – it's just what these people do. Would Rhys Jones, the 11-year-old Liverpudlian shot in 2007 in crossfire between rival gangs, be written off as a victim of "white-on-white" violence? No, there must have been some kind of reason for it. We must find out what happened. If only those last two sentences applied more often when black people make the news.

With overseas stories too, one often gains only a one-dimensional impression of events. When sporadic fighting broke out in Kenya over the disputed election results of December 2007, many of the press dusted off their tired old "tribes fighting each other" line to report what was mainly a politically based conflict. The word "tribe", evocative of those spear-carrying "natives" from the old Tarzan movies, is also racially loaded shorthand. It says: they're savages, they're irrational, and they'll fight over anything; so there's little need to explain any details, or any complex history. Compare the coverage of similar conflicts in Europe, such as Northern Ireland or the Balkans – which could equally be described as tribal warfare but never are. Europeans don't walk around carrying shields and wearing grass skirts – and neither do Kenyans.

Foreign reporting, though, has to be more than just about disasters, or wars. We hear of white people – be they in Australia, South Africa, Europe or, of course, the United States – when they have surfing accidents, when the sprinklers on their golf courses run dry, or when they have embarrassing TV incidents. All of these serve to bring us closer to the citizens of those countries: we see them in their full humanity – as more than just victims of atrocities or natural disasters. People of colour, however, seem to make news only when the four horsemen arrive in town.

'Fitting in'

If our media reported internal American news the same way as they do Africa's, which stories would we have heard this century? Probably only that the centre of one of its major cities was reduced to rubble by a terrorist attack; and that when another city was flooded, with its homes destroyed and a thousand dead, the dominant tribe left the minority tribe to rot. Doesn't exactly provide the full picture, does it?

So why, despite the fact that black and Asian journalists are playing a role in our national newspapers, does this kind of reporting still happen? Obviously, the low numbers are a key factor. Despite the reticence of newspapers to give figures, I'm willing to bet with any of them that their minority journalists could be counted on the fingers of one or two hands. Their responses are reminiscent of the comments one would receive ten or so years ago: "We can't have a racism problem here – we don't have any black journalists!" Another factor is the lack of seniority. Given that many minority journalists have joined their papers only in the last decade, they are not able significantly to affect their newspaper's editorial line. Having said that, anecdotal evidence is that black and Asian journalists, who've been around for many more than 10 years, haven't risen up the career ladder as quickly as their white colleagues. There are several white editors who have been in the industry less than a decade.

In a way, this mirrors the situation with black footballers. Two decades ago, they were seen as not having the right attributes to make it as professionals – "not enough strength of character, not quite the right temperament", the managers and pundits would say. Today, black footballers are at the highest levels everywhere, yet they still face the same old prejudices if they want to move into management. Despite the large number of black players, in the entire 92-club Premier and Football Leagues there is only one black manager – and there has only ever been one, short-lived, black British boss in the top division. So do today's newspapers really trust us minority journalists yet? It seems they now feel reasonably OK about sending us out to cover stories, but giving us real responsibility for managing staff and deciding tomorrow's news agenda is another matter.

Added to that is the need felt by so many journalists to fit in. National newspaper offices can be very intimidating to those either straight out of university or who have worked only on small publications. Imagine you're the only brown face in an all-white office: you're likely to feel inhibited suggesting ideas about the latest Bollywood film or black theatre production. Your first contacts are likely to be with junior editors who know that the best way to move upwards is to get to understand the boss and give him or her what they want. The higher up the chain – as a 2006 survey by the Sutton Trust educational charity confirmed – the more middle-class, public school and Oxbridge the structure becomes. Would they prefer a story from Peckham or Purley? Brixton Academy or the Royal Academy? After a few rejections (and I've had this conversation with several black and Asian colleagues), many minority journalists are left wondering whether they should simply keep their individualism quiet. Moreover, what do you say when you see a particularly negative and misleading example of reporting of your own community? Speak up, or shut up? Risk your career by alienating your bosses, or live a lie and take the misery home with you? All of this calls into question the very meaning of the word "diversity" within the print industry.

Do we want our newspapers to reflect properly the communities they cover? Or is it just about having brown faces covering the same stories, from the same angles, as before? Aside from the editors, the major newspaper power figures are columnists and critics – the so-called opinion formers. On politics, books, music CDs, cinema, theatre, DVDs, concerts, restaurants, these are the people paid to tell the readers what to think. And their exclusive club is even whiter than the editors'. Across the press there are literally hundreds of pundits with a regular space to air their views, yet the number from a minority background does not even reach double figures. Gary Younge of the *Guardian*, the *Independent*'s Yasmin Alibhai-Brown, and *Daily Mail* showbusiness columnist Baz Bamigboye are rare exceptions to the rule. In fact, as I write, a visit to the "Our columnists" section of Britain's national quality newspaper websites reveals only two non-white faces from a total of over 100.

In the earlier reference to police chief Ian Blair, every one of the columnists so quick to condemn his comments was white, and few of them even bothered to examine the grounds for his claim of media bias. Might it not have been interesting to see a black or Asian perspective on this issue – or did commissioning a different voice require too much creative thought, too much thinking outside the box?

A little while ago I had a call from actor/writer/director Kwame Kwei-Armah, whose play, *Statement of Regret*, was then running at the National Theatre. He couldn't understand why many of his black acquaintances had been complimentary about it, yet the national paper reviews had been mixed. So he organised a separate viewing evening for black journalists, many of whom worked in the national press (but, obviously, not as critics). I went along and thought that the play was entertaining and raised many significant and thought-provoking issues about the relationship between British Africans and British Caribbeans. Many others present that evening thought likewise.

Reading those press reviews afterwards, it was as if I'd seen a completely different play. One reviewer couldn't get over the fact that it was set in a black think-tank (such a thing, he surmised, was beyond the bounds of possibility); another wondered why anyone would be at all interested in such an internal black issue; yet another was annoyed that it left his mind "swimming" with thoughts (I always assumed that this was the sign of a good production – would a visit to a Picasso exhibition be seen as irritating too?). I'm not claiming that every white critic will automatically pan black productions, only that sometimes you need a little knowledge to understand exactly what it is you're critiquing.

Moving forward

In the current context, having a black Fleet Street editor would almost certainly make little difference beyond symbolism. Would anyone with a significantly different outlook be able to work their way up to a position where they could seriously be in the running for such a post? If we really are to make our press more fair and representative in its coverage, we need to get beyond mere "diversity" and move towards inclusion – where members of staff feel equally valued whatever their background; where they wouldn't feel it damaging to their career to query the selection of stories, the columnists' lazy stereotyped assumptions, or their paper's leader line; where the difference of their culture, religion or global origins is seen as an asset, and a way of reaching new readers, rather than a threat to the established order.

In modern-day Britain, papers retaining a mono-cultural outlook could soon begin to appear outdated and out of touch to their readers and risk missing out on major stories. On July 7, 2005, as London was ravaged by bombings, how many news editors were pleading: "Is there a Muslim in the house?" And as global issues become more and more local, how much of an advantage would it be to be able to call on someone with, say, a Zimbabwean or Middle Eastern family connection?

After all, what personal qualities make for a good journalist? The ability to spot a story; to think creatively; to be tenacious; to analyse the facts; to be a thorough researcher? Are these specific to one ethnicity or one background type?

As newspapers face more and more intense competition, both in print and online, surely they can't afford to ignore Britain's growing minority populations. The assumption that things can continue as they always have, with a wealthy, well-connected elite handing down news from above, expecting their underlings to try to imitate them, just doesn't fit with a twenty-first-century world. Ultimately, surely what we all want is for all sections of society to feel they are properly represented in the range, variety and balance of stories written about them. In other words, extend the overall treatment afforded to white people in the press – as journalists, readers, and those reported – to the whole population. But how many newspaper organisations will genuinely commit themselves to reaching that goal?

* This chapter draws on material from my article, 'Ethnic Balance: Race Against the Tide', published in the *British Journalism Review* (www.bjr.org.uk) in 2008 (19(1): 23-31). It is used here with permission.

Further reading

Ainley, B. (1998) *Black Journalists, White Media*. Stoke on Trent: Trentham.

Campbell, C.P. (1995) *Race, Myth and the News*. London: Sage.

Cottle, S. (ed.) (2000) *Ethnic Minorities and the Media*. Buckingham: Open University Press.

Cottle, S. (2004) *The Racist Murder of Stephen Lawrence: Media Performance and Public Transformation*. New York: Praeger.

Dennis, E.E. and Pease, E.C. (eds) (1997) *The Media in Black and White*. New Brunswick, NJ and London: Transaction.

Downing, J and Husband, C. (2005) *Representing Race: Racism, Ethnicity and the Media*. London: Sage.

Entman, R. and Rojecki, A. (2001) *The Black Image in the White Mind: Media and Race in America*. Chicago: University of Chicago Press.

Ferguson, R. (1998) *Representing 'Race': Ideology, Identity and the Media*. London: Arnold.

Gabriel, J. (1998) *Whitewash: Racialized Politics and the Media*. London: Routledge.

Gandy, Jr, O.H. (1998) *Communication and Race*. London: Arnold.

Gonzalez, J. and Torres, J. (2009) *White News: the Untold Story of Racism in the American Media and the Journalists Who Fought it*. New York: The New Press.

Heider, D. (2000) *White News: Why Local News Programs Don't Cover People of Color*. Hillsdale, NJ: Lawrence Erlbaum.

Jacobs, R.N. (2000) *Race, Media and the Crisis of Civil Society*. Cambridge: Cambridge University Press.

Karim, K.H. (2000) *Islamic Peril: Media and Global Violence*. Montreal: Black Rose.

Larson, S. G.. (2005) *Media and Minorities: The Politics of Race in News and Entertainment*. New York: Roman & Littlefield.

Law, I. (2002) *Race in the News*. London: Palgrave.

Newkirk, P. (2000) *Within the Veil: Black Journalists, White Media*, New York and London: New York University Press.

Poole E. & Richardson, J. E. (eds) (2006) *Muslims and the News Media*. London: IB Tauris.

Rodriguez, A. (1999) *Making Latino News*. Thousand Oaks: Sage.

30

GETTING IT STRAIGHT: GAY NEWS NARRATIVES AND CHANGING CULTURAL VALUES

Marguerite Moritz

Biblical literalists will disagree, but the Bible is a living document, powerful for more than 2,000 years because its truths speak to us even as we change through history. In that light, Scripture gives us no good reason why gays and lesbians should not be (civilly and religiously) married – and a number of excellent reasons why they should.

Lisa Miller
Newsweek, 15 December 2008

Newsweek hit a cultural nerve when it argued "The Religious Case for Gay Marriage" in an opinion piece that included the image of a Bible bookmarked with a miniature Rainbow Flag on the magazine's cover. Their opinion, coming just weeks after ballot initiatives against gay marriage carried in four different states, sent 40,000 readers to their computers. The magazine had to temporarily suspend its electronic in-box, so heavy was the email traffic to its website. When the predicted firestorm of opposition started appearing in the blogosphere as well, the reaction was heavily covered on newsweek.com, complete with quotes condemning the article ("If *Newsweek* actually intended to be an honest mediator of this issue, they should have published pro and con articles by respected Bible scholars rather than engage in such blatantly obvious opinion journalism.") and links to the full texts of the criticisms ("The Good Book and Gay Marriage", 16 Dec 2008, http://www.newsweek.com/id/175223).

The civil rights of LGBT people are affected by culture as well as by law. In this case, even after decades of debate in the popular press, the culture clash over marriage (and military service) can still get readers' blood boiling and sell magazines in the process. With so many print properties trying to attract a shrinking audience, that is no small matter. More than ever before, the bottom line is now a central concern of the journalistic enterprise and no longer something for the sales department to deal with. It's hard to imagine an opinion piece matching the drama of the US presidential election that dominated the news just a month earlier, but if anything could do it, coming out for marriage between same sex couples might just be the ticket. And it was.

While hardly thinkable in an earlier era, LGBT issues are now a familiar and largely accepted topic in American journalism. I am focusing on the US media because they are what I consume and observe, but also because they have been a highly influential model, providing content used around the globe for the last 50 years. During that time, mainstream newspapers, magazines, and broadcast news entities in the United States have moved from a position of condemnation and scorn to one of familiarity and even support for gay people as we emerged from the social margins into the mainstream.

I begin this chapter by looking back and asking how and why this change happened.[1] As journalists, researchers, scholars and citizens, we need to understand this history if we are to influence and critique the role of news in creating more equitable societies. I end by looking forward: in a time of wide ranging and perhaps fundamental changes in journalism, what should the future agenda for research and scholarship on gays and the news media look like? These kinds of large questions call for collective, collaborative answers. I offer some suggestions as a way of adding to a conversation in which many others are already engaged. My initial point is simply that the creation, growth and success of the American gay rights movement has been affected by many factors; in today's media saturated world, the news narrative has been and is likely to remain among the most significant.[2]

Why news matters

As readers and viewers, we may approach news reports as discrete entities about specific events or issues. But taken from a broader perspective, the vast array of words and images that constitute "the news" also exists as a set of on-going narratives. Collectively, they create a discourse that heavily influences our vision of self and others. Like their counterparts in the entertainment industry, the narratives of news are not reality, but representations of reality, created according to professional codes and practices that typically rely on familiar templates. Journalists may claim that they don't make the news, they just report it, but communication research has made clear the constructed nature of news (see, for example, Epstein 1973; Gans 1979; Tuchman 1978).

Far from being neutral observers, journalists come to their work with racial, gender, sexual orientation, class, geographic and generational identities that deeply affect not only what they select to cover but also how they choose to cover it. By drawing on longstanding stereotypes that resonate deeply with their audiences, media workers can reduce complex issues to simplified binaries of right and wrong, strong and weak, normal and perverted.

Hollywood films and entertainment television alike, arguably two of the most significant cultural touchstones for Americans in the post-World War II period, have a long history of suppressing gay themes. As Fiske noted in *Media Matters*, because the mere mention of gay existence created "immense anxiety" in American culture, "overt references are typically repressed from public or popular discourse, except, of course, when they are the subject of a news report" (Fiske 1994: 57). In the decades when gays were invisible in entertainment media, news depictions were unapologetically negative in the extreme, "framed alternatively as a sickness, perversion or crime" (Fejes and Petrich 1993: 402).

Headline references to queens, faggots and fairies may be hard for today's readers to imagine. But at the time they were being published, pejorative news stories were not particularly remarkable and in fact conformed quite seamlessly with widely held beliefs that thrived in an era of ignorance. The most typical discursive devices for journalists were deviance and abnormality, concepts the American public accepted without much questioning.

News frames our vision

Framing theory helps us understand the multiple ways in which journalists display value judgments in the products they create. The selection of what to cover, the prominence given to that coverage in terms of headline size or minutes of airtime, as well as the choice of words, images, audio and video all play a role in framing a story and thereby in influencing audience perceptions of content and meaning. Ross shows that media frames are most powerful when they describe "people, places or issues about which we have no direct information. Media frames tend to be most influential when they provide a means for us to interpret and understand the unknown. The frames we encounter in media provide a template for our vision of the foreign, the marginal, the other" (Lester and Ross 2003: 32).

Well into the 1980s, gay identity was often a closely guarded secret, kept from co-workers, friends and even family members. As a result, news stories about gay people were generally a primary source of information for straight America. But news coverage relied on damaging, inaccurate and sensational stereotypes. When they were not ignored altogether, gays – like racial and ethnic minorities – were typically framed as outside of mainstream acceptability, formulated routinely as the discursive other.

Frames direct readers to develop meanings that go well beyond the words and pictures on the page or the television screen. They shape the news narratives by suggesting connections of "… each story to others and to a wealth of cultural myth and legend, to cultural beliefs of how the world works, and of how stories end. Framing connects today's news/issues with our personal and social histories and with the myriad of images and stereotypes we use to represent reality" (Lester and Ross 2003: 31). In this way, news frames help to formulate the larger discourse. Entman points out that, while the specific facts of an individual news account may be accurate, the cumulative impression of repeated news stories may none the less lead to distortions and misrepresentations.

> [T]he specific realities depicted in single stories may accumulate to form a summary message that distorts social reality. Each in a series of news stories

may be accurate, yet the combination may yield false cognitions within audiences (Entman 1994: 509).

Entman was writing about crime reporting and race, but his point very much applies to the coverage of gays that also drew heavily on stereotypes and on the deviance frame. Stories showing gay people as functioning members of society were absent from news coverage. What was reported about gays continually directed readers and viewers toward negative conclusions. In this way, mainstream institutions like newspapers help to reinforce rather than challenge conventional assumptions and beliefs. Entertainment narratives draw on the same cultural mythologies, and hence it is no accident that fictional depictions of gays have had a great deal in common with stories ripped from the headlines.

Media, society transformed

No single transformative moment changed reporting practices. Coverage of LGBT communities evolved over decades due to a complex and dynamic set of interacting economic, technological, social and cultural forces. The most significant milestones are recounted here only briefly to provide an overview of what was a very different time.

In broad societal terms, change was seemingly everywhere in post-World War II America. The era of sex, drugs and rock & roll was shattering notions of the idealized nuclear American family. Movements against the Vietnam War and for Black Civil Rights and Free Speech provided both inspiration and templates for mobilization and strategic action. Women's Liberation challenged gender conventions and effectively argued that the personal was political. When gays began to organize and press for changes in the law, they also saw the importance of social and cultural recognition. One of the earliest objectives of gay rights groups was the elimination of media representations dominated by negative stereotypes. As the 1960s drew to a close, their work was starting to pay off and "gay and lesbian demands for equal protection began to be viewed as legitimate news, although the legitimacy of their demands still was viewed as questionable" (Fejes and Petrich 1993: 402).

In media terms, change was widespread as well. By the mid-1970s, television had replaced newspapers as the dominant source of information for most Americans. Cable news came of age a decade later and opened the era of 24/7 coverage, in which news content was not only expanding but also becoming increasingly sensational. And corporate owners no longer regarded news departments solely as a public service. Instead, they were increasingly viewed as a critical part of the commercial imperative. With the right kind of approach, news programming could bolster the bottom line.

TV talk shows had demonstrated that previously forbidden topics could produce eager audiences and impressive ratings. *People* magazine was a moneymaker for Time, Inc., and showed the commercial power of celebrities. The border between news and entertainment and between public and private discourse began to fade into media history. Even elite journalistic enterprises saw the successes and followed suit. In this milieu, gay content emerged as culturally cutting edge, controversial, and commercially viable.

Impact of AIDS and advocacy

The AIDS crisis became a major mainstream news story in the mid-1980s. While reporting on AIDS further stigmatized gay men in particular, it also raised the visibility of gay communities whose grassroots efforts to cope with a national epidemic were valiant. Journalists who reported these stories were suddenly confronted with their own bias:

> ... reporters and their readers were exposed to a view of gay and lesbian life very different from the 1970s hedonistic stereotypes of gay life. ... Particularly in large urban communities with gay and lesbian communities that were mobilized against AIDS, editors and other media professionals began to learn more about the gay and lesbian community and thereby became sensitized to the homophobic slant of much of their previous accounts. Professional news journals such as ASNE Bulletin, Presstime, and the Columbia Journalism Review began to carry articles commenting on some of the more obvious examples of homophobic news coverage of AIDS. (Fejes and Petrich 1993: 404)

In fact, homophobic stories about AIDS in *The New York Post* prompted activists to create the Gay and Lesbian Alliance Against Defamation in 1985. Two years later, GLAAD persuaded the *New York Times* to use the word gay instead of homosexual.[3] GLAAD successfully used multiple strategies with editors around the country to push for elimination of stereotypes and for a greater inclusion of gays in everyday news coverage. The National Gay and Lesbian Journalist Association (NLGJA) was founded in 1990 and became a significant force for change by working inside newsrooms to offer story ideas, critiques of coverage that did not meet professional standards of fairness, and contextual details that were often missing from reporting.

Throughout the 1990s – often called the gay 90s because of such prominent LGBT media content – gay issues and events became an increasingly familiar feature of news and public discourse. The debate over gays in the US military, for example, led the television news and made front page headlines on a daily basis during the first months of Bill Clinton's presidency. Clinton did not end the ban on military service, but he none the less was viewed as "a friend in the White House" and the first official meeting between an American president and a group of homosexuals took place during the Clinton administration (Fiske 1994: 59). In 2000, NLGJA's longitudinal study of "Lesbian and Gays in the Newsroom: Ten Years Later" tracked the prevalence of mainstreaming gays as story sources and subjects. Defined as representing gays "regularly in subjects not confined to gay or lesbian issues," mainstreaming "is getting more common," the study concluded (Aarons and Murphy 2000: 21). Of the journalists who responded to the national survey, 59 percent said that their news organizations mainstreamed LGBT people in some or much of their reporting. "There was a time when gay people jumped for joy at any mention at all," the study quotes one respondent as saying. "Now I think people … want our lives integrated into mainstream coverage" (Aarons and Murphy 2000: 29).

Reframing gay issues

It took several decades but the narrative frame had shifted. In 2002 the *New York Times* began to include gay couples on its Weddings/Celebrations pages. By then, hundreds of smaller newspapers around the country had already adopted that practice, clearly including gays in the discourse of relationships and families. In so doing, it became increasingly hard to argue that gays destroy family values. As Fiske had noted, "far from wanting to weaken the family, gays and lesbians want to become families" (Fiske 1994: 61). In 2004, the *Times* endorsed marriage for same sex couples on its editorial page, and a lead in *Newsweek* followed in a more provocative way in 2008 by putting its opinion piece on the cover and by centering its arguments on religion and the Bible rather than law and the US Constitution.

While critiques of media coverage are still very much a part of today's agenda for GLAAD, NLGJA and other advocacy groups, the gay rights movement in the United States has moved its most crucial battles from the arena of discourse to that of law. This is precisely why the success of anti-gay ballot initiatives in the 2008 elections was both stunning, and as noted in an open letter to the newly elected president, ironic.

> On Nov. 4, 2008, millions of gay, lesbian, bisexual and transgender Americans of all races proudly cast their ballots for Barack Obama, helping to elect the first African American president of the United States. On that same day, voters in Arizona, Arkansas, California and Florida approved initiatives denying basic civil rights to GLBT citizens (Jones and Black, 14 November 2008).

The specific concern was the passage of initiatives prohibiting marriage, and in the Arkansas case prohibiting adoption, for same sex couples. But their broader point was to call for federal legislation to protect the rights "of gay, lesbian, bisexual and transgender citizens in all areas, including civil marriage, military service, adoption, Social Security, taxation, immigration, employment, housing and access to health care, social services and education." This agenda could hardly have been imagined in an earlier era, much less been given a hearing in a mainstream American newspaper. Improved and expanded coverage has helped change attitudes and perceptions, but equal protection under the law remains a central challenge in the twenty-first century, something that is particularly true when looking at gay rights in the global context.

Future research

News may be said to have a common set of features regardless of its geographic origin. TV news in particular is regularly dominated by violence and disaster. But norms and values regarding LGBT issues are culturally specific, and this has major implications for journalistic reporting and for scholarship. As we look toward a future agenda in both of these arenas, I would argue that there is no universal discourse for LGBT people. Even in the US case, the preponderance of news and scholarly writing has focused on gay men who are white, urban and economically advantaged. Lesbians, bisexuals and transgendered people – whose issues are often quite different from those of gay men – are largely absent from the US news media's coverage. LGBT people of color are similarly on the media margins. As media scholars, we need to look at the diversity within our communities across categories of race, class, age, geography and religion. We need to study the policies and practices of ethnic presses, which often publish in languages other than English and serve growing immigrant populations.

Much remains to be learned about news reporting on LGBT people in the non-Western world. Iranian president Mahmoud Ahmadinejad made headlines when he told Columbia University students, "In Iran we don't have homosexuals like in your country. We don't have that in our country" ("Iran Sites Omit Leader's Homosexuality Remarks." See at http://www.msnbc.msn.com/id/20999705/ Ahmadinejad, 24 September 2007, Columbia University). But in fact, same sex contact in Iran is a criminal offense punishable by imprisonment or by execution. Muslim countries differ widely in their laws regulating sexual expression. In more secular societies such as Turkey, homosexuality is legal, and gay life is a visible part of the culture, especially in major cities. In neighboring Iran, conditions are quite different. As the second largest religion in the world, with more than one billion adherents in dozens of Muslim-majority countries, Islam's gay populations are critically important and offer a largely untapped site of study for scholars and journalists interested in expanding our collective knowledge of media practices and impacts.

China also offers a vast terrain for study. Homosexuality is not prohibited by law but, because strong cultural stigmas persist, gay topics are not in the headlines, on television nor are they easily accessible on the highly filtered Internet. None the less, gay life is emerging in all major Chinese cities just as LGBT scholarship is emerging in its universities. These developments offer exciting possibilities for collaborative work including comparative international case studies that examine similarities and differences in professional journalistic practice, governmental policy, and other causal mechanisms that impact media constructions.

In the digital era, we need to study interactivity, social networking and the content production by an increasingly sophisticated global citizenry. Multi-dimensional news and information and their increasingly complex distribution patterns require multiple methodologies for study. At the same time, we need to remain alert to the ways in which historical patterns, prejudices and stereotypes against LGBT people remain embedded in news narratives – and may even be enhanced by distribution patterns of new technologies.

The 21st century media landscape

Digital media, social networking, blogs, websites, user-generated content and proliferating hand-held devices are all helping to change the ways in which news is conceptualized, produced, circulated and consumed. Audiences are global as well as local; many no longer look to traditional media for their news and information. Social networks are essential for a generation of readers and viewers who are far more attached to their laptops, cell phones and iPods than they are to the morning paper or the evening news.

Changing business models have had a huge impact on the creation and distribution of news, adding to both its velocity and its reach. In this 24/7 all-news-all-the-time culture, bloggers may be as influential as news reporters in setting agendas and shaping values, particularly among young people. Contrary to the conventional wisdom that describes the youth audience as basically uninterested in news, they are "heavy consumers of media – not old media, but new media. Their media, which is to say cell phones, digital cameras, text messages, websites, message boards, Internet blogs, vlogs and podcasts" (Moritz and Kwak 2009 forthcoming). In this arena, traditional journalism is only one part of a much bigger media-saturated world. Activists and communication scholars alike have focused much of their work on traditional media. But the territory that remains to be explored on the Internet is enormous and largely untraveled, and its relevance cannot be understated, particularly for the generation currently coming of age.

Hate speech

Although gays have become more accepted and visible in American culture, hostile rhetoric against them is far from abolished, particularly in the world of news-talk television and radio. TV evangelist Jerry Falwell, for example, used his cable TV show to accuse gays and lesbians (along with feminists and abortionists) of being responsible for the 9/11 terror attacks. He apologized after a blizzard of protest. In 2003, cable TV talk show host Michael Savage flew into an on-air rage ("You should only get AIDS and die, you pig") and referred to a gay caller as a sodomite and piece of garbage. NBC subsequently dismissed him (Moritz 2007b: 123). But Savage remains a prominent player in what Rory O'Connor (2008) describes as the "politicized and often factually challenged world of talk radio that dominates a sizable portion of America's airwaves…"

The Internet is another haven for hate speech. American courts have ruled that Internet expressions are protected by First Amendment guarantees of free speech and therefore cannot be restricted. In contrast, international laws view hate speech as a crime. In France, Germany, Sweden and Canada, websites that engage in such expressions are shut down. But cyber communication crosses national borders with ease and hate groups have found a hospitable digital home base in the United States. Today, hate sites have become a common location for the expression of hostilities that cannot be easily advanced in more controlled cultural spaces. As a result the Internet has become, according to the US-based Human Rights Information Network, "a utopia for all kinds of hate groups, from new-Nazis to anarchists" (Moritz 2007b: 124).

> In the last decade, the Internet has emerged as a powerful new tool not only for spreading hate but also for mobilizing a highly organized opposition movement. Indeed, the Internet provides a unique opportunity for linking huge numbers of individuals, for providing them with e-mail connections, contact information, prescribed protest letters and other resources, which are used to vilify gay people ... (Moritz 2007b: 124).

Some sites, such as godhatesfags.com, are blatant in their language and approach, "opposing the fag lifestyle of soul-damning, nation-destroying filth" (homepage of website). Others, such as the American Family Association's site, have a much more civil and sophisticated tone. They offer so-called expert testimony from individuals identified as doctors, authors, pastors and educators who promote scientifically discredited reparative therapies to cure gays of their afflictions. AFA's messages serve as a reminder that "hate can be cloaked in civility ... language does not have to be visceral to inflict harm" (cited by Moritz 2007b: 130).

With technology that is not only widely available but also simple to use, individuals and groups can become overnight publishers. Resistance Records, for example,

> contains graphics, downloadable white power music and a message from its founder describing the state of crisis in the White world, and is a prominent example of the technical sophistication many of these websites display (Moritz 2007b: 130).

Once moving and still images, speeches, interviews and recordings are sent into cyberspace, their re-distribution potential is enormous. They can be accessed by journalists, researchers, writers, and producers – any of whom are in a position to further the distribution process, and more importantly, to seemingly certify the validity of the information simply by appropriating it for incorporation into more mainstream discourse. This circulation of uninformed and hateful materials was problematic before the advent of the Internet and is even more so now. This is particularly relevant to vulnerable populations in places where gays are still highly stigmatized and where journalists themselves have limited knowledge and training.

Conclusion

The US case demonstrates that media play a critical role in shaping public perceptions about LGBT people and in helping to foster support for socially just policies. A national survey commissioned by GLAAD just after the 2008 elections suggested that most Americans are strongly supportive of gay rights. Fully 75 percent said they favored either marriage, domestic partnerships or civil unions for gay and lesbian couples; 69 percent said they opposed laws that banned qualified gay and lesbian couples from becoming adoptive parents; 63 percent said they favored extending hate crime laws to cover gay and transgendered people.

In releasing the survey results, GLAAD president Neil Giuliano underscored the importance of "increasing the visibility of our stories in the media … this work is changing hearts and minds and must continue." (Harris Interactive2008).

This call for fair, accurate and inclusive treatment in the ever-changing, ever-present journalistic arena must become a global agenda addressed across platforms by multiple constituents. Journalists have an obligation to be informed as well as inclusive and impartial. Perhaps most importantly, they need to appreciate the consequences of prejudice on the safety and civil rights of the people they portray.

Gay people themselves have been in the forefront of creating change. Advocacy groups like the Human Rights Campaign, Gay Pride, The National Gay and Lesbian Task Force, ACT UP, Queer Nation and many others work in various venues to make LGBT voices heard. Because GLAAD's mission specifically targets media portrayals, its impact in terms of face-to-face meetings with reporters, editors, media managers and community leaders is especially noteworthy. Similarly, NLGJA members are in-house resources who have addressed issues ranging from workplace equity to appropriate use of language. Their stylebook, for example, identifies pejorative and problematic terms (transvestite, special rights), medical terms relating to HIV and AIDS, and discusses editorial policy issues. It is available online in English and in Spanish.

In the contemporary digital environment, scholars must assess not only issues of access but also of content, production, distribution and governmental policies, influence and interventions. We need to unpack the systemic nature of discrimination and demonstrate the linkages between misogyny, racism and homophobia. Analyses of culturally specific issues of place, politics and religion along with issues of power related to race, class and gender are all critically important to this research agenda. And we should not forget to record the fascinating media histories that are being created every decade in every region of the world.

Notes

1 The author was a member of the Board of Directors of the Gay and Lesbian Alliance against Defamation (GLAAD) from 1996–99. She was on GLAAD's National Research Advisory Board from 1999–2005. She has also been an advisor to the National Lesbian and Gay Journalists Association (NLGJA).

2 Here I am using the term gay to refer to lesbians, bisexuals, transgendered and queer people, but as I will discuss later in the chapter, there are distinct and important differences among these groups that need to be articulated and that often get lost glossed over in more general discussions of "gay" issues. Similarly, I am using news and news media initially as a reference to mainstream journalism in the United States, including major daily newspapers, all-news radio and cable television, network and local television news programs and weekly news magazines. Here too there are dangers in generalizations and in suggesting that all news products are alike, a topic that I address later in the chapter.

3 According to GLAAD's media reference guide, the term homosexual is offensive and its use is restricted by the Associated Press, *The New York Times* and *The Washington Post*. "Because of the clinical history of the word 'homosexual,' it has been adopted by anti-gay extremists to suggest that lesbians and gay men are somehow diseased or psychologically/emotionally disordered – notions discredited by both the American Psychological Association and the American Psychiatric Association in the 1970s."

References

Aarons, L. and Murphy, S. (2000) *Lesbian and Gays in the Newsroom: ten years later*. Report from the Annenberg School for Communication, University of Southern California, and the National Lesbian and Gay Journalists Association. Online. Available HTTP: <http://www.usc.edu/schools/annenberg/asc/projects/soin.old/NGLJA.pdf>.

Ahmadinejad, M. (24 September 2007) Columbia University.

Barnhurst, K. G. and Henderson, L. (2007) *Media/Queered: Visibility and Its Discontents*, New York: Peter Lang.

Entman, R. M. (1994) "Representation and reality in the portrayal of blacks on network television news." *Journalism Quarterly*, vol. 71, no. 3, 509-520.

Epstein, E. (1973) *News from Nowhere: television and the news*, New York: Random House.

Fejes, F. (2008) *Gay Rights and Moral Panic: the origins of America's debate on homosexuality*, New York: Palgrave Macmillan.

Fejes, F. and Petrich, K. (1993) "Invisibility, homophobia and heterosexism: lesbians, gays and the media." *Critical Studies in Mass Communication*, vol. 10, no. 4: 396-420.

Gans, H. (1979) *Deciding What's News: a study of CBS evening news, NBC nightly news, Newsweek, and Time*, New York: Pantheon Books.

Harris Interactive (2008) *Pulse of Equality: a snapshot of US perspectives on gay and transgender people and policies* .8 December. Online. Available HTTP: <http://74.125.47.132/custom?q=cache:sl4hoqufKYkJ:www.glaad.org/2008/DOCUMENTS/HarrisPoll120308.pdf+pulse+of+equality:+a+snapshot+of&hl=en&ct=clnk&cd=2&gl=us&client=google-coop-np> (accessed 21 January 2009).

Jones, C. and Black, L. (2008) "Letter to the Editor." *The San Francisco Chronicle*. 14 November.

Lester, P. M. and Ross, S. D. (2003) *Images That Injure: pictorial stereotypes in the media*, 2nd edn, Westport, Connecticut: Praeger.

Miller, L. (15 December 2008) "Our mutual joy," *Newsweek*. Online. Available HTTP: <http://www.newsweek.com/id/172653> (accessed 21 January 2009).

Moritz, M. (2007a) "Say I do: gay weddings in mainstream media." In Barnhurst, K. G. and Henderson, L., *Media/Queered: visibility and its discontents*, New York: Peter Lang.

Moritz, M. (2007b) "Hate speech made easy: the virtual demonisation of gays," In Prum, M., Deschamps, B. and Barbier, M. (Eds), *Racial, Ethnic and Homophobic Violence: killing in the name of otherness*, New York and London: Routledge Cavendish.

Moritz, M. and Kwak, S. (forthcoming) "Students as Creators and Consumers of e-News: The Case of Virginia Tech." In Kiran Prasad (Ed.). "E-journalism: New directions in New Media and News Media." New Delhi: BRPC.

Newsweek (2008) The Good Book and Gay Marriage." 16 December. Online. Available HTTP: <http://www.newsweek.com/id/175223> (accessed 21 January 2009).

O'Connor, R. (2008) *Shock Jocks: hate speech and talk radio: America's ten worst hate talkers and the progressive alternatives*, San Francisco: AlterNet Books.

Tuchman, G. (1978) *Making News: a study in the construction of reality*, New York: Free Press.

31

THE BROADCAST NEWS INTERVIEW: QUESTIONS OF DISCOURSE

Martin Montgomery

This chapter explores the broadcast news interview. It identifies a variety of different types of interview in order to suggest that it is a mistake to regard the accountability interview with a public figure as the principal or defining form, despite its public salience and despite the way in which broadcasters themselves routinely regard it as the cornerstone of their public-service remit. Instead, this chapter will show how broadcast news interviews help to shape the news by providing space for the presentation of expert knowledge and personal experience and in doing so offer different perspectives on the news for the broadcast audience.

The media interview and the news interview

One significant characteristic of media interviews as a generic form lies in the way that they work as talk for an overhearing audience. Interviewers and interviewees know that what they say will be appraised not just by their immediate interlocutor but by who-knows-how-many beyond. This is not merely a matter of pressure towards increased circumspection in one's choice of words, though that must undoubtedly exist. It is also a matter of the public performance of talk – of talking adequately for the public purposes of the encounter and of acquitting oneself well in public.

A second significant aspect of the media interview as a genre is the way in which it is characterised by clear differentiation or pre-allocation of roles: one speaker asks questions and the other answers them. The speaker who asks questions does so from an institutionally-defined position – one in which they hold some responsibility for setting the agenda, the terms or the topic of the discourse. Nor is it a case of simply asking questions; the media interviewer also controls the length, shape and even the style of the encounter. Conversely, the interviewee has not achieved that role by accident. In some way or other they have earned, by virtue of a distinctive attribute, their 'communicative entitlement' as material for a documentary case study, as witness, as celebrity. And the nature of the entitlement is always 'evidenced' or consti-tuted in practice within the interview: in other words, witnessing, 'celebrity-ness', or 'documentary-ness' (Corner, 1995) is an outcome of the kinds of interrogation pursued within the interview.

The broadcast news interview itself provides a particular manifestation of a widely available mediated public genre, but distinct in the way that it offers journalists a crucial device for supplying quotable material to underpin the news. In doing so, we may distinguish four principle sub-genres: (1) interviews with correspondents (reporting and commenting); (2) interviews with ordinary people affected by, or caught up in, the news (witnessing, reacting, and expressing opinion); (3) interviews with experts (informing and explaining); and (4) interviews with 'principals' – public figures with some kind of responsible role in relation to the news event (accounting). These four sub-genres may be defined – as here – by characterising the social identity and role of the person being interviewed and their characteristic contribution to the interview; but they could equally have been described in terms of the kinds of lead-in that set the agenda of the interview or the kinds of question that form its spine. For instance, a prototypical question to a correspondent is "can you tell us more about what is going on?" (see Haarman, 2004), whereas prototypical questions to an ordinary witness or bystander include "What could you see … ?", or "What did/does it feel like …?".

Amongst these main sub-genres of news interview, the broadcast encounter with a public, often political, figure has received by far the greatest attention (Harris, 1991; Clayman, 1991, 1992; Heritage, 1992; Clayman and Heritage, 2002; Hutchby, 2005, 2006; Blum-Kulka, 1983; Fetzer, 2002; Fetzer and Weizman, 2006; Lauerbach, 2006) – in part because they are seen as instances of the classic public sphere in action. The focus of discussion in treatments of interviews of this type is on topics such as bias/neutrality, adversarialness, 'holding to account', and evasion. Indeed, the amount of attention devoted to political interviews might be seen as disproportionate, especially since it leads to this one sub-type coming to define the genre and practice of the news interview as a whole (see, for instance, Hutchby, 2005, and Clayman and Heritage, 2002) even though they are in practice extremely rare within mainstream news programming as represented by the standard bulletin news programme. On the contrary, they are the rather exclusive preserve of those extended news programmes that aim to offer in depth coverage of current affairs, such as ABC's *Nightline*, BBC2's *Newsnight*, BBC Radio 4's *Today*, Channel 4 *News*, *Frost on Sunday* or NBC's *Nightly News*. Accordingly, to focus on the political interview as if it were typical of news interviewing in general is neither supported by the history of the journalistic interview nor justified by a survey of current broadcasting practice.

The aim of this chapter, therefore, is to offer a general typology of the broadcast news interview and thereby to situate the interview with a political or public figure as merely one type amongst the major kinds of interviews that make up the news. The four main generic types of interview are: the *accountability interview*, the *experiential interview*, the *expert interview* and the *news interview* with a correspondent, reporter, or editor, which we term the *affiliated interview*.[1]

This chapter will discuss specific instances of the main sub-genres of news interview. In order to clarify the position of a specific interview within the typology of news interview genres it is useful to distinguish between four broad parameters or axes. The first parameter defines the interviewee as affiliated with the news institution or not. The second parameter defines the interviewee as involved with the news event as an actor or responsible agent. The third parameter defines the interviewee as having first hand knowledge of the event or holding knowledge about it. And the fourth stipulates the nature of their presumed alignment with the audience set up by the interview – whether with the interviewee or not.

On this basis, the following matrix can be constructed.

	Affiliation	*Knowledge*	*Agency*
Accountability interview	–	(of)	+
Experiential interview	–	(of)	–
Expert interview	–	(about)	–
Correspondent interview	+	(of/about)	–

Although this matrix generates a set of ideal-typical classifications to which many actual broadcast news interviews unproblematically correspond, there are in practice some instances of mixed or indecidable cases, or instances where an interview starts out as one type and shifts into another. None the less, such typifications are associated with recognisable differences in interview both in terms of broad purpose (within the overall discursive economy of the news) and particular discursive practice (for instance, type of lead-in or question), even though it must be accepted that part of the difficulty in defining the sub-generic types is that the roles of participants may on occasion be re-defined through shifts of discursive practice.

The accountability interview with a public figure

In news interviews of this type the emphasis falls upon calling a public figure to account in relation to an issue or event of the moment, either for their own deeds or words or for the actions/statements of the institution with which they are associated. While the interviewer seeks to query the basis of a statement or action, typically the interviewee seeks to justify it. Interviewees are public figures in the sense that they hold institutional positions and by their official status are treated as 'having some locus' on the matter at hand. Perhaps the clearest examples of this kind of interview involve politicians being interviewed in relation to a relevant current news event or topic. The example cited below is from a news item broadcast on Channel 4 News the day before a scheduled meeting between Prime Minister Blair and Colonel Gaddafi in Libya. Relations between Libya and the UK had been strained for over a decade by events such as the shooting of a police officer (WPC Yvonne Fletcher) outside the Libyan Embassy in London, the bombing of Tripoli by US planes flying from bases in Britain and the destruction of a transatlantic flight over Lockerbie, Scotland. Latterly, however, relations between Libya and the West (e.g. Italy, France, UK, US) had improved following the curtailment of her nuclear weapons programme and the payment of financial compensation for the victims of the Lockerbie bombing. In Extract 1 Baroness Symon, 'the foreign office minister responsible for the Middle East', is being interviewed by the *presenter* (or programme anchor), Jon Snow.

Extract 1

1 Interviewer: in Westminster now the foreign office minister responsible for the Middle

2 East (.) Baroness(t) Symon (2.0) hh

3 Minister (1.0) er the Prime Minister is is is gonna go ahead

4 and do the: (.) the handshake (.)

5 do we not need more time (.) to:: (.) check Gaddaffi out

6 Symon: (.) hhh (1.0) I think you know there's been a great deal of time

7 I think that was very clear from (.) what Mr Mosey was just telling us

8 in what I thought was er uh a very hh (.) moving er piece that he did just now

9 (.) the fact is that this has been a process (.)

10 there have bee:n (.) many things (.) asked (.) of the Libyans

11 in relation to what happened in Lockerbie (.) hh

12 and they have met (.) those points that have been raised (0.5)

39 but but the enormous thing of course has been Libya's willingness to deal

40 with their weapons of mass destruction programme

41 and that has been (.) the big breakthrough (.) hhh

42 and of course it is er that that has been the major building block

43 for taking the relationship forward

44 Interviewer: put in the most crude terms

45 I mean it is an extraordinary state of affairs isn't it

46 that that a er er er a sponsor of terrorism (.)

47 who: probably killed more Brits than Saddam Hussein did

48 we're going to go and shake the hand of

49		but (.) Saddam Hussein we went to war with and (.) arrested
50	Baroness S:	well you know I think if Mr Mosey (.)
51		can er say that he would shake the hand
52		then probably it isn't for the rest of us to turn round and say no
53		we're not going to do this you don't (.) make break-throughs (.)
54		in foreign relationships by only talking to your friends (.)
55		it's by talking to those with whom you disagree that you manage
56		to make some some real progress
57		and [my point about this is that only ( ) if I could just make the point
58	Interviewer:	[er in a sense that was exactly the point I was asking you whether
59		why we didn't do that with Saddam Hussein
60	Baroness S:	hhh hhh Saddam Hussein was
61		over eighteen years refused all cooperation that was er that was asked of him
62		from the er from the United Nations he deliberately er turned his face away
63		from all those mandatory United Nations Security Council Resolutions
64		and refused all cooperation
65		here we have the exact reverse of that
66		that is the whole point (.)
67		because Colonel Gaddaffi has cooperated
68		Colonel Gaddaffi has come forward
69		and offered up his weapons of mass destruction
70		he has had the International Atomic Energy Authority in there
71		verifying dismantling those weapons of mass destruction
72		if we had seen that sort of action er from Saddam Hussein
73		things might have been very different
74	Interviewer:	[Baroness Symon
75	Baroness S:	[but in fact of course
76		it is the positive action of Colonel Gaddaffi that has led us to this position
77	Interviewer:	thank you very much for joining us
78	Baroness S:	thank you

There are various markers of this as an accountability interview. In programmes where the whole news interview is broadcast, interviewees are always introduced at or just prior to the onset of the interview. This is not just by proper name (Baroness Symon) but also by an *identifier* – a specification of the grounds on which they speak for the purposes of the interview at hand. She could have been introduced using any or all of the following identifiers:

of Vernham Dean
of the British-American Project
a government spokeswoman
a junior foreign office minister
Deputy Leader of the House of Lords
Minister of State for the Middle East, International Security, Consular and Personal Affairs in the Foreign and Commonwealth Office

The identifier adopted, however, is 'the foreign office minister responsible for the Middle East' and this establishes the relevance of her contributions for the interview at hand where the surrounding news item explores the wisdom of an imminent visit by Blair to Libya. Identification in this way also grants a specific kind of communicative entitlement (see Myers, 2000) as part of setting up the accountability interview: her contributions are elicited on the grounds that she by implication shares responsibility for the actions of the government and is accountable to the public on whose behalf she – like the Prime Minister – holds office. Jon Snow's frequent references to *we/us* (see ll. 5, 48, 49 and 59) invoke not only the UK government but also the audience/public on whose behalf the government acts and on whose behalf Jon Snow presents himself as speaking. This lends his questions the force of 'request justification of a statement, decision, policy or course of action'.

Indeed, the questions which he asks are built around propositions that are disputable (or 'D-events' in Labov and Fanshel's 1977 terms): see 45–49 for example. The questions also have an inbuilt preference and may therefore be considered coercive. For example:

45 I mean it is an extraordinary state of affairs isn't it
5   do we not need more time (.) to:: (.) check Gaddaffi out

Furthermore, there are two distinctive features of turn-by-turn talk in a public accountability interview. One of them is the absence of in-turn vocalisations by the interviewer such as *mmhum, yeh, oh, I see* (sometimes described as *receipt tokens*, Atkinson, 1992; Clayman and Heritage, 2002) that routinely occur as indications of attention in non status-marked, co-present encounters. Broadly these receipt tokens signal acknowledgement by the hearer of what the speaker is saying. One reason that the interviewer withholds them is that they may be interpreted as affiliative: in other words, they may be heard as indications of agreement by the hearer with the speaker's position. In withholding such behaviour the interviewer maintains a neutral position (Atkinson, 1992) with respect to what the speaker is saying. This in part, then, is a way of performing that official impartiality that the broadcasting of current affairs as a public service requires.

However, if receipt tokens are withheld by interviewers, this does not mean that turns by the interviewee are met with silence by the interviewer. On the contrary, among accountability interviews we encounter a high incidence of overlap at the boundaries of turns. Indeed, here, Baroness Symon hardly finishes a turn before Jon Snow begins his. Since, in these cases, he is producing a new (or a re-phrased) question which runs across what is from her a yet unfinished answer, he gives the impression that she has not provided an adequate response to what has gone before. Or, alternatively, that there is a conflict about agendas – that he, for instance, considers that she should be talking about something else. Certainly, the following exchange registers a difference of view about what is the main point at issue:

55	Symon:	it's by talking to those with whom you disagree that you manage
56		to make some some real progress
57		and [my point about this is that only ( ) if I could just make the point
58	Interviewer:	[er in a sense that was exactly the point I was asking you whether
59		why we didn't do that with Saddam Hussein

As with other news interviews, accountability interviews are cued or occasioned by the surrounding *news item*. It is noticeable, for instance, in this interview how both participants orient at points to previous news discourse in the programme.

More so, perhaps, than other news interviews, however, accountability interviews can also prime the news. In other words, they not only develop out of a news item but also have the potential to feed into subsequent coverage – particularly by providing a topical resource in the form of quotation for a later news item (see Ekstrom 2001). This may be exemplified by the following exchange on Al Jazeera's *Frost over the World* between David Frost as interviewer and Prime Minister Blair.

Extract 2

15	Blair:	the idea that Iraqis should be faced with the situation
16		where they either have (0.5) a brutal (0.5) dictator . in Saddam
17		or alternatively . a sectarian religious conflict .
18		why can't they have in Iraq what their people want .
19		which is a non-sectarian government .
20		a government that is elected by the people
21		and the same opportunities and the same rights
22		that we:: enjoy in countries such as this .
23	In'viewer:	but but . so far it's been (1.5) you know . pretty much of a disaster
24	Blair:	it it it it
25		HAS but you see what I say to people is .
26		why is it difficult in Iraq
27		it's not difficult because of some . accident in planning .

28	it's difficult because . there is a deliberate strategy (0.5)
29	al-Qaeda with Sunni insurgents on the one hand .
30	erm . Iranian-backed . elements with Shia militia on the other
31	to create a situation in which the will of the majority of Iraqis
32	which is for peace .
33	is displaced by the will of the minority for war

This interview was broadcast on 17 November 2006 and formed the basis for widespread reports that Blair had admitted that Iraq was/had been a disaster. By the next day newspapers in the UK carried headlines such as 'Iraq is a "disaster" admits Blair' (*Mail*) or 'Iraq invasion a disaster, Blair admits' (*Telegraph*) with CNN on 18 November subsequently commenting that: Blair's 'Iraq disaster' interview provokes storm. BBC Online used the headline: 'Blair accepts "disaster" in Iraq'. Al-Jazeera subsequently ran the recorded interview with the caption 'Blair admits Iraq "a disaster"'.

Blair's own words themselves were hardly salient at the time. And it hardly matters that Blair does not in any case say exactly: 'Iraq has been a disaster'. As lines 23–25 of the transcript show, what actually happens is that Blair agrees elliptically with Frost's utterance, 'so far it's been (1.5) you know . pretty much of a disaster', where the reference for Frost's 'it' has to be recovered from some way back in the discourse (and Frost's turn itself is full of hesitancy including the hedge 'pretty much', which is omitted from all subsequent quotation). It is also worth noting that Blair's own turn-initial component, 'it has' (subsequently treated as his admission), begins even before

Frost's turn had concluded with 'disaster'. None the less, as long as the subsequent loose quotations (often in headlines, which by convention allow a degree of imprecision) are difficult to refute, this accountability interview has done substantive work in priming subsequent news coverage. This, accordingly, is the rubric under which the accountability interview runs: not only may the interviewee be held to account within the interview for actions and words prior to it; but it is also the case that the interview may generate material that can be used subsequently in its aftermath for accountability purposes. Faced with clear potential for discursive pitfall it is not perhaps surprising that politicians (the principle, though not the only focus of the accountability interview) become a byword for evasiveness. Indeed, we must at least entertain the possibility that evasion is on occasion a produced consequence of the discourse practices of the accountability interview, as much as a quality inherent in the interviewee's performance (or character).

The experiential/witness interview with an ordinary member of the public

The experiential interview provides news programmes with personal reactions to issues or events and, where appropriate, with eyewitness accounts. As with the accountability interview there is a clear demarcation of roles between questioning and answering. There are, however, particular differences in the way these actions are performed that mark the encounter as a case of the 'experiential' interview. The interviewee is presented in the role of an observer, victim or survivor rather than as an active agent in relation to the news and is interviewed not to answer for the event but to answer about it.

A principal class of experiential interview includes those that depend upon having had a first hand experience of an event or issue. For these interviews the entitlement is more direct and may be seen as dependent upon an act of witnessing. This is particularly relevant in relation to a whole class of 'bad news' events such as accidents, disasters and emergencies. In broadcasting bad news, the tales of survivors offer something similar to reportage: they provide a significant counterweight to the core element of these news events – the accounts of fatalities.

A significant component of news coverage of the London bombings of July 2005, for instance, was precisely this kind of witnessing. At the core of interviews with survivors – overwhelmingly pervasive across the domain of broadcast news – were accounts which routinely conformed to Labov's description of narratives of personal experience (Labov, 1972b; Labov and Fanshel, 1977; Labov and Waletsky, 1967). Indeed, a striking aspect of the London accounts is their sheer similarity: for all the unique awfulness of individuals' experiences, the forms through which this was mediated to the broadcast audience were highly uniform (see Montgomery, 2007).

The example for discussion here, however, is of a rather different kind where the interviewee is invited to express feeling, opinion or judgement on the basis of an indirect connection to the news event. It took place just prior to the interview with Baroness Symons, transcribed as Extract 1, and as part of the same *news item*. (Symons herself refers to it in her own interview as a very hh (.) moving er piece.). The interviewer is again the *presenter* (anchor) of the programme, Jon Snow.

Extract 3

1	Interviewer:	John Mosey lost his daughter Helga in the Lockerbie crash
2		he joins us now from Malvern (.) .hh
3		erm John Mosey (1.5)
4		d'you have every reason to believe Colonel Gaddafi now
5	John Mosey:	(2.5)
6		er to believe him (.)
7		erm well (.) we have to accept
8		that he's (.) jumped over all the hurdles that the United Nations
9		have placed in front of him (.).hh
10		and if your erstwhile enemy:: (.) says he wants to change
11		and shows (.).h verifiable (.).h er evidence of changing (.)
12		only a (.) fool I think would (.) put their foot in his face at the last minute (.)
13	Int'viewer:	what will your thoughts be:: (.) tomorrow
14	Mosey:	(2.5)
15		er I I can't see any negative side to this
16		erm I'm not sure about the timing (.).h
17		I'm not a politician (.).h
18		but it can only be a good thing only good can come out of it
19		erm when as I've said your enemy has done all that's been demanded of him
20		by the United Nations (.).h
21		er surely we also have a responsibility to keep our side (.).h of the bargain
22		and (.) and er (.) welcome these people back into the:: community of nations
23		if we don't (.)
24		what sort of signal do we send to the: (.) erm (.) dangerous world out there (.)
25		do we send a signal that says
26		don't do deals with the West (.).h they can't be trusted
27		they won't keep their side of the bargain (.)
28		we must maintain our integrity
29	Int'viewer:	d'you think he is the man who (.) ultimately killed your daughter
30	Mosey:	(2.5)
31		I don't know (1.0)
32		I sat through the whole of the ten months trial (0.5)
33		I have some reservations (0.5)

34		erm but we (.) said that we would (.) accept the verdict of the: Scottish court
35		and that's what we (.) have to do (.)
36	Int'viewer:	and if you had to would you shake his hand
37	Mosey:	(3.0)
38		huphh (.)
39		I'm not eager to become (.) a friend of his (.)
40		erm (.) but if I had to yes it wouldn't trouble me at all (.).h
41		er (.) thank God there's forgiveness for all of us (.)
42	Int'viewer:	John Mosey thank you so much for joining us
43		(2.5)

Although this example displays the standard question-answer structure of the interview this is clearly different from an accountability interview. For one thing Mosey is *identified* in a very different kind of way to Baroness Symon.

1 Interviewer: John Mosey lost his daughter Helga in the Lockerbie crash

In contrast to Symons who is addressed as someone with an implied obligation to answer questions and who can represent an aspect of government, Mosey is identified and addressed as an ordinary individual who has an entitlement to speak based upon a personal and particular connection with the news material, which the interview will provide an opportunity to develop. John Mosey is not precisely a witness to an event. For one thing Blair has not yet met Gaddafi, so the event at the heart of the interview hasn't even happened. And, in any case, John Mosey will not be there when it does take place. At the core of his answers, none the less, we find some statement of personal experience:

29	Int'viewer:	d'you think he is the man who (.) ultimately killed your daughter
30	Mosey:	(2.5)
31		I don't know (1.0)
32		I sat through the whole of the ten months trial (0.5)
33		I have some reservations (0.5)

John Mosey is treated as speaking simply on his own behalf (as the father of the victim). Indeed, at the heart of the interview is quite simply an invitation to him to state his own personal views; and in offering his views (in the first person) he is responding to questions that are very different in kind from those of the accountability interview.

4	Int'viewer:	d'you have every reason to believe Colonel Gaddafi now
13	Int'viewer:	what will your thoughts be:: (.) tomorrow

These questions are directed to the personal beliefs, thoughts and feelings of the recipient rather than to issues of the interviewee's responsibility or liability. It is noticeable also that they are short and simple in construction. Indeed, Jon Snow's turns in the two interviews contrast sharply in kind. Here each turn has just one turn-component. In the accountability interview they sometimes contain two or more. There is also no overlap between turns in this interview. Despite John Mosey's pauses there are no occasions where Snow speaks across his turn. It is not just that Mosey is not held to account for his views but these are treated as if they were by definition indisputable. This is an important point of difference between the accountability interview and the experiential interview. Whereas in the accountability interview interviewers routinely pursue a (satisfactory) response to questions by repeating or rephrasing them, in the experiential interview answers are rarely treated as unsatisfactory. Note, for instance, the way in which Snow moves from question to question, each of which represents a shift of topic.

If we examine Mosey's answers closely, however, it is not obvious that he has in each case answered the question which was put to him. In answer to the question about what his thoughts will be tomorrow he says we should keep our side of the bargain. In answer to the question of whether Gaddaffi killed his daughter he says we should accept the verdict of the Scottish court. If Snow's questions are addressed to Mosey's thoughts, emotions and beliefs, the latter's answers invoke instead what might loosely be called 'principled bases for action' – Mosey says in effect that we should treat others' actions and words at face value, we should keep our side of a bargain, and we should remember that forgiveness is universal. And yet despite the apparent gap between the question and the answer there is little or no sense of any conflict of agendas here or of questions being evaded.[2]

The two types of interview – the accountability interview and the experiential interview – are thus very different in character. The former is built upon questions designed to seek justifications from the recipient for their statements or lines of action and to challenge them. The latter is designed to elicit perspectives on an event or an issue. The most obvious kind of experiential interview is one involving a witness to an event, or a survivor of it. But some kind of (non-responsible) connection to the event may be enough to warrant the interview.

The generic differences between these two types of interview are partly at the level of opening 'lead in' or introduction, partly at the level of question type and type of follow-up question from the interviewer. But they also invite a different kind of attention from their audience. The accountability interview, as currently practised, invites the audience to identify with the interviewer as their spokesperson: it proceeds as if the interviewer is asking questions on behalf of components of the public. The experiential interview, however, occupies a quite different relationship to the audience. This kind of interview is shaped to give us the experiential flavour of the event and the audience is situated on the side of the interviewee who has been invited to articulate a version of what we might think, see, or feel if we too were close up in some way to the event. Whereas in the accountability interview the interviewer speaks as if for us and the interviewee is presented as estranged from the audience ('an evasive politician'), in the experiential interview the interviewee is treated as one of us.

The expert interview

After the accountability and the experiential interview, the third main type of interview – the *expert interview* – is designed to elucidate the event or topic of the news by providing 'background' through eliciting supplementary information, clarifying unfamiliar concepts, spelling out the implications of a development or providing independent comment. They are most likely to be used when technical or semi-technical issues are involved and typically figure interviewees who are 'not affiliated' to the broadcast institution itself as a way of projecting a sense of the disinterested, non-partisan nature of the information, evidence or explanation being offered. Although not affiliated to the news organisation itself they do of course often have some kind of institutional affiliation or professional status which confirms their expert credentials. As with other news interviewees this information will be referenced at the onset of the interview by the interviewer as part of the identifier.

Here is an example of an expert knowledge interview being used in order to cast light on an issue in the news – in this case whether or not to re-classify cannabis as a dangerous drug. It is *focused* at the outset and the interviewee is introduced not only by name ('Matthew Atha') but with a particular, topically relevant credential ('the director of the Independent Drug Monitoring Unit') which provides for his commu-nicative entitlement in this particular context.

Extract 4 BBC Radio 4 *Today*

1	Int'viewer:	cannabis is not going to be re-classified as a more dangerous drug
2		even though many say that it is far more potent these days than it was
3		well is that true
4		Matthew Atha is the director of the Independent Drug Monitoring Unit
5		and joins us from Liverpool
6		good morning
7	Int'viewee:	good morning Sarah
8	Int'viewer:	(hhhen) first of all what is skunk
9	Int'viewee:	skunk
10		well it depends how you define skunk
11		skunk technically is a trade mark variety
12		er supplied by a (hhhh) ho. a Dutch seed bank
13		but it has become come to be known
14		as any loose form of cannabis female flowering tops
15		erm grown indoors under lights
16		so which tend to be more potent than indeed cannabis resin
17		or imported cannabis bush that's been carried half way round the world

18		and.er
19	Int'viewer:	and presumably also more likely to be grown at home
20	Int'viewee:	yes in . the vast majority of cases it is grown by by the users themselves
21		or by their friends etcetera
22	Int'viewer:	and is it more powerful
23	Int'viewee:	(hhh) again it depends
24		erm in general it will
25		if we compare cannabis resin
26		the typical range of potencies of cannabis resin is about
27		three to seven per cent
28		the typical er potency range of skunk is about eight to fifteen per cent
29		very occasionally up to twenty per cent
30		and on extremely rare occasions over twenty per cent
31		so it's on average about twice as as potent as as cannabis resin
32		but it's that's not the whole picture
33		cannabis resin has got other compounds in it notably cannabidiol or CBD
34		which tends to take the edge off the high
35		whereas skunk doesn't have that
36		so it tends to intensify the high rather more
37	Int'viewer:	so so broadly it is a lot more powerful
38	Int'viewee:	it is more powerful than can- cannabis resin er commercial cannabis resin

. . . .

50	Int'viewer:	so so should it have been up been re-classified
51		cannabis should have been re-classified
52		to be a more dangerous drug do you think
53	Int'viewee:	no can- no the class-
54		cannabis doesn't become more or less of a dangerous dr- drug
55		depending on its classification
56	Int'viewer:	I- I appreciate that
57		but the decision not to re-classify
58		was that the right one
59	Int'viewee:	no I think the decision not to reclassify was the right one
60		er primarily because so far re-classification
61		seems to have been an unqualified success
62		in that not only has usage not increased
63		it's actually seen to have decreased particularly among young people
64		and one could say that

65		the forbidden fruit when it's less forbidden loses much of its sweetness
66	Int'viewer:	not cool any longer
67		Matthew Atha thank you

Two kinds of overlapping alternation of perspectives are apparent in this interview: (a) between a frame of reference derived from 'the life-world' (cf. Schutz, 1989; Fairclough, 1995) and a framework of reference identifiable as 'scientific' – or, at least, one which is evidence-based; and (b) between the news frame of the interviewer and the expert frame of the interviewee. On several occasions during the interview a formulation offered by one party is re-formulated by the other. So, for instance, when Sarah Montague, the interviewer, offers the formulation 'more likely to be grown at home', Matthew Atha apparently concurs but reformulates it as 'yes in . the vast majority of cases it is grown by by the users themselves or by their friends etcetera'. (See also ll. 37–38.) The interviewee, rather than simply accept the unqualified comparative 'more powerful', supplies a precise term for the comparison. Indeed, there has up to this point been an alternation between 'potency' and 'powerful' in the interview, Montague offering 'powerful' twice in questions (though 'potent' when focusing at the outset) whereas Atha on the other hand offers 'more potent', 'range of potencies', 'potency range' and 'twice as potent'.

However, whereas re-formulations in an accountability interview will typically be seen as 'evasive', and routinely treated as such by interviewers, here the overall effect might be described as one of 'striving for accuracy'. The selection and alternation of expressions or formulations is nuanced by the perspective of the speaker. Montague speaks to some extent on behalf of a common-sense perspective in which drugs are, broadly speaking, more or less powerful and more or less dangerous as a result. Her contributions mediate between that position and the informed perspective of the expert. Atha speaks instead to a set of (presumably) systematically gathered evidence underpinning statements of fairly precise proportions of potency (see 26–32).

Indeed, the interview as a whole elaborates and refines a distinction between 'skunk' and 'cannabis resin'. Significantly, in its closing it moves away from the adducing of evidence (about potency) to the elicitation of an expert opinion on the merits of the policy of re-classification itself (ll. 59–67).

One of the paradoxes of expert interviews is that while they are ostensibly about knowledge – data, evidence, or science – they may well incorporate or build to a definite view in favour of one position on an issue or another. And positions may be advocated in ways quite immune from contradiction or interrogation. In other words, experts in the context of news are almost by definition not there to be held accountable by the broadcaster (unlike a fully public figure such as a politician). It is noticeable, for instance, that in moving to close the interview the interviewer reformulates in a manner that affiliates with the interviewee (ll. 65 and 66) rather than calls into question the interviewee's viewpoint. In a curious way, expertise – like experience in the experiential interview – is elicited in a manner which takes it beyond question.

The interview fragment

Extended interviews with political or public figures are an important feature of in-depth, analytic, background news programmes, such as *Newsnight*, *Today*, *Panorama*, *Channel 4 News* in the UK and *ABC 20/20*, *CBS 60 Minutes*, *CBS Evening News* and *NBC Nightly News* in the United States. In bulletin programmes, however, the news interview as a complete, live speech event is a diminishing element. Increasingly interviews are used instead – throughout news output – as inserted fragments in other elements such as reports. Here, for instance, part of a report about drink driving includes three fragments of speech from sources other than the reporter – two customers in pub, and a senior police officer:

Extract 5 BBC *News at Ten*

1	REPORTER:	But what happens if your wine comes in a large glass or the lager you're drinking happens to be a strong continental type.
3		Each of these on their own will put you over the limit
4		and merely adds to the confusion
5	CUSTOMER 1:	"This a Stella Artois which ah know is quite strong.
6		It's heading towards a whole one and half to two units.
7		So again it's probably a pint is as much.
8		But the best thing is not to do it."
9	CUSTOMER 2:	"Everybody is different innit they? (...)
10		It's what ye limitations are, I suppose, or what ye think are yer limitations."
11	REPORTER:	Every year government sponsored adverts
12		ram home the dangers of drink driving.
13		It works for many motorists but for others the police are the deterrent.
14	POLICE OFFICER:	"The core message is 'don't drink and drive'. you can see the results behind me.
16		If ye are gonna drink and drive, we're gonna do our damnednest to catch ye."

The practice here amounts to a form of direct quotation. The main and framing discourse is that of the reporter. But embedded seamlessly within it are utterances from members of the public and from a police officer. These speakers are not introduced by the reporter using a reporting clause or by a caption but are presented directly by video-clip extract, edited into the body of the report. Thus we see each speaker saying their piece – presumably in response to questioning by the reporter. It is difficult to make sense of these elements except as embedded fragments of larger interviews conducted by the reporter in preparing the report.

In running news, especially when dominated by a single major event, short on-the-spot interviews amongst bystanders – vox pops – play an important role in offering a range of emotional reactions to the event. Here, for instance, are some fragments from the coverage of the funeral of Diana, Princess of Wales.

1	REPORTER:	You were saying earlier
2		some of what Earl Spencer had to say you thought might be a bit political
3	CLAIRE:	yes
4		and I felt when I was listening to it
5		it didn't feel like er er a speech I expected at a funeral

Reactions to the Queen's televised speech, broadcast earlier, had been solicited in similar fashion in vox pops with bystanders in public spaces outside Buckingham Palace:

1	REPORTER:	do you think the Queen struck a chord
2	BYSTANDER 1:	she sounded very sincere
3		and she looked as though she were very moved
4		and I think that will satisfy everyone
5	BYSTANDER 2:	I thought she said everything that she should have said
6		can't think of anything that she left out at all

The focus of these vox-pops is clearly on the personal reactions – the thoughts and feelings of an interviewee who has heard or witnessed something. In these cases, what gives the interviewee their entitlement to speak is simply their capacity to provide in a reasonably fluent and articulate manner some kind of personal experience of something which has happened in the public eye – one that will be seen as representative of what anyone might feel or think in those circumstances. Interviewees are being asked to offer a view, their view. But there is no sense that they are going to be held accountable for it, asked to justify it, or have their view forensically disproved. Indeed, in marked contrast to the accountability interview these interviews are presented to the audience in a way that offers possible points of identification (or dis-identification), along the lines of: 'yes: that is how I felt, or how I might feel in their position', or even 'that is not how I felt'.

Conclusions

Leading news presenters or news anchors may pride themselves on holding political figures evenly to account in a 'no-nonsense', non-deferential manner. But this is only one kind of news interview – one that relies heavily on the relation of politicians to the public and how broadcasters mediate between them. Another way of considering the news interview is as part of a different history in which broadcast news constantly seeks to discover appropriate forms of discourse for a mass audience who are mostly watching or listening to the news at home (or on the commute). The prevalence of the news interview and changes to its forms can be as well understood as part of what commentators have called variously the personalisation, informalisation, or conversationalisation of public discourse (Scannell, 1996; Cameron, 2000; Fairclough, 1992). It is no longer appropriate for news to be delivered (if ever it was) in the form of a single-voiced monologue by a man dressed in a dinner suit. It has become a thing of many voices – orchestrated by the institution admittedly – but often presented in dialogue with each other. In this process, the news interview itself is the primary mechanism for dramatising or making palpable the news as an interactional, dialogic discourse.

News in general depends upon sources. A crucial tool in the process of gathering and assembling the news from a range of sources is the interview. The role of the fully-fledged extended interview may increasingly have become reduced to a brief insert or quotations in the smooth surface of a broadcast news report. But it survives by quotation or occasionally as the news item itself. The broadcast news interview, and the practices of direct quotation derived from it, take us – the news public or audience – closer to the sources of the news. The incorporation or embedding of interviews, or fragments from them, into the news displaces news discourse away from the single-voiced enunciation of the event and draws us closer to the event itself and to typical reactions to it and opinions about it. In this it represents a shift in news discourse from narration to dramatisation, in which what is dramatised is in part the making of the news itself, but also in which a society or community can be seen in conversation with itself about matters of the moment.

Notes

* This chapter is based on material from Montgomery, M. (2007) 'The broadcast news interview' in *The Discourse of Broadcast News* London: Routledge, pp. 144–181 and on 'The Discourse of the Broadcast News Interview' in *Journalism Studies* 9(2), 2008, pp. 260–277.

1 Because of reasons of space, this last type will not feature further in this discussion. A full treatment of the live 2-way may be found in Montgomery 2006.
2 Strictly speaking, of course, Snow's questions in any case are almost impossible to answer. How can one have *every* reason to believe anyone? How can anyone know what their thouts will be tomorrow? The last question ('if you had to would you shake his hand') looks tautological.

References

Atkinson, J.M. (1992) 'Displaying neutrality: formal aspects of informal court proceedings' in Drew, P. and Heritage, J. (eds.) *Talk at Work*, Cambridge: Cambridge University Press
Bell, M. and van Leeuwen, T. (1994) *The Media Interview: confession, contest, conversation*, New South Wales University Press
Blum-Kulka, S. (1983) 'The dynamics of political interviews', Text, 3(2): 131-53.
Cameron, D. (2000) *Good to Talk*, London: Sage.
Clayman, S. (1991) 'News interview openings: aspects of sequential organisation' in Scannell, P. (ed) *Broadcast Talk*, London: Sage

Clayman, S. (1992) 'Footing in the achievement of neutrality: the case of news interview discourse' in Drew, P. and Heritage, J. (eds) Talk at Work Cambridge: Cambridge University Press pp 163–198

Clayman, S. and Heritage, J. (2002) The News Interview: journalists and public figures on the air, Cambridge: Cambridge University Press

Corner, J. (1995) Television Form and Public Address, London: Arnold

Ekstrom, M. (2001) 'Politicians interviewed on television news', Discourse and Society, 12 (5): 563–84

Ellis, J. (2002) Seeing Things: television in the age of uncertainty, London: I.B. Tauris

Fairclough, N. (1992) Discourse and Social Change, Oxford: Blackwell

Fairclough, N. (1995) Media Discourse, London: Arnold

Fetzer, A. (2002) '"Put bluntly, you have something of a credibility problem": Sincerity and credibility in political interviews'. In Politics as Text and Talk, Chilton, Paul and Christina Schäffner (eds,) 173–201

Fetzer, A. and Weizman, E. (eds) (2006) Pragmatic Aspects of Political Discourse in the Media. Special Issue of Journal of Pragmatics 38(2).

Garfinkel, H. (1967/1984). Studies in Ethnomethodology, Malden MA: Polity Press/Blackwell Publishing.

Haarman, L. (1999) (ed.) Talk about Shows, Bologna: CLUEB

Haarman, L. (2004) '"John, what's going on?": some features of live exchanges on television news' in A. Partington, J. Morley and L. Haarman (eds) Corpora and Discourse, Bern: Peter Lang

Harris, S. (1991) 'Evasive action: how politicians respond to questions in political interviews'. In Scannell, P. (ed.) Broadcast Talk, pp. 76–99. London: Sage.

Heritage, J. and Greatbatch, D. (1991) 'On the institutional character of institutional talk: the case of news interviews' in Boden, D. and Zimmerman, D. H. (eds) Talk and Social Structure, Cambridge: Polity Press.

Hutchby, I. (2005) 'News talk: Interaction in the broadcast news interview.' pp. 210–223 in S. Allan (ed.) Journalism: Critical Issues. Buckingham, UK: Open University Press.

Hutchby, I. (2006) Media Talk, Maidenhead: Open University Press.

Kumar, K. (1975) 'Holding the Middle Ground: The BBC, the Public and the Professional Broadcaster' in Sociology, 9(1), 67–88.

Labov, W. (1972b) 'The transformation of experience in narrative syntax' in Language in the Inner City, pp. 354–398.

Labov, W. (1972a) Language in the Inner City, Philadelphia: University of Pennsylvania Press.

Labov, W. and Fanshel, D. (1977) Therapeutic Discourse: psychotherapy as conversation, New York: Academic Press.

Labov, W. and Waletsky, J. (1967) 'Narrative analysis: oral versions of personal experience' in Helm, J (ed.) pp. 12–44.

Lauerbach, G. (2006) "Discourse representation in political interviews: The construction of identities and relations through voicing and ventriloquizing" Volume 38, Issue 2, Pages 196–215(February 2006).

Montgomery, M. (1999a) 'Televised Talk: Face Work, Politeness and Laughter in the Mrs Merton Show". Working with Dialogue: proceedings of the 7th International Association of Dialogue Analysis Conference. Max Niemeyer Verlag.

Montgomery, M. (2006) 'Broadcast news, the live two way and the case of Andrew Gilligan', Media, Culture & Society, 28(2), 233–259.

Montgomery, M. (2007) The Discourse of Broadcast News, London: Routledge.

Myers, G. (2000) 'Entitlement and sincerity in broadcast interviews about Princess Diana' Media, Culture & Society 22: 167–185.

Scannell, P. (1996) Radio Television and Modern Life, Oxford: Blackwell.

Schutz, A. (1989) Structures of the Life World, Northwestern University Press.

Tolson, A. (1991) 'Televised chat and synthetic personality' in Scannell (ed.), Broadcast Talk London: Sage.

32

TABLOIDIZATION OF NEWS

David Rowe

There are few words (both adjectives and nouns) in the field of News and Journalism Studies that are likely to attract more viscerally negative responses than 'tabloid', and few processes more commonly used to signify the decline of the contemporary news media than 'tabloidization'. Why should a concept that, at its most elementary, refers only to the size of a newspaper, have such pejorative connotations and provoke such trenchant critiques? In seeking to answer this question, we are engaging with the whole field of debate that has concentrated on what is happening to the practice of journalism and the quality of news, under conditions where the news media have proliferated at the same time as the industrialized production of entertainment, enhanced by rapid technological change, has burgeoned (McChesney, 2007). At an historical moment where the state in most countries (at least in liberal democracies) has been retreating from direct involvement in news production in favour of a deregu-lated commercial media sector, there is anxiety that market values will overwhelm those of the public interest; that trivial, media-supplied distractions will supplant those of serious new gathering and communication; and that the resultant conflation of news, information and entertainment (as encapsulated by the negative neolo-gisms 'infotainment' and 'newszak') will degrade the public sphere and erode the conditions for a robust democracy of well informed, vigilant and demanding citizens (Franklin, 1997).

It would be misleading to suggest that tabloidization is always presented as the pivotal process both describing and explaining such diagnoses of the state and trajectory of the contemporary news media and journalism. For example, the journalist Nick Davies (2008), in his excoriation of the news media in his book *Flat Earth News*, applies his critique of the increasing incidence of what he calls 'churnalism' (the rapid-fire recycling by journalists of information received from news agencies and public relations companies that they have not checked) across broadsheet and tabloid newspapers, and public and commercial broadcasters and websites, in the now-dominant 'news factories'. However, it is common for such developments to be attributed to a leakage of concerns, techniques and genres from the tabloid media to a generalized 'news system', as Bennett (2003: 10) puts it:

Topics that were once relegated to gossip columns and the screaming headlines of the tabloids are now increasingly the stuff of mainstream news. The key question about this somewhat chaotic information form is how well it serves the needs of democracy.

Analogous notions of a broader tabloidization of media that typify a range of developments – including the sensationalization of news, the abbreviation of news stories, the proliferation of celebrity gossip, and the more intensive use of visual material such as large photographs and illustrations – are similarly deployed in many works of contemporary media analysis (Sparks and Tulloch, 2000; Bromley, 2001; Page, 2003; Hallin and Mancini, 2004). This chapter sets out to explore the key questions that surround the concept of the tabloid, and, in particular:

- Why has 'the tabloid' taken on such negative connotations in both News and Journalism Studies, and in wider public discourse?
- How can the tabloid and tabloidization be effectively defined and utilized?
- Is tabloidization actually occurring?
- Does tabloidization inevitably have a destructive impact on the news media and the health of contemporary citizenship and democracy?

The main concern here is to distinguish between two rhetorics: at their polar ends, the first exhibits cultural prejudice against popular cultural forms and a vague, overgeneralized attachment of a stigmatized label to the tabloid. The second celebrates the tabloid as a more open and liberating engagement of news media with everyday life, and so can be accused of a populist pandering to commercial exploitation and of abandoning a critical impulse in favour of an apolitical, functionalist acceptance of current trends and tastes. Finding a sustainable analytical pathway between these starkly differing positions is difficult given the dynamism of contemporary news and journalism. This task requires theoretical consistency, conceptual clarity and empirical evidence – qualities that have tended to be conspicuous by their absence in many debates about the condition of media organizations, the integrity of journalists, and the influence of the ethos of the tabloid.

Although some spirited defences of the tabloid have been mounted with varying degrees of qualification (for example, Fiske, 1992; Glynn, 1990; Hartley, 1996; Lumby, 1999), it is fair to argue that in the field of News and Journalism Studies the burden of argument has tended to lament tabloidizing trends (Langer, 1998; Sparks and Tulloch, 2000). For this reason, there will be greater concentration on the critique of tabloidization in this chapter. The concept of the tabloid and the process of tabloidization can be approached within two main domains. The first is mainly confined to the media sphere, and hinges on the notion that the media can be divided into 'quality' and 'tabloid' media, with a widening divide between the two as the latter depart increasingly from approved methods, purposes and subjects of journalism. Here there is a striking contrast between the 'serious' news media with traditional media concerns and the tabloid forms that increasingly depart from what can be recognized as news gathering and analysis in favour of the trivial and the diverting. Second, though, is a much more wide ranging conception that sees tabloidization as a general socio-cultural process extending beyond the media sphere to typify entire societies, with what is seen as a coarsening and trivialization of all media and the societies that they represent. Here, sober organizations like major newspapers and broadcasters are represented as 'infected' by the tabloid 'bug'. In this chapter, both media-specific and the societal-general analyses of tabloidization will be addressed.

Tabloidization is a process that has been a focus for, and bearer of, anxieties about developments in the contemporary, 'mediatized' world. Hallin (2000: 231) summarizes a widely held concern that tabloidization debauches the news media and has wider, deleterious implications:

> The trend from 'hard news' to 'sensationalism' is often referred to as 'tabloidi-zation', and it makes sense to consider specifically the influence of the new television tabloids. Appropriately enough, these shows tend to generate debates among media critics which resemble the shouting matches of the Geraldo Rivera and Jerry Springer shows. For journalism traditionalists they are the purest manifestation of evil; for some popular cultural theorists of postmodern bent they represent, 'a place where ideological forces of the powerful may be challenged by oppositional or popular forces' (Glynn, 1990: 32; see also Fiske, 1992) ...
>
> ... Like their print forerunners, the supermarket tabloids (Bird, 1992), they tend to be quite traditional in their worldview: they focus, to be sure, on transgressors of social norms, but typically with strong condemnation ... There are plenty of reasons to worry about the effect of tabloidization on the wider culture. The tabloids, to give just one example, depend heavily on the exploitation and amplification of fear.

Debates about tabloidization, then, have a direct bearing not only on trends in the media and their analysis (for example, Hallin's invocation above of disputation between political economy and postmodern theory), but also on matters concerning their impact on society at large, and their positive and negative implications. A prior question, though, is empirical – is tabloidization actually happening, and if so where?

Tabloidization and the news pages

The study on which this chapter is based[1] examined developments in the principal news pages of selected newspapers in Australia. The condition and role of the media in Australia have much in common with those prevailing in other countries, and some distinctive elements. The Australian media framework has, like that of Britain, Canada and most European countries, a strong public service broadcasting tradition, and a vigorous print and commercial broadcasting sector. Its ownership structure is both local and international (with controls, recently relaxed somewhat, on cross-media and foreign ownership). Newspapers are, as in other places, powerful organs of news, but subject to the commercial pressures caused by falling sales and circulation, and levels of classified advertising, and competition from other media, especially broadcasting and the Internet. As a result, Australian newspapers, which are predominantly regionalized, are diversifying into other media and modes of advertising, especially online.

In examining two newspapers – a broadsheet and a tabloid – from the same publishing stable (the Rupert Murdoch family-controlled News Corporation) that is Australia's most powerful in print (challenged only by the Fairfax company), any incipient or accentuated tabloidization development can be tracked. The *Australian* is the country's only daily national broadsheet (first published in 1964), while the *Daily Telegraph* is the only daily tabloid and the largest selling newspaper in Australia's largest and most plausibly 'world' city, Sydney. The content analysis component of the research, supplemented by industry and interview data, covered the period 1992–2002, a decade of major change in Australian newspapers and other media (Cunningham and Turner, 2005).[2]

There is no absolute consensus about what constitutes the tabloidization of news, but some characteristics are frequently invoked when it is described (Rowe, 2000). One of these is the 'space budget' of the principal news pages, so that a way of establishing whether tabloidization is actually occurring is to examine trends of this aspect of newspapers, irrespective of their size and format. If, for example, there was a detectable decrease in the amount of text in the main pages, then this change would be likely to lend support to criticisms that newspapers are 'dumbing down', producing simple stories in 'bite-size' chunks in their most important, prominent place for news (Franklin, 1997). If there was a corresponding increase in the size of visual material (especially so-called 'impact' photographs, as well as diagrams, tables and cartoons) it might similarly be claimed that textual depth is being sacrificed in the interests of visual attraction and, perhaps, distraction (McChesney, 2007). A bigger masthead, more space allocated to an index that enhances 'navigability', and other non-news items, as well as more 'white space' that would give a 'cleaner' appearance while reducing the amount of text, are also conventional indicators of tabloidization. Larger headlines, especially those of the 'screaming' nature for which newspapers like the British tabloids the *Sun* and the *Daily Mirror* are notorious (although sometimes admired for their wit and economy – see Essery, 1993), would also be largely consistent with a tabloidization trend as markers of sensationalist attention grabbing at the expense of serious journalistic analysis. Similarly, greater space devoted to advertising would signify for many critics the triumph of commercial over journalistic values (McChesney, 2008).

In looking at the sampled news space budget of a tabloid paper, the *Daily Telegraph* (pages 1–6 between 1992 and 2002), any differences between broadsheet and tabloid formats can be discerned, as well as whether an actual tabloid is undergoing further tabloidization as measured by reductions in text, greater space for images, and so on. In Figure 32.1 a general trend, though not an entirely consistent one, is evident. Article text space actually increased by 2.5 per cent, although it was rather higher in 1997. Proportional image space rose by 5.9 per cent between 1992 and 2002, but actually fell slightly from a peak of 32 per cent five years earlier. The masthead proportion also fluctuated slightly, again moving upwards overall but falling from a peak in 1997. Yet advertising space actually fell by 9.3 per cent over the decade, having plummeted in 1997, while headlines and index were proportionately consistent overall. It would be unwarranted to advance ambitious conclusions based on a newspaper sampled at intervals over a decade, and there has been no attempt here to analyse the qualitative nature of the text as opposed to its quantitatively measured structural features. But in trend terms they reveal that the suggestion of a consistent tabloidization process involving a relentless reduction of text, increase in visual material, and ascendancy of advertising is not supported. This is not to deny that a range of changes may be occurring that do not represent tabloidization, but rather that it is more uneven and complex than is often suggested by News and Journalism Studies scholars and critics.

Figure 32.1 Components of the *Daily Telegraph* as a percentage of pages 1–6 News Space Budget, 1992–2002, sampled at five-year intervals

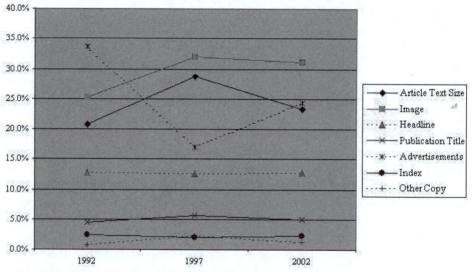

In pursuing these questions, it is useful to compare news space budget proportions and trends between the tabloid and broadsheet newspapers. Figure 32.2 opposite, in tracking proportions and changes in the principal news pages of the *Australian* between 1992 and 2002, reveals clear differences compared with the *Daily Telegraph*.

There is much more article text, both absolutely and relatively, in historical terms. For example, in the 1992 sample the *Australian* published 14,580.56 cm² (45.2 per cent) of principal news space text, compared with the *Daily Telegraph*'s 6,907.92 cm² (20.8 per cent). Similarly, in the same year's sample advertising in the broadsheet's news page was 5,423.00 cm² and 11,165.38 cm² for the tabloid. However, if tabloidization is occurring generally across the media, it would be expected that the trend would be for the broadsheet to become more like the tabloid across the decade in question. In the *Australian* there was, indeed, an overall reduction in text space by 6.8 per cent between 1992 and 2002, but it was lower in 1997 than in 2002, while in the same

Figure 32.2 Components of the *Australian* as a percentage of pages 1–3 News Space Budget, 1992–2002, sampled at five-year intervals

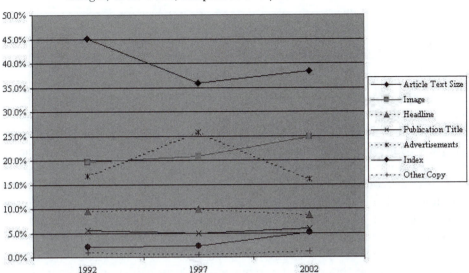

period, as noted above, the *Daily Telegraph* actually increased the proportion of article text (although, in this case, it had fallen from a peak in 1997). In other words, by one test of tabloidization, the broadsheet had become more tabloid – and the tabloid less so. In the same period, the tabloid's image component had risen (though unevenly) by 5.9 per cent and the broadsheet's image space had risen (and consistently) by 5 per cent, while masthead size rose (though unevenly) for both – so supporting a proposition of general tabloidization by this measure. But other component trends were less clear: headline size was generally consistent for the tabloid but rose and then fell for the broadsheet, and the index space fell for the tabloid but more than doubled for the broadsheet. Most strikingly, the advertising component was very volatile in both cases, but falling across the decade – by 9.3 per cent for the tabloid and 0.7 per cent for the broadsheet.

It could be suggested, then, that Australia's most important national broadsheet has been 'going tabloid' in some respects, aping the easy readability, striking appearance and simplified journalism of the tabloids. But in other regards tabloidization is not occurring – such as in the increasing placement of display advertising in the principal news pages. Furthermore, few of the changes were major and many uneven in the case of both newspapers, and contrast significantly with some of the more apocalyptic pronouncements on tabloidization (Page, 2003). As noted, headlines and advertisements have remained fairly consistent when comparing the 1992 and 2002 samples, while other trends have evidenced considerable fluctuation. For the *Australian* half way through the sample period, advertising space in the principal news pages rose considerably (+8.9 per cent) and news text fell by an even greater proportion (−9.3 per cent), but five years later less space was allocated to advertising than a decade before, and news text had risen again (+2.5 per cent), though still below the figure for 1992

(−6.8 per cent). The rhetoric of tabloidization theory, then, needs to be tempered by empirical evidence that challenges some of its more sweeping diagnoses of relentless, one-dimensional change.

Adjusting to new conditions? News article types

The above findings from a segment of a study of two newspapers showed that evidence of tabloidization in a formal sense (the composition of the principal news pages) was equivocal. Other areas examined were likewise – for example, when the sampled articles in the principal images were classified by type. Table 32.1 opposite demonstrates the patterns in the analysed broadsheet and tabloid newspapers of story type across the period that most closely align with what is usually described as tabloid news. The *Daily Telegraph* consistently carried a much larger proportion of stories about accidents and disasters than the *Australian*, although there was also a considerable decline in such stories in its news pages. Of course, sometimes (as with other categories) such news stories correspond to 'hard' news – for example, in the case of a natural disaster (like a tsunami) or a major civilian incident (such as an industrial accident causing many fatalities). But they also often represent the 'personalization' of distant events that may be regarded as a key part of the 'armoury' of the tabloid (Fiske, 1992). Crime/ court coverage, by contrast, became less prominent in the tabloid off a higher base (although spiking significantly in 1997), and by the end of the decade encompassed by the study was higher in the broadsheet than the tabloid after a consistent rise, while the same pattern was evident for stories classified as human interest/personalities. Intriguingly, popular culture/entertainment and sport stories were entirely absent from the principal news pages of both newspapers in 1992, but sport had begun to feature subsequently (with greater sport coverage conventionally regarded as a major index of tabloidization – see Rowe, 2004), although it was notable that popular culture/ entertainment registered only in the broadsheet. Thus, once again, some evidence can be found that tabloidization is happening in general and that it is a clear feature of developments in the broadsheets, but also that it is not occurring consistently (as in the case of the accident and disaster stories) and that in some areas the tabloids may be moving in a different or less predictable direction (as, again, with accident and disaster stories, and popular culture/entertainment).

The kind of interpretive analysis presented immediately above provides some more detail for the picture already sketched concerning the tabloidization of news in contemporary newspapers and media. Apart from the questions surrounding trends in media content and appearance, there are further ones concerning the extent to which editors and journalists themselves subscribe to the broadsheet/quality and tabloid/ popular classification, its associated value set, and also their assessment of whether tabloidization is in train. Hence it is useful to turn briefly (drawing on the interview-based aspect of the reported research) to the perspectives of those engaged in the production of news texts.

Table 32.1 Major articles in the principal news pages of the *Australian* and the
Daily Telegraph by selected type as a percentage of total article space,
1992–2002, sampled at five-year intervals

	Australian		
Story Type	**1992**	**1997**	**2002**
Accidents/Disasters	1.1%	4.6%	1.9%
Crime/Courts	4.1%	11.6%	16.8%
Human Interest/Personalities	2.9%	12.1%	17.9%
Popular Culture/Entertainment		0.5%	5.2%
Sport		5.1%	5.9%
	Daily Telegraph		
Story Type	**1992**	**1997**	**2002**
Accidents/Disasters	23.4%	8.1%	10.9%
Crime/Courts	10.0%	27.6%	14.8%
Human Interest/Personalities	12.3%	24.0%	15.5%
Popular Culture/Entertainment		0.0%	0.0%
Sport		1.5%	6.9%

Tabloid pros and cons: some journalists' perspectives

In the newspaper industry journalists have different professional histories and
trajectories. Some work exclusively for broadsheets or tabloids, and some move
between the two (especially broadsheet journalists who have trained on tabloid
newspapers). Some journalists – an increasingly large group – work on a broadsheet that goes to a tabloid format, such as those working for the *Independent*
and the *Times* in the UK, or at least to a mid-size, such as the so-called 'Berliner'
(the *Guardian* (UK) and *New York Times* (USA)), or are becoming progressively
narrower, like the *Sydney Morning Herald* (Australia). Others work on newspapers
that are classified as broadsheets but are involved in the proliferating tabloid
sections that they contain. As a result there is no absolute divide that enables
a precise measurement of tabloidization. For example, Martin (names of interviewees and some newspapers have been disguised to protect agreed anonymity),
a journalist on an Australian broadsheet, works in a tabloid section, and rejects
any clear-cut quality distinctions between newspapers based on size and format,
but also recognizes the connotation of the word tabloid. When asked what he

associates with the tabloid, Martin responded in both technical and value-relevant terms:

> Probably two things spring to mind, one is purely tabloid as in the shape of the paper and that can apply to newspapers like the *Daily Telegraph* as much to a section I work in, which is a tabloid format. But obviously the word 'tabloid' also brings to mind a certain type of journalism which I guess probably originated with the tabloid newspapers in Britain, and I would associate sensationalist, police rounds type stories coming to the fore, one story on the front page, one big headline, attention grabbing headlines, the lowest common denominator in journalism.

Martin recognized the advantages of ease of use for commuters of the tabloid format, and was open to his whole newspaper changing to it:

> 'I would, if I ruled the world and if I were in management, I would say, let's go to tabloid and make this a tabloid newspaper, now show me the reasons why we shouldn't, show me the advantages of a broadsheet, and we 'll say broadsheet if you can convince ...
>
> ... What you can lose, and what would be really damaging for a paper like the *Sydney Morning Herald* going tabloid is if it did things like the Sunday papers do, which is litter the front page with competitions and, you know, commercial furniture on the front, which would be hugely damaging to the *Herald* if it went tabloid.

Martin, like several other journalists interviewed, saw tabloidization in format terms as a necessary adjustment to modern styles of living, but believed that it did not necessarily mean a change towards the style associated 'with tabloid newspapers in Britain'. Jill, a journalist who'd joined a tabloid from a broadsheet after doing a cadetship on a tabloid newspaper, similarly observed that:

> people use the term tabloid in different ways. I guess if I think tabloid I think it's maybe a bit more accessible, it's maybe written a bit clearer. I think the tabloid media has a lot of positive attributes that the broadsheets could learn from.

Jill also makes a distinction between serious news in the broadsheets and some of the less reputable content of tabloids:

> I guess if you want to be crude about it and use 'dull but worthy',' 'slug boring but important', so it's the stuff [in broadsheet journalism] you should know and need to know, and then there's the stuff that everybody is interested in. It's a bit more salacious, it's a bit more voyeuristic, and that's what people tend to think of as tabloid. Stuff you want to read but you don't want to admit necessarily that that's what you read.

Here it can be seen that a professional journalist is fully aware of the moral economy of newspapers. Jacqueline, working on a tabloid regional newspaper, connected tabloidization to the anxious, calculated search for readers caused by falling circulation and sales:

> Circulation is becoming more important, chasing circulation, chasing readership, and that's really been pushed right down to journalists' level. To be aware of what readers want and give readers what they want, not what we think they want – 'broccoli journalism' as someone described it.

The motive force behind tabloidization of news is here laid bare – the survivalism of the once dominant media form of the newspaper when confronted with competing broadcast and online media forms, and with audiences that are harder to know, understand and secure.

Conclusion: tabloidization as process and metaphor

The tabloid phenomenon can be read as both a sign of critical and professional anxiety about finding a media audience without substantial loss to a sophisticated political democracy, and a product of that anxiety when converted, in the media industry, to systematic attempts to connect with audiences by all available means. The many current pressures on newspapers are both cause and effect of the signs of tabloidization, or may be unrelated to it. For example, technological changes, such as the digitization of photography and the enhancements to colour occasioned by new printing infrastructure, encouraged the use of more visual material. Making newspapers more visibly appealing counters competition from other media with an audio-visual capacity, especially television, and increasingly the Internet, which can speedily deliver textual, photographic and moving news images and messages. At the same time, sober, worthy forms of television – sometimes lampooned as 'radio with pictures' – might be enlivened without a necessary loss to the quality and function of news provision and analysis. Such an approach may be denounced as tabloidization, or seen as a necessary adjustment to the presentation of the news media by adapting to the perceived needs and demands of new audiences less wedded to traditional news media consumption patterns. While commercial media organizations have obvious economic interests, neither private nor public media can preserve or enhance democracy if financially unviable and/or ignored by audiences. As Sparks (2000: 35) observes, 'The social composition and patterns of life of the news audiences in advanced societies is changing. There is a perceived crisis in representative democracy marked by low participation rates and declining party membership'. Under these circumstances, what is described as tabloidization can also be interpreted as part of a search for 'the right sort of news mix for commercial success' (p. 36) and, among public media, for the legitimacy conferred by relevance to their citizen audiences (Born, 2005).

The power of media organizations to set their own agenda should not be exaggerated. For example, the fluctuations in levels of advertising in the principal news pages in the newspapers sampled above may have been caused not by publisher–editor deliberations, but by a weakening of the advertising market occasioned by external circumstances (a drift to other media, an economic recession, or, as in the case of 2002, the 'post 9/11' climate of business pessimism). Similarly, changes in government have profound implications for media organizations funded or regulated by the state – that is, virtually all of them. Yet the power of the popular tabloid press in the political sphere cannot be underestimated – as the case of the UK's *Sun* during the years of the Thatcher Government in the late twentieth century conspicuously reveals (Chippindale and Horrie, 1992). Debates about tabloidization of the news media, therefore, are always about media power and the responsibilities of journalism – both to enhance and to degrade democracy in making diurnal choices about the rendering of the world.

Notes

1 This research project was funded by an Australian Research Council Discovery Grant 'Disposing of the Tabloid? A Critical Analysis of Contemporary Developments in the Print Media'. Drs Peter Wejbora and Ruth Sibson are thanked for their research assistance, and Professors Colin Sparks and Toby Miller for their academic advice and research facilitation.

2 A comparative section of equivalent print space across broadsheet and tabloid newspapers was taken as the sample size in the base year of analysis (1992) and replicated in the 1997 and 2002 sample years. Six issues per annum of the first three pages of broadsheet newspapers and the first six pages of the tabloid newspaper were sampled on a rolling week basis. Article composition; total news pages space budget; average size of article (all-text); number of articles/images; number of page one articles; spatial location of news (for example, national, international); mode of reader address and article reporting style; and news focus (for example, crime, politics, sport), were all subjected to content analysis. Newspaper sales and circulation trends were also analysed, and over 30 journalists interviewed (using semi-structured method) in Australia, with over 20 additional interviews in the UK and USA for comparative purposes. Editors and broadcast journalists were interviewed as well as 'beat' and general rounds journalists.

References

Bennett, W.L. (2003) *News: The Politics of Illusion* (fifth edition). New York: Longman.

Bird, S. E. (1992) *For Inquiring Minds: A Cultural Study of Supermarket Tabloids*. Knoxville, TN: University of Tennessee Press.

Born, G. (2005) *Uncertain Vision: Birt, Dyke and the Reinvention of the BBC*. London: Vintage.

Bromley, M. (ed.) (2001) *No News is Bad News: Radio, Television and the Public*. Harlow, UK: Pearson Education.

Chippindale, P. and Horrie, C. (1992) *Stick it up your Punter! The Rise and Fall of the Sun*. London: Mandarin.

Cunningham, S. and Turner, G. (2005) *The Media and Communications in Australia* (second edition). Sydney: Allen & Unwin.

Davies, N. (2008) *Flat Earth News: As Award-Winning Reporter Exposes Falsehood, Distortion, and Propaganda in the Global Media*. London: Chatto & Windus.

Essery, J. (ed.) (1993) *Gotcha: Classic Headlines from The Sun*. London: Signet.

Fiske, J. (1992) 'Popularity and the Politics of Information', in P. Dahlgren and C. Sparks (eds), *Journalism and Popular Culture*. London: Sage, pp. 45–63.

Franklin, B. (1997) *Newszak and News Media*. London: Arnold.

Glynn, K. (1990) 'Tabloid Television's Transgressive Aesthetic: A *Current Affair* and the "Shows that Taste Forgot"', *Wide Angle* 12(2): 22–44.

Hallin, D.C. (2000) 'Commercialism and Professionalism in the American News Media', in J. Curran and M. Gurevitch (eds) *Mass Media and Society* (third edition). London: Arnold, pp. 218–37.

Hallin, D.C. and Mancini, P. (2004) *Comparing Media Systems: Three Models of Media and Politics*. New York: Cambridge University Press.

Hartley, J. (1996) *Popular Reality: Journalism, Modernity, Popular Culture*. London: Arnold.

Langer, J. (1998) *Tabloid Television: Popular Journalism and the 'Other News'*. New York: Routledge.

Lumby, C. (1999) *Gotcha: Life in a Tabloid World*. Sydney: Allen & Unwin.

McChesney, R. (2007) *Communication Revolution: Critical Junctures and the Future of the Media*. New York: The New Press.

McChesney, R. (2008) *The Political Economy of Media: Enduring Issues, Emerging Dilemmas*. New York: Monthly Review Press.

Page, B. (2003) *The Murdoch Archipelago*. London: Simon & Schuster.

Rowe, D. (2000) 'On Going Tabloid: A Preliminary Analysis', *Metro*, 121/122: 78–85.

Rowe, D. (2004) *Sport, Culture and the Media: The Unruly Trinity* (second edition). Maidenhead, UK: Open University Press.

Rowe, D. (2009) 'Tabloidization: Form, Style and Socio-Cultural Change' in V. Rupar (ed.) *Journalism and Sense-making: Reading the Newspaper*. New Jersey, NJ: Hampton Press (forthcoming).

Sparks, C. (2000) 'Introduction: The Panic over Tabloid News', *Tabloid Tales: Global Perspectives on the Popular Media*. Boulder, CO: Rowman and Littlefield, pp. 1–40.

Sparks, C. and Tulloch, J. (eds) (2000) *Tabloid Tales: Global Perspectives on the Popular Media*. Boulder, CO: Rowman and Littlefield.

33
TELEVISION NEWS IN THE ERA OF GLOBAL INFOTAINMENT

Daya Kishan Thussu

Despite the astonishing growth of the Internet worldwide (about one quarter of the planet's population is now online), television remains the most global and powerful of media. Its imagery crosses linguistic and national boundaries with relative ease, making it the most important purveyor of public information. This is particularly so in developing countries, where large sections of the population cannot read or write, yet holds true in Western contexts as well. The influence of television news on how everyday life is lived, from London to Washington, to Dhaka to São Paulo, is so profound it is difficult to comprehend.

The changing contours of television news have been a longstanding area of concern for critical scholars. News is not merely a media product, they point out, but a vehicle for engagement in the democratic process, one with significant implications for the conduct of domestic politics and international relations. A recent international public opinion poll, commissioned by GlobeScan in conjunction with the BBC, Reuters and the Media Centre, reported that national television news was the most trusted source of news (by 82 per cent) in ten major countries in 2006. International satellite TV news was trusted by 56 per cent of those surveyed, who similarly deemed this medium to be the most 'important' news source available to them (GlobeScan, 2006).

This chapter examines the growth of what has been aptly termed 'infotainment' – that is, the convergence of information and entertainment – found to varying degrees in the editorial output from television newsrooms across the globe. Part of the reason for this growth appears to be that private, commercially driven broadcasting, with its epicentre in the United States, has come to dominate television journalism globally. In the first instance, I shall briefly map the globalization of the commercial model of television news, arguing that in a market-driven, 24/7 broadcasting environment, television news tends towards infotainment. Soft news, lifestyle and consumer journalism have become pre-eminent. On this basis, I shall proceed to make the case that infotainment is contributing to the corporate colonization of the public sphere, undermining public journalism as well as public service broadcasting. This 'soft' news has engendered an important ideological dimension, in my view, helping to legitimize a neo-liberal ideology predicated on the superiority of free-market democracy.

Global news

The growing commercialism of the airwaves is the result of a number of factors – among them the privatization of global communication hard and software, together with the deregulation of broadcasting and the technological convergence between television, telecommunication and computing industries – which, taken together, have dramatically changed the ecology of broadcasting. The general shift from public to a ratings-conscious television, dependent on corporate advertising, has implications for news agendas and editorial priorities. While marketization has brought new energy and vitality to the broadcasting sector – evident in the mushrooming of news networks – it has also exposed journalism to the rules of the market to an ever greater extent, thus commodifying news and information.

One result of the proliferation of news outlets is a growing competition for audiences and, crucially, advertising revenue, at a time when interest in mainstream forms of news appears to be waning. As a report from the Project for Excellence in Journalism (2006) in the US indicates, the audiences for network television peak-time news bulletins there have declined substantially, from 85 per cent of the television audience in 1969 to 29 per cent in 2005. The reasons for this decline are complex, but are partly a result of many – especially younger – viewers opting to receive their news from alternative sources, including bloggers (Project for Excellence in Journalism, 2006).

Coincidental with the growing commercialization of television news is a perceived need to make it more entertaining. Indeed, this has become a crucial priority for broadcasters as they scramble to borrow and adapt characteristics from entertainment genres and modes of conversation that privilege an informal communicative style with its emphasis on personalities, style, storytelling skills and spectacle. News-gathering, particularly foreign news, is an expensive operation requiring high levels of investment and, consequently, media executives are under constant pressure to deliver demographically desirable audiences for news and current affairs programming to contribute to profits or at least avoid losses. In the US, the major news networks are controlled by conglomerates whose primary interest is in the entertainment business: Viacom-Paramount owns CBS News; ABC News is part of the Disney empire; CNN is a key component of AOL-Time-Warner (the world's biggest media and entertainment conglomerate). Even Fox News, owned by Rupert Murdoch's News Corporation, finds itself under the same corporate umbrella as Hollywood's Twentieth Century Fox, amongst a vast array of other entertainment interests. This shift in ownership is similarly reflected at the level of content, that is, in extensive news coverage concerned with celebrities from the world of entertainment. These are supplemented by the new genre of reality TV and its relatives – docudramas, talk shows, court and crime enactments and rescue missions. In the process, symbiotic relationships between the news and new forms of current affairs and factual entertainment programmes have developed, blurring the boundaries between news, documentary and entertainment. Such hybridized ratings-driven programming feeds into and benefits from the 24/7 news cycle: providing a feast of visually arresting, emotionally-charged infotainment which sustains audience interest and keeps production costs low.

Infotainment – a neologism which emerged in the late 1980s to become a handy catchall for all that was wrong with contemporary television news – refers to an explicit genre-mix of 'information' and 'entertainment' in news and current affairs programming. According to the *Oxford English Dictionary*, infotainment is 'broadcast material which is intended both to entertain and to inform.' The phenomenon of infotainment denotes a type of television news where style triumphs over substance, the mode of presentation becoming more important than the content. This new news cannibalizes visual forms and styles borrowed from postmodernist TV commercials and an MTV-style visual aesthetics. Fast-paced visual action, computer-animated logos and eye-catching visuals are combined with sensationalist headlines, more often than not delivered by a glamorous anchor person. Such news, particularly on the rolling 24/7 channels, appears to be the answer to attracting the 'me' generation of media users, prone to channel hopping and zapping, with a preference for on-line and mobile news. This style of presentation, with its origins in the ratings-driven commercial television news culture of the US, is becoming increasingly global, made possible by a liberalized and privatized broadcasting environment and the creation of an international infrastructure for communication hardware.

Epicentre of infotainment

Though the word infotainment is of relatively recent origin, the phenomenon it represents has a long tradition, from the broadside ballad to the 'yellow' and 'tabloid press,' as attested in most standard histories of journalism. Equally, the tension between informing and educating the public, on the one hand, and entertaining the crowd in the market place, on the other, has a venerable history.

The United States is widely perceived to be the home of the infotainment industry, starting with the penny press in the 1830s, exemplified by such publications as the New York-based *Sun* with a high quota of human interest stories – and which was sold for one penny (one cent) at a time when all other newspapers cost six cents (Mott, 1962). The penny press provided diversions for working people, as Neal Gabler has observed. 'For a constituency being conditioned by trashy crime pamphlets, gory novels and overwrought melodramas,' he writes, 'news was simply the most exciting, most entertaining content a paper could offer, especially when it was skewed, as it invariably was in the penny press, to the most sensational stories.' Moreover, he adds, 'one might even say that the masters of the penny press *invented* the concept of news because it was the best way to sell their papers in an entertainment environment' (cited in Gitlin, 2002: 51).

Schudson (1978), in his history of journalism in the US, notes that from the nineteenth century onwards a 'journalism of entertainment', with its distinct formats and style – accessible language and more pictures – became increasingly popular. This 'journalism of entertainment', underpinned by the rise of the advertising industry in the US, was exported to Europe and then to the rest of the world, as part of the globalizing American mass culture that began to circulate in the mid-nineteenth century. By the end of the century, advertising had become a powerful element in the making of the world's most consumerist society, and in 1899, US-based advertising company J. Walter Thompson had established 'a sales bureau' in London. By the 1920s, the United States already boasted an advanced network of culture industries – including its formidable motion picture factories – that served to promote consumerist values.

From its very inception, broadcasting in the United States had a commercial remit: the US Radio Act of 1927 defined radio broadcasting as a commercial enterprise, funded by advertising. It was argued that public interest would be best served by largely unfettered private broadcasting; therefore the Act made no provision for supporting or developing non-commercial broadcasting (McChesney, 1993). Television, too, followed the market model, driven by advertising and dependent on ratings with the trio of television networks – CBS (Columbia Broadcasting System), NBC (National Broadcasting Corporation) and ABC (American Broadcasting Corporation) – providing both entertainment and information. As the networks' revenue was based on audience ratings, entertainment was an important ingredient of their programming (McChesney, 1993; Barkin, 2002). It is no coincidence that one of the world's oldest celebrity talk programmes, *The Tonight Show*, has been successfully running on NBC since 1954.

In this television culture, the notion of the citizen as consumer is deeply entrenched. The idea that the 'public interest' should be defined only by market logic was clear during the first Reagan Presidency. In 1982, the Federal Communications Commission (FCC) chairman, Mark Fowler, wrote:

> Communication policy should be directed toward maximizing the services the public desires. Instead of defining demand and specifying categories of programming to serve this demand, the Commission should rely on the broadcasters' ability to determine the wants of their audience through the normal mechanisms of the marketplace. The public's interest, then, defines the public interest' (cited in Calabrese, 2005: 272).

By the late 1980s, concern was being expressed about declining political interest among citizens, leading to an apathetic or cynical public which some commentators believed was undermining quality journalism. The steady loss of audience and advertising forced US networks to adapt to the new multi-channel broadcasting environment, preferring soft' features to hard news. Evidence of such trends was also found in a major study conducted in 1997 by the Project for Excellence in Journalism, which examined the US mass media over the previous two decades. The study noted: 'There has been a shift toward lifestyle, celebrity, entertainment and celebrity crime/scandal in the news and away from government and foreign affairs'. Looking specifically at television networks, it reported:

> The greatest new shift in emphasis of network news was a marked rise in the number of stories about scandals, up from just one-half of one per cent in 1977 to 15 per cent in 1997. The next biggest shift in emphasis in network news is a rise in human interest and quality of life stories. On network TV, human interest and quality of life stories doubled from 8 per cent of the stories that appeared in 1977 to 16 per cent in 1997 (Project for Excellence in Journalism, 1998).

The commercialization of the US news media intensified during the 1990s, marking 'a period of unprecedented decay in broadcast journalism', when the networks 'greased the slippery slope with pointed suggestions for news stories that were little more than promotions for upcoming entertainment shows' (Marc and Thompson, 2005: 121). Consultants with backgrounds in marketing and advertising were employed by broadcast networks to spruce up news programmes, including 'more soft-feature stories, more emotive delivery, more use of graphics, and the close attention to the youthful and attractive appearance of (female) on-air talent' (Calabrese, 2005: 278). One major example of the encroachment of entertainment into news was the infamous O. J. Simpson story, marking, in the words of Kellner (2003) the 'shift from journalism to infotainment'. Between 1 January and 29 September 1995, Kellner noted, the nightly news programmes on ABC, CBS, and NBC devoted 1,392 minutes to covering the Simpson trial, exceeding by a vast margin the reporting of the war in Bosnia (2003: 100–101).

Global growth of 24/7 news networks

The deregulation, liberalization and privatization of the airwaves that started in the late 1980s has had a profound impact on media systems across the globe, with the US-originated commercial model of television defining broadcasting globally in a post-Cold War world. Examining media systems in different cultural and political contexts, Hallin and Mancini (2004) noted the 'triumph of the liberal model', effectively adopted across the world 'because its global influence has been so great and because neo-liberalism and globalization continue to diffuse liberal media structures and ideas' (2004: 305). They noted that the differences among national media systems were 'clearly diminishing', and in their place a 'global media culture is emerging, one that closely resembles the Liberal Model', which is represented by central features of the American media system (2004: 294).

One key component of this change is the notion of choice reflected in the number of dedicated news networks – by 2009, there were more than 120 of them operating in the world. Economic globalization, with its attendant flexible and mobile workforce, contributed to a large and growing diasporic televisual market, which private networks have been quick to exploit, benefiting from the extension of satellite footprints and the growth of DTH (Direct-to-Home) broadcasting to feed into transnational geo-cultural spaces. Unlike state broadcasters, which tend to address traditional, territory-bound citizens, private networks are more interested in subscription-paying consumers, irrespective of nationality and citizenship (Chalaby, 2005).

State and regional broadcasting organizations have also jumped on the 24/7 news bandwagon, ensuring a presence on the global media scene and a vehicle for political public relations and diplomacy. While it would be going too far to describe some of these less than slick productions as infotainment, with their cheap and cheerful production values, their presence indicates the importance of being visible on the global image marketplace (see Table 33.1).

Table 33.1 Leading global 24/7 TV news networks

Network	Where based	Launch year
CNN International	US	1985
Sky News	UK	1989
BBC World Television	UK	1992
EuroNews	France	1993
Aljazeera	Qatar	1996
Globo News	Brazil	1996
Fox News	US	1998
Star News	India	1998
NHK World TV	Japan	1999
Channel NewsAsia	Singapore	2000
CCTV-9	China	2000
Star News Asia	Hong Kong	2000
Phoenix Infonews	Hong Kong	2001
NDTV 24x7	India	2003
DD News	India	2003
Telesur	Venezuela	2005
Russia TV	Russia	2005
France 24	France	2006
Aljazeera English	Qatar	2006
Press TV	Iran	2007

Source: Compiled from company websites

Among these are such regional networks as EuroNews (the 24/7 multi-lingual news consortium of Europe's public service broadcasters) and the pan-Latin American TV channel Telesur launched in 2005. English-language news networks continue to have a privileged position in the production and distribution of global TV news, as shown by a spate of new English-language networks outside the Anglophone world: Russia Today, France 24, NDTV 24x7, Channel NewsAsia and Aljazeera English, are some key examples of this trend. Germany's international broadcaster, Deutsche Welle TV, regularly broadcasts news bulletins in English, while Iran launched an English language channel, Press TV, in 2007. The expansion of CCTV-9, the English language 24-hour news network of China Central Television, reflects the recognition by the Beijing authorities of the importance of the English language as the key to success for global commerce and communication and their strategy to bring Chinese public diplomacy to a global audience.

Globalization of infotainment

As television news is an expensive business – especially of the 24/7 variety – and demands huge resources for programming, only large media conglomerates or well-funded state organizations can hope to run successful global news channels. Even some well-established brands have struggled to survive. Britain's Independent Television News (ITN), for example, had to close down the ITV News Channel (a round-the-clock digital news channel) in 2005 for lack of sufficient revenue. Fierce competition between proliferating news networks for ratings at a time when broadcasters are struggling to increase market share, as well as a bigger slice of a diminishing advertising cake, has prompted them to provide news in an entertaining manner. Broadcasters have had little choice but to adapt their news operations to this changing ethos in order to try to retain their viewers or to acquire them anew.

In Western Europe, excessive commercialism has posed a threat to public-service monopolies or duopolies, with an explosion of new private channels. News television, including business news channels, have proliferated in one of the world's richest media markets – from 6 in 1990 to 119 in 2005 – while documentary channels have grown from just 2 in 1990 to 108 in 2005. In Britain, with a well-established tradition of public-service broadcasting – exemplified by the BBC but including commercial broadcasters such as Independent Television (ITV) and Channel 4 – and a record of providing quality programmes on national and international public affairs, TV journalism has also been affected by the trend to infotainment. The role of entertainment – the last of the Reithian triad of 'informing, educating and entertaining' the public – gained ever greater prominence during the 1990s. One indication of this occurred when the BBC's flagship current affairs series *Panorama* (broadcast since 1953 and which set the standards for current affairs reporting for half a century) was shifted to a late weekend slot, its content diluted in an effort to retain a steadily declining viewership (though it was re-launched in 2007, in a prime time slot, albeit reduced by ten minutes to 30 minutes). For its part, ITV replaced long-running and respected current affairs and investigative programmes such as *World in Action* (1963–65 and 1967–98) and

This Week (1955–92) with more popular peak-time programming – drama and reality TV slots. In other parts of Europe, commercialism was deftly exploited for political power. In Italy, infotainment-driven private television catapulted Silvio Berlusconi from a businessman to the office of the Prime Minister, elected first in 1994 (for seven months); in 2001; and then again in 2008.

In Eastern Europe and parts of the former Soviet Union, the triumph of market capitalism has inevitably undermined the state-driven model of public broadcasting. State broadcasters were exposed as little more than propaganda networks, losing all credibility. The idea of news operating in a marketplace was normalized in a new world shaped by the market. As a former press secretary to the president of the Czech Republic noted, 'most of the formerly serious Czech journalism has moved into infotainment. Many relevant media have traded a comprehensive, analytical coverage for a soft-news, entertainment approach driven by television culture …' (Klvana, 2004: 40–41). A study of journalism in Russia found that the 'media aggressively implants hedonistic morals, paying huge attention to the entertainment genre' with young journalists 'willingly accepting' the 'role of entertainer' (Pasti, 2005: 109).

In India, the world's most crowded television news bazaar (by 2009, the country had 65 dedicated news channels), infotainment is rampant. Deregulation of the Indian television news sector has partly been responsible for this boom, as private investors – both national and transnational – have sensed new opportunities for revenue and influence by going into the television news business. The growing competition among these channels has contributed to the tendency to tabloidization of television news, encapsulated by what I have described elsewhere as the three Cs – cinema, crime and cricket – of Indian infotainment (Thussu, 2007b). Prominent among these, and one which reflects infotainment trends elsewhere in the world, is the apparent obsession of almost all news channels with celebrity culture, which in India centres on Bollywood – the world's largest film industry in terms of number of films produced annually. The power of Bollywood to sell television news is perhaps most clearly demonstrated by the way Rupert Murdoch's Indian entertainment network Star Plus used the Bollywood superstar Amitabh Bachchan as the host of *Kaun Banega Crorepati*, an Indian version of the successful British game show *Who Wants to be a Millionaire?*, giving its launch in 2000 extensive coverage on Star News. The show dramatically changed Murdoch's fortunes in India, securing an average of 40 out of the top 50 shows every week for Star Plus. The third series of the programme, launched in 2007 and hosted by the leading Bollywood star Shah Rukh Khan, retained very high ratings, thanks partly to the unprecedented publicity, including on Star News, making Star Plus the most popular private channel in the country. Other networks have realized the selling power of Bollywood and most now broadcast regular programmes about its glamour and glitz. Star News has a daily programme, *Khabar Filmi Hai* (The News about Cinema), full of celebrity-obsessed reporting and film-based gossip. Such 'Bollywoodization' is an increasing trend across the news channels.

In China, where the transition from Maoist state-controlled and propagandist media to a state-managed marketization has had a different trajectory to that of former communist countries in Europe, new 'capitalist ways' have prompted the media to 'soften the propagandist edges' and replace it with 'soft', entertaining and apolitical news. This type of news is perceived to be particularly appealing to a mass audience and 'sets the stage for profit' (Chan, 2003). Phoenix infonews channel, partly owned by Murdoch's News Corporation, regularly runs an infotainment programme, 'Easy Time, Easy News', which the company labels as 'soft and diverting news'. Meanwhile in the Arab world, where television has traditionally been controlled by governments, globalization of infotainment has brought what one commentator has called a 'liberal commercial television', adding that 'Arab viewers are exposed to American-style news formats and orientations that draw on sensational and technically alluring features' (Ayish, 2002: 151).

The primacy of ratings-driven media, as this brief selection of examples suggests, is well established across the world. Infotainment, with its privileging of soft stories as sensationalist spectacles, translates into handsome revenues.

Diluting or democratizing television news?

Here it is worth pausing to pose some key questions. Is this 'populist' version of news, with its emphasis on consumer journalism, sports and entertainment, diluting television news? To what extent is it fair to claim that this tendency to move away from a public-service news agenda to privatized infotainment – privileging information and education over the entertainment value of news – is actually harmful for democratic discourse? Or is this type of broadcast news, in fact, contributing to what might be regarded as a democratization of the public sphere, as some supporters of popular communication paradigms have argued. In their view, claims about 'tabloidization' or a 'dumbing down' of news content risk reaffirming an elitist view of journalism (Hartley, 1999).

Such debates have exercised media theorists for generations. Years before debates about the globalization of infotainment emerged, critics such as Adorno (1991) warned that the 'mechanisms of television' were creating a false global 'feel good' factor, predicated on the supremacy of the market as defined by the West. Postman (1985), in his influential book *Amusing Ourselves to Death*, formulated the thesis that public discourse in the United States was assuming the form of entertainment. He argued that the 'epistemology of television' militated against deeper knowledge and understanding since television's conversations promote 'incoherence and triviality'. Television, he believed, 'spoke in only one persistent voice – the voice of entertainment' (Postman, 1985: 84).

I would argue that global infotainment works as a powerful, seductive discourse of diversion, taking attention away from – and thereby displacing from the airwaves – such grim realities and excesses of neo-liberal capitalism as witnessed in the US invasion and occupation of Iraq. At the same time, it contributes to the globalization of a profligate and unsustainable consumerist lifestyle. With the global circulation of Americana and its localized versions, this capacity to divert and deflect has in fact increased many fold, despite appearances to the contrary (Thussu, 2006; Thussu 2007c).

'Soft news' as soft propaganda

Jacques Ellul (1965), in his excellent study of propaganda, makes an important distinction between an overtly political rendering of it and a subtler conception – namely, a propaganda of 'integration' represented by popular cinema, television, advertising and public relations – which unconsciously moulds individuals to conform to dominant societal ideas (Ellul, 1965). The growing power of global media conglomerates and their local clones can promote a softer version of corporate propaganda masquerading as infotainment, reaching billions of people in their living rooms. Governments across the globe appear to be unconcerned by the growth of infotainment, perhaps because it can keep the masses diverted with various versions of 'reality TV' and consumerist and entertaining information, displacing serious news and documentaries, which might focus on the excesses of neo-liberalism. In India, for example, the woeful lack of coverage of rural poverty, of regular suicides by small farmers (more than 100,000, between 1993 and 2003, the decade of neo-liberal 'reform', according to government figures), and the negligible reporting of developmental issues, such as health and hygiene, educational and employment equality (India has the world's largest population of child labour at the same time as having a vast pool of unemployed young people), demonstrates that such grim stories do not translate into ratings and are displaced by the diversion of infotainment.

The national elites – part of a transnational class in its infancy in many developing countries and in transition economies – play a critical role in the establishment and popularity of global infotainment. The transnational elite is susceptible to the charms of neo-liberalism, as it benefits from having closer ties with the powerful core of this tiny minority, largely based in the West, as the *Fortune 500* listings annually attest. The media system, as McChesney (1999) has reminded us, 'is not only closely linked to the *ideological* dictates of the business-run society, it is also an integral element of the economy' (1999: 281, italics in original). Infotainment conglomerates are part of the dominant economic forces in neo-liberal societies and operate within what Ellul (1965) refers to as a 'total' and 'constant' propaganda 'environment', which can render the influence of propaganda virtually unnoticed. He noted that although the educated classes believed that they are not affected by propaganda, in fact, they were more vulnerable as they consumed a greater quantity of news than the general population, and engaged regularly with processes of political communication. In the context of globalization of infotainment, it is the Westernized, mostly young and middle-class social groups, with aspirations to a consumerist lifestyle, which engage with neo-liberal media. Infotainment is more conducive to this new generation with its individualistic worldview, social and geographical mobility and transnational working environment.

The growing presence of what I have described elsewhere as 'glocal Americana' (Thussu, 2007c) is feeding into and creating a media culture in which neo-liberalism is taking deep roots. And it is because of this 'constant' and soft propaganda that neo-liberalism has been embraced, almost universalized by dominant sections of the global elites, who have come to regard its basic tenets – private (efficient and therefore preferable) vs. public (corrupt and inefficient); individualism (to be applauded) vs.

community (to be decried); market (good) vs. state (bad) – as undisputed opposites which fall within the rubric of 'commonsense'.

As Harvey (2003) has argued, neo-liberalism has become a hegemonic discourse with pervasive effects on ways of thought and political-economic practices, making it part of the commonsense view of the world. The globalization of neo-liberal ideology and the near global reach and circulation of televised infotainment have provided neo-liberalism with a powerful opportunity to communicate directly with the world's populace, as more and more global infotainment conglomerates are localizing their content to reach beyond the 'Westernized' elites.

At a time when infotainment becomes entrenched in news conventions around the world, the US experience is likely to become widely acceptable. This will be to the considerable benefit of the right-wing political agendas, predicated on the supremacy of the market. The German media sociologist Niklas Luhmann, who saw the mass media as one of the key cognitive systems of modern society, posed a crucial question: '*How* is it possible to accept information about the world and about society as information about reality when one knows *how* it is produced'? (Luhmann, 2000: 122, italics in original). As the global financial crisis, unleashed in 2008, exposes the limitations of neo-liberal ideology, Luhmann's question acquires added salience and urgency.

References

Adorno, Theodor (1991) *The Cultural Industry: Selected Essays on Mass Culture*. London: Routledge.

Ayish, Mohammed (2002) Political Communication on Arab World Television: Evolving Patterns. *Political Communication*, 19:137–154.

Barkin, Steve (2002) *American Television News: The Media Marketplace and the Public Interest*. New York: M.E. Sharpe.

Calabrese, Andrew (2005) The Trade in Television News, in Janet Wasko (ed.) *A Companion to Television*. Oxford: Blackwell.

Castells, Manuel (2004) *The Information Age: Economy, Society and Culture*, vol. 2: *The Power of Identity*, second edition. Oxford: Blackwell.

Chalaby, Jean (ed.) (2005) *Transnational Television Worldwide – Towards a New Media Order*. London: I. B. Tauris.

Chan, Joseph Man (2003) Administrative Boundaries and Media Marketization: A Comparative Analysis of the Newspaper, TV and Internet Markets in China', pp. 159–76 in C.C. Lee (ed.) *Chinese Media, Global Contexts*. London: Routledge.

Ellul, Jacques (1965) *Propaganda: The Formation of Men's Attitudes*. New York: Knopf, originally published in French as *Propagandes* in 1962.

Gitlin, Todd (2002) *Media Unlimited: How the Torrents of Images and Sounds Overwhelms Our Lives*: New York: Metropolitan Books.

GlobeScan (2006) *BBC/Reuters/Media Center Poll: Trust in the Media*, released 3 May. Available at: www.globescan.com/news_archives/bbcreut.html

Hallin, Daniel and Mancini, Poulo (2004) *Comparing Media Systems*. Cambridge: Cambridge University Press.

Hartley, John (1999) *Uses of Television*. London: Routledge.

Harvey, David (2003) *The New Imperialism*. Oxford: Oxford University Press.

Kellner, Douglas (2003) *Media Spectacle*. New York: Routledge.

Klvana, Tomás (2004) New Europe's Civil Society, Democracy, and the Media Thirteen Years After: The Story of the Czech Republic. *Harvard Journal of Press/Politics*, 9(3):40–55.

Luhmann, Niklas (2000) *The Reality of the Mass Media*. Cambridge: Polity.

Marc, David and Thompson, Robert (2005) *Television in the Antenna Age – A Concise History*. Oxford: Blackwell.

McChesney, Robert (1993) *Telecommunications, Mass Media and Democracy: The Battle for the Control of US Broadcasting, 1928–1935*. New York: Oxford University Press.

McChesney, Robert (1999) *Rich Media, Poor Democracy – Communication Politics in Dubious Times*. Champaign, IL: University of Illinois Press.

Mott, Frank Luther (1962) *American Journalism: A History: 1690–1960*, third edition. New York: Macmillan.

Pasti, Svetlana (2005) Two Generations of Contemporary Russian Journalists. *European Journal of Communication*, 20(1): 89–115.

Postman, Neil (1985) *Amusing Ourselves to Death: Public Discourse in the Age of Show Business*. New York: Viking.

Project for Excellence in Journalism (1998) *Changing Definitions of News*, March 6, Available at: http://www.journalism.org/resources/research/reports/

Project for Excellence in Journalism (2006) *The State of the News Media: An Annual Report on American Journalism, 2006*. Journalism.org. Available at http://stateofthemedia.org/2006

Schudson, Michael (1978) *Discovering the News: A Social History of American Newspapers*. New York: Harper.

Thussu, Daya Kishan (2006) *International Communication – Continuity and Change*, second edition. London: Hodder Arnold.

Thussu, Daya Kishan (2007a) *News as Entertainment: The Rise of Global Infotainment*. London: Sage.

Thussu, Daya Kishan (2007b) The 'Murdochization' of News? The Case of Star TV in India. *Media, Culture & Society*, 29(3): 593–611.

Thussu, Daya Kishan (2007c) Mapping Global Media Flow and Contra-Flow, in Daya Kishan Thussu (ed.) *Media on the Move: Global Flow and Contra-Flow*. London: Routledge.

34

REAL NEWS/FAKE NEWS: BEYOND THE NEWS/ENTERTAINMENT DIVIDE

Geoffrey Baym

To hear the comedian Jon Stewart and his colleagues tell it, the curious hybrid program *The Daily Show* is *fake news*: a "nightly half-hour series unburdened by objectivity, journalistic integrity or even accuracy." Claiming "zero credibility," they insist that watching the show is no substitute for attending to the news – it's "even better than being informed" (Comedy Central, 2007). Certainly their show is more entertaining than most journalistic forms, but the label of fake news, which has been so carefully cultivated by the show producers and readily adopted by most commentators in the popular and academic press is, at heart, misleading. As I consider in this chapter, the concept of fake news rests on a host of assumptions that deserve, but are rarely subject to, careful scrutiny. As such, it obscures more than it reveals, inadequately describing *The Daily Show* (TDS) and its spin-off *The Colbert Report*, and masking the deeper implications these programs contain for the practice and study of public-affairs journalism.

At the least, fake news fails to recognize the quite *real* role TDS, *Colbert*, and other comedy news sources now play in the contemporary news environment. In recent years, large numbers of people – especially, but not only, the younger ones – have been turning away from traditional sources of news, while many more are tuning out "the news" altogether (Buckingham, 2000; Mindich, 2005; Prior, 2007). Even in the midst of Barack Obama's historic run for the presidency in 2008, more than a third of 18–24-year-old Americans reported paying no attention to news on an ordinary day. Older people likewise have become less interested in news, with as many as 22% of people aged 30–34 also saying they go "newsless" most days (Pew, 2008a).

By contrast, the fake news continues to grow in appeal. In 2008, for example, the number of Americans who said they learned at least something about the presidential campaign from comedy programs such as TDS rose considerably, with 28%

of the general population and nearly 40% of those under 30 saying they learned real information from the fake news (Pew, 2008b). In the fall of 2008, both TDS and *Colbert* were reaching their largest audiences ever (1.8 and 1.4 million respectively), an increase for both shows of 16% over the previous year (Lafayette, 2008). Those numbers undoubtedly underestimate the total audience, neglecting the domestic viewership for the programs' multiple reruns and their increasing international following. Neither do they include the many thousands who view full programs and individual clips on the Internet.

What's more, both shows reach audiences diverse in age and higher in education and political knowledge than either the general population or the audiences for most other forms of news and public affairs (NAES, 2004; Pew, 2008a). For those reasons, the fake news has become a near-mandatory booking for authors trying to sell works of political non-fiction and for politicians hoping to influence the national conversation. Senator John McCain, for example, used multiple visits to TDS to revive his flagging campaign for the 2008 Republican presidential nomination. Hillary Clinton likewise appeared on the show for a 10-minute interview the night before the critical Ohio and Texas Democratic primaries, and Barack Obama appeared less than a week before he would win the presidency. For his part, Colbert insisted he gave Republican Mike Huckabee the "Colbert Bump," helping lift the former governor of Arkansas from political obscurity and to his own talk show on Fox News.

If the label of fake news neglects the serious role these programs are playing in public political discourse, it has another, more significant problem. Any notion of "fake" depends upon an equal conception of a "real." To label TDS or *Colbert* as fake news is to assume that one can identify an *authentic* or *legitimate* kind of news: a journalism of objectivity and accuracy, public service and professional integrity. Although for many these ideals remain compelling, a lap around the contemporary dial of news media, at least in the United States, reveals that they have become difficult to identify. Lacking a codified set of professional guidelines, standardized entrance examination, or supervisory guild, news instead is defined by a shifting set of practices, informal and often implicit agreements about proper conduct, style, and form. As many of the chapters in this volume attest, those practices are in flux; multiple, debatable, and open for reconsideration. In the face of rapidly changing technological, economic, and cultural contexts, we are seeing a marked proliferation in journalistic forms – professional, public, citizen, tabloid, alternative, and convergent, to name but a few – overlapping and interwoven approaches that complement, contradict, and always complicate one another.

The emergent kind of journalism too often dismissed as "fake news" has become one of the more significant, but largely misunderstood of these. In this chapter, I seek to clarify the nature of the so-called fake news, exemplified – but not reducible to – *The Daily Show*. My goal is not to analyze specific programs or performances, work that has been conducted elsewhere (e.g. Baym, 2005, 2007a, 2007b; Jones, 2005). Here I extrapolate from TDS and *Colbert* to make sense of "fake news" more broadly – to explore what distinguishes it from the kind of news more often assumed to be "real." My starting premise is that fake news is not, nor could be, fake in and of itself – that is, it is not fake because it *misrepresents* its subject matter or somehow exists at a greater distance to *the actual* than do other forms of news. Rather, fake news is "fake" to the extent that it rejects the conventional practices widely accepted as defining "the news." For that reason, fake news may be better understood not as fake, but rather as a quite real and much-needed effort to reinvent public-interest journalism in ways that have the potential to reinvigorate both the Fourth Estate and popular engagement with politics.

Organizing logics

Many commentators are quick to label the fake news as fake because it readily criss crosses the boundary between news and entertainment, thus violating the assumption that the informative is somehow, and necessarily, distinct from the entertaining. That assumption, although long culturally enshrined, fails to stand up to careful analysis. News has always been a particular kind of narrative art, one that arranges the events of the phenomenal world into neatly defined stories – dramatic tales rich with heroes and villains, conflict and suspense. So too has entertainment often grappled with serious issues, providing the citizenry with a largely unacknowledged source of information and socio-political orientation. The dividing line between news and entertainment is fundamentally porous, if not entirely arbitrary, and difficult to define with any meaningful measure of precision (Delli Carpini & Williams, 2001).

Like the similarly vague boundary between the serious and the silly, the distinction between news and entertainment can be understood as a product of modernity, the social epoch that gave rise to the kind of journalism, at least in its "high-modern" variety, that forged our current assumptions about "real news" (see Baym, 2009; Carey, 1993; Hallin, 1992). Building on the work of Max Weber, Habermas (1983) has argued that modernity itself largely was a project of *social rationalization*, the dividing of social and cultural activity into autonomous spheres, each entrusted with advancing a particular aspect of the human condition. For the modern mind, the *political-normative* – that arena of politics, policy, and the social good – was clearly distinct from the *aesthetic-expressive* – the realm of art and affect, pleasure and play. Each sphere in turn was assumed to contain, without overlap, particular types of cultural activities and concerns, and gave rise to clearly demarcated sets of institutions, practices, and discourses.

Thus Richard Salant, the president of CBS News at the apex of the high-modern, could confidently proclaim that "our field is journalism, not show business," and demand that his employees avoid using any televisual techniques that might blur the line between news and entertainment, and thus he assumed, between fact and fiction (quoted in Schaefer, 1998, p. 8). In recent years, however, media genres and public performances of all kinds have become profoundly intertwined and the lines between news and entertainment, politics and show business, the serious and the silly, have been largely obscured. Although I hesitate to endorse the whole of *postmodern* theory, we clearly live now in an age of "de-differentiation," of the melding of once-distinct "field logics and system codes" (Corner & Pels, 2003, p. 8). Elsewhere I have described this as a process of *discursive integration* (Baym, 2005). In a media landscape marked by the fluidity of content and the permeability of form, genres have become deeply hybrid and the very conceptual frames through which we make sense of public life inseparably conflated. Politics has become indivisible from poplar culture, the "real news" all-too-often a kind of postmodern "infotainment" indistinguishable from other styles of reality-based TV, and the fake news a consistent and quite serious source of information and public conversation.

Institutional parameters

Perhaps, then, fake news is fake because it is produced from within a markedly different institutional context than is the real news. That, of course, is the running joke on TDS, which certainly is not broadcast, despite its continual claim, from "Comedy Central's World News Headquarters in New York." Instead the fake news is shaped by the production parameters of the entertainment industry, which frees it from both the expectations and the constraints that over determine the daily output of the real news business.

For example, unlike most forms of journalism, the fake news has no obligation to follow the *news cycle* – that daily attention focused on a small number of events and issues – sometimes significant, sometimes trivial – that move rapidly in and out of journalistic focus. With a remarkable degree of homogeneity, the mainstream media ape one another each day, relying on the same narrowly articulated understanding of "news value" to report on a largely identical set of topics. The fake news, however, maintains a far greater degree of editorial independence. Of course, it largely shadows the "real" news, drawing on the output of various mainstream media outlets for its content, but it is also free to ignore the natural disasters, child abductions, celebrity foibles, and other tabloid topics that periodically saturate the real news. With greater control over its own editorial agenda, the fake news can focus more consistently on the kinds of *high-modern* topics – national politics, federal policy, and foreign affairs – that are often obscured in the age of infotainment. Indeed, The Project for Excellence in Journalism (2008) itself has confirmed the suspicion that TDS covers such "hard news" with more regularity than do the mainstream media.

The fake news is also free from the constraints of the 24-hour timeframe that structures the production of real news. Unlike other forms of daily journalism, TDS isn't even a *daily* show. Both it and *Colbert* are produced only four days a week and, even more unlike the real news, take several weeks off during the year. Similarly, neither show, with but a few exceptions, is broadcast live. Instead they are taped in the afternoon and then aired several hours later. Both shows are also rerun multiple times throughout the following day, and in some instances, re-aired several weeks after their original production. So too is all of their content now always available on-line through a continuously expanding digital collection.

In practice this means little emphasis on *immediacy*, the measure of professional journalistic competition that privileges speed of reporting over all else. Structurally prohibited from covering "breaking news" – that bit of news jargon that has become increasingly clichéd – the fake news can be more reflective. Never the breathless effort to be first on the scene, it instead can engage in a more thoughtful exploration of issues and their contexts, one that transcends a journalistic system that must find a new episode or a new angle every 24 hours. The fake news is able to explore the archive, revisiting significant moments, comments, and claims from previous days, months, or even years. Although such material may shed valuable light on current events, it often lies beyond the purview of the real news, whose lack of memory systematically prevents it from explicating the context of the daily episodes on which it reports. Fake news likewise is free to devote air time to explaining background and basic institutional processes, the kind of base knowledge essential to understanding current events and participating in politics, but largely elided by the mainstream news.

To be sure, fake news' positioning outside the parameters of mainstream journalistic institutions also means it lacks any real institutional credentials. Although TDS has been able to obtain media credentials to attend recent major political events such as the 2008 party conventions and presidential debates, the fake news lacks the kind of inside access to the White House and the halls of Congress, or the ability to command comment from public officials, that demarcates the real news as such. This may be one of the most significant distinctions between real and fake, and it most certainly leaves the fake news dependent on the real. At the same time, though, it also means that the fake news exists independently of the wider press/politics axis, the dominant system of mutual dependence between journalists and public officials in which journalists are simultaneously enabled and constrained by their access to the corridors of power (Bennett, Lawrence, & Livingston, 2007).

As was demonstrated particularly clearly in the United States during the Bush years, the real news' dependence on access too easily can become an over-eagerness to report on the scripts of power – consider Judith Miller's reporting in the *New York Times* on Saddam Hussein's alleged weapons of mass destruction – and an equal refusal to engage in the kind of critical inquiry that the ideals of the Fourth Estate would require. The result is a symbiotic relationship between the mainstream press and political power, one that too often converts the news media from an *institution* committed to holding government accountable to an *instrument* to be used by the government in the effort to manage public opinion (Bennett, Lawrence, & Livingston, 2007). Never having had access, fake news can never lose that access, and thus it is able to preserve its autonomy from the power structure – a critical distance that enables it to more consistently issue a call for democratic accountability than one hears from the mainstream media.

Journalistic methods

The fake news may be fake, therefore, because it pursues this distinctly democratic labor, and does so through a markedly different set of journalistic methods than does the real news. Some might suggest that by definition, the fake news has no journalistic methods. Like the real news, however, it too is the craft of obtaining, packaging, and disseminating public information. Enabled by the sheer availability of news and information in the contemporary media environment, it functions as a content aggregator, a synthesis of news reports from a variety of television, print, and web-based sources. To that, the fake news adds its own summaries of presidential press conferences, Congressional hearings, and other public proceedings – material now regularly broadcast in its entirety on CSPAN, 24-hour cable news, and a number of other media outlets.

In its presentation of this "real news" content, however, the fake news stands several journalistic conventions on their head. Its selection of soundbites, for example, rejects standard approaches to quoting in ways that often lead to far greater insight than one finds in the real news. With its emphasis on brevity and clarity, the mainstream news narrative requires a particular kind of quote – the eight-to-12 second morsel containing a clean beginning and end, an easily discernible focus, and a measure of character-revealing emotion. Well aware of this, professional speech writers and media handlers have long scripted soundbites for media consumption, designing one-liners and talking points intended to seed public discourse with spectacle and spin. The fake news, while replaying many of the same prefabricated soundbites that occupy the real news, also mines the outtakes – the vast majority of public speech that does not make it into the daily news – to confront the talking point and offer contrary perspectives. It seeks out soundbites that do not always fit the narrative, that demonstrate uncertainty, contradiction, or blatant repetition, and thus help expose the construction of political rhetoric – the strategic effort to plant preferred interpretations of the real into the popular imagination.

The primary method here is *juxtaposition*, the central technique in the art of satire, but one largely considered illegitimate in the field of news. There, soundbites are seamlessly woven into the daily narrative, presented as the authoritative word, imposing narrative closure, and limiting further avenues of inquiry. The kind of juxtaposition practiced by the fake news, however, forces soundbites and talking points into critical exchange. Statements that are allowed to stand in isolation in the real news are instead confronted with previous statements and counterfactual claims, often from the very same people who now appear in back-to-back clips offering both arguments and their own rebuttals. Soundbites are juxtaposed in the same way with the fake newscasters' own interpretations. Unlike the real journalists, the fake ones never claim to be neutral conduits through which authoritative information and official proclamations are allowed to pass. Instead, they are explicitly situated, refusing to mimic the real news' tenuous claim to objectivity and willfully interrogating soundbites and their speakers.

If the real news' insistence on objectivity can become too easily the non-reflexive amplification of scripted spin (Bennett, Lawrence, & Livingston, 2007), the fake news instead challenges the claims offered by those in power, examining both their logic, and at times the very morality upon which they rest. Rejecting the modernist divide between fact and value, the fake news locates public political speech within a coherent moral framework, covering *what is*, while equally attending to *what is right*. Particularly during the Bush Administration, for example, the fake news regularly returned to the question of the treatment of detainees in Iraq and at Guantanamo Bay, which it discussed in explicitly moral terms. In the wake of the Abu Ghraib scandal, TDS would broadcast a statement from then-US Defense Secretary Donald Rumsfeld, who clearly voiced the administration's chosen frame. "I'm not a lawyer," he asserted, but "my impression is that what has been charged thus far is abuse, which I believe, technically, is different from torture, and therefore I'm not gonna address the torture word." As the audience groaned in the background, Stewart retorted: "I'm also not a lawyer, so I don't know, technically, if you're *human*, but as a fake news person, I can tell you, what we've been reading about in the newspapers, the pictures we've been seeing … it's f***ing torture" (see Baym, 2005).

For Stewart, it was the fact that he was *not* a journalist, but a "fake news person," that allowed him to engage in a kind of moral inquiry the "real news person" could not – to unequivocally label US conduct as "torture," and both it and Rumsfeld's dissembling as violations of human decency. Conventions of objectivity disallow comment: the real journalists can reiterate Rumsfeld's troubling quote in the hope it will "speak for itself," but they cannot confront it as does Stewart. Not surprisingly, Bennett et al.'s research finds that most of the "real" journalists did indeed parrot the administration's frame, also avoiding "the torture word" for the far safer label of "abuse" (see also Bennett, this volume). Perhaps that explains why, as Stewart has often noted, journalists regularly tell him they wish they could say the things he does.

If the fake news reworks soundbites into critical exchange, its interviews with public figures provide a platform for a wider ranging conversation about public affairs than one finds in the mainstream news media. There, a narrow set of governmental insiders and media pundits are allowed to shape the terms of the debate. Although many of those same people appear as interview guests on both TDS and *Colbert*, the fake news also regularly features a broader diversity of experts, authors, and activists, many of whom are rarely afforded the opportunity to speak in the mainstream media. Through the fake news, though, they are able to address critical topics often overlooked by daily journalism and voice counter-positions that at times strain the boundaries of the mediated public sphere (Baym, 2007a). Similarly, people who do often appear in other mediated spaces are able to diverge from their primary public personas they construct elsewhere. Thus when she appeared on TDS, CBS Foreign Correspondent Lara Logan could offer harsh criticism of US news coverage of the wars in Afghanistan and Iraq, something she could never do on the CBS News (see Baym, 2009). Similarly, even the hyper-partisan conservative John Bolton, who briefly served as George Bush's ambassador to the UN, could (in his *second* interview with Stewart) relax the ideological rigidity he displays elsewhere to engage in a thoughtful discussion of US foreign policy.

Discursive voice

To be sure, these conversations are not always the kind of *rational* exchange the modern mind would have expected of "the news." The fake news might be fake, therefore, because it is not always literal, nor necessarily linear. Unlike the real news, which is assumed to be expository – a discourse of fact and explanation – fake news draws on a wider range of voices and standpoints. It is at times expository and often rational-critical, offering cogent argument and erudite discussion, but it is also silly, crass, and sophomoric. Likewise, it is always satirical and ironic, assuming a host of non-literal stances, differing rhetorical postures that allow it to function in more complex ways than does the traditional news.

Like all good satire, the fake news is in part a discourse of *play* – a celebration of laughter, joy, and wit (see Griffin, 1994). Its humor, its bursts of the playful and the irrational, function as aesthetic style, providing the initial appeal especially for those who, in an entertainment-saturated age, have grown less committed to the citizenly rite of attending to the news. In a time when many now dismiss "the news" as *boring*, the fake news simply makes following the news *fun*. On a deeper level, though, it more profoundly melds the domains of politics and play, blending the political-normative with the aesthetic-expressive. As such, it helps confront the wider cultural problematic that although some may "like" politics and "enjoy" the news, for many news and politics are entirely divorced from pleasure and play, contained within a distant, if not foreign, discursive realm. For them, political attention and participation are marginalized, increasingly seen as irrelevant to the lifeworld and unable to compete with more enjoyable leisure-time activities (Prior, 2007; Van Zoonen, 2005). From such a perspective, the fake news' discourse of play contains the power to overcome the cleavage many perceive between news, politics, and everyday life (Baym, 2007b; Jones, 2005).

The multiple voices of fake news also make it more *critically engaging* than the real news often is. The latter is largely *monologic* in the Bakhtinian sense, a hierarchical, unidirectional discourse that claims to "possess a ready-made truth" (Griffin, 1994, p. 42). By contrast, the fake news is *dialogic* – the juxtaposition of voices and perspectives, but also and equally, the interaction between the *said* and the *unsaid*. Unlike the real news, whose voice is both literal and often void of nuance, the meaning of the fake news, for whom the double voice of irony is a primary discursive modality, always remains at a measure of interpretive distance. Satire and irony demand that the audience actively fill in the blanks; to get the joke necessitates reading between the lines. As such, the fake news engages the audience in its discourse of inquiry, less providing its viewers with authoritative information and interpretation than inviting them to participate in an always-ongoing and cooperative search for truth.

The fake news thus ultimately functions not just as an informational source, but as a *rhetorical resource*. In contrast to the real news, which is structured to be passively consumed by isolated individuals, the fake news is designed to be shared. It lends itself to citation and re-creation, offering conversational bits and teaching tools that resonate with many and wind their way through a variety of inter-personal, pedagogical, and organizational settings. In a convergent age, one sees this quite literally on the Internet, where every clip from TDS and *Colbert* is housed in a publicly accessible archive, both searchable and sharable. Here the fake news readily facilitates its own reappropriation, inviting technologically enabled audiences, now reconceptualized as *users*, to seize and interweave it within their own digital media creations and commentary. A resource for the audience's own performance of rhetorical citizenship, the fake news has become a critical component in a fundamentally new and remarkably hybrid form of *public voice* (Baym, 2009).

Fake news: the way of the future?

In many ways, the "real news" is in a state of crisis, faced with a range of challenges that include rapidly declining audiences, decreasing profits, and a wider loss of credibility. Having repackaged themselves as various versions of infotainment, the mainstream news media not only fail to appeal to much of the citizenry, but also have too readily abdicated their watchdog function – that modernist impulse that many would suggest defines the *real news* and that democracy demands. That point provided the subtext for Jon Stewart's interview with Paul O'Neill, the former US treasury secretary who was the first administration insider to speak out against both the Bush White House and the national news media. The latter in particular, he said, were no longer interested in reasoned discourse, and "hammered me really hard for telling the truth." To that, Stewart gleefully proclaimed: "This is why, and I hate to toot our own horn, that fake news is the way of the future." O'Neill's response was telling. "I like what you're doing," he said. "Keep making fun."

The suggestion here is intriguing – that by "making fun," fake news is at the same time engaged in the serious exploration of political issues; an exploration that is vital to the conduct of democracy but all too often missing in the contemporary news. As O'Neill may have recognized, the fake news represents the *flip side* of infotainment. It is neither a "dumbing down" of the news, nor the corruption of serious information by the logic of entertainment. Instead, it is in part the injection of news and politics into previously non-political spaces. More importantly, though, it represents the harnessing of the power of entertainment in pursuit of an older set of journalistic ideals. The fake news thus reminds us that *entertainment* is a doubly articulated concept. On one hand, "to entertain" means to *amuse* and to *give pleasure*. On the other, it means to *engage with* and to *consider*. The fake news does both. It makes the news pleasurable, but more than that, it continuously calls on its viewers to consider.

Lying just beneath, or perhaps interwoven with the laughter, is a serious exercise in critical inquiry: a demand for governmental accountability, a performance of democratic dialogue, and a resource for citizen engagement. In an age when the "real news" too often fails on all of those accounts, the fake news stands at the leading edge in the effort to reimagine the possibilities of journalism. Its increasing popularity and its growing significance in the serious world of news and politics support the suggestion that it is not really fake at all. Rather, embracing an alternative organizing logic, originating from a differing institutional context, and employing a range of experimental journalistic methods and discursive voices, fake news may indeed be "the way of the future."

References

Baym, G. (2005) *The Daily Show*: Discursive Integration and the Reinvention of Political Journalism. *Political Communication*, 22: 259–276.

Baym, G. (2007a) Crafting New Communicative Models in the Televisual Sphere: Political Interviews on *The Daily Show*. *The Communication Review*, 10: 93–115.

Baym, G. (2007b) Representation and the Politics of Play: Stephen Colbert's *Better Know a District*. *Political Communication*, 24: 359–376.

Baym, G. (2009) *From Cronkite to Colbert: The Evolution of Broadcast News*. Boulder, CO: Paradigm Publishers.

Bennett, W.L., Lawrence, R.G., and Livingston, S. (2007) *When the Press Fails: Political Power and the News Media from Iraq to Katrina*. Chicago: University of Chicago Press.

Buckingham, D. (2000) *The Making of Citizens: Young People, News and Politics*, New York: Routledge.

Carey, J.W. (1993) The Mass Media and Democracy: Between the Modern and the Postmodern. *Journal of International Affairs*, 47: 1–21.

Comedy Central (2007). *The Daily Show*. Retrieved October 22, 2007 from http://www.thedailyshow.com/about.html

Corner, J. and Pels, D. (2003) *Media and the Restyling of Politics*. Thousand Oaks, CA: Sage.

Delli Carpini, M.X. and Williams, B.W. (2001) Let Us Infotain You: Politics in the New Media Environment. In W.L. Bennett & R.M. Entman (Eds.), *Mediated Politics: Communication in the Future of Democracy* (pp. 160–181). New York: Cambridge University Press.

Griffin, D. (1994) *Satire: A Critical Reintroduction*. Lexington, KY: University Press of Kentucky.

Habermas, J. (1983) Modernity – An Incomplete Project. In H. Foster (Ed.), *The Anti-Aesthetic: Essays on Postmodern Culture* (pp. 3–15). Seattle: Bay Press.

Hallin, D.C. (1992) The Passing of the "High Modernism" of American Journalism. *Journal of Communication*, 42: 14–25.

Jones, J.P. (2005) *Entertaining Politics: New Political Television and Civic Culture*. New York: Rowman & Littlefield.

Lafayette, J. (2008) "Political Parodies Pay in Election Year," *Television Week*, October 6.

Mindich, D.T.Z. (2005) *Tuned Out: Why Americans under 40 Don't Follow the News*. New York: Oxford University Press.

National Annenberg Election Survey (2004) Daily Show viewers knowledgeable about presidential campaign. Retrieved February 24, 2005 from http://www.annenbergpublicpolicycenter.org/naes/2004_03_late-night-knowledge-2_9-21_pr.pdf

Pew Research Center for the People and the Press (2008a) Audience Segments in a Changing News Environment. Retrieved October 26, 2008 from http://people-press.org/reports/display.php3?ReportID=1354

Pew Research Center for the People and the Press. (2008b) Social Networking and Online Videos Take Off: Internet's Broader Role in Campaign 2008. Retrieved February 7, 2008 from http://people-press.org/reports/ display.php3?ReportID=384

Prior, M. (2007) *Post-Broadcast Democracy: How Media Choice Increases Inequality in Political Involvement and Polarizes Elections*. New York: Cambridge University Press.

Project for Excellence in Journalism (2008) Journalism, Satire or Just Laughs? Retrieved 10 May, 2008 from www.journalism.org/files/Daily%20Show%20PDF_3.pdf

Schaefer, R.J. (1998). The Development of the CBS News Guidelines during the Salant Years. *Journal of Broadcasting and Electronic Media*, 42: 1–20.

Van Zoonen, L. (2005) *Entertaining the Citizen: When Politics and Popular Culture Converge*. New York: Rowman & Littlefield.

35

JOURNALISM IN THE CINEMA

Brian McNair

This chapter explores the representation of journalism in one of the most important popular culture forms, cinema. It advocates the use of movies about journalism in journalism studies teaching and research, and reviews the existing literature on the subject.

A good tradition of love and hate

Cinema is the main location in our culture (apart from the news media themselves), where journalists have regularly been represented, their role and functions discussed and their performance scrutinised. Which is to say not only that more people encounter journalists in the cinema than in any other medium, but that cinematic representations of journalism tend to have greater cultural resonance than those contained in novels, TV drama, theatre or other popular cultural forms. There have been many great novels and non-fiction books written about journalism, to be sure, and one could easily write a substantial book's worth of essays on those representations alone. TV drama, too, has frequently addressed the subject of journalism in sit coms, one-off plays, and series such as ITV (UK)'s 2008 production starring James Nesbitt, Midnight Man.[1] Theatre has produced one of the all time classic stories of journalism, frequently adapted and remade for cinema – 1928's The Front Page, written by Ben Hecht and Charles MacArthur – as well as more recent productions such as Pravda (David Hare and Howard Brenton, 1985) and Frost/Nixon (Peter Morgan, 2006).

But theatre and TV drama tend to be localised within one country. Movies, by contrast, particularly those made by the dominant US industry and involving popular stars such as George Clooney, Angelina Jolie and Kate Winslet (all of whom have played screen journalists in recent times) are prominent and much-in-demand elements in an increasingly globalised culture.

Novels and other forms of literary work, meanwhile, are hugely important as texts,[2] and have been the source material for many of the greatest movies about journalism ever made (All the President's Men perhaps being the best-known example), but in a predominantly televisual culture books are read by less people than will see a reasonably successful movie on the big screen (or later on TV and DVD). Woodward's and Bernstein's book sold millions, but Alan J. Pakula's 1976 film of All The President's Men has been seen by tens if not hundreds of millions worldwide, and took more than $70 million at the US box office in its initial cinema run. When we think of the Watergate scandal, it is more likely to be the forever-young 1970s faces of Redford and Hoffmann we see, not the actual journalists who broke the story and are now ageing gracefully on the proceeds.

The importance of cinema in the representation of journalism goes beyond the question of 'bums on seats'. If journalists are, as they like to believe and we non-journalists expect, a Fourth Estate charged with the critical scrutiny of political and other elite groups in liberal democratic societies, film-makers have the function of scrutinising the scrutineers, watching over the watch dogs, whistle blowing on the whistle blowers, measuring journalistic performance against the normative standards which are built into our democratic DNA. Cinema is the conscience of the journalistic profession, the key location in culture where its role and functions are held up to broad public inspection. Movies like The Insider (Michael Mann, 1998) and Good Night, and Good Luck (George Clooney, 2005) engage their audiences in thinking about how the news media operate in a world where commercial and political pressures abound, and media freedom is always under strain. They remind us what it is that journalists are *supposed* to do in a democracy, and then present scenarios in which how they *actually* perform is interrogated (often, as in both of the aforementioned movies, scenarios based on actual events). They are, in this sense, teaching tools for a mass mediated culture – educating, exposing errors and malfunctions in the smooth working of a core element of the democratic infrastructure, and in some cases advising on how to correct those errors. Jack Lule writes about "the mythological role of journalism" (2001), of how news media tell stories which are, in an anthropological sense, timeless and deeply functional for social reproduction. Movies about news, in turn, are a source of the legitimation myths of liberal journalism, dramatising and articulating those shared values and ideas about how news works which, alongside many other myth systems, bind us together as citizens in a democracy.

Cinema has been called the 'dream factory', and with good reason. Here, more than anywhere else in the cultural domain, issues circulating in the public sphere around the performance of journalism are played out before a mass, mainstream audience, most of whom will never have had direct experience of working in or with the profession, or have read scholarly books such as this one at college or university. Cinema is the key popular medium of the electronic era. It tells its stories by means of narrative shortcuts, stereotypes and the employment of familiar, attention-grabbing actors performing up there on the big screen in a darkened auditorium where the audience may lose itself for an hour or two. This escapist quality is the reason for its mass appeal, its iconicity the source of its myth-making power.

The myth-making quality of cinema is true as a generality, but the importance of journalism in our societies makes movies about news media of particular cultural significance. Barbie Zelizer's 2004 book urges us to take journalism seriously, and that is precisely what movies do. In 1994 I introduced a book on News & Journalism In the

UK with a chapter called 'Why journalism matters' (McNair, 2009). Journalism *does* matter, in a way that few other forms of cultural expression do, because it is directly bound up with the maintenance of the democratic polity and the wider social system. Cinema is a space where we are reminded of that fact, again and again from the 1920s and the birth of Hollywood to the most recent example of a journalism movie released in cinemas before this essay was sent to the printers – Ron Howard's Frost/Nixon (2008), based on Peter Morgan's play. Note that this reconstruction of the famous TV interview between British journalist David Frost and former US president Nixon was titled Frost/Nixon rather than Nixon/Frost, an order of billing which may be thought to reflect the relative cultural status of the two figures.

The dualities of screen journalism

Journalism matters because of its watchdog functions in a democracy, and in a system of free market capitalism prone to excess and abuse. But journalism is not just about the serious issues of politics and the economy. Journalism is also, and has always been, a form of entertainment, providing readers, listeners, viewers and now online users with information intended to facilitate rest, relaxation, recreation and pleasure. News is entertainment when it shocks and scandalises with coverage of Britney Spears' latest escapades. The early newspapers entertained with gory headlines about witch burnings and public executions. Today's journalistic media are packed with 'human interest', and information about cooking, interior decoration, health and lifestyle, book and film reviews, sport, art and celebrity. The degree to which journalism entertains is key to its success as a cultural commodity, and to the survival of news organisations as businesses. With some exceptions, such as the public service broadcasters, news media are engaged above all in selling information, attracting customers, and selling those customers on again to advertisers. This has been the case since the very first news books, and journalism has always been required to strike a balance between the provision of information for the public good, and information which in one way or another provides an audience with pleasure (even the perverse pleasure of reading about crime and other horrors). In the century of cinema, however, many believe that the balance has been distorted, so that entertainment has become more important as a goal of journalism than the normatively preferred coverage of politics, business, foreign affairs. Journalism, it is argued by these critical observers, has become dominated by infotainment. Journalism has been commercialised, degraded, vulgarised, corrupted by market forces and the need to sell news.

This is not a chapter about the flaws of contemporary journalism, or a critique of the news values which govern media organisations. That there is intense and long-lasting debate around these questions does, however, help to explain the cultural schizophrenia which surrounds the figure of the journalist in cinema, as it structures public perceptions. He, or she, exists in the public imagination, and on the silver screen, as both a hero and a villain; as an admired celebrity at one moment, akin in some cases to a rock star, and a reptile at another, loathsome and repellent (which is unfair to reptiles, I know, but bear with me). Journalism is perceived, and represented in cinema, as both glamorous and grimy, sexy and sleazy – a good tradition of love and hate, indeed. Hunter S. Thompson, the subject of a big screen documentary released in 2008, summed up this duality when he said:

> Journalism is not a profession or a trade. It is a cheap catch-all for fuckoffs and misfits – a false doorway to the backside of life, a filthy piss-ridden little hole nailed off by the building inspector, but just deep enough for a wino to curl up from the sidewalk and masturbate like a chimp in a zoo-cage.[3]

Thompson was famous for his ferocious literary style, directed in this case at his own journalistic peers. He was also a prime example of the glamour and celebrity which attaches to some journalists, and which makes journalism studies one of the most in-demand subjects in higher education. That glamour, juxtaposed with the 'fear and loathing' in which so many journalists are held (to use another Thompsonian phrase) infuses cinema and makes movies a rich source of knowledge and debate not just about how journalism works, but how it is perceived to work. Movies articulate the dualities of liberal journalism – the tensions between the production of knowledge for the public interest on the one hand and, and for personal pleasure and private gain on the other.

Journalism in the movies

In all, more than 2000 films have been made for the cinema in which journalism is a significant plot element (in some more significant than others, of course. Richard Ness' filmography [1996], from which this figure is taken, makes the point that journalists often play bit parts in the movies, or act as a kind of Greek chorus moving the narrative along – as in Cinderella Man [Ron Howard, 2005], about the media-driven rise and fall and rise again of 1930s boxer James J. Braddock). Not all of those 2000 films will be 'about' journalism, therefore. There is no doubt, however, that the subject of journalism has fascinated film-makers throughout the history of the medium, and engaged some of the industry's best talents.

Both their quantity, and in many cases their quality, mean that films about journalism are an expanding and increasingly valuable resource for students, teachers and researchers of journalism. As a journalism educator for more than two decades I have always found movies in which journalists feature as central characters to be a catalyst for engaging students in discussion and critical thought about often complex and demanding issues. What does it mean for journalists to be independent of political and business elites, and why is it important? Let's refer to Good Night, and Good Luck, or The Insider. How should the correspondent behave in a war zone – should they be detached and objective, as normative values declare, or become a participant, such as Michael Henderson in Welcome To Sarajevo (Michael Winterbottom, 1997, and based on the true story of ITN's Michael Nicholson and his rescue-adoption of a Bosnian orphan). Was Daniel Pearl right to interpret his role as an objective foreign correspondent to include interviewing *jihadis* to get their side of the story – a decision which cost him his life? Let's see what Michael Winterbottom's A Mighty Heart has to say about it. What happens to journalistic trust when an ambitious young features writer such as Stephen Glass can fabricate dozens of articles for a leading US periodical of record such as the *New Republic*? Part of the answer to that very timely question can be found in Billy Ray's film about the case, Shattered Glass (2004).

Films, of course, like journalism itself, are only versions of reality, and even at their best can only ever be part of the story of journalism which a society tells to itself; a part, moreover, which is by definition aestheticised, dramatised, invented, exaggerated. Even the words 'true story', or 'based on true events' on the credits of a movie signify only an interpretation or 'creative reimagining' of what happened, inflected by the subjective input of directors, writers, actors, as well as the production constraints imposed by the fact that movie-making is an industry with a product to sell, and investors hungry for profit. So Woodward and Bernstein become Redford and Hoffman, and Stephen Glass becomes that guy out of Star Wars (great performances all, but rather more photogenic than the actual people they portrayed, it is no great insult to say). To render them more palatable to a broad audience, and constrained by cinematic conventions of narrative, style and structure, even films based on well-documented stories such as that of tobacco industry whistle blower Jeffrey Wigand (The Insider) compress episodes, add scenes which did not happen, or create combinatory characters made up of bits of several real people who on their own would not pack the required dramatic punch. Films – even those made with aspirations to stylistic realism and narrative authenticity such as All the President's Men – represent journalism in a manner which is as subjective as the best journalists aspire to be objective. There is nothing wrong with that. On the contrary, the subjectivities of others are what makes art appealing, but we must be aware of their status as constructions when approaching the subject as scholars.

Studying journalism in the movies

Recognition of the potential of movies for educating the public and engaging debate about journalism, and of their cultural role as a second order, meta-media myth-making system for societies which take their journalism seriously (watchdogs over the watchdogs, to repeat) is not new, but scholarly studies of the subject are surprisingly thin on the ground. I have occasionally referred to movies such as Ace In the Hole (Billy Wilder, 1954) and The Sweet Smell of Success (Alexander Mackendrick, 1957) in books and essays where I am addressing the topics they explore – the tendency of popular journalism to manipulate events and 'manufacture reality' for the sake of a good story, and the excessive power of celebrity journalists respectively (McNair, 2005). Others have done so too, in similarly anecdotal and non-systematic manner. Morris and Goldsworthy's 2008 book on PR: *a persuasive industry?* refers to The Sweet Smell of Success and its representation of press agent Sydney Falco (Tony Curtis), columnist JJ Hunsecker's lackey and source. There is to date, however, no book-length study of journalism in the movies by a British or European author, despite the growth of journalism studies as an academic discipline in recent years.

The best (indeed only) scholarly work in this emerging sub-sector of the field comes out of the United States, where the academic study of movies about journalism goes back some decades. This might be explained by the fact that the USA is both the global centre of the film industry, and a country where the democratic necessity of liberal journalism is inscribed in the founding constitution with all the force of a religious dogma. Liberal journalism matters in the USA (as it does in many other countries, of course), but the notional importance of the news media as a check and balance against other institutions exists, as nowhere else, alongside a huge film-making industry employing many people who genuinely seem to care about how those roles are played out in practice. It has been noted by several commentators that some of the greatest films ever made in America have been films about journalism – Citizen Kane, obviously (Orson Welles, 1941); Howard Hawks' His Girl Friday (1940); All the President's Men (Alan J. Pakula, 1976), of course, and Alexander Mackendrick's The Sweet Smell of Success (1957) – and while the question of what is or is not a great film is a matter of personal judgement, there can be no doubt that some of the most talented of that country's cinematic artists have been drawn to the subject of journalism.

Perhaps this is because many have themselves been victims of celebrity journalism, and of the media circus which now routinely accompanies success in the popular arts, and wish to strike back. This is the explanation advanced for a film called Paparazzi (Paul Abascel, 2003), produced by Mel Gibson and widely panned by reviewers who saw it as a misguided attempt to avenge his own treatment at the hands of US hacks.

It may also be due to the fact that film-makers are immersed daily in the workings of the media, and more than a few have liberal political convictions making them predisposed to an interest in how journalists relate to power in their society. George Clooney's father was a journalist, which by his own admission has fuelled his interest in the subject. Clooney had, as of this writing, directed two films about journalism (Good Night, and Good Luck; and Leatherheads, his less successful 2007 homage to screwball comedy of the 1930s) and starred in two: Three Kings (David O. Russell, 1998) in which journalism (and a passable impersonation of CNN celebrity reporter Christiane Amanpour in particular) features as a key plot element; and Steven Soderbergh's The Good German (2005). Robert Redford has shown a similar interest in the Fourth Estate, most recently with Lions for Lambs (2005), his study of a political journalist (Meryl Streep) under pressure to collaborate with a pro-war Senator (played by Tom Cruise). Angelina Jolie has played Mariane Pearl, a reporter for French public radio and wife of the murdered Daniel Pearl in A Mighty Heart (Michael Winterbottom, 2006), and a TV news reporter in the romantic comedy Life Or Something Like It (Stephen Herek, 2002). Richard Gere has also played a journalist in a comedy (Runaway Bride, Gary Marshall, 1998), as well as in a more serious, based-on-actual-events drama (The Hunting Party, Richard Shepard, 2007).

Many of these films have won awards, stimulated public debate, and achieved significant commercial success both in the US and internationally. They have become part of the mythology not just of American journalism, but of American society and culture more broadly. We think of Cary Grant, or James Stewart, or Rosalind Russell, and we see in our minds those classic screwball comedies in which they played wise-cracking, sexy journalists with clothes to die for and lines to match. We think of George Clooney, and see his quietly understated portrayal of Fred Friendly, Ed Murrow's producer in Good Night, and Good Luck.

Given the importance of film in American and global culture, then, and of journalism as a subject for American film-makers down the years, it is probably not surprising that journalism studies in the US has pioneered the study of the journalism movie, producing a body of work which remains essential for the contemporary student of the subject. Richard M. Ness's encyclopedic filmography, From Headline Hunter To Superman (1996) is an invaluable reference work, documenting every film made about journalism in the USA (and some in other countries) since the 1920s, ending in 1996. Alex Barris (1976), Thomas Zynda (1979) and Lynda Ghiglione (2004) have addressed the subject, while Howard Good has written a series of books on The Drunken Journalist (2000), The Girl Reporter (1998) and Media Ethics Goes to the Movies (2002, with Michael J. Dillon). Matthew Ehrlich's Journalism in the Movies (2004) is the most recent book-length study by an American author (see also Ehrlich, 2006).

In addition there are a number of useful scholarly articles, some journalism about journalism-in-the-movies[4] and, last but not least, an online journal based within the Annenberg School for Communication, The Image of the Journalist in Popular Culture (http://www.ijpc.org/). According to its website:

> The mission of the Image of the Journalist in Popular Culture is to investigate and analyze, through research and publication, the conflicting images of the journalist in film, television, radio, fiction, commercials, cartoons, comic books, music, art, demonstrating their impact on the American public's perception of newsgatherers.

Led by Joseph Saltzman, Professor of Journalism at the University of Southern California, IJPC publishes scholarly articles, as well as making available archives, lists and other resources for research and teaching.

This mainly US work above has examined the stereotypes which have evolved in American film-making about journalism (such as the drunken journalist, a figure seen most recently in George Clooney's Leatherheads. The character of Suds is always drunk, often asleep, yet never bad tempered or in the least depressed by his obviously chronic alcoholism, and surprisingly efficient in delivering his copy). It has explored the mythological role of Watergate and All the President's Men not just to subsequent generations of US journalism but to American society as a whole (Schudson, 1992, 1995; Brennen, 2003; Ghiglione, 2004). Some films about journalism, notably Citizen Kane, have been judged sufficiently ground-breaking and important as texts to be written about within academic film studies (Mulvey, 1994). Welles' film continues to be voted the greatest of all time by authoritative panels of judges such as those organised by Cahiers Du Cinema and Sight & Sound.

As noted above, the approach of those US-based authors has been focused on the identification of generic stereotypes such as the 'drunken journalist', or tracing the evolution of gender roles and other aspects of the professional environment of the journalist. As such, they present a valuable record of historical change within the profession.

On the first point, movies represent a particular place and time which may now have passed, such as the 1930s newsroom, with its noise and smoke and bottles of strong alcohol stashed away in desk drawers. The difference between the newsroom depicted in His Girl Friday and the air-conditioned, health-and-safety approved sterility of Rag Tale (Mary McGuckian, 2004), and the story of how we got there as reflected in movies like All the President's Men (1976) and Broadcast News (1983), could be the subject of a fascinating lecture for students who know only mobile phones, wireless lap tops and the Internet. As for the 'drunken' journalist, or Lunchtime O'Booze as we have known him in Britain, he (and indeed she) still exists here and there, but is a much rarer beast in the contemporary professional culture of journalism.

In the area of gendered journalism representations we can see in cinema, as one would expect a steady increase in the number and status of female journalists as the impact of feminist ideas and workplace politics has been felt. Strong, senior women feature in the aforementioned Rag Tale (though that film was so savagely reviewed by most critics – unfairly, in this writer's view – that Jennifer Jason Leigh, Kerry Fox and Sarah Stockbridge who play the women in question may prefer not to be reminded of it).

Sexism in the journalistic profession has been a long-standing concern of both scholars and professionals,[5] especially as the success of feminist politics since the 1970s has raised expectations about the imminent shattering of the 'glass ceiling' which has held women back in media organisations (Chambers et al., 2004; Djerf-Pierre, 2007). For today's female students of journalism, who frequently outnumber men in the lecture theatre, cinematic representations can be both inspirational and depressing, sometimes ahead of their time, sometimes deeply reactionary. One of the very first female journalists on screen – Rosalind Russell as Hildy Johnson in His Girl Friday – appears to the contemporary gaze as a rare example from that period in American culture of a strong, powerful woman working extremely effectively in a man's world, combatting patriarchal prejudice with exemplary professional ability, and balancing her own desire for family with that for a successful career. As Laura Mulvey has observed in a review of the film, 'Hildy is a perfectly credible professional journalist, equal in the male group.'[6]

Made more than 70 years ago, and with no conscious articulation on the part of the male producers of anything we would recognise today as 'feminism',[7] Hildy Johnson can none the less be seen as a radical, positive role model for women working in the news media, ahead of her time and pointing the way to the post-feminist future. And when one looks at representations of women journalists in films of that period and since, one sees a remarkable number of such portrayals – Torchy Blane in the seven-film series of the 1930s; Jean Arthur as a tough reporter in Mr Deeds Goes To Town (Frank Capra, 1936), Jane Fonda as a TV news reporter in The China Syndrome

(James Bridges, 1979). In general, as Saltzman and others have noted, portrayals of journalists have been one sub-genre of the movies where women have often had access to complex and satisfying roles which challenge patriarchal stereotypes of femininity. Women have, of course, also been presented in movies about journalism as super-bitches, manipulating and destroying all around them, including quality journalism (Faye Dunaway in Network; Gina Gershon in The Insider; Nicole Kidman in To Die For), or as fluffy creatures in search of nothing more than a wedding ring and a designer frock (Sarah Jessica Parker as Carrie in Sex & the City).

Then again, if women have advanced in capitalist societies as a result of feminism, one measure of that change is the extent to which they can be portrayed in negative as well as positive terms. There is a gap in the journalism studies literature for a substantial, book-length study of the complex and often contradictory ways in which the representation of female journalists has changed over the decades since Torchy Blane and Hildy Johnson. As a male author and a film-lover, my sense is that movie makers have with some sincerity sought to include more realistic and politically correct images of women journalists in films which, after all, are marketed to young women impatient with being patronised. Katie Bosworth's portrayal of Pulitzer Prize-winning single mother Lois Lane in Superman Returns (Bryan Singer, 2006) is very different in tone from that of earlier Superman films. Angelina Jolie's Mariane Pearl is a tribute to the courage not only of the growing number of women journalists working in war zones, but to the dignity and strength of women in their grief when they lose loved ones in those wars. Meryll Streep's style mag editor in The Devil Wears Prada (David Frankel, 2006) may be a super-bitch, but underneath the tough surface we are permitted see a woman only too aware of the sacrifices she has made for her career.

Conclusion

The representation of female journalists is just one example of how cinema can provide a narrative or running commentary on the changes going on in the journalistic profession. The films listed above reflect the changing status of women in journalism, and of women's journalism – that is, the journalism of style and fashion – within the public sphere. Once dismissed as 'women's issues' and 'new girl journalism' (even by feminist scholars – see Chambers et al., 2004), The Devil Wears Prada can also be viewed as a film about style journalism premised on the counter-argument – that what women want in their newspapers and magazines matters, and that it is part of journalism's function to deliver it, without shame or apology. Anne Hathaway's character in Prada eventually abandons the world of style journalism, but not before she has been firmly apprised of the importance of fashion in modern life, and warned against the snobbery of those who dismiss it as trivial. The film is a feminist text, in that it takes femininity seriously.

One could undertake similar analyses of the changing representation of the war correspondent as the world has moved from cold war, to ethnic conflict, to war on terror. Or of the investigative journalist in an era when many fear for the future of this key specialism. Journalism in the movies remains a rich terrain of exploration, and the work of excavating it has just begun.

Notes

1 For an interview with Nesbitt, and a discussion of some key movies about journalism, see Armstrong, Stephen, 'From hero to zero ', *Guardian*, May 12 2008 (http://www.guardian.co.uk/media/2008/may/12/itv?gusrc=rss&feed=media).

2 Novels about journalism range from Evelyn Waugh's *Scoop*, through Graham Greene's *The Quiet American* (1955) to Sebastian Faulks' *Engleby* (2007) and *Born Yesterday: the news as a novel* by Gordon Burn (2007).

3 Quoted in Wise, Damon, 'Gonzo's back', *Guardian*, December 6 2008.

4 See for example James, Caryn, 'The decline and fall of journalists on film', *New York Times*, July 19 2005. (http://www.nytimes.com/2005/07/19/movies/19jame.html).

5 See the work of the Fawcett Society for research and other resources on the representation of women in journalism, and their status as journalists (http://www.fawcettsociety.org.uk/).

6 Mulvey, L., *Sight & Sound*, volume 7, number 3, 1997.

7 Mulvey recounts Howard Hawks' explanation of how the male character of The Front Page became a female. "I asked a girl to read Hildy's part and I stopped and I said, 'Hell, it's better between a girl and a man than between two men'" (Mulvey, L., *Sight & Sound*, volume 7, number 3, 1997).

References

Barris, A. *Stop the Presses! The Newspaperman in American Films*, New York, Barnes and Company, 1976.

Brennen, B.'sweat and melodrama: reading the structure of feeling in All the President's Men', *Journalism*, volume 4, number 1, 1998, pp 115–133.

Chambers, D., Steiner, L., Fleming, C. *Women and Journalism*, London, Routledge, 2004.

De Burgh, H., ed., *Making Journalists*, London, Routledge, 2005, pp 15–25.

Djerf-Pierre, M. 'The gender of journalism', *Nordicom Review*, volume 28, 2007, pp 81–104.

Ehrlich, M. *Journalism in the Movies*, Urbana and Chicago, University of Illinois Press, 2004; 'Facts, truth and bad journalists in the movies', *Journalism: theory, practice and criticism*, volume 7, number 4, 2006, pp. 501–19.

Ghiglione, L. 'The American journalist: Fiction versus Fact', unpublished paper, 1990 (ijpc.org/ghiglione.htm).

Good, Howard *Outcasts: the image of journalists in contemporary film*, Lanham, Md., Scarecrow, 1989; *Girl Reporter: gender, journalism and movies*, Lanham, Md., Scarecrow, 1998; *The Drunken Journalist: biography of a film stereotype*, Lanham, Md., Scarecrow, 2000.

Good, Howard, Dillon, Michael J. *Media Ethics Goes to the Movies*, New York, Praeger, 2002.

Keeble, R., Wheeler, S., eds. *The Journalistic Imagination: literary journalists from Defoe to Capote and Carter*, London, Routledge, 2008.

Lule, J. *Daily News, Eternal Stories: the mythological role of journalism*, New York, Guilford, 2001.

McNair, B. 'What is journalism?', in De Burgh, H., ed., *Making Journalists*, London, Routledge, 2005, pp 15–25; *News & Journalism in the UK*, 5th edition, London, Routledge, 2009.

Morris, T., Goldsworthy, S. *PR: a persuasive industry?*, Houndmills, Palgrave Macmillan, 2008.

Mulvey, L. *Citizen Kane*, London, British Film Institute, 1994.

Ness, Richard M. *From Headline Hunter to Superman: a Journalism Filmography*, Lanham, Md., Scarecrow, 1997.

Saltzman, J. 'Analyzing the images of the journalist in popular culture: a unique method of studying the public's perception of its journalists and the news media', *IJPC*, 2003. (http://www.ijpc.org/AEJMC%20Paper%20San%20Antonio%20Saltzman%202005.pdf)

Schudson, Michael *Watergate in American Memory*, New York, Basic Books, 1992; *The Power of News*, Cambridge, Mass., Harvard University Press, 1995.

Zelizer, B. *Taking Journalism Seriously*, London, Sage, 2004.

Zynda, T. 'The Holywood Version: movie portrayals of the press', *Journalism History*, volume 6, number 2, 1979, pp 16–25.

PART V
MAKING SENSE OF THE NEWS

36

JOURNALISM AND THE QUESTION OF CITIZENSHIP

Toby Miller

Classical political theory accorded representation to the citizen through the state. The modern, economic, addendum was that the state promised a minimal standard of living. The postmodern, cultural guarantee is access to the technologies of communication. In essence, then, the last two hundred years have produced three zones of citizenship, with partially overlapping but nevertheless distinct historicities. These zones of citizenship are the political, covering the right to reside and vote; the economic (the right to work and prosper); and the cultural (the right to know and speak). The first category concerns political rights; the second, material interests; and the third, cultural representation.

This chapter summarizes the impact of these three principal forms of citizenship on journalism, with particular reference to the contemporary United States. At first glance, one might assume that the three terms simply refer to three distinct news beats, respectively the congress or parliament (politics), the stock exchange or board room (economics), and the theatre or cinema (culture). There is a germ of truth in this distinction, but the three categories in fact inflect and overdetermine one another as their relative importance shifts over time. They help to account for the deplorable condition of US journalism today, along with the pressures imposed by new kinds of shareholder and new kinds of technology.

Political citizenship and journalism

Political citizenship gives the right to vote, to be represented in government, and to enjoy physical security. Democracy is conventionally said to arise and thrive in the interactions of governments and populations, with its model the French and US Revolutions. The polity is bounded by countries whose inhabitants recognize one another as political citizens, and use that status to invoke the greater good.

The journalistic corollaries of political citizenship are regular reportage of domestic political affairs, with a focus on lawmakers' deliberations and judicial review; the associated notion that representative government depends on an open press that explains social-policy issues as defined by social movements and parliamentary parties; election coverage; and a concentration on international relations in terms of local and global security. The intent is to draw citizens into a vital part of the policy process – informed public comment, dissent, and consent. I focus here on the declining US television and print coverage of foreign affairs, which I suggest has been trumped by an emphasis on economic and cultural questions.

Given the expansion of US power over the last quarter of a century, it is noteworthy that TV coverage of governmental, military, and international affairs dropped from 70% of network news[1] in 1977, to 60% in 1987, and 40% in 1997. In 1988, each network dedicated about 2000 minutes to international news. A decade later, the figure had halved, with about 9% of the average newscast covering anything "foreign." Between May 2000 and August 2001, just 22% of network news was international – ten points below, for example, British and South African equivalents, and 20 points below Germany. Just 3% of US coverage addressed foreign policy. In 2000, three stories from beyond the US (apart from the Olympics) made it into the networks' 20 most-covered items. And all three were tightly linked with domestic issues: the Miami-Cuba custody dispute over Élian Gonzales, the second Intifada, and the bombing of the USS Cole off Yemen. The main broadcast networks have closed most investigative sections and foreign *bureaux*, other than in Israel. ABC News once maintained 17 offices overseas. Now it has seven. CBS has one journalist covering Asia, and seven others for the rest of the world (Miller, 2006).

The reaction to September 11, 2001 temporarily reversed this autotelic trend, but that catastrophe's news impact was short-lived, despite the subsequent invasions of Afghanistan and Iraq. And extensive content analysis discloses that September 11 saw coverage of terrorism differ very minimally from existing, narrowly-focused news norms. There was no significant documentary investigation. A study of articles carried in *US News and World Report* indicates that in the seven months after September 11, explanations for the attacks focused entirely on Al Qaeda and domestic security failings, avoiding US foreign policy as an element. The *New York Times* was intellectually unprepared to report on the phenomenon. Because terrorism mostly occurred outside the US prior to 2001, it was not rated as newsworthy. Throughout the 1970s and 1980s, reportage of overseas terror took up less than 0.5% of the paper (Gerges 2003: 79, 87 n. 9; Love 2003: 248).

It should come as no surprise, then, that from September 2001 to December 2002, network-news coverage of the attacks and their aftermath basically ignored a stream of relevant topics: Zionism, Afghanistan after the invasion, and US foreign policy and business interests in the Middle East (McDonald and Lawrence 2004: 336–37; Traugott and Brader 2003: 183–84, 186–87; *Tyndall Report* 2003). And that corporate influence pushed hard to distort the US public's knowledge of the geopolitical situation. Viacom, CNN, Fox, and Comedy Central refused to feature paid billboards and commercials against the invasion of Iraq, and UN activities in the region, including weapons inspections, were the least-covered items on network news (Hastings 2003; Huff 2003). During the occupation, General Motors – the country's biggest advertiser at the time – and other major corporations announced that they 'would not advertise on a TV program about atrocities in Iraq' (quoted in McCarthy 2004). And when US authorities finally admitted in January 2005 that no weapons of mass destruction had been found in Iraq, only ABC made it a lead story. Fox News barely touched on the topic, and CBS and NBC relegated it to a minor item – fewer than 60 words on the nightly news. The *New York Times* cravenly claimed that the admission was "little noted" around the world (Whiten 2005). Clearly, US journalism has turned away from a central element of political citizenship. The country that has the greatest global impact of any nation in world history is simply not committed to informing its residents of basic geopolitical facts.

Economic citizenship and journalism

Like political citizenship, economic citizenship has been alive for a very long time, via the collection and dissemination of information about the public through the census and related statistical devices. This became an interventionist category during the nineteenth-century transformation of capitalism when paupers came to be marked as part of the social. Their wellbeing became a right, a problem, a statistic, with society more than a market.

Economic citizenship developed in the Global North during the Depression and the Global South during decolonization. It redistributed capitalist gains to secure employment, health, and retirement, and the state invested in areas of market malfunction. The great task of the New Deal was "to find through government the instrument of our united purpose" against "blind economic forces and blindly selfish men," via "a new chapter in our book of self government" that would "make every American citizen the subject of his country's interest and concern" (Roosevelt 1937).

After the Second World War, the state effectively said "we are asking you to get yourselves killed, but we promise you that when you have done this, you will keep your jobs until the end of your lives" (Foucault 2008: 216). Two historic promises were made by established and emergent governments: to secure the political sovereignty of citizens, and their economic welfare. Universal sovereignty required concerted international action to convince colonial powers that the peoples they had enslaved should be given the right of self-determination. The ensuing postcolonial governments undertook to deliver economic welfare via state-based management of supply and demand and the creation of industries that would substitute imports with domestically-produced items. But these new nations remained dependent on the metropole, and were unable to grow economically. Formal *political* postcoloniality rarely became *economic*, apart from some Asian states that pursued a more trade-based capitalism.

After the global economic crises of the 1970s, even those Western states that had *bourgeoisies* with sufficient capital formation to fund a social welfare system could no longer hedge employment against inflation, while development policies were dismantled as state socialism eroded. Economic citizenship was turned on its head through policy renegotiations conducted by capital, the state, and their intellectual servants in economics. Anxieties over unemployment were trumped by anxieties over profits, with workers called upon to identify as stakeholders in business or as consumers. Reforms redistributed income back to domestic *bourgeoisies* and First World metropoles. Corporations became privileged economic citizens, and individual citizens were conceived of as self-governing consumers. I focus next on how this shifting discourse has affected journalism.

English-language media references to "the economy" as a subject, with needs and desires, derive from the Great Depression. Press attention shifted from relations between producers and consumers of goods (a labor-process discourse of the popular newspapers which dissented from conventional economics) and onto relations between different material products *of* labor, with a similar change in emphasis from use-value to exchange-value. The discursive commodities "the economy" and "the market" were anthropomorphized and valorized (Emmison 1983; Emmison and McHoul 1987). With the crisis of the 1930s and the diffusion of Keynesianism, "the economy" entered popular knowledge.

Today's journalistic corollaries of economic citizenship, however, focus on national and multinational corporations and the stock market, along with a residual, romantic account of small business and a barely-breathing labor beat. There is saturation coverage of the discourse of life as a competition and the self as a rational subject ready to build its capacities, with Gary Becker (1993) an informal deity. Each person is intelligible through the precepts of selfishness, because people are supposedly governed through market imperatives. The market becomes "the interface of government and the individual" (Foucault 2008: 253). At the same time, consumption is turned on its head. Internally divided – but happily so – each person "is a consumer on the one hand, but ... also a producer" (Foucault 2008: 226). Foucault identifies cash-operated think tanks like the American Enterprise Institute as the intellectual handservants of this practice, vocalists of a "permanent criticism of government policy" (2008: 247). Today they do "research" in order to pen op-eds in the newspapers and provide talking-points on cable news.

The result? TV parrots the market's specialized vocabulary; assumes a community of interest and commitment to fictive capital; and takes the deep affiliation and regular participation of viewers in stock prices as watchwords. The heroization of business executives by fawning journalists became part of a doubling of time dedicated by television news to the market across the 1990s. In 2000, finance was the principal topic on ABC, NBC, and CBS nightly news, and second only to terrorism in 2002. Promoting stocks where one had a personal financial interest became *de rigueur* for anchors and pundits. By 2002, even the New York Stock Exchange was worried, and called for regulation requiring reporters to disclose their investments, so egregious had been their complicity with the dotcom overinvestment of the 1990s (Miller 2007).

This trend is international: leading sources of wholesale video news, such as Reuters, make most of their money from finance reporting, which infuses their overall delivery of news. But the influence of economic discourse on news has special poignancy in the US. Business advisors dominate discussion on dedicated finance cable stations like CNBC and Bloomberg, and are granted something akin to the status of seers when they appear on cable-news stations and the networks. During his time as Chair of the Federal Reserve, the now-discredited and always laughable Alan Greenspan was filmed getting in and out of cars each day as if he were *en route* to a meeting to decide the fate of nations, each upturned eyebrow or wrinkled frown subject to hyper-interpretation by a bevy of needy followers. The focus fell on stock markets in Asia, Europe, and New York; reports on company earnings, profits, and stocks; and portfolio management (Martin 2002; Martin 2004). The obsessive pattern is repeating as a farce in the latter part of the decade, as financial markets crumble into self-indulgent, infantile fury and tears.

Along the way, economic and labor news have been reduced to corporate and shareholder news, with politics measured in terms of its reception by business. There is a sense of markets stalking everyday security and politics, ready to punish political activities that might restrain capital. Journalists' veneration of the market is ever-ready to point to infractions of this anthropomorphized, yet oddly subject-free sphere, as a means of constructing moral panics around the conduct of whoever raises its ire. Meanwhile, the leftist media, which had investigated Enron and other sites of malfeasance for years, were either ridiculed or ignored.

Cultural citizenship and journalism

And cultural citizenship, which seems to have trumped, or perhaps incorporated, these other two categories? Of course, citizenship has always been cultural. For instance, the Ottoman Empire offered rights to non-Muslims, and the first constitutional guarantees of culture appear in Switzerland in 1874. But that was unusual until after the Second World War. Today, cultural provisions are standard in post-dictatorship charters, blending artistry and ethnicity. Concerns with language, heritage, religion, and identity are responses to histories structured in dominance through cultural power and the postcolonial incorporation of the periphery into an international system of "free" labor.

The ideal citizen is frequently understood as a clear-headed, cool subject who knows when to set aside individual and sectarian preferences in search of the greater good. This sounds acultural. But it has frequently corresponded, in both rhetorical and legal terms, to male, property-owning subjects protecting their interests from the population in general. The specificity of this apparent universalism has been called into question. Similarly, many philosophical liberals insist on a common language and nation as prerequisites for effective citizenship. But cultural differences bring this into question, because nations are split and remade by migrant languages, religions, and senses of self. Malaysia, for instance, has been a predominantly Islamic area for centuries. Colonialism brought large numbers of South Asian and Chinese settlers, along with their religions. The postcolonial Constitution asserts a special status for ethnic Malays and Islam. Muslims are the only people who can evangelize, and they have religious courts. Other varieties of superstition are tolerated, but may not proselytize, and are governed by secular rule. In the Netherlands, Sudan, Yemen, Slovenia, Bahrain, and Portugal, citizenship rests on language skills. In Sweden, it depends on leading "a respectable life" and in Sudan having "good moral character." "Attachment" to local culture is a criterion in Croatia, and knowledge of culture and history in Romania. Liberia requires that citizens "preserve, foster, and maintain the positive Liberian culture," something it avows can only be done by "persons who are Negroes or of Negro descent." This racialization also applies in Sierra Leone, and Israel restricts citizenship to Jews plus Arabs who lived there prior to 1948 and their descendants. Partial racial and religious preferences also rule in Bahrain and Yemen (Miller 2007).

These new sovereign realities are influenced and indexed by the wider political economy, which has seen a turn to culture not just as a pleasurable pastime or article of faith, but a core material concern. The First World recognized in the 1980s that its economic future lay in finance capital and ideology rather than agriculture and manufacturing, and the Third World sought revenue from intellectual property as well as minerals and masses. Changes in the media and associated knowledge technologies over this period have been likened to a new Industrial Revolution or the Civil and Cold Wars. They are touted as routes to economic development as much as cultural and political expression. Between 1980 and 1998, annual world exchange of electronic culture grew from US$95 billion to US$388 billion. In 2003, these areas accounted for 2.3% of Gross Domestic Product across Europe, to the tune of €654 billion – more than real estate or food and drink, and equal to chemicals, plastics, and rubber. The Intellectual Property Association estimates that copyright and patents are worth US$360 billion a year in the US, more than aerospace, automobiles, and agriculture. And the cultural/copyright sector employs 12% of the US workforce, up from 5% a century ago. Global information technology's yearly revenue is US$1.3 trillion. PriceWaterhouseCooper predicts 10% annual growth in the area (Miller 2009; Collins 2008).

The journalistic corollaries in the US are an increased focus on the cultural/service side of the economy; mixed lamentations and celebrations of the loss of agriculture and manufacturing; expanded but still restricted access of readers to news – so old-style newsroom tips and letters to the editor have turned into almost-live images from cell phones of dramatic events and comments on blogs (great sources of free intellectual property); and more and more space dedicated by journalists to such topics as cuisine and health. I investigate these tendencies here with a look at the way that newspaper coverage of food has changed over this period, alongside various moral panics about diagnoses of Attention Deficit Hyperactivity Disorder (ADHD) and its preferred treatment, Ritalin®.[2] In each case, lifestyle trumps politics.

In 1940, the *New York Times* published 675 food stories, of which just 4% were light background fare (what is now known as "foodie" news, such as profiles of chefs or recipes). The remainder reported on food poisoning, nutrition, or famine. Twenty years on, the corollary proportion of "foodie" news had doubled to 9%. But 20 years after that, in 1980, 36% of food stories in the *New York Times* were lifestyle-related. Approximately 25% of US newspapers added "Style" pages between 1979 and 1983, of which 38% had circulations of more than 100,000. Fairly rigorous distinctions were being drawn between *dining* out (costly, occasioned, planned, and dressed for) and *eating* out (easy, standardized, and requiring minimal presentational effort). By 2000, 80% of the *New York Times'* 1927 food stories were on chefs and recipes. The "foodie" trend in reportage and interest is celebrated as a response to affluent consumers, a skilled working class, efficient and effective transportation, and cosmopolitanism (Jones 2003; Barnes 2004; Danford 2005; Harris 2003: 55; Makala 2005; Finkelstein 1989: 38; Fine and Leopold 1993: 167; O'Neill 2003).

Consider the shifting discourse on cuisine in the *Philadelphia Inquirer* and the *Philadelphia Magazine*. In the early 1960s, the *Inquirer* ran recipe columns and advertisements related to home dining, with women the target. Functional aesthetics articulated with home economics: simplicity and thrift were called for, other than on special occasions. In the 1970s, a section appeared in the Sunday *Magazine* on places to go, dramatically displacing "Food and Family." The restaurant was now described as a public, commercial, and cultural site of urban sophistication. By the 1980s, the Sunday food section included a wine guide. Food writers were dubbed "critics," and they offered instruction on enjoyment rather than production. Aesthetics had displaced functionality (Hanke 1989).

This trivialization comes at a time of serious public-health crises: 30 years ago, food-borne disease was rare in the US, and generally attributable to cutesy-pie events like church picnics. Now, 76 million people are laid low through infected food each year. Five thousand die, and 325,000 are hospitalized, at a public-health cost of US$10 billion. The Federal Government makes a quarter of the food-safety inspections compared to two decades ago, with the percentage of imported food examined dropping from 8% in 1993 to 2% ten years on. Under George Bush Minor, it provided links between fast-food outlets and the President's Council on Physical Fitness, and attacked the World Health Organization's findings that fruit and vegetables help ward off obesity and diabetes. As rewards, Republican politicians receive 80% of campaign contributions handed out by the livestock and meat-processing industries, and the National Cattlemen's Beef Association endorsed Bush Minor in 2004 – its first such decision in a century of promoting death and despoliation. But the proportion of food stories that engage the political economy has become minuscule by contrast (Miller 2007).

And serious conflicts of interest are generated by interlocking directorates between media and food corporations. General Electric (owner of NBC) and the *Washington Post* share company directors with Coca-Cola, and Pepsi's board has people from the equivalent group within the *New York Times*, Gannett, and the Tribune Company. Tribune also has directors in common with McDonald's and Quaker Oats, while General Electric is represented at Anheuser-Busch and Kellogg. Attempts by investigative journalists to reveal corporate malfeasance in the food sector are met with the delightful new domain of litigation public relations. Potential jurors, attorneys, judges, and journalists are targeted by corporations seeking to discredit revelations of their venality by focusing on clandestine newsgathering. This sounds perfect fodder, as it were, for investigative journalism. But why bother when your column inches are dedicated to culinary tourism and critique?

This culturalist shift leads us to another area spurred on by the media's recent uptake of citizenship. By the late 1960s and early 1970s, popular magazines were locked in a contest for audiences with color television. They reacted by addressing young people both as readers (through stories on popular culture) and as problems (through generational stereotyping). This practice continued as the cultural industries promoted the existence of catchy-sounding generational cohorts to advertisers ("the Greatest Generation," "Baby Boomers," "Generation X," "Generation Y," and "Generation Rx") with supposedly universal tendencies and failings. When the Partnership for a Drug-Free America® (free of recreational drugs, not corporate ones) released a report on teens in 2005, the *bourgeois* media leapt at the neologism "Generation Rx" as part of an emergent moral panic over prescription abuse – without noting this was just the second occasion such substances had been included in the national survey (Miller, 2008a).

Recognizing the media's power, the pharmaceutical corporation Ciba-Geigy spread the gospel of brain disorders as the key to depression and other abnormalities wherever possible, for example by financing public television's series *The Brain* during George Bush the Elder's celebration of the brain, when ADHD became known as the "diagnosis of the decade." Across the 1990s, there was a veritable explosion of stories, mostly credulous, in popular periodicals from *Better Homes & Gardens* to *Seventeen* (Miller and Leger 2003; Miller 2008c).

Because of the desire to address young people and spread anxieties about them, and despite corporate concerns, from the 1970s, horror stories about Ritalin® began appearing in the *bourgeois* US press, as part of its drive to identify appealing topics unrelated to old definitions of news. In the late 1980s, there were articles skeptical of ADHD and critical of Ritalin® in the *New York Times*, the *Wall Street Journal*, the *Washington Post*, and the *Los Angeles Times*, and a segment on ABC's *Nightline* (Miller 2008b). *Good Housekeeping* magazine queried "the rush to Ritalin," dubbing it "kiddie cocaine" and lamenting that "at the slightest sign of trouble – a child keeps running back and forth to the water fountain, has an unruly week pushing other kids on the playground, or plays drums on his desk with pencils – parents are circled by the school's teachers, psychologists, and even principals, all pushing Ritalin." *Newsweek* went from an unfortunately-worded endorsement of Ritalin® as "one of the raving successes in psychiatry" to warning that it "may be causing some hidden havoc … in an impatient culture" (quoted in Miller 2008a).

Congressional hearings were prompted in 2000 by a story in the *Washington Post* that raised the specter of mind control and merged with popular concerns about diet to suggest a more "natural" treatment. Over the next three years, Ritalin® made guest appearances on *Dateline NBC*, CNN's *Larry King Live* (featuring Bush Minor's dyslexic brother and ADHD-diagnosed nephew explaining why Ritalin® must be abjured), *48 Hours* and *Eye on America* from CBS, and Cleveland's WKYC-TV. These programs screened investigative reports and idiot punditry on Ivy-League Ritalin® abuse and drug dealing, emergency-room visits, and school complicity. PBS and A&E ran documentaries (Sussman *et al.*, 2006). But minimal attention, if any, was paid to the political economy of the pharmacorps, their investment in marketing versus research and development, their direct-to-consumer commercials, their corruption of medical academia, and the like.

Conclusion

So what can we conclude about cultural citizenship and journalism? I have emphasized the culturalist turn's impact on US coverage of political and economic issues – how conventional politics has shifted from the centre of the news, especially international relations; how the shift in economic discourse from rights to responsibilities and the shift of the economy itself to a culturalized one has changed the way finance is discussed; and finally, how cultural topics themselves have been transformed to suit the demographic calculations of media corporations about audiences and their marketability to advertisers. The positive sides to citizenship that I outlined, across the three forms, are barely relevant to contemporary US journalism.

It doesn't have to be like that, of course, and the vast, loose, rhizomatic network of alternative news outlets across the nation offers very different stories, from Al Jazeera on Livestation to *Democracy Now* on radio and *Left Business Observer* in print. But even as the nightly news and the daily paper slide into desperate waters across the country, they decline to address their failures through a reintegration of citizen address across the three zones I have outlined.

Journalism education and research stand at what should be a wonderful point in their history. The mass extension of literacy worldwide sees readership at levels one could barely have imagined five years ago. New outlets are emerging all the time – in the Global South. Sadly and ironically, the cultural nationalism and neoliberalism of US journalism professionals ill-equips them for life in this providential world, so tied are they to the fiscal fortunes of their own country and its stockmarket fetishes. We can only hope that a truly internationalist perspective, of political, economic, and cultural citizenship, will inspire them anew.

Notes

1 Defined as the nightly news on the major broadcast English-language networks.
2 For more on cultural citizenship in this context, see Harrington 2008; Hermes 2006; and Stevenson 2003.

References

Barnes, Bart. (2004) 'Giving Americans Entrée to Cuisine.' *Washington Post*, August 14 A1.

Becker, Gary. (1993) 'Nobel Lecture: The Economic Way of Looking at Behavior.' *Journal of Political Economy*, 101, no. 3: 385–409.

Collins, Luke. (2008) 'YouTube Generation No Match for the Man.' *Engineering & Technology*, 3, no. 9, May 24–June 6: 40–41.

Danford, Natalie. (2005) 'Video Made the Cookbook Star.' *Publishers Weekly*, March 21: 24–26.

Emmison, Mike. (1983) 'The Economy: Its Emergence in Media Discourse', in Howard Davis and Paul Walton (eds) *Language, Image, Media*, Oxford: Basil Blackwell. 139–55.

Emmison, Mike and Alec McHoul. (1987) 'Drawing on the Economy: Cartoon Discourse and the Production of a Category.' *Cultural Studies*, 1, no. 1: 93–111.

Fine, Ben and Ellen Leopold. (1993) *The World of Consumption*, London: Routledge.

Finkelstein, Joanne. (1989) *Dining Out: A Sociology of Modern Manners*, New York: New York University Press.

Foucault, Michel. (2008) *The Birth of Biopolitics: Lectures at the Collège de France, 1978–79*, trans. Graham Burchell, ed. Michel Senellart, Houndmills: Palgrave Macmillan.

Gerges, Fawaz A. (2003) 'Islam and Muslims in the Mind of America.' *Annals of the American Academy of Political and Social Science*, 588: 73–89.

Hanke, Robert. (1989). 'Mass Media and Lifestyle Differentiation: An Analysis of the Public Discourse about Food.' *Communication*, 11, no. 3: 221–38.

Harrington, Stephen. (2008) 'Popular News in the 21st Century: Time for a New Critical Approach.' *Journalism: Theory, Practice and Criticism*, 9, no. 3: 266–84.

Harris, Lis. (2003) 'The Seductions of Food.' *Wilson Quarterly*, 27, no. 3: 52–60.

Hastings, Michael. (2003) 'Billboard Ban.' *Newsweek*, February 26.

Hermes, Joke. (2006) 'Citizenship in the Age of the Internet.' *European Journal of Communication*, 21, no. 3: 295–309.

Huff, Richard. (2003) 'Blitz of War Coverage on Nightly News.' *Daily News*, March 24.

Jones, Richard. (2003) 'The New Look – and Taste – of British Cuisine.' *Virginia Quarterly Review*, 79, no. 2: 209–31.

Love, Maryann Cusimano. (2003) 'Global Media and Foreign Policy', in Mark J. Rozell (ed) *Media Power, Media Politics*, Lanham: Rowman & Littlefield. 235–64.

Makala, Jeffrey. (2005) 'The Joys of Cooking.' *Chronicle of Higher Education*, February 18: B19.

Martin, Christopher R. (2004) *Framed! Labor and the Corporate Media*, Ithaca: ILR Press/Cornell University Press.

Martin, Randy. (2002) *Financialization of Daily Life*, Philadelphia: Temple University Press.

McCarthy, Michael. (2004) 'Violence in Iraq Puts Advertisers on Edge.' *USA Today* May 18: 2B.

McDonald, Ian R. and Regina G. Lawrence. (2004) 'Filling the 24 x 7 News Hole.' *American Behavioral Scientist*, 48, no. 3: 327–40.

Miller, Toby. (2006) 'US Journalism: Servant of the Nation, Scourge of the Truth?' in Benjamin Cole (ed.) *Conflict, Terrorism and the Media in Asia*, London: Routledge. 5–22.

Miller, Toby. (2007) *Cultural Citizenship: Cosmopolitanism, Consumerism, and Television in a Neoliberal Age*, Philadelphia: Temple University Press.

Miller, Toby. (2008a) *Makeover Nation: The United States of Reinvention*, Columbus: Ohio State University Press.

Miller, Toby. (2008b) 'Panic Between the Lips: Attention Deficit Hyperactivity Disorder and Ritalin®', in Charles Krinsky (ed.) *Moral Panics Over Contemporary Children and Youth*, Farnham: Ashgate Publishing. 143–65.

Miller, Toby. (2008c) 'Ritalin®: Panic in the USA.' *Cultural Studies Review*, 14, no. 2: 103–12.

Miller, Toby. (2009) 'Can Natural Luddites Make Things Explode or Travel Faster? The New Humanities, Cultural Policy Studies, and Creative Industries', in Jennifer Holt and Alisa Perren (eds) *Media Industries: History, Theory, and Method*, Malden: Wiley/Blackwell. 184–98.

Miller, Toby and Marie Leger. (2003) 'A Very Childish Moral Panic: Ritalin.' *Journal of Medical Humanities*, 24, nos. 1–2: 9–33.

O'Neill, Molly. (2003) 'Food Porn.' *Columbia Journalism Review*, 42, no. 5: 38–45.

Roosevelt, Franklin Delano. (1937) Second Inaugural Address', January 20 <millercenter.org/scripps/archive/speeches/detail/3308>.

Stevenson, Nick. (2003) 'Cultural Citizenship in "the Cultural" Society: A Cosmopolitan Approach.' *Citizenship Studies*, 7, no. 3: 331–48.

Sussman, Steve, Mary Ann Pentz, Donna Spruijit-Metz, and Toby Miller. (2006) 'Misuse of "Study Drugs": Prevalence, Consequences, and Implications for Policy.' *Substance Abuse Treatment, Prevention, and Policy* 1, no. 15 <substanceabusepolicy.com/content/1/1/15>.

Traugott, Michael W. and Ted Brader. (2003). 'Explaining 9/11', in Pippa Norris, Montague Kern, and Marion Just (eds) *Framing Terrorism: The News Media, the Government, and the Public*, New York: Routledge. 183–201.

Tyndall Report. (2003) *On Aftermath of September 11*. <tyndallreport.com/0911.php3>.

Whiten, Jon. (2005) '"The World Little Noted": CBS Scandal Eclipses Missing WMDs.' *Extra!*, March/April: 7.

37

NEWS, AUDIENCES AND THE CONSTRUCTION OF PUBLIC KNOWLEDGE

Greg Philo

Much of the work of the Glasgow University Media Group, of which I am a longstanding member, has highlighted the role of media in relation to the development of social attitudes and beliefs. In the UK, this has gone against a trend in media and cultural studies which emphasised the active nature of audiences and their capacity to resist messages as well as to create their own. Our work did in fact show that audiences can indeed sometimes be active and critical but we also found strong evidence pointing to the power and influence of media. This dimension of media power is often neglected in current scholarship. In this chapter, I will examine some of the major arguments which have led to this 'reduced' view of media effects and then re-evaluate these in relation to contemporary evidence on the nature of reception processes.[1]

Encoding/decoding

One of the major stimuli for the development of active audience theory was Stuart Hall's (1980) well-known encoding/decoding model. The discussion around it has often been very confused so I will return to it first and then explain what actually happens when messages are produced and received. The main elements of Hall's thesis are well known. In essence he is concerned with 'the class struggle in language'. Following Barthes, he uses the concept of the 'code'. This is a system of meaning which relates visual signs and spoken and written language (linguistic signs) to the different ideological positions by which a cultural order is either legitimised or contested. As he puts it, codes 'contract relations for the sign with the wider universe of ideologies in a society'. The codes:

> refer signs to the 'maps of meaning' into which any culture is classified; and those 'maps of social reality' have the whole range of social meanings, practices and usages, power and interest 'written in' to them.

The point is that what is being written constitutes a 'dominant cultural order', which imposes a 'taken for granted' knowledge of social structures (Hall, 1980, p. 134).

This is what he terms a 'hegemonic' viewpoint. This 'carries with it the stamp of legitimacy – it appears coterminous with what is 'natural', 'inevitable', taken for granted about the social order' (Hall, 1980, p. 137). Hall argues that television news or a current affairs programme will be 'encoded' within this viewpoint. The language and visual images that it uses will be organised within this taken for granted knowledge.[2] At the time of his writing there were major conflicts between British governments and trade unions. Inflation was high and, to reduce it, the official policy was to hold wages down. The state presented this policy as being in the national interest, but the trade unions' perspective was that they were being made to pay for a crisis they had not produced. Some believed that the policy simply preserved an economic and class structure from which they did not benefit.

In our own work, we analysed these conflicts and the manner in which they were presented on television. We showed how words such as 'reasonable' and 'rational' were used in news coverage to describe what was presented as acceptable behaviour by trade unionists. They could be seen as 'code' words within Hall's formulation and as linked to an overall system of meaning (an ideology) which legitimised a dominant order. For example, in an exchange between a journalist and trade unionists, the latter say that they are only trying to hold wages level (i.e. they were not asking for anything 'excessive' or 'unacceptable '). To this, the journalist replies:

> But as reasonable men and responsible citizens can you say that is all you are trying to do and all you are interested in when you hear warnings from the Chancellor to the effect that increases of this sort are going to wreck the national economy? (ITN 13.00 24.2.95 in Philo et al., 1982, p. 60).

Hall's main concern was to show how the 'hegemonic viewpoint' would then be 'de-coded' by viewers.[3] He sets out three positions. The first is the 'dominant hegemonic position' where the viewer takes the meaning 'full and straight' – i.e. de-codes the message in the same terms within which it was encoded (p. 136). Here the message relates directly to what the viewer sees as normal, natural and as 'taken for granted'. The second is the 'negotiated' position which contains a mixture of 'adaptive and oppositional' elements. Here viewers might accept the hegemonic viewpoint at a general level, but seek particular exceptions in terms of their own beliefs or behaviour. So a trade unionist might believe that there is a 'national interest' and that it is wrong to have 'excessive inflationary wage demands' but this belief might co-exist with the view that his/her own wages are very low and therefore the person is willing to go on strike to get a better settlement.

The third of the positions is what Hall terms the 'oppositional code'. Here the viewer decodes the message in a 'globally contrary way'. The message is 're-totalised' within an alternative frame of reference. As Hall writes:

> This is the case of the viewer who listens to a debate on the need to limit wages but 'reads' every mention of the 'national's interests' as 'class interest' (Hall, 1980, p. 138).

This is an important paragraph since it had the effect of sending a large number of people in media and cultural studies up a very long and ultimately pointless path. In particular it encouraged the belief that the language of news texts (visual and verbal) was polysemic – that it could have a variety of meanings to different groups. So viewers of the same news could be seeing and hearing it differently. What they saw and heard would be defined by their own class, gender or ethnicity. The assumption was that people would thus be 'closed off' from the intended (encoded) message and could in fact create their own meanings. A crude example of what was being suggested was the supposed behaviour of football supporters who do not 'see' the fouls of their own side but only those of the other team. The assumption was also justified by pointing to cross cultural studies, which suggested that people from various cultures would receive TV messages differently. In a soap opera, for example, behaviour seen as villainous in one culture might be interpreted as heroic in another. The conclusion of some theorists was that meanings were created in the encounter between the reader and the text and that each new encounter could potentially create a new meaning.[4]

The theory that texts were polysemic and subject to divergent meanings swept through cultural studies. In this example Oliver Boyd-Barrett (2002) describes the work of Hall and its later development by David Morley:

> (Hall) developed a theory of ideology which allows that texts are 'polysemic', which is to say that they offer the possibility of a diversity of readings, even if a 'preferred reading' is inscribed within the text by its producers. Through the work of Morley, in particular, this crucial insight has been further explored to reveal the divergent meanings that different groups, whether defined in terms of social class, gender or ethnicity, could draw from texts (2002: 45).

There is a fundamental error here, it seems to me, in what is being suggested about how audiences can reject messages. It might be that people from very different cultures do not understand each other's cultural symbols, as for example when Western explorers appropriated artefacts, which had deep religious significance and thought they would make nice wall decorations. It is also the case that some media, literary or artistic products are deliberately made to be open to a variety of interpretations, as in a poem or work of art. But our work on TV news showed that audiences within a culture do not typically create a new meaning with each 'reading' or encounter with an encoded message. Rather, they are likely to criticise the content of the message in relation to another perspective, which they hold to be correct. They are therefore aware of the encoded meaning and the manner in which it has been constructed – they just don't agree with it. We studied audience perceptions of the miners' strike in 1984/5 in Britain. At this time, TV news repeatedly showed images of miners and pickets in violent clashes with police. People from different class and political backgrounds saw these images and understood in the same way what was being shown (i.e. that the miners and pickets were responsible for the trouble). Thus, a politically conservative person in our sample commented on what she saw as the bad behaviour of 'this rabble'. The miners who we interviewed did not 'see' the images differently in the sense that they thought they were looking at news pictures and language about pickets being kind to police. There was no new meaning created in this sense. The miners understood the encoded message but they thought that the news had left out images which showed their perspective (which was that the police had started the trouble).

We can now look back to Hall's hypothetical example of the oppositional viewer. Here again the person may understand the hegemonic view that a wages policy is supposed to be in the national interest, but simply not believe it and instead think that it will mainly benefit the rich.[5] Crucially, it is also possible for someone who *accepts* the hegemonic view to be aware of the alternative 'radical' view and even to see how such a perspective is being excluded by the encoded message. My argument is then that (1) viewers do not typically construct a new meaning with each encounter with a news text but rather, they can share an understanding of what is being presented and differ in their responses to it (acceptance or rejection), and (2) viewers do not necessarily occupy their own 'sealed off' cultural space, unaware of the values and definitions offered by others. The second of these points was actually confirmed by Morley's work (against his own expectations) when he tried to test Hall's model. Hall had suggested that people who accepted the encoded message would be 'living within' the taken-for-granted hegemonic ideology. They would therefore be unaware of the processes by which the ideology was being 'preferred'. Following this position, Morley (1980) writes that:

> For some sections of the audience the codes and meanings of the programme will correspond more or less closely to those which they already inhabit in their various institutional political, cultural, and educational engagements, and for these sections of the audience their dominant readings encoded in the programme may well 'fit' and be accepted (1980, p. 159).

Morley believed that such people would see the television account as being simply commonsense – and also that the alternatives which television has excluded will be 'invisible' to them. But his own evidence in fact showed examples of both conservative and radical groups who were clearly aware of alternative positions on the economy. In one case, a group of bank managers who were politically conservative actually criticised a programme they were shown, for promoting the conservative position without giving what they saw as a proper 'balance' of views. In Morley's terms they were able to 'deconstruct' the programme. In this case the programme had included an interview with an accountant who was presented as a neutral commentator. In the event this 'expert' gave a very conservative view of economic policy, focusing on the need for tax cuts to provide incentives and the need for cuts in public expenditure. The group of bank managers who watched this commented that:

> Particularly that accountant from Birmingham ... was ... very much taking a view very strongly, that normally would only be expressed with someone else on the other side of the table ... (1980, p. 106).

Morley, in fact, found many examples of audiences being able to de-construct programmes by, for example, 'seeing through' loaded questions. But this ability to de-construct did not necessarily mean that the audience members rejected the view that was being promoted. As he wrote:

> The recognition of 'preferring' mechanisms is widespread in the groups and combines with either acceptance or rejection of the encoded preferred meaning; the awareness of the construction by no means entails the rejection of what is constructed (1980, p. 140).

But not everyone is aware of the 'preferring' mechanisms, so Hall's original depiction of some people who live within a taken for granted ideology is still useful.

This leaves us with three central questions on the relationship between media, audiences and ideologies (which we take to mean perspectives which are linked to and legitimise social interests). The first question is what are the conditions under which people accept or reject a perspective when they are aware of the range of alternatives? This is a very fundamental issue and relates in part to how humans choose between value systems. Such choices are affected by many factors including our class and cultural history, by notions of self interest or more altruistic beliefs, by our accumulated experience of attempts at social change and by the immediate economic and political conditions which we face. All these can influence preferences for social democracy or free market capitalism or socialism or whether people decide that no change is possible or simply take to drink or drugs or consult astrologers or in other ways try to forget all about it. So it does not follow that just because people know the range of alternatives they will necessarily choose the radical, oppositional one. Still, one factor in the choices that are made and in attitudes which are formed is whether people do actually know of alternative ways of understanding and of a range of possible actions.

The second question is then, what are the conditions under which information about these alternatives is either made available or is limited in public discourse, and what happens to Hall's group of people who are living within the hegemonic ideology if they are given different information? We have argued in our work that the media are a key element in the construction of public understanding. When we studied attitudes to tax and redistribution of income, we found that most people in our focus groups did not know that in Britain 10 percent of the population owned well over half of the private wealth or that it was the poor who paid the highest proportion of tax relative to their income. Some participants were angry when they found out that this was the case. This does not mean that such responses necessarily transform into political action but none the less it was felt by people in the groups that TV news was not properly informing the public when it discussed government policy on tax spending and budgets (ESRC 2004). Another example from our work was of how understandings of the Israeli–Palestinian conflict were affected by news accounts of the motives and actions of those involved. We showed how the news gave very little explanation of the history of the conflict. This history was contested by both sides, but the Palestinian perspective rested crucially on their claim that they had lost their homes and land when Israel was established and also that they were now living under Israeli military occupation. Without knowledge of this, there was no apparent rationale for Palestinian actions when they attacked Israelis. The Palestinians could thus be seen as 'starting' the violence. The Israelis were portrayed in the news as 'responding' to these attacks that had been made upon them and some in the audience clearly took this message from what they saw. As one participant expressed it:

> You always think of the Palestinians being really aggressive because of the stories you hear on the news. I always put the blame on them in my own head ... I always think the Israelis are fighting back against the bombings that have been done to them. (cited in Philo and Berry, 2004, p. 222).

But when people did encounter new information on the history of the conflict, this could then affect their understanding:

> I just thought it was disputed land. I wasn't under the impression that the Israeli borders had changed or that they had taken land from other people.

And another:

> The impression I got was that the Palestinians had lived around that area and now they were trying to come back and get some more land for themselves – I didn't realise they had been actually driven out (Philo and Berry, 2004, pp. 216–217).

It is clear that how actions are perceived and the legitimacy of different positions can be dramatically affected by the context in which they are understood and the information which is given. Inasmuch as the media influence this information flow, then they do have a key role in sustaining and developing some ideologies.[6]

The third question is under what conditions can such ideologies (in the encoded message) be critiqued by audiences. For Hall and Morley the key issue is the class and cultural location of the viewer (at least in the periods of their work which I am discussing here). As Morley put it, the hegemonic meanings encoded in a television programme will jar 'with those produced by other institutions and discourses in which they are involved – trade union or deviant subcultures for example' (1980, p. 159). In our own work we also found evidence of this. For example, one of our interviewees rejected television images of violence in the miner's strike, because she had direct experience of being involved in another strike at Chrysler, the car company. She believed that TV had misrepresented this strike and then generalised her experience to what she saw later of the miners' dispute (Philo, 1990, p. 63). But it was not always the case that a cultural and class affiliation was sufficient to produce such a rejection. We also interviewed a group of retired people, many of whom had trade union experience and were sympathetic to the miners. Yet these also had a high regard for television as an information source and some expressed their sadness at how the 'violence' reflected on the miners' cause (Philo, 1990, p. 93). None of these people had actually attended a picket line. This turned out to be a crucial variable and we found that everyone who had actually seen a picket line (whatever their politics or class) rejected the television depiction (p. 150).[7]

Another key variable in terms of audience criticism was the use of conceptual processes such as logic. Thus when people were asked if they believed that picketing was mostly violent, some reasoned that it could not have been so, given the huge numbers of people involved. As one noted, 'if they had been really violent, the police couldn't have coped, it would have been the army'. Their conclusion was that television images of violence must have been very selective. Such a use of logic could occur in different groups and was not necessarily related to support for the miners. Another participant who said she 'would have shot' striking miners also argued that 'because of the amount who were actually on strike ... it can't all have been violent' (Philo, 1990, p. 151). We found the same phenomenon of the use of logic in our study of beliefs about the Israeli–Palestinian conflict. We asked large samples of people about the casualties suffered by each side. In fact, many more Palestinians had been killed than Israelis (about 2–3 times as many). But TV news coverage had focused disproportionately on Israeli casualties with extensive coverage of suicide bombing. Many people did in fact take their beliefs from this presentation and accepted the TV account rather uncritically. They believed either that the Israelis had had the highest casualties or that the numbers were about equal for the two sides. In this example, a participant describes the source of her belief as being TV news:

> Well basically on the news coverage they do always seem to make the Palestinians out to be the ones who are the suicide bombers, so it's like, I would imagine, it's going to be more casualties on the Israeli side, but it is purely from television, that's where I'm getting my info from, that's how it is being portrayed on television (cited in Philo and Berry, 2004, p. 234).

Only a minority of those interviewed actually believed at this time that Palestinians had significantly more casualties than the Israelis. For these participants, one of the key factors in making this judgement was the use of logic.[8] These participants commented on the contrast between Palestinians with 'sticks and stones' and Israelis with 'guns and tanks'. The conclusion was:

> If that's all they have got to fight with, presumably they are killed more often than someone with a gun (cited in Philo and Berry, 2004, p. 235).

This is a dimension of audience activity which is completely missing from the encoding/decoding approach. The model as offered by Hall and Morley was in some ways useful in that it focused attention on how class and cultural factors could produce different responses to encoded messages. In his later work Morley (1986) writes of how a range of 'experiences of life' can incline people to different readings (1986, pp. 42–43). But the model is weak both in that it misses important dimensions of audience activity but also underestimates the power of the media in shaping 'taken for granted beliefs'. The conceptual arrangements appropriate to a class position are seen in the model as the key variable in evaluating a new message from the media. However, this neglects the issue that the conceptual structures include 'knowledges' about what typically occurs and assumptions about the rationality and legitimacy of action which may already have been subject to prior exposure to media messages. There is little room in the encoding/decoding model to investigate such a possibility. In one noteworthy case, Morley in his own work showed the response of audience groups to TV images of car workers. The workers had actually won £600,000 on the football pools. But soon as the image of the factory was shown, several of his audience groups assumed the story was about a strike. One person commented that 'first thing you think, whenever you hear of British Leyland (the car manufacturer) is "who's on strike this time?"' Morley (1980) comments on the groups responses that:

> Their decoding of this item is informed by, and leads into a generalised exposition of, a stereo-type of the 'greedy car worker/mindless union militants' presumably derived, at least in part, from the media (1980, p. 127).

But Morley does not then pursue this with his interviewees to trace the constituent elements of the belief systems or their origins, as the research design does not really permit this.

However, the main problem which I have with the encoding/decoding model is the impact which it had on the subsequent development of media and cultural studies. The view which many took from it was that audiences could resist messages, safe in the conceptual boxes of their class and culture, and renegotiating an endlessly pliable language. This led eventually to the serious neglect of issues of media power. In contrast, the Glasgow University Media Group has resisted the tendency to underestimate the capacity of audiences to actively engage with texts. Today there is a powerful body of evidence which shows the influence of media messages on the construction of public knowledge as well as the manner in which evaluations are made about social action and what is seen as necessary, possible and desirable in our world. For us, media power is still very much on the research agenda.

Notes

1 An earlier version of this chapter appeared as: Philo, G. (2008) 'Active audiences and the construction of public knowledge', *Journalism Studies*, 9(4): 535–544.

2 Theorists such as Fairclough have shown how this can work in relation to news and other texts. Fairclough analysed the speeches of Tony Blair and showed how they gave preference to right wing, neo-liberal views. Fairclough used concepts such as hyponymy (meaning a presupposed semantic relationship) to show how 'globalisation' and 'economic progress' might be treated as hyponyms

(2003: 213). Van Dijk in other work has looked at the importance of headlines, story structures, and issues such as 'agency, responsibility and blame for actions' (1998: 44). For a further account of these studies, see Philo (2007).

3 The term 'hegemonic' is used here in discussing Hall's original model. It implies the legitimising of a dominant perspective but we should not assume that media output in contested areas of social and political life consists only of the promotion and reproduction of such perspectives. There is some space for alternative accounts. When we studied TV news coverage of the Israeli–Palestinian conflict, we found for example that the Israeli perspective was heavily featured but some news such as that on Channel 4 featured more critical commentary of Israeli spokespeople than did the BBC news. Journalists certainly felt very pressured when covering this area but there were instances such as in the deaths of the Palestinian children where strong criticisms were made of Israeli policy across various news outputs including the BBC. We describe media in our work as a 'contested space' though the contest is certainly not equal and structures of access and power have a strong influence on media content. For a fuller account of this see Philo (2007).

4 See, for example, Fiske (1987). For a critique of this position see Philo (1990) pp. 190–199.

5 This understanding of Hall's model is tenable within his original formulation as he says of the opposi-tional position that it is possible for the viewer 'to understand both the literal and connotative inflection' (plus their own oppositional understanding). In his later work Hall moved towards a discursive approach in which language was constitutive of the real and speakers occupied different positions in relation to 'truth'. The exchange of meaning becomes a 'process of translation' between different speakers. For a critique of this perspective see Philo and Miller (2001, pp. 33–35).

6 This is not their only function since the media also endorse value systems as well as influencing how we understand action in relation to such systems. So media references to being 'reasonable' and 'respon-sible' are actually the advocacy of a value system, while the reporting of what unions are asking for, shaped the information which viewers can use to decide whether the unions are acting in accordance with these values. (For a further discussion of this see Philo, 1990, pp. 4–6).

7 This was such a strong research result that we took it to be almost axiomatic that direct experience would overrule a contrary media image or presentation. This was until we undertook work on mental distress and media. In this study we asked people whether they associated mental illness with violence. We found that such was the level of fear generated by media images such as in horror films, that in some cases these associations overruled direct experience. For example, a young woman working in a special hospital with elderly people who were not in any way violent, none the less made this association and was scared of them because of what she had seen in films and plays (Philo, 1996, p. 104).

8 Other groups of people also judged correctly the ratio of casualties for each side. This was because they had studied the subject and/or had an intense support for one or other side in the conflict. So both those who were strongly pro-Palestinian and as those who were pro-Israeli stated that Palestinians had the highest numbers of deaths. They did not of course agree on everything and many events were highly contested, but it is interesting that both accepted the 'facts' in this case.

References

Boyd-Barrett, O. (2002) 'Theory in Media Research' in Newhold, C., Boyd-Barrett, O. and Van Den Bulck, H., *The Media Book*, London: Arnold.

ESRC study (2004) *Audience Receptions of Television News, Current Affairs and Documentary Programmes End of Award Report*, ESRC R/000/23/9669.

Fairclough, Norman (2003) *Analyzing Discourse*, London: Routledge.

Fiske, J. (1987) *Television Culture*, London: Methuen.

Hall, Stuart (1980) 'Encoding/decoding', in Hall, Stuart, Hobson, Dorothy, Lowe, Andrew and Willis, Paul (eds) *Culture, Media, Language*. London: Hutchinson/CCCS.

Morley, D. (1980) *The Nationwide Audience*, London: BFI Television Monograph.

Morley, D. (1986) *Family Television; Cultural Power and Domestic Leisure*, London: Comedia.

Ofcom (2007) *New News, Future News*. Office of Communications, London.

Philo, G. (1990) *Seeing and Believing*, London: Routledge.

Philo, G. (1996) *Media and Mental Distress*, London: Pearson/Longman.
Philo, G. (2007) 'Can discourse analysis fully explain journalistic practice', in *Journalism Studies*, April, London: Sage.
Philo, G. and Berry, N. (2004) *Bad News from Israel*, London: Pluto.
Philo, G., Hewitt, J., Beharrell, P. and Davis, H. (1982) *Really Bad News*, London: Writers and Readers.
Philo, G. and Miller, D. (2001) *Market Killing*, London: Pearson/Longman.
Van Dijk, Teun (1998) 'Opinions and Ideologies in the Press', in Bell, A. and Garrett, P. (eds) *Approaches to Media Discourse*, Oxford: Blackwell.

38
NEWS PRACTICES IN EVERYDAY LIFE: BEYOND AUDIENCE RESPONSE

S. Elizabeth Bird

Although the concept of "news practices" clearly relates to the idea of the news "audience," I leave a more detailed discussion of direct audience response to other contributors. In this chapter, my goal is to address a more diffuse question – something akin to "what does news mean in everyday life?" For many people, discussions about current events are an important part of their daily routines; for others, the importance of news is more personal, less shared, but may nevertheless help structure their lives.

To explore this question, I draw on two related strands of literature. First, I discuss scholarship that examines, for want of a better word, news consumption as a "habit" that affects people's sense of connection. Second, I look at what we know about "news talk" – how do people talk about news in their daily lives, and how do they make meaning from news texts? In this context, I will address how the new online environment may have changed both daily news habits and the quantity and quality of everyday discourse about the news, which in turn may have implications for civic participation.

As ethnographically-informed scholarship on media 'audiences' moves away from studies of direct engagement with texts towards a consideration of broader cultural context, this approach is increasingly being framed in terms of media "practices" – what people do and say around and about media (Bird *forthcoming*; Couldry 2004). Anthropologist Mark Hobart captures this in his description of realizing that to understand how media operate in contemporary Bali, he had to explore practices that "only partly overlap with direct engagement in the medium (reading the newspapers, watching the box) and have as much to do with anticipating, chatting about, criticising, understanding and so on" (Hobart 1999: 12). Scholars from various disciplines (e.g. Abu-Lughod 2000; Gauntlett 2007; Hoover et al. 2004; Peterson 2009) are looking increasingly at such things as everyday talk about media, everyday activities that involve media, and ways in which media help provide scripts for everyday behaviour (Bird *forthcoming*). These arguments echo Carey (1975) who long ago advocated a "ritual" model of communication, arguing similarly that much media consumption is less about textual content, and more about activities surrounding reception. As he wrote, "culture must first be seen as a set of practices" (1975: 19), some of which are the habitual activities surrounding news.

The news habit

Academic interest in the news "habit" has a long history, dating back before Carey to Berelson's classic study of "what missing the newspaper means" (1949). Berelson researched people's sense of emotional loss when their morning newspapers disappeared because of the 1945 newspaper strike, concluding that the loss was less about missing specific information, and more about an interruption in their daily schedule, and a sense of being disconnected from public discourse. Berelson talks about a "non-rational" attachment to news that prefigured more recent discussions of "practices" around news (although later interpretations would not frame this is such overtly psychological terms). Decades later, Bentley (2001) conducted in-depth interviews with people who for various reasons had not received their daily paper. He summarizes older literature that explored the daily functions of news, from the uses and gratifications approach in which Berelson was working, through media dependency theory, ritual theory, and play theory. He concludes that while people find it very difficult to articulate what reading the newspaper really means to them,

> The unifying function of the newspaper buried in the comments of the respondents was of social integration. Whether it was by providing them news of their neighbors, helping them cope with the death of a friend or simply telling them that tuna was on sale at the market, the newspaper made survival in their community much easier and more enjoyable, a function of the community building ability of the press (p. 14).

Jeffres et al. (2007) develop this notion of the unifying function of news reading. Through survey research, they concluded that those who read newspapers and talk regularly about current events reported in the media are much more connected to their community, more politically active, and more socially tolerant. Anthropologist Mark Peterson (2009) uses a more ethnographic approach to explore this broader context of news consumption as a habit with a significant social dimension – in this case, in urban India. He draws attention to:

> the wide range of possible discoveries ethnography of news consumption may produce once we abandon the nearly ubiquitous a priori assumption that news consumption is primarily about the transmission of content, and that contexts of consumption merely affect the nature of reading and interpretation. Instead ... contexts of consumption constitute social fields in which people engage in narrative and performatory constructions of themselves, reinforce social relations with other actors, negotiate status, engage in

economic transactions, and imagine themselves and others as members of broader imagined communities.

These researchers generally tie the sense of connectedness directly to the form of the newspaper, but similar claims have been made about the role of television news in maintaining a sense of community. Bourdan (2003), in an unusual study, used life history techniques to show how consumption of television, including news, has moved in predictable cycles: "Changes in viewing habits are associated with major changes in the life cycle. Being a child, coming of age, leaving one's parents, marrying, divorcing, losing one's spouse: all these changes are naturally evoked by viewers when they recall changes of viewing habits" (p. 17). In particular, attention to news increases with maturity. Bourdan's respondents recalled special news "flashbulb" moments, when major news events were first known, often in a communal setting. Gauntlett and Hill's (1999) unique longitudinal study, using self-reported diaries, shows that watching the news is frequently very much part of a daily routine. Within the family, teenagers and young adults develop an interest in the news from the example of parents, and eventually take up the "news habit" as they mature. And of course the larger issue here is the assumed connection between regular news consumption and a commitment to civic participation.

The end of the news habit?

Today, however, we know that both newspaper reading and TV news viewing are declining, as younger generations are abandoning both and turning to the Internet. Barnhurst and Wartella (1998) suggest that the traditional life stages of news consumption, as people move to newspapers and serious TV news later in life, no longer hold true. Indeed, the changing news environment has precipitated something of a crisis for the profession of journalism, with grand assumptions being made about new generations of uninformed, distracted young people. Other research is suggesting that what may be happening is a reconceptualizing about what news is and how it is delivered, rather than a rejection of news in itself. Barnhurst and Wartella argued that changes do not necessarily mean young people do not want the sense of connectedness that news provides. "Whatever it means to them to be citizens, to be political does not seem to require the services of television news" (Barnhurst and Wartella, 1998, p. 304). More recently, Meijer (2007) acknowledges that young people are not likely to become traditional news consumers, because they live in a totally different news environment:

> Because young people are almost permanently in contact with their peers, siblings or parents through various new means of communication, they feel no need to watch the news all the time. They will soon be informed about important news anyway (p. 105).

Thus the habitual patterns of morning newspaper reading or evening TV newscast viewing are disappearing because they are no longer necessary to stay informed. Meijer studied news habits in a large sample of Dutch young people, using an impressive array of techniques that ranged from surveys to diaries, and concluding:

> Young people do not watch news as part of a daily routine ... Instead, young people watch news because TV is on and others are watching, because they happen to have nothing else to do at that moment. If while zapping they happen to run into news, some may watch it for a few minutes, but most will move on to another station after they have seen the headlines (p. 104).

Meijer's respondents still have a clear sense that news is important to keep them informed about what is going on in the world. However, in a media environment in which almost every form of communication comes virtually (whether through computers, cell phones, or other devices), genres are even more blurred than on other media; news, entertainment, gossip, reality programming and so on are all intertwined. Young people, like older generations, link citizenship and community with news, but may express it very differently, depending, for example on virtual communities for support and action on political issues, rather than connecting with their immediate geographical neighbours.

News talk in everyday life

The study of newsreading as a "habit" or a "practice" is one way to approach the role of news in everyday life. From this perspective, the content of the news itself is less important than the sense of connectedness and social participation that comes with attention to the news. In practical terms, the news habit can be studied quite effectively through self-reporting; people can be asked about how and how often they access news, with the emphasis being on the routine, rather than the content. However, another (if closely-related) dimension of everyday interaction with news is the engagement of people with the information in news, through what we might call "news talk." Again, the rise of ethnographic approaches to media response has moved the emphasis away from the "effects" tradition, with its interest on how effective messages are in reaching the intended audience. Rather, we are interested in what audiences do with media messages. An extensive body of scholarship has developed around the idea of the "active audience," showing how readers make their own meanings from texts, inflected through the life experiences, personal identity and so on (see Alasuutari 1999; Abercrombie and Longhurst 1998; Bird 2003).[1] Martin (2008), for example, shows how racial identity is a key filter through which news is passed. News talk, then, is the informal and often very active way that news stories are communicated among people, and meanings are made that may have more or less to do with the original intent of the journalist who created the text.

My own work (Bird 1992; 2003) suggests that "the stories" of news emerge as much through interpersonal communication as from the specific texts. However, there is relatively little scholarship done in this area, partly because of the difficulty of actually capturing everyday news conversations in natural settings. In many ways, the ideal is the kind of long-term ethnography described by anthropologists like Hobart (1999) and Peterson (2009), in which media practices emerge naturally in the course of observation. However, this is rarely a practical way for most scholars with limited time. Self-reporting methods, such as the diaries used by Gauntlett and Hill (1999) or Markham and Couldry (2007) go some way to addressing this gap, but again they tend to shed light more on the "habit" than the actual engagement with news. Several researchers have tried to create situations that as far as possible mimic everyday conversations (e.g. McCallum 2009; Bird 2003; Martin 2008). However, as Tewkesbury (2003) writes, "The upshot of all this is that communication researchers have an incomplete picture of how people receive the news" (2003: 695).

However, perhaps the most exciting development in capturing everyday news talk has been the rise of the Internet. As Tewkesbury comments, "New technologies are changing the nature of news reading and providing new opportunities for studying ... behavior" (2003: 695). As newspaper reading and TV news-watching decline, and people move to the Internet, there may be fewer opportunities for people to talk in person about news – Internet news consumption use is generally solitary, not tied to specific times, and is often tailored closely to individual tastes and interests. At the same time, the rise of newsgroups and other online forums offers new possibilities for everyday news-related interactions. Some scholars have suggested that the future of newspapers lies in encouraging reader involvement through interactive environments associated with virtual versions of their print edition. An interesting study by Gray (2007) suggests that news "fan" communities are vibrant forums where news is energetically discussed, and where civic awareness and interest in "trivial" news may not be mutually exclusive. Rosen (2006) in a much-blogged statement, claims that the new media environment has finally destroyed the concept of "the audience" for news:

> The people formerly known as the audience are those who *were* on the receiving end of a media system that ran one way, in a broadcasting pattern, with high entry fees and a few firms competing to speak very loudly while the rest of the population listened in isolation from one another – and who *today* are not in a situation like that *at all*.

Can the Internet, then, provide us with an opportunity to peek into the everyday news talk that has shifted from the living room to the virtual world? Is it possible that the decline of newspaper reading and TV news watching can actually lead to the creation of new, informed communities in which news has a different, but equally significant role? Gray's work suggests this, and Rosen argues that "Now the horizontal flow, citizen-to-citizen, is as real and consequential as the vertical one."

While optimistic about this possibility, I would also like to sound a note of caution, based on some preliminary study of online comment sections associated with newspaper sites. I found these forums interesting because they appear to resemble everyday conversations about news, possibly akin to the kind of "water cooler" conversations we might seek to capture through ethnographic observation. However, my analysis of both the content and tone of the online discourse suggests that they are very different from face-to-face conversation.

I use two groups of data to discuss this. First, I use data gathered as part of a larger ongoing study of public discourse on the teaching of human evolution in US public schools. Public debate about this peaked in the state of Florida as the State Board of Education debated whether to mandate the teaching of evolution as part of revised science standards in schools – an action it approved in February 2008, against considerable opposition. This decision was then followed by attempts by conservative legislators to introduce bills allowing teachers to offer both their own criticisms and alternative positions (such as "intelligent design") in the classroom. In addition to doing interpretive content analysis of news stories, I also studied online comment sections in two newspapers, the *St. Petersburg Times* and the *Tampa Tribune*, in the months following the decision. A total of 23 stories was analyzed. Second, I have also been studying the online comments associated with generally popular stories in the *Tribune*. My goal in both cases was to try to develop a sense of the nature of this news talk. Did the commenters engage with the content of the stories, and debate them, and what was the quality of that debate? How was online discussion like or unlike personal conversation? And more broadly, can we learn anything from this about the future of civic engagement?

In both cases, I found there was relatively little discussion of news content. Indeed, many contributors do not even address the particular story, but simply use it as a catalyst to express an opinion. Stories about evolution, for instance, consistently caused contributors to divide into distinct evolution/creation camps. A typical example is a *Tampa Tribune* story (April 24, 2008) that reported on the narrow passage in the Florida Senate of the bill to allow "academic freedom" to teachers to criticize evolution (the measure was later defeated by the entire legislature). The story triggered four pages of comments that remained on the site, as well as many more that were removed because of abusive language. Almost none debate the central issue of the article; instead, participants begin stating and restating their existing positions on evolution generally, in the identical terms they use in all stories about the topic. Many postings are quite long – the longest is 495 words – as representatives from each camp detail their "evidence," as well as their characterizations of their opponents. Some excerpts illustrate the way the insults develop (online screennames removed):

- Why are Darwinists so afraid of debate when they can't even prove their theory in a scientific laboratory? Evolution is a religion in itself.
- Do you folks never tire of the same tedious and specious arguments? … C'mon, think a little. If you bring pre-existing beliefs about invisible intelligences, you don't get to play.
- By stating that the Theory of Evolution is a religion, you have proven your ignorance of science and said theory. You should be ashamed of yourself for your un-American behavior. It is this exact kind of thing that caused the Founding Fathers to include the clause prohibiting the establishment of a state religion. You would undo the history of America and its founding principles. You, sir, are a traitor.

- The anti-Godly Theory of Evolution relies quite a bit on "belief" and could not be taught without Freedom of Speech ... the anti-Godly want to deny Freedom of Speech in the classroom so that those theories cannot be heard or taught. Sounds like Soviet Communism all over again.
- Perhaps you should go to a creationist doctor and tell him you do not wish to be availed of any medical technology that has grown out of science ... It was nice of you to provide an article showing how vicious, underhanded so-called Christians will do anything to suppress the truth.
- I guess all that talk about being tolerant of others' views was really just baloney just like the theory of evolution is baloney.
- For those of you who really believe in the bubbles of Evolution because it was taught as fact in school, I'm sorry for popping your bubbles but the truth will make you free. For those of you who are anti-God zombies marching to Marxist/Leninist Communism, I pity you.

Although I have presented these comments in a kind of "count-pointercount" format, these comments are not being traded between one pair of posters, but actually represent several contributors. The tone of the "debate" is not collaborative, building on the various views expressed. Rather it resembles the type of debate structure often seen between US political candidates – each one states a position and neither engages directly with the other.

The evolution/creation issue is perhaps untypical because the opposing positions have become so entrenched in US culture, and in this case news does not function to enlighten, but simply to stimulate constant restating of the same discussion, often in abusive terms. What about the more random, daily flow of stories that are read and commented on each day in the *Tampa Tribune* and online editions of other newspapers across the country? First, the lists of most viewed stories are revealing. Tewkesbury (2003) notes that while people typically report paying most attention to news about public affairs, when tracked online, this is not the case. Rather, readers seek out stories about entertainment, crime, and various human interest topics. That certainly is true on the *Tribune*, which regularly lists the "most viewed" and "most commented" stories.

To reach a sense of the most popular kinds of stories, I read all the "top three" stories in the Metro (city news) section of the paper for the month of October, 2008, along with the accompanying comments (I avoided the national news section, which was dominated by coverage of the upcoming Presidential election; local and state elections, however, were the domain of the Metro section). Since space is limited, I will discuss here only the top three (not rank-ordered) stories for 31 October, which seemed very typical. None was about public affairs. These were: 1) "Tampa woman charged with felony child neglect," a brief story that reported on the arrest of a woman whose home and children were reportedly found in a filthy and neglected state; 2) "Missing teeth gum up relationship," which described a knife fight between a woman and her live-in boyfriend, whom she accused of stealing her false teeth; 3) "Gunman robs girl at school bus stop," about an armed robber stealing from a 15-year-old girl waiting at a bus stop.

It could certainly be argued that none of these stories was especially informative, but each was apparently quite entertaining. In fact, they are very much like the stories that participants in my earlier study (Bird 2003) found most memorable, and which spurred them into enthusiastic conversation. As I wrote then, "from an audience point of view, the best stories are those that leave room for speculation, for debate, and for a degree of audience 'participation'" (p. 41). And to some extent, we see the same process online, as people bring their own experiences to bear on the story at hand. However, it was striking that the collaborative quality of face-to-face communication seems to disappear online. In my earlier study, participants talked about how their sense of the story was reached through conversation. As one participant noted, "I want to hear everyone's opinion about what's going on in the news. There's something in their view that I can use, and hopefully there's something in my view that can contribute to making theirs better" (p. 42).

The tone of the online discussions is markedly different – much more aggressive, and quite often hateful. The most vitriolic comments are typically removed by site staff almost immediately, especially those that are overtly racist, but many still remain. I will look briefly at each of the "top three" stories to illustrate this. Comments on the first story are characterized by assumptions about the woman's status as a welfare freeloader, and frequently address race indirectly (the accompanying photo shows that she is African-American):

- She's a filthy nasty two-bit ho!
- Thank god they arrested her today, on Tuesday we will be sharing the wealth with her (this refers to the Nov. 4 election; Black candidate Barack Obama had made a widely-quoted comment about the need to "share the wealth" through tax changes).
- By "socializing with friends" do ya mean, hookin? I have no doubt she's been on the receiving end of our redistributed wealth for a couple generations already. I'll bet she gets her nails done every week!

The second story elicited nine pages of comment, all derisory in the extreme.

- This took place in a mobile home? Hmmmm??
- Can you imagine the fracas if she had misplaced her diaphragm?
- What a typical bunch of trailer trash. Do any of them see a shrink?

While the commenters were united in their mockery, they also began to snipe at each other, with people claiming that "white trash" people like this are natural Obama voters, while others noted the plethora of signs for Republican candidate John McCain in such "trailer trash" areas. Thus the discussion moves away from the story itself, and into often mean-spirited characterizations of fellow-contributors, based on stereotypes.

The third story, perhaps unexpectedly, became a major opportunity for political name calling and insults. A few commenters began with fairly innocuous comments about the need to be vigilant while waiting alone at dawn or dusk, or simply bemoaned the declining state of civility. The tone soon changed:

- When Obama isn't elected, the thugs will all be coming for you. Lock and load.
- If Obama is not elected no one will have any money to steal, we will be in a depression waiting for jobs and wages to trickle down, just like workers in China, we will probably have to join the Buddhist religion too.
- It's fortunate this girl wasn't hurt or killed. Since Obama wants to "spread the wealth around" the middle class will be supporting more people. "Spreading the wealth" – isn't that the same as living in a commune? Everyone better run, not walk, to your nearest gun store ...
- When McCain wins the election, all the Obama supporters will riot & claim bias against the candidate. The foolishness of the school bus robbery is just the beginning.

One might argue that this story became an opportunity to debate politics – but in reality, it simply devolved into a flurry of virtual insults that one could not imagine happening "around the water cooler." This pattern occurs repeatedly in the online comments. A story about a civic award for a person working with migrant families spurs readers to vitriolic attacks on the supposed evils of illegal immigration. Stories about crime routinely produce racist diatribes, and so on. Such forums actually free people to talk in ways they would not do face-to-face, which of course has some advantages in terms of facilitating open discussion. However, it does tend to change the nature of talk about news, producing rapid polarization rather than thoughtful discussion – or even the empathetic, personal responses I found in my earlier study.

Conclusion: The future of news in everyday life

As yet, I am not offering firm conclusions, because the nature of the news environment is changing so rapidly, and my current study is very preliminary. It certainly appears that the "news habit," as documented by researchers with a primary interest in newspapers and television news, is changing. Younger people are consuming their news differently, and, as Meijer (2007) and Martin (2008) suggest, they are not necessarily making the same kind of generic distinctions between news and other forms of information that older generations and journalists find familiar. Furthermore, the Internet has opened up a whole new environment, not only for the creation of news, but also for its consumption, offering numerous opportunities actively to participate in daily "news talk."

For me, the biggest question now is whether this new audience environment will contribute to civil, democratic participation. As I have long argued, I do not believe that talk about public affairs and politics is the only kind that contributes to a sense of shared community. "Trivial" news allows us to interrogate morality and dialogue with others about shared values, cementing community connectedness. And there is actually growing evidence that online participation has contributed to increased political activity, as the stunning success of the Internet-savvy Obama campaign demonstrates. At the same time, I believe the daily online environment may also be contributing to a rise in incivility and intolerance, in contrast to research on newspaper reading and interpersonal newstalk, which seems to be correlated with greater levels of tolerance (Jeffres et al. 2007). The result could be everyday patterns of news consumption that are less like a civil debate and more like a public shouting match. There is much still to be learned.

Note

1 This is not to say that study of news texts and their direct reception is unimportant. As Philo (2008) argues, the active audience approach alone often pays inadequate attention to the authorative power of those who produce and write the news.

References

Abercrombie, N. and B. Longhurst (1998). *Audiences*. London: Sage.

Abu-Lughod, L. (2000). "Locating ethnography," *Ethnography* 1(2): 261–67.

Alasuutari, P. (ed.) (1999). *Rethinking the media audience*. London: Sage.

Barnhurst, Kevin. G. & Wartella, Ellen (1998) "Young Citizens, American TV Newscasts and the Collective Memory", *Critical Studies in Mass Communication* 15,279–305.

Bentley, C. (2001). "No newspaper is no fun – even five decades later, *Newspaper Research Journal*, 22(4): 2–15.

Berelson, B. (1949). "What 'missing the newspaper' means," in P.F. Lazarsfeld and F.N, Stanton (eds) *Communications Research, 1948–1949*, New York: Harper.

Bird, S.E. (1992). *For enquiring minds: A cultural study of supermarket tabloids*, Knoxville: University of Tennessee Press.

___. (2003). *The audience in everyday life: Living in a media world*, New York: Routledge.

___. (forthcoming). "Mediated practices and the interpretation of culture," in J. Postill and B. Braeuchler (eds) *Theorising Media and Practice*, Oxford: Berghahn.

Bourdan, J. (2003). "Some sense of time: Remembering television." *History and Memory* 15(2): 5–35.

Carey, J.W. (1975). "A cultural approach to communication," *Communication* 2, 1–10; 17–21.

Couldry, N. (2004). "Theorising media as practice," *Social Semiotics*, 14 (2): 115–32.

Gauntlett, D. (2007). *Creative explorations: New approaches to identities and audiences*, London: Routledge.

Gauntlett, D. and A. Hill (1999). *TV living*. London: Routledge.

Gray, J. (2007). "The news: You gotta love it," in J. Gray, C. Sandvoss and C.L. Harrington (eds), *Fandom*, New York: New York University Press.

Hobart, M. (1999). "After Anthropology? A view from too near," Anthropology Department Seminar, S.O.A.S., University of London. Online. Available <HTTP://www.criticalia.org/Articles/After%20 Anthropology.pdf (accessed 4 September 2007).

Hoover, S., L.S. Clark, D.F. Alters, J.G. Champ, and L. Hood (2004). *Media, home and family*, New York: Routledge.

Jeffres, L.W., J. Lee, K. Neuendorf, and D. Atkin (2007). "Newspaper reading supports community involvement," *Newspaper Research Journal*, 28(1): 6–23.

Markham, T. and Couldry, N. (2007). "Tracking the reflexivity of the (dis)engaged citizen: some methodological reflections," *Qualitative Inquiry*, 13(5): 675–695.

Martin, V. (2008). "Attending the news: A grounded theory about a daily regimen," *Journalism* 9(1): 76–94.

McCallum, K. (2009). "News and local talk: Conversations about the 'crisis of indigenous violence,' in Australia," in S.E. Bird, (ed.), *The anthropology of news and journalism: Global perspectives*, Bloomington: Indiana University Press.

Meijer, I.C. (2007). "The paradox of popularity," *Journalism Studies*, 8(1) 96–116.

Peterson, M.A. (2009). "Getting the news in New Delhi: Newspaper literacies in an Indian mediascape," in S.E. Bird, (ed.), *The anthropology of news and journalism: Global perspectives,* Bloomington: Indiana University Press.

Philo, G. (2008). "Active audiences and the construction of public knowledge," *Journalism Studies*, 9(4): 535–44.

Rosen, J. (2006). "The people formerly known as the audience." Online. Available <HTTP:journalism. nyu.edu/pubzone/weblogs/pressthink/2006/06/27/ppl_frmr.html, June 27> (accessed 1 November 2008).

Tampa Tribune (no author) (2008a). "Tampa woman charged with felony child neglect," 31 October. Online. Available HTTP://www2.tbo.com/content/2008/oct/31/tampa-woman-charged-felony-child-neglect/c_2/#comments (accessed 31 October, 2008).

Tampa Tribune (no author) (2008b). "Tampa police: Missing teeth gum up relationship." 31 October. Online. Available <HTTP://www2.tbo.com/content/2008/oct/31/311634/tampa-police-womans-missing-teeth-gum-relationship/news-metro/ (accessed 31 October, 2008).

Tampa Tribune (no author) (2008c). "Tampa police: Gunman robs girl at school bus stop." Online. Available <HTTP://www2.tbo.com/content/2008/oct/31/tampa-police-gunman-robs-girl-school-bus-stop/news-metro/ (acessed 31 October 2008).

Tewkesbury, David (2003). "What do Americans really want to know? Tracking the behavior of news readers on the Internet," *Journal of Communication*, 694–710.

White, N.M. (2008). "Senate approves evolution bill," *Tampa Tribune*, 24 April. Online. Available <HTTP://www2.tbo.com/content/2008/apr/24/me-senate-approves-evolution-bill/> (accessed 15 August, 2008).

39

LIVING WITH NEWS: ETHNOGRAPHIES OF NEWS CONSUMPTION

Mirca Madianou

The discussion about ethnography and news consumption is not just a matter of methodological choice, but has implications for theory. Ethnographic approaches to the study of news audiences are located in the developments in media anthropology (Bird 1992), but also in the broader approach that understands news as mediation (Silverstone 2005) and communication as ritual as opposed to transmission (Carey 1989). Although discussions about ethnography in media studies have largely focused on questions of method and the legitimacy of transposing ethnography from social anthropology, this chapter will only briefly consider these debates. Our main concern here is to address what is distinctive about an ethnographic perspective on news consumption and what such a perspective can contribute to the understanding of the phenomenon of news.

In defining ethnography, authors often refer to participant observation as the distinctive approach of ethnographic inquiry which requires a long term immersion in the culture studied. Others have used the term in a more liberal way, referring primarily to a set of qualitative methods, where the 'ethnographer is participating, overtly or covertly, in people's daily lives for an extended period of time, watching what happens, listening to what is said, asking questions' (Hammersley and Atkinson 1995: 1). However, apart from referring to a method or set of methods, ethnography has a second meaning in anthropology: it refers both to the process of collecting the data, but also to the end product which is ethnographic writing, the books and articles written by ethnographers. Ultimately, according to Geertz, what defines ethnography is not so much the techniques used, but the kind of intellectual effort that it represents, which is an endeavour for 'thick description' (Geertz 1973).

This chapter addresses the intellectual project that the ethnography of news consumption is by considering the distinctive features of ethnographic inquiry and how they contribute to the understanding of the social and cultural phenomenon of the news and its place in everyday life. Particular attention will be paid to how ethnography can uncover the practices surrounding news consumption and the ways in which they are implicated in wider processes of identity, citizenship and power. The chapter will place emphasis on the ways in which ethnography can offer a nuanced perspective in addressing questions of power. This is done through widening the remit of analysis to consider people's direct experiences with the media frame (Couldry 2000) and through the contrasting of discourses (what people say about the news) and practices (what people actually do with the news). Finally, the bottom up perspective of ethnography contributes to the quality of data collected, while it also guards against essentializing audiences especially in those cases when audiences represent ethnic or cultural groups. The holistic perspective of ethnography shares similarities with the theory of mediation as advanced by the late Roger Silverstone (1999, 2005) which the chapter also considers. But before embarking on the discussion of what ethnography brings to the study of news audiences we will briefly consider the debates surrounding the application of ethnography in the study of media; these debates are, of course, also relevant to ethnographies of news audiences more specifically.

Media ethnographies: contestations, (some) resolutions and interdisciplinarity

Traditionally associated with the discipline of social anthropology, ethnography has become a popular approach in the study of media over the past three decades (for ethnographies of media production, see among others Born 2004; Hannerz 2004; for consumption, Mankekar 1999). Recent years have also marked an increased interest in media amongst anthropologists themselves (Ginsburg, Abu Lughod and Larkin 2002; Miller and Slater 2000) and an intensification of the interdisciplinary dialogue between anthropologists and media researchers leading some to define a new field of media anthropology (Rothenbuhler and Coman 2005) although there is no universal agreement on a paradigmatic shift. Despite this increased interest in ethnography, news consumption remains relatively understudied although there are some exceptions (Bird 1992 and 2003; Gillespie 1995; Madianou 2005a and 2005b).

Despite its popularity the import of ethnography in media studies has not been uncontested. Some criticisms referred to the fact that the term has been used to indicate qualitative methods in general (Lull 1988; Nightingale 1993), while only a few researchers have actually conducted participant observation, which requires a long immersion in the culture studied. Another area of concern has been the narrowness of the inquiry and the explicit focus on a particular medium or genre (Radway 1988). Finally, critics have addressed the lack of attention paid by media ethnographers to the problem of studying one's own culture (Press 1996) which matters as it is through the ethnographers' own interactions that they come to understand the culture under study.

Interestingly, the discussions over ethnographic purity within media studies took place at a time when anthropologists themselves had already questioned the traditional approach. The postmodern shift in anthropology (Marcus and Fischer 1986; Clifford and Marcus 1986) emphasized subjectivity, reflexivity and, most importantly, the awareness that (ethnographic) knowledge is historically, culturally and socially defined (Marcus and Fischer 1986: 87, 113). Recent anthropological theory considers the concepts of culture, of the 'self' and the 'other', not as fixed entities, but rather as categories of thought (Abu-Lughod 1991; Hastrup 1995). As a consequence, doing ethnography 'at home', or 'auto-anthropology' (Strathern 1987), is now considered a valid approach as long as the researcher can be aware of their position in the culture under study (Loizos 1992: 170) and embody the distance needed to look for otherness within the familiar (Marcus and Fischer 1996: 111–136). Furthermore, the requirement that an ethnography needs to research a culture in *all* its aspects, as Malinowski (1960) had originally stipulated, has been criticized as anthropologists realized the inherent incompleteness of ethnographic endeavours (see Agar 1996; Geertz 1973). However, the requirement for long term immersion is still valid as it is through longer term contact that the depth that characterizes ethnographic inquiry can emerge. Although the traditional golden rule for one year long fieldwork is not always kept or seen as necessary, what distinguishes ethnography from other qualitative approaches is that research knowledge is based on a rapport which is built up over time.

Ethnography of news consumption

If we accept the earlier definition of ethnography as an intellectual endeavour in thick description, what kind of intellectual project is the ethnography of news audiences? First of all, an ethnographic perspective understands news as a process and a ritual (Carey 1989) rather than an act of transmission. The effort here is to understand news not just as a text and thus reception, but also as a cultural form, a social phenomenon and institution. An ethnographic perspective is well suited to examine the double articulation of media as texts and as technologies and objects (Silverstone 1994). An ethnographic approach may well include the point of contact between audiences and texts, but will also extend beyond reception to examine the wider practices in which news audiences engage in. In this sense, consumption which is a more encompassing concept (Miller 1987) than reception can better capture the complex ways in which people engage with the news. Ultimately, an ethnographic perspective is an attempt to understand what the sheer presence of news means in everyday life.

So what can an ethnographic perspective contribute to the understanding of the place of news in everyday life? At an initial level, it can uncover the various practices associated with news consumption which often reveal the non-informational uses of the news. News programmes, because of their regular scheduling, provide a fixed point of reference in people's everyday lives which provides reassurance (Silverstone 1994). News is often about violence, conflict and risk, but the ritual of viewing the news every evening at the same time represents a 'dialectical articulation of anxiety and security' (Silverstone 1994: 16). Elsewhere Silverstone had argued:

> Our nightly news watching is a ritual, both in its mechanical repetitiveness, but much more importantly in its presentation, through its fragmentary logic, of the familiar and the strange, the reassuring and the threatening. In Britain, no major news bulletin will either begin without a transcendent title

sequence [...] nor end without a 'sweetener' – a 'human story' to bring viewers back to the everyday (Silverstone 1988: 26).

Conversely, the absence of news can be experienced as terrifying. In my study of news consumption in domestic and work environments in London, several informants recalled the anxiety they experienced on September 11 after their unsuccessful attempts to access news online as most news sites collapsed under the immense demand. The momentary lack of news added to the perception of the magnitude of the crisis (Madianou forthcoming).

Although ethnography can uncover such uses that transcend the traditional informational dimension of news reception, it needs to be noted that similar observations have already been made by qualitative studies such as the pioneering one by Berelson who studied readers' responses to the 17-day newspaper strike in New York in 1945 in order to find 'what missing the newspaper means' (Berelson 1949). What Berelson found is that people did not miss factual information, but rather the sense of security that newspapers provided in a disturbing world (Berelson 1949).

However, what ethnographies can do is add further depth to the understanding of the uses of news for purposes other than informational. For example, studies have revealed the ways in which citizens use news media in order to amplify their voices and visibility in the public domain. Canclini has observed that in Mexico people resorted to radio and television to obtain recognition and justice that the traditional citizen institutions did not provide (Canclini 2001) while an ethnography of news consumption in Greece has shown how television news programmes often become the vehicle for voicing complaints and criticisms in the absence of adequate civil society institutions (Madianou 2005c: 103). News, quite literally, mediated between public institutions and private interests as members of the public sought to appear on television and radio news programmes in order for their complaints to be taken seriously by the state and other public organizations (Madianou 2005c).

Ethnographic research has also linked news consumption to the performance of identity. In Gillespie's study of British Asian teenagers in London's neighbourhood of Southall, watching the news is 'perceived as a marker of becoming an adult and as a way of gaining access to a world beyond [the teenagers'] immediate or local experiences' (Gillespie 1995: 109). The teenagers in Gillespie's study would translate British news for their parents, a practice that would 'confer status and a degree of responsibility among those who were able to act as an interpreter' (Gillespie 1995: 109). For members of an ethnic minority in Greece, the viewing of Greek news was a way to make a symbolic statement about their citizenship and being part of the 'country in which they live' (Madianou 2005a: 531). Therefore the practice of 'watching the news' constitutes more than simply 'watching' as it can signify one's identity, aspirations and desire to participate in a cultural or political narrative.

If news becomes meaningful at so many different levels (from the cognitive to the emotional and from the instrumental to the ontological), it is no surprise then that audiences almost universally express a desire to 'keep up' with the news as a number of studies from across the world have indicated (see Jensen 1998 for an international comparative study; also Hagen 1997 and Martin 2008) and even describe themselves as 'addicted to the news' and 'news junkies' (Madianou 2005b: 58).

Moreover, an ethnography of news in everyday life can widen the remit of the analysis. An ethnographic study of news in everyday life can, for example, include an analysis of people's personal experiences with journalists. Such personal experiences with the media frame, as Couldry has found (2000), are revealing of the symbolic power attributed to the media. Couldry has proposed that the investigation of people's direct contact with journalists (or other media institutions) is a productive way to capture the diffuse nature of media power (Couldry 2000). Similarly, a study of news consumption in a Turkish speaking neighbourhood in Athens revealed that it was in people's personal experiences with journalists when evidence of media power became particularly poignant (Madianou 2005a: 533). While many of the informants were keen to watch the news on Greek national television networks as a means of asserting their citizenship and desire to participate in public life, their personal experiences of being interviewed by journalists were tainted by the profound dissatisfaction about how their community was systematically misrepresented in the media (Madianou 2005a). Such negative experiences with journalists generated a lot of anger among those who felt unable to control their own mediated representation and contributed to a wider sense of disenfranchisement and exclusion which would not have been evident if the research had only centred on the reception of some news programmes (Madianou 2005a).

Perhaps more crucially what ethnography can uncover is the discrepancy between discourses (what people say about the news content in an interview context) and practices (what people do with the news which is revealed through participant observation). My research has observed a discrepancy between the two which has been crucial in understanding the ways in which people engage with the news. For example, in my research with news audiences both in Greece and the UK, differences between discourses and practices have revealed much about people's emotional involvement with the news (Madianou 2005b and forthcoming). While audiences in an interview context were often very critical towards the news, sometimes to the point of appearing cynical, when looking into their practices I found that people were avid news watchers and had daily rituals of news viewing, reading, or listening which often revealed an affective connection with the news.

Discrepancies between discourses and practices also reveal contested moral values and norms about taste. For example, in my study of consumption of news in Greece, viewers were keen to stress during interviews that the news programmes of commercial television networks were 'unwatchable' because of their populist and vulgar character. However, in practice most of my informants were watching the news on these very channels, confirming the trends suggested by audience ratings. In the same vein, interviewees often declared that the only news programmes worth watching were those of the public service broadcaster. Despite such statements, in my visits to their homes I never saw a television set tuned to the public service channels, an observation which again concurs with audience ratings (Madianou 2005b: 60–1).

Such discrepancies between practices and discourses reveal not only the ambivalence that characterizes news consumption (Hagen 1997), but also the power of media. What people say about the news is often informed by what is a dominant and widely accepted view which links news viewing with being a good citizen (Graber 1984). The idea that watching the news should be one's duty is so internalized (Graber 1984) that people express embarrassment or feel the need to apologize (Hagen 1997; Madianou forthcoming) when they are seen not to have been in touch with current affairs. Such observations reveal the extent to which news is taken for granted and ultimately constitute compelling evidence of its power.

The discrepancy between interview based findings and data based on participant observation suggests that different methodologies can yield different results. To illustrate this with an example from my recent research, in my study of news consumption in London I observed a near absence of talk about political issues in work environments. Given that talk is considered the foundation of deliberative democracy (Habermas 1989) its absence could be interpreted as 'avoiding politics' (Eliasoph 1998) and a confirmation of the decline in civic engagement (Putnam 2000). However, the interview based data revealed a different picture: on the whole interviewees expressed well informed and often critical views about current affairs which did not indicate ignorance, or apathy. Interviewees also acknowledged that they did talk about current affairs, only that this did not take place where I had been seeking to find it. People preferred to talk about politics in friendly environments such as the domestic, suggesting that people are reluctant to discuss controversial issues in non-friendly environments in order to avoid conflict (see Martin 2008). Had I only relied on participant observation, or interviews, the understanding of the political talk news consumption generates would have been considerably different (Madianou forthcoming).

Ethnography is also evident in and can make a productive contribution to the analysis of research data as it allows for the categories of analysis to be derived from the bottom up, rather than top down. This does not mean that an ethnographic perspective replaces theory, but rather that the collection of data and their analysis allow for the voice of the participants to be heard. Such an approach matters, for example, in the study of processes of political participation and engagement. Instead of presupposing the meaning of the categories 'engagement' and 'participation' an ethnographic approach can reveal the meaning which people themselves attribute to such processes (Couldry, Livingstone and Markham 2007). This way it is possible to develop a definition of civic engagement which reflects the way in which people engage with the political, including, for example, alternative politics. The problem with a top down definition of 'civic engagement' is that by presupposing a narrow set of variables (see Putnam 2000) one misses out on all the practices that people engage with which can be ascribed as political. The ethos of ethnography allows for issues which matter to people, but which the research design does not always anticipate, to emerge. Such surprises can deepen our knowledge and contribute to new theoretical developments.

The bottom up perspective of ethnographic inquiry can also guard against essentializing the audience especially when the audiences studied are ethnically or nationally defined. Such an approach proved particularly useful in my study of news consumption in Greece as part of a wider concern with the question of the reproduction of nation-alism and identities (Madianou 2005b). Instead of presupposing people's identities as fixed, adopting a perspective from the bottom up allowed for the dynamic nature of people's identifications to come to light. Crucially, because such a perspective allowed for people's own discourses and practices about belonging to emerge, it became possible to observe the ways in which people moved from one identity positioning to another according to context, whether mediated or not. The observation of such shifts over time is again facilitated by the longitudinal nature of ethnographic data. As it is in relation to someone, or something else (including the news text) that identities are articulated, this dynamic and relational understanding of identity highlighted the boundary-making capacity of the news media to create symbolic communicative spaces that either include or exclude (Madianou 2005a and 2007).

The long term involvement that ethnography necessitates facilitates a relationship of trust between the ethnographer and their subjects through which a deeper understanding can emerge. This matters specifically when the people concerned are members of minorities or marginalized in any way as ethnographies allow them to express in their own words what it means to be in touch with the media and what it means to be excluded by the media (Gillespie 1995; Madianou 2005a). Ultimately, the ethnographic endeavour represents a commitment to recording the voice of the people.

To argue for an ethnographic perspective of news consumption does not in any way render the news text and its reception redundant. An ethnographic approach, as I have outlined it here, is still concerned with the text as one of the means of examining the vertical dimension of communication and ultimately, media power. Depending on the research questions, an ethnography of news audiences can take place in parallel to a study of reception or incorporate it as studies have done (Bird 2003; Gillespie 1995; Madianou 2005b). The study of the text is immensely important if we want to under-stand processes of representation, power and resistance which are an inextricable part of the understanding of the place of news in everyday life.

Ethnography and mediation

The ethnographic perspective on news discussed in this chapter shares many similar-ities with the theory of mediation advanced by the late Roger Silverstone (1999; 2002; for a discussion of his application of mediation to news see Silverstone 2005). Both ethnography and mediation represent a holistic attempt to understand news not just as a genre or a text, but as a cultural and social phenomenon. Silverstone defined mediation as the fundamentally, but unevenly dialectical process in which institutionalized media of communications are involved in the general circulation of symbols in social life (Silverstone 2002: 762). Mediation, according to Silverstone:

> requires us to understand how processes of communication change the social
> and cultural environments that support them as well as the relationships that
> participants, both individual and institutional, have to that environment and

to each other. At the same time it requires a consideration of the social as in turn a mediator: institutions and technologies as well as the meanings that are delivered by them are mediated in the social processes of reception and consumption (Silverstone 2005: 3).

To study this 'circulation of meaning' in media and social life (Silverstone 1999: 13) audiences need to be examined together with the other moments that constitute the mediation process, namely media production, media texts, media technologies and the social and cultural context. An ethnographic perspective is well suited to do so, especially in the form of a multi-sited ethnography which moves from the single sites and local situations of conventional ethnographic research 'to examine the circulation of cultural meanings, objects and identities in diffuse time-space' (Marcus 1995: 96). Multi-sited ethnographies are particularly well suited to capture the increasingly transnational nature of news production and the consequences of transnational media texts in audiences' lives (for an example of a study of transnational audiences for September 11 news, see Gillespie 2006).

Silverstone's formulation of mediation may be broad, but it is so in a helpful way as it provides a flexible framework for thinking about the dialectic transformation of the media and the social (Couldry 2008). The flexibility of mediation allows for it to be easily combined with an ethnographic perspective as outlined above, while it can offer ethnography a more explicit concern with the ways in which consumption is linked to other dimensions of the mediation process.

Conclusions

This chapter has reflected on what an ethnography of news consumption can contribute to the understanding of the news as a social and cultural phenomenon. First of all, ethnographies, through their longitudinal and in depth engagement with audiences, can uncover the myriad practices associated with news and the ways in which such practices are implicated in processes of citizenship and identity and thus the very fabric of social life. Moreover, ethnography can contribute to a nuanced understanding of media power. This chapter highlighted two ways in which this can be achieved: the first is by widening the remit of analysis through investigating people's direct experience with the media frame (Couldry 2000), while the second is by drawing attention to the discrepancies between discourses (what people say, or feel they ought to say, about the news in an interview context) and practices (what people do with the news which is revealed through participant observation). Ethnography is also evident in the analysis of data, allowing for unanticipated themes to emerge and therefore enriching the understanding of the process of consumption. Furthermore, by focusing on the ways in which people themselves reflect on the relevance of news in their everyday lives, ethnography can guard against essentializing the audience. The commitment to recording people's voices reflects the rapport and empathy through which ethnographic knowledge is generated and, at a wider level, represents an ethical stance in research.

So does the contribution of an ethnographic perspective signal a paradigm shift in the ways in which we study the consequences of news? It is true that there has recently been a lot of discussion through publications, conferences, but also online initiatives about media anthropology[1] (see Gisburg, Abu Lughod and Larkin 2002; Rothenbuhler and Coman 2005, among others). However, it is not clear whether media anthropology is a distinct and coherent field of inquiry in the strict term of the word: a bounded field with its own concepts and theories.[2] It seems more likely, and this may actually be a more productive way to move forward, that although media anthropology represents an intense dialogue between anthropologists and researchers of the media, a new canon has not yet been invented. Moreover, it is not entirely clear how new this inquiry is. Ethnography has been used within media studies from the 1980s (Lull 1988; Morley 1986; Silverstone and Hirsch 1992) and some of the key concepts, such as consumption and practice have a long history (Miller 1987). Moreover, as indicated above, ethnography is not rendering reception obsolete. On the contrary, the study of the text and its reception needs to be part of and complement an ethnographic inquiry. As the mediational approach suggests, consumption needs to be investigated in conjunction with the other dimensions of mediation in order to understand the consequences of the (news) media in social life (Silverstone 2005). But the lack of an immediately recognizable paradigm shift is good news from the point of view of suggesting continuing (productive) ferment in the field which will hopefully address what is an uncontestable observation: the lack of a sufficient number of ethnographies of news audiences.

Notes

1 I am particularly referring to the highly successful initiative of the interdisciplinary media anthropology network of the European Association of Social Anthropologists (EASA) which regularly debates such matters and also holds e-seminars (see: http://www.media-anthropology.net/).
2 Although admittedly, there seems to be a new agenda emerging amongst those participating in the interdisciplinary debate focusing on topics such as media rituals (Couldry 2002; Rothenbuhler and Coman 2005).

References

Abu-Lughod, L. (1991) 'Writing against culture', in R. Fox (ed.), *Recapturing Anthropology*. Santa Fe: School of American Research Press, pp. 137–161.

Agar, M. (1996) *The professional stranger: an informal introduction to ethnography*. London: Academic Press.

Berelson, B. (1949) 'What missing the newspaper means', in P. Lazarsfeld and F. Stanton (eds.) *Communications Research 1948–9* (pp. 111–128). New York: Harper and Brothers.

Bird, E. S. (1992) *For inquiring minds: A cultural study of supermarket tabloids*. Knoxville, TN: University of Tennessee Press.

Bird, E. S. (2003) *The audience and everyday life: living in a media world*. London and New York: Routledge.

Born, Georgina. (2004) *Uncertain Vision: Birt, Dyke and the Reinvention of the BBC*. London: Secker and Warburg.

Canclini, N. G. (2001) *Consumers and citizens: Globalization and multicultural conflicts*. Minneapolis: University of Minnesota Press.

Carey, J. (1989) *Communication as culture: Essays on media and society*. New York: Routledge.

Clifford, J. and Marcus, G. (eds.) (1986) *Writing culture: The poetics and politics of ethnography*. Berkeley: University of California Press.

Couldry, N. (2000) *The place of media power: Pilgrims and witnesses in a media age*. London: Routledge.

Couldry, N. (2002) *Media rituals*. London: Routledge.

Couldry, N. (2008) 'Mediatization or mediation: alternative understandings of the emergent space of digital storytelling', *New Media and Society*, 10(3): 373–391.

Couldry, N., Livingstone, S. and Markham, T. (2007) *Media consumption and public engagement: Beyond the presumption of attention*. London: Palgrave.

Eliasoph, N. (1998) *Avoiding politics: how Americans produce apathy in everyday life*. Cambridge: Cambridge University Press.

Geertz, C. (1973) *The interpretation of cultures*. New York: Basic Books.

Gillespie, M. (1995) *Television, ethnicity and cultural change*. London: Routledge.

Gillespie, M. (2006) Transnational Television Audiences after September 11, *Journal of Ethnic and Migration Studies*, Vol. 32(6): 903–921.

Ginsburg, F., Abu-Lughod, L. and Larkin, B. (2002). *Media worlds: Anthropology on new terrain*. Berkeley: University of California Press.

Graber, D. A. (1984). *Processing the news: how people tame the information tide*. New York: Longman.

Habermas, J. (1989 [1962]) *The structural transformation of the public sphere*. Cambridge: Polity.

Hagen, I. (1997) 'Communicating to an ideal audience: News and the notion of the "informed citizen,"' *Political Communication*, 14: 405–419.

Hammersley, M. and Atkinson, P. (1995 [1983]) *Ethnography: principles in practice*. New York: Tavistock Publ.

Hannerz, U. (2004) *Foreign news: exploring the world of foreign correspondents*. Chicago: Chicago University Press.

Hastrup, K. (1995) *A passage to anthropology: between experience and theory*. London: Routledge.

Jensen, K. B. (ed.) (1998) *News of the world: World cultures look at television news*. London: Routledge.

Loizos, P. (1992) 'User friendly ethnography?', in Pina-Cabral, J. and J. Campbell (eds.), *Europe observed*. Oxford: Macmillan, pp. 167–187.

Lull, J. (ed.) (1988) *World families watch television*. Newbury Park, CA: Sage.

Madianou, M. (2005a) 'Contested communicative spaces: identities, boundaries and the role of the media', *Journal of Ethnic and Migration Studies* 31(3): 521–541.

Madianou, M. (2005b) *Mediating the nation: News, audiences and the politics of identity*. London: UCL Press/Routledge.

Madianou, M. (2005c) 'The elusive public of television news', In Livingstone, S. (ed.), *Audiences and publics: When cultural engagement matters to the public sphere*. Bristol: Intellect Press.

Madianou, M. (2007) Shifting identities: banal nationalism and cultural intimacy in Greek television news and everyday life. In Mole, R. (ed.), *Discursive constructions of identity in European politics* (pp. 95–118). London: Palgrave.

Madianou, M. (forthcoming) The emotional life of news. Manuscript in preparation.

Malinowski, B. (1960 [1922]) *Argonauts of the western Pacific*. London: Routledge and Kegan Paul.

Mankekar, P. (1999) *Screening culture, viewing politics: an ethnography of television, womanhood, and nation in Postcolonial India*. Durham, NC, and London: Duke University Press.

Marcus, G. E. (1995) 'Ethnography in/of the world system: The emergence of multi-sited ethnography', *Annual Review of Anthropology* 24: 95–117.

Marcus, George. E. and Michael M. Fischer (1986) *Anthropology as Cultural Critique: An experimental moment in the human sciences*. Chicago: University of Chicago Press.

Martin, V. B. (2008) 'Attending the news: A grounded theory about a daily regiment', *Journalism: theory, practice and criticism*. 9(1): 76–94.

Miller, D. (1987) *Material culture and mass consumption*. Oxford: Blackwell.

Miller, D. (1998) 'Introduction: Why some things matter', in Miller, D. (ed.) *Material cultures* (pp. 3–24). London: UCL Press.

Miller, D. and Slater, D. (2000) *The Internet: an ethnographic approach*. Oxford: Berg.

Morley, D. (1986) *Family television*. London: Comedia.

Nightingale, V. (1993) 'What's ethnographic about ethnographic audience research?', in Turner, G. (ed.), *Nation, culture, text: Australian cultural and media studies*. London: Routledge, pp. 164–177.

Press, A. (1996) 'Toward a qualitative methodology of audience study: using ethnography to study the popular culture audience', in J. Hay, L. Grossberg and E. Wartella (eds.), *The audience and its landscape*. Boulder, CO.: Westview Press, pp: 113–130.

Putnam, R. (2000) *Bowling alone: the collapse and revival of American community*. New York: Simon and Schuster.

Radway, J. (1988) 'Reception study'. *Cultural Studies*, vol. 2(3): 359–376.

Rothenbuhler, E. and Coman, M. (eds) (2005) *Media anthropology*. London: Sage.

Schudson, M. (2000) 'The sociology of news production revisited (again)', in Curran, J. and Gurevitch, M. (eds), *Mass media and society* (3rd ed). London: Edward Arnold, pp. 175–200.

Silverstone, R. (1988) 'Television, myth and culture', in Carey, J. (ed.), *Media, myths and narratives*. Newbury Park, CA.: Sage, pp. 20–47.

Silverstone, R. (1994) *Television and everyday life*. London: Routledge.

Silverstone, R. (1999) *Why study the media?* London: Sage.

Silverstone, R. (2002) 'Complicity and collusion in the mediation of everyday life', *New Literary History*, 33(5): 745–764.

Silverstone, R. (2005) 'Mediation and communication', in Calhoun, C., Rojek, C. and Turner, B. (eds.), *Handbook of sociology*. London: Sage, pp. 188–207.

Silverstone, R. and Hirsch, E. (eds.) (1992) *Consuming technologies: media and information in domestic spaces*. London: Routledge.

Strathern, M. (1987) 'The limits of auto-anthropology', in Jackson, A. (ed.), *Anthropology at home*. London: Tavistock, pp. 16–37.

40
NEWS INFLUENCE AND THE GLOBAL MEDIA SPHERE: A CASE STUDY OF AL-JAZEERA ENGLISH

Mohammed el-Nawawy and Shawn Powers

News media have become an integral part in any discussion of globalization and global politics today. Since CNN's coverage of the Gulf War in 1991, satellite news networks have sprung up across the globe at an incredible pace. In regions where the freedom of the press has not always been a privilege, satellite news networks have made waves, particularly in the Middle East. This chapter is a brief overview of the rise of global media, a summary of the debates surrounding the influence of contemporary international news broadcasters, an introduction to a recent broadcast giant – Al-Jazeera English – and an examination of its influence amongst audiences across six countries.

More specifically, we discuss the broad question of whether the news media, particularly global news networks, contribute to shaping public opinion about current events. In doing so, we present the various arguments surrounding the "CNN effect" and the relationship between today's expanding global news media and the "global public sphere." We also test the impact of Al-Jazeera English – whose mission and identity are different from its Western counterparts – on the global mediascape. Our findings show that the broadcast news media are more likely to reinforce already existing opinions and attitudes regarding politically salient topics than to change opinions, but that viewing Al-Jazeera English may have a positive impact on facilitating less dogmatic and more open-minded thinking amongst its viewers.

The CNN effect and beyond

During the last decade of the twentieth century, several communication scholars attributed much power to the news media role in constructing a mediated reality about current affairs on both local and global levels. In this context, Chris Paterson (1998) argued that "mass media are almost wholly responsible for shaping that reality, and among mass media international television news agencies are especially influential (for they alone provide contemporary visual representations of most of the world to the entire world)" (1998: 82). According to Paterson, this strong media impact could be applicable on a global level, where "The globalization of television news is producing an international public sphere, but one dominated by mainstream Anglo-American ideologies conveyed in the texts of internationally distributed television news" (1998: 95).

Along the same lines, Ingrid Volkmer (1999: 1) argued that "The media, in their function of shaping, sustaining and diversifying global stratification, influence a worldwide formation of 'communities', 'identities', 'democracy' and other forms of social organization." Volkmer noted that some news channels play a remarkable role in formulating a "global media sphere of 'political news' and 'political infor mation' ... Their activities mediate the diverse global 'worlds' of ideas and create a new mediating sphere with various models of participation: symbolic, representative or real" (1999: 224).

One news channel in particular, Cable News Network International (CNNI), stood out thanks to its wide reach and impact on the global political scene and thanks to its role in setting new standards as a pioneer in the global 24-hour news reporting. "CNNI has reshaped the conventional agenda of international or 'foreign' news and created a platform for worldwide communication ... [Moreover, it] has altered the focus of global news in an interrelationship of changing political centers and peripheries, and has given a new meaning to news, journalistic values, the setting of a global agenda" (Volkmer 1999: 2). In this context, a CNNI reporter was quoted in Volkmer (1999: 154) as saying that "The fact that television is becoming more powerful was attributed especially to CNN's worldwide political influence."

CNN's coverage of the 1991 Gulf War, which was the first war where coverage of the conflict was instantaneously broadcast into millions of homes, highlighted the enhanced role played by news networks in today's networked society and led many scholars and media analysts to coin the phrase "CNN effect" (Robinson 2002: 1). "Since then the phrase has become the generic term" (Robinson 2002: 2) that refers to the tremendous power of the news media, particularly satellite channels, in shaping the audiences' opinions about current events and even accelerating the political and diplomatic processes by providing a platform through which political leaders can communicate with each other via television. This media power has been subject to fierce debate by media scholars and critics. "Debate has not only centered on the role and impact of CNN but also on the impact of the news media in general upon both foreign policy formulation and world politics. In other words, the CNN effect is not synonymous with CNN" (Robinson 2002: 2).

Within the perimeters of the debate around the "CNN effect," some communication scholars such as Volkmer (1999) have gone as far as arguing that CNNI, by setting new journalistic standards and affecting the domestic and international political processes, has contributed to the formulation of a "global public sphere"

(1999: 4) in a way that has given "a homogeneous global shape to diverse news events" (1999: 6). According to Volkmer, "CNNI has inaugurated a market-force-oriented process which shifts global communication onto a new level by mixing the conventional reference-system of national news presentation, with its 'home' and 'foreign' news ... with a global juxtaposition of the 'internal' and the 'external', a substantial new inter-relationship which can shape political action" (1999: 3).

On the other side of the debate, scholars such as Piers Robinson (2002) and Eytan Gilboa (2005) are more cautious and conservative in attributing power to the global news networks, particularly CNN, whose influence on the political scene, they argued, has been overstated and exaggerated. It can be argued that such cautious approach to media power has started in the early years of the twenty-first century which have witnessed a complication in the global political environment, coupled by a proliferation of media technologies, particularly satellite television. "Despite the radical claims of some, new communication technologies have not transformed world politics and media-state relations" (Robinson 2002: 129).

Robinson did not totally rule out the influence of media coverage on politics, but he argued that the media ought to be perceived as one of several factors that affect political decisions rather than a main cause for such decisions. In other words, the politicians, according to Robinson, base their final political decisions on several considerations, one of which is the media coverage (2002). "But in no way [can] media coverage drive or compel policymakers into taking action where they would have otherwise not" (Robinson 2002: 71).

Kai Hafez (2007) has taken an even more conservative approach, compared to Robinson, in his criticism of the global impact of satellite news channels. He described the global media system as a "utopia" (2007: 13), and argued that the "CNN effect" is a "myth" (2007: 51). "There are many 'CNNs', but no complete global programme. Through the proliferation of satellite programmes in the last decade, CNN has lost its elevated position and is now merely a decentralized variant of an American television programme, whose country of origin remains easily recognizable in its agenda and framing. CNN tends to be a mixture of characteristics of the American system and the target system of the specific window; it is thus at best a multinational but not a global programme" (Hafez 2007: 13).

Hafez questioned the role played by satellite television channels in trying to homogenize the global public sphere. He argued that there is not enough evidence to show that satellite television has played a significant factor in changing people's cultural norms and values or their domestic social fabrics. "How is one to interpret the fact that while nowadays a significant chunk of humanity has the technology to access foreign broadcasters at its disposal, it almost never makes use of it? People's media habits and how they organize their lives are not changing as radically as has frequently been assumed" (Hafez 2007: 2–3).

According to Hafez, "the media *follow* rather than *lead*. The true strength of the media consists not in its capacity to influence politics, as evoked in the 'CNN effect', but in the affirmation and legitimation of national politics" (Hafez 2007: 54). To further illustrate his point, Hafez argued that the differences in news agendas and viewing habits of satellite news channels such as Al-Jazeera Arabic and CNN have reinforced the argument that the impact of such networks is local at the nation and state level rather than global. "... Given the differences in these networks' world-views, one would also have to reflect upon whether CNN and Al-Jazeera [Arabic] are not in fact merely the harbingers of an ever more divided media world, characterized not by more, but by ever less cross-border exchange" (Hafez 2007: 3). Satellite networks, according to Hafez, have the ability to cross national borders, but this ability is curtailed, to a large extent, by the cultural nuances and the social and historical intricacies that characterize and identify each society (2007: 75). Hafez argued that the news content provided by satellite channels is often "domesticated" (2007: 173) to serve the interests and address the concerns of particular culturally and politically aligned audience members rather than the general interests of the global audience at large. "Who could expect global media diplomacy from such provincial systems?" (Hafez 2007: 173). Hafez's argument is drastically different from that of what Robinson referred to as the "radical technological optimists [who predicted that the news networks would] erode people's identification with the state and instead 'mold a cosmopolitan global consciousness'" (Robinson, 2002).

News in a New Media Ecology

As it turns out, neither prediction of the news media as creating a new "global public sphere," nor their "affirmation and legitimation of national politics" offers a compelling explanation for today's highly complex news media environment. Contemporary news broadcasters operate in an over-saturated media environment that presents a new set of challenges for global news networks, as well as those that study these networks. Whereas CNN was the only game in town during the first Gulf War, today there are hundreds of satellite news broadcasters available via satellite across the globe (Cottle & Rai 2008). Moreover, the rise of the Internet society presents an additional challenge for global news giants, as audiences have an added means of consuming information that, at its very core, can provide information faster, with more depth and tailored to meet the needs of its users. As a result, news organizations are adapting to today's changed media ecology. Whereas traditional media of old were integral to the formation of national identity, today's successful new media systems are focused on community and network forming, oftentimes across borders.

As globalization continues to create conditions of "manufactured uncertainty" (Beck 2000) and "ontological insecurity" (Giddens 1990), people continue to turn to the news media to make sense of an otherwise increasingly fragmented world. According to Hjarvard (2002: 70–1), while "the vocabulary of contemporary analysis and theories provide a clear illustration of the ... disembedding role of new media," contemporary news media in particular have functioned as a "re-embedding social mechanism, i.e. a mechanism that reconstructs and institutionalizes patterns of social interaction and thereby provides trust."

An important question for scholars of the news media is how do today's audiences choose between different mediums and sources of news. Hjarvard (2002) argues that new news media lack a level of influence that was often associated with the media of old. In today's world of relative social disorder and competing news narratives, it is becoming more difficult for audiences to grasp all of the facts all of the time, and use objective standards to evaluate the trustworthiness of news media. Rather, similar to how consumers choose between brand products that they know little about, they rely on brands to determine which news organizations they trust and don't trust. "The communication of a brand name plays a much more prominent role in global media, almost to the extent that the presentation of a brand name is equally important as relying on the brand name itself" (Hjarvard 2002: 80). Thus, brands – and symbols associated with media brands – are the essential landmarks by which trust is gauged in today's decoupled and decentralized media environment.

Importantly, another essential ingredient is the "personification of the message," in terms of both form and content (e.g. is the message framed in a way that I can relate to?). Thus, questions of identity construction, promotion and identification have become increasingly central to analyzing and understanding how media become trusted means for accessing information about the world.

Along these lines, Bennett's (2004: 141) research found that "changes in citizenship may account for a large part of the difficulty in delivering standard mass society news format ... to audiences whose members are increasingly parsing information in highly personal terms. This identity shift means ... that news and information systems cannot simply go back in time to the seemingly rosier days of mass news audiences."

This past decade has seen the rise of a number of international and regional news broadcasters, most of which have been tethered to a geopolitical power or multi-national corporation. Among the mix of news channels, one news network – Al-Jazeera English – stands out as transcending the 'nation-state' based paradigm of old while also promising a highly personalized, journalistically sound and culturally connected perspective on global events. Below is a brief synopsis of a study of Al-Jazeera English's influence in today's new news media ecology.

Al-Jazeera English

Al-Jazeera English (AJE), a subsidiary of Qatar's Al-Jazeera Arabic network, represents a new form of transnational media that has the declared purpose of revolutionizing the global mediascape. Launched on November 15, 2006, AJE, which is the world's first global English language news channel to be headquartered in the Middle East, is already accessible in over 110 million households worldwide, and has also agreed to provide distribution (oftentimes free of charge) via multiple video sharing websites, making it accessible to anyone with a connection to the World Wide Web. With over 25 bureaus worldwide, AJE is hyped as "the voice of the South." Importantly, AJE is trying to bridge the gap between old and new media paradigms, covering global issues, but always from a "local" perspective.

According to its proponents, AJE presents a tremendous opportunity for a new direction in the discourse of global newsflow. With its avowed promise of giving a "voice to the voiceless," AJE's launch and growing popularity represent a new style of media structure and content that provide an important test case for existing research regarding the influence of transnational media organizations in today's highly particularized and saturated media environment.

Serving as a "voice to the voiceless" represents a phenomenon that has not been familiar among many Western news media networks. In this context, AJE's deputy manager for news and programs, Ibrahim Helal (2008), told the authors: "The AJE way of journalism is a bit different from the West because we tend to go faster to the story and to go deeper into communities to understand the stories, rather than getting the [news] services to give us the information … We try to do our best to set the agenda by searching for stories others cannot reach or don't think of." According to Helal, the nature of AJE stories and the angles they focus on contribute to their standing out as a network compared to Western television stations. "We were in Myanmar exclusively during the tensions last year. We covered Gaza from within Gaza by Gazan correspondents. We looked into why Gazans are united behind Hamas despite the suffering. These kinds of stories are not easily covered by other media" (Helal 2008).

With a budget of over U.S.$ 1 billion, mostly coming from the emir of Qatar, AJE has opened up four broadcasting centers (in Qatar, the UK, Malaysia and the United States) and 21 supporting bureaus in Africa, Latin America and Asia – parts of the world that have often been marginalized or altogether neglected by the mainstream Western media. Thanks to its sizable and remarkably market-independent resources, AJE is not subject to the economic pressures that control and have resulted in a decline in the quality of the many Western media (McChesney 2000).

Thus, AJE represents an interesting test case for media scholars. While encompassing many of the traditional journalistic strengths of traditional broadcast news media, its identity, mission and brand are cloaked in a message that personifies its message to a "global south." Compared to BBC World and CNNI, both of which are largely considered to have Western agendas, AJE's agenda is not associated with any particular region or politics but rather a global audience of the historically and currently disenfranchised.

Method

In order to evaluate AJE's influence in today's new news media environment, we conducted a cross-sectional survey on a purposive sample of audiences of global news in Malaysia, Indonesia, Qatar, Kuwait, the United Kingdom and the United States to analyze the demographics, worldviews, and cultural, political, civic and cognitive dispositions of viewers of AJE. A purposive sample is a type of non-probability sample that "includes subjects or elements selected for specific characteristics or qualities and eliminates those who fail to meet these criteria" (Wimmer & Dominick 2006: 91–92). Purposive samples are not meant to be representative of the population. Drawing from existing research, all of the countries were chosen due to their relative levels of viewership of AJE as well as their ability to signify existing cultural perspectives in the context of growing resentment between the "Islamic" and "Western civilizations." The total sample size surveyed was 597 participants, approximately 100 participants surveyed at each of the proposed locations. The survey focused on sampling existing viewers of AJE only, though the sample included participants who had just started watching AJE as well as those who had been watching since it was first broadcast. Accordingly, the survey data provides an empirical record of the numerous dispositions of viewers of AJE that are examined, relative to the participants' dependence on AJE as a source of information, as well as how often and how long they had been viewing AJE. In order to allow for comparative analysis, the survey also asked participants about their levels of dependence on two other global news networks: CNN International and BBC World.

In order to determine the levels of importance that AJE had on the opinions and attitudes of participants, compared to other international news broadcasters, we drew from Media System Dependency theory. In order to measure cultural and cognitive dispositions, we drew from scales and questions to measure each participant's level of cognitive dogmatism. Moreover, the survey asked questions about participants' opinions of the United States culture, people and foreign policies.

Results and Discussion

Our findings present an interesting set of answers, and several more questions, in terms of what role news plays in today's global mediasphere. The first set of results have to do with the impact that viewership of global news outlets had on participants' levels of cognitive dogmatism, defined as "a relatively closed cognitive organization of beliefs and disbeliefs about reality, organized around a central set of beliefs about absolute authority which, in turn, provides a framework for patterns of intolerance and qualified tolerance toward others" (Rokeach & Fruchter 1956: 356). Our second set of findings have to do with the relationship between how dependent a participant was on a certain source for news and their opinions of the U.S. polices and culture. Our findings demonstrate a nuanced answer to the question of how much influence global news media have in the current media environment. While people today are likely tuning into news programming which they find helps them reaffirm their already existing opinions on current affairs, the news media – when they provide depth and context, draw on experienced but local correspondents, and serve as a microphone for those that have been largely ignored – may be able to foster lower levels of dogmatism, and thus produce a latent but substantial media effect.

First, the results showed that participants that reported they were dependent on either AJE, BBC World or CNNI as a source of information for following global news events or for determining their political behavior were more likely to be considered "dogmatic," according to an 11-item scale measuring each participant's level of cognitive dogmatism. While this finding may be surprising at first, a likely explanation is that any viewer who is "dependent" on any particular source of news – global or local – is already, in a certain sense, being dogmatic in the way they approach information gathering. Indeed, this finding confirms previous literature suggesting that "individuals high in dogmatism attempt to avoid information that is inconsistent with their belief systems, and they react to inconsistent information by minimizing or ignoring it"

(Shearman & Levine 2006: 276). Thus, it is unlikely that viewers that were found to be dependent on any particular medium for global news would change their opinions based upon information they gathered via the news media. Moreover, media system dependency, one of the scales used to measure how important particular news outlets were in forming the participants' opinions and behaviors, may be a poor indicator to measure how viewing a particular news broadcaster can influence someone's levels of dogmatic thinking.

Another indicator – how many months the participant had been watching AJE – proved to be more interesting. While it was the case that those viewers that were dependent on AJE were found to be more dogmatic, the more months a viewer had been watching AJE, the less dogmatic they were in their thinking. This finding was found to be significant both amongst participants that relied heavily on AJE as their primary source for information and political behavior, as well as those that were less dependent on AJE. Moreover, the relationship was significant regardless of gender, religion or socio-economic status. Since levels of dogmatism are strongly related to how people behave in confrontational situations, as well as levels of political and cultural tolerance (Shearman & Levine 2006), we argue that AJE viewership may be able to positively impact viewers' behaviors over the long term. AJE may prove to fulfill a socially valuable function in that audiences that tune in for longer periods of time will more likely be receptive to new types of information, arguments and perspectives.

The second set of results demonstrated a strong relationship between the participants' attitudes toward the U.S. policies and culture and the particular broadcaster they depended on for news and information. Participants were asked how supportive/ unsupportive they were of: (1) America's War on Terror, (2) U.S. policy in Iraq, (3) U.S. policy toward the Palestinian–Israeli conflict, (4) purchasing American-made brands and products; as well as how in favor/not in favor they were of (5) American cultural values, (6) U.S. foreign policy in general and (7) American people. Respondents who were dependent on BBC World and especially on CNNI were more supportive of U.S. foreign policy generally. Moreover, those dependent on BBC World were more favorable of American cultural values, while those dependent on CNNI were more likely to support America's war on terror. Finally, participants dependent on CNNI were more likely to support U.S. policy in Iraq and U.S. policy toward the Palestinian–Israeli conflict, while those dependent on AJE were more critical of both.

Given that AJE brands itself on showing the "other side" of the war in Iraq and the oppression of the Palestinian people, these findings are not surprising. It is unlikely that a viewer who is in favor of the U.S. policy in Iraq or the Palestinian–Israeli conflict would likely report him/herself dependent on AJE, especially given the Al-Jazeera network's history of reporting on both those issues. Rather, these findings likely suggest that people seek out news media that reinforce their predetermined ideologies and opinions. In other words, viewers use the media to be affirmed rather than informed. So, for example, the viewers who oppose the U.S. policies in Iraq and Palestine may have been found to be more dependent on AJE because they felt it would likely provide them with information to further substantiate their already established opinions. Similarly, viewers who support the U.S. foreign policy may start watching CNN since they believe its reporting operates along a similar ideology to theirs.

Importantly, while viewers likely choose to watch international news broadcasters that will tell stories in ways that reinforce their opinions, we found that the more frequently a participant watched AJE, the less supportive they were of U.S. policy towards the Palestinian–Israeli conflict. Similarly, the longer a participant had been tuning into AJE, the more critical they were of U.S. policy in Iraq. Thus, while the news media are unlikely to change one's opinion on politically salient issues, it may often be the case that they do reinforce and deepen already held opinions. These findings seem to provide strong evidence for Hafez's argument that the media appeal to their particular constituencies rather than to a universal audience. According to Hafez (2007: 25), "When all is said and done, the mass media are not in the least oriented towards a 'world system,' but in fact concentrate upon national markets, whose interests and stereotypes they largely reproduce. Moreover, the influence of the media on politics is negligible, particularly in relation to international conflicts that touch upon vital national interests." While AJE presents a challenge to Hafez's suggestion that today's news media concentrate on national markets given its cross-regional and global focus, our findings do support the argument that the news media are more likely to reinforce existing opinion of current events rather than challenge them.

Moving Forward

In terms of news media today, AJE is an anomaly when it comes to its role, mission and identity. It stands out from its competitors in that it presents a challenge to the existing paradigms guiding international news broadcasters. It is dominated by neither geopolitical nor commercial interests, and is the first of its kind to have the resources, mission and journalistic capacity to reach out to ideologically and politically similar audiences throughout the world.

Our results here provide evidence for a number of arguments reviewed in the literature. First, brand recognition and the personification of the message do matter. AJE's strength in connecting audiences from Bangladesh to Burlington, VT, stems from its ability to consistently approach issues from the perspective of the "global south." By connecting the inequalities that exist in very different parts of the world, AJE has created a niche perspective, one that the networks' overall brand – largely created by AJ Arabic news broadcasters – relies on for attracting audiences around the globe. Both in Malaysia and Indonesia, viewers told us that they tuned into AJE at first because they liked what they had seen of its Arabic counterpart when Al-Jazeera Arabic had been dubbed into local Bahasa and rebroadcast on local television stations in the early stages of the 2003 Gulf War.

Second, viewers tune into global media that are likely to further support the already determined opinions with regard to current affairs. Given the number of state-based and commercially driven news broadcasters available around the world, it is unlikely that viewers will tune into a network that is constantly challenging opinions formed based on years of media consumption and personal experience. Our findings demonstrated that, to a certain extent, viewers' opinions of pertinent foreign policy issues determined which news broadcaster they were likely to depend on for information. For instance, viewers dependent on CNN or the BBC were more likely to be supportive of U.S. policy in the Middle East compared to viewers dependent on AJE. Moreover, it was not surprising to find that viewers highly dependent on AJE were more critical of U.S. policies towards the Palestinian–Israeli conflict, nor was it surprising that the longer viewers watched AJE, the more critical they were of the U.S. policy in Iraq. These are flagship issues, both tied to the image of the Al-Jazeera network, and the Al-Jazeera network approaches both issues differently than either CNNI or the BBC.

The assumption that viewers seek reinforcement of their views through the media does not rule out the media potential to affect people's cognitive level of thinking. The fact that the longer people watched AJE, the less dogmatic they had become is a strong indication that the media can affect how people approach new issues where their opinions have not already been formed. What remains to be seen is how decreased levels of dogmatism from viewing AJE will actually impact viewers' behaviors.

Having mentioned that, we believe that the political situation on the ground may play a bigger role than the media outlets in shaping people's opinions, particularly when it comes to complicated and highly sensitive problems such as the Palestinian–Israeli conflict or the situation in Iraq. In other words, the news media by themselves are unlikely to have an immediate and drastic impact on viewers' opinions with regard to old, complicated issues as long as those viewers do not see improvements or changes on the ground.

References

Beck, U. (2000) The risk society revisited: theory, politics and research programmes. In *The Risk Society and Beyond*, (Eds, Adam, B., Beck, U. & Von Loon, J.) Sage, London, pp. 211–229.

Bennett, W.L. (2004) Global Media and Politics: Transnational Communication Regimes and Civic Cultures. *Annual Review of Political Science*, 7, 125–148.

Cottle, S. & Rai, M. (2008) Global 24/7 news providers: Emissaries of global dominance or global public sphere? *Global Media and Communication*, 4, 157–181.

Giddens, A. (1990) *The consequences of modernity*. Polity Press, Cambridge.

Gilboa, E. (2005) The CNN Effect: The Search for a Communication Theory of International Relations. *Political Communication*, 22, 27–44.

Hafez, K. (2007) *The Myth of Media Globalization*, Polity: London.

Helal, I. (2008) Personal interview, April, Doha, Qatar.

Hjarvard, S. (2002) Mediated encounters: An essay on the role of communication media in the creation of trust in the 'Global Metropolis'. In *Global encounters: Media and cultural transformation*, (Eds, Stald, G. & Tufte, T.) University of Luton Press, Luton, pp. 69–84.

McChesney, R.W. (2000) *Rish Media, Poor Democracy: Communication Politics in Dubious Times*. University of Illinois Press, Champaigne.

Paterson, C. (1998) Global Battlefields, In *The Globalization of News* (Boyd-Barrett, O. & Rantanen, T. eds), pp. 79–103, Sage Publications: London.

Robinson, P. (2002) *The CNN Effect: The Myth of News, Foreign Policy and Intervention*, Routledge: London.

Rokeach, M. & Fruchter, B. (1956) A Factorial Study of Dogmatism and Related Concepts. *The Journal of Abnormal and Social Psychology*, 53 (3), 356–360.

Shearman, S. & Levine, T. (2006). Dogmatism Updated: A Scale Revision and Validation. *Communication Quarterly*, 54 (3), 275–291.

Volkmer, I. (1999). *News in the Global Sphere: A Study of CNN and its Impact on Global Communication*, University of Luton Press.

Wimmer, R. & Dominick, J. (2006). *Mass Media Research: An Introduction* (8th ed.). Wadsworth: Boston, MA.

41
YOUNG CITIZENS AND THE NEWS

Kaitlynn Mendes, Cynthia Carter and Máire Messenger Davies

In liberal, democratic societies, citizens have rights, but also responsibilities – one of the most important being to keep oneself informed on key public issues and debates. It is only in so doing that citizens are able to form sound judgements and opinions that form the basis of their contribution to democratic processes, most notably during elections when they are choosing politicians to represent them. In order to undertake this role, it is the responsibility of news organisations to provide trustworthy, fair and accurate reporting upon which citizens may make sensible political decisions. This symbiotic relationship is widely regarded as central to the health of democratic societies (Allan, 2004; Lewis, Inthorn and Wahl-Jorgensen, 2005).

Before examining how children's news fits into a broader discussion around news and citizens, we begin this chapter by briefly considering the thorny question of children's citizenship. Do news organisations in the UK view children as citizens or, at the very least, as 'citizens in the making' (Buckingham, 2000a)? If so, why is it that children have so few news outlets that directly address them and their interests and concerns as young citizens? If journalists don't see children as citizens, perhaps it is not surprising, as previous research has suggested, that by the time children become adults, few are participating in the parliamentary political system by voting in general elections (Carter and Allan, 2005; Cushion, 2006).[1] 'Children' can be defined in many ways, but for the purpose of our study we focused on young people between the ages of 8 and 15.

From there, we turn our attention to a consideration of research on children's news, where it has been noted that such programmes tend to contradictorily provide children greater depth and understanding of news events while also sometimes oversimplifying or evading certain stories their producers deem to be too sensitive or boring for their audience (Buckingham, 2000a; Matthews, 2009; Messenger Davies, 2007). We then report on preliminary findings of a study we have conducted with over 200 primary and secondary school children across the UK in which we explored their views on children's news and its relationship to children's citizenship. The chapter concludes by calling for greater interaction between children's news and its audiences to make the news more engaging and relevant to young citizens.

Children as citizens

When examining academic research regarding the relationship between children and citizenship, Bennett (2008) has proposed that there are two distinct paradigms that emerge. Researchers in the first paradigm suggest that children are politically 'disengaged' or 'apathetic', an accusation that has been levelled at citizens in general, not just children (Bennett, 2008; Iyengar and Jackman, 2003; Putnam, 2000). Yet, it is difficult to build a culture of participation when children feel that issues about which they care most are not addressed (Kirby et al., 2003 cited in Cockburn, 2007: 447). For some young people, their sense of exclusion from the adult public sphere of political debate results from feelings of powerlessness over unfolding political events – they are rarely given a space to voice their opinions. Children pick up on this and some react by declaring that they find the news to be 'boring', a term that needs to be unpacked. We would argue that 'boring' often means that the news doesn't speak to them in a language that they can understand, on the issues about which they care most (Carter, 2007; Messenger Davies, 2007). This point serves to highlight the continuing importance of a children's news media in which children's concerns and interests are reflected, where they can discover other children's opinions, and where they are enabled to discuss issues in what might be regarded as a children's public sphere.

Studies with children and young people that ask them about their levels of political engagement actively challenge the view that they are apathetic (Buckingham, 2000a, 2000b; Chekoway et al., 2003; Cushion, 2006; Hine, 2004; MacKinnon, 2008). This research belongs to Bennett's (2008) second paradigm where children and young people are seen to be both politically engaged and 'disconnected.' That is to say, government and mass media are seen to be failing children as citizens because they don't know how to speak to them in a way that will tap into their willingness to participate in the public sphere (Bennett, 2008: 2). Although many children are already engaged in a wide range of collective projects in their schools and communities, adults often fail to view these activities as 'political' or constituting children as politically 'engaged,' since they rarely connect to a more traditional (party-based) notion of politics. A claim sometimes made is that children are more interested in being passively entertained than in being politically active. In our view, this is an assumption that clearly needs sustained interrogation. After all, politics and entertainment are not necessarily mutually exclusive; games, music, and other forms of popular culture can be useful methods for teaching and experiencing a growing sense of citizenship (Sweetser and Kaid, 2008).

Educators, according to Buckingham (2000a: 223), must enable young people to build connections between the personal and political in order to prepare them for participatory forms of citizenship. We argue that the news media also have a critical role to play, providing children with opportunities to express themselves publicly and to see their interests reflected in the news. Politics, in this sense, necessarily extends beyond the bounds of Whitehall,[2] highlighting issues and events that affect children directly or indirectly as citizens of local and global communities.

News formats, features and the child citizen

Much is being made of the potential of online environments to draw children to the news, thus enhancing their citizenship. For instance, a now substantial area of research has focused on issues of children's increasing access to and use of online communication (Buckingham, 2007; Livingstone, 2002; Livingstone and Bovill, 1999; van der Voort et al., 1998). Issues that arise include a growing 'digital divide' amongst children and what role gender, age and economic status might play in creating and exacerbating social inequalities (Livingstone and Helsper, 2007), the ways in which new technologies may help maintain social links and identity (Wilska, 2003), the everyday use of technology located in children's local and global worlds (Holloway and Valentine, 2003), and how ICTs might be impacting children's experiences and practices of citizenship (Coleman et al., 2008; Hermes, 2006; Livingstone, 2007).

Although it may be tempting to think that children who use the internet for information automatically become engaged in civic life, research has so far suggested that this is not necessarily the case. Instead, it has been proposed that children first need to be socialised in their everyday lives in order to develop the necessarily critical tools to engage with politics (Buckingham, 2000a, 2000b). This is particularly the case, it is argued, when talking about online forms of engagement (Livingstone et al., 2007: 12). Hermes (2006: 295), for example, has noted that ICTs do not necessarily produce new citizens. Instead they may provide new and important citizenship practices that bridge the public and private spheres, and can be variously used for information, entertainment, consultation and communication.

Children's news

While much has been written about adult news, when examining the media research literature, it becomes apparent that few studies have investigated the structure and content of children's news programmes or their audiences (Matthews, 2003: 131). Scholars have examined children's representation in adult news (Carter and Messenger Davies, 2005; Wayne et al., 2008), the potential negative emotional effects of adult news on children, with particular attention paid to stories about violence (for an overview of this research see Villani, 2001; see also Carter, 2004; Carter and Messenger Davies, 2005; Lemish and Gotz, 2007; van der Molen, 2004), children's newspaper reading habits (Raeymaeckers, 2004), and the potential of news to politically socialise young people (Buckingham, 2000a, 2000b; Chaffee and Kanihan, 1997).

Cowling and Lee's (2002) report analysing television schedules over a 50-year period from 1952 to 2002 for the UK Institute of Public Policy Research states that children's news programmes, as a proportion of total programmes, decreased so much in the last 20 years of their study that by 2002 only 0.2% of all children's television could be classified as 'news.' Despite the fact that broadcasters have been seen to theoretically support children's news provision, current affairs programmes and other educational content, in practice very little of this type of content is currently produced.

Some media critics such as Hirst (2002) have pointed out that the dearth of children's news programmes is due, in part, to their high cost compared to dramas, cartoons or other types of shows, all of which can be sold, resold and almost endlessly repeated worldwide, thereby reducing overall production costs quite substantially. In addition, Hirst suggests that advertisers in the commercial broadcast services appear to prefer to advertise in a slot next to a 'fun' programme rather than a 'serious' one, thereby providing even less incentive to create non-fiction programmes. Whereas this stance does not seem to be as pronounced with public service broadcasters, in his study of the British Broadcasting Corporation's (BBC) children's news programme, *Newsround*, Matthews (2008) found that in order to maximise the audience, producers often chose to highlight 'entertaining' stories over 'serious ones' (2008: 269). What this seems to indicate is that even public service providers cannot escape what are, in effect, commercial pressures to maintain (and hopefully increase) audiences. Extending this point, Buckingham (2000a: 45) has argued that one of the strengths of children's news programmes is that they tend to emphasise understanding and context in relation to the stories they report. At the same time, it is also true that they sometimes oversimplify or evade stories that they judge to be either too sensitive or uninteresting for their audience.

Although commercial interests might be a major factor in the paucity of children's news programmes, various studies have concluded that this is not because children are indifferent to the news. Barnard (2007: 7) asked young people between the ages of 15 and 29 in 10 countries about their news media use, and found that most are curious about the world and actively follow the news (although more tend to trust their families and friends more than the news media). A recent Portuguese study of 500 children of different ages, classes and social backgrounds also concluded that children avidly follow the news 'not only because it allowed them to be "updated" but also as a way of occupying their time' (Ponte, 2008). Because assumptions regarding children's news are often made on professional intuition and short term market research rather than on sustained academic study (Wartella, 1994), children's programming 'frequently says much more about adults' and children's fantasy investments in the *idea* of childhood than they do about the realities of children's lives' (Buckingham, 2002: 7–8). This highlights the importance of asking young people what sort of news stories and formats engage them, instead of simply relying upon adults to speak for them. Rather than assuming that young people are not interested in what is happening in the world, or are disengaged or apathetic about politics, it is important for researchers to listen to what children and young people say about their views on a range of political issues.

Researching *Newsround*

In recent years, there have been a number of studies examining *Newsround*, the UK's only children's television news programme, and its associated website (Buckingham,

2000a; Carter, 2007; Messenger Davies, 1997, 2001, 2007; Harrison, 2000; Matthews, 2003; 2005; 2008; 2009). On the subject of the programme's production values and news selection criteria, Matthews (2003: 138; 2008) contends that, like most children's television shows, it is based on a view about what is appropriate for the age range of its target audience (in the case of *Newsround* this is 8–12-year-olds). While Matthews identifies several production values shaping *Newsround* content, we will focus on three pertaining to the issues raised in this chapter. The first one is that of personalisation, where children's voices are used to attract larger audiences. Stories tend to include children's emotional, more often than reasoned, reactions to the events reported, argues Matthews, because *Newsround* editors and journalists believe emotions stimulate greater programme interest from their audience (2008: 272).

Secondly, Matthews contends that *Newsround* stories are always simplified for the child audience. At times, this results in de-contextualising events, making them more 'palatable' rather than 'intelligible.' Complex or potentially 'boring' information is removed (2008: 274). This simplification often goes hand in hand with the third criterion, choosing stories that *Newsround* producers believe to be of primary interest to children, based on the desire to maintain good audience ratings. While these characteristics might result in an oversimplification of news, Matthews notes some benefits. For instance, the producer's desire to highlight how local, national and international events might impact on children's lives means that children are often represented in relation to stories where they might be completely excluded in adult news (2003: 139). Still, Matthews suggests that *Newsround* sometimes has the tendency to exaggerate children's participation thus creating a false impression of their contribution to public discussion (2005; 2008). That said, Buckingham (2000a: 54) suggests that out of various UK and US children's news programmes that he examined in his research in the late 1990s, *Newsround* was the least likely to give children a voice.[3] When children's voices were included on the programme, he found that they tended to take the forms of witness testimony and vox pops. Children are rarely afforded the opportunity to directly engage in public discussion, Buckingham contends, even within a news programme that is specifically designed for them. When voices of 'the public' are included on *Newsround*, he found, they are often those of adults expressing concern about or plans for children (2000a: 54).

Our research on *Newsround* tends to challenge this last point, recognising that the programme made a number of changes in its production style in the period between Buckingham's research in the late 1990s, and 2007–8 when we conducted our study (Milani, 2008).[4] Many of the children with whom we have spoken feel that *Newsround* generally does a very good job when it comes to giving them a chance to speak (although there is, of course, always room for improvement), while also confirming that the same is not true with adult news. Additionally, many of our over 200 respondents from England, Scotland, Wales and Northern Ireland, between the ages of 8 and 15, stated that adults shouldn't just assume that because children have not yet reached voting age their views are necessarily uninformed or what they have to say is unimportant to public debates. As 13-year-old Karishma from Bournemouth told us:

I think that even though we can't vote, kids our age have important things to say, for example we have things to say about education and how it can be improved, transport, how it could be cheaper or free for us, and we do have opinions on the government and how they could change or improve services for young people.

While some researchers' assessments of *Newsround* seem rather negative, others have found more positive things to report. For instance, Carter (2007: 122) has examined young people's use of *Newsround*'s website message board 'In the News.' She found that it successfully engages some young people (particularly teenagers) in discussions with each other on a wide range of issues and events, demonstrating their knowledge and enthusiasm for critical, public debate. Our study has produced similar results, with a sizable majority of those in *Newsround*'s target audience agreeing that the programme and its website makes them feel that their views are being taken seriously and consistently engages with their interests.[5] According to 10-year-old Kathryn from Portrush in Northern Ireland, *Newsround* is largely successful in its attempts to connect with its core audience, 'because all of the other news programmes don't listen, and they focus on adults, and children are just as important as adults.'

Additionally, we have found that many of the younger children we have spoken to respond well to 'entertainment' features such as games, polls and quizzes which can be found on *Newsround*'s website, as a way to enhance their learning. Though as previously stated, some might argue such features cannot possibly provide serious avenues for civic involvement, children in our study have suggested ways that these 'entertainment' features could be used in politically meaningful ways. Proposals include having a quiz after each news story to see how much children have learned from it, using data from online polls to demand political change, or using the red button on the television remote control to find out more information on a topic. Such features could be used as effective means of drawing them to civic websites that they might not otherwise have visited.

Children's voices

Before we conclude this chapter, we want to focus on what we believe to be one of the more important features of children's news – that is, that such programmes provide children with opportunities to share their ideas, thoughts and feelings as young citizens. Returning to Buckingham's (2000a) study of children's television news programmes in the US and UK, he established that some routinely asked children to contribute content or interact with journalists via e-mails, letters, or phone calls. Nevertheless, while certain programmes offer children these types of 'access,' it appears that children rarely have much control over the choice of content or editing (2000a: 54).

Although we agree that children ideally should take a more active role in children's news production, it is perhaps unrealistic to expect that they (or any audience member, regardless of age) could be consulted in depth on every news item broadcast or published online. Likewise, one should bear in mind that most children probably don't want to contact children's news producers. For example, in their study examining the ways in which Finnish children tend to interact with the news, Hujanen and Pietkainen (2004: 394) note that although children are aware of techno-logical opportunities to contact newsrooms, they generally feel that contact should be made by 'someone else,' or 'others,' and not themselves. When children interact with children's news, they are most likely to do so by taking part in competitions, polls, and questionnaires (2004: 394) – a finding our own research supported. So while children may lack real 'access' to children's news production, or they may not be interested in gaining such access, it is perhaps more important to judge a programme based on how 'in tune' it is with issues that interest its audience.

That said, many of the children in our study insisted that children's news producers should continue to encourage greater interaction with their audiences, through further development and promotion, for example, of their website message boards, feedback emails, and user generated content/citizen journalism. Additionally, a further suggestion for improving *Newsround* was mentioned by several children, clearly expressed by 9-year-old Flora from Glasgow, who says 'I think my ideas are important, but *Newsround* doesn't make me feel they are. To change this, maybe they could have child presenters on the show.' A similar point is made by 12-year-old Amina in Glasgow who offers a number of constructive ideas for improving the television programme and website. For example, she suggests that '*Newsround* should have news competitions for the best articles and they could be put up on the website occasionally. Kids should be involved more in *Newsround*. I think they should get kids to present more as well.'

Conclusion

In our view, much more could be done to improve and extend the provision of news for children (and teenagers) around the world in order to engage them, as early as possible, as young citizens. To support this position, the chapter began by first exploring the relationship between children and citizenship, identifying two paradigms that tend to shape much of the research – one assuming that young people are largely politically apathetic or disengaged, as evident in their withdrawal from civic activities such as voting once they are eligible; and the other concluding that children are politically engaged but largely 'disconnected' from mainstream politics. Although researchers have noted that children are often politically active, these activities tend to differ somewhat from those of previous generations. For many young people, political activism on global and local issues tends to be more interesting for them than traditional party politics.

The chapter then went on to discuss how new media technologies could be used to politically engage children, helping them to express themselves as citizens. New technologies and forms of entertainment such as polls, quizzes and games can be employed to draw children into news and citizenship websites by offering entertaining ways to learn. Finally, the chapter ended with a discussion of research examining children's news, including a few of the findings from our study with primary and secondary school children across the UK. While some researchers suggest that children's news often does little to make space for children's voices, others have shown that children, especially those in *Newsround's* target audience, are largely content with the current provision, and that it engages with them in meaningful ways. This view is certainly consistent with our research.

We conclude this chapter by urging researchers to recognise the importance of including children's perspectives in the development of children's news programmes and websites so as to sharpen academic insights into the ways in which children's news might enhance their civic engagement. This necessitates rethinking certain assumptions about children's intellectual capacities and their rights, envisaging a more active, political role for them in the public sphere. There is similarly a need for researchers to make the case for a renewed citizenship-based commitment to media education in schools to help children become more critical media consumers and to equip them with the skills and confidence needed to contribute, should they want to do so, as young 'citizen journalists.' Children's news that extends children's right to speak, helping their voices to be heard and taken seriously, will make an important contribution to the richness and diversity of our democracy.

Notes

1 Amongst 18–24-year-old voters in the 2005 UK General Election, a mere 37% voted, down from 39% in 2001.
2 The term 'Whitehall' is often used to refer to the UK Parliament and associated ministries and departments of government that are located along Whitehall in Westminster, London.
3 *Nick News* and *Channel One News* in the USA and *Wise Up, First Edition* and *Newsround* in the UK.
4 This project was funded by the UK Arts and Humanities Research Council (AHRC) and the BBC as part of a 'Knowledge Exchange Programme' funding pilot studies to encourage partnerships between academics and the BBC. Partners in our project include Stuart Allan, Bournemouth University, Cynthia Carter, Cardiff University, Kaitlynn Mendes, De Montfort University, Máire Messenger Davies, University of Ulster, Roy Milani, BBC and Louise Wass, BBC.
5 The same cannot be said for the teenagers we interviewed, many of whom suggested that the BBC ought to have a news programme or website aimed at their age group.

References

Allan, S. 2004. *News Culture*, Second Edition. Maidenhead: Open University Press.
Barnard, R. 2007. *Youth Media DNA: Decoding youth news and information consumers globally*. Phase two report World Association of Newspapers (WAN) Report (May).
Bennett, W.L. 2008. Changing Citizenship in the Digital Age. Civic Life Online: Learning How Digital Media Can Engage Youth. In Bennett, W.L. (ed). *The John D. and Catherine T. MacArthur Foundation Series on Digital Media and Learning*. Cambridge, MA: The MIT Press. pp. 1–24.
Buckingham, D. 2000a. *The Making of Citizens: Young People, News and Politics*. London: Routledge.
Buckingham, D. 2000b. *After the Death of Childhood: Growing Up in the Age of Electronic Media*. Cambridge: Polity.
Buckingham, D. (ed). 2002. *Small Screens: Television for Children*. London: Leicester University Press.
Buckingham, D. 2007. *Beyond Technology: Children's Learning in the Age of Digital Culture*, Cambridge: Polity.
Carter, C. 2004. Scary news: Children's Responses to News of War, *Mediactive* 3: 67–84.

Carter, C. 2007. Talking About My Generation: A Critical Examination of Children's BBC Newsround Web Site Discussions about War, Conflict, and Terrorism. In Lemish, D. and Gotz, M. (eds). *Children and Media in Times of War and Conflict*. Cresskill, NJ: Hampton, 121–142.

Carter, C. and Allan, S. 2005. Hearing their Voices: Young People, Citizenship and Online News, in Williams, A. and Thurlow, C. (eds). *Talking Adolescence: Perspectives on Communication in the Teenage Years*. New York: Peter Lang, 73–90.

Carter, C. and Messenger Davies, M. 2005. 'A Fresh Peach is Easier to Bruise': Children and Traumatic News, in Allan, S. (ed). *Journalism: Critical Issues*. Maidenhead: Open University Press, 224–235.

Chaffee, S.H., and Kanihan, S.F. 1997. Learning about Politics from the Mass Media. *Political Communication*: 14: 421–430.

Checkoway, B. Richards-Schuster, K. Abdullah, S., Aragon, M. Facio, E. Gigueroa, L., Reddy, E., Welsh, M., and White, A. 2003. 'Young People as Competent Citizens, *Community Development Journal* 38 (4): 298–300.

Cockburn, T. 2007. Partners in Power: A Radically Pluralistic Form of Participative Democracy for Children and Young People. *Children and Society* 21: 446–457.

Coleman, R., Lieber, P., Mendelson, A.L. and Kurpius, D.D. 2008. Public Life and the Internet: If You Build a Better Website, Will Citizens become Engaged? *New Media and Society*, 10 (2): 179–201.

Cowling, C. and Lee, K. 2002. *They Have Been Watching – Children's TV 1952–2002*, London: Institute for Public Policy Research.

Cushion, S. July 2006. Protesting their Apathy? Young People, Citizenship and News Media, unpublished PhD Thesis, Cardiff University.

Harrison, J. 2000. *Terrestrial TV News in Britain: The Culture of Production*. Manchester: Manchester University Press.

Hermes, J. 2006. Citizenship in the Age of the Internet, *European Journal of Communication*, 21(3): 295–309.

Hine, J. 2004. *Children and Citizenship*. Home Office: London.

Hirst, C. 2002. Watch out John Craven, Here's Jimmy Neutron: Why Isn't Commercial TV Interested in News Programmes for Children? The *Independent*, 8 February, http://www.independent.co.uk/news/media/watch-out-john-craven-heres-jimmy-neutron-641552.html

Holloway, S.L. and Valentine, G. 2003. *Cyberkids: Children in the Information Age*. London and New York: Routledge Falmer.

Hujanen, J. and S. Pietkainen. 2004. Interactive Uses of Journalism: Crossing between Technological Potential and Young People's News-Using Practices, *New Media and Society* 6: 383–401.

Iyengar, S. and Jackman, S. 2003. Technology and Politics: Incentives for Youth Participation, Presentation at the International Conference on Civic Education Research. New Orleans, November 16–18.

Lemish, D. and Gotz, M. (eds) 2007. *Children and Media in Times of War and Conflict*. Cresskill, NJ: Hampton.

Lewis, J., Inthorn, S., and Wahl-Jorgensen, K. 2005. *Citizens or Consumers?: What the Media Tell us about Political Participation*. Maidenhead: Open University Press.

Livingstone, S. 2002. *Young People and New Media*. London: Sage.

Livingstone, S. 2003. Children's Use of the Internet: Reflections on the Emerging Research Agenda, *New Media and Society* 5(2): 147–166.

Livingstone, S. 2007. The Challenge of Engaging Youth Online: Contrasting Producers' and Teenagers' Interpretations of Websites, *European Journal of Communication* 22(2): 165–184.

Livingstone, S. and Bovill, M. 1999. *Young People, New Media*. Report of the Research Project Children Young People and the Changing Media Environment. London: London School of Economics and Political Science.

Livingstone, S. and Helsper, E. 2007. Gradations in Digital Inclusion: Children, Young People and the Digital Divide, *New Media and Society* 9(4): 671–696.

Livingstone, S., Couldry, N. and Markham, T. 2007. Youthful Steps Towards Civic Participation: Does the Internet Help? in Loader, B.D. (ed.). *Young Citizens in the Digital Age: Political Engagement, Young People and New Media*. London: Routledge, 21–34.

MacKinnon, M.P. 2008. Talking Politics, Practicing Citizenship, *Education Canada*, 48(1): 64–66.

Matthews, J. 2003. Cultures of Production: Making Children's News, in Simon Cottle, S. (ed.). *Media Organisation and Production*. London: Sage, 131–146.

Matthews, J. 2005. 'Out of the Mouths of Babes and Experts': Children's News and What it Can Teach us about News Access and Professional Mediation, *Journalism Studies*. 6(4) 2005: 509–519.

Matthews, J. 2008. A Missing Link? *Journalism Practice* 2(2): 264–279.

Matthews, J. 2009. Negotiating News Childhoods: News Producers, Visualized Audiences and the Production of the Children's News Agenda, *Journal of Children and Media*, 3(1): 2–18.

Messenger Davies, M. 1997. *Fake, Fact, and Fantasy: Children's Interpretations of Television Reality*. Mahwah, NJ: Lawrence Erlbaum.

Messenger Davies, M. 2001. '*Dear BBC*': *Children, Television Storytelling and the Public Sphere*. Cambridge: Cambridge University Press.

Messenger Davies, M. 2007 'And what good came of it at last?' Ethos, Style and Sense of Audience in the Reporting of War by Children's News Programs, in Lemish, D. and Gotz, D. (eds). *Children and Media in Times of War and Conflict*. Cresskill, NJ: Hampton.

Milani, R. 2008. Personal interview, February 8th.

Ponte, C. 2008. Children in the News, Children and the News – Notes from a Portuguese research project. *News on Children, Youth and Media: International Clearinghouse* (1).

Putnam, R. 2000. *Bowling Alone: The Collapse and Revival of American Community*. New York: Simon and Schuster.

Raeymaeckers, K. 2004. Newspaper Editors in Search of Young Readers: Content and Layout Strategies to Win New Readers, *Journalism Studies* 5(2): 221–232.

Sweetser, K.D., and Kaid, L.L. 2008. Stealth Soapboxes: Political Information Efficacy, Cynicism and Uses of Celebrity Weblogs among Readers, *New Media Society* 10 (1): 67–91.

van der Molen, J.W. 2004. Violence and Suffering in Television News: Toward a Broader Conception of Harmful Television Content for Children, *Paediatrics*, 112(6), June: 1771–1775.

van der Voort, T.H.A., Beentjes, J.W.J., Bovill, M., Gaskell, G., Koolstra, C.M., Livingstone, S. and Marseille, N. 1998. Young People's Ownership and Uses of New and Old Forms of Media in Britain and the Netherlands. *European Journal of Communication* 13 (4): 457–477.

Villani, S. 2001. Impact of Media on Children and Adolescents: A 10-Year Review of the Research. *Journal of the American Academy of Child & Adolescent Psychiatry*. 40(4):392–401.

Wartella, E. 1994. Producing Children's Television Programs. In Ettema, J.S. and Whitney, D.C. (eds), *Audiencemaking: How the Media Create the Audience*. Thousand Oaks, CA: Sage.

Wayne, M., Henderson, L., Murray, C., Petley, J. 2008. Television and the Symbolic Criminalization of Young People, *Journalism Studies* 9(1): 75–90.

Wilska, T.A. 2003. Mobile Phone Use as Part of Young People's Consumption Styles, *Journal of Consumer Policy* 26: 441–463.

42

NEWS AND MEMORY: OLD AND NEW MEDIA PASTS

Andrew Hoskins

News media, particularly television news, seem to shape in an ongoing way an historical consciousness of today's events. The unfolding details of everyday life – our personal biographies – intersect with larger society through the aperture of the news media. Just as personal memory works through the matching of the here-and-now with an intelligible there-and-then, by shifting context, re-framing meaning and massive selectivity, news media function in a similar fashion. The discourses, sounds, and images of news simultaneously mediate our ongoing experience of the world out there as they revivify certain pasts and particular elements of those pasts and always at the expense of others (see also Hoskins, 2004a). Despite this, there is surprisingly little sustained academic study exploring the role of news and journalism in shaping individual, social and cultural memory. For instance, as Zelizer (2008: 80) states: 'decades into the systematic scholarly study of collective memory, there is still no default understanding of memory that includes journalism as one of its vital and critical agents'. Thus, the who, how, and why of the continual re-articulation of the past as and in news has been buried by an amnesiac scholarship and by journalists themselves who as Zelizer maintains are not very conscious of their agency in social remembering and forgetting.

There are some notable exceptions, including, for example: Kitch (2005); Edy (2006) and Volkmer (ed.) (2006). The commonality of these accounts and other studies of the relationship between media and memory (see, for example, Erll and Rigney (eds.) (2009) are that they are undertaken principally in the fields of media and communication studies and the broader social sciences. This in itself is not surprising. However, in those disciplines – notably the human sciences and particularly psychology – which dominate the field of individual memory – there is relatively little work studying the impact of mass media on human remembering and forgetting. Moreover, there is very little cross-fertilization of theories and methods between the human and social sciences brought to bear on a collaborative interrogation of the media shaping of memory.

In this chapter, I examine some of the challenges for the interdisciplinary study of memory in the period identified as the 'memory boom' (Huyssen, 2003) and which is marked by a rapid and ongoing transformation in all-things-media. Notably, there is underway a simultaneous and paradigmatic shift in two landscapes, or rather 'ecologies': media and memory. It is not merely that the transformations in and of media are drivers of the memory boom, but that there is a need for a reassessment of the nature and the very value of remembering subject to the technologies of and the discourses disseminated by media. News and journalism are part products and part engines of this ecological shift, and their memorial value requires significant exposition for any holistic understanding of how societies remember and forget.

Moreover, a supremely significant and consequential shift for memory (individual, social, and cultural) as well as news is embedded in the move from the broadcast to the post-broadcast age. None of the 'what', 'how', 'why' and 'when' of remembering and forgetting, are untouched by the advent of the digital media. What I have called the 'mediatization of memory' (Hoskins, 2009) is premised upon our being at that very juncture of transition from an ordered mediascape to a disordered media ecology. There is an emergent tension between a perspective overwhelmingly informed by the theories, models and methods of an era of unambiguously 'mass' media (including the idea of 'media events') a corollary of which is the re-establishment of the notion of 'collective' memory, and a diverse if somewhat fragmented scholarship that adopts a more radical position. Notably, the latter envisages a paradigmatic shift to a 'new media ecology' (Hoskins and O'Loughlin, 2009) that necessitates a critical re-evaluation of the legacy of mass communication/media studies, and proposes a more dynamic and diffused model of 'the mediation of everything' (Livingstone, 2009). In terms of the study of memory, this is something of a double-whammy. It was already challenging enough to advocate the study of news and journalism, for instance, into research on why and how individuals, groups and societies remember and forget, in the broadcast era. Today, however, this challenge extends to addressing the impact of the fluidization of digitized content, the revelation of a 'long tail' (Anderson, 2007) of the past, the new modes of participation in semi-public memory through the increasingly affordable and available tools of digital recording and dissemination. This entails the 'inter-medial' and 'trans-medial' (Erll, 2008) dynamics of old and new media, and thereby the related rise of a 'convergence' culture (Jenkins, 2006).

News generations

Nodal news events are often constructed (in news and popular culture) as synonymous with a particular decade or generation. Yet, it is easy to dismiss as technologically deterministic those proclaiming that paradigmatic shifts in the technologies that produced the news of each generation somehow shape different kinds of remembering and forgetting. However, Volkmer's (2006) pioneering transnational and trans-generational study provides important evidence of the co-evolution of media and memory. The 'Global Media Generations' project launched in 1998 applied Mannheim's (1952) 'theory of generations' to a study of three cohorts selected on the basis of their experience of media particular to their 'formative' years. Thus the corpus was divided into (1) those born between 1924 and 1929, their formative years being 1935–1945, the 'print/radio' generation, (2) those born between 1954 and 1959, their formative years being 1965–1975, the 'black-and-white television generation', and (3) those born 1979–1984, their formative years being 1989–1999, which were labelled the 'Internet generation' (Volkmer, 2006: 6–7). The importance of 'formative years' to memory is termed 'the reminiscent bump' by some psychologists and relates to the memories drawn from the lifespan between the ages of 10 and 30, for all subjects aged over around 35 years (Rubin et al., 1998). Knowledge acquired during this period has been found to be highly accessible and includes the recall of public events and popular culture as well as more personal and autobiographical memories (Williams et al., 2008: 59). So, if we accept that the sharing of public memories is related to the mechanisms and extent of mediation of the subject of those memories, then not only is the medium of the original event and experience significant, but also its potential for technological translation into different media (i.e. 'remediation'). Put another way, what are the shifting means through which, when and to what extent mediated events come to be experienced by particular generational cohorts?

The Global Generations Media project employed a framework of generational 'entelechies' (Mannheim, 1952), notably: the structuring of the common experiences of each generation, thus the creation of 'incessantly superseded, creatively willed generational world-views' (Kettler and Loader, 2004: 163). So, from their work on this project, Kumar et al. (2006: 218) argue:

> The process of collective elaboration of memories itself seems to create such 'generational units'. There is a certain kind of connectivity among those who share some knowledge or experiences. They are able to connect with one another and to understand each other. In the media age, then, generations do not only appear as sociodemographic units (as contemporaries, for instance) but as groups of people who share knowledge, preferences, habits, beliefs, experiences, and memories. Media generations, then, are widening because more and more people of different age groups and from different ethnic and cultural contexts share the same or similar media experiences; they know the same mediated events as they are reported worldwide, presented, and repeated, put on the Internet, or stored on tape, CD, DVD, etc.

So, whereas in the older cohorts of the Global Generations Media project, 'media memories were specific to a technology ... younger generations were awash in media product. As media become more enveloping, the source became less important' (Slade, 2006: 207). In this way, the digital media literacy of the young is an important differentiator of their emergent generational entelechy, and perhaps radically so in comparison to the development and shifts in mass media experienced by preceding generations. This is precisely the challenge I introduced earlier in the need to assess the impact of the fluidization of digitized content, the revelation of a 'long tail' of the past, and the availability of new modes of digitally-afforded participation in new kinds of public spheres. Unfortunately, it is difficult to assess the digital generation's memories of their formative years, given that their reminiscent memory bump is not clearly discernible for most subjects until they are aged into their thirties.

Moreover, I wish to suggest that it is the temporal transformations ushered in by new media which require investigation as much as the spatial (a key emphasis of the Global Generations project) in shaping and restricting the potential of memory forged through the technologies of our everyday digital media. For instance, the Internet does not merely avail an interweaving of past and present, but a new networked 'coevalness', of connectivity and data transfer, that mediatizes memory in new ways. In this respect I differentiate between the broadcast and the post-broadcast eras as suggestive of the formation of two intersecting but none the less distinct formations of memory beyond-the-individual, namely 'collective' and 'connective' memory, respectively. To do this I identify the (mostly psychological) study of so-called 'flashbulb memory' as indicative of a generational orientation to news or 'media events' particular to the televisual or broadcast era, as well as such mass-mediated events being seen as synonymous with assumptions as to the formation of collective memory. Instead, I contend that memory in the post-broadcast age is more effectively characterized through its digital 'connectivity' and its 'diffusion' through and across everyday media consumption and practices.

Collective memory in the broadcast age

To the extent that one can identify an era of modern news media there is also seen to be a related period of modern mass and 'collective memory'. The term 'collective' (rather than 'social') has been most attached to the study of memory beyond the individual. This is attributable in part to the 1980 translation into English of Maurice Halbwachs's (1914–1945) *The Collective Memory* (which was first published in 1950 as *La Mémoire Collective*, but was written in the 1930s). It is easy to identify the age of mass media as the age of collective memory. Radio's and later television's capacity to mediate simultaneously to a national and now routinely global audience provided in this way a common and shared experience, and thus arguably memories, of nodal news events. In the academic study of so-called 'media events', i.e. when programming schedules are interrupted and 24-hour news channels move to continuing extended coverage of a major news story, these are seen as extraordinarily powerful in shaping memory. Dayan and Katz (1992: 213), for example, argue: 'media events and their narration are in competition with the writing of history in defining the contents of collective memory. Their disruptive and heroic character is indeed what is remembered, upstaging the efforts of historians and social scientists to perceive continuities and to reach beyond the personal'.

In fact there is something of a paradox to the ways in which news media and specifically journalists are presumed to shape our understandings of the past. To cite Dayan and Katz: 'Where academic historians see events as projective of underlying trends, journalists prefer a stroboscopic history which flashes dramatic events on and off the screen' (1992: 22). So, one can see a strong correlation between that which drives news agendas ('news values') and the features that are claimed to shape enduring memories such as surprising or shocking events; newsworthiness is translated into collective memory through striking images and accounts. These elements of nodal news events and strong visual memories are brought together in psychology in the study of so-called 'flashbulb memory' (FBM) (Brown and Kulik, 1977; Winograd and Neisser (eds), 1992; Conway, 1995). FBM describes human memory that can apparently be recalled very vividly and in great detail, as though reproduced directly from the original experience. Such memories are said to possess a 'photographic' quality, owing to the apparent visual clarity of the reproduction of the image in the mind's eye. For instance, events that elicit a greater emotional response (e.g. from surprise or shock) and that are deemed to have greater (private and/or public) consequentiality, are frequently noted in psychological studies as key factors in strengthening FBMs (see e.g. Finkenauer et al., 1997).

FBMs of public happenings are linked directly with the hearing (and also viewing) of the news of momentous events and often mark historical memory (an assassination of a political leader, a natural catastrophe, or a terrorist attack, for example). Despite the photographic metaphor, most studies of FBMs have taken television and television news as their modus operandi. Consequently, the most studied public FBMs are those defined by their 'televisuality' (Caldwell, 1995) and also the concept of the 'media event' (Dayan and Katz, 1992), for example: the 1986 explosion of the Space Shuttle *Challenger*; the 1997 death of Diana, Princess of Wales, and the terrorist attacks of September 11, 2001 (see Winograd and Neisser (eds), 1992; Julian et al., 2009; and Hirst and Meksin, 2009, respectively).

However, the origins of the study of FBM do appear to predate the advent of the modern mass media. For example, writing in an 1899 issue of the *American Journal of Psychology*, F.W. Colegrove details his testing of 'a well known pedagogical principle ... that vivid impressions are easily recalled' through comparing individual memories of the hearing of the news of the assassination of a nineteenth-century American president (1899: 247). He asked 179 people: 'Do you recall where you were when you heard that Lincoln was shot'? (p. 247) Even though the question was put some 33 years after the death of President Lincoln, 127 of Colegrove's respondents claimed to remember and provided full details of what they said was the context of their learning of the news for the first time. The surprise, consequentiality and emotional response to an event are frequently noted in psychological studies as key factors in strengthening FB memories so catastrophic events deemed of national, international and historical magnitude tend to predominate in these studies, for example, the 1967 assassination of President John F. Kennedy; the 1986 explosion of the US Space Shuttle *Challenger*; and the terrorist attacks on the United States on September 11, 2001.

Ironically, perhaps, the *Challenger* catastrophe does not have the memorial resonance of the other two of these examples, and resides more in the academic literature of FBM than in the wider public memory it seeks to illuminate! However, one consistent cross-medial commonality of FBMs (and those selected for study) is their real-time or 'live' quality. The shock of witnessing the unfolding of a catastrophic event via television news seems seductive to memory. For instance, a majority of Americans polled at the time believed that they had seen the Kennedy assassination live on television. Yet, the original Zapruder film had been stored in a vault at *Time-Life* until five years after the event, and had only been available as photographs during this period (Esch, 1999).

But the very same processes of the recycling, repetition and remediation of news images and footage that effect a shift in the memory of the experiential context of an event (the 'where were you when' question) can also be seen to restrict, to inure, to deaden the memory. The iconic footage of the planes crashing and the collapse of the Twin Towers in New York on 9/11 was obsessively repeated on (especially US) television news for hours, days, and months following the attacks, including being played in slow-motion and even backwards (on ABC News). In this way the perpetual remediation of the once mesmerizing event as and in news (and across other media genres) produces a 'collapse of memory' (Hoskins, 2004b).

An important question to pose then is, if these events had not been visually documented, what would their original public dissemination have looked like and, given their much diminished potential for reproduction, mediation and remediation, how would this have restricted their historical trajectories in collective memory (and its subsequent collapse) as it undoubtedly would. Without the pathway into the future that is constructed through both inter- and intra-generational media, events are more likely to flicker and fade in memory.

In addition to a general absence of the employment of the literature and theories of media and communication studies in these psychological accounts, a detailed and systematic analysis of media content itself appears to be seen as mostly beyond their remit. However, given the fact that the study of FBM is so embedded in the era of broadcast television news, there is not sufficient consideration of the extent to which there is a 'co-evolution' (see Grusin, forthcoming) of media and memory. And it is this dynamic that I consider is part of the process of the mediatization of memory. Namely, this involves a generational renewal of the experiencing and remembering of public events in relation to the technological and cultural shifts in media and journalism.

Diffused memory in the post-broadcast age

Even within the broadcast era, flashbulb news events were – and still are – particularly vulnerable to repetition, rehearsal, and recycling, by the medium of their 'production'. Massively increased competition amongst news producers and providers over the past decade has driven a greater promotional (and emotional) attachment to the product of news as a means of standing out in a crowded and highly globalized (in terms of presentational format and style) market. Correspondents, programmes and networks have shifted their orientation to events on which they report from 'here is the world', to 'we bring you the world', and now even to 'welcome to *our* world'. The discursive relationships constructed by reporters with the subject of their reporting have become much more self-reflexive, as they position themselves increasingly as witnesses to, if not participants in events. Indeed the role of journalists as 'witnesses' to the events on which they report has attracted a great deal of attention in recent years (see Peters, 2001; Zelizer, 2002; and Frosh and Pinchevski (eds), 2009). Yet, the very same technologies and media that have availed greater mobility and thus immediacy and proximity for journalists and other news-workers to the event on which they report, have also opened up similar opportunities for anyone and everyone, be they in pursuit of the dramatic and the catastrophic, or accidental bystanders.

Just as events are appropriated as 'news' by networks, producers and correspondents, affording them a certain authorial status premised upon the news values of immediacy, proximity, and a certain exclusivity in terms of publication and broadcast space, so this is at the very same time being challenged by the new 'pro-sumers' who routinely record their co-presence to events deemed publicly nodal (*and* those previously restricted to the domain of the personal and the familial) and who publish indiscriminately on websites, blogs, and social networking sites, for example.

The trinity of authorship, ownership and witness was formerly the journalists' guarantor in their shaping of a 'metamemory'[1] or 'metahistory' of events, in other words those who have control or ownership of that medium or media are potentially able to powerfully influence the future trajectory and continuance (or discontinuance) of the public memory of a given event. Yet, today, there is something of a paradox in the idea that there is a breakdown in an institutionalized metamemory of events, given the rise of digital media (for instance, as proclaimed in the title of Clay Shirky's (2008) book: *Here Comes Everybody*) and that of the notion of repetition and saturation as indicative of the memory-shaping power of the intensity of the mass-mediated experience (see, for example, Gitlin, 2001).

So, whereas the influence of the news media and particularly television (the era in which most of the studies of FBM have emerged) is seen in terms of the nodal, the dramatic and the extraordinary, paradoxically, the function of news in memory is also a consequence of its repetition, saturation, and today, its 'remediation' (Bolter and Grusin, 1999). Thus, as psychologists argue that memory works through 'the rehearsal' (Parkin, 2003) it can be argued that mass media are a prime shaper of memory as Hirst and Meksin (2009: 213) observe: 'Media coverage is the quintessential externally driven act of rehearsal'. In this way, the idea of the news media as producing, using and reinforcing an ongoing repertoire or archive of images, sounds, events, so that journalism involves a kind of 'translation' of collective memory, is quite compelling.

One of the metaphors sometimes used in support of this argument is that of the 'archive'. It is sometimes seen as synonymous with the 'mass media' and detrimental in terms of its capacity to replace or overburden the dynamics of human memory (Nora, 1989). Furthermore, the accumulation of media data in the form of archives, or a 'turn to' the past, is viewed as a response to uncertainties and insecurities of the present (nostalgia, for example). Notably, the need or desire to preserve the past as a necessary element of remembering that the same past is a key sign of this trend. The vast archival capacities delivered by new technologies and their use by the mass media have fundamentally transformed the politics of memory in relation to both what of the past is remembered and how it is remembered. One can point to the extensive accumulation of archives as also partly responsive to a fear of the 'loss' of the past.

However, the permanency (of storage and availability) associated with the archive has become more porous: media and technologies not only translate what has been called 'cultural memory' (notably that which exists after and beyond generational memory) is dying or has died out. Rather, diffused memory is a 'living memory' that is articulated through the everyday digital connectivity of the self (with others and with the past) that can be continually produced, accessed and updated, but which also is subject to different although none the less highly significant modes of 'forgetting'.

The popular usage of metaphors of memory are often based upon technologies and media (written, photographic, taped), notably a comparison with some permanent medium of storage (Neisser, 2008: 81). However, digital media introduce different equations of ephemera into our remembering processes and capacities as well as a new means to preserve, restore and to represent the past. Indeed, digital memory technologies also effect what Bowker (2005) calls 'inaugural acts' where the old is overwritten by the new. The mediatized diffusion of memory is thus the ongoing negotiation of the self through and interplay with the emergent technologies of the day to shape a past that is, to borrow from Gitelman, 2006, 'always already new'.

For instance, to take Merrin's (2008) excellent characterization of a paradigm shift from mass media to a new post-broadcast age:

> In place of a top-down, one-to-many vertical cascade from centralised industry sources we discover today bottom-up, many-to-many, horizontal, peer-to-peer communication. 'Pull' media challenge 'push' media; open structures challenge hierarchical structures; micro-production challenges macro-production; open-access amateur production challenges closed access, elite-professions; economic and technological barriers to media production are transformed by cheap, democratised, easy-to-use technologies; the single expert voice is threatened by the 'long tail' of expertise; the 'lecture' is replaced by the 'conversation'; the individual as consumer is complemented by the individual as producer and user and broadcasting to a mass-market is challenged by niche and nano-publishing. The contrast may be too heavily drawn and big media remain present and powerful but the rise of me-casting, my-casting and me-dia represents a significant and very real transformation of the broadcasting era.[2]

Merrin's qualification in the final sentence of this extract is an important one, although not just because it signals a note of caution for any approach that seeks to highlight transformation over continuation in any present and unfolding context. Rather it is precisely these emergent tensions and complexities that need illumination as shapers of new mediatized forms of memory. One can go further to suggest that Merrin's articulation of new 'structures' of 'micro' and 'amateur' media production can be seen to fit with accounts that identify new 'principles' of organization underlying our new media ecology.

For instance, Knorr Cetina draws upon John Urry's (2003) notion of 'complexity' to argue: 'Global systems based on microstructural principles do not exhibit institutional complexity but rather the asymmetries, unpredictabilities and playfulness of complex (and dispersed) interaction patterns' (Knorr Cetina, 2005: 214). This, I wish to contend, can be applied to the underlying structure of the common experiences – the 'entelechy' (Volkmer, 2006: 7) – of the digital generation, and this would include growing up in an ecology in which media production and consumption have become de-differentiated.

News and journalism seen as constitutive of the organizations and archives of the broadcast era are thus also being reshaped through (as much as shaping of) the contingencies of 'microstructural principles'. In this way, the future of the authority and authenticity of journalists as mediators of memory in this system is uncertain. The slippage in the exclusivity of the traditional journalistic production of news that powerfully shaped 'collective memory' at the very least suggests a need for an interdisciplinary re-evaluation of work around 'flashbulb memory' and other products of the broadcast age. Rather, the diffused and digital practices and prisms of the emergent new media entelechy will shape and reshape new 'connective memories' going forward. Of course, there is some deep convergence ongoing between the sometimes seemingly dichotomous broadcast and post-broadcast cultures and media. Ultimately, however, the media that produce, reproduce, and remediate increasingly digital content, contribute to a more fluid, diffused and unpredictable ecology, that appear to enable the genesis of new 'microstructures of memory'.

Notes

1 Here I draw loosely on the common psychological usage of the term metamemory as 'knowledge about one's memory capabilities and strategies that can aid memory, as well as the processes involved in memory self-monitoring' (Jasmeet Pannu and Alfred Kasniak, 2005: 105).
2 William Merrin (2008) 'Media Studies 2.0' available at: http://twopointzeroforum.blogspot.com/ (accessed January 2008).

References

Anderson, Chris (2007) *The Long Tail: How Endless Choice is Creating Unlimited Demand*, London: Random House Books.
Assmann, Jan (1995) 'Collective Memory and Cultural Identity', *New German Critique*, 65: 125–133.
Bolter, Jay David and Grusin, Richard (1999) *Remediation: Understanding New Media*, Cambridge, MA: The MIT Press.
Bowker, Geoffrey C. (2005) *Memory Practices in the Sciences*, Cambridge, MA: MIT Press.
Brown, Roger and Kulik, James (1977) 'Flashbulb Memories', *Cognition* 5, 73–99.
Caldwell, John Thornton (1995) *Televisuality: Style, Crisis, and Authority in American Television*, New Brunswick: Rutgers University Press.
Colegrove, F. W. (1899) 'Individual Memories', *American Journal of Psychology*, 10(2), 228–255.
Conway, Martin (1995) *Flashbulb Memories*, Hove: Lawrence Erlbaum.
Dayan, Daniel and Katz, Elihu (1992) *Media Events: The Live Broadcasting of History*, Harvard: Harvard University Press.
Edy, Jill (2006) *Troubled Pasts: News and the Collective Memory of Social Unrest*, Philadelphia, PA: Temple University Press.
Erll, Astrid (2008) 'Literature, Film, and the Mediality of Cultural Memory' in Erll, Astrid and Nünning, Ansgar (eds.) *Cultural Memory Studies: An Interdisiplinary Handbook*, Berlin: Walter de Gruyter: 389–398.
Erll, Astrid and Rigney, Ann (eds.) (2009) *Mediation, Remediation, and the Dynamics of Cultural Memory*, Berlin: Mouton de Gruyter.

Esch, Deborah (1999) 'No time like the present' at http://www.pum.umontreal.ca/revues/surfaces/vol3/esch.html (accessed March 2003).

Finkenauer, Catron et al. (1998) 'Flashbulb memories and the underlying mechanisms of their formation: Toward an emotional-integrative model', *Memory and Cognition*, 26(3): 516–531.

Frosh, Paul and Pinchevski, Amit (2009) *Media Witnessing: Testimony in the Age of Mass Communication*, New York: Palgrave Macmillan.

Gitelman, Lisa (2006) *Always Already New: Media, History and the Data of Culture*, Cambridge, MA: MIT Press.

Gitlin, Todd (2001) *Media Unlimited: How the Torrent of Images and Sounds Overwhelms Our Lives*, New York: Metropolitan Books.

Grusin, Richard (forthcoming) *Premediation*.

Halbwachs, Maurice (1980) *The Collective Memory*, London: Harper & Row.

Hirst, William and Meksin, Robert (2009) 'A social-interactional approach to the retention of collective memories of flashbulb events' in Luminet and Curci (eds) (see entry below), pp. 207–225.

Hoskins, Andrew (2004a) *Televising War: From Vietnam to Iraq*, London: Continuum.

Hoskins, Andrew (2004b) 'Television and the Collapse of Memory', *Time & Society*, 13(1) 109–127.

Hoskins, Andrew (2009) 'The Mediatization of Memory' in Garde-Hansen, Joanne, Hoskins, Andrew and Reading, Anna (eds.) *Save As . . . Digital Memories*, Basingstoke: Palgrave Macmillan.

Hoskins, Andrew and O'Loughlin, Ben (forthcoming) *War and Media: The Emergence of Diffused War*, Cambridge: Polity Press.

Huyssen, Andreas (2003) *Present Pasts: Urban Palimpsests and the Politics of Memory*, Stanford: Stanford University Press.

Jenkins, Henry (2006) *Convergence Culture: Where Old and New Media Collide*, New York: New York University Press.

Julian, Megan et al. (2009) 'Measures of flashbulb memory: Are elaborate memories consistently accurate?' in Luminet and Curci (eds.) (see entry below), pp. 99–122.

Kettler, David and Loader, Colin (2004) 'Karl Mannheim and problems of historical time', *Time & Society*, 13(2/3): 155–172.

Kitch, Carolyn (2005) *Pages from the Past: History and Memory in American Magazines*, Chapel Hill: University of North Carolina Press.

Knorr Cetina, Karin (2005) 'Complex global microstructures: The new terrorist societies, *Theory, Culture & Society*, 22(5): 213–234.

Kumar, Keval J. et al. (2006) 'Construction of Memory' in Volkmer, Ingrid (ed.) (see entry below), pp. 211–224.

Livingstone, Sonia 'On the Mediation of everything': ICA Presidential Address; Journal of Communication, 59: 1–18.

Luminet, Olivier and Curci, Antonietta (eds.) (2009) *Flashbulb Memories: New Issues and New Perspectives*, New York: Psychology Press.

Mannheim, Karl (1952) *Essays in the Sociology of Knowledge*, London: Routledge & Kegan Paul.

Merrin, William (2008) 'Media Studies 2.0', at: http://mediastudies2point0.blogspot.com/

Neisser, Ulric (1982) *Memory Observed: Remembering in Natural Contexts*. New York: W.H. Freeman and Company.

Neisser, Ulric (2008) 'Memory with a Grain of Salt' in Wood, Harriet Harvey and Byatt, A. S. (eds.) *Memory: An Anthology*, London: Chatto & Windus, pp. 80–88.

Nora, Pierre (1989) 'Between Memory and History: *Les Lieux de Mémoire*', translated by Marc Roudebush, *Representations*, 26: 7–25.

Pannu, Jasmeet and Kaszniak, Alfred (2005) 'Metamemory Experiments in Neurological Populations: A Review', in *Neuropsychology Review*, 15 (3): 105–130.

Parkin, Alan J. (1993) *Memory: Phenomena, Experiment and Theory*, Oxford: Blackwell.

Peters, John Durham (2001) 'Witnessing', *Media, Culture & Society*, 23(6): 707–723.

Rubin, David C. et al. (1988) 'Autobiographical Memory Across the Lifespan' in Rubin, David C. (ed.) *Autobiographical Memory*, Cambridge: Cambridge University Press, pp. 202–224.

Slade, Christina (2006) 'Perceptions and Memories of the Media Context' in Volkmer, Ingrid (ed.) (see entry below), pp. 195–210.

Shirky, Clay (2008) *Here Comes Everybody: The Power of Organizing Without Organizations*, London: Allen Lane.

Urry, John (2003) *Global Complexity*, Cambridge: Polity.

Volkmer, Ingrid (ed.) (2006) *News in Public Memory: An International Study of Media Memories Across Generations*, New York: Peter Lang.

Williams, Helen L. et al (2008) 'Autobiographical Memory' in Cohen, Gillian and Conway, Martin, A. (eds.) *Memory in the Real World*, Hove: Psychology Press, pp. 21–90.

Winograd, Eugene and Neisser, Ulric (eds.) (1992) *Affect and Accuracy in Recall: Studies of 'Flashbulb' Memories*, Cambridge: Cambridge University Press.

Zelizer, Barbie (1992) *Covering the Body: The Kennedy Assassination, the Media, and the Shaping of Collective Memory*, Chicago: University of Chicago Press.

Zelizer, Barbie (2002) 'Photography, journalism, and trauma' in Zelizer, Barbie and Allan, Stuart (eds.) *Journalism After September 11*, London: Routledge, pp. 48–68.

Zelizer, Barbie (2008) 'Why Memory's Work on Journalism Does Not Reflect Journalism's Work on Memory', *Memory Studies*, 1(1): 79–87.

PART VI

CRISIS, CONFLICT AND CONTROVERSY

43

GLOBAL CRISES AND WORLD NEWS ECOLOGY

Simon Cottle

... the cosmopolitan outlook means that, in a world of global crises and dangers produced by civilization, the old differentiations between internal and external, national and international, us and them, lose their validity and a new cosmopolitan realism becomes essential to survival.

Ulrich Beck (2006) *The Cosmopolitan Vision*, p. 14

We live in the global age. We live in a world that has become radically interconnected, interdependent and communicated in the complex formations and flows of news journalism. We also inhabit a world increasingly defined by global crises. From climate change to the global war on terror, from financial meltdowns to forced migrations, from pandemics to world poverty, and from humanitarian disasters to the denial of human rights, global crises represent the dark side of our 'negatively globalized planet' (Bauman 2007: 25). Global crises are endemic to our globalized and globalizing world; they are *spawned* by it. Through processes of news mediation they can also *shape* it; deepening a sense of globality and helping to forge a 'cosmopolitan outlook' or the shared recognition that global threats to humanity and the planet demand coordinated and cooperative global responses. This is what Ulrich Beck means when he speaks of a new 'civilizational community of fate' (Beck 2006: 13).

In today's world, global crises cannot be regarded as exceptional or aberrant events only, seemingly erupting without rhyme or reason or dislocated from the contemporary world (dis)order. They are not confined within particular national borders, nor are they best accounted for through national prisms of understanding. Their impacts register across 'sovereign' national territories, surrounding regions and beyond and they can also become subject to systems of governance and forms of civil society response that are sometimes no less encompassing or transnational in scope. Global crises also depend, in large measure, on how they become signaled and defined, constructed and contested in the complex flows and formations of today's world news ecology.

In exercising their symbolic and communicative power, the world's news media can variously inform processes of public understanding and political response and so too can they variously distance and dissimulate the nature of the threats that confront us, marginalizing those views and voices that seek to build wider public recognition and mobilize forces for change. The scale of death and destruction involved or the potentially catastrophic consequences of global threats are no guarantee that they will register prominently, if at all, in the world's news media, much less that they will be defined therein as a global crisis. We know that 'hidden wars' and 'forgotten disasters' still abound in the world today and, because of their media invisibility, may command neither global recognition nor wider political response (AlertNet 2008).

Global crises, then, can become differently *constituted within* the news media as much as *communicated by* them. It is both surprising and regrettable, therefore, with too few exceptions, researchers of media and communications have thus far failed to concertedly theorize and empirically examine today's endemic, proliferating and often overlapping global crises or their complex dependencies on the world's news media. This chapter, based on more detailed discussion elsewhere (Cottle 2006, 2009a, 2009b), argues that the complex of communication flows and differentiated formations of the world's news media, termed here the 'world news ecology', now enters into and conditions the communication of global crises and often does so in consequential ways, from the outside in, and inside out, defining their nature and contributing to their course and conduct. To help ground these claims the discussion that follows makes reference to a number of recent global crises and discerns three analytically distinguishable modalities of global crisis reporting within today's world's news ecology. This serves to illuminate something of the representational complexities that lie behind the seeming 'cultural chaos' of global journalism (McNair 2006) and hopefully encourages the need for closer empirical engagement when reflecting on the nature of global communications in a crisis world (Lull 2007).

The chapter considers the enhanced *surveillance* capacity of the global news ecology in spotlighting struggles for human rights and democracy around the world and how this conditions both forces of reaction and progressive change. We also address how the world's news ecology can transform national humanitarian disasters into *global focusing events*, circulating competing national discourses and geo-political voices of criticism and dissent – worldwide. Finally, we turn to how the news media can themselves, on occasion, adopt a more performative stance towards some global crises, such as climate change, 'spectacularizing' them through the deliberate production of spectacular and dramatic images deployed to raise awareness and mobilize concern. Here we also consider how the performative use of *mediated spectacle* can sometimes assume a much less benign function when deployed, for example, in the 'global war on terror'. In this context, images of 'symbolic violence' and 'violent symbolism', defined below, have been deliberately staged and choreographed by governments, military and insurgents in pursuit of their strategic goals and disseminated by the world's news media.

In and across these different modalities of global crisis reporting, as we shall hear, it is possible to detect political control and discursive closure as well as political opportunities and discursive openings. These complexities have yet to be recognized, comparatively studied and properly theorized in respect of the world's endemic, proliferating global crises and threats. But first a few more words on world news ecology, a defining feature of our global age.

World news ecology: enveloping, complexly structured, interpenetrating

Such is the centrality of the world's news ecology within processes of problem definition, awareness, legitimation and mobilization today, that for a global crisis to exist it must generally be seen to exist in the news media by a great number of people, not all of whom may be directly involved. Global crises, then, are communicated and in important respects constituted in and through today's world news ecology. This communicative space comprises overlapping and interpenetrating communication flows, traditional mainstream and alternative news media, and new interactive technologies of news dissemination and user-generated content. Its political economy, ownership structures, and leading news agencies and 24/7 global news services all reinforce the dominant positioning of Western media corporations, interests and agendas (Thussu 2007) but today's world news ecology is complexly structured none the less (Rai and Cottle 2007). Regional and national news formations, both established and emergent, as well as contra-news flows from the 'rest to the West', the local to the global, and new oppositional and alternative sources of news and crossover journalism productions all make for a far more complex communicative space of world news than could have been envisaged even a few years ago (see Figure 43.1).

Traditional newspapers and mainstream broadcasting still predominate within this news ecology but they are increasingly contiguous with the ubiquitous internet and its enhanced connectivity, interactivity and invigoration of new forms of online journalism and blogosphere(s), and indeed most have felt compelled to establish their own online presence. For the most part, however, mainstream journalism organizations, news outlets and associated ideas of professionalism continue to enact traditional ideas and practices of editorial control, agenda-setting and source access, selecting who enters 'their' news domain and how and when – though they increasingly make use of forms of citizen journalism and growing blogosphere (Allan and Thorsen 2009).

The following now pursues some of the complex ways in which different global crises including political conflicts and the struggle for human rights, major (*un*)natural disasters, climate change, and the war on terror, have variously registered in and through this world news ecology, attending to different modalities of crisis reporting and the latter's globalizing impacts.

Global news surveillance, human rights and the march of democracy

In September 2007 Burmese monks dressed in traditional saffron robes defied the Burmese authorities and led mass protests against the appalling poverty and human rights abuses in their country. In 1988 when a similar popular uprising had been attempted it was brutally suppressed by the Burmese junta with the loss of nearly three thousand lives. In 1988 little was known outside Burma of this crushed revolt as the witnesses to these events had no way of communicating them to the outside world. In 2007, in contrast, the so-called 'saffron revolution' palpably registered around the world. Graphic scenes and sounds recorded by mobile phone cameras and camcorders and relayed to the internet and weblogs, in turn, often made their way into the mainstream press and broadcasting news media.

Figure 43.1 *World News Ecology*

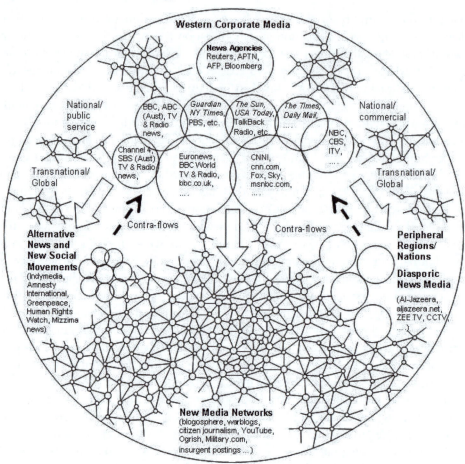

By such means the world's global and nationally-based news media witnessed the progress of the revolt and then its brutal repression via smuggled videos distributed to news agencies and television networks and by online blogs written by dissidents in Rangoon and Mandalay. Images of troops beating demonstrators and firing into unarmed crowds circulated widely. The world also witnessed the last moments of the Japanese video-journalist, Kenji Nagai, being shot at point blank range by a soldier – giving the lie to the official Burmese response that he had died from a stray bullet. The power of these and other images as well as the graphic testimonies of the protestors posted on the internet and picked up by the mainstream Western news media, summoned condemnation from the UN, political leaders and different publics around the world. The words of one blog placed on the front page of a British newspaper, for example, and superimposed over an image of a fleeing monk and subtitled 'Inside the Saffron Revolution', read:

> '...Riot police and soldiers are beating monks ... I saw a truck full of police
> with guns ... They are using tear-gas bombs against the crowd ... Buddhist

monks are now chanting: "All humans be free from killing and torturing" ...
A monk was beaten to death while he was praying ... the military have been
ordered to shoot ... About 200 people were hauled off on to the trucks and
driven away ... One patient died on arriving in hospital – four are still in a bad
way ... They are starting a crackdown ... The junta is reducing the internet
connection bandwidth ... I think they will cut off communication ... We are
so afraid.'

The *Independent*, 27 September 2007, p. 1

Visceral accounts such as these poured out of Burma at the height of the crack-down,
demonstrating the capacity of the internet and its so-called blogosphere to infuse
traditional mainstream news media with first-hand, experiential accounts and vitalize
global news reporting (Allan 2006, Pallister 2007, Reese et al. 2007).

This flood of powerful testimonies, accounts and images conveyed around the
world by new and old means of communication undoubtedly caused consternation
in the Burmese junta which quickly sought to regain control of the communications
environment. The regime had quickly barred TV crews from entering the country, it
then pulled the plug on all but the state-run television service, closed down telephone
lines and the country's principal internet server and forced internet cafes to close under
threat of reprisals. It finally set about tracking down computers and video-cameras
smuggled into the country by external dissidents. Dissidents and alternative news
sites based in exile none the less continued to disseminate flows of information and
eye-witness accounts. The Democratic Voice of Burma, originally an opposition short-
wave radio station, for example, continued to operate out of Norway; Mizzima News,
established by a group of independent Burmese journalists in 1998, and based in Delhi,
ran a news bureau in Thailand that provided an email news service and online video
site with updates and eyewitness testimonies; and an Irrawaddy magazine also run by
exiles in Thailand provided 'citizen reporter' accounts online – all in defiance of the
regime's attempted stranglehold on Burmese communications (Pallister 2007: 5).

These examples help to illustrate the complex communication flows between
different regions, across national borders and different mainstream and independent
news services and sources and how, together, they have enhanced the capability for
news surveillance, throwing a world spotlight on a repressive regime and the struggle
for democracy and human rights. Though, in this instance, the Burmese junta managed
to regain communication control relatively easily (only 1% of the Burmese population
ordinarily have access to the internet for example) this was not before some of the
most damaging images and accounts of brutal repression had been captured, circulated
internationally and condemned by political leaders around the world. Even though
largely suppressed, the reporting of human rights violations in Burma at the height of
the crack-down and covertly and intermittently since, underlines how an embryonic
'global public sphere' can emerge on the basis of multiple infusions from different
communication networks and the wider news ecology. These communication flows are
no longer simply coincident with or confined behind national borders (see also Shaw
1996, Serra 2000).

Repressive regimes around the world are increasingly cognizant of the 'soft power' of this new communications environment with its capacity to capture and communicate human rights violations around the globe, potentially incriminating them and galvanizing world opinion and opprobrium (Giddens 2002: 72–73). The power relations that constitute the foundation of all societies as well as those processes that challenge institutionalized power, argues Manuel Castells, 'are increasingly shaped and decided in the communications field' (Castells 2007: 239). This is not to suggest that this is only where relations of power are conducted and contested, as the images of indiscriminate shooting from the bloodied streets of Rangoon attest. But it is to say that this is where such images can register with wider political force and impact, in the world news ecology and its interlinkage with diverse national and transnational networks.

Global focusing events, 'natural' disasters and geo-political dissent

When mediated in the news media some national-based disasters can become the site for discursive contention and political dissent or, in the terms of Jeffrey Alexander and Ronald Jacobs (1998), they can become 'mediatized public crises'.

> Celebratory media events of the type discussed by Dayan and Katz tend to narrow the distance between the indicative and the subjunctive, thereby legitimating the powers and authorities outside the civil sphere. Mediatized public crises, on the other hand, tend to increase the distance between the indicative and the subjunctive, thereby giving to civil society its greatest power for social change.
>
> (Alexander and Jacobs 1998: 28)

In today's world news ecology this power immanent within national civil societies can become territorially extended and transnational in scope, turning some national-based disasters into 'global focusing events'. News reporting of Hurricane Katrina that swamped New Orleans in 2004 represents a case in point.

A national-based analysis by Kathleen Tierney, Christine Bevc and Erica Kuligowski (2006), documents how US press reporting of Hurricane Katrina perpetuated a number of 'disaster myths' including characterizing disaster victims as 'opportunistic looters and violent criminals' and presenting 'individual and group behaviour through the lens of civil unrest'. Later this framing shifted to 'metaphorically represent the disaster-stricken city of New Orleans as a war zone and to draw parallels between the conditions in that city and urban insurgency in Iraq'. The overall effect of this national media coverage, they argue, was that 'Hurricane Katrina may well prove to be the focusing event that moves the nation to place more faith in military solutions for a wider range of social problems than ever before' (Tierney et al. 2006: 78). Through time some sections of the mainstream media in the US also gave vent to criticisms of city officials, failed evacuation plans, inadequate relief efforts and the seeming abandonment of some of the poorest people in American society to their fate (Bennett et al. 2007; Durham 2008). The President of the United States, George Bush, was identified as a source of blame as Hurricane Katrina exposed the normally invisible inequalities of 'race' and poverty in American society.

Hurricane Katrina, then, became an opportunity for political appropriation by different national discourses and political projects; it became, in the terms of Tierney et al. (2006), a 'focusing event'. Its reverberations were not only confined within US civil society however, and it also became a 'global focusing event'. The BBC online news website, for example, positioned itself as a portal for world opinion and exhibiting critical views and perspectives from newspapers around the world, providing hyperlinks to most of them. It is instructive to examine just a few of these here.

Bush is completely out of his depth in this disaster. Katrina has revealed America's weaknesses: its racial divisions, the poverty of those left behind by its society, and especially its president's lack of leadership.

Phillipe Grangereau in France's *Liberation*

The biggest power of the world is rising over poor black corpses. We are witnessing the collapse of the American myth. In terms of the USA's relationship with itself and the world, Hurricane Katrina seems to leave its mark on our century as an extraordinary turning point.

Yildrim Turker in Turkey's *Radikal*

Hurricane Katrina has proved that America cannot solve its internal problems and is incapable of facing these kinds of natural disasters, so it cannot bring peace and democracy to other parts of the world. Americans now understand that their rulers are only seeking to fulfill their own hegemonic goals.

Editorial in Iran's *Siyasat-e Ruz*

Co-operation to reduce greenhouse gas emissions can no longer be delayed, but there are still countries – including the US – which still do not take the issue seriously. However, faced with global disasters, all countries are in the same boat. The US hurricane disaster is a 'modern revelation', and all countries of the world including the US should be aware of this.

Xing Shu Li in Malaysia's *Sun Chew Jit Poh*

This tragic incident reminds us that the United States has refused to ratify the Kyoto accords. Let's hope the US can from now on stop ignoring the rest of the world. If you want to run things, you must first lead by example. Arrogance is never a good advisor.

Jean-Pierre Aussant in France's *Figaro* (http://news.bbc.co.uk/1/hi/world/ americas/4216142.stm)

As we can see, differences of geo-political interests and cultural outlooks clearly register in these very different national views from around the world and here relayed on the global media stage. The exposure of America's continuing racial divides and depth of poverty for some sullied its projected international image as a 'free democracy'. Countries normally regarded as political pariahs or as economic supplicants by the US government turned the tables and offered their support to the world's mightiest power in its evident failure to respond to its home-grown humanitarian disaster. And yet others took the opportunity to make the connection to climate change and the irony of the US position having not signed up to the Kyoto treaty.

The world's press reporting of Hurricane Katrina, then, provided a diverse range of nationally inflected responses and these became circulated and available via web pages and the blogosphere (see: Allan 2006: 156–165). In such ways, Hurricane Katrina was extensively and intensively mediated around the globe, reverberating across this wider geo-political terrain and becoming infused with diverse national discourses and political projects. In today's world news ecology, the flows of news and commentary traversing continents, countries and cultures can infuse different views and values into the field of disaster communication and some major disasters evidently become 'global focusing events'.

Global spectacle, performative media and the production of violent images

The Intergovernmental Panel on Climate Change (IPCC), established by the United Nations to assess the impact of human activity on climate change, published its Fourth Assessment Report in 2007. Based on an overwhelming consensus of the world's scientists, the report concluded, 'Warming of the climate system is unequivocal, as is now evident from observations of increases in global average air and ocean temperatures, widespread melting of snow and ice and rising global average sea level' (IPCC 2007: 5). This unequivocal conclusion by the world's scientists about anthropogenic or human-induced climate change received prominent exposure across the world's news media. For many it seemed to be a wakeup call.

Newspaper front-pages accompanied by images of environmental devastation from around the world proclaimed, for example, 'Worse than We Thought: Report Warns of 4C rise by 2100, Floods and Food and Water Shortages Likely' (*Guardian*), 'World Wakes to Calamity', 'UN Issues Global Warming Alert: Burning Fuel to Blame' (*Sydney Morning Herald*), 'Deal With Warming, Don't Debate It, Scientists Warn' (*Los Angeles Times*), 'Grim Warning of Climate Change' (*China Daily*). The environmental debate about global warming had seemingly entered a new phase. What many had warned about for years was now being visualized as front-page news; climate change, previously contested by a small but influential group of sceptics, had become a legitimate public and political concern. Sceptics would no longer be given such an easy ride in the media as calls for international and global responses became more urgent.

News media images of melting glaciers and ice-caps, drying lakes, vast swathes of the Amazon rain forest laid bare and the effects of drought and encroaching desertification on people and endangered species around the world, as well as pictures of extreme weather events including cyclones, floods and fires (all of which now appeared not quite so 'natural') became more common as correspondents and camera crews were dispatched from the Amazon to the Arctic to capture scenes of the effects of climate change. Images of the Earth taken from outer space also now figured prominently as well as time-series photographs mapping the planetary scale of the environmental changes that now confront us all. In such imagistic and performative ways, the news media sought to spectacularize and 'bring home' to readers and audiences the consequences of climate change. Such images helped to invoke a sense of the world as a planet under threat, a shared space inhabited perhaps by Beck's 'civilizational community of fate'. Evidently, the mainstream news media including press and broadcasting can, on occasion, promote awareness of certain global crises, performatively enacting them on the media stage and deploying spectacular and affective images to help dramatize their consequences and impacts (Cottle 2006: 130–137; Lester and Cottle forthcoming).

The performative use of news mediated spectacle in the war on terror has proved no less visible in the global news ecology, and points to how images of 'symbolic violence' and 'violent symbolism' (Cottle 2006: 152–162) can enter, tactically and strategically, into the war of images. This is so whether in respect of attempts to build public support and legitimacy for war (through aestheticized spectacles and other forms of *'symbolic violence'* that occlude or deny the human carnage of war) or those deliberate productions of violence designed to disseminate public fears (through staged mediated acts of terror or *'violent symbolism'*). As Michael Ignatieff has observed, 'When war becomes a spectator sport the media becomes the decisive theatre of operations' (Ignatieff 2001: 207).

The global War on Terror unleashed by the US administration in the aftermath of '9/11' pitched the world into a vortex of political violence and killing that has continued long after the 'successful' invasions of Afghanistan (2001) and Iraq (2003). The war of images has become a salient feature of this bloody turn in world history, from the aestheticized spectacle of the televised 'shock and awe' bombing of Baghdad to the dreadful DIY 'shock and awe' of videotaped beheadings circulated by insurgents on the internet and designed and executed to 'send a chill down the spine of the world' (Ignatieff 2004: 2); from the US administration's no-expense-spared staged announcement of 'victory' by the US president in military fatigues on the deck of the USS *Abraham Lincoln* to the choreographed violent symbolism of stripped, tortured and sexually degraded bodies produced by low-grade US military personnel at Abu Ghraib.

These and many other staged and recorded images point to the prominent role of images in contemporary warfare where insurgents and soldiers as well states and military machines have access to recording technologies and, via the world wide web, the world news ecology. This extended network of news media could possibly be construed as democratizing in so far as the availability of new digital technologies, ease of visual recording and access to communication systems seemingly enfranchises everyone, from ordinary citizens and human rights activists to foot soldiers and even torturers who can bear witness to their own and others' acts of inhumanity anywhere in the world. But it also proves tyrannical in so far as these same communication technologies and developments have produced a new 'amoral economy' in which the production and circulation of acts of violence have increasingly become performed for the news media in pursuit of strategic war aims.

News mediated spectacles of war, then, raise questions about the evolving forms of socially organized violence as well as the latter's growing dependency on the news media in processes of public opinion formation and public legitimation (see also Tumber and Webster 2006). News images of war as spectacle may provide more visceral if ideologically opaque means of communicating war than in the past, but it is too soon to disregard the continuing efficacy of traditional forms of news management and propaganda in the manufacture of consent and dissemination of fears. And some wars in the world today, as already noted, shun both cameras and spectacle, preferring to go about their inhumane business by stealth, killing and maiming unseen and undeterred by the news media. In all cases, none the less, the world-encompassing news ecology has become not only integral to the communication of contemporary war *outside* of the field of conflict but insinuated *inside* its very conduct.

Conclusions

Global crises emanate from the dark side of a 'negatively globalized planet' (Bauman 2007: 25) but in crucial respects, as we have heard, become constituted and even conducted in and through today's world news ecology, whether through general modalities of *global surveillance*, *global focusing events* or *global spectacle*. When conducted through the circulating flows and communications cross-traffic of today's news ecology (see Figure 43.1), an expanded array of views and voices – global–local, West–rest, elite–ordinary, expert–lay, military–civilian – can now sometimes enter the frame and challenge the parameters and preferred terms of public discourse – though often with differing degrees of access and possibilities of success. The blogosphere is not coincident with the mainstream news media, nor does it simply map onto the traditionally conceived 'public sphere'. Transnational activist networks are certainly not comparable to transnational corporate news organizations in terms of organizational power, available resources or public communications reach, and nor do they aim to be. They none the less sometimes manage to inject new flows and agendas, images and accounts into the global news ecology, as we have heard, and may even, on occasion, infiltrate and influence mainstream public discourse and debate (Cottle 2008). And transnational terrorism has become no less news adept in its performative choreographing of spectacles of violence deliberately designed to be recorded, uploaded and disseminated via the internet and interlinked world news ecology.

None of this should be taken to suggest that much of the mainstream news media remains anything but steadfastly wedded to national outlooks and sees through national prisms and frames of reference. When reporting on distant disasters and humanitarian emergencies, for example, national news media often seek out stories populated by their own 'nationals', whether embodied as 'heroes', 'saints', 'saviors', 'victims' or 'concerned celebrities' (Cottle and Nolan 2007). This stock news cast of *dramatis personae* serves to 'nationalize', personalize and 'bring back home' the meanings of distant events and tragedies. The global crisis of climate change has now moved into a new phase of contention as countries, corporations and citizens seek to negotiate their respective responsibilities whether in terms of national policies of mitigation and adaptation or through governmental support of developing countries confronting the worst effects of global warming. But again these various actions and contentions are frequently reported in and through national news prisms. And the global war on terror, inevitably, becomes reported through blood-flecked glasses tinted by national interests and returning coffins draped in the national flag.

It would be hard, then, to underestimate the continuing 'pull of the national' that *claws back* global crises and frames in ways consonant to national news prisms or the formidable stumbling bloc that this poses to Beck's envisaged 'cosmopolitan vision', even when the latter is forced upon the world through the intensifying inter-dependency-crises of ecology, terror and economy. Even so, as we have encountered above, today's world news ecology and its different modalities of global crisis reporting can none the less also give expression to counter-trends and transnational develop-ments that speak simultaneously to the possible emergence of a 'global public sphere' and the 'meta-power of global civil society' (Beck 2005: 64–71). How different global crises become communicated, contested and *constituted* within the world's media formations and communication flows – within its evolving world news ecology – may not only be the harbinger of a new (forced) cosmopolitanism but also prompt the *re-imagining of the political* within an increasingly interconnected, inter-dependent and *crisis-ridden* world.

References

AlertNet (2008) *AlertNet: Alerting Humanitarians*. Thompson Reuters Foundation (http://www.alertnet.org/)

Allan, S. (2006) *Online News: Journalism and the Internet*. Maidenhead: Open University Press.

Allan, S. and Thorsen, E. (eds) *Citizen Journalism: Global Perspectives*. New York: Peter Lang.

Alexander, J. C. and Jacobs, R. N. (1998) 'Mass Communication, Ritual and Civil Society', pp. 23–41, in T. Liebes and J. Curran (eds.) *Media, Ritual and Identity*, London: Routledge.

Bauman, Z. (2007) *Liquid Times*. Cambridge: Polity.

Beck, U. (2005) *Power in the Global Age*. Cambridge: Polity Press.

Beck, U. (2006) *Cosmopolitan Vision*. Cambridge: Polity Press.

Bennett, L., Lawrence, R., and Livingston, S. (2007) *When the Press Fails: Political Power and the News Media from Iraq to Katrina*. Chicago: University of Chicago Press.

Castells, M. (2007) 'Communication, Power and Counter-Power in the Network Society', *International Journal of Communication*, 1: 238–266.

Cottle, S. (2006) *Mediatized Conflict: Developments in Media and Conflict Studies*. Maidenhead: Open University Press.

Cottle, S. (2008) 'Reporting Demonstrations: The Changing Media Politics of Dissent', *Media, Culture and Society*, 30(6): 853–872.

Cottle, S. (2009a) *Global Crisis Reporting: Journalism in the Global Age*. Maidenhead: Open University Press.

Cottle, S. (2009b) 'Global Crisis Reporting: The Forgotten Dark Side of Globalization' (*forthcoming*).

Cottle, S. and Nolan, D. (2007) 'Global Humanitarianism and the Changing Aid-Media Field: "Everyone was Dying for Footage"' *Journalism Studies*, 8(6): 862–878.

Durham, F. (2008) 'Media Ritual in Catastrophic Time: the Populist Turn in Television Coverage of Hurricane Katrina', *Journalism*. 9(1): 95–116.

Giddens, A, (2002) *Runaway World*. Profile Books: London.

Ignatieff, M. (2001) *Virtual War: Kosovo and Beyond*. London: Chatto and Windus.

Ignatieff, M. (2004) 'The Terrorist as Film Director', *The Age* (Melbourne) November 20: 2.

International Institute of Strategic Studies (IISS) (2007) *Strategic Survey 2007: The Annual Review of World Affairs*. London: IISS.

International Panel on Climate Change (IPCC) (2007) *Climate Change 2007: The Physical Science Basis. Summary for Policy Makers*. IPCC Secretariat: Geneva. (Available at: http://www.ipcc.ch/sp)

Klein, N. (2007) *The Shock Doctrine: The Rise of Disaster Capitalism*. Allen Lane: London.

Lee, C., Chan, J., Pan, Z. and So, C. (2005) 'National Prisms of a Global "Media Event"' pp. 320–335, in J. Curran and M. Gurevitch (eds) *Mass Media and Society*. London: Edward Arnold.

Lester, L. and Cottle, S. 'Visualizing Climate Change: Television News and Ecological Citizenship' (*forthcoming*).

Lull, J. (2007) *Culture-On-Demand: Communication in a Crisis World*. London: BFI Publishing.

McNair, B. (2006) *Cultural Chaos: Journalism, News and Power in a Globalised Age*. London: Routledge.

Oxfam (2007) *From Weather Alert to Climate Change*. Oxfam: Briefing Paper 108.

Oxfam (2008) *Food Prices*. London: Oxfam.

Pallister, D. (2007) 'Junta Tries to Shut Down Internet and Phone Lines', *Guardian*, September 27, p. 5.

Rai, M. and Cottle, S. (2007) 'Global Mediations: On the Changing Ecology of Satellite Television News', *Global Media and Communication*, 3(1): 51–78.

Reese, S., Rutigliano, L., Hyun, K. and Jeong, J. (2007) 'Mapping the Blogosphere: Professional and Citizen-based Media in the Global News Arena', *Journalism*, 8(3): 235–261.

Serra, S. (2000) 'The Killings of Brazilian Street Children and the Rise of the International Public Sphere', pp. 151–172 in J. Curran (ed.) *Media, Organization and Society*. London: Arnold.

Shaw, M. (1996). *Civil Society and Media in Global Crises*. London: St Martin's Press.

Thussu, K. (2007) *News as Entertainment: The Rise of Global Infotainment*. London: Sage.

Tierney, K., Bevc, C. and Kuligowski, E. (2006) 'Metaphors Matter: Disaster Myths, Media Frames and Their Consequences in Hurricane Katrina', *The Annals of the American Academy*, 604: 57–81.

Tumber, H. and Webster, F. (2006) *Journalists Under Fire: Information War and Journalistic Practices*. London: Sage.

44

REPORTING THE CLIMATE CHANGE CRISIS

Anabela Carvalho

Climate change is one of the most serious threats that humankind will have to deal with in the coming decades. There is every indication that it will engender a significant upheaval in the climate patterns of the world regions, with corresponding impacts on agriculture, ecosystems and human health. This may entail unpredictable weather events, like storms and tornados, while posing significant risks for human security, destruction of housing and economic structures, and flooding of low lying countries, among other effects (IPCC 2007).

The enhanced greenhouse effect is a complex, multi-dimensional issue, both in terms of causes and effects. The production of greenhouse gases (GHGs), which strongly influence the Earth's climate, is deeply embedded in the way in which modern societies work: in transportation, heating, the production of goods, and so forth. Climate change has strong links with powerful economic activities and organizations, such as the oil industry. Therefore, tackling the problem requires an unprecedented level of coordination between governments, industry and consumers in a short time-scale.

The precise definition of the problem is itself a battlefield, where different actors – NGOs, corporations, scientific community, etc. – attempt to make their views prevail. This conceptual struggle will have material consequences, since the solutions are conditioned by what is understood to be the problem. The news media, as a key space for the production, reproduction and transformation of meanings, play an important role in this process, influencing both social representations and policy-making on this issue (see Cabecinhas, Lázaro and Carvalho 2008; Corbet and Durfee 2004; Wilson 1995).

This chapter focuses on the roles that the mainstream media have played in the last two decades in the social construction of climate change and in the relations between science, policy and public opinion. By mainstream media I mean the major television networks, newspapers and magazines with high circulation, and radio channels with significant audiences.[1] Alternative media, such as community media, blogs, social movements' online news and other citizen-produced content on the internet, continue to grow in importance; however, the fragmented nature of the audiences of these media complicates the evaluation of their social impact and turns them into more difficult research objects than the traditional media. The chapter will discuss the challenges that climate change poses to the media, the dominant public and political discourses, and some of the emerging issues and questions to be addressed by researchers.

The emergence and discursive control: a novel global risk

Although there were sporadic appearances of the 'greenhouse effect' in the media before 1988, that year was a turning point. This was due to a confluence of factors: a heat wave and intense drought in the USA; James Hansen's testimony to the US Senate Energy Committee that he was 99% certain that global warming was underway; and Margaret Thatcher's sudden interest in the issue (perhaps motivated by conflicts with the coal unions and the plan to invest in nuclear power) with dramatic statements made in a speech to the Royal Society. It was also in 1988 that the Intergovernmental Panel on Climate Change (IPCC) was formed. Levels of media attention paid to the issue fluctuated quite dramatically until 1997, the year of the Kyoto Protocol, when it reached a peak in the last decade (Mazur 1998; Carvalho and Burgess 2005). Since 2000, levels of media coverage reached new heights all around the world, spurred by factors such as the Sixth Conference of the Parties to the United Nations Framework Convention on Climate Change at The Hague and later the hurricane Katrina, Al Gore's documentary 'An Inconvenient Truth' and the Stern Review on the economics of climate change (see Boykoff and Roberts 2007). Even China has now decided to give prominence to this issue in its state-owned media. The English-language newspaper *China Daily*, for example, published over 600 articles in 2007, up from around 15–20 articles five years before.

Although the publication of the 4th IPCC Assessment Report in 2007 gained a significant prominence in the media, throughout the last two decades the main triggers for media coverage seem to have been political factors. Particularly salient in this regard were the pronouncements of top level politicians on the issue and international summits, such as Rio's Earth summit in 1992, the Kyoto summit in 1997 and The Hague summit in 2000. This suggests that policy-makers have a strong power in setting the media agenda on climate change.

In fact, while scientists were the most frequent social actors present in the media (and the most frequent sources) in the mid-1980s, politicians quickly acquired greater visibility in the news about climate change (Trumbo 1996; Carvalho and Burgess 2005). Given what is at stake in climate change, it is not surprising that a variety of social actors have tried to shape the media debate with multiple arguments, proposals and worldviews being played in this arena. However, official discourses and political actors have been almost constantly dominant. Since early on in its public career, climate change has been appropriated by political figures to advance various types of agendas and in many cases to justify stalling on necessary action. Research indicates that the media have been an important ally in this process (e.g. Carvalho and Burgess 2005; Olausson 2009). While there have been some instances of critique and progressive thinking, the media have mainly been a forum to award visibility and legitimacy to the arguments of decision-makers.

News-making and postnormal science

Funtowicz and Ravetz (1993) forged the concept 'postnormal science' to refer to those cases where facts are uncertain, and where there is dispute over values. The stakes are high and the decisions urgent. Climate change fits this description neatly, thereby representing a number of challenges for news media reporting. This is a domain where forecasting is crucial: unlike other issues where what matters is knowing how things *are*, in climate change it is essential to have an idea of how things *will be*. Futurology necessarily involves a degree of uncertainty. Moreover, cause–effect links are not always as simple and linear in climate change as media discourse requires; a variety of causes are inter-related in a complex fashion, resulting in a number of different effects, some of which are diffuse. The time-frame of this slow unravelling issue does not easily match the frequency of news in the media either. Finally, its space-frames are at odds with a typical media division between 'national' and 'foreign' news.

It is worth inquiring how different factors in the news-making process interact with these characteristics of climate change. In one of the earliest studies on the media and the greenhouse effect, Wilkins and Patterson (1990) found that in order to make the news, slow-onset environmental hazards (which also included acid rain, ozone depletion, and Rhine River pollution) 'had to "find" an event' (1990: 16). Their conclusions pointed out that media representation was event-oriented, official sources-based, and tended to frame risk in terms of human activity rather than social and political contexts.

Smith (2005), in his research with television news professionals and environmental issues, has observed that those involved tend to rely on a 'myth of detachment': that is, the belief that their role is to just to find the 'facts' and let people know about the 'truth'. This perception of the professional self is incompatible with the features of postnormal science. It may translate into a troubled communication of uncertainty, and thereby into a tendency to avoid reflecting upon the choices and values associated to mitigating climate change.

Research indicates that there have been significant international differences in the representation of uncertainty in climate change, with implications on the interpretation of different proposals for action (or inaction). In the US, a very significant aspect of media coverage is the prominence that has been awarded to the so-called climate sceptics or contrarians (at least until recently). Boykoff and Boykoff (2004) have shown that between 1995 and 2004, 53% of newspaper stories in the so-called prestige press and 70% of TV segments on climate change in American news networks were 'balanced' in the presentation of the consensus views represented by the IPCC and those of the sceptics. This means that a small group of individuals, often lacking in scientific credibility (see Oreskes 2004) but resorting to loud marketing tactics, were awarded about the same time and prominence as a scientific community composed of thousands of scientists (whose work is regularly reviewed by the IPCC) and that has consistently maintained that the greenhouse effect is being enhanced by human activities. Boykoff and Boykoff have called this 'balance as bias', that is to say a 50/50 type of representation of scientific claims on climate change does not correspond to the size and/or professional authority of the two parts and in fact constitutes a biased representation of reality.

While Boykoff and Boykoff have highlighted the role of journalistic norms in the production of this image of controversy (see also Boykoff and Boykoff 2007), other explanations can be ventured. McCright and Dunlap (2000) point outside the media to the role of claims-makers and their pro-activity. The active engagement of the anti-environmental movement in the construction of alliances between conservative think tanks, fossil fuel interests and 'sceptic' scientists probably contributed to the disproportionate weight of 'contrarian' views in the media.[2]

In a comparison between France and the US, Brossard, Shanahan and McComas (2004) found that in the coverage of climate change, Le Monde gave more emphasis to international relations issues than the New York Times, which tended to focus on domestic politics and give more attention to conflicts between scientists. The authors maintain that those differences reflect two distinct news-making cultures, with American journalism having a stronger tradition of 'objectivity' – and hence of hearing the two sides of an argument – and Le Monde having a tradition of favouring political over scientific issues.

In Germany, Weingart, Engels and Pansegrau (2000) found that there was a tendency for reporting the problem in catastrophist terms since the mid-1980s, attributable to the media's preference for 'sensationalism, negativity and unequivocal clearness' (2000: 275) but also to the German scientific and political discourses on climate change. A debate on uncertainty developed only later. More recently, Peters and Heinrichs (2008: 34) have demonstrated that in the last few years the German media 'construction' of climate change has been defined by a proximity to science and the IPCC, and that there is a 'great consonance in characterizing the risks of global climate change'. This symbolic environment turns climate change into a 'legitimate field for political action'.

In the United Kingdom, climate change 'sceptics' have gained some visibility in the conservative press (Carvalho 2007). Analyses of this country's media discourses have shown important differences in media representations of climate change. The ideological culture of each news organization appears to have shaped many aspects of media coverage with right wing news outlets often displaying positions of resistance to the changes that would need to be put in place to mitigate GHG emissions (Carvalho and Burgess 2005; Carvalho 2007). Besides professional news-making norms and the agency of social actors, the media's depictions of climate change may therefore also depend on the institutional ethos of news organizations (including their perceived audiences' expectations, preferences and values). The wider ideological and symbolic environments of each country may also play a role. Dispensa and Brulle (2003) have argued that the type of government, economic structures and industrial interests may as well lead to different forms of media coverage of climate change across countries.

Scale, engagement and modes of representation

Studies indicate that media representations of climate change in France (Brossard, Shanahan and McComas 2004), Sweden (Olausson 2009) and Portugal (Carvalho and Pereira 2008) have been dominated by the international politics of climate change. While this can be expected when we think about the relevance of international negotiations for the management of climate change, it can also be argued that the national and the local are the appropriate levels to act upon the sources of the problem. Yet, sustained analysis of the possibilities for local policy-making on climate change is featured in the media only rarely. Hence, while climate change may be represented as a tragic threat, debate on the climate impacts of a new road or a new housing development does not necessarily take place in a meaningful way. There is an apparent disconnect between climate change and specific sources of GHG emissions, and between the global and local scales.

Lorenzoni, Nicholson-Cole and Whitmarsh (2007) have demonstrated that many of the barriers to citizen engagement with climate change are related to information, such as a perceived information overload or lack of access to relevant details. While the media have privileged the global level for action on climate change and emphasised 'distant' effects, such as ice retreating in the polar regions, representing climate change as more tangible (and thus more manageable) has been shown to be useful for the common citizen. For instance, O'Neill (2008) has concluded that non-experts prefer climate change 'icons' that are locally relevant, such as flooding in the Norfolk Broads in the case of British public opinion. While the cognitive aspects of communication have been traditionally considered most important, she shows that affective engagement is also crucial.

This takes us to visual depictions of climate change, a key area that has been relatively under-researched. Environmental problems are not easily captured by the human senses, which makes efforts to improve public awareness – let alone mobilize collective action to address their causes – much more difficult. Climate change is particularly 'invisible', given the nature of the problem and the temporal and spatial scales that characterize it. Therefore in a culture where visual communication is not only pervasive but often profoundly shapes the meaning of an issue, product or idea, it is not surprising that many have felt the need to find visual representations of climate change.

To date, a diverse imagery has been associated with climate change issues; for example, meteorological phenomena (e.g. droughts, storms, flooding); sources of GHGs (e.g. cars, factories, power stations); and 'season'-related elements (e.g. early flowers). Organizations like Greenpeace have used photography to provide visual 'proof' that climate change is taking place: pictures of retreating glaciers are one of the striking examples of this. Doyle (2007) has pointed out certain tensions involved in trying to represent climate change through photography, however. For example, because photographs can only document what has already happened, efforts to make the issue depend on the 'truth effect' of images risk undermining preventive actions. Doyle argues that given the 'representational limitations of the visual [...], rather than proving that climate change is real through visible means, it might be more useful for environmental NGOs, and environmental scientists, to persuade the public that not all environmental problems can be seen' (2007: 147).

Between catastrophism and ecological modernization

We will now turn to a brief analysis of the prevailing tones, ideas and values in media discourses on climate change. In a study of the British media (Ereaut and Segnit 2006), it has been found that there are two main 'discursive repertoires': one alarmist and one optimistic. Hulme (2007) and other scholars have also called attention to the media emphasis on fear in representing climate change. In fact, examples abound, in the UK's media and in other countries, of visions of imminent doom associated with climate change (e.g. New York flooded by the Atlantic Ocean; the planet going up in flames; the end of life on Earth). Some analysts have labelled this kind of media imagery 'climate porn' (Ereaut and Segnit 2006) and have linked it to excessive sensationalism and commercialism.

Research has shown that a focus on catastrophe and fear may lead to paralysis. Some people may be led to think that climate change is out of their control and that there is nothing they can do. Instead of attempting to cut down emissions, they may adopt reactive behaviours, such as purchasing more air-conditioners in anticipation of potential heat waves. Others may have reactions of disbelief when faced with very dramatic scenarios (see Lowe 2006). The conclusion to be derived from this is not that the negative impacts of climate change should be removed from the public sight, however. Rather, it is recognized that this kind of imagery plays a role in terms of maintaining a sense of urgency. As such, it is a form of pressure that can be placed upon politicians to encourage them to address the problem, albeit one that has to be handled carefully so as to avoid public apathy, fatalism or scepticism. In this line, it is worth mentioning that Ereaut (2008) has noted that between 2006 and 2007 there has been a move in the British media towards moderation in language: that is, a move from 'alarmism' to 'alarm'.

Situated against the alarmist discourse is a more optimistic reading of climate change in the media. It comes in many shades, from the conviction that warming will be good for us to a faith in human ability to act in a rational way to avoid climate change. One of the most pervasive optimistic discourses is 'ecological modernization', which is a belief in a win-win scenario where economic and technological investment oriented to mitigating GHG emissions leads to economic gains and the creation of jobs (see Hajer 1995). This is an idea that is commonly advanced by governments, to whom the prospect of economic growth resulting from environmental protection is obviously highly attractive. The problem with this discourse is that it may lead us to believe that no transformations are required in our forms of consumption, mobility and lifestyles, more generally, which is certainly not realistic.

Still, this is a rhetorically powerful discourse. Indeed, the corresponding notion of sustainable development, with its ambiguities and open texture (Torgerson 1995), has been highly influential as well. To a large extent it has rendered climate change into something amenable to international management and technological solutions. Thus climate change has been commodified (for instance by emissions trading plans), and subjected to a techno-managerial approach – instead of remaining as a crucial political matter, subject to ideological debate, scrutiny and contention.

It is readily apparent that the news media have aided the institutionalization (see Hajer 1995) of these discourses. In most countries, there is little to be found in the mainstream media in terms of critical debate in relation to these hegemonic views. Olausson (2009) has pointed out that in the Swedish print media the construction of climate change 'takes place in a largely uncontested discursive setting' with the media discourse essentially reproducing and legitimating the political discourse. Carvalho and Pereira (2008) have shown that there is a similar situation in Portugal. In the UK, while there has been some dispute in discourses on climate change on the pages of the quality newspapers, for example (Carvalho and Burgess 2005), the general tendency has been to stay inside the parameters of free-market capitalism, industrialism and neo-liberalism.

The internet is the space where most alternative voices can be found. A myriad of websites offer critical insight, advance specific policy proposals, and create opportunities for discussion and empowerment of citizens (e.g. Global Climate Campaign; Global Commons Institute; Rising Tide). Nevertheless, this is an area that is largely under-researched. Analyzing these discursive practices and understanding their social, cultural and political effects is a key goal for communication researchers in the next few years.

Entertainment, advertising and the evolving meanings of climate change

Up until this point, this chapter has focused mainly on the media genre of news and associated 'information-type' discourses. Based on the analysis of non-news types of media messages, Shanahan and McComas (1999) have argued that rather then environmental consciousness, the media, as a whole, reinforce values like progress, materialism and technology. Television, magazines and other media contribute to creating a social environment that is at odds with environmental protection. Rather, they are seen to contribute to the maintenance of the status quo, thereby dissuading audiences that they can or should play a role in solving environmental problems.

A long-term cultivation-type analysis of a person's exposure to all types of media would reveal an image irreconcilable with climate protection. In fact, the media constantly spread appeals to consumption and mobility. Most forms of fictional and entertainment content refer to a lifestyle characterized by material comfort and wellbeing, and tend to instil a desire for purchasing more and more goods and for 'getting away' all the time.

In the omnipresent field of advertising, discourses addressing climate change are increasingly common. As public expectations grow in relation to the environmental performance of business, many companies have engaged in greening their image or brands. Green marketing is no longer the exclusive of Body Shop: almost every car-maker now suggests that we can save the climate by purchasing their new cars (and most fuel companies seem to have now gone Beyond Petroleum). Behind these messages, the degree of substantive action taken by companies towards avoiding harm to the environment is certainly variable, but the discursive hegemony of 'green growth' is in itself a revealing sign of the current times.

In these dynamic processes, climate change keeps gaining new meanings, sometimes involving a true symbolic subversion (Linder 2006). One example of this can be found in a campaign for the clothes brand Diesel, entitled 'Global warming ready'. The campaign uses climate-altered scenarios, like Venice with red araras or a flooded London, not to generate concern or to call attention to the consequences of some forms of consumption, but to promote more consumption in a 'cool' new world where models wear Diesel's clothes and sunglasses in defiance of change.

The future of media practice and research

The speed at which the media field continues to change is remarkable, opening up new opportunities to develop strategies for communicating climate change. Technology has been creating possibilities for 'richer storytelling and more prominent and fuller expression of diverse public voices' (Smith 2005: 1480). Greater inter-activity, programming that mixes different genres and media, 'the capacity to build future scenarios and to represent affective dimensions as well as "the facts"' (ibid), are among the potential to be explored by media practitioners and researchers alike.

An important scope for social debate and for research is presented by alternative media, especially the internet. In recent years, an array of citizen movements on climate change has emerged and made creative uses of online communication. As mentioned above, it is important that scholars turn their attention to the struggles over meaning transpiring in this vast arena and seek to contribute to understanding how its uses have been shaping social and political action.

For both 'new' and 'old' media, as well as for research, a number of professional and ethical issues deserve continuous rethinking. For instance, the media could play an important role in monitoring the performance of corporations in terms of GHG emissions, exposing the climate impacts of big corporations, and making news about the emissions cuts that corporations could be making and are not making. Instead, these aspects are almost completely absent from the news coverage. The same kinds of checks could be made on government policies, which should be scrutinized in cross-sectoral ways. Promoting the public accountability of institutions could help to engage and empower citizens.

The relation between the media, public opinion and policy action is complex and dynamic, with successive circuits of production and circulation of messages – as well as multiple forms of decoding and appropriation of meanings in everyday life – traversing public life. It is a process where numerous factors play, from journalistic pressures to economic drivers to political contexts (see Carvalho and Burgess 2005). Analyzing the evolution of media representations of climate change will remain an important goal for research as it helps us to better comprehend the dynamics of mediation. That is, how – and why – certain definitions of climate change become hegemonic, however fleetingly, while others are suppressed or reduced to marginal positions in public debates.

It is extremely unusual for an issue to sustain such an intense and prolonged mediatization as climate change has done in the last two decades. Neverla (2008) has argued that it has become a new 'grand narrative', a sort of journalistic 'meta-perspective' or 'superframe', which facilitates greater connectivity across otherwise disparate issues. There is little doubt that climate change has become associated with a variety of questions, problems and themes, such as energy, security, resource-management, technological innovation and many others. Spelling out and interpreting these connections is an important responsibility for media professionals. It is similarly worth paying even closer attention to the ways in which journalism itself is evolving in this regard, and what implications this may entail for our future.

Acknowledgement

This chapter builds on research for the project 'The Politics of Climate Change: Discourses and Representations', funded by the Portuguese Fundação para a Ciência e a Tecnologia (POCI/COM56973/2004).

Notes

1 For ease of access, the majority of studies have focused on the print media, especially newspapers, so references to those will be overrepresented.
2 This kind of representation of climate change has contributed to confuse the public, with 40% of citizens saying that they think that there is a lot of disagreement among scientists about whether global warming is happening (Pew Research Center for the People and the Press 2001). It has also contributed to citizen and political inaction, and fed a tendency for American citizens to disregard political responsibility on this issue: opposition to George W. Bush's decision to abandon the Kyoto protocol in 2001 was much bigger in other countries than in the USA (Yale/Gallup/ClearVision 2007).

References

Boykoff, M. and Boykoff, J. (2004) 'Balance as bias: Global warming and the US prestige press', *Global Environmental Change*, 14: 125–136.
Boykoff, M. and Boykoff, J. (2007) 'Climate change and journalistic norms: A case-study of US mass-media coverage', *Geoforum*, 38: 1190–1204.
Boykoff, M. and Roberts, J. T. (2007) *Media Coverage of Climate Change: Current Trends, Strengths, Weaknesses*, United Nations Development Report, Occasional paper, 2007/3.
Brossard, D., Shanahan, J. and McComas, K. (2004) 'Are issue-cycles culturally constructed? A comparison of French and American coverage of global climate change', *Mass Communication & Society*, 7 (3): 359–377.
Cabecinhas, R., Lázaro, A. and Carvalho, A. (2008) 'Media uses and social representations of climate change', in A. Carvalho (ed.) *Communicating Climate Change: Discourses, Mediations and Perceptions* (e-book), Braga: Centro de Estudos de Comunicação e Sociedade, Universidade do Minho (e-book available from <http://www.lasics.uminho.pt/ojs/index.php/climate_change>): 170–89.

Carvalho, A. (2007) 'Ideological cultures and media discourses on scientific knowledge. Re-reading news on climate change', *Public Understanding of Science*, 16 (2): 223–243.

Carvalho, A. and Burgess, J. (2005) 'Cultural circuits of climate change in UK broadsheet newspapers, 1985–2003', *Risk Analysis*, 25 (6): 1457–1469.

Carvalho, A. and Pereira, E. (in press) 'Communicating climate change in Portugal: A critical analysis of journalism and beyond', in A. Carvalho (ed.) *Communicating Climate Change: Discourses, Mediations and Perceptions* (e-book), Braga: Centro de Estudos de Comunicação e Sociedade, Universidade do Minho (e-book available from <http://www.lasics.uminho.pt/ojs/index.php/climate_change>): 126–56.

Corbett, J. and Durfee, J. (2004) 'Testing public (un)certainty of science: Media representations of global warming', *Science Communication*, 26 (2): 129–151.

Dispensa, J. M. and Brulle, R. J. (2003) 'Media's social construction of environmental issues: Focus on global warming – A comparative study', *International Journal of Sociology and Social Policy*, 23 (10): 74–105.

Doyle, J. (2007) 'Picturing the Clima(c)tic: Greenpeace and the Representational Politics of Climate Change Communication', *Science as Culture*, 16:2, 129–150.

Ereaut, G. (2008) 'Warm Words. The UK discourse of climate change: implications for *what*–and *how*–we can communicate', paper presented at the workshop 'Engaging the public in climate change and energy demand reduction', UKERC, Oxford, 7–8 October.

Ereaut, G. and Segnit, N. (2006) *Warm Words: How are we telling the climate story and can we tell it better?* London: Institute for Public Policy Research.

Funtowicz, S. and Ravetz, J. (1993) 'Science for the Post-Normal Age', *Futures*, 25:7, 739–755.

Global Climate Campaign. Online. Available < http://www.globalclimatecampaign.org//> (accessed 10 October 2008).

Global Commons Institute. Online. Available <http://www.gci.org.uk//> (accessed 10 October 2008).

Hajer, M. (1995) *The Politics of Environmental Discourse. Ecological Modernization and the Policy Process*, Oxford: Clarendon Press.

Hawkins, A. (1993) 'Contested ground: international environmentalism and global climate change', in R. Lipschutz and K. Conca (eds) *The State and Social Power in Global Environmental Politics*, New York: Columbia University Press.

Hulme, M. (2007) 'Newspaper scare headlines can be counter-productive', *Nature* 445 (22 February): 818.

IPCC (2007) *Climate Change 2007: Synthesis Report*. Online. Available: <http://www.ipcc.ch/ipccreports/ar4-syr.htm> (accessed 4 September 2008).

Linder, S. (2006) 'Cashing-in on risk claims: On the for-profit inversion of signifiers for "global warming"', *Social Semiotics*, 16 (1): 103–132.

Lorenzoni, I., Nicholson-Cole, S., and Whitmarsh, L. (2007) 'Barriers perceived to engaging with climate change among the UK public and their policy implications', *Global Environmental* Change, 17: 445–459.

Lowe, T. D. (2006) *Is this climate porn? How does climate change communication affect our perceptions and behaviour?*, Tyndall Centre Working Paper 98, Norwich.

Mazur, A. (1998) 'Global Environmental Change in the News', *International Sociology*, 13 (4): 457–472.

McCright, A. and Dunlap, R. (2000) 'Challenging global warming as a social problem: An analysis of the conservative movement's counter-claims', *Social Problems*, 47 (4): 499–522.

Neverla, I. (2008) 'The IPCC reports 1990–2007 in the media. A case-study on the dialectics between journalism and natural sciences', paper presented in the panel 'A global dialogue on climate change?', ICA Conference 'Global Communication and Social Change', Montreal, 22–26 May.

Olausson, U. (2009) 'Global warming-global responsibility? Media frames of collective action and scientific certainty', *Public Understanding of Science*, 18: 421–436.

O'Neill, S. (2008) *An Iconic Approach to Representing Climate Change*, Unpublished PhD thesis, University of East Anglia

Oreskes, N. (2004) 'Beyond the ivory tower: The scientific consensus on climate change', *Science*, 306 (5702): 1686.

Peters, H. P. and Heinrichs, H. (2008) 'Legitimizing climate policy: The "risk construct" of global climate change in the German mass media', *International Journal of Sustainability Communication*, 3: 14–36.

Pew Research Center for the People and the Press (2001) 'Bush Unpopular in Europe, Seen as Unilateralist'. Online. Available <http://pewglobal.org/reports/print.php?PageID=39> (accessed 21 October 2001).

Rising Tide. Online. Available <http://risingtide.org.uk/> (accessed 10 October 2008).

Shanahan, J. and McComas, K. (1999) *Nature Stories: Depictions of the Environment and their Effects*, Cresskill, NJ: Hampton Press.

Smith, J. (2005) 'Dangerous news: Media decision making about climate change risk', *Risk Analysis*, 25 (6): 1471–1482.

Torgerson, D. (1995) 'The uncertain quest for sustainability: public discourse and the politics of environmentalism', in F. Fischer and M. Black (eds) *Greening Environmental Policy. The Politics of a Sustainable Future*, Liverpool: Paul Chapman.

Trumbo, C. (1996) 'Constructing climate change: Claims and frames in US news coverage of an environmental issue', *Public Understanding of Science*, 5: 269–273.

Weingart, P., Engels, A., and Pansegrau, P. (2000) 'Risks of Communication: Discourses on Climate Change in Science, Politics, and the Mass Media', *Public Understanding of Science*, 9: 261–283.

Wilkins, L. and Patterson, P. (1990) 'Risky business: covering slow-onset hazards as rapidly developing news', *Political Communication and Persuasion*, 7: 11–23.

Wilson, K. (1995) 'Mass media as sources of global warming knowledge', *Mass Communication Review*, 22 (1–2): 75–89.

Yale/Gallup/ClearVision (2007) 'American opinions on global warming'. Online. Available < http://environment.yale.edu/news/5305/american-opinions-on-global-warming/> (accessed 22 September 2008).

45

NEWS AND FOREIGN POLICY: DEFINING INFLUENCE, BALANCING POWER

Philip Seib

News professionals are observers and reporters of, not participants in, the events they cover and have no interest in affecting outcomes. That is a nice definition of objectivity and it is nonsense.

When a television newscast or website presents graphic rather than sanitized video from a famine-stricken country, when a newspaper puts reports of a bloody civil war on page one rather than page twenty, those who deliver the news are making choices that will affect how at least some members of the public look at the world. Doing so might create a tiny ripple that soon vanishes in the vast ocean of information. Or it might produce a tidal wave of activism that policymakers cannot ignore.

The news media are de facto players in foreign affairs, just as they are in electoral politics and other matters. They help set the public's agenda in terms of what issues receive attention and this, in turn, may affect policymakers' decisions. It is important to not overstate the significance of this role. It is influential rather than determinative, an important distinction that transcends semantics. Nevertheless, it is a force to be reckoned with, and policymakers ignore it at their peril.

This chapter relies primarily on examples from the United States, but the lessons that can be drawn from these cases are applicable elsewhere and may prove valuable to policymakers, journalists, and academics throughout the world. To define the news media's role in the foreign policy process, several historical examples are cited to illustrate that this sometimes contentious relationship has deep roots. On a more theoretical level, the notion of the press as a "fourth branch" of government is examined, as is the influence news coverage may exert through the framing process. A principal theme in the chapter is the duty of the news media to maintain what may be called a "constructively adversarial" relationship with government. Some examples from the post-9/11 years underscore the importance of this. The chapter also considers how new technologies are reshaping the news–foreign policy nexus. Interactivity of new media may pull the public into a more participatory role in journalism and the policy process. Scholars, students, and others should begin considering the potential ramifications of this change now, rather than trying to catch up later. The intellectual challenges involved in doing so are exhilarating.

Some history

As policymakers and scholars grapple with the role of the news media in the foreign policy process concerning the Iraq War and other contemporary instances, it is useful to remember that virtually nothing is new. Informative precedents are not difficult to find.

Mr. Hearst's War

If you were a regular reader of the *New York Journal* in 1898, you would have frequently seen stories about atrocities perpetrated by Spanish forces occupying Cuba. The stories were basically true, although they were dressed up in lurid details that were difficult to verify. When the U.S. battleship *Maine* blew up in Havana harbor on February 15, 1898, the *Journal's* publisher, William Randolph Hearst, told the editor working on the next morning's paper, "Please spread the story all over the page. This means war" (Swanberg 1961: 160). During the next week, headlines in the *Journal* included, "The Whole Country Thrills With the War Fever," and "The *Maine* Was Destroyed by Treachery."

To this day, the sinking of the *Maine* remains unexplained, although an accidental explosion is presumed a more likely cause than "treachery." Hearst, however, was intent on war. The *Journal* organized a letter-writing campaign aimed at Congress and announced in its pages, "There will be a war with Spain as certain as the sun shines unless Spain abases herself in the dust and voluntarily consents to the freedom of Cuba" (Swanberg 1961: 168).

President William McKinley was not eager for war. Soon after the *Maine* exploded, he said, "I don't propose to be swept off my feet by the catastrophe" (O'Toole 1984: 125). But he recognized the effect the press coverage was having on public opinion and gradually moved into the pro-war camp. Hearst and others in the press, including his rival Joseph Pulitzer, soon had the war they had so loudly endorsed.

The conflict lasted only four months. Shortly after the fighting ended, Hearst smugly described his view of the role of the press in a signed editorial in the *Journal*: "The force of the newspaper is the greatest force in civilization. Under the republican government, newspapers form and express public opinion. They suggest and control legislation. They declare wars ... The newspapers control the nation because they REPRESENT THE PEOPLE" (Swanberg 1961: 201).

Mr. Hearst's appraisal of news media power has its flaws. In the case of the Spanish–American War, the amount of "control" exercised by the press was due in large part to the failure of McKinley to push back against the pro-war publishers and to rein in the likes of his impetuous assistant secretary of the Navy, Theodore Roosevelt (who had told friends during the run-up to war that the president "has no more backbone than a chocolate éclair") (Pringle 1956: 124).

This and other cases have demonstrated that if a president fails to exercise leadership and allows a vacuum to exist, the news media may move to fill it (Seib 1997: 1–13).

Mr. Murrow's War

During the summer of 1940, Great Britain was reeling. The phony war had given way to the German blitzkrieg. Germany had invaded Norway and Denmark in April, had rolled into Belgium, the Netherlands, and Luxembourg in early May, and by mid-June German troops had entered Paris. More than 300,000 British and French troops had to be evacuated from the beaches of Dunkirk as Adolf Hitler tightened his grip on Western Europe.

In the United States, forecasts of Britain's doom – coming from the likes of Charles Lindbergh and Joseph Kennedy – were widely believed and strengthened isolationist sentiment. President Franklin D. Roosevelt was inclined to help Britain, but his highest priority was winning re-election. From England, Winston Churchill's heroic rhetoric stirred Americans but not to the point at which they were willing to ride to the rescue as they had done little more than two decades before.

One of Britain's principal allies in the battle for American public opinion was a journalist, Edward R. Murrow. Broadcasting from London rooftops during air raids and reporting how Britons went about their lives in their rubble-strewn neighborhoods, Murrow presented a portrait of courage in the midst of horror that reached millions of Americans every evening through their radios. Implicitly, and sometimes explicitly, Murrow urged his listeners to consider Britain's battle for survival as crucial to America's own security. Murrow believed – and his broadcasts made this clear – that if Britain were to fall the United States would soon find itself standing alone against Hitler.

Unrestrained by the political pressures Roosevelt felt and more credible than any British spokesperson, Murrow was an effective advocate for intervention. He used journalism as a tool to shape public opinion, which allowed Roosevelt and other pro-intervention policymakers to move with increasing assertiveness. Shortly before the United States entered the war, Archibald MacLeish, America's foremost political man of letters, said of Murrow's vivid radio reports: "You burned the city of London in our houses and we felt the flames that burned it. You laid the dead of London at our doors and we knew the dead were our dead" (MacLeish 1941: 6–7).

Murrow's London broadcasts merit analysis as well as praise. His commitment to saving Britain and standing up to Hitler transcended journalism. Although "objectivity" and "detachment" are considered core journalistic values, Murrow believed that they should not impede a reporter's ability to deliver fundamental truth, in this case about the evils of Nazism and the political realities of the war. Murrow's approach to journalism in this case showed he believed that in extraordinary times, professional responsibility might need to be redefined.

History proved him right. Murrow knew that war is always terrible but sometimes necessary. That knowledge shaped his work and had lasting effect on the role of the news media as a player in the foreign policy process (Seib 2006).

These examples are not isolated ones. Plenty of stories can be told about how news coverage influenced public opinion and then policy. Sometimes policymakers were complicit in this; sometimes they tried to obstruct it. This leads to the need to consider just how much "power" the news media wield.

The "Fourth Branch" fallacy

The Hearst and Murrow cases might be cited as evidence of news media power based on a simple continuum: reporting affects public opinion, which in turn affects policy. That is nice and neat, and sometimes it may happen that way. But as is noted in the discussion above about William Randolph Hearst's muscular journalism, this influence is meaningful only if policymakers allow it to be so by not asserting their own prerogatives. As a practical matter, news media have no power to govern and are dependent on government for everything from cues about events' significance to access to those events. In this context, the "independence" of the news media is at least partly illusory.

Also, news organizations tend to be uncomfortable when crossing the line from observer to participant (although some descendents of the Hearst approach remain today). In fact, for every case in which a news organization seems to be leading public opinion, there are many more when journalists are simply tagging along, with their news agendas and even their reporting heavily influenced by policymakers.

The complexity of political dynamics should not be underestimated. Interaction among policy, public opinion, and news coverage is affected by numerous variables. As Daniel Hallin observed about U.S. coverage of the Vietnam War, "whether the media tend to be supporting or critical of government policies depends on the degree of consensus those policies enjoy, particularly within the political establishment." The media as institutions, Hallin added, "reflect the prevailing pattern of political debate: when consensus is strong, they tend to stay within the limits of political discussion it defines; when it begins to break down, coverage becomes increasingly critical and diverse in the viewpoints it represents, and increasingly difficult for officials to control" (Hallin 1984: 21).

Hallin's argument is important because it illustrates that change in the tone of coverage of the war was not the product of the news media changing their collective mind about the conflict but rather reflected the diminishing of consensus about U.S. policy related to Vietnam. This was a political failure that began during Lyndon Johnson's administration and became particularly acute after the 1968 Tet offensive. In February 1968, Walter Cronkite, the most respected U.S. broadcast journalist at the time, presented an analysis of the Vietnam situation that concluded: "It is increasingly clear to this reporter that the only rational way out will be to negotiate, not as victors but as an honorable people who lived up to their pledge to defend democracy, and did the best they could" (Oberdorfer 1972: 288).

At first look this may seem to be evidence of oppositional press asserting itself. David Halberstam wrote, "It was the first time in history a war had been declared over by an anchorman" (Ranney 1983: 5). But that appraisal disregards the failures of governance by the Johnson administration that opened the door through which Cronkite and others proceeded. Clark Clifford, who was Secretary of Defense during the last months of the Johnson presidency, later wrote: "Reporters and the antiwar movement did not defeat America in Vietnam. Our policy failed because it was based on false premises and false promises" (Clifford 1991: 474). Those "false premises and false promises" could hold up only so long, and when they collapsed so too did the consensus that had encompassed most of the public and most of the news media.

The press did not bring about the end of the war. Halberstam's observation about Cronkite declaring the conflict over was very wrong; fighting continued for another seven years, until the fall of Saigon in 1975. But debate about how to end the war – fuelled in part by news coverage – dominated American politics, shaping the bitter presidential campaign of 1968 and producing a surge of cynicism.

Policymakers learned from this, and in later administrations efforts were undertaken to develop and sustain consensus. Robert Entman (2003) wrote about the care exercised by the George W. Bush administration to frame its foreign policy after the September 11, 2001 attacks on the United States in ways that would use news coverage to enlist public support. In his public statements, President Bush repeatedly used "evil" to describe the perpetrators of the attacks and those who supported them, and "war" to define the steps to be taken against terrorism. Most news coverage adopted these terms as part of the framing of the larger story, although a few journalists endorsed viewpoints that differed from those of the administration.

"Framing," wrote Entman, "is the central process by which government officials and journalists exercise political influence over each other and over the public." Entman added that framing entails "selecting and highlighting some facets of events or issues, and making connections among them so as to promote a particular interpretation, evaluation, and/or solution" (Entman 2003: 415–17). Entman developed a "cascading activation" model that illustrates how opinion may be affected as a report or image moves from the government to other elites to the media and through news frames to the public. Then reaction-opinion may climb back up the sequence, perhaps affecting, for example, how the administration continues to frame a matter (Entman 2003: 417–18).

These and other theories indicate that there is constant interaction and often dynamic tension in the relationship between the news media and policymakers. The public is sometimes content to remain in the passive role of spectator (with varying degrees of attentiveness) but sometimes assumes a more participatory role through voting or other forms of activism. The tripartite relationship is affected by an array of factors. Some events, such as the 9/11 attacks, capture the attention of almost the entire U.S. public (and people throughout the world), while in other instances, much of the public remains uninterested and uninvolved.

During events such as the Russia–Georgia conflict in mid-2008, the global public – except in areas directly affected by the fighting – becomes only slightly engaged. This can change, however, if policymakers and/or the news media provide a compelling frame for what is happening. Two examples: conflict in the Kurdish areas of Iraq in 1991 and in Somalia in 1992. In both cases an insurrection or civil war that was of little interest to much of the world became far more salient when it was framed as a humanitarian emergency. Instigation for the reframing in the Iraq case came mainly from NGOs and the news media, and led reluctant Western governments to provide humanitarian relief and military protection for the Kurds. In the latter case, impetus originated with aid agencies and members of the U.S. Congress who alerted journalists to the situation in Somalia. News coverage caught the attention of policymakers, including President George H. W. Bush, and with his support humanitarian and military assistance from the United States and the United Nations increased.

Such multifaceted participation in the policy–press nexus is not uncommon. Sometimes coverage by a single, influential news organization can lead to policy change, as was seen in reports carried by the BBC about famine in Ethiopia in 1984 and coverage by the *New York Times* of the war in Darfur during the early years of the 21st century. Coverage in such cases might have its roots in lobbying by humanitarian aid organizations or even in a reporter's chance encounter with someone who has witnessed events. No encompassing formula exists that governs these matters.

Yet another aspect of this process is seen when policymakers use news coverage to build public support for a course of action that otherwise might lack such backing. During Bill Clinton's presidency, coverage of the plight of Albanians in Kosovo helped generate the domestic political support he needed to bring the power of NATO to bear against the Serbian government.

It is difficult to prove the existence of a "CNN effect," the assumption that news coverage – especially graphic television images – significantly affects policy in the ways discussed here. Some case studies of events such as the Kosovo War indicate that the "CNN effect" plays a role in decision making, but in many other instances the news media's influence is less pronounced and policymakers' decisions are attributable to non-media factors (Bahador 2007). Sometimes a "CNN effect backlash" is reflected in policymakers' pronouncements, such as British Foreign Secretary Douglas Hurd's comment about taking action in Bosnia: "We have not been and are not willing to begin some form of military intervention which we judge useless or worse, simply because of day by day pressures from the media" (Gowing 1994: 85).

If all these examples seem to lack a unifying characteristic, that is because there are none that can be said to be present in every instance. Furthermore, it may be difficult to establish where the "cascade" of influence actually begins. A policymaker may favor a course of action and then cultivate media coverage that helps generate political support. Or, news coverage might nudge a cautious policymaker toward taking a new approach to an issue. Discerning where a cyclical process begins and where power truly resides is not always possible.

The question of duty

Determining the extent of news media influence is secondary to defining the fundamental duty of the press to provide accurate, thorough information about what is at stake, what the costs (human and economic) are, and how the public will be affected. A democracy cannot function properly if the news media do not fulfill this responsibility.

Gathering news requires persistence, skepticism, knowledge of the subject, and willingness to challenge the powerful and resist the tug of popular opinion. Sometimes, however, the press gets off track and fails to do its job properly. A striking example of such failure was coverage of the run-up to the 2003 invasion of Iraq, when too few journalists were asking tough, pertinent questions and too few news organizations were willing to seem "unpatriotic" while the 9/11 attacks set the tone for debate about national security matters.

Two of the world's best newspapers, the *New York Times* and *The Washington Post*, looked back at their reporting and found it flawed. In a "From the Editors" column in May 2004, the *Times* admitted that "we have found a number of instances of coverage that was not as rigorous as it should have been. In some cases, information that was controversial then, and seems questionable now, was insufficiently qualified or allowed to stand unchallenged" ("From the Editors" 2004).

Writing that same week, Daniel Okrent, the public editor (ombudsman) of the *Times*, was more critical. "To anyone who read the paper between September 2002 and June 2003," he wrote, "the impression that Saddam Hussein possessed, or was acquiring, a frightening arsenal of W.M.D. [weapons of mass destruction] seemed unmistakable. Except, of course, it appears to have been mistaken." He added that some of the paper's coverage "was credulous; much of it was inappropriately italicized by lavish front-page display and heavy-breathing headlines," and good stories, such as one about CIA analysts feeling pressure as they prepared reports about Iraq, were buried deep inside the paper. "War", wrote Okrent, "requires an extra standard of care, not a lesser one. But in the *Times*'s W.M.D. coverage, readers encountered some rather breathless stories built on unsubstantiated 'revelations' that, in many instances, were the anonymity-cloaked assertions of people with vested interests." Some stories, he noted, "pushed Pentagon assertions so aggressively you could almost sense epaulets sprouting on the shoulders of editors" (Okrent 2004).

At *The Post*, executive editor Leonard Downie Jr. said that "voices raising questions about the war were lonely ones. We didn't pay enough attention to the minority." Downie also said that some of the people opposed to the war "have the mistaken impression that somehow if the media's coverage had been different, there wouldn't have been a war" (Kurtz 2004). Perhaps, but that is beside the point. *The Post* was not responsible for whether there was to be a war. Its job was to deliver accurate information that represented an appropriately broad spectrum of viewpoints about the impending conflict. Instead, like many other American news organizations, the paper saluted rather than reported and failed to properly serve the public.

This did not happen by accident. The Bush administration was aware that news coverage would be a crucial element in winning public support for war. With considerable skill, administration officials made speculation sound like solid facts and equated support for war with patriotism. Journalists' skepticism should have come into play and the administration should have been challenged to provide better evidence of the need for war, but the news media failed to do so.

A related journalistic failure occurred in coverage of the treatment of prisoners at the American-run Abu Ghraib prison in Iraq. The news media acquired graphic photos of American service personnel mistreating Iraqi prisoners. A strong case could be made that the prisoners were being tortured, but rarely did the mainstream news media use the word "torture" to characterize what was going on.

This was another instance of the Bush administration asserting its version of events and a mostly complacent press corps not forcefully enough challenging official pronouncements. In their study of this case, W. Lance Bennett, Regina G. Lawrence, and Steven Livingston found, "For all the photos and available evidence suggesting a possible policy of torture laid bare at Abu Ghraib, the story quickly became framed as regrettable abuse on the part of a few troops. The early limited appearance of the torture frame followed by its quick demise suggests that event-driven frames, particularly in matters of high consequence, are seriously constrained by mainstream news organizations' deference to political power ... As it turned out in this case, the photos may have driven the story, but the White House communication staff ultimately wrote the captions" (Bennett, Lawrence, and Livingston 2006: 482).

In this instance, not only were the news media not influencing policy, they were not even presenting the public with an appropriately forceful discussion of the issues involved in the Abu Ghraib scandal. One of the roles of news coverage is to facilitate public debate about important issues, but U.S. news organizations were slow to acknowledge the possibility that officially condoned torture was being tolerated or perhaps encouraged. Later in the war, the Bush administration's use of certain interrogation techniques, kidnapping, and other extralegal measures began to receive more consistent coverage by news organizations, but the failure to treat the Abu Ghraib case with greater seriousness was, like the flawed coverage of the run-up to the war, a failure of the news media to fulfill their responsibilities to the public.

New media, new issues

New media – principally satellite television and Internet-based media – have altered the relationship between news coverage and foreign policymaking in profound ways. The speed at which information travels, the pervasiveness of that information, and the interactive/participatory attributes of new media raise issues that journalists, governments, and publics must address.

The Arab satellite news channel Al Jazeera, created in 1996, is a symbol of this new media world. With an audience of about 35 million, it affects global politics and culture, particularly by enhancing the clout of the Islamic world. As it delivers its programming in Arabic and English (and perhaps eventually in additional languages), and as its message meshes with content from Islamic websites, blogs, and other on-line offerings, Al Jazeera helps foster unprecedented cohesion in the worldwide Muslim community.

While ten years ago, there was much talk about the influence of "the CNN effect," today "the Al Jazeera effect" redefines media influence. The concept encompasses the use of new media as tools in global affairs ranging from democratization to terrorism, and including the concept of "virtual states."

The de facto nation of Kurdistan is a good example of the virtual state. It is not officially recognized by governments and does not appear on commonly used maps, but it exists, knitted together largely by a combination of radio and television stations and an array of websites and online communication. Common media reach Kurds who live in Iraq, Turkey, Syria, and elsewhere, sustaining the Kurdish identity and accelerating its political maturation. The phenomenon of the virtual state may someday encompass entities far larger than Kurdistan, such as the *ummah*, the global Islamic community. The rise of the virtual state is made possible by new media (particularly news providers) and requires policymakers to adjust their worldviews.

The growth of new media has been explosive. In the Middle East, Al Jazeera has plenty of company on the airwaves. From a mere handful of stations a few years ago, more than 400 Arab satellite channels are now on the air providing ample alternatives to Western news organizations such as CNN and the BBC. Similarly in Latin America, the regional channel Telesur was created by Venezuela's president Hugo Chavez as a means of "counteracting the media dictatorship of the big international news networks" (Forero 2005). Similar ventures may appear in other underserved areas such as sub-Saharan Africa.

These emerging media tend to be dismissed by their critics (including Western governments) because they are not "objective" providers of information and therefore presumably have little clout with their audiences. But to use Western standards of journalistic objectivity to judge the effectiveness of these media misses the point of why they are so influential. They are credible; that's what matters. As Telesur's managing director put it, there is an "urgency to see ourselves through *our own* eyes and to discover *our own* solutions to our problems" ("Telesur" 2005). Similar sentiments have been expressed by Arab viewers watching Al Jazeera's coverage of the Palestinian *intifada* or anti-Syrian demonstrations in Lebanon.

New, popular sources of information create challenges for those who govern. In Egypt, opposition groups that are ignored by state-run media are sustained by blogs. The United States, professing concern about winning support for its policies on the "Arab street," finds its public diplomacy efforts overwhelmed by the flood of messages generated by regional and local media. China tries to monitor Internet traffic within its borders, but by late 2006 there were 137 million Internet users in China, more than 20 million blogs, and 360 million daily search engine queries. The government's watchers cannot keep up.

This kind of thing is happening around the world. In the past, governments could control much of the information flow and therefore keep tight rein on political change. No longer.

New media are also factors in larger issues, such as prospects for a "clash of civilizations" that could cast a shadow on the world for decades to come. The 2006 Danish cartoon controversy, which initially spread on the Internet, seemed to illustrate inescapable conflict between the Islamic world and the West. "News" about the cartoons was primarily provided not by traditional news organizations but rather by e-mails, text messaging, websites and other populist alternative media.

New media are changing the relationship between public and news providers. In the past, news consumers have passively received whatever news organizations offered, whenever they chose to deliver it. When Ted Turner created CNN in 1980, he let his viewers get news when they wanted it. This has been taken to the next level by web-based news content, which provides a nearly infinite variety of news products available at all times. The Internet also allows more people to become part of the "culture of information," as can be seen by the success of South Korea's OhmyNews, which has featured tens of thousands of bylines and has had tens of millions of daily page views.

"The media" are no longer just the media. They have a larger popular base than ever before and, as a result, have unprecedented impact on international politics. The media can be tools of conflict and instruments of peace; they can make traditional borders irrelevant and unify peoples scattered across the globe. (Seib 2008)

Less than a century separated William Randolph Hearst's American jingoism and the birth of pan-Arab Al Jazeera. During that time, the technologies of mass media evolved spectacularly, creating a "global village" more complex than that envisioned by Marshall McLuhan and featuring news providers whose numbers and diversity generate political power that challenges traditional mechanisms of governance.

Journalism is woven into these new media, using a blend of old and new technologies to reach publics with expanding appetites for information. Given their increasing pervasiveness and technology-based relationships with their audience, the news media in their various incarnations will have renewed opportunity to influence foreign affairs and will be challenged to prove they can do so responsibly.

References

Bahador, Babak (2007) *The CNN Effect in Action: How the News Media Pushed the West Toward War in Kosovo*, New York: Palgrave Macmillan.

Bennett, W. Lance, Lawrence, Regina G. and Livingston, Steven (2006) "None Dare Call It Torture: Indexing and the Limits of Press Independence in the Abu Ghraib Scandal," *Journal of Communication*, vol. 56, no. 3.

Clifford, Clark (1991) *Counsel to the President*, New York: Random House.

Entman, Robert M. (2003) "Cascading Activation: Contesting the White House's Frame After 9/11," *Political Communication*, vol. 20, no. 4.

Forero, Juan (2005) "And Now, the News in Latin America's View," *New York Times*, May 16.

"From the Editors" (2004), *New York Times*, May 26.

Gowing, Nik (1994), "Real-time Television Coverage of Armed Conflicts and Diplomatic Crises," Working Paper 94–1, Joan Shorenstein Barone Center, John F. Kennedy School of Government, Harvard University.

Hallin, Daniel (1984) "The Media, the War in Vietnam, and Political Support: A Critique of the Thesis of an Oppositional Media," *The Journal of Politics*, vol. 46, no. 1.

Kurtz, Howard (2004), "*The Post* on WMDs: An Inside Story," *Washington Post*, August 11.

MacLeish, Archibald (1941) "A Superstition Is Destroyed," in "In Honor of a Man and an Ideal: Three Talks on Freedom," New York: CBS (self-published booklet).

Oberdorfer, Don (1972) *Tet*, New York: Avon.

Okrent, Daniel (2004) "Weapons of Mass Destruction? Or Mass Distraction?" *New York Times*, May 30.

O'Toole, G. J. A. (1984) *The Spanish War*, New York: W. W. Norton.

Pringle, Henry F. (1956) *Theodore Roosevelt*, New York: Harcourt, Brace, and World.

Ranney, Austin (1983) *Channels of Power*, New York: Basic Books.

Seib, Philip (1997), *Headline Diplomacy: How News Coverage Affects Foreign Policy*, Westport, CT: Praeger.

Seib, Philip (2006) *Broadcasts from the Blitz: How Edward R. Murrow Helped Lead America into War*, Washington: Potomac.

Seib, Philip (2008) *The Al Jazeera Effect: How the New Global Media Are Reshaping World Politics*, Washington: Potomac.

Swanberg, W. A. (1961) *Citizen Hearst*, New York: Scribners.

"Telesur: A Counter-hegemonic Project To Compete with CNN and Univision" (2005), *La Jornada* (Mexico), February 27.

46
ICONIC PHOTOJOURNALISM AND ABSENT IMAGES: DEMOCRATIZATION AND MEMORIES OF TERROR

John Tulloch and R. Warwick Blood

Figure 46.1: South Vietnamese forces follow terrified children fleeing down Route 1, near Trang Bang, South Vietnam, June 8 1972, after an accidental aerial napalm strike. © AP/PA Photos/Huynh Cong/Nick Ut

Figure 46.2: © Abdul Hamid Raihan/ Drik/Majority World.

This chapter focuses on iconic photojournalism, especially images of war and terror. Our objective is to contrast iconic photojournalism in the mainstream Western press

with what is absent from the global news agenda. In a challenge to professional journalism, Rebecca Narracott (2008: 10) writes:

> Even with the advent of the internet and digital photography, photographers from the developing world (or majority world as it is increasingly being called) are still not presenting their reality in the global media.

This position contrasts sharply with Hartley's (2007: 561) generalized assertion that in late capitalist societies 'the democratization and monetization of photojournalism has reached its logical conclusion: now we are all paparazzi' – the concluding comment in Brennen (this volume). Narracott's position, which represents many majority world photojournalists, is about a distinct lack of democratic process and representation in the photojournalism industry internationally; and her comment follows on directly from one significant move to begin to put that right – the *Bangladesh 1971* exhibition at Rivington Place, London and the Side Gallery, Newcastle-upon-Tyne in 2008. We analyze this majority world exhibition in the context of current research on iconic photojournalism, public culture and democracy in the 'minority world' of the West.

Iconic photojournalism

American scholars Hariman and Lucaites (2001; 2003; 2007) have led the way in elaborating a theory of iconic photojournalism within the context of U.S. public culture. They define iconic photojournalism as photographic images:

- recognized by everyone within a public culture;
- understood to be representations of historically significant events;
- evoking strong emotional identification or response; and
- regularly reproduced or copied across a range of media, genres and topics (Hariman and Lucaites, 2007: 27).

There are various ways, ranging across theoretical traditions, of defining and understanding 'iconic' in the photojournalism context; and we are currently engaged in writing about that (Tulloch and Blood, forthcoming). But Hariman and Lucaites' work is powerful conceptually, well accepted in the field, and appropriate as a sounding board for our argument here, in so far as, drawing strongly on theories of visual rhetoric, they define iconic photojournalistic images as 'moments of visual eloquence' that acquire exceptional importance in public life and are believed to 'motivate public action on behalf of democratic values' (Hariman and Lucaites, 2003: 38). Perlmutter (1998: 11) offers a similar typology including:

- importance of the event depicted;
- metonymy (or how the image is used to stand for or represent the greater event);
- celebrity of the image (often promoted by press elites, and academic researchers who analyze it);

- prominence of display;
- frequency of use; and
- primordiality (themes embedded in specific visual and literary culture).

Thus, these scholars suggest, iconic photojournalism is important to study because of its portrayal of democratic societies, especially at war, its ability to encapsulate and define an historical moment, its ability to promote emotive responses in diverse audiences, and its potential impact on society, policy and cultural understandings.

Key issues

Photojournalism in the press and on the internet has long been of scholarly interest, as recent accounts by Hariman and Lucaites (2007), Tirohl, (2000), Taylor (1998), Perlmutter (1998) and Brennan (this volume) document show.

At one level, the limits on photojournalism in a democratic society centre on taste, decency, tone and propriety in keeping with the press's self image as the 'fourth estate' (Taylor, 1998: 4–7) as well as on mainstream news processes, routines and values, such as timeliness, objectivity, selection, cultural sensitivity, exclusivity, fit with the news agenda, the role of international photographic libraries, etc (see, for example, Yung and Kelly, 2008; *Journalism*, 2004; Taylor, 1998: 22; Craig, 1995, 1994; Banks, 1994; Jensen, 1992; Evans, 1991; Jarecke, 1991). Other forces influence photojournalism through direct censorship and, more subtly, through denial of, or control of, access in covering events. Military (and government) censorship and 'information control' in democracies during wartime are the prime examples, as Taylor's (1998: 160) analyses of news in the Vietnam, Falklands and Gulf wars illustrate. (Also see: Konstantinidou, 2008; Wells, 2007; Spratt, Peterson and Lagos, 2005).

But, at another level, limiting publication of photojournalism may have profound implications for knowledge in local and global societies (Taylor, 1998: 6). Arguably, *absences* in the photojournalistic record shape the meanings of events, as much as the iconic circulation of images, significantly influencing news agenda and democratic debate. We focus on two differing examples of photojournalism – the first, *iconic* of the Vietnam War; and the second, *absent* and hidden for decades from public gaze, but presented at the *Bangladesh 1971* exhibition.

Iconic photographs in war – 'Memories of terror'

In June 1972, Nick Ut's photograph (*Phan thi kim phuc*, 2008; Fig. 46.1) of the naked 'napalmed girl', Kim Phuc, hit the front page of newspapers around the world and became iconic. Hariman and Lucaites (2003: 40) observe that the photograph could not have been effective simply because of its news values. It is not especially horrific, the caption of 'accidental napalm' sets limits on its documentary value, South Vietnam not U.S. forces executed the napalm strike, and the young girl was treated immediately and taken to hospital. How could a photograph – a still image – come to dominate collective memory and democratic debate of a war that is still generally considered as the first televisual war (Hariman and Lucaites, 2003: 40; Hallin, 1986: 4)?

That is one question, but another is: why, did a photograph taken only six months earlier in December 1971, by photojournalist Abdul Hamid Raihan, of other naked children surrounded by the horrific detritus of war during Bangladesh's struggle for independence (after the Pakistan military government ignored the result of democratic elections) not become iconic internationally (*Guardian*, 2008, image 11; Fig. 46.2)? Why did we not even see this image? In the final month of this war of independence the Pakistani government unleashed state terror to the point of genocide. Up to three million Hindu, Christian, Muslim and Buddhist civilians were killed, an estimate of up to 400,000 women were brutally raped by the military, and hundreds of thousands of citizens fled their homes to neighbouring India.

In April and May 2008, this photograph was in the exhibition *Bangladesh 1971* at the Rivington Place gallery, London (Alam, 2008). Near it was another photograph of a child taken in Bangladesh at the same time. It shows a young girl staring frightened at the camera while her mother hugs herself separately in silence amongst the ruins of their home. The image is symptomatic of the silence that surrounded the ravaged girls and women of Bangladesh, then and for years later, and of the terrifying isolation and vulnerability of the children seen in the other photograph. More than 100 photographs were shown at the exhibition (Anam, 2008: 12) organized by the photographic agency Autograph ABP and Bangladeshi photojournalist Dr Shahidul Alam, director of the Drik picture library in Dhaka and curator of the exhibition. He has written (Alam, 2008) of these photographers, both named and unknown:

> They had risked all to hold on to this moment in history. The scarred negatives, hidden from the military, wrapped in old cloth, buried underground, also bore the wounds of war. These photographers were the only soldiers who preserved the tangible memories of our war of liberation. A contested memory that politicians fight over, in their battle for supremacy. These faded images, war weary, bloodied in battle, provide the only record of what was witnessed. Nearly four decades later, they speak.

So why was it that only one of these images of a child terrified in war, of the 'napalmed girl' in Vietnam, became iconic? Only some of the *Bangladesh 1971* images were buried in the ground. How do we account for lasting visual media coverage in one case, complete absence, until recently, in another?

Hariman and Lucaites (2007) argue that the 'accidental napalm' photograph of 1972 represents in the U.S. 'the point at which the balance in the public culture shifts from appeals for democratic solidarity to a discourse of liberal individualism' (2007: 22). They analyze five vectors of potential influence of importance for iconic photojournalism: reproducing ideology, communicating social knowledge, shaping collective memory, modelling democratic citizenship, and providing figural resources for communicative action (Hariman and Lucaites, 2007: 9). These five vectors of influence, they argue, explain *how* the image operates in U.S. public culture.

Ideologically Hariman and Lucaites' understanding is significantly premised on Barthes' account of myth as a 'set of beliefs that presents a social order as if it were a natural order' (Hariman and Lucaites, 2007: 9). They contend that Kim Phuc's image is impoverished as personal history, a 'combination of naked expressiveness and personal anonymity' (2007: 199). But at the same time as the photograph empties her personal/social history in war-torn Vietnam, they argue it is also 'expressive' of the fragmentation already occurring in U.S. public culture as part of a democratic process during the war. Thus not only does Kim Phuc tear off her clothes, 'she tears the conventions of social life ... The image shows what is hidden by what is being said in print – the damaged bodies behind the U.S. military's daily "body counts", "free fire zones", and other euphemisms' (Hariman and Lucaites, 2007: 176).

The 1968 Tet offensive, and the 1970 Kent State shootings (Hariman and Lucaites, 2001) had already suggested to many citizens in the U.S. that 'their government was waging a war without purpose, without legitimacy, and without end' (Hariman and Lucaites, 2007: 176–177). They argue that the 'accidental napalm image mediated a figural-rhetorical aesthetic of fragmentation'. This sense of a fragmented strategy was amplified by the rhetorical media practices of journalists reporting the war:

> Day after day the public saw a jumble of scenes – bombings, firefights, helicopter evacuations, patrols moving out, villages being searched, troops wading across rivers – that could seemingly be rearranged in any order.

Into this sense of visual/governmental fragmentation exploded the image of Kim Phuc. As the authors note (2007: 176), girls should not be shown stripped bare in public; and civilians should not be bombed:

> Likewise, U.S. soldiers ... are supposed to be handing out candy to the children in occupied lands, and the United States is supposed to be fighting just wars for noble causes. Just as the photograph violates one form of propriety [about child nudity] ... the photograph ruptures established narratives of justified military action, moral constraint, and national purpose.

The Western media Vietnam War environment was largely televisual but it reinforced the most significant effect that photography can have on an understanding of war – giving specific events a significance but leaving larger articulations of purpose outside the photographic frame (see Perlmutter and Wagner, 2004: 102 on the police shooting to death of an anti-globalization activist at the July 2001 G8 summit in Genoa).

The history of an icon, however, is never static and the original Vietnam photograph has produced several subsequent narratives. Hariman and Lucaites (2007: 184–185; 186–187) discuss the social knowledge communicated by a 'sequel' photograph of Kim Phuc as an adult peace activist in the West. This time it is her back that is naked, showing healed napalm scars, and now she holds her new baby:

> [T]his sequel to the iconic photo inculcates a way of seeing the original image and the history to which it bears witness. A record of immoral state action has

become a history of private lives ... Questions of collective responsibility – and of justice – have been displaced by questions of individual healing ... [and] a narrative of ... a new, unblemished, innocent generation ... [T]he reinscription of the iconic image by the second image ... reinvokes a therapeutic discourse that has become a symptomatic and powerful form of social control in liberal-democratic, capitalist societies.

Hariman and Lucaites' comparison of the two images of the 'napalmed girl' is part of their argument emphasizing a shift in U.S. public and political culture from the 'democratic' to the 'liberal' (which we read as 'neoliberal') taking place in the 1970s and 1980s. Most photojournalism focuses on the present, but iconic images reconfigure public memories of past history, and it is clear that Hariman and Lucaites (2007: 187) read the 'sequel' image of Kim Phuc as part of a dominant trend in modelling citizenship in the U.S.A.:

The icons of U.S. public culture increasingly underwrite liberalism more than they do democracy, and we believe this imbalance threatens progressive social and economic policies and ultimately democracy itself.

Hariman and Lucaites' analyses offer a useful social-rhetorical-theoretical map with which to begin exploring the *Bangladesh 1971* images. But their entirely U.S. focus tells us nothing of issues of agency and structure in photojournalism's majority world. So we will use their map here simply as a launch point for our further observations about iconicity and absence in international photojournalism.

Reproducing ideology

The ideological code produces a way of talking about the world but one that is necessarily "impoverished" in order to sustain its own contradictions (Hariman and Lucaites, 2007: 9).

As in the 'napalmed girl' image, a combination of personal anonymity and naked expressiveness operate in Raihan's photo (*Guardian*, 2008, Image 11) of the two small boys in *Bangladesh 1971*. In one way the image is 'impoverished': we know nothing about the boys personally. But as they stand alone in human communion, one completely naked, his arm round the younger boy wearing only a t-shirt, the photographer's local knowledge renders them extraordinarily expressive. To local viewers of this image, what is absent here from the frame – their parents, the millions of dead and dispossessed, the countless thousands of raped women – would be as powerful as what is included. The photographer was recording what he was politically commissioned to do as a war volunteer: portraying symbolically as well as naturalistically the human rights devastation conveyed by continuous acts of state terrorism. The boys are small physically, and visually in the absolute centre of the frame – a lingering site of preciously vulnerable human rights – while the rocket shells clutter the entire lower half of the frame, their foregrounding making them almost as large as the smaller boy. In the background is the ravaged ground: their homes abandoned and ruined, the tree bomb-blasted, the crops burnt, the villagers gone. It is a powerful image of almost complete powerlessness: of naked presence in absence.

This photojournalism was not absent from the world's media because of seemingly 'poor' news values. It was absent because of harsh war conditions, the Pakistani military's embargo on Western journalists, and a predisposition of news agencies in the West for 'icons of poverty' images – what Hicks (2008) and Harriman and Lucaites (2007: 49–67) trace from the 1936 iconic 'Migrant Mother' photojournalism of mother and suckling child in the American Great Depression to the present; for example, the front cover of *Time* magazine of April 1999, during the NATO bombing of Kosovo, portraying a Kosovar Albanian woman, amongst a crowd of displaced people, breast-feeding her child.

Significantly, when Bangladesh's independence was achieved a contradictory silence surrounded many of the photographic images. In *Scattered Memories of 1971*, Antara Datta (cited in 24 Hour Museum, 2008) speaks of another image of a woman photographed by Naib Uddin Ahmed (*Brave Women*) and also shown at the *Bangladesh 1971* exhibition (*Guardian*, 2008, Image 10). Against an indeterminate light background, the woman's head and upper body form a dominant triangle in the frame – as solidly 'classical' a pose as any Madonna and Child by Bellini. But this is no spiritualized Madonna. It is an image of a girl or young woman (we cannot tell which) who has been repeatedly raped. Her long hair covers the entire triangle of her upper body. Her face is completely hidden by this unfettered hair, conventionally symbolizing lust or, as here, shame. Her hands in front of her face peep through the hair. But the bangled wrists, beneath each clenched fist, look more like shackles. Datta (24 Hours Museum, 2008) writes that there have been no histories written of this episode of the war:

> The new Bangladeshi state tried to incorporate these women into national life by calling them birangonas, or heroines, but simultaneously refused to grant citizenship to the children born of rape ... the ambiguous figure of the birangona (the shamed one) cannot be easily contained within a generalised glorious narrative of the nation.

For years these photographs were not widely recognized so could have little distinctive influence on public opinion, except those shown personally to liberation fighters during the war itself. Instead, Bangladeshi schoolbooks, representing the politics of different governing factions, were dominated by the images of 'war heroes'. Further, the burying and silencing of these terror images – an extreme version of visual impoverishment – not only effaced an everyday history but enabled a contradictory political and public policy, as the tension between a 'free, democratic Bangladesh' and continuing U.S. support for dictatorships in both Pakistan and Bangladesh drowned out appeals for democratic solidarity behind globalizing discourses of market individualism – the global shift towards 'liberalism' that Hariman and Lucaites worry about.

Datta (24 Hour Museum, 2008: 10) at the end of his notes for the London exhibition says:

the Bangladeshi dream has not quite gone the way it was originally envisioned, and Bangladesh has spent many years under military rule up to the present day. Perhaps the final question to ponder has to do with the legacies of 1971 … why has Bangladesh's history, in the … years since independence, begun to resemble that of Pakistan?

Communicating social knowledge

With the iconic image, social knowledge is fused with a paradigmatic scene, say of poverty or war (Hariman and Lucaites, 2007: 10).

'To be put to work', as Hariman and Lucaites (2007: 203) argue, iconic images need 'to have remained in circulation'. But the Bangladesh photographs were not in circulation in 1971. Instead images of poverty, disease and war were circulating in Western media during the war. Our survey of British newspaper coverage at this time reveals two tiny children clutching hands 'on a bare hospital bed. And that is how they died soon afterwards … holding hands' (*Daily Mail*, 7 June, 1971); two mothers pushing their young, prostrate children 'on a handcart into Karimpur to be treated for cholera, but at the first-aid centre all were found to be dead' (*Guardian*, 5 June, 1971); the skull-like, 'anguished face of a mother watching the life of her cholera stricken child fade away in a refugee camp' (*Daily Mail*, 8 June, 1971). All of these Western images emblemize Hariman and Lucaites' sense of the iconic image's 'paradigmatic scene'; and represent also Alam's criticism of the Western 'development' image-agenda. Here the merging of 'poverty' and 'catastrophe' is combined in the West's tacit social knowledge of 'developing countries', and has become a conventionalized conduit for humanitarian aid discourse. But these are the kinds of images that photojournalism Alam describes, of a Western 'helping hand … blocking the sun' of politics (Narracott, 2008: 10).

To challenge this 'development' paradigm, in 1990 a small group of media professionals, including Alam, set up a Dhaka picture agency, Drik. Alam also helped establish Pashshala, the South Asian Institute of Photography. In 2006 Drik, in collaboration with Kijiijivision World Photography U.K. created a new global website with the aim of providing a platform for indigenous photographers from the majority world to gain fair access to global image markets (Narracott, 2008). In addition, continuous *local* circulation of the images of 1971 is a crucial aspect of the Institute's policy of communicating social knowledge. As Alam says (Kolhatkar, 2007):

we put the images on rickshaws … we take them into the streets, on boats, to school fields, to football playgrounds, and it is open to a much wider public [in Bangladesh] than art or journalism would conventionally be.

In contrast to his local, everyday sites in Bangladesh, the *Bangladesh 1971* exhibition in London and Newcastle was Alam's *Western-local* presentation of the images of genocide for young, hybrid-identity Bangladeshis in Britain. Hence, the exhibition focused on retelling the history, seeking to make the images active and iconic both internationally and locally, and it was visited by many mixed-culture school parties. *Guardian* reviewer Tahmina Anam (2008: 12) emphasized the novelty of these photographic images, and the hope for greater recognition in London, including areas close to Rivington Place where Indians, Pakistanis and Bangladeshis live and gather.

> By highlighting the images ... the curators have created an intimate, reflexive portrait of a war ... And as Londoners walk past Rivington Place, perhaps they will find a new window into the history of their neighbours on Brick Lane, a visual testament to the trauma and hope of independence.

Shaping collective memory

> Although most photojournalism ... is highly oriented towards the present, the iconic photographs assume special significance in respect to the past (Hariman and Lucaites, 2007: 11).

It is the repeated cultural performance of iconic photographs, Hariman and Lucaites argue, which establishes active historical memory. But within Bangladesh's media industry – and authoritarian politics – 'repeated memory' is produced in a different way. Drik's public policy of presenting majority world images via circulating rickshaws and boats, at school sports grounds, as well as at free public galleries in the U.K. and on the internet is designed to repeat and redesign memories of the history of independence, both within Bangladesh and throughout the diaspora. The images compete amongst those same children at the sports grounds with school textbooks, which, also repetitively, have been emphasizing the 'true' claims of this or that male-hero initiator of independence rhetoric. In contrast to masculinist war rhetoric, Drik's policy has been to indigenize photographic production, while emphasizing different identities and politics among majority world journalists. Its policy has also been to feminize its photographic texts both through its *Bangladesh 1971* images, and through Alam's own photographs of women workers and leaders in majority world countries.

Hariman and Lucaites (2007: 197) have pondered over the iconic re-gendering of the public sphere in comparing Vietnam War icons: for example, the image of the silent 'self-immolating monk' (where 'Male suppression of pain ... becomes the vector for projecting a power', 2007: 197) and the 'napalmed girl' (who screams in pain).

> [S]uch gendering hardens a number of dangerous alignments among power, violence, and masculinity, and against discourse, deliberation, and social reciprocity. Worse yet, as women only cry out and scream while remaining helpless [as in the 'napalmed girl' and Kent State iconic photos], public speech becomes hysterical and without agency, and as their meaning is transferred to the visual medium that is featuring a woman's body, the public becomes subject to the male gaze while being reduced to the politics of spectacle.

In contrast, the *Bangladesh 1971* images challenge these gendered polarities. On the one hand, the cover of the Rivington Place exhibition catalogue featured Rashid Talukder's photograph, *Students on the street during the non-cooperation movement of 1970*. *Guardian*'s reviewer Anam (2008: 13) commented:

> It is in its attempt to challenge our expectations that the exhibition is most successful. In the flagship piece, displayed against the window of Rivington Place, a group of women march in perfect formation through the middle of a busy road, rifles cupped in the palms of their hands. Another photograph is a seemingly idyllic image of two women wading through a pond with a basket of flowers. But the caption reads: 'During the liberation war, female freedom fighters would smuggle grenades in baskets covered with water hyacinth.' (See *Guardian*, 2008, Images 2 and 8.)

There is no screaming, nothing hysterical, plenty of deliberation, and a merging of public and private spheres among the women in these photographs. On the other hand, where there are images at the exhibition of brutalized women still alive, as in Ahmed's *Brave Woman* covering her face with her hair, there is no screaming either. Rather the emotional effect is conveyed by the silence, the determined screening of the face, and the classically triangular monumentality of the framed body. This is not a woman for the male gaze; not now.

Modelling citizenship

> By its location in the public media and its focus on public events, photojournalism is a premier visual practice for articulating democratic life ... [T]he iconic photo ... may be the leading edge of globalization on U.S. terms (Hariman and Lucaites, 2007: 18–19).

Citizenship within globalization *on U.S. terms* is what many countries experience in the majority world. Alam cites, as examples, the U.S. refusal to sign the Kyoto climate protocol (especially significant for low-lying Bangladesh, where disastrous floods are already endemic) and its active support of multinationals selling baby milk powder in the face of Bangladesh's promotion of breast-feeding.

For us, as media academics, as well as Data's 'final question' about the links of U.S. neoliberalism with military/authoritarian regimes, there is another 'final question' to ponder. This is about photojournalism's 'icons of poverty'; about the relationship between the 'minority world' assemblages of militaries, corporations, media, World Bank, NGOs and donor organizations that new wars theorists describe as part of the 'development-security paradigm' (Duffield, 2001); and about mainstream newspaper images that we did get to see in the West from Bangladesh in 1971. As the recto–verso of governments like the U.S. fighting 'the war against terror' via supporting military regimes in Pakistan and Bangladesh, this rhetorical media practice of those reporting the majority world via photos of poverty, sickness and war extend what Hariman and Lucaites call 'therapeutic state' images of citizenship across a so-called 'failed state' world.

Providing figural resources for communicative action

The uniformed soldier has an identity; the naked body has been stripped of conventional patterns of recognition, deference, and dismissal ... The girl's naked vulnerability is a call to obligation ... A fragmented world is still a world of moral demands (Hariman and Lucaites, 2007: 178).

Images of naked vulnerability from Bangladesh, 1971 failed to generate international 'obligation' because of their invisibility for decades; but also because that obligation was conventionalized via the 'development' photo-images of dying children and starving mothers we have described. In contrast, Alam (2006) has continued to photograph children because he found that even when they were without food, their homes washed away by floods or destroyed by armies, and without parents who had died, 'the children surrounded me. They wanted a picture.'

Alam (2006) argues that because the stakeholders, owners and editors of Bangladeshi newspapers are the urban elite, for them, as in the West, village people 'exist only as numbers, generally when plagued by some disaster' – exist, in other words, as 'development' images in Bangladesh too. But as he continues to take photographs of children in disaster areas, Alam says:

My thoughts are far away ... I remember the children screaming on the night of Mar. 25, 1971, during the Indo–Pakistan War of 1971, when I watched in helpless anger as Pakistani soldiers shot the children trying to escape their flamethrowers. The United States had sent their seventh fleet to the Bay of Bengal in support of the genocide that was Operation Searchlight, which led to the deaths of 3 million Bengalis in what was then East Pakistan (Alam, 2006).

Discussing globalized time and space, Terhi Rantanen (1997: 618–619) has noted that:

According to Relph (1976: 58) mass media produce mass-identities of places that are the most superficial identities of place, offering no scope for empathetic insideness and eroding existential insideness by destroying the bases for identity with places. In the global news flow, places could easily become phantasmagoric non-places, that only refer to an event that has taken place there and lose their local ... identity. This leads us again to the issues of inequality and dominance that are easily neglected when we talk about 'abstract' things like time and space ... a space in which frontiers and boundaries have become permeable.

It is precisely those phantasmagoric non-places – or 'development' photojournalism – that Alam challenges through his photography of children in trauma locations, and via the *Bangladesh 71* images circulating in public spaces in Dhakha, London and Newcastle.

Conclusions

Hariman and Lucaites' (2007) thesis is that iconic photojournalism separates itself out from other journalistic images via the sedimentation of time and holistic cultures. That is one way of looking at iconic images. Another, which is what we have been pointing towards, is to consider the iconic and the absent image together in terms of agency, dominant conventions, and structure. Our suggestion has been that, in the absence of Western (or even local) circulation, the *Bangladesh 1971* images have been part of an active agency in reproducing, foregrounding, and circulating, locally and internationally, images of terror and brutality to human beings, to *make* them have an iconic meaning by constructing memories. Theoretically, this means a challenge to conventionalized minority world media spaces via empathetic 'insideness of place' (Rantanen, 1997: 618).

These images, representing richness and diversity of place in the majority (not 'failed state') world, speak back to Barthes' notion of the impoverishment of photojournalism's icons. These photographs – and there are many more on the website from majority world photojournalists – speak of an agency within new media structures establishing powerful figural resources to challenge autocratic-militaristic ideology, communicate knowledge of cultural richness and diversity, shape collective memory out of silence and injustice, and model a citizenship of place alternative to that of the minority world's ownership of 'globalization' of space.

References

24 Hour Museum (2008) 'Images of the 1971 Bangladeshi war at Rivington Place'. Available at: http://www.24hourmuseum.org.uk/nwh_gfx_en/ARTS56200.html (accessed 19 August 2008).

Alam, Shahidul (2006) 'I hear the screams', Asia Media. Available at http://www.asiamedia.ucla.edu/print.asp?parentid=51509 (accessed 30 July 2008)

Alam, Shahidul (2008) 'Musings by Shahidul Alam'. Available at: http://shahidul.wordpress.com/2008/02/22/bangladesh-1971 (accessed 8 August 2008).

Anam, Tahmima (2008) 'The War that Time Forgot', *Guardian*, 10 April, G2: 12–14. Available at: http://www.guardian.co.uk/world/2008/apr/10/bangladesh.photography (accessed 15 July 2008).

Banks, Anna (1994) 'Images Trapped in Two Discourses: Photojournalism codes and the international news flow', *Journal of Communication Inquiry*, 18 (1): 118–134.

Carter, Bill, Rutenberg, Jim and Sink, Mindy (2004) 'Pentagon Ban on Pictures of Dead Troops is Broken' *New York Times* (23 April 2004). Available at: http://query.nytimes.com/gst/fullpage.html?res=980CE6DD153AF930A15757C0A9629C8B63 (accessed 24 January 2009).

Craig, Geoffrey (1994) 'Press Photographs and News Values: Analysis of the West Australian and the Australian newspapers 17 January to 12 February 1994', *Australian Studies in Journalism*, 3: 182–200.

——. (1995) 'Press Photography, Pixel Technology and Questions of Representation', *Australian Journalism Review*, 17(1): 70–78.

Domke, David, Perlmutter, David and Spratt, Meg (2002) 'The Primes of our Times? An examination of the "power" of visual images', *Journalism*, 3 (2): 131–159.

Duffield, Mark (2001) *Global Governance and the New Wars: The Merging of Development and Security*. London: Zed Books.

Evans, Howard (1991) 'Facing a Grim Reality', *American Photo*, July/August: 48.

Guardian (2008) '1971 Bangladesh War of Independence, (12 pictures). Available at: http://www.guardian.co.uk/world/gallery/2008/apr10/10/bangladesh1971? picture=333462

Hallin, Daniel (1986) *The "Uncensored War": The Media and Vietnam*. Berkeley, California: University of California Press, 1986.

Hariman, Robert and John Louis Lucaites (2001) 'Dissent and Emotional Management in a Liberal-Democratic Society: The Kent State iconic photograph', *Rhetoric Society Quarterly*, 31(3): 4–31.

——. (2003) 'Public Identity and Collective Memory in U.S. Iconic Photography: The image of "Accidental Napalm", *Critical Studies in Media Communication*, 20(1): 35–66.

——. (2007) *No Caption Needed: Iconic Photographs, Public Culture, and Liberal Democracy*. Chicago: University of Chicago Press.

Hartley, John (2007) 'Documenting Kate Moss. Fashion photography and the persistence of photojournalism,' *Journalism Studies*, 8: 555–565.

Hicks, Jim (2008) 'Narrowing the Range of Permissible Lies: recent battles in the international image tribunal', *Postmodern Culture*, 17(3). Available at: http://muse.jhu.edu/journals/pmc/v017/17.3hicks.html (accessed 12 August 2008)

Jarecke, David (1991) 'The Image of War: The story behind a horrific and controversial photo', *American Photo*, July/August: 41–46, 120.

Jensen, Robert (1992) 'Fighting Objectivity: The illusion of journalistic neutrality in coverage of the Persian Gulf War', *Journal of Communication Inquiry*, 16(1): 20–32.

Journalism (2004) 'Special Issue. Photojournalism: Professional Work and Cultural Expression.', 5(4): 379–518.

Kolhatkar, Sonali (2007). 'Conversation with Photo-Journalism Shahidul Alam'. Available at: http://uprisingradio.org/home/?p=1577 (accessed 8 August 2008)

Konstantinidou, Christina (2008) 'The Spectacle of Suffering and Death: The photographic representation of war in Greek newspapers', *Visual Communication*, 7(2): 143–169.

Lucaites, John Louis and Hariman, Robert (2001) 'Visual Rhetoric, Photojournalism, and Democratic Public Culture', *Rhetoric Review*, 20(1): 37–42.

Narracott, Rebecca (2008) 'Majorityworld.com', *Autograph Archive Issue Spring 2008* (Rivington Place, London).

Perlmutter, David (1998) *Photojournalism and Foreign Policy: Icons of Outrage in International Crises*. Westport, CT: Praeger.

Perlmutter, David and Wagner, Gretchen (2004) 'The Anatomy of a Photojournalistic Icon: Marginalization of dissent in the selection and framing of "a Death in Genoa"', *Visual Communication*, 3(1): 91–108.

Phan Thi Kim Phuc (2008). Available at: http://en.wikipedia.org/wiki/Phan_Th%E1%BB%8B-Kim_Ph%C3%BAc (accessed 8 August 2008).

Rantanen, Terhi (1997) 'The Globalization of Electronic News in the 19th Century', *Media, Culture and Society*, 19: 605–620.

Relph, E. (1976) *Place and Placelessness*. London: Pion.

Spratt, Meg, Peterson, April and Lagos, Taso (2005) 'Of Photographs and Flags: Uses and perceptions of an iconic image before and after September 11, 2001', *Popular Communication*, 3(2): 117–136.

Taylor, John (1998) *Body Horror: Photojournalism, Catastrophe and War*. New York: New York University Press.

Tirohl, Blu (2000) 'The Photo-journalist and the Changing News Image', *New Media & Society*, 2 (3): 335–352.

Tulloch, J. and Blood, R.W. (forthcoming) *Images of War, Terror and Risk*. London: Open University Press.

Wells, Karen (2007) 'Narratives of Liberation and Narratives of Innocent Suffering: The rhetorical uses of images of Iraqi children in the British press', *Visual Communication*, 6(1): 55–71.

Yung, Soo Kim and Kelly, James (2008) 'A Matter of Culture: A comparative study of photojournalism in American and Korean newspapers', *International Communication Gazette*, 70(2): 155–173.

47

JOURNALISM AND THE VISUAL POLITICS OF WAR AND CONFLICT

Lilie Chouliaraki

This chapter focuses on the visual politics of journalism by thematising the image as a crucial resource for the symbolic definition of world events. This is so not only in the sense of making visible but, in fact, rendering intelligible places and people otherwise not available to us through immediate experience (Zelizer 2004: 115–33). It is, in particular, the capacity of the image to go beyond simply enhancing our knowledge of distant others and to actually shape our orientation towards these others that raises the demand for journalistic reflexivity as an ethical obligation (Silverstone 2006).

The clearest manifestation of this ethical obligation is the unique responsibility of journalists to manage our encounter with distant but potentially traumatic events such as war and conflict (Allan 2004: 347–65). The symbolic power of news journalism, in this sense, can be conceptualised as the power of the image to render spectacles of war and conflict a cause of engagement for media publics and thereby to constitute these publics as 'imagined communities' – as 'deep horizontal comradeships' sharing dispositions to emotion and action (Anderson 1989: 6–7).

Focusing on two equally illustrative but radically different cases of war and conflict reporting, the 'shock and awe' bombardment of Baghdad (2003) and the killing of a Greek-Cypriot in the green zone of Cyprus (1996), I illustrate how the visual politics of each piece contributes to construing a particular type of imagined community for its viewing publics – respectively, a trans-national and a national community.

The two reports deliberately differ in many respects[1]: in their historical contexts, a Western alliance in the 'war against terror' and a local conflict; in their importance, a global media event and a regional drama; in their journalistic culture, a trans-national (BBC World) and a national (Greek) network; in visual content, a cityscape in flames and the actually-occurring death of one person. Despite these differences, there is a significant similarity: both reports rely on a set of visual strategies, what we may call 'strategies of sublimation' (the phantasmagoria of cityscape in flames or the human body fatally wounded) in order to activate regimes of emotion that orient viewers towards particular imaginations of community. In Iraq war reporting, this is the transnational community of Western spectators contemplating a war without victims, whereas in the Cyprus killing, this is the national community of Western civility protesting against Oriental barbarism – both imaginations inevitably presupposing and producing particular conceptions of the enemy as an Other (Silverstone 2006: 56–79).

The point of the chapter is, therefore, to demonstrate how journalism participates in the imagination of community and the production of Otherness not only through public argument and rational discourse, but also through aesthetic performance and affective discourse. Journalistic reflexivity, in this context, is a matter of becoming aware of the choices of image and language involved in war and conflict reporting and about developing an understanding of the implications that these choices may have on the dynamics of collective belonging. In juxtaposing two different news reports, this chapter draws on their similarities to problematise the assumptions that inform the aesthetic staging of war and conflict and discuss their contribution to the making of community.

Journalism and the politics of pity

Journalistic reflexivity in the context of war and conflict can be productively approached through the concept of a politics of pity (Boltanski 1999: 6–7). Journalists in such contexts are faced with the challenge of reporting on human suffering in ways that are compatible with Western principles of public presentation: such spectacles should protect viewers from trauma but, simultaneously, they should also invite them to a moral response. The politics of pity, therefore, refers to those journalistic choices of image and word that manage the emotional potential of viewers vis à vis the spectacles of suffering, in ways that motivate particular orientations to a response as if these viewers were present in the scene of action, yet without overexposing them to the horror of the scene.

My claim is not that journalists consciously enact a politics of pity, in the sense that they always act on the basis of explicit knowledge of these requirements of Western publicity. It would be more accurate to say that the requirement to represent suffering through the moral response of pity has historically informed the textual genres of the public representation of suffering and today remains an unarticulated but constitutive principle in the authoring of journalistic reports. Pity, in this respect, should not be seen as the natural sentiment of human empathy but rather as a discursive accomplishment, something that we can be invited to feel, as a consequence of the ways in which journalistic reports render suffering a particular kind of 'fact' for viewers.

The strategic role that routine practices of reporting play in the imagination of communities lies precisely in investing the imagery of suffering with certain ethical norms of what is legitimate and fair to feel and do towards such imagery, thereby also mobilizing processes of collective belonging and Othering. Whereas these normative discourses may take either the form of denunciation against the injustice of suffering, in the presence of a persecutor, or the form of care and philanthropic sentiment, in the presence of a benefactor, war and conflict reporting often resorts to a third possibility that turns away from action and renders the scene of suffering an object of aesthetic appreciation.[2]

Operating within the cultural field of Western journalism, such ethical norms are routinely produced through what Campbell calls a number of key 'economies of regulation': an economy of 'taste and decency', which bans the imagery of suffering from the screen thereby responding to the public's aversion to atrocity, and an economy of 'display', whereby images of death are domesticated by the use of language and montage that frame the meaning of depictions of atrocity (Campbell 2004:70).[3] Even though these economies of regulation can be seen as particular manifestations of the requirement of pity to avoid shocking viewers with spectacles of suffering, a consequence of their intersection is that the imagery of death is excluded from Western media. In so doing, Campbell claims, they come to restrict the *possibility for an ethical politics exercising responsibility in the face of crimes against humanity* (2004: 5).

What I wish to argue is that a third economy of regulation, what I call an economy of 'witnessing', is also always in operation in the journalistic presentation of war and suffering – an economy that controls the boundaries of taste and decency and the linguistic practices of display in ways that are politically, rather than morally or aesthetically, motivated.[4] Witnessing functions as an economy of regulation by drawing on strong religious and cultural traditions of the West and, thereby, investing the imagery of war and conflict with a force of authentic testimony that leaves little space for questioning the 'truth' of the reported event. Operating in close articulation with the other two economies, witnessing may not altogether exclude atrocity from the media but rather make different claims to the authenticity of atrocity: it may come too close to it, showing actually-occurring death along the lines of a 'pathos' aesthetics characteristic of tragic heroism (Greek-Cypriot conflict) or it may keep us at a distance, presenting the scene of war along the lines of a cinematic aesthetics of phantasmagoria (Iraqi footage). In both cases, without being explicitly political, witnessing produces forms of pity that primarily rely on the beautification or sublimation of suffering,[5] thereby strategically participating in the political project of imagining community.

The analytics of mediation

In order to empirically explore the question of the politics of pity in the cases under study, I introduce the 'analytics of mediation' (Chouliaraki 2007c). This is a framework for the study of television as a mechanism of representation that construes war and conflict within specific regimes of pity, that is within semantic fields where emotions and dispositions to action vis à vis suffering others are made possible.

The analytics of mediation thus conceptualises the broadcast reports under study as discursive structures of witnessing that, following the economy of display, combine specific visual (camera work) and linguistic (voiceover) choices to invite a particular moral response on the part of viewers. The assumption behind the analytics of mediation is that such choices over how suffering is portrayed, where, when and

with whom the suffering is shown to occur always entail broader ethical dispositions, throwing into relief the norms of taste and decency that inform the authoring
of suffering in journalistic reports. The value of the analytics of mediation, in this
respect, lies in its capacity to re-describe the discursive constitution of the imagery of
war and conflict and, in so doing, to explicate its moral implications for the mobilisation of emotion and action in the service of imagining community.

My discussion of the two types of footage is organised around two categories of
the analytics of mediation: the *aesthetic quality* of the footage, that is the choices of
language and image that construe witnessing as a dominant mode of seeing in war and
conflict reports, and the impact of these reports on the forms of *moral agency* that the
footage makes possible for the audiences of the broadcast.

Greek-Cypriot conflict

This case study refers to footage on the 22nd anniversary of the Turkish invasion of
Cyprus (August 1996), where demonstrations and protests took place on the green
zone that separates the Southern from the Northern occupied part of Cyprus (August
14–15). In the course of these demonstrations, which turned into riots, two Greek-
Cypriots were killed. The footage under study, referring to the second death, is unique
not only in the sense of capturing actually-occurring, rather than accomplished or
impending death (Zelizer 2005: 26–55), but also because it is one of the first examples
of 'networked journalism', in the sense that the recording was amateur and accidental
rather than professional (Beckett 2008). The footage follows last movements of the
the victim, Solomon Solomou, as he broke away from a protesting crowd and ran
into the buffer zone of the island, forbidden to civilians, and started to climb up the
Turkish flag pole.

Aesthetic quality

Filmed in medium-range and broadcast in slow motion, this footage captures some of
the background of the scene with the figure of a gunman standing in the balcony of a
near-by building. As the victim is hit by bullets on the flag pole, his body jerks back,
the cigarette in his mouth falls out and his grip of the flag pole is loosened; he slides
down, turns to the side and falls on the ground.

Slow motion situates the footage within a particular aesthetic register, that of
the pathos formula. Even though, historically, the pathos formula refers to a specific
artistic tradition, whereby visual representation depicts the dying body as something
willingly alienated by the victim for the sake of pleasure and aggrandizement of the oppressor
(Eisenman 2007: 16), today the pathos formula reappears in the repertoire of war
photojournalism as evidence of contemporary forms of martyrdom.[6] By focusing on
the singular figure of the dying man inviting his own death and by construing death
as service to a higher cause, love for the country, the pathos formula essentially
sublimates suffering: it seeks to remove suffering from the order of lived experience,
thereby protecting the spectator from the horror of death, and presents it as 'beautiful
suffering', allowing us to indulge in its aesthetic value from a position of safety

(Reinhardt et al. 2007). Slow motion turns death into spectacle by magnifying every movement and amplifying every second of the act of dying: the slight jerk of the body, the cigarette falling out, the gentle sliding down the pole.

In parallel to the footage, the newsreader's text moves away from the pathos formula and introduces the political theme of denunciation: *Into a rally of denunciation of the monstrosities of Attila was transformed the funeral of Solomon Solomou ... Whereas the* first clause of the text is about the funeral-as-denunciation, the other two sentences are about reactions to the killing from the European Union and the US State Department: *At the same time, in Brussels, the Irish President of the European Union was condemning the two assassinations by the occupation forces, calling them barbaric murders. Whereas in Washington, the press representative of State Department, Nicholas Burnes, used for the first time harsh language to condemn the assassinations ... The protection of the flag cannot justify the incidents of the 15th of August, said Mr Burnes, adding emphatically that human life and its sanctity are, in any case, more important than the protection of a piece of cloth.*

What we have here is a group of vocabulary choices that work together to consolidate denunciation as the dominant discourse of the international community towards the event of the killing. This discourse, first, signifies identicality of opinion among Greek-Cypriots, the US administration and the EU presidency, who all condemn the killing, and, second, stresses an intensity of emotion which all three parties are sharing through the act of condemnation ('occupation forces', 'barbaric murders', 'harsh language'). A set of evaluative norms is thus presupposed in the discourse, whereby Greece and the rest of the world are seen to form a moral front in defence of human rights whereas Turkey is seen to be diplomatically condemned and morally isolated (particularly in the contrast between the *sanctity of human life* and the protection of the flag as a *piece of cloth*).

At the same time, by attributing denunciation to a range of institutional actors, the report evokes a discourse of impartial authority: it is the trans-national community, rather than just the Greeks, which speaks out against the killing. This aura of objectivity that the international verdict lends to the report is further consolidated visually: the Turkish gunmen in the background are being circled, at the moment of the shooting, as if to disclose the identity of the 'assassins'.

Moral agency

The pathos formula, the denunciatory language and the displacement of moral evaluation onto external sources show the ways in which the economy of witnessing endows Solomon's killing with a strong claim to authenticity. It does so by appealing to two different but simultaneously enacted journalistic modes of seeing: *being an eye-witness* of the killing and *bearing witness* to the killing (Oliver 2004: 79–88; Zelizer 2004: 115–35). Being an eye-witness to the killing entails watching the event as it happens and engages with the objective depiction of historical truth; bearing witness entails watching the event as a universal truth that transcends the fact of killing and engages with a traumatic moment that borders the unrepresentable. The imagination of the nation arises out of a complex politics of pity that the witnessing of Solomon's death makes possible: the bearing witness of the sublimation of a national martyr and the eye-witnessing of a human rights crime denounced by an international community of civility.

Bearing witness as a mode of seeing is reflected in the slow motion, the frontal view and the focus on detail, in short in the pathos formula that recognises death and suffering to be, at once, the beautification of death as martyrdom and the authentic manifestation of the national psyche. The regulative economy of witnessing here relies on the capacity of the pathos formula to use a traumatic spectacle so as to produce collective imaginations of the nation as a source of heroic action. It is this productive capacity of the pathos formula to celebrate the national body politic that overrules the norms of taste and decency and renders the footage of actually occurring death not only legitimate but, in fact, strategic in the context of conflict reporting.

Eye-witnessing is reflected in the documentary aesthetic of the recording combined with the reporting on international reactions to the killing. Unlike bearing witness, the eye-witness involves a mode of seeing that approaches the scene of dying as actually-existing reality that requires an urgent response. The regulative economy of witnessing here relies on this testimonial element of the report, which hints at the juridical dimension of journalism: providing objective evidence in the service of a just cause.[7] The voiceover further participates in this juridical procedure by setting up a contrast between the values of the West (construed as an alliance between Greece, EU and US) and the values of Turkey, thereby producing a national imagination of Western civility sharply juxtaposed to its Other: the 'monstrosities of Attila'.

If the moral claim of a nation traumatized by the death of a martyr is the proto-typical claim of journalism as bearing witness, the eye-witness proposes an explicitly political form of national imagination driven by the desire to restore justice in the name of international law.

Iraqi war footage

The shock and awe bombardments of Baghdad (BBC World, March–April 2003), one of the most visually arresting spectacles of warfare, were broadcast live on BBC World and they were, subsequently, inserted as regular 'updates' in the channel's 24–7 live footage flow – the examples described here focusing on the updates' common patterns throughout their three-week broadcast span.[8]

Aesthetic quality

The imagery of Iraqi warfare is the exact opposite of the Greek-Cypriot footage: without a sign of human presence, the point of view is from afar and above with a steadycamera capturing the Baghdad cityscape in its visual plenitude. Bombing action animates this imagery through camera tracks and zooms that capture the hectic movement of weapon fire. The outcome is a structure of visualization reminiscent of the 'tableau vivant', an art form that relies on the physical re-enactment of culturally familiar pictorial representations of other cityscapes, fuzzing the line between live performance and still image (Rosengarten 2007). As a tableau vivant, the war becomes visualised as an explosion of shapes and colours against the dark background of the cityscape: the bomb explosions themselves, which appear as random orange-coloured flashes that temporarily amplify the sense of onscreen space, and of Iraqi anti-aircraft fire, which appears on screen as a tiny, round, fluorescent whiteness that glows in the dark on its way towards the sky. This pictorial composition, a shape and colour panorama, is often accompanied by the sound effect of rattles and blasts that amplify the visual effect of unrelenting bombing action.

In terms of language choices, both the bomber and the Iraqi sufferer are represented in non-human terms. This happens through word choices such as *'the plane'* and *'the strikes'*, for the persecutor, and *'the compound'*, *'the city'* or *'Baghdad'* for the sufferer. These collective wordings parallel the visual effect of the long shot: they diffuse the figures of pity away from a politics of justice or care and invite us to indulge in the spectacle of warfare as a game to be studied: '... *we saw this building take a direct hit. Look carefully and you'll see ...'*, *'this is what shock and awe looked like ...'* or *'Then we heard ... we looked up ... above us a buster ... it swooped down ... And it blasted'*.

On the whole, the bombardments of Baghdad are a spectacle of rare audio-visual power but without perpetrators or victims. Its visual effect is that of a digital game, endowing the spectacle of war with a fictional rather than a realist quality – a similar quality to the Gulf War visuals that made Baudrillard (1995) famously conclude that the war never happened.

Moral agency

As in the piece on Solomon's death, these journalistic choices invite us both to experience 'reality as it is', in the position of the eye witness, and to take a moral stance vis à vis this reality, in the position of bearing witness to the horrific fact of warfare. This happens through the combination of the tableau vivant with the two narrative types of the voiceover: description and exposition, or evaluation (adapted from Chatman 1991). The 'this-is-what-happened' function of description uses language in the first person to put words into visual action and invites us to experience the spectacle 'as if' we were there. This is obvious in expressions such as '... *we saw this building take a direct hit ...'*; *'this is what shock and awe looked like ...'*; *'then we heard ... we looked up ...'* etc. This combination both authenticates the report as objective reality and invites viewers to study the war as spectacle.

This same language of eye-witnessing simultaneously allows for sporadic elements of evaluation to be dispersed across the reports: *a terrible deafening sound as though the earth was being ripped open ... anti-missile flare spewing out of its wing ..., let loose a ferocious barrage*. Such quasi-literary use of adjectives and metaphors, such as *spewing, let loose* and *as though the earth*, frames the sight of bombing action with a sense of the horrific and the extraordinary, moving beyond description to introduce a bearing witness position vis à vis the spectacle of war – the proliferation of sound effects further magnifying the 'shock and awe' experience that visuals and voiceover seek to evoke.

Through an imagery of panoramic phantasmagoria and a language that is devoid of human agency but full of commentary on the detail of action, the 'updates' propose an approach to war primarily as a cinematic spectacle to be appreciated rather than a humanitarian catastrophe to be denounced. This perspective resembles the idea of beautiful or sublime suffering that I associated with certain features of the footage of Solomon's death, including the slow motion and the focus on subtle detail in movement. Similarly here, the footage of the bombings invites viewers to engage with the scene of suffering through reflexive contemplation – slow motion being replaced by the camera's zooms and close-ups as well as by the journalist's analytical voiceover.

Unlike Solomon's report, however, which quickly passes from the aestheticisation of death to the denunciation of the 'assassination', thereby providing the resources for the collective imagination of a national community, this one insists on presenting the war as an aesthetic spectacle to be studied rather than as a political fact that requires a response. Consequently, whereas the Greek news relies on a politics of justice that enables an action-oriented disposition vis à vis Solomon's death, witnessing warfare as a work of art is founded upon the condition of inaction (Boltanski 1999: 127).

This is because the choice of the tableau vivant eliminates the humanness of civilian victims from the imagery of the reports and draws attention away from the destructive consequences of the bombings – euphemistically called 'collateral damage'. Whereas this elimination of human suffering from these journalistic reports fully resonates with the Western economy of taste and decency, it simultaneously works to construe the Iraqi sufferer as the West's Other, a figure undeserving of Western pity.

Released from the responsibility to take sides, the trans-national community of BBC viewers is oriented towards reflecting upon its own experience of 'watching itself seeing' (Boltanski 1999: 119) – an experience well-orchestrated by the analytical voiceover. It is this introverted process of analytical self-contemplation over the evils of warfare that invites these viewers to join an indefinite and undefinable type of community united solely by its 'common humanity' – a humanity that discovers itself in its shared judgement of the war as 'shock and awe' about which, however, nothing can be done.

The imagination of such trans-national, yet resolutely Western, community arises then out of an economy of witnessing, which co-ordinates the viewers' 'feeling together' through the detached and analytical observation of bombing action (eye-witnessing) and through the invitation to contemplate the visual aesthetics of, rather than takes sides on, the destruction of Baghdad (bearing witness).[9] This is, simultaneously, a community that comes into being at the expense of recognising the humanity of the Iraqi sufferer: invisible in this war footage, suffering is construed as irrelevant to our political and moral concerns.

Journalistic reflexivity: the ethics and aesthetics of witnessing

Whereas all war and conflict journalism inevitably balances rival concerns, namely objectivity and partiality or patriotism and humanity, the question of this chapter is how journalistic discourse reflexively manages these balancing acts in specific cases of reporting. I sought to address this question by proposing a conceptualisation of war and conflict reporting as a politics of pity. The politics of pity, let us recall, refers to those journalistic choices of image and word that seek to present the spectacles of war and conflict as authentic and as demanding a response, without over-exposing viewers to the horrors of suffering.

Placing emphasis on witnessing as an economy of regulation that proposes particular modes of seeing suffering as authentic, I discussed two radically different journalistic reports, a 'global' war and a local conflict. My aim was to show how, despite their differences, both reports strategically use the imagery of war and conflict in the service of imagining community. I specifically focused on strategies of sublimation as the predominant repertoire of aesthetic resources, which manages the act of witnessing by performing two functions at once: to protect viewers from the trauma of war and to construe bonds of belonging along the lines of a West/Other distinction.

The function of sublimation to protect viewers from traumatic witnessing responds to the Western prohibition of the public display of death as a morally unacceptable and culturally sanctioned spectacle. Regulated through the economy of taste and decency, the journalistic imagery of war and conflict can only become legitimate under the condition that it is elevated to beautiful suffering – here construed by use of the pathos formula and the tableau vivant. Both strategies, each in their own way, seek to aestheticise suffering through a range of choices of display: the magnification of detail though slow motion and analytical language, or the objectification of the scene of suffering through editing devices (circling the persecutors) and first person language (what I/we see) or reported speech (what others say about the event).

Such choices render death and suffering morally acceptable for public viewing, yet they risk blurring the line between fact and fiction, between historical world and mediated virtuality. In seeking to manage what Ellis (2001) calls the psychological process of 'working through' traumatic events, journalistic stories enact economies of display which represent war and conflict both as a reality-out-there and as a de-realised filmic sequence. Several criticisms of war reporting as Hollywood entertainment find justification in photojournalistic routines similar to the 'shock and awe' bombardments of Baghdad, where the moral dilemmas and political tensions of war are suppressed in favour of a contemplative aesthetics of inaction.[10]

Journalistic reflexivity, in this context, entails an awareness of the fact that war and conflict reporting is not simply about how journalists remain objective whilst acting patriotically, but about how concepts such as objectivity, patriotism or humanity are themselves produced in the course of reporting and are inherently linked to the aesthetic effects of imaging war. As our two cases demonstrate, the use of strategies of sublimation may, in fact, combine the tendency to fictionalise death, in the pathos formula or the tableau vivant, with simultaneous references to objective truth, through the use of the documentary or an appeal to first and third party testimonies.[11] Central to these unresolved (and perhaps unresolvable) tensions is the duality of journalistic reporting as both eye-witnessing and bearing witness, pointing simultaneously to another boundary that war and conflict reporting continuously negotiates – the boundary between friend and enemy, self and Other.

This leads me to the second function of the sublimation of suffering in journalism: imagining community. Aesthetic choices of war and conflict reporting, as we saw, also have important implications as to who we care for and who we do not, thereby configuring collective dispositions to emotion and action that exclude Others who lie outside this boundary. Differences in the communities they imagine granted, a significant similarity between the two cases is that they employ the aesthetics of pathos and the tableau vivant in order to strategically move the self/Other boundary in terms of a West/non-West distinction – thereby subjecting the Other to the discursive trope of *annihilation: the denial of both a common humanity and closeness* between us and them (Silverstone 2002: 14).

In the Greek-Cypriot conflict, annihilation is ethical and cultural: the enemy is construed as an Other on the basis of a sharp distinction between Western civility and Oriental barbarism, which places the Turkish 'assassins' beyond the pale of civilised humanity, progress or reason. In the Iraq war case, annihilation is semiotic: the Iraqi population, a sufferer as well as an enemy, is physically absent from the war footage and linguistically suppressed through non-human terms such as 'city', 'compound' or 'building' – thus removing this population from the order of 'our own' humanity and the scope of our empathy and care.

Journalistic reflexivity, in this context, entails an awareness of the fact that strategies of sublimation do not lie beyond political questions and the power relations of conflict and belonging but are, in fact, constitutive of these questions. Specifically, we saw that aesthetic choices, such as the death of a hero or the war in Baghdad, strategically balance out the two journalistic requirements, to record (eye-witnessing) and to evaluate reality (bearing witness), in politically productive ways. In the Baghdad footage, the position of bearing witness subordinates the fact of bombing civilians to a cinematic spectacle, promoting a view of the war as a game and so construing a community of contemplation without action. In the Greek-Cypriot footage, in contrast, the contemplative position of the death of the hero quickly gives way to a politics of justice, introducing the perspective of denunciation in the name of human rights, and so imagining a community of action.

The crucial difference here seems to be one not between fact and fiction or objectivity and patriotism, but between a purely aesthetic politics of pity leading to inaction and one that makes an explicitly political demand for action – thereby framing the imagery of war and conflict within a discourse of denunciation in the name of international law. In the light of such differences in journalistic witnessing, we need to revisit the criticism that reporting on war and conflict one-sidedly excludes the spectacle of suffering from Western media at the expense of enabling an ethical politics of responsibility (Boltanski 1999; Campbell 2005). We could argue instead that such reporting capitalises on various synergies between the journalistic economies of regulation and their politics of pity in order to make distinct claims to authenticity – not supporting one constant 'truth' but selectively upholding many. The pathos formula, on the one hand, is strategically used to sideline 'taste and decency'-related offences in order to re-imagine an already-existing national community as a community of political action, where Greeks protest against the killing of a fellow citizen. The tableau vivant, on the other, conveniently stages a controversial war as a spectacle without victims, at the service of a political agenda that imagines the trans-national community, deeply torn over this war, as united in its silent contemplation of evil and humanity – rather than active in denouncing this war as illegal in line with UN Security Council resolutions and international law.

Journalistic reflexivity, in this respect, involves an increased awareness of the aesthetic choices through which these multiple 'truths' come into being and of the political implications they may have in terms of the kinds of communities they bring into being. Central to this political project of imagining community is the requirement for action, either against injustice or in support of human needs, as a possible response of these communities in contexts of war and conflict. As public controversies over other examples of reporting, such as the Lebanon (2006) and Gaza (2009) wars, have shown, the systematic analysis of the aesthetic staging of action constitutes an important priority in the critical study of war and conflict reporting. Such analysis can positively contribute to our understanding of the interplay between journalistic discourse and the dynamics of collective belonging and can increase reflexivity over the ways in which economies of regulation may be selectively used not only to reproduce but also to challenge existing West/Other distinctions in war and conflict reporting.

Conclusion

In this chapter, I used the 'analytics of mediation' in order to discuss how war and conflict reporting participates in the imagination of (Western) community. Drawing on the concept of a politics of pity to identify the aesthetic strategies used in two radically different cases of reporting, I conclude that the imagination of community occurs through a moral economy of journalistic witnessing that regulates the boundaries of journalistic discourse between fact and fiction, as well as between us and the Other.

The ethical obligation of journalists here consists not simply in following the professional codes of conduct in terms of proper 'display' or 'taste and decency'. In a fundamental manner, it consists in the obligation to recognise the responsibility they have in constituting media viewers as moral and political communities at the moment that they appear to simply inform – or entertain them.

Notes

1 Flyvebjerg (2001: 79) for the maximum variation principle in case study selection.
2 Boltanski (1999: 46–8) for the three 'tropes of suffering'; Zelizer (2004: 120–25) for the historical iteration of aesthetic motifs in war photography; Machin (2007: 123–42) for the contemporary dominance of the 'symbolic photograph' at the expense of realistic depictions of war.
3 Campbell's third economy, 'indifference', already presupposes a particular public attitude towards spectacles of war and conflict. Indifference, I argue, is not a regulative mechanism of journalistic reports but instead a consequence of the intersection between the economies of display, taste and decency and witnessing (see also Fishman 2002: 53–70).
4 For journalism as witnessing, Allan & Zelizer (2004b: 3–22), Zelizer (2004: 115–35); for witnessing as central to journalism Peters (2001), Frosh & Pinchevski (2008); for a shift from journalism as dangerous profession to traumatic witnessing, Rentschler (2008).

5 The multidisciplinary uses of the term the 'sublime' granted, I here take it to refer to a regime of pity that constitutes suffering less through emotions towards the sufferer and primarily through aesthetic appreciation derived from the horror of suffering (Boltanski 1999: 121).

6 Exemplars including the death-in-action shot of the Civil War soldier (Robert Kappa 1936); and the death of a French First World War soldier captured on film (Stepan 2000:30 quoted in Zelizer 2004: 124).

7 The killing as a human rights crime is confirmed in the judgement of the European Court of Human Rights, which, upon visual testimony and UN Peacekeepers accounts, found the incident to constitute a violation of Article 2 ECHR (verdict, July 1, 2008).

8 Examples drawing on 27 March and 8 April reports (Chouliaraki 2007a;c).

9 This stands in contrast to Al Jazeera: *Al Jazeera television . . . showed bloody pictures of civilian casualties night after night. An Egyptian parliamentarian observed: 'You can't imagine how the military strikes on Baghdad and other cities are provoking people every night'.* (Nye 2004: 29).

10 Lewis (2004: 305) claims that the quality of UK Iraq war footage *could make war seem too much like fiction, and make it too easy to forget people are dying.*

11 Tumber & Prentoulis (2004: 215-30) for objectivity in war reporting; Tuchman (1972: 660–79; Schudson 2002: 149–70) for objectivity as a ritual and the public norms of objectivity in US and European press.

References

Allan S. (2004) *The Culture of Distance* in Allan S. & Zelizer B. (2004a) *Reporting War. Journalism in Wartime* pp. 347–65.

Allan S. & Zelizer B. (eds) (2004a) *Reporting War. Journalism in Wartime* Routledge, London.

Allan S. & Zelizer B. (2004b) *Rules of Engagement: Journalism and War* in Allan S. & Zelizer B. (eds) *Reporting War. Journalism in Wartime* pp. 3–22.

Anderson B. (1989) *Imagined Communities* Verso, London.

Beckett C. (2008) *Supermedia* Blackwell, London.

Boltanski L. (1999) *Distant Suffering. Morality, Media and Politics* Cambridge University Press, Cambridge.

Baudrillard J. (1995) *The Gulf War Never Happened* Polity, Cambridge.

Campbell D. (2004) *Horrific Blindness: Images of Death in Contemporary Media* in *Journal for Cultural Research* Vol. 8 No. 1 pp. 55–74.

Chatman S. (1991) *Coming to Terms: The Rhetoric of Narrative in Fiction and Film* Cornell University Press, Ithaca NY.

Chouliaraki L. (2000) *Political Discourse in the News: Democratizing Responsibility or Aestheticizing Politics* in *Discourse & Society* Vol. 11, No. 3, 293–314.

Chouliaraki L. (2007a) *The Aestheticization of Suffering on Television* in *Visual Communication* Vol. 5 No. 3 pp. 261–85.

Chouliaraki L. (2007b) *Towards an Analytics of Mediation* in *Critical Discourse Studies* Vol. 4 No. 2.

Chouliaraki L. (ed) (2007c) *The Soft Power of War* Benjamins Publications, Philadelphia and Amsterdam.

Eisenman S. (2007) *The Abu Graib Effect* Reaktion Books, New York.

Ellis J. (2000) *Seeing Things: Television in an Age of Uncertainty* IB Tauris Books, London.

Fishman J. (2002) *On News Norms and Emotions: Pictures of Pain and Metaphors of Distress* in Gross L. et al. (eds) *Image Ethics in the Digital Age* University of Minnesota Press, pp. 53–70.

Flyvebjerg B. (2001) *Making Social Science Matter* Cambridge University Press, Cambridge.

Frosh P. & Pinchevski A. (2008) *Witnessing in the Era of Mass-mediated Communication* Palgrave, London.

Machin D. (2007) *Visual Discourses of Iraq War* in Hodges A. & Nilep C. (eds) *Discourse, War and Terrorism* Benjamins, Philadelphia and Amsterdam.

Nye J. (2004) *Soft Power: The Means to Success in World Politics* Public Affairs, New York.

Oliver K. (2004) *Witnessing and Testimony* in *Parallax* Vol. 10 No. 1 pp. 79–88.

Peters J.D. (2001) *Witnessing* in *Media, Culture and Society* Vol. 23 No. 6, pp. 707–27.

Reinhardt M. et al. (eds) (2007) *Beautiful Suffering. Photography and the Traffic of Pain* Chicago University Press.

Rentschler C. (2008) From Danger to Trauma: Affective Labour and the Journalistic Discourse of Witnessing in Frosh P. & Pinchevski A. (eds) *Witnessing in the Era of Mass-mediated Communication* Palgrave, London.

Rosengarten R. (2007) The Painting of Modern Life: Contemporary Photography and the Everyday (http://www.londongrip.com/LondonGrip/Art:_Ruth_Rosengarten_Painting.html)

Silverstone R. (2006) *Media and Morality. On the Rise of the Mediapolis* Polity, Cambridge.

Taylor J. (1998) Body Horror: Photojournalism, Catastrophe and War, New York University Press.

Tumber H. and Prentoulis M. (2004) *Journalists Under Fire: Subcultures, Objectivity and Emotional Literacy* in Thussu D. and Freedman D. (eds) *War and the Media* Sage, London.

Zelizer B. (2004) *When War is Reduced to a Photograph* in Allan S. & Zelizer B. (eds) *Reporting War. Journalism in Wartime* Routledge, London pp. 113–35.

Zelizer B. (2005) *Death in Wartime. Photographs and the 'Other War' in Afghanistan* in The *Harvard International Journal of Press/Politics* Vol. 10 No. 3 pp. 26–55.

48

JOURNALISTS AND WAR CRIMES

Howard Tumber

In recent years, prosecution of war crimes has become widespread.[1] The setting up of ad hoc tribunals to try war criminals in the former Yugoslavia 1993 and Rwanda 1994 and the advent of the International Criminal Court in July 2002 has put the issue of international justice in the spotlight.[2] One consequence of this is the increasing awareness of human rights workers and journalists of conflict zones as potential crime scenes. Photojournalists, in particular, are becoming acutely aware of the need to take pictures of the surrounding area of a killing scene in order to document evidential material. Their material is used as the basis for potential prosecution of war crimes and sometimes for locating a murder scene many years later.

This chapter looks at developments in international justice, the relationship between journalist and human rights workers and the changing role of journalists covering conflict. The dilemmas facing journalists in determining whether to testify in international trials and tribunals are deserving of close attention (Tumber, 2008). Some journalists, such as Jackie Rowlands, then of the BBC, and Lindsey Hilsum of the UK's Channel 4, willingly testified before the war crimes tribunals for Yugoslavia and Rwanda. Others (such as those employed by United States news organisations), although willing to provide information to the tribunal investigators, either tended to see the subpoena power of the tribunals as a threat to first amendment journalistic freedoms or were specifically prevented from testifying by their employers (see, in particular, the case of Jonathan Randall; Tumber, 2008: 264–266).[3] Apart from the important area of testimony, there are further aspects of the relationship between journalists and international justice that merit examination here.

Journalists and human rights workers

Journalists who cover conflict are essential contributors to public understanding of the war. They operate in conditions of danger and discomfort, where threats to their safety are commonplace and traumatic experiences are routine. They risk death, injury and kidnap and have to work in inhospitable locations with significant risks. The same is true for the human rights workers, who work in similar conflict zones to the journalists, documenting human rights violations.

During the course of the last twenty years, a new relationship has developed between the journalists covering conflict and the human rights workers often working alongside them. For many human rights workers, the kind of traditional human rights methodology developed by organisations such as Amnesty International and Human Rights Watch – where they would go out into the field, do the research and come back and write their reports, releasing them two months later – is not very effective in intervening in fast moving, complex situations such as Kosovo, Sierra Leone, Congo, and Iraq.

The new methodology that these organisations developed and adopted was for them to be present on the ground for longer periods when events are happening so that they can document, investigate, and produce information in a much quicker way, without prejudicing the quality of their reports. In Kosovo, for example, the day after massacres, agencies put out detailed reports with the names of the people who were killed and some details about who was responsible.

In the past, the view was that human rights researchers worked from a relatively safe distance, thereby limiting their impact in contrast to the journalists doing similar work who were getting to the story much quicker, and a lot closer. The human rights organisations tried to develop a methodology that mirrored that of the journalists particularly in terms of access.[4]

Similarly to news organisations, especially the broadcasters, human rights organisations now provide specialist security training to allow their employees to operate safely in conflict zones using the services of organisations such as AKA and Centurion, as well as their own internal training procedures and security procedures. Following the pattern of news organisations they also employ consultants from these organisations to advise on security procedures.

Human Rights NGOs have had to think clearly about what they want to achieve from their missions in conflict zones. Questions may include: are they aiming to generate evidence for the purposes of litigation? Are they ultimately looking to provide information to an international court or tribunal in some form, either as a friend of the court or in cooperation with the prosecutor or cooperation of another party? Or are they intending to produce a more journalistic type of NGO report, which they hope will get out to a wide audience and subsequently be covered by more traditional news sources? In each of these sets of circumstances, there is a different legal regime that will apply. There are diverse obligations owed to those people that the NGOs encounter. They may engage with them either as potential witnesses or as sources of one form or another. 'Journalists have a primary role, but they are not the only people focused on the brutality of contemporary conflict,' as Gutman and Reiff (1999) note. 'Groups such as Human Rights Watch, Amnesty International and the German Society for Threatened Peoples increasingly have turned their focus to violations of humanitarian law' (1999: 12).

The human rights organisations' new 'emergencies programmes' have led to very close relationships developing between human rights workers and journalists. Moving from one crisis conflict to another, the two groups become very well acquainted and awareness of their different requirements often leads to providing briefings for each other. It is a very fruitful symbiotic relationship. The journalist, with a day-to-day deadline, who may come across a victim of torture or a family which has been killed, will write the story and then pass on the information to the human rights worker so they can interview the victims and witnesses in more depth. In contrast, many stories in war zones require more in-depth research than journalists can accomplish in a day and it is the human rights workers who specialise in these aspects of the story. Once the more detailed research is complete, the human rights workers provide the journalists with the names of victims and witnesses willing to talk. The two groups travel together to and within dangerous places and often share resources such as armoured cars and personnel – translators, sometimes sources. At times, the two occupational groups also use the same drivers and fixers. War reporting undoubtedly has its rewards, but it requires an ethical calling from journalists (and human rights workers) prepared to risk life and limb (see Tumber & Webster, 2005; Tumber, 2002).[5]

The human rights workers may find they are working for weeks alongside magazine journalists and roaming war correspondents of the major US and European papers. Journalist stories will often mirror human rights organisations' investigations because they will have accompanied them for a number of days taking notes of their interviews. This is not to suggest that these journalists are lazy but more a case of these journalists trusting and understanding the human rights methodology. These interviews can take anything up to two or three hours compared to journalistic ones of twenty to thirty minutes. The sharing of translators can pose problems for the two groups. Translators are a scarce resource. There are very few people who have the kind of professional experience required and who are willing to take the risks of working in a war zone. Many of the translators are used to working with journalists, they know what kind of questions the journalists are going to ask and they cut short the interview because they are mainly looking for a quote. They find it very difficult to adjust to the human rights workers' lengthy interview process, which is trying to determine a chronology of events.

It is important to note that the testimonies of witnesses interviewed previously by reporters are open to contestation at war crimes trials. Journalists may be the first people to arrive at the scene of a killing and therefore are vital when it comes to informing and alerting the world to what had transpired. Owing to the extreme trauma they experience, witnesses and victims often have trouble remembering the details of events (Human Rights Watch, 2001: xxiii). Further problems may arise when different journalists ask the same questions to the same victims and witnesses. Following the arrival of journalists to the scene, human rights investigators then ask further questions of victims. Witnesses may be reluctant to retell their experiences again. A further difficulty, which can hamper a successful prosecution, is the difference in the manner of a journalist's questioning of a witness compared to the manner of an investigator. Statements of witnesses can look inconsistent, and their testimony can be totally discredited by a defence council. The more people who ask the same question, or even different questions, the greater the risk of contamination and the undermining of a witness's credibility (Tumber, 2008: 266).

Human rights workers' relationships with local journalists are also very important. They often work in a context where the professionalism of local journalists is in question and the human rights organisation's impartiality is in doubt. It is therefore important for them to work with local journalists exposing them to their methodology and providing access to their stories.[6]

The closeness of the journalists' working relations with aid workers is revealed in the testimony of Lindsey Hilsum of Channel 4, one of the journalists who agreed to testify in the Prosecutor v. Akayesu case at the International Criminal Tribunal for Rwanda (ICTR) (UNorg).

> 160. *Lindsey Hilson, a journalist, testified that she was in Kigali from 7 February 1994 to mid-April 1994. Following the aeroplane crash of 6 April 1994 in which the Presidents of Rwanda and Burundi were killed, she said she heard from others and saw for herself the ensuing killings of Tutsi in the capital. On the third day after the aeroplane crash, she toured Kigali with aid workers and saw victims suffering from machete and gunshot wounds. In Kigali central hospital, where she described the situation as "absolutely terrible", wounded men, women and children of all ages were packed into the wards, and hospital gutters were "running red with blood". At the morgue she saw "a big pile like a mountain of bodies outside and these were bodies with slash wounds, with heads smashed in, many of them naked, men and women". She estimated that the pile outside the morgue contained about five hundred bodies, with more bodies being brought in all the time by pickup trucks. She stated that she also saw teams of convicts around Kigali collecting bodies in the backs of trucks for mass burial, as well as groups of armed men roaming the city with machetes, clubs and sticks.*
> (from http://sim.law.uu.nl/sim/caselaw/tribunalen.nsf/2dffba7eb96617eec 12571b5003d5f3f/2f2e10bb4e3e4fc2c12571fe004fa1f9?OpenDocument).

The war photographer as forensic journalist

The recent conflicts in the Balkans and Africa had a profound effect on the journalists and photojournalists reporting from those regions. Many who reported from the conflict and witnessed acts of atrocity believed that it was important there was a pressure, part of a checks and balance system, an active voice to protect innocent civilians who are the ones who suffer the most in these civil conflicts. Through their work, some photojournalists became more and more dedicated and focused on providing that voice. They became more purposeful in trying to document what was happening. Part of the motivation was the disillusionment with the lack of intervention by the international community. The photojournalists lost their naivety that photography could have an impact, as they believed it had done in previous interventions. Instead, they began to understand photography as having another role, the role of creating evidence, work that would hold people accountable, and not allow the perpetrators or politicians to deny or say that they did not know this was happening. It was this change in occupational values that motivated them to keep reporting in conflict zones, not only in the Balkans, but also in Africa and other places.

These changes of motivation in work practices are largely under-researched by communication scholars, a general trend of neglect identified by Hanno Hardt (2004) in a special issue on photojournalism in the academic journal *Journalism: Theory, practice and criticism*. Photojournalism, he writes, 'remains marginalised in its historical and contemporary roles as suggested by the modest amount of analytical literature addressing the actual contributions of photojournalists to the narratives of their respective societies and the place of documentary photograph as a cultural and political phenomenon' (2004: 379).

The despair felt by journalists at the lack of intervention in Bosnia[7] was tempered to some extent by the intervention in Kosovo a few years later. Some of the photojournalists believe that their presence, albeit as a small group in Bosnia, added to the pressure for intervention in Kosovo. It was the publication of the same kind of stories and photographs of ethnic cleansing and atrocities, which, they believed, persuaded Western politicians, particularly President Clinton and Prime Minister Blair, that action was required.[8] The journalists' belief in the so-called CNN effect, in which global broadcasting organisations can prompt changes in foreign policy and humanitarian intervention by Western governments by reporting and transmitting pictures of human suffering, is understandable.[9] The need to believe that their work has an effect is important to their motivation. Their critics, though, insist that they were following a selective human rights agenda that coincided with the perspectives and policies of Western governments rather than exercising critical independence (Hammond 2002: 4).

One question often asked of photojournalists at work is whether they intervene in situations where they may be photographing some violent or potentially violent incident. Nearly all of the time it is impossible for them to stop it from happening. The change in culture, though, has stopped them from leaving the scene without having a piece of evidence, a document or photograph of what happened making it more difficult for the perpetrators to dispute it.

Paradoxically the advent of the International Criminal Court and the setting up of various International Tribunals is making the work of journalists more difficult. The international community hoped that the development of these institutions for dispensing international justice would affect the behaviour of soldiers and paramilitaries through compliance with the Geneva Conventions. However, in some cases, the threat of criminal proceedings has led to an increased risk to journalists as soldiers and paramilitaries are careful to cover up atrocities and make sure there is no documentary evidence of their crimes.

Through experience and education, photojournalists have learned and understood a great deal more about what they find in their work. To put matters in context they have to comprehend what they see.

The dilemmas were set out succinctly by Roy Gutman and David Reiff (1999). Whilst acknowledging that journalists who cover conflict and humanitarian emergencies know far better than their audiences or indeed critics 'how much they are operating in unchartered territory' (1999: 11), their comprehension of the situation is anything but simple as they try to navigate their way through the 'havoc, confusion and disinformation' (1999: 11). It is difficult for reporters 'to make the necessary distinctions between legal, illegal, and criminal acts. Is it a war crime under international law or a horrible, destructive, but legal act of war when one sees a hospital being shelled in Sarajevo, a humanitarian aid convoy blocked at a checkpoint on the Dagestan–Chechen border, or combat in which no prisoners are taken in Sri Lanka? (1999: 11)

The photojournalist's first task is informing – telling the world – and trying to effect change on the ground, as Alex Levac (1999) remarked 'every photojournalist wants to make an impact, wants his picture to be worth a thousand words' (1999: 146). The 'new' next stage is the collection or photographing potential evidence and the discussions amongst themselves about documenting evidence. The increased contact and proximity to human rights workers has enhanced the photojournalist's awareness of documenting evidence of a potential crime scene. An example of this is the photographing of the position of bodies and graves and the surrounding area including the position of shell casings.[10]

A good example to illustrate the work of a photojournalist and his consequent testimony was the case of Simon Cox. The following are two paragraphs taken from the Trial Chamber decision in the Prosecutor v. Akayesu at the International Criminal Tribunal for Rwanda (ICTR).

> 161. Simon Cox, a cameraman and photographer, testified that he was on an assignment in Rwanda during the time of the events set forth in the indictment. He said he entered Rwanda from Uganda, arriving in the border town of Mulindi, in the third week of April 1994. Thence he headed south with an RPF escort and found evidence of massacres of civilian men, women and children, whom it appeared from their identity cards were mostly Tutsi, in church compounds. En route to Rusumo, in the south-east of the country, he visited hospitals where Tutsi civilians suffering from machete wounds were being treated, some of whom he interviewed. At the Tanzanian border, near Rusumo, by the Kagera river which flows towards Lake Victoria, Mr. Cox saw and filmed corpses floating by at the rate of several corpses per minute. Later, at the beginning of May, he was in Kigali and saw more bodies of dead civilians on the roads. The Chamber viewed film footage taken by Mr. Cox.

> 162. On a second trip, in June 1994, Mr. Cox visited the western part of Rwanda, arriving in Cyangugu from Zaire (now the Democratic Republic of Congo) and travelling north towards Kibuye. On that journey, he visited orphanages populated by Tutsi children whose parents had been massacred or disappeared. He visited a church in Shangi where a Priest described how the whole of his congregation who had been Tutsi had been hiding inside the church, because they had heard disturbances, and they were eventually all killed by large armed gangs of people, some of whom were equipped with hand grenades. The church had previously survived five repeated attacks. Mr. Cox himself examined the church and outbuildings and found graves,

much blood and other evidence of killings. On the way to Kibuye, he saw further evidence of freshly dug mass graves in churchyards. Later, in the hills of Bisesero, he saw some 800 Tutsi civilians "in a desperate, desperate state", many apparently starving and with severe machete and bullet wounds, and with a great many corpses strewn all over the hills.

(from http://www.un.org/ictr/english/singledocs/jpa_summary.html).

For prosecutors, working for the tribunals, this kind of testimony is enormously helpful. Photographs and film footage can be powerful pieces of evidence. They can provide further evidence to substantiate horrific events that witness after witness may have described. Sometimes the testimony may be so horrific that it is very hard to visualise. Having the journalist describe what he saw through his own eyes – the bodies on the ground, the piles of machetes, the bloody identity cards – can strike a powerful chord. Human rights organisations use photojournalists because they want to cause an impact and make people think about images. The photographers and the camera operators are the ones who have to be there and see it.

Trouble can later emerge though over the verification of journalist stories.[11] The debate over journalists testifying in international criminal courts and tribunals has led some reporters to suggest that the written or spoken report might not be believed if a reporter was not willing and ready to testify in a court. This doubt over the verification of journalist stories could have profound implications for journalism in general, were it deemed essential for reporters to sign a declaration of 'truth' every time they wrote a story. The position adopted by those agreeing to testify – 'I may be a journalist but I am also a human being' and a 'time must come when journalists' rules are outweighed by moral conscience' – is opposed by some journalists.

The problem is an acute one and has become a particular line of attack on journalists who testified in the tribunals from defence lawyers who questioned their credibility as witnesses (Tumber, 2008: 266). In one particular trial case at the International Criminal Tribunal for Rwanda (ICTR) the defence counsel accused two European journalists of exaggeration, sensationalism and second hand reports (Tumber, 2008: 266). The problem for the journalistic profession is that it opens itself up to wider scrutiny. Journalists who testify not only have to stand up to interrogation and cross examination by lawyers with regard to their own stories, testimony and witness statements, but also have to defend their profession (Tumber, 2008: 266).[12]

The involvement of journalists with international justice is fraught with difficulty. Questions of moral responsibility are at the forefront of war reporters' practice. The internalisation of the ethical and moral duties places enormous pressure on journalists. The attempt to attract world attention and evoke sympathy towards war crimes does not necessarily end with the accomplishment of journalistic work (Tumber & Prentoulis, 2003). As journalist Tom Gejelten (2008) remarked:

We journalists have always had a difficult time deciding whether professional ethics require that we care about the people we cover or remain indifferent to their plight [. . .] we need to think more carefully about the responsibilities we have, individually and professionally, when we find ourselves in a place where crimes of war are occurring and where our actions as journalists and as people may change the course of events (Gejelten, 2008).

In view of this heightened reflexivity by journalists in the implications of their actions, journalists will need to take account of their safety, their relationships with sources and human rights workers, the verification of their stories, and the nature of their objectivity.

Notes

1 This article is based on research carried out under the auspices of an ESRC grant (RES-000-22-1648) (Journalists and War Crimes). I am very grateful to all those who agreed to be interviewed and provided invaluable information during the course of the research.

2 The ICC was established in 2002 to prosecute individuals for crimes against humanity, crimes of aggression, genocide and war crimes. The tribunal can only prosecute crimes committed on or after 1 July 2002, the date the Rome Statute entered into force.

3 For the US press, journalists are seen not as an extension of the Justice System, but as an independent system, with their gathering of information for the benefit of the general public, and not for that of prosecutors or defence attorneys. All major news organisations resist subpoena, but under the threat of penalty most will allow reporters to testify. The requirement of testifying is minimal to any case, and usually courts do not compel testimony.

4 Human Rights Watch, for example, began documenting human rights violations in Kosovo in 1990 and over a number of years produced a series of reports based primarily on field missions to the area. With the start of the conflict, the nature of their research changed. Their missions focus on documenting violations of humanitarian law by all sides in the conflict (see Human Rights Watch 2001: xxi).

5 The Protection of Journalists was a subject highlighted in Section III (Professional integrity and standard), of the McBride Report 1980 'Many Voices, One World'. Recognising the 'dangers that journalists are subject to in the exercise of their profession: harassment, threats, imprisonment, physical violence, assassination,' the report acknowledged that 'continual vigilance was required to focus the world's attention on such assaults on human rights and recommended that the professional independence and integrity of all those involved in the collection and dissemination of news, information and views to the public should be safeguarded'.

6 In terms of accountability, it is also very important because *Notice* is one of the issues that Human Rights organisations often testify on in The Hague. Notice is when the accused know about the crimes committed by their inferiors. The proof can be in the form of letters sent by the Human Rights organisation to the accused informing them of the publication of a particular report on police abuse, and providing the FedEx receipt from that day. Proof can also be in the form of articles in the local press, where it is assumed that the accused has read the content of the local newspapers. Human rights organisations tend to testify more about the Notice issue than about the actual crimes.

7 David Reiff, for example, states: 'by the summer of 1993, people in Bosnia had grown weary of the press and cynical about its ability to change anything, which finally was the only criterion which made any sense. Journalists who were once greeted as trusted friends and in whom Bosnians, generally but Sarajevans in particular, had placed such hopes were greeted more dispassionately. It was not that Bosnians believed they had failed to tell the story; it was that it had done no good' (1995: 223–224).

8 This is part of a wider debate surrounding the 'journalism of attachment' and the broader human rights discourse which is supported by some as an important factor leading to the humanitarian/military intervention in Bosnia and Kosovo and criticised by others as legitimating barbarism. (see Tumber, 2008: 263).

9 For a review of the literature on the CNN effect see Gilboa (2005); see also Beck (2005: 65), Hawkins (2002), Jacobsen (2000) and Robinson (2002).

10 Photojournalists are employed both by news organisations and by human rights organisations and this can potentially lead to complications for them regarding testifying or providing evidence to international tribunals. If they are contracted to work for the *New York Times* for example, should they adopt the position of the journalist and refuse to testify? If they are contracted by Human Rights Watch for example, should they adopt the position of the human rights worker and agree to testify? The occupational values may differ in each case.

11 The debate over verification of reporters' stories is not one that occurs very frequently. Apart from cases of libel and defamation, the most recent high profile issue in the UK was when Andrew Gilligan, the former BBC journalist, was subjected to intensive questioning by lawyers during the Hutton enquiry set up to investigate the circumstances surrounding the death of a government scientist (see Tumber and Palmer, 2004: 139–159, 167–172).

12 Depending on the legal system, journalists may also be subject to discovery once they act as a witness.

References

Beck, U. (2005). *Power in the Global Age*, Cambridge: Polity.

Gilboa, E. (2005). The CNN effect: The search for a communication theory of international relations. *Political Communication*, 22, 27–44.

Gejelten, T. Professionalism in War Reporting: A Correspondent's View, URL (consulted 23 November 2008) http://www.wilsoncenter.org/subsites/ccpdc/pubs/gj/gjfr.htm

Gutman, R. and D. Reiff (1999). Preface in Gutman, R. and D. Reiff (eds.) *Crimes of War*, London: W.W. Norton & Company, 8–12.

Hammond, P. (2002). 'Moral Combat; Advocacy Journalists and the New Humanitarianism', URL (consulted 31 January 2007) http://myweb.1sbu.ac.uk/phillip hammond/2002.html

Hardt, H. (2004). Photojournalism: Professional Work and Cultural Expression Introduction, *Journalism*, Vol. 5(4): 379–380.

Hawkins, V. (2002). The Other Side of the CNN Factor: The media and conflict. *Journalism Studies*, 3(2), 225–240.

Human Rights Watch (2001) *Under Orders: war Crimes in Kosovo*, New York; Human Rights Watch

Jacobsen, P. V. (2000). Focus on the CNN Effect Misses the Point: The real media impact on conflict management is invisible and indirect. *Journal of Peace Research* 37(5), 547–562.

Levac, A. (1999). 'The Camera as Witness', in Gutman, R. and D. Reiff (eds.) *Crimes of War*, London: W.W. Norton & Company, 8–12.

Reiff, D. (1995). *Slaughterhouse; Bosnia and the Failure of the West*, London: Simon & Schuster.

Robinson, P. (2002). The CNN Effect. London: Routledge.

Tumber H. and J. Palmer (2004) *Media at War: the Iraq Crisis*, London: Sage Publications.

Tumber, H and F. Webster (2005). *Journalists under Fire*, London: Sage.

Tumber H. (2002) Reporting under Fire: The physical safety and emotional welfare of journalists, in B. Zelizer and S. Allan, (eds.) Journalism After September 11, London: Routledge 247–262

Tumber, H. (2008). Journalists, War Crimes and International Justice, *Media War & Conflict* 1(3): 261–269.

United Nations ICTR URL consulted 4 January 2008. (http://www.un.org/ictr/english/singledocs/jpa_summary.html)

49
PEACE JOURNALISM
Jake Lynch

Peace journalism is a set of distinctions in the reporting of conflict and a fund of evaluative criteria for media monitoring and content analysis. It has been, variously, the rallying cry in campaigns for media reform, a focus for the training of editors and reporters in conflict zones, and latterly a subject of academic inquiry. This chapter explains the origin of the concept, and examines some of the controversies arising out of its introduction to what Zelizer (2004) calls the 'interpretive communities' of journalism and critical humanities scholarship respectively. It considers peace journalism in the context of global news 'flow', and as a social artefact of larger struggles over the definition and representation of issues in conflict, both historical and present-day. And it maps out, briefly, two particular areas where further research is warranted.

Origins

The present wave of interest in peace journalism, among journalists, researchers and media activists, builds on an original concept from Johan Galtung, known as the 'father' of peace studies and giver of many of its key concepts. Galtung also contributed the first significant conventionalist account of journalism about conflict, *The Structure of Foreign News* (Galtung and Ruge, 1965/1980). Media research had already dwelt on the mismatch in size between 'the facts' and 'the news' – journalism, in other words, inescapably involves 'gatekeeping' (White, 1950). The Galtung-Ruge study showed that this is a systematic process. Gatekeeping decisions create discernible patterns of omission and inclusion – not random, but structured, according to five key criteria:

- Threshold: A big story is one that has an extreme effect on a large number of people.
- Frequency: Events that fit well with the news organization's schedule.
- Negativity: Bad news is more exciting than good news.
- Unexpectedness: If an event is out of the ordinary it will have a greater effect.
- Unambiguity: Events whose implications are clear make for better copy.

Galtung later added 'upstream filters' to propose a 'four-factor news communication model' (1992). In general, negative events, befalling elite individuals in elite countries, are news stories. Positive processes, benefiting non-elite groups in non-elite countries, are non-stories. His adumbration of 'war journalism', introduced at a conference at Taplow Court, in southern England, in 1997 (and subsequently published in Galtung, 1998) can be understood as an adaptation of these insights, that the mainstream of reporting, in most places at most times, tends to be biased in favour of:

- violence, with conflicts represented in dualistic terms, two parties contesting the single goal of victory;
- elites, with 'official sources' – political and military leaders – dominating definitions of issues at stake in both war and peace;
- propaganda, with particular attention to exposing 'their' untruths while ignoring 'ours';
- and victory, so media typically pack their bags and leave when weapons fall silent.

Peace journalism, then, is:

- conflict- or peace-oriented, reaching out in time and space to represent parties to conflict as both multiplicitous and variegated, pursuing many goals and with many opportunities for intervention;
- people-oriented, recognizing that conflict issues may look very different when examined along cross-cutting angles and in terms of how they are experienced in everyday life by those at the 'grassroots';
- truth-oriented, determined to expose self-serving pronouncements and representations on all sides;
- and solution-oriented, being prepared to seek and ventilate peace initiatives from whatever quarter.

Anyone who hoped, and wished to advocate, for changes in the media representation of conflicts, now had a readymade binary opposition to work with. And opposition was plentiful, notably from journalists, who, in rich Western countries with liberal traditions, tend to be immediately suspicious of such calls. One of them, David Randall – a former colleague of mine on the London *Independent* – is also the author of a standard journalism textbook, in which he declares:

> There is only good and bad journalism. And the two are universal ... Good journalists wherever they are will be attempting the same thing: intelligent fact-based journalism, honest in intent and effect, serving no cause but the discernible truth, and written clearly for its readers whoever they may be (Randall, 1996: 2).

The BBC correspondent, David Loyn (2007), likewise calls for the minimum range of journalistic endeavour to be proscribed – by libel laws, 'taste and decency' regulations and suchlike – whilst resisting attempts to 'prescribe' what should be reported. The tools of journalism, he adds, should be 'sharpened, not altered'. In academic circles, too, critics whetted their knives. For Hanitzsch (2007), journalism can be defined, indeed, as a category of 'public communication', by its preoccupation with 'internal goals'. Journalists simply want to do what they and their peers think of as good journalism, defined, typically, according to values such as 'fairness' and 'accuracy'. The political campaigner or advertising executive, on the other hand, may launch many a tendentious slogan, in bad prose and accompanied by crude images, without a qualm, so long as the external goals – getting votes or increasing sales figures – are met. Adding an external goal – peace – to journalism therefore threatens to cross an important line.

Peace journalism finds a foothold by inquiring into how particular parts of 'the truth' come to be 'discerned', in Randall's terms, whilst others are habitually ignored. Journalists typically judge 'threshold', for instance, according to readily identifiable conventions, notably in nationalistic terms. Nossek finds the alignment of news with nation still applies, in reporting of political violence, even after 'the accelerated technological development of 1990s, which left its mark on the communication map' (2004: 343), and McNair adds that 'while … the relevance of *political* borders has been substantially weakened by the expansion of new information and communication technologies, most of what we consume as media is still national in origin and orientation' (2006: 8).

Then, research on news flow, pioneered by the MacBride report in 1980, the study commissioned by UNESCO on 'communication problems', shows rich countries – a list headed by the United States – as the chief sources of international news. Wu (2004) confirms these findings in a study drawing on data gathered in 1995. At the time, millions of refugees from the slaughter in Rwanda, barely a year earlier, were hunkered down in giant refugee camps, but their plight figures nowhere, he finds, in the international news in media from 44 countries.

In this and other aspects of the Galtung-Ruge list, it is when events mesh with the preoccupations of officials in their own country that journalists tend to discern particular parts of the truth about the world around them. Frequency and unambiguity also predispose the news in favour of officialdom as prime sources:

> Journalism's criteria of newsworthiness and factuality, and its routines of newsgathering anchored in bureaucratic institutions with designated spokes-people and prescheduled routines, are mutually constitutive. Taken together, they tend to ensure routine and privileged access for bureaucrats and agency officials, who provide the 'hard facts', credible claims and background information for objective reporting (Hackett & Zhao, 1998: 78).

Bagdikian (1997) shows how the primacy of officialdom, as a source for definitions and representations in news, emerged, and hardened into convention, in response to commercial imperatives. To be able to sell journalism, to consumers of all political views and none, it was necessary to devise ways to present it as unexceptionable. Quoting officials could pass as 'neutral'. Reflecting the extent of dissension between the two major parties in a representative democracy, the habit of 'indexing', could serve to define the bounds of 'legitimate controversy' (Hallin, 1989).

The general problems to which this gives rise have been much discussed. Important issues tend to drop off the edge of the news agenda if it does not suit the two major parties to discuss them. Then, in Bagdikian's words, officials 'issue a high quotient of self-serving declarations' (2000: 176). There are also particular problems when it comes to representing conflicts. For obvious reasons, political leaders seldom, if ever, originate moves to peace. Their position demands that they be seen to respond to an established public mood, or risk being isolated and undermined. Long before that, however, such developments may be underway. The peace researcher, John Paul Lederach, remarks:

> I have not experienced any situation of conflict, no matter how protracted or severe, from Central America to the Philippines to the Horn of Africa, where there have not been people who had a vision for peace, emerging often from their own experience of pain. Far too often, however, these same people are overlooked and disempowered either because they do not represent 'official' power, whether on the side of government or the various militias, or because they are written off as biased and too personally affected by the conflict (1997: 94).

For such people to be overlooked by journalism, unless and until their visions are finally taken up by journalists' usual sources, means that readers and audiences often receive a picture of the conflict which is less 'peaceful' than is warranted by the facts – inaccurate, in other words. Then, states are defined, in terms originally supplied by Max Weber, as political organizations that successfully claim a monopoly on the legitimate use of force in a given territory – so, if news anoints the leaders of those states as the most important sources, there is bound to be a general, ongoing bias towards force as a response to conflict, certainly over international law, for instance. Friel and Falk (2004) surveyed 70 editorials in the *New York Times*, dealing with the prospective invasion of Iraq, in 2003, and found no mention of the words 'UN Charter' or 'international law'.

Taken together, negativity, unambiguity and unexpectedness also install two further biases – in favour of event over process, and in favour of dualism as a basic underlying model for reporting conflicts. The first has left journalism vulnerable, in recent years, to what I have characterized as 'the signature propaganda ploy for the "war on terrorism"' (Lynch, 2008: 145) – namely that to seek to explain political violence is tantamount to justifying it. With explanation effectively prohibited, representations of conflict become automatically more receptive to the proposition that further violence will prove an appropriate and effective response. (A recollection – in the days following the '9/11' attacks in the US, a former assistant secretary of state being interviewed on BBC World, and challenged by the presenter: 'But isn't terrorism like a multi-headed hydra?' Answer: 'Yes, and we're going to cut off all the heads.') The second, dualism, insulates the reporter against allegations of partiality because s/he has 'heard both sides'. But it also constructs a zero-sum, 'tug of war' pattern in which 'anything that is not, unequivocally, "winning", can only be "losing"; and risks being interpreted, indeed reported, as such' (Lynch, 2006).

Peace journalism, then, is conceived as a remedy for these biases, to 'give peace a chance' in public debate. It is taking place whenever 'editors and reporters make choices – of what stories to report, and how to report them – that create opportunities for society at large to consider and value non-violent responses to conflict' (Lynch & McGoldrick, 2005: 5). It comes with no matching commitment to ensuring that violent responses get a fair hearing, because the conventions of news mean they seldom struggle for a place on the agenda. But, if society is presented with non-violent options, and rejects them, then there is little else journalism can do about it, while remaining journalism. In other words, peace is added, as an external goal, on an instrumentalist basis – the better to deliver on internal goals of fairness and accuracy.

Counter-currents

To account for the journalistic conventions, which predispose conflict reporting in some places, at some times, in favour of a dominant strain of war journalism, as belonging to a 'tradition', and having 'emerged' in response to market conditions, risks glossing over discontinuities and ignoring counter-currents.

In England, for one, Curran (1988) reminds us that market forces were pre-empted, in the nineteenth century, by politically motivated censorship. Punitive taxation was used to curtail the increasingly subversive 'penny press' – the medley of small-circulation publications read by the newly literate lower-middle and working classes. And the rich tradition of alternative media, exemplified in the UK by the long-running *Peace News* and now flourishing in the abundance of net-based journalism, has grown and sustained itself alongside commercial media. The history of the press, even in one of its heartlands, cannot be satisfactorily mapped in terms of 'the irreversible processes, the constant readjustments, the underlying tendencies that gather force' (Foucault, 1972), nor can its dimensions be captured in purely structuralist terms, by identifying 'sociological constants', despite the importance of Galtung-Ruge in doing just that.

To attempt, instead, what Foucault calls a 'general history', entails considering different traditions, and 'what vertical system they are capable of forming; what interplay of correlation and dominance exists between them; what may be the effect of shifts, different temporalities, and various rehandlings' (1972).

Peace journalism has been more readily accepted in the 'majority world' (Rogers, 2008). Many journalists in Indonesia, for instance, took up peace journalism, or *jurnalisme damai*, in the period following the fall of the Suharto regime, when horizontal and vertical conflicts entered a more violent phase, and the lifting of restrictions on coverage of community tensions drew allegations that media were fanning the flames. The country's biggest newspaper, *Kompas*, adopted *jurnalisme damai* as an editorial policy; the Jakarta newspaper, *Sinar Harapan* – banned under the New Order – relaunched with the slogan, 'peace journalism represents the hope that we can live together', and AJI, the journalists' union, helped to set up a safe space for reporters to meet in Ambon, where they could keep in touch with the point of view of the other side, in order to contribute to mutual understanding.

The Philippines' biggest newspaper, the *Philippine Daily Inquirer* (PDI), was launched in 1985 with the avowed aim of helping to end martial law under President Ferdinand Marcos – which, indeed, it did (Coronel, 2000). It has since been found to be doing more peace journalism, according to evaluative criteria based on the Galtung schema, than most other Asian newspapers (Lee & Maslog, 2005; Lee et al., 2006); and in comparison with Australian media, and international media (both in Lynch, 2008).

The latter two studies examine the *PDI's* coverage in the context of the 'global war on terrorism': a template applied, by the Philippines government, to the long-running insurgency by the communist rebels, the New People's Army (NPA), which was blacklisted as a 'terror grouping' by both the State Department and the European Union. This is an interplay, in Foucault's words, of correlation and dominance. The Marcos regime was backed by the US, and after its fall, the new government of Corazon Aquino immediately drew up a new law prohibiting the siting of foreign military installations on Philippines soil – obliging the Pentagon to dismantle the Clark airbase and Subic naval base, anchor and symbol of American power. Alliance with Washington in one global conflict narrative – the Cold War – had become irremediably tainted, and, latterly, alliance in another – the 'war on terrorism' – has gone the same way. The Philippines was the first country to pull its troops out of Iraq, after some of its nationals were kidnapped and killed. Given the specific content of the 'war on terrorism' ideology, discussed earlier, the chief evaluative criterion for studies of the *PDI* in this period is the iteration of what Shinar (2007: 200) calls 'backgrounds and contexts' – re-opening the distinction between explaining and justifying the armed struggle of, in this case, the NPA. The extent of peace journalism is therefore, in Lynch's words, 'a qualitative indicator, in social artefact, of the degree of resistance to the "war on terrorism" in one of its strategic target countries' (2008: 148).

Indeed, peace journalism can, in this respect at least, be understood as a form of resistance to what the MacBride report identifies as the 'world information and communication order'. Journalism of the minority world, compiled according to the conventions identified by Galtung and Ruge, is likely to foreground 'dispositional' explanations for behaviour in conflict over 'situational' ones (Zimbardo, 2003: 4). It thus downplays the effect of structural violence as an analytical factor in representing and explaining the world around us, and is automatically less receptive to propositions for responding to conflict with effective measures to address systematic disadvantage and injustice. To illuminate backgrounds and contexts, to seek out and explore suggestions and initiatives for non-violent responses to conflict issues and equip us to negotiate our own readings of dominant definitions and representations – all aspects of peace journalism – is to challenge, in the information and communication domain, relations of dominance in the world economic, political and social order.

In Western corporate media, I have argued elsewhere (Lynch, 2008) that 'possessive individualism' is a default ideological recourse for conceptualizing the reader, listener or viewer, and his/her relations with both the media themselves and the world in general. In this, according to the political philosopher, C.B. Macpherson, who coined the phrase, the individual sells labour and skills on the open market, owing nothing to society. In the different temporality of countries that struggled against colonialism, such as those discussed here, discursive practices in general, and journalism in particular, may draw on an opposite tradition, in which the alignment of news with nation takes on the explicit connotation of solidarity against oppression.

Journalists in the Philippines inherit a 'legacy of a century-long tradition of a fighting, anti-colonial press' (Coronel, 2000: 149). Through the twentieth century (the period when the US itself was the colonial power) 'clandestinely distributed newspapers helped raise awareness of the evils of nearly 400 years of colonial rule, germinating the idea of an independent Philippine nation' (2000: 149–150). And it is from his study of the rise and spread of *Bahasa Indonesia* – in large part through the founding and circulation of newspapers – that Benedict Anderson coins his aphorism: 'print-language is what invents nationalism' (1991: 134). The process is fictionalized in a famous Indonesian novel, *Child of all Nations* (1984), by the late Pramoedya Ananta Toer. The hero is a journalist, Minke, who is urged to write in his own native language, to rouse his people in the struggle for liberation: 'Just think about it – who will urge Natives to speak out if their own writers, such as yourself, won't do it? ... He who emerges at the top of his society will always face demands from that society – it is his society that has allowed him to rise'.

If there are specific contextual reasons why news about conflict in the majority world is likely to prove more open to peace journalism, then there is abundant evidence of various rehandlings in Western journalism as well. Shinar (2008) is one of several researchers to examine coverage of the war between Israel and Lebanon in 2006. In comparing the reporting offered by one Israeli and one Canadian newspaper, he operationalizes the model into evaluative criteria, finding peace journalism 'overshadowed, but not entirely excluded', with considerable attention to 'people-oriented sources' and a notably limited penetration by 'military discourse'. Hackett and Schroeder (2008) examine coverage of the same conflict, along with the war in Afghanistan, taking place at the same time and involving Canadian troops. Their content analysis of more than 500 articles (from Canadian, US, Israeli, and al-Jazeera online and print news outlets) finds each of a list of ten war journalism criteria occurring in about half the articles studied, while the peace journalism criteria crop up in an average three out of ten, with the most frequent, the inclusion of multiple parties in the conflict picture rather than a reduction to just two.

A paradigm shift?

The Galtung-Ruge essay was one of a clutch of early structuralist texts, in a range of disciplines, as varied as Northrop Frye's *Anatomy of Criticism* (1957); *Structural Anthropology* by Claude Levi-Strauss (English translation in 1963) and Thomas Kuhn's *Structure of Scientific Revolutions* (1962). Kuhn popularized the phrase 'paradigm shift', arguing that, in science, it is when anomalies proliferate under an existing paradigm that a new one can be asserted. Notable examples of peace journalism often emerge in such circumstances, when official discourses part company with the perceptions of a critical mass of readers and audiences.

Two instances, among many, will serve to illustrate the point. In 2007, the *Sydney Morning Herald* led its own campaign for 'earth hour' – one sixty-minute spell in which everyone in the city was encouraged to switch off appliances including electric lights. The paper publicized the results as a way of underlining what was already known about the effects of anthropogenic climate change – and efforts, effectively peace initiatives, to minimize and alleviate them – in the face of attempts by the then Liberal (conservative)-led government of John Howard, to downplay them. The idea caught on and has since been replicated in other cities around the world. In another example, from some years earlier in Northern Ireland, when peace talks entered the agenda, the biggest party, the Ulster Unionists, were publicly haggling over whether they should join in, the future of the peace process effectively in their hands. Then the main newspaper of the protestant community in Belfast, the *Newsletter*, published an opinion poll which revealed overwhelming support for the UUP to enter the talks; which they immediately did.

Journalism cannot afford to appear less well-informed than its public. In Michael Schudson's words, 'the media are formally disconnected from other ruling agencies because they must attend as much to their own legitimation as to the legitimation of the capitalist system as a whole' (1995: 270). The rapid and conspicuous unraveling of propaganda over the US-led invasion of Iraq in 2003 has led to the brink of a 'journalistic abyss' (Lynch, 2006), since official pronouncements and representations, traditionally the prime sources of news, have lost a significant, perhaps decisive portion of their credibility, at least when it comes to mediating international conflict.

This is manifest in a crisis of military legitimacy, in which the publics of allied countries are notably sceptical towards both the principle and the actuality of their governments sending troops to join military adventures led by the US. In this, public opinion is often out of step with political opinion. In Australia, in September 2008, a poll published by the Lowy Institute, a foreign affairs think-tank, revealed that the country's armed intervention in Afghanistan had lost public backing (by 56% to 44%) for the first time, after a long slide from an initial position of strong support. But both main parties – Labour, by now in government, and the Liberal/National coalition – continued to back the intervention and its reinforcement. Rogers argues:

> The occupation of countries in the middle east and southwest Asia by western military forces is no longer politically feasible. The starting-point for any new policy will have to be complete withdrawal. Any other approach has been rendered obsolete by the cumulative effects of the last six years. That thought is at present beyond Washington and London's reach, but it is a reality that one day they will simply have to face (2008).

It poses a potential problem for US military planners because, as Kay (2000) found Americans 'favor the use of force' only when certain criteria are met, notably the presence of 'allies to share the risk and cost' – a finding supported by polling in the latter months of 2002 on the then proposed invasion of Iraq (in Lynch & McGoldrick, 2005). Schudson's (1995) observation implies that Rogers's reality will have to be faced by the media before the political classes denoted in his formula of 'Washington and London'. Politicians in US-allied states can, in some cases, behave as if nothing is amiss, when (for instance) lectured by the likes of Secretary of State Condoleezza Rice and then-presidential candidate John McCain, on the wickedness of 'invad[ing] other countries ... in the 21st Century'. These strictures, in 2008, came in connection with events in the southern Caucasus. But readers and audiences, having witnessed the events of the previous few years, may very well say 'that's rich coming from you' – and the programmes, websites and newspapers they are consuming may feel they need to prove they are up to speed.

David Loyn responds to my suggestion (2007), that much of his own reporting for the BBC exhibits characteristics of peace journalism, by offering, as a crucial distinction, that 'it was not my *intention* to commit peace journalism' [emphasis in the original]. The anomalies clustering around the old paradigm may now transcend intentionality, I have argued, to a point where we inhabit a 'peace journalism condition' in which an 'increased level of debate and contestation over journalistic representations of conflict' has made room for 'more conflict-orientated, people-orientated and solution-orientated coverage and ... vantage points from which to inspect propaganda on the outside' (Lynch & Galtung, 2010).

Exponents and critics alike have pondered how peace journalism is supposed to 'work', in the sense of creating or finding a space in actual journalistic practice. It represents an 'overly individualistic and voluntaristic perspective', Hanitzsch (2007) says, taking too little account of the structures, institutions and routines of day-to-day reporting in media industries. Hackett and Carroll (2006) offer a typology of three main types of 'media activism' – change journalists, change the audience, create more media. In pursuit of the first, Hackett, in a separate work (2007), considers how the newsmaking process can be conceptualized so as to allow scope for journalistic 'agency': seeing the content of news as, perhaps, governed, rather than determined, by the 'structure' in which it is produced. Pierre Bourdieu's notion of journalism as an autonomous institutional system, or 'field', is preferable, according to Hackett, to 'reductionist' models which 'risk obscuring the specificity and coherence of journalism as a cultural practice and form of knowledge-production'.

Shinar identifies the most promising elements of the peace journalism model to emphasize in exhortatory or pedagogical initiatives with journalists: 'People-oriented sources, lesser use of victimizing language and military discourse, and a win-win orientation can be promoted more easily than other dimensions as viable professional peace journalism practices. Like other components of conflict coverage, these findings might serve to steer efforts at promoting peace journalism' (2008: 24). When it comes to the second of Hackett and Carroll's categories, Wenden spots a significant gap – and opportunity – in efforts to change audiences, which she calls 'critical language education', with peace journalism identified as a precursor:

> Despite the fact that discourse can indirectly contribute to practices that lead to social and ecological violence and despite its potential for effecting reconciliation and promoting social harmony, it remains a neglected variable in the analysis of problems that present obstacles to a comprehensive peace and in the prescription for solutions (Wenden, 2007: 165).

And Tehranian (2002) presents what is still, perhaps, the most inspiring vision for creating more media, even among the proliferation of recent years: the call for a dedicated UN agency, a Media Development Bank, to be financed from taxes on the two global communication commons, the geo-stationary orbit and the electro-magnetic spectrum, and based on peace journalism as 'a system of global media ethics'. It amounts to a call to revive the MacBride vision of a New World Information and Communication Order, or 'NWICO'. Shinar (2007) helpfully updates the original prescriptions, to include the establishment and support of indigenous institutions to monitor the media; organizing networks of independent radio/TV stations to help pool programming resources; training for both journalists and audiences in media literacy, and supporting equal access, particularly to new media, by marginalized groups.

New frontiers

Where research into peace journalism has, perhaps, had too little to say, is in the area of media effects. Calculations, about likely media responses, clearly play a part in the actions and motivations of parties to conflict, both large and small. Sources for stories can only know what to do or say, in order to obtain the kind of coverage they believe will redound to their benefit, on the basis of their experience of previous coverage. 'The facts of tomorrow bear the ineradicable imprint, or residue, of the reporting of today ... [there is] a feedback loop of cause and effect, connecting journalists, their sources and audiences' (Lynch & McGoldrick, 2005: 218).

To trace the influence of *particular* trends in media representation on *particular* departures in responses to conflict is, however, a challenge of a different order. Accounts by journalists such as Gowing (1997) and Strobel (2001) are flawed by methodology, relying, as they do, chiefly on privileged access to key political and policy-making figures, with the respective authors asking them, in as many words, whether their decisions were influenced by the media. Their conclusion – that such influence is, at best, limited – was predictable. To go further would entail both a cannier approach to setting interview protocols, and perhaps some effort to map the distinctions of peace journalism onto models of policy decision-making from international relations, such as the theory that the perceived scope for governmental actions is derived from the assessment of successive institutional and other 'constraints' (Linklater, 2000).

If that is one path across the hitherto under-explored territory of examining effects on source behaviour, then the collection and analysis of data on differentials in the respective effects of war journalism and peace journalism on audience response – both cognitive and, latterly, psychological – is at least a little more advanced. McGoldrick's (2008) study found that war journalism is a significant stressor, indeed, that 'immersion in news representations of conflict, in the prevalent mode of war journalism, can be seen ... as a contributory factor to the interiority of subjects in therapy comparable – in the nature of its impact, if not in scale – with the experiences of childhood and family life'. It is, perhaps, a discernible further step to the proposition that war journalism is bad for us. Cross-referenced on to the method, established by several of the researchers whose work is cited in this chapter, of cross-national comparative content analysis, based on evaluative criteria derived from the peace journalism schema, it could give us the basis for setting a global standard in conflict coverage, as a tool for consumer protection and touchstone for media activists. And that could, indeed, represent a challenge to what are still the dominant patterns of representation in global media.

References

Ananta Toer, Pramoedya, (1984) *Child of All Nations*, trans. M. Lane, Sydney: Penguin Australia.

Anderson, Benedict, 1991: *Imagined Communities* 2nd ed, New York: Verso.

Bagdikian, Ben, 1997: *The Media Monopoly* 5th ed, Boston: Beacon Press.

Bagdikian, Ben, 2000, The Media Monopoly 6th ed, Boston.

Coronel, Sheila S., 2000: 'Free as a mocking bird', in L. Williams and R. Rich (eds), *Losing Control – Freedom of the Press in Asia*, Canberra: Asia Pacific Press, pp. 147–168.

Curran, James and Seaton, Jean, 1988: *Power Without Responsibility*, London: Routledge (Third Edition)

Friel, Howard and Falk, Richard, 2004: *The Record of the Paper*, New York: Verso.

Foucault, Michel, 1972: *The Archaeology of Knowledge*, London: Routledge (trans: A.M. Sheridan Smith)

Galtung, Johan, 1992: *Peace by Peaceful Means*, London: Pluto Press.

Galtung, Johan, 1998: 'High Road, Low Road – Charting the Course for Peace Journalism', *Track Two*, vol. 7, no. 4, Centre for Conflict Resolution, South Africa.

Galtung, Johan and Ruge, Mari H., 1965/1980: 'The Structure of Foreign News', *Essays in Peace Research*, Ejlers: Copenhagen, vol. IV, pp. 118–151.

Gowing, Nik, 1997: *Help or Hindrance? The media's role in conflict prevention*, New York: Carnegie Commission for the Prevention of Deadly Conflict

Hackett, Robert A., 2007: 'Is Peace Journalism Possible? Three frameworks for assessing structure and agency in news media', in D. Shinar and W. Kempf (eds.), *Peace Journalism – the State of the Art*, Berlin: Regener, pp. 75–96.

Hackett, Robert A. and Zhao, Yuezhi, 1998: *Sustaining Democracy? The Politics of Objectivity*, Toronto: Garamond Press.

Hackett, Robert A. and Carroll, William K., 2006: *Remaking Media – The Struggle to Democratise Public Communication*, Abingdon: Routledge.

Hackett, Robert A and Schroeder, Birgitta, 2008: 'Does anybody practice peace journalism?' in Peace and Policy, vol 13, pp 26–46.

Hallin, Daniel C., 1989: *The 'Uncensored War': the Media and Vietnam*, Berkeley: University of California Press.

Hanitzsch, Thomas, 2007: 'Situating Peace Journalism in Journalism Studies: a critical appraisal', *Conflict and Communication Online*, vol. 6 no. 2.

Kay, Alan, 2000: 'When Americans Favor the Use of Force', *International Journal of Public Opinion Research*, vol. 12, no. 2, pp. 182–190.

Lederach, John Paul, 1997: *Building Peace – Sustainable Reconciliation in Divided Societies*, Washington DC: United States Institute of Peace Press.

Lee, S.T. and Maslog, C.C., 2005: 'War or Peace Journalism in Asian Newspapers', *Journal of Communication*, vol. 55, no. 2, pp. 311–329.

Lee, S.T., Maslog, C.C. and Kim, H.S., 2006: Asian Conflicts and the Iraq War – a comparative framing analysis. *International Communications Gazette*, vol. 68, no. 5–6, pp. 499–518.

Linklater, Andrew, 2000: *International Relations: Critical Concepts in Political Science*, London: Taylor & Francis.

Loyn, David, 2007: 'Peace journalism or good journalism?' in *Conflict and Communication Online*, vol 6 no 2

Lynch, Jake, 2006: 'What's So Great About Peace Journalism?', *Global Media Journal, Mediterranean Edition*, vol. 1, no. 1.

Lynch, Jake, 2008: *Debates in Peace Journalism*, Sydney: Sydney University Press.

Lynch, Jake and Galtung, Johan, 2009: *Reporting Conflict: New Directions in Peace Journalism*, Boulder: Paradigm Press (forthcoming).

Lynch, Jake and McGoldrick, Annabel, 2005: *Peace Journalism*, Stroud: Hawthorn Press.

McGoldrick, Annabel, 2008: 'Psychological effects of war journalism and peace journalism' in Peace and Policy, vol 13, pp 86–98.

McNair, Brian, 2006: *Cultural Chaos – Journalism, News and Power in a Globalised World*, Abingdon: Routledge.

Nossek, Hillel, 2004: 'Our News and their News: The Role of National Identity in the Coverage of Foreign News', *Journalism*, vol. 5, pp. 343–368.

Randall, David, 1996: *The Universal Journalist*, London: Pluto Press.

Rogers, Paul, 2008: 'The Iraq Project', *OpenDemocracy*, January 31.

Schudson, Michael, 1995: *The Power of News*, Cambridge, MA: Harvard University Press.

Shinar, Dov, 2007: 'Peace Journalism State of the Art', in eds. Wilhelm Kempf and Dov Shinar, Peace Journalism State of the Art, Berlin: Regener.

Strobel, Warren P, 1997: Late-breaking foreign policy, Washington: United States Institute of Peace Press

Tehranian, Majid, 2002: 'Peace Journalism: Negotiating Global Media Ethics', *Harvard International Journal of Press/Politics*, vol. 7, no. 2, pp. 58–83.

Wenden, Anita L., 2007: 'Educating for a Critically Literate Civil Society: incorporating the linguistic perspective into peace education', *Journal of Peace Education*, vol. 4, no. 2, pp. 163–180.

White, David Manning, 1950: 'The Gatekeeper: A Case Study in the Selection of News', *Journalism Quarterly*, vol. 27, pp. 383–390.

Wu, Denis H., 2004: 'The World's Windows to the World: an overview of 44 nations' international news coverage', in A. Sreberny and C. Paterson (eds.), *International News in the 21st Century*, Eastleigh: John Libbey Publishing, pp. 95–110.

Zelizer, Barbie, 2004: Taking Journalism Seriously: News and the Academy. Thousand Oaks, CA: Sage.

Zimbardo, Philip G., 2003: A *Situationist's Perspective on the Psychology of Evil: Understanding How Good People are Transformed into Perpetrators*, in A. G. Miller (ed.) The Social Psychology of Good and Evil, New York: Guilford Press, pp. 21–50.

PART VII
JOURNALISM'S FUTURES

50

NEWS IN THE DIGITAL AGE

Natalie Fenton

Many commentators on the nature and state of journalism have claimed that it is undergoing a fundamental transformation. One of the key reasons cited for this transformation is the changing nature of technology that is claimed to impact directly upon the practice of journalism and access to the profession. The particular characteristics of the Internet marked out as creating the most impact can be summarized as speed and space; multiplicity and polycentrality; interaction and participation. Within these organizing themes, the nature of the transformation is considered variably as a negative and a positive development. Both approaches usually base their judgments upon the perceived contribution of news media to fully functioning modern democratic systems and hence upon journalism's role in contributing to the public sphere (Habermas, 1989). Whatever the approach, what is described, in one way or another, is the dismantling of the structures of news media as we know them.

On the face of it there has certainly been a step change in the nature of news productivity. The Office of Communications – the independent regulator and competition authority for the UK communications industries (Ofcom, 2007: 34), report that the:

> Daily Telegraph launched the first UK on-line national news operation – Electronic Telegraph – in 1994, followed three years later by the BBC's news website. The last major UK national newspaper to launch its website was the Daily Mail, in 2004. Within the last decade, web-based operations have come to be viewed as essential for newspapers – national, regional and local – and for all major broadcasters and news agencies.

Though technology may frequently be the target of derision or delight, the nature of change is not attributable to technology alone. This particular technological wave of change is deeply embedded in and part of a complex convergence of economic, regulatory and cultural forces that are contingent upon local circumstance at any one time. None the less it would be wrong to underestimate the impact of technology. There is little doubt that the Internet in particular is a key constitutive element of contemporary newsrooms – but it is critical to stress the continuum between the online and offline worlds that exist in a relationship of mutuality and interdependence. Online news merges traditional ways of producing the news with the web's new potentials in an on-going process in which different local conditions have led to different outcomes. Although this chapter is a general discussion of news production and journalism there are very real differences between media – be it print or broadcast; the funding model – be it public, private or mixed; the ethos – be it public service or commercial; and the locality – be it local, national or international news that should be borne in mind when reading the general debates referred to in this chapter.

Much of what is argued either for or against the changes described and forecast have historical precedents. Journalism and journalists have faced a long history of criticism. The decline of journalistic integrity and the professional standards of journalism have been accused variously of egomania, being parasitic, exploitative of human tragedy and generally of being squalid and untrustworthy. Hargreaves (2003: 12), a former journalist, writes:

> Journalism stands accused of sacrificing accuracy for speed, purposeful investigation for cheap intrusion and reliability for entertainment. 'Dumbed down' news media are charged with privileging sensation over significance and celebrity over achievement.

It is no surprise that new media have offered a fresh means of anxiety and an extension of these concerns but the concerns are not new. Similarly, other forms of new technology have in the past also invited eulogizing on their democratic potential, their ability to become a tool of the people wresting power from the elite structures of society. Once more, the debates echo the praises of plurality, accessibility and participation. Importantly then, we should re-emphasize from the outset that these concerns do not arise because of the technology per se. Rather they are part of a more complex socio-economic, political and cultural history.

Since the mid-1990s a number of studies have explored the implications of the Internet for journalistic practice. These studies report that the Internet brings new ways of collecting and reporting information into the newsrooms (Fenton, 2009; Miller, 1998; Reddick and King, 1997; Singer, 1998, 2001; 2003; Deuze, 1999). They have looked at the nature of news content, the way journalists do their job, the structure of the newsroom and shifting relationships between journalists, news organizations and their publics. In their quest to make sense of the impact of new media on the news they have considered the interactive nature of the Internet; the complexity of its content in volume and variety as well as its accessibility and convergence across previously distinct media.

In this chapter, I trace the contours of these debates under the themes of speed and space; multiplicity and polycentrality; interactivity and participation. At one end are those who regard the digital age (and the Internet, in particular) as the route to reinvigorated democracy, wherein the complex network of news is fragmented, participatory, non-hierarchical and de-centred. On the other end are those who see the Internet as detrimental to democracy – that is, where technology is used as no more than a fix for economic efficiency, resulting in more competition, as well as more space to fill, but with fewer professional journalists to do it. This leads to desk-bound, administrative, cut and paste journalism.

New media and the news: reinvigorated democracy

In general, claims for the democratization of the public sphere relate to the accessibility of the Internet to producers and users. In these debates, new media is claimed to be a dynamic tool for enhanced democracy (Whillock, 1997). The ability to bypass a news intermediary to get information means that people communicate with people rather than be filtered out through the mainstream news media (Gillmor, 2004). The Internet is invested with the ability to be empowering; to spread civic networks; to aid access to information and discussion of social and political issues (Beckett, 2008; Hargreaves, 2003, Rivas-Rodriguez, 2003).

Speed and space: expanding news platforms and increasing timeliness

The argument begins simply enough: more space equals more news. The sheer space available online is said to open up new possibilities for news presentation that cannot be found in hard copies. Through archiving facilities the ability to provide more depth of coverage is increased exponentially. Similarly the ability to update regularly is vastly improved. The space for multimedia formats also allows for news to be presented in innovative and interesting ways (Gunter, 2003).

Space is also linked to geographical reach. Reach is further enhanced by speed. The Internet has enabled journalists to get to data without having to leave the newsroom (Quinn, 2002). Reports can be downloaded in seconds, public databases interrogated in a fraction of the time it would have taken previously (Phillips, 2009).

Multiplicity and polycentrality: bringing diversity and challenging news dominance

The space available also translates into a plurality of news providers that removes the monopoly of provision from the major transnational corporations and opens it up to all citizens able to get access to a computer and the right software. In a mass system a few voices speak to the masses – the public becomes a media market; in online environments communities speak to each other. Citizens, it is claimed, become netizens followed by the creation of rhizomes of news and citizen journalism. The Internet provides a many-to-many model of information dissemination putting the smaller and the smallest news providers on an equal footing with the transnational conglomerates (Rheingold, 1993). This in turn opens up the possibility for smaller online news providers providing spaces for minority views and news that do not make it into the dominant news media because of their apparent lack of appeal to a mass audience (Rivas-Rodriguez, 2003).

Journalism, it is claimed, is diversifying in an unprecedented manner. This diversity reaches out to the range of publics in terms of economic structures, gender, class, ethnicity, age, geography etc. In the past, the sheer economics and scale of publishing news prevented all but a small number of companies from being the privileged gatekeepers of information dissemination. Hargreaves (2003) cites the example of Wales, with a population of 3 million people of whom about 20 per cent are Welsh-speaking, who as a result of investment by BBC Wales in an online news service now have, for the first time, a Welsh language daily news service online. This is a development that would not have been commercially possible with traditional media.

Related to issues of multiplicity and diversity, McNair (1999: 213) states that a proliferation of news platforms calls into question the notion of the public as a single, monolithic construct 'defined and serviced by a metropolitan elite, and encourages its replacement with a vision of multiple publics, connected in key ways'. As a result online journalism is claimed to offer audiences a view of the world that is more contextualized, textured, and multidimensional than traditional news media.

In this space it is more difficult for journalists to claim privilege and it is difficult to control. The Internet offers a space where interested readers can check the validity of one news report against another and even access the news sources referred to. The nature of news gathering is exposed like never before, undercutting the notion of journalistic objectivity. These changes have put the notions of journalistic objectivity and impartiality under scrutiny. In online journalism these normative anchors become dislodged in favour of the acknowledgment of the impossibility of objectivity and an increased awareness of subjectivity. The ability of audiences to go online, check reports and substantiate mainstream news perspectives for themselves is argued to lead to increased media literacy. The apparent multiplicity of views and voices from a diversity of cultures and viewpoints helps to keep the mainstream news 'on its toes' and render its construction more transparent.

Similarly, on-line news media frequently supply their users with further sources of information via hyper links which is another way in which the authority of the news provider shifts 'becoming in effect a network of a variety of news sources, rather than the undisputed bearer of "the news" or "the truth"' (Hargreaves, 2003: 53) introducing a more relativistic view of what constitutes the 'facts'. Perspective and point of view suddenly become important in striving to understand or make sense of what is fed to us as 'the news'. The notion of objectivity starts to fall apart in this environment. And as more people have access to more stories that claim partiality and subjectivity as their modus operandi and even as the route to 'truthfulness' so too does a 'journalism of attachment' begin to emerge (see Brayne, 2004). This journalism of attachment brings a more personal style of reporting that is claimed to better reflect the 'complexities and nuances of an increasingly diverse and pluralistic society' (Pavlik, 2001: 23).

Interactivity and participation:
increasing civic intervention and citizen journalism

The interactive and participative nature of the web suggests that everyone or anyone can be a journalist with the right tools. Interactivity and participation have led to three main changes for those traditionally conceived of as 'the audience'. Firstly, civic journalism is increasing; secondly, citizen access to public information and government services is expanding; and thirdly, citizens are more and more able to get information directly from political and government sources themselves (Pavlik, 2001). Citizen journalism bleeds into mainstream journalism and vice versa. Boczkowski (2004) argues that because of the interactive and participatory characteristics of the web the content and form of news (in his case, news that originates from American mainstream newspapers) is becoming more audience centered and this in turn changes the nature of news. The blogosphere has been credited with taking on the major news corporations through instant feedback that is often lively, openly subjective and highly critical. In the more renowned cases bloggers have been attributed with helping to topple Senator Trent Lott and the *New York Times* editor, Howell Raines, from their offices; helping to organize and coordinate protests over the Iraq war; boosting the presidential hopes of Howard Dean and Barack Obama with followers and cash contributions (Hachten, 2005).

Journalism now works in a world of email, text-messaging, multi-media story-telling, blogging etc. Ofcom (2007) state that there was a one-hundred-fold increase in weblogs from 2004–2007. This has been claimed as a positive enhancement of democracy – allowing citizens to break through the mainstream media's stranglehold on what is and what should be news. Allan (2004) notes that the 2003 Iraqi war has seen an unprecedented amount of news and information available online including the hard hitting commentary from one Iraqi blogger, Salaam Pax, who gained international recognition for his accounts of what was happening on the ground that eventually became a column in the UK daily national newspaper, the *Guardian*. It would appear that journalism has indeed had to adapt to a more inclusive, open and interactive communication environment. In 1973 Sigal wrote, 'News is consensible: newspaper audiences, by their responses to news, actively shape its content. Yet the average reader has little impact on the consensual process.' In the online environment it is argued that readers can have a greater impact on the news through an increase in the intensity of their exchanges with journalists and the presentation of their own views in online papers. News online is thus open to a higher degree of contestation than is typical of traditional print media.

However, many of the positive claims for new media reside in a small set of extra-ordinary examples and rest largely on the *potential* of new media alone to re-invigorate democracy rather than a consideration of technology in an economic, cultural and technological context. Considered in this vein, the picture begins to change.

New media and the news: the depression of democracy

Speed and space: increasing pressures on a decreasing work force

In a nutshell, the negative appraisal of new media and the news can be summed up by the description – speed it up and spread it thin. Researchers describe how established news organizations are encouraged by the speed of the Internet to release and update stories before the usual checks for journalistic integrity have taken place (Gunter,

2003; Silvia, 2001). The increasing emphasis on immediacy in news coverage is frequently satisfied by the news agencies (Ofcom, 2007) to the detriment of reportage (Scott, 2005). Hargreaves (2003) notes that journalists are concerned that new media technologies are turning them into 'robohacks', rather than reporters and editors.

Intensification of pressure in the newsroom is claimed to have led to fewer journalists gathering information outside of the newsroom (Phillips, 2009). For some the entire production process is a desk-top activity with journalists not only writing but also composing a complete presentation package on-screen. This form of multi-skilling is common in other deregulated industries and has been argued to lead to a reduction in levels of professionalism associated with standards as individuals are expected to do everything from get the pictures, to write the copy, to design the page (Gunter, 2003).

The increase in space has clearly brought intensified commercial pressures (Cohen, 2002). Every mainstream newspaper has gone online but none to date have managed to make it a consistently profitable enterprise. In the fiercely competitive world of news it is likely that the voices on the web will be dominated by the larger, more established news providers that will duplicate the same commercial interests according to the same understanding of how news fits those commercial concerns leading to anything but increased diversity. After all, Internet news is generally free and a threat to traditional commercial news industries that operate business models based on sales of advertising space and hard copies (Picard, 2002). As mainstream news providers plough more resources into online operations that are generally loss makers, journalism, or more accurately journalists suffer the consequences of reduced investment, increasing the temptation in the newsroom to rely on news agencies and cheaper forms of news-gathering to the detriment of original, expensive, time-consuming, in-depth journalism (Freedman, 2009; Schechter, 2004).

Multiplicity and polycentrality: more of the same

True, there is now more news available to more citizens than ever before. Quantity of course has never been a predictor of quality. Finding information can be an ever more difficult task as people attempt to navigate their way through a morass of search engines and news sites. Many have argued that the sheer abundance of news across a range of different media platforms is nothing more than sophisticated marketing and ever increasing commodifi-cation of the news product (Scott, 2005). This, it is argued, leads us irredeemably down the path of tabloidization and infotainment. More, simply means more opportunities for the news market to sell its wares – in a manner that maximizes profit rather than public interest. Issues of political discourse become assimilated into and absorbed by the modes and contents of entertainment. News, we are warned, will be transformed into a discourse of personalization, dramatization, simplification and polarization. The idea that person-alization will increase in an age of online social networking is argued to have a negative impact on the processes of rational democratic thought processes. Sunstein (2001: 192) writes that 'a market dominated by countless versions of "Daily Me", would make self government less workable [and] create a high degree of social fragmentation.'

In this argument more translates into more of the same. The major news sites online are said to provide little by way of original material and have a heavy reliance on the limited news spread of the major news agencies (Lewis et al., 2007; Redden and Witschge, 2009). Far from providing a diversity of views we are left with an homogenizing of public discourse. Hoge (1997) argues that the Internet provides information aplenty on the news agendas as fixed by the dominant news players but little on subjects of which we may know hardly anything. Ofcom (2007: 3) also report that despite the proliferation of news sources 'news outlets of all kinds often tell the same stories, from the same perspective, using much the same material.'

Studies that have completed content analyses of online news found that mainstream newspapers that developed an online version used a fraction of their print stories in the online edition, used mostly the same news stories with similar news judgments and operated under similar financial constraints (Singer, 1997). In other words news online does not automatically result in news diversity – it is often more of the same (Redden and Witschge, 2009).

The issues of ownership have been chronicled by news production studies (Schlesinger, 1987; Halloran et al., 1970; Epstein, 1974). Three corporations, Reuters, AP and AFP, dominate international wholesale news delivery and supply most source material for international stories on television and the Internet, while six operate the majority of major websites, commercial broadcasting/cable casting and newspapers worldwide (News Corporation, Bertelsmann, Vivendi, AOL-Time Warner, Disney and Viacom). With the further deregulation of US broadcasting in 2003 concentration of ownership shows no sign of slowing (McChesney, 2000). More news, faster news, prettier news via digital satellite, Internet and mobile phones do little to change the traditional news landscape when the same few corporations dominate news provision and the same standard storylines persist (Paterson and Sreberny, 2004: 14).

Criticism has been directed at international news in particular. A study by Paterson (2005 cited in Ofcom, 2007) on international news pointed to a major search engine boasting 4,500 news sources updated continuously. On closer inspection almost all of these sources from around the world were posting the same news stories, in the same words lifted from one of the four key international sources – BBC, AP, Reuters and AFP. More, it would seem, also translates into more control of search engines. In a study by Fenton et al. (2009) on UK news this outcome was repeated across a range of news stories from celebrities to earthquakes.

Interactivity and participation: limited and thin

Neither is the open and iterative world of online commentary seen to be taking journalism to new heights. Rather, the limitless opportunities for anyone to have their say on anything is decreed to result in opinion and vitriol replacing the hard-won gains of investigative journalism. One-off fragmentary responses are the norm rather than sustained analysis. 'Old news' values are argued to be replaced by populist ranting or those more interested in self publicity than the ethics of public value. Spaces for online discussion blur into the wider provision of news. The lack of accountability and anonymity of those responding online also introduces concerns of verification, accountability and accuracy. There are criticisms of the blogosphere as doing nothing more than opening the floodgates to unverified, de-professionalized gossip (Silvia, 2001). Similar concerns are voiced regarding consumer-generated video and audio material. There is also some evidence that online journalism differs little from traditional journalism in terms of interactivity as journalists have little time or inclination to interact with their audience (Phillips, 2009).

Conclusion

The history of communications technology shows us that if innovative content and forms of production appear in the early stages of a new technology and offer potential for radical change, this is more often than not cancelled out or appropriated by the dominant institutions operating within dominant technological and socio-political paradigms. 'Newness' of form and content is quickly smothered by predominance, size and wealth (Winston, 1995). Any 'newness' that is apparent is better described as novel or unprecedented – a description that fits more comfortably with the awareness that new media emerges out of old and existing socio-political and material infrastructures. But we should also be wary of economic reductionism.

Analyzing the practices that enact apparent technological and social/political transformation helps us to understand them and contemplate their potential consequences. Social histories of the press have demonstrated how institutional and technological factors have shaped the news over the last 200 years (Schudson, 1978; Blondheim, 1994) establishing that news is constitutive – it is social, political, economic, cultural and technological. Our understandings of the new news environment should not forget the lessons well learnt from these earlier studies. But the nature of news and the nature of news production have changed massively over the last two decades. We have seen the globalization of news take hold (Boyd-Barrett, 1998; Campbell, 2004); the concentration of ownership increase (McNair, 2006); and technology transform (Allan, 2006). To make sense of the complexity of contemporary formations of news we must combine macro-societal level analyses of news media and micro-organizational approaches to understanding contemporary formations of news.

A non-technologically deterministic approach to understanding news in a digital age suggests that studying new media and news still purports that news is what those contributing to its production make it. And this is precisely the point – those who contribute to its production are changing. The social actors' involvement in the construction of news has expanded and extended outside of the newsroom. This has resulted in the expansion of the locus of news production. Journalism is no longer a monologue; rather it increasingly consists of multiple voices. The extension of voice is all too often seen as expanding democratic practice – where voice is attributed to news users and seekers who by voicing opinions in chat rooms, forums and interactive news pages can shape what is seen as newsworthy and how it is reported. But, in an era of electronic news media marked by economic liberalism and globalization with a technology that has enabled a space for convergence between broadcasters and newspapers which compete with each other directly on the web (Hargreaves, 2003) other crucial voices enter the fray with ever more importance – those of advertising and marketing, design and technical personnel influence what gets covered via topic selection and budget allocation as online news sites strive to be profitable. The coordination and prioritization of the tasks, roles and values of these various groups will shed light on the nature of future news. But as news is a business, the business of news is increasingly not the business of journalists.

The nature of news journalism is changing and challenging the identities of the occupations and organizations that constitute the news industry. It is easy to wax lyrical about the *potential* of a digital age to change news for the better. For now, the reality appears somewhat different.

Note

This chapter draws upon research on new media and the news undertaken (January 2007–July 2009) in the Goldsmiths Media Research Centre: Spaces, Connections, Control and funded by the Leverhulme Trust. The research team consisted of James Curran, Aeron Davis, Natalie Fenton, Des Freedman, Peter Lee-Wright, Angela Phillips, Joanna Redden and Tamara Witschge.

References

Allan, S. (2004) 'Conflicting Truths: Online News and the war in Iraq' in C. Paterson and A. Sreberny *International News in the 21st Century*, Luton: John Libbey Press pp. 285–301.

Allan, S. (2006) *Online News: Journalism and the Internet*, Milton Keynes: Open University Press.

Beckett, C. (2008) *Supermedia: Saving Journalism So It Can Save the World*. London: Blackwell.

Boczkowski, P. (2004) *Digitizing the News*, Cambridge, MA: MIT Press.

Boyd-Barrett, O. (1998) 'Global News Agencies' in O. Boyd Barrett and T. Rantanen (eds.) *The Globalization of News*. London: Sage.

Blondheim, M. (1994) *News Over the Wires: The Telegraph and the Flow of Public Information in America, 1844–1897*. Cambridge MA: Harvard University Press.

Brayne, M. (2004) 'Emotions, Trauma and Good Journalism' in C. Paterson and A. Sreberny *International News in the 21st Century*, Luton: John Libbey Press, pp. 275–285.

Campbell, V. (2004), *Information Age Journalism: Journalism in an International Context*, Oxford: Oxford University Press.

Cohen, E. L. (2002). 'Online Journalism as Market-driven Journalism'. *Journal of Broadcasting and Electronic Media*, 46(4), 532–548.

Deuze, M. (1999) 'Journalism and the Web: An Analysis of Skills and Standards in an Online Environment'. *Gazette*, 61 (5): 373–390.

Epstein, E. (1974) *News from Nowhere*. New York: Vintage Books.

Fenton, N. (ed.) (2009) *New Media: Old News: Journalism and Democracy in the Digital Age*. London: Sage.

Freedman, D. (2009) 'The Political Economy of the New News Environment' in N. Fenton (ed.) *New Media: Old News: Journalism and Democracy in the Digital Age*. London: Sage.

Garrison, B. (2000) 'Diffusion of a New Technology: On-Line Research in Newspaper Newsrooms', *Convergence: The Journal of Research into New Media Technologies* 6(1): 84–105.

Gillmor, D. (2004) *We, The Media: Grassroots Journalism, By the People, For the People*. California: O'Reilly Media.

Gunter, B. (2003) *News and the Net*, London, New Jersey: Lawrence Erlbaum.

Habermas, J. (1989) *The Structural Transformation of the Public Sphere. An Inquiry into a Category of Bourgeois Society*. Cambridge, MA: The MIT Press.

Hachten, W. A. (2005) *The Troubles of Journalism: A Critical Look at What's Right and Wrong with the Press*. Third Edition, London: Lawrence Erlbaum.

Halloran, J., Elliott, P. and Murdock, G. (1970) *Demonstrations and Communication: A Case Study*. Harmondsworth: Penguin.

Hargreaves, I. (2003) *Journalism: Truth or Dare*. Oxford: Oxford University Press.

Hazen, D. (2003) 'Salon Goes for Broke' Alternet.org. http://www.alternet.org/story/15016/salon_goes_for_broke/ last accessed October 13 2008.

Hoge, J. (1997) 'Foreign News: Who Gives a Damn?' *Columbia Journalism Review* Nov/Dec pp. 1–4.

Lewis, J., Williams, A., Franklin, B., Thomas, J. and Mosdell, N. (2007) *The Quality and Independence of British Journalism*. Cardiff: Cardiff University.

McChesney, R. (2000) 'The Titanic Sails On: Why the Internet won't sink the media giants' *Extra!* March/April.

McNair, B. (1999) *News and Journalism in the UK*, London: Routledge.

McNair, B. (2006): *Cultural Chaos: Journalism, News and Power in a Globalised World*, London: Routledge.

Miller, L.C. (1998) *Power Journalism: Computer Assisted Reporting*. Fort Worth, TX: Harcourt Brace.

Ofcom (2007) *New News, Future News: The Challenges for Television News After Digital Switchover*. London: Ofcom.

Paterson, C. and Sreberny, A. (eds.) (2004) *International News in the 21st Century*. Luton: John Libbey Press.

Pavlik, J. V. (2001) *Journalism and New Media*, New York: Columbia University Press.

Phillips, A. (2009) 'Old Sources in New Bottles' in N. Fenton (ed.) *New Media: Old News: Journalism and Democracy in the Digital Age*. London: Sage.

Picard, R. G. (2002) *The Economics and Financing of Media Companies*. New York: Fordham University Press.

Quinn, S. (2002) *Knowledge Management in the Digital Newsroom*, St Louis, MO: Focal Press.

Redden, J. and Witschge, T. (2009) 'A New News Order? Online News Content Examined' in N. Fenton (ed.) *New Media: Old News: Journalism and Democracy in the Digital Age*. London: Sage.

Reddick, R. and King, E. (1997) *The Online Journalist: Using the Internet and other Electronic Resources*. Fort Worth, TX: Harcourt Brace.

Rheingold, H. (1993) *The Virtual Community: Homesteading on the Electronic Frontier*. Reading, MA: Addison-Wesley.

Rivas-Rodriguez, M. (2003) *Brown Eyes of the Web: Unique Perspectives of an Alternative US Latino Online Newspaper*, London: Routledge.

Schechter, D. (2004) 'Slaying the Media Beast: The MediaChannel as an Act of Personal Responsibility and Political Mission', C. Paterson and A. Sreberny, *International News in the 21st Century*, Luton: John Libbey Press, pp. 243–261.

Schlesinger, P. (1987) *Putting Reality Together: BBC News*. London: Methuen.

Schudson, M. (1978) *Discovering the News*. New York: Basic Books.

Scott, B. (2005) 'A Contemporary History of Digital Journalism'. *Television & New Media*, 6(1): 89–126.

Sigal, L. (1973) Reporters and Officials: The Organization and Politics of Newsmaking. London: Heath.

Silvia, T. (ed.) (2001) Global News: Perspectives on the Information Age, Iowa: Iowa State University Press.

Singer, J. (1997) 'A New Front Line in the Battle for Readers? Online Coverage of the 1996 Election by Denver's Competing Newspapers', Electronic Journal of Communication / La Revue Electronique de Communication 7(3). Available at: http://www.cios.org/www/ejc/v7n397.htm

Singer, J. (1998) 'Online Journalists: Foundation for Research into their Changing Roles'. *Journal of Computer Mediated Communication* 4(1), Available at http://www.asusc.org/jcmc/vol4/issue1/singer.html

Singer, J. (2001) 'The Metro Wide Web: Changes in Newspapers Gatekeeping Role Online'. *Journalism and Mass Communication Quarterly*, 78(1): 65–80.

Singer, J. (2003). Who Are These Guys? The online challenge to the notion of journalistic professionalism. *Journalism: Theory, Practice and Criticism*, 4(2): 139–168.

Sunstein, C. (2001) *republic.com*. Princeton, NJ: Princeton University Press.

Whillock, R. (1997) 'Cyberpolitics: The online strategies of '96' *American Behavioural Scientist* 40(8): 1208–1225.

Winston, B. (1995) 'How are Media Born and Developed?' in Downing, J. et al., (eds.) *Questioning the Media: A Critical Introduction*. Thousand Oaks: Sage.

51
REASSESSING JOURNALISM AS A PROFESSION

Henrik Örnebring

What is journalism? A common-sense definition of what journalism is would likely place *newsgathering* and *newswriting* at the core of the occupation – and so would most journalists, going by the large-scale surveys of the profession that exist (e.g. Delano & Henningham, 1995; Weaver, 1996, 1998; Weaver & Wilhoit, 1986). In that sense journalism is a fairly new invention – most historians of media and journalism agree that the consolidation of a coherent occupation occurs in the second half of the nineteenth century (Chalaby, 1998; Conboy, 2004; Edwards, 1998; Elliott, 1978; Schudson, 1978, 2001; Wiener, 1988).

The emergence and rise of a distinct occupation is commonly analyzed using the concept of *professionalization*. Like most social science concepts, professionalization is contested, not least when it comes to journalism. Many journalists have resisted labeling theirs as a profession, preferring instead to call it a trade or craft, and this ambivalence (or even antipathy) towards the idea of journalism as a profession is reflected in scholarship on the professionalization of journalism as well (e.g. Kimball, 1965) – more than one scholar has characterized journalism as 'semi-professional' or some other version of not-quite-a-profession (e.g. Schiller, 1979; Tumber & Prentoulis, 2005; Tunstall, 1971). In fact, given that journalism is considered a key part of democratic society, journalism could never be considered a profession according to some of the key criteria from the professionalization literature: licensing journalists or otherwise limiting the practice of journalism would be anathema to democracy, for example (Asp, 2007, p. 239).

Using the word professionalization implies *process*. It should be theoretically possible for professionalization to halt and even reverse: an occupation could become less professional over time, not just more. Wilensky criticizes the idea of a 'natural history' of professionalization, where more or less all occupations are considered to follow a path towards a *greater* degree of professionalization (Wilensky, 1964).

Some scholars argue that journalism is going through a reverse professionalization in the contemporary era: a *de-professionalization* of journalism (e.g. Bromley, 1997;

Liu, 2006; Nygren, 2008; Tunstall, 1996). These scholars claim that journalism is becoming less of a coherent and autonomous occupation which in turn is thought to have negative effects on the status of journalism in society, the quality of journalism available to audiences, and, perhaps most importantly, the role of journalism as an institution of democracy (related arguments can be found in Davies, 2008; Franklin, 2005; Ursell, 2004, though these authors do not explicitly use the term de-professionalization). The aim of this chapter is to assess the evidence available for this de-professionalization thesis by tracing some key elements generally thought to be important in the history of professionalization of journalism. We cannot properly judge the merits of the *de-professionalization* argument unless we also look at how *professionalization* is generally conceieved.

Aspects of journalistic professionalization

The literature available on professionalization is enormous, and scholars have suggested many different criteria for what constitutes a profession and for what professionalization involves. Any generalization on such a vast body of literature is bound to be found lacking, but I will make the attempt regardless: criteria for professionalism seem to fall into three broad categories: *knowledge*, *organization*, and *autonomy*. Criteria related to knowledge include the notion that a profession is connected to a specialized body of knowledge (sometimes referred to as the *cognitive base* of a profession) and to a specific, non-ambiguous domain of skill and expertise; the notion that a profession requires formal knowledge generally acquired through special education, and that this knowledge is applied in concrete situations and cases. Organization refers to, among other things, how a profession may require membership of professional associations that legitimately represent the profession as a whole, how practitioners must be able to earn a living from engaging full-time in their profession, and how formal codes of ethics organize the profession. Autonomy, finally, refers to such things as professionals being able to do their job with a great amount of individual discretion, that professional standards and professional sanctions should be decided on from within the profession rather than outside it, and that external influences over the work process itself should be non-existent or minimal.

I will focus here on *knowledge* and *autonomy*, not because they are more important but simply because the evidence in these domains is more contradictory. In terms of organization, the de-professionalization of journalism is clear-cut: in most Western countries there has been a substantial weakening of journalists' unions (according to many the key form of professional organization, see for example Hallin & Mancini, 2004, p. 171f) since the 1980s, both in terms of membership figures and in terms of formal recognition and legal protection (Gall, 1993, 1997; Marjoribanks, 2000; McKercher, 2002; see also Smith & Morton, 1990, 1992). In this, journalism follows a general trend of falling union membership and weakening of the position of unions in the labour market. Union derecognition has taken place parallel with the transformation of journalism into a mass occupation (Ursell, 2004), something that in turn seems to indicate that an oversupply of labour is driving wages down (Becker,

Stone, & Graf, 1996). While the professionalization vs. de-professionalization argument has many levels and different aspects, in one key aspect the evidence is wholly on the side of de-professionalization: the weakening of unions. However, as this is something journalism shared with almost all other professions, I will leave this aspect aside in this text and instead focus on the aspects of professionalization where trends, changes and conflicts are more unique to journalism.

Knowledge, domain, skill: journalism as distinct occupation

When the word 'journalism' was coined in English in the early 1830s, it was a neologism borrowed from French used to describe newspaper reportage (King & Plunkett, 2005, p. 293). It did not come into wide usage until the second half of the nineteenth century. 'Journalist' (someone who practised journalism) thus primarily referred to someone who wrote a particular type of texts (news) for a particular medium (newspapers) and who therefore needed a particular set of skills (both newsgathering skills and the skill to write in a particular genre) not necessarily shared by other writing occupations (I have covered this development in an earlier text, see Örnebring, 2007). A simplified version of the history of journalism is that journalism first had to become distinct from printing, and then from other forms of writing.

In the early history of the press, gathering and disseminating news was a form of craft labour, not yet distinct from the craft of printing. The labour of collecting, presenting and distributing information was all done by one person, the printer. Schudson refers to early nineteenth century newspapers as still being essentially 'one-man bands' (Schudson, 1978, p. 65). Up until the mid-to-late nineteenth century, newsgathering was often an ad hoc process, where printers and publishers could not necessarily rely on a predictable supply of material. During the nineteenth century, however, it became increasingly common that the printer employed others to produce text, or that those interested in producing and disseminating texts simply employed printers. In other words, *writing* gradually became distinct from *printing*. A group of people emerged who made their living as writers for the mass media of the day.

Several scholars (e.g. Brake, 2001; Brake, Madden, & Jones, 1990; Cross, 1985; Sutherland, 1995) have noted how these nineteenth-century media professionals routinely produced many different types of texts and for many different types of media: they wrote commentaries, criticism, poetry, fiction, they wrote for all kinds of period-icals, books, dictionaries, etc., they wrote serials, notices, essays – and sometimes even news. The key to success as a jobbing writer was not to specialize but to be able to write anything.

Over the course of the nineteenth century, writing gradually became more specialized, as writers adapted to a more diverse media landscape where different publications catered for different audiences and focused on different types of text. One of the new specialisms was writing for the newspaper press (King & Plunkett, 2005, p. 291f). The market demands associated with the industrialized press and its print and distribution technologies placed demands on journalism to fit particular formats:

'news' gradually became defined as brief snippets of factual and ideally entertaining information, suitable for filling a newspaper page with shorter blocks of text (Brown, 1985, p. 80; Høyer, 2003, p. 455; Örnebring, 2007, pp. 76, 80).

The modern era has seen a definite increase in this aspect of professionalization, as journalism has become more and more specialized. Early specialisms such as political reporting and crime reporting have been followed by (among others) sports journalism, labour journalism, and entertainment journalism. Not long ago, a journalistic subject area specialism was something a journalist entered into late in his/her career, but now specialization also happens much earlier in the career history of journalists (compare Tunstall, 1971, 1996). Specialization is also evident in the provision of education for journalists, as universities and other educational institutions now offer study programmes focusing on many different types of journalism: sports, travel, and fashion to mention just a few. Journalism now includes sub-specialisms in much the same way as medicine, law, and engineering do, and these sub-specialisms increasingly demand specialized education. This would point to an ongoing process of professionalization rather than de-professionalization. On a more general note, perhaps the most powerful indicator of ongoing professionalization is the fact that journalism is now a *de facto* graduate occupation, with some form of higher education a nigh-necessary requirement for entry. In the last 50 years, there has been a big increase in the educational level of journalists (Delano & Henningham, 1995; Frith & Meech, 2007; Tunstall, 1996) – not only in the UK but everywhere (e.g. Edström, 2007; Weischenberg, Malik, & Scholl, 2006).

However, there are also trends pointing in the opposite direction. Ursell notes that the British Press Association (the oldest domestic news agency in Britain) now has sharply differentiated between their newsgathering operation and their news processing operation – news process employees, or 'production journalists', are tasked to convert gathered information into saleable news products, and are not required to have journalism training (but must have good writing skills and be proficient in digital production technologies) (Ursell, 2004, p. 45f). News *writing* thus becomes more strictly separated from news *gathering*. And in a study of Slovenian journalists, Krasovec and Zagar note that there is an important dividing line between those journalists employed on permanent full-time contracts and those working freelance: the freelancers are increasingly like the Victorian 'common writer' (as described by Cross, 1985) in that they may produce PR text or advertising copy one day, features the next and hard news the third (Krasovec & Zagar, 2009, forthcoming). This state of affairs is hardly unique for Slovenia (see for example Walters, Warren, & Dobbie, 2006). For those journalists without permanent employment, the distinctness of the occupation is eroding – if it was ever there to begin with.

Finally, some scholars also note that ongoing processes of convergence in the media landscape also contribute to making journalism less distinct and thereby more and more de-professionalized: journalists are not the only ones with access to the media anymore, and thus have a weaker claim on having a distinct cognitive base, and on journalism demanding any particular skills. Journalism is just another form of media content, which you do not necessarily have to be a journalist to produce – and that non-journalists are increasingly producing (Henry, 2007, p. 23; Nygren, 2008, p. 158f).

On the one hand, the cognitive base of journalism seems healthy enough to support many different sub-specialisms that are still part of the same main profession, and the same cognitive base is increasingly in the domain of higher education. On the other hand, for some journalists the work they do is not at all distinct from other forms of writing-for-hire. Processes of convergence also contribute to blurring the distinction between journalism and other forms of text as well as between journalists and non-journalists – the latter a development that according to some is worrying (e.g. the two writers referenced in the previous paragraph) and for others a sign of hope (e.g. Benkler, 2006; Gant, 2007).

Autonomy: from what and whom?

Autonomy – referring to the freedom to shape one's own work without being controlled by internal or external forces – is a key concept in the research on professionalization (e.g. Freidson, 1970; Wilensky, 1964). A high degree of autonomy is generally considered to be of paramount importance in order for journalism to fulfil its democratic functions, but as Scholl and Weischenberg point out, journalistic autonomy is 'Janus-faced' as it has several different levels that may come into conflict with each other:

> Journalists (individuals) ought to be free in selecting information and in covering stories; newsrooms (organizations) ought to be independent from external influences, such as commercial and political constraints; media systems (society) ought to have guaranteed press freedom and ought to be free from all kinds of censorship (Scholl & Weischenberg, 1999, p. 2).

The Janus-like character or autonomy does not end with these different levels: there is also the less-than-straightforward issue of what exactly are the external and internal forces that journalism should be autonomous *from?*

Historically, there is no doubt that the first force journalism wished to be autonomous from was that of government. We know, of course, that those fighting for a press independent of government were not always doing so for purely unselfish reasons (Boyce, 1978; Lee, 1976; Wiener, 1969), but the fact remains that autonomy from government was a defining drive in the nascent history of journalism as a profession.

After freedom from government interference (censorship, taxation) had been achieved, there was less agreement on what kind of autonomy was most important. In the second half of the nineteenth century, members of the profession primarily argued for 'independence', by which they mostly meant independence/autonomy from political interests and political parties, but also independence from business interest (Cronin, 1993; Dicken-Garcia, 1989; Hampton, 2008, p. 483f; Marzolf, 1991). The argument was that in order to fulfil its watchdog function, journalism should be autonomous from other organized societal interests. This type of independence or autonomy was not embraced by all journalists, as many journalists saw no contradiction in speaking explicitly and passionately in support or condemnation of specific issues or interests (again, see Hampton, 2008). In many countries, the links between journalism and political parties in particular were viewed as natural and appropriate, and 'autonomy' in this regard did not become a prominent feature of journalism as a profession until the second half of the twentieth century (Hadenius & Weibull, 2003, p. 88ff; Hallin & Mancini, 2004).

Regardless of the differences between different nations in whether links to political interests were deemed acceptable or not, the global, comparative trend has been clear: journalism in the Western world is becoming more and more autonomous from other organized political interests, a 'secularization' of journalism (Hallin & Mancini, 2004, p. 263ff). This has given rise to the issue of whether journalism also needs greater autonomy from the market – commonly framed in terms of commercialization. Some scholars and journalists are critical of how news selection and story coverage are increasingly subjected to management control in order to maximize audience figures and profitability (Hallin, 2000; McManus, 1994; Underwood, 1993). While this critique is powerful and the authors have good evidence for their assertions, they are usually more vague when it comes to how this increased autonomy from market forces should be achieved – common answers include appeals to a stronger commitment to professionalism, however defined (Carey, 1993; Hallin, 2000) or appeals to owners to simply spend more on 'quality journalism' (Davies, 2008).

According to several scholars, journalism has become more autonomous in other, perhaps more subtle ways during the second half of the twentieth century and the beginning of the twenty-first. Not only has journalism become more autonomous from political parties and political organizations, but it has also become more autonomous from the political sphere as a whole. Political actors are treated more aggressively and subjected to a higher degree of scrutiny, and journalists are clearly exercising more autonomy in how they cover the news (news of politics in particular). Journalists are also more actively *interpreting* the news and engaged in setting the media agenda (Benson, 2008; most notably Bourdieu, 1997; Djerf Pierre & Weibull, 2001; Ekecrantz, 2005; Lloyd, 2004).

But yet again, the evidence is contradictory. A recent study by Lewis, Williams and Franklin showed that nearly one in five newspaper stories (in UK national quality dailies) and 17 per cent of broadcast stories were verifiably derived from PR materials or PR activity (Lewis, Williams & Franklin, 2008, p. 7) – pointing to decidedly less autonomy from news sources than one might think. The power of PR to influence and even control news selection has been known for some time (Gandy, 1982), and the power of sources over journalism has also been studied by others (Gans, 1979; Jones, 2006; Reich, 2006). Many of those studying this issue think that source influence and source control are on the increase, and that journalistic autonomy, and, in turn, professionalism are concomitantly decreasing. The increased influence of sources over news is often linked to commercialization – source dependency being a consequence of diminishing resources in newsrooms (this is the conclusion of Lewis, Williams, & Franklin, 2008, for example).

It is difficult to come up with definite answers. While journalistic autonomy from government and organized political and business interests has increased through a general secularization of journalism, government, parties and business have found other ways to influence and control journalistic work through PR material. However, this latter development could well be viewed as a response to journalism's increasingly autonomous relationship with other societal spheres or fields. And finally, of course, even though increased autonomy is often viewed as a normative good (at least among journalists), autonomy of journalists on the individual or organizational level does not necessarily translate to the autonomy on the societal level that is needed for democracy to function: a high degree of autonomy might lead journalists to become cut off from their audiences, or even to start disliking them (Donsbach, 1981; Lichter, Rothman, & Lichter, 1986), severely reducing the legitimacy of journalism.

Rise – or fall?

In its strong form, the de-professionalization argument cannot be sustained. Historians of professionalization emphasize the role of formal education and the link between the cognitive base of the profession and the academy, and in this respect the professionalization of journalism is continuing apace, even accelerating. The 'secularization' of journalism has also led to increased autonomy from political and business interests.

However, using a more fine-grained definition of (de-)professionalization, it does seem like journalism is de-professionalizing in other aspects. A cognitive base of newsgathering and newswriting skills is no longer self-evident in parts of the profession, and likewise much newsgathering and newswriting is today done by people who would not describe themselves as journalists (e.g. bloggers). Furthermore, while journalism as a profession has freed itself considerably from the government, organized political interests and indeed the political sphere as a whole, it has also become increasingly dependent on external sources for content.

For those concerned with the quality of journalism and the role of journalism in democracy, this simultaneous professionalization/de-professionalization may sadly represent the worst of two worlds: creating a journalism that on the individual level is increasingly dominated by the middle class (as education requirements become more exacting, the class-based barriers of entry to the profession increase – again, see Edström, 2007) and aggressively asserting its autonomy from the political sphere (and other societal spheres), but which on the organizational level is highly dependent on external sources because it lacks the resources for active newsgathering. In other words, a simultaneous rise and fall of the profession: the rise of journalism as a profession autonomous from the institutions it once served, and the fall of journalism as a profession engaged in the independent gathering and presentation of news.

References

Asp, K. (2007). En profession på gott och ont [A profession for good or ill]. In K. Asp (Ed.), *Den svenska journalistkåren [Swedish Journalists]* (pp. 239–246). Göteborg: JMG.

Becker, L. B., Stone, V. A., & Graf, J. D. (1996). Journalism Labour Force Supply and Demand: Is Oversupply an Explanation for Low Wages? *Journalism and Mass Communication Quarterly*, 73(3), 519–533.

Benkler, Y. (2006). *The Wealth of Networks: How Social Production Transforms Markets and Freedom*. New Haven, CT: Yale University Press.

Benson, R. (2008). *Framing Immigration: How the French and American Media Shape Public Debate*. Cambridge: Cambridge University Press.

Bourdieu, P. (1997). *Sur la television [On television]*. Paris: Liber-Raisons d'Agir.

Boyce, G. (1978). The Fourth Estate: The Reappraisal of a Concept. In G. Boyce, J. Curran & P. Wingate (Eds.), *Newspaper History: From the 17th Century to the Present Day* (pp. 19–40). London: Constable.

Brake, L. (2001). *Print is Transition, 1850–1910: Studies in Media and Book History*. Basingstoke: Palgrave.

Brake, L., Madden, L., & Jones, A. (Eds.), (1990). *Investigating Victorian Journalism*. Basingstoke: Macmillan.

Bromley, M. (1997). The End of Journalism? Changes in Workplace Practices in the Press and Broadcasting in the 1990s. In M. Bromley & T. O'Malley (Eds.), *A Journalism Reader* (pp. 330–350). London: Routledge.

Brown, L. (1985). *Victorian News and Newspapers*. Oxford: Clarendon Press.

Carey, J. W. (1993). The Mass Media and Democracy: Between the Modern and the Post-modern. *Journal of International Affairs*, 47 (1), 1–21.

Chalaby, J. (1998). *The Invention of Journalism*. Basingstoke: Palgrave Macmillan.

Conboy, M. (2004). *Journalism: A Critical History*. London: Sage.

Cronin, M. M. (1993). Trade Press Roles in Promoting Journalistic Professionalism, 1884–1917. *Journal of Mass Media Ethics*, 8(4), 227–238.

Cross, N. (1985). *The Common Writer: Life in Nineteenth-century Grub Street*. Cambridge: Cambridge University Press.

Davies, N. (2008). *Flat Earth News: An Award-winning Reporter Exposes Falsehood, Distortion and Propaganda in the Global Media*. London: Chatto & Windus.

Delano, A., & Henningham, J. (1995). *The News Breed: British Journalism in the 1990s*. London: London Institute.

Dicken-Garcia, H. (1989). *Journalistic Standards in Nineteenth Century America*. Madison, WI: University of Wisconsin Press.

Djerf Pierre, M., & Weibull, L. (2001). *Spegla, granska, tolka: aktualitetsjournalistik i svensk radio och TV under 1900-talet [Mirror, Critic, Interpreter: Current affairs journalism in Swedish radio and TV in the 20th century]*. Stockholm: Bonnier Prisma.

Donsbach, W. (1981). Journalisten zwischen Publikum und Kollegen. Forschungsergebnisse zum Publikumsbild und zum in-group-Verhalten [Journalists Between Audience and Colleagues. Empirical Results in Image of Audience and on In-group Behavior of Journalists]. *Rundfunk und Fernsehen*, 29(2–3), 168–184.

Edström, M. (2007). Journalisters arbete och utbildning – omstrukturering pågår [Work and education of journalists – ongoing restructuring]. In K. Asp (Ed.), *Den svenska journalistkåren [Swedish journalists]* (pp. 55–66). Göteborg: JMG.

Edwards, P. (1998). *Dickens's Young Men: George Augustus Sala, Edmund Yates and the World of Victoria Journalism*. Aldershot: Ashgate.

Ekecrantz, J. (2005). News Paradigms, Political Power and Cultural Contexts in 20th Century Sweden. In S. Høyer & H. Pöttker (Eds.), *Difussion of the News Paradigm, 1850–2000* (pp. 93–104). Göteborg, Sweden: NORDICOM.

Elliott, P. (1978). Professional Ideology and Organisational Change: the journalist since 1800. In G. Boyce, J. Curran & P. Wingate (Eds.), *Newspaper History: From the 17th Century to the Present Day* (pp. 172–191). London: Sage.

Franklin, B. (2005). McJournalism: the local press and the McDonalization thesis. In S. Allan (Ed.), *Journalism: Critical Issues*. Maidenhead: Open University Press.

Freidson, E. (1970). *Professional Dominance: The Social Structure of Medical Care*. New York: Atherton Press.

Frith, S., & Meech, P. (2007). Becoming a Journalist: Journalism education and journalism culture. *Journalism: Theory, Practice, Criticism*, 8(2), 137–164.

Gall, G. (1993). The Employer's Offensive in the Provincial Newspaper Industry. *British Journal of Industrial Relations, 31*(4), 615–624.

Gall, G. (1997). The Changing Relations of Production: union derecognition in the UK magazine industry. *Industrial Relations Journal, 29*(2), 151–161.

Gandy, O. (1982). *Beyond Agenda Setting: information subsidies and public policy.* New York: Ablex.

Gans, H. J. (1979). *Deciding What's News.* New York: Pantheon.

Gant, S. (2007). *We're All Journalists Now: The Transformation of the Press and Reshaping of the Law in the Internet Age.* New York: Free Press.

Hadenius, S., & Weibull, L. (2003). *Massmedier: En bok om press, radio och TV* (8th ed.). Stockholm: Albert Bonniers förlag.

Hallin, D. C. (2000). Commercialism and Professionalism in the American News Media. In J. Curran & M. Gurevtich (Eds.), *Mass Media and Society. 3rd Edition.* London: Arnold.

Hallin, D. C., & Mancini, P. (2004). *Comparing Media Systems: Three Models of Media and Politics.* Cambridge: Cambridge University Press.

Hampton, M. (2008). The 'Objectivity' Ideal and its Limitations in 20th Century British Journalism. *Journalism Studies, 9*(4), 477–493.

Henry, N. (2007). *American Carnival: Journalism under Siege in an Age of New Media.* Los Angeles: University of California Press.

Høyer, S. (2003). Newspapers Without Journalists. *Journalism Studies, 4*(4), 451–463.

Jones, N. (2006). *Trading Information: Leaks, Lies and Tip-offs.* London: Politicos.

Kimball, P. (1965). Journalism: Art, craft, or profession? In K. S. Lynn (Ed.), *The Professions in America.* Boston: Houghton Mifflin.

King, A., & Plunkett, J. (Eds.). (2005). *Victorian Print Media: A Reader.* Oxford: Oxford University Press.

Krasovec, P., & Zagar, I. Z. (2009). Divisions and Struggles of the Slovenian Journalistic Guild: A Case Study of Contemporary European Journalism. *Journalism Studies, 10*(1).

Lee, A. J. (1976). *The Origins of the Popular Press in England, 1855–1914.* London: Croom Helm.

Lewis, J., Williams, A., & Franklin, B. (2008). A Compromised Fourth Estate? UK news sources, public relations and news sources. *Journalism Studies, 9*(1), 1–20.

Lichter, S. R., Rothman, S., & Lichter, L. S. (1986). *The Media Elite: America's New Power Brokers.* Bethesda, ML: Adler & Adler.

Liu, C.-d. (2006). De-skilling Effects on Journalists: ICTs and the Labour Process of Taiwanese Newspaper Reporters. *Canadian Journal of Communication, 31*(3), 695–714.

Lloyd, J. (2004). *What the Media are Doing to our Politics.* London: Constable.

Marjoribanks, T. (2000). The 'anti-Wapping'? Technological innovation and workplace reorganization at the Financial Times. *Media, Culture & Society, 22*(5), 575–593.

Marzolf, M. (1991). *Civilizing Voices: American press criticism, 1880–1950.* New York: Longman.

McKercher, C. (2002). *Newsworkers Unite: Labor, Convergence, and North American Newspapers.* Lanham, MD: Rowman & Littlefield.

McManus, J. H. (1994). *Market-driven Journalism: let the citizen beware?* Beverly Hills, CA: Sage.

Nygren, G. (2008). *Yrke på glid: om journalistrollens deprofessionalisering [Profession on the skids: The de-professionalization of journalism].* Stockholm: Institutet för mediestudier.

Örnebring, H. (2007). A Necessary Profession for the Modern Age? 19th century news, journalism, and the public sphere. In R. Butsch (Ed.), *Media and Public Spheres* (pp. 71–82). Basingstoke: Palgrave Macmillan.

Reich, Z. (2006). The Process Model of News Initiative: Sources lead first, reporters thereafter. *Journalism Studies, 7*(4), 497–514.

Schiller, D. (1979). An Historical Approach to Objectivity and Professionalism in American News Reporting. *Journal of Communication, 29*(4), 46–57.

Scholl, A., & Weischenberg, S. (1999). Autonomy in Journalism: How It Is Related to Attitudes and Behaviour of Media Professionals [Electronic Version]. *Web Journal of Mass Communication Research (WJMCR), 2.* Retrieved April 24, 2008 from http://www.scripps.ohiou.edu/wjmcr/vol02/2-4a.htm.

Schudson, M. (1978). *Discovering the News: A Social History of American Newspapers.* New York: Basic Books.

Schudson, M. (2001). The Objectivity Norm in American Journalism. *Journalism: Theory, Practice, Criticism, 2*(2), 149–170.

Smith, P., & Morton, G. (1990). A Change of Heart: Union Exclusion in the Provincial Newspaper Sector. *Work, Employment and Society*, 4(1), 105–124.

Smith, P., & Morton, G. (1992). New Technology in the Provincial Newspaper Sector: A Comment. *British Journal of Industrial Relations*, 30(2), 325–328.

Sutherland, J. (1995). *Victorian Fiction: Writers, Publishers, Readers*. London: Macmillan.

Tumber, H., & Prentoulis, M. (2005). Journalism and the Making of a Profession. In H. de Burgh (Ed.), *Making Journalists: Diverse Models, Global Issues* (pp. 58–73). London: Routledge.

Tunstall, J. (1971). *Journalists at Work*. London: Constable.

Tunstall, J. (1996). *Newspaper Power: The New National Press in Britain*. Oxford: Clarendon Press.

Underwood, D. (1993). *When MBAs Rule the Newsroom: how the marketers and managers are reshaping today's media*. New York: Columbia University Press.

Ursell, G. (2004). Changing Times, Changing Identitites: a case study of British journalists. In T. Elgaard Jensen & A. Westenholz (Eds.), *Identity in the Age of the New Economy*. Cheltenham: Edward Elgar.

Walters, E., Warren, C., & Dobbie, M. (2006, April 2006). The Changing Nature of Work: A Global Survey and Case Study of Atypical Work in the Media Industry. Retrieved April 29, 2008, from http://www.ifj.org/default.asp?Index=3965&Language=EN

Weaver, D. H. (1996). Journalists in Comparative Perspective. *The Public*, 3(4), 83–91.

Weaver, D. H. (Ed.). (1998). *The Global Journalist: News People Around the World*. Cresskill, NJ: Hampton Press.

Weaver, D. H., & Wilhoit, C. G. (1986). *The American Journalist*. Bloomington, IN: University of Indiana Press.

Weischenberg, S., Malik, M., & Scholl, A. (2006). *Die Souffleure der Mediengesellschaft. Report über die Journalisten in Deutschland [The Prompters of Media Society: Report on Journalists in Germany]*. Konstanz: UVK Verlagsgesellschaft.

Wiener, J. H. (1969). *The War of the Unstamped: The Movement to Repeal the British Newspaper Tax, 1830–1836*. Ithaca, NY: Cornell University Press.

Wiener, J. H. (Ed.). (1988). *Papers for the Millions: The New Journalism in Britain, 1850s to 1914*. New York: Greenwood Press.

Wilensky, H. L. (1964). The Professionalization of Everyone? *The American Journal of Sociology*, 70(2), 137–158.

52

CITIZEN JOURNALISM: WIDENING WORLD VIEWS, EXTENDING DEMOCRACY

Mark Glaser

What is Citizen Journalism? The idea behind citizen journalism is that people without professional journalism training can use the tools of modern technology and the global distribution of the Internet to create, augment or fact-check media on their own or in collaboration with others. For example, someone might write about a city council meeting on a blog or in an online forum. Or they could fact-check a newspaper article from the traditional media and point out factual errors or bias on their blog. Or they might snap a digital photo of a newsworthy event happening in their town and post it online. Or they might videotape a similar event and post it on a site such as YouTube.

All these might be considered acts of journalism, even if they don't go beyond simple observation at the scene of an important event. Because of the wide availability of so many excellent tools for capturing live events – from tiny digital cameras to videophones – the average citizen can now capture the news and distribute it globally, an act that was once the province of established journalists and media companies.

There is some controversy over the term *citizen journalism*, because many professional journalists believe that only a trained journalist can understand the rigors and ethics involved in reporting the news. And conversely, there are many trained journalists who practice what might be considered citizen journalism by writing their own blogs or commentary online outside of the traditional journalism hierarchy.

One of the main concepts behind citizen journalism is that traditional media reporters and producers are not the exclusive center of knowledge on a subject – the audience knows more collectively than the reporter alone. Now, many of these traditional media outlets are trying to harness the knowledge of their audience either through comments at the end of stories they post online or by creating citizen journalist databases of contributors or sources for stories. Plus, many online newspapers and broadcast outlets ask their audience to send in on-the-scene video reports when a hurricane hits a coastal town or any other breaking news event happens in their locality.

To better understand citizen journalism, we will need to view it in the context of history. This chapter will look at the history of citizen journalism before the Internet; efforts to come up with alternative terminology to the oft-maligned phrase "citizen journalism"; examples of citizen journalism over the years; how political coverage has been shaped by citizen journalism; and the rise of hyper-local news and its many forms.

History of citizen journalism

There's a common expression: "If you look in the dictionary for such-and-such definition, you should see a picture of so-and-so." Well, if you look in the dictionary for the term *citizen journalism*, you should see a picture of Dan Gillmor. Gillmor wrote the first blog at a newspaper website, while he was a technology columnist at the San Jose Mercury News; wrote the seminal book, *We the Media*, on the subject of grassroots media; and later ran the Center for Citizen Media, a joint project of the Graduate School of Journalism at UC Berkeley and Harvard's Berkman Center for Internet & Society. Later, Gillmor became the director of the Knight Center for Digital Media Entrepreneurship at Arizona State University's Walter Cronkite School of Journalism and Mass Communication.

In *We the Media*, Gillmor traces the roots of citizen journalism to the founding of the United States in the eighteenth century, when pamphleteers such as Thomas Paine and the anonymous authors of the Federalist Papers gained prominence by printing their own publications. Further advances such as the postal system – and its discount rates for newspapers – along with the telegraph and telephone helped people distribute news more widely.

In the modern era, video footage of the assassination of President John F. Kennedy in the 1960s and footage of police beating Rodney King in Los Angeles in the 1980s were both captured by citizens on the scene. Plus, the rise of talk radio and even the do-it-yourself stylings of cable access TV and 'zines gave average folks the chance to share their views with a much larger audience. In newspapers, there were letters to the editor and op-ed pieces submitted by citizens, while pirate radio stations hit the airwaves in the U.S. without the permission of the Federal Communications Commission. The advent of desktop publishing on computers in the late 1980s allowed many more people to design and print out their own publications, but distribution was still limited.

With the rise of the World Wide Web in the 1990s, anyone could set up a personal home page to share their thoughts with the world. Chris Anderson, a doctoral student at Columbia University, wrote a useful timeline for citizen journalism that includes the advent of personal websites as well as the launch of the Indymedia site in 1999 after the World Trade Organization protests in Seattle that year. At Indymedia, anyone can share photos, text and video with other activists and the world. Here is how Anderson, on his blog, describes the importance of Indymedia in citizen journalism's history:

> The fact that Indymedia was dedicated to providing "real-time" information to readers as part of a larger anti-capitalist movement had several major consequences regarding its relationship to traditional journalism. First, the relaying of specific information from "newsworthy" events immediately brought Indymedia into a closer relationship with journalistic activity. Second, Indymedia was grounded in a larger, much more radical critique of the corporate (and, I argue, the professional) press than many of the "citizen journalism" projects that came before it, or after it. Third, while we can trace personal homepages back to 'zine form, Indymedia journalism is more directly linkable to the tradition of "alternative media" and "alt.journalism" that has existed for hundreds of years, ever since the start of journalism itself. This puts it far outside the mainstream, even in the American blogging world in the U.S.

Also in the 1990s, NYU journalism professor Jay Rosen helped spearhead the public journalism or civic journalism movement, focused on getting mainstream reporters to serve the public. But right as that movement started to fade, the citizen journalism meme caught on after the 9/11 terrorist attacks in the U.S.

At that time in 2001, the earliest weblogs were more focused on reacting to the news and were written and read by a tech-savvy audience. But after 9/11, many ordinary citizens became on-the-spot witnesses to the attacks, and their stories and images became a major part of the story. Popular conservative political blogger Glenn Reynolds, who writes Instapundit, rose to great influence in the charged atmosphere after 9/11.

Other important milestones in the recent history of citizen journalism include eyewitness bloggers in Iraq such as Salam Pax giving stunningly detailed early accounts of the war. Plus, at the 2004 U.S. political conventions, bloggers were given press passes for the first time. Later, in 2005, the earliest photos on the scene of the London bombings on 7 July were taken by ordinary citizens with their camera phones. Mainstream media sites run by the BBC and MSNBC accepted photos, video and text reports – a practice that continues to this day among many major broadcasters and newspapers.

Citizen journalists and bloggers also helped in the worldwide reaction and relief efforts to the tsunami and flooding in Southeast Asia in late 2004 and to damage wrought by hurricanes Katrina and Rita in the U.S. in 2005. They provided eyewitness reports to tragedy in locations which mainstream reporters could not reach because of the broad swathe of destruction. Some of the most striking video of the tsunami's damage in Thailand came from tourists who were visiting the country and had video cameras with them to capture the scene.

Eventually, it wasn't just Average Joe citizens running blogs and independent media sites online. Big-time entrepreneur billionaire Mark Cuban ran his own blog to share his viewpoints directly with the public, and celebrities helped put the group blog Huffington Post on the map – leading to a similar effort in the U.K. by the *Guardian*, Comment Is Free.

Inexact terminology

The terms *citizen journalism* and *citizen journalist* are not popular among traditional journalists or even the people who are doing citizen journalism at the ground level because they are imprecise definitions. Aren't professional journalists citizens as well? What if you're an illegal alien and not really a citizen – does that invalidate your work?

The New West website has chosen to use the term "Unfiltered" for its citizen journalism contributions, and runs the following instructions for people to contribute: "Don't let the 'citizen journalism' title scare you. Your post doesn't have to be a structured article. It can be a rant, a rave, a rhyme, a short comment, a novel – anything you feel like writing. We just want to hear what's on your mind."

Other media thinkers have suggested alternate terms for citizen journalism. Here's a list of some of those terms:

grassroots journalism
networked journalism
open source journalism
citizen media
participatory journalism
hyperlocal journalism
bottom-up journalism
stand-alone journalism
distributed journalism.

Max Kalehoff, an executive at Nielsen BuzzMetrics, wrote this comment on Jeff Jarvis' BuzzMachine blog on a post about changing the term citizen journalism to networked journalism:

> Why not just call journalism "journalism" – a word the citizens, amateurs, networks, distributors and professionals can understand? Journalism can be "practiced" in all sorts of ways, and by virtually anyone. You don't even have to be a citizen or a professional; you could be a foreigner, or even an alien from outer space. But I do agree with your overall beat: journalism is not some exclusive club; it's something that takes many forms, including all the ones you describe.

Ad hoc examples

When a traditional media outlet covers a story, the editor usually assigns the story to a reporter, the reporter does the work and turns in a story that gets edited and published. But in the case of ad hoc citizen journalism, a blogger or observer might see something happening that's newsworthy and bring it to the attention of the blogosphere or the online public. As more people uncover facts and work together, the story can snowball without a guiding editor and produce interesting results – leading to the mainstream media finally covering it and giving it wider exposure.

Here are some examples of ad hoc citizen journalism:

- Trent Lott resigns as majority leader of the U.S. Senate in December 2002 after blogs keep up pressure over a racist remark he made.
- Conservative bloggers helped discredit documents related to President Bush's National Guard service used in an episode of "60 Minutes II" in 2004. This became known as Rathergate.
- Various people worked together online to help identify the star of the Lonelygirl15 videos on YouTube as a New Zealand actress. That included teenagers and the *Los Angeles Times*.
- A former Lockheed Martin engineer takes his story about security flaws with Coast Guard ships straight to YouTube after the mainstream media ignored his entreaties. Later, the *Washington Post* wrote about it.
- People in the ePluribus Media community make a timeline of key events around the 29 August 2005 landfall of Hurricane Katrina in New Orleans, with more than 500 events included, which are fact-checked and sourced by the group alone. The timeline stretched all the way until July 2006.

Hybrid examples

While the rise of citizen journalism largely happened outside of traditional media in the U.S., there are some exceptions and cases of hybrid efforts that mix the on-the-scene reports from citizens with professional editing. One of the pioneering efforts in citizen journalism was the OhMyNews site in South Korea, launched in early 2000, which has become a popular mainstream news source in that Asian country. The site is a hybrid of professionally reported and citizen reported stories, with citizen journalists being paid small sums for the more popular work they do.

OhMyNews was successful in South Korea because it provided an alternative view of politics in a country that had been dominated by a conservative press. The site was an important hub of the opposition party during the December 2002 presidential election, won by Roh Moo Hyun, who gave his first post-election interview to OhMyNews.

The site has gone on to introduce a more globally focused English-language site called OhMyNews International, with nearly all its content coming from citizen journalists. In 2006, the site launched OhMyNews Japan with an influx of funding from the investment firm Softbank. But those efforts to expand have not been successful business ventures outside of Korea, and the site started to lose momentum in 2007 as other media sites started to use the same tactics that OhMyNews made famous.

In the U.S., newspaper publishers have created some of the more viable citizen media sites, from the Northwest Voice in Bakersfield, California, to the series of Your Hub sites out of Denver. Plus, Minnesota Public Radio has built a database of citizen contributors to help give reporters a more informed view of society with a project called Public Insight Journalism.

More hybrid projects have launched with paid professional editors, reporters or "network wranglers" helping to shape the story ideas while interested citizen journalists help do the research and dig up facts they know locally. Liberal political blogger Josh Marshall has launched one such effort called TPMmuckraker, and led the way reporting and using citizen journalists to cover the firings for political reasons of eight U.S. attorneys by the Department of Justice. That reporting – which included readers sifting through thousands of documents released by the government – won Josh Marshall a George Polk Award for investigative journalism, the first time a blogger had won a Polk award.

Political inroads

The Sunlight Foundation has also created numerous projects that combined professional editors with citizen input to help make the U.S. Congress more transparent. In 2006, the group brought together conservative and liberal bloggers in an "Exposing Earmarks" campaign to track all the legislative "earmarks" in a labor bill. These earmarks are used by members of Congress to send money to their own pet projects at home with little oversight by the public. That campaign led to the Coburn-Obama bill, a bi-partisan effort to create an online database of all earmarks on all bills before Congress. The bill was signed into law by President Bush on 26 September 2006.

During the 2008 presidential campaign in the U.S., there were many efforts to combine professional editors or producers with citizen journalist coverage. MTV hired 50 citizen journalist/videographers in 50 states to report on how the election affected those areas. The "Street Team '08" site gave each of the citizen journalists the space to blog, post audio, photos and videos and interact with readers to decide what aspects of regional politics they should cover. The citizen journalists were paid by MTV and were given direction by veteran producers at MTV.

PurpleStates.tv also combined professional TV producers with citizen reporters, who reported on the U.S. presidential campaign during the primary season. The five citizen reporters were supposed to represent a range of political opinions, but none of them had prior on-air training before becoming the focal point of this reality-TV type series of video vignettes online. The video series ran on the *New York Times* website during the primaries and on the *Washington Post*'s website in the fall campaign.

Another hybrid effort was called "Off the Bus," hosted by the Huffington Post group blog, and including citizen reports that were edited by professional journalists.

The initial idea for the project was that hundreds of citizens would follow various candidates and report on their every move. But Huffington Post learned that getting people to do complex reporting without training was a difficult task. Marc Cooper, the editorial coordinator of Off the Bus, told PBS MediaShift:

> Where we've had the biggest problem is assuming that untrained citizen reporters can quickly and adequately replace professional and trained reporters. We do ourselves a lot of damage if we underestimate the training and professional rigors of journalism. I'm talking about the standards and training that go into building a journalist. Journalists don't just come off the shelf.

Though many old-school journalists have been wary about the power wielded by citizen journalists, some of the more enlightened members of the journalism elite are starting to catch on. Kenneth Neil Cukier, a technology correspondent for *The Economist* in London, told the OpenBusiness blog these eye-opening thoughts on citizen journalists:

> I acknowledge the problems but welcome the development of the 'amateur journalist', akin to the 'gentleman scientist' of the 18th century, which did so much to advance knowledge. I believe journalism is undergoing its 'reformational moment'. By that I mean that the Internet is affecting journalism just as the printing press affected the Church – people are bypassing the sacrosanct authority of the journalist in the same way as Luther asserted that individuals could have a direct relationship with God without the intermediary of the priest. The Internet has disintermediated middlemen in other industries, why should journalism be immune?
>
> The tools of broadcast media have gone from owning paper mills, presses, million-dollar transmitters and broadcast licenses, to having a cheap PC or a mobile phone in one's pocket. That gives everyone the ability to have a direct rapport with the news as either a consumer or a producer, instantaneously. This is like the advent of literacy: it threatened elites and sometimes created problems. But it empowered individuals and led to a far better world. The new literacy from digital media will do the same, even as it creates new problems. Ultimately, I believe it is a positive thing for journalism, because it enables something journalism has lacked: competition from the very public we serve.

In countries such as Iran, Burma and Egypt, bloggers have played an important role as citizen journalists reporting on subjects that the state-controlled media wouldn't allow professional journalists to cover. In Iran, bloggers have for years been rated as the most trustworthy source of news because they have been difficult to control by the Islamic government.

In Burma, when monks took to the streets to protest against the military junta in September 2007, it was up to citizen journalists on the scene to blog, snap photos and videos and distribute them online so the world could see what was happening when the government killed and rounded up protesters.

An anonymous blogger in Bangkok who went by the online name Jotman went into Burma to talk to monks who were in hiding in safe houses. Jotman interviewed them and then posted the videos and their stories on his blog, sharing information that many traditional journalists couldn't get because the Burmese government is hostile to foreign journalists. Later, Jotman won an award from the press freedom group, Reporters Without Borders, for his work as a solo citizen journalist covering the Burmese uprising and crackdown.

In Egypt, blogger/activists have helped to organize protests against the government, and have often provided the only coverage of those protests and resulting arrests. When one prominent blogger, Alaa Abd El-Fatah, was arrested in May 2006, the Egyptian blogosphere spread the word to tell outside media about what happened, leading to foreign pressure on the Egyptian government to release him. During his time in jail, Alaa passed out messages to visitors, who then posted the messages on his blog, effectively allowing him to blog from jail and tell his supporters how he was doing.

Hyper-local news

Hyper-local news is the information relevant to small communities or neighborhoods that has been overlooked by traditional news outlets. Thanks to cheap self-publishing and communication online, independent hyper-local news sites have sprung up to serve these communities, while traditional media have tried their own initiatives to cover what they've missed. In some cases, hyper-local sites let anyone submit stories, photos or videos of the community, with varying degrees of moderation and filtering. Pioneers such as Northwest Voice in Bakersfield, California, and YourHub, which started in Denver, actually reverse publish select material from their websites in print publications. Both of them are run by mainstream newspaper publishers.

The motivation for starting independent hyper-local sites is often to tell the previously untold stories of communities, while also bringing like-minded people together online. Mainstream news outlets that have created hyper-local sites are trying to engage their readers, while also creating a place for smaller, niche advertisers who want to reach a highly geographically targeted audience.

The business models for hyper-local news sites are still evolving, and some independent sites are run as labors of love by their publishers and communities. Venture-funded startups Backfence and Bayosphere tried and failed to make a business out of creating a series of hyper-local sites, while Pegasus News was bought by Fisher Communications.

Methods for collecting hyper-local news

In the past few years, people have used a variety of methods to capture hyper-local news, from assigning professional journalists to hyper-local beats to collecting stories from interested citizens, to a combination of the two. In terms of presentation, the storytelling format has included everything from articles and videos to blogs, wikis, and annotated maps. The following is a list of some of the ways that traditional and independent media have gathered hyper-local news.

Self-moderated citizen media

Perhaps the least work-intensive approach to a hyper-local news site is simply allowing people to post their stories with minimal moderation. The moderation could depend on users flagging submissions as inappropriate, or on a publisher who might check the site for obscenities or spam. A common challenge with these sites is getting people to contribute content on a regular basis, and then filtering or highlighting the best material.

Strengths: Open format invites more participants.
Weaknesses: Takes hard work to get people to contribute; varying quality of submissions.
Examples: Philly Future, BeniciaNews.com, IndyMoms, iBrattleboro, NowPublic

Reverse publishing citizen media in print

Many sites ask people to tell the stories of their community, with a mixture of text, photos and videos. But if the site is associated with a traditional news outlet – most likely a local newspaper – there are usually more stringent rules for moderation. Eventually the best of the online content is reverse published into a regular print publication that goes out to people who live in that community. Professional editors might eliminate submissions that contain libelous or offensive content, and could spend time filtering and highlighting important issues.

Strengths: Higher quality content and filtering of stories; increased distribution in print with more ad revenues.
Weaknesses: Contributors don't get equal exposure across platforms, and the excerpted content may exclude some points of view.
Examples: Northwest Voice, YourHub, Bluffton Today

Involved proprietors on blogs

Rather than opening up the editorial to citizens, many place-specific blogs are written by people who review local happenings with a unique voice. These blogs might include polls or comments so others can contribute, but the main focus is on the voice of the bloggers. Some of these blogs cover small suburban areas, while others are focused on urban life.

Strengths: Stronger editorial voice and consistent publishing schedule vs. citizen media efforts.

Weaknesses: Personal viewpoint does not represent the variety of voices in a community.
Examples: H2otown, Baristanet, Gothamist network, Metroblogging network, WestportNow

Aggregation sites

These sites include very few original stories, and simply aggregate and link to stories found on other news outlets or blogs for that locality. Some do include ways for people in the community to share their views on stories with comments or forums. Topix, for example, has had success reaching small rural areas by being the only online outlet for news in those communities.

Strengths: Low overhead and largely automated operations.
Weaknesses: Not enough local flavor or voice, except through outside links.
Examples: Topix, Placeblogger, Outside.in

Mobile journalism

A few traditional news organizations are experimenting with having their reporters go out as "one-man bands" who write up quick reports, take photographs or video and file them from the road. Gannett has tried to do more coverage of community events, while Reuters is working with Nokia to outfit reporters with gear to get raw footage of live events as they happen.

Strengths: Quick coverage of more events on the fly.
Weaknesses: Lower quality video and photos; not enough time for thoughtful work.
Examples: Reuters Mobile Journalism, Gannett's MoJos

Email lists and online forums

Perhaps the most overlooked way that communities can stay in touch and share news is through email lists and online forums. Many of these are ad hoc lists created by citizens, with the content coming directly from them. These email lists let you get a daily digest of all the content in one email and allow you to respond or post your own items. The subject matter can be intensely local to your neighborhood,

Strengths: Very local information helps neighbors get to know each other.
Weaknesses: Usually not a lot of moderation so content quality can be low.
Examples: Front Porch Forums, DCWatch

Evolving Business Models

While no one disputes that the Internet and new technology can help small geographical communities share news, the open question is whether these connections will lead to profitability for news organizations or startups. And what's also unclear is whether independent startups have an advantage or disadvantage to existing traditional local news outlets. Northwest Voice and YourHub have been financially successful for their parent news organizations, but most of their revenue comes from reverse published print editions. Hyper-local startups with venture capital funding such as Backfence and Bayosphere have failed because they couldn't get enough locals online – nor the advertising to support their businesses.

Two newer hyper-local startups, YourStreet and EveryBlock, are aiming to use more aggregation and annotated maps to show what's happening in a locale, without having high-cost editorial from reporters. But there remains a tough balancing act between using amateur or automated information and on-the-ground reporting by professional journalists. Journalist Steve Outing, who helped start The Enthusiast Group as a series of niche sites about sports, wrote about his lessons learned when his business failed and how that could apply to hyper-local sites:

> We believed that having a core level of professional content – from our site editors – would be enough to attract a loyal following even if the user-submitted content wasn't enough on its own. But I think we didn't have nearly enough of that. If I had any money left to throw at the business, I'd hire more well-known athletes and adventurers, so that the core was a larger pool of professional content – and I'd mix that in with the best user content.
>
> I'm not saying that user-submitted content isn't worthwhile, let me be clear about that. I am saying that I think you can't rely too much on it. And you need to filter out and highlight the best user content, while downplaying the visibility of the mediocre stuff.

While the online business model is being sorted out, newspaper publishers have been making money by selling print ads into special editions that are stocked with the best of the online content. Travis Henry, the editor of YourHub at the *Rocky Mountain News*, wrote about that paper's experience running various hyper-local news sites since 2005:

> YourHub has registered over 34,000 members in the Denver metro area alone. We have 18 print sections just in Colorado. YourHub is now live in eight states and poised to launch in more, admittedly with varied results. In Colorado alone we have more than 3,000 stories posted a month and more than 3,000 events a month. Our biggest achievement has been the creation of an awesome online community that has become a large family of sorts. User gatherings we have held have been powerful and prove that this is an experiment worth going forward.

We have been in the black since our first year. Most of our revenue comes from print advertising.

J-Lab, an incubator of news experiments at the University of Maryland, conducted a survey of 191 hyper-local sites in early 2007 and found that most sites are simply labors of love, funded by founders who are not out to make a fortune. Of those surveyed, 51% said they don't need money to keep the operation going, and 42% said revenues didn't cover their expenses. But they were largely happy with the local impact their sites had made, with 73% saying their sites were successful.

Whether hyper-local sites are run as an adjunct to a traditional media outlet, run as a labor of love or non-profit, what's most important for the public's interest is that the community feels connected to a news source or website that engages them and lets them discuss intensely local issues. The same could be said for citizen journalism, a pursuit that has been done mainly by passionate people who aren't professional journalists, but who feel they can contribute to the media conversation. Both hyper-local websites and citizen journalism are key to bringing in more voices to traditional journalism, and broadening a world view that was once the exclusive domain of the professional media.

Note

This chapter uses material previously published on PBS MediaShift in the following entries:
- Your Guide to Citizen Journalism
  http://www.pbs.org/mediashift/2006/09/digging_deeperyour_guide_to_ci.html
- Your Guide to Hyper-Local News
  http://www.pbs.org/mediashift/2007/12/digging_deeperyour_guide_to_hy.html

References

Anderson, Chris (31 July 2006) "'Actually Existing'" Citizen Journalism Projects and Typologies: Part I on the Unpacking My Library blog http://indypendent.typepad.com/academese/2006/07/actually_existi.html

Citizen Media Cookbook by Hartsville Today http://www.jour.sc.edu/pages/fisher/hvtd/HVTDyear1.pdf (PDF File)

CyberJournalist.net's List of Citizen Media Initiatives http://www.cyberjournalist.net/news/002226.php

Fowler, Geoffrey A. (28 September 2007) "'Citizen Journalists' Evade Blackout On Myanmar News" in the Wall Street Journal http://online.wsj.com/article/SB119090803430841433.html

Gillmor, Dan (2004) We the Media, O'Reilly We Media Report for The Media Center at the American Press Institute http://www.mediacenter.org/pages/mc/research/we_media_report/

Glaser, Mark (4 April 2007) "Sunlight Foundation Mixes Tech, Citizen Journalism to Open Congress" on PBS MediaShift http://www.pbs.org/mediashift/2007/04/digging_deepersunlight_foundat.html

Glaser, Mark (8 October 2007) "Can Internet, Blogs Sustain the Saffron Revolution?" on PBS MediaShift http://www.pbs.org/mediashift/2007/10/burma_unrestcan_internet_blogs.html

Glaser, Mark (17 November 2004) "The New Voices: Hyperlocal Citizen Media Sites Want You (to Write)!" at Online Journalism Review http://ojr.org/ojr/glaser/1098833871.php

Katrina Timeline at ePluribus Media http://timelines.epluribusmedia.net/timelines/index.php?&mjre=KATR&table_name=tl_katr&function=search&order=date&order_type=DESC

Outing, Steve (15 June 2005) "The 11 Layers of Citizen Journalism by Steve Outing" at Poynter Online http://www.poynter.org/content/content_view.asp?id=83126

Potts, Mark (16 July 2007) "Co-Founder Potts Shares Lessons Learned from Backfence Bust" on PBS MediaShift http://www.pbs.org/mediashift/2007/07/postmortemcofounder_potts_shar.html

SourceWatch's Tools for Citizen Journalists http://www.sourcewatch.org/index.php?title=Tools_for_citizen_journalism

53

NEWSPAPERS, LABOR AND THE FLUX OF ECONOMIC UNCERTAINTY

James R. Compton

In the spring of 2008 the trade journal *Advertising Age* published an online poll asking its readers a simple yet revealing question: How long will newsprint continue to exist? Respondents were pessimistic. A majority, 54 percent, said newsprint would die within 20 years or less; 23 percent said within 10 years. The remaining 46 percent chose the third and final option of 20 years or more. The results of the unscientific survey (newsprint will never die was not offered as a choice) are not surprising. Newsmagazines and journalism trade journals have, in recent years, repeatedly warned readers that their favorite morning routine of reading the home-delivered local newspaper along with a cup of coffee may be short lived. In fact, the chorus of publications announcing the coming demise of the newspaper age has been short of deafening. Even the usually sober newsmagazine *The Economist* passed judgment in August 2006 with a cover story that asked provocatively: "Who killed the newspaper?" (*The Economist* 2006).

Indeed, *The Economist* is not alone. It is a widely held view among media pundits that the end is near. The reasons given are well rehearsed: declining circulation, slumping advertising and classified revenue, stalled stock values, and an aging readership. But perhaps the most often cited reason is that the Internet has delivered a death blow to newspapers. It is on the Web, we are told, that most young people search for information, news and entertainment; and without young readers there is no future. Steve Outing, a widely-read columnist for *Editor and Publisher*, confessed in April 2008 that, after much thought, he cancelled his local newspaper subscription. "A print edition is no longer as relevant to our lives. We're flooded with information – most of it free – from the Web, e-mail, RSS feeds, podcasts, phone alerts, TV and radio news." Outing concluded, without guilt, that continuing to support his regional paper's print edition "would just delay the inevitable" (Outing 2008).

Outing's fin de siècle tone is shared by techno-enthusiast Jeff Jarvis, a journalist, university instructor and blogger. Jarvis, known in the blogging community as buzz-machine, says the newspaper industry has reached its "iPod moment," by which he means the moment when a portable mass-market electronic device supplants newsprint. He argues that moment arrived with the launch of Apple's iPhone. "Everything you can do on the web," says Jarvis, "you can do with media on the iPhone, anywhere, any time." The challenge now facing the newspaper industry, he continues, is to learn how to take advantage of these efficiencies (Jarvis 2007).

Not all critics are as optimistic. Pulitzer Prize winning journalist Chris Hedges is deeply concerned about the future of newspapers, but he dismisses the suggestion that the Internet is simultaneously newsprint's killer and savior. "The decline of newspapers is not about the replacement of the antiquated technology of news print with the lightning speed of the Internet. It does not signal an inevitable and salutary change. It is not a form of progress" (Hedges 2008). Hedges acknowledges that daily newspapers are facing difficulties, but he suggests these challenges cannot be understood without understanding the role of capital and newspapers' historical relationship to the liberal-bourgeois public sphere, itself understood as a social space that has undergone a transition from a modern print to a post-modern image culture. Hedges, I believe, correctly directs our attention away from a reified fixation on the technological delivery system of news and back to the newspaper as a journalistic institution that, in the main, is also a capitalist enterprise.

The newspaper is not simply an ink-on-paper publication; it is a newsgathering institution with its own political economy and social history. This chapter is a modest attempt to historicize some of the problems currently facing the newspaper industry. The Internet has indeed had an impact on newspapering, but this relationship must be understood, I argue, within the context of a broader neoliberal restructuring of the global economy, the disciplining of labor, and capital's not always successful struggle to harness protean changes in networked communication to the purpose of extracting surplus value. A fixation on technology naturalizes the very real economic, social and cultural difficulties facing newspapers. They are enormous. No more so than for the labor of reporting – the work of collecting information, synthesizing it and presenting it for public consumption via storytelling.

Neoliberal restructuring and labor

Neoliberalism, in its most broad terms, is a political economic theory that prescribes a set of practices stressing marketplace efficiencies, pro-capitalist regulations and the privatization of public assets, all applied (supposedly) to advance the production of both wealth and individual well-being. At least since the 1970s, under neoliberal policies, national and regional economies have been subject to financial deregulation involving the globalization of financial markets, itself made possible by the wide diffusion of information and communication technologies. These changes have facilitated an unprecedented mobility of capital and a disciplining of corporations who now, more than ever, are compelled to react swiftly to the vagaries of the market or risk losing the support of stockholders.

In this political economic environment, the power of workers has waned. Among other dynamics, the use of new media changes capital's relationship to labor. Capital – because it is relatively "flexible" in relation to labor's relative immobility – has become more agile; better able to redeploy its resources to those locales where workers have become both more pliable and disposable (Bauman 2000: 120). "It is the blend of merger and downsizing strategies that offers capital and financial power the space to move and move quickly, making the scope of its travel ever more global, while at the same time depriving labor of its bargaining and nuisance-making power" (Bauman 2000: 122). One outcome is a widespread sense of insecurity and anxiety which has been rationalized through a discourse of self responsibility (Sennett 2006: 52).

Such neoliberal developments have had a particular impact on media. In the United States regulation of broadcasting content was eased through the elimination of the Fairness Doctrine in 1987, while the 1996 Telecommunications Act lowered barriers to corporate mergers. In Europe public service broadcasters were either privatized or forced to commercialize. The relaxation of foreign ownership restrictions and pressure to privatize has led over the past two decades to a significant "neoliberal transnationalization" of media (Yong Jin 2008). The most affected sectors are broadcasting, advertising and telecommunications. Prior to the 1980s the newspaper industry remained tied to regional and national markets. "However, the situation has substantially changed since the 1990s, and the press industry has become part of the global M&A market" (Yong Jin 2008: 364). The majority of the 3467 mergers and acquisitions in the newspaper industry from 1983 to 2005 occurred after 1996. The biggest players, by country, were the United States, the United Kingdom, Germany, France, Canada and Australia (2008: 363). A tension is created – while circulation and advertising for print remain tied to national and regional markets (Picard 2008), North American and European newspapers are integrated into transnational capital. These companies now command large cross-media empires. Gannett, the largest publisher of newspapers by circulation in the United States including *USA Today*, also owns 19 newspapers in the United Kingdom and more than 20 U.S. television stations. News Corporation owns newspapers in the United States, the United Kingdom and Australasia, including the influential *Wall Street Journal* and *The Times* of London. In addition, News Corporation has substantial interests in television, direct broadcast satellite (DBS), cable, film, children's books, and with its purchase of the social networking site MySpace, the Internet.

In a survey of research on the effects of corporate media mergers, C. Edwin Baker concludes that "Corporate mergers often create direct *structural* pressures that exacerbate the undesirable emphasis on profit maximization" (Baker 2007: 35). The increasing size of cross-media conglomerates enhances their ability to cut costs through vertical and horizontal integration, an ability that is only enhanced by the Internet (McChesney 2004: 79). These developments have had an impact on the relative autonomy of the journalist profession. An intensification of market forces in broadcasting and print journalism contribute to, what Robert McChesney calls, a "hyper-commercialism." One impact has been an emphasis on attracting and holding readers through crime, celebrity gossip and human interest. Secondly, efforts are ramped up to control costs through labor rationalization. McChesney cites a 2002 survey by the Project for Excellence in Journalism that found U.S. journalists to be "a grumpy lot" largely due to newsroom cut backs, low salaries and job insecurity (2004: 79). Newsroom staff reductions started in the 1980s – well before the mid 1990s expansion of the Internet into a popular medium – have continued to the present day putting pressure on professional standards and reducing the resources required for investigative reporting. Consequently, reporters increasingly become reliant on "news subsidies" provided by PR firms (2004: 80–81). Baker cites studies that found "newspaper quality relates positively to staff size, in particular, the number of journalists employed" (Baker 2007: 36). Moreover, research has "found that the reduction in newsroom employees more than doubled for those publically traded papers or chains whose profit margins were greater than the average profit margins for privately owned papers" (2007: 36). Quantitative changes in budgets have resulted in qualitative changes in the work of reporters.

New media and flux in the newspaper industry

Pronouncements on the end of newspapers have a long history. The first known instance may date back to 1914; that's the year in which the film trade journal *The Bioscope* predicted that the new technology of the newsreel would soon put illustrated newspapers out of business (Thussu 2007: 19). The newsreel was never a serious threat. As Mike Gasher (2007) points out, the newspaper industry has survived competitors before. Similar predictions of a coming fall were made in the 1920s and 1930s with the emergence of radio and then again in the 1950s and 1960s with television, which some predicted would also kill radio and cinema. It never happened. The historical record shows that "old media" do not die. They adapt to a continuously changing political economy, culture and technological environment. Following Martin Conroy and John Steel's research into the history of newspapers, we can say that new technologies don't signal "dramatic and revolutionary change" for newspapers as much as they are a "part of the continuous development of capitalist production relations" (Conroy and Steel 2008: 655).

Newspapers began to test alternative forms of electronic distribution in the 1980s. Experiments were launched in videotex, teletex, audiotex and fax papers. They were all eventually abandoned. These experiments were a defensive move against the uncertainty of capital accumulation amidst technological change and a fragmenting audience/readership, but importantly they followed in the wake of a range of developments affecting newspapers. Pablo J. Boczkowski argues, contrary to popular discourse, that the development of online newspapers is a response to "broader socioeconomic trends" dating back to the 1960s, "such as rising newsprint and distribution costs, growing segmentation of consumption patterns, and the increased appeal of audiovisual media among younger generations" (Boczkowski 2005: 4). Newspapers were beginning to face competition for readers. Supper-time television news hastened the end of afternoon delivery (well before the arrival of the Internet); newspapers began searching for consumer-oriented alternatives in lifestyle and entertainment sections.

Indeed, newspapers continue to re-launch titles using new layouts, sections and color to retain a fragmenting audience. Newspapers finally took the plunge into electronic publishing in 1995 after it became clear that the Internet was a "settled" popular medium.

Newspapers' *annus horribilis*?

The *New York Times* rang alarms in early February 2008 with a report that the newspaper industry was in peril. "The talk of newspapers' demise is older than some of the reporters who write about it, but what is happening now is something new, something more serious than anyone has experienced in generations" (Pérez-Peña 2008). Profits were down and share prices were shrinking. Circulation for papers such as *The San Francisco Chronicle*, *The Boston Globe* and *The Los Angeles Times*, was reportedly plummeting. A main culprit was said to be a shift to advertising on the Internet – in particular for classified ads, which historically account for up to 20 percent of newspaper revenue. The *Times* reported that "Adjusted for inflation, 2007 ad revenue was more than 20 percent below its peak in 2000," just prior to the 2001 recession (Pérez-Peña 2008). Companies responded with layoffs. The numbers are staggering: 250 jobs lost at *The Los Angeles Times*, including 150 editorial staff, or 17 percent of newsroom jobs (Strupp 2008). Its owner, Tribune, extended cuts across its papers by as much as 20 percent. The *New York Times* cut 3.8 percent of its staff; the San Jose *Mercury News* newsroom was reduced to 200, half the size it employed in 2000. At the Gannett chain 1000 job cuts were announced across its Community Publishing Division, while McClatchy, publisher of 30 daily newspapers including the *Miami Herald*, slashed close to 10 percent of its work force, or 1400 jobs (Adams 2008a); and industry job losses continued in 2009.

Was 2008 the newspaper industry's *annus horribilis*? One might conclude that layoffs sweeping the industry in the United States and the UK were a necessary adjustment to save a mature industry on the brink of extinction. This would be incorrect. Newspapers remain highly profitable. Gannett's newspaper division did indeed report a 10 percent decline in operating profit for 2007; however, it enjoyed a healthy 21 percent operating profit margin. Media General, a large southern U.S. chain that owns the *Tampa Tribune*, had a 17 percent margin (Pérez-Peña 2008). In 2006 U.S. newspaper industry profits averaged 19 percent. These are not the numbers of an industry in a death spiral. By the *New York Times*' own admission they exceed profits at Fortune 500 companies (cited in Baker 2007: 33). Large dailies enjoyed profit margins above 20 percent during the 1980s and 1990s (Picard 2008: 705). In the UK, regional publishers posted considerable earnings in 2007 – Johnston Press reported an operating profit of £178m, with a profit margin of 29 percent; Trinity Mirror £196m, with a margin of 20 percent (Luft 2009). The layoffs were capital's response to a relative decline in an extremely profitable industry.

The World Association of Newspapers (WAN) reports that, from a global perspective, "newspapers are a growth business" (2008). Situations vary across countries, but the most recent data gathered from 2007 indicate that paid circulation was up 2.57 percent over the year and 9.39 percent over five years. That five-year tally rises to +14.3 percent when free dailies are included. Circulation is up in three-quarters of the countries surveyed and is particularly strong in the world's two largest newspaper markets: China (+20.69 percent over five years) and India (+35.51 percent over five years). Paid circulation is indeed down for 2007 in North America (−2.14 percent) and the United Kingdom (−3.46 percent). It is down 2.37 percent in the European Union (EU), but when free dailies are included circulation rose 2 percent in 2007, 9.61 over a five-year period.

Drilling deeper reveals variation among sectors. In the UK circulation is off steeply over a 40-year period for daily and Sunday titles – down from 38.4 million in 1965 to 22.7 million in 2007. However, most of the loss has been experienced by weekday and Sunday tabloids. The so called "quality" dailies "have enjoyed +27.5 percent circulation growth from 2.03 million in 1965 to 2.6 million in 2007," (Franklin 2008: 632). North American newspapers have experienced a gradual slide in circulation over the past 20 years. Circulation in the USA fell 3.03 percent in 2007; but most of the decline is attributed to evening dailies. "Over the past five years, evening dailies declined −25 percent, compared with a −5.08 percent drop for morning newspapers" (WAN 2008). Paid circulation has remained relatively steady over the past few years at top national dailies in the USA, including USA Today, The Wall Street Journal, and New York Times (Pérez-Peña 2007).

Gasher argues the newspaper industry is not in a state of crisis, but a period of "restructuring characterized by convergence, concentration and commercialism, bringing with it considerable change and uncertainty" (Gasher 2007: 5). He gives three reasons why newspapers have survived the emergence of new media: adaptation to change, newsprint's relative advantages (portability, ease of use), and the relative resilience of readership.

The large cross-media empires to which many of the newspapers in North America and the UK belong provide long-term security through cost sharing, multi-platform ad deals and cross promotion among proprietary brands. "This strategy of 'media convergence,' by which a company's media properties work as commercial complements to one another, means that economic success cannot be measured by looking at any single piece of the puzzle, but instead by looking at the entire corporate enterprise" (Gasher 2007: 23).

A decline in print circulation does not necessarily mean fewer people are reading newspapers because of the Internet. In fact research indicates there was no major change in print circulation in the five years before and after 1995 – the year newspapers broke out onto the Internet. Online publications were instead viewed as opportunities to make circulation gains (Cao and Li 2006, pp. 133–135, cited in Gasher 2007). A 2007 report by Editor and Publisher observed: "While the overall print numbers don't look so hot, there's another story that gets buried every time print circulation figures are released. When a newspaper's Web site is taken into account, it gains a healthy number of readers" (Saba 2007). The Boston Globe Sunday print readership is off, but over a seven-day period 17 percent of surveyed adults say they read Boston.com. In the UK, the Guardian has lost many daily print readers over a 20-day period, and yet "the online *Guardian Unlimited* claims 16 million readers and 147 million page impressions every month" (Franklin 2008: 632). The emergence of free dailies is another case in point. The rise in circulation for ad-supported free dailies in North America and the UK (containing re-purposed content) brings in added revenue for their larger corporate parents (Franklin 2008: 632; Gasher 2007: 6).

Overall advertising revenue remains strong. The WAN reports that globally it grew 12.84 percent from 2002 to 2007; and that newspapers remain the second largest advertising medium in the world, after television. Newspaper advertising revenues in the United States, "decreased by 3 percent in 2007 but increased by +8 percent over the last five years" (WAN 2008). Newspaper markets in the EU saw a 9.91 percent increase over five years. The UK was one of only three newspaper markets in the EU where advertising revenue fell – off 5.18 percent over five years. A 55-year survey of advertising revenue in the United States newspaper industry found that both national and retail advertising revenue rise and fall with the economy and are particularly hurt during recessions, such as occurred in 1955, 1960, 1991 and following the 2000 dot-com meltdown (Picard 2008). Advertising revenue declines during 2007–2009, I suggest, should be viewed in the broader context of a global recession ignited by volatile oil prices and the collapse of housing markets in the USA and UK – both crises having been fueled, in part, by financialization of the global economy.

> Although the shifts in newspaper advertising are removing the unusually high profitability of the industry, they are not yet dooming it to demise or altering the basic structural element of the local newspaper markets in the United States. The changes, however, would seem to be moving the industry back to a period in which the newspaper industry was less financially interesting to investors who were primarily interested in profits and asset growth (Picard 2008: 715).

Audiences are fragmenting in a multi-media environment flooded with new mobile technologies. Classified advertising has been affected by online alternatives; ad growth is not keeping pace with inflation and, while online ad revenue is growing fast, it remains a very small portion of the overall advertising pie. These changes notwithstanding, they cannot fully explain the massive rationalization of labor taking place in newsrooms in the UK and USA. I suggest a key contributor is pressure from investors to increase profits.

Rationalizing flexible labor

Shareholder pressure for short term profit increases is enormous. Stock values drop as capital searches for more stable returns. When the UK's Trinity Mirror group reported 10 percent lower earnings in July 2008 the market reaction was swift: more than a quarter of its stock-market value was wiped out in one day (Tryhorn and Sweney 2008).

The decline was part of a larger trend. Johnston Press, which publishes 18 daily and 300 weekly local UK newspapers, lost nearly three quarters of its share value over 2007–2008 (Price 2008). Share prices also tumbled in the USA. In two years the McClatchy Holding Company, one of America's largest newspaper chains, saw its share price nose-dive 80 percent, from $50 to less than $9 (Toughill 2008).

In an economic environment characterized by great uncertainty, capital searches for ways to reduce risk. The three strategies of multi-media convergence – repurposing resources, cross-promotion, and the creation of new synergistic business opportunities – are part of that response (Compton 2004: 115–127). As mentioned above, newsroom layoffs are not new phenomena. Broadcast and print media corporations have been paring labor costs through layoffs and buyouts since the early 1980s. More recent newsroom layoffs, I believe, must be viewed as attempts to maintain double-digit profit margins to appease fickle investors and not as a direct result of online media. In addition to cuts, Gannett announced it would freeze its employee pension plan in a bid to save up to $90 million in 2009 (Adams 2008b). The day following the cuts the company's stock rose 10 percent (Ahrens 2008). The pressure pushed McClatchy to announce a year-long wage freeze starting in September 2008 (Adams 2008a). At least one financial analyst in the UK predicted shareholders and investors would lobby regulators to allow more mergers in an attempt to shore up stock values (Tryhorn and Sweney 2008). Labor cuts at privately held companies, such as Tribune, are also related to the merger boom. Tribune's layoffs came as the company struggled to finance an enormous debt load accrued as a direct result of its M&As, including the 2000 merger with Times Mirror, the publisher of the *Los Angeles Times*. Tribune was a profitable company in 2007 – posting profits of $87m on sales of $5.1bn – when new owner Sam Zell saddled the company with roughly $13bn in debt to take the company private (O'Shea 2008). Unable to cover its short-term debt during a recessionary downswing, Tribune declared bankruptcy in December 2008. Similarly onerous short-term debt loads led the *Philadelphia Inquirer* and the *Journal Register* to file for so-called Chapter 11 debt restructuring in February 2009 (Pilkington 2009).

Media convergence of newsrooms requires flexible labor. What is occurring is a fundamental restructuring of the division of newsroom labor. "Virtually all print journalists are now required to work across multiple media platforms which involves not only delivering copy for print and online editions of their newspapers, but also shooting brief video clips, reading pieces to camera, as well as recording podcasts which can be downloaded from the newspaper's website" (Franklin 2008: 635). These changes work to discipline labor and threaten communal professional standards.

Along with job cuts, the UK's *Daily Express* announced the introduction of a Woodwing editorial system. The new technology allows reporters to write "stories directly on to pages, rather than send their stories to subeditors first" (Brook 2008). Close to 300 journalists working for Trinity Mirror papers were told in August 2008 to re-apply for their jobs following news the company was building two multimedia newsrooms in Birmingham and Coventry. The facilities would provide content for five papers, including the *Birmingham Post* and the *Coventry Telegraph*. "People are scared about whether they'll have a job later this year," said Jeremy Dear, the general secretary of the National Union of Journalists. Moreover, Dear suggests the greater burden of work that will inevitably be shouldered by the remaining workers will affect "the long-term future of quality journalism at the titles" (Luft 2008). C. Edwin Baker argues that there will always be examples of quality editorial produced as a result of moments of inspired creativity.

> Most creation of quality content, however, involves regular application of considerable labor, talent, often costly production services, and other inputs including past mental or cultural creations that themselves may be costly if previously transformed into 'intellectual property.' That is, quality content ... requires money" (Baker 2007: 115).

The issue of paid labor is essential. The expanding multimedia environment has produced an overall increase in the amount of available information. But looks can be deceiving. There are millions of weblog writers, but there is little evidence to suggest that they produce original reporting (Haas 2005; Drezner and Farrell 2004). Research indicates that, in the main, weblogs reproduce and comment upon reporting produced by traditional reporters. The Project for Excellence in Journalism's State of the News Media (2008) report is blunt: "Even with so many new sources, more people now consume what old-media newsrooms produce, particularly from print, than before. Online, for instance, the top 10 news Web sites, drawing mostly from old brands, are more of an oligarchy, commanding a larger share of audience than they did in the legacy media." The Internet is primarily a distribution mechanism that makes it possible for more people than ever to access information. Despite this democratic gain, "search engines do not create content" (Baker 2007: 118).

James Carey reminds us that public life cannot exist without some form of collective memory (Carey 2007: 11). There must be some form of accessible record-keeping on which strangers can focus debate and discussion. Newspapers and journals have historically provided this service. Critical scholarly research has drawn attention to the failings of the institution and how particular social interests (owners and advertisers) are more equal than others (Herman and Chomsky 1988), but this criticism is leveled precisely because the work of reporters is seen as crucial to a democratic society.

Newspaper workers are the canaries in the coal mine of journalism, and by extension of the modern public sphere. Outside of large public service broadcasters, such as the BBC, newspapers are the largest employers of reporters and editors. Television remains the principal source of news for most people in developed Western societies; but despite the resilience of television and the rise of the Internet as news platforms it is the labor of men and women employed by newspapers that produces the vast bulk of reportage. More people watch television and the power of the image has deeply influenced public life, yet newspapers, because of their larger staffs, continue to do the heavy lifting of original newsgathering, investigative and critical reporting. It is because of this fact that spreading layoffs and labor rationalization at newspapers is critical; for what is at risk arguably goes well beyond a failed business model.

References

Adams, R. (2008a) "Gannett to Cut 1,000 Jobs As Revenue Drops 10%," *The Wall Street Journal*, 15 August, Online. Available at: <http://online.wsj.com/article/SB121873506239441307.html> (accessed 15 August).

Adams, R. (2008b) "Gannett Will Freeze Employee Pension Plan," *The Wall Street Journal*, 12 June, B7.

Ahrens, F. (2008) "Gannett to Eliminate 1,000 Newspaper Jobs," *The Washington Post*, 15 August, D03.

Baker, C. E. (2007) *Media Concentration and Democracy: Why Ownership Matters*, New York: Cambridge University Press.

Bauman, Z. (2000) *Liquid Modernity*, Cambridge: Polity.

Boczkowski, P. J. (2005) *Digitizing the News: Innovation in Online Newspapers*, Cambridge, MA: MIT Press.

Brook, S. (2008) "More than 80 Jobs to Go in Express Cull," *Guardian*, 10 September, Online. Available at: <http://www.guardian.co.uk/media/2008/sep/10/dailyexpress.richarddesmond> (accessed 11 September, 2008).

Cao, Z. and Z. Li (2006) "Effect of Growing Internet Newspapers on Circulation of U.S. Print Newspapers," In X. Li (ed.), *Internet Newspapers: The Making of a Mainstream Medium*, Mahwah, NJ: Lawrence Erlbaum Associates.

Carey, J. (2007) "A Short History of Journalism for Journalists: A Proposal and Essay," *Harvard International Journal of Press/Politics*, 12, 3–16.

Compton, J. (2004) *The Integrated News Spectacle: A Political Economy of Cultural Performance*, New York: Peter Lang.

Conroy, M. and J. Steel (2008) "The Future of Newspapers: Historical Perspectives," *Journalism Studies*, 9 (5), 650–661.

Drezner, D. and H. Farrell (2004) "The Power and Politics of Blogs," paper presented to the Annual Convention of the American Political Science Association, Chicago, Illinois, September.

Economist, The (2006) "Who Killed the Newspaper?" *The Economist*, 26 August, Online. Available at <http://www.economist.com/opinion/displaystory.cfm?story_id=7830218> (accessed 9 September 2006).

Franklin, B. (2008) "The Future of Newspapers," *Journalism Studies*, 9 (5), 630–641.

Gasher, M. (2007) "Crisis? What Crisis? A Report on the Restructuring of the Daily Newspaper Industry in Canada," Unpublished report prepared for the law firm Trudeau, Morissette & Saint-Pierre.

Haas, T. (2005) "From 'Public Journalism' to the 'Public's Journalism'? Rhetoric and Reality in the Discourse on Weblogs," *Journalism Studies*, 6 (3), 387–396.

Hedges, C. (2008) "Bad Days for Newsrooms – and Democracy," 21 July, *Truthdig.com*, Online. Available at: <http://www.truthout.org/article/the-internet-is-no-substitute> (accessed 5 August 2008).

Herman, E. and Chomsky, N. (1988) *Manufacturing Consent: The Political Economy of Mass Media*, New York: Pantheon.

Jarvis, J. (2007) "The iPod Moment has Arrived for Newspapers," *Guardian*, 8 October, Media Pages, 6.

Luft, O. (2008) "Trinity Mirror: 300 Midlands Staff Told to Reapply for Jobs," *Guardian*, 20 August, Online. Available at: <http://www.guardian.co.uk/media/2008/aug/20/trinitymirror.pressandpublishing> (accessed 21 August 2008).

Luft, O. (2009) "NUJ to Hold Day of Action over Newspaper Job Cuts," *Guardian*, 26 January, Online. Available: http://www.guardian.co.uk/media/2009/jan/26/nuj-day-of-action-newspaper-job-cuts> (accessed 26 February 2009).

McChesney, R. W. (2004) *The Problem of the Media: U.S. Communication Politics in the 21st Century*, New York: Monthly Review Press.

O'Shea, James (2008) "The Tribune Tragedy," *Guardian*, 15 December, Media Pages, 1.

Outing, S. (2008) "Life Without the Print Edition," *Editor and Publisher*, 1 April, Online. Available: <http://www.editorandpublisher.com/eandp/columns/stopthepresses_display.jsp?vnu_content_id=1003783560> (accessed 1 April 2008).

Pérez-Peña, R. (2007) "Newspaper Circulation in Steep Slide Across Nation," *New York Times*, 1 May, C10.

Pérez-Peña, R. (2008) "Paper Cuts An Industry Imperiled by Falling Profits and Shrinking Ads," *New York Times*, 7 February, C1.

Picard, R. G. (2008) "Shifts in Newspaper Advertising Expenditures and their Implications for the Future of Newspapers," *Journalism Studies*, 9 (5), 704–716.

Price, S. (2008) "Still Fit to Print," *The Sunday Times*, 20 July, F12.

Pilkington, Ed. (2009) "Philadelphia Inquirer Placed under Bankruptcy Protection," *Guardian*, 24 February, International Pages, 23.

Project for Excellence in Journalism (2008) "The State of the Media," 17 March, Online. Available at: <http://www.stateofthenewsmedia.org/2008/> (accessed 17 March, 2008).

Saba, J. (2007) "Behind the Numbers: The 'Other' Side of Today's FAS-FAX," *Editor and Publisher*, 30 April, Online. Available at: <http://www.editorandpublisher.com/eandp/news/article_display.jsp?vnu_content_id=1003578427> (accessed 1 May, 2008).

Sennett, R. (2006) *The Culture of the New Capitalism*, New Haven: Yale University Press.

Strupp, J. (2008) "L.A. Times Cuts 250 Jobs, 15% of Pages," *Editor and Publisher*, 2 July, Online. Available at: <http://www.editorandpublisher.com/eandp/news/mailto:jstrupp@editorandpublisher.com> (accessed 2 July 2008).

Thussu, D. K. (2007) *News as Entertainment: The Rise of Global Infotainment*, London: Sage.

Toughill, K. (2008) "Battling over Newspaper Spoils," *The Toronto Star*, 15 March, AA04.

Tryhorn, C. and M. Sweney (2008) "Media: Press the Panic Button," *Guardian*, 7 July, Media Pages 1.

World Association of Newspapers (2008) "World Press Trends: Newspapers Are a Growth Business," 2 June, Online. Available at: <http://www.wan-press.org/article17377.html>.

Yong Jin, D. (2008) "Neoliberal Restructuring of the Global Communication System: Mergers and Acquisitions," *Media, Culture and Society*, 30 (3), 357–373.

54

IMPARTIALITY IN TELEVISION NEWS: PROFITABILITY VERSUS PUBLIC SERVICE

Julian Petley

Within public service broadcasting systems, journalists are generally required by law to be impartial. On the other hand, newspaper journalists, however much they may personally believe in the value of impartiality, can find themselves working for a publication whose political partisanship is one of its main selling points. Indeed, one of the main arguments for impartiality in broadcasting is that it counterbalances the partiality of much of the press.

This is most certainly the case in Britain, where the press is not simply partisan but, historically, has always been heavily skewed to the right. None the less, in recent years there have been a number of calls for the repeal of the impartiality regulations in broadcasting, for three main reasons.

The first is that ever since the partial 'de-regulation' of British television ushered in by the 1990 Broadcasting Act, and the consequent arrival of the satellite broadcaster BSkyB as a major player, there has been a massive increase in the number of channels. Here the argument runs that, since audiences are now able to choose from a wide range of programmes, the content regulations necessary when news was produced only by the BBC and ITN are no longer appropriate. Unsurprisingly, this line is frequently taken by newspapers whose owners would like to be able to broadcast programmes as politically and ideologically partisan as their newspapers. The most important of these is Rupert Murdoch, who has made no secret of the fact that he would like to be able to turn the currently impartial Sky News into the UK equivalent of the far from impartial Fox News.

The second factor is research carried out by the BBC and Ofcom (a regulatory body covering both telecommunications and broadcasting, which was created by the Communications Act 2003) which consistently shows that viewing figures for news and current affairs programmes amongst the young, the working class and the minority ethnic communities are relatively low. As one of the principles of public service broadcasting laid down in that Act is that there should be 'a suitable quantity and range of high quality and original programmes for children and young people', and as another is that there should be 'a sufficient quantity of programmes that reflect the lives and concerns of different communities and cultural interests and traditions within the United Kingdom', it thus appears that the public service broadcasters are not adequately fulfilling their remit in terms of audience reach. One suggestion for reaching these 'disconnected' sections of the population is to offer them more 'opinionated' news and current affairs programmes.

The third factor concerns wider political and ideological changes which may have rendered the impartiality regulations not simply redundant but counter-productive. Traditionally, impartiality was thought to be achieved by balancing the views of the main parties on the issues of the day as perceived by Westminster. Today, however, for many people, for example those concerned with the wars in Iraq and Afghanistan, animal rights, climate change and so on, the play of forces within Parliament no longer constitutes what they regard as politics. As Damian Tambini and Jamie Cowling explain:

> Impartiality regulation in the UK has traditionally been highly focussed on party balance and the formal institutions of democracy. As a result, we are ill-prepared to cope with the complexity of politics in the new century, and the institutions of impartiality regulation run the risk of becoming irrelevant or, worse, obliging journalists to focus on ritualised formal politics when the real story, and the real challenge for public information, is elsewhere. (2002: 84).

This chapter will begin by outlining the current rules on impartiality and then summarise the research which has led some to suggest that these rules should be abolished for certain channels. It will argue that such a conclusion is not actually borne out by the research itself, and will go on to examine the 2007 BBC report *From Seesaw to Wagonwheel*, which suggested that what the rules really need is re-interpretation if broadcasters are to reach a wide range of audiences and if news and current affairs programmes are to deal adequately and fairly with a changed political and ideological landscape. The chapter will endorse and extend this critique, and conclude by arguing that abolishing the impartiality rules could, paradoxically, result in *less* diversity of viewpoints in public service broadcasting.

The current situation

Currently, the impartiality regulations established by the BBC and Ofcom forbid broadcasting institutions from expressing an opinion on current affairs or matters of public policy. They also operate on the principle of balance. Thus for example the BBC *Editorial Guidelines* state that:

> We seek to provide a properly balanced service consisting of a wide range of subject matter and views broadcast over an appropriate time scale across

all our output. We take particular care when dealing with political or industrial controversy or major matters relating to current public policy. We strive to reflect a wide range of opinion and explore a range and conflict of views so that no significant strand of thought is knowingly unreflected or under represented (http://www.bbc.co.uk/guidelines/editorialguidelines/edguide/impariality/index.shtml).

The *Ofcom Broadcasting Code* insists that 'news, in whatever form, is reported with due accuracy and presented with due impartiality', stressing that, 'in dealing with matters of major political and industrial controversy and major matters relating to current public policy an appropriately wide range of significant views must be included and given due weight in each programme or in clearly linked and timely programmes. Views and facts must not be misrepresented' (http://www.ofcom.org.uk/tv/ifi/codes/bcode/undue/).

An early warning sign

It was in a report published in 2002 by two of Ofcom's predecessors, the Independent Television Commission (ITC) and the Broadcasting Standards Commission (BSC), that the continuing viability of the impartiality regulations was first questioned at the regulatory level. The research which served as the basis for this report showed that the overall level of television national news consumption had fallen by 5.6 per cent since 1994, in spite of an 80 per cent increase of supply on the five main terrestrial channels. ITV had experienced a 23 per cent decline, and the biggest fall-offs in overall news viewing (14 per cent) had been among the 25–34-year-old age group and social groups C2DE.

On the other hand, no fewer than 95 per cent of those questioned stated that they were either very or fairly satisfied with broadcast news, although 20 per cent of black people expressed dissatisfaction. Nor did the research itself actually suggest that the impartiality of television news was a factor in audience disengagement from it. Indeed, 91 per cent agreed that impartiality was a good thing, although this fell very slightly to 88 per cent amongst 16–34-year-olds, and more dramatically to 64 per cent in the black community. The research also uncovered the fact that 88 per cent of those in multi-channel homes thought impartiality a good thing, compared to 93 per cent in non-multi-channel homes, and the report argues that this finding

> add[s] weight to the view that there may be the first signs of a growing volume of dissent from this long-established principle as viewers enjoy greater choice. This may be an early warning sign that Parliament and regulators should be ready to understand and respond to a shifting view and to encourage innovation rather than stifle it (Hargreaves and Thomas 2002: 69).

Taking into account these various factors, the report suggested that it may be that a more opinionated style of broadcast news, originated from well outside the UK broadcasting mainstream, is helpful in the overall news mix, so long as consumers are aware what they are getting and which services conform to impartiality rules and which do not. The time has come when a range of experimentation should be encouraged (2002: 105).

It thus concluded that in the case of minority interest channels, and as long as no threat is posed to the central, impartial reputation of mainstream UK television news:

In the interests of achieving greater diversity of television news, to serve a wider range of audience interests, Ofcom could use its freedom to interpret the principle of 'due impartiality' and might be given the power to recommend to the Secretary of State the terms on which particular television and radio services might be authorised to depart from standard rules and codes on issues such as impartiality (2002: 106).

However, the empirical research on which the report was based fails to justify such a conclusion. Firstly, it clearly demonstrated that support for the impartiality regulations across the broadcasting spectrum was extremely high. Second, the fall-off of that support in multi-channel homes is too small to be of any real significance. And finally, and most importantly, the slight fall in support amongst the young, and the larger fall amongst black people, not necessarily mean that these groups value impartiality less highly than does the population as a whole; instead they could well suggest that some members of these groups simply do not believe that television news is impartial in the way that it represents them and the issues with which they are concerned. Indeed, this could well be interpreted as an argument for more, not less, impartiality in television news. (For further discussion of this report see Petley 2003.)

Partial news

However, Ofcom returned to the future of the impartiality regulations in 2007 in a report arguing that 'universal impartiality may become less enforceable in a digital environment, where regulated and unregulated services exist side by side on the same platform' (2007: 71). For this reason, it concluded that news on the PSB channels should continue to be subject to the impartiality regulations, but also asked whether, 'for channels other than the main PSBs, is impartiality still important, or is it a barrier to diversity in an era with a wide range of services available to viewers?' (2007: 71) and enquired whether 'other channels [should] be allowed to offer partial news in the same way that newspapers and some websites do at present?' (2007: 71).

Like the previous report, this drew on research showing that support for the impartiality regulations remains high at 87 per cent of adults. However, this drops to 73 per cent in the case of 16–24-year-olds, and the report used this to suggest a possible link between the regulations and the disengagement from news among certain sections of society. In particular it wondered if the way in which the impartiality requirements have operated has affected not only the way in which news stories have been told, but also the selection of the stories, resulting in a middle-of-the-road news culture and a tendency to cluster around a narrow news agenda. It thus contended that:

> It may be an unintended consequence that rules on impartiality serve to stifle the expression of views that are not part of the established mainstream, such as those of the young; of some ethnic minorities; and others. It arises because news broadcasters may feel compelled to offer a traditional 'both-sides-of-the-argument' approach, to the exclusion of more diverse voices. Thus the issue of impartiality is linked to the broader question of disengagement. Impartiality, if applied across the board, may come to be seen as a possible hindrance to a truly diverse news supply (2007: 2).

More specifically, the research on which the report is based revealed that 46 per cent of people from minority ethnic groups felt that they received too little airtime, with 60 per cent of black Caribbean and 61 per cent of black African respondents feeling this to be the case. 64 per cent of 16–24-year-olds thought that much of the content of television news was irrelevant to them, whilst 53 per cent thought that young people did not appear onscreen enough in news programmes (interestingly, 45 per cent of 35–54-year-olds agreed with them).

However, although the research did indeed reveal a worrying degree of disengagement from television news amongst young people and members of the minority ethnic communities, there was nothing in it which suggested that the problem lies with the impartiality regulations per se. Again, the main complaint appeared to be that many members of these groups regard television news as treating them decidedly *partially*. The idea, then, that the solution to the problem of disengagement might be a relaxation of the impartiality rules, even if only on certain non-PSB channels, seems distinctly at odds with the report's empirical base.

'Radical impartiality'

There is, of course, nothing new in the idea that equating impartiality with balance, and then balancing a range of views drawn entirely from within the Westminster political spectrum, is exclusionary and results in a distinct democratic deficit in broadcasting. This is a criticism of broadcasting made familiar through the work of Ralph Miliband, Stuart Hood, Stuart Hall, Philip Schlesinger, the Glasgow University Media Group and others. However, this is not an argument for abolishing the impartiality regulations, but for interpreting them differently – an idea which broadcasters have traditionally resisted. It was thus refreshing that, in a lecture in November 2006, the BBC's Head of News, Peter Horrocks, signalled a change of tack on this vexed issue.

According to Horrocks (2006), the Corporation's purpose in the new broadcasting environment is 'to provide the widest range of information and views to all – so that the bulk of the population sees its own perspective reflected honestly and regularly.

We must also provide the opportunity for people to regularly come across alternative information and perspectives that provide a wider viewpoint'. He also argued that:

> the days of middle-of-the-road, balancing left and right, impartiality are dead. Instead I believe we need to consider adopting what I like to think of as a much wider 'radical impartiality' – the need to hear the widest range of views – all sides of the story. So we need more Taliban interviews, more BNP interviews – of course put on air with due consideration – and the full range of moderate opinions. All those views need to be treated with the same level of sceptical inquiry and respect. The days are over when the BBC treated left wing or pro-diversity views as 'loony' or interviewed anti-Europe or anti-immigration spokesmen insufficiently often. We lost considerable credibility with some of our audience by excluding views that significant parts of the population adhere to. So please get used to hearing more views that you dislike on our airwaves. This wider range of opinion is a worthwhile price to pay to maintain a national forum where all can feel they are represented and respected.

The value of the impartiality regulations, and the sheer wrong-headedness of the suggestion that broadcasters should be allowed to report the news in as partisan a fashion as newspapers, were all too starkly illustrated by the manner in which these eminently sensible views were reported by sections of the press. Thus the *Mail*, 1 December 2006, under the headline 'Radical impartiality: That's BBC-speak for why they want to give terrorists a platform', put its own highly distinctive spin on Horrocks' words:

> The BBC triggered outrage yesterday by calling for the views of extremists and fundamentalists to be given the same weight as those of mainstream politicians. The corporation's head of television news, Peter Horrocks, said groups such as the Taliban and the far-Right BNP need more airtime at the expense of moderate opinion. He said all views need to be treated with the same respect, describing his proposals as 'radical impartiality'.

Meanwhile in the *News of the World*, 5 December, Fraser Nelson argued that Horrocks 'wants to give the Taliban more of a platform (when they're not busy trying to kill our troops). It's a duty, he says – as if propaganda for Islamo-fascists was part of the BBC charter. If Nazi poodle Lord Haw Haw were alive today he'd get his own show'.

Fortunately, however, the BBC was not swayed by such tendentious nonsense, and in June 2007 it published a report which developed Horrocks' ideas. This stated that 'impartiality involves a mixture of accuracy, balance, context, distance, even-handedness, fairness, objectivity, open-mindedness, rigour, self-awareness, transparency and truth. But it is also about breadth of view and completeness. Impartiality in programme-making is often achieved by bringing extra perspectives to bear, rather than limiting horizons or censoring opinion' (BBC Trust 2007: 5–6). Admitting, with refreshing candour, that 'impartiality today requires a greater subtlety in covering and counterpointing the varied shades of opinion – and arguably always should have done' (2007: 36), and that the BBC had sometimes found difficulty in 'addressing opinion that that has not emerged through Parliament or other formal institutions', it continued:

> The growth of inter-party agreement at Westminster and unofficial cross-party alliances – whether on the invasion of Iraq, the funding of higher education, the detention of terrorist suspects, or global warming – complicates the impartiality equation. There are many issues where to hear 'both sides of the case' is not enough: there are many more shades of opinion to consider. Indeed, the principal linkage of impartiality to 'matters of party political or industrial controversy' has a very dated feel to it: there are many other areas where controversy is now much fiercer … Parliament can no longer expect to define the parameters of national debate: it can sometimes instigate it, but more often it has to respond to currents of opinion already flowing freely on the internet and in the media. The world no longer waits on parliamentary utterance, and parliamentary consensus should never stifle the debate of topical issues on the BBC – because it does not always correspond with the different strands of public opinion (2007: 34).

The report thus concluded that:

> Factual programming should not normally be built simply round a 'for' and 'against' proposition. Opinion is more complex and subtle than that. All rational shades of opinion should be covered, though not necessarily in equal proportions. Maverick or minority views should not necessarily be given equivalent weight with the prevailing consensus, but it is not the role of the BBC to close down debate. (2007: 80-1)

Like the ITC/BSC report, this drew on research which showed considerable public support for the impartiality principle. Thus 84 per cent of respondents agreed that, whilst impartiality is difficult to achieve, broadcasters must try very hard to do so. However, a noticeably lower level of support for this was expressed by those aged 24 or under, those of non-white ethnicity, and those in social classes D and E. But on the question of whether broadcasters should stay neutral and not give their own view, 33 per cent said it was vital, 47 per cent very important and 14 per cent fairly important – with little variation across age, class and ethnicity. Regarding diversity, 83 per cent agreed that broadcasters should report all views and opinions, however unpopular or extreme. The only sharp variation in this pattern was among those from ethnic minorities, where 61 per cent agreed and 10 per cent disagreed. But again, there was no evidence to suggest that relaxing the impartiality rules, or abolishing them altogether for certain channels, would make television news and current affairs programmes more attractive to currently hard-to-reach groups.

The clear difference, then, between the ITC/BSC and Ofcom reports, on the one hand, and the BBC report on the other, is that the former suggest that 'disconnected' audiences might better be served by channels which are not obliged to broadcast impartial news and current affairs programmes, whilst the latter argues that what is needed is a reinterpretation of the impartiality requirements so as to admit a wider and more diverse range of views.

A diminution of diversity

However, it is possible to go further and to argue that relaxing the impartiality regulations, or abolishing them for certain channels, could well result in not an increase but a diminution of diversity. Evidence to back up this point of view is not hard to find. For example, when in 1987 in the US Federal Communications Commission abolished the 'Fairness Doctrine', this certainly contributed to the process whereby talk radio became increasingly dominated by rabidly right-wing 'shock-jocks', as well as paving the way for the blatantly biased Fox News. Or take the example of the notoriously partisan British daily press where, with the exception of the small circulation 'qualities', the *Guardian*, *Independent* and *Financial Times*, illiberal opinion is quite remarkably hegemonic, and majoritarian (if the venerable British Social Attitudes survey is to be believed) liberal opinion finds itself not only woefully underrepresented (and more often than not, quite simply unrepresented) but routinely travestied, traduced and trashed. Similarly, whilst the Web has undoubtedly allowed many voices once silenced by the mainstream media to be heard, there is little evidence to suggest that the majority of users employ it to access a wide and diverse range of views on current affairs. Indeed, quite the reverse, as Andrew Keen argues:

> Instead, we use the Web to confirm our partisan views and link to others with the same ideologies. Bloggers today are forming aggregated communities of like-minded amateur journalists … where they congregate in self-congratulatory clusters. They are the digital equivalent of online gated communities where all the people have identical views and the whole conversation is mirrored in a way that is reassuringly familiar. It's a dangerous form of digital narcissism; the only conversations we want to hear are those with ourselves and those like us. (Keen 2007: 55).

Furthermore, specifically British political blogs, far from counterbalancing the dominance of right wing views in the press, actually mirror it: *Iain Dale's Guide to Political Blogging* (Dale 2007) shows that, of the top ten political blogs, five are Conservative, one UK Independence Party (UKIP), and one otherwise right wing. Interestingly, a favourite, not to say obsessive, theme of many right wing blogs is precisely the need to abolish the impartiality regulations, which are seen as a means of shoring up a perceived 'left-liberal' hegemony within broadcasting. But as Horrocks correctly pointed out: 'the increasing shouts of bias against public broadcasters are more a reflection of the distorted information environment the complainants themselves live in. They are so conditioned to their own self-reinforcing perspectives that they are more inclined than before to see impartiality as bias' (2006).

Not that one needs to visit websites to find these kinds of rants – British newspapers have long been stuffed with them. To take but one example, when the ITC/BSC published their report, *The Sunday Times*, 17 November 2002, ran a piece by Andrew Sullivan headlined 'Let's hear it for prejudiced television news' and calling for 'an injection of honest bias, US-style'. In Sullivan's view, BBC news reflects an 'effortless left-liberal viewpoint', leading him to conclude that whilst

> there's room for a left-leaning network in Britain … what's wrong is the pretence that the BBC is somehow neutral, objective or balanced. And what makes this doubly wrong is that it's paid for by the licence fee. I can't see why people in a free society should tolerate a television channel that promotes a viewpoint with which they disagree. I don't see why they should also be forced to pay for it and then be denied the opportunity to have an alternative by specious regulations over something ludicrously called balance.

Profit in populism

Of course, it could be argued that the provision of a right-leaning news service to counterbalance a left-leaning one is actually a form of public service broadcasting. However, this would depend on accepting that the BBC is indeed left-leaning, which, as we have seen, is not a view shared by the vast majority of the population. Furthermore, when newspapers owned by Murdoch remorselessly peddle this kind of line, one suspects a commercial as well as an ideological motive. Indeed, former *Sun* pundit Richard Littlejohn let this particular cat out of the bag when he complained that when working at Sky News 'we'd never been able to make the programme we intended. If Sky News could emulate its US sister Fox News, which has wiped the floor with CNN with opinion-driven "fair and balanced" coverage, ratings would soon shoot past the Astra satellite. But the regulators won't allow it' (Littlejohn 2002: 68). And according to the minutes of a meeting in September 2007 at which Murdoch himself testified to the House of Lords Select Committee on Communications, he made it clear that 'he believed that Sky News would be more popular if it were more like the Fox News Channel'.

More popular, and thus, of course, more profitable. In the US, research carried out by Matthew Gentzkow and Jesse M. Shapiro for the National Bureau of Economic Research showed that 'consumer demand responds strongly to the fit between a newspaper's slant and the ideology of potential readers, implying an economic incentive for newspapers to tailor their slant to the ideological predispositions of consumers' (2006: 43), whilst the Harvard economists Sendhil Mullainathan and Andrei Shleifer concluded similarly from their research that 'competition forces newspapers to cater to the prejudices of their readers, and greater competition typically results in more aggressive catering to such prejudices as competitors strive to divide the market' (2005: 1042). As we have seen, the vast majority of British television viewers still expect news and current affairs programmes to remain impartial, but in an ever more competitive broadcasting environment, the demands from purely

[handwritten margin note: populism: the claim that they side with the people]

commercial broadcasters such as Murdoch for the abandonment of regulations which prevent his channels from pandering to his target audiences' prejudices in the same manner as the *Sun* and *News of the World*, are bound to become ever more strident.

British television is a fragile and complex ecology, and it is impossible to introduce changes into one part of it without setting off others elsewhere. So consider the following scenario. Ofcom abolishes the impartiality regulations for non-PSB channels and Murdoch is finally able to turn Sky News into a UK version of Fox News. Like the latter, it's extremely popular with certain sections of the audience (even if loathed by others), and its success in audience terms is greatly aided by massive cross-media promotion from elsewhere in the Murdoch empire – including, quite possibly, a Murdoch-owned Five. As its audience share grows, others realise that there's profit in populism, and begin to follow suit. Thus is repeated in broadcasting the process by which Murdoch has done such incalculable damage to the British press, namely forcing his rivals to compete with him on his own terms. Nor would the BBC be immune – already far too prone to shadowing press-set news agendas, it would risk being swept along in the populist slipstream emanating from the revamped Sky. Indeed, if it stood out against this, it would soon find Sky adding its voice to the press campaign against the 'left-liberal' BBC. If the Corporation's pusillanimous reaction to that campaign is anything to go by, it would become increasingly defensive and reactive – and thus, ineluctably, broadcasting in the UK would fall prey to the same process of 'Foxification' that Murdoch has so successfully initiated in the States.

It was therefore encouraging that a recent Lords Select Committee report stated that:

> We believe that any weakening of the impartiality requirements as they apply to UK broadcasters would have a negative impact in the quality and trustworthiness of the country's news. Such a move would not benefit the public or journalists and could run the risk of undermining the most important medium for news (House of Lords 2008: 94).

Equally encouraging was Ofcom's admission that 'on the basis of responses received [to its report discussed above], the benefits of required impartiality on all TV news appear to outweigh any reservations, beyond the point of switchover at least' and that 'there appear to be no strong arguments for rules to be relaxed at present' (2008: 9).

Also encouraging was the government response, which stated that:

> The Government fully endorses the Committee's view of the importance of the impartiality requirements especially on PSBs, and considers them an essential part of the regulatory framework safeguarding the informational needs of citizens. They will remain part of the regulatory framework for television content. However, the increasing blurring of distinctions between different media platforms will provide a challenge for content regulation in future and we will continue to examine the implications of this for regulation and policy (DCMS 2008: 7).

Deeply discouraging, however, was a Conservative discussion document which argued that 'impartiality should remain a central public service obligation on public service broadcasters. However, impartiality requirements should be relaxed for broadcasters not receiving public funds or spectrum subsidies' (Conservative Research Dept. 2008: 16). This threatens to make the future of the impartiality regulations a party political issue, and to introduce the distinct possibility that Murdoch will bestow his newspapers' political favours on whichever party enables him to 'Foxify' Sky – or any other UK-based television channel which he may acquire.

As noted at the start of this chapter, as society becomes more fragmented, it is harder to set the parameters within which impartiality in broadcasting is exercised. But never has this been a more important task, as impartial sources of news are one of the key means by which people construct a sense of shared understanding of the society, and indeed of the world, in which they live. As David Cox puts it: 'the forces threatening broadcasting impartiality make its practice all the more necessary. The more society atomises, the more important a common thread of meaning becomes' (2007: 38). Clearly, then, the future of the broadcasting impartiality regulations in Britain is far too important to be allowed to become a party political football or a cynical ploy in a political beauty contest presided over by Murdoch.

References

BBC Trust (2007) *From Seesaw to Wagonwheel: Safeguarding Impartiality in the 21st Century*, London: BBC.

Conservative Research Department (2008) *Plurality in a New Media Age: the Future of Public Service Broadcasting*, London: The Conservative Party. Available http://www.shadowdcms.co.uk/pdf/Plurality InANewMediaAge.pdf (accessed 4 December 2008).

Cox, D. (2007) 'Impartiality imperilled', *Prospect*, September, 36–9.

Dale, Iain (ed.) (2007) *Iain Dale's Guide to Political Blogging*, Petersfield: Harriman House Ltd.

Department for Culture, Media and Sport (DCMS) (2008), *Government Response to the Report of the House of Lords Select Committee on Communications on the Ownership of News (HL122–1) Session 2007–08*, London: TSO.

Gentzkow, M. and Shapiro J. (2006) 'What drives media slant? Evidence from U.S. daily newspapers', National Bureau of Economic Research Working Paper no. 12707. Available http://www.nber.org/papers/w12707.pdf (accessed 4 December 2008).

Hargreaves, I. and Thomas, J. (2002) *New News, Old News*, London: Independent Television Commission/ Broadcasting Standards Commission.

Horrocks, P. (2006) 'Finding TV news' lost audience'. Available http://www.st-annes.ox.ac.uk/fileadmin/STA/Documents/About_-_Lectures/Peter_Horrocks_Lecture_28xi06.pdf (accessed 1 December 2008).

House of Lords Select Committee on Communications (2008) *The Ownership of the News: Volume 1: Report*, London: TSO.

Keen, Andrew (2007) *The Cult of the Amateur: How Today's Internet Culture is Killing Our Culture and Assaulting Our Economy*, London: Nicholas Brealey Publishing.

Littlejohn, Richard (2002) 'Why I'll never give up the day job', *British Journalism Review*, 13: 3, 65–70.

Mullainathan S. and Shleifer, A. (2005) 'The market for news', *The American Economic Review*, 95: 4, 1031–53.

Ofcom (2007) *New News, Future News: the Challenges for Television News After Digital Switchover*, London: Office of Communications.

Ofcom (2008) 'Ofcom response to the House of Lords Select Committee on Communications report on the ownership of the news (HL 122–I) session 2007–8'. Available http://www.parliament.uk/documents/upload/Ofcom response.doc (accessed 4 December 2008)

Petley, J. (2003) 'The wrong medicine', *British Journalism Review*, 14: 1, 81–5.

Tambini, D. and Cowling, J. (2002) 'News regulation and the transition to digital: taking the long view', in D. Tambini and J. Cowling (eds), *New News: Impartial Broadcasting in the Digital Age*, London: Institute for Public Policy Research.

55

COMPARATIVE NEWS MEDIA SYSTEMS: NEW DIRECTIONS IN RESEARCH

Rodney Benson

Long hampered by American chauvinism, comparative research on news media is finally coming out of its long slumber. Presuming the inferiority of journalism as practiced anywhere other than in the land of Watergate and the Pentagon Papers, U.S. researchers for many years were little inclined to explore conditions elsewhere. More surprisingly, this U.S.-centric worldview was often embraced by legions of Europeans and others who rejected their own journalistic traditions in favor of an American ideal that was often ill-suited to their own country (Mancini 2000). Promoted by the State Department and private foundations (Wrenn 2008), U.S. notions of a market-driven "free press" were also long reinforced by the classic textbook, *Four Theories of the Press* (Siebert, Peterson, and Schramm 1956). *Four Theories* celebrated the U.S. and U.K. "liberal" and "social responsibility" models, reviled the "authoritarian" and "Soviet-communist" alternatives, and simply ignored the possibility of anything in between. In short, one had to choose: the "American Way," or the Highway (to the Gulag). Clearly, this stark dichotomy effectively removed from view the range of western European democratic press traditions, as well as the diverse panoply of non-Western media.

Fortunately, in recent years, a growing tide of cross-national comparative research has begun to challenge this American-centric narrative. After the pioneering essay by Blumler and Gurevitch (1975), new journals emerged, such as the *European Journal of Communication* and the *International Journal of Press/Politics*, which emphasized comparative research. Important anthologies were edited by Blumler, McLeod, and Rosengren (1992) and Curran and Park (2000), the latter attempting to more fully incorporate non-Western media, and important comparative case studies were conducted by Alexander (1981), Hallin and Mancini (1984), Chalaby (1996), Åsard and Bennett (1997), Esser (1998, 1999), Benson (2000), Ferree et al. (2002),

Deuze (2002), Donsbach and Patterson (2004), Strömbäck and Dimitrova (2006), among many others. In 2004, Daniel Hallin and Paolo Mancini's *Comparing Media Systems* presented a landmark synthesis of this emerging research field, replacing the American-centric normative approach of *Four Theories* with an original framework for open-ended empirical research.

In a very short period of time, *Comparing Media Systems* has become an essential point of reference for comparative news media research, but as Hallin and Mancini themselves concede, it is far from the last word. Their classification of national media systems into broader regional political/journalistic "models" – a North Atlantic "liberal" model, a Northern European "democratic corporatist" model, and a southern European "polarized pluralist" model – is admittedly not fully able to capture the diversity of media within and across each model. Likewise, their identification of four key factors shaping news production (to be discussed below), while immensely useful, needs to be interrogated in relation to other theoretical traditions, such as the sociology of news, new institutionalism, and field theory. Finally, important questions scarcely explored by Hallin and Mancini are now arguably the most crucial: first, the extent to which even an "expanded" understanding of Western media (beyond the American paradigm) is adequate to fully account for the wide variety of media found in Latin America, Africa, Asia, and Eastern Europe, and second, whether the internet is dissolving or exacerbating or creating new kinds of cross-national differences.

These are of course big questions, and I do not intend to settle them in this chapter. Instead, I will focus on the challenge of employing comparative research for testing hypotheses about the effects of system-level variables on news content and form, and limit myself to a few concluding remarks about the "new frontiers" of research on non-Western media and internet journalism. In my view, comparative research needs to be more self-conscious about seeking out national cases that vary on system-level variables (such as concentration of ownership, political party system, specific media policies, etc.) rather than on the basis of regional or topical interest. Because the French and U.S. news media differ so systematically – in their relations to political and economic power, and in their journalistic professional traditions – many communication scholars and sociologists have found this comparison to be especially fruitful in theory-building (see, Alexander 1981; Lemieux and Schmalzbauer 2000; Brossard et al. 2004; Starr 2004). For this reason, my own research has focused on French–American comparisons, and I will draw upon some of my recent findings to illustrate the theory-building potential (and limitations) of comparative research.

There are some positive signs that journalists are paying increasing attention to this research (see, Nordensen 2007), providing them with new ideas about reporting practices and ways to resist excessive market or governmental pressures. Moreover, to the extent that publics and policy-makers can understand better the factors that shape journalistic production, they are in a better position to demand changes that will help journalism better serve the needs of democratic societies. Comparative research is now poised, more than ever, to honestly and directly answer such questions.

Reconceptualizing the sociology of news

Institutional and organizational scholars (e.g., DiMaggio and Powell 1991) have posited that contemporary societies are composed of a number of competing and semi-autonomous institutional orders or "fields." Journalism is clearly a "field" in most if not all Western democratic nation-states in that it has developed some limited amount of autonomy from the state and the capitalist market and that it is an arena of contestation and struggle operating according to "rules of the game" consciously or unconsciously enacted by actors in the field. Such a structural conception of journalism suggests that news content will be shaped first of all by the journalistic field's positioning vis-à-vis other powerful fields, chiefly the political and economic fields, and second of all, by factors internal to the field itself, such as historically-shaped cultural logics of practice and social class differentiation. This "field-level" conceptualization of journalism – simultaneously analyzing political, economic, and internal "journalistic field" constraints on the production of news – builds upon the classic sociology of news while offering a more parsimonious and comprehensive systems-level framework that will be especially useful for cross-national comparative research.[1]

The first type of structural constraint is political. It is hypothesized that the state powerfully constrains (or enables) the diversity of voices and views in the press, as well as the amount and types of criticism and critical reporting, through its power to regulate or subsidize the media, provide official information to the press, and shape the system of parties and elections (Kuhn 1995; Starr 2004); in Bourdieu's terms, this factor concerns the journalistic field's relation to the "political field" (Bourdieu 2005).

The second type of structural constraint is commercial, or in Bourdieu's terms, the journalistic field's relation to the economic field. Such economic influences are often portrayed as a unitary phenomenon when in fact they encompass different, potentially conflicting elements. At least four distinct kinds of economic pressures can be identified: concentration of ownership (Klinenberg 2007; Baker 2007), profit pressures related to type of ownership (Cranberg et al. 2001), type of funding such as advertising versus paying audiences (Baker 1994; or type of advertising, see Benson 2003), and level and intensity of market competition, which may be closely related with non-economic forms of competition among journalists, as discussed below.

A third claim is that while economic and political factors establish the broad context for press performance, it is journalistic norms and practices historically emerging out of a particular national journalistic field that directly shape news content and form (Bourdieu 1998, 2005). As Bourdieu (1998: 39) insists, a field is a "microcosm with its own laws ... [which is to say] that what happens in it cannot be understood by looking only at external factors." A field's "rules of the game" are established when the field is founded, and once "routinized" tend to persist over time. Field internal "logics" may thus tend to persist even when conditions external to the field change. Field logics may be expressed in a number of ways, in taken-for-granted assumptions about what constitutes "news" and the purpose of journalism, the relationship between fact and opinion, modes of news story construction and sourcing practices, or dominant genres and news design formats. Journalistic fields may also differ cross-nationally in class stratification and organizational ecology, specifically in their degree of concentration or fragmentation, which can affect the amount and types of information flows and the level and intensity of competition, both economic and professional.

This framework of three broad types of structural forces shaping the production of news – political, economic, and journalistic fields – should not be taken as precluding the possibility of other fields shaping the news; in some nation-states and under certain historical conditions, the religious, social scientific, or civil society associational fields may exert significant influences. In order to understand any given case of news coverage, all of these fields and their leading individual or organizational actors need to be taken into account. This framework overlaps to a certain degree with Hallin and Mancini's "four factor" model, though again I believe that the three factors I have outlined offer a broader model for comparative research as it seeks to analyze media outside of western Europe and North America. Hallin and Mancini identify four relevant "dimensions" of media systems: (1) historical development of a strong or weak mass circulation press, (2) political parallelism or the extent to which the media system reflects the major political currents, (3) journalistic professional training and tradition, and (4) type and extent of state intervention in the media sector.

Dimension 1 is one type of commercial constraint, but as noted there are others that could be relevant to explaining cross-national differences in news content. Dimensions 2 and 4 are both types of political constraints, and Dimension 3 is one aspect of journalistic field dynamics that as noted could also include the class characteristics of journalists and their audiences (see Bourdieu 1984; Benson 2006, 2009a; Hovden 2008), enduring cultural logics of practice, and organizational ecologies of both economic and symbolic (prestige) competition.

Having identified the potential universe of influences on the news, the crucial question then becomes: How do these factors shape the news in ways relevant to various democratic aspirations? In what ways do they contribute to journalistic content that is more or less ideologically diverse, more or less critical, more or less reasoned? Based on previous and emerging research, I offer six partially competing hypotheses about the ways in which these three structural factors – economic field, political field, and journalistic field – may work together or at cross-currents to produce variable effects on the production of news.

Commercial, political and field effects: some hypotheses

1 Greater dependence on advertising is likely to contribute to more positive (or less negative) coverage of business, more critical (or sparse) coverage of labor unions, as well as a pro-consumerist depoliticization and ideological narrowing of the news (Tasini 1990; Baker 1994).
2 Government regulations, particularly via legal definitions of defamation and libel, may crucially shape patterns of news coverage. In particular, we might suppose that more restrictive defamation and libel laws will contribute to lesser public discussion of the private lives of government or other officials (Saguy 2003: 93), and perhaps

less critical and cynical coverage. Likewise, stricter laws and regulations concerning journalistic access to confidential government information are likely to contribute to fewer revelations about governmental corruption or mismanagement.

3 Depending on the specific policy and kind of subsidy, the state as "enabler" could actually contribute to a range of media "public goods" (Baker 2002), a broader representation of groups and ideologies in the news, greater attention to government and political life in general, and more sustained, in-depth debate of issues (Curran 1991; see also Murschetz 1998).

4 Such subsidies, however, also may place particular news outlets and the media system as a whole in the uncomfortable position of financial dependency on the government. For this reason, other scholars (de Tarlé 1980: 146) suggest that state "enabling" intervention has a chilling effect on news coverage of politics, or at least, on the party or leaders in power.

5 Field-specific cultural logics will generally express and reinforce extra-field influences. However, to the extent that such field logics are "path dependent" (Powell 1991) and subject to "cultural inertia", thus tending to perpetuate the political and economic constraints at the time the field was first formed, the congruence between internal field logics and external forces may vary, especially during periods of rapid societal change. Field cultural logics will also tend to exert relatively uniform effects across the field, smoothing out to a certain degree differences among media outlets based on their ownership, funding, or audience demographic composition.

6 Finally, the internal organizational ecology of fields may play a role in encouraging or discouraging the kind of direct competition that leads to more sensationalistic or dramatized news coverage. For instance, Esser (1999) finds that national press coverage of politics is more "tabloidized" (defined here as more cynical toward politicians and more scandal-oriented) in the United Kingdom than in Germany, in part because of the U.K.'s more direct and intense competition among national newspapers as opposed to Germany's regionally-based system press.

Comparative research as hypothesis testing: French–U.S. comparisons

Of course, this list is far from exhaustive, and others might produce a different set of hypotheses. Yet any attempt to systematically link media system characteristics and news content would be a significant improvement on the all-too-frequent framing study with methodological sophistication to spare but which ignores system-level causal linkages (see my specific critiques in Benson 2004).

Given the complexity and multiplicity of factors involved, it is certainly fair to say that news discourses are over-determined. In other words, since multiple factors often push the media in the same direction (e.g., both state and commercial factors potentially contributing to ideological narrowing), it simply may not be possible to identify the one or two most important factors. Gamson and Modigliani (1989: 5) even challenge the appropriateness of "the language of dependent and independent variables" for a constructionist account of media discourse, instead favoring what they term a "value-added process." I share their uneasiness over a strictly linear regression approach that would ignore how forces shaping news production are often intertwined and inter-related. Nevertheless, the simple lumping together of factors as encouraged by such a value-added model offers little hope of any insight into cross-national variations.

Comparative research, at least initially, may be less able to resolve questions about causality than to punch holes in the existing assumptions.[2] But this alone would be an impressive step forward. Let us consider just a few of the preceding hypotheses. What can comparative research tell us? Given that the French and U.S. media present in many ways opposite "ideal" types, and since this is my own area of research expertise, several of my examples will derive from this case study comparison. Within-country comparisons (across media outlets, differing in various characteristics) will also be used to contextualize and qualify cross-national findings.

Dependence on advertising funding varies significantly across national media systems. Is it true that media outlets that are more dependent on advertising will be less ideologically diverse or less critical of business? The French national press receives about half as much of its revenues from advertising as does the U.S. press. My case study comparison of immigration news coverage in seven U.S. newspapers and seven French newspapers shows that the French national press is in fact the more ideologically diverse, both at the level of individual newspapers and across the media system as a whole (Benson 2009a); another study (Benson and Hallin 2007) that analyzed random samples of political news articles in the 1960s and 1990s likewise showed that *Le Monde* and *Le Figaro* offered a wider range of civil society viewpoints than the *New York Times* (see Väliverronen and Kunelius 2008 for an extension of this research to include the "democratic corporatist" media system in Finland). An earlier comparison of Italian national public television and the U.S. national commercial networks likewise found a broader representation of diverse political and civil society viewpoints in the Italian media (Hallin and Mancini 1984). Certainly, political system factors – for instance, the existence of multi-party systems and the use of state subsidies to support ideological diversity, especially in the case of France – help explain these cross-national differences. Advertising's "value-added" negative causal influence, however, seems to be demonstrated by the fact that the most ideologically diverse newspapers in each country in my immigration news study tended to be among those least dependent on advertising: in the U.S. case, the *Christian Science Monitor* (just 10 percent of revenues from advertising); and in France, *Libération* (just 20 percent of revenues) (Benson 2009a).

What about critical coverage of business? Is coverage of business more critical in news media systems that rely less on advertising? French–U.S. comparisons, at least, offer little evidence that this is the case. In another article drawing on my immigration news case study (Benson 2009b), I find that critical statements, either by journalists or the sources they quote, directed at business are rare in both the French and U.S. press, appearing in just 5 percent of French news stories and 7 percent of U.S. stories. Business criticism is higher than average at less advertising dependent outlets like the communist *L'Humanité* (not surprisingly!), the left-leaning *Libération*, and again, in the U.S., the *Christian Science Monitor*, but it is also relatively high at the *New York*

Times (just as high as at the *Monitor*, and higher than at most French newspapers), so advertising cannot be the entire story. Obviously, journalists are not so mechanically controlled by a dollop more or less of advertising; it may be that across most capitalist societies, powerful businesses will tend to be absent from the general news pages, thus precluding critical coverage, except during relatively rare moments of crisis or scandal (Davis 2002). Moreover, the amount and intensity of business criticism may vary by issue. But that is just the point. Mechanistic claims – about advertising, or ownership, and the like – are frequently made in both scholarly and popular venues. Cross-national research, because it allows for variation across multiple dimensions, helps us test and sort out the complex, overlapping, or contradictory avenues of influence on journalistic production.

Critical coverage of government, on the other hand, has often been assumed to be inversely related to the degree of state intervention in the media sector. Given the relatively higher degree of state intervention in the French media system, a French–U.S. comparison is illustrative. It does seem to be the case that there is more investigative reporting in the United States than in France (Chalaby 2004), though it is important to emphasize that the amount of investigative reporting is relatively low even in the U.S. In my immigration case study, using a generous indicator of "investigative reporting," only about 5 percent of U.S. news coverage could be considered to fall into this category (compared to about 2 percent in the French sample). However, using the indicator of frequency of critical statements about government, or of dominant parties of the left or right, the French press was at least as or more critical than the U.S. press (Benson 2009b).

Finally, how might the cultural logic of journalistic fields offer additional explanatory power for differences in news form and content? In answering such a question, I hope to go beyond what has been done so often in the past, that is, to simply assert the primacy of "cultural" practices without also considering additional contextual factors, such as the aforementioned political and commercial influences, that may also be shaping the news. At the same time, I also want to search for evidence that might show that such practices are not simply "mechanisms," that is, means through which external political and economic forces shape the news, but rather are semi-independent causal factors in their own right.

The "form of news" (Barnhurst and Nerone 2001), I would like to suggest, is a key means through which the internal logics of journalistic fields are expressed. The journalistic form of "dramatic narrative" has been highlighted by Darnton (1975), Schudson (1995) and Pedelty (1995), among others. There is no reason to assume, however, that narrative is necessarily a "universal" characteristic of journalistic practice. Ferree et al. (2002) show that German journalists are significantly less likely than U.S. journalists to construct their news articles as "narratives," instead preferring to focus on reasoned debate among elites; likewise Hallin and Mancini (1984) found that Italian television journalists emphasized the presentation of opposing party viewpoints rather than personalized narratives. In France, there seems to be a similar emphasis on journalism as polemical "debate" rather than personalized narrative (Benson 2006, 2009a, 2009b; Boudana 2008). French debate oriented news is enabled by a distinct journalistic format – the "debate ensemble" – which is given various labels by newspapers ("événement" [today's big news] at *Libération*, "le fait du jour" [fact of the day] at *Le Parisien*, etc.) The debate ensemble format packages one or more of the page one news stories of the day into collections of related articles of various genres – breaking news, analyses, transcripts of interviews, background context articles, editorials, guest commentaries, and simple lists of quotes (often headlined "reactions") from various officials, activists, experts, or ordinary citizens. In contrast, a page one news story in an American newspaper tends to be packaged as a single and often lengthy article authored by one or two journalists (though of course, there are exceptions when the "news" is extraordinary), and rarely mixes genres on the same page.

Dramatic narrative would seem to be highly compatible with investigative reporting, thus offering an additional explanation of its relatively greater prominence in the United States. On the other hand, it seems reasonable to suppose as Wessler (2008: 8) hypothesizes, that narrative-driven formats actually "restrict the room for deliberative exchange of ideas." At the qualitative level, the virtual absence of narrative-driven articles in the French immigration coverage as opposed to the overwhelming predominance of narrative-inflected articles in the U.S. coverage offers an additional explanation both for relatively greater ideological diversity and greater density of critical statements.

Future challenges

It is important to acknowledge that two-country case study comparisons are limited in their capacity to definitively sort out the explanatory power of causal factors which are sure to over-determine any given national-level outcome. For this reason, another important approach not discussed in this chapter are ambitious multi-country studies, such as Shoemaker and Cohen's recent *News around the World* (2006), though these kinds of studies sometimes attain scope at the sacrifice of contextual nuancing and depth. The best of both approaches might be combined via carefully designed multi-country comparisons that hold constant certain variables (e.g., level of advertising, or ownership concentration) in order to test more effectively for others (such as the effects of libel or other government policies); in order not to lose sight of contextual, historical factors, however, it might be advisable to keep the number of nation-states to a manageable number (i.e., three to ten).

As I noted at the outset, two crucial challenges remain. The first is to extend comparative news media research beyond Europe and North America. Building on the legacy of Curran and Park's *De-westernizing Media Studies* (2000), there have been a number of worthwhile recent studies of news media in the Arab world (Ayish 2005), Mexico (Hughes 2006), Indonesia (Hanitzsch 2006), India (Rajagopal 2001), Japan (Freeman 2000, Krauss 2000), and elsewhere. While some of this work is explicitly comparative, much of it is not: the "comparisons" in these cases will have to be made by the reader, or even better, by the scholar who can put them to use via creative syntheses of these case studies.

A great deal of this research on the "developing world" demonstrates the ways in which European and North American news models have shaped local practice. For example, Silvio Waisbord's *Watchdog Journalism in South America* (2000) finds much of South American journalism to be a "hybrid" of Anglo-American and French/Spanish traditions. However, Waisbord also emphasizes local influences, and indeed, one must be careful not to simply "apply" Western models, either empirical (e.g., Hallin and Mancini 2004) or democratic normative (Jürgen Habermas's "discursive" model, among others, as elaborated in Ferree et al. 2002), onto non-Western societies. Without going to the extremes of an absolute relativism, it is crucial that one attempt to acknowledge and understand the difference of the "Other" rather than too quickly eliding it (Silverstone 2007). At the same time, comparative research would be impossible if we gave up on the possibility of attaining some level of cross-cultural understanding and some level of impartial knowledge of empirical similarities and differences. In order to keep the number of potential causal variables manageable, however, it would seem advisable to compare media systems that share cultural and linguistic traditions. This principle means that comparisons of Western and non-Western media should be undertaken with care (with the purpose of the comparison clearly specified), and certainly cases should be selected to carefully control for as many factors as possible.

Finally, the project of comparative research as outlined in this article obviously presumes the continuing importance of the nation-state. I am willing to defend that choice; the nation-state is not going to disappear any time soon (Morris and Waisbord 2001). At the same time, globalization and internet communication networks may be accelerating the integration of what Joseph Straubhaar (1998) has called "geo-linguistic" global markets. The internet may be reshaping journalism primarily through its effects on the "ecology" of competition and information flows within and across national journalistic fields. That is, by breaking down barriers of space and time, and making diverse types of media equally available anywhere via a single medium, the internet in some ways "centralizes" formerly fragmented media fields. Paradoxically, this American-led technology could thus serve as a Europeanizing rather than Americanizing force for global journalistic convergence (contra Hallin and Mancini 2004). Barnhurst and Nerone (2001: 294) observe that online media are breaking down local information monopolies that were crucial in establishing American-style non-partisan media (since a single urban newspaper had to appeal to audiences across partisan divides). For example, now that residents of Portland, Oregon can (and increasingly do) access the *New York Times*, the *Washington Post*, and London's *Guardian* (Thurman 2007; see also Reese et al. 2007) just as easily as their hometown newspaper website, ideological differences among leading media outlets – within a given "geo-linguistic" global circuit – may become more distinct as a means of developing and maintaining loyal audiences. Globalization and the internet may or may not be leading to significant cross-national convergence; in my reading of the literature, it is the continuing differences rather than the emerging similarities that seem striking (see van der Wurff 2005). Certainly the process is uneven, and we cannot presume that convergence will necessarily be towards the "American Way." As good comparativists, we simply have to put the question to the test.

Notes

1 While the sociology of news has been hampered by its myopic focus on the United States and the United Kingdom (but see Neveu [2004] and Brin, Charron and de Bonville [2004] for broader analyses that take into account French, Canadian, and other European cases and theorizing), there have been several notable attempts to identify the key "types" of factors that shape the news, including Gans (1979), Gitlin (1980: 249–51), Shoemaker and Reese (1991), and Schudson (2000). See Benson (2004) for a critique of these typologies, in which I argue that they tend to either focus too much on the microlevel (individual journalists, individual news organizations) or the broad societal level (political culture, ideology, or political economy in which "political" and "economic" logics are not kept analytically distinct), missing entirely the mezzo-level "fields" in which social action takes shape.

2 For more extensive discussions of the virtues and limits of comparative methodology, see Blumler et al. (1992), Hallin and Mancini (2004, especially chapter one), Wirth and Kolb (2004), and Livingstone (2003).

References

Alexander, J.C. (1981) 'The mass news media in systemic, historical and comparative perspective', in E. Katz and T. Szecsko (eds.) *Mass Media and Social Change*, Beverly Hills, CA.: Sage.

Åsard, E. and Bennett, L.W. (1997) *Democracy and the Marketplace of Ideas: Communication and Government in Sweden and the United States*, Cambridge: Cambridge University Press.

Ayish, M.I. (2005) 'Media Brinkmanship in the Arab World: Al Jazeera's The Opposite Direction as a Fighting Arena', in M. Zayani (ed.) *The Al Jazeera Phenomenon: Critical Perspectives on New Arab Media*, Boulder, CO: Paradigm Publishers.

Baker, C.E. (1994) *Advertising and a Democratic Press*, Princeton, NJ: Princeton University Press.

Baker, C.E. (2002) *Media, Markets, and Democracy*. Cambridge: Cambridge University Press.

Baker, C.E. (2007) *Media Concentration and Democracy*, Cambridge: Cambridge University Press.

Barnhurst, K.G. and Nerone, J. (2001) *The Form of News: A History*, New York: The Guilford Press.

Benson, R. (2000) 'Shaping the public sphere: Journalistic fields and immigration public debates in France and the United States, 1973–1994', Ph.D. Dissertation, Department of Sociology, University of California, Berkeley.

Benson, R. (2003) 'Commercialism and Critique: California's Alternative Weeklies', in N. Couldry and J. Curran (eds.) *Contesting Media Power: Alternative Media in a Networked World*, Lanham, MD: Rowman and Littlefield.

Benson, R. (2004) 'Bringing the Sociology of Media Back In', *Political Communication*, 21, 3: 275–92.

Benson, R. (2006) 'News Media as a "Journalistic Field": What Bourdieu adds to New Institutionalism, and Vice Versa', *Political Communication*, 23, 2: 187–202.

Benson, R. (2009a) 'What Makes News More Multiperspectival? A Field Analysis', *Poetics*, 37, 5–6 (winter issue).

Benson, R. (2009b) 'What Makes For a Critical Press? A Case Study of French and U.S. immigration News Coverage', *Press/Politics* (fall issue).

Benson, R. and Hallin, D.C. (2007) 'How States, Markets and Globalization Shape the News: The French and American national press, 1965–1997', *European Journal of Communication*, 22, 1: 27–48.

Blumler, J.G. and Gurevitch, M. (1975) 'Towards a Comparative Framework for Political Communication Research', in S.H. Chaffee (ed.), *Political Communication: Strategies and Issues for Research*, Beverly Hills, CA: Sage.

Blumler, J.G., McLeod, J.M., and Rosengren, K.E. (1992) 'An Introduction to Comparative Communication Research', in J.G. Blumler, J.M. McLeod, & K.E. Rosengren (eds.) *Comparatively Speaking: Communication and Culture Across Space and Time*, Newbury Park, CA: Sage.

Boudana, S. (2008) 'Le Spectateur Engagé: Detachment versus Involvement Among French War Correspondents', Paper presented to the International Communication Association annual conference, Montreal, May.

Bourdieu, P. (1984) *Distinction*, Cambridge, MA: Harvard University Press.

Bourdieu, P. (1998) *On Television*, New York: New Press.

Bourdieu, P. (2005) 'The Political Field, the Social Scientific Field, and the Journalistic Field', in R. Benson and E. Neveu (eds.) *Bourdieu and the Journalistic Field*, Cambridge: Polity.

Brin, C., Charron, J., and de Bonville, J. (2004) *Nature et transformation du journalisme: Théorie et recherches empiriques*, Saint-Nicolas, Quebec: Les Presses de L'Université Laval.

Brossard, D., Shanahan, J. and McComas, K. (2004) 'Are Issue-Cycles Culturally Constructed? A Comparison of French and American Coverage of Global Climate Change', *Mass Communication & Society*, 7, 3: 359–77.

Chalaby, J.K. (1996) 'Journalism as an Anglo-American Invention: A Comparison of the Development of French and Anglo-American Journalism, 1830s–1920s', *European Journal of Communication*, 11, 3: 303–26.

Chalaby, J.K. (2004) 'Scandal and the Rise of Investigative Reporting in France', *American Behavioral Scientist* 47, 9: 1194–207.

Cranberg, G., Bezanson, R., and Soloski, J. (2001) *Taking Stock: Journalism and the Publicly Traded Newspaper Company*, Ames, IA: Iowa State Press.

Curran, J. (1991) 'Rethinking the media as a public sphere', in P. Dahlgren and C. Sparks (eds.) *Communication and Citizenship: Journalism and the Public Sphere in the New Media Age*, London: Routledge.

Curran, J. and Park, M.L. (eds.) (2000) *De-Westernizing Media Studies*, London: Routledge.

Darnton, R. (1975) 'Writing News and Telling Stories', *Daedelus* 104: 175–94.

Davis, A. (2002) *Public Relations Democracy: Public relations, politics and the mass media in Britain*, New York: Manchester University Press.

De Tarlé, A. (1980) 'The Press and the State in France', in A. Smith (ed.), *Newspapers and Democracy: International Essays on a Changing Medium*, Cambridge, MA: The MIT Press.

Deuze, M. (2002) 'National News Cultures: A Comparison of Dutch, German, British, Australian, and U.S. Journalists', *Journalism and Mass Communication Quarterly*, 79, 1: 134–49.

DiMaggio, P.J., & Powell, W.W. (1991) 'Introduction', in W.W. Powell & P.J. DiMaggio (eds.), *The New Institutionalism in Organizational Analysis*, Chicago: University of Chicago Press.

Donsbach, W. and Patterson, T. (2004) 'Political News Journalists: Partisanship, Professionalism, and Political Roles in Five Countries', in F. Esser and B. Pfetsch (eds.) *Comparing Political Communication: Theories, Cases, and Challenges*, New York: Cambridge University Press.

Esser, F. (1998) 'Editorial Structures and Work Principles in British and German Newsrooms', *European Journal of Communication*, 13: 375–405.

Esser, F. (1999) '"Tabloidization" of News: A Comparative Analysis of Anglo-American and German Press Journalism', *European Journal of Communication*, 14, 3: 291–324.

Ferree, M.M., Gamson, W.A., Gerhards, J., and Rucht, D. (2002) *Shaping Abortion Discourse: Democracy and the Public Sphere in Germany and the United States*, Cambridge: Cambridge University Press.

Freeman, L.A. (2000) *Closing the Shop: Information Cartels and Japan's Mass Media*, Princeton: Princeton University Press.

Gamson, W. and Modigliani, A. (1989) 'Media Discourse and Public Opinion on Nuclear Power: A Constructionist Approach', *American Journal of Sociology*, 95: 1–37.

Gans, H. (1979) *Deciding What's News*, New York: Pantheon.

Gitlin, T. (1980) *The Whole World is Watching: Mass Media in the Making and Unmaking of the New Left*, Berkeley, CA: University of California Press.

Hallin, D.C. and Mancini, P. (1984) 'Speaking of the President: Political Structure and Representational Form in U.S. and Italian TV News', *Theory and Society*, 13: 829–50.

Hallin, D.C. and Mancini, P. (2004) *Comparing Media Systems: Three Models of Media and Politics*, Cambridge: Cambridge University Press.

Hanitzsch, T. (2006) 'Mapping Journalism Culture: A Theoretical Taxonomy and Case Studies from Indonesia', *Asian Journal of Communication*, 16, 2: 169–86.

Hovden, J.F. (2008) 'Profane and Sacred: A Study of the Norwegian Journalistic Field', Ph.D. Dissertation, University of Bergen, Norway.

Hughes, S. (2006) *Newsrooms in Conflict: Journalism and the Democratization of Mexico*, Pittsburgh: Pittsburgh University Press.

Klinenberg, E. (2007) *Fighting for Air*, New York: Basic Books.

Krauss, E.S. (2000) *Broadcasting Politics in Japan: NHK and Television News*, Ithaca: Cornell University Press.

Kuhn, R. (1995) *The Media in France*, London and New York: Routledge.

Lemieux, C. and Schmalzbauer, J. (2000) 'Involvement and detachment among French and American journalists: to be or not to be a "real" professional', in M. Lamont and L. Thévenot (eds.) *Rethinking Comparative Cultural Sociology: Repertoires of Evaluation in France and the United States*, Cambridge: Cambridge University Press.

Livingstone, S. (2003) 'On the Challenges of Cross-National Comparative Media Research', *European Journal of Communication*, 18, 4: 477–500.

Mancini, P. (2000) 'Political Complexity and Alternative Models of Journalism: The Italian Case', in J. Curran and M-J. Park (eds.) *De-Westernizing Media Studies*, London: Routledge.

Morris, N. and Waisbord, S. (eds.) (2001) *Media and Globalization: Why the State Matters*, Lanham, MD: Rowman and Littlefield.

Murschetz, P. (1998) 'State Support for the Daily Press in Europe: A Critical Appraisal', *European Journal of Communication*, 13, 3: 291–313.

Neveu, E. (2004) *Sociologie du journalisme*, Paris: La Découverte.

Nordenson, B. (2007) 'The Uncle Sam Solution: Can the government help the press? Should it?', *Columbia Journalism Review* (September/October).

Patterson, T.E. and Donsbach, W. (1996) 'News Decisions: Journalists as Partisan Actors', *Political Communication*, 13: 455–68.

Pedelty, M. (1995) *War Stories*, London: Routledge.

Powell, W.W. (1991) 'Expanding the Scope of Institutional Analysis', in W.W. Powell and P.J. DiMaggio (eds.) *The New Institutionalism in Organizational Analysis*, Chicago: University of Chicago Press.

Rajagopal, A. (2001) *Politics After Television: Hindu Nationalism and the Reshaping of the Public in India*, Cambridge: Cambridge University Press.

Reese, S.D., Rutigliano, L., Hyun, K., and Jeong, J. (2007) 'Mapping the blogosphere: Professional and citizen-based media in the global news arena', *Journalism*, 8, 3: 235–61.

Saguy, A.C. (2003) *What is Sexual Harassment? From Capitol Hill to the Sorbonne*, Berkeley, CA: University of California Press.

Schudson, M. (1995), *The Power of News*, Cambridge, MA: Harvard University Press.

Schudson, M. (2000) 'The Sociology of News Production Revisited (Again)', in J. Curran and M. Gurevitch (eds.) *Mass Media and Society*, London: Arnold.

Shoemaker, P.J. and Reese, S.D. (1991) *Mediating the Message: Theories of Influence on Mass Media Content*, New York: Longman.

Shoemaker, P.J. and Cohen, A.A. (eds.) (2006) *News Around the World*, London: Routledge.

Siebert, F., Peterson, T., and Schramm, W. (1956) *Four Theories of the Press*, Urbana: University of Illinois Press.

Silverstone, R. (2007) *Media and Morality: On the Rise of the Mediapolis*, Cambridge: Polity.

Starr, P. (2004) *The Creation of the Media*, New York: Basic Books.

Straubhaar, J. (1998) 'Distinguishing the global, regional and national levels of world television', in A. Sreberny-Mohammadi, D. Winseck, J. McKenna and O. Boyd-Barrett (eds.) *Media in Global Context*, Oxford: Oxford University Press.

Strömbäck, J. and Dimitrova, D.V. (2006) 'Political and Media Systems Matter: A Comparison of Election News Coverage in Sweden and the United States', *Press/Politics*, 11, 4: 131–47.

Tasini, J. (1990) 'Lost in the Margins: Labor and the Media', *Extra!*, 3, 7.

Thurman, N. (2007) 'The globalization of journalism online: A transatlantic study of news websites and their international readers', *Journalism*, 8, 3: 285–307.

Väliverronen, J. and Kunelius, R. (2008) 'On the Emergence of a Journalistic Field in Democratic Corporatism', Paper presented at the International Communication Association annual conference, Montreal, May.

Van der Wurff, R. (2005) 'Impacts of the Internet on Newspapers in Europe: Conclusions', *Gazette*, 67, 1: 107–20.

Waisbord, S. (2000) *Watchdog Journalism in South America: News, Accountability, and Democracy*, New York: Columbia University Press.

Wessler, H. (2008) 'Investigating Deliberativeness Comparatively', *Political Communication*, 25: 1–22.

Wirth, W. and Kolb, S. (2004) 'Designs and Methods of Comparative Political Communication Research', in F. Esser and B. Pfetsch (eds.) *Comparing Political Communication*, Cambridge: Cambridge University Press.

Wrenn, M. (2008) 'Inadvertent Architects of 20th Century "Media Convergence": Private Foundations and the Reorientation of Foreign Journalists', in W. Buxton (ed.) *Patronizing the Public: The Impact of American Philanthropy on Communication, Culture, and the Humanities*, Lanham, MD: Rowan and Littlefield.

56
STUDYING JOURNALISM: A CIVIC AND LITERARY EDUCATION

G. Stuart Adam

In the 100 years since Missouri launched its program, the field of journalism studies in the university has developed and prospered throughout the world. In the United States and Puerto Rico alone, there are currently more than 110 accredited programs and roughly 470 non-accredited schools where journalism and mass communication programs are offered. In 2006–2007, an estimated 49,930 students earned bachelor's degrees and 3,790 took master's degrees (Vlad *et al.* 2008: 4). There has also been a steady stream of doctoral students at the major centers and, in this respect, the discipline has generated a remarkable body of knowledge and commentary. It would be difficult to quantify the collection with any precision, but it is fair to say it is vast.

Nevertheless, a continuing rumble of discontent and uncertainty has marked the field. In the 1980s, that discontent was expressed in the US in the Oregon Report (1984), which sought to connect the study of journalism and mass communication more firmly to the scholarly and pedagogical practices of the university. The report said forthrightly that many of the units under study were simply trade schools and, in light of this, its principal author asked in a separate document if journalism should even be offered as a university subject (Dennis 1986: 1). Such a question may no longer be moot, but it has been succeeded by a conversation reflecting similarly-inspired discontent. If the authors of the Oregon Report sought to promote a clearer conception of the scholarship supporting journalism studies, later reports and task forces have proposed alternatives to established practices. For example, the Public Journalism movement focused on democracy and governance. It promoted forms of journalism supporting a strong civic culture and its influence has been extensive and lasting.

In a similar but independent vein, Lee Bollinger, the President of Columbia University, turned up as an advocate on the stage of reform when he called for a full reconsideration of the program at Columbia. He struck a task force in 2002 whose work would constitute a first step in a process leading to the appointment of a new dean. President Bollinger's view was that a school should immerse its students in the intellectual culture of the university as they acquire and master the skills of craft. He believed, sensibly, that journalism is thickened – is richer and more useful – if it constitutes in part the application of discipline-based knowledge to the description and interpretation of the events that mark the here and now (Adam, 2004). President Bollinger said forthrightly that "[i]t is the superficial skipping from event to event that produces both sophomoric journalism and unfulfilled journalists." He also said that journalism "may be moving increasingly to a system in which reporters have an underlying expertise, and to the extent that is true, universities ought to provide opportunities for journalism students to develop that expertise" (Bollinger, 2003). He called for a comprehensive review of the curriculum.

By contrast, the reforms introduced at the Medill School at Northwestern in this decade have been sponsored in part by a belief that journalism education should be tailored to the needs of the news industry, which, as everyone in the field acknowledges, has been experiencing severe economic problems as the digital revolution invades its territory. The architects of Medill's curriculum sought to connect the practices of journalism to a better understanding of business practices and marketing. Medill's new curriculum, rolled out in 2005 following a fifteen-month strategic planning process, sought to foster forms of journalism that would stem "the tides of circulation loss for newspapers and declining viewership for broadcasting" (Claussen, 2008: 337).

Finally, an ongoing initiative announced in 2005 by the Carnegie and Knight Foundations is seeking ambitiously to change the basic way in which journalism is taught in the United States. The term "basic" is telling. The initiative includes an experimental online news incubator that recognizes the changed technological environment. It also includes a task force that promotes policy-oriented research. But more fundamentally, it includes a goal of curricular enhancement that would aim at enhancing the intellectual horizons of journalism students. Like the proposals advocated by Columbia's president, the Carnegie-Knight declaration promotes steps that will enable schools to face up to the emerging character of the craft and, at the same time, to engage with the sturdy disciplines of the university. So there is a vein of doubt that marks the field and has kept alive a longstanding desire to place journalism studies on a more stable and intellectually-demanding foundation. The question is how should this be done?

This chapter seeks to provide an answer. It proposes an approach to the development of curricula, based in part on the philosophy of the late James W. Carey, that seeks to stock and strengthen the minds of students as it prepares them for vocational and, above all, democratic work. I start with a review of where Carey's philosophical pragmatism leads and then argue for a specific curricular architecture that brings such courses – in general arts and science, media studies, and professional practices – into a functional and productive relationship with one another. I conclude with observations on how such a curriculum should be managed so that stocking and strengthening the minds of apprentice journalists is blended thoughtfully into the more strictly technical skills that mark journalism practice. In short, I advocate in the name of the improvement of schools of journalism and journalism practice that students receive what can be thought of broadly as a civic and literary education.

Philosophical pragmatism

In many respects, the outline of an inspirational model has already been spelled out. In a number of essays and speeches over a long career, the late James Carey, as Dean of the College of Communications at the University of Illinois and, later, as Professor of Journalism at Columbia University, articulated a point of view, which he hoped would guide such reform. He believed profoundly in the role journalism plays in democratic life and, with equal force, he believed in the university as a potential storehouse of what he called journalism's "intellectual soil" (Carey & Shedden, 1991).

Carey's point of view was an expression of the philosophical pragmatism associated with John Dewey. He thought that educational and journalistic institutions, through their instructional and curricular methods, should foster the formation of communities and a moral order. So they should be measured by the success with which they promote a vibrant (and deliberative) democratic order. Carey once said that every act of teaching is an act of citizenship (Carey, 1978: 114). On another occasion, he said that journalism and democracy are two words for the same thing (Carey, 2000: 67).

It does not follow from the foregoing that all of journalism, or all of journalism teaching, should be dedicated to the examination and analysis of legal, government and democratic events and practices. The forms of journalism studied in such lights should be interpreted generously and in the light of an understanding that the task of the journalist, through the exercise of independent judgment, is to construct pictures of and commentary on the life of a democratic society in all its variability and complexity. Carey's view, which he spelled out most famously in his essay "A Plea for the University Tradition" (1978), was that the principle mission of journalism – and therefore of journalism education – is to invigorate and facilitate democratic life by sponsoring a democratic conversation. It follows that an education in journalism should be a civic education in which the student masters, amongst other things, the languages of public life. To put the matter a little more precisely, journalism education should involve centrally the study of disciplines that formalize our understanding of the elements of American democratic experience and life. It is important to note that Carey's model of education is democratic not classical. It features American more than European experience. In Carey's world, the Cathedral is Congress; scripture is American writing and thought. The trick of curricular reform is to stitch his understanding into university programs in journalism.

The subject of journalism

More often than not the basic structure of a journalism program at the undergraduate level comprises a series of courses in each of the following broad areas: a) general arts and sciences; b) media studies; and c) professional practices. The general arts and sciences component includes courses in such fields as politics, literature, economics, film, and modern languages. Media studies comprises such subjects as journalism history, law, ethics, and communication or media theory. Professional practices include all the reporting and writing courses and studio offshoots in graphics and illustration, radio and television broadcasting, online reporting, multi-media, and photography. They are the courses whose character and purposes define the project as a whole.

The liberal arts and sciences portion of the program reflects a continuing and healthy belief that preparation for the vocation of journalism should include general education. Current accreditation criteria require that roughly 65 per cent of the overall time allocation in the curriculum be dedicated to such studies (ACEJMC, 2005). So, compulsory studies in the arts and sciences constitutes a first and primary point of contact between the academic culture of the university and the study of journalism. Is it sufficient? The answer, measured quantitatively, is yes. Perhaps it is more than enough. But the requirement should be stated more precisely and require, following Carey, specific obligatory courses. For example, an insistence on courses in literature including, for example, the novel, the short story, and poetry would turn on a belief that journalism shares (and can gain) much from contact with other arts of narrative and language. An insistence on the study of numbers including, above all, statistics turns on the observation that journalism is an empirical craft and, as a professional matter, is deeply concerned with fact, evidence, and truth.

Just as courses in literature and the philosophy of evidence provide foundations in matters of craft and journalistic method, so, too, do courses in history, law, economics, politics, and sociology provide a critical foundation for journalism's content. Speaking of history, Carey once said that it represents the underlying stratum of consciousness out of which news judgments are made (Carey, 1993: v). More generally, the study of history and the humanistic social sciences promote knowledge of the world. They provide a textured backdrop to a journalistic reading of the world.

So the accreditation criteria need not call for more room in the curriculum. Rather, they should steer student journalists more firmly towards study in the disciplines containing the elements out of which journalism is constructed. To put the matter more directly, there should be a compulsory humanistic core in a journalism program that is chosen for the practical and, in the end, democratic benefits it confers. To do so requires that the arts and sciences be regarded not simply as 'good' or as sources of virtue and understanding for their own sakes. Rather, they should be read as sources of indispensable practical goods that in due course will strengthen the practice of journalism and promote the maintenance of a democratic culture. For example:

- The study of poetry and literature strengthens students' capacities for self expression. An immersion in literary studies shapes and invigorates the vocabularies of students and promotes the forms of eloquence called for by journalistic tasks.
- The study of visual art enables students to see the world more clearly – through the visions of our best painters, photographers, and film-makers.
- The study of history formalizes memory. It attaches an empirical and reflective dimension to human experience and thus enables our students to live in time as well as in space.

- The study of politics, economics, and society equips us to navigate through and understand our major institutions.
- Philosophy sharpens our capacity to reason – a necessary skill on the job as well as in the political arena; it sharpens our moral sense.
- Democratic theory situates journalism in the complex artifice of belief and procedure that marks advanced democracies.

So arts courses are practical in their effects – all the more so when they are taken by students who will make their livings as reporters and writers.

Theory

Media studies comprises the second axis organizing the curriculum and it embraces minimally the study of journalism ethics, journalism law, and media theory (including policy studies). In a pragmatist's world, it could include journalism history as an incorporated or independent element, although, as Carey (1974) pointed out in one of his most widely circulated essays, the scholarship and teaching of that subject was specially fraught and problematic in its early years. It may be said now that the scholarship in journalism history, law and ethics is in good, even excellent, shape with a full array of scholarly journals and books in print to support teaching. In recent years, journalism professors have approached ethics and law as applied fields where, for example, the systematic organization and accumulation of knowledge has been carefully articulated to case studies. Furthermore, these subjects have increasingly reflected the forms of understanding that mark their sponsoring disciplines. Journalism history can be seen in this context as a branch of social and political history; journalism law can be seen as a branch of constitutional law; journalism ethics can be seen as a branch of applied ethics. In the best curricula, constitutional law and applied ethics would be appropriate prerequisites for such journalism courses. Regardless, the points of intellectual contact are firm in these areas.

Media theory is more problematical. It is a literature of remarkable proportions which, for present purposes, starts in 1922 with the publication of Walter Lippmann's *Public Opinion*. In many respects, its situation resembles the situation of journalism history when Carey wrote his commentary on journalism history. It is still captured by old ideas and practices that speak past the central concerns of journalists. The problem has two faces: one involves the matter of how it is articulated to practice. Much of it does not illuminate problems in practice. Furthermore, it has been dominated by "scientism," research marked by a rigorous attachment to measurement and the protocols of science. Its prestige is related more to its methods than its relevance to questions of craft. When Lee Bollinger proposed to reform the journalism curriculum at Columbia, one widely-circulated commentary forecast the "academization" of journalism – namely, the abandonment of journalism or its subordination to the models of scholarship born in the mainstream social sciences (Kurtz 2002).

That such a prediction was made is not surprising. Professors of professional practices routinely think of the scholarship and research blessed by university promotion and tenure committees as narrow-gage empirical studies. A smaller number, but with the same spirit of estrangement, think of dense theorizing that subordinates the practitioner and his or her work to concepts of ideology and systems of power – where journalism is seen less as a form of democratic expression that expands consciousness and more as a piece of a very large ideological machine. Paradoxically, the scholarship occupying the place of media studies on the axes of learning has been dominant in journalism studies as it derives its authority and prestige from science (Carey 1979). Nevertheless, this body of knowledge represents, though it could be reformed by incorporating the helpful pragmatism represented by Carey's thinking, a point of contact with the university culture. It contributes to the education of journalists as students of media and society and for that reason it should be represented, though it should not dominate, the broad field of journalism studies itself. What may be said confidently, is that media studies – history, law, ethics, and theory – represent continuing opportunities for firm connections with the intellectual culture of the university.

Practice

Professional practices comprise the third axis of the curriculum of an undergraduate program in journalism. The courses offered along this axis make sense of all the rest and they include reporting and writing, graphics and news design, photography, online journalism, and radio and television broadcasting. They represent in whole and in part the range of expressive forms that mark journalism. But at the same time, they are likely to create an unnecessary and destructive distance from the intellectual culture of the university. They do this by virtue of the excitement and busy-work they call for (and for the time they consume) and by virtue of the way they are conceptualized.

The second of these observations should be emphasized. Skills courses tend to be conceptualized in relation to technologies or media – as print, radio, television, or online. Such naming and conceptualization is akin to the practice of referring to journalism as 'media'. The problem with so doing is that the term 'media' blends (and blurs) concepts of culture and technology. It folds journalism into an ill-defined media environment and buries the reality that journalism is a distinctive cultural practice and form of expression. Thought of as a cultural practice, journalism is a method for apprehending and representing events in the here and now. It involves, independent of the medium through which it is circulated, the making of news judgments, the gathering of evidence, the creation of narrative structures, and the contextualization and conferral of meaning. While there is no doubt that the practice developed and evolved first in newspapers, that it established itself later in broadcast media, and that it is now establishing itself on the internet, it is nevertheless a distinctive form of expression on which modern democratic societies depend.

So there is a core of intellectual and professional work defined by journalism that should constitute the spine of the portion of the program dedicated to professional practices. Professional practices should be seen first and foremost as vehicles for methodological and intellectual growth. To put the matter more definitively, the principal task of journalism education involves learning to make thoughtful news judgments, to exercise a strong and responsible sense of evidence, to master the use of language, narrative and other representational techniques, and, to the extent it is possible in junior reporters, to reveal and interpret the meaning of events. To develop such capacities, the courses in reporting and writing should be mandatory and stratified in three tiers.

Tier one reporting is probably the most familiar and successful course in journalism schools. It normally involves a workshop or news lab that meets at least once a week for two terms. Its pedagogical method follows an apprenticeship model. The instructor constitutes him- or herself as a city editor in relation to a group of junior reporters. The process of assignment and critique (with auxiliary support from reporting textbooks and style manuals) moves the novice reporters toward an understanding of and practice in making news judgment, writing news, and engaging in basic reporting. Tier two, variously called in-depth or advanced reporting, similarly occupies two terms and, in the best cases, involves continuing work on news judgment, and such added layers as investigative techniques, the use and assessment of evidence (including numbers), and narrative technique derived as much from the examination of the best work in journalism as from purely literary sources.

Tier three – specialized reporting – involves an area or beat defined in part by an academic subject such as politics, economics, fine arts or science and defined in part by the practices of journalists covering specialized subjects. In constructing a curriculum that maximizes the practical use of academic study, the trick is to require students to dovetail their studies in academic fields with studies in reporting and writing. In other words, the ideal student following an ideal curriculum, would major in two fields – journalism and one mainstream discipline such as politics, economics, fine arts, or a science – that dovetail in subject matter with his or her course in specialized reporting. The payoff, once again, is that the student would continue to be immersed in the university culture as he or she completes the requirements of the journalism curriculum.

Curricular choices

The argument of this chapter points to a curricular structure that limits choices while at the same time expanding opportunities for a strong education. The method proposes, regardless of how elementary and self-evident it may seem, an understanding that follows from the belief that as a first step the study of grammar and literature are essential to the education of those who seek to make their living as writers. When the task is to build a curricular structure spread over a four-year period, parallel questions should be asked of the sturdiest disciplines of the arts, humanistic social sciences, and sciences. The question that guides the enterprise is how should a program in journalism nest within the larger intellectual culture of the University? How should the connection between journalism and the university culture be forged?

The architects of journalism curricula should be inspired by the example of those who design programs in other applied fields. It is elementary, for example, that an engineer must study calculus, that an architect must study structures, and that a business student must study finance. Similarly, scientific specializations like biology, chemistry, and physics depend on the contributions of other sciences and mathematics. Is it not equally elementary to say that student journalists should study democratic theory and literature – that they should receive a civic and a literary education?

Of importance to the educator is the way in which each element of journalism is articulated to a wider landscape of human expression. Reporting is naturally articulated to the manifold methods of evidence gathering and fact assessment that mark scholarly disciplines, narration and language similarly are linked to the literary world of poetry and prose, and analytical methods to the systems of explanation and interpretation that mark the humanities and social sciences. These elements point to investigative techniques, statistical analysis, and forensics, to English composition and to literary and visual forms of representation, to manifold notions of meaning and critical understandings of cause and effect located in the human sciences.

So journalism can be articulated to territories of reflection and practice that mark other academic disciplines. In other words, the points of contact with the academic culture can be guided by a broadened and enriched concept of journalism in which it is seen not as a bureaucratic function but as a form of expression through which we draw portraits of and seek to understand the here and now. This is not to suggest that news in its bureaucratic incarnation and the daily newsroom in which it is generated are not important examples of what journalism is and does. Nor is it to suggest that specialist studies in broadcast and online should be set aside. Journalism is a rich form of expression and the pedagogy marking it in a university school should reflect that richness. To do so, it needs to be first decoupled from technological categories before being returned to them.

So there should also be news labs, studio courses in broadcasting, workshops in graphics and design, and (perhaps above all these days) courses in online methods. It is a feature of journalism school that they need elaborate and expensive infrastructure to complete their tasks. So the method guiding the construction of the curriculum and creating its priorities does not imply the suspension of hands-on classes. The point is to position the workshops and studio courses in a way that prevents them from casting a long shadow over the academic side. One set of courses stocks the mind and that takes time and patience; the other set – the studio-based set – allows the mind to express itself in realistic journalism settings. The trick is to manage the mix and prevent the busy work from interfering with the work that takes time and patience.

A common democratic culture

The first major position paper on the subject of journalism education was written in 1904 by Joseph Pulitzer and published in *The North American Review*. It was a clear and uncomplicated, although lengthy, meditation on the goals and curriculum of a school he was proposing to endow at Columbia. To take him at his word, Pulitzer sought in that essay to describe a school where the study of journalism practices would be combined with the careful study of such subjects as law, economics, literature, history, and politics. He believed that such study would lead to a higher level of literacy and judgment in working journalists; he believed that an education in such subjects would provide an appropriate foundation for a civic vocation.

James Carey's vision was not so different. It was born in a deep attachment to democratic life. He, too, was an advocate of something akin to a civic and a literary education, but mainly he emphasized the civic part. He believed that universities had a responsibility to shape a common democratic culture. As he wrote in one of his several essays on education:

> The core of humane learning is the possession of a common culture with enough durability to transform today's students into tomorrow's leaders, persons who feel a sense of care and responsibility for their fellow citizens and for the noblest of our democratic traditions. That is still the essence of university life and any humane program of education even in the age of high-tech (Carey, 1987: 198).

Other reformers have sought in a variety of ways to add strength and substance to the more technical dimensions of journalism practice and there are many models of success available to guide their further development. But the attempts to reform the whole package will falter unless the program it proposes functions in "intellectual soil." The key is to understand and then to incorporate into the curriculum the elements of a civic and literary education and then to manage carefully the manner in which these elements are articulated to professional practices.

References

ACEJMC (2005) Accrediting Standards; Standard 2 – Curriculum and Instruction

Adam, G. S. (2004) "The Events at Columbia, the Design of Journalism Programs and the Sources and Nature of Professional Knowledge," *Australian Journalism Review*, 26: 1

Bollinger, L. C. (2003) "Discussion Draft," March 21 2003

Carey, J. (1974) "The Problem of Journalism History," *Journalism History* 1: 1

Carey, J. (1978) "A Plea for the University Tradition," *Journalism Quarterly* 55:4, pp. 846–55.

Carey, J. (1979) "Graduate Education in Mass Communication," *Communication Education* 28: 4

Carey J. (1985) "Putting the World at Peril': A Conversation with James W. Carey," *Journalism History* 12: 2

Carey, J (1987) "High Technology and Higher Education," in *Technological Change and the Transformation of America*, edited by Steven E. Goldberg and Charles R. Strain. Carbondale: Southern Illinois University Press (Revised as "Salvation by Machines: Can Technology Save Education?" in *James Carey: A Critical Reader*.)

Carey, J. (1993) "Foreword," to Adam, G.S., *Notes Toward a Definition of Journalism; Understanding an old craft as an art form*, The Poynter Papers: No. 2; (St. Petersburg: The Poynter Papers); v

Carey, J. (2000) "Journalism and Democracy are Names for the Same Thing," *Nieman Reports* 54: 2

Carey, J. and Shedden, D. (1991) "An interview with Jim Carey," Poynter Institute Oral History Program. St. Petersburg, Florida

Carnegie-Knight initiative on the future of journalism education, 2006–2008; http//newsinitiative.org/

Claussen, D. (2008) "Medill 2020: 411 or 911?" *Journalism & Mass Communication Educator*, Winter: Vol. 62, Issue 4.

Dennis, E. (1986) *Commentaries on Journalism Education*, New York, Gannett Center for Media Studies

Kurtz, B. (2002) August 10, *Editor and Publisher* on line, "Don't Academize Columbia J-School"

Pulitzer, J. (1904) "Planning a School of Journalism – The Basic Concept in 1904," *The North American Review*; 178: 5

Vlad, T., Becker, L., Vogel, M., Hanisak, S., and Wilcox, D. (2008) "Annual Survey of Journalism and Mass Communication Graduates," *AEJMC News*, 42: 4

57

THE POWER OF FRAMING: NEW CHALLENGES FOR RESEARCHING THE STRUCTURE OF MEANING IN NEWS

Brian Baresch, Shih-Hsien Hsu and Stephen D. Reese

Starting in late 2010 and through the first several months of 2011, a series of protests in Tunisia, Egypt, and other nations in the Middle East toppled authoritarian governments and put pressure on others. The wave of action eventually came to be widely known in English-language media as the Arab Spring – a perspective which, by evoking both the season of rebirth and the Prague Spring of 1968, places the protests in a frame of beneficence and hope. By this reckoning, the actions reflect popular striving for self-determination in the face of oppression, a social value of Western culture. The "Arab Spring" frame thus places these events in a favorable, democratic light.

That is the sort of thing news frames do: They highlight some aspects of the events behind a story and downplay others, often with the effect of supporting a certain way of looking at the world. This is accomplished by word choice (e.g. using language of "awakening" rather than "chaos" to describe the Middle East uprisings) and by source selection (e.g. quoting more democracy activists than state security officers).

In another example, social "progress" has been a popular news frame in nuclear energy policy since the 1940s and was dominant in the 1960s (Gamson & Modigliani, 1989). On the surface, this frame presents nuclear power as the most effective way to solve the energy crisis, making its "powerful" and "efficient" aspects salient while omitting other options and negative consequences. Moreover, the "progress" frame aligns with the deeply rooted social value that technology and talented experts are capable of solving social problems.

Occasionally a journalist or news organization deliberately adopts a specific ideology, but often their work routines and source availability lie behind these choices. In any case, news frames lay the foundation on which we citizens build our collective understanding of our world.

Thus, news and journalism researchers have often used the concept of framing since Goffman (1974) introduced the approach. Goffman described a frame as a "schema of interpretation" that allows people to "locate, perceive, identify, and label a seemingly infinite number of concrete occurrences defined in its limits" (p. 21). Derived from social psychology, the core of framing research has aimed to understand "how people reply on expectations to make sense of their everyday social experience" (Reese, 2001, p. 7). These expectations about daily life – that is, the frames in one's head – are constructed socially, a dynamic process involving the social contexts and the actors who generate the frame. The means to develop and transmit the frames, and the individual cognitive mechanism to perceive and assess them, must be considered. This dynamic interaction between social contexts and individuals attracts scholars from sociology, psychology, communication, political science, and journalism studies.

News media are no doubt the most important actors in the framing process: They are frame generators, organizers, and transmitters, linking social structure and the individual. News content is not mere combinations of words; it carries embedded social meaning and reflects the prevalent organizing principles in society through journalists' selection of words, news sources, and metaphors. This process sets the boundary of an issue, reduces a complex situation to a simple theme, and shapes people's interpretations by making some elements salient while ignoring others. In the "Arab Spring" and nuclear "progress" frames, news content is not unproblematic but contains social values and conveys ideologies, thus wielding significant social power.

In analyzing this power of news framing, researchers often emphasize one or the other side of the process, focusing on how news media frame an issue or how audiences perceive it. These two approaches, using both qualitative and quantitative methods, map the traditional research territory. New media, meanwhile, have challenged framing research in terms of how we reconcile and adjust these approaches to "shaping" and "effects" in the provider-receiver relationship. In the new media environment, a networked, multidirectional relationship has replaced the traditional linear and unidirectional relationship between media and audience, and the term *actor*, which represents the active role of participants and a blurred boundary between producer and users, has replaced *audience*, which connotes a passive receiver. As a result, researchers have more difficulty identifying the source of any given news frame as it steers public discourse. The traditional mass media environment offers each perspective a spot to rest on and a place to simplify many complex relationships and effects. However, the rich but fragmented information environment and interlocking networks make the influence of social structures and networked society, which until recently were latent and easily ignored by much framing research, more and more influential and important. In this chapter, we examine the challenges that the changing media environment brings to news-framing research, and re-evaluate the theoretical "framework" in order to capture the ongoing movement of the framing research project.

Framing

News-framing research territory

Framing scholars have their own interests in analyzing different levels in the framing process, resulting in multiple definitions and research perspectives. To map the territory, scholars have categorized framing research in terms of the focus and level of analysis (i.e. the social structure that generates a frame or the effect a frame has on individuals). D'Angelo (2002) categorizes framing research into cognitive, critical, and constructionist paradigms, and the images best describing these paradigms are respectively negotiation, domination, and co-optation.

- Cognitive framing research is interested in the process of interaction and negotiation between the media frame and the individual's existing schemas and knowledge. In short, it primarily focuses on framing effects (e.g. Price, Tewksbury, & Powers, 1997; Iyengar & Kinder, 1987; Cappella & Jamieson, 1997).
- The critical paradigm regards news frames as the outcomes of both journalistic routines and the values of the elites who oversee the news-reporting structures that in turn sway the audience (e.g. Entman & Rojecki, 1993; Gitlin, 1980; Martin & Oshagen, 1997; Reese & Buckalew, 1995).
- The constructionist perspective treats frames as "interpretive packages" and "tool kits," collections of rhetorical devices that sponsors and journalists use to understand the social world; its sociological focus is the interaction among media packages, public opinion, and the socialization process (e.g. Gamson & Modigliani, 1989; Pan & Kosicki, 1993).

The critical and constructionist perspectives each emphasize the cultural and political context of frames and the shared social meanings.

Reese (2010) maps the news framing territory with two perspectives, the "what" and the "how," which are roughly aligned with qualitative and quantitative orientations. The "what" perspective centers on the frame-building process, while the "how" focuses on the individual's cognitive process. The "what" orientation examines latent framing devices in texts to capture the embedded meaning and tie them to the cultural and social structures where ideological and power practices are carried out. Therefore, identifying the reasoning devices (e.g. Gamson & Modigliani, 1989) and the cluster of concepts (Cappella & Jamieson, 1997) in the narratives matters to the "what" framing study – for example, the problem-definition and moral-evaluation functions that a frame plays in public discourse (Entman, 1993).

The "how" orientation takes explicit frames as the starting point and, in emphasizing the social-psychological perspective, addresses how individuals adopt frames and process information received from media; however, its focus on regarding the frame as an outcome of various predetermined actors (e.g. elites competing over health-care policy; see Pan & Kosicki, 1993) often takes for granted the existing power and cultural structure where a frame is embedded. In a world where everyone is highly connected and is part of the social meaning creating and enhancing process, the tendency of the "how" perspective to limit the news frame to a term or slogan created by a political actor is reductive and misses the macro influence that cultural and structural factors play. For example, in the United States the "War on Terror" frame was built on a term used by the George W. Bush administration for describing its foreign policy, but it was reified through various social actors through various means (media routines, political parties, surveys of public opinion) and has become a naturalized common sense, an ideology, and a "way of life" to see the world (see Reese, 2010). Fixing the frame and examining "how" it yields effects on receivers misses the broader cultural dynamic.

Framing definition and the bridging model

Many scholars have sought a unified model of news framing research, but consensus in reconciling the disparate elements in the framing "project" has remained elusive. Framing research is attractive because it crosses various paradigms and perspectives, but that makes any unified model impossible. Yet without striving to conduct research within a unified model that covers the whole framing process, or without missing the values other approaches possess, news framing researchers can provide insights by carefully identifying their research positions and concerns in the broader field and joining the conversation with other perspectives. Instead of pinning it down to a single function (e.g. the effect of a salient frame) or seeking a mended paradigm (e.g. Entman, 1993), we see framing as a multiparadigmatic research field (following D'Angelo, 2002) and a model that bridges various interlocking approaches: quantitative and qualitative, empirical and interpretive, psychological and sociological, and academic and professional. This bridging function is like the nature of the framing concept itself, connecting various aspects in the social world and providing identifiable patterns to see the world we live in.

Many scholars have defined framing, and a noted definition is Entman's:

> To frame is to select some aspects of a perceived reality and make them more salient in a communicating text, in such a way as to promote a particular problem definition, causal interpretation, moral evaluation, and/or treatment recommendation.
>
> (Entman, 1993: p.52)

This points out the functions of framing for a certain issue, but how it is done, and what determines "in such a way," are also of interest. Reese's definition emphasizes the underlying organizing principle that determines "in such a way," and captures the theoretical diversity and the bridging nature of framing:

> Frames are *organizing principles* that are socially *shared* and *persistent* over time, that work *symbolically* to meaningfully *structure* the social world.
>
> (Reese, 2001: p.11, emphasis in the original)

This captures framing as a dynamic and evolving process, not simply fixing on an individual frame sponsor, topic, or issue stance. A frame is instead a macro way of thinking. Framing's organizing function goes beyond the immediate information and spreads across discourses in a broader cultural realm. For instance, the perspective "War on Terror" did not stay limited to policy debates, or remain used by only the US administration, but crossed the political realm and became a predominant part of American culture. The information this frame organized has seemed unproblematic and natural because people have been used to seeing the world without knowing the frame existed. Reese's definition suggests that framing research not only examine the manifest or most salient content but also strive to catch the structure and pattern hidden in the media texts, and search for what makes people take this latent structure and a way of thinking for granted – that is, the naturalization and routinization process in which an organizing principle emerged.

Thus, to map the news-framing research territory, Reese proposes a question model:

> What power relationships and institutional arrangements support certain routine and persistent ways of making sense of the social world, as found through specific and significant frames, influential information organizing principles that are manifested in identifiable moments of structured meaning and become especially important to the extent they find their way into media discourse, and are thus available to guide public life.
>
> (Reese, 2001: p.19)

This approach seems to better fit the new media environment in which news frames circulate, to which we now turn.

Reese (2001, 2007, 2010) has articulated the news-framing concept and how to apply his definition of framing to reality, examining the dominant organizing principle and its naturalized features. It takes time and a wide range of observations for researchers to dig into news discourse until an organizing principle emerges, a challenge made more difficult by the fragmented media ecosystem. News text is not a neutral sphere that only contains competing issue stances, and this type of framing research involves moving beyond taking text at face value, listing topics and citations, and seeing certain individuals as the sole sources of the discourse. It is a dynamic process and a web of culture that involves various social actors and publics. It is like a network in which all aspects are interlocking, and it is hard to examine the structure of the network by reducing it to a unidirectional media-effects relationship or limiting it to the competition of issue stances (Reese, 2007). New media have changed the way people communicate and build discourse, and society has become more highly connected and networked. Traditional news media have lost much of their hegemonic status in producing and transmitting news text. Online space provides means for individuals to voice opinions and interact with one another, and abundant information for them to actively select and engage with.

The challenges of the new media landscape, in which the source and direction of effects is less clear, provide news-framing research with an opportunity, to take the networked structure and relationships into consideration and move toward untangling the complex reality to reveal the embedded organizing principles.

New media and framing challenges

The complex news environment

American framing research was simpler in its early decades, from Goffman (1974) until the beginnings of the digital era in the mid-1990s: The news consumer was limited to a much smaller set of media – a local newspaper, a small group of national newspapers (e.g. the *New York Times*, *The Wall Street Journal*), local TV news broadcasts, a few network news shows, and a couple of news magazines. Whether taking a critical approach or a more constructionist one, the framing researcher had a limited number of sources and story forms to deal with. These US news outlets had comparable corporate structures and processes, the newsgathering routines of their reporters and editors were in large part the same, as was the balance of reportorial autonomy and institutional imperatives. The framing researcher, whether examining content or the forces behind it, thus had a finite, manageable number of points of entry.

But with the arrival of the digital revolution, news content and influence have diffused across a range of new media. Blogs, social network sites, Twitter, podcasts, and video sharing have complicated both the forms of content and the structures of authority. At the same time, especially since the mid-2000s, most news organizations have streamlined (shortened) their editorial processes, so reporters' copy gets fewer interventions from newsroom managers before it is released to the public. Many people outside the legacy news organizations engage in journalistic activity and must not be ignored. The "article" or "story" as the unit of analysis is no longer the default choice. Framing researchers must attend to new story forms and new conditions of creation.

Thus, analyzing texts also has become more problematic now that there are exponentially more texts, and more kinds of texts, and they are more scattered. A frame researcher must decide whether to account for institutional blogs (the *New York Times*, for example, has dozens of them) and Twitter feeds as part of the news product. Including these media makes analysis more complicated: Unlike news articles, which researchers have generally treated as standalone products, blog posts and especially tweets often refer, explicitly or implicitly, to previous posts, or to other blogs. A sample of media content must account for not only that diversity but also the way the components relate to each other. (This is especially true of tweets; the 140-character limit forces an economy of expression in which many of these relations are implied but not stated, and the researcher must account for these devices.) A series of tweets may be taken individually or as a collective opus. Also, the retweet – passing along another's tweet, often without comment – often implies support for the retweeted sentiment, but not always. This also complicates the landscape for the careful scholar.

Researchers also must deal with new habits of audience interaction. In 2008, the *New York Times* (Stelter, 2008) quoted a college student in a study who said he or she can stay abreast of the news without looking for it: "If the news is that important, it will find me" (para. 7). Stelter called this strategy the "social filter" (para. 6) and contrasted it with the better-known "professional filter" (para. 4) that characterized the traditional relationship of news providers to their audiences. With many news users now monitoring media less and social networks more, information is taking a variety of paths from source to destination in a variety of forms – becoming, in effect, a new type of news medium, paid attention to in various ways, and the framing scholar must account for it. Certainly, the search for news frames should not be limited to traditional texts.

Meanwhile, engagement with "the people formerly known as the audience" (Rosen, 2006) becomes another previously unaccounted influence; frames don't originate solely in the newsroom or among elites, and this is more true than ever. News organizations have also been creating internal structures devoted specifically to engaging the public through social media (Garber, 2010). And many American journalists do not work for large news organizations on a regular basis. The journalist Christopher Allbritton (2003), without an employer or sponsor, raised money from readers to pay his reporting expenses at the beginning of the Iraq War. Reporters and columnists maintain blogs and engage readers in the comments sections. Journalists who use Twitter not only promote their work there but also test out ideas, solicit feedback, and search for sources. Beginning in early 2011, Andy Carvin at NPR essentially created a new model of the journalist with his intensive aggregation and reporting on Middle East and North Africa protests on Twitter.

Thus, one could once count institutional controls and professional norms as significant influences on the US news product (and they still are, of course); but with the fragmentation of institutional oversight as reporters gain autonomy in various new media, journalists find themselves in new situations where new practices and sets of norms are taking shape. Reporters like Allbritton can function outside any journalistic organization; Carvin had support from his employer, but an enterprising freelancer may be able to support a similar endeavor with donations direct from the public. Many part-time bloggers become part of the news ecosystem with no budget or boss at all (see for example Buttry, 2010). Thus, a researcher who hunts for frames only in "mainstream" publications risks missing larger news territories.

Challenges to news-framing research

Institutional authority also has become fragmented and its oversight weakened. Individual journalists now often maintain blogs and micro-blogging Twitter accounts, and engage readers in comments sections attached to their product. Different publications exert control over their blogs and tweets to varying degrees; blog entries may get some editing, or they may go straight to the web; journalists' tweets are rarely scrutinized before being posted. The relationship between reporters' social media presence and the parent news organization may also be uneasy or ill-defined. For example, on the night of May 1, 2011, the earliest notice by the *New York Times* of Osama bin Laden's apparent death (and, for many readers, the first time they heard the news) was a tweet at 10:25 p.m. Eastern time by reporter Brian Stelter, who followed up with two more tweets in the next eight minutes. Yet in a later recounting of the night's reporting, the Times wrote that its first publication was a news alert posted at nytimes.com at 10:40 (Salmon, 2011). This omission of Stelter's work indicates a complicated and possibly contradictory vision by Times managers of its various news products, and of the lines of authority connecting them.

We are accustomed to regarding news articles as produced with an institutional voice established through both socialization of the reporter into newsroom practices, and a collaborative editing process; in other words, we once could infer much about frame construction from this context. Blogs and tweets, however, lend themselves to individualization, and bloggers may be encouraged to develop a particular "voice" distinct from the institutional tenor. And even as visual framing remains under-researched, developing digital journalistic forms such as interactive graphics and other data visualizations add to the challenges for the researcher analyzing selection and omission of data sets and samples, and the choice of display and analysis tools.

The new media also make identifying frame sponsors more challenging. Straightforward long-form news articles generally name the sponsors, often government officials such as the US president. A 15-word tweet, however, poses a greater challenge of interpretation: Is the reporter transmitting a source's frame, or the news institution's, or constructing her own? Again, clues may come from examining the interrelations among texts.

When facing this sort of interpretive challenge, the framing researcher may have to deal with notions of agency and autonomy. That is, where certain elites (government officials, business leaders, newspaper executives) once had a great deal of control over news frames (which is not to say they were always in consensus), now many journalists have more leeway in story selection and production than the more tradi-tional reporter.[1] A critical frame analysis of a new-media text must take into account the agency and nature of frame creators, and as the news production environment evolves, the power relationships become more and more tangled.

New directions and theoretical framework

In a networked and fragmented ecosystem, we ask whether framing power is more concentrated across these platforms or more fragmented itself. In this environment, the "organizing principle" approach to framing becomes much more important. With the content so scattered, the relationships among individual texts and the persistence of concepts across texts help to reveal the underlying intellectual and ideological framework, which "do[es]n't stop with organizing one story, but invite[s] us to marshal a cultural understanding and keep on doing so beyond the immediate information" (Reese, 2001, p. 13). Such an underlying principle, if it is widely recognized in a given audience, may be evoked with only a brief mention or even implicitly, by allusion. Similarly, situational irony employed to reinforce a frame may be transparent to a text producer's regular audience but more opaque to the researcher dropping in to gather a sampling of texts. These devices will be difficult to spot, but the researcher must account for them.

Returning to a recent example of an organizing principle, consider the "War on Terror" frame. Immediately after hijacked jetliners crashed into the World Trade Center and the Pentagon in September 2001, US President George Bush described the attacks as a heinous crime. Shortly, though, he changed his approach and framed the events as an act of war (Lakoff, 2004). This shift had lasting consequences for the nation and the world, as it provided a rhetorical basis for subsequent invasions of Afghanistan and later Iraq (Reese & Lewis, 2009). For years after the attacks, US news media adopted the "War on Terror" frame as their own. (Bush's successor Barack Obama's movement away from the phrase signaled his emphasis on a more multilateral and less "us versus them" approach to foreign policy.)

Reese and Lewis (2009) investigated the "War on Terror" framing by searching news texts for key words and then carefully reading the relevant texts for context and meaning. This reading was possible in large part because the texts themselves – newspaper articles, editorials, columns, and letters – were long enough to support such analysis, and the key words and phrases could be counted on to appear in articles that involved this frame. Many blog posts are long enough to be treated similarly. But individual tweets, and blog posts as brief as tweets, do not submit as readily to such analysis; the "story" cuts across these smaller units of text. At this early stage in new media scholarship, the enterprising frame researcher must innovate methods for identifying, sampling, and analyzing data sets that will yield meaningful results.

The proliferation of news products also creates challenges for frame-effects researchers: How much effect does an outlet or a story or a blog post have in the end? Who reads a given blog or Twitter stream, and what influence does it carry? The classic agenda-setting study involves comparing public opinion about priorities with the news media's story mix. Similar studies in the framing tradition analyze the transmission of news frames, often by showing texts to research subjects. But with so many more news pathways, determining the news mix and then gauging outlets' relative influence has become more difficult. Divided attention means divided effects.

Conclusion

The continuing transformation of journalism and the roles of journalists and the "people formerly known as the audience" is also transforming journalism studies and especially framing research. New actors have joined old ones, new forms of news have established their beachheads, and new theories are beginning to emerge. In this environment framing research can exert a centripetal force to pull together the expanding universe of texts and analyses.

Content analyses will be needed to survey this sprawling new landscape and produce the beginnings of maps of the territory. But frame research must take yet more ambitious approaches. The growing network of news contains many actors and complicated patterns of texts, and researchers must do it justice. The organizing principles that drive our understanding of the world are scattered, dispersed through an expanding web of articles, images, videos, radio shows, podcasts, infographics, and visualizations. Some of these texts are produced by established news organizations; many are not. This complicates the questions of frame sponsorship and journalistic agency. Scholars must work hard to pull it all together and make sense of the underlying narratives.

Framing operates through news, but our definition of "news" must be fluid: It is no longer enough to say that news is current information selected, collected, assembled, and transmitted by professional news organizations. Today's news diet includes, for example, science blogs supplementing science news, church blogs interpreting political news, one-writer blogs reporting on local issues, and other grassroots intermediaries. The average American doesn't draw a bright line between news and not-news, and we hamstring our own efforts if we make such artificial distinctions without clear justification.

Thus, to gather in content-based studies the texts that spring from the framing's organizing principles, we must gather all sources, follow all links, search all engines, examine tweets, and network socially. We can map networks and identify influencers to guide us to the most relevant texts, burrow down to the sources to hunt the genesis of the frames, and surf to the far reaches of information's spread.

One source of organizing frames, often overlooked but ripe for research, is news-talk radio. Especially for those commonly described as political conservatives, talk radio transmits and reifies frames and schemas relating to political ideologies frequently not represented in "mainstream" media, but journalists and scholars rarely plumb these depths, so this source of organizing principles is poorly understood. Yet these frames serve to organize the social understanding of life and politics for millions of Americans and, to some extent, for the elected officials they support. Researchers who examine a polarized political ecosystem must reach out to the actors whose schemas incorporate the views largely hidden from the mainstream.

As the number of influential texts increases along with their interconnectedness online and the roster of actors grows longer, frame research becomes ever more important to assessing the news and information ecosystem from which we build our pictures of our world. Framing researchers uncover the structure and patterns connecting the diffuse yet interlocking texts that we use to make sense of the world. To fully understand our world we must first discover and understand its organization in the media and the mind.

Note

1 "Here on the Forbes blogs, we decide what to write about, for the most part. We function relatively autonomously" (Breslin, 2011).

References

Allbritton, C. (2003). Blogging from Iraq. Retrieved from http://www.nieman.harvard.edu/reports/article/101075/Blogging-From-Iraq.aspx

Breslin, S. (2011, April 20). How your journalism sausage gets made, part one. [Web log post]. Retrieved from http://blogs.forbes.com/susannahbreslin/2011/04/20/how-your-journalism-sausage-gets-made-part-one/

Buttry, S. (2010, January 16). Pew doesn't understand news ecosystem well enough to study it. [Web log post]. Retrieved from http://stevebuttry.wordpress.com/2010/01/16/pew-doesnt-understand-news-ecosystem-well-enough-to-study-it/

Cappella, J.N. and Jamieson, K.H. (1997). The spiral of cynicism: The press and the public good. New York: Oxford University Press.

D'Angelo, P. (2002). News framing as a multiparadigmatic research program: A response to Entman. Journal of Communication, 52, 870–88.

Entman, R.M. (1993). Framing: Toward a clarification of a fractured paradigm. Journal of Communication, 10, 231–42.

Entman, R.M. and Rojecki, A. (1993). Freezing out the public: Elite and media framing of the U.S. anti-nuclear movement. Political Communication, 10, 155–73.

Gamson, W.A. and Modigliani, A. (1989). Media discourse and public opinion on nuclear power: A constructionist approach. American Journal of Sociology, 95, 1–37.

Garber, M. (2010). What Voice of San Diego wants in an "engagement editor." Retrieved from http://www.niemanlab.org/2010/03/what-voice-of-san-diego-wants-in-an-engagement-editor/

Gitlin, T. (1980). The whole world is watching: Mass media in the making and unmaking of the New Left. Berkeley: University of California Press.

Goffman, E. (1974). Framing analysis: An essay on the organization of experience. Boston: Northeastern University Press.

Iyengar, S. and Kinder, D.R. (1987). News that matters: Television and American opinion. Chicago: University of Chicago Press.

Lakoff, G. (2004). Don't Think of an Elephant!: Know Your Values and Frame the Debate. White River Junction (Vermont): Chelsea Green Publishing.

Martin, C.R. and Oshagen, H. (1997). Disciplining the workforce: The news media frame a General Motors plant closing. Communication Research, 24, 669–97.

Pan, Z. and Kosicki, G.M. (1993). Framing analysis: An approach to news discourse. Political Communication, 10, 55–76.

Price, V., Tewksbury, D. and Powers, E. (1997). Switching trains of thought: The impact of news frames on readers' cognitive responses. Communication Research, 24, 481–506.

Reese, S.D. (2001). Prologue – Framing public life: A bridging model for media research. In S.D. Reese, O.H. Gandy and A.E. Grant (eds.), Framing public life: Perspectives on media and our understanding of the social world (pp. 7–31). Mahwah, New Jersey: Lawrence Erlbaum Associates.

Reese, S.D. (2007). The framing project: A bridging model for media research revisited. Journal of Communication, 57, 148–154.

Reese, S.D. (2010). Finding frames in a web of culture: The case of the War on Terror. In P. D'Angelo & J. A. Kuypers (eds.), Doing news framing analysis: Empirical and theoretical perspectives (pp. 17–42). New York: Routledge.

Reese, S.D. and Buckalew, B. (1995). The militarism of local television: The routine framing of the Persian Gulf War. Critical Studies in Mass Communication, 12(1), 40–59.

Reese, S.D. and Lewis, S.C. (2009). Framing the War on Terror : The internalization of policy in the US press. Journalism, 10, 777–97.

Rosen, J. (2006, June 27). The people formerly known as the audience. [Web log post]. Retrieved from http://archive.pressthink.org/2006/06/27/ppl_frmr.html

Salmon, F. (2011, May 8). The hermetic and arrogant New York Times. [Web log post]. Retrieved from http://blogs.reuters.com/felix-salmon/2011/05/08/the-hermetic-and-arrogant-new-york-times/

Shoemaker, P.J. and Reese, S.D. (1996). Mediating the message: Theories of influences on mass media content (2nd ed.). New York: Longman.

Stelter, B. (2008, March 27). Finding Political News Online, the Young Pass It On. The New York Times, from http://www.nytimes.com/2008/03/27/us/politics/27voters.html

58

'NO LONGER CHASING YESTERDAY'S STORY': NEW ROLES FOR NEWSMAGAZINES IN THE 21ST CENTURY

Heidi Mau and Carolyn Kitch

'We've all heard the argument that a weekly newsmagazine has no role in today's relentless, 24/7 news culture, in which digital blizzards of information come at us at blinding speed. ... What a magazine can offer readers is a path to understanding, a filter to sift out what's important, a pause to learn things that the Web has no time to explain, a tool to go back over the things we think we know but can't make sense of.'

(Brown, 2011: 5)

Observers have been declaring the impending death of the newsmagazine medium since at least the 1980s (Burton, 2007; Clurman, 1992). Recent years have seemed especially grim, with one of the three major American newsmagazines ceasing print publication and another, burdened with more than $50 million of debt, sold for a dollar ('An Audio,' 2010). Yet the category's two most prominent titles, *Time* and *Newsweek*, have survived into the second decade of the 21st century, as have other weekly magazines that provide news, such as *The Economist*. And the success of a recent entry into the field, *The Week*, suggests that the concept of the newsweekly may indeed have a future.

When Tina Brown became the newest editor of *Newsweek* in early 2011, industry buzz predicted major change. A staffer declared, 'It's slick, contemporary and feels like something out of the new millennium – sort of *New York* mag meets *GQ* ...' (quoted in Pompeo, 2011). Commentators veered between hope that just such 'slick' modernization could save the newsweekly genre and hand-wringing over the celebri-fication of news, especially considering Brown's celebrity-journalism background as a former editor of the British *Tatler* and the American *Vanity Fair*. Others predicted a new editorial style because, given her most recent job as editor of the website *The Daily Beast*, she was coming to the position from the world of online journalism. Her first issue made clear another point that had received less attention: under the skyline '150 Women Who Shake the World' stood Secretary of State Hillary Clinton, with a coverline reading, 'How she's shattering glass ceilings everywhere.' Brown unveiled this cover, one day before its news-stand debut, on the ABC News program *This Week with Christiane Amanpour*, as part of a segment on the role of women in Middle East political revolutions. Here was a reminder that, for the first time in its long history, a woman finally had shattered the glass ceiling of the American newsmagazine industry (Just, 2011).

Nevertheless, Brown's 'editor's letter' inside her first issue (quoted above) made a more general case for the need for newsmagazines – and it was remarkably consistent with the rationale offered by Henry Luce and Briton Hadden nearly 90 years earlier when *Time* debuted. The current era is not the first time that newsmagazine editors have proclaimed the special value of their work in an age of information overload and competition from new media. This chapter assesses the current state of newsmagazines as well as their longer-term survival, focusing primarily, though not solely, on the American sector of this genre.

'All the news of the world' once a week: foundings, dominance, and prominence

When they founded *Time* in 1923, Luce and Hadden, lamenting the little 'time which busy men are able to spend on simply keeping informed,' promised to 'organize the world's news and give it to readers in short, easily digestible doses' (*Time* prospectus quoted in Tebbel & Zuckerman, 1991: 160). Yet they also promised to do something more: to provide explanation, interpretation, and opinion, to 'sift through the clutter, synthesize what was important and preach their cheeky prejudices,' as *Time* managing editor Walter Isaacson recalled on the magazine's seventy-fifth anniversary (1998: 96). By the 1930s, Luce[1] had broadened his reach through new media – a newsreel series and a radio program, both called *The March of Time* – but had maintained his mission. The radio show promised listeners, 'you can depend on one magazine to summarize for you at the end of the week all the news of the world' (quoted in Brinkley, 2010: 181).

Launched in 1933, *Newsweek* (then *News-week*) similarly defined its work as a process of 'sifting, selecting, and clarifying the significant news of the week. ... [It] does not take the place of a newspaper ... it is an indispensable complement to newspaper reading, because it explains, expounds, clarifies' (Untitled advertisement, 1933: n.p.; 'A Letter', 1933: 33). A third title became a serious competitor in 1948, when conservative political columnist David Lawrence merged two publications he had founded in the 1930s – a weekly newspaper, *U.S. News*, and a weekly magazine, *World Report*.

These three magazines dominated the American newsweekly market for the following six decades.[2] Their editorial voices were authoritative, evaluative, and national, making sweeping editorial gestures on behalf of history and on behalf of the country.

Time began its annual tradition of naming a 'Man of the Year' in 1927, just four years after the magazine's founding. In 1941, Henry Luce made his famous declaration that the 20th century was 'the American Century' and offered a proposal not only for US entry into World War II but also for the nation's place in the world afterwards.[3] In 1950, *Time* named a 'Man of the Half-Century' (Winston Churchill[4]), and it began to make broader cultural statements with its 'Man of the Year' feature – choosing, for instance, 'The American Fighting Man' for 1950 and 'The Middle Americans' for 1970. *U.S. News & World Report* did not engage in summary journalism until the 1980s, though in 1983 it inaugurated an evaluative practice that would later become its editorial bread-and-butter, its annual ranking of colleges and universities. In that same year, *Newsweek* marked its fiftieth anniversary by publishing 'The American Dream,' a gold-covered special issue that told 'the true story of America' through the lens of 'five heartland families' living in the representative town of Springfield, Ohio. It also was *Newsweek* that made what may have been the most memorable editorial gesture of any journalistic medium just after September 11, 2001: its cover featuring three firemen raising the American flag on the site of the World Trade Center, an image that conjured popular memory of the famous World War II photograph of Allied soldiers raising the flag on Iwo Jima.

Indeed, newsmagazines' finest moments may come after extraordinary events, whether they are shocking disasters (such as an act of terrorism or a devastating flood) or a cultural or historic milestone (such as the death of a beloved celebrity or the election of the first African-American US President). On such occasions, these publications often do some of their best journalism, offering explanation – what James Carey (1987) famously called the 'how' and 'why' of journalism that are too often missing from breaking news coverage – for a national audience that seems to be at least temporarily unified. These issues also tend to produce the magazines' highest news-stand sales, thanks to the continuing phenomenon that readers still want tangible evidence of major events.[5]

Coverage of such events has been one common focus of academic examinations of this medium, and the extent of continuing scholarship on newsmagazines suggests that researchers still presume their journalistic importance and national prominence. Most recently, quite a few studies have used the newsmagazines as a lens through which to understand news coverage of the events of September 11 (e.g., Clark & Hoynes, 2003; Deveau & Fouts, 2005; Fried, 2005; Hutcheson et al., 2004; Kitch & Hume, 2008). Other research has considered who and what have appeared on the magazines' covers over the years (e.g., Cardoso, 2010; Christ & Johnson, 1985), their coverage of wars (e.g., Landers, 2004; Nikolaev, 2009; Patterson, 1984), and their articulation of American attitudes on various social issues (e.g., Ashley & Olson, 1998; Gilens, 1996; Kitch, 2005; Lentz, 1990; Covert & Washburn, 2007). Most book-length studies of the newsmagazine medium have been historical profiles of the institutions themselves and of their famous editors (e.g., Baughman, 2001; Brinkley, 2010; Elson, 1973; Herzstein, 1994; Swanberg, 1972; Walker, 2006).

Some of these studies have confirmed that the newsmagazines' ambitious missions and authoritative status have remained intact even decades after their founding. In making this point, some scholars have used the same kind of grand language as the magazines themselves. For instance, in his examination of the three major newsweeklies' coverage of the Vietnam War, James Landers concluded: 'The editors and correspondents of the newsmagazines were journalists, but they regarded themselves as observers whose job was to provide insight and perspective on the war, not to merely report what happened. The psychological ebb and flow of the American experience in Vietnam, from confidence to wariness to despair, appeared in the pages of *Newsweek*, *Time*, and *U.S. News & World Report*' (2004: 5).

The 'young tiger' and an 'aggregator with an attitude': recent challenges

During the middle decades of the 20th century, the newsweeklies competed, in function if not form, with other kinds of successful weekly magazines that covered many of the same subjects they did. Chief among those weekly competitors were two corporate siblings of *Time*, first the photojournalism magazine *Life*, beginning in 1936, and then America's first major celebrity magazine, *People*, beginning in 1974 (two years after *Life* had succumbed to the competitive pressures of television). During the 1960s and 1970s, *Time* and *Newsweek* expanded their definitions of 'news' from the acts of political figures to a broader array of individuals and events representing trends in popular culture as well as politics.

Historian James Baughman contends that the latter editorial shift signaled the newsweeklies' departure from 'opinion leadership' and thus the beginning of their demise (1998: 125). James R. Gaines, editor of *People* during the late 1980s and of *Time* during the early 1990s, makes this point in somewhat different language, calling *People* 'the young tiger that ... over time subtly changed the sense of what news is' (2010: 64). Former *Time* staffer Richard Clurman (1992) dates the newsweeklies' editorial decline to the 1990 corporate merger between Time Inc. and Warner Communications that resituated the genre's leading publication within an entertainment company.

In 2001, US newsmagazines gained a new competitor in *The Week*, a British import published by Felix Dennis, that uses a different editorial formula: not original reporting, but rather a digest of brief reports based on other news sources, delivered in a self-described 'fresh' style. (Ironically, notes Gaines, this was the original mission of *Time*, which vowed to report news in a modernly no-nonsense way amid the information overload of the 1920s; it was meant to be 'an aggregator with an attitude' [2010: 64].) *The Economist*, another British weekly with significant US readership, similarly runs short and often unbylined news summaries.

As these imports gained ground in the US market during the first decade of the 21st century, the fortunes of the more established magazines were declining. Editorially the major titles still had national prominence, and as recently as 2006, *Time* won the National Magazine Award for General Excellence, the industry's highest honor, for its coverage of Hurricane Katrina during the previous year (Seelye, 2006). Yet both

Time and *Newsweek* made deep cuts to their editorial staffs and closed many of their international as well as domestic bureaus.

The financial picture was worse. In less than a decade, the leading two magazines' advertising pages decreased by more than half, falling as much as 25 percent in a single year (as was the case for *Newsweek* in 2009) (Moses, 2010c). In 2007, *Time* cut its rate base (the number of copies a magazine guarantees to its advertisers that it will sell with every issue) from 4 million to 3.25 million while raising its news-stand copy price by $1, to $4.95 – a high price for a magazine that was sometimes fewer than 50 pages long. This strategy was defended (to advertisers) on the grounds that *Time*'s readers were of better 'quality' than those of other news publications, a claim also made about the magazine's online edition, which its editor at the time called '24-hour news for smart people' (John Tyrangiel, quoted in Smolkin, 2007: 20; also see Fiore, 2006). *Newsweek* followed suit, cutting its own rate base, and the combination of this move with additional losses in paid readership resulted in a 2010 circulation of 1.5 million, half of what it had been just two years earlier. Meanwhile, the US circulations of the other weeklies that provide news – *The Economist*, *The New Yorker*, and *The Week* – continued their gradual growth, although none of them exceeds one million (Matsa, Rosenstiel & Moore, 2011).

The most dramatic change of 2010 was the decision of *U.S. News & World Report* to abandon newsmagazine journalism in print. It had switched from weekly to semi-monthly and then to monthly during 2008, and in the following year it had begun publishing a digital version of its newsmagazine, which it emailed to subscribers in PDF format ('*U.S. News* Launches,' 2009). Today its only print publications are its well-known 'special' issues ranking various kinds of institutions, especially in the fields of health care and education. A *New York Times* report on this change quoted from a memo sent to the staff by the magazine's management: 'Our emphasis on rankings and research content is the right path, making us an essential information source' ('*U.S. News &*,' 2010: B3).

'Extending the brand': The move toward new editorial products

While it always emphasized what it called 'news you can use,' *U.S. News & World Report* is now quite firmly in the business of selling 'essential information' – defined not as news, but as data on which people base buying decisions. The company's rankings, which are available online, in print, and as videos, now assess not only schools and hospitals, but also travel, mutual funds, law firms, cars, and insurance companies, as well as questions such as 'best places to live' and 'best affordable places to retire.' *US News & World Report* has taken what used to be a 'bonus' aspect of the publication's work and made it central to its identity (and its income) in the 21st century. *Newsweek* and *Time* also have created new kinds of editorial products that offer readers – or entirely new audiences – something more.

Partnering with test-preparation company Kaplan, *Newsweek*, too, has entered the college-rankings business. It also publishes books, some unrelated to its news opera-tions (with titles like *100 Places to Remember Before they Disappear*), but most written by its high-profile columnists and editors. When political reporter Evan Thomas penned a post-mortem assessment of campaign strategy in the 2008 Presidential election, the book carried *Newsweek*'s logo, and its jacket touted the magazine's 'remarkable access to the candidates ... The result is a story that reads like no other coming off the campaign trail' (2009). Even before the election's conclusion, *Newsweek* had drawn from its own reporting to create book-length profiles of the Democratic and Republican candidates and their running mates, selling them for $9.99 apiece as e-books via Amazon.com. 'Turning this kind of collection into books is an old idea,' the magazine's then-editor Jon Meacham told the *New York Times*. 'This is competing in the digital space with our traditional strengths, and that's been hard to do' (Perez-Pena, 2008: 6).

As Meacham noted, repackaging newsmagazine content is not a new strategy, and no company has done more of it than Time Inc.[6] The practice of 'extending the brand' through 'ancillary media products' – seemingly new buzzwords in the journalism business – began for *Time* in 1931 with its 'March of Time' radio show; the Time-Life Books Division, which long has repackaged the contents of corporate-sibling magazines *Time* and *Life*, was formed in 1961 (Elson, 1973: 480). Throughout the 20th century, *Time* and *Life* issued not just year-end and decade-end summaries, but also book sets telling history for a popular audience, and their favorite theme was World War II. Correspondingly, it was that 'Good War' and the 'Greatest Generation' who fought it that sparked *Time*'s serious and regular enterprise of 'magabook'[7] publishing beginning in the early 1990s, when the magazines published 'keepsake' issues that coincided with the fiftieth anniversaries of that war's milestones. By then, the company was equally as interested in constructing social memory for the Baby Boomers, creating magabooks on anniversaries of events of the 1960s, ranging from the Kennedy assassination to the 'Summer of Love.' This theme remains a popular seller: as recently as 2010, *Time* issued a new magabook titled *Visions of the 1960s: The Images that Define the Decade* (and the present tense of the verb is a hint that, in commemorative media products, the 1960s live on).

During the late 1990s, *Time* published a series of magabooks summing up the 20th century, beginning with *Time's Great Events of the 20th Century* (1997) and culminating in a six-part series on the century's 100 most important people, arranged into six categories. The latter project was eventually published in partnership with CBS News, whose then-anchor, Dan Rather, wrote the book's Foreword. Rather declared that 'these stories and images should serve as a reminder of where we have been, and where we can go. The rough draft of history now has a smoother, more definitive shape' (1999: 19).

Despite that declaration, *Time* has continued to offer *new* 'definitive' definitions of history in coffee-table-book format with grand titles such as *America: An Illustrated History* (2007) and *History's Greatest Events: 100 Turning Points that Changed the World: An Illustrated Journey* (2010). Also published in 2010 was perhaps the most telling artifact of the magazine's self-presentation in a new-media world, a history of *Time* itself. Weighing in at six pounds, this 431-page, $50 hardcover book, which is on sale nationally in bookstores, is boldly titled *Time: The Illustrated History of the World's Most*

Influential Magazine (Angeletti & Oliva, 2010). Its sections recount episodes of the magazine's past in terms of their historical backdrops (e.g., 'From Civil Rights to the Space Race' [122]), and the magazine's launch is recalled in a chapter titled 'Writing History Every Seven Days' (16). Such pomposity earned the sarcasm of a *Wall Street Journal* reviewer who described the book's voice as 'the tone of a man at a bar, or perhaps on his deathbed, insisting that he once steered the planet through the stars,' adding, in a parting shot, 'this book does have the size and heft of a small tombstone' (Shiflett, 2010).

Surfing, feeding, trending, and tweeting: negotiating the internet and social media

While it continues to publish material products meant as history books, *Time* insists that it has found a new editorial and corporate life on the internet. The company reports having more than 3 million users of its mobile app as well as 2.6 million followers on social media sites (in 2010, *Time* was the second-most-followed magazine on Twitter, behind *People*). Combined with a total of 22 million[8] people reading the print magazine, 'the magazine's reach [is] at an all-time high' claims a 2010 report on the state of the industry (Matsa, Rosenstiel, & Moore, 2011). Monthly web traffic is at 4.9 million for *Time* and at 3.7 million for *Newsweek*. While those numbers are considerably higher than their print circulations even before the readership cuts of the past decade, they pale in comparison to the 40 million monthly visitors to the aggregator Yahoo! News (news.yahoo.com) (Matsa, Rosenstiel, & Moore, 2011).

Critics say that newsmagazines' traditional format is their greatest challenge on a new-media landscape. *Adweek* columnist Bob Greenberg (2007) declares, 'The editorial role of magazines in curating the best content on a particular subject and distilling it down to what fits into the weekly or monthly print run is being replaced by machines (e.g., search, personalization) and social networks (e.g., sites where users tell other users what's good, useful or popular).' This problem is partly a matter of space (what will fit inside a magazine) and partly a matter of the greatly increased availability of 'curation.'

Since the internet began to make inroads on both fronts, offering not only aggregation of information but also many new analytical voices, newsmagazine editors have continued to insist that *their* choices and analysis are simply superior. 'I would argue that the information explosion now is so tumultuous and so varied, that people … need a trusted guide, someone to help sort out the wheat from the chaff,' *Time* editor Richard Stengel said in 2007, adding: 'It's not somebody … sucking their thumb or scratching their chin. It's someone who does a huge amount of reporting to come to a conclusion about something' (quoted in Smolkin, 2007: 18). Nonetheless, it is apparent that the newsweeklies must offer something new and different.

U.S. News & World Report has most clearly differentiated its web content by focusing on its rankings enterprises. As a result, by mid-2010, the company's two websites, *USNews.com* and *rankingsandreviews.com*, together had more than 10 million unique users, and some 60 percent of the company's revenue was coming from digital content ('USNews.com,' 2010; Moses, 2010a and 2010b). The others are becoming heavily involved in social media and other new technologies. By April 2011, *Time.com*, *Newsweek.com*, and *TheWeek.com* were engaged in online news norms such as listing their most popular (or 'trending') stories, noting their most emailed stories, and encouraging the sharing of their online content through social media – ways in which these sites can spread their digital brand and attempt to build loyal readership. Each of these sites works differently to promote its authors as potential guides to content. *Time.com* prominently features bylines alongside the headlines for its news content and blog links. *Newsweek.com* features bylines and additionally offers an alphabetical listing of contributing-author names and a related search function. *TheWeek.com* offers, alongside its aggregated content, a boxed section of its own 'exclusive opinion makers.'

The newsmagazine websites feature multimedia material, mostly in the form of videos and photo slideshows. *Time.com* and *Newsweek.com* produce some of their own online short videos, also featured on their YouTube channels. *TheWeek.com* curates videos, hosted within its site. Whereas *TheWeek.com* also curates photo slideshows from other sources, *Time.com* and *Newsweek.com* feature material from their extensive print and online photo archives. *Time.com*, *Newsweek.com*, and *TheWeek.com* each offer a free daily newsletter via email inclusive of links that lead readers back to online newsmagazine content.[9] Each site offers mobile apps that reformat its website for easier navigation on smartphones, most including customization options so users can configure their news according to interests. As of April 2011, most of these apps are available free of charge or at low cost and are particular to online content.[10]

The relationship between online content and print content varies per newsmagazine. *TheWeek.com* curates work from other sources both online and in print, but limits online access to its weekly newsmagazine to print subscribers only. *Time.com* partners with *CNN*, providing online content separate from its print material. In early 2011, *Time.com* visitors could still find about half of the content of *Time's* current print issue in the site's 'magazine' section and sometimes as online material under adapted headlines. Articles were unabridged but embedded with links to other *Time.com* material. At the same time, stories featured on the home page and section headers of *Newsweek.com* were often unabridged material from the magazine's current newsstand issue, and a majority of that issue was accessible online for free.

Whereas the amount of online access to print material varies per newsmagazine, all the websites continue to feature persistent and prominent ads for print subscription offers. Even with the various technologies available to connect with online news via social media, RSS tools, email, and mobile apps, newsmagazines still hope to connect with readers through a magazine format – currently in print, but perhaps increasingly via digital platforms.

Back to the future: the digital newsmagazine experience

The newsmagazines continue adapting their print magazines for digital platforms, most notably electronic readers and tablet computers, each new platform bringing its own set of challenges. Electronic book readers, or e-readers, initially came on to the market with books and newspapers in mind – a predominantly black-and-white world with few images. Early models and current lower-end models cannot easily navigate writing and images as experienced in a magazine layout. Newsmagazine issues for the e-reader platform often do not include the full content of their print counterparts, but they offer price value and newsmagazine content.[11] In early 2011, rates hovered around $2.99 per month for Amazon's Kindle and Barnes and Noble's Nook subscriptions to *Newsweek* and *Time* and for the *Kindle* edition subscription to *U.S. News Weekly*.[12] Some magazines are adapting their material for e-reader/tablet hybrids, which can better incorporate a magazine layout view.[13]

The tablet platform receiving most of the newsmagazine application development in 2010 was Apple's iPad, although Apple has frustrated magazine publishers (in all categories) with its difficulty in negotiating subscription rates. Initial single issues of *Time* for the iPad cost the same as the print issue, a cost highly criticized by consumers posting feedback in the Apple app store. Google mentioned interest in creating a digital news-stand that would give magazine publishers the option of selling subscriptions as well (Peters, 2011; Tsukayama, 2011). By late 2010, *Newsweek* was offering its iPad app, and introductory subscription rates of 12 weeks for $9.99 and 24 weeks for $14.99.[14] The consumer responses, in this instance, were overwhelmingly positive to this development. It is still unclear how subscriptions and advertising will work in the tablet platform, and when other tablet applications will be available (as of the end of March, 2011, *U.S. News Weekly* and *The Week* had yet to offer an iPad app).

Time has collaborated with a digital design company and a software developer to build an iPad app that resembles a print-magazine reading experience while incorporating the interactive and touchscreen technologies of the iPad tablet platform.[15] The transition from print to tablet platform seems the closest translation of the print-magazine experience so far. The size of an iPad tablet is close to the size of most weekly newsmagazines. Tablets are relatively lightweight, portable, and easy to carry around. Touchscreens often allow readers to scroll through pages with a finger-flip movement. Color resolution is good and continues to improve, as does battery life. Although still not the same sensory and tactile experience as holding and reading a print magazine, reading newsmagazines via the tablet platform may be the closest experience yet to being able to slow down, perhaps comfortably lounge on a couch, and engage in the more in-depth reading experience newsmagazines proclaim they want their readers to have.

'Stopping a frantic world': an old defence in new language

While they proudly forge a path into new media, newsmagazines simultaneously praise their form of journalism as an *antidote* to – as Tina Brown put it in her first issue of *Newsweek* – the 'digital blizzards of information that come at us at blinding speed' and the 'quick zap of news on the Web.' When reporters are 'no longer chasing yesterday's story,' she writes, they, and their readers, can 'pause to learn things that the Web has no time to explain' (Brown, 2011: 5). Brown's argument is a direct engagement with the most common criticism of print media, the charge that they no longer can deliver news in a timely fashion. She is not alone in taking this tack, which is an attempt to redefine the terms of debate by redefining the meaning of time itself.

The new line of defense of the newsmagazine medium is that readers today wish for *slower* news, or at any rate, a less-frantic presentation of it. 'Counterintuitively, perhaps, the weekly cycle is a promising one in a world running at a digital pace,' wrote Brown's predecessor, Jon Meacham, in 2009 (9). This also was the premise of *Time*'s decade-in-review issue published at the end of 2010, which offered what it called 'TimeFrames.' The magazine, its editor explained, offered a 'longer view' of the passage of time in an age when news reports are too often 'casualties of hit-and-run journalism, measured in second-by-second spikes of traffic' and when 'information ... is a commodity [and] understanding is scarce' (Stengel, 2010: 4). The introduction to this issue's set of cover stories explained:

> The first decade of the 21st century moved so fast that it was easy, as the poet said, to have the experience but miss the meaning. It's hard to find the truth about the age of truthiness. ... So TimeFrames is our attempt to stop the clock, slow down, look back, see what comes into focus only from a distance. We know what happened in the past 10 years. But what really happened? ... how do we find the music or the meaning in the noise of the news?
>
> (Gibbs, 2010: 33)

Even as it discontinued its print newsmagazine, *U.S. News & World Report* used much the same language in explaining the value of its digital edition of the magazine, which is issued as a PDF file that readers can print and which employs the layout of a print publication ('designed horizontally, to be read easily on a computer screen' instead of 'the typical Web page filled with blinking images and endless headlines'). Then-editor Brian Kelly promised readers when the online version debuted: 'What's not so different is the journalism. We're still doing what a news weekly (*sic*) does best: stopping a frantic world for a moment to take stock of events and sift out the meaning from the meaningless' (Kelly, 2009: 6).

This newest rationale echoes the credo of the genre's inventors nearly a century ago. Without question, today's information landscape makes it a challenge for 'busy men' (and busy women) to 'simply keep informed,' as Luce and Hadden wrote in 1923. Newsmagazines' survival in a new-media world will determine whether that mission is, as critics claim, obsolete – or, as editors proclaim, timeless.

Notes

1 Luce's partner, Briton Hadden, died in 1929. A new biography of Hadden contends that he was the true 'genius' behind the idea and style of *Time* and that Luce later unfairly took the lion's share of credit (Walker, 2006).

2 During this period, two of the magazines came under new ownership. *Newsweek* was an independent company until 1961, when it was bought by *The Washington Post*; it was sold again in 2010 to entrepreneur Sidney Harman. *U.S. News & World Report* was independent until 1984, when it was bought

by Mortimer Zuckerman. *Time* remains the flagship publication of Time Inc., which merged with Warner Communications in 1990; that combined company acquired the Turner Broadcasting System in 1996 and then was merged with America Online from 2000 to 2009. These ownership changes are documented in many sources, including Smolkin (2007).

3   This article actually appeared in *Life* magazine, by then *Time*'s corporate sibling (Luce, 1941).

4   The choice of Churchill was surely a snub to the recently deceased former US President Franklin Delano Roosevelt, of whom the conservative Luce long had been a political foe.

5   *Time*'s four best-selling issues to date are, in order, two of its special reports on September 11 and the commemorative issues it published after the deaths of John F. Kennedy, Jr. and Princess Diana (Angeletti & Oliva, 2010: 414–15).

6   For an overview of Time Inc.'s marketing of 'special' issues and other ancillary products across all of the company's magazine titles, see Kitch, 2006.

7   'Magabooks' or 'bookazines' are perfect-bound (glued, not stapled) softcover books that cost between $10 and $15 and remain on sale for extended periods.

8   This figure represents total readership, not paid circulation. Readership figures are based on data showing how many readers-per-copy (or 'pass-along rate') a magazine has.

9   *Newseek.com*'s daily newsletter link leads to *TheDailyBeast.com*, where readers can sign up for *TheDailyBeast*'s newsletter.

10 *Newsweek.com* charged $1.99 for its various mobile apps, while *Time.com* and *TheWeek.com* offered their mobile apps for free. *Newsweek.com* additionally promotes iPhone apps for ancillary products such as *Newsweek's 100 Places to Remember Before they Disappear* and *Flashback by Newsweek*, featuring an image archive of *Newsweek* magazine covers.

11 It is unclear whether the offering of partial content was due to limitations of technology, a platform/tier pricing strategy, or other unknown reasons.

12 Prices as advertised on Amazon.com and BarnesandNoble.com, accessed online 4 April 2011.

13 Barnes and Noble debuted their 'NOOK Color,' an e-reader/tablet hybrid for the 2010 holiday season. Some magazines are set up to appear on a NOOK Color as they would in print, but since the size of the reader is so small (approximately 5" x 7"), it has to use a function that allows the reader to pop up the text in a separate window for easier reading. This reader was priced halfway between the base Kindle e-reader and the base iPad tablet (The-ebook-reader.com).

14 Prices as advertised in the Apple App Store, accessed through iTunes, 4 April 2011.

15 *Time* collaborated with The Wonderfactory of New York and WoodWing Software of the Netherlands in creating the debut 'Time Magazine' iPad app. The overall design is intended to mimic the *Time* magazine print reading experience while incorporating optional multimedia such as slideshows, video clips, and links to online updates (Wonderfactory, 2010).

References

'A Letter to News-Minded People' [advertisement] (1933). *News-week*, 25 March: 33.

'An Audio Pioneer Buys Beleaguered *Newsweek*' (2010). *New York Times*, 3 August, p. B1.

Angeletti, N. and Oliva, A. (2010). *Time: The Illustrated History of the World's Most Influential Magazine*. New York: Rizzoli.

Ashley, L. and Olson, B. (1998). 'Constructing Reality: Print Media's Framing of the Women's Movement, 1966–1986.' *Journalism & Mass Communication Quarterly*, 75(8): 263–77.

Baughman, J.L. (1998). 'The Transformation of *Time* Magazine.' *Media Studies Journal*, 12(3): 120–7.

Baughman, J.L. (2001). *Henry R. Luce and the Rise of the American News Media*. Baltimore: Johns Hopkins University Press.

Brinkley, A. (2010). *The Publisher: Henry Luce and His American Century*. New York: Alfred A. Knopf.

Brown, T. (2011). 'Notebook: A New *Newsweek*.' *Newsweek*, 14 March: 5.

Burton, L.W. (2007). 'Still Going.' *American Journalism Review*, April/May: 19.

Cardoso, C.R. (2010). 'The Future of Newsmagazines.' *Journalism Studies*, 11(4): 577–86.

Carey, J. (1987). 'Why and How?: The Dark Continent of American Journalism,' in R.K. Manoff and M. Schudson (eds), *Reading the News*. New York: Pantheon, 146–96.

Christ, W.G. and Johnson, S. (1985). 'Images through *Time*: Man of the Year Covers.' *Journalism Quarterly*, 62(4): 891–3.

Clark, C. and Hoynes, W. (2003). 'Images of Race and Nation after September 11.' *Peace Review*, 15(4): 443–50.

Clurman, R. (1992). *To the End of* Time: *The Seduction and Conquest of a Media Empire*. New York: Simon & Schuster.

Covert, T.J.A. and Washburn, P.C. (2007). 'Measuring Media Bias: A Content Analysis of *Time* and *Newsweek* Coverage of Domestic Social Issues, 1975–2000.' *Social Science Quarterly*, 88(3): 690–706.

Deveau, V.L. and Fouts, G.T. (2005). 'Revenge in U.S. and Canadian News Magazines Post-9/11.' *Canadian Journal of Communication*, 30(1): 99–109.

Elson, R.T. (1973). *Time Inc.: The Intimate History of a Publishing Enterprise, 1941–1960*, vol. 2. New York: Atheneum.

Fiore, M. (2006). '*Time* Magazine Slashes Rate Base, Raises Newsstand Price.' *www.foliomag.com*. Posted 10 November; accessed 2 April 2011.

Fried, A. (2005). 'Terrorism as a Context of Coverage before the Iraq War.' *The Harvard International Journal of Press/Politics*, 10(3): 125–32.

Gaines, J. (2010). 'Where the Newsweeklies Went Wrong.' *Folio: The Magazine for Magazine Management*, 39(6): 64.

Gibbs, N. (2010). 'TimeFrames.' *Time: Special Timeframes Issue: What Really Happened, 2000–2010*, 6 December: 33.

Gilens, M. (1996). 'Race and Poverty in America.' *Public Opinion Quarterly*, 60(4): 515–41.

Greenberg, B. (2007). 'The Digital Dialogue.' *Adweek.com*, 11 February; accessed 26 March 2011 via LexisNexis database.

Herzstein, R.E. (1994). *Henry R. Luce: A Political Portrait of the Man Who Created the American Century*. New York: Scribner's.

Hutcheson, J., Domke, D., Billeaudeaux, A. and Garland, P. (2004). 'U.S. National Identity, Political Elites, and a Patriotic Press Following September 11.' *Political Communication*, 21(1): 27–50.

Isaacson, W. (1998) 'Luce's Values – Then and Now.' *Time: 75th Anniversary Issue*, 9 March: 96–7.

Just, S. (2011). 'Tina Brown Reveals New *Newsweek* Magazine.' *ABC News* [online], accessed 6 March 2011, <http://abcnews.go.com/Politics/tina-brown-reveals-newsweek-magazine-hillary-clinton-abc/story ?id=13068817>.

Kelly, B. (2009). 'The Weekly, and the Monthly.' *U.S. News & World Report*, March: 6.

Kitch, C. (2005). *Pages from the Past: History and Memory in American Magazines*. Chapel Hill: University of North Carolina Press.

Kitch, C. (2006). '"Useful Memory" in Time Inc. Magazines: Summary Journalism and the Popular Construction of History.' *Journalism Studies*, 7(1): 105–22.

Kitch, C. and Hume, J. (2008). *Journalism in a Culture of Grief*. New York and London: Routledge.

Landers, J. (2004). *The Weekly War: Newsmagazines and Vietnam*. Columbia: University of Missouri Press.

Lentz, R. (1990). *Symbols, the News Magazines, and Martin Luther King*. Baton Rouge: Louisiana State University Press.

Luce, H.R. (1941). 'The American Century.' *Life*, 17 February: 61–5.

Matsa, K.-E., Rosenstiel, T. and Moore, P./Pew Project for Excellence in Journalism (2011). 'Magazines: A Shake-Out for News Weeklies.' *The State of the News Media 2011: An Annual Report on American Journalism*. Accessed 14 March 2011, <http://stateofthemedia.org/2011/magazines-essay/>.

Meacham, J. (2009). 'Top of the Week: A New Magazine for a Changing World.' *Newsweek*, 25 May: 9.

Moses, L. (2010a). 'Digital Blueprint: Is *U.S. News*' Web Success a Model for Newsweeklies?' *Media Week*, 20(19), 10 May: 26.

Moses, L. (2010b). 'Some Good News from *U.S. News*.' *Brandweek*, 51(19): 26.

Moses, L. (2010c). 'Surviving the Week: With Rival *Newsweek* in Peril, Can *Time* Be Saved?' *Media Week*, 17 May: 6.

Nikolaev, A.G. (2009). 'Images of War: Content Analysis of the Photo Coverage of the War in Kosovo.' *Critical Sociology*, 35(1): 105–30.

Patterson III, O. (1984). 'Television's Living Room War in Print: Vietnam in the News Magazines.' *Journalism Quarterly*, 61(1): 35–9, 136.

Perez-Pena, R. (2008). 'Campaign Articles from *Newsweek* Become E-Books for Amazon Kindle.' *New York Times*, 13 October: 6.

Peters, J.W. (2011). 'For Magazines, a Bitter Pill.' *New York Times*, 17 January, p. B1.

Pompeo, J. (2011). 'Redesigned *Newsweek* on Stands Monday'. *The Cutline* [blog]/*Yahoo! News* [online], Accessed 14 March 2011, <http://news.yahoo.com/s/yblog_thecutline/20110305/ts_yblog_thecutline/redesigned-newsweek-on-stands-monday>.

Rather, D. (1999). 'The Reporter's Century' [foreword]. In *Time*/CBS News, *People of the Century: 100 Men and Women Who Shaped the Last 100 Years*. New York: Simon & Schuster.

Seelye, K.Q. (2006). '*Time* Wins Top Award for Magazine Excellence.' *New York Times*, 10 May, p. C7.

Shiflett, D. (2010). 'The Glossies.' *The Wall Street Journal*, 22 May. Accessed 19 April 2011 via ProQuest database.

Smolkin, R. (2007). 'Finding a Niche.' *American Journalism Review*, April/May: 16–25.

Stengel, R. (2010). 'To Our Readers: The Long View.' *Time: Special Timeframes Issue: What Really Happened, 2000–2010*, 6 December: 4.

Swanberg, W.A. (1972). *Luce and His Empire*. New York: Scribner's.

Tebbel, J. and Zuckerman, M.E. (1991). *The Magazine in America, 1741–1990*. New York: Oxford University Press.

The-eBook-Reader.com. 'Nook Color Review' [weblog]. Accessed 8 April 2011, <http://www.the-ebook-reader.com/nook-color.html>.

Thomas, E., with reporting by the staff of *Newsweek* (2009). '*A Long Time Coming': The Inspiring, Combative 2008 Campaign and the Historic Election of Barack Obama*. New York: Public Affairs Press.

Time: America: An Illustrated History (2007). New York: Time Books.

Time: History's Greatest Events: 100 Turning Points that Changed the World: An Illustrated Journey (2010). New York: Time Books.

Time/CBS News (1999). *People of the Century: 100 Men and Women Who Shaped the Last 100 Years*. New York: Simon & Schuster.

Time's Great Events of the 20th Century (1997). New York: Time Inc. Home Entertainment.

Tsukayama, H. (2011). 'Faster Forward: Google May Launch Digital Newsstand for Android.' *Washingtonpost.com*, 3 January. Accessed 19 April 2011 via Business & Industry database.

Untitled advertisement (1933). *News-week*, 25 February 25: n.p.

'*U.S. News* Launches Weekly Online Pub' (2009). *B to B*, 94(2): 6.

'*U.S. News & World Report* to End Monthly Publication' (2010). *New York Times*, 6 November, p. B3.

'USNews.com Audience Reaches Record High in August 2010' (2010). *PR Newswire*, 9 September 9. Accessed 26 March 2011 via Proquest database.

Walker, I. (2006). *The Man Time Forgot: A Tale of Genius, Betrayal, and the Creation of Time Magazine*. New York: HarperCollins.

Wonderfactory (2010). 'Time Magazine iPad App Demo' [online video]. Uploaded 5 April 2010; accessed 15 April 2011, <http://www.youtube.com/watch?v=avM3Aor7Ptg>.

59

HEAR TODAY AND ON TOMORROW: THE FUTURE OF NEWS AND 'NEWS TALK' IN AN ERA OF DIGITAL RADIO

Guy Starkey and Andrew Crisell

In a volume which covers the general theory and practice of journalism, a chapter that focuses on its particular manifestations in radio might seem unnecessary. The key principles of journalism manifest themselves in any and every medium because they relate to a set of core issues around truths about the world we live in and the ways of selecting and presenting those truths. Because 'truth' is controversial, because facts and their meanings can be disputed, some of these core issues relate to a journalist's ability to verify them and the ethics of the way in which they are presented (Starkey, 2007: 1–20).

Nevertheless, we would argue that an understanding of nothing more than these key principles would be an inadequate preparation for the practice of journalism in radio. The medium makes unique demands on the journalist, imposing practices which have been tried and tested over a long period of time. Yet the medium is changing: other practices are relatively new or still emerging, and one important catalyst for change has been the transition from analogue to digital technology. In this chapter we will examine the potential impact of digital technology on radio journalism, specifically news and news-related content, and venture some predictions which are at once conservative and optimistic.

Digital technology as a force for radical change

It will be helpful to begin with an outline of the ways in which digital technology has affected the medium itself. First, by reducing transmissions to a stream of data expressed as a series of zeros and ones it enabled a much greater number of stations to share the available broadcasting spectrum: instead of one channel per frequency, each frequency could accommodate several channels. Second, and even more significant, it made possible the internet and so created a new habitat for radio as for every other medium. Third, it was the precondition of mobile communications, most obviously in the form of the telephone and portable computer, which could create a valuable production tool in terms of the recording, editing and transmission of audio. Finally, digital technology resulted in an expansion in the modes of radio reception. In addition to dedicated receivers (known as DAB radios), it allowed listeners to consume radio on television sets, desktop and laptop computers and mobile communications – iPhones, iPods and the like.

The collective impact of these developments has been twofold. First, there has been a fall in the cost of broadcast transmission and thus a widening of access to it. Now almost anybody can start a radio station and reach a worldwide audience. Moreover, and particularly in respect of the news, there has been a potential increase in content: with mobile media almost anybody can be a news-gatherer, either by sending reports and sound actuality to the radio station or by broadcasting it directly. Second, and inevitably in view of the expansion in the modes of reception, there has been something of a convergence of radio with other media. Nearly every radio station has its own website, and many provide video clips containing material that is supplementary to the broadcasts or webcams that deliver to the listener's computer images of the broadcasters in the studio. For the time-shifted consumption of programmes there are also podcasts, special programmes which can be downloaded to iPods, and in the United Kingdom iPlayer, a device that allows the listener to hear BBC programmes on her computer – alongside much of the output of BBC television – for up to a week or so after they have been transmitted.

Some of this convergence is in a sense not new: in the guise of audio-cassette recording and replay, time-shifted consumption pre-dated the digital revolution by more than twenty years. The forms of convergence that digital technology has introduced have been between radio and *visual* media. In 2011 the UK radio industry launched something called Radioplayer, essentially an online platform which allows rapid access to the streamed output of every participating radio station in the country. But Radioplayer enables stations to add parallel visual content to the streamed audio, including exhortations to follow links to other online content which is not necessarily characteristic of radio. Even the conventional DAB receivers incorporate information – in the form of rolling text – that the listener can look at. But what will all these changes mean for radio in general and radio news in particular? We will offer two views of the future: a radical one in which new technology will transform and in effect reduce the medium; and our own more conservative and sceptical view, which sees the new technology as having an evolutionary rather than revolutionary impact.

From a radical perspective the proliferation of radio channels will mean an expansion of news sources – room for lots of different perspectives on the news and, indeed, for different understandings of what news is. In the past, nation-states subjected broadcasting to tight regulation primarily because they felt that it could wield considerable political influence, and, practically speaking, because they could do so very easily. The spectrum was limited and so broadcasting was a scarce commodity and more easily policed than, for instance, scores of publishers and booksellers (Starkey, 2007: 23–4). But in the form of the internet, digitisation has abolished scarcity. Stations can be easily started, they transcend national boundaries and, indeed, have worldwide reach: they can evade the political and legal controls of particular states. This new freedom from regulation could lead to forms of 'news' in which hard facts are mingled with propaganda, surmise, rumour and innuendo, with everything enhanced by those devices of the 'citizen journalist' that we have just described: mobile phones, laptops and so on. Once upon a time the 'grapevine' – the circulation of rumours and unofficial information – was one resource that the journalist could use in gathering news which would then be properly verified and combined with other information to make a balanced and coherent whole. In future, however, the grapevine itself could be what passes for news on many radio stations.

These developments could have major professional and institutional consequences. As we have just implied, the rise of the citizen journalist could threaten the livelihood of the professional by circumventing the latter's news-gathering and editorial skills. Journalism has never, of course, been wholly professionalised: news stories can originate from casual witnesses; articles, sometimes political, are written by individuals from other walks of life. But whereas until now the journalistic contribution of what we might call 'ordinary people' has always been controlled by a kind of priesthood of professionals, a revolution could occur. Owning, or with access to, their own web stations, operating their own equipment and gathering and reading their own news, many ordinary people could become radio journalists, and it may often be hard to distinguish them from those who have been professionally trained.

We might nevertheless feel that the traditional, publicly sanctioned broadcasting institutions would continue to guarantee the integrity of the news. In the United Kingdom, to take one example, a dual system of broadcasting persists. The licence-funded BBC, providing both network and local radio, is still the central feature of the landscape, but surrounded, so to speak, by a sprawling commercial sector (sometimes still known as 'Independent Radio' (IR) in order to dissociate it from a BBC that is dependent on public money). IR operates at national, regional and local levels. However – and unlike newspapers – both kinds of broadcaster are required to be accurate and impartial in their reportage of the news. This is essentially a public service requirement, also dating from a time when broadcasting was both scarcer and arguably more influential than it is today. The BBC has always been bound by it and it is also imposed on IR by the independent regulator, Ofcom, the Office of Communications: 'News, in whatever form, must be reported with due accuracy and presented with due impartiality' (Ofcom Broadcasting Code, February 2011, Section 5.1).

Nevertheless, the global proliferation of radio stations, most of them also streaming on the web, could make considerable inroads into the audience for both BBC radio and IR – with financial and editorial consequences. Governments are unwilling to make the public pay for a broadcasting organisation which loses significant audience share, and private companies will not place advertising with stations that attract few listeners. It is perhaps unlikely that this will mean the end of the present system of sound broadcasting (adieu Auntie! au revoir IR!) but reduced income would surely impact on the ability of both sectors to provide properly mediated and authoritative news. Even more insidious would be the development of a situation in which the majority of the public no longer turned to radio as one of its primary, trusted sources of news and information.

A radical view of radio's future would also posit a highly active audience, one which is not merely listening to live sound-only broadcasts on dedicated receivers, laptops, desktops, TV sets and mobile phones, but also to podcasts and webcasts. At the same time it will be scouring station websites and watching the video clips these carry, as well as peering via webcams at the radio broadcasters in their studios. There is something at once reassuring and disquieting about this prospect. Throughout its existence radio has always been very largely a 'secondary' medium, one which is listened to while the listener is doing something else such as driving or cleaning her car or lying in the bath. In other words, her primary activity would have nothing to do with the radio. However, it is likely that the primary activity of the newer, active listener will more often be radio-related, in that sense making her more attentive: if she is listening on her computer or mobile phone, she may be tempted, at least occasionally, to glance at the video or webcam images the station is offering or to scan the pages of its website.

Yet the prospect is also disquieting. It is true that the traditional listener was sometimes so absorbed in her primary occupation that she would be paying scant attention to what she heard, but there was nevertheless a certain self-sufficiency in radio's messages. Should she choose to, she could listen to messages that did not depend for part of their meaning on extraneous material but were complete in themselves. But if the primary occupation of the active listener is radio-related she may well, paradoxically, pay less attention to the medium itself, for the material she absorbs from the website and webcams is likely to dilute the impact of what she hears. Conscious of this fact, will sound broadcasters then be tempted to express some of the meaningful content of their programmes in printed words and images? When that happens radio will be on the point of extinction: it will be little more than a soundtrack, and we will be arguing shortly that this would be particularly unfortunate in respect of the news.

Digital technology as a force for gradual change

There is, however, a more sceptical view of radio's future which is also more sanguine. Stations may multiply but the global audience for radio will not. Hence the ability to fund them will not increase proportionately, and it is likely that many of them will be run by amateur broadcasters and be ephemeral and of unpredictable quality. For these reasons, they are unlikely to attract very large audiences. In search of reliably good programmes, most of us will prefer to remain with the traditional kinds of radio station staffed by trained professionals, and will thus ensure their continued funding. Among the professionals will be journalists – people who, amid all the hubbub of fact, rumour, allegation and sheer invention, will be able to mediate the news for us in a trustworthy way. It is therefore ironic that those 'gatekeepers' of the news (White, 1950; Carter, 1958) who were once regarded with scholarly suspicion could shortly be hailed as angels of mercy. Moreover in order to reach the largest audiences, even citizen journalists will prefer to submit their stories and sound actuality to the traditional networks, something they already do.

In all this, branding is crucial: it is a way of confirming the veracity of the news. The BBC's brand is arguably one of the strongest in the world, and it is in large part the BBC's radio journalism that has made it so. Since the beginning of the Empire Service in 1932 it has reached millions of overseas listeners, many of them grateful for the relatively impartial account of the world that it offered. Its successor, the BBC World Service, found equal favour. A trusted brand is also one that domestic audiences turn to, especially in times of uncertainty, in order to make sense of events outside their personal experience. Naturally, most citizen journalists would prefer to contribute to a service with this kind of reputation than to shout into a void.

Even the idea of the highly active audience needs to be qualified, in respect of radio at least. It is true that a lot of listening is time-shifted, but as we have already observed, this activity was common well before the arrival of digital technology and probably focuses on other, less ephemeral and ubiquitous kinds of programming than news. It is true that digital technology makes time-shifting easier to set up: few radio cassette recorders allowed users to set recording start and end times in advance. The recordings made online or on personal video recorders (PVRs) today are also easier to navigate, as every second is time-coded and fast-forward and rewind actions can be performed almost instantly. But radio listening remains far more rooted in linear, real-time consumption than television, and because radio journalism is dynamic and able to be quickly updated, there seems little point in accessing outdated news bulletins when the latest, more up-to-date version is never far away. There are of course more durable forms of radio journalism, including the documentary and the specialist magazine programme focusing on a specific subject area such as medicine or economics. Nevertheless, to speak of a highly active listener is in essence to speak of multi-media consumption, and at this point it will be helpful to examine it more closely and draw some distinctions that are important in respect of radio.

First, we should remember that for many people the consumption of news has always been a multi-media activity. Typically we listen to the radio news when we awake, then, and in no particular order, turn to newspapers, television and online forms of news. In other words, radio has for most if not all of its existence been part of a broader news diet, though this is not to imply that in communicative terms it lacks self-sufficiency. What is new is the potential or actual *simultaneity* of consumption – that is to say, the phenomenon of the listener consuming radio news at the same time as scanning web pages, webcams, video clips, and so on. However, we would suggest that such behaviour is relatively unusual, that for the most part radio continues to be consumed in a singular and secondary way and that this is not simply a matter of convenience – of enabling us to access the news while we are lying in a bath or driving the car – but a recognition that the medium in general, and the news in particular, has no need of vision in order to convey its messages.

Though circumstantial, the evidence for this assertion is persuasive and is to be found in the listening figures for digital radio which are compiled at quarterly intervals by Radio Joint Audience Research (RAJAR). Despite the variety of means by which one can listen to it – on television sets, on the internet via desktop or laptop computers or mobile media – dedicated radio receivers, DAB sets, continue to account for more than 60 per cent of all digital consumption. Indeed, between the third and fourth quarters of 2010 their share increased by 1.5 per cent (RAJAR, February 2011). Moreover, although radio is indeed changing in reaction to digital technology, analogue consumption still outstrips all digital forms of listening by a ratio of two to one. RAJAR has recorded record levels of *listening*, but found that listening through the internet accounts for only three per cent of the whole. Indeed, DAB has proved more popular in the UK than in most countries of the world: elsewhere listening to radio *broadcasts* remains stubbornly 'analogic' (Jauert et al., 2010). Hence the fact that large numbers of people are continuing to use receivers that are *incapable* of providing them with images of anything more than minimal text suggests that they like radio *because*, not in spite of, its lack of vision. Since the most popular radio content is acoustic – music – this is hardly surprising, but radio news and radio talk are sufficiently popular for us to seek other reasons for this acquiescence in the non-visual.

In fact, such an attitude is eminently reasonable. However vividly they may be shown on television, events are easily – and concisely – described on the radio. Moreover, 'events' of the finite, visible kind are only one element of the news: crucial to an understanding of them are the causal connections between them, the reactions to them, the context of them, all of which are essentially invisible. Moreover, their visible manifestations are, from a cognitive point of view, just so much distracting clutter: in a technical sense, 'noise'. Words are the main currency of understanding and the primary code of radio, even music radio (Crisell, 1994: 53–5). It is, indeed, arguable that they are the main currency of understanding in *any* medium, including television (Crisell, 2003: 7–9).

This need to 'intellectualise' the news – felt both by journalists, who often believe that they can report it only by locating it within the bigger picture, and by listeners, who need to better understand its causes and implications and may wish to voice their own views of it – has given rise in recent years to a supplementary radio genre of 'news talk' alongside the more conventional news coverage. Since news and news talk are carefully distinguished, they should not be confused with the conflation of news and hearsay that might develop in webcasting, nor should the need to intellectualise that the distinction expresses be perceived as exclusively highbrow: it is universal. Extended discussions of contemporary affairs can be encountered not only on BBC Radios 3 and 4 but on 5 Live and, chaired by Jeremy Vine, on Radio 2, not to mention the commercial station talkSPORT. This is good radio not simply because it allows the listener to perform some other activity while listening but because it enables her to contemplate ideas and issues without having to view imagery which is at once germane to them and a distraction from them.

Journalistic practice in the era of digital radio

With this essentially traditional concept of the medium in mind, what are the specific demands of radio journalism, and to what extent have they already changed in response to the development of digital technology? They are inextricably linked to the nature of the medium and the manner of its consumption we have just begun to explore. Without the ability – or the inclination – to pause, rewind or replay the spoken word which makes up the bulk of its content, listeners have to assimilate in real time what is being said. Whereas written text can be consumed at the reader's own pace, re-read if necessary and dwelt on at leisure, the radio journalist probably has only one opportunity to convey the essence and the detail of a story in a way that will be heard and understood over the sights and other sounds which might be clamouring for the listener's attention (Starkey and Crisell, 2010). Utterances therefore tend to be short and pithy, avoiding the complication of parentheses. Because this journalism is conveyed verbally, some stations apply a fairly colloquial house style, including elided forms such as *he'll*, *there's* and *we're*. The journalist who writes the copy is often the same person who delivers it to the microphone, either live or as part of an item inserted into a longer news bulletin. Whatever the format, clarity of diction and an ability to colour a phrase through the appropriate use of 'light' and 'shade', rises and falls in intonation and even implied seriousness or lightheartedness are all essential to the creation of something not only which the audience can understand but which it will *wish to listen to*.

Depending on the radio station, its target audience and the prevailing sense of how much formality is required of it, radio journalism is also susceptible to tabloidization. The brevity that is associated with the tabloids is perhaps not surprising in a medium that exists in time rather than space, for time, as the saying goes, is precious. But the tabloid character may also extend to the prioritising of lighter stories from the worlds of entertainment and sport over potentially more challenging hard news, foreign affairs, politics, economics and regional or local administration. In its efforts to 'hook' the audience to a story, it may make that blatant appeal to their self interest which is also characteristic of the tabloids. An example might be copy which begins with the words: 'Your pay packet may feel lighter from today, with the raising of the income tax rate'. However, such tabloidization is less a direct consequence of digital technology than of the increasingly competitive market we have already identified.

Quite apart from the use of voice to convey paralinguistic meaning, one of the main illustrative resources on which radio journalism continues to draw is actuality. This may take the form of live or recorded *atmosphere* (the 'sound' of a place, an event or a process) or simply the additional use of the voices of protagonists in, or commentators on, a story. Extraneous noise should be avoided, but sound which illustrates a location can be a bonus. Interview material should be focused and edited without misrepresenting interviewees because with airtime at a premium it will almost inevitably need to be used sparingly. Short-form items, such as illustrative clips used to break up the live delivery of journalistic copy by the newsreader, are inevitably subject to high levels of selection and editing. A number of such clips may be used in a 'package' which provides a more detailed account of a news story and – depending on its length – may be intended for use within a longer bulletin or to be incorporated into the programming of the station.

This blend of illustrative sound and authoritative comment characterised radio news journalism for many years before the arrival of digital technology: what has changed is the *ease* with which it can be created. The editing of source material, the removal of mistakes in the delivery of the recorded script and the blending of sound from different sources are all far quicker and simpler than the cumbersome manipulation of analogue recordings that was commonplace just a decade and a half ago. Today's roving radio reporter is likely to carry a laptop, a smartphone or a tablet in order to carry out post-production tasks and send the finished recording back to the newsroom: gone are the days of tape recorder, razor blade, chinagraph pencil and splicing tape. Moreover a notable recent development has been the widening of the radio journalist's brief to encompass other media. Both when planning and gathering source material and during post-production, the journalist may also be preoccupied with the role of the web and with parallel visual content that will be broadcast digitally or posted online. As well as creating a radio report, she might, for instance, produce copy as a visual text which contains headlines and even photographic images.

The erosion of localism in the digital era

What, though, are the implications for radio journalists of some of the other developments in recent years, whether technological or otherwise? What is their likely impact on the development of the medium in the present and in the future? One of the most significant trends since the introduction of IR has been its dislocation from the communities it was intended to serve. In its original form it was a network of separate locally owned and operated companies, each being able to connect with its listeners in a way that could not be achieved by regional or national radio (Starkey, 2011). By the beginning of the last decade the number of independent local radio (ILR) stations far exceeded the sixty that were envisaged in the election promise which brought about the end of the BBC's monopoly of radio in 1973 (Conservative Party, 1970). But by 2008, when the number of local broadcasting licences approached three hundred, a period of mergers and takeovers had already elapsed, and the vast majority of stations belonged to one or another of the large radio groups which dominated the commercial sector.

In that year the formation of Global Radio was one of the most significant events of the decade for the commercial sector, coinciding as it did with Ofcom's latest reinterpretation of the frequently rewritten rules governing ownership and the origination of content. No longer would locally relevant content have to be produced in the locality, and neighbouring stations would be allowed, if the circumstances were judged appropriate, to 'co-locate' in shared premises which might even be outside the editorial areas of one or more of the stations. The production of local news at a distance was also trialled, with some local newsrooms being reduced to only a minimal presence (Crisell and Starkey, 2006). Then Global pulled off a magnificent coup, rebranding most of its stations, irrespective of their location, as either Heart or Capital and networking and syndicating programming as much as it could.

Other developments in journalism in the digital era

While consolidation in the commercial sector has left bulletin-driven news journalism intact in many locations around the country, it has had little effect on news talk.

This has remained largely the preserve of the BBC, although an enduring example of forays into the genre is London's Biggest Conversation, LBC 97.3. Compared to the cost of playing virtually non-stop music between advertisements and news bulletins, this is a relatively expensive form of radio to produce. With its inherently higher production values, documentary making for radio is now almost exclusive to the BBC, and a recent, outstanding history of its 'intelligent speech' network, Radio 4, provides a real flavour of the richness of long-form radio journalism as it is practised there (Hendy, 2007). At many times during its history, the BBC's journalism has appeared unassailable – certainly from within the corporation – and notably under the news-driven approach to governance of one of its most controversial Directors-General, John Birt (Born, 2004).

Times change even at the BBC, however, and although the World Service continues to provide a high standard of radio journalism for the benefit of numerically and geopolitically significant audiences overseas, changes to its funding are behind a new tightening of budgets. Thanks to a disadvantageous licence fee settlement agreed with the Conservative–Liberal Democrat coalition government in 2010, the BBC's domestic services also face cuts, and one of the solutions being mooted at the time of writing is a severe scaling back of the output of its local radio network, perhaps reducing it outside peak time to a relay of 5 Live. This would have the effect of restricting the output of all those local radio newsrooms to the production of the harder news demanded by the breakfast and drive-time slots and abandoning the softer journalistic material which fills much of the rest of the day. While many deplore such moves to downgrade its radio journalism, critics of the BBC would argue that compared to the commercial sector the corporation's news operation remains relatively handsomely resourced.

Despite the need to balance budgets and cope with the constraints imposed by the wider economy, the news about radio news is not all negative. The record listening figures recorded by RAJAR in recent years suggest that two of radio's greatest strengths, its portability and its secondariness, might make it one of the more durable of the 'old' media in the 'new' media age. If radio combines with other media it will almost certainly dwindle to a soundtrack, but if it stays true to its pristine blindness, news and news talk will help to ensure its future.

References

Born, G. (2004) *Uncertain Vision: Birt, Dyke and the Reinvention of the BBC*, London: Vintage.

Carter, R.E. (1958) 'Newspaper gatekeepers and the sources of news', *Public Opinion Quarterly*, 22.

Conservative Party (1970) *1970 Conservative Party General Election Manifesto: A Better Tomorrow*, London: Conservative Party.

Crisell, A. (1994) *Understanding Radio*, 2nd edn, London: Routledge.

— (2003) 'Look with thine ears: BBC Radio 4 and its significance in a multi-media age' in Crisell, A. (ed.) *More than a Music Box: Radio Cultures and Communities in a Multi-Media World*, Oxford: Berghahn Books.

Crisell, A. and Starkey, G. (2006) 'News on local radio' in Franklin, B. (ed.) *Local Journalism and Local Media: Making the Local News*, London: Routledge.

Hendy, D. (2007) *Life on Air: A History of Radio Four*, Oxford: Oxford University Press.

Jauert, P., Ala-Fossi, M., Lax, S., Nyre, L. and Shaw, H. (eds) (2010) *Digital Radio in Europe: Technologies, Industries and Cultures*, Bristol: Intellect Books.

Ofcom (2011) *Broadcasting Code*, London: Office of Communications. Available online: www.ofcom.org.uk.

RAJAR (2011) *Quarterly Summary, Third and Fourth Quarters*, London: Radio Joint Audience Research Limited.

Starkey, G. (2007) *Balance and Bias in Journalism: Representation, Regulation, and Democracy*, Basingstoke: Palgrave Macmillan.

— (2011) *Local Radio, Going Global*, Basingstoke: Palgrave Macmillan.

Starkey, G. and Crisell, A. (2010) *Radio Journalism*, London: Sage.

White, D. M. (1950) 'The "Gatekeeper": a case study in the selection of news', in D. Berkowitz (ed.) *Social Meanings of News: A Reader*, Thousand Oaks, CA: Sage.

60

TWEET THE NEWS: SOCIAL MEDIA STREAMS AND THE PRACTICE OF JOURNALISM

Alfred Hermida

The first signs that a major news story was about to break on May 1, 2011, came in a terse message on Twitter from the communications director at the White House, Dan Pfeiffer. "POTUS to address the nation tonight at 10:30 p.m. Eastern Time," said the tweet sent at 9.45 EST, referring to a surprise appearance by President Barack Obama. Less than an hour later came the first credible report on what the president was set to announce: the death of Osama Bin Laden.

The news did not come from a news agency or a 24/7 news channel, but on Twitter in the form of a message sent at 10:25 EST by Keith Urbahn, the chief of staff for the former defense secretary Donald Rumsfeld: "So I'm told by a reputable person they have killed Osama Bin Laden. Hot damn." (Urbahn, 2011). The tweet reverberated across social media, triggering a flood of reactions and discussions on Twitter. Just over an hour later, at 11.35 EST, a somber President Obama confirmed that US special forces had killed Bin Laden in Abbottabad, a Pakistani city about two hours from the capital Islamabad. The flow of messages on Twitter reached fever pitch, with the company recording more than 4,000 tweets per second as the president spoke (Twitter Comms, 2011). Among the messages were those of Pakistani IT consultant Sohaib Athar, who unwittingly live-tweeted the US raid on Bin Laden's compound (Butcher, 2011).

The death of Bin Laden led one commentator to say that Twitter had experienced its "CNN moment" (Rosof, 2011), a reference to how the 24-hour news channel broke through into the mainstream during the first Gulf War with its live broadcasts of the aerial bombing raids on Baghdad. But this was far from the first time that Twitter played a significant role in the flow and spread of breaking news.

Figure 60.1 *Keith Urbahn's tweet*

 @keithurbahn
Keith Urbahn

So I'm told by a reputable person they have killed Osama Bin Laden. Hot damn.

1 May via Twitter for BlackBerry®   ☆ Favorite ⇄ Retweet ↩ Reply

The social messaging service has been in the media spotlight for its role in coverage of major events such as the earthquake in the Sichuan province of China in May 2008, the terrorist attacks in Mumbai in November 2008 (BBC News, 2008), the crash of a US Airways plane on the Hudson River in January 2009 (Kwak et al., 2010), the protests following the Iranian election in June 2009 (Grossman, 2009) and the uprising in Egypt (Crovitz, 2011). In its brief five-year history, Twitter has developed as the default media network for real-time news, accelerating flows of information, leading one commentator to note that "news no longer breaks, it tweets" (Solis, 2010).

Twitter is one of a range of digital communication tools and services, usually identified by the catch-all phrase of social media, that are transforming the way news is gathered, disseminated and consumed, and influencing the direction and practice of journalism. Social media platforms build on notions of a participatory media culture, where the people formerly known as the audience (Rosen, 2006) can do more than simply read the news. The technologies allow citizens and organizations to take on some communication functions that were previously largely in the hands of media institutions. It has become common for the first reports, photos and video of a breaking news event to come from people caught up in the incident. As a result, the media circulating in the social media has become an integral part of newsgathering by news organizations.

Making sense of Twitter

Twitter has come a long way since its launch in August 2006 by a San Francisco start-up, asking its users the question "What are you doing?" later changed to "What's happening?" Towards the end of 2010, it had a reported 175 million registered users (Cain Miller, 2010). According to its own figures, an average of 140 million messages were being sent daily on the service by March 2011 (Penner, 2011). Twitter now describes itself as "a real-time information network that connects you to the latest information about what you find interesting" (Twitter, n.d).

The free service brings together aspects of text messaging, blogging and social interaction. Twitter is usually described as microblogging but it is perhaps more accurate to refer to it as a social messaging technology that extends our ability to communicate. Users can share short messages of 140 characters or less that are sent out to their followers – people who subscribed to receive the tweets. Since accounts are public by default, the messages can be seen by anyone, regardless of whether or not they have signed up to Twitter.

There is a conversational aspect as users can send a public message directed at another person by using the @username convention. People can also resend a message by someone else to their social circle by retweeting it, generally using the "RT @ username" format to acknowledge the original source. The @username convention is also used when a person is mentioned in a message. Thus, it is easy to see recent messages in which a user was replied to, retweeted or mentioned.

Twitter supports a hash annotation format that allows users to tag a message. The hash sign, #, is used to indicate the topic of a tweet. The hash convention means discussions on issues such as the uprising in Egypt in early 2011 could be tracked using the tag #Jan25, a reference to the day when mass protests started against the then president Hosni Mubarak. Twitter uses an algorithm to identify and rank keywords or hashtags that are immediately popular, creating a list of trending topics. These trending topics reflect what new or newsworthy topics are occupying the most people's attention on Twitter at any one time, exposing the aggregate interests and attention of global and local communities.

Twitter and related social media platforms such as Facebook that allow users to share streams of content, from short status messages to links, photos and videos are social awareness streams (Naaman et al., 2011). Initial research into the content of these streams on Twitter identified four main activities: daily chatter, conversation, sharing information and reporting news (Java et al., 2009). Sharing information and reporting news are directly relevant to journalism, but so too are daily chatter and conversation.

By providing a means for millions to communicate, share and discuss events in real time, Twitter can provide a constantly updated live representation of the lives, interests and opinions of its users. Sankaranarayanan et al. go as far as saying that "Twitter, or most likely a successor of it, is a harbinger of a futuristic technology that is likely to capture and transmit the sum total of all human experiences of the moment" (2009: 51). Of course, the topics range from the trivial to the ridiculous to the momentous. For example, at the time of writing, a trending topic worldwide was a rumor, later confirmed, that actor Ashton Kutcher was replacing Charlie Sheen in the popular TV sitcom *Two and a Half Men*. In contrast, at the same time one of the preoccupations of Twitter users in Vancouver, Canada, was the recent election of the provincial premier Christy Clark.

Twitter and journalism

The streams of data on social media such as Twitter can be described as ambient journalism (Hermida, 2010a; 2010b). Ambient journalism posits that journalism itself has become omnipresent, like the air we breathe, due to the emergence and uptake of social awareness communication systems. Twitter is part of an ambient media system where users are able to dip in and out of flows of news and information from both established media and from each other.

Social awareness streams create a multifaceted and fragmented news experience, marking a shift away from the classical paradigm of journalism as a framework to provide reports and analyses of events through narratives. The immediacy and velocity of microbursts of data can strain the cognitive abilities of journalists and audiences to spot the important amongst the trivial and obtain a developed picture of events. The problem is exacerbated during breaking news events. For example, during the protests against the Iranian election results in June 2009, the volume of tweets mentioning Iran peaked at 221,774 in one hour, from an average of between 10,000 and 50,000 an hour (Parr, 2009).

The overwhelming nature of the messages on Twitter is one of the most common critiques by journalists. In their analysis of US media coverage of the first three years of its existence, Arceneaux and Schmitz Weiss found critics commonly mocked the service for unleashing "a torrent of useless information upon users" (2010: 1271). At other times, the media expressed skepticism about Twitter. Remarks by journalists such as "it's like searching for medical advice in an online world of quacks and cures" (Goodman, 2009) and "Twitter? I won't touch it. It's all garbage" (quoted in Stelter, 2009) reflect the intensity of derision from some in the profession. Even the renowned *New York Times* columnist Maureen Dowd described Twitter as "annoying," suggesting to its founders that they had created "a toy for bored celebrities and high-school girls" (2009).

The negative reactions to Twitter reflect what Arceneaux and Schmitz Weiss call "the contested process of technological adoption in response to new forms of media," (2010: 1263), such as the telegraph, radio and the internet. There are parallels with the initial reaction of journalists to another form of social media, blogs, in the early 2000s when established news outlets regarded them as "amateurish, filled with errors and not credible" (Tremayne, 2007: 261). What makes journalists and others uneasy about technologies such as Twitter is that "they disrupt established concepts of communication, prevailing notions of space and time and the distinction between public and private spheres" (Arceneaux and Schmitz Weiss, 2010: 1265).

Despite some vocal critiques of the social media platform, Arceneaux and Schmitz Weiss conclude that USA media coverage was primarily positive about Twitter, with most stories mentioning at least some benefit. This might go some way towards explaining the rapid adoption of the service by journalists and newsrooms. The number of media professionals signing up prompted the American Journalism Review (AJR) to publish an article in April 2009 entitled "The Twitter Explosion." It pointed out that some well-known media figures had followings that are almost as large as the circulation of their newspapers or viewership of their TV show, but also mused whether Twitter "is more than just the latest info-plaything" (Farhi, 2009).

Since then, the Twitter explosion has reached more journalists and newsrooms. Research in the US found that by 2010 all but one of the top 198 newspapers and TV stations in the US had an official Twitter account (Messner et al., 2011). Some news organizations have encouraged their staff to sign up for the service, while others have created a new post of social media editor to engage with audiences and teach reporters how to make the most of Twitter (Gleason, 2010).

Every new communication technology, from radio to TV to the internet, has played a role in influencing how journalists think and go about their work. We are still in the early stages of understanding how Twitter and similar real-time social messaging tools are affecting well-established journalistic norms and practices. But there is a growing body of work into how mainstream journalists are figuring out how to integrate what Lasorsa et al. label as "a new media format that directly challenges them" (2011: 1). Twitter is one of a range of technologies that undermine the traditional gatekeeping role of journalists by allowing anyone to gather, publish and distribute news and information to a broad audience. I have previously argued that social media platforms are "creating new forms of journalism, representing one of the ways in which the Internet is influencing journalism practices and, furthermore, changing how journalism itself is defined" (Hermida, 2010a: 4).

Journalists' use of Twitter

When media take up a new communication technology, there is a process of negotiation as newsrooms incorporate novel tools and techniques into time-honored ways of working. Journalists have tended to transfer their organizational norms to digital media rather than rethink established routines and conventions. There is an emergent body of literature into what journalists are doing on social media platforms, and how these new practices are interacting with journalistic conventions.

Initial research suggests that journalists are extending existing practices to social media. There are four main ways that journalists have been using Twitter: to report the news, to drive traffic to websites, to gather the news and to find sources. The ability to send short bursts of information in real time has been embraced by journalists as a way to post snippets of news and to share and send links to their material. As Farhi (2009) notes, "reporters now routinely tweet from all kinds of events – speeches, meetings and conferences, sports events." Twitter has even become a factor in court reporting, with tweets from the courtroom offering virtually contemporaneous accounts of proceedings. One particularly notable case was the trial in Canada of convicted murderer Colonel Russell Williams, where the graphic nature of the evidence led to questions about the appropriateness of Twitter as a reporting tool (Zerbisias, 2010). Similar questions were raised in 2008, when a US reporter provided real-time updates from the funeral of a three-year-old boy, prompting a wave of criticism (Degette, 2008).

News outlets have tapped into the ability to reach a broader audience by incorporating social media platforms as distribution networks for stories. Both news organizations and individual journalists have used Twitter to promote their work and build the online audience. In their analysis of the official Twitter accounts of the top newspaper and TV organizations in the US, Messner et al. (2011) found that most tweets were links back to their websites. In effect, Twitter was being used as an alternative to an automated RSS feed of the latest news stories. One study found that many newsrooms automatically generated a tweet with a link anytime a story was published on their website (Blasingame, 2011). "The use of the news organisation's official Twitter channels has not yet developed beyond the utilization as a promotional tool to drive traffic to websites," suggest Messner et al. (2011: 20). A study of the use of Twitter by regional news outlets in Portugal reached similar conclusions (Jerónimo and Duarte, 2010). As for individual journalists, an analysis of the tweeting habits of US journalists by Lasorsa et al. (2011) found that 42 percent of the tweets contained an external link, with half of these to the journalist's own host news organization.

There are mixed indications as to the effectiveness of Twitter as a platform for journalists and newsrooms to promote their work. Following an analysis of 80 US media sources on Twitter in 2009, An et al. (2011) suggested that social links increase the reach of a news organisation, particularly for those with smaller audiences. However, a study by the Project for Excellence in Journalism found that Twitter accounted for a small percentage of the total traffic sent to the top news sites in the US, especially when compared to visitors coming via Google or to the news sites directly (Olmstead et al., 2011). Links to news stories posted on Twitter.com made up just over 1 percent of traffic to top news sites such as the *New York Times*, *New York Post* and the *Huffington Post*.

But news organizations do see value in extending their newsgathering operations to Twitter and related social media platforms. Time and again, Twitter has demonstrated its potential as a platform for eyewitness reports of events as they unfold in real time.

For example, one of the first reports from Haiti when the devastating earthquake struck in January 2010 came in a tweet from Frederic Dupoux just seven minutes after the tremor, followed by dozens more (Bruno, 2011). "Once again social media took charge of 'breaking the news' to the world about a major crisis event," wrote Bruno (2011: 13).

At the time of the quake, the only two foreign correspondents on Haiti were an Associated Press reporter and a Reuters local stringer. While news outlets rushed to get their correspondents to Haiti, many newsrooms turned to Twitter, Flickr and YouTube for first-hand reports from witnesses on the ground. A senior TV news editor in the UK, Ed Fraser, remarked that "for the first time really, certainly in online terms but also for broadcast, Twitter was one of those vehicles which had a life of its own. It gave us real time information as to what was going on on the ground" (quoted in Bruno, 2011). In these types of situations, Twitter users take on the role of social sensors of the news (Sakaki et al., 2010). The network functions as a detection system that can provide early warning of breaking news, and then provide a stream of real-time data as events unfold.

By extension, journalists have turned to social media platforms to find and develop a range of sources and contacts. A reporter can choose to follow specific people relevant to their beat or create lists of users, based on topic or location. *We the Media* author Dan Gillmor recommends that journalists "follow people who point them to things they should know about" (quoted in Farhi, 2009). Twitter enables journalists to create a personalized news wire, with potentially thousands of sources relevant to the focus of their professional work. A survey of nearly 500 journalists across 12 countries found that nearly half of respondents said they used Twitter to source new story angles, compared to 35 percent who used Facebook (Oriella PR Network, 2011). Now, in journalism classes, students are being taught how to monitor the chatter on social networks on issues in their areas and connect with key sources (Hermida, 2010c).

By and large, journalists have been adopting social media tools like Twitter on their terms. In his analysis of how prominent news outlets such as the BBC, the *Guardian* and the *New York Times* were using social media, Newman concludes:

> So far at least, the use of new tools has not led to any fundamental rewrite of the rule book – just a few tweaks round the edges. As with so many aspects of the Internet, social media are providing a useful extra layer of functionality, enabling stories to be told in new ways, not changing the heart of what journalists do. "Same values, new tools", sums up the core thinking in most newsrooms.
>
> (Newman, 2009: 39)

However, there are indications that decades old norms and practices are bending as social media plays an increasingly prominent role in journalism.

New roles, new rules

The use of social media by journalists raises questions about key tenets of the profession. Journalism is built on the basis of verify first, then publish. In their seminal 2001 work *The Elements of Journalism*, Kovach and Rosenstiel state, "the essence of journalism is a discipline of verification" (71). Through the discipline of verification, the journalist establishes jurisdiction over the ability to objectively parse reality to claim a special kind of authority and status. However, the emergence of Twitter as a source for breaking news, and the speed at which information is disseminated on the network, is challenging the "verify first, then publish" premise of journalism.

One of the early examples of these tensions came in November 2008 when gunmen carried out a series of coordinated attacks in Mumbai. The BBC adopted a collaborative style of newsgathering that combined reports from its own correspondents with contributions from ordinary citizens. The venerable news organization published unverified tweets on its news website as part of its 24-hour rolling news coverage of the bombings (BBC News, 2008). The decision to publish unsubstantiated, and at least in one case, false, information circulating on Twitter was heavily criticized. While acknowledging the need to check tweets for authenticity, BBC News website Editor Steve Herrmann argued "there is a case also for simply monitoring, selecting and passing on the information we are getting as quickly as we can, on the basis that many people will want to know what we know and what we are still finding out" (Herrmann, 2008).

The use of social media content by mainstream media came to the fore a year later during the Iranian election protests of June 2009. With severe reporting restrictions on foreign correspondents on the ground in Tehran, newsrooms turned to social media to fill the news vacuum. Leading news organizations, from the *New York Times* in the US to the *Guardian* newspaper in the UK, published constantly updated accounts that relied on unverified videos and Twitter messages, complemented with reports from their journalists in Tehran (Stelter, 2009). Since then, the blend of professional and amateur content has become a feature of how breaking news is reported.

News organizations are in the process of figuring out how to marry established practices with the notion of "publish first, verify later," given fears that it may erode public trust in the media. There are signals of a shift in the standards of verification applied in the real-time coverage of ongoing, fast-moving events. The discussions at a BBC social media conference in May 2011 suggested that there is "a view within the mainstream media that audiences have lower expectations of accuracy and verification from journalists' and media outlets' social media accounts than they do of 'appointment TV' or the printed page" (Posetti, 2011).

Research by Italian journalist Nicola Bruno into the rolling news coverage of the 2010 Haiti earthquake by three major news outlets found that only the BBC consistently sought to verify information on social media before publication (Bruno, 2011). The two other organizations, the *Guardian* and CNN, chose speed versus verification, at least some of the time. As a consequence, the BBC used less content from social media than other outlets that chose to "tweet first, verify later."

One technique adopted by news organizations is to differentiate between material produced by its journalists and content drawn from social media. The publication of unverified material has tended to take place within live blogs, a commonly used online story-telling format that is distinct from more traditional journalism. Matthew Weaver at the *Guardian* suggested that audiences have a different set of expectations from a live blog compared to an article authored by a correspondent. "On a live blog you are letting the reader in on what's up there, and say: look, we're letting you in on the process of newsgathering. There's a more fluid sense of what's happening" (quoted in Bruno, 2011: 44).

The integration of social media content into the newsgathering process is giving rise to an emerging role of the journalist as curator. Their primary role is to navigate, sift, select and contextualize the vast amounts of data on social awareness streams such as Twitter. The most well-known example of the journalist as curator is Andy Carvin, a social media strategist at NPR in the US. He rose to prominence during the uprisings in Tunisia in December 2010 and Egypt at the start of 2011 when he turned to Twitter to find and reach out to credible sources, carry out real-time fact-checking and aggregate news as it happened.

Carvin's Twitter stream has been described as "a living, breathing real-time verification system" (Silverman, 2011). The verification process, though, differs from standard journalistic practice, as it takes place in the open on Twitter. In his messages, Carvin would regularly turn to his online social network to verify or confirm a piece of information, a process he himself described as an "open newsgathering operation" (quoted in Farhi, 2011). In the role of journalist as curator, the media professional lays bare the manner through which a news story is constructed, as fragments of information are reported, contested, denied or verified. Journalism is transformed from a final product presented to the audience as a definitive rendering of events to a tentative process where contested accounts are examined and evaluated in real time. In commenting on Carvin's work, the head of NPR's digital media division, Kinsey Wilson, makes this distinction clear, stating "it's not positioned as the definitive sort of piece that you might hear on NPR. It's a different form" (quoted in Farhi, 2011).

This different form of journalism on social media is also challenging another key tenet in journalism: objectivity. Journalists are expected to keep their personal opinions out of their reporting (Kovach and Rosenstiel, 2001), yet new media formats such as blogs have enabled the personality of the author to be more visible (Singer, 2005; Domingo and Heinonen, 2008; Hermida, 2009). Social awareness streams can exacerbate the tensions between professional and personal behavior for a number of reasons. Accounts can be set up in both the name of a news organization and an individual journalist. The messaging activity takes places on a platform beyond the framework of a news organization's website.

There is also an ethos on Twitter and similar platforms of life sharing, with users expected to discuss personal aspects of their lives. "In an emerging communication space like Twitter, which can be used for everything from breaking news to banality, journalists have far greater license to write about whatever strikes their fancy, including the mundane details of their day-to-day activities" (Lasorsa et al., 2011: 6). The extent to which social media is chipping away at the divide between the personal and professional in journalism is unclear. Lasorsa et al. found that US journalists deviated from traditional expectations of objectivity by offering opinions in their tweets. They conclude:

> J-tweeters appear both to be adopting features of Twitter in their micro-blogging and adapting these features to their existing norms and practices. Specifically, much like other Twitter users, j-tweeters are offering opinions quite freely in their microblogs, which deviates from their traditional professional conventions.
>
> (2011: 12)

The journalists also talked about their personal lives on Twitter, but significantly, they were less likely to take part in a conversation with the audience. Other studies suggest that engaging in an exchange with readers on social media is not part of the journalist's toolkit (Garcia de Torres et al., 2011). Attitudes and practices to contend with the blurring of the personal and professional on social media are evolving. Newsrooms have drawn up specific editorial policies out of concerns about trust and credibility to aid journalists in negotiating their interactions on social media. The introduction to guidelines issued by the American Society of News Editors (ASNE) reflects the tensions:

> Putting in place overly draconian rules discourages creativity and innovation, but allowing an uncontrolled free-for all opens the floodgates to problems and leaves news organizations responsible for irresponsible employees.
>
> (Hohmann, 2011).

Conclusion

A degree of hyperbole tends to accompany new technologies and Twitter is no exception. The social media platform itself may be "the app du jour that will fade from the limelight, or it could become a staple of daily life," (Arceneaux and Schmitz Weiss, 2011: 1263). Communication services are subject to shifting social and cultural habits. It is important to consider the affordances of a technology that provides for real-time diffusion of short bursts of data from individuals and institutions in a highly connected and public social space.

Twitter is part of an array of Web 2.0 technologies that are enabling forms of interpersonal communication online that have an impact on how citizens gain the news and information they require to be free and self-governing, transforming how journalists and audiences relate to the news. Even skeptical voices such as *New York Times* executive editor Bill Keller concede "Twitter is a brilliant device – a megaphone for promotion, a seine for information, a helpful organizing tool for everything from dog-lover meet-ups to revolutions" (2011). There is growing research into understanding of how traditional functions of journalism – informing citizens, holding the powerful to account, providing analysis and mobilizing public opinion – are being transformed.

The changes impact how the news is reported and distributed, together with who is doing the reporting. Social awareness streams such as Twitter present the ultimate unbundling of the news into its individual components, where the journalism itself becomes fragmented, omnipresent and ambient. Contradictory reports, rumors, speculation, confirmation and verification circulate via social interaction in a compressed news cycle on digital networked platforms, laying bare the processes of journalism.

Twitter is affecting how news organizations respond to breaking news, how journalists go about their reporting and whose voices are heard. New journalistic genres are emerging as news outlets incorporate social media services into daily routines. A process of negotiation is taking place, as traditional ways of working bump up against social, cultural and technological practices that disrupt established journalistic norms. The role of the journalist has evolved, and continues to evolve, as a vital node in a networked media environment that is trusted to authenticate, interpret and contextualize information flows on social awareness streams.

References

An, J., M. Cha, K. Gummadi and J. Crowcroft (2011) 'Media Landscape in Twitter : A World of New Conventions and Political Diversity,' Association for the Advancement of Artificial Intelligence. Retrieved from http://www.cl.cam.ac.uk/~jac22/out/twitter-diverse.pdf

Arceneaux, N. and A. Schmitz Weiss (2010) 'Seems Stupid Until You Try It: Press Coverage of Twitter, 2006–9,' *New Media & Society*, 12 (8), 1262.

Blasingame, D. (2011) 'Twitter First: Changing TV News 140 Characters at a Time,' International Symposium on Online Journalism, UT Austin. Retrieved from: http://online.journalism.utexas.edu/2011/papers/Dale2011.pdf

BBC News (2008, Nov. 27) 'Mumbai Rocked by Deadly Attacks,' BBC News.com. Retrieved from: http://news.bbc.co.uk/2/hi/south_asia/7751160.stm

Bruno, N. (2011) 'Tweet First, Verify Later: How Real-Time Information is Changing the Coverage of Worldwide Crisis Events,' Reuters Institute for the Study of Journalism. Retrieved from: http://reutersinstitute.politics.ox.ac.uk/fileadmin/documents/Publications/fellows__papers/2010-2011/TWEET_FIRST_VERIFY_LATER.pdf

Butcher, M. (2011, May 1) 'Here's The Guy Who Unwittingly Live-Tweeted The Raid On Bin Laden,' TechCrunch. Retrieved from: http://techcrunch.com/2011/05/01/heres-the-guy-who-unwittingly-live-tweeted-the-raid-on-bin-laden/

Cain Miller, C. (2010, Oct. 30) 'Why Twitter's C.E.O. Demoted Himself,' New York Times. Retrieved from: http://www.nytimes.com/2010/10/31/technology/31ev.html

Crovitz, G. (2011, Feb. 14) 'Egypt's Revolution by Social Media,' Wall Street Journal. Retrieved from: http://online.wsj.com/article/SB10001424052748703786804576137980252177072.html

Degette, C. (2008, Sept. 10) 'RMN 'Tweets' the Funeral of 3-Year Old Boy Killed in Ice Cream Shop,' Colorado Independent. Retrieved from: http://coloradoindependent.com/7717/rmn-tweets-the-funeral-of-3-year-old-boy

Domingo, D. and A. Heinonen (2008) 'Weblogs and Journalism. A Typology to Explore the Blurring Boundaries,' Nordicom Review, 29 (1), 3–15.

Dowd, M. (2009, April 22) 'To Tweet or Not to Tweet,' New York Times. Retrieved from: http://www.nytimes.com/2009/04/22/opinion/22dowd.html?_r=3&ref=opinion

Farhi, P. (2009) 'The Twitter Explosion,' American Journalism Review, April-May. Retrieved from: http://www.ajr.org/article.asp?id=4756

Farhi, P. (2011, April 12) 'NPR's Andy Carvin, Tweeting the Middle East,' The Washington Post. Retrieved from: http://www.washingtonpost.com/lifestyle/style/npr-andy-carvin-tweeting-the-middle-east/2011/04/06/AFcSdhSD_story.html

Garcia de Torres, Elvira, L. Yezers'ka, A. Rost, M. Calderin, M. Bello, C. Edo, E. Sahid, P. Jerónimo, C. Arcila, A. Serrano, J. Badillo and L. Corredoira Alfonso (2011) 'See You on Facebook or Twitter? How 30 local News Outlets Manage Social Networking Tools,' International Symposium on Online Journalism, UT Austin. Retrieved from: http://online.journalism.utexas.edu/2011/papers/Elvira2011.pdf

Gleason, S. (2010) 'Harnessing Social Media,' American Journalism Review 32(1), 6–7.

Goodman, E. (2009, July 5) 'Journalism Needed in Twitter Era,' Columbia Daily Tribune. Retrieved from: http://www.columbiatribune.com/news/2009/jul/05/journalism-needed-in-twitter-era/

Grossman, L. (2009, June 17) 'Iran Protests: Twitter, the Medium of the Movement,' Time.com. Retrieved from: www.time.com/time/world/article/0,8599,1905125,00.html

Hermida, A. (2009) 'The Blogging BBC,' Journalism Practice, 3 (3), 1–17.

Hermida, A. (2010a) 'Twittering the news,' Journalism Practice, 4 (3), 297–308.

Hermida, A. (2010b) 'From TV to Twitter: how ambient news became ambient Journalism,' Media-Culture Journal, 13 (2).

Hermida, A. (2010c, Aug. 30) 'How to Teach Social Media in Journalism Schools,' PBS Mediashift. Retrieved from: http://www.pbs.org/mediashift/2010/08/how-to-teach-social-media-in-journalism-schools242.html

Herrmann, S. (2008, Dec. 4) 'Mumbai, Twitter and Live Updates.' BBC The Editors. Retrieved from: http://www.bbc.co.uk/blogs/theeditors/2008/12/theres_been_discussion_see_eg.html

Hohmann, J. (2011, March) '10 Best Practices for Social Media.' American Society of News Editors. Retrieved from: http://asne.org/portals/0/publications/public/10_Best_Practices_for_Social_Media.pdf

Java, A., X. Song, T. Finin and B. Tseng (2009) 'Why we twitter: An analysis of a microblogging community,' Advances in Web Mining and Web Usage Analysis, 118–38.

Jerónimo, P. and A. Duarte (2010) 'Twitter e Jornalismo de Proximidade: Estudo de Rotinas de Produ{cc}{at}o nos Principais Titulos de Imprensa Regional em Portugal's' Prisma.com, 12.

Kwak, H., C. Lee, H. Park and S. Moon (2010) 'What is Twitter, a Social Network or a News Media?' Proceedings of the 19th international conference on World wide web, 591–600.

Keller, B. (2011, May 18) The Twitter Trap, New York Times. Retrieved from: http://www.nytimes.com/2011/05/22/magazine/the-twitter-trap.html

Kovach, B. and T. Rosenstiel (2001) The Elements of Journalism. New York: Crown Publishers.

Lasorsa, D.L., S.C. Lewis and A.E. Holton (2011) 'Normalizing Twitter: Journalism practice in an emerging communication space,' Journalism Studies, first published on 21 April 2011 (iFirst).

Messner, M, M. Linke and A. Esford (2011) 'Shoveling Tweets: An Analysis of the Microblogging Engagement of Traditional News Organizations,' International Symposium on Online Journalism, UT Austin. Retrieved from: http://online.journalism.utexas.edu/2011/papers/Messner2011.pdf

Naaman, M., H. Becker and L. Gravano (2011) 'Hip and Trendy: Characterizing Emerging Trends on Twitter,' *Journal of the American Society for Information Science and Technology*, 62(5), 902–18.

Newman, N. (2009) 'The rise of social media and its impact on mainstream journalism,' Reuters Institute for the Study of Journalism Working Paper. Oxford: University of Oxford.

Olmstead, K.A. Mitchell and T. Rosenstiel (2011, May 9) 'Navigating News Online,' Project for Excellence in Journalism. Retrieved from: http://www.journalism.org/analysis_report/twitter_0

Oriella PR Network (2011) 'The State of Journalism in 2011,' Oriella. Retrieved from: http://www.oriel-ladigitaljournalism.com/

Parr, B. (2009, June 17) 'Mindblowing #IranElection Stats: 221,744 Tweets Per Hour at Peak,' *Mashable*. Retrieved from: http://mashable.com/2009/06/17/iranelection-crisis-numbers/

Penner, C. (2011, March 14) 'Numbers,' Twitter blog. Retrieved from: http://blog.twitter.com/2011/03/numbers.html

Posetti, J. (2011) 'BBC Social Media Summit Fixates on Creating 'Open Media,'' PBS Mediashift, 7 June, 2011, accessed 7 June 2011 http://www.pbs.org/mediashift/2011/06/bbc-social-media-summit-fixates-on-creating-open-media158.html

Rosen, J. (2006) The People Formerly Known as the Audience, PressThink. Retrieved from: http://archive.pressthink.org/2006/06/27/ppl_frmr.html

Rosoff, M. (2011) 'Twitter Just Had its CNN Moment,' *Business Insider*. Retrieved from: http://www.businessinsider.com/twitter-just-had-its-cnn-moment-2011-5

Sakaki, T., M. Okazaki and Y. Matsuo (2010) 'Earthquake shakes Twitter users: real-time event detection by social sensors,' *Proceedings of the 19th international conference on World Wide Web*, ACM, New York, NY, USA, 851–60.

Sankaranarayanan, J., H. Samet, B.E. Teitler, M.D. Lieberman and J. Sperling (2009) 'TwitterStand: news in tweets,' *Proceedings of the 17th ACM SIGSPATIAL International Conference on Advances in Geographic Information Systems*, 42–51.

Silverman, C. (2011, April 8) 'Is This the World's Best Twitter Account?' *Columbia Journalism Review*. Retrieved from: http://www.cjr.org/behind_the_news/is_this_the_worlds_best_twitter_account.php

Singer, J. (2005) 'The Political J-blogger: 'Normalizing' a New Media Form to Fit Old Norms and Practices,' *Journalism* 6 (2), 173–98.

Solis, B. (2010). The information divide between traditional and new media, Feb 10, 2010. http://www.briansolis.com/2010/02/the-information-divide-the-socialization-of-news-and-dissemination/

Stelter, B. (2009, June 2009) 'Journalism Rules Are Bent in News Coverage From Iran,' *New York Times*. Retrieved from: http://www.nytimes.com/2009/06/29/business/media/29coverage.html

Tremayne, M. (2007) 'Harnessing the active audience: Synthesizing blog research and lessons for the future of media,' in M. Tremayne (ed.) *Blogging, citizenship, and the future of media*, New York: Routledge. 261–72.

Twitter Comms, (2011, May 1) Twitter. Retrieved from: http://twitter.com/#!/twitterglobalpr/status/64917013851680768

Twitter, (n.d.) About, Twitter. Retrieved from: http://twitter.com/about

Urbahn, Keith (2011, May 1) Twitter. Retrieved from: http://twitter.com/#!/keithurbahn/status/64877790624886784

Zerbisias, A. (2010, Oct. 22) 'Murder She Wrote: In 140 Characters or Less,' *Toronto Star*. Retrieved from: http://www.thestar.com/news/insight/article/880020--murder-she-wrote-in-140-characters-or-less

INDEX